COMPARATIVE COUNTER-TERRORISM LAW

Terrorism law is as international as it is regionally distinct and as difficult to define as it is essential to address. Given recent pressures to harmonize terrorism laws from international organizations such as the United Nations Security Council, the Financial Action Task Force, and the Council of Europe, this book presents readers with an up-to-date assessment of terrorism law across the globe. Covering twenty-two jurisdictions across six continents, the common framework used for each chapter facilitates national comparisons of a range of laws, including relevant criminal, administrative, financial, secrecy, and military laws. Recognizing that similar laws may yield different outcomes when transplanted into new contexts, priority of place is given to examples of real-world application.

Including an extensive introduction to the field as well as a detailed final chapter on common themes and future challenges, this book will help establish comparative counter-terrorism law as an emerging discipline crossing traditional boundaries in legal scholarship.

Kent Roach is a professor of law at the University of Toronto. He served as General Reporter on counter-terrorism law at the XIX Congress on Comparative Law as well as Director of Research for the Air India bombing inquiry. His most recent book, *The 9/11 Effect: Comparative Counter-Terrorism* (2011), was co-recipient of the Mundell Medal for contributions to legal writing.

Comparative Counter-Terrorism Law

Edited by

KENT ROACH
University of Toronto

CAMBRIDGE
UNIVERSITY PRESS

CAMBRIDGE
UNIVERSITY PRESS

32 Avenue of the Americas, New York, NY 10013-2473, USA

Cambridge University Press is part of the University of Cambridge.

It furthers the University's mission by disseminating knowledge in the pursuit of education, learning, and research at the highest international levels of excellence.

www.cambridge.org
Information on this title: www.cambridge.org/9781107057074

First published 2015

A catalog record for this publication is available from the British Library.

Library of Congress Cataloging in Publication Data
Comparative counter-terrorism law / edited by Kent Roach.
pages cm
ISBN 978-1-107-05707-4 (hardback)
1. Terrorism – Prevention – Law and legislation. 2. Terrorism – Prevention.
I. Roach, Kent.
KZ7220.C64 2015
344.05′32517–dc23 2015004872

ISBN 978-1-107-05707-4 Hardback

Contents

Notes on Contributors

Kent Roach, FRSC, holds the Prichard Wilson Chair in Law and Public Policy at the University of Toronto. He is the author of twelve books, including *The 9/11 Effect: Comparative Counter-Terrorism*, published by Cambridge University Press in 2011 and co-winner of the 2012 Mundell Medal. He has published widely on counter-terrorism matters in Australia, Canada, Hong Kong, Singapore, Sweden, the United Kingdom, and the United States and served as General Reporter on Counter-Terrorism Law at the XIV Comparative Law Conference in Vienna in July 2014. He served on the research advisory committee of the Commission of Inquiry into the Actions of Canadian Officials in Relation to Maher Arar from 2004 to 2006 and as Director of Research for the Commission of Inquiry into the Bombing of Air India Flight 182 from 2006 to 2010. In 2013, he was one of four academics awarded a Trudeau Fellowship for his academic and policy contributions. With Craig Forcese, he has analyzed Canada's current counter-terrorism bills at www.antiterrorlaw.ca.

George Antoniu (Romania) was University Professor and editor-in-chief of the *Revue de Droit Pénal*. His many publications include *La culpabilité pénale*, IIe édition (Éditions de l'Académie, Bucharest, 2003) and *La réforme pénale* (a collaboration) (Éditions de l'Académie, Bucharest, 2003). Professor Antoniu passed away in August 2014.

Veronika Bílková (the Czech Republic) is a Research Fellow at the Institute of International Relations in Prague, a lecturer in international law at the Law Faculty of the Charles University in Prague, and a member of the European Commission on Democracy Through Law (Venice Commission) on behalf of the Czech Republic. Graduated from the Law and Philosophical Faculties of the Charles University (JUDr., PhDr., Ph.D.) and from the European Master's Degree in Human Rights and Democratisation (E.MA), she holds the diploma in international law from the University of Cambridge. Bílková's work focuses on international law (especially the use of force, international humanitarian law, international criminal law, and human rights) and international relations (mainly security topics and the United Nations).

Miguel Ángel Boldova (Spain) has been Professor (*Catedrático*) of Criminal Law at the University of Zaragoza (Spain) since 2010. His main research interests include the study of the fundamental problems of the general part of criminal law, the system of legal consequences of crime, juvenile delinquency, and corporate criminal liability, as well as the study of various offenses, including falsification of documents and human trafficking. He is the principal investigator of a research team funded by the government of Aragon and the University of Zaragoza.

Céline Cocq (Belgium) has obtained a law degree (2005), a master's degree in international humanitarian law (2010), and two university diplomas in criminology and criminal studies (2005 and 2011), and graduated with an L.L.M. in international public law (2012) from the Center of International Law (Université Libre de Bruxelles, Belgium). She is currently a Ph.D. researcher at the Legal Section of the Institut d'Etudes Européennes and a researcher on the SURVEILLE project studying surveillance technologies of different legal frameworks. Her research focuses mainly on substantive criminal law and criminal procedure, dealing with serious crime, at national and regional levels, including the European Union and the Association of South East Asian Nations, in order to conduct comparative analysis within and between regional organizations.

Piotr Daranowski (Poland) is Chair of International Public Law and International Relations at the University of Lodz in Poland. He is the author of the monograph *International Protection of Civil and Political Rights* in statu nascendi – *The International Pact of Human and Political Rights* (1993), which received an award for the best *habilitationsschrift* monograph from the Manfred Lachs Foundation (1994).

Fergal Davis (Australia) is a senior lecturer and member of the Australian Research Council Laureate Project: Anti-Terror Laws and the Democratic Challenge in the Gilbert + Tobin Centre of Public Law in the University of New South Wales. He is well published in the area of terrorism and democracy, including in major international journals such as the *Oxford Journal of Legal Studies* and *POLITICS*.

José Francisco de Faria Costa (Portugal) is Chair Professor of Criminal Law at the College of Law of Coimbra University, where he teaches doctorate, master, postgraduate, and degree courses. He also serves currently as president of the Institute for Economical and European Criminal Law, as a designated member of the Supreme Judicial Council, and as an elected member of the General Council of the University of Coimbra. He regularly teaches master courses in countries such as Brazil (Porto Alegre), China (Macau), and Angola (Luanda). In 1998, he was visiting professor at the University of Trento. His current research focuses on criminal punishment, economical criminal law, criminal law philosophy, criminal law and ethics, and medical criminal law. He is the author of more than one hundred publications, including *Danger in Criminal Law* (1992); *Lines of Criminal Law and Philosophy* (2005); *Notions of Criminal Law*, 3rd ed. (2012); and *Criminal Law and Globalization* (2010).

Rodrigo de Souza Costa (Brazil) is a criminal law professor at the University of the State of Rio de Janeiro in Rio de Janeiro, Brazil. He is also Deputy Secretary General of the Brazilian group of the International Association of Penal Law. He coordinates the research group Criminal Law and Constitution, which is primarily focused in international and comparative criminal law and violence against women.

Robert Diab (Canada) is an assistant professor in the Faculty of Law at Thompson Rivers University in British Columbia. He holds a Ph.D., LL.M, and LLB from the University of British Columbia and is the author of *Guantanamo North, Terrorism and the Administration of Justice in Canada* (2009). His areas of interest include counter-terror law, public order policing, and criminal law.

Maša Kovič Dine (Slovenia) is a Ph.D. candidate and teaching assistant at the Chair of International Law, Faculty of Law, University of Ljubljana. After receiving her graduate law degree in Slovenia, she obtained her LL.M. degree from the Faculty of Law at the University of Toronto and worked at the University of Toronto G8 Research Group, analyzing G8 countries' compliance with their summit commitments. Her research interests include cyber security and responsibility to protect.

Julien Gafner (Switzerland) is an attorney at law and partner in the law firm LEGENTIS Avocats (previously named Trivelli, Pelot, Sutter, Hahn, Genillod & Gafner) in Lausanne. Her publications include *Blanchiment d'argent, financement du terrorisme et nouvelles technologies*, contribution presented and edited within the seminar *E-banking et E-trading* held on February 15, 2006, by the Centre du Droit de l'Entreprise at the University of Lausanne.

Takeyoshi Imai (Japan) is a professor of criminal law and attorney at law at the Graduate School of Law in Hosei University in Japan. He serves as a member of the Justice Ministry's Legislative Council Criminal Law Subcommittee and is the Japanese representative (examiner) to the Organisation for Economic Co-operation and Development Working Group on Bribery, as well as the Japanese representative to the International Institute of Higher Studies in Criminal Sciences of the United Nations. He has been a visiting scholar at the universities of Cambridge and Geneva.

Shiri Krebs (Israel) is an international lawyer from Israel, specializing in international humanitarian law (law of war) and terrorism. From 2005 to 2010, she worked at the Israeli Supreme Court, where she served as legal advisor on international law matters in the chief justice's chambers. After leaving the Supreme Court, Krebs joined the Israeli Democracy Institute as a researcher, working on "Terrorism and Democracy" projects. She is completing her doctoral dissertation at Stanford Law School, and her publications include "Lifting the Veil of Secrecy: Judicial Review of Administrative Detentions in the Israeli Supreme Court," 45 *Vanderbilt Transnational Law Journal* 639–703 (2012). This article is an empirical analysis of preventive detention cases and won the Steven M. Block Civil Liberties Award.

Nicola McGarrity (Australia) is a lecturer and member of the Australian Research Council Laureate Project: Anti-Terror Laws and the Democratic Challenge in the Gilbert + Tobin Centre of Public Law in the University of New South Wales. McGarrity's research interests relate to the intersection of public and criminal law. She has published extensively in Australian and international journals on the human rights implications of antiterrorism law and policy and, in particular, the prosecution of suspected terrorists in Australia. She is a coeditor (with Andrew Lynch and George Williams) of *Counter-Terrorism and Beyond: The Culture of Law and Justice after 9/11* (2010). McGarrity has also practiced as a barrister in Australia in the fields of administrative, constitutional, and antiterrorism law.

Raluca-Ioana Mocanu (Romania) is Junior Lecturer on Criminal Law, Special Part, Department of Criminal Law and Criminology, Faculty of Law, at the University of Bucharest in Romania. She received her Ph.D. in law in 2010 for writing "Terrorism: Legal Aspects of National and International Criminal Law," under the direction of Professor Constantin Mitrache, Ph.D. Faculty of Law, University of Bucharest. Her publications include *Drug Trafficking and Abuse: Criminal Cases*, Hamangiu Ed. (2007).

Jamil Ddamulira Mujuzi (South Africa) is an associate professor of law in the Faculty of Law at the University of the Western Cape, Cape Town, South Africa. He has published more than eighty articles and chapters in books on various aspects of criminal law, criminal justice, and human rights that have appeared in some of the most prestigious peer-reviewed law journals in Africa, Asia, Europe, and North America. Some of his articles have been cited by the South African Supreme Court of Appeal and High Court. His publications have also been cited by human rights and international criminal law scholars in books, articles, and reports published in languages such as English, French, Italian, Czech, Danish, and Spanish. His article was also cited in the 2010 *United Nations Secretary General's Report on the Death*

Penalty, E/2010/10, December 28, 2009. Mujuzi is the editor-in-chief of the Faculty of Law's journal, *Law, Democracy and Development.*

Luz E. Nagle (Colombia) is a professor of law at Stetson University College of Law, where she specializes in international law, international criminal law, and national security law. Nagle's scholarship probes the realities of law, society, transborder crime, and armed conflict in the Americas. Her distinguished career includes having been a judge in Medellín, Colombia, during the so-called War on Drugs in the 1980s; clerking for the Supreme Court of Virginia; and pursuing software pirates as a member of Microsoft Corporation's Latin America Copyright Enforcement Practice. Nagle has participated in rule of law, judicial reform, and hemispheric security projects sponsored by the U.S. departments of Defense, Justice, and State throughout Latin America, and she is a regular presenter on various topics of international law and the rule of law for the State Department's Distinguished Foreign Visitors' Program. She is an El Centro Fellow of the Small Wars Foundation and an external researcher in the Strategic Studies Institute of the U.S. Army War College. An elected member of several learned legal societies, including the American Law Institute, Nagle currently sits on the International Bar Association's Legal Practice Division Council. Nagle holds an LL.D. from the Universidad Pontificia Bolivariana, her J.D. from the College of William & Mary, an LL.M. in international law and an M.A. in Latin American studies from the University of California at Los Angeles, and two certifications in national security law from the Center for National Security Law at the University of Virginia School of Law.

Bertrand Perrin (Switzerland) is a professor of criminal law, University of Fribourg, Switzerland. He holds a doctor of law degree, is an attorney at law, and holds an M.A. in economics. He received his Doctor of Law degree from the University of Fribourg (*summa cum laude*) in 2008 and won the Joseph Vigener Award in 2010. His publications include Isabelle Augsburger-Bucheli and Bertrand Perrin (dir.), *Les enjeux juridiques du secret bancaire* (2010); Étienne Blais and Bertrand Perrin (dir.), *La lutte contre la criminalité économique: réponses interdisciplinaires à un défi global* (2010); and "L'incrimination du financement du terrorisme en droits canadien et Suisse" (2012) 42 *Revue générale de droit (Ottawa)* 213.

Sabrina Praduroux (Italy) is Research Fellow at the University of Torino. She holds a Ph.D. in comparative law from the University of Palermo, and in May 2012 she obtained a Ph.D. in European law from the University of Helsinki. She has spent training and working periods at both the European Court of Human Rights in Strasbourg and the European Agency for Fundamental Rights in Vienna. Her main fields of interest concern human rights law, constitutional law, and European law, and much of her work is comparative and interdisciplinary.

Maria Ángeles Rueda (Spain) is Profesor Titular on Criminal Law at the University of Zaragoza and accredited Professor (*Catedrática*) since 2011. Rueda has carried out her teaching activity at the University of Zaragoza since the academic year 1993–1994. She has conducted research in organized crime, cyber crime, and the protection of privacy. Rueda has taken part in different research projects sponsored by the Spanish Ministry of Science and Education and is a member of the consolidated research group of the Autonomous Community of Aragon and of the University of Zaragoza, called Grupo de Estudios Penales.

Vasilka Sancin (Slovenia) is an assistant professor of public international law at the Faculty of Law, the University of Ljubljana, and a researcher at the Institute for Comparative Law at the same faculty. She is also a director of the Centre for International and Business Law. Sancin is a member of the Nuclear Weapons, Non-proliferation and Contemporary International Law Committee of the International Law Association, a member of the Chaudfontaine Group researching legal regulation of the export of dual-use items; she is also a member of the International Nuclear Law Association. She is an author of numerous articles and books on the area of international law.

Sudha N. Setty (The United States) is the associate dean for faculty development and intellectual life and a professor of law at Western New England University School of Law in Springfield, Massachusetts. She teaches law and terrorism, comparative constitutional law, constitutional law, civil rights, and contracts, and she was awarded the Catherine J. Jones Professor of the Year Award in 2009. Her scholarly work focuses on comparative analysis of separation of powers, rule of law, and national security issues. Her most recent article, "National Security Interest Convergence," was published in the *Harvard National Security Journal*. She was a visiting professor at the University of Connecticut School of Law in 2011. Prior to joining the faculty of Western New England in 2006, Setty served as defense counsel in civil, regulatory, and criminal matters involving national security issues, including terrorism financing investigations and lawsuits, and a *pro bono* matter challenging sentencing guidelines for those convicted of terrorist acts. Setty graduated as a Harlan Fiske Stone Scholar from Columbia Law School and received her A.B. in history (concentration in comparative civil rights) with honors from Stanford University.

Marissabell Škorić (Croatia) graduated from the Faculty of Law, the University of Rijeka, in December 1995. In 2000, she was conferred a master of law at the Faculty of Law, Zagreb University. She defended her doctoral dissertation at the Faculty of Law University of Zagreb in 2005, on the topic "The Prosecutor in

International Criminal Tribunals." She has published articles in internationally recognized publications and has presented papers at several international scientific conferences. Currently she works as an assistant professor at the Faculty of Law, Department of Criminal Law, University of Rijeka. Her main scientific and research interests are concerned with criminal law.

Keith Syrett (The United Kingdom) joined Cardiff Law School as Professor of Public Health Law in September 2012, having previously worked at the universities of East Anglia and Bristol. He has an LL.B. degree in jurisprudence from Oxford University, an M.A. in international relations from Yale University, and a Ph.D. in government from the London School of Economics. He is also a solicitor of the Supreme Court of England and Wales, having trained with Clifford Chance LLP. His publications include *Law, Legitimacy and the Rationing of Health Care* (2007) and *The Foundations of Public Law: Principles and Problems of Power in the British Constitution* (2011).

Eugene K. B. Tan (Singapore) is an assistant law professor at the School of Law, Singapore Management University. He is a graduate of the National University of Singapore, the London School of Economics and Political Science, and Stanford University, where he was a Fulbright Fellow. His interdisciplinary research interests include the mutual interaction of law and public policy, the regulation of ethnic conflict, and the government and politics of Singapore. He has published in internationally refereed journals, including the *Australian Journal of Asian Law*, *China Quarterly*, *Citizenship Studies*, *Ethnic and Racial Studies*, *Ethnopolitics*, the *Hong Kong Law Journal*, the *Israel Law Review*, the *Singapore Year Book of International Law*, and *Terrorism and Political Violence*. Tan is completing a book-length manuscript on the management of ethnic relations in Singapore. He also writes a regular column on law, society, and politics for a Singapore newspaper. In February 2012, he was appointed a nominated member of parliament.

Georgios Triantafyllou (Greece) is Assistant Professor of Criminal Law and Criminal Procedure at the School of Law, the University of Athens. He has published in the areas of criminal law, criminal procedure, and international criminal law. A member of the Athens Bar Association, Triantafyllou practices as defense counsel in all fields of criminal litigation.

Anne Weyembergh (Belgium) is Professor at the Université Libre de Bruxelles (ULB) and President of the Institute for European Studies of the ULB. She founded and coordinates the European Criminal Law Academic Network. Weyembergh is the coordinator of the ULB team on European criminal law and is co-coordinator of the research team RECL (University of Brussels – European Criminal Law), which is common to ULB and Vrij Universiteit Brussel. She has published numerous scientific articles and coedited several collective books in the field of EU criminal law. Weyembergh has presented at many conferences in Belgium and abroad and given lectures in various countries. She is one of the chief editors of the *New Journal of European Criminal Law*.

George Williams (Australia) is Anthony Mason Professor, Scientia Professor, and Foundation Director of the Gilbert + Tobin Centre of Public Law at the Faculty of Law, the University of New South Wales. As an Australian Research Council Laureate Fellow, he is engaged in a five-year international project on antiterror laws and democracy. Williams has written and edited thirty-one books, including *Australian Constitutional Law and Theory* and *The Oxford Companion to the High Court of Australia*. Williams was made an Officer of the Order of Australia in 2011 "For distinguished service to the law in the fields of anti-terrorism, human rights and constitutional law as an academic, author, adviser and public commentator."

Li Zhe (China) is an assistant professor of criminal law at the Faculty of Law of the University of Macau (UM). She finished her Ph.D. degree at China University of Political Science and Law in July 2005, and her Ph.D. thesis was published by the Peking University Press in 2008; she was awarded as the Second-Grade Award on Excellent Monographs of Young and Middle-Aged Scholars by the Chinese Criminal Law Society in 2009. Before joining UM, she worked as a Research Fellow in the Policy Branch of the Supreme People's Procuratorate of P.R. China for five years. Her publications include one monograph, four coauthored monographs, one edited book, chapters in sixteen books, and more than forty papers in journals and edited books.

Acknowledgments

I wish to thank the organizers of the XIX International Congress on Comparative Law held in Vienna in July 2014 for selecting comparative counter-terrorism law as a topic and for giving me the great privilege of serving as General Reporter on the topic. I thank all the national reporters for their hard work on their reports and subsequently on their chapters and for their helpful comments on my general report. I also thank Professor Ulrich Sieber, Director of the Max Planck Institute for Foreign and International Criminal Law in Freiburg, Germany, for chairing the session in Vienna and for his wise comments.

My work on this project has been made possible by the support of the Faculty of Law, University of Toronto, and in particular by the excellent organizational work of my assistant Nancy Bueler and by the dedicated and creative research assistance of the staff of the Bora Laskin Law Library. My work has also been greatly assisted by the generous funding and other support provided by the Pierre Elliott Trudeau Foundation by way of the award to me of a 2013 Trudeau Fellowship.

Kent Roach
April 2015

1

Comparative Counter-Terrorism Law Comes of Age

Kent Roach

I. INTRODUCTION

The essays in this collection were originally prepared as general and national reports for the XIX International Congress of Comparative Law held in Vienna in July 2014. Counter-terrorism law was included for the first time as a subject in this important conference held every four years. This represents an important recognition of comparative counter-terrorism law as a discipline. In the years since the 9/11 terrorist attacks on the United States, interest in and knowledge about counter-terrorism law has greatly expanded. This collection adds to this knowledge by providing structured information about the counter-terrorism laws of twenty-two countries and by reflecting on the nature of the subject of comparative counter-terrorism law. The conclusion of this volume identifies similarities and divergences between counter-terrorism law in countries drawn from the all the continents. It also examines common challenges and analytical themes as counter-terrorism law continues to evolve most recently in response to the challenges of foreign terrorist fighters.

II. THE FIELD OF STUDY

Counter-terrorism law is a challenging and complex subject within one jurisdiction, let alone compared over multiple jurisdictions. It covers a wide swath of domestic law and regulation. It is often centered in criminal law, but includes various forms of administrative regulation relating to diverse matters such as finance and immigration. Counter-terrorism law is focused on the state, but also interacts with the private sector, as financial institutions play an important role in attempting to identify and stop the financing of terrorism, and telecommunications companies play an important role with respect to surveillance. The technology that both the private and public sectors can apply to these issues intensifies what is at stake in terms of both privacy and security.

In many countries, police and intelligence agencies are given special powers to investigate terrorism, and these powers may involve limitations or infringements of human rights. Counter-terrorism law is thus deeply intertwined with constitutional law. In particular, courts have been increasingly willing to enforce human rights in the national security context, but opinions differ as to how effective such judicial interventions have been, given the tendency of the legislature to reassert the need for security laws.[1] Countries also differ in the extent to which legislation restrains or empowers the executive, with the United States often allowing the executive to act without explicit legislative authorization. In short, counter-terrorism law now frequently involves important constitutional questions about the relations among courts, the legislature and the executive.

The important role of intelligence in counter-terrorism brings with it problems relating to respect for human rights, including privacy rights. Intelligence also implicates many of the dilemmas posed by secrecy. For example, secrecy can threaten the fairness of legal proceedings where intelligence is used as evidence, and secrecy can make it difficult to conduct terrorism prosecutions or to hold governments accountable for the propriety or the efficacy of counter-terrorism activities. The military is also sometimes involved in counter-terrorism, and this also raises questions concerning human rights and the interaction of the laws of crime and war.

Even if only examined in one country, it is impossible to understand counter-terrorism law without understanding the demands supra-national laws and institutions place on states. In the immediate aftermath of 9/11, the UN Security Council used its mandatory powers under Chapter VII of the UN Charter to enact Security Council Resolution 1373, which required all states to ensure that terrorism and terrorism financing were treated as serious crimes without offering any guidance on how to define terrorism or seriously contemplating whether terrorism financing and travel bans based on executive listing of known terrorists would be fair or effective.

Although Resolution 1373 was criticized as international legislation beyond the Security Council's powers and even as "anti-constitutional,"[2] the Security Council

[1] For arguments that courts have had little effect, see Keith Ewing and Joo-Cheong Tham "The Continued Futility of the Human Rights Act" (2008) *Public Law* 668; Jenny Martinez "Process and Substance in the 'War on Terror'" (2008) 108 *Columbia Law Review* 1013. See also Kent Roach "Comparative Constitutional Law and the Challenges of Terrorism Law" in Tom Ginsburg and Rosalind Dixon eds. *Comparative Constitutional Law* (Cheltenham: Edward Elgar, 2011). See generally Fergal Davies and Fiona de Londras eds *Critical Debates on Counter-Terrorism Judicial Review* (Cambridge: Cambridge University Press, 2014).

[2] Kim Lane Scheppele "The Migration of Anti-Constitutional Ideas: The Post 9/11 Globalization of Public Law and the International State of Emergency" in Sujit Choudhry ed. *The Migration of Constitutional Ideas* (Cambridge: Cambridge University Press, 2006).

in September 2014 enacted a strikingly similar Resolution 2178 to require all states to ensure that travel to plan, prepare, provide or receive terrorist training, or participate in or perpetuate terrorist acts be treated as serious criminal offences.[3] This Resolution affirms a commitment to the problematic practice of terrorist listing[4] despite the far greater numbers that are joining the Islamic State compared to al Qaeda. Resolution 2178 has set off another round of expansion of terrorism offences even though, like Resolution 1373, the Security Council offers no guidance on the definition of terrorism and enhances the potential breadth of the term by linking it with "violent extremism" and "radicalization… which can be conducive to terrorism."[5] The supra-national drivers of domestic counter-terrorism law are not limited to these momentous Security Council Resolutions. The huge impact of 2002 and 2008 EU Guideline Decisions on terrorism laws will become clear in the chapters of this collection examining counter-terrorism law in European states. The Arab Convention for the Suppression of Terrorism has been a powerful influence in convincing many countries in the Middle East to enact broad definitions of terrorism that can be applied to both those prepared to use violence and those who simply dissent from authoritarian regimes.[6]

Counter-terrorism law is a broad field. It spans criminal, administrative, immigration, constitutional, military and foreign affairs law. It involves the interaction of domestic and supra-national law. The breadth of the domain of counter-terrorism law is extremely challenging for scholars.[7] It is, however, necessary to study the field in all its breadth to understand the multiple counter-terrorism instruments available to the state and the state's ability constantly to adjust the emphasis it places on different interventions. The state is not limited to the use of one type of law when countering terrorism. Hence, scholars must abandon their traditional comfort zones if they are to understand and evaluate the state's constantly evolving approach to terrorism.

3 S/Res/2178 (2014) at para 6.

4 Ibid at paras 7–10, 20–4.

5 Ibid at para 15.

6 Lynn Welchman "Rocks, Hard Places and Human Rights: Anti-Terrorism Law and Policy in Arab States" in Victor Ramraj et al. *Global Anti-Terrorism Law and Policy* 2nd ed (Cambridge: Cambridge University Press, 2012).

7 This may make it difficult for comparative counter-terrorism law to be merged with the distinct and developed field of terrorism studies. For an argument that comparative constitutional law needs to be merged with social studies of such matters, see Ran Hirshl *Comparative Matters: The Renaissance of Comparative Constitutional Law* (Oxford: Oxford University Press, 2014) ch. 4. Although this volume is focused on law, it is not "court- centric" (ibid at 163) because of the importance of statutes in counter-terrorism law.

A. *The Need for Comparative Study of Counter-Terrorism Law*

Why examine the already broad field of counter-terrorism law in a comparative manner? The nature of both international terrorism and international efforts to combat terrorism means that it is often not sufficient just to understand one jurisdiction's response to terrorism. A significant number of countries use immigration law as a means to detain suspected terrorists, but many find deportation is made difficult because of the harsh manner in which some states practice counter-terrorism. The same is true of extradition. There has been a trend to greater counter-terrorism co-operation between many countries, including intelligence sharing, but this requires understanding of how co-operating countries respond to terrorism. Counter-terrorism can rarely be practiced in isolation from other states. There is thus a practical need to understand the counter-terrorism laws and practices of the broadest range of countries.

The comparative study of counter-terrorism law also provides an excellent context to study strong supra-national demands for the harmonization of law. As mentioned previously, the UN Security Council and other supra-national bodies have since 9/11 devoted much effort to encouraging all states to enact counter-terrorism law. As will be seen throughout this collection, there has been a trend to the enactment of broad definitions of terrorism and broad terrorism offences, especially in relation to terrorism financing. At the same time, there are also interesting differences in even the formal law, and we are a long way from having one global form of counter-terrorism law. A few countries such as Brazil have so far resisted supra-national pressures to enact terrorism laws.[8] There is also much divergence in whether states have been prepared to use immigration and military laws against suspected terrorists, with many countries in Europe resisting both trends.

There are strong supra-national demands, including the use of Chapter VII powers by the United Nations Security Council, most notably in the sweeping Resolutions 1373, enacted in response to 9/11, and Resolution 2178, enacted in September 2014 in response to the rise of the Islamic State. Framework Decisions by the Council of the European Union enacted in 2002 and 2008 also were powerful forces for the harmonization of counter-terrorism law in Europe and another Framework Decision will likely emerge as a response to the Paris and Copenhagen terrorist attacks in early 2015. These are significant drivers towards convergence that at the extreme would only be satisfied by a uniform and homogeneous global counter-terrorism law.

At the same time, the inherently controversial nature of counter-terrorism law, as well as the increasing influence of domestic constitutional norms, serve as significant forces for divergence in counter-terrorism law. Such law is often responsive to local

[8] Chapter 5, "Brazil" infra at 148.

conditions, history, and norms. For example, both Canada and South Africa have borrowed heavily from British law when defining terrorism in post-9/11 laws, but as will be seen in this chapter, each country has placed the stamp of its own history and constitutional norms on its definition of terrorism. Indeed, the distinctive nature of their approaches casts doubt on whether the quest for harmonization of European counter-terrorism law is realistic given the different experiences of European states with terrorism and their own domestic norms. In any event, counter-terrorism law is an excellent field to evaluate the competing pulls toward convergence and divergence and between universal and functional demands as they compete with cultural and expressive concerns.

A strict focus on the law in the books as compared to the law in action may falsely suggest that there is more convergence than actually exists. For example, terrorism financing laws look strikingly similar in many countries, a phenomena that is encouraged by pressure and assistance provided by the Financial Action Task Force originating from the G7 states but spreading throughout the world. The contributors to this volume, however, have been asked whenever possible to provide information about the actual use of such laws. What emerges from this examination of the law in action is a sense of increased divergence, with many countries reporting no terrorism financing prosecutions and others such as the United States and Italy reporting higher levels of prosecutions. This underlines that it is especially important not to ignore the law in action in the study of comparative counter-terrorism law.[9]

It is also important to study counter-terrorism comparatively to understand the complex processes of migration and borrowing. This chapter will explore the influence that a few definitions of terrorism have had on counter-terrorism laws in many parts of the world. Comparative lawyers need, however, to go beyond simply noting examples of borrowing or influence in the crafting of laws. They need to examine and explain why similar laws may have very different effects and consequences in different jurisdictions because of the operation of domestic background factors, including those that influence the law in action. The evolution of counter-terrorism law since 9/11 also provides an excellent vehicle to examine migration as a more complex process over time that involves multiple actors,[10] including those operating at the supra-national level.

Comparative lawyers should be attentive to substantive borrowing as concepts developed in administrative fields, such as freezing the assets of suspected terrorists,[11] or in the intelligence field,[12] such as watchlisting, migrate into the criminal law. They

9 Victor V. Ramraj "The Impossibility of Global Anti-Terrorism Law?" in Ramraj *Global Anti-Terrorism Law and Policy* supra.

10 Margit Cohn "Legal Transplant Chronicles" (2010) 58 *American Journal of Comparative Law* 583.

11 Laura Donohue "Transplantation" in Ramraj *Global Anti-Terrorism Law and Policy*.

12 Kent Roach "Terrorism" in Markus Dubber and Tatjana Hornle eds. *The Oxford Handbook of Criminal Law* (Oxford: Oxford University Press, 2014).

also need to be aware that the migration of even identical laws from one country may have very different effects once those laws are transplanted into a different legal, political, or social environment.[13] The study of migration of law, unlike earlier studies of legal transplants, does not load the dice toward convergence, but instead facilitates an examination of the competing pulls of the universal and the particular.

In short, the study of comparative counter-terrorism law has a practical value because of the fluid and international nature of both terrorism and counter-terrorism. International terrorism may be global, but borders still matter in how we respond to terrorism. Courts determining whether counter-terrorism laws impose justified and proportionate limits on human rights are often interested in the laws used in other countries. Counter-terrorism co-operation means we need to understand how many other nations practice counter-terrorism.

The rapid development of counter-terrorism law since the 9/11 attacks and more recently the rise of foreign terrorist fighters makes the field an important one to advance our approach to the study of comparative law. The study of comparative counter-terrorism law forces us to break down neat distinctions among criminal, administrative, constitutional and international law that have persisted in the academic study of law, but which are blurred in practice. The high publicity that often accompanies acts of terrorism and counter-terrorism also allow comparative lawyers who focus on terrorism to examine the law in action as well as the law on the books. Finally, counter-terrorism law is an excellent field to critically evaluate the processes of migration and harmonization that are crucial to so many fields of comparative law.

B. A *Common but Flexible Format for Country Reports*

A traditional practice in comparative law is to ask national reporters to respond to detailed questionnaires about the laws of their specific country. This approach does not require national reporters to be expert in the laws of other countries. This facilitates the accumulation of information about many countries and allows readers to make their own comparisons. At the same time, the questionnaire can obscure important questions of context and can present a misleading impression of the respective importance of various measures. It can also frustrate the project of comparing different jurisdictions.

The questionnaire approach used for the national reports contained in this volume attempted to address some of the shortcomings of the traditional approach. The authors were asked to comment on the experience of terrorism in their country

[13] Andrew Lynch "Control Orders in Australia: A Further Case Study of the Migration of British Counter-Terrorism Law" (2008) 8 *Oxford Universities Commonwealth Law Journal* 159.

in order to provide context. They were also asked to report where possible not only on the enactment of laws but their actual use. Many countries report little experience with terrorism and few terrorism prosecutions, but the enactment of many counter-terrorism laws.

The authors were also asked to address the extent to which new counter-terrorism laws were enacted in response to various supra-national demands and whether they were influenced by other countries. The result hopefully will give readers a fuller picture of the process of migration and harmonization and provide material to make judgments about what laws were enacted mainly to satisfy supra-national demands and what laws have actually been used.

In order to ensure that the reports reflect on the full range of comparative counter-terrorism instruments, reporters were asked to comment on criminal law, immigration law, administrative measures, military and extra-territorial measures used for counter-terrorism measures.[14] In some cases, most notably with respect to military and administrative measures, this resulted in report of no or minimal use of such measures in their countries. This in itself represents an important finding.

The breadth of the questionnaire also allows for an examination of how some counter-terrorism actions, such as targeted killing by the United States, may have substituted for other practices such as military detention and trial.

Each chapter includes a detailed discussion of how terrorism is defined in that country's law. The definition of terrorism lies at the heart of terrorism laws both in defining various offences and special investigative powers. The next part examines criminal offences against terrorism, including both terrorism-specific offences and those available under the ordinary criminal law. It would be a mistake to ignore the role of the ordinary criminal law in countering terrorism, and indeed some countries such as Brazil and Japan rely almost exclusively on the ordinary law. This part of each chapter will also discuss the actual use of terrorism laws in terrorism prosecutions. This glimpse of the law in action will reveal that while some countries have many terrorism prosecutions, such prosecutions are extremely rare in other countries.

Each country reporter then examines the investigative powers available in terrorism cases with an emphasis on whether they depart from ordinary investigative powers available to police and prosecutors. Many countries, especially in continental Europe, rely on investigative powers available in ordinary criminal cases, though some countries such as China, Portugal and South Africa have special investigative powers for organized crime that can also be used in terrorism investigations.

The related topics of the proscription and listing of terrorist groups and individuals associated with terrorism and the regulation of terrorism financing are next examined

[14] A copy of the questionnaire given to national reporters is contained in the appendix of this volume.

in each chapter. Terrorism financing regimes that rely on the private sector reporting of suspicious transactions and the freezing of assets must rely on the administrative expedient of lists of suspected terrorists. The fairness of the use of secret intelligence to compile such terrorist blacklists has increasingly been challenged. Each chapter examines the available evidence about the enforcement of terrorism financing laws. We hope this places readers in a position to evaluate both the propriety and efficacy of the elaborate terrorism financing regimes.

The next two sections of each chapter examine the use of administrative measures, with the first section being devoted to the use of immigration law as anti-terrorism law and the second examining the role of the military, including the related question of extra-territorial counter-terrorism activities. As will be seen, there are significant differences within the twenty-two countries examined in this collection in the use of less restrained alternatives to the criminal law to combat terrorism.[15] Even if we may be moving towards one global counter-terrorism law (and there is considerable evidence of divergence), the actual reliance that each nation places on this formal law would be different.

One of the weaknesses of the questionnaire approach is its tendency to focus on the formal law. In an attempt to counteract this weakness, national reporters were asked where possible to describe real cases where counter-terrorism laws were applied and to use available statistical data to capture the use of counter-terrorism laws. In many countries, such statistics are not readily available in part because of the secrecy of many counter-terrorism activities. Nevertheless, the data presented in the national reports contained in this volume present interesting information especially with respect to terrorism financing, which has been a particular focus of many post-9/11 counter-terrorism laws. As will be seen, most countries have terrorism financing laws, and financial intelligence units often report many suspicious transactions. At the same time, most of suspicious transaction reports relate to suspected money laundering and not terrorism financing. Moreover, many countries have recorded few if any terrorism financing convictions. This provides vital information about the law in action that can help assist in making judgments about the success of terrorism financing laws based on listings. These findings are especially important given that the Security Council has recently in Resolution 2178 confirmed its commitment and significant investment in terrorist listing and travel and financing bans as a means to combat foreign terrorist fighters joining the Islamic State.

Another weakness of the questionnaire approach is its tendency to downplay the author's own assessment of the importance of various measures and of the values

[15] Kent Roach "The Criminal Law and Its Less Restrained Alternatives" in Ramraj ed. *Global Anti-Terrorism Law and Policy*.

that are represented in the law. The questionnaire attempted to respond to these potential shortcomings by asking each national reporter to reflect on the influences of his or her country's counter-terrorism law and to make evaluative judgments about whether the country's laws reflect the appropriate balance of competing state interests in preventing terrorism and respecting human rights. The length of each chapter was expanded beyond the norm in order to facilitate some of the more demanding aspects of the questionnaire used to compile this collection.

The questionnaire format will also be reflected in the last chapter of this collection that compares and synthesizes the information provided in the chapters based on the national reports and discusses common challenges and themes. As will be seen, I have not hesitated to make evaluative and normative conclusions even in cases where national reporters were more reticent in doing so.

C. *Counter-Terrorism Law and Supra-National Influences*

Although counter-terrorism law reflects a country's own history and experience with terrorism, it is increasingly influenced by the demands of supra-national institutions, such as the United Nations Security Council and the Financial Action Task Force (FATF), and regional bodies, such as the Council of Europe. These supra-national demands for counter-terrorism laws have increased since the 9/11 terrorist attacks on the United States. Many of the chapters in the collection report that a desire to comply with international and regional mandates has been the prime motivation behind the enactment of many counter-terrorism laws. At the same time, however, other states, including the United States, the United Kingdom, Israel and Colombia, seem to be primarily motivated by responding to their own country's traumatic experiences with terrorism. Brazil emerges as an outlier in this collection that has so far resisted supra-national demands that it enact counter-terrorism law despite the increased pressure brought on that country as host of the 2014 World Cup and 2016 Olympics. With an increase in recent terrorist attacks in China, that country has proposed a sweeping draft anti-terrorism law in November 2014. It responds to domestic issues with Uighurs in Xinjiang, but also uses concepts of targeting "threats," "speech" and attempts to "influence" the government taken from Western anti-terrorism law as well as the concept of "extremism" referred to in Security Council Resolution 2178, albeit without the qualification in the Resolution that the extremism must be "violent."

The authors in this collection have been asked to reflect on the influence of such supra-national influences on their countries' counter-terrorism law, and many have concluded that their countries laws, especially those enacted after 9/11, are a direct response to such supra-national pressures. A particularly strong theme in chapters dealing with European countries is the influence of 2002 and 2008 Framework Decisions on counter-terrorism law.[16] The role of these Framework Decisions raise important issues about the desirability of harmonization of counter-terrorism law, which often impinges on domestic constitutional norms and domestic democratic debate.

The tension between the values of harmonization and international good citizenship and between allowing each country to shape its counter-terrorism laws in accord with its own experience and its own democratic and constitutional demands is particularly intense with respect to supra-national initiatives that are intended to be mandatory. These including Security Council Resolutions enacted under Chapter VII of the United Nations Charter and EU Framework Decisions. The tensions between the universal and the particular are also present in cases where states voluntarily borrow from the counter-terrorism laws of other countries.

D. *Counter-Terrorism and Human Rights*

Counter-terrorism law is also complex and interesting because state efforts to prevent terrorism inevitably raise questions about the need to preserve a wide range of human rights. These include most basic rights, including the right to be free from torture and degrading treatment. As is well known, these basic rights were violated by some post-9/11 counter-terrorism activities. They include extreme interrogation in a number of venues, including in the American military base at Guantanamo Bay, Cuba, and in American "black sites" in European states such as Poland. They also include extraordinary and extra-legal rendition of terrorist suspects to a number of countries such as Egypt and Syria that are notorious for torturing suspected Islamic extremist terrorists. All countries continue to struggle with torture issues, and as will be seen, they do not all take the same position on their obligations not to deport people to face torture. For example, Canada has reserved the right to deport a suspected terrorist to face torture in other countries in "exceptional circumstances,"[17] while the European Court of Human Rights has maintained the absolute ban on refoulement to torture[18] while also showing increased interest in the possibility of deportation with assurances[19] despite the difficulty of monitoring and enforcing such assurances.

Offences against membership and participation in terrorist groups raise issues of the appropriate balance between preventing terrorism and respecting expressive and associational freedoms. Demands to use intelligence as evidence but to keep it

[16] There is a growing literature on EU counter-terrorism. See for example Cian Murphy *EU Counter-Terrorism Law Pre-Emption and the Rule of Law* (Oxford: Hart, 2012); Maria O'Neill *The Evolving EU Counter-Terrorism Legal Framework* (London: Routledge, 2012).

[17] Suresh v. Canada [2002] 1 S.C.R. 3 at para 78.

[18] Saadi v. Italy [2008] ECHR 179.

[19] Othman v. The United Kingdom (2012) ECHR 817.

secret raise questions of fair trials in both criminal and administrative proceedings. Counter-terrorism offences relating to the incitement or provocation of terrorism raise issues concerning freedom of expression. Not all the authors in the collection agree on whether such laws strike an appropriate balance between freedom of expression and the compelling state interest in preventing terrorism. The recent rise of the Islamic State in parts of Syria and Iraq and the many people from Western democracies who have been recruited to the organization's brutal cause may well result in democracies strengthening measures against extremism, including those that target expression. There will be a need to evaluate such measures both with respect to their compliance with human rights and democratic freedoms but also with respect to their efficacy. The possibility that some counter-terrorism measures may be counterproductive should not be discounted.

The protection of human rights involves the separation of powers and interactions among the judiciary, the executive and the legislature. International and regional bodies dominated by the executive have often asked states to enforce travel bans and asset freezes on listed terrorist groups and individuals, but some affected persons have challenged such listings on the basis that they have been made without a fair hearing.[20] The courts have made a number of important decisions vindicating human rights in the post-9/11 era, but they have not always had the last word when they have done so. Indeed, legislatures and executives have often been quick to assert the need for robust measures to prevent terrorism. These episodes allow comparative lawyers to study important and high-stakes dialogues or interactions between courts and governments.

E. *Multiple Counter-Terrorism Instruments and Substitution Effects*

The multiple instruments available to states to prevent terrorism also create a risk that states will simply shift emphasis from one counter-terrorism instrument to another if the protection of human rights makes any particular instrument difficult to employ. As will be seen, the courts have insisted on some human rights standards with respect to military detention and trial at Guantanamo Bay, but in recent years there appears to be a shift in American counter-terrorism policy towards increased use of targeted killing, a practice that so far has resisted judicial review. The United Kingdom has placed less emphasis on administrative measures such as control orders after the courts restricted the duration of such measures and their use of secret evidence. Increased regulation of surveillance by public authorities may lead to more reliance on the state's ability to use information collected and held by

[20] Kadi I 2008 C 402 /05 P; Kadi II (2013) Joined Cases C-584/10 P, C-593/10 P and C-595/10 P.

private companies. The multiple and shifting instruments used to prevent terrorism makes counter-terrorism law particularly dynamic.

The use of private telecommunications systems for counter-terrorism purposes is not the first use of the private sector as an instrument of counter-terrorism. Since 9/11, there has been a global explosion of attempts to regulate terrorism financing, and most terrorism financing schemes effectively deputize financial institutions to collect information about the financial dealings of suspected terrorists. The ability of governments to use multiple departments of government, transnational alliances and the private sector to combat terrorism strains traditional accountability mechanisms for state conduct perhaps to the breaking point.[21]

F. *The Experimental Nature of Post-9/11 Counter-Terrorism Law*

Some recent counter-terrorism law has taken on an experimental character that has challenged a number of traditional distinctions. For example, distinctions between intelligence that must generally be kept secret in order to protect sources and methods and evidence that must generally be made public and subject to adversarial challenge have eroded in many jurisdictions. New institutions such as the use of security-cleared lawyers to challenge secret evidence have emerged in the United Kingdom and Canada, but remain controversial.

The criminal law has been expanded in an attempt to prevent terrorism, but in a manner that leaves some wondering whether what remains is truly criminal law or a new preventive form of "enemy criminal law."[22] The new criminal law criminalizes associations and preparation that are remote from acts of violent terrorism and that verge on status crime. It also builds on broad definitions of terrorism and the assertion of universal jurisdiction. Broad criminal laws designed to prevent even remote risks of terrorism combined with the understandable need to denounce and deter violent terrorism also challenge theories of proportionate punishment. At times, the new criminal law incorporates executive determinations of the enemy in the form of terrorist listings.

Another form of "enemy criminal law" may be the use of immigration law as anti-terrorism law, including long-term detention of non-citizens suspected of terrorism, possible refoulement to a risk of torture or degrading treatment. As will be discussed in the last chapter, some of the technologies of immigration law are now

[21] This issue will be examined Kent Roach "Thematic Conclusions and Future Challenges" infra Chapter 24 infra 688–92.

[22] Gunther Jakobs "On the Theory of Enemy Criminal Law" at http://www.law-lib.utoronto.ca/bclc/crimweb/foundation/Jakobs%20current.pdf, translated version of "Zur Theorie des Feindstrafrechts," in Henning Rosenau & Sanyun Kim eds. *Straftheorie und Strafgerechtigkeit* (*Augsburger Studien zum Internationalen Recht*, vol. 7), 2010, at 167–82.

being applied by states to their citizens in response to the rise of foreign terrorist fighters primarily associated with the Islamic State. Such measures include various forms of travel restrictions, including passport revocations that are designed to prevent radicalized citizens from travelling to Iraq, Syria or other places where foreign terrorist fighters train and fight. There are increased attempts to strip citizenship so that even citizens can be deported. Finally, various measures are being invented to prevent citizens from returning home from foreign terrorist fights or to monitor their re-entry.[23] These are all forms of experimental law in which nations seek to treat their citizens in ways that have previously been reserved for non-citizens. It remains to be seen whether courts will resist such experimental law. They may to the extent that such new counter-measures restrict traditional freedoms, such as the right to travel, or result in state complicity in exposing citizens to mistreatment or death in foreign lands. Such judicial decisions will produce legislative and administrative replies, including the substitution of some counter-terrorism measures with others.

Traditional distinctions between the law of crime and the law of war have also been challenged. Both Israel's 2002 Unlawful Combatants Law and the 2006 and 2009 Military Commissions Act in the United States are based on the implicit premise that terrorists and their supporters are a third category separate from the traditional law of war categories of combatant and civilians. The post-9/11 US war on terror has blurred traditional distinctions between the law of war and law of crime in a manner that has, at times, dispensed with the safeguards of both forms of law. As will be seen, the courts have been somewhat resistant to some of this experimentation and have asserted habeas corpus review over the Guantanamo detentions and invalidated some of the non-traditional war crimes, such as conspiracy and material support for terrorism, that the United States claimed could be subject to military trial.[24] The experimental nature of much recent counter-terrorism laws helps explain both its dynamic nature and its adverse impact on human rights.

III. THE CENTRALITY OF THE DEFINITION OF TERRORISM IN COUNTER-TERRORISM LAW

A recurring issue in all counter-terrorism law is the difficulty – or, some would argue, the impossibility – of defining terrorism in a legally and politically satisfactory manner. The United Nations has long struggled with the difficulty of whether to include state terrorism and whether to exempt freedom fighters from a general definition of

[23] See the UK's Counter-Terrorism and Security Act, 2015 c. 6 ss.1–15 providing for passport seizure and renewable temporary exclusion orders with controlled re-entry conditions as discussed in Chapter 24, "Thematic Conclusions and Future Challenges" infra at 745.

[24] Chapter 2, "United States" infra at 68.

terrorism. For this reason, the international community has only prohibited specific acts of terrorism such as hijackings and hostage takings in various international conventions. Some countries somewhat similarly rely on predicate offences or even the international conventions themselves in their definitions of terrorism. Nevertheless, many countries have enacted much broader general definitions of terrorism.

Article 2(1) of the 1999 International Convention on the Suppression of the Financing of Terrorism contains a general definition of terrorism as acts covered by the specific conventions or:

> any other act intended to cause death or serious bodily injury to a civilian, or to any other person not taking an active part in the hostilities in a situation of armed conflict, when the purpose of such act, by its nature or context, is to intimidate a population, or to compel a government or an international organization to do or to abstain from doing any act.[25]

After 9/11, the Security Council used its mandatory Chapter VII powers in Resolution 1373 to require all states to ensure that terrorism and terrorism financing be treated as serious crimes. The Security Council, however, did not attempt to define terrorism or promote the preceding rather restrained general definition of terrorism. It essentially allowed each state the freedom to enact its own definitions of terrorism. In 2004, the Security Council did provide some guidance for defining terrorism in Resolution 1566, but by that time many states as well as the EU Council had opted for definitions that were broader than the 1566 definition, which focused on criminal acts causing death or serious bodily injury or taking hostages in order to provoke a state of terror, intimidate a population or compel a government or international organization to act.[26]

In September 2014, the Security Council again used its Chapter VII powers in Resolution 2178 to call on all nations to ensure that the "perpetration, planning, or preparation of, or participation in, terrorist acts, or the providing or receiving of terrorist training" are "serious criminal offences."[27] The Resolution called for many other measures including listing of terrorists and travel bans to stop the movement of "foreign terrorist fighters." It also affirmed the expansion of counter-terrorism law and listing to include those who use "information and communications technologies"[28] to recruit terrorists. As with Resolution 1373, terrorism was still not defined. Indeed, the Security Council did not even bother to recall its previous attempts at definition in Resolution 1566. Resolution 2178 increases definitional ambiguity by targeting not only all undefined "terrorism," including presumably

[25] U.N. Doc. A/RES/54/109; 39 ILM 270 (2000).
[26] S/Res/1566 (2004) at para 3.
[27] S/Res/2178 at para 6.
[28] Ibid at para 7.

domestic terrorism, but also "violent extremism" and "radicalization."[29] Broad definitions of terrorism, especially those linked with the even vaguer concepts of extremism and radicalization mentioned in Resolution 2178, will increase the risk that dissenters will be investigated and punished as terrorists. This may undermine the legitimacy of some counter-terrorism efforts.

A. *Comparative Law in Action: The Global Migration of Three Influential Definitions of Terrorism*

Although a few states such as Japan looked to the 1999 International Financing Convention for guidance as it defined terrorism while enacting a 2002 law against terrorism financing,[30] many other states looked elsewhere for guidance on how to define terrorism. This process underlines the importance of the study of comparative counter-terrorism law as countries borrowed aspects of other countries' definitions of terrorism while often making changes to suit their own circumstances.

Three definitions of terrorism appear to have been extremely influential. One was a broad definition of terrorism found in the UK's Terrorism Act, 2000, which influenced many definitions of terrorism in the Commonwealth of states associated with the former British Empire. As will be seen, however, states such as Australia and Canada adapted the British definition to their own circumstances and constitutional norms. Other states such as Malaysia and Pakistan also borrowed from the UK's Terrorism Act, 2000, but placed elements of that definition into a very different and more repressive context than found in the United Kingdom.

Egypt's 1992 definition of terrorism was influential in the Arab world, in part by influencing regional definitions of terrorism such as the Arab Convention on the Suppression of Terrorism. The Egyptian definition is notable because of its breadth and vagueness and its ability to be used to target dissenters. As will be seen, many countries influenced by the Egyptian example also defined terrorism in a manner that criminalized speech and peaceful dissent and secessionist movements.

Another influential definition of terrorism is found in a 2002 Framework Decision of the European Union Council. It contained a broad definition of terrorism, with concerns about capturing legitimate expressive and associational activities being relegated to the preamble. Many European countries simply copied this definition into their laws in an attempt at harmonization. At the same time, some European countries, including Germany, Italy and the United Kingdom, have not done so. This raises interesting questions about competing interests in convergence and

[29] Ibid at para 16.

[30] Chapter 20, "Japan" infra at 570.

divergence and whether complete European harmonization of counter-terrorism law is possible or desirable.

The focus on the migration of three influential definitions facilitates a variety of comparisons. They facilitate a "most similar case" approach that allows small differences to be identified among countries in the EU and the Commonwealth and among Arab and Middle Eastern countries that were influenced by the three definitions. At the same time, comparison between these groups, especially those between Arab and Middle Eastern countries and more established democracies, follows a "most different case" approach that is particularly useful in identifying a global trend to broader definitions of terrorism. Finally, I will examine a few countries that are "outliers" to the global trend towards broad definitions of terrorism.[31] American definitions of terrorism tied to particular predicate offences were surprisingly not influential and more restrained than many other definitions. Brazil and China will also be examined as important outliers because they have yet to define terrorism in their domestic law.

B. *The Influence of the United Kingdom's Terrorism Act, 2000*

As Keith Syrett reminds us in Chapter 6, a concern about politically motivated violence has long been a concern in the United Kingdom. The modern British experience with terrorism was formulated in the context of the Irish troubles where over 3500 deaths were incurred between 1969 and 2001. During this time, the UK used a fairly minimalist definition of terrorism that focused on violence for political ends. This definition also included violence for the purpose of putting any section of the public in a state of fear.[32]

In 2000, the UK opted for a greatly expanded definition that would prove to be extremely influential, especially in the Commonwealth of former British colonies. Section 1 of the Terrorism Act, 2000,[33] as enacted, provided:

In this Act "terrorism" means the use or threat of action where –

(a) the action falls within subsection (2),
(b) the use or threat is designed to influence the government or to intimidate the public or a section of the public, and
(c) the use or threat is made for the purpose of advancing a political, religious or ideological cause.
(2) Action falls within this subsection if it –

[31] These strategies are identified and discussed in Hirschl *Comparative Matters* supra at 244–67.
[32] Prevention of Terrorism (Temporary Provisions) Act 1989, s.20(1).
[33] c.11.

(a) involves serious violence against a person,
(b) involves serious damage to property,
(c) endangers a person's life, other than that of the person committing the action,
(d) creates a serious risk to the health or safety of the public or a section of the public, or
(e) is designed seriously to interfere with or seriously to disrupt an electronic system.
(3) The use or threat of action falling within subsection (2) which involves the use of firearms or explosives is terrorism whether or not subsection (1)(b) is satisfied.
(4) In this section –
(a) "action" includes action outside the United Kingdom,
(b) a reference to any person or to property is a reference to any person, or to property, wherever situated,
(c) a reference to the public includes a reference to the public of a country other than the United Kingdom, and
(d) "the government" means the government of the United Kingdom, of a Part of the United Kingdom or of a country other than the United Kingdom.
(5) In this Act a reference to action taken for the purposes of terrorism includes a reference to action taken for the benefit of a proscribed organisation.

In a signal to the emphasis placed in many laws on preventing terrorism, this definition includes not only actions, but the undefined concept of a "threat of action." It includes actions designed not only to intimidate the public but "to influence the government." It singles out religiously and politically motivated actions, including those that only involve serious damage to property or any use of firearms or explosives or serious interferences with electronic systems. It also includes any "action taken for the benefit of a proscribed organization" as a form of terrorism. As will be seen, a number of countries provided some exemptions for protesters, strikers and freedom fighters even while adopting the broad British definition.

The British definition includes terrorism aimed at influencing all governments. The UK Supreme Court in *R. v. Gul*[34] has recognized with some regret that this provides protection for the most repressive governments. The problem of drawing a line between freedom fighters and terrorists is well known, but the Terrorism Act, 2000, did not attempt to draw such a line. In the course of upholding the nine-hour detention of a man suspected of involvement in the Edward Snowden leaks, a British court has concluded that politically motivated leaks of information also fall within the broad definition of terrorism if they endanger life.[35]

[34] 2013 UKSC 64 [62–7].
[35] Miranda v. SSHD [2014] EWHC 255.

The British definition did not until 2006[36] include attempts to influence international governmental organizations even though such actions are included in many international conventions. In 2008, the definition was amended to include the actions taken pursuant to a "racial" as well as a "political, religious or ideological cause."[37] These terms are vague. As will be seen, the EU Council encouraged European states to distinguish terrorism from ordinary crime without relying on proof of political or religious motive, but the British template proved influential in parts of Africa, Asia and the Caribbean as well as Australia and Canada. Views are divided on the religious and political motive requirement, with some arguing that it reflects the reality of terrorism and restrains the ambit of terrorism laws, and others arguing that it can encourage the investigation of Islamic radicals who may share political or religious views with terrorists but are not prepared to engage in violence.[38] Supra-national definitions have generally avoided reference to political or religious motive, but the Security Council's focus in Resolution 2178 on "violent extremism" and "radicalization" has religious overtones.

Many countries in the former British Empire and current members of the Commonwealth were influenced by the broad definition of terrorism contained in s.1 of the Terrorism Act, 2000. This definition had the advantage of being brand new after 9/11. It also benefited from the reputation of the UK as a steady and experienced hand with terrorism. The migration of the UK definition, however, was very much a voluntary process and can be contrasted with the more hierarchical process used by the EU Council to impose the broad definition of terrorism contained in the 2002 Framework Decision. The voluntary process of migration and transplantation is of special interest because it reveals how countries can shape definitions of terrorism to their own legal, political and social conditions.

As Robert Diab makes clear in Chapter 3,[39] Canada was influenced by the UK's Terrorism Act, 2000, as it quickly enacted its first Anti-Terrorism Act in December 2001. In addition to a provision incorporating various offences that applied outside Canada to the extent that those offences implemented Canada's international commitments with respect to various conventions against terrorism, Canada enacted a general definition similar to s.1 of the Terrorism Act, 2000.

At the same time, there were some important differences. Canada would require that terrorist actions be designed to "compel" governments or international

[36] Terrorism Act 2006 c. 11 s.34.

[37] Terrorism Act 2008 c. 28 s.75.

[38] Compare Ben Saul "The Curious Element of Motive in Definitions of Terrorism" and Kent Roach "The Case for Defining Terrorism with Restraint and Without Reference to Political or Religious Motive" in Andrew Lynch et al. eds. *Law and Liberty in the War on Terror* (Sydney: Federation Press, 2008).

[39] Chapter 3, "Canada" infra at 80ff.

organizations, whereas the British definition only required that they be designed to "influence" governments. Canada took a more restrained approach to property damage and provided that politically or religiously motivated property damage would be considered terrorism only if it endangered life. This provision should be read in conjunction with a Canadian innovation of providing an exemption for protests and strikes that did not endanger human life. This exemption was likely devised in the knowledge that protests and strikes would be protected under Canada's constitutional bill of rights and that the government would have to justify the proportionality of any restrictions on fundamental freedoms. The terrorism bill as originally introduced in mid-October 2001 exempted only lawful protests and strikes, but was amended to exempt all protests and strikes that did not endanger life by the time the bill became law in December 2001. This demonstrates the importance of democratic debate about terrorism laws, a debate that may be restrained by the more mandatory nature of the EU Framework Decisions examined later in this chapter.

The Canadian law also included an interpretative clause that the expression of political or religious belief would generally not constitute a terrorist activity. This sensitivity could be related to widespread concerns about religious and racial profiling in Canada as well as Canada's constitutional commitments to protect both fundamental freedoms and multiculturalism. In 2006, a trial judge in the first prosecution under Canada's new Anti-Terrorism Act found that the requirement of proof of religious and political motive was a disproportionate and unnecessary limit on freedom of expression and freedom of religion. This ruling was reversed by the Supreme Court of Canada. It ruled that fundamental freedoms would not protect terrorist-related activities.[40] The Canadian interpretative clause designed to affirm expressive and religious freedoms has not been influential in legislation adopted in other countries. At the same time, many definitions of terrorism, including those in international conventions, European Union definitions and those used in many Islamic states, as well as in states such as Singapore, with a large Muslim minority, do not use political or religious motive as a means of differentiating terrorism from other crimes.

The Canadian experience also reveals how many countries employ multiple definitions of terrorism as they use different forms of law to combat terrorism. In 2002, the Supreme Court of Canada adopted the general definition of terrorism in the 1999 Terrorism Financing Convention into an undefined reference to terrorism in Canadian immigration law that was being used to detain and deport suspected terrorists.[41] This international definition was more restrained than Canada's 2001 criminal law definition because it focused on causing death or serious injury to

[40] R. v. Khawaja [2012] 3 S.C.R. 555.

[41] Suresh v. Canada [2002] 1 S.C.R. 3.

those not involved in armed conflict. The adoption of such a restrained definition may reflect the judiciary's particular concern with human rights. As will be seen, the general definition in the 1999 Convention has not found much favor in legislatures that have adopted their own definitions of terrorism, though as will be seen it was used in a 2007 Slovenian law on money laundering and terrorism financing. Slovenia, like Canada, uses the 1999 Convention definition in one law but not its main Penal Code.[42]

Canada's 2001 Anti-Terrorism Act was more expansive than the UK's Terrorism Act, 2000, in one respect. The reference to serious interference or disruption of electronic services in the UK act was expanded in the Canadian law to apply to serious interference and disruption "of an essential service, facility or system, whether public or private...."[43] This expansion was influential, and similar phrases occur in counter-terrorism laws enacted in Australia in 2002[44] and in South Africa in 2004.[45] The Canadian law, like the UK law, was influential as many other countries scrambled after 9/11 to enact their own laws against terrorism and terrorism financing and found that these laws assisted them in confronting the challenges of defining terrorism.[46]

The Canadian approach to providing an exemption for protests and strikes was also influential. It appears in subsequent anti-terrorism laws enacted in Australia, Bahamas, Kenya, South Africa and Tanzania. Fergal Davis, Nicola McGarrity and George Williams argue that much of Australia's explosion of aggressive post-9/11 counter-terrorism legislation can be explained in part by the absence of a constitutional bill of rights.[47] The Australian adoption of the Canadian protest and strike exemption may, however, be something of an exception, though it too can perhaps be explained by a willingness of Australian courts to protect freedom of expression as a constitutional value. The Green Party and independent reviewers have expressed reservations about the Australian definition, including its reference to "threats of harm," the requirement for proof of political or religious motive and the absence of any exemptions for armed conflict governed by international law. Nevertheless, the broad Australian definition remains unchanged.

[42] Chapter 14, "Slovenia" infra at 402.
[43] Criminal Code of Canada s.83.01(b)(ii) (E).
[44] Chapter 23, "Australia" infra at 651.
[45] Chapter 19, "South Africa" infra at 545.
[46] On the concept of laws being at hand and countries engaging in a form of bricolage when drafting laws, see Mark Tushnet "The Possibilities of Comparative Constitutional Law" (1999) 108 *Yale L.J.* 1225; Kent Roach "Sources and Trends in Post 9/11 Anti-Terrorism Laws" in Benjamin Goold and Liora Lazarus eds. *Security and Human Rights* (Oxford: Hart, 2007).
[47] Chapter 23, "Australia" infra at 680.

The Australian experience with a broad definition of terrorism as well as other aggressive investigative powers and administrative measures reveals the difficulty of amending terrorism laws to take a more restrained approach. To be sure, there are some notable examples of recent repeal of broad terrorism laws, including the UK's repeal in 2005 of a 2001 law providing for indeterminate detention of non-citizens suspected of terrorism, India's repeal in 2004 of its Prevention of Terrorism Act, 2000, and Malaysia's 2012 repeal of its Internal Security Act. In all of these cases, however, legislatures have subsequently enacted other terrorism laws to fill the perceived void. One recurring theme in this collection is the profound degree of legislative activism in counter-terrorism law as legislatures enact multiple and overlapping terrorism laws both to reassure the public and to respond to international and regional demands for counter-terrorism laws.

a. South Africa's Surprising Acceptance of a Broad Definition of Terrorism

If any country might have resisted the global post 9/11 demand for counter-terrorism laws, it might have been South Africa. Apartheid-era South Africa featured a broad terrorism offence under an Internal Security Act[48] that defined terrorism to include the commission, aiding, threatening, advising or encouraging of violence to "overthrow or endanger state authority in the Republic"; to achieve or promote "any constitutional, political, industrial, social, or economic aim or change"; to induce the government to act; or to "put in fear or demoralize the general public" or "induce" the public or part thereof to "do or to abstain from doing any act." Chapter 19 by Jamil Ddamulira Mujuzi indicates how despite the historical use of terrorism offences against the African National Congress (ANC), South Africa enacted broad terrorism offences in 2004. Indeed, South Africa has some of the broadest definitions of terrorism, at least among countries influenced by the Terrorism Act, 2000.

The 2004 law stressed South Africa's international commitments to combat terrorism, but its definition of terrorist activity drew heavily on the UK's Terrorism Act, 2000, by requiring proof of "political, religious, ideological or philosophical motive" and by requiring intimidation of the public. It also required undue compulsion of a government or international organization, something as will be seen that is also required under the 2002 EU Framework Decision and is more restrained than the controversial reference to influencing governments in the UK legislation.

South Africa also expanded terrorist purposes to include those that could "reasonably be regarded as being intended.... to threaten the unity and territorial integrity of the Republic."[49] As will be seen, threats to national unity are also

48 Law No 74 of 1982 s.54(1).

49 Protection of Constitutional Democracy Act s. 1 (xxv)(b) (i).

included in the definition of terrorism of some Arab states, including states in North Africa. They create a risk, however, that even peaceful secessionist movements may be investigated, tried and punished as terrorists. Proposed security legislation in Hong Kong would have criminalized secession as well as treason, sedition and subversion, but was withdrawn in 2003 after widespread public protests.[50] A proposed anti-terrorism law released by China in 2014, however, includes within its definition of terrorism attempts "to divide the country by means of violence, destruction or intimidation,"[51] raising concerns that if enacted it could be used to put down secessionist movements in Xianjing or Tibet.

The South African definition included all politically motivated property damage, as did the Terrorism Act, 2000. Although s.1(3) of the South African act has a Canadian-style exemption for protests and strikes, it is narrower than the Canadian law because it does not exclude intentional and politically motivated substantial damage to property. The reference to interference with electronic systems in the Terrorism Act is, as in the Canadian law, expanded in the South African law to include serious interference with all essential services, facilities or systems whether private or public. South Africa also added causing "any major economic loss" and creating "a serious public emergency situation or a general insurrection in the Republic" as prohibited harms.[52] The reference to emergencies may, however, be restrained by South Africa's widely praised constitutional restrictions on declarations of emergencies.

Other vague harms prohibited in the South African law include, as in Canada, harms to "economic security,"[53] a neo-liberal phrase that complements the criminalization of damage to private critical infrastructure as well as a reference to actions causing "feelings of insecurity."[54] It is somewhat surprising that a country with both a recent history of abuse of terrorism laws and a constitutional bill of rights would enact such vague and sweeping provisions. It may well be that these terms if ever used in a terrorism prosecution in South Africa would be invalidated or at least read narrowly by the South African Constitutional Court.[55] As will be seen, however, there has only been one use of South Africa's broad law since its

[50] Fu Hualing, Carole Petersen and Simon Young *National Security and Fundamental Freedoms: Hong Kong's Article 23 Under Scrutiny* (Hong Kong: Hong Kong University Press, 2005).

[51] Human Rights Watch "China Draft Counterterrorism law a recipe for abuse" January 20, 2015 at http://www.hrw.org/news/2015/01/20/china-draft-counterterrorism-law-recipe-abuses.

[52] Ibid s.1 (xvv) (a) vi and vii.

[53] Ibid s. 1(1)(b) (ii).

[54] Ibid s.1(1)(b) (ii).

[55] Kent Roach "A Comparison of South African and Canadian Anti-Terrorism Legislation" (2005) 18(2) *South African Journal of Criminal Justice* 127 at 136.

enactment in 2004,[56] suggesting that the law may have been intended primarily for external consumption.

b. South Africa's Distinct Freedom Fighter Exemption

An important focus in the study of comparative law is an assessment of the respective influence of forces that favour convergence and harmonization of the law and forces that push towards divergence and diversity based on the distinct experiences of different countries. South Africa's enactment of a broad anti-terrorism law in 2004 demonstrates the pressures that all countries, including those with many reasons to be suspicious about the abuse of terrorism laws, were under to respond to post 9/11 global demands to combat terrorism. At the same time, however, we are far from a future where there is one harmonized global anti-terrorism law, and South Africa's distinct history is reflected in a broad freedom fighter exemption. Section 1(4) of the Protection of Constitutional Democracy Act exempts:

> any act committed during a struggle waged by peoples, including any action during an armed struggle, in the exercise or furtherance of their legitimate right to national liberation, self-determination and independence against colonialism, or occupation or aggression or domination by alien or foreign forces, in accordance with the principles of international law....

This section reflects the history of the ANC going from being a proscribed terrorist organization to South Africa's governing party. To my knowledge, this exemption for freedom fighters acting for "national liberation, self-determination and independence against colonialism" or against occupation and aggression by foreign powers is quite unique.

Most of the counter-terrorism laws examined in this collection do not have exemptions for freedom fighters or even armed conflict. Switzerland, Greece and Canada have much more limited exemptions than South Africa's. Canada's exemption, though praised by the UK Supreme Court in *R. v. Gul*, is quite limited and applies only to acts in armed conflicts that are "in accordance with customary international law or conventional international law" and acts undertaken by state military forces that "are governed by other rules of international law."[57] This exemption was unsuccessfully argued in a case where the accused was involved in plots against Coalition forces in Afghanistan.[58] It also seems to exempt state military acts as terrorism even if they violate international law, so long as they are governed by international law. The Swiss exemption has a similar armed conflict exemption

56 Chapter 19, "South Africa" infra at 547.
57 Criminal Code of Canada RSC 1985 c. C-34 s.83.01(b) (ii).
58 R. v. Khawaja [2012] 3 S.C.R. 555.

for actions that "do not violate the rules of international law on the conduct of armed conflict."

Swiss law has a broader exemption for acts "carried out with a view to establishing or re-establishing a democratic regime or a state governed by the rule of law or with a view to exercising or safeguarding human rights."[59] Greece has a similar exemption for acts that exercise any fundamental human, political or trade union freedom or any right protected in the European Convention of Human Rights in its terrorism legislation. The Greek exemption has been criticized for its vagueness. In Chapter 7, Bertrand Perrin and Julien Gafner suggest that the Swiss courts have already narrowed the freedom fighter exemption. They suggest that while any freedom fighter exemption will inevitably be complex and involve "fine distinctions," proportionality principles can play an important role in crafting an exemption for freedom fighters.[60]

Freedom fighter exemptions demonstrate the continued influence of the particular even while there is a global trend towards broad definitions of terrorism. South Africa's reference to "national liberation, self-determination and independence against colonialism" reflects very much the history of the ANC. Canada's exemption reflects its acceptance of international law, and the Swiss and Greek exemptions more consciously reflect their self-definitions as European democracies that respect human rights.

c. The Influence of the Terrorism Act, 2000, in Pakistan, Malaysia and Singapore

The migration of terrorism law is not necessarily a benign process, and there are legitimate concerns that countries that abuse terrorism laws may seek to claim legitimacy by borrowing from the laws of the UK or other respected democracies. One of the first countries to be influenced by the UK's Terrorism Act, 2000, was Pakistan, which in August 2001 amended its counter-terrorism laws[61] to provide that terrorism would include actions or "threat of action" that

> involves the doing of anything that causes death; (b) involves grievous violence against a person or grievous bodily injury or harm to a person; (c) involves grievous damage to property; (d) involves the doing of anything that is likely to cause death or endangers a person's life…, (i) creates a serious risk to safety of the public or a section of the public, or is designed to frighten the general public and thereby prevent them from coming out and carrying on their lawful trade and daily business,

59 Chapter 7, "Switzerland" infra at 205.

60 Ibid.

61 Available at https://www.unodc.org/tldb/pdf/Pakistan_Anti-terrorism_Act_1997.pdf. See Pakistan report to the Counter-Terrorism Committee S/2003/307.

> and disrupts civic life…, (l) is designed to seriously interfere with or seriously disrupt a communications system or public utility service.[62]

Although some wording is changed, these provisions track the broad range of harms contained in s.1 of the Terrorism Act. To be sure, Pakistan's terrorism law also contains other subsections (e to n) covering acts such as inciting hatred or contempt on "religious, sectarian or ethnic basis," "stoning," "brick batting" and "firing on religious congregations" that reflect the distinct circumstances of that country, including its sectarian violence. It is also notable that the Pakistani definition does not rely on the British example of requiring proof of political or religious motive.

One significant difference between the Pakistani and UK laws was that the former only applies to acts "designed to coerce and intimidate or overawe the Government" whereas s.4(d) of the Terrorism Act, 2000, applies to acts of terrorism against all domestic or foreign governments. The UN Security Council's Counter-Terrorism Committee has raised concerns about the exclusively domestic focus of Pakistan's definition. These concerns are understandable given Pakistan's practice of harboring terrorists, including Osama bin Laden, who focus on attacking the governments of other countries such as neighboring Afghanistan. The Pakistani approach to this matter, however, suggests that all of the differences between the law in the Global South and the Global North may not be related to the law in action[63] but can also be found in the text of the law.

In 2003, Malaysia amended its Penal Code to define a terrorist act in a manner that closely mirrored the UK definition. As in the UK, a threat of action was included as well as all serious damage to property, health and safety and electronic systems.[64] The 2003 Malaysian law, influenced by the Internal Security Act, also contains vaguer notions of prejudice to national security or public safety[65] not found in the Terrorism Act, 2000.

As noted by Eugene Tam in Chapter 22, Singapore continues to rely on its Internal Security Act (ISA) to deal with suspected terrorists, but it also enacted legislation after 9/11 that was influenced by the Terrorism Act, 2000.[66] Singapore enacted terrorism financing laws that defined terrorist activities as "the use or threat of action where the action (i) involves serious violence against a person; (ii) involves serious damage to property; (iii) endangers a person's life; (iv) creates a serious risk to the health or the safety of the public or a section of the public" and "where the

62 https://www.unodc.org/tldb/pdf/Pakistan_Anti-terrorism_Act_1997.pdf.

63 Ramraj "The Impossibility of Global Anti-Terrorism Law" supra.

64 Penal Code of Malaysia s.130B at https://www.unodc.org/tldb/showDocument.do?documentUid=6805&q=.

65 An alternative definition of a terrorist under the ISA, one which also indicates some of the antecedents to modern terrorism financing laws, is one who demands, collects or receives supplies for those who act "in a manner prejudicial to public safety or the maintenance of public order." Ibid s.2.

66 Chapter 22, "Singapore" infra at 614.

use or threat is intended or reasonably regarded as intending to (i) influence the Government or any other government; or (ii) intimidate the public or a section of the public."[67] This part of the definition follows the UK's definition closely, including in its reference to influencing the government and its application to acts that are designed to influence any government or intimidate any public in the world. As in Malaysia, however, the definition also borrowed from the Internal Security Act by including terrorism as acts or threats of actions involving the use of firearms or explosives or that "involves prejudice to public security or national defence." The end result is a definition of terrorism even broader than that used under the infamous ISA, but one that would have much more legitimacy given its more modern British pedigree.

The migration of the UK's Terrorism Act, 2000, to Pakistan, Malaysia and Singapore underlines the complexity of the oft-noted process of "borrowing," "transplantation" or "migration" in comparative law,[68] especially when laws migrate from established democracies such as the UK to developing democracies with different traditions. Assumptions that security officials are politically neutral cannot be applied universally.[69] British laws that are subject to challenge in the European Court of Human Rights will not be subject to such challenges when they migrate outside of Europe.[70] At the same time, borrowing from the laws of established democracies may make it more difficult for the judiciary or even civil society to challenge overbroad terrorism laws. Comparative lawyers should be attentive to the processes of migration but also aware of how laws change when transplanted into different contexts. This also underlines the imperative of studying the law in action as well as the law on the books.

d. The Competing Influence of Old and New Visions of Security in Malaysia, Singapore and Israel

The breadth of modern terrorism laws raise the intriguing possibility that jurisdictions with repressive histories may be able to repeal older security laws and replace them with modern counter-terrorism laws which provide almost as much power to the state. Old style repression of dissent could be legitimized through the language of modern counter-terrorism.[71]

67 Terrorism (Suppression of Financing) Act Cap 325, 2003, s.2.

68 See for example Choudhry *The Migration of Constitutional Ideas*; R.A. Macdonald "Three Metaphors of Norm Migration in International Context" (2009) 34 *Brooklyn J. of International Law* 603; Laura Donohue "Transplantation" in Ramraj et al. *Global Anti-Terrorism Law and Policy*.

69 Ramraj "The Impossibility of Global Anti-Terrorism Law?"

70 Lynch "Control Orders in Australia."

71 See Kent Roach *The 9/11 Effect* 441–2.

Malaysia provides an interesting test of this hypothesis. As previously examined, Malaysia borrowed from the UK's Terrorism Act, 2000, when it amended its Penal Code in 2003 to include broad terrorism offences. In 2012, Malaysia repealed its Internal Security Act, which was inherited from British colonial rule and allowed indeterminate preventive detention of those the state subjectively deemed to be security threats. The ISA was a much criticized symbol of repression in Malaysia,[72] and its repeal may seem to be an unqualified good. Malaysia replaced the Internal Security Act with the Security Offences (Special Measures) Act 2012,[73] which seems to have been inspired by modern terrorism laws from many democracies. Following the UK, the new Malaysian law has twenty-eight days maximum preventive detention. Following Canada, the new law provides that people should not be arrested simply because of their political beliefs.[74] The 2012 law allows anonymous witnesses, as is allowed in Europe, and has provisions modeled on American legislation to allow for the non-disclosure of state secrets while also giving the state stronger powers to protect secrets and the identity of informers. The 2012 law was not perfect, but it was more rights-friendly than the ISA.

Alas, old habits of preventive detention die hard. In 2013, midnight amendments to a 1959 Prevention of Crime Act[75] were pushed through the Malaysian legislature over the resistance of civil society and the bar. These amendments, now consolidated in the Prevention of Terrorism Act, 2015, allow an executive board to authorize indeterminate preventive detention for renewable two-year periods, as was available under the ISA. The 1959 act originally designed to deal with triads and organized crime can now apply to "organized violence," including suspected terrorism. The amendments update powers of police supervision through control orders by allowing the use of electronic monitoring. They also restrict the availability of judicial review as was done under the ISA. In essence, Malaysia repealed its ISA in 2012 only to resurrect it in 2013 and to consolidate it in 2015.

[72] Therese Lee "Malaysia and the Internal Security Act: The Insecurity of Human Rights After September 11" [2002] *Singapore Journal of Legal Studies* 56.

[73] Act 747 of 2012.

[74] Ibid s.4. In Canada, see s.83.01(1.1) of the Criminal Code RSC c.C-34 providing that the expression of "a political, religious or ideological thought, belief or opinion" does not in itself satisfy the broad definition of terrorist activities.

[75] Act 297 of 1959. The Malaysian bar criticized the amendments as a re-introduction of preventive detention and "a great blow to the rule of law in Malaysia." Malaysian Bar Press Release "Amendments to the 1959 Prevention of Crime Act are Regressive and a Blow to the Rule of Law in Malaysia" October 3, 2013, at www.malaysianbar.org.my/press_statements/press_release_amendments_to_the_prevention_of_crime_act_1959_are_regressive_and_a_blow_to_the_rule_of_law_in_malaysia.html. Part IV of the Prevention of Terrorism Act, 2015 authorizes indeterminate detention as under the ISA and was defended in its explanatory statement as a response to UN Security Council Resolution 2178.

The Malaysian experience does not suggest that modern counter-terrorism laws will eclipse older and more starkly authoritarian laws. The same is true in Singapore, which has not abolished its Internal Security Act despite enacting some post-9/11 modern legislation on terrorist financing, bombing and hostage taking. Singapore continues to rely on the ability of the executive indeterminately to detain people under its Internal Security Act "with a view to preventing that person from acting in any manner prejudicial to the security of Singapore or any part thereof or to the maintenance of public order or essential services therein."[76] As Eugene Tam notes, Singapore's government has shown no interest in repealing the ISA. Indeed, it has attempted to justify the continued need for the ISA in relation to the detention of about forty citizens said to be part of the terrorist group Jemaah Islamiyah.[77]

Israel is another country that has enacted some modern counter-terrorism laws while not abandoning older laws, including those established when it was under British rule. Israel enacted a 2004 terrorism financing law that contained a UK-influenced definition of terrorist activities as politically or religiously motivated actions designed to coerce governments or threats of actions that endanger life, public health or security or involve serious damage to property or serious disruption of vital infrastructures or systems. Like the UK definition, the Israeli definition provides no exemptions for armed conflict. In Chapter 18, Shiri Krebs describes this 2004 definition as a "modern, narrower and more refined definition for a terrorist act"[78] compared to the 1948 definition British mandate–era Prevention of Terrorism Ordinance that included all acts or threats to commit violence calculated to cause death or injury to a person. The 2004 Israeli definition is certainly more modern and distinguishes terrorism from other crime better than the 1948 definition. At the same time, it also applies to acts beyond violence, such as serious property damage and serious disruptions of essential services.

A draft of a comprehensive anti-terrorism bill that would replace some older measures inherited from British colonial rule is still before the Knesset.[79] The bill would expand the 2004 definition of terrorism to include attempts to motivate rather than coerce governments or international organizations and all acts done to benefit proscribed terrorist groups. This would bring the Israeli law even closer to the UK's Terrorism Act, 2000, in its reference to influencing rather coercing governments and its presumption that acts taken to benefit a proscribed organization are actions taken for the purposes of terrorism.[80] The Israeli example

76 Internal Security Act 18 of 1960 s.8.

77 Chapter 22, "Singapore" infra at 611. See also Sundaresh Menon "International Terrorism and Human Rights" 2014 4 *Asian Journal of Int Law* 1 at 25–33.

78 Chapter 18, "Israel" infra at 514.

79 Chapter 18, "Israel" infra at 516.

80 Terrorism Act, 2000 c.11 s.1(5).

raises interesting questions of whether modern and broad definitions of terrorism might eventually replace older definitions, including those found in British colonial emergency legislation.[81] In contrast, the experience in Singapore and Malaysia suggests that states may be unwilling to abandon older security concepts. In terms of comparative law, the competing visions of old and new security are an important reminder of the need to examine the evolution and migration of security legislation in a historical context.

C. *The EU Framework Decision Approach to the Harmonization of Counter-Terrorism Law*

The influence of the definition of terrorism in the UK's Terrorism Act, 2000, was voluntary. Nothing forced countries in the Commonwealth, much less republics such as Israel and South Africa, to borrow from the UK law. This process of voluntary migration of the law can be contrasted with the process started by a 2002 Framework Decision by the European Council. Although not all member states transposed the Framework Decision's definition of terrorism and terrorism offences into their domestic laws, many did. The result is a certain uniformity in European counter-terrorism law that is not seen in the laws of those states that borrowed from the UK's Terrorism Act, 2000, or, as will be seen, from those that borrowed from Egypt's 1992 definition of terrorism. The uniformity of the European approach can be seen as harmonization that will inspire greater counter-terrorism co-operation between European states. At the same time, the harmonization may have detracted from genuine democratic debate about and determination of European counter-terrorism law.

The 2002 Framework Decision was an important impetus to the growth of counter-terrorism law in European states. Cian Murphy reports that only six of fifteen states had counter-terrorism laws in 2002, but by March 2007 twenty-two of twenty-seven member states had such laws.[82] This is an explosive growth, indeed what some might call a viral propagation of anti-terrorism laws in Europe. As will be seen, many of these laws were strikingly similar. To the extent that EU Framework Decision challenged human rights or criminal law principles, its influence spread quickly throughout the EU.

Article 1 of the EU Framework Decision defined terrorism as follows:

> Each Member State shall take the necessary measures to ensure that the intentional acts referred to below in points (a) to (i), as defined as offences under national

[81] See Roach *The 9/11 Effect* at 440–2.

[82] Murphy *EU Counter-Terrorism Law* at 55.

law, which, given their nature or context, may seriously damage a country or an international organisation where committed with the aim of:

1) seriously intimidating a population, or
2) unduly compelling a Government or international organisation to perform or abstain from performing any act, or
3) seriously destabilising or destroying the fundamental political, constitutional, economic or social structures of a country or an international organisation, shall be deemed to be terrorist offences:
    (a) attacks upon a person's life which may cause death;
    (b) attacks upon the physical integrity of a person;
    (c) kidnapping or hostage taking;
    (d) causing extensive destruction to a Government or public facility, a transport system, an infrastructure facility, including an information system, a fixed platform located on the continental shelf, a public place or private property likely to endanger human life or result in major economic loss;
    (e) seizure of aircraft, ships or other means of public or goods transport;
    (f) manufacture, possession, acquisition, transport, supply or use of weapons, explosives or of nuclear, biological or chemical weapons, as well as research into, and development of biological and chemical weapons;
    (g) release of dangerous substances, or causing fires, floods or explosions the effect of which is to endanger human life;
    (h) interfering with or disrupting the supply of water, power or any other fundamental natural resource the effect of which is to endanger human life;
    (i) threatening to commit any of the acts listed in (a) to (h).[83]

This definition of terrorism is less broad than that found in the Terrorism Act, 2000. The EU approach applies only if governments and international organizations are "unduly compelled"[84] and not simply "influenced" as in the UK legislation. The EU directive also provided some recognition of the freedom to strike and to assemble, albeit only in the preamble. It did not rely on proof of political or religious motive as a means to distinguish terrorism from other crimes. Property damages and damage to electronic systems must be of such a magnitude as to endanger human life or result in "major economic loss." The latter harm is quite vaguely defined and indicates how the EU definition might potentially be directed at some elements of protests against globalization. The preamble of the 2002 Framework Decision also indicated that acts in armed conflict would be governed by relevant international law and not considered to be terrorism, something not contained in the Terrorism Act, 2000.

Member states were obliged to report their progress on implementation by the end of 2002, but only two had implemented the legislation by that time. These

[83] 2002/475/JHA 13 June 2002.
[84] Ibid.

delays can be contrasted with the speed with which anti-terrorism legislation was enacted in North American jurisdictions. The slower European pace might have been justified had it opened space for full democratic debate and deliberation, but this opportunity seems to be constrained by the binding nature of the Framework Decision. Although member states participate in EU Council decisions, this is participation by the executive and it does not allow full legislative debate with its ties to civil society and the media.

A 2007 report reveals more compliance with the 2002 Decision, but also quite a bit of non-compliance, and singled out:

> The deficient implementation of Article 1 in Germany, Italy, Lithuania, Luxembourg, Poland, Slovenia and the United Kingdom. This provision is of crucial importance not only for the Framework Decision but for counter-terrorism policy in general. A common definition of terrorism constitutes the basis on which all other provisions in the Framework Decision are built and allows for the use of law enforcement co-operation instruments.[85]

Cian Murphy suggests that this means that "merely half of EU residents are subject to a criminal law that defines terrorism in accordance with the framework decision."[86] The low form of compliance may suggest that the EU's hierarchical vision of requiring member states to transpose or copy draft framework laws is not realistic given political and cultural differences among member states and their different experiences of and reactions to terrorism.

a. Harmonization: Laggards or Legitimate Legal Nationalism?

One recent study of EU counter-terrorism policy repeatedly criticizes states that have not transposed the Framework Decision as "laggards." In my view, this ignores the possibility that differences in counter-terrorism laws may reflect different legal, political and historical experiences. For example, the same study quotes one EU Council official who recognized that "even the Danes or the Swedes" never implemented the participation in a terrorist organization offence "because they don't have the concept" because guilt of the basis of membership "is an awkward concept for their legal system."[87] A desire to maintain the integrity of domestic legal systems and comply with domestic constitutional laws may be legitimate justifications for

85 Report from the Commission based on Art 11 of the Council Framework Decision of 13 June 2002 (Com) 2007 681 final at 10 at http://eur-lex.europa.eu/legal-content/EN/TXT/PDF/?uri=CELEX:52007DC0681&from=EN.

86 Murphy *EU Counter-Terrorism Law* at 60.

87 As quoted in Javier Argomaniz *The EU and Counter-Terrorism* (London: Routledge, 2011) at 131.

falling short of full compliance with EU Framework Decisions. In my view, it makes a country different, not a "laggard."

Some countries were non-compliant with the 2002 EU Framework Decision simply because they enacted laws before the 2002 Decision was finalized. Romania enacted an emergency ordinance and subsequent legislation, only to have to amend this law in 2004 to comply with the 2002 Decision. As Raluca-Ioana Mocanu and George Antoniu explain, "the Ordinance and the Law have been elaborated under the deep emotion raised after 9/11 events," but had to be reshaped after the EU Framework Decision in June 2002.[88] In any event, Romania's 2004 definition of terrorism still seems to depart from the 2002 EU Framework Decision by defining terrorism in relation to "public risk" affecting "national security" and motivated by "extremist conceptions and attitudes" and "following specific political objectives" and intended to have "a powerful psychological impact" on the population and to be "premeditated." Mocanu and Antoniu note that the reference to "extremism" (one now found in Security Council 2178) is subjective and vague. They also argue that terrorism should be punished even if it does not reach a magnitude that creates a "public risk" to "national security" as required under the present Romanian definition. From their perspective, the transposition of the EU definition would have been an improvement.

Germany was one of the non-compliant countries, but its non-compliance also seems minor. The relevant provisions of the German Penal Code refer to a variety of predicate offences and then more or less faithfully implement the 2002 EU Framework Decision.[89] Similarly, Italy has been deemed non-compliant, even though, as Sabrina Praduroux indicates in Chapter 9, a 2005 law "reproduces almost word for word the definition of conduct for terrorist purposes in the terrorist offence of Article 1 of the EU Council Framework Decision. . . ."[90] The Italian offence includes conduct prohibited by international conventions binding on Italy.[91] The Italian courts have interpreted the law to include acts during armed conflicts that target or harm civilian non-combatants. This approach is consistent with the

88 Chapter 7, "Romania" infra at 484.

89 German Penal Code article 129A as translated at https://www.unodc.org/tldb/showDocument.do?documentUid=943&node=docs&cmd=add&country=GER.

90 Chapter 9, "Italy" infra at 273.

91 Article 270 sexies of the Italian Penal Code provides defines terrorist purposes as "those conducts which, due to their nature or context, can cause considerable damage to a Country or international organization and are committed in order to intimidate the population and force public authorities or an international organization to perform or restrain from performing any deed or destabilize or destroy the fundamental political, constitutional, economic and social structures of a Country or international organization, as well as the other conducts defined as terrorist or committed for the purpose of terrorism by conventions or other international law provisions which are binding on Italy." As translated at https://www.unodc.org/tldb/showDocument.do?documentUid=8863&q.

general definition of terrorism in Article 2 of the 1999 International Convention on the Suppression of Terrorism Financing, but apparently not the 2002 EU Framework Decision. Another difference is that Italian courts have required that terrorist acts be committed for political, religious or ideological motives. This seems to be a reasonable choice in light of the influence of the UK's Terrorism Act, 2000 as discussed earlier in this chapter. There is considerable evidence of convergence even in those jurisdictions that are labeled by EU authorities to be deficient and non-compliant. The EU Framework Decision may inhibit the type of expression of small differences seen in countries that have used either British or Egyptian definitions of terrorism as templates.

Poland crafted 2004 amendments to its Penal Code with an eye on complying with the EU's 2002 Framework Decision and securing membership in the EU. It faithfully reproduced the requirements of serious intimidation and compulsion of governments and international organizations, but added, as a terrorist intent, the intent to "cause serious disturbance to the constitutional system or to the economy of the Republic of Poland. . . ."[92] The value of the inclusion of harm to the economy as one of the prohibited harms or aims of terrorism is debatable, but it is a choice that a number of other countries, including Canada and South Africa, have made. The EU Framework Decision approach seems particularly inapt for imposing something as important and as debatable as a definition of terrorism.

Vasilka Sancin and Maša Kovič Dine reveal in Chapter 14 how the definition of terrorism in Article 108 of Slovenia's Penal Code has much in common with the 2002 Framework Decision, but also in a gesture to legal nationalism includes as terrorist intent actions against "the constitutional, social or political foundation of the Republic of Slovenia." The Slovenian legislators[93] choose to use a general definition of terrorism taken from Article 2 of the International Convention for the Suppression of Terrorism Financing rather than from the EU when it enacted a 2007 law against money laundering and terrorism financing. Sancin and Kovič Dine raise concerns about the differences between the definition of terrorism in Slovenia's Penal Code and its terrorism financing legislation. They suggest that harmonization towards the broadest definition would be in order.[94]

Greece tried to avoid the difficult task of defining terrorism and took a minimalist approach to complying with the 2002 Framework Decision. This may reflect the turbulent history of terrorism law in that country. The Greek approach is based on predicate offences already existing in the Penal Code that cause serious damage

[92] Article 115 s 20 Polish Penal Code as translated at https://www.unodc.org/tldb/showDocument.do?documentUid=7424&q=economy&edit_btn=SEARCH.

[93] Chapter 14, "Slovenia" infra at 401.

[94] Ibid.

to countries or international organizations and with the intent either seriously to intimidate a population or unduly compel a public authority or an international organization to perform or abstain from performing any act.[95] This seems to layer a harmonized European approach over the existing structure of criminal offences in Greece.

Many of the countries examined in this book are among those that fully transposed the 2002 Framework Decision. For example, Chapter 13 indicates that Croatia has "achieved complete harmonization with Framework Decisions on combating terrorism" despite the fact that the country previously had its own indigenous definitions of international and domestic terrorism.[96] Veronika Bílková suggests in Chapter 16 that the definition of terrorism "is not a controversial issue in the Czech Republic" because it follows the definition in the 2002 EU Framework Decision. The lack of controversy over the definition of terrorism could produce a situation where democratic legislative debate may be truncated because of the felt need to comply with the Framework Decision.

The difficulty of transposing the EU definition into domestic law should not be underestimated. José de Faria Costa indicates that three amendments between 2003 and 2011 have been made to Portugal's definition of terrorism in order to achieve compliance with the 2002 EU Framework Decision. These amendments have had the effect of expanding the definition of terrorism to include various forms of international terrorism. In another gesture to legal nationalism, the Portuguese definition retains its original concern with acts that "have the intent to harm national integrity or independence" or that subvert "the functioning of State institutions" as contemplated in the Portuguese constitution. This approach suggests the durability of differences based on the expression of domestic norms even in jurisdictions that are eager to harmonize their counter-terrorism laws with the rest of Europe.

Belgium did not have terrorism offences until it enacted them in 2003 in order to comply with the 2002 Framework Decision. Compliance required the creation of crimes concerning threats, preparation and associations that would otherwise be quite foreign to Belgium's indigenous approach to defining crimes. Comparative law scholars need to be aware of the pressure that supra-national demands place on the structure of each country's laws. The Belgian approach to defining terrorism offences was challenged as unconstitutionally vague, but upheld by Belgian courts, which emphasized that it was not possible to remove all judicial discretion when applying broad terms such as terrorism.[97] At the same time, the fact that such a

95 Chapter 12, "Greece" infra at 349.
96 Chapter 16, "Croatia" infra at 366.
97 Chapter 8, "Belgium" infra at 240.

challenge was made reveals potential conflicts between EU demands and the domestic constitutional norms of its member states.

The question of harmonization is a significant one for comparative lawyers. The EU experience raises questions about whether the definition of terrorism imposed in the Framework Decisions can be subject to meaningful democratic debate before being copied into the laws of member states. Countries such as Canada were free to make their own changes from the starting point of the broad definition of terrorism in the Terrorism Act, 2000. In many but by no means all cases in the European Union, the starting point of the Framework Decisions was also the end point.

Harmonization may help set aside lingering concerns that terrorism might be considered a political crime not subject to extradition, and it may promote greater counter-terrorism co-operation. The European Arrest Warrant is a symbol of such co-operation and dispenses with the need for establishing double criminality in extradition proceedings. Some commentators, however, note that the European Arrest Warrant still works in the absence of full harmonization of counter-terrorism law in Europe.[98] Regardless of one's views on its merits, counter-terrorism law is an excellent context to study the migration and harmonization of law across borders and the increasing role of supra-national influences on the development of domestic law.

D. *The Influence of Egyptian Definitions of Terrorism*

Lynn Welchman has outlined how the broad definition of terrorism enacted in Egypt in 1992 influenced subsequent definitions of terrorism found in the 1998 Arab Convention on the Suppression of Terrorism and in other Arab states.[99] The 1992 Egyptian definition of terrorism includes:

> all use of force, violence, threatening, or frightening, to which a felon resorts in execution of an individual or collective criminal scheme, with the aim of disturbing public order, or exposing the safety and security of society to danger, if this is liable to harm the persons, or throw horror among them, expose their life, freedom or security to danger, damage the environment, cause detriments to communications, transport, property and funds, buildings, public or private properties, occupying or taking possession of them, preventing or obstructing the work of public authorities, worship houses, or educational institutions, or interrupting the application of the constitution, laws, or statutes.[100]

[98] Murphy *EU Counter-Terrorism Law* at 186–96.

[99] Welchman "Rocks, Hard Places and Human Rights" supra.

[100] Penal Code Article 86 as translated at https://www.unodc.org/tldb/showDocument.do?documentUid=2512&country=EGY.

This is an extremely broad definition of terrorism that includes protests that have "the aim of disturbing public order" or "exposing the safety and security of society to danger." It also includes various forms of property damage and actions that obstruct public authorities and even religious institutions and educational institutions. It is supplemented in Article 86bis by an even broader definition of terrorist groups that includes those with the aims of "impairing national unity or social peace."[101]

In 2003, Tunisia under President Ben Ali enacted a new terrorism law that featured a definition that borrowed the broad concept of "disturbing public order" from the Egyptian law, but added a post-9/11 twist of prohibiting actions aimed at "disturbing international peace and security." Like the Egyptian law, the Tunisian law protected a broad range of harms to property and infrastructure. Given its comparatively successful "Arab spring," it is not surprising that Tunisia is now considering a reformed law. Alas, a 2014 draft law still defines terrorism broadly as activity that:

> First: kills a person or several people, or inflicts considerable physical damage; Second: causes damages at facilities of diplomatic and consular missions, and international organizations; Third: does substantial damage to the environment, putting residents' lives and health at risk; Fourth: Harms public or private property, vital resources and infrastructures, transportation means, communication networks, information and computer systems or public facilities; or aims by its nature and context to terrorize the population or to force a state or an international organization to carry out or refrain from carrying out an action.[102]

Human Rights Watch and other groups have criticized this definition of terrorism and recommended a narrower definition focused on intentional infliction of death and bodily harm and hostage taking. Nevertheless, the fact remains that the draft law's reference to infrastructure and computer structures and forcing states or international organizations to act finds support in definitions of terrorism used by long-established democracies. It will likely be included in a legislative response to the March, 2015 terrorist attack in Tunis.

a. Threats to National Unity as Terrorism?

Qatar enacted a counter-terrorism law in 2004. Its definition of terrorism followed the Egyptian model by relying on the broad concepts of

> breaching the public order or exposing the public safety and security to danger or damaging the national unity that results or could have resulted in injuring the

101 Penal Code Article 86 bis as translated at https://www.unodc.org/tldb/showDocument.do?documentUid=2512&country=EGY.

102 As translated in Human Rights Watch *An Analysis of Tunisia's Draft Counter Terrorism Laws* July, 7, 2014.

> public, or terrifying them, exposing their life, liberty or security to danger, harming the environment, public health, the national economy, public or private utilities, establishments, or properties, or seizure thereof or hindering their functions, or obstructing or hindering the public authorities from exercising their duties.[103]

The characterization of damage to national unity as a terrorist purpose in Qatar's 2004 law is particularly worrying as it creates a risk that even peaceful separatism will be investigated and punished as terrorism. It is not entirely unprecedented, however, because as discussed previously, South Africa's 2004 anti-terrorism law had a similar inclusion of threats to national unity.

The equation of threats to national unity with terrorism is also found in the 2005 counter-terrorism law of Iraq. The law defines terrorism as a:

> criminal act committed by an individual or an organized group targeting an individual, a group of individuals, communities, official or non-official organizations, causing damage to public or private property for the purpose of breaching the security situation, stability and national unity or of causing panic, fear and alarm among people or of causing chaos and disorder in order to attain terrorist ends.[104]

The broad definition of terrorism in the 2005 Iraqi terrorism law is striking in light of long-standing demands by the Kurds for autonomy and because a terrorism financing law enacted a year earlier employed a much more restrained general definition taken from the 1999 UN Convention on Terrorism Financing.[105] The incoherence and inconsistency of the Iraqi approach is an important reminder that observers must be cautious about reading too much into differences in counter-terrorism laws. Although some differences may reflect distinct legal, political and social cultures, they may also only reflect the influence of foreign advisors and groups such as the Financial Action Task Force, which placed pressures on many states to enact terrorism financing laws.[106]

Jordan enacted a temporary law in October 2001 that broadly defined terrorism with reference to concepts such as disturbing public order, infringing safety and security, spreading fear and frightening people all found in the 1992 Egyptian definition. The 2001 law also regulated speech in the interest of "national unity."[107] A permanent 2006 Jordanian law retains but softens some of these qualities. It defines

[103] Law No 3 of 2004 On Combating Terrorism article 1 as translated at https://www.unodc.org/tldb/showDocument.do?documentUid=6338&country=QAT.

[104] Law on Combating Terrorism, 2005 Article 1 as translated at https://www.unodc.org/tldb/showDocument.do?documentUid=6740&country=IRQ.

[105] Anti-Money Laundering Law of 2004 Article 4.2 available at https://www.unodc.org/tldb/pdf/Iraq/IRQ_AML_2004_EN.pdf.

[106] Zaid Al-Ali "Constitutional Drafting and External Influence" in Ginsburg and Dixon eds. *Comparative Constitutional Law* supra.

[107] Welshman "Rocks, Hard Places and Human Rights" supra at 642–3.

terrorism as intentional acts against persons, property or infrastructure "intended to disturb public order, endanger public safety and security, cause suspension of the application of the provisions of the Constitution and laws, affect the policy of the State or the government or force them to carry out an act or refrain from the same, or disturb national security by means of threat, intimidation or violence."[108] In 2014, Jordan's definition of terrorism was further expanded to include disturbing relations with a foreign state.[109] The recent focus in Jordan has been on procedural reforms that have allowed Abu Qatada to leave the UK to face trial in Jordan, but procedural reforms cannot nullify the effects of overbroad definitions of terrorism.

The trend to broad definitions of terrorism that include damage to national unity and stress subjective notions of acts inspiring fear or terror is also seen in a 2006 law enacted by Bahrain that refers to the concept of "disrupting public order" and "threatening the Kingdom's safety or security." Bahrain's law also includes "damaging national unity or security of the international community if this would result in harming persons, terrorizing and intimidating them and endangering theirs lives, freedoms or security or causing damage to the environment, public health, national economy or public utilities, facilities or properties or seizing them and obstructing the performance of their business activities, preventing or obstructing the government authorities, places of worship or academic institutions from carrying out their activities."[110] Bahrain's law is also administered in a context where special and ordinary courts condone the use of torture to produce confessions from terrorist suspects.[111] This is a reminder that even identical laws will be enforced in different ways in different countries.

b. Another Round of Expansion?

The metaphor of a chain novel captures some of the process of the growth of counter-terrorism law. A number of different Arab and Islamic countries started with the 1992 Egyptian definition of terrorism but often expanded on that definition.[112] In turn, this has inspired Egypt to enact a law at the end of 2014

[108] Anti-Terrorism Law No 55 of 2006 Art 2 as translated at https://www.unodc.org/tldb/showDocument.do?documentUid=8459&country=JOR.

[109] Human Rights Watch Jordan Terrorism Law Amendments Threatens Rights May 18, 2014 at http://www.hrw.org/news/2014/05/17/jordan-terrorism-amendments-threaten-rights.

[110] Law 58 of 2006 with Respect to Protecting the Community Against Terrorist Act, Article 1 as translated at http://www.hrw.org/news/2014/05/17/jordan-terrorism-amendments-threaten-rights https://www.unodc.org/tldb/showDocument.do?documentUid=8520&country=BAH&pageNum=2.

[111] Report of the Bahrain Independent Commission of Inquiry 10 December 2011, available at http://files.bici.org.bh/BICIreportEN.pdf.

[112] Roach "Sources and Trends in Post 9/11 Anti-Terrorism Laws."

that allowed the listing as a terrorist group of "any group which disrupts public order or threatens the safety, security or interests of society, or harms or frightens individuals or threatens their lives, freedoms, rights or security or harms national unity."[113] This definition adopts the idea that threats to national unity can be a form of terrorism, as seen in Qatar's 2004 law and Bahrain's 2006 anti-terrorism law, as well as in South Africa's 2004 law. An expanded Egyptian counter-terrorism law could place pressure on other states in the region to again expand their own counter-terrorism laws. As in other countries, there is a danger of an endless ratchet of expanding concepts of terrorism.

E. *American Exceptionalism and Complexity*

American exceptionalism is a recurring but often misunderstood theme in the study of comparative counter-terrorism law. The USA Patriot Act enacted immediately after 9/11 is often held out as a symbol of aggressive or overreaching legislation. For example, some of the debate in France in the wake of the two terrorists attacks in January, 2015 that left 13 people dead was whether France would, rightly or wrongly, enact its own Patriot Act. Leaving aside surveillance, the USA Patriot Act did not authorize many of the post 9/11 abuses and is actually more restrained than many other terrorism laws.[114] Its approach to the definition of terrorism is no exception.

Domestic and international terrorism was defined in the USA Patriot Act enacted shortly after 9/11 as "violent acts or acts dangerous to human life" that violate the criminal laws of the federal government or the states and "that appear to be intended to intimidate or coerce a civilian population; to influence the policy of a government by intimidation or coercion; or to affect the conduct of a government by mass destruction, assassination, or kidnapping."[115] The American definition built on a wide range of existing predicate offences in both state and federal criminal law. This meant that the American definition was not as easily exportable as the British or Egyptian definitions that did not rely on specific predicate offences. The Patriot Act did, however, distinguish terrorist crimes from other crimes by focusing on the intimidation or coercion of civilians and governments. Perhaps reflective of its First Amendment culture, the Patriot Act did not follow the UK by relying on proof of political or religious motive or include membership-based offences. The extensive

[113] Ryan Suto "Egypt's New Anti-terrorism Law" December 12, 2014 at http://www.atlanticcouncil.org/blogs/egyptsource/egypt-s-new-terrorism-law. Another terrorism law building on this definition, expanding terrorist crimes and increasing punishment, is expected to be enacted in Egypt. "Egypt to Issue New Terrorist Entities Law" February 4, 2015 at http://www.aawsat.net/2015/02/article55341101/egypt-to-issue-new-terrorist-entities-law-sources.

[114] Roach *The 9/11 Effect* at 180–98.

[115] 18 USC s.2331 as amended by Patriot Act s.801.

influence of the United States on counter-terrorism in other countries lies not so much in the migration of American laws, which are often dauntingly complex and as such not easily transplanted, but rather in pressure to co-operate with a range of counter-terrorism programs, such as spying and rendition, which themselves are not specifically authorized in American legislation.

F. *Brazil's Wavering Reluctance to Define Terrorism*

Brazil and Argentina are "outliers in the international community by resisting pressures to create and implement laws that criminalise terrorist acts."[116] Rodrigo de Souza Costa outlines how Brazil, perhaps suspicious of its authoritarian past where laws "that often lacked a precise definition of the prohibited activity" were used against dissenters, still has not enacted a general definition of terrorism. Professor Costa notes the influence in Brazil of commentary that argues that it is impossible to define terrorism especially with regards to freedom fighters and state terrorism. It is interesting to contrast the Brazilian experience with that of South Africa, which enacted a broad definition of terrorism in 2004 despite the past misuse of terrorism laws. A key factor in South Africa's approach was a desire to comply with international mandates to co-operate in the battle against international terrorism.

Costa suggests that the absence of a definition of terrorism has not provided a barrier to counter-terrorism in Brazil. For example, Brazilian courts have been able to extradite suspected terrorists under the double criminality requirement despite the absence of a crime of terrorism. Terrorism can also be dealt with under laws enacted to combat organized crime and money laundering. The essence of terrorism – political violence – is criminal in most countries without the enactment of specific laws against terrorism.

Despite reservations about defining terrorism and the workability of using other crimes to prosecute terrorism, as well as the 2010 election of President Rousseff, who had been held and tortured by the military as a terrorist in 1970, Brazil seems to be moving towards defining terrorism. There are a number of bills before the legislature proposing different definitions of terrorism, and Brazil is under international pressure to enact a counter-terrorism regime if only because of its role in hosting the 2014 World Cup and the 2016 Olympics.

Some of the Brazilian proposals follow the UK approach in stressing the political or religious motivation of terrorism while others stress the intent to cause panic. One law reform project proposes a relatively broad definition of terrorism that includes sabotage of both critical infrastructure and computer systems. This proposal

[116] Rebecca Welsh "Understood but Undefined: Why Do Argentina and Brazil Resist Criminalising Terrorism?" (2013) 7 *ICL Journal* 327.

distinguishes terrorism from other crimes by having a purpose of forcing national or foreign authorities to act, by involving actions "against the constitutional order or Rule of Law" or by taking actions motivated by prejudice on the basis of religion, nationality, gender or sexual identity or actions motivated for political or religious reasons. These latter two phrases demonstrate how counter-terrorism law can be presented as a form of protection of a democratic constitutional order and even as anti-discrimination legislation. Such an approach recognizes the connection between religiously motivated terrorism and hatred of other religions. The proposed Brazilian definitions share the breadth of many modern definitions of terrorism, but also provide some exemptions for protest.

Brazil's refusal to criminalize terrorism can also be contrasted with Colombia's approach. As Luz Nagle outlines in Chapter 4, the criminalization of terrorism has been part of a strategy to deny the Revolutionary Armed Forces of Colombia (better known as FARC) the legitimacy of belligerent status in what has often amounted to a literal war between FARC and the Colombian state. Article 144 of the Colombian Penal Code recognizes that "indiscriminate or excessive attacks ... with the principal objective of terrorizing the civilian population" should be treated as a serious crime even during "an armed conflict."[117] This provision also demonstrates some of the blurring of the laws of war and crime also seen in the Military Commissions Acts used in the United States to prosecute some of those detained at Guantanamo Bay.

G. *China's Evolving Approach to Defining Terrorism*

Until recently, China has not attempted to define terrorism. Article 120 of the 1997 Penal Code of China prohibits the commission of "terrorist activities" and the financing of a "terrorist organization" but does not attempt to define these terms. China did, however, agree along with Russia in June 2001 to the Shanghai Convention on Combating Terrorism, Separatism and Extremism. The Shanghai Convention provided a general definition of terrorism as any "act intended to cause death or serious bodily injury to a civilian, or any other person not taking an active part in the hostilities in a situation of armed conflict or to cause major damage to any material facility, as well as to organize, plan, aid and abet such act, when the purpose of such act, by its nature or context, is to intimidate a population, violate public security or to compel public authorities or an international organization to do or to abstain from doing any act." This definition has some resemblance to the general definition in the 1999 Terrorism Financing Convention, but is broader in including "major damage to any material facility" and the violation of "public security." In any event, this definition has not been incorporated into Chinese domestic law.

[117] As translated at https://www.unodc.org/tldb/showDocument.do?documentUid=1825&country=COL.

If China, perhaps like Brazil, is moving towards defining terrorism, a key question may be the respective emphasis it places on supra-national instruments such as the Shanghai Convention and the emphasis it places on domestic concerns, including national unity and the desires in some parts of China for greater autonomy and religious freedom.

In October 2011, a Standing Committee of the National People's Congress issued a decision on strengthening anti-terrorism work. This decision defined terrorism as "activities conducted by violence, destruction, intimidation, and other means to create social panic, endanger public security or threaten state organization; cause or attempt to cause casualties, grave property loss, damage to public facilities, disruption of social order, and other severe social harm." Although influenced by the definition in the Shanghai Convention, this decision contains a much broader definition of terrorism that includes vague references to "disruption of social order" and "other severe social harm" with no exemptions for dissent or freedom fighting.

China released a draft terrorism law in November 2014. It provides a broader definition of terrorism than found in the October 2011 Standing Committee's decision. The 2014 draft law defines terrorism as "any thought, speech, or activity that, by means of violence, sabotage, or threat, aims to generate social panic, influence national policy-making, create ethnic hatred, subvert state power, or split the state."[118] Before the draft law was debated in the National People's Congress, however, it was modified to apply to "any speech or activity that, by means of violence, sabotage or threat, generates social panic, undermines public security, and menaces government organs and international organisations."[119]

The draft law also equates terrorism with extremism in several proposed new crimes targeting various forms of speech including teachings, writings and recordings.[120] This borrows from the reference to "extremism" found in UN Security Council

[118] Chapter 21 "China" infra at 583. Zunyou Zhao "How China Defines Terrorism" *The Diplomat* February 13, 2015 at http://thediplomat.com/2015/02/how-china-defines-terrorism/. Dr. Zhao concludes, after comparing the definition in the draft law to UN, EU and American definitions, that "the Chinese definition lacks more restrictive words such as 'compel,' 'seriously,' and 'unduly' to set terrorism apart from other serious crimes. Of all the definitions, the Chinese one is clearly the broadest." Note that the definition in China's November 2014 draft law has been translated in a similar but somewhat different manner by Human Rights Watch as "the ideology, speech or action with the intent to cause social panic or terror, influence national decision-making, create racial hatred, subvert state power, or divide country by means of violence, destruction or intimidation." Human Rights Watch "China Draft Counterterrorism Law a Recipe for Abuse" January 20, 2015 at http://www.hrw.org/news/2015/01/20/china-draft-counterterrorism-law-recipe-abuses.

[119] "China Narrows Definition of Terrorism by Deleting 'Thought' from List of Crimes" *South China Morning Post* February 26, 2015 at http://www.scmp.com/news/china/article/1723625/changes-needed-chinas-counter-terrorism-law-avoid-human-rights-abuses-say.

[120] Chapter 21 "China" infra at 586.

Resolution 2178, but without the important qualification of targeting only "violent extremism." If China adopts such an anti-terrorism law it would follow global trends to broader definition of terrorism. Indeed, China's draft terrorism law is considerably broader than both the UK's Terrorism Act, 2000 and the Framework Decisions of the EU, though it does echo the former's focus on "threats" and its concern with attempts to "influence" rather than to "compel" or "intimidate" the government.[121] The definition in China's draft law is most similar to the extremely broad and similarly evolving Egyptian approach to the definition of terrorism, especially in its references to terrorism as including splitting the state and causing panic.

The proposed definition in the November 2014 draft law also includes "thought and speech." This reflects the trend to criminalizing speech associated with terrorism, but raises troubling issues about the impact of attempting to criminalize speech and even thought. The draft also includes the creation of ethnic hatred as a form of terrorism. The conflates the social harmony and counter-terrorism rationales for the law, but finds precedent in Pakistan's approach. China's draft law also echoes older security concepts by including the subversion of state power as a form of terrorism. In any event, the extremely broad definition of terrorism in its draft law suggests that China is not immune from the frequent trend of reactive expansion of terrorism laws in response to twelve well-publicized terrorist attacks in China in 2013 and 2014 that killed over 180 people.[122]

Legislative definitions of terrorism may be less important in China than in countries with a strong sense of rule of law. Directives issued by political organs in China may play a role similar to legislative definitions in other countries. Pre-textual application of different laws to suspected terrorists may also play an important role. The power of both these alternatives is demonstrated in a September 2014 directive that reminded Chinese police, prosecutors and courts that "religious extremism" could constitute crimes of terrorism or succession.[123] Although this directive could be fitted within the focus on violent extremism and radicalization of UN Security Council Resolution 2178, it also suggests that China's evolving response to terrorism may be influenced by contextual issues relating to the Muslim Uighurs in Xinjiang. As Li Zhe notes, however, China has not yet defined terrorism in relation to religious or political motives or included threats to national unity in its definition of terrorism.[124] Indeed, Professor Li Zhe suggests that terrorism laws

[121] The Terrorism Act, 2000 influenced Hong Kong's anti-terrorism law, which is some respects was broader than the definition used in mainland China until the 2014 draft anti-terrorism law. See Chapter 21, "China" infra at 605.

[122] See Chapter 21, "China" infra at 580.

[123] "China Focus: Judicial Explanation Clarifies Law on Terrorism" *Shanghai Daily* September 21, 2014.

[124] Chinese academics, however, have done important work laying the basis for the adoption of a legislative definition that would be informed by international and comparative experience. See Zhao

in both Hong Kong and Macau are somewhat broader than terrorism law on the mainland before the November 2014 draft law.[125] Any restraint in Chinese terrorism law may, however, be illusory given the ability of the Chinese state to convict and sentence to life imprisonment a Uighur academic, Ilham Tohti, for "separatism" and recent attempts in Xinjiang to provide financial incentives for Muslims who marry non-Muslims.[126] As always, comparative law scholars need to be attentive not just to the law in the books, but the broader legal, social and political structures in which the law is put into action.

IV. CONCLUSION

This chapter has defined the broad domain of counter-terrorism law and has suggested that comparative counter-terrorism law has come of age since the 9/11 terrorist attacks. Increased international co-operation in counter-terrorism has underlined the need to understand the counter-terrorism laws and practices of the broadest range of countries possible. Supra-national pressures for harmonization of counter-terrorism law make this area a particularly fertile one for examining trends towards convergence and divergence in counter-terrorism law. The high stakes of counter-terrorism laws in terms of security and human rights should encourage scholars to examine not only the law on the books, but the law in action. This should help us better understand how even similar counter-terrorism laws can have very different effects when transplanted to different legal, political and social environments. The final chapter of this collection will systematically address convergence, divergence, trends and challenges with respect to a wide variety of counter-terrorism issues.

This chapter has focused on defining the field of counter-terrorism law and on evolving and migrating definitions of terrorism. Some might argue that too much attention has been devoted to parsing the language of definitions of terrorism, but it should be remembered that such definitions are the heart of counter-terrorism laws. They often trigger a broad array of criminal offences and investigative powers

Bingzhi and Du Miao *Research on the Rule of Anti-terrorism Laws in China* (Beijing: Chinese People Public Security University Press, 2010).

[125] Chapter 21, "China" infra at 580. Hong Kong in its United Nations (Anti-Terrorism Measures) Ordinance Ord. no 27 of 2002 s.1 defines terrorism in a manner similar to the definition found in the UK's Terrorism Act, 2000, but also includes some exemptions for protest, dissent or industrial action patterned after Canadian exemptions. Macao has its own distinct definition of terrorism that applies to two or more people who commit a broad array of harms in order "to impede, alter or subvert, by means of violence, the operation of the political, economic or social system" of the Macao Special Administrative Region. Prevention and Suppression of the Crimes of Terrorism Law no 3/2006.

[126] "A Lone Voice Silenced" *The Economist* September 27, 2014; Edward Wong "China Offers Incentives for Ethnic Intermarriage" *New York Times* September 14, 2014.

that will be examined in subsequent chapters. This chapter has identified a distinct global trend to broader definitions of terrorism that go beyond violence to humans and include property destruction, serious disruptions of essential services and threats to national unity. At the same time, however, this chapter has also identified considerable diversity. Some countries, including Brazil and China, have so far avoided the seeming imperative of defining terrorism in their laws, but this may soon change in both countries.

American definitions of terrorism have had much less influence on the laws of other countries than the UK's Terrorism Act, 2000, Egypt's 1992 definition and the European Council's 2002 Framework Decision. Even while these definitions have formed the basis for many definitions in the Commonwealth, Middle East and European countries, there are still some small but revealing differences as countries have placed their own stamp on the definitions. Some countries have restrained the broad definitions of terrorism through exemptions for protesters, strikers and freedom fighters while others have broadened them by including references to national unity and economic interests. The reluctance of a number of European states to copy the Framework Decision into their law also raises questions about whether complete harmonization is possible or desirable. Those influenced by Egypt's definition generally have the broadest laws, and such laws often single out expressive activities and threats to national unity, as does a draft anti-terrorism law released in China in November 2014. However tempting, it may be difficult for those in the West to criticize such laws. As will be seen in the chapters that follow, laws in Europe, Australia and Canada are targeting speech associated with terrorism, and UN Security Council Resolution 2178 is encouraging states to expand counter-terrorism laws to address violent extremism and radicalization.

PART ONE

North America

2

The United States

Sudha N. Setty

I. INTRODUCTION

The terrorist attacks of September 11, 2001, which killed almost three thousand civilians, led to profound changes in societal viewpoints, political agendas, and the legal authority to combat terrorism and threats of terrorism. The United States, like all other democratic nations that have suffered terrorist attacks, continues to struggle with questions of how to keep its population safe while maintaining the principles of democracy and the rule of law that are essential to the nation's character.

In the twelve years since the attacks of September 11, Congress, the executive branch, and the judicial system have reacted strongly to the need to protect against future national security threats by giving more powers to the police, military, and intelligence forces to investigate potential threats and neutralize them before another attack occurs. Some of the these changes occurred in response to United Nations Security Council resolutions,[1] but many have been domestically motivated shifts that reflect the will of politicians and the polity as a whole. The expanded powers accorded to these counterterrorism programs have – in the view of many critics – allowed for government infringement on civil liberties and human rights in significant and corrosive ways, with little or no accountability for such overreaching.

In the years immediately following the attacks of September 11, the Bush administration asserted both inherent presidential authority and broad powers conferred under the Authorization for the Use of Military Force[2] and the USA

The author thanks Matthew H. Charity and Lauren Carasik for thoughtful comments and suggestions, and Kelly Heuser for fine research assistance.

[1] UN Security Council Resolution 1373 has played a strong role worldwide in developing a concerted counter-terrorism effort. The United States played a significant role in supporting the language and passage of Resolution 1373 and encouraging its worldwide mandate. *See* Kim Lane Scheppele, *Other People's Patriot Acts: Europe's Response to September 11*, 50 LOY. L. REV. 89, 91–2 (2004).

[2] Authorization for Use of Military Force (AUMF), Pub. L. 107–40, codified at 115 Stat. 224 (Sept. 18, 2001).

PATRIOT Act.[3] The government conducted warrantless wiretapping surveillance, detained thousands of individuals – almost all of whom were Muslim – who were later released based on lack of evidence of any connection to terrorism, conducted extraordinary renditions to capture and transport suspected individuals from one country to another without judicial oversight, and resorted to torture on some detainees as an interrogation and control technique.

Some of these issues were eventually resolved – through public pressure, judicial intervention, and/or a change in political branches – in ways that improved the individual rights of detainees, suspects, and the public. Yet robust presidential authority and extremely high levels of secrecy continue to be the norm, and the nation's policy makers still struggle with how best to maintain security, accountability, and the rule of law.

II. THE DEFINITION OF TERRORISM

Terrorism is defined in numerous ways under U.S. law, but contains several basic elements: premeditation, political or religious motivation, perpetration of violence, noncombatant targets, and actors as subnational groups or clandestine agents.[4] The United States has not made any exceptions to this definition based on the activity being expressive in character or with regard to national liberation struggles.[5]

The USA PATRIOT Act, passed in the weeks immediately following the September 11 attacks, offers both greater counterterrorism resources and more flexibility in implementation to the government, including increased surveillance powers,[6] increased government authority to conduct intelligence-gathering operations in matters of suspected terrorism,[7] the power of civil seizure of assets based only on

3 Uniting and Strengthening America by Providing Appropriate Tools Required to Intercept and Obstruct Terrorism Act of 2001, Pub. L. No. 107–56, 115 Stat. 272 (codified as amended in scattered sections of U.S.C.) (hereinafter PATRIOT Act).

4 E.g., 22 U.S.C.A. § 2656f(2)(d) (2) (WEST) (defining terrorism for the purpose of the State Department's annual report to the Speaker of the House and the Senate Committee on Foreign Relations as "premeditated, politically motivated violence perpetrated against noncombatants by subnational groups or clandestine agents"); see *Third Mutual Evaluation Report on Anti-Money Laundering and Combating the Financing of Terrorism: United States of America* (Financial Action Task Force, Paris, France) June 2006, at 40, available at http://www.fatf-gafi.org/countries/u-z/unitedstates/documents/mutualevaluationoftheunitedstates.html (offering similar elements of a definition of terrorism for the purposes of evaluation under the Immigration and Nationality Act [Title 8 USC 1182(a)(3)(B)(iv)]).

5 See Sudha Setty, *What's in a Name: How Nations Define Terrorism Ten Years After 9/11* (2011), 33 U. PA. J. INT'L L. 1.

6 See PATRIOT Act § 218 (amending the Foreign Intelligence Surveillance Act of 1978 such that electronic surveillance and physical searches need only be justified in "significant" part by the goal of obtaining foreign intelligence).

7 PATRIOT Act § 901.

probable cause,[8] and heightened punishments for any of the underlying crimes related to the newly broadened understanding of "domestic terrorism," which includes:

> [A]cts dangerous to human life that are a violation of the criminal laws of the United States or of any State [that] appear to be intended to intimidate or coerce a civilian population; to influence the policy of a government by intimidation or coercion; or to affect the conduct of a government by mass destruction, assassination, or kidnapping; and occur primarily within the territorial jurisdiction of the United States.[9]

This definition of domestic terrorism was the result of intense pressure on Congress[10] to amend various existing criminal statutes to broaden and strengthen the government's resources before another attack potentially took place.[11]

The PATRIOT Act amended the definition of terrorism from 18 U.S.C. § 2331 to broaden its scope and application further,[12] but included an important sunset provision – added in part because of the haste with which the legislation was passed – that forced Congress to reexamine the legislation at intervals of several years.[13] Although Congress debated the renewal of certain parts of the PATRIOT Act in 2005 – none of which involved the definition of terrorism – in March 2006, Congress renewed most provisions, removed the safeguard of a sunset provision, and made the provisions permanent.[14]

8 PATRIOT Act § 806.

9 PATRIOT Act § 802. Critics of this broad definition have noted that such language could encompass numerous activist groups, including Greenpeace, protestors of the World Trade Organization, Operation Rescue, and protesters of bomb-testing facilities on the island of Vieques. See *How the USA PATRIOT Act Redefines "Domestic Terrorism,"* AM. CIV. LIBERTIES UNION (December 6, 2002), available at http://www.aclu.org/national-security/how-usa-patriot-act-redefines-domesticterrorism.

10 See Laura K. Donohue, THE COST OF COUNTERTERRORISM: POWER, POLITICS AND LIBERTY 11(New York, Cambridge University Press, 2008) (arguing that the legislative role in safeguarding civil liberties is hampered by political imperatives).

11 See Robert O'Harrow, Jr., *Six Weeks in Autumn*, WASHINGTON POST MAGAZINE, October 27, 2002, at 6, 10 (describing the pressured deliberations of Congress and the executive branch in drafting the Patriot Act).

12 See 18 U.S.C. § 2331 (including "mass destruction" as a means by which terrorists operate).

13 See 18 U.S.C. § 2510 (commenting that Section 801 of Pub. L 90–351 provided a sunset provision for various counter-terrorism tools, including those related to wiretapping and surveillance).

14 See James Beckman, *Comparative Legal Approaches to Homeland Security and Anti-Terrorism* 31 (Farnham, UK: Ashgate, 2007) (describing how sunset provisions were adopted, extended, and then removed). Only three provisions not dealing with the definition of terrorism were still kept subject to the sunset provisions. Those provisions were extended in May 2011 until 2015. See Paul Kane & Felicia Somnez, *PATRIOT Act Amendments Signed into Law Despite Bipartisan Resistance from Congress*, washpost.com, May 27, 2011, http://www.washingtonpost.com/politics/patriot-act-extension-signed-into-law-despite-bipartisan-resistance-incongress/2011/05/27/AGbVlsCH_story.html (describing the extension of surveillance provisions of the PATRIOT Act).

The current PATRIOT Act definition of terrorism has a broad scope, and its reach exacerbates the uncertainty surrounding the application of conflicting definitions of terrorism, including the potential lack of notice to individuals as to whether they will be categorized as a terrorist and exactly what kind of conduct is prohibited.[15]

III. CRIMINAL LAWS AND PROSECUTIONS

A. *Criminal Law*

Terrorist acts are often prosecuted using the ordinary criminal justice system, particularly when the alleged crime occurred domestically. Statutes such as the Anti-Effective Death Penalty Act (AEDPA) of 1996[16] and the PATRIOT Act were enacted as specific responses to terrorist acts and to enable investigation and prosecution of activities that were not previously criminalized.

A serious constitutional issue has been raised with regard to a number of U.S. statutes that criminalize speech-related conduct that supports or encourages violent acts, including terrorist acts. The federal criminal solicitation[17] and sedition statutes,[18] for example, authorize such prosecution. However, the most widely used statute in this

[15] See Subcomm. on Terrorism and Homeland Sec. & House Permanent Select Comm. on Intelligence, 107th Cong., Counterterrorism Capabilities and Performance Prior to 9–11: A Report to the Speaker of the House of Representatives and the Minority Leader (2002), available at http://www.fas.org/irp/congress/2002_rpt/hpsci_ths0702.html (reviewing alternative ways to combat terrorism in order to prevent future attacks). The subcommittee's recommendation that a single definition of terrorism be agreed upon by all U.S. agencies was predicated on a concern that a lack of uniform definition would lead to terrorist acts being treated identically under the law as ordinary criminal acts. Id.

[16] Antiterrorism and Effective Death Penalty Act of 1996 (AEDPA), Pub. L. No. 104–132, 110 Stat. 1217 (codified in scatter sections of 8, 18, and 28 U.S.C.).

[17] See 18 U.S.C. § 373(a) (criminalizing solicitation of crimes). See also Letter from the Chairman of the Security Council Committee Established Pursuant to Resolution 1373 (2001) Concerning Counter-terrorism Addressed to the President of the Security Council (June 15, 2006), Enclosure: Response of the United States of America to the Counter-Terrorism Committee: United States implementation of Security Council resolution 1624 (2005), at 5–6, available at http://daccess-dds-ny.un.org/doc/UNDOC/GEN/N06/395/24/PDF/N0639524.pdf?OpenElement (hereinafter "U.S. CTC Response 2006") (citing the availability of 18 U.S.C. § 2332[b] [acts of terrorism, such as murder, maiming, or kidnapping, transcending national boundaries], 18 U.S.C. § 2332f [bombings of places of public use], and 49 U.S.C. § 46502 [aircraft piracy] in prosecuting support of terrorism).

[18] 18 U.S.C. § 2384 prohibits seditious conspiracy (plotting to use force to overthrow the government). 18 U.S.C. § 2385 proscribes teaching or advocating the duty or necessity of overthrowing or destroying the government of the United States by force or violence; publishing or circulating literature which so teaches or advocates; joining or organizing any group which so teaches or advocates, knowing the purposes thereof; or conspiring to do any of the foregoing. See U.S. CTC Response 2006, supra note 17 (discussing the availability of these statutes in the counterterrorism context); *U.S. v. Rahman*, 189 F.3d 88, 116–117 (2nd Cir. 1999) (upholding the solicitation conviction of Sheik Omar Amad Ali Abdel Rahman based on his exhortations for others to bomb New York City facilities and to assassinate certain persons).

area criminalizes material support of terrorism. Sections 2339A and 2339B of Title 18 of the U.S. Code prohibit knowingly or intentionally providing, attempting to provide, or conspiring to provide material support or resources to a terrorist organization, defining the term "material support or resources" to include

> ... any property, tangible or intangible, or service, including currency or monetary instruments or financial securities, financial services, lodging, training, expert advice or assistance, safehouses, false documentation or identification, communications equipment, facilities, weapons, lethal substances, explosives, personnel (1 or more individuals who may be or include oneself), and transportation, except medicine or religious materials.[19]

Material support charges have been used extensively to try terrorism suspects or to exert pressure toward a plea bargain and are often successful.[20] Unlike other crimes often invoked to prosecute terror suspects, such as continuing criminal enterprise[21] and violations of the Racketeer Influenced and Corrupt Organizations Act,[22] which require at least some predicate act for criminal liability to attach,[23] the material support statute does not require the defendant to have had a specific intent to support a terrorist act; knowing support of a designated terrorist organization without intent is sufficient to convict.[24] The scope and flexibility offered by the material support statute has made it an often-used tool for prosecutors and was used to convict John Walker Lindh,[25] Ahmed Omar Abu Ali,[26] and the "Lackawanna Six,"[27] among others.

In 2010, the U.S. Supreme Court decided that the statute does not unconstitutionally infringe on the expressive rights of individuals.[28] In some respects, this decision

19 See 18 U.S.C. §§ 2339A and 2339B.

20 See Press Release, Dep't of Justice, Fed. Bureau of Investigation, Minneapolis, Minneapolis Man Sentenced for Conspiracy to Provide Material Support to al Qaeda (July 9, 2009), available at http://minneapolis.fbi.gov/dojpressreVpressrel09/mp070909.htm (last visited October 19, 2010) (describing the guilty plea of Mohammed Abdullah Warsame to charges of material support for al Qaeda, which resulted in a prison sentence of ninety-two months); Philip Coorey, *Hicks Case Flawed All Along; Prosecutor*, SYDNEY MORNING HERALD (April 30, 2008), available at http://www.smh.com.auJarticlesI2008/04/29/1209234862811.htrnl (last visited October 19, 2010) (detailing David Hicks' guilty plea to material support charges).

21 21 U.S.C. § 848 (2008).

22 18 U.S.C. §§ 1961–1968 (2000).

23 See, e.g., 18 U.S.C. § 1961(5) (2008) (defining racketeering as involving at least two acts in furtherance of the illegal plan).

24 18 U.S.C. § 2339B(a)(I) (2000).

25 *United States v. Lindh*, 227 F. Supp. 2d 565 (E.D. Va. 2002) (entering guilty plea in violation of, among other things, the material support statute).

26 *United States v. Abu Ali*, 528 F.3d 210 (4th Cir. 2008), cert. denied, 129 S. Ct. 1312 (2009).

27 "Press Release, U.S. Dep't of Justice, U.S. Attorney, W. Dist. of N.Y., United States Attorney's Office Successfully Concludes Terrorism Case with Sixth Conviction of al Qaeda Supporter," May 19, 2003 (announcing the conviction of Muhktar al-Bakri).

28 See *Holder v. Humanitarian Law Project*, 130 S. Ct. 2705 (2010).

promoted additional uncertainty as to what individuals and organizations will be prosecuted under the material support statute and on what basis.[29] The United States government maintains, however, that the majority of the terrorist propaganda found on the Internet today could not be prosecuted under U.S. criminal law, and that even a website advocating committing acts of terrorist violence likely lacks (at least without proof of additional facts) the potential to produce imminent lawless action that could be criminalized.[30]

B. *Terrorism Prosecutions*

The United States has historically shied away from specialized trials for terrorist attacks, instead relying on the criminal justice system.[31] In part, this policy is intended to affirm the rule of law in the United States and to maintain the United States' reputation in the international community for fairness toward criminal defendants[32] regardless of the crime committed or the national origin or religion of the defendant.[33]

One critique of the criminal justice system with regard to terrorism prosecutions has been the de facto unavailability of the entrapment defense. In evaluating an entrapment defense, most courts will consider whether the defendant was induced into illegal acts by law enforcement or had, to the contrary, a predisposition to commit the crime even if law enforcement had not intervened. In the context of a terrorism prosecution, a defendant's predisposition toward terrorist acts is often inferred from the defendant's political and religious views or sympathies toward those of the same political bent or religious background who have engaged in terrorist activities.[34] In the post-9/11 context, there has not been one publicly known

[29] See Peter Margulies, *Advising Terrorism: Hybrid Scrutiny, Safe Harbors, and Freedom of Speech* (2011) 63 *HASTINGS L.J.* 455 at 498 (arguing that the majority opinion failed to specify how much coordination with a foreign terrorist organization would lead to a violation of the federal statute prohibiting material support to these organizations).

[30] U.S. CTC Response 2006, supra note 17, at 4–5.

[31] Sudha Setty, *Comparative Perspectives on Specialized Trials for Terrorism* (2010) 63 *ME. L. REV.* 131.

[32] This reputation for a justice system with exceptionally strong protections for defendants is open to critique. See James Forman, Jr., *Exporting Harshness: How the War on Crime Helped Make the War on Terror Possible* (2009) 33 *N.Y.U. REV. L & SOC. CHANGE* 331 at 337 ("we hav[e] one of the most punitive systems in the world while believing we have one of the most liberal").

[33] Deborah Colson, THE CASE AGAINST A SPECIAL TERRORISM COURT, HUMAN RIGHTS FIRST, at 3 (2009 ("Unjust detentions and trials at Guantanamo have fueled animosity toward the United States. These decisions also have undermined U.S. efforts to advance the rule of law around the world, which is critical to confronting the threat of terrorism. Creating a special terrorism court… would perpetuate these errors").

[34] Wadie E. Said, The Terrorist Informant (2010) 85 Wash. L. Rev. 687 at 698–711.

instance of a successful entrapment defense in a terrorism case,[35] despite ample evidence of law enforcement inducing defendants toward illegal activities.[36]

Since September 2001, numerous alternative venues to criminal trials have been proposed and sometimes used. The creation of a specialized national security court has been advocated by some on the political left and right as a means to professionalize and depoliticize the process of adjudicating terrorism trials while also protecting the classification of secret documents.[37] However, such proposals have been met with concern and have not been implemented. The Bush administration made a decision soon after September 2001 to use military commissions to try those who were designated by the administration as "enemy combatants." The military commission system has been through several iterations in the intervening thirteen years, but relatively few defendants have actually been tried in this system.[38]

C. *Punishment of Terrorism*

Prior to the passage of the AEDPA in 1996, sentencing for crimes involving terrorism fell within the range dictated under ordinary criminal law, since defendants usually faced charges based on violent criminal activity, regardless of any political motivations. Upon the passage of the PATRIOT Act, Congress authorized enhancements to the sentencing for numerous terrorism-related crimes.[39] As a result, sentences for such crimes increased significantly, even in situations where there was no direct link to an act of violence, such as material support for terrorism.[40] The existence of a terrorism sentencing enhancement also serves as a statutory basis for appellate courts to overturn sentences as too lenient, as has occurred in high-profile prosecutions, such as those of Ahmad Abu Ali, Lynne Stewart, and Jose Padilla.[41]

[35] See *Ctr. on Law & Security*, N.Y. *Univ. Sch. of Law, Terrorist Trial Report Card: September 11, 2001–September 11, 2011*, 26 (2011), available at http://www.lawandsecurity.org/Portals/0/Documents/TTRC%20Ten%20Year%20Issue.pdf.

[36] See Paul Harris, *Fake Terror Plots, Paid Informants: The Tactics of FBI 'Entrapment' Questioned*, theguardian.com, November 16, 2011, available at http://www.theguardian.com/world/2011/nov/16/fbi-entrapment-fake-terror-plots (arguing that the FBI has concocted terrorism plots, lured and enabled individuals to participate, and then arrested them in order to justify the expansion of the government's counter-terrorism powers).

[37] See Jack Goldsmith and Neal Katyal, *The Terrorists' Court*, nytimes.com, July 11, 2007, available at http://www.nytimes.com/2007/07/11/opinion/11katyal.html?_r=0.

[38] See Part IX.A, infra, for a discussion of the U.S. military commission system.

[39] See *U.S. Sentencing Guidelines Manual*, appendix A (sentencing table) (2011).

[40] The penalty for conviction is a sentence of up to fifteen years in prison, rising to life in prison if the material support results in death. 18 U.S.C. § 2339B (2006).

[41] See *United States v. Stewart*, 686 F.3d 156 (2d Cir. 2012); *United States v. Abu Ali*, 528 F.3d 210 (4th Cir. 2008).

IV. INVESTIGATIVE POWERS

A. *Police Powers*

The USA PATRIOT Act and other legislation in the post-9/11 context increased the powers of federal law enforcement authorities such as the Federal Bureau of Investigation (FBI). This has led to increased surveillance and investigation, as well as a significant number of arrests of alleged terrorists. The government has maintained that its efforts have prevented planned terrorist acts from occurring[42] and has elicited valuable counterterrorism and intelligence information as part of the interrogation, negotiation, and plea bargain process.[43] The federal material witness statute, which empowers the government to detain and question individuals without charge,[44] has enhanced the ability of law enforcement to detain individuals with potentially relevant information for terrorism prosecutions, but it has also increased the potential for abuse of discretion and abuse of executive power.[45]

For most[46] covert counterterrorism-related surveillance, the FBI is obligated to follow requirements under the Foreign Intelligence Surveillance Act (FISA) to seek judicial approval from the Foreign Intelligence Surveillance Court (FISC). Under FISA, law enforcement officials must meet the standard of probable cause to garner a warrant for surveillance, a standard that the government meets in almost all cases.[47] Law enforcement officers must undertake a minimization process by which they attempt to ensure that individuals and communications that are not targets of

42 See, e.g., Sarah Kershaw, *Terrorist in '99 U.S. Case Is Sentenced to 22 Years*, N.Y. TIMES, July 28, 2005, available at http://query.nytimes.com/gstlfullpage.htrn1?res=9A07E7DCI03FF93BAI5754COA9639 C8B63 (describing the detention of Ahmed Ressam two weeks prior to the execution of his planned attack).

43 See Jeff Zeleny and Charlie Savage, *Official Says Terrorism Suspect Is Cooperating*, N.Y. TIMES, February 3, 2010, at A11 (noting that Umar Farouk Abdulmutallab, arrested in conjunction with his alleged attempt to use explosives on a United States–bound airline flight on December 25, 2009, cooperated with law enforcement and offered valuable information pertaining to al-Qaeda).

44 See 18 U.S.C. § 3144 (2000).

45 The government used the material witness statute broadly after the terrorist attacks of September 11, 2001, arresting hundreds of people and detaining them for up to several months. See, e.g., *al-Kidd v. Ashcroft*, 580 F.3d 949 (9th Cir. 2009); *Elmaghraby v. Ashcroft*, No. 04 CV 01809 JG SMG, 2005 WL 2375202, at *2 (E.D.N.Y. September 27, 2005).

46 National Security Letters, used over one hundred thousand times by the Bush administration, circumvented judicial oversight altogether. Instead, they were subpoenas by the FBI seeking information on a target from third parties such as banks or employers, while implementing a gag order on the recipients of the subpoenas. See generally Shirin Sinnar, *Protecting Rights from Within? Inspectors General and National Security Oversight* (2013) 65 STAN. L. REV. 1027.

47 *See* David Kravets, *Domestic Surveillance Court Approved All 1,506 Warrant Applications in 2010*, wired.com, May 6, 2011, available at http://www.wired.com/threatlevel/2011/05/domestic-surveillance/.

investigation are excluded from surveillance.[48] Much of the information garnered pursuant to an FISC warrant is usable in court. FISA has been amended several times since its enactment in 1978, with the most recent amendments in 2008 allowing for broader surveillance authority and immunizing telecommunications companies that work with law enforcement to enable surveillance from civil liability.[49]

The FBI's police powers have also generated a high level of scrutiny of immigrant populations within the United States. The lowered due process protections accorded to immigrants allow for a more searching and a less privacy-protective approach. Lawyers cite the presence of FBI agents during immigration proceedings, Immigration and Custom Enforcement's (ICE) reliance on statements made in old FBI interviews in its decisions, and the FBI's submission of prejudicial affidavits raising national security concerns without providing the basis of the allegations. FBI agents have used the structural power imbalances inherent in the immigration processes to coerce Muslim immigrants into becoming informants or to retaliate if they refuse.[50]

State and local police agencies have worked on counterterrorism issues, often in conjunction with federal law enforcement agencies. Joint Terrorism Task Forces (JTTFs)[51] are arrangements in which a local police department assigns a number of officers to work on a terrorism-related task force with FBI agents;[52] federal agents offer access to powerful investigative tools, whereas police departments offer local knowledge and engagement in community policing.[53] Over one hundred American cities participate in JTTFs,[54] despite occasional concerns that the JTTFs engage in

48 See, e.g., 50 U.S.C. § 1801(h) (2006) (directing the use of minimization procedures to "minimize the acquisition and retention, and prohibit the dissemination, of nonpublicly available information concerning unconsenting United States persons").

49 Foreign Intelligence Surveillance Act of 1978 Amendments Act of 2008, Pub.L. 110–261 (enacted July 10, 2008).

50 Ctr. for Human Rights and Global Justice, Asian Am. Legal Def. and Educ. Fund, *Under the Radar: Muslims Deported, Detained, and Denied on Unsubstantiated Terrorism Allegations* 8 (2011), available at http://aaldef.org/UndertheRadar.pdf.

51 See Federal Bureau of Investigation, *Protecting America from Terrorist Attack: Our Joint Terrorism Task Forces*, fbi.com, available at http://www.fbi.gov/about-us/investigate/terrorism/terrorism_jttfs (describing the role and structure of JTTFs).

52 See Tung Yin, *Joint Terrorism Task Forces as a Window into the Security vs. Civil Liberties Debate* (2012) 13 FLA. COASTAL L. REV. 1 at 3; Fed. Bureau of Investigation, *Boston Joint Terrorism Task Force Memorandum of Understanding* (2006), available at https://www.aclu.org/files/pdfs/spyfiles/ma_attachment3_attach_MSP&FBI2.pdf.

53 See James Forman, Jr., *Community Policing and Youth as Assets* (2004) 95 J. CRIM. L. & CRIMINOLOGY 1 at 9. For a cogent critique of the use of community policing in the counterterrorism context, see Sahar F. Aziz, *Policing Terrorists in the Community* (2014) 5 *Harvard National Security Journal* 147.

54 See FBI, *Protecting America from Terrorist Attack*, supra note 51.

unconstitutional racial and religious profiling.[55] Municipalities such as New York City have engaged in expansive counterterrorism work in the post-9/11 years that has raised significant concerns as the infringement of civil liberties.[56] Fusion centers are state and local entities meant to enhance the ability of the federal government to garner and synthesize information from local communities,[57] but have been criticized for undermining civil liberties and wasting taxpayer funds.[58]

B. *Intelligence Agencies*

The Central Intelligence Agency (CIA) and the National Security Agency (NSA), the leading intelligence-gathering organizations for the U.S. government, have operated with much greater latitude in the post-9/11 era than previously.[59] The CIA has worked extensively to capture, detain, and interrogate suspected terrorists abroad. It operated various secret detention facilities, known as "black sites," throughout the world to accomplish this goal, prompting criticism from international and domestic groups that people were being disappeared by the CIA.[60] In 2009, the use of those black sites was curtailed by President Barack Obama.[61]

In the post-9/11 era, the NSA has, among other programs, allocated tremendous energy and resources to massive data collection of electronic communications of U.S. and foreign persons.[62] The NSA defends its collection of telephone call

55 See William Yardley, *Portland, Ore, Votes to Rejoin Task Force After Terrorism Scare*, nytimes.com, April 30, 2011, available at http://www.nytimes.com/2011/05/01/us/01portland.html?_r=2&ref=us& (visited September 27, 2013) (describing the civil liberties concerns behind the temporary refusal of Portland, Oregon, to work with the FBI as part of a JTTF).

56 See generally Matt Apuzzo and Adam Goldman, Enemies Within: Inside the NYPD's Secret Spying Unit and *Bin* Laden's Final Plot Against America (New York, Touchstone, 2013) (offering evidence of systematic religious profiling and discrimination by the New York City Police Department's counterterrorism unit).

57 See Department of Homeland Security, *State and Major Urban Area Fusion Centers*, available at http://www.dhs.gov/state-and-major-urban-area-fusion-centers.

58 See Senators Carl Levin and Tom Coburn, *Federal Support for and Involvement in State and Local Fusion Centers*, United States Senate Permanent Subcommittee on Investigations Committee on Homeland Security and Governmental Affairs, October 3, 2012.

59 The CIA is prohibited from conducting surveillance within U.S. borders. See Executive Order 12333, 46 Fed. Reg. 59941 (December 4, 1981); National Security Act of 1947. However, the CIA has justified its surveillance within the United States by focusing its efforts on foreign targets that have contact with domestic sources, as well as assigning CIA officers on unpaid leave to work on domestic efforts. See Inspector General David B. Buckley, *Review of CIA-NYPD Relationship*, December 27, 2011, available at https://www.documentcloud.org/documents/717864-cia-nypd-ig.html).

60 See Dafna Linzer and Julie Tate, *New Light Shed on CIA's 'Black Site' Prisons*, washpost.com, February 28, 2007, available at http://www.washingtonpost.com/wp-dyn/content/article/2007/02/27/AR2007022702214.html (visited September 27, 2013).

61 Exec. Order No. 13,491, 74 Fed. Reg. 16,4893 (January 22, 2009).

62 Timothy B. Lee, *Here's Everything We Know About PRISM to Date*, washpost.com, June 12, 2013, available at http://www.washingtonpost.com/blogs/wonkblog/wp/2013/06/12/heres-everything-we-know-about-prism-to-date/ (visited September 27, 2013).

metadata and electronic communications based on the FISC's interpretation of section 215 of the PATRIOT Act. The FISC has created a nonpublic body of law that has allowed the NSA to amass the metadata (time, location, duration, and other information not containing content) for all domestic and some international phone calls.[63] From June 2013 onward, as details of the breadth and depth of the NSA's surveillance programs continue to leak to the public,[64] questions have arisen as to whether the scope of the NSA's surveillance is an unconstitutional intrusion into the privacy of U.S. citizens, whether congressional oversight of the NSA must be strengthened,[65] and whether the FISC provides an effective mechanism to curb potential abuse by the NSA.[66]

These debates continue to be robust, largely due to the impact of these counterterrorism programs on a vast swath of the U.S. public and because of the seeming inability of the public to understand the program and unwillingness to pressure the political branches to curtail it. This opacity stems from the executive branch secrecy surrounding the program, Congress's inability to disclose the extent of its knowledge to the public or exercise substantial oversight, the FISC not being able to take an adversarial position with regard to government assurances of the necessity of such surveillance, and the extent of NSA access to the data stored by telecommunications companies, even without their consent.[67] Thus far, Congress has failed to pass legislation to curtail NSA data collection practices, and reforms to limit the NSA's data collection practices have been modest and have stemmed from the executive branch itself.[68]

63 Jennifer Valentino-Devries and Siobhan Gorman, *Secret Court's Redefinition of "Relevant" Empowered Vast NSA Data-Gathering*, WALL ST. J., July 8, 2013, available at http://online.wsj.com/article/SB10001424127887323873904578571893758853344.html.

64 Former CIA contractor Edward Snowden began disclosing numerous aspects of NSA surveillance practices in June 2013. See Glenn Greenwald, *NSA Collecting Phone Records of Millions of Verizon Customers Daily*, theguardian.com, June 5, 2013, available at http://www.theguardian.com/world/2013/jun/06/nsa-phone-records-verizon-court-order.

65 See Spencer Ackerman, *Intelligence Committee Withheld Key File Before Critical NSA Vote, Admid Claims*, guardian.com, August 12, 2013, available at http://www.theguardian.com/world/2013/aug/12/intelligence-committee-nsa-vote-justin-amash (noting that congressional leaders had not shared the relevant information with their colleagues prior to voting for PATRIOT Act reauthorization).

66 See Carol D. Leonnig, *Court: Ability to Police U.S. Spying Program Is Limited*, washingtonpost.com, August 15, 2013, available at http://www.washingtonpost.com/politics/court-ability-to-police-us-spying-program-limited/2013/08/15/4a8c8c44-05cd-11e3-a07f-49ddc7417125_story.html (citing U.S. district judge Reggie Walton and noting that "the court lacks the tools to independently verify how often the government's surveillance breaks the court's rules…[and] it also cannot check the veracity of the government's assertions that the violations its staff members report are unintentional mistakes").

67 See Nicole Perlroth, Jeff Larson, and Scott Shane, *N.S.A. Able to Foil Basic Safeguards of Privacy on Web*, N.Y. TIMES, September 6, 2013, at A1 (discussing NSA efforts to make encryption software vulnerable and noting that much of this activity has been sanctioned by the FISC).

68 *See* Office of the Director of National Intelligence, *Signals Intelligence Reform 2015 Annual Report*, IC on the Record, available at http://icontherecord.tumblr.com/ppd-28/2015/privacy-civil-liberties (visited February 7, 2015) (detailing some curtailing of the NSA's domestic and foreign data collection

V. PROSCRIPTION/LISTING OF TERRORIST GROUPS/INDIVIDUALS

A. *Proscription Mechanisms*

The ability of the secretary of state to designate "foreign terrorist organizations" (FTOs) as such for the purposes of prohibiting material support, increasing surveillance, and freezing financial assets has been an important tool for U.S. counterterrorism efforts.[69] In particular, U.S. law provides that incitement to commit a terrorist act (under circumstances indicating an intention to cause death or serious bodily injury) is a basis for designating a group as either an FTO[70] or a terrorist organization for immigration purposes.[71] Even if a group has not been formally designated as an FTO, if the requisite incitement standard is met, that automatically triggers treatment as a terrorist organization for immigration purposes.[72] Observers suggest that the FTOs fall into one of two categories: those that genuinely threaten the national security of the United States in a direct way, and those that challenge the foreign relations or economic interests of the United States.[73]

Under the AEDPA, a specific process must be undertaken to designate an organization as an FTO.[74] It is a process that is open to critique as being insufficiently rights-protective, but also incorporates some safeguards against abuse.[75] Once the State Department has made the FTO designation, limited procedural safeguards are available, after which the designation is finalized.[76]

and retention practices); Dan Roberts and Dominic Rushe, *Proposed Changes to US Data Collection Fall Short of NSA Reformers' Goals*, theguardian.com, February 3, 2015, available at http://www.theguardian.com/us-news/2015/feb/03/proposed-changes-us-data-collection-nsa-reformers (describing changes to NSA data collection practices as modest).

69 U.S. 2006 CTC Report, *supra* note 17, at 8.

70 8 U.S.C. § 1189.

71 8 U.S.C. § 1182(a)(3)(B)(vi)(II) (provided that other relevant legal criteria are met).

72 8 U.S.C. § 1182(a)(3)(B)(vi)(III).

73 Wadie E. Said, *The Material Support Prosecution and Foreign Policy* (2011) 86 IND. L.J. 543 at 568.

74 See AEDPA §§ 219(a)(1)(A)-(C), 219(a)(2)(C) (codified in 8 USC §1189(a)) (finding that anyone who interacts with FTOs is violating the statute, and authorizing the secretary of the treasury to freeze the assets of entities designated as FTOs); Exec. Order No. 12,947, 3 C.F.R. 319 (1995) (establishing authority for the secretary of state and the secretary of the treasury to limit property rights of designated terrorists). See also Exec. Order No. 13,224, 3 C.F.R. 786 (2002) (finding it necessary to utilize financial sanctions against foreign terrorists).

75 See AEDPA § 219(a) (codified as 8 U.S.C. § 1189(a)) (establishing both the procedure used for designation as a terrorist organization as well as congressional and judicial means available to pursue designations review and revocation); see also Julie B. Shapiro, *The Politicization of the Designation of Foreign Terrorist Organizations: The Effect on Separation of Powers* (2008), 6 CARDOZO PUB. L. POL'Y & ETHICS J. 547 at 556–8 (arguing that the designation process contravenes due process guarantees).

76 Under AEDPA, the secretary of state notifies leaders in Congress and gives notice to designees in the Federal Register. AEDPA § 302(a)(2)(A) (codifed as 8 U.S.C. § 1189(a)(2)(A)). FTOs then have thirty days to challenge their designation in the U.S. Court of Appeals for the District of Columbia Court. § 302(b).

Because the consequences of FTO designation can be severe, including the ability of financial intuitions to block or freeze assets of an FTO,[77] the barring of FTOs from entry into the United States,[78] and potential material support charges,[79] the procedural safeguards are even more important.[80] FTO designation carries with it mandatory review and renewal process for the secretary of state.[81]

B. *Challenges to Proscriptions and Listings*

Another such safeguard in the FTO designation process is the opportunity to contest the designation proposed by the State Department. This layer of judicial review protects against arbitrariness in the designation[82] and requires some disclosure of the basis upon which the State Department made its determination.[83]

Designated groups may challenge their designations by seeking judicial review before the D.C. Circuit Court within thirty days of the designation being published in the Federal Register. The court may rely only on the administrative record generated by the secretary of state, who may supplement this record on an *ex parte* basis with classified information used in making the designation.[84] The D.C. Circuit has the right to reverse if the designation is found to be not in accord with the procedures required by law. The FTO designation remains in force until it is

Such cases, usually based on allegations of an abuse of discretion by the State Department or a lack of substantial support for the FTO designation, are largely unsuccessful. E.g., People's Mojahedin Org. of Iran v. Dep't of State, 327 F.3d 1238, 1244 (D.C. Cir. 2003) (upholding FTO designation based on classified evidence and emphasizing deference to the State Department in the FTO designation process).

77 18 U.S.C. § 2339B(a)(2) (2006).

78 8 U.S.C. §§ 1182(a)(3)(B)(i)(IV)-(V) (2006).

79 18 U.S.C. § 2339B(a)(1) (2006). The constitutionality of the FTO designation process authorized by Executive Order No. 13,224 and various statutes was upheld by the U.S. Supreme Court in *Humanitarian Law Project v. Holder. Holder v. Humanitarian Law Project*, 130 S. Ct. 2705 (2010).

80 See Nat'l Council of Resistance of Iran v. Dep't of State, 251 F.3d 192, 196 (D.C. Cir. 2001) (discussing the severe impact of FTO designation).

81 8 U.S.C. § 1189(a)(4)(C), (a)(6) (2006). If no review has been made of an FTO designation for five years, the secretary of state must review the listing to determine whether it should be revoked due to a change in the organization's mission and actions or due to a change in the national security assessment by the United States. See id.

82 Under the AEDPA, courts have the power to set aside the State Department designation of an FTO if it is arbitrary, capricious, and an abuse of discretion or if it is not based on substantial evidence. AEDPA § 302(b)(3) (codified as 8 U.S.C. § 1189(c)(3)). Courts have, however, been extremely deferential to the State Department, choosing not to review classified evidence in some instances, but relying instead on State Department affirmations of substantial evidence to support its designation decision. E.g., *People's Mojahedin Org. of Iran*, 327 F.3d at 1244.

83 E.g., *People's Mojahedin Org. of Iran v. United States Dep't of State*, 613 F.3d 220, 231 (D.C. Cir. 2010) (holding that the government had violated due process by failing to give an FTO the opportunity to view unclassified evidence prior to making a final decision denying petition to revoke designation as an FTO).

84 See Said, *Material Support Prosecution*, supra note 73, at 559.

revoked by either judicial or administrative review. In either case, the burden lies with the FTO to challenge its designation.

VI. REGULATION OF TERRORISM FINANCING

A. *The Regulatory Regime to Counter Terrorism Financing*

Executive Order 13224 was signed by President George W. Bush in September 2001 with the stated purpose of disrupting and destroying financial support for al-Qaeda.[85] A number of policies designed to minimize and disrupt terrorist financing have become important tools in U.S. counterterrorism strategy. These policies are implemented largely by the Treasury Department,[86] with support from the State Department and Justice Department. The Office of Intelligence and Analysis (OIA) within Treasury Department was created in 2004, making the Treasury Department the only finance ministry in the world with its own in-house intelligence unit. Separately, Treasury Department's Office of Terrorism and Financial Intelligence (TFI) members chair the U.S. delegation to the Financial Action Task Force, an intergovernmental body that develops and promotes policies to combat illicit finance.[87]

Title III of the PATRIOT Act amended the Bank Secrecy Act to require certain financial institutions and businesses to establish anti–money laundering programs.[88] The government also sought to encourage transparency, good corporate governance, and strong anti–money laundering programs through suggesting that public and media attention will cause social stigma to attach to businesses that engage with entities that are associated with criminal or terrorist activity.[89] U.S. authorities have prioritized the investigation and disruption of funding to nonprofit organizations and have used the material support statutes as an effective, if highly controversial, tool to hinder the ability of terrorist groups to maintain their finances. The robust use of material support statutes has caused such solicitation to wither or, in some cases, go further underground.[90]

85 Executive Order 13224 of September 23, 2001: Blocking Property and Prohibiting Transactions with Persons Who Commit, Threaten to Commit, or Support Terrorism (citing both domestic authority and United Nations Security Council Resolution (UNSCR) 1214, UNSCR 1267, UNSCR 1333, and UNSCR 1363 as supportive authority).

86 The Treasury Department's Office of Terrorism and Financial Intelligence (TFI) coordinates these efforts. The TFI consists of four subgroups: the Financial Crimes Enforcement Network (FinCEN), the Office of Foreign Assets Control (OFAC), the Office of Terrorist Financing and Financial Crimes (TFFC), and the Office of Intelligence and Analysis (OIA).

87 *Third Mutual Evaluation Report on Anti-Money Laundering and Combating the Financing of Terrorism: United States of America* (Financial Action Task Force, Paris, France), June 2006, at 4 (hereinafter "June 2006 Financing Report"), available at http://www.fatf-gafi.org/countries/u-z/unitedstates/documents/mutualevaluationoftheunitedstates.html.

88 Id.

89 Id. at 5.

90 Id. at 8.

The Department of Justice is the principal government entity responsible for overseeing the investigation and prosecution of money laundering and terrorist financing offenses at the federal level, whereas the State Department represents the U.S. government in several multilateral institutions, including those exercising sanctions related to U.N. Security Council Resolution 1267 and Counter-Terrorism Committees.[91]

The State Department's Office of the Coordinator for Counterterrorism leads its efforts to designate FTOs in order to freeze assets and prepare Executive Order 13224 designations to block assets and prohibit contributions of terrorists and terrorist organizations.[92]

B. *Criminal Offenses of Terrorism Financing*

The issues of what standards of knowledge and intent are necessary to sustain a conviction for material support of terrorism have been extensively litigated. The 2010 Supreme Court decision in *Holder v. Humanitarian Law Project* affirmed the constitutionality of the material support statute, thereby upholding the congressional intent to criminalize almost all support to FTOs, even if the funds were earmarked for humanitarian – not terrorism – purposes.[93]

The four federal offenses deal directly with financing of terrorism or terrorist organizations and criminalize the provision of material support for the commission of certain offenses,[94] provision of material support or resources to designated FTOs,[95] provision or collection of terrorist funds,[96] and the concealment or disguise of either material support to FTOs or funds used or to be used for terrorist acts.[97]

VII. IMMIGRATION MEASURES

A. *Immigration Detention*

The government is authorized to detain any person for whom it has certified that reasonable grounds exist to believe that the person has engaged in espionage,[98] opposition

91 Id. at 17.
92 Id. at 19.
93 *Holder v. Humanitarian Law Project*, 130 S. Ct. 2705 (2010).
94 18 USC 2339A (enacted in 1994, effective in 1996).
95 18 USC 2339B (enacted by Congress and signed by the president in April 1996 and implemented with State Department designations of FTOs on October 8, 1997).
96 18 USC 2339C(a) (enacted June 25, 2002).
97 18 USC 2339C(c) (enacted June 25, 2002).
98 Immigration and Naturalization Act (INA) §237(a)(4)(A)(i) (authorizing detention for those suspected of engaging in espionage, sabotage, or export control).

by violence,[99] or terrorist activity[100] or is involved with an organization that is suspected of terrorist activity.[101] The attorney general may detain the suspect for up to seven days prior to placing the suspect in removal proceedings or charging the suspect criminally.[102] If the suspect is not placed in removal proceedings or criminally charged, the attorney general must release him or her, but if placed in proceedings, the attorney general must detain the person even if he or she is eligible for relief or obtains relief until the attorney general determines that there is no longer any reason to believe that the person falls under one of the bases for certification.[103] The attorney general is obligated to review the certification subjecting the person to mandatory detention every six months, and the detainee may request review every six months and may submit documents and other evidence in support of his or her request.[104] A detainee who has been ordered removed, but whose removal is unlikely in the reasonably foreseeable future, may be detained for additional six-month periods only if the government believes that release will threaten national security or the safety of the community or any person.[105]

Since September 11, 2001, the federal government has relied heavily on immigration law and policy to detain, interrogate, control, and remove suspected terrorists.[106] With fewer checks and balances, it is much easier for the government to arrest, detain, and investigate an individual under immigration law than criminal law. Unlike the U.S. criminal justice system, where defendants have the right to an attorney, the right to a speedy trial, and the presumption of innocence until guilt is proven beyond a reasonable doubt, immigration law does not afford detainees ample protections. For example, a noncitizen is permitted to have an attorney in immigration proceedings, but counsel is not provided for the 80 percent of detainees in removal proceedings who are indigent. Furthermore, a noncitizen can be mandatorily detained for months, or even years, before being released or

99 INA §237 (a)(4)(A)(iii) (authorizing detention for those expressing opposition by violence or overthrow of the U.S. government).

100 INA §212(a)(4)(B) (authorizing detention for those suspected of terrorist activity); 8 U.S.C. § 1182(a)(3)(B)(i)(III) and (iv)(I) (authorizing removal of those indicating an intention to cause death or serious bodily harm or who have incited terrorist activity); 8 U.S.C. § 1182(a)(3)(B)(i)(VI) (making inadmissible aliens who endorse or espouse terrorist activity or persuade others to endorse or espouse terrorist activity).

101 See 8 U.S.C. § 1182(a)(3)(B)(vi)(II) or (III). See also U.S. CTC Response 2006, *supra* note 17, at 8 (noting that "if a group is designated or treated as a terrorist organization for immigration purposes, aliens having certain associations with the group [including persons who knowingly provide material support to the group] become inadmissible to and deportable from the United States").

102 INA §236(a)(5).

103 INA §§236(a)(2), (5).

104 INA §236A (a)(7).

105 INA §236A (a)(6).

106 In 2009, Immigration and Customs Enforcement (ICE) had over 1.6 million aliens in its scope of monitoring: in ICE detention centers, in other jails or prisons, or under a released monitoring system. See Department of Homeland Security Office of the Inspector General, *Supervision of Aliens Commensurate with Risk*, OIG 11–81 (December 2011) (hereinafter DHS 2011 IG Report), at 3.

removed from the United States, and the standard for removal is that of "clear and convincing evidence," a much lower standard than that of reasonable doubt.[107]

These lesser protections have allowed federal officials to undertake several initiatives that have targeted immigrants, primarily those from Muslim-majority countries, in the name of national security. Muslims in the immigration system have been subjected to possibly abusive[108] preventive detention,[109] exclusion based on political views, heightened surveillance, and arguably unconstitutional racial profiling.[110] Detainees in the immigration system face serious hurdles in challenging the government's case for removal due to the lower removal standard of "clear and convincing evidence" as well as the inability to access and challenge the secret evidence presented and alleged by the government.[111]

The government has, to some extent, conflated immigration and counterterrorism programs and has encouraged use of the immigration system as an important tool in counterterrorism efforts.[112] The result has been a system that, although legal under U.S. law,[113] arguably violates international law and norms with regard to the treatment of migrants.[114]

[107] Immigration and Naturalization Act §240(c)(3)(A).

[108] See *Ashcroft v. Iqbal*, 556 U.S. 662, 667–9 (2009).

[109] Another category of detained aliens are those subject to an additional interagency screening called Third Agency Check. This system screens aliens in ICE custody who are from specially designated countries (SDCs) that have "shown a tendency to promote, produce, or protect terrorist organizations or their members." See DHS 2011 IG Report, *supra* note 105, at 5. The SDC list is largely comprised of majority Muslim nations. See *ICE List of Specially Designated Countries (SDCs) that Promote or Protect Terrorism*, publicintelligence.net, July 2, 2011, available at http://publicintelligence.net/specially-designated-countries/ (listing the SDCs that were originally part of the DHS 2011 IG Report, but which were subsequently removed from that publication).

[110] See Ctr. for Human Rights and Global Justice, Asian Am. Legal Def. and Educ. Fund, UNDER THE RADAR: MUSLIMS DEPORTED, DETAINED, AND DENIED ON UNSUBSTANTIATED TERRORISM ALLEGATIONS 4 (2011) (hereinafter "Under the Radar"), available at http://aaldef.org/UndertheRadar.pdf (discussing various programs targeting noncitizens, including Absconder Apprehension Initiative, NSEERS special registration policy, and Operation Frontline). Another controversial immigration policing program is Secure Communities, which requires state and local police to send fingerprints of arrestees to ICE so that undocumented immigrants can be identified and possibly detained, prosecuted and removed. See Immigration and Customs Enforcement, *Secure Communities*, ice.gov (describing the Secure Communities program), available at http://www.ice.gov/secure_communities/ (visited September 13, 2013).

[111] See "Under the Radar," supra note 110, at 4.

[112] See, e.g., Attorney General John Ashcroft and INS Commissioner Jim Ziglar, Announcement of INS Restructuring Plan (November 14, 2001), available at http://www.justice.gov/archive/ag/speeches/2001/agcrisisremarks11_14.htm ("The INS will also be an important part of our effort to prevent aliens who engage in or support terrorist activity from entering our country.").

[113] See DHS 2011 IG Report, supra note 106, at 1 (noting that immigration authorities had generally complied with applicable domestic laws).

[114] See "Under the Radar," supra note 110, at 18 (citing the conclusion of the U.N. Special Rapporteur on the Rights of Migrants that U.S. immigration enforcement policies violate international laws that bar arbitrary detention).

VIII. ADMINISTRATIVE/EXECUTIVE MEASURES

The AUMF and PATRIOT Act cemented the government's authority to determine whether information was too sensitive to disclose and then punish those who disclosed such information.[115] More recently, Congress enacted the National Defense Authorization Act of 2012, which empowered the president to take extraordinary national security measures unilaterally and enabled further nondisclosure of information by the administration and military.[116]

One area in which the tensions between secret, unilateral executive action and the desire for a public, multibranch course of action has been most prominent is that of targeted killings. The U.S. use of unmanned aerial vehicles ("drones") for targeted killings[117] of suspected terrorists has expanded significantly since President Obama took office in 2009.[118] The Obama administration has consistently emphasized the necessity, efficacy, and legality of targeted killings. However, the program has prompted much debate over its existence,[119] the moral calculus[120] and legal parameters and authorities for such a program,[121] and specific questions

[115] See USA PATRIOT Act of 2001, Pub. L. No. 107–56, § 215, 115 Stat. 272 (codified in scattered sections of 50 U.S.C.) (disallowing the dissemination of information regarding any business records that are sought pursuant to terrorism investigations); id. § 223 (codified in scattered sections of 18 U.S.C.) (permitting civil liability and administrative disciplinary measures against individuals who make unauthorized disclosures of information); id. § 116 (prohibiting disclosure to individuals involved in suspicious activities that such activity was reported pursuant to the issuance of a National Security Letter).

[116] National Defense Authorization Act for Fiscal Year 2012, Pub. L. No. 112–81, §1025 (2011) (limiting the types of information, forms of communication, and representation available to detainees).

[117] Although "targeted killings" are not defined under international law, they are often considered to encompass "premeditated acts of lethal force employed by states in times of peace or during armed conflict to eliminate specific individuals outside their custody." See Jonathan Masters, *Targeted Killings*, Council on Foreign Relations, May 23, 2013, available at http://www.cfr.org/counterterrorism/targeted-killings/p9627 (visited July 18, 2013). Although the governments that utilize targeted killings differentiate them from assassinations (see Harold Hongju Koh, *The Obama Administration and International Law*, March 25, 2010, available at http://www.state.gov/s/l/releases/remarks/139119.htm), critics view them as similar actions in terms of illegality. See, e.g., Complaint, *Al-Aulaqi, et al. v. Panetta*, at ¶1, Case 1:12-cv-01192-RMC (D.D.C. July 18, 2012).

[118] *See* New America Foundation, Drone Database, available at http://natsec.newamerica.net/about (visited July 18, 2013) (detailing the number of drone strikes by the United States in Yemen and Pakistan since 2004).

[119] See, e.g., Philip Alston, *Report of the Special Rapporteur on Extrajudicial, Summary or Arbitrary Executions: Study on Targeted Killings*, A/HRC/14/24/Add.6, May 28, 2010 (questioning the legality of the CIA drone program).

[120] See generally Samuel Isaacharoff and Richard H. Pildes, *Drones and the Dilemma of Modern Warfare*, available at http://ssrn.com/abstract=2268596 (visited July 31, 2013) (theorizing the moral dilemma of drone use in the context of warfare in which geographic and other traditional boundaries of violence are distorted).

[121] See Alston, *supra* note 119, at Add.6, May 28, 2010 (discussing international law of war principles with regard to targeted killings); e.g., Eric Holder, *Attorney General Eric Holder Speaks at Northwestern*

regarding the legality of its scope in terms of geographic location of the target and citizenship of the target.[122] The parameters and future of the targeted killings program should be considered in the context of two Obama administration positions as to the nature of the battle being fought: first, the assertion that the theater of war for U.S. counterterrorism efforts is not restricted geographically and, therefore, encompasses the entire globe;[123] and second, statements made by administration officials in early 2013 that although the country should not remain on a war footing permanently, current counterterrorism efforts will likely last another ten to twenty years.[124]

The parameters of the targeted killing program remain largely shielded from public view, with limited information disclosed during President Obama's first term[125] and the leak of a classified Department of Justice memorandum detailing some of the legal bases for the program.[126] In early 2012, Attorney General Holder's public statement on drone use made clear that the administration was not bound geographically, that U.S. citizenship was no protection against being included on the list of targets for a drone strike, and that no judicial process was constitutionally necessary to target U.S. citizens so long as the administration followed its own careful procedures of determining whether to target a citizen.[127]

In May 2013, President Obama gave his second[128] major national security policy speech, discussing a number of national security and foreign policy priorities, but

University School of Law, March 5, 2012, available at http://www.justice.gov/iso/opa/ag/speeches/2012/ag-speech-1203051.html (outlining the parameters used by the Obama administration to determine whether a targeted killing comports with international and domestic legal obligations).

122 See *Al-Aulaqi v. Obama*, 727 F. Supp. 2d 1 (D.D.C. 2010) (dismissing, based on standing grounds, the suit of Nasser al-Aulaqi to enjoin the U.S. government from keeping his son, U.S. citizen Anwar al-Aulaqi, on its targeted killing list).

123 Spencer Ackerman, *Spec Ops Chief Sees '10 to 20 Years' More for War Against al-Qaida*, wired.com, May 16, 2013, available at http://www.wired.com/dangerroom/2013/05/decades-of-war/ (visited July 18, 2013) (discussing the Senate testimony of Michael Sheehan, the assistant secretary of defense for special operations and low-intensity conflict, with regard to the global theater of war).

124 Id. (relating the Senate testimony of Michael Sheehan, the assistant secretary of defense for special operations and low-intensity conflict, with regard to the probable duration of the U.S. counterterrorism effort against al-Qaida).

125 E.g., John O. Brennan, *Remarks of John O. Brennan: Strengthening Our Security by Adhering to Our Values and Laws*, September 16, 2011, available at http://www.whitehouse.gov/the-press-office/2011/09/16/remarks-john-o-brennan-strengthening-our-security-adhering-our-values-an (visited July 24, 2013); Koh, *The Obama Administration and International Law*, supra note 117.

126 Department of Justice White Paper, *Lawfulness of a Lethal Operation Directed Against a U.S. Citizen Who Is a Senior Operational Leader of Al-Qa'ida or an Associated Force*, available at http://msnbcmedia.msn.com/i/msnbc/sections/news/020413_DOJ_White_Paper.pdf (visited July 24, 2013) (hereinafter "DOJ White Paper").

127 See Holder, *Attorney General Eric Holder Speaks*, supra note 121.

128 President Obama gave his first major speech on national security in 2009. See Remarks by the President on National Security, May 21, 2009, available at http://www.whitehouse.gov/the-press-office/remarks-president-national-security-5-21-09 (hereinafter "2009 National Archives Speech").

focusing in large part on the parameters of the administration's targeted killing program.[129] In it, he argued that the use of drones to kill suspected terrorists is effective, legal and necessary, yet also acknowledged legal, foreign policy and political constraints on the program.[130] Some critics were disappointed that the speech did not place additional meaningful limits on the president's authority to use drones, and that the president's promises of transparency and adequate oversight were unsupported by specific details or plans.[131]

IX. ROLE OF MILITARY AND EXTRATERRITORIAL COUNTERTERRORISM ACTIVITIES

A. *Military Courts and Detention*

The Bush administration decided immediately after the September 11 attacks to detain suspected terrorists as unlawful enemy combatants – often at the U.S. military facility in Guantanamo Bay, Cuba – and to try them, if at all, before a military commission.[132] Such detention would not necessarily comport with international standards, and any commissions would be administered by the executive branch and would not necessarily include the protections mandated by the Uniform Code of Military Justice for the courts-martial system.[133]

129 Remarks by the President at the National Defense University, May 23, 2013, available at http://www.whitehouse.gov/the-press-office/2013/05/23/remarks-president-national-defense-university (hereinafter "May 2013 NDU Speech").

130 Id.

131 E.g., Glenn Greenwald, *Obama's Speech: Seeing What You Want to See*, theguardian.com, May 27, 2013, available at Fred Kaplan, *Obama's Post-9/11 World*, slate.com, May 23, 2013, available at http://www.theguardian.com/commentisfree/2013/may/27/obama-war-on-terror-speech (visited August 12, 2013) (arguing that President Obama's speech was mostly rhetoric meant to appease critics from a variety of political perspectives); http://www.slate.com/articles/news_and_politics/war_stories/2013/05/barack_obama_national_defense_university_speech_nothing_new_about_drones.html (visited July 18, 2013) (noting that President Obama's speech outlined limits that were almost identical to those already in place and that the Justice Department had defined those limitations in ways that rendered the restrictions "meaningless"). Some politically conservative critics asserted that President Obama's speech consisted largely of rhetoric to appease liberal voters concerned about the administration's use of drones, but that Obama's substantive policy and approach to executive power was similar to that of President George W. Bush. See, e.g., Benjamin Wittes, *The President's Speech: A Quick and Dirty Reaction – Part 1 (Are We At War?)*, Lawfare Blog, May 23, 2013, available at http://www.lawfareblog.com/2013/05/the-presidents-speech-a-quick-and-dirty-reaction-part-1/.

132 Military Order of November 13, 2001, 66 Fed. Reg. 57833 (November 13, 2001).

133 See Setty, *Specialized Trials*, supra note 31, at 142–3 (discussing the ways in which the procedural protections offered to detainees in the military commission system deviated from the Uniform Code of Military Justice).

a. Detention at the Guantanamo Bay Facility

In designating the Guantanamo Bay, Cuba, military facility[134] to hold detainees, the Bush administration made an overt choice to seek to evade the domestic legal protections that would run to detainees held on U.S. soil,[135] including access to habeas corpus hearings.[136] The government further denied the applicability of international human rights and humanitarian norms and international law more generally, as applied to the detainees held at Guantanamo.[137] When the Supreme Court held that the U.S. habeas corpus statute encompassed the indefinite detention of detainees at Guantanamo,[138] the administration convinced Congress to amend that statute to deny all detainees the right to habeas corpus, even those who had already filed claims in court.[139] In the 2008 *Boumediene v. Bush* decision, the Supreme Court ruled that Congress and the president could not decide that detainees at Guantanamo had no access to the law.[140] Since then, most captured detainees have been taken to other locations, such as the Bagram Air Force base in Afghanistan, where courts have held that detainees have no habeas rights.[141]

Since 2002, 779 men have been taken to the naval base in Guantanamo Bay, Cuba,[142] and 164 remained there as of September 2013.[143] There have been consistent reports of widespread abuse, torture, and violations of the prisoners' human rights.[144]

[134] For a thoughtful and detailed assessment of the role of the Guantanamo Bay military facility in U.S. history and foreign policy, see Ernesto Hernandez-Lopez, *Guantánamo as Outside and Inside the U.S.: Why Is a Base a Legal Anomaly?* (2010) 18 AM. U. J. GENDER SOC. POL'Y & L. 471.

[135] See *Rasul v. Bush*, 542 U.S. 466, 497–8 (2004) (Scalia, J., dissenting).

[136] David Cole, *The Taint of Torture: the Roles of Law and Policy in Our Descent to the Dark Side* (2012) 49 *HOUS. L. REV.* 53, 65.

[137] See Memorandum from Jack L. Goldsmith III, Assistant Attorney Gen., Office of Legal Counsel, to Alberto R. Gonzales, Counsel to the President, *"Protected Person" Status in Occupied Iraq Under the Fourth Geneva Convention* 23 (March 18, 2004), available at http://www.justice.gov/olc/2004/gc4mar18.pdf.

[138] See *Rasul v. Bush*, 542 U.S. 466, 484 (2004).

[139] See Military Commissions Act of 2006, Pub. L. No. 109–366, §7, 120 Stat. 2600, 2635–36 (codified as amended at 28 U.S.C. §2241(e) (1) (2006)).

[140] See *Boumediene v. Bush*, 533 U.S. 723, 785 (2008). ("The Constitution grants Congress and the President the power to acquire, dispose of, and govern territory, not the power to decide when and where its terms apply.")

[141] See *Al-Maqaleh v. Gates*, 605 F.3d 84 (D.C. Cir. 2010).

[142] Amnesty Int'l, *USA: "I Am Fallen into Darkness." Obaidullah, Guantánamo Detainee in His 12th Year Without Trial* 1 (2013), available at http://www.amnestyusa.org/sites/default/files/amr510512013en.pdf.

[143] See Karen McVeigh, *US Sends Two Guantánamo Bay prison Detainees Home to Algeria*, theguardian.com, August 29, 2013, available at http://www.theguardian.com/world/2013/aug/29/us-guantanamo-bay-detainees-algeria (visited September 22, 2013) (detailing the recent release of two Algerian detainees, bringing the total number of Guantanamo detainees to 164).

[144] See, e.g., Ctr. for Constitutional Rights, *Report on Torture and Cruel, Inhumane, and Degrading Treatment of Prisoners at Guantánamo Bay, Cuba* (2006), available at http://ccrjustice.org/files/Report_ReportOnTorture.pdf.

Almost two-thirds of the prisoners joined an ongoing hunger strike in February 2013, which has led to military resorting to force-feeding several prisoners.[145] Federal district courts have declined to intervene on behalf of the prisoners, despite widespread condemnation by the United Nations and international human rights groups that the force-feeding constitutes torture.[146] President Barack Obama recommitted to closing Guantanamo Bay in May 2013[147] after failing to fulfill the promise to do so when he took office in 2009.[148]

b. Access to Justice

The United States Supreme Court, in a series of cases from 2004 to 2008,[149] found various aspects of the administration's detention and military commission model to be unconstitutional. However, the Supreme Court consistently found that the use of military commissions instead of the ordinary criminal justice system was constitutionally acceptable.[150]

Supreme Court jurisprudence set a minimum guarantee of constitutional rights to be available to detainees, such as that of habeas corpus, but curtailing certain procedural and substantive protections in a military commission system is acceptable.[151] After initially suggesting that military commissions were not necessary

[145] Ann E. Marimow, *Judge Rejects Request to Block Force-feeding of Guantanamo Bay Detainees*, WASH. POST (July 16, 2013), http://articles.washingtonpost.com/2013-07-16/national/40606715_1_hunger-strike-detainees-force-feeding.

[146] See United Nations Human Rights, *IACHR, UN Working Group on Arbitrary Detention, UN Rapporteur on Torture, UN Rapporteur on Human Rights and Counter-Terrorism, and UN Rapporteur on Health Reiterate Need to End the Indefinite Detention of Individuals at Guatánamo Naval Base in Light of Current Human Rights Crisis*, May 1, 2013, available at http://www.ohchr.org/EN/NewsEvents/Pages/DisplayNews.aspx?NewsID=13278&LangID=E (decrying the force-feeding of the detainees as contrary to international law).

[147] See President Barack Obama, *Remarks by the President at the National Defense University* (May 23, 2013), available at http://www.whitehouse.gov/the-press-office/2013/05/23/remarks-president-national-defense-university.

[148] See President Barack Obama, *Closure Of Guantanamo Detention Facilities* (January 22, 2009), available at http://www.whitehouse.gov/the_press_office/ClosureOfGuantanamoDetentionFacilities . (visited September 22, 2013).

[149] See *Boumediene v. Bush*, 553 U.S. 723 (2008) (demanding improved procedural protections for detainees to comport with constitutional due process requirements); *Hamdan v. Rumsfeld*, 548 U.S. 557 (2006) (demanding congressional authorization for military commissions); *Hamdi v. Rumsfeld*, 542 U.S. 507, 538 (2004) (finding the lack of due process protections in the military commission system to be unconstitutional).

[150] See *Hamdi v. Rumsfeld*, 542 U.S. 507, 538 (2004) (acknowledging "the possibility that the [due process] standards [the Supreme Court] ha[s] articulated could be met by an appropriately authorized and properly constituted military tribunal"); see also *Boumediene v. Bush*, 553 U.S. 723 (2008) (same).

[151] See *Hamdi*, 542 U.S. at 538.

to try detainees, President Obama in 2009 revived the military commission system,[152] citing the long history of their use and military necessity.[153] A July 2009 protocol noted that detainees are entitled to the presumption of trial in an ordinary criminal court, but numerous objective and subjective factors could warrant a change in venue, including strength of interest, efficiency, and "other prosecution considerations" such as the available sentence and the ability to use certain evidence in a given forum.[154]

Under the Military Commissions Act of 2009, evidence from torture or cruel, inhuman, or degrading interrogations is disallowed, the use of hearsay is limited, defendants are granted greater latitude in selecting their counsel, and protections against self-incrimination were instituted.[155] Nonetheless, significant deviations exist among the military commissions, the courts-martial system, and ordinary criminal courts. Defendants in military commissions are guaranteed neither the right to remain silent or the right to the exclusion of their previous coerced statements,[156] nor the right to a speedy trial.[157] Trial for ex post facto crimes is permissible in a military commission.[158] Guilty verdicts in noncapital cases can be rendered by two-thirds of the jury.[159] Hearsay evidence is more easily admissible, and access to classified information is significantly curtailed.[160] The controversial and problematic curtailing of these due process protections is further compounded by the Obama administration's reservation of the right to continue to imprison anyone acquitted

[152] See David E. Sanger, *Obama After Bush: Leading by Second Thought*, N.Y. TIMES, May 15, 2009, at A3 (discussing President Obama's changing stance on the utility of military commissions).

[153] Press Release, the White House, Office of the Press Secretary, Statement of President Barack Obama on Military Commissions (May 15, 2009), http://www.whitehouse.gov/the_press_office/Statement-of-President-Barack-Obama-on-Military-Commissions/ (last visited October 21, 2010).

[154] See Department of Defense and Department of Justice Protocol, Determination of Guantanamo Cases Referred for Prosecution, at 2 (July 20, 2009).

[155] See Jennifer K. Elsea, *Comparison of Rights in Military Commission Trials and Trials in Federal Criminal Court*, Congressional Research Service, February 28, 2013, available at http://www.fas.org/sgp/crs/natsec/R40932.pdf (offering a detailed comparison of the rights guaranteed under the Military Commissions Act of 2009 and those offered in ordinary criminal courts).

[156] Compare Military Commissions Act § 949a(b)(2)(c) with Unif. Code of Military Justice, art. 31, §§ (a), (b), & (d) (guaranteeing freedom from self-incrimination, and which are specifically made inapplicable to military commissions) and U.S. Const., amend. V (guaranteeing freedom from self-incrimination).

[157] Military Commissions Act § 949a. A speedy trial is guaranteed in both Article III courts and courts martial. U.S. Const., amend. VI (giving the right to a speedy trial); 18 U.S.C. § 3161(d)(2) (2008) (mandating commencement of trials within seventy days of indictment or original appearance in court). Unif. Code of Military Justice, art. 10.

[158] Military Commissions Act §§ 948d, 950p. Cf. U.S. Const., art. 1, § 9, cl. 3 ("No ex post facto law shall be passed.").

[159] Military Commissions Act § 949m. Cf. Fed. R. Crim. P. 31 (requiring unanimous jury verdicts for conviction).

[160] Military Commissions Act §§ 949a(b)(3)(D), 949p-1- 949p-7.

under the military commission system if security interests suggest that continued detention is necessary.[161]

A number of military commission trials have taken place at the Guantanamo Bay detention facility,[162] despite critiques that the trials are both unnecessary given the availability of ordinary criminal courts and the courts-martial system and fundamentally unfair, and despite irregularities and setbacks. For example, Omar Khadr was first detained in 2002 at the age of fifteen, subjected to problematic interrogation, and eventually pled guilty to various terrorism-related charges.[163] Salim Hamdan, a driver to Osama bin Laden, was convicted of conspiracy in a military commission, a charge that was overturned by an appellate court in 2012 based on the fact that conspiracy was not considered a war crime at the time that Hamdan was detained.[164]

c. Torture and Accountability

The United States has long been party to international treaties prohibiting torture as well as cruel, degrading, and inhuman treatment. Among them are the Universal Declaration of Human Rights,[165] the Geneva Conventions,[166] the International Covenant on Civil and Political Rights,[167] the American Convention on Human Rights,[168] and the Convention Against Torture.[169] On the domestic level, the Fifth, Eighth, and Fourteenth Amendments to the U.S. Constitution have been interpreted as prohibiting torture,[170] and various domestic laws codify the obligations

161 Jess Bravin, Detainees, Even If Acquitted, Might Not Go Free, WALL ST. J. (July 8, 2009), http://online.wsj.com/article/SB124699680303307309.html (last visited September 21, 2013).

162 See *Military Commissions Cases*, Office of Military Commissions, available at http://www.mc.mil/CASES/MilitaryCommissions.aspx (visited September 21, 2013).

163 See Charlie Savage, *Deal Averts Trial in Disputed Guantanamo Case*, nytimes.com, October 25, 2010, available at http://www.nytimes.com/2010/10/26/us/26gitmo.html (visited September 21, 2013).

164 See *Hamdan v. United States*, 696 F.3d 1238 (D.C. Cir. 2012).

165 Universal Declaration of Human Rights, G.A. Res. 217A (III), U.N. Doc A/810, at 71 (December 10, 1948).

166 Geneva Convention Relative to the Treatment of Prisoners of War, August 12, 1949, 6 U.S.T. 3316, 75 U.N.T.S. 135 (entered into force October 21, 1950); Geneva Convention Relative to the Protection of Civilian Persons in Time of War, August 12, 1949, 6 U.S.T. 3516, 75 U.N.T.S. 287 (entered into force October 21, 1950).

167 International Covenant on Civil and Political Rights, December 16, 1966, 999 U.N.T.S. 171 (entered into force March 23, 1976).

168 American Convention on Human Rights, O.A.S. Treaty Series No. 36, 1144 U.N.T.S. 123 (entered into force July 18, 1978), reprinted in Basic Documents Pertaining to Human Rights in the Inter-American System, OEA/Ser.L.V/II.82 doc. 6 rev.1 at 25 (1992).

169 Convention Against Torture and Other Cruel, Inhuman or Degrading Treatment or Punishment, December 10, 1984, 1465 U.N.T.S. 85 (entered into force June 26, 1987) (hereinafter "Convention Against Torture").

170 See generally Seth F. Kreimer, *Too Close to the Rack and the Screw: Constitutional Constraints on Torture in the War on Terror* (2003) 6 U. PA. J. CONST. L. 278.

in the Convention Against Torture: the federal Torture Statute,[171] the Torture Victim Protection Act of 1991,[172] the Alien Tort Claims Act,[173] and the Foreign Affairs Reform and Restructuring Act of 1998.[174]

In late 2003, evidence surfaced of abuse and torture of detainees held at the Abu Ghraib prison in Iraq at the hands of members of the U.S. military.[175] Similar reports surfaced from the detention facility at Guantanamo Bay.[176] Memos prepared by the Office of Legal Counsel in 2002 and 2003 advised the president and the military that detainees who were suspected members of al Qaeda were not protected by international and domestic prohibitions against torture and, furthermore, that abuse of detainees would not constitute "torture" unless the interrogators intended to cause the type of pain associated with death or organ failure.[177] Those memos were subsequently rescinded, and several members of the military were convicted at courts-martial for detainee abuse.[178] Congress subsequently cemented the U.S. prohibition of the abuse and torture of detainees with the Detainee Treatment Act of 2005.[179]

In 2009, President Obama signed an executive order banning the use of enhanced interrogation techniques and limiting interrogation techniques to those permitted in the *Army Field Manual*.[180] Such limitations were reinforced with the Military Commissions Act of 2009.[181] Despite Obama's campaign rhetoric on the need for a full accounting of torture, President Obama has not pursued prosecution and

[171] Foreign Relations Authorization Act, Fiscal Years 1994 and 1995, Pub. L. No. 103–236, § 506, 108 Stat. 382 (codified at 18 U.S.C. §§ 2340-2340B (2006)).

[172] Torture Victim Protection Act of 1991, Pub. L. No. 102–256, 106 Stat. 73 (codified at 28 U.S.C. § 1350 note (2006)).

[173] Alien Tort Claims Act, 28 U.S.C. § 1350 (2006).

[174] Foreign Affairs Reform and Restructuring Act of 1998, Pub. L. No. 105–277, § 2242(a), 112 Stat. 2681 (codified at 8 U.S.C. § 1231 (2006)).

[175] Seymour M. Hersh, *Torture at Abu Ghraib*, THE NEW YORKER (May 10, 2004) available at www.newyorker.com/archive/2004/05/10/040510fa_fact.

[176] See, e.g., Center for Constitutional Rights, *Report on Torture and Cruel, Inhumane, and Degrading Treatment of Prisoners at Guantánamo Bay, Cuba* (2006) available at http://ccrjustice.org/files/Report_ReportOnTorture.pdf.

[177] Memorandum for Alberto R. Gonzales, Counsel to the President, from Jay S. Bybee, Asst. Atty. General, Standards of Conduct for Interrogation Under 18 U.S.C. §§ 2340-2340A (Aug. 1, 2002); Memorandum from Jay S. Bybee, Asst. Atty. General, regarding Standards of Conduct for Interrogation Under 18 U.S.C. §§ 2340-2340A (August 1, 2002).

[178] Scott Shane, David Johnston, and James Risen, *Secret U.S. Endorsement of Severe Interrogation*, N.Y. TIMES, October 4, 2007, available at http://www.nytimes.com/2007/10/04/washington/04interrogate.html?pagewanted=all.

[179] Detainee Treatment Act of 2005, Pub. L. No. 109–148 §§ 1001–1006, 119 Stat. 2739 (codified at 42 U.S.C § 2000dd (2006)).

[180] Exec. Order No. 13,491, 74 Fed. Reg. 16,4893 (January 22, 2009).

[181] Military Commissions Act of 2009, Pub. L. No. 111–84, § 1802, 123 Stat. 2190, 2608 (codified at 10 U.S.C. § 950t(11)).

has precluded a full investigation of those who created the policies that arguably allowed torture to occur.[182]

d. Non-refoulement

The non-refoulement obligation in Article 3 of the Convention Against Torture[183] applies to U.S. extraordinary rendition practices and the movement of detainees from the Guantanamo detention facility. With regard to the former, when Canadian-Syrian dual citizen Maher Arar was rendered to Syria, the United States was obligated to seek assurances that he would not be mistreated there. However, evidence suggests that Arar was subjected to prolonged abuse and torture by his captors in Syria.[184] With regard to Guantanamo, several detainees have been cleared for release, but under the obligation of non-refoulement, the United States continues to hold them because of fear of torture upon return to their countries of citizenship.[185]

B. *Extraterritorial Terrorism Law Enforcement*

Since the attacks of September 11, extraordinary rendition has been used to capture over one hundred suspected terrorists in foreign countries and remove them to other nations for interrogation and control purposes. Some such detainees suffered extreme abuse and torture at the hands of their interrogators.[186] Several have brought suits in U.S. courts seeking compensation for their treatment. Despite substantial evidence that citizens of Canada,[187] Germany,[188] and the United Kingdom,[189] among others, were rendered by the United States government to other nations and were

[182] Scott Shane, *No Charges Filed on Harsh Tactics Used by the C.I.A*, nytimes.com, August 30, 2012, available at http://www.nytimes.com/2012/08/31/us/holder-rules-out-prosecutions-in-cia-interrogations.html?pagewanted=all (visited September 27, 2013).

[183] Convention Against Torture, supra note 168, Art. 3.

[184] See Human Rights Watch, *Torture and Non-refoulement*, January 29, 2004, available at http://www.hrw.org/news/2004/01/28/torture-and-non-refoulement (detailing Arar's situation).

[185] International Committee of the Red Cross, *Persons Detained by the US in Relation to Armed Conflict and Counter-terrorism – the Role of the ICRC*, June 18, 2013, available at http://www.icrc.org/eng/resources/documents/misc/united-states-detention.htm.

[186] See Amrit Singh, *Globalizing Torture: CIA Secret Detention and Extraordinary Rendition* (2013), Open Society Foundations, at 13–15 (describing the history and use of extraordinary rendition).

[187] See Commission of Inquiry into the Actions of Canadian Officials in Relation to Maher Arar, *Report of the Events Relating to Maher Arar: Analysis and Recommendations* (2006). See also Kent Roach, *Review and Oversight of National Security Activities and Some Reflections on Canada's Arar Inquiry*, 29 CARDOZO L. REV. 53 (2008).

[188] See Jane Mayer, *The Dark Side* 282–87 (New York, Anchor, 2008) (detailing Khalid El-Masri's plight).

[189] See Sudha Setty, *Judicial Formalism and the State Secrets Privilege* (2012) 38 WM. MITCHELL L. REV. 1630 at 1634–5 (detailing the claims of Binyam Mohamed).

subsequently abused by the security forces in the nations to which they were rendered, all such suits have been dismissed on procedural bases.[190]

In 2009, the Obama administration created a task force to study the practice of extraordinary rendition with the aim of ensuring compliance with domestic and international human rights standards and legal norms.[191] Renditions are believed to be continuing under this articulated standard.[192]

X. SECRECY AND TERRORISM

A. *Secrecy Claims and Secret Evidence*

The Classified Information Procedures Act (CIPA) is a 1980 law that established procedures for the use of classified and secret information in criminal trials.[193] CIPA outlines a comprehensive set of procedures for the treatment of evidence in criminal cases that implicate classified information or rely on evidence that is classified. For example, CIPA allows the government, under limited circumstances, to substitute unclassified summaries of classified evidence.[194] The Supreme Court in *Boumediene v. Bush* acknowledged the need to deal with classified information in a sensitive and thoughtful manner and expressed confidence that ordinary criminal courts would be able to manage the task successfully.[195]

B. *Secrecy in the Courtroom and Anonymous Witnesses*

The state secrets privilege is a common law evidentiary privilege that enables the government to prevent disclosure of sensitive state secrets in the course of litigation. The claim of privilege by the government, if upheld by a court, can result in consequences ranging from the denial of a discovery request for a particular document to the outright dismissal of a suit. Although a balancing test for assessing claims of privilege was established in the 1950s,[196] a meaningful assessment has

[190] E.g., *Mohamed v. Jeppesen Dataplan, Inc.*, 614 F.3d 1070, 1092–93 (9th Cir. 2010) (en banc); *Arar v. Ashcroft*, 585 F.3d 559, 565 (2d Cir. 2009), cert. denied, 130 S. Ct. 3409 (2010); *El-Masri v. United States*, 437 F. Supp. 2d 530 (E.D. Va. 2006), aff'd, 479 F.3d 296 (4th Cir. 2007), cert. denied, 128 S. Ct. 373 (2007).

[191] See Executive Order 13,491, *Ensuring Lawful Interrogations* at § (5)(e)(ii) (January 22, 2009).

[192] See David Johnston, *U.S. Says Rendition to Continue, but with More Oversight*, nytimes.com, August 24, 2009, available at http://www.nytimes.com/2009/08/25/us/politics/25rendition.html?_r=0 (visited September 22, 2013).

[193] Classified Information Procedures Act of 1980, Pub. L. No. 96-456,94 Stat 2025.

[194] Classified Information Procedures Act of 1980, Pub. L. No. 96-456,94 Stat 2025, § 6.

[195] *Boumediene v. Bush*, 553 U.S. 723, 128 S. Ct. 2229, 2276 (2008).

[196] *United States v. Reynolds*, 345 U.S. 1 (1953).

often been precluded by the judicial tendency to uphold claims of privilege without engaging in a substantial analysis of the underlying evidence or of the government's claimed need for nondisclosure.[197] In 2009, the Obama administration promised to reform the use of the state secrets privilege to allow for greater government accountability.[198] However, the administration's continued aggressive use of the privilege, seeking and winning dismissal of suits alleging serious government abuse such as torture,[199] suggests only continuity in the use of the privilege to prevent meaningful accountability through civil suits.

XI. CONCLUSION

U.S. counterterrorism policy has shifted in some significant ways, such as ending the use of abusive interrogation practices and accepting that international law applies to U.S. counterterrorism practices. However, the continuity between the Bush and Obama administrations in the substance of many counterterrorism programs, the assertion of high levels of presidential power, and the continued high level of secrecy have created a bipartisan imprimatur of the robust counterterrorism programs that exist today, as well as the many problematic aspects of those programs. Congress, the judiciary, and the public, all grateful that no large-scale terrorist attacks have occurred since 2001 and cognizant that threats still exist, have been largely acquiescent despite significant costs to human rights and civil liberties in the form of racial and religious profiling, indefinite detention, expansive and seemingly poorly controlled surveillance, extrajudicial killings, torture, and other abuses for which there has been a pronounced lack of accountability.

The government's aggressive counterterrorism stance has influenced actions and policies outside of the U.S. federal government: the work of domestic local and state-level law enforcement has been altered through federal programs mandating vertical information sharing and coordination; the United States has exerted significant influence on the United Nations Security Council in shaping and promoting resolutions that have had a worldwide impact on counterterrorism programs; and the United States has exerted its soft power to attempt to influence other nations to shape their own counterterrorism policies in ways that promote

197 See Setty, *Judicial Formalism*, supra note 189.

198 See Memorandum from Eric Holder, Attorney Gen., on Policies and Procedures Governing Invocation of the State Secrets Privilege to Heads of Exec. Dep'ts & Agencies (September 23, 2009), available at http://legaltimes.typepad.com/files/ag-memo-re-state-secrets-dated-09-22-09.pdf (establishing layers of internal review within the Department of Justice and including a new executive branch policy to report to Congress any invocations of the state secrets privilege).

199 See *Mohamed v. Jeppesen Dataplan*, 614 F.3d 1070 (9th Cir. 2010) (en banc) (dismissing a suit seeking compensation for extraordinary rendition and torture based on the government's invocation of the state secrets privilege).

U.S. interests.[200] Furthermore, the U.S. stance on issues such as foreign surveillance and the use of drones for targeted killings in areas that are not active theaters of war has set a dangerous precedent with regard to other nations attempting to develop and use the same technology.[201] It may be that the muscular stance of the United States on such issues will promote a similar response in other nations as their technology and power develops.

Future challenges for U.S. counterterrorism law are manifold. The driving imperative will continue to be recognizing and confronting continuing threats posed by al-Qaeda, other foreign terrorist groups, domestic terrorism, and cyberterrorism. However, the United States would do well to improve its transparency and accountability mechanisms to comport with the rule of law and maintain democratic values. Such initiatives are unlikely to stem from the executive branch, which means that the judiciary, Congress, and public must engage more fully to insist upon open debate, accountability, and further oversight and constraint.

The U.S. response to terrorism has been multifaceted and expansive, reflective of the U.S. role in global security, and is an ongoing work in progress. Branches of the federal government and the public question and redefine their obligations and roles in upholding security while safeguarding the rule of law, and the debate over the appropriate course of action on these matters will no doubt continue for the foreseeable future.

[200] See, e.g., Setty, *Judicial Formalism*, supra note 189, at 1643–5, 1652–3.

[201] See, e.g., Andrew Erickson and Austin Strange, *China Has Drones. Now What?* foreignaffairs.com, May 23, 2013, available at http://www.foreignaffairs.com/articles/139405/andrew-erickson-and-austin-strange/china-has-drones-now-what (raising questions as to how China will deploy its military drone capability).

3

Canada

Robert Diab

I. INTRODUCTION

Since 2001, Canada's Parliament and courts have developed a large body of law on counter-terrorism, giving rise to a range of issues and an often passionate and enduring public debate. Much of the focus has been on criminal and immigration law. The key features of Canada's legal framework were shaped in large part by UN Security Council Resolution 1373,[1] including an emphasis on preventing terror financing, the use of new terror-related offences in the *Criminal Code*,[2] and the imposition of stiffer punishments. Canada has also increased the scope of state secrecy and surveillance and the powers of various agencies to gather and share information. A salient problem in cases applying these new laws has been how to balance the need to protect the secrecy of information often obtained from other states with assurances and the need to be fair and transparent. Areas for improvement moving forward include the need for more effective central coordination and oversight of the agencies involved in counter-terrorism, given their enhanced powers, their often overlapping mandates and the greater secrecy under which many of them operate.

Canada's recent history with terrorism lends context to much of the law explored in this chapter. Among the most significant of our past experiences with terrorism were the October crisis of 1970 and the Air India bombing of 1985. In the earlier case, the Front de Liberation du Quebec kidnapped a British diplomat and a provincial cabinet minister and murdered the latter. The federal government declared a state of emergency, deployed six thousand troops in the streets of Montreal, detained close to five hundred people and suspended habeas corpus.[3] The experience bolstered public support for the adoption of the *Canadian Charter of Rights and Freedoms*

1 United Nations Security Council S/Res/1373 (2001) ["Resolution 1373"].

2 RSC 1985, c C 34 ["*Criminal Code*" or "*Code*"].

3 Kent Roach, *The 9/11 Effect: Comparative Counter-Terrorism* (New York: Cambridge University Press, 2011), at 365–7.

in 1982,[4] which curtailed police powers and in times of emergency allowed for a suspension of fundamental freedoms only with a constitutional override.[5] Lessons learned from the crisis also led to the creation of the Canadian Security and Intelligence Service (CSIS), a civilian agency that gathers intelligence on threats to national security and is separate from law enforcement.[6] Yet, the Royal Canadian Mounted Police (RCMP) also gained explicit authority to investigate and prevent threats to national security. The overlap in these services' mandate gives rise to a tension between the two in the gathering and use of intelligence and evidence in terrorism cases.

The tension was central to the efforts to prevent the Air India bombing of 1985, one of the largest acts of aviation terrorism to date,[7] and in the prosecutions that followed. Sikh-Canadian extremists in Vancouver had placed bombs on planes bound for India, killing 331 people.[8] The prosecutions were beset by various problems. CSIS had destroyed early wiretap evidence. Witnesses were murdered. The Crown refused to reveal confidential sources resulting in trials being stayed.[9] By 2005, only a single guilty plea had been entered (to manslaughter), and the two remaining principals were acquitted. In 2010, the Air India inquiry pointed to various flaws in aviation security to explain the failure to prevent the bombing. It also found deficiencies on the part of both CSIS and the RCMP in terms of their collection and sharing of information in a timely fashion.[10]

The events of 9/11 have also played a role in Canada's experience of terrorism due to its direct impact on many fronts. Twenty-three Canadians were killed in the attacks.[11] The southern border with the United States was closed for several days, with significant economic consequences.[12] And while none of the 9/11 hijackers had entered the United States through Canada, the impression of Canada as a likely point of entry for terrorists would remain, exerting a pressure on Canadian lawmakers with consequences extending beyond the domain of border security.

Canada's primary legislative response to 9/11, and Resolution 1373, was the *Anti-terrorism Act* (ATA)[13] of December 2001. It added to the *Criminal Code* a

[4] *Canadian Charter of Rights and Freedoms*, Part I of the *Constitution Act*, 1982, being Schedule B to the *Canada Act 1982* (U.K.), 1982, c. 11.

[5] *Ibid* s 33.

[6] Roach, *supra* note 3, at 365.

[7] *Ibid* at 369.

[8] *Ibid.*

[9] *Ibid* at 369–72.

[10] Commission of Inquiry into the Investigation of the Bombing of Air India Flight 182, *Air India Flight 182: A Canadian Tragedy* (Ottawa: Public Works, 2010) ["Air India Report"], vol. 1, at 22–3.

[11] Kent Roach, *September 11: Consequences for Canada* (Montreal: McGill-Queen's University Press, 2003) at 3.

[12] Roach, *supra* note 3, at 374.

[13] S.C. 2001, c 41 ["*Anti-terrorism Act*"].

definition of terrorism, provisions for the listing of terrorist entities and several new offences, such as financing, facilitating and participating in terrorist activity. It gave police and prosecutors new powers, including preventive arrests and "judicial investigations," and expanded surveillance powers of police and intelligence agencies with and without a warrant. The act also significantly expanded the scope for national security privilege.

But while prosecution was a crucial tool in countering terrorism, in cases involving non-citizens the government tended to favour the use of immigration detention. Pre-dating 9/11, Canada's *Immigration and Refugee Protection Act*[14] allowed for detention pending deportation on secret evidence. Together, the five men who were subject to these provisions for much of the decade generated extensive litigation (some still ongoing) that resulted in various limits and qualifications to the detention regime.

A first wave of terror prosecutions has resulted in significant sentences for those involved in serious plots, but also a directive from the Supreme Court that rehabilitation remains an important potential consideration in all terrorism sentencing. The experience in these early cases, including immigration, has helped to incline the government to proceed in a recent case involving non-citizens by way of criminal prosecution. Yet state secrecy and expanded powers of surveillance remain important to Canada's security policy. And the government has thus far resisted calls for more effective central coordination and oversight of national security agencies.

II. THE DEFINITION OF TERRORISM

Prior to the passage of the *Anti-terrorism Act* in 2001, Canadian law had lacked a definition of terrorism. Drafters of the *ATA* drew upon the definition in the United Kingdom's *Terrorism Act 2000*.[15] Although Canada's definition differs in many respects, it follows the UK's approach in defining terrorism to include harm to essential services in addition to persons and property.[16]

The definition in Canada's *Criminal Code* contains two general parts. The first part deems any one of a series of *Code* offences to be a "terrorist activity" if committed in or outside of Canada. These include hijacking, hostage taking and bombing – most of which were included in the *Code* prior to 2001 pursuant to various international conventions.[17] The second part of the provision sets out a substantive definition, which in turn contains several parts.

14 SC 2001 c 27.
15 *Terrorism Act 2000 (U.K.)*, c 11 ss 1; Roach, *supra* note 3, at 377.
16 Roach, *ibid.*
17 *Criminal Code*, *supra* note 2, s 83.01(1)(a).

First, a "terrorist activity" is any act committed in or outside of Canada that is committed for a "political, religious or ideological purpose, objective or cause."[18] Concerns about police profiling against ethnic or religious groups in Parliamentary debates led to a qualifying provision which indicates that "the expression of a political, religious or ideological thought, belief or opinion" does not fall within the scope of terrorist activity unless it satisfies the other criteria of the definition, including the intent requirements.[19] The act must also be committed

> in whole or in part with the intention of intimidating the public, or a segment of the public, with regard to its security, including its economic security, or compelling a person, a government or a domestic or an international organization to do or to refrain from doing any act, whether the public or the person, government or organization is inside or outside Canada [...].[20]

Notable aspects here are the high degree of subjective culpability required – intent rather than recklessness – and the variety of cases in which this intent might be applied. In distinction to the UK definition, which is confined to conduct aimed at influencing governments or the public, Canada's definition extends to a segment of the public or single individuals, along with corporations and organizations.[21] The definition also extends to acts meant to impact *economic* security, such as violent acts of protest aimed at banks or corporations.

The activity must also intentionally cause death or serious bodily harm "by the use of violence," endanger a person's life, cause a serious risk to the health or safety of the public or a part of it, or cause serious disruption of an essential service or facility, public or private.[22] The definition excludes forms of disruption that result from "advocacy, protest, dissent or stoppage of work" not intended to endanger life or cause serious risk to public health or safety. It therefore excludes a form of protest that intentionally disrupts an essential service or aims to influence a corporation or government – but does not endanger life or cause serious risk to public health or safety.[23]

The definition also includes as terrorist activity the counselling, conspiracy, attempt, or threat to commit any of the acts defined, along with being an accessory

18 *Ibid* s 83.01(1)(b)(i)(A). A constitutional challenge to this provision is discussed later in this chapter.
19 *Ibid* s 83.01(1.1).
20 *Ibid* s 83.01(1)(b)(i)(B).
21 Roach, *supra* note 11, at 33.
22 *Criminal Code*, *supra* note 2, s 83.01(1)(b)(ii).
23 Roach, *supra* note 11, at 34 notes that an earlier version of the definition excluded only "lawful" forms of politically inspired protest that caused disruption and did not pose a serious risk to public safety. Concerns were raised about the broad sweep of such a provision, with the final version now contemplating the exclusion of forms of protest that may involve minor criminal offences or infractions of provincial or municipal law.

after the fact.[24] The *Criminal Code* had already contained separate offences for each of these contemplated forms of involvement, except threatening to commit a terrorist activity, which creates a new and distinct threatening offence.[25] The *ATA* thus captures as terrorism a wide range of conduct at a significant remove from actual acts of terror in both space and time. The critical safeguard here is the high level of intent required to contribute to terrorist activity of some kind – a point explored further later in this chapter.

Finally, the definition excludes acts committed "during an armed conflict" if carried out "in accordance with customary international law or conventional international law applicable to the conflict."[26] It also excludes acts committed "by military forces of a state in the exercise of their official duties" consistent with international law.[27] This was intended to capture acts of assistance or involvement in civil or inter-state conflicts, but not violent acts by armed insurrectionaries not respecting laws of war: for example, those targeting civilians. Yet, it remains unclear where this line is to be drawn and whether it would exclude forms of assistance with revolutionary groups against dictatorships abroad.[28]

The definition is therefore broad in its potential scope, yet it requires a high degree of subjective intent, and intent of a specific nature: politically or religiously motivated and intended to intimidate, significantly disrupt, or endanger life or pose a serious risk to health and safety. The potential scope of the definition can be further understood by considering its operation in relation to the new set of terrorism offences in the *ATA*.

III. CRIMINAL LAWS AND PROSECUTIONS

A. *Criminal Law*

In addition to setting out a definition of "terrorist activity," the *ATA* added a series of new offences, including financing, participating, facilitating and instructing terrorism. The new crimes draw upon the definition of terrorist activity and of a terrorist group (discussed later in this chapter) and carry more severe punishments.

Notably, Canada chose not to criminalize membership in a terrorist organization due in part to concerns about the constitutionality of such a law, given the protection of free association in the *Charter*. Parliament instead added the offence of participating

[24] *Criminal Code, supra* note 2, s 83.01(1)(b).

[25] The existing offence of "uttering threats" in section 264.1 of the *Criminal Code* is aimed more generally at conveying a threat to cause death, bodily harm, or damage to property.

[26] *Criminal Code, supra* note 2, s 83.01(1)(b).

[27] *Ibid.*

[28] Roach, *supra* note 11, at 31.

or contributing to terrorism, which has a potentially wider scope than a membership offence. Section 83.18 requires proof that a person has *knowingly* participated in or contributed to any activity of a terrorist *group* for the purpose of enhancing its ability to carry out a terrorist activity.[29] Participation is defined to include a range of conduct, such as recruiting, training, travelling, waiting, or providing a skill or expertise for the group's benefit. Participation may also be established regardless of whether a terror group carries out a terrorist activity, whether the person's involvement enhances the terror group's ability to carry out the activity, or whether the person knows of the specific nature of the activity.[30] Challenged as overbroad in *Khawaja*, the Supreme Court upheld the provisions by applying a purposive interpretation.[31] The purpose of the act is to prevent terrorism rather than punish minor or incidental acts not intended to contribute to terrorism. A conviction therefore requires a specific intent to enhance a group's ability to carry out a terrorist activity (rather than recklessness or wilful blindness),[32] and conduct that a reasonable person would believe to be "capable of materially enhancing the abilities of a terrorist group to facilitate or carry out a terrorist activity."[33]

The offence "facilitating terror" in section 83.19 is potentially broader in scope, requiring only that a person "knowingly facilitate a terrorist activity."[34] It may therefore apply to terror involving an individual or a group. Similar to the participation provision, facilitation involves a subjective but discrete form of intent. The accused must intend to facilitate a terrorist activity, but need not know that a "particular terrorist activity is facilitated" or carried out, that "any particular terrorist activity was foreseen or planned at the time it was facilitated," or that "any terrorist activity was actually carried out."[35] The offence thus requires an intent to assist with terrorist activity of a more generalized nature. Presumably, trial courts will apply the Supreme Court's reading of section 83.18 in *Khawaja* to section 83.19, given the similarity in their wording. In summary, both the participation and facilitation provisions allow for significant penalties to result in a case where an accused specifically intended to assist a terrorist group in its general terrorist goals but *without discriminating as to the potential severity* of the terrorism that the group carries out.

Other new offences in the ATA include instructing and harbouring terrorism, and more recently Parliament has criminalized the act of leaving Canada with the intent of carrying out a terrorism offence.[36] A person is guilty of "instructing" when he or she

[29] *Criminal Code*, *supra* note 2, s 83.18(1).
[30] *Ibid* s 83.18(2).
[31] *R v Khawaja*, 2012 SCC 69.
[32] *Ibid* para 46.
[33] *Ibid* para 52.
[34] *Criminal Code*, *supra* note 2, s 83.19(1).
[35] *Ibid* s 83.19(2).
[36] *Ibid* ss 83.21, 83.22, 83.23 and ss 83.191, 83.201 and 83.202.

instructs another to carry out an activity in association with a terrorist group for the purpose of enhancing its ability to carry out terrorist activity.[37] The offence is potentially broader in scope than the older counselling offence in the *Code* given the lack of a requirement to instruct a particular person or to know their identity.[38] This provision provides the closest equivalent to the offence of inciting terror. Canada has not passed an inciting offence in response to UN Security Council Resolution 1624 in part due to concerns about the constitutional validity of such a provision given the protection of free speech in the *Charter*. Harbouring or concealing involves the knowledge that one harbours or conceals a person likely to carry out a terrorist activity for the purpose of enabling that person to carry out the activity.[39]

As Kent Roach has noted, the need for these new offences was not clear in the fall of 2001, given that most if not every conceivable act of terrorism was already an offence in Canadian law (*e.g.*, murder, hijacking, and possessing or setting off an explosive device), and many carried life sentences.[40] The *Code* had also contained a series of inchoate offences such as counselling, conspiracy and attempts, and it provided for party liability for those aiding and abetting or those acting as accessories after the fact. There are, however, two distinct features of the new provisions. One is that many involve more limited knowledge of the terrorist activity to which a person is contributing, in ways noted previously. The other is that they involve different rules on sentencing.

Although none of the new terrorism offences carry mandatory minimums, many carry life sentences. For those that do not carry a life sentence, the *ATA* added a provision of general application that provides that any indictable offence can be punished with up to life if "the act or omission constituting the offence also constitutes a terrorist activity."[41] The *ATA* also mandated consecutive sentences for multiple counts of terrorism offences[42] and allowed for increased periods of parole ineligibility.[43] Given the operation of a common law rule, accused persons are protected from multiple convictions for the same conduct, precluding, for example, convictions for facilitating terrorism and acting as a party to murder for the same actions.[44]

37 *Ibid* s 83.21.
38 Roach, *supra* note 11, at 44.
39 *Criminal Code*, *supra* note 2, s 83.23.
40 Roach, *supra* note 11, at 22–3.
41 *Criminal Code*, *supra* note 2, s 83.27. The Crown is required to provide the accused with notice of intent to proceed under the provision, but there are no other conditions to its application.
42 *Ibid* s 83.26.
43 *Ibid* s 743.6(1.2).
44 *R v Kienapple*, [1975] 1 SCR 729.

B. *Terrorism Prosecutions*

Terrorism prosecutions proceed in the superior courts of Canada's provinces, which are the normal courts for serious criminal cases such as murder. Constitutional protections in Canada's *Charter* apply, as do common law defences and rules of evidence. However, in ways to be explored in section X below, questions of national security privilege in these cases are dealt with in separate but parallel proceedings in Canada's Federal Court system – a court that does not handle criminal law matters and deals primarily with administrative matters of federal jurisdiction. In ways to be explored later in this chapter, the *Canada Evidence Act*[45] allows for the granting of national security privilege in a criminal trial, but contains various safeguards of the accused's right to a fair trial. The *Criminal Code* also explicitly prohibits the use in any proceeding in Canada of evidence obtained through torture or degrading treatment.[46]

Thus far, the terrorism provisions of the *ATA* have been tested in two sets of cases. The most common charges were participating in or facilitating terrorism, along with older offences related to bomb making. The first prosecution under the *ATA* resulted in the conviction of Mohammad Khawaja in 2008 for participating in a terrorist group and facilitating terrorist activity in Canada, the UK and Pakistan.[47] Khawaja assisted the group by building a prototype for a remote bomb detonator, with a view to building thirty more. The group had intended to use one of the detonators to bomb an office building in London. Khawaja also provided funds, accommodations in his parent's home in Pakistan for co-conspirators and possessed various weapons and cash in his Ottawa home. The court found that Khawaja lacked knowledge of the specifics of the UK bomb plot but had knowingly facilitated terrorist activity. Khawaja sought to rely on the armed insurgency exception in the *ATA*'s definition of terrorism, claiming that his intent throughout was only to assist with the Taliban and Mujahedeen insurgency in Afghanistan. The court rejected this defence on the basis that the groups in question were not acting in accordance with international law, as required by the definition of terrorism in the *ATA*.

Khawaja's case was also important for raising a number of challenges to new terrorism laws. He was successful at trial in arguing that the motive provision was an unreasonable limit on free speech, belief and expression, although, as noted, this holding was overturned on appeal.[48] He was not successful in challenging the *mens rea* requirements of the participating and facilitation provisions, with the Supreme

[45] *Criminal Code*, *supra* note 2, s 269.1(4).
[46] RSC 1985, c C-5 ["CEA"].
[47] *R v Khawaja* [2008] 238 CCC (3d) 233.
[48] *R v Khawaja* 2012 SCC 69.

Court holding that a generalized intention to assist with terrorist activity sufficed.[49] Khawaja received a 10.5 year sentence at trial, which the Court of Appeal raised to a life sentence and the Supreme Court upheld.[50]

In 2006, eighteen people, including four youths, were arrested in two terror plots, one involving a plan to storm Parliament and murder MPs and another to carry out bombings at various buildings in Toronto. The case involved large amounts of wiretap evidence and two informers within the Muslim community who worked closely with the RCMP.[51] Four accused chose to go to trial, resulting in convictions for various offences; seven pled guilty, and the Crown stayed the remaining charges.[52] One of the two principal figures, Amara, twenty years old at the time, received a life sentence for participating in a rural terrorist training camp and for committing explosives offences for a terrorist purpose.[53] Sentences in the other cases ranged widely, though in two of them the Court of Appeal raised the sentences by several years.[54]

Two terror-related prosecutions are currently unfolding in Canada. One involves two non-citizens who were plotting to bomb a passenger train outside of Toronto. Another involves two Canadian citizens who were attempting to set off bombs at the Canada Day gathering outside of British Columbia's Legislative Assembly in Victoria in July 2013.

C. *Punishment of Terrorism*

Sentences under the *ATA* have generally been more severe than might have been the case for similar conduct prior to 2001.[55] In reviewing the sentences in four of the early terrorism prosecutions, the Ontario Court of Appeal held that, categorically, terrorism offences warranted a primary emphasis upon denunciation and deterrence.[56] In affirming Khawaja's sentence, the Supreme Court rejected the ratio of the lower court's decision, holding that rehabilitation remains a potentially significant consideration in all terrorism cases, including the more serious ones.[57]

49 *Ibid* paras 34–64.

50 *Khawaja*, *supra*, note 43.

51 Roach, *supra*, note 3, at 408.

52 *Ibid.*

53 *R v Amara*, 2010 ONSC 441, upheld on appeal, 2010 ONCA 858.

54 *R v Gaya*, 2010 ONCA 860; *R v Khalid*, 2010 ONCA 861.

55 See, for example, Roach's discussion of sentences imposed against those involved in the murder of Pierre Laporte in the October crisis, *supra* note 3, at 367.

56 *R v Khawaja*, 2010 ONCA 862, para 238.

57 *R v Khawaja*, 2012 SCC 69, para 124. See also Robert Diab, "*R v Khawaja* and the Fraught Question of Rehabilitation in Terrorism Sentencing" (2014) 39:2 *Queens Law Journal*.

Code provisions also allow courts to take into account a person's cooperation with authorities as a mitigating circumstance at sentencing, and in one of the Toronto 18 cases, the court did so.[58]

IV. INVESTIGATIVE POWERS

A. *Police Powers*

The *Anti-terrorism Act* gave police special powers for investigating terrorism offences, not all of which are available in ordinary criminal investigations. Two that are unique to the context of terrorism are the preventive arrest and judicial investigation provisions. Originally included in the ATA, they were subject to a sunset clause and lapsed in 2007, but were re-enacted in 2013.

Under the preventive arrest provisions, police may obtain a warrant to arrest a person not charged with an offence and to detain the suspect for up to seventy-two hours.[59] The warrant may be issued where there are reasonable grounds to believe that a terrorist activity will be carried out and there is reasonable suspicion that the arrest is necessary to prevent it.[60] Kent Roach has drawn a contrast here between the standard of reasonable suspicion and the need for "reasonable and probable grounds to believe" an indictable offence has been committed for a warrantless arrest in ordinary criminal cases.[61] Where a preventive arrest has occurred, the subject can be compelled to enter a recognizance of up to a year, placing him or her on conditions of release (a kind of "control order" as is used in the UK).[62] If a person refuses to enter into the recognizance, the court may commit the person to custody for up to a year.[63]

The ATA also added provisions that allow the court to carry out a kind of judicial interrogation of a terrorism suspect.[64] Police begin the process by applying *ex parte* for a subpoena-like order compelling a person to appear before the court to be questioned. The order may be issued where there are reasonable grounds to believe

[58] *Gaya*, *supra* note 54.

[59] *Criminal Code*, *supra* note 2, ss 83.3(2), (6) and (7).

[60] *Ibid* s 83.3(2). In order to seek a warrant, police first require the approval of the attorney general of Canada, but may proceed without a warrant in exigent circumstances (section 83.3(1) and (4)).

[61] *Ibid* s 495(2); Roach, *supra* note 11, at 48.

[62] *Criminal Code*, *supra* note 2, s 83.3(8).

[63] *Ibid* s 83.3(9). Section 810.01 of the *Code* provides for an analogous one-year recognizance where there are "reasonable fears" that a person may commit a terrorism offence, with up to a year of committal for refusal to enter into it.

[64] *Ibid* s 83.28.

a terrorism offence has been or will be committed, the person has information relating to it and reasonable attempts have been made to obtain the information by other means.[65] A person is obliged to answer any question asked of him or her, aside from matters of privilege or matters otherwise protected from disclosure by law.[66] The section also protects a person from self-incrimination by precluding the use of any statements made (or evidence derived from the person) except in a prosecution for perjury.[67]

In 2004, the Crown brought an *ex parte* application under these provisions in a proceeding that took place alongside the Air India trial. The Crown had sought to obtain an order for the judicial examination of a potential Crown witness in the trial. The court ordered the proceedings to be held *in camera*, with defence counsel becoming aware of them only inadvertently. In response to a *Charter* challenge, the Supreme Court of Canada upheld the provisions, but extended the scope of the use immunity and derivative use immunity protections to immigration and extradition hearings.[68] In dissent, two justices (LeBel and Fish JJ.) held that the provisions violate the independence of the judiciary, contemplating a role in which the judge "takes part in and facilitates the police investigation without having real power to act as a neutral arbiter."[69] In a companion decision, the majority read in to the provisions a presumption in favour of open court hearings.[70]

The *Anti-terrorism Act* also extended the scope of police powers of surveillance that had been recently expanded in cases involving organized crime. As in that context, police investigating terrorism offences could now obtain a wiretap warrant lasting a year rather than the normal sixty days without needing to demonstrate that other, less invasive, methods are unlikely to succeed.[71] Nor do police need to inform the subject of the warrant of the fact of the surveillance for up to three years.[72] More generally, police investigating terrorism offences may seek to rely on the powers set out in section 25.1 of the *Criminal Code* to engage in unlawful conduct short of causing bodily harm or death intentionally or by criminal negligence.

65 *Ibid* s 83.28(3) and (4).

66 *Ibid* s 83.28(8).

67 *Ibid* s 83.28(10).

68 *Application Under s. 83.28 of the Criminal Code (Re)*, 2004 SCC 42.

69 *Ibid*, para 188.

70 *Vancouver Sun (Re)*, 2004 SCC 43.

71 *Criminal Code*, *supra* note 2, ss 185(1.1) and 186.1.

72 *Ibid* s 196(5). The court in *R. v. NY*, 2008 CanLII 15908 (Ont SC) has held that investigative necessity is not a requirement of a reasonable search under section 8 of Canada's *Charter*. For a contrary view, see Steven Penny, "National Security Surveillance Powers in an Age of Terror" (2010) 48 Osgoode Hall LJ 247.

B. *Intelligence Agencies*

Intelligence agencies in Canada have important but distinct roles to play from the police in countering terrorism. Chief among these agencies are Canadian Security Intelligence Service (CSIS) and the Communications Security Establishment (CSE). The CSIS is a civilian agency tasked with gathering intelligence pertaining to terrorism, espionage and other threats to national security. The Communications Security Establishment collects foreign signals intelligence.

Turning to the first of these, notably, Parliament did not add to CSIS's powers or its investigative scope with the *ATA*. Earlier legislation had already mandated CSIS to collect "to the extent that is strictly necessary" and analyze and retain information relating to activity that "may on reasonable grounds be suspect of constituting threats to the security of Canada."[73] CSIS was also able to apply to a Federal Court judge to obtain a sixty-day warrant to intercept communications or carry out other forms of search or seizure where there are reasonable grounds to believe it necessary for CSIS to "investigate a threat to the security of Canada."[74] But unlike the police under the expanded warrant provisions of the *ATA*, CSIS must also establish that other investigative means are not practicable or that the urgency of the matter renders other methods impractical.[75] Oversight of CSIS activity is conducted by the Security Intelligence Review Committee, consisting of a group of between two and four members of the Privy Council who are not also Parliamentarians. The committee has access to confidential materials and provides Parliament an annual review.

In many cases, intelligence gathering begins and ends with CSIS, but in some cases, the service may work with police or other state or foreign agencies, giving rise to the possible use of intelligence in terrorism prosecutions or administrative matters in ways that directly affect a person's liberty. Section 19 of the *CSIS Act* contemplates the sharing and use of intelligence in other contexts, including a criminal prosecution.[76] Thus far, in terrorism prosecutions after 2001, the Crown has not attempted to rely upon CSIS intelligence as primary evidence in a given case. The Crown has instead tended to rely on police evidence based on investigations that have been informed to varying degrees by CSIS intelligence. The defence has sought disclosure of the intelligence, and CSIS or the Crown has opposed this on

73 *Canadian Security Intelligence Service Act*, S.C. 1984, c. 21, s 12 ["*CSIS Act*"].

74 *Ibid* s 21.

75 *Ibid* s 21(2)(b).

76 In *Charkoaui v Canada*, 2008 SCC 38, a case involving immigration detention, the Supreme Court held that where CSIS gathers intelligence involving individuals or groups, it has a duty to retain material pertaining to it that may, upon review, be disclosed to the detainee. The logic would seem to extend to information that might be used in criminal proceedings.

one or more of several grounds: national security privilege (explored later in this chapter); that the information was not obtained for the purpose of the prosecution; that it is not essential to proving the accused's innocence; or that it is not subject to the usual disclosure requirements in criminal law.[77]

Although the CSE had been collecting foreign signals intelligence prior to the ATA, the act gave clear legislative definition to the agency's scope.[78] Prior to the ATA, the *Criminal Code* prevented the CSE from intercepting communications that either originated or terminated in Canada.[79] The ATA amended the *National Defence Act* to authorize interceptions involving individuals located in Canada, so long as the interceptions are "directed at foreign entities located outside Canada."[80] The act requires the minister to confirm that "satisfactory measures are in place to protect the privacy of Canadians and to ensure that private communications will only be used or retained if they are essential to international affairs, defence or security."[81] Roach suggests that this last qualification would pose an obstacle to the use of such intelligence as evidence in a criminal trial.[82] Yet the act still contemplates a form of mass warrantless surveillance similar to what is permitted in the United States under section 702 of the *Foreign Intelligence Surveillance Act.*[83] A civil liberties group has brought a *Charter* challenge to these provisions, citing evidence of numerous ministerial authorizations for the collection of metadata from non-suspected persons in Canada from 2002 to the present.[84]

V. LISTING OF TERRORIST ENTITIES OR INDIVIDUALS

A. *Proscription Mechanisms*

There are two primary means under Canadian law to proscribe or list individuals or groups as terrorist entities, with various legal consequences. One method for listing

77 See, for example, the use of CSIS intelligence as part of the police investigation of the Toronto 18 and the application for disclosure in *R. v. Ahmad*, 2009 Canlii 84776. The issue also arose in the Khawaja prosecution, where the defence sought disclosure of information that the RCMP had obtained from UK intelligence: *Attorney General v. Khawaja*, 2007 FCA 342 and *Canada v Khawaja*, 2008 FC 560.

78 Martin Friedland, "Police Powers under Bill C-36," in Ronald Daniels et al., *The Security of Freedom: Essays on Canada's Anti-terrorism Bill* (Toronto: University of Toronto Press, 2001) 269, at 275.

79 *Ibid.*

80 *National Defence Act*, RSC, 1985, c N-5 ["*NDA*"], s 273.65.

81 *Ibid* s 273.65(2)(d).

82 Roach, *supra* note 3, at 389.

83 (1978), Pub.L. 95–511, 92 Stat. 1783, 50 U.S.C. ch. 36. Roach, *supra* note 3, at 389.

84 See the British Columbia Civil Liberties Association's Notice of Civil Claim, online: http://bccla.org/wp-content/uploads/2013/10/2013-10-22-Notice-of-Civil-Claim.pdf.

pre-dates the *ATA* and is found in regulations to the *United Nations Act*.[85] The other was added to the *Criminal Code* by the *ATA*. The two methods continue to function. To understand their distinct purposes, it may help to consider the context in which they were created.

The earlier method for listing draws authority from the *United Nations Act*, which was passed in 1945 to provide a vehicle through which Canada could comply with UN resolutions in short order through the passage of regulations to the act.[86] In 1999, cabinet passed an earlier version of what is now called the *United Nations Al-Qaida and Taliban Regulations*[87] in response to UN Security Council Resolution 1267. This called upon member states to pass law prohibiting forms of financial assistance to the Taliban and related entities, a call that was expanded in Security Council Resolution 1333 to include al Qaida and associated persons defined on a list kept by the UN's 1267 Committee. The Canadian regulations did not create a separate list. It set out consequences for those engaged in prohibited conduct with persons or entities on the UN list.

Resolution 1373, passed September 28, 2001, required member states to pass law prohibiting the financing of terrorism and allowing for the seizure of funds and property relating to a wider range of entities and individuals across the globe.[88] Four days later, cabinet passed the *Suppression of Terrorism* regulations.[89] These created a separate list in Canadian law with two sources: the UN's 1267 list and a schedule to the regulations to which cabinet could add names upon the recommendation of the minister of foreign affairs. Later amendments have limited the source to cabinet alone. The governor in council may add to the list where there are reasonable grounds to believe that an entity or person has (a) carried out, participated in, facilitated or attempted terrorist activity, or (b) is acting on behalf of, at the direction of or in association with any person conducting such activities.[90] The specific prohibitions of both regulations are discussed in the section VII.

As a further response to Resolution 1373 and the *Convention on the Suppression of Terrorism Financing*,[91] Canada added a further means for listing in the *Criminal Code*.[92] Listing under the *Code* is significant for its potential function with the

85 *United Nations Act*, RSC, 1985, c U-2 ["*UN Act*"].
86 Alexandra Dosman "For the Record: Designating 'Listed Entities' for the Purposes of Terrorist Financing Offences at Canadian Law" (2004) 62 *U.T.Fac.L.Rev*. 1.
87 (SOR/99–444) ["*Al-Qaida* regulations"].
88 Dosman, *supra*, note 86, at 10.
89 *Regulations Implementing the United Nations Resolutions on the Suppression of Terrorism*, SOR/2001–360 ["*Terrorism Suppression* regulations"].
90 *Ibid* s 2.
91 UN General Assembly, *International Convention for the Suppression of Terrorist Bombings*, 15 December 1997, No. 37517.
92 *Criminal Code, supra* note 2, s 83.05.

previously surveyed terrorism offences in the *Code*. Along with defining "terrorist activity," the *ATA* defined a "terrorist group" as "an entity that has as one of its purposes or activities facilitating or carrying out any terrorist activity," an association of such entities, or a listed entity.[93] A number of the terrorism offences in the *Code* – participating, instructing, providing property and financial services for terrorist purposes – require a form of association with a "terrorist group." The provisions therefore make it easier for the Crown to establish proof of these offences, since one of the essential elements of the offence – the character of a person or a group as a "terrorist group" – is established on the basis of their having been listed.[94]

The process by which persons or groups may be added to the *Code* list is similar to that under the *Terrorism Suppression* regulations, with a slightly more stringent test. In this case, acting upon the recommendation of the minister of public safety and emergency preparedness, the governor in council may add groups or persons if there are reasonable grounds to believe the entity has *knowingly* carried out a "terrorist activity"; if they have facilitated, participated in, or attempted such activity; or if they have *knowingly* acted at the direction of, in association with, or on behalf of such an entity.[95] Thus, under both the *Code* and the *Terrorism Suppression* regulations, a person or group may not be listed solely on the basis of speech or advocacy of terrorism. However, under both the regulations and the *Code*, a person or group may be listed without prior notice or a chance to oppose the listing before it occurs.

B. *Challenges to Proscriptions and Listings*

Both the *Terrorism Suppression* regulations and the *Code* contain similar provisions to allow a listed entity to apply in writing to be delisted.[96] In the case of the *Code*, where the minister of public safety receives an application, he or she must decide whether there are "reasonable grounds to recommend" that cabinet delist the entity.[97] The decision not to recommend delisting may be reviewed by a judge of the Federal Court within sixty days on the relatively low standard of whether the

93 *Ibid* s 83.01(1). Note that this section defines "entity" to mean a person, group, trust, partnership, fund, or unincorporated association or organization.

94 David Paciocco queries the constitutional validity of this aspect of the provisions on the basis that they may violate the presumption of innocence: "Constitutional Casualties of September 11" (2002) 16 SCLR (2d) 199.

95 *Criminal Code*, *supra* note 2, s 83.05(1). By contrast, s 2(1) of the *Terrorism Suppression* regulations, *supra* note 89, does not contain a knowledge requirement.

96 Section 5.3(1) of the *Al Qaida* regulations, *supra* note 87, also provides an analogous means for requesting that the minister of foreign affairs petition the UN's 1267 Committee for delisting (since, as noted, those regulations set out consequences for UN listing but do not contain a separate list).

97 *Criminal Code*, *supra* note 2, s 83.05(2). See sections 2.1 and 2.2 of the *Terrorism Suppression* regulations, *supra*, note 89, for the equivalent process.

decision is "reasonable on the basis of the information available to the judge."[98] The court may privately examine secret intelligence on which the decision was based and may receive Crown submissions in the absence of the applicant or his or her counsel where disclosure would "injure national security or endanger the safety of any person."[99] In addition, the court may receive into evidence "anything that, in the opinion of the judge, is reliable and appropriate," and the decision upon review may be based on such evidence.[100] Notably, there is no provision under either the *Code* or the *Terrorism Suppression* regulations for the use of special advocates. The review procedure in both cases contemplates only a limited form of adversarial challenge, reliant upon whatever information counsel for the applicant happens to be provided – which may not even include a summary of the information on which the cabinet has relied.[101]

After listing six groups in early 2002 upon the *Code* provisions coming into force, the list has grown to forty-seven at present, with thirty-six listed under the *Terrorism Suppression* regulations.[102] The only challenge to inclusion in any of these lists has been brought by a Somali-Canadian, Liban Hussein, who had been mistakenly added to the *Terrorism Suppression* list by the cabinet, following his addition to a list under the Bush administration (and, soon after, by the 1267 Committee) in late 2001. In the course of extradition proceedings brought by the United States, Hussein brought a *Charter* challenge to the *UN Act* regulations.[103] In June of 2002, prior to the hearing of the matter, Canada determined that Hussein had not been involved in terrorist activity, abandoned the intent to extradite him and delisted him from the *Terrorism Suppression* regulations. Canada then asked the 1267 Committee to remove Hussein, which occurred in July 2002.

VI. REGULATION OF TERRORISM FINANCING

A. *The Regulatory Regime to Counter Terrorism Financing*

As a founding member of the UN's Financial Action Task Force (FATF), Canada has sought to implement its recommendations regarding the prevention of terrorism financing in a number of ways. In addition to the regulations under the *UN Act*,

[98] *Criminal Code*, *supra* note 2, s 83.05(6)(d).
[99] *Ibid* s 83.05(6)(a).
[100] *Ibid* s 83.05(6.1).
[101] Roach, *supra* note 11, at 38.
[102] The *Code* list is published online by the Ministry of Public Safety: http://www.publicsafety.gc.ca/cnt/ntnl-scrt/cntr-trrrsm/lstd-ntts/crrnt-lstd-ntts-eng.aspx. The Office of the Superintendent of Financial Institutions publishes a consolidate list of entities under all three lists discussed here: http://www.osfi-bsif.gc.ca/Eng/fi-if/amlc-clrpc/atf-fat/Pages/default.aspx.
[103] For an account of this litigation, see Dosman, *supra* note 86, at 18.

discussed earlier in this chapter, which prohibit financial dealings with listed entities, the *ATA* added new terrorism finance offences to the *Criminal Code*. Some of them depend on proscription or listing, but a number rely on the *Code*'s definition of terrorism and thus have a broader possible scope. The *ATA* also amended the *Proceeds of Crime (Money Laundering) Act* to include terrorism financing, and expanded the mandate of the Financial Transactions and Reports Analysis Centre (FINTRAC) of Canada.[104] FINTRAC is the agency that oversees compliance with the reporting requirements that the act imposes on a range of financial institutions and entities. The *ATA* also added the *Charities Registration (Security Information Act)*,[105] which allows for the use of secret information to monitor and revoke an entity's charitable status under the *Income Tax Act* where there are reasonable grounds to believe that an organization is using funds to finance terrorism. Finally, in 2006, as a further response to FATF recommendations, Parliament passed Bill C-25.[106] This required registration and reporting of a wider range of financial service entities, mandated more extensive identification for wire transfers and provided greater scope for the Canada Revenue Agency (CRA) to disclose information to law enforcement and intelligence agencies in relation to registered charities.[107]

Canada has followed other countries in modeling its terrorism financing regulation on earlier money laundering legislation.[108] The merits of this approach have been questioned, given the small costs of many significant terrorist acts and the many informal channels through which funds may be raised.[109] Yet, as the Final Report of the Air India Inquiry noted, "much of Canada's anti-terrorist financing initiative is based on a money laundering model that focuses on transactions over $10,000."[110]

[104] The act is now titled *Proceeds of Crime (Money Laundering) and Terrorism Financing Act*, SC 2000, c 17 ["*PCMLTFA*"].

[105] SC 2001, c 41, s 113 ["*CRSIA*"].

[106] *An Act to Amend the Proceeds of Crime (Money Laundering) and Terrorist Financing Act and the Income Tax Act and to Make a Consequential Amendment to Another Act*, S.C. 2006, c. 12 ["Bill C-25"].

[107] Air India Report, *supra* note 10, vol. 5, at 67; on the CRA provisions, see David Duff, "Charities and Terrorist Financing: A Review of Canada's Legal Framework," in Air India Report, *supra* note 10, *Research Studies – Volume 2: Terrorism Financing, Charities, and Aviation Security* (Ottawa: Public Works, 2010), 199 at 231–5.

[108] Air India Report, *supra* note 10, vol. 5, at 55–6.

[109] *Ibid* vol. 1, at 185.

[110] *Ibid*. One exception to this is the broad scope of possible application of the *Code*'s terrorism financing provisions, discussed later in this chapter. Aside from these, and the broader range of entities required to register under the *PCMLTFA* pursuant to Bill C-25, *supra* note 106, Canada has not directly attempted to subject smaller, informal money transfer systems, such as "hawalas" to the terrorism financing regime

These limitations are evident in the work of FINTRAC, a primary agency responsible for tracking terrorism financing, given the extensive reporting it oversees under the *PCMLTFA*. The Centre receives roughly 7 to 8 million large cash transaction reports annually, along with roughly 11 million electronic funds transfer reports from various financial institutions and from entities tracking cross-border transfers of funds.[111] Only a small portion of the reports involve "suspicious transactions" – some sixty thousand to eighty thousand per year.[112] Yet, as the Air India report notes, "[a]bout 90 per cent of the terrorist financing cases that come to FINTRAC's attention do so because law enforcement agencies or CSIS made voluntary reports to FINTRAC. The number of terrorist financing cases discovered solely by FINTRAC is minimal."[113] The Air India report also notes that despite the central role that both FINTRAC and the CRA are meant to play in preventing terror financing, neither is "sufficiently integrated into the intelligence cycle to detect terrorism financing or to provide the best financial intelligence to CSIS and the RCMP."[114]

B. *Criminal Offences of Terrorism Financing*

As noted previously, Canada has passed a number of criminal offences relating to terror financing. In response to Security Council Resolutions 1267 and 1333, the *Al Qaida* regulations prohibit anyone in Canada from dealing with property or providing financial services to the Taliban, al Qaida, or any associated entities listed by the 1267 Committee.[115] The regulations also placed a duty on Canadian financial institutions to "determine" whether to disclose when they are in possession or control of money or property belonging to listed entities.[116] Similarly, the *Terrorism Suppression* regulations prohibit dealing with property or providing financial services to entities listed by cabinet, and impose a similar duty to determine and disclose possession or control of listed entity funds.[117] Violations of either regulations are punishable as offences under the *United Nations Act*, with penalties of up to ten years in prison.[118]

The *Criminal Code* terror financing offences added by the *ATA* include knowingly dealing with property or providing financial services to a listed entity under the

111 Financial Transactions and Reports Analysis Centre of Canada, *Results Through Financial Intelligence: FINTRAC Annual Report 2013* (FINTRAC Canada, 2013) at 9–10.

112 *Ibid* at 10.

113 Air India Report, *supra* note 10, vol. 1, at 188.

114 *Ibid* at 186.

115 *Al Qaida* regulations, *supra* note 87, ss 3, 4, and 5.

116 *Ibid* ss 5.1, 5.2.

117 *Terrorism Suppression* regulations, *supra* note 89, ss 3, 4, 7 and 8.

118 *UN Act, supra*, note 85, s 3.

Code.[119] The *Code* also imposes a continuous duty on various financial institutions to determine and report on possession of property belonging to or held on behalf of a listed entity[120] and a broader duty on every person in Canada to disclose to the RCMP or CSIS any property in their possession that they know is owned or controlled by or on behalf of a listed entity.[121] In addition, the *Code* includes a series of more general terror finance provisions that are not dependent on listed entities. These include wilfully and without lawful excuse providing or collecting property knowing or intending it to be used for terrorist activities;[122] providing property or financial services intending or knowing it to be used to carry out a terrorist activity;[123] or possessing property for the purpose of facilitating or carrying out a terrorist activity.[124] Each of these offences carries a ten-year maximum prison term. Finally, the *Code* contains provisions for the seizure and forfeiture of property or funds related to terrorism. These require the Crown to prove on a balance of probabilities that the property or funds are owned or controlled by or on behalf of a listed entity or will be used to facilitate or carry out a terrorist activity.[125]

Further offences or sanctions can be found in the *PCMLTFA* (proceeds of crime) and the *CRSIA* (charities). The former act requires financial institutions such as banks, trust companies and securities brokers to report to FINTRAC transactions that they reasonably suspect involve a "terrorist activity financing offence," which the act defines as any of a number of terror financing offences under the *Criminal Code*.[126] A violation of this requirement carries a fine of up to $500,000 or six months in prison for a first-time offence.[127] Under the *CRSIA*, the ministers of public safety and national revenue may sign a certificate revoking an entity's status as a registered charity under the *Income Tax Act* where there are reasonable grounds to believe the entity has made or will make available any resources to a list entity under the *Code*.[128] As David Duff notes, the act requires no knowledge or fault element on the part of the charity and does not allow for a due diligence defence.[129] The act

119 *Criminal Code*, *supra* note 2, s 83.08.
120 *Ibid* s 83.11.
121 *Ibid* s 83.1.
122 *Ibid* s 83.02.
123 *Ibid* s 83.03.
124 *Ibid* s 83.04. Terror financing may also be caught by the facilitation, participation, or instruction provisions discussed earlier in this text (ss. s. 83.18, 83.19, 83.21), in addition to s 83.2, which makes it an offence punishable by up to life imprisonment to commit an indictable offence in association with a terrorist group.
125 *Ibid* s 83.13 and 83.14; see also sections 462.32(4) and 462.35 for other instances in which terrorist funds or property may be forfeited.
126 *PCMLTFA*, *supra* note 104, s 7(1).
127 *Ibid* s 75(1).
128 *CRSIA*, *supra* note 105, ss 4(1) and 8(1).
129 Duff, *supra* note 107, at 240.

sets out a process for seeking review of the minister's decision that is closely analogous to those for delisting under the *Criminal Code* and *UN Act* regulations. Applications are reviewed in Federal Court and may involve secret intelligence to assess whether the decision to issue the certificate was "reasonable on the basis of the information and evidence available."[130] Despite the fact that until recently no charities had their status revoked under the act, concerns had been raised about the possible chilling effect the provisions would have on charities considering work in war zones and other troubled regions.[131] Two charities have now had their status revoked as a consequence of concerns of involvement in terror financing.[132]

At present, there has been only a single prosecution for a terrorism financing offence in Canada not coupled with other terrorism charges. The accused was forty-six years old, with no criminal record. He pled guilty to a single count of providing financial services knowing they would benefit a terrorist group, the Liberation Tigers of Tamil Eelam (LTTE), a listed entity under the *Code*. He received a six-month custodial sentence, which the Crown appealed. The appeal court upheld the decision partly on the basis that the Crown had taken the position at sentencing that the accused's conduct was "at the extreme low end of the continuum with respect to this type of conduct."[133]

VII. IMMIGRATION MEASURES

A. *Immigration Detention*

Following 9/11, immigration detention had become an important tool in Canada's counter-terror efforts, due in part to the extraordinary powers it affords the government. It allows for lengthy detention on a standard lower than proof beyond a reasonable doubt, on mere suspicion of association with terrorist groups, and through the use of secret evidence. Canada used these provisions to detain five non-citizens from between 2001 to 2003, for periods of between two and seven years, along with a group of some twenty-three students from South Asia for a brief period in 2003 in what Canadian officials called Operation Thread.[134]

[130] *CRSIA*, *supra* note 105, s 7(1).
[131] See, for example, Duff, *supra* note 107, at 227, and Terrance S. Carter, "Charities and Compliance with Anti-Terrorism Legislation: The Shadow of the Law" (2004), 19:1 *The Philanthropist* 43 at 44 [cited in Duff].
[132] According to bulletins of the Canada Revenue Agency, the Canadian Foundation for Tamil Refugee Rehabilitation had its status revoked in 2010 and the ISNA Development Foundation had its status revoked in 2013; CRA online: http://www.cra-arc.gc.ca/nwsrm/rlss/2011/m12/nr111209-eng.html; http://www.cra-arc.gc.ca/nwsrm/rlss/2013/m09/nr130920-eng.html.
[133] *R v Thambaithurai*, 2011 BCCA 137, para 9.
[134] Kent Roach, "Counter-Terrorism In and Outside Canada and In and Outside the *Anti-Terrorism Act*" (2012) 16:2 *Review of Constitutional Studies* 243 at 255.

Long-term detention is authorized through the use of "security certificates" under the *Immigration and Refugee Protection Act*.[135] A part of the act since 1978, the certificate provisions mandate that the ministers of immigration and of public safety sign a certificate for the arrest and detention of non-citizens pending their deportation where there are reasonable grounds to believe they have engaged in terrorism, are a member of an organization that has or will engage in terrorism, or that they generally pose "a danger to the security of Canada."[136] The certificate is reviewed in Federal Court, where a judge assesses whether the decision to issue it was "reasonable," and once affirmed, the certificate becomes a removal order.[137] In advance of the hearing, the detainee receives only a brief summary of the information that forms the basis of the certificate.[138] The court may hear evidence *in camera* and in the absence of the detainee or his or her counsel where disclosure would be injurious to national security or to the safety of any person.[139] As Kent Roach has noted, the provisions do not require the court to engage in a balancing between the state's interest in non-disclosure and interests in disclosure to the detainee, by contrast to analogous provisions in the *Canada Evidence Act* for assessing national security privilege in other proceedings.[140] Therefore, in contrast to a criminal case, a person may be detained under a security certificate entirely on the basis of secret evidence.

In 2007, the Supreme Court of Canada ruled that the certificate provisions violated the *Charter*'s guarantee not to be deprived of liberty or security of the person except in accordance with the principles of fundamental justice.[141] The regime did so by depriving a detainee of a fair hearing, which includes the right to know the case to meet. The *Charter* requires that the hearing process provide either disclosure of material evidence or a "substantial substitute."[142] The Court held that special advocates could serve as such a substitute – counsel who could view the intelligence and consult with the detainee but not disclose the intelligence to him or her. As the court noted, special advocates had first been used in the 1980s by Canada's Security Intelligence Review Committee, a body tasked with oversight of CSIS, and were used again to challenge secret evidence during the Arar Commission and in

135 2001, SC, c 27 ["*IRPA*"].
136 *Ibid* s 34 and 77.
137 *Ibid* s 80.1.
138 *Ibid* s 77(2). As Craig Forcese notes, in "Assessing Secrecy Rules" (2009) *Institute for Research on Public Policy: Choices*, 15:5, at 15, in some cases, the summary provided has been "of the most general sort."
139 *IRPA*, *supra* note 135, s 83(1)(c).
140 *CEA*, *supra* note 46, s 38.06, discussed later in this chapter; Kent Roach, "Secret Evidence and Its Alternatives," in Aniceto Masferrer ed., *Post 9/11 and the State of Permanent Legal Emergency: Security and Human Rights in Countering Terrorism* (New York, Springer: 2011), at 184.
141 *Charkaoui v Canada (Citizenship and Immigration)*, 2007 SCC 9.
142 *Ibid* para 61.

immigration detention hearings in the UK. They seemed an adequate compromise despite the significant differences between the parties and their interests in these various contexts.

The court suspended the effect of the judgment for a year, declining to cancel any of the outstanding certificates. Parliament amended *IRPA* to allow for the use of special advocates, but it chose one of the more restrictive of the many possible frameworks for structuring the role of special advocates.[143] After viewing the secret information, the special advocate must maintain confidentiality but may not consult with the detainee without the court's permission.[144] The constitutionality of the revised scheme has been challenged and upheld.[145]

B. *Immigration Proceedings and Torture*

Canada's *Criminal Code* makes torture an offence and prohibits the use of evidence obtained through torture or cruel and degrading treatment in any legal proceedings.[146] Provisions in *IRPA* confirm that this applies in security certificate reviews.[147]

Canada does not maintain an absolute ban on *refoulement* or deportation to torture. Before being deported, security certificates detainees and others deemed inadmissible to Canada on security grounds may seek a "pre-removal risk assessment" under the *IRPA*, which may result in a stay of their removal. The act requires the minister to decide whether the detainee's risk of torture or cruel and unusual treatment in the receiving country is outweighed by the "danger that the applicant constitutes to the security of Canada."[148] In its 2002 decision in *Suresh*, the Supreme Court confirmed the constitutional validity of this balancing test.[149]

Suresh involved a Sri Lankan refugee detained under a security certificate in 1995 on the basis of membership in the Tamil separatist group the LTTE. Canada considered the LTTE a terrorist group but knew that Sri Lanka had a record of torturing the group's members. The Court acknowledged that torture is absolutely prohibited under various international treaties to which Canada is a signatory and held that deportation to torture was generally prohibited under the *Charter*. Yet it also held that "in exceptional circumstances, deportation to face torture might

[143] For assessments of the revised scheme, see Kent Roach, "Charkaoui and Bill C-3" (2008) 42 *Supreme Court Law Review* 281, and Craig Forcese and Lorne Waldman, "A Bismarkian Moment: Charkaoui and Bill C-3" (2008) 42 *Supreme Court Law Review* 355.

[144] *IRPA*, *supra* note 135, s 85.4(2).

[145] *Harkat v Canada*, [2014] 2 S.C.R.33.

[146] *Criminal Code*, *supra* note 2, s 269.1(4).

[147] *IRPA*, *supra* note 135, s 83(1.1).

[148] *Ibid* s 113(d)(ii).

[149] *Suresh v. Canada (Minister of Citizenship and Immigration)*, 2002 SCC 1.

be justified, either as a consequence of the balancing process mandated by s. 7 of the *Charter* or under s. 1."[150] The exception was not applied in *Suresh*, but the government continues to rely in part on the balancing test in the *IRPA* and the *Suresh* exception as a basis for its position that remaining certificate detainees may be deported despite concerns about torture.[151]

The Federal Court has applied the *Suresh* exception in *Nlandu-Nsoki v. Canada* (2005).[152] Nsoki was a refugee claimant from Angola found inadmissible to Canada on the basis of his membership in an Angolan terror group. The minister ordered his removal despite an opinion issued by a "pre-removal risk-assessment officer" concluding that there was a "very serious risk of torture and severe sanctions" if he were returned. Dismissing Nsoki's challenge to the order, Justice Shore applied *Suresh* in notably broad terms: "In this case exceptional circumstances do exist, namely the need to protect Canada's security."[153]

However, *Nlandu-Nsoki* runs against the grain of judicial approaches to the problem of deportation to torture after *Suresh*, in particular on the issue of whether seeking diplomatic assurances from receiving countries can adequately address *Charter* concerns. The Supreme Court in *Suresh* was sceptical of the merits of such assurances. It held that in the future, a minister's decision to deport a detainee in reliance on such assurances could be reviewed in light of the receiving nation's human rights record, that government's record in upholding its assurances and its "capacity to fulfill the assurances" in light of doubts about its control over its security forces.[154] Canada's attempt to deport on the basis of assurances was then challenged in *Mahjoub*,[155] a case involving a security certificate detainee to be sent to Egypt, and *Sing*,[156] a case involving deportation to China on the basis of serious criminality. The court in each case set aside the minister's decision based on the failure to consider adequately the historical record of the nation in question and the lack of a requirement for an effective monitoring mechanism.

Where concerns about deportation to torture have persisted, courts have chosen to release the detainee on conditions or to cancel the certificate. The Supreme Court held in *Charkaoui* that over time, the state's onus to justify detention becomes greater and may become harder to meet as information on which a certificate is based ages.[157] In all five post-9/11 security certificate cases, the detainees were eventually

[150] *Ibid* para 78.
[151] Roach, *supra* note 3, at 403.
[152] *Nlandu-Nsoki v. Canada (Minister of Citizenship and Immigration)*, 2005 FC 17.
[153] *Ibid* at para 22.
[154] Roach, *supra* note 3, at 403.
[155] *Mahjoub v. Canada*, 2006 FC 1503.
[156] *Sing v. Canada*, 2007 FC 361.
[157] *Charkaoui*, *supra* note 76, para 112–13.

released on conditions, with two of the certificates being cancelled. Yet the release conditions have been among the most restrictive in Canadian law, including house arrest (with exceptions); continuous surveillance, including phone calls; and the use of electronic bracelets and other tracking devices.[158]

Canada's use of security certificates as a primary tool for counter-terrorism has been controversial among the public and has provoked a considerable amount of litigation, often favourable to the detainee. Partly as a consequence, no new security certificates have been issued since 2003, and the government has expressed a reluctance to return to them for counter-terror purposes.[159]

VIII. ADMINISTRATIVE AND EXECUTIVE MEASURES

Apart from security certificates, Canada has not used other executive or administrative measures as an alternative counter-terror measure to criminal sanctions. Within the criminal law, as an alternative to prosecution and punishment, the *ATA* added an equivalent to UK-style control orders in the form of a recognizance with conditions, including electronic monitoring device. The court may order a person to enter into a recognizance of up to one year where there are reasonable grounds to fear that the person will commit a terrorism offence.[160] Breach of any of the conditions is an offence with a penalty of up to two years in prison.[161] If a person refuses to enter into the recognizance, they may be held in custody for up to a year.[162] The provisions do not contemplate the use of secret evidence, but do not preclude the assertion of national security privilege under the *Canada Evidence Act*, discussed in the following section.

IX. ROLE OF MILITARY AND EXTRA-TERRITORIAL COUNTER-TERRORISM ACTIVITIES

A. *Military Courts and Detention*

The military does not play a role in Canada's domestic enforcement of terrorism law. Nor does Canada detain terror suspects on a law of war basis, though Canada

[158] See the discussion of release conditions in *Charkaoui*, *supra* note 76, at para 103.

[159] Michelle Shepard and Tonda MacCharles, "Man Hounded by Ottawa Loses 'Terrorist' Tag at Last," *Toronto Star* (December 15, 2009).

[160] *Criminal Code*, *supra* note 2, s 810.01. Where a person has been previously convicted of a terrorism offence, the recognizance may be for up to two years: s. 810.01(3.1).

[161] *Ibid* s 811.

[162] *Ibid* s 810.01(4).

has accepted the transfer of former Guantanamo detainee Omar Khadr, who is serving the remainder of an eight-year sentence for war crimes.

B. *The Extra-Territorial Treatment of Citizens Suspected of Terrorism*

The detention of Canadian citizen Omar Khadr in Guantanamo and now in Canada has been the subject of much controversy and litigation since his capture by U.S. forces in 2002 in Afghanistan when he was fifteen years old. Canadian officials interrogated Khadr in Guantanamo in 2003, acting with the knowledge that he had been sleep-deprived by U.S. authorities. Fruits of the interrogation were shared with the United States for use in a military prosecution of Khadr for war crimes. In 2008, Canada's Supreme Court held that Khadr's detention violated international human rights law and the *Charter*. It ordered the Crown to disclose some of the transcripts of the interrogation but held that portions should remain confidential.[163]

Khadr then sought an order in Federal Court compelling Canada's prime minister to seek his return from Guantanamo. The court granted the order, recognizing that Canada had a duty to protect Khadr under section 7 of the *Charter*. The Supreme Court then overturned the order in early 2010, holding that although the government's involvement in the case provided a sufficient nexus to establish a *Charter* breach, the appropriate remedy was to declare Khadr's *Charter* rights violated and leave to the government "how best to respond in light of current information."[164] In the fall of 2010, Khadr pled guilty to five war crimes, including the murder of a U.S. military medical aid, and received an eight-year prison sentence. Khadr was finally returned to Canada in September of 2012 following a request by the U.S. government for Khadr to serve the remainder of his sentence in Canada.[165] Khadr is now eligible to seek parole, but the present Conservative government, which has resisted the view of Khadr as a child soldier, vigorously opposes his release.

C. *Extra-Territorial Terrorism Law Enforcement*

A number of recent cases have explored the issue of whether domestic law, including the *Charter*, limits the actions of Canadian officials acting abroad. The Supreme Court has held that the *Charter* does not constrain the conduct of Canadian officials acting outside of Canada, except where their involvement with a foreign state (or its agents) entails conduct that is "contrary to Canada's international obligations or

[163] *Canada v Khadr*, 2008 SCC 28.
[164] *Canada (Prime Minister) v Khadr*, 2010 SCC 3.
[165] Michele Shephard and Tonda MacCharles, "Omar Khadr Back in Canada" *Toronto Star* (September 29, 2012).

fundamental human rights norms."[166] The Court applied this exception in *Canada v Khadr* (2008), in light of the fact that the U.S. Supreme Court had found the military commission regime under which Khadr was being prosecuted to be contrary to international human rights law.[167]

It is difficult, however, to reconcile these holdings with the outcome of litigation relating to detainees of Canada's military in Afghanistan. Canadians were concerned that their military was transferring detainees to Afghan authorities despite the risk of torture. Amnesty International and other groups challenged the transfers as contrary to the *Charter*. The Federal Court held that the *Charter* did not apply on the basis that Canadian forces lacked "effective control" over the territory in question, and because Afghanistan had consented to the application of Canadian law to Canadian personnel but not to Afghan nationals.[168]

Finally, Canada has extradited persons accused of involvement in terrorism to face prosecution in other countries, including France and the United States.[169] But it has not had cause in these cases to seek assurances from receiving countries that the death penalty not be sought or that military detention or trial be avoided. However, in the criminal context, the Supreme Court has held that in "all but exceptional cases," the government is required to seek assurances against the death penalty where extradition may result in such an outcome.[170]

X. SECRECY AND TERRORISM

A. *Secrecy Claims and Secret Evidence*

As noted earlier, criminal prosecutions for terrorism offences are conducted in the superior courts of Canada's provinces. Trial judges in criminal cases have the power to adjudicate claims of police informer privilege at common law and public interest immunity under section 37 of the *Canada Evidence Act*.[171] Under the latter provisions,

[166] *Khadr* (2010), *supra* note 164, at para. 14, paraphrasing the rule in *R v Hape*, 2007 SCC 26.

[167] *Khadr* (2008), *supra* note 163, at para. 26.

[168] *Amnesty International v Canada*, 2008 FC 336, aff'd 2008 FCA 401, leave to the SCC denied. On the conflict between these cases, see Kent Roach, "The Supreme Court at the Bar of Politics: the Afghan Detainee and Omar Khadr Cases" (2011) 28 *National Journal of Constitutional Law* 115.

[169] Examples include the case of Abdellah Ouzghar, a Moroccan-Canadian extradited to France in 2009 and sentenced to four years for having forged passports for terrorist organizations. Notably, the Ontario Court of Appeal upheld a stay of extradition against Khadr's older brother Abdullah, sought by the United States for material support for terrorism. Having been subject to extensive abuse at the hands of Pakistani intelligence acting in concert with U.S. authorities, the court affirmed the trial court's holding that to permit the proceedings would constitute an abuse of process: *United States of America v Khadr*, 2011 ONCA 358.

[170] *United States v Burns*, 2001 SCC 7, para. 8.

[171] CEA, *supra* note 46, s 37.

evidence may be privileged on the basis that the public interest in disclosure is outweighed by one or more specific interests in non-disclosure, including the safety of informers and the protection of ongoing investigations or investigative techniques. These provisions might be applied to shield sources of information in affidavits used to obtain warrants under the *Criminal Code* or the *CSIS Act*, discussed earlier in this chapter.

Where claims of national security privilege arise in the course of a terrorism prosecution, or any other judicial proceeding in Canada, the *Canada Evidence Act* requires that they be heard in separate, parallel proceedings by a judge of the Federal Court.[172] The matter is adjudicated without the Federal Court judge having heard the evidence in the criminal case, and his or her decision as to privilege is binding on the judge in the criminal trial. Secret evidence not disclosed to the accused may not be used in the criminal trial. Where the accused is denied disclosure of evidence on national security grounds and that evidence may be essential to his or her defence, the trial judge in the criminal case may order a stay of proceedings.[173]

On a hearing under section 38, the court must first decide whether the disclosure of the information would be injurious to international relations, national defence, or national security.[174] If it would be, the judge must then decide whether "the public interest in disclosure outweighs in importance the public interest in disclosure."[175] The court may order partial disclosure or impose conditions on an order granting privilege. For example, the court might require the Crown to provide a summary of the evidence or make an admission of fact. When deciding on privilege under section 38, the court may also hear evidence *in camera*, and either the Crown or defence may make submissions *ex parte*. A defence may thus be revealed without disclosing it to the Crown. The act also imposes a duty on the accused or any participant in a judicial proceeding to disclose to the Crown its intent to call evidence that is "potentially injurious," defined as "information of a type that, if it were disclosed to the public, could injure international relations or national defence or national security."[176] The duty also extends to any party intending to disclose "sensitive information," which is defined with sweeping breadth as "information relating to international relations or national defence or national security that is in the possession of the Government of Canada, whether originating from inside or

[172] *Ibid* s 38.04. The constitutional validity of the dual court provisions were challenged and upheld in *R. v. Ahmed* 2011 SCC 6, in part due to the power of the superior provincial (or criminal trial) court to remedy abuses of process or fair trial right violations.

[173] CEA, *supra* note 46, s 38.14.

[174] *Ibid* s 38.06.

[175] *Ibid* s 38.06(2).

[176] *Ibid* s 38.01.

outside Canada, and is of a type that the Government of Canada is taking measures to safeguard."[177]

The decision of a Federal Court judge under section 38 may be appealed, which may cause further delay in the criminal trial. If the Federal Court of Appeal orders disclosure, the *CEA* allows the attorney general of Canada to personally issue a certificate prohibiting the disclosure – acting, therefore, as a kind of trump card.[178] The certificate may be reviewed by a single appeal judge, but only on a test of whether the evidence at issue *relates to* national defence or security.[179] As noted, the trial judge is bound by the holdings of the Federal Court under section 38, but may grant various remedies to protect the accused's right to a fair trial. For example, he or she may dismiss counts on the indictment or order a stay of proceedings.[180]

Despite the Supreme Court upholding the dual court process contemplated under section 38, commentators have noted a number of shortcomings with the process.[181] When weighing the merits of disclosure, a judge in the Federal Court will not have heard evidence in the criminal trial and is not therefore in a strong position to assess the importance of disclosure. Nor are defence counsels in a strong position to argue for disclosure given the lack of information they possess in relation to the evidence.[182] Moreover, without access to the privileged material, the trial judge in the criminal case is not in the best position to assess the merits of an application to stay a trial or order some other fair trial remedy. As a consequence, evidence may be disclosed in Federal Court when not truly warranted, or the trial judge might stay a criminal prosecution when not truly necessary.[183]

B. *Secrecy in the Courtroom and Anonymous Witnesses*

There are also a number of mechanisms to protect state secrets in the course of a trial or other proceeding. The *Criminal Code* allows for part or all of a terrorism prosecution to be subject to a publication ban and also to be held *in camera*, if these are necessary in a trial judge's view to "prevent injury to international relations

177 *Ibid.*
178 *Ibid* s 38.13.
179 *Ibid* ss 38.131(8), (9) and (10).
180 *Ibid* s 38.14.
181 See Kent Roach's summary of criticisms in Air India Report, *supra* note 10, *Research Studies – Volume 4: Towards a Workable Relation Between Intelligence and Evidence* (Ottawa: Public Works, 2010), 192–5; see also the Air India Report, *supra* note 10, vol. 3, at 165–7.
182 See the discussion of the possible use of special advocates in this context in Air India Report, *supra* note 10, vol. 3, at 167–9.
183 Kent Roach, "The Unique Challenges of Terrorism Prosecutions: Towards a Workable Relation Between Intelligence and Evidence," in Air India Report, *supra* note 10, *Research Studies – Volume 3: Towards a Workable Relation Between Intelligence and Evidence* (Ottawa: Public Works, 2010), at 358–9.

or national defence or national security."[184] Section 38 hearings under the *CEA* are generally subject to a publication ban.[185] And evidence at inquiries and in final reports may also be privileged or redacted pursuant to section 38.[186]

The extent to which witnesses, including members of intelligence services, may protect their identity in the course of a terrorism prosecution is limited in Canadian law by various rules. Police informer privilege at common law protects the identity of police informants who provide information on condition of preserving their anonymity. The court does not engage in a balancing here between interests; where it applies, the privilege is absolute, except if the accused's innocence is at stake (if disclosure is the only way to prove it).[187] But police informer privilege does not apply to state agents or operatives who become material witnesses to the crime being tried. It would therefore not extend to CSIS agents.[188] What is unclear in Canadian law at present is whether informer privilege may extend to informers who provide information to CSIS that is then turned over to the RCMP pursuant to section 19 of the *CSIS Act*.[189]

Intelligence agents, and others not subject to police informer privilege, may still testify under rules allowing for partial anonymity. In addition to allowing for publication bans and *in camera* hearings, the *Criminal Code* allows for witnesses in a terror prosecution to testify outside the courtroom and behind a screen so as not to see the accused. The witness would still be visible to the accused, the judge and the jury.[190] Finally, at common law, judges may permit a witness to testify under a pseudonym.[191] The Air India Commission has suggested that amendments to Canadian law permitting a prosecution that placed primary or crucial reliance on evidence from fully anonymous witnesses would likely violate the fair trial rights under the *Charter*, and not be found to be a reasonable limit on those rights under section 1.[192]

184 *Criminal Code, supra* note 2, s 486.1.

185 *CEA, supra* note 46, s 38.02. In *obiter*, Lufty J. of the federal court, in *Ottawa Citizen Group Inc. v. Canada (Attorney General)*, 2004 FC 1052 (CanLII), paras 34–45, has queried whether these are consistent with the open court principle affirmed in *Vancouver Sun (Re), supra* note 70.

186 *(Canada (Attorney General) v. Canada (Commission of Inquiry into the Actions of Canadian Officials in Relation to Maher Arar)* (F.C.), 2007 FC 766.

187 *R. v. Leipert*, [1997] 1 S.C.R. 281.

188 Air India Report, *supra* note 10, vol. 3, at 131.

189 In the main Air India prosecution, information that was turned over in this fashion was not found to be subject to informer privilege partly on the basis that CSIS gave no indication when providing the information to the RCMP that informer privilege was a condition of obtaining it or providing it to police: *R v Malik and Bagri*, 2004 BCSC 554, para 18. See also *Harkat (Re)*, [2014] 2 S.C.R. 33, holding, in the context of security certificates, that CSIS sources were not subject to informer privilege but to public interest immunity at common law.

190 *Criminal Code, supra* note 2, s 486.2.

191 *Vancouver Sun, supra* note 70, at para 91.

192 Air India Report, *supra* note 10, vol. 3, at 204–21.

XI. OTHER MATTERS

In the decade following 9/11, much of the discussion about national security in Canada has focused on terror prosecutions and administrative detention. From 2004 onward, however, Canada's counter-terror efforts have comprised only one part of a larger policy on national security premised upon protecting human security broadly understood.[193] The earlier Liberal government had thus sought to address terrorism as one among a range of concerns that include emergency preparedness (for medical and natural disasters), transportation and border security and the regulation of sensitive sites and materials. To fulfill this mandate, the government created a new Ministry of Public Safety and passed the *Public Safety Act*,[194] which bolstered the regulation of sensitive materials and aviation security and allowed for greater information sharing among domestic intelligence agencies and their international partners. The present Conservative government has remained committed to approaching terrorism as one of several threats to human security broadly conceived.[195]

A further important aspect of Canadian counter-terrorism after 9/11 involves the use of inquiries to examine human rights abuses and other aspects of security law and policy.

From 2004 to 2006, Canada held an inquiry into the role of Canadian officials in the ordeal of Syrian-Canadian citizen Maher Arar. In 2002, the RCMP provided U.S. officials with information that prompted them to detain Arar on a stopover in New York, on his way back to Canada from a vacation in Tunisia.[196] The United States sent him to Syria, where he was tortured and imprisoned for almost a year, then released upon Canada's intervention. The Commission found that the RCMP had provided U.S. officials with inaccurate information, violated the RCMP's own screening policies for relevance and reliability and provided the information without caveats as to its use.[197] It was also critical of the lack of interagency coordination and

[193] Canada, *Securing an Open Society: Canada's National Security Policy* (Ottawa: Privy Council Office, 2004).

[194] SC 2004, c 15.

[195] Public Safety Canada continues to define its basic function as "a centralized hub for coordinating the work in counter-terrorism, critical infrastructure, cyber security and transportation security" ("National Security," online: http://www.publicsafety.gc.ca/cnt/ntnl-scrt/index-eng.aspx). This multifaceted approach can also be discerned across a series of recently published strategies statements on security, including the Ministry's *Building Resilience Against Terrorism: Canada's Counter-Terrorism Strategy*, its latest global policy statement on point: online http://www.publicsafety.gc.ca/cnt/rsrcs/pblctns/index-eng.aspx?t=ntnl-scrt.

[196] Commission of Inquiry into the Actions of Canadian Officials in Relation to Maher Arar, *Report of the Events Relating to Maher Arar: Analysis and Recommendations* (Ottawa: Public Works and Government Services Canada, 2006) ["Arar Commission Report"] at 27.

[197] *Ibid* at 13–14.

found that Canadian officials had not been sufficiently cautious in their reception and internal distribution of information obtained from Syrian officials through torture. Following the inquiry, the government paid Arar $10.5 million in settlement of a civil action and issued an apology in the House of Commons.

A second inquiry looked into Canada's role in the detention and torture of three Canadian citizens traveling in Syria and Egypt in 2002. Headed by former Supreme Court Justice Frank Iacobucci, the inquiry, reporting in 2008, found that Canadian officials had indirectly contributed to the detention of two of the three men and indirectly contributed to the mistreatment of all three.[198] The inquiry pointed to various "deficiencies" in protocols for sharing information with Syrian and Egyptian authorities, and in their dealings with those authorities to obtain information from the detainees.[199]

Only the first of these inquiries was tasked with making recommendations for improving counter-terror practices. The Arar Commission recommended that CSIS and the RCMP should abide by clearer divisions of labour in terms of intelligence gathering and law enforcement; that training and protocols for the RCMP's national security work (such as information sharing) be improved; and that the RCMP and other agencies with national security mandates (Canada Border Services, FINTRAC, the Department of Foreign Affairs, among others) be subject to a centralized review body with similar powers to access confidential information to those exercised by the Security Intelligence Review Committee that oversees CSIS.[200] In response, the government has recognized the need for more central coordination of agencies in national security, but has thus far resisted the implementation of a central review body with powers to assess the efficacy of such coordination or access to confidential information commensurate to the task.[201]

The government also ordered an inquiry into issues surrounding the failure to prevent the Air India bombing of 1985 and the investigation and prosecutions that followed. In addition to assessing causes of the failure to prevent the bombing (noted earlier in this chapter), the Commission made a series of recommendations relating to terror investigations and prosecutions. Among them were suggestions about how intelligence might be more effectively gathered with a view to its use as evidence and how to improve information sharing, witness protection and aviation security.[202] In

[198] Commissioner Frank Iacobucci, *Internal Inquiry into the Actions of Canadian Officials in Relation to Abdullah Almalki, Ahmad Abou-Elmaati, and Muayyed Nurredin* (Ottawa: Public Works and Government Services Canada, 2008), at 35–9.

[199] *Ibid.*

[200] Arar Commission Report, *supra* note 191, at 363–9; see also the Commission of Inquiry into the Actions of Canadian Officials in Relation to Maher Arar, *A New Review Mechanism for the RCMP's National Security Activities* (Ottawa: Public Works and Government Services, 2006).

[201] Roach, *supra* note 3, at 417.

[202] Air India Report, *supra* note 10, vol. 1, chapter VII.

response, the government has published an "Action Plan," setting out its intention to make changes on several fronts.[203] Notably, the government has declined to respond to two of the Commission's key recommendations: enhancing the role of the prime minister's national security advisor in the coordination of national security agencies and giving trial judges in terrorism prosecutions the power to decide on disclosure requests for secret intelligence.[204]

XII. CONCLUSION

In the fall of 2001, the *Anti-terrorism Act* was controversial, both during its brief period as a bill before Parliament and in the early years following its passage. Canada followed the United Kingdom by entrenching a broad definition of terrorism, and it followed the United States in expanding powers of state secrecy and surveillance. There were concerns that the definition of terrorism, provisions for listing, terror financing and charities would place a chill on free speech, hinder fundraising or be misapplied. There were concerns about the overreach of the new offences and the possible misuse of the preventive arrest or judicial interrogation provisions. Yet with the benefit of hindsight and a growing body of jurisprudence, many of these concerns have subsided. The RCMP, working in coordination with CSIS and other agencies, has succeeded in disrupting a number of plots in early stages. Early prosecutions under the *ATA* have unfolded without a pattern of misuse of police powers or an overbroad application of new offences in the *Code*.

However, concerns about the fundamental unfairness of the use of immigration detention have been borne out. Security certificate detainees have spent significant time in custody without charge on secret evidence. Doubts remain as to whether special advocates are indeed a "substantial substitute for disclosure" or whether there can be such a thing. Fortunately, Canada appears to have abandoned the use of immigration detention as a substitute for prosecution. It may be following the lead of the United Kingdom and the United States in shifting a focus back to prosecution and a closer adherence to conventional approaches to due process.

Concerns also remain about the overuse of privilege. In a number of cases, claims of privilege have coincided with sensitive issues of accountability of state agents, as in the Arar case, the Afghan detainees case and some of the security certificate cases. In addition to this, there is a concern that expansive claims of national security privilege will become normalized in a wider range of areas of Canadian law through

203 Canada, *Action Plan: the Government of Canada Response to the Commission of Inquiry into the Investigation of the Bombing of Air India Flight 182* (Ottawa, 2010).

204 Roach, *supra* note 3, at 373.

the spread of the use of special advocates as a kind of global solution to the problem of secrecy and fairness.

Among the challenges for Canada going forward will be to restrain the use of secrecy, carefully limit and oversee the use of surveillance and institute more effective central coordination and review of the various agencies involved in national security – possibly through enhanced powers of the national security advisor to the prime minister and a parallel review body.

XIII. POSTSCRIPT

At the time of this writing, the government of Canada has tabled two bills that contemplate significant changes to Canada's counter-terrorism law. The bills come in the wake of two events in October of 2014 that brought terrorism to the fore of public discussion. In Quebec, a radicalized individual, acting alone, struck two soldiers with his car, killing one of them. Three days later, in Ottawa, another radicalized, lone-wolf actor shot a soldier guarding a war memorial and entered Parliament attempting to claim more lives before he was shot dead.

Later that month, the government tabled bill C-44, the *Protection of Canada from Terrorism Act*. Now in third reading and likely to pass, the bill will allow CSIS to obtain a warrant to use measures outside of Canada that may violate the laws of a foreign state – including surveillance contrary to foreign privacy laws. The bill also extends the doctrine of informer privilege to CSIS informants, but allows the privilege to be lifted in a criminal case where it is essential to establishing the accused's innocence.

In January of 2015, following the attacks in Paris and with a federal election in Canada on the horizon, the government tabled bill C-51, the *Anti-terrorism Act, 2015*. Currently in first reading, the bill contains the most extensive set of revisions to Canada's counter-terror law since 2001 and is likely to pass in substantially similar form, given the governing party's majority status and recent policy pronouncements.

The bill adds a new offence to the *Criminal Code* of advocating or promoting terrorism. It prohibits knowingly communicating statements that advocate or promote the "commission of terrorism offences in general" knowing they will be committed or being reckless as to whether they may be committed. It carries a penalty of as much as five years in prison. Concerns have been raised about the overbroad scope of the offence given the uncertainty as to the meaning of the phrase "terrorism offences in general" and its application to terrorism that "may" be carried out. A related provision allows police to obtain a warrant to seize or destroy "terrorism propaganda," which is defined as any representation that advocates the commission of "terrorism offences in general."

The bill also contains a new *Secure Air Travel Act* that allows for the creation of a no-fly list of a broader scope than the ones discussed earlier in this chapter. The minister of public safety may add individuals to the list where there are "reasonable grounds to suspect" the person will "threaten transportation security" or commit a terrorism offence in Canada or abroad. The minister may direct airlines to "do anything … reasonable and necessary to prevent" the acts from occurring, including denying a person transportation or screening them. A listed person may make recourse to the minister or appeal his or her decision to a judge, who must assess whether any ministerial direction was reasonable.

Bill C-51 also lowers the threshold for preventive detention and orders placing a person on a recognizance with conditions. Whereas at present police may detain without charge where they reasonably suspect it to be "necessary" to prevent a "terrorist activity," they may do so under the bill where it is "likely to prevent" such activity. Similarly, a terrorism recognizance order may be imposed not only where a terrorist act "will be carried out" and is "necessary to prevent" such an act – as is currently the case – but where it "may be carried out" and is "likely to prevent" the act. The bill will extend the limit on pre-trial detention from three to seven days and introduces a new terrorism peace bond that may last as long as five years and require electronic monitoring, surrendering a passport and travel restrictions.

Perhaps most controversially, bill C-51 amends the *Canadian Security Intelligence Service Act* to include a provision stating that where the service has reasonable grounds to believe an activity constitutes a threat to "the security of Canada," its agents may "take measures within or outside Canada to reduce the threat." The measures may not infringe a Charter right or be contrary to law unless CSIS obtains a warrant. A key consideration in granting the warrant is whether the measures are reasonable and proportionate – though regardless of whether they obtain a warrant, CSIS may not take measures that cause death or bodily harm, obstruct justice or "violate the sexual integrity of an individual." By assuming this power, Parliament has blurred the clear separation between CSIS's role as a civilian intelligence gathering agency and the RCMP's role as a law enforcement body. Yet the bill does not include any substantial new oversight mechanisms for CSIS to accompany these new powers.

Finally, the bill introduces a new *Security of Canada Information Sharing Act*, which allows for greater sharing among federal agencies of information "relevant … in respect to activities that undermine the security of Canada." The latter phrase is defined broadly to include any activity that may undermine the "sovereignty, security or territorial integrity of Canada" and may also include "interference" with the government's "economic or financial stability." No oversight mechanisms have been added that might enable more effective review of information sharing beyond the purview of single-agency review bodies.

PART TWO

South America

4

Colombia

Luz E. Nagle

I. INTRODUCTION

Terrorism in Colombia is a continuum of violent conflict straddling several generations and sustained by a sense of unease that never quite dissipates from the sociopolitical landscape. Its impact includes unprecedented population displacements, environmental degradation and illegal exploitation of natural resources, and large areas of national territory where there is little or no government authority. The proliferation of landmines by terrorist groups has rendered many areas of Colombia too dangerous for occupation, and indiscriminate bombings have devastated communities and transportation systems in both rural and urban settings. Kidnapping and other forms of extortion to fund terrorist activities cause constant stress throughout the civil society, and crimes related to terrorism, such as money laundering and weapons smuggling, result in a loss of trust in government institutions. Efforts by the government and military forces to counter terrorist groups have often resulted in serious human rights abuses against civilian populations and have brought international condemnation and ridicule upon the Colombian state. Foreign assistance in Colombia by the United States has redefined the fight against terrorism, not only in Colombia but throughout Latin America, as Colombian terrorist groups have spilled over into neighboring states and set up shop to continue the criminal activities that fund their continued existence. Indeed, the illegal armed groups that once preached insurgency against the Colombian state have evolved into sophisticated transnational crime organizations and have landed on the lists of terrorist organizations of several countries.

Terrorism against the Colombian government and the civil society is primarily the result of two sets of actors: narcotraffickers fighting extradition to the United States during the 1980s and 1990s, and various insurgent groups and private armies engaged in an armed conflict against the Colombian state reaching back six decades.[1] Over time, the nature of the sources and methods for countering both terrorist threats has shaped corresponding changes in the national legislation and more recently has influenced the way Colombia participates in the global war against terrorism.

The Colombian people have endured a level of political violence worse than nearly any other state in Latin America. Forced civilian displacements, proliferation of landmines, indiscriminate bombings, kidnapping, and crimes related to and in support of terrorism have sustained a sense of unease across the Colombian landscape.

Despite many ups and downs and the inflow of billions of dollars in aid for rule of law, civil society, and military programs, the Government of Colombia (GOC) has yet to gain the upper hand on the nation's security situation. This is due to many factors having less to do with any diminution in terrorism and more with the inability of the state to contend with problems that continue to inhibit the enforcement of constitutional protections and human rights for the society. For all intents, Colombia is a de facto narcoplutocracy. The economy, commerce, political alliances, and the ability of the nation's civil society to sustain itself are based heavily on the billions upon billions of narcodollars that have fueled the formal economy over the last four decades. Also, corruption from drug trafficking and illegal armed groups pervades every aspect of Colombian life and Colombia's government institutions such that in many ways corruption is not a plague on the political system; it *is* the political system.

The tenacity of illegal armed groups has enabled them to infiltrate the Colombian government at all levels, including the government agencies tasked with combating them and with protecting the security and constitutional rights of Colombian citizens: the Department of Administrative Security (DAS), loosely, Colombia's counterpart to the United States Federal Bureau of Investigation; and the Directorate of Criminal Investigation and Interpol (DIJIN), a part of the National Police responsible for citizen security and investigation of special crimes.

This infiltration has resulted in a term called "FARC politica," which expresses the success that Colombia's most powerful illegal armed group, the Revolutionary Armed Forces of Colombia (known by the acronym FARC), has achieved in embedding its influence within government institutions, in the private business sector, and even in higher education. The FARC has also actively sought through bribery and blackmail to corrupt government officials and Colombia's professional class to be informants and to provide the technical expertise needed to sustain

[1] Diego Fernando Tarapués Sandino, *An Overview of the Terrorism in Colombia: Context, National Legislation and Anti-Terrorism Measures* (2012), 1 [CON]TEXTOS 29–37.

and increasingly anti-American populist president, Rafael Correa.[6] lso continues to enjoy ideological and possibly logistical support from ie FARC's 57th Front overtly uses jungle regions in Panama to maintain s for staging supplies and weapons into Colombia and to conduct drug nd human trafficking operations, including sex slavery, in Central beyond.[7]

: is a sophisticated transnational criminal organization with significant nd support networks in several foreign countries, including nearly all ican states, nations in Central America, and a number of countries in western Africa.[8] The FARC has known ties to the Irish Republican ıal organizations worldwide, and radical Islamic terrorist organizations, ssibly al-Qaeda.[9]

C's organizational structure is based on a supreme command council ty over "bloques" that divide the national territory. Within the "bloques" lozen smaller units, called "frentes" (fronts), operating in both rural ıreas, and mobile columns that have the ability to move quickly to nts where needed. The combat strength of FARC fronts is typically hundred combatants plus support personnel and "camp followers."[10] ; order of battle has proved a successful formula, with fronts assigned pecific duties, such as urban fronts tasked with conducting extortions, dnappings, money laundering, and intelligence gathering, and rural ıed to tactical operations against government forces and supervising drug production and trafficking, cattle rustling, illegal mining, weapons ınd human trafficking empire. There is no region within the national ably free of FARC influence.

C intimidates political adversaries through violence and prosecutes ıst the government on multiple levels, using terrorist tactics such as ıte bombings against civilian targets, deployment of landmines in

ı his third term in office, Correa is seen by many political experts in the region as the Hugo Chavez in the Bolivarian movement. See Jose R. Cardenas, *Meet Latin America's Chavez*, WASHINGTON TIMES, April 6, 2012, http://www.washingtontimes.com/news/2012/ latin-americas-next-hugo-chavez/.

rite Cawley, *Former Panama Policeman Is a FARC Leader*, InSightCrime.org, October 1, www.insightcrime.org/news-briefs/panama-policeman-new-farc-leader.

Senator Diane Feinstein Before Hearings of the U.S. Senate Caucus on International Control, May 16, 2012, http://drugcaucus.senate.gov/r-west-africa-hearing-statement-5-16-12

ıj, *Colombian FARC Rebels, al-Qaeda Joining Forces to Smuggle Cocaine into ys DEA*, NY DAILY NEWS, January 5, 2010, http://articles.nydailynews.com/2010-01-05/ 446_1_al-qaeda-smuggle-colombian-farc-rebels.

ng: *The FARC Is Not Finished Yet*, THE ECONOMIST, July 7, 2011, http://www.economist 18928504.

FARC operations. Skills ranging from engineer
arts, finance, and computer programming, forei
after by the FARC.

II. ABOUT THE I

The FARC is the oldest active leftist revolutio
with its roots going back to communist-foment
in the 1950s.[2] The FARC has been listed on th
International Terrorist Organizations since Oc
reports emanating from the Colombian govern
press releases that the FARC's military capacity l
both a well-organized military organization a
criminal and terrorist organization numbering b
ten thousand members within Colombia and ove
that the FARC has strengthened and changed tact
loss of key members of its high command. Its ta
efforts to infiltrate student groups at several camp
bring well-educated young adults into the leader
of women and children under fifteen years of age
as well as concubines for FARC commanders.[5]

The FARC exerts hegemony over large portions
continued overt support from beyond the Colon
anti-imperialist, democratic socialist Bolivarian
tacit support from Bolivarian populist president

[2] For a thorough overview of modern Colombia history, see
Colombia: A Nation in Spite of Itself (Berkeley: University

[3] See Office of the Coordinator for Counterterrorism, *Forei*
30, 2013, http://www.state.gov/j/ct/rls/crt/2012/209989.htm. T
are designated as foreign terrorist organizations: the Nation
Self-Defense Forces of Colombia (AUC). The AUC formall
and former commanders have formed new criminal orga
and are active in poor urban areas in the larger Colomb
BACRIMs, see Luz E. Nagle, *How Conflict and Displacem*
Vulnerable Groups: The Case of Colombia and Opportuniti
(2014), 1 GRONINGEN J. INT'L L. 1.

[4] *FARC Terror Group Infiltrating Colombian Student Movem*
FORUM, November 11, 2011, http://americasforum.
colombian-student-movement-captured-evidence-shows.

[5] Human Rights Watch, *You'll Learn Not to Cry: Child Co*
http://dspace.cigilibrary.org/jspui/bitstream/123456789/18
Cry%20Child%20combatants%20in%20Colombia.pdf?1.

left-leaning
The FARC
Cuba, and
support bas
smuggling
America an

The FAR
operations
South Ame
Europe an
Army, crim
including p

The FAI
with autho
are several
and urban
reinforce f
sixty to on
The FARC
to perform
terrorism,
fronts assig
FARC's vas
smuggling,
territory re

The FA
its war aga
indiscrimi

[6] Currently
successor
Next Hug
apr/6/mee

[7] See Marg
2013, http:

[8] Remarks
Narcotics
.html.

[9] Neil Nag
Europe, S
news/1794

[10] *Never En*
.com/nod

populated rural areas, kidnapping, extortion, and armed assaults and sabotage against government infrastructure, private property, and industrial sites and against military forces and the national police. The FARC also wreaks havoc by forcibly recruiting child soldiers, thereby fragmenting close-knit communities, and foments mass displacements of rural populations to cause stress on the GOC's social services and administrative infrastructure. In 2010 alone, more than 280,000 civilians were forcibly displaced due to the internal armed conflict,[11] and it is estimated that as December 2013 more than 5.2 million people are now internally displaced, due in large measure to the FARC.[12]

The FARC is not realistically capable of achieving military superiority of any kind, long term, over the Colombian state. Therefore, FARC attacks are often indiscriminate and intended primarily to create terror and keep military and national police units off balance. The FARC combatants are particularly fond of low-precision explosive devices and use them to devastating effect.[13] Since at least 2001, the FARC has been training for increased capabilities to wage urban warfare and terrorism, especially in the national capital of Bogotá. In August 2001, a group of individuals suspected of being members of the Irish Republican Army were arrested in Bogotá's international airport for traveling with false passports as they were preparing to board a flight to Paris after spending five weeks in FARC-held territory. The three men were subsequently accused of training the FARC in the use of explosives in urban settings, especially car bombs and mortars. The most recent terrorist act blamed on the FARC was a devastating car bomb attack on a police station in Cauca Province in December 2013 in which at least five people were killed, including five soldiers and one police officer.[14] This terrorist act occurred even as FARC representatives were engaged in peace talks with the Colombian government in Cuba.

The group's transformation from Marxist insurgents to a sophisticated transborder criminal/terrorist organization stretches back to 1982, when the FARC leadership, convening during the Seventh Guerrilla Conference, decided to tax coca farmers in territory under FARC control.[15] According to one report, the FARC "transformed from a traditional guerrilla group into a full-fledged insurgency because of its ability to effectively convert the proceeds derived from illegal narcotics trafficking

[11] Amnesty International, *Annual Report: Colombia 2011*, http://www.amnestyusa.org/research/reports/annual-report-colombia-2011.

[12] See 2014 UNHCR Report on Colombia, http://www.unhcr.org/cgi-bin/texis/vtx/page?page=49e492ad6.

[13] Amnesty International, *Annual Report: Colombia 2011*, http://www.amnestyusa.org/research/reports/annual-report-colombia-2011.

[14] *See Deadly Colombia Bomb Attack Blamed on FARC Rebels*, BBC News Latin America & Caribbean, December 7, 2013, http://www.bbc.co.uk/news/world-latin-america-25287046.

[15] Thomas R. Cook, *The Financial Arm of the FARC: A Threat Finance Perspective* (2011), 4 J. OF STRATEGIC SECURITY 19 at 21–2.

into operational funds."[16] As the lucrative possibilities became more apparent, the FARC leadership selected for occupation and control areas of the national territory where coca production was especially high. Based on proceeds from its coca revenue stream, the FARC began making "strategic investments" to improve its organizational structure.[17] This included establishing ties to countries such as Russia and Vietnam to obtain training for FARC commanders, purchasing sophisticated communications and surveillance hardware, and establishing trafficking corridors throughout South America and across the Atlantic. Ironically, the successful counter-narcotics operations by the United States and the Colombian government in the 1990s and 2000s actually played into the hands of the FARC, which moved quickly to fill the vacuum left by the downfall of the Medellín and Cali drug cartels, and made the FARC far stronger as an international criminal organization and global terrorist entity.

In January 2012, the group's current leader, Timoleón Jiménez (a.k.a. Timochencko), called for peace talks with President Juan Manuel Santos Calderón.[18] As part of his overture to the government, Jiménez announced that the FARC would no longer kidnap civilians (non-military targets and politicians) and would consider releasing FARC hostages.[19] Several hostages were released in early 2012, but it is estimated that several hundred remain in FARC captivity.[20] The FARC's statement on kidnapping is just another in a very long line of false overtures the FARC has made over the decades, and it is not expected that such peace negotiations will move beyond a hypothetical stage.[21] It also comes with several provisos and insincerities, the most significant being that while it will no longer kidnap "for financial ends," kidnapping will still remain a tool to gain political leverage. This means that while private citizens and business executives may no longer be targeted, politicians and military personnel remain fair game, and since the FARC central command does

[16] Thomas R. Cook, *The Financial Arm of the FARC: A Threat Finance Perspective* (2011), 4 J. OF STRATEGIC SECURITY 19 at 21–2.

[17] Thomas R. Cook, *The Financial Arm of the FARC: A Threat Finance Perspective* (2011), 4 J. OF STRATEGIC SECURITY 19 at 26.

[18] *See Colombia Rebel Leader Denies Talks Imply Surrender*, AGENCE FRANCE PRESSE, April 20, 2012.

[19] The FARC also continues to attack and murder local officials, police, and politicians, and such political violence can occur at any time, in any location in Colombia. In July 2011, for example, two mayoral candidates were abducted and murdered in northern Colombia in the department of Antioquia by FARC guerrillas. The candidates were from different parties – a clear indication that no political party is exempt from being targeted by the FARC. See Patrick Corcoran, *FARC Murders Mayor Candidates in North Colombia*, InsightCrime.org, May 31, 2011, http://insightcrime.org/insight-latest-news/item/1010-farc-murders-mayor-candidates-in-north-colombia.

[20] *Colombia's FARC Announces It Will Halt Kidnapping*, USA TODAY, February 26, 2012, http://www.usatoday.com/news/world/story/2012-02-26/colombia-farc-halt-kidnapping/53257458/1.

[21] Jack Kimball, *Colombia Rebels Call for Peace Negotiations*, NEWS DAILY, January 10, 2012, http://www.newsdaily.com/stories/tre8091qm-us-colombia-conflict/.

not have full control over its nationwide network of fronts and cells, there is no way to determine if semi-independent FARC units will toe the line with the central command's edicts.

If the FARC is abandoning kidnapping as a terrorist tactic against the Colombian people and the GOC, this should not be taken as a sign of weakness or of deteriorating presence anywhere in the national territory. All it demonstrates is what most experts on the FARC have known for many years – that the FARC does not need to kidnap people to gain revenue because the FARC's primary income comes from having emerged as a multimillion dollar international crime organization with its tentacles reaching well beyond Colombia.

The FARC's revenues as of August 2011 were estimated to be between $80 and $350 million dollars, placing it third among the world's wealthiest terrorist organizations.[22] With no realistic hope of actually overthrowing the GOC, and due to the success of its transborder criminal enterprises, the FARC has no incentive either to disarm or even declare a cease-fire. This alone renders the peace talks currently under way as little more than political theater, a stalling tactic in which the FARC has engaged quite successfully for more four decades. By reading the comments of readers in Colombian news magazines and publications, not even the Colombian people think the FARC is serious about peace or that the GOC is capable of reaching a peace agreement with the FARC.[23]

In addition to drug trafficking, the FARC is engaged in weapons smuggling,[24] trafficking in human beings,[25] money laundering, and cattle rustling. The FARC is believed to run the largest illicit cattle ranching operation in Colombia, bringing in some $22 million annually from tens of thousands of stolen cattle grazing on tens of thousands of hectares of land throughout Colombia.[26] While the GOC noted in 2010 that the FARC was selling livestock because it was stretched for revenues, most experts dismissed the government's claims as ludicrous. The FARC is also one of the largest stakeholders in illegal mining operations throughout Colombia, profiting

[22] *The World's Five Richest Terrorist Groups*, Money Jihad blog, August 29, 2011, http://moneyjihad.wordpress.com/2011/08/29/the-worlds-5-richest-terrorist-groups/.

[23] See Carlos Andrés Barahona, *Colombians Skeptical About the FARC's Desire for Peace*, Infosurhoy, May 16, 2012, http://infosurhoy.com/en_GB/articles/saii/features/main/2012/05/16/feature-02.

[24] See, for example, Marguerite Cawley, *Colombian Police Capture Arms Trafficking Brother-in-Law of FARC Alias "Gafas,"* COLOMBIA REPORTS, June 23, 2011, http://colombiareports.com/colombia-news/news/17173-colombian-police-capture-arms-trafficking-brother-in-law-of-farc-alias-gafas.html.

[25] Don Winner, *FARC Trafficking Humans, Drugs, Weapons – Recruiting Panamanians as Sex Slaves in the Darien*, Panama-Guide.com, November 4, 2011, http://www.panama-guide.com/article.php/20111104131623379 (reporting that the FARC is involved in trafficking illegal aliens from Asian and African countries through the border area between Colombia and Panama).

[26] See Luz E. Nagle, *Cattle Rustling and Ranching by Illegal Armed Groups and Organized Crime* (2013) 29 No. 6 *INT'L ENFORCEMENT L. REP.* 177, *and* Luz E. Nagle, *The FARC: Doing What Any Multinational Corporation Would Do – Diversify* (2012) 28 No. 5 *INT'L ENFORCEMENT L. REP.* 178.

directly from illegal gold and coltan mining and profiting from surcharges to miners for leasing claims and mining equipment.[27] The FARC's mining and cattle ranching operations are being carried out in the open throughout the Colombian territory. It is inconceivable that the GOC would not know that these illegal activities are occurring and expanding, and this would suggest that significant government corruption and collusion among the political elites are present.

III. THE "FARC POLITICA" PHENOMENON

The FARC's success as a highly successful and long-enduring international crime organization and illegal armed group is due to its organizational characteristics and its ability over the course of several decades to establish a highly sophisticated intelligence gathering and surveillance network comprised of domestic servants, groundskeepers, taxicab drivers, bank employees, shopkeepers, and government officials who collude with or are coerced into cooperating with the FARC. The group maintains an extensive electronic communications grid via computer-based wireless and cellular networks and has surveillance capabilities throughout the national territory, as well as overseas. The organization can track a person's physical whereabouts through any number of paper trails and financial transactions, including through airlines and travel agencies and, increasingly, through the illegal use of GPS tracking devices, easily concealed handheld scanners, and facial recognition software downloaded onto smartphones. The FARC is believed capable of tracking a person through activities as seemingly benign as using a debit card to buy groceries in a local market.

The FARC recruits, coerces, and forcibly conscripts into its ranks individuals it deems to be useful. The FARC targets university campuses in Bogotá and nationwide, women and children living in poor communities (known as *comunas*), and disaffected members of Colombia's professional and intellectual classes. For instance, in 2003, the perpetrator of a FARC terrorist attack on Bogotá's public transportation system turned out to be a female medical student.

The FARC has placed operatives in key government agencies to track the daily affairs of business and commerce throughout Colombia. Among the more notable incidences is the case of one Freddy Escobar Moncada, a political associate of former Medellín mayor Sergio Fajardo (now governor of the department of Antioquia and a perennial presidential candidate). Escobar was a prominent university professor who sat on the board of the city's utilities authority (Empresas Publicas de Medellín), was involved in social improvement organizations, and managed a multimillion

[27] Edward Fox, *FARC Set to Exploit Venezuela "Conflict Mineral,"* INSIGHT ORGANIZED CRIME IN THE AMERICAS, March 12, 2012, http://insightcrime.org/insight-latest-news/item/2336-farc-set-to-exploit-venezuela-conflict-mineral.

dollar budget. He was also for more than twenty-six years a clandestine member of the FARC in Medellín and one of its leading ideologues. His arrest in 2006 took many of the political elites by surprise,[28] and then-Mayor Fajardo's public relations machine had to work overtime to mitigate the damage to his reputation and political aspirations.[29]

There is no solid evidence that the FARC has infiltrated police forces at the national, department, or municipal levels, since the FARC and police forces are bitter and implacable enemies.[30] However, *corruption* within the military and national police and within the other internal security groups does exist, and the FARC does exploit and benefit from corruption within the ranks. Moreover, security forces are believed to downplay the number of reports and investigations they handle related to FARC assaults and persecution because the GOC needs to show the United States and other nations giving foreign aid to Colombia that the security situation in Colombia is under control. This is a misleading tactic solely for political gain and utterly fails to recognize that security for the civil society and protection of the rule of law in much of Colombia remains tenuous.[31]

[28] *El alcalde de Medellín desconocía nexus de directive de EPM con las FARC*, CARACOL, August 8, 2006, http://www.caracol.com.co/noticias/actualidad/el-alcalde-de-medellin-desconocia-nexos-de-directivo-de-epm-con-las-farc/20060808/nota/317832.aspx.

[29] Two other troubling recent examples of the FARC Politica in the GOC are worth noting. One concerns the 2011 appointment by the Juan Manuel Santos administration of Viviane Morales as Colombia's attorney general. As the *Wall Street Journal* reported it, Dr. Morales "remarried her ex-husband Carlos Alonso Lucio, who happens to be a former member of the M-19 [guerrilla group] and a former adviser to both the ELN and the paramilitary. He was in jail when they married the first time. In other words, the attorney general's husband has spent years cavorting with the type of people she is supposed to be investigating." The other example concerns longtime Colombian politician, legal activist, and former senator Piedad Córdoba Ruiz. Córdoba has long been part of the extreme left and an unapologetic advocate for FARC interests in Colombian political affairs. She was part of a humanitarian exchange effort with the FARC in the early 2007 that proved politically controversial. In 2008, files found on the captured computer of FARC commander Raúl Reyes following his demise in Ecuador at the hands of a Colombian military raiding party further established Córdoba's close political ties to the FARC, including revealing her FARC code name of "Teodora de Bolivar." Córdoba later met with FARC leaders under the patronage of Hugo Chavez in Venezuela, and in 2010, the inspector general of Colombia revoked Córdoba's senatorial credentials due to her involvement in supporting and promoting the FARC. Relationships such as these demonstrate that nothing in Colombian political life is black and white and that the gray is a constantly changing shade of alliances and political maneuverings. See Mary Anastasia O'Grady, *Colombia's Compromised Courts*, WALL STREET JOURNAL, December 12, 2011, at A17.

[30] Although in 2003, fifteen suspected ELN members were discovered to have enrolled in the José María Córdoba Military School.

[31] We do know that drug traffickers have infiltrated the government at high levels and it is conceivable that infiltration could include FARC operatives who are engaged in drug trafficking. One instance of infiltration made international headlines in 2006 when ten members of the Colombian Judicial Police (DIJIN) and an informant were ambushed by army soldiers moonlighting for a wanted drug trafficker. According to reports, the Colombian Army labeled the killings as a "friendly fire" incident and

In the *2012 Country Report on Colombia*,[32] the U.S. State Department's Bureau of Western Hemisphere Affairs asserted that the GOC had greatly improved internal security and the rule of law during 2011, that drug trafficking had been significantly impacted, and that the threat of the FARC and other illegal armed groups toward the civil society had been greatly reduced. The report credited the Santos administration with having made great strides in maintaining "positive trends in security consolidation," which included the capture, killing, or demobilization of more the 4,500 guerrillas and members of criminal gangs.[33]

One year later in May 2013, however, the State Department reported that, "Despite significant successes in its campaign against the Revolutionary Armed Forces of Colombia (FARC) and the beginning of peace talks, Colombia experienced a year of increased terrorist activity in 2012."[34] The increase was actually a 53 percent jump over the prior year, and the FARC was to blame for many of the terrorist acts.

The same *2012 Country Report* came on the heels of ratification of the Colombia Free Trade Agreement (CFTA), which took effect on May 15, 2012. In order for the CFTA to succeed, it must be demonstrated that (1) the security situation in Colombia is under control and the economic climate is favorable for doing business, and (2) that the judicial system has implemented reforms necessary to ensure that commercial contracts can be properly enforced in court. This means that data and

attempted to cover up the investigation under a military tribunal. But Colombia's attorney general called it a massacre and took the investigation of the shootings away from the military tribunal to be carried out by the government prosecutor's office. The head of the DIJIN at the time, General Oscar Naranjo, stated that, "In some cases, they (police and soldiers) are passive participants. In other cases, there is a direct criminal penetration of the public institutions that basically conceal[s] the activities of the mafia don by allowing him to do his work or, in some cases, being active participants with him in his work." See Steven Dudley, *Drug Mafia's Infiltration of Military Grows Clearer*, MIAMI HERALD, July 5, 2006.Other illegal armed groups such as the AUC were known several years ago to have infiltrated the attorney general's office. This was revealed during the investigation of an AUC death squad operative who was recorded in a government wiretap providing details about his assassination of a prosecutor's office investigator in 2004. According to intelligence reports revealed to the press at the time, "[I]nternal memos and interviews with investigators, former prosecutors and human rights observers, illegal paramilitary groups responsible for killing thousands of suspected leftist guerrillas and supporters have the power to steer investigations and influence personnel decisions." In one internal investigation, it was discovered that fifty-two prosecutors had spoken to paramilitary members as many as two hundred times. See Frances Robles, *Militias Said to Corrupt Prosecutors*, MIAMI HERALD, April 18, 2004.

32 See *Report on Colombia*, March 6, 2012, http://www.state.gov/outofdate/bgn/colombia/199006.htm.

33 In early March, a FARC commander, Alexander Beltran Herrera, was extradited to the United States to face charges of kidnapping three American contractors whose plane crashed in FARC-held territory while on a drug interdiction surveillance flight in 2003. See Frederic J. Frommer, *Alleged Member of FARC Extradited to US*, AP, March 12, 2012, http://abcnews.go.com/US/wireStory/alleged-member-farc-extradited-us-15902174.

34 See Office of the Coordinator for Counterterrorism, U.S. State Department, *Country Reports: Western Hemisphere Overview, Country Reports on Terrorism 2012*, chapter 2, May 30, 2013, http://www.state.gov/j/ct/rls/crt/2012/209984.htm.

reports produced by the GOC and endorsed by the United States have been issued regarding conditions that in several cases cannot be substantiated by what one actually sees on the ground, especially beyond the nation's capital of Bogotá.

The *2012 Country Report* also depicted that the FARC was on the run and maneuvering to sue for peace negotiations, which began in 2013. However, one might argue that based on prior experience, the picture of progress promoted by the State Department and by the GOC is largely a myth intended to justify the vast sums of aid and military materiel the United States has provided to Colombia since the implementation of Plan Colombia back in 2000. Moreover, an earlier 2011 report issued by the Corporación Nuevo Acro Iris, a Colombian non-government human rights organization, noted that FARC activity increased significantly in 2011, and that the army was "crippled by corruption" and unable to provide security in areas in which the FARC operates or operated. Moreover, notes the Coporación, in areas where the military has taken control away from FARC, human rights organizations have reported an increase in human rights abuses.[35]

Currently the peace talks are an ebb and flow of the FARC making demands and the Colombian government making concessions, while the Colombian people continue to be skeptical that any peace will come from the process. There is also considerable public acrimony over the idea that the FARC could be allowed to become a recognized political party in the government. In the final analysis, the FARC has little to gain by demobilizing, and the organization is not quaking in its combat boots that the GOC is bearing down on them. In fact, the character of the ongoing peace talks in Cuba is perplexing at best, as news organizations broadcast images of FARC negotiators being treated like rock stars and even relaxing on a sailing yacht during one of the frequent breaks in talks. Now well into its fifth decade in existence, there is no reasonable evidence to indicate that the FARC's existence is in any immediate danger of collapse.

IV. ASSESSING THE GOC'S CAPACITY TO RESPOND TO TERRORIST THREATS

In the eight years that former president Alvaro Uribe served in the presidency (2002–2010), the GOC confronted the FARC through military, law enforcement, and judicial means and by pitting right-wing paramilitary groups under an umbrella organization called the United Auto-Defense Forces of Colombia (AUC) against FARC and other leftist groups. While Uribe proved himself to be a staunch ally of the United States and a grateful beneficiary of billions of dollars in military and

[35] See *Report Shows Increase in FARC Activity This Year*, JusticeforColombia.org, July 25, 2011, http://www.justiceforcolombia.org/news/article/1045/report-shows-increase-in-farc-activity-this-year.

legal assistance under Plan Colombia (formulated originally by his predecessor, Andrés Pastrana), narcoguerrilla drug trafficking and FARC terrorist operations were not substantively reduced. Moreover, Mr. Uribe and his family members have themselves long been linked to drug trafficking, as well as to forced population displacements and extreme political violence for personal gain and enrichment. This paradox underscores how complicated the political landscape in Colombia is and why it is so difficult for Colombia to achieve sustainable security. Further complicating matters is that Mr. Uribe became the first former president to be elected to the Colombian Senate, taking office in July 2014 as a representative of the Democratic Center, a "big tent coalition" that vehemently opposes President's Santos' peace process with the FARC.[36]

Despite claims that the Colombian military and national police are better trained and better equipped to confront terrorism and illegal armed groups, enforcement of Colombian law and protection of civil society from terrorist threats are only as good as the capabilities of government forces. In many precincts, equipment is seriously degraded or unusable, understaffing is a constant problem, morale is low, salaries are poor, and officers continue to lack ongoing professional training and command leadership. Moreover, antagonism among law enforcement branches, particularly between the Colombian military and the national police, places the law enforcement apparatus in disarray in some areas. While the Colombian people have a high regard for the Colombian military, they have less confidence in the national police, and most do not feel that the GOC, overall, is capable of protecting citizens proactively from terrorist attacks. As one taxi cab operator told me during a visit to Colombia in 2103, "The police are only good for picking up the pieces and counting bodies and not for deterring crime before it happens." In fact, in 2012 the GOC reported that the nation continued to see a rise in criminal organizations connected to the FARC and other illegal armed groups and that violence associated with such groups "spilled over into many of Colombia's major cities, leading to an increase in the murder rates within some urban centers and the mass displacement of thousands of rural citizens in 2011."[37]

The state of the Colombian judicial system also raises significant concern with regard to protecting the security of Colombian citizens. Despite the system having been "reformed" and invested with hundreds of millions of dollars and technical

36 Mr. Uribe campaigned on the slogan of "No more impunity," and his message has been favored by many Colombians who see Santos' negotiations with the FARC as an act of treason against the Colombian state. See *Colombia Voters Give Lukewarm Support for Peace Process*, TIMES OF OMAN, March 11, 2014, available on Westlaw at 2014 WLNR 6606870. Uribe's entry into the Congress has factionalized the legislative branch to the point that little progress is now being made with regard to coalition building and political cooperation.

37 See United States Department of State Bureau for International Narcotics and Law Enforcement Affairs, 2012 *International Narcotics Control Strategy Report* 170, http://www.state.gov/documents/organization/184314.pdf.

assistance by the United States under Plan Colombia during the 2000s,[38] the conversion from a civil law system of inquisitorial process to the Anglo-American form of accusatory (or adversarial) adjudication imposed by the United States has not gone well.[39] In point of fact, the Colombian judiciary is in turmoil. In a letter to the United States House Foreign Affairs Committee in late 2011, a former Colombian senator warned of the infiltration of illegal armed groups and narcoterrorists in the Colombian judiciary and non-government organizations, where operatives disguised as human rights defenders orchestrate and support actions to attack democratic institutions.[40]

The manner in which reform of the criminal justice system was implemented has resulted in serious inequities in the delivery of justice. Many Colombian criminal law professors have asserted that government prosecutors received the best training first and that whatever funding and resources remained went much later to training the judges and defense lawyers. The result has been that the judges don't understand the system in which they are now hearing cases, and the defense lawyers do not understand how the accusatory process is supposed to work. The rules of evidence are unclear; taking testimony is problematic; and the notion of plea bargaining, which was also introduced into the criminal justice process, has yet to be properly integrated or even fully understood. It is far easier for some judges to throw up their hands in frustration and toss cases out, or not try them at all, because they do not understand or believe in a criminal justice system that is not part of their continental legal tradition. Other judges simply do not want to put in the time necessary to make the system work. Moreover, the mafias and illegal armed groups continue to intimidate the courts, and judges and prosecutors are not willing to risk their lives challenging powerful forces over which they have no control. For this reason, criminals walk, impunity is rampant, and the citizens have no faith in the delivery of justice.

An assessment by the United States Department of State in 2012[41] concluded that:

> Judicial impunity remains a major impediment to deterring violence. President Santos acknowledged that less than 10 percent of arrested BACRIM members

[38] See Luz E. Nagle, *The Search for Accountability and Transparency in Plan Colombia: Reforming Judicial Institutions – Again*, IMPLEMENTING PLAN COLOMBIA SPECIAL SERIES (Carlisle, PA: Strategic Studies Institute, U.S. Army War College, 2001).

[39] For a thorough analysis of the current state of the judiciary in Colombia, see Luz E. Nagle, *Process Issues of Colombia's New Accusatory System* (2008) 14 *SW. J. L. & TRADE AM.* 223 (providing an informed examination of how the Colombian judiciary is in far greater disarray following the introduction of adversarial procedures in criminal court cases).

[40] Mary Anastasia O'Grady, *Colombia's Compromised Courts*, WALL STREET JOURNAL, December 12, 2011, at A17.

[41] See United States Department of State Bureau for International Narcotics and Law Enforcement Affairs, *2012 International Narcotics Control Strategy Report* 172, http://www.state.gov/documents/organization/184314.pdf.

> actually serve jail time. One former municipal security advisor estimated Bogota's conviction rate for homicide at less than 10 percent; other major cities appear to rank similarly. Lower conviction rates in rural areas are likely due to more limited investigative capacity and lack of protection for judges, investigators, and witnesses. In June, the news media widely reported on a perceived deterioration in public security while the Santos government defended its efforts to rein in violent crime more effectively.

In the 1980s, the term "narcoterrorism" emerged from wanton deadly attacks against government and civilian targets by the infamous Medellín Drug Cartel, run by a career criminal from the working class named Pablo Escobar, and the equally fierce and unpredictable Cali Cartel, run by a highly educated family that was well regarded among the political and social elites of that southwestern Colombian city. Narcoterrorist attacks included bombings of government buildings, police stations, the U.S. embassy, newspaper offices, nightclubs, and pharmacies, and even a Colombian airliner was blasted from the sky.[42]

The attacks were highly destructive and intended entirely to spread fear in order to sabotage the plans of executive branch of the Colombian government to send Colombian drug traffickers to the United States to stand trial and face heavy prison sentences. At the same time, other Marxist-Leninist guerrilla groups such as the M-19, the ELP, and ELN and right-wing paramilitary opponents such as the AUC used terrorist attacks to promote their political agendas, disrupt security throughout the nation, cause displacements of large populations, and take control of large areas of Colombian territory.

Even with the promulgation of anti-terrorism decrees and statutes (some at the expense of civilian freedoms), terrorism continued to escalate into the 1990s. Between 1988 and 1990, more than fourteen thousand Colombians were killed by terrorist attacks. Assassinations of officials and leaders included the murders of twelve judicial officers of the Public Order Court, other judges and prosecutors, a national police colonel, and three presidential candidates, including the popular front runner in the presidential elections, Senator Luis Carlos Galán. More alarming still was the fact that despite the best efforts of government officials, agencies, and the judiciary to investigate and prosecute narcoterrorist murders, the perpetrators of most of the killings enjoyed total impunity, thanks to legislation formed with an eye toward appeasing narcoterrorists in order to gain some respite from terrorist acts.[43]

[42] See *All 107 Aboard Killed as Colombian Jet Explodes*, NY TIMES, November 28, 1989, http://www.nytimes.com/1989/11/28/world/all-107-aboard-killed-as-colombian-jet-explodes.html.

[43] Luz E. Nagle, *Global Terrorism in Our Own Backyard: Colombia's Legal War Against Illegal Armed Groups* (2005), 15 *TRANSNT'L L. & CONTEMP. PROB*. 5.

Despite rounds of peace negotiations, a shaky cease-fire, and a successful democratic security policy that reduced the guerrillas' combatant strength during the last decade, terrorist attacks still pose a constant threat to civilians.[44] This threat has resulted in far-reaching developments in Colombian anti-terrorism law,[45] which also aligns with the global war on terror.

According to former Ambassador Alfonso Valdivieso, Colombia's twenty-fourth permanent representative to the United Nations, "The acts, methods and practices of terrorists are criminal acts that are unjustifiable and contrary to the purposes and principles of the United Nations.... Colombia is of the view that international terrorism differs from other serious crimes because its aim is to sow terror among the population and to destabilize or force a government or an international organization to take or refrain from taking some action."[46] From this statement, one can understand the Colombian state's attempt to (1) render domestic terrorism a crime that is by nature international or with international effects, and (2) remove it from the political context in which the "armed conflict" is recognized.

V. ANTI-TERRORISM LEGISLATION

Analysis of the current legislation requires a review of the main instruments that were used to fight "terrorist acts" in Colombia's past. A long-standing tool to address a security or national crisis is to declare a state of emergency (*estado de sitio*). The state of emergency conveys broad powers to the executive branch and the law enforcement agencies to confront threats to public safety and state stability. Decreed by the president, the state of emergency is often related to terrorist actions[47] and can entail the temporary suspension of many individual rights and constitutional guarantees, such as freedom of movement and freedom of assembly. The state of emergency power was first included in Article 121 of the Colombian Constitution of 1886. It was the main instrument to fight the "occasional" terrorist acts[48] and was invoked during the so-called drug war against the criminal cartels during the last decades of the twentieth century.

[44] Rafael Nieto Navia, *¿Hay o no hay conflicto armado en Colombia?* (2008) 1 ACDI 139–59.

[45] Aljure Salame, Antonio, *El Conflicto Armado Interno y el Derecho Internacional*, in DERECHO INTERNACIONAL CONTEMPORÁNEO: LO PÚBLICO, LOS PRIVADO, LOS DERECHOS HUMANOS (Bogotá, Colombia: Editorial Universidad del Rosario, 2006).

[46] Item 166: Measures to Eliminate International Terrorism, Statement by Ambassador Alfonso Valdivieso, Permanent Representative of Colombia, New York, October 2, 2001, http://www.colombiaun.org/English/Security%20Council/Colombia%20Non%20Permanent%20Member/Int_Ter_Statements/StatementINT_Oct02_01.html.

[47] Nicolás Orejuela Botero, *Los estados de excepción en Colombia* (Cali, Colombia: USABU, 2011).

[48] Constitución Política 1 de 1886 Asamblea Nacional Constituyente, http://www.alcaldiabogota.gov.co/sisjur/normas/Norma1.jsp?i=7153.

The state of emergency provision was adopted into the Political Constitution of 1991. However, the implementation of modern legislation to contend with terrorism has diminished its application. Nevertheless, decree powers continue to allow the president to exercise considerable political control over matters of state security and in response to terrorist threats. It was an executive decree issued in 1988 (Decree 180)[49] that defined terrorism under Colombian law as crimes against state security and public tranquility rather than against property or people and established lengthy prison sentences and fines for acts that "provoke a state of anxiety or terror to the public or a section of it, through acts that endanger the life, physical integrity or liberty of persons or buildings or means of communication, transportation, processing or fluid handling or drivers using means capable of causing havoc."

The decree power granted by the Constitution to the executive branch allows the president to respond quickly to a national crisis without having to go through what can often be a lengthy deliberative process in the Colombian Congress. Although a decree can address an imminent threat, its continuation is subject to judicial review, and Congress retains the discretion to convert the decree into a permanent law.

A presidential decree can also establish a unique judicial authority for dealing with threats against the state. One such example was Decree 2970 of 1990,[50] which established subject matter jurisdiction for special crimes related to terrorism, including kidnapping, extortion, terrorist acts, and related terrorist acts.[51]

VI. THE DEFINITION OF TERRORISM

In the Colombian system, both the executive and the legislative branches draft criminal policy, select the corresponding penalties, and establish which criminal conducts are the biggest concern for the civil society and for the legal system. Under the recent political conditions in which the terrorist threat has come from guerrilla insurgency, the GOC opted to recognize the "internal armed conflict" under international humanitarian law to avoid conferring the status of belligerents on illegal armed actors such as the FARC and other guerrilla combatants.

There is some controversy to this maneuver. In any internal armed conflict, the applicable international law is embodied in Common Article 3 of the four 1949

49 Decreto 181 de 1988, Diario Oficial No. 38.191, de 27 de enero de 1988, ftp://ftp.camara.gov.co/camara/basedoc/decreto/1988/decreto_0181_1988.html.

50 Decreto 2970 de 1990, Diario Oficial No. 395, de 20 de noviembre 1990, http://juriscol.banrep.gov.co/contenidos.dll/Normas/Decretos/1990/decreto_2790_1990.

51 Art. 9(4), Decree 2970 de 1990, Diario Oficial No. 395, de 20 de noviembre 1990, http://juriscol.banrep.gov.co/contenidos.dll/Normas/Decretos/1990/decreto_2790_1990.

Geneva Conventions,[52] Protocol II of 1977,[53] and Article 8 of the Rome Statute of the International Criminal Court.[54] Common Article 3 articulates standards of humane treatment by which warring parties must abide, while Article 3 applies to the conducts and safeguards armed forces must observe during conflict. The Rome Statute applies "when there is protracted armed conflict between governmental authorities and organized armed groups or between such groups." Protocol II, Article 1(1), defines internal conflicts as "those taking place in the territory of a High Contracting Party between its armed forces and dissident armed forces or other organized armed groups which, under responsible command, exercise such control over a part of its territory as to enable them to carry out sustained and concerted military operations and to implement this Protocol."

In Colombia, guerrilla groups, particularly the FARC, have long had a command structure, exert control over part of the territory, and have sufficiently intense combat activities that cannot be dismissed as isolated and sporadic acts of violence. Protocol II should, therefore, apply to this type of command. But when Colombia ratified the four Geneva Conventions on August 11, 1961, and acceded to Protocol II on August 14, 1995, the principle of state sovereignty made the application of the rules of internal armed conflict difficult in Colombia and placed the true status of Colombian guerrilla groups in question. In the decades prior to the adoption of Protocol II, the government depicted the political crisis in Colombia as little more than an ongoing series of internal disturbances with occasional acts of violence that did not meet the conditions necessary for the application of Protocol II. The GOC also believed that Protocol II, if embraced, would upgrade the status of the guerrillas to that of belligerents – something the guerrilla groups long hoped to achieve in order to gain status as a legitimate political entity struggling for a place at the table of Colombian government. The GOC and the military, however, maintained that ratification of Protocol II was unnecessary and inappropriate because its adoption would open the door to international intervention, including the possibility of intervention on the side of the guerrillas.[55] As the crisis persisted and intensified heading into the 1980s, however, internal pressures on the government by the guerrillas and the channeling

[52] Geneva Convention relative to the Treatment of Prisoners of War, 75 U.N.T.S. 135 (entered into force October 21, 1950), http://www1.umn.edu/humanrts/instree/y3gctpw.htm.

[53] Protocol Additional to the Geneva Conventions of August 12, 1949, and Relating to Protection of Victims of Non-International Armed Conflicts, June 8, 1977, 16 I.L.M. 1442 (entered into force December 7, 1978), http://www1.umn.edu/humanrts/instree/y6pagc.htm.

[54] Statue of the International Criminal Court, U.N. Doc. A/CONF.183/9 (1998), http://unispal.un.org/UNISPAL.NSF/0/26D5982060C2D2AD85256B3B0074F5F8.

[55] See Jorge L. Esquirol, *Can International Law Help? An Analysis of the Colombian Peace Process* (2000) 16 CONN. J. INT'L L. 23, 40.

of resources into fighting an increasingly violent campaign against international drug traffickers forced the ratification of the Protocols.[56]

In trying to diminish the belligerent nature of the illegal armed groups, the GOC enacted several pieces of anti-terrorist legislation. Crimes against public security and crimes of terrorism are codified primarily under articles 144, and 340 through 349, respectively, of the Colombian Penal Code (Law 599 of 2000).[57] Terrorism is considered as a singular crime (systematical and group-oriented) and terrorist acts as individual acts carried out for a terrorist purpose (for example, kidnapping, sabotage, and armed assault carried out with terrorist purpose). This issue of the status of illegal armed groups remains problematic for the GOC.

VII. FIGHTING TERRORISM WHEN IT IS NOT POLITICAL IN NATURE

The legislation relating to terrorism is based on a policy of keeping terrorism from being labeled a political crime. Within the Colombian Penal Code, terrorism is a crime against the juridical good *(bien jurídico tutelad)*, a civil law expression referring to a protected juridical interest, such as the sustaining of life, wealth, progress, public finances, or public health. This categorization of terrorism differentiates it from political crimes, thereby allowing the application of extradition treaties and other international conventions and also allowing it to be not only an independent crime, but also an aggravating condition for other conducts when they are committed with the intent to disrupt public order. Under the scenario of a recognized internal armed conflict[58] and a crime of terrorism that is nonpolitical and can be committed by various forms of illegal conduct, Colombian legislation does not contemplate any exceptions to the crime for reasons of political struggle, freedom of speech, or liberation movements.

VIII. TERRORISM UNDER THE COLOMBIAN PENAL CODE

The so-called Global War on Terror following the al-Qaeda attacks in the United States on September 11, 2001, and subsequent recommendations and actions of United Nations in response have effectively informed Colombian legislation by the addition of "supplementing laws" modifying and complementing the criminal code,

[56] Luz E. Nagle, *Placing Blame Where Blame Is Due: The Culpability of Illegal Armed Groups and Narcotraffickers in Colombia's Environmental and Human Rights Catastrophes* (2004) 29 WM. & MARY ENVTL. L. & POL'Y REV. 1, 38–40.

[57] Código Penal Colombiano, Diario Oficial No. 44.097, del 24 de julio del 2000, http://perso.unifr.ch/derechopenal/assets/files/legislacion/l_20130808_01.pdf.

[58] Juan Manuel Valcárcel Torres, *Beligerancia, terrorismo y conflicto armado: No es un juego de palabras* (2008) 13 REV. COLOMB. DERECHO INT. 363–90.

raising the punishments for terrorism acts, and giving more investigative powers to government authorities. Terrorism under Colombian criminal law appears as an independent crime in the Penal Code and includes crimes supporting terrorist activities as an aggravating punitive condition, such as financing terrorism. The inclusion of terrorism itself may be considered a breakthrough in Colombia law since it is an individual crime, complementary but independent of "acts of terrorism" crimes.[59]

Terrorism, as an individual crime, is based on the act of producing and maintaining societal fear and distress by any means, including threatening life, government infrastructure, transportation, public services, and power generation sources. The notion of "maintaining in fear" gives Article 343 a scope of "permanence in time" that other provisions of the Colombian penal code do not provide, therefore, rendering this article of law the most relied upon to prosecute high-profile guerrilla combatants.

Acts of terrorism are covered under article 144 of the Penal Code. Article 144 is an explicit application to prosecute whoever commits acts with terrorist goals, despite standing or permanence in an organization created with such a goal. An additional anti-terrorism legislation addressing the "permanence in time" is Law 733 de 2002,[60] which increases the imprisonment time for criminal acts such as kidnapping. It also includes an important provision that no pardon or amnesty shall be granted to anyone convicted for terrorism, terrorist acts, and crimes linked with terrorism. Since terrorism is understood as an unlawful goal (keeping the society in fear), the punitive consequences of committing any other crime in conjunction with advancing a terrorist goal becomes greater. In this way, crimes of terrorism in Colombia are not limited only to participation in a terrorist organization, but include the commission of multiple crimes that can become part of a terrorism prosecution. This assists the prosecution because participation in a terrorist organization or in the planning of a terrorist goal is not necessary for a conviction.

IX. TRAINING, FINANCING, AND MEMBERSHIP IN A TERRORIST GROUP

Colombian law also contains provisions for punishing the training for membership and participation in terrorist groups. Article 340 criminalizes participation in a terrorist organization and provides for increased penalties where there are aggravating circumstances. Article 14 of Law 890 of 2004[61] modifies article 340 by providing for

[59] Ley 599 de 2000, Diario Oficial No. 44.097, de 24 de julio del 2000, ftp://ftp.camara.gov.co/camara/basedoc/ley/2000/ley_0599_2000.html.

[60] Ley 732 de 2002, Diario Oficial No 44.693, de 31 de enero de 2002, http://www.cartagena.gov.co/Cartagena/secplaneacion/Documentos/pages/pot/files/normograma/Ley_732_de_2002.pdf.

[61] Ley 890 de 2004, Diario Oficial No. 45.602, de 7 de Julio de 2004, http://www.refworld.org/pdfid/46d686a72.pdf.

sentences of two to three years imprisonment for anyone who organizes, instructs, trains, or equips persons in tactics, techniques, and military procedures for carrying out terrorist acts or for participating in illegal armed groups. The intentions of Law 890 are twofold: (1) to deter terrorist recruitment, which in Colombia has been a widespread phenomenon in impoverished and displaced communities; and (2) to deter midlevel and lower-ranking members of terrorist organizations from participating in indoctrinating new members or new combatants.

Colombia has enacted legislation addressing the financing of terrorism financing and participation in terrorist groups via two specific provisions in article 345, which criminalizes providing financing or logistical aid to terrorist groups, national and international alike, as well as administering and processing funds for terrorist groups. Prosecutors follow a formula for determining charges of terrorism for individual crimes and aggravated circumstances. The formula is essentially any crime (for example, murder, sabotage, extortion) plus an aggravating element and terrorism as a stand-alone crime. In addition, under international instruments, a suspect could be charged for violations of human rights plus crimes against humanity.

In September 2014, the GOC implemented a new regulation to comply with emerging international principles called "Know Your Client" to confront the financing of terrorism. The regulation is intended to assist the business community in combating money laundering and related illegal activities.[62]

> Know your client (KYC) is an international standard that companies can implement to help mitigate such risks. The "Know" implies a due diligence to any client, provider or company determining a risk level and also helps to prevent involvement in fraud, money laundering and terrorist financing.[63]

The Colombian regulation mandates that any companies with revenue above 160,000 pesos in minimum monthly wages must implement internal procedures to monitor risk of money laundering and terrorism financing activities. In addition to introducing client-tracking software to identify risks, companies are now required to retain experts to analyze information to determine the safety of working with potentially risky companies.[64] In complying with the new regulation, issued by the Superintendencia de Sociedades, companies must show that they are working within the "parameters for prevention of money laundering, fraud and terrorism financing" and "undertake periodic checks on existing clients and suppliers."[65]

[62] Maria Arango, *New Compliance Regulation In Colombia Calls On Companies To Verify Clients And Providers Information*, MONDAQ, September 10, 2014.

[63] Maria Arango, *New Compliance Regulation in Colombia Calls on Companies to Verify Clients and Providers Information*, MONDAQ, September 10, 2014.

[64] Maria Arango, *New Compliance Regulation in Colombia Calls on Companies to Verify Clients and Providers Information*, MONDAQ, September 10, 2014.

[65] Maria Arango, *New Compliance Regulation in Colombia Calls on Companies to Verify Clients and Providers Information*, MONDAQ, September 10, 2014.

X. SUPPORTING INCITEMENT OF TERRORISM

A crime for incitement of criminal acts related to terrorism is not directly contemplated under Colombian law. While laws have been proposed to criminalize such conduct, human rights and freedom of speech concerns have been raised.[66] However, article 184 of the Penal Code criminalizes the act of obligating others through any kind of coercion to participate in terrorist organizations.

XI. INVESTIGATION OF TERRORISM

Colombia participates in the Anti-terrorism Assistance (ATA) program funded by the United States throughout Latin America and is also a member state of the Financial Action Task Force of South America Against Money Laundering. According to the U.S. State Department, Colombia is a "leader in the fight against terrorist financing and has become a key part of a regional Financial Intelligence Unit initiative aimed at strengthening information sharing among Latin American countries."[67] Through the ATA, Colombia has received technical training and support in the form of instructor development and crisis-response training "to expand its role both as a regional provider of counterterrorism training to other countries in the Western Hemisphere, and as a senior participant in joint trainings with other ATA partner nations."[68]

Three government ministries, foreign affairs, finance, and justice, entered into a memorandum of understanding that authorizes the Prosecutor General's Office to implement the necessary seizure orders under existing Colombian asset forfeiture law against the assets of individuals and entities on the UNSC 1267/1989 and 1988 Sanctions Committees' consolidated list and to freeze assets of terrorists, terrorist financiers, and terrorist groups.[69] The Prosecutor General's Office Justice and Peace Division created a special asset forfeiture unit in May 2011 to identify and seize assets belonging to armed illegal groups, such as the AUC and the FARC (both U.S.-designated terrorist organizations). Intelligence gathering on terrorist groups in

66 A draft article existed, but was not enacted due to human rights concerns. See *No habrá delito de apología al terrorismo*, EL ESPECTADOR, October 4, 2010, http://www.elespectador.com/impreso/articuloimpreso-227862-no-habra-delito-de-apologia-al-terrorismo.

67 U.S. State Department Office of the Coordinator for Counterterrorism, Country Reports: Western Hemisphere Overview, Country Reports on Terrorism 2012, chapter 2, May 30, 2013, http://www.state.gov/j/ct/rls/crt/2012/209984.htm.

68 U.S. State Department Office of the Coordinator for Counterterrorism, Country Reports: Western Hemisphere Overview, Country Reports on Terrorism 2012, chapter 2, May 30, 2013, http://www.state.gov/j/ct/rls/crt/2012/209984.htm.

69 U.S. State Department Office of the Coordinator for Counterterrorism, Country Reports: Western Hemisphere Overview, Country Reports on Terrorism 2012, chapter 2, May 30, 2013, http://www.state.gov/j/ct/rls/crt/2012/209984.htm.

Colombia is handled primarily by the National Directorate of Intelligence (DNI) and a special unit within the national police, the Policía Judicial, which exercises special powers under the new criminal procedural law regarding investigation of high-profile crimes such as terrorism.[70] The Colombian military, too, maintains a special unit for combating terrorism, the Agrupación de Fuerzas Especiales Antiterroristas Urbanas (Urban Counter-Terrorism Special Forces Group, AFEUR) which is trained as a rapid response force for combating terrorist threats. Within the judicial branch, article 35 of the Code of Criminal Procedure[71] has established special tribunals throughout the national territory to hear cases of terrorism crimes and related conduct. These special courts have jurisdiction over crimes such as genocide, crimes against international humanitarian law, kidnapping for extortion, torture, and money laundering.

Law 1621 of 2013[72] was recently enacted to define more clearly the framework of cooperation between counterterrorism agencies and to set limits on intelligence and counterintelligence gathering activities. Law 1621 also establishes mechanisms for control and supervision of agents involved in intelligence gathering.

XII. EVIDENCE AND HUMAN RIGHTS

Colombian criminal procedure is heavily influenced by the emphasis on human rights in the Political Constitution of 1991. During court proceedings, one judge observes that a defendants human rights are protected *(juez de garantías)*, and a subject matter judge *(juez de conocimiento)* oversees the proceedings of the case. Evidentiary rules proscribe any kind of forced interrogation or torture methods used to obtain evidence or confessions, even in terrorism matters, and evidence obtained through such means is inadmissible according to article 23 of the Code of Criminal Procedure.

Colombian law provides for restorative justice and rehabilitation in sentencing practices. Law 975 of 2005[73] provides a way for members of illegal armed groups to be reincorporated into the civil society in a manner that conforms to promoting national peace and humanitarian practices. However, while sentencing reductions are available to the judge for convicted criminals, reductions are not applicable to terrorism crimes related to offenses that can be considered crimes against humanity.

[70] *See* Iván Andrés Astwood Romero, *Función de policía judicial y sistema acusatorio* (2005) 48 REV. CRIMINALIDAD 250, http://www.policia.gov.co/imagenes_ponal/dijin/revista_criminalidad/vol48/13.pdf.

[71] Código de Procedimiento Penal, Ley 906 de 2004, Diario Oficial No. 45.657, de 31 de agosto de 2004, http://www.oas.org/dil/esp/Codigo_de_Procedimiento_Penal_Colombia.pdf.

[72] Ley 1621 de 2013, Diario Oficial No. 48.764, de 17 de abril de 2013, http://wsp.presidencia.gov.co/Normativa/Leyes/Documents/2013/LEY%201621%20DEL%2017%20DE%20ABRIL%20DE%202013.pdf.

[73] Ley 975 de 2005, Diario Oficial No. 45.980, de 25 de junio de 2005, http://www.eclac.cl/oig/doc/col2005ley975.pdf.

A very important ruling of the Constitutional Court, Sentencia C-095/7, stated that this prohibition is constitutional.[74]

Under article 441 of the Colombian Penal Code, failure to notify the authorities of terrorist criminal activity is a crime, called "Omisión de denuncia de particular." This provision was intended to conform to international law and can be used in relation to all unreported crimes.

XIII. UNDERCOVER INVESTIGATIONS

Infiltrating a criminal organization and performing undercover operations has been one of the most effective ways to fight terrorism. In Colombia, the complex activity of undercover operations is regulated in the Code of Criminal Procedure under articles 241, 242, and 243, respectively. The prosecutor, based on previous evidence, can authorize the judicial police to perform such operations to obtain evidence and capture members of terrorist groups. This prosecutorial power gives broad leeway to the agents to perform functions necessary to maintain undercover surveillance and investigation.

XIV. ELECTRONIC SURVEILLANCE

Surveillance of communications on the World Wide Web and other computer-based systems is a recently addressed topic under Colombian law. Article 54 of Law 1453 of 2011,[75] in particular, amends article 239 of the Code of Criminal Procedure, by establishing the provisions by which national prosecutors may authorize electronic surveillance of suspects based on preliminary evidence. Only evidence obtained from authorized electronic surveillance is admissible in court.

XV. TERRORIST LISTS

The current peace process and terrorism legislation make the proscription process in Colombia a difficult system that mixes politics and legislation. The most significant legislative act, Law 782 of 2002,[76] defined the process of negotiating with terrorist groups and addressed the power of certain elements within the GOC to enter into negotiations without granting such groups the political status that would pave the way to gaining belligerent status. Combined with the criminal legislation that defines terrorist acts, Law 782 helps to categorize as a terrorist anyone suspected or

[74] Available at http://www.corteconstitucional.gov.co/relatoria/2007/c-095-07.htm.

[75] Ley 1453 de 2011, Diario Oficial No. 48.110, de 24 de junio de 2011, http://www.secretariasenado.gov.co/senado/basedoc/ley_1453_2011.html.

[76] Ley 782 de 2002, Diario Oficial No. 45.043, de 23 de diciembre de 2002, http://www.alcaldiabogota.gov.co/sisjur/normas/Norma1.jsp?i=6677.

searched in connection with terrorist or terrorist-related crimes. A prior law, Law 418 of 1997,[77] enacted during peace negotiations that subsequently failed, granted terrorist groups recognition under international humanitarian law.

XVI. TERRORISM FINANCING

Law 1121 of 2006[78] is the controlling law criminalizing the financing of terrorism. Investigating terrorist financing activities falls under the authority of the GOC agency, Unidad de Información y Análisis Financiero (UIAF), and its powers are articulated in Law 526 of 1999.[79] Under the recommendations of the GOC's Grupo de Acción Financiera Internacional de Sudamérica (GAFISUD), the government created the Integrated Center for Fighting the Financing of Terrorism (Centro Integrado para la Lucha contra las Finanzas del Terrorismo), which is charged with extending financial surveillance to economic activities such as money laundering and the "black market peso" money exchanges.[80]

XVII. FORFEITURE OF TERRORIST PROPERTY

Any goods and resources that are the product of or directly linked to terrorist activities can be seized by authorities as a punitive measure. Forfeitures can also be used for restitution to victims. The description of the proceeding is found in the Code of Criminal Procedure at article 82.[81]

XVIII. COLOMBIAN LAWS AND EXECUTIVE ACTIONS TO COMBAT TERRORISM

In sum, anti-terrorism legislation in Colombia is a constantly evolving process such that current legislation is a progressive extension of prior legislative acts and executive actions created over the last sixty years. The following table lists in chronological order the relevant domestic legislation and executive decrees intended to combat terrorism within Colombia.

[77] Ley 418 de 1997, Diario Oficial No. 43.201, de 26 de diciembre de 1997, http://www.javeriana.edu.co/pensar/sitio/juridico-minas/LEY%20418%20DE%20DICIEMBRE%2026%20DE%201997.pdf.

[78] Ley 1121 de 2006, Diario Oficial No. 46.497, de 29 de diciembre 29 de 2006, http://www.elabedul.net/Documentos/Leyes/2006/Ley_1121.pdf.

[79] Ley 526 de 1999, Diario Oficial No. 43.667, de 15 de agosto 15 de 1999, http://www.alcaldiabogota.gov.co/sisjur/normas/Norma1.jsp?i=6288.

[80] *Cacería a finanzas de los terroristas*, DIARIO OCCIDENTE, July 7, 2012, http://www.occidente.co/caceria-a-finanzas-de-los-terroristas/.

[81] Pedro Bordugo, *Código de procedimiento penal* (Bogotá, Colombia, Defensor del Pueblo, 2008), at 135.

Legislation	Description
Decree 180 of 1988	The "Anti-Terrorist Statute." Crafted to deal with narcoterrorism and politically motivated crimes. Includes "any statements, news, or conferences on security problems" to be potentially considered incitement of terrorist acts. Authorized military forces to arrest anyone merely suspected of terror activities and to hold without court order for up to ten days. Also authorized the now defunct Departamento Administrativo y Securidad (Department of Administration and Security, DAS) and the military to search and arrest without warrants. Subsequently declared unconstitutional (except for provisions that dealt with expanding jurisdiction of Public Order Courts).
Decrees 678 and 679 of 1988	Allowed the government to declare parts of Colombia zones of emergency and military operation in order to replace civilian authority with military authority. Subsequent decrees curtailed freedom of association and freedom of expression, barred workers from participating in strikes, and imprisoned labor leaders who sought to mobilize workers. It was later folded into Decree 474.
Decree 474 of 1988	Organized the jurisdiction of Public Order Courts and reassigned jurisdiction to include the Special Tribunal of Criminal Instruction.
Decrees 3030 and 2047 of 1990	Attempted to appease drug dealers and reduce violence. The government conferred reduced sentences and guaranteed nonextradition to drug traffickers who turned themselves in and confessed to at least one offense. Extradition was automatic, however, for suspects who escaped, attempted escape, retracted a confession, or gave a false confession.
Law 04 of 1991	Declared internal public order, civic local police, and other norms.
Decree 2265 of 1991	Permanently adopted legislation enacted under state of siege.
Law 07 of 1991	Issued some dispositions on criminal procedure.
Decree 264 of 1993	Granted concession of benefits for collaboration with justice.
Decree 649 of 1994	Geared toward seeking peace. Granted dispositions regarding registration of birth certificates of members of armed groups that have demobilized and are linked to a peace process.
Decree 715 and 716 of 1994	Facilitated reincorporation of demobilized guerrilla groups engaged in a peace process.
Decree 1059 of 1994	Attempted to facilitate reincorporation of popular militias with political character that are in the peace process.
Decree 1901 of 1995	Issued norms on public order throughout the national territory.

(*continued*)

Legislation	Description
Law 282 of 1996	Attempted to eradicate crimes against personal freedom, especially kidnapping and extortion.
Law 288 of 1996	Established mechanisms to compensate victims of human rights violations.
Decree 1635 of 1997	Delimited high-risk zones in the national territory for reasons of public order in fulfillment of Article 17 of Decree 2329 of 1995.
Decree 2008 of 1997	Granted guarantees for the democratic participation of citizens in the electoral process.
Decree 2500 of 1997	Created conservation of public order during the elections period.
Decree 2548 of 1997	Modified Decree 2500 of 1997.
Law 418 of 1997	Contained instruments for the search for *convivencia* (social harmony) and improvement of the efficacy of justice.
Decree 1015 of 1998	Created Comisión para la busqueda de la verdad (Truth Commission).
Decree 2233 of 1998	Reestablished and conserved public order in the departments of Vaupés, Guainía, and Guavíare.
Decree 395 of 1998	Created conservation of public order during elections.
Resolution 83 of 1998	Declared the initiation of a peace process and acknowledged the political character of an armed organization.
Decree 13 of 1999	Issued measures for public order.
Executive Resolution 01 of 1999	Modified Resolution 85 of 1998 regarding the FARC zona de distensión (distension zone).
Executive Resolution 38 of 1999	Designated government representatives in dialogs with FARC.
Executive Resolution 39 of 1999	Adopted decisions to contribute to the search for peace.
Executive Resolution 40 of 1999	Acknowledged certain people as representative members of FARC.
Executive Resolution 092 of 1999	Extended the deadline established by Article 1 of Executive Resolution 39 of 1999.
Decree 1254 of 1999	Issued measures to preserve public order.
Decree 1980 of 1999	Modified Decree 1254 of 1999.
Decree 2281 of 1999	Issued measures to preserve public order.
Law 548 of 1999	Extended the application term of Law 418 of 1997.
Ministerial Resolution 001 of 2000	Established the organization, administration, financing, and operation of Grupos de Acción Unificada por la Libertad Persona (Groups of Unified Action for Personal Liberty, GAULA).

(*continued*)

Legislation	Description
Decree 1091 of 2000	Adopted the 1993 Paris Convention on Chemical Weapons.
Decree 149 of 2000	Organized the Fondo de Inversión para la Paz (Peace Investment Fund).
Decree 324 of 2000	Created Centro deCoordinacion de la Lucha contra los Grupos de Autodefensas Ilegales y Demas Grupos al Margen de la Ley (the Center of Coordination in the Fight Against Illegal Autodefense Groups and Other Groups Outside of the Law).
Decree 1592 of 2000	Implemented Article 6 of Law 199 of 1995.
Law 554 of 2000	Adopted the 1997 Oslo Convention on Antipersonnel Mines.
Law 684 of 2001	Established a new security and national defense system. Later declared unconstitutional.
Decree 1837 of 2002	Declared a state of internal commotion and listed twenty-five reasons for declaring internal unrest.
Decree 1838 of 2002	Permitted the imposition of a wealth tax designed to preserve the democratic security of the nation.
Decree 2002 of 2002	Took measures for the control of public order and defined zones of rehabilitation and consolidation.
Resolution 129 of 2002	Delineated zones of rehabilitation and consolidation and assigned commanders.
Legislative Act 02 of 2003	Attempted the "constitutional reform" of Articles 15, 24, 28, and 250 of the Colombian Constitution. Later declared unconstitutional Constitutional Court Sentencia C-816-04, August 30, 2004.
Law 898 of 2004	Approved the Inter-American Convention Against Terrorism as signed in Bridgetown, Barbados. The subject of the convention relates to international crime, money laundering, extradition, etc.

XIX. COLOMBIA'S INTERNATIONAL COMMITMENTS TO COMBAT TERRORISM

Colombia is a signatory of many international instruments for fighting terrorism. Most are domesticated under Colombian law and subject to review by the Colombian Constitutional Court. The following table lists the relevant United Nations agreements that have been domesticated into Colombian law.

The next table lists the relevant Organization of American States agreements that have been domesticated into Colombian law.

Signed	Ratified/Enacted	Title
1963	October 4, 1973 Law 14 of 1972	Convention on Offenses and Certain Other Acts Committed on Board Aircraft (Tokyo Convention)
1966	October 29, 1969	International Covenant on Civil and Political Rights
1970	July 3, 1973 Law 14 of 1972	Convention for the Suppression of Unlawful Seizure of Aircraft (Hague Convention)
1971	December 4, 1974 Law 4 of 1974	Convention for the Suppression of Unlawful Acts Against the Safety of Civil Aviation (Montreal Convention)
1973	January 16, 1996 Law 169 of 1994	Convention on the Prevention and Punishment of Crimes Against Internationally Protected Persons and Diplomatic Agents
1979	Not yet ratified Law 837 of 2003	International Convention Against the Taking of Hostages
1988	January 14, 2004 Law 764 of 2002	Protocol for the Suppression of Unlawful Acts of Violence at Airports Serving International Civil Aviation
1991	April 14, 2003 Law 831 of 2003	Convention on the Marking of Plastic Explosives for the Purpose of Detection
1997	September 14, 2004 Law 804 of 2003	International Convention for the Suppression of Terrorist Bombings
1998	August 5, 2002 Law 742 of 2002	Rome Statute of the International Criminal Court
1999	September 14, 2004 Law 808 of 2003	International Convention for the Suppression of the Financing of Terrorism
2000	August 4, 2004 Law 800 of 2003	Convention Against Transnational Organized Crime (CATOC)
2003	October 27, 2006 Law 970 of 2005	Convention Against Corruption
2005	Signed Nov. 1, 2006 Not yet ratified	International Convention for the Suppression of Acts of Nuclear Terrorism

Colombia is currently a delegate member of the Sixth Committee of the United Nations tasked with drafting a comprehensive convention on international terrorism.[82] The Committee began work in October 2013 on forming a clear definition of terrorism that required that delegate states show flexibility and political will in order to reach consensus. Some delegates "spoke of the need to distinguish

[82] *As Sixth Committee Commences Session, Delegates Once Again Call for Clear Definition of Terrorism, Consensus on Draft Comprehensive Convention*, STATES NEWS SERVICE, October 7, 2013.

Signed	Ratified	Title
1971	August 13, 1996 Law 195 of 1995	Convention to Prevent and Punish the Acts of Terrorism Taking the Forms of Crimes Against Persons and Related Extortion that Are of International Significance
1996		Declaration of Lima to Prevent, Combat, and Eliminate Terrorism
1996		Plan of Action on Hemispheric Cooperation to Prevent, Combat, and Eliminate Terrorism
1996	January 19, 1999 Law 412 of 1997	Inter-American Convention Against Corruption
1998		Second Specialized Conference on Terrorism convenes in Argentina and results in the "Commitment of Mar del Plata," which established the Inter-American Committee Against Terrorism (CICTE), later ratified by the General Assembly in June 1999. The purpose of the Committee is to coordinate cooperation between member states to "prevent, combat, and eliminate terrorist acts and activities." Composed of "competent national authorities of all member states of the OAS," the CICTE draws its authority from both international and OAS treaties and resolutions. CICTE is also charged with establishing a framework for technical cooperation between member states, providing assistance to any member state requesting it, and "establish[ing] mechanisms of coordination with other competent international entities."
1999		Hemispheric Cooperation to Prevent, Combat, and Eliminate Terrorism
2002	Currently inexecutable Law 898 of 2004	Inter-American Convention Against Terrorism

between terrorism and the legitimate effort for self-determination by people under foreign domination."[83] In October 2014, delegates began their session with a stronger sense of urgency to complete drafting a comprehensive convention in light of the rapid escalation of terrorism and terrorist acts worldwide in the last year.[84]

[83] The Iranian delegation stressed, for example, that "brutalization of peoples under foreign occupation should continue to be denounced as the gravest form of terrorism." Ibid.

[84] *Speakers Urge That Differences Be Resolved in Draft Comprehensive Convention on International Terrorism as Sixth Committee Begins Session*, STATES NEW SERVICE, October 7, 2014. The Sixth

Colombia appears to be an active participant among the Sixth Committee delegates and has stressed that a global strategy to address international terrorism requires a balanced approach, particularly with regard to the payment of ransoms as a source for funding terrorist organizations. The Colombian delegate, Emma Mejía Vélez stated that:

> It must be made clear that victims of kidnapping were at risk of losing their lives and, at least temporarily, their freedom. Those trying to aid the victims should not be made criminals for doing so. In addition, the increased number of foreign fighters greatly affected the stability of certain regions in the world. The radicalization that led to violent extremism must be addressed. However, all measures must be in line with all aspects of international law and must respect human rights. Stereotyping and restrictions on travellers must be avoided. The international community must also adopt measures to address money laundering, as well as the illicit transfer of arms.[85]

XX. CONCLUSION

Colombia's violent history shapes Colombian society and political institutions in many ways. There is an element of audacity among antigovernment groups that in their own minds renders illegal acts against the state as legitimate rights of protest. A key example of this is the seizure of the Colombian Supreme Court in 1985 by a group of disaffected intellectuals known as the M-19[86] guerrilla organization. Their foolish act, which some would argue was the result of arrogance within the far left movements, resulted in consequences that continue to shape the Colombian political landscape thirty years later. First, the attack, which resulted in the death of most of Colombia's top jurists, eviscerated a generation of the nation's best and brightest legal minds. Second, the incendiary destruction of the Palace of Justice created iconic, gut-wrenching images that would define Colombian political violence in the 1980s. Third, the overt assertion of the armed forces over the civilian government after the Betancur presidency demonstrated woeful ineptitude in dealing with the crisis showed the Colombian people in no uncertain terms what the military class is capable of doing during a national/constitutional crisis. Fourth, the fiery martyrdom of leftist ideologues created populist sympathy that would later allow surviving members of the M-19 to assume important political positions within subsequent governments.[87]

Committee was set to consider the UN Secretary-General's report on Measure to Eliminate International Terrorism (UN Doc. A/69/209).

85 *Speakers Urge That Differences Be Resolved in Draft Comprehensive Convention on International Terrorism as Sixth Committee Begins Session*, STATES NEW SERVICE, October 7, 2014.

86 Formally known as the 19th of April Movement.

87 For example, former M-19 commander Antonio Navarro Wolff later held several positions in government, including mayor of Pasto, representative and then senator of the Colombian Congress,

Colombian governments have taken an almost schizophrenic approach to confronting antigovernment movements. One president will attempt to deal with insurgent groups through military confrontation, while another president will appease guerrilla groups to the point of ceding large parts of national territory to insurgents as distention zones where illegal armed groups declare autonomy over the hapless populations within that territory. Another president will rely on citizen militias and paramilitary forces to confront insurgent groups,[88] only to leave a successor to contend with feudal warlords in totalitarian control of important Colombian territory. Some presidents have sought amnesty for illegal armed groups only to be confounded by the groups transforming into new criminal organizations and illegal armed groups or becoming subject to vigilante fury of Colombian citizens who seek redress and revenge from the illegal armed combatants who committed outrages against them.

The current so-called peace talks between the present government and the FARC guerrillas are yet another attempt at appeasement, but in reality are viewed by a majority of Colombians as little more than folly by the government and an opportunity by the FARC to solidify its standing as a potent transborder criminal organization and illegal armed group whose influence now extends to nearly every continent.

Colombia's government has a duty to protect its citizens from domestic and foreign terrorist threats and it has ample military and law enforcement means to do so. But no amount of laws, decrees, and policy making can overcome terrorism, secure the peace, or extend security and safety to the entire national territory if there is no political will. In particular, political will is necessary to disperse resources to critical areas beyond the major urban and suburban population centers, to fortify military and local law enforcement capacity in a way that protects all members of Colombian society, and to hold accountable the civilian branches of government most responsible for preserving the constitutional and human rights of Colombian citizens.

governor of Nariño Department, and more significantly, co-president of the Constituent Assembly that drafted the 1991 National Constitution.

88 And any other entity viewed by the political right as antigovernment, such as labor organizers, social workers, and even homosexuals.

5

Brazil

Rodrigo de Souza Costa

I. INTRODUCTION

Brazil is a recent democracy. Between 1964 and 1985, the country experienced a long period of authoritarian government. Democracy was restored only in 1988, with the promulgation of a new democratic constitution.

During the authoritarian period, the terrorist phenomenon was viewed as a matter of national security. Most actions of the government at the time were marked by the expansion of the concept of national security, extended in such a way as to cover also common offenses and opponents of the regime, all within exceptional legislation that abolished the guarantees of the due process of law.

During this period, Brazil enacted three national security laws, and all of them brought new offenses relating to terrorism: Decree-Law no. 314/67,[1] later amended by Decree-Law no. 510/69,[2] Law no. 6,620/78,[3] and Law no. 7,170/83.[4]

1 Art. 25. Practicing massacre, devastation, looting, robbery, kidnapping, setting fire to or vandalism, personal attacks, sabotage or terrorism act; preventing or hindering the operation of essential services administered by the State or by means of public utility or permission: Penalty – imprisonment, 2–6 years.

2 Art. 25. Practicing devastation, looting, robbery, kidnapping, setting fire to or vandalism; act of sabotage or terrorism, also against a credit or financing institution, massacre, personal attack; preventing or hindering the operation of essential services administered by the State or by means of public utility or permission. Penalty: Imprisonment, 2–6 years.Art. 40. Importing, manufacturing, having on deposit or under its possession, buying, selling, donating or transferring, transporting or carrying firearms or private gadgets of the Armed Forces, or any instruments of destruction and terror. Penalty: Imprisonment, 1–3 years.

3 Art. 26. Ravaging, plundering, robbing, stealing, kidnaping, setting fire to, vandalizing or practicing personal attack, sabotage or terrorism, with purposes of attacking National Security. Penalty – imprisonment, 2–12 years.Sole Paragraph – Serious injury or death as a consequence due to the performance of the act. Penalty – imprisonment, 8–30 years.Art. 43. Importing, manufacturing, having on deposit or under its possession, buying, selling, donating or transferring, transporting or carrying firearms or private gadgets of the Armed Forces, or any instruments of destruction and terror, without the previous consent of the competent official. Penalty – imprisonment, 1–6 years.

4 Art. 20. Ravaging, looting, extorting, robbing, kidnaping, maintaining a false imprisonment, setting fire to, vandalizing, causing an explosion, practicing personal attack or act of terrorism due to political

These laws did not define terrorism but rather specified a wide array of criminal offenses that could be used against criminals and opponents of the regime. These offenses often lacked a precise definition of the prohibited activity.

Another issue appeared at the end of the authoritarian period, in the early 1980s: state terrorism. Unhappy with the political opening initiated in Brazil with the enactment of Law no. 6,683/79, which granted amnesty for political crimes committed against national security, conservative military elements began a series of deadly bombings. Perhaps the most famous of such cases were those of the letter bomb at the Brazilian Bar Association (OAB) and the RioCentro bomb.

The case of OAB occurred on August 27, 1980, when the Bar's presidency secretary, Lyda Monteiro da Silva, was killed while opening a letter bomb addressed to the president of the Bar, Eduardo Seabra Fagundes. The Bar had actively participated as an instrument of pressure to bring more democracy to Brazil.

The case of RioCentro occurred on April 30, 1981, when two soldiers, Sergeant Guilherme Pereira do Rosário and Captain Wilson Dias Machado, took a bomb to the convention center known as RioCentro, where thousands of people were celebrating Labour Day. At around 9 PM, with the event already under way, one of the bombs exploded inside the soldiers' car. The sergeant was killed and the captain was wounded before they could finish the attack.

It is noteworthy that in both cases, there was no punishment for those responsible. Moreover, until now, there have been no punishments for human rights violations committed by members of the Brazilian government during the civil-military dictatorship in Brazil.

In this context, the Democratic Constitution of 1988 confronted the human rights violations recently committed by the Brazilian state. At the same time, it did not discard the need to suppress terrorism. Apart from recognizing that "the fundamental objectives of the Federative Republic of Brazil are to build a free, just and solidary society" (Art. 3, item I, Brazilian Federal Constitution) and "to promote the well-being of all, without prejudice as to origin, race, sex, color, age and any other forms of discrimination" (Art. 3, item IV, Brazilian Federal Constitution), the 1988 constitution made two express references to terrorism.

When dealing with the governing principles of the international relations taken by Brazil, the authors of the constitution listed not only human rights but also the repudiation of terrorism and racism.[5]

nonconformity or to obtain funds for maintaining clandestine or subversive political organizations. Penalty – imprisonment, 3–10 years.Sole Paragraph – If the fact results in serious bodily injury, the penalty will increase up to the double; in case it results in death, it will increase up to three times.

[5] Art. 4. The Federative Republic of Brazil is governed in its international relations by the following principles: II – prevalence of human rights; VIII – repudiation of terrorism and racism.

In Article 5, which addresses rights and guarantees, the Constitution included a requirement of criminalization, effectively ordering the ordinary lawmaker to punish terrorism and consider it a particularly serious crime.[6]

Despite this constitutional obligation, the ordinary lawmaker, up to this moment, has not complied with this requirement of criminalization, and certainly there is no legal definition of a crime of terrorism in Brazil.[7] Thus both before and after the transition to democracy, there remains no definition of terrorism in Brazilian law.

II. THE DEFINITION OF TERRORISM

There is no definition of terrorism or crime of terrorism in Brazil for a number of reasons.

The first reason is that most of the Brazilian doctrine says it is nearly impossible to come up with a concrete definition of terrorism. Heleno Cláudio Fragoso, writing for the most important legal publication on the matter, argues that "all those who write about terrorism work under difficulties resulting from the fact that no one has been able to develop a definition of terrorism which was completely satisfactory."[8]

There are those who say that such task is truly impossible. In a report meant for the examination of a bill on the matter, the director of the Institute of the Attorneys of Brazil, Ricardo Pieri Nunes, argued that "the conceptual flow [it] is characterized for, hinders the establishment of objective elementary issues with the precision demanded by the principle of legality, in order to meet the scope of legal security which the criminal rule must comply with."[9]

Even with this understanding, many bills pending in the Brazilian Congress attempt to achieve such legal definition.

Bill no. 2,462/91 defines a terrorist action as one that aims at "devastating, looting, robbing, exploding bombs, kidnapping, setting fire to, vandalizing or practicing a personal attack or sabotage, resulting in effective damage or danger to people or property, with the purpose of coercing any one of the Powers of the Republic."[10]

[6] Art. 5. XLIII. The law will consider as unbailable crimes and not entitled to executive pardon or amnesty any practices of torture, illegal trafficking of narcotics and similar drugs, terrorism and crimes defined as heinous crimes. The ones who ordered these crimes, their performers, and those who could have avoided them, but omitted to do so, will be responsible for them.

[7] It is true that some authors defend that Article 20 of Law no. 7,170/83, the last one on national security, would still be in force today, as it was never formally repealed. In spite of that, the majority understanding is that the National Security Law would have been incompatible with the 1988 Constitution.

[8] FRAGOSO, Heleno Cláudio, *Terrorismo e Criminalidade Política*, Rio de Janeiro: Forense, 1981, pages 5–6.

[9] NUNES, Ricardo Pieri – Report to IAB (mimeo), 2011.

[10] http://www.camara.gov.br/proposicoesWeb/fichadetramitacao?idProposicao=18156.

On the other hand, Bill no. 149/2003[11] defines the conduct as "practicing a crime in reason of political, religious, philosophical or ethnic factionalism, with the purpose of hindering the national integrity or independence, preventing, changing or subverting the operation of State institutions, forcing officials to practice an illegal act, to refrain from practicing what the law determines, or, moreover, intimidating people, a group of people or the general population, causing insecurity, fear, panic or physical, moral or psychological damage."

More recently, Bill no. 7,485/2006[12] proposed defining terrorism using the old Law of National Security, by means of an amendment in its Article 20, with the following wording: "Paragraph 2 – Those who loot, break in, vandalize or set fire to any third party property or who keep anyone who is there in false imprisonment, with the purpose of stating political dissatisfaction or pressuring the government to do or stop doing something, will be held accountable under the same penalties."

Bill no. 7,765/2010[13] defines the matter as "any act practiced by means of violence, or threatening a person or a group of people, aiming at causing panic, through actions dealing with explosives or firearms, with the purpose of unbalancing State institutions." All of these different bills demonstrate the difficulty of defining terrorism and the diverse approaches that can be taken to defining terrorism.

Finally, the reform project of the Brazilian Criminal Code,[14] which started in 2013 and is also pending in Congress, defined a terrorism crime in the proposed new Article 239 of the Code:

Terrorism

Art. 239. To cause terror in the population by means of the conducts described in the paragraphs of this article, when:

I they have as purpose to force public, national or foreign authorities or people who act on their behalf, to do what the law does not demand or stop doing what the law does not forbid;

II they have as purpose to obtain resources for the maintenance of political organizations or armed groups, composed of civilians or the military, who act against the constitutional order or the Rule of Law; or

III they are motivated by prejudice in regards to race, color, ethnic group, religion, nationality, gender, sexual identity or option, or in regards to political, ideological, philosophical or religious reasons.

§ 1 Kidnapping or holding someone in false imprisonment;

[11] http://www.camara.gov.br/proposicoesWeb/fichadetramitacao?idProposicao=104916.

[12] http://www.camara.gov.br/proposicoesWeb/fichadetramitacao?idProposicao=333936.

[13] http://www.camara.gov.br/proposicoesWeb/fichadetramitacao?idProposicao=484837.

[14] http://www.senado.gov.br/atividade/materia/detalhes.asp?p_cod_mate=106404.

§ 2 Using or threatening to use, transporting, keeping or carrying explosives, toxic gases, poison, biological content or other means capable of causing damage or promoting mass destruction;
§ 3 Setting fire to, vandalizing, looting, exploding or breaking in any public or private property;
§ 4 Interfering, sabotaging or damaging computer systems and databases; or
§ 5 Sabotaging the operation or taking possession, with serious threat or violence to people, of the total or partial control (even if temporarily) of means of communication or transport, of ports, airports, railway stations, bus stations, state-owned and private hospitals, schools, sports stadiums, public or local installations where essential public services are rendered, installations of generation or transmission of energy and military installations:

Penalty – imprisonment, from eight to fifteen years, apart from sanctions corresponding to threat, violence, damage, bodily injury or death, attempted or consummated.

Aggravated Form

§ 6 If the conduct is practiced by means of use of mass destruction weapons or another mean capable of causing great damage:

Penalty – imprisonment, from twelve to twenty years, apart from penalties corresponding to threat, violence, damage, bodily injury or death, attempted or consummated.

Crime Exclusion

§ 7 The individual or collective conduct of people motivated by social or claiming purposes, provided that their goals and means are compatible and adequate to their purpose, does not constitute a crime of terrorism.

This complex proposed definition lacks precision or limits in its prohibited purposes in Articles I through III. The prohibited purposes include forcing a broad range of public authorities to act. It also includes obtaining resources for those who "act against the constitutional order or Rule of Law." Finally, it includes those who commit crimes motivated by political, ideological, philosophic, or religious reasons or for reasons related to prejudice.

Subsections 1 through 5 contain specific crimes but fail to include homicide. The proposals also provides for harsh penalties of between eight and fifteen years imprisonment apart from other penalties that may apply to crimes committed. In cases of mass destruction, the penalty would be between twelve and twenty years.

Perhaps a reason why terrorism is not yet a crime is that many concluded that terrorism is not a relevant topic for Brazil. At a meeting promoted in 2004 by the Brazilian government, it was concluded that

> A priori, the possibility of Brazil becoming a stage or even a target for terrorist actions is not excluded, for the country or Brazilian organizations have not been directly or indirectly involved in international controversies in which the component of terror is present, so as to convert Brazilian citizens, installations and interests, both in their own territory or abroad, in immediate or priority targets of international terrorism.[15]

Violent urban criminality, much more than terrorism, is the focus of concerns about crime in Brazil.

Taking into consideration the international instruments signed by Brazil and absorbed in its legal system, it is not possible to say that there is not a definition of terrorism in the Brazilian law.

Law no. 10,744/03,[16] which deals with the assumption, by the federal government, of civil liability before third parties in cases of terrorist attacks, acts of war, or similar events against aircraft of Brazilian registry, operated by Brazilian companies of public air transportation, with the exception of air taxi companies, defines a terrorist act in Article 1, paragraph 4, as "any act of one or more people, agents of sovereign power or not, with political or terrorist purposes, being their resulting loss or damage accidental or intentional."

As a signatory of the Inter-American Convention Against Terrorism,[17] the Brazilian state eventually will absorb the Convention's concepts. The Convention makes reference to other international instruments for fighting terrorism, providing a list of crimes that may be considered typical of a terrorist activity, including the following:

- The Convention for the Suppression of Unlawful Seizure of Aircraft, signed in The Hague on December 16, 1970
- The Convention for the Suppression of Unlawful Acts Against the Safety of Civil Aviation, signed in Montreal on December 23, 1971
- The Convention on the Prevention and Punishment of Crimes Against Internationally Protected Persons, Including Diplomatic Agents, adopted by the UN General Assembly on December 14, 1973
- The International Convention Against the Taking of Hostages, adopted by the UN General Assembly on December 17, 1979
- The Convention of the Physical Protection of Nuclear Material, signed in Vienna on December 3, 1980
- The Protocol for the Suppression of Unlawful Acts of Violence at Airports Serving International Civil Aviation, complementary to the Convention for

15 http://geopr1.planalto.gov.br/saei/images/publicacoes/2004/2_encontro_de_estudos_terrorismo.pdf.
16 http://www.planalto.gov.br/ccivil_03/Leis/2003/L10.744.htm.
17 http://www.planalto.gov.br/ccivil_03/_Ato2004-2006/2005/Decreto/D5639.htm.

the Suppression of Unlawful Acts Against the Safety of Civil Aviation, signed in Montreal on December 24, 1988

- The Convention for the Suppression of Unlawful Acts of Violence Against the Safety of Maritime Navigation, held in Rome on December 10, 1988
- The Protocol for the Suppression of Unlawful Acts Against the Safety of Fixed Platforms Located on the Continental Shelf, held in Rome on December 10, 1988
- The International Convention for the Suppression of Terrorist Bombing, adopted by the UN General Assembly on December 15, 1997
- The International Convention for the Suppression of the Financing of Terrorism, adopted by the UN General Assembly on December 9, 1999

Extradition is governed by Law no. 6,815/80[18] and requires the so-called double criminality rule:[19] in other words, crimes for which extradition is sought by a foreign country must also be a crime in Brazil. Throughout its history, the Brazilian Supreme Court (also known as the Superior Tribunal Federal or the Federal Supreme Court) has analyzed fourteen requests for extradition[20] that in some way dealt with acts of a terrorist nature. For most of them, terrorism was an incidental issue, therefore the Brazilian Supreme Court did not have any case of double criminality. In extraditions 493 (Argentina) and 694 (Italy), the request made was denied, since the Brazilian Court considered the crimes to be of a political nature, and the Brazilian law does not authorize extradition in these cases.[21]

One can see that the main issue faced by Brazilian law in these cases is the distinction between acts of a terrorist nature (and therefore those considered common crimes) and political crimes.

One can note a trend to use one criterion: "the violent nature or not of the acts themselves, as well as the condition or qualification of victims of such actions, depending on the system of atrocity of the environment."[22] The notion of atrocity, to be better understood, consists of a crime being considered "of unjustifiable cruelty or evil"[23] – basically, crimes involving violence or a serious threat to a person.

[18] http://www.planalto.gov.br/ccivil_03/leis/l6815.htm.

[19] Art. 77, II of Law no. 6,815/80.

[20] Extradition 162 (Bolivia), Extradition 399 (France), Extradition 412 (Italy), Extradition 417 (Argentina), Extradition 493 (Argentina), Extradition 615 (Bolivia), Extradition 694 (Italy), Extradition 700 (Germany), Extradition 855 (Chile), Extradition 974 (Argentina), Extradition 994 (Italy), Extradition 1008 (Colombia), Extradition 1085 (Italy), and Extradition 1150 (Argentina). They are all available at http://www.stf.jus.br/portal/jurisprudencia/pesquisarJurisprudencia.asp.

[21] Art. 77, VII of Law no. 6,815/80.

[22] SOUZA, Artur de Brito Gueiros. *As novas tendências do Direito Extradicional*. 2ª ed. Rio de Janeiro: Renovar, 2013, p. 191.

[23] HUNGRIA, Nélson. A criminalidade política no direito brasileiro. In *Revista Forense*, vol. 188, March–April 1960, p. 10.

In one specific case, Extradition 855 (Chile), the Federal Supreme Court analyzed an extradition request based on terrorism and overcame the issue of double criminality, granting extradition.[24] In fact, the solution given by the court was to focus on the underlying offenses (homicide, extortion by means of kidnapping, and armed conspiracy), all with equivalents in Brazilian law, but more importantly to reaffirm the necessity of repression on the part of Brazil of that type of crime. Thus, although there is no legal specific crime of terrorism, it can be said that the Brazilian Supreme Court treats terrorism as a crime.

III. CRIMINAL LAW AND PROSECUTIONS

As mentioned in the previous section, the substantive criminal law lacks a specific definition of what constitutes the crime of terrorism, despite the constitutional law requirement that the legislature enact such laws. Nevertheless, in August 2013, Law no. 12,850[25] was enacted. This law dealt with organized crime in a manner that included terrorist organizations.

Article 1 of the Law states:

> **Art. 1.** This Law defines a criminal organization and provides for the criminal investigation the means of obtaining evidence, related criminal offenses and criminal procedure to be applied.
>
> § 1 It is considered a criminal organization any association of four (4) or more persons structurally ordered and characterized by the division of tasks, albeit informally, in order to obtain, directly or indirectly, an advantage of any kind through the practice of criminal offenses whose maximum penalties are greater than four (4) years, or that have a transnational character.
>
> § 2 This Law also applies to:
>
> I the criminal offenses provided for in international treaties or conventions when, once the execution starts in the country, the result has or should have occurred abroad, or vice versa;
>
> II international terrorist organizations, recognized according to the rules of international law, by a court which Brazil is part of, whose acts supporting terrorism, as well as the preparatory and execution acts of terrorism, occur or are likely to occur in the Brazilian territory.

[24] It is true that in Extradition 417 (Argentina), the Supreme Court granted extradition for terrorist acts; however, this decision was made in 1984, during the Brazilian military regime, and the issue of double incrimination was solved under Article 20 the Law of National Security, which, as explained earlier in this chapter, is considered as not approved by the Brazilian Constitution of 1988.

[25] http://www.planalto.gov.br/ccivil_03/_Ato2011-2014/2013/Lei/L12850.htm.

The criminalization itself comes under Article 2, which refers to the preceding quoted provision:

> **Art. 2.** To promote, establish, finance or integrate, personally or through an intermediary, a criminal organization:
>
> Penalty – imprisonment from three (3) to eight (8) years and a fine, without prejudice to the penalties corresponding to other criminal offenses committed.
>
> § 1 The same penalties apply to those who prevent or in any way hinder the investigation of a criminal offense involving a criminal organization.
>
> § 2 The penalties increase up to half of their terms if, during the activities of the criminal organization, there is use of any firearm.
>
> § 3 The penalty is increased for those who exercise individual or collective control of the criminal organization, even if they do not personally practice execution acts.
>
> § 4 The penalty is increased by one-sixth (1/6) to two-thirds (2/3):
>
> I if there is involvement of children or adolescents;
>
> II if there is participation of a civil servant, and the criminal organization makes use of this condition for the practice of a criminal offense;
>
> III if the product or avail of the criminal offense is intended, in whole or in part, overseas;
>
> IV if the criminal organization maintains connection with other independent criminal organizations;
>
> V if the circumstances of the fact evidence a transnational organization.
>
> § 5 If there is sufficient evidence that the civil servant integrates the criminal organization, the judge may determine their precautionary removal from office, employment or position, without prejudice to their compensation, when the measure becomes necessary for the investigation or procedural instruction.
>
> § 6 The unappealable conviction will lead to the civil servant losing their office, function, employment or term and the interdiction of exercising a public function or office for a period of eight (8) years following the completion of the sentence.
>
> § 7 If there is evidence of police involvement in the crimes mentioned in this Law, the Office of Internal Affairs will initiate a police investigation and notify the Prosecution Office, which will appoint a member to accompany the issue until its conclusion.

Although there is no specific offense of the crime of terrorism, belonging to an organization of terrorist type is criminalized as a form of organized crime.

In this matter, two issues are worth clarifying: the criminalization of terrorist behaviors and the definition of a terrorist organization.

Brazil punishes acts of a terrorist nature with common crimes of homicide,[26] kidnapping for ransom,[27] and bodily injury,[28] all provided for in the criminal law.

According to the law, the definition of terrorist association is at the discretion of the judge. This can be facilitated based on several international treaties to which Brazil is a signatory and whereby it undertakes to fight terrorist activities, such as the Inter-American Convention to Prevent and Punish Acts of Terrorism That Constitute Crimes Against Persons and Related Extortion When They Have International Relevance of March 8, 1973, signed by Brazil on February 5, 1999, and enforced by Decree 3018 of April 6, 1999; the Inter-American Convention Against Terrorism,[29] signed by Brazil on June 3, 2002, and enforced by the Legislative Decree 890 of 2005 and Decree 5639/05; and the International Convention for the Suppression of the Financing of Terrorism,[30] signed by Brazil on November 10, 2001, and enforced by Decree 5640/05.

IV. INVESTIGATIVE POWERS

As previously explained, despite having no criminal category for classifying terrorist acts, Brazilian law prohibits participation in terrorist organizations by virtue of Law no. 12,850/13. This 2013 law aimed at criminal organizations also regulates new powers of investigation and finding of evidence in cases involving criminal organizations in general, including those of a terrorist nature.

These exceptional measures are state's evidence; monitoring and reception of electromagnetic, optical, or acoustic signals; controlled response; access to the records of telephone and telematic calls, to data filed in public or private databases, and to commercial or electoral information; interception of telephone and telematic communications pursuant to specific legislation; removal of financial, banking, and tax secrecies under specific legislation; police infiltration in investigations; and cooperation among institutions and agencies of federal, district, state, and municipal levels for finding evidence and information relevant to the investigation or the evidentiary stage.

In regard to state's evidence,[31] or plea bargaining agreements, the judge may grant pardons (exemption from punishment), reduce sentences by as much as two-thirds, or replace with an alternative punishment to imprisonment for those who have cooperated effectively and voluntarily with the investigation and the

[26] Article 121 of the Brazilian Criminal Code.
[27] Article 159 of the Brazilian Criminal Code.
[28] Article 129 of the Brazilian Criminal Code.
[29] http://www.planalto.gov.br/ccivil_03/_Ato2004-2006/2005/Decreto/D5639.htm.
[30] http://bo.io.gov.mo/bo/ii/2006/26/aviso26.asp#ptg.
[31] Article 4 of Law no. 12.850/13.

criminal prosecution. To qualify for such reduced punishment, such cooperation must entail one or more of the following results: identification of accomplices and other participants in the criminal organization and of criminal offenses committed by them; disclosure of the criminal organization's hierarchical structure and division of tasks; prevention of criminal offenses arising from the activities of the criminal organization; full or partial recovery of the product or proceeds derived from criminal offenses committed by the criminal organization; or the location of any victims with their physical integrity preserved.

Broadly speaking, Brazil already had a general provision for state's evidence provided in Articles 13 and 15 of Law no. 9,807/99.[32] Despite the similarity of the provisions, it is worth highlighting that the specific provision applicable to terrorist organizations gives rise to a broader scope of application, because it provides for the possibility of sentencing alternative punishment if the accused reveals the hierarchical structure and division of tasks within a criminal organization, including a terrorist organization.

Controlled response refers to delaying police or administrative intervention against offenses committed by a criminal organization or otherwise related to it, provided that these activities are kept under observation and monitoring, so that legal measures are undertaken in a timely manner for the production of evidence and collection of information.

Special authorization of a controlled or delayed response is necessary because of Article 301 of the Brazilian Code of Criminal Procedure,[33] ordinarily requires immediate police intervention at the commission of a crime. Delay in police or administrative intervention must be disclosed in advance to the competent court, which, if necessary, will set forth its limits and report to the Prosecution Office. Should the controlled response involve boundary crossing, such delays will be possible only with the cooperation from authorities of countries that are likely to be a potential route or destination for the suspect, in order to reduce risk of escape and loss of product, object, instrument, or proceeds of crime.

Police infiltration[34] will be allowed only if no evidence can be produced by other available means. This measure might be authorized by a judge for a period of six months, without prejudice to any renewal, provided its need is duly proven. The infiltration encompasses the authorization given to the state agent to commit any crime together with the criminal organization, provided such action is necessary for the smooth conduct of the investigation.[35]

[32] http://www.planalto.gov.br/ccivil_03/leis/l9807.htm.

[33] http://www.planalto.gov.br/ccivil_03/decreto-lei/del3689compilado.htm.

[34] Articles 10 to 14 of Law no. 12850/13.

[35] Article 13, sole paragraph, of Law no. 12.850/13.

Brazilian law distinguishes access to records of telephone and telematic calls from the access to registration information filed in public or private databases and to commercial and electoral information, as well as the interception of telephone and telematic communications.

The first option, supported by a special provision in the law of criminal organizations, presumes the access, regardless of judicial authorization, only to the suspect's data that exclusively present his or her personal qualification, filiation, and address kept by the Electoral Court System, telecoms carriers, financial institutions, and credit card companies.

On the other hand, the interception of telephone and telematic communications is regulated by Law no. 9,296/96[36] and may be authorized only by a court order in case of severe offenses and when evidence cannot be produced by any other means.[37] This measure may be authorized for a period of fifteen days and renewed for a similar period provided its indispensability as evidence is proven.[38]

The removal of financial, banking, and tax secrecy is governed by Supplementary Law no. 105/01,[39] with special provision for removal, by means of a court order, in the event of terrorism.[40]

The Brazilian intelligence system is led by the Brazilian Intelligence Agency (ABIN), regulated by Law no. 9,883/99[41] and Decree 4,376/2002.[42] The intelligence system consists of the following:

- The Civil House of the Presidency of the Republic, through its Executive Secretariat
- The Institutional Security Bureau of the Presidency of the Republic, the coordinating authority of federal intelligence activities
- The ABIN of the Institutional Security Bureau of the Presidency of the Republic, the primary authority of the system
- The Ministry of Justice, through the National Public Security Secretariat, the Police Intelligence Directorate of the Federal Police Department, the Federal Road Police Department, the National Penitentiary Department, the Department of Assets Recovery and International Legal Cooperation, and the National Secretariat of Justice

36 http://www.planalto.gov.br/ccivil_03/leis/l9296.htm.

37 Article 2 of Law no. 9.296/96.

38 Article 5 of Law no. 9.296/96.

39 http://www.planalto.gov.br/ccivil_03/leis/lcp/Lcp105.htm.

40 Article 1, paragraph 4, I of Supplementary Law no. 105/01.

41 http://www.planalto.gov.br/ccivil_03/Leis/L9883.htm.

42 http://www2.camara.leg.br/legin/fed/decret/2002/decreto-4376-13-setembro-2002-476380-norma atualizada-pe.html.

- The Ministry of Defense, through the Office of Strategic Intelligence, the Operational Intelligence Advisory Board, the Military-Strategic Intelligence Division of the Strategy Office of the Army Staff, the Navy Intelligence Center, the Army Intelligence Center, the Air Force Intelligence Center, and the Operating and Managing Center for the Amazonian Protection System
- The Ministry of Foreign Affairs, through the General Secretariat for Foreign Affairs and the General Coordination for Combat of Transnational Illicit Acts
- The Ministry of Finance, through the Executive Secretariat of the Financial Activities Control Board, the Secretariat of the Federal Revenue of Brazil, and the Central Bank of Brazil
- The Ministry of Labor and Employment, through the Executive Secretariat
- The Ministry of Health, through the Office of the Minister of State and the Brazilian Health Surveillance Agency (ANVISA)
- The Ministry of Social Security, through the Executive Secretariat
- The Ministry of Science and Technology, through the Office of the Minister of State
- The Ministry of Environment, through the Executive Secretariat and the Brazilian Institute of Environment and Renewable Natural Resources (IBAMA)
- The Ministry of National Integration, through the National Secretariat of Civil Defense
- The Office of the Comptroller General, through the Executive Secretariat
- The Ministry of Agriculture, Livestock, and Food Supply, through its Executive Secretariat
- The Civil Aviation Secretariat of the Presidency of the Republic, through its Executive Secretariat
- The Ministry of Transportation, through its Executive Secretariat and the National Department for Transport Infrastructure (DNIT)
- The Ministry of Mines and Energy, through its Executive Secretariat
- The Ministry of Communication, through its Executive Secretariat

It is noteworthy that intelligence agencies in Brazil have no precedence over the police, hence their investigation activities are governed by the same legal provisions.

V. PROSCRIPTION AND LISTING OF TERRORIST GROUPS AND INDIVIDUALS

Brazil does not have any lists at the national level for naming terrorist groups or individuals.

Nevertheless, it has made effective the UN Security Council Resolution 1267 by means of Decree 3,267/99, adopting, even directly, the list therein. Even so, such lists were used only at the administrative level by the Brazilian financial intelligence agency, as discussed further in section VI.

VI. REGULATION OF TERRORISM FINANCING

Although Brazil has been a signatory since 2001 to the International Convention for Suppression of the Financing of Terrorism enforced by the United Nations, the Brazilian law does not have a specific provision to punish terrorism financing.

The most similar crime to it would be that of money laundering, under Law no. 9,613/98,[43] committed through a criminal organization, in the form aforementioned in Law no. 12,850/13, also including terrorist organizations in its scope.

Moreover, Brazil has a financial intelligence agency, the Council for Financial Activities Control (COAF),[44] an institution affiliated to the Brazilian Central Bank.

COAF approached the subject in March 2007 by issuing resolution 15,[45] which sets forth a special procedure to report financial transactions involving the following: (a) Osama Bin Laden, al-Qaeda, and the Taliban members, and other individuals, groups, companies, or entities related to them; (b) the former government of Iraq or its state bodies, corporations, or agencies outside Iraq, as well as funds or other financial assets or economic resources that have been taken from Iraq or acquired by Saddam Hussein or other senior officials of the former Iraqi regime and by the closest members of their families, including privately owned or controlled entities, whether directly or indirectly, by them or by persons acting on their behalf or under their command; (c) people who perpetrate or attempt to perpetrate terrorist acts or participate in or facilitate the commission of such acts, or entities owned or controlled, directly or indirectly, by these people, as well as individuals and entities acting on their behalf or under their command; and (d) financial transactions that may constitute strong evidence of acts of financing of terrorism, according to the International Convention for the Suppression of the Financing of Terrorism.

It is worth mentioning that COAF has been receiving a significant amount of reports of suspicious situations, as shown in the following table:[46]

43 http://www.planalto.gov.br/ccivil_03/leis/l9613.htm.

44 http://www.coaf.fazenda.gov.br/.

45 http://www.coaf.fazenda.gov.br/legislacao-e-normas/normas-do-coaf/coaf-resolucao-no-015-de-28-de-marco-de-2007-1.

46 http://www.coaf.fazenda.gov.br/estatisticas/comunicacoes-recebidas-por-uf.

	2008	2009	2010	2011	2012	2013
Reports of suspicious transactions	645,785	1,802,865	1,038,505	1,289,087	1,587,450	1,286,233

These reports of suspicious transactions are not limited to those related to terrorism but include other crimes connected with money laundering.

VII. IMMIGRATION MEASURES

Brazil does not have any preventive immigration measure regarding terrorism. The Brazilian migration policy is determined by the National Immigration Council,[47] an agency subordinated to the Ministry of Labor, and the National Secretariat of Justice, through its Department of Foreigners,[48] an agency affiliated with the Ministry of Justice.

Recently, due to economic advancement, Brazil has resumed the tradition of being a receiving country of migrants. As a regional power, Brazil endeavors to help its neighbors and their citizens in difficulty. This can be measured by the number of permanent visas granted by the Brazilian government between 2012 and the third quarter of 2013 (7,637) compared to 1,466 visas granted in the years of 2010 and 2011.

Note that from the 7,637 permanent visas granted, 6,477 are resident visas on humanitarian grounds, underscoring the Brazilian government's immigration policies, mainly for Haitian refugees.[49] There is no apparent concern that refugees will also be terrorists, as there is in some countries.

VIII. ADMINISTRATIVE AND EXECUTIVE MEASURES

Brazil has no tradition of applying administrative measures to control the activities of suspects of terrorism. Even though the law that punishes any kind of participation in terrorist organizations came into force in September 2013, there is still no criminal proceeding regarding the issue within the Brazilian territory.

47 http://portal.mte.gov.br/cni/.

48 http://portal.mj.gov.br/main.asp?View=%7B1842B341-E821-4631-93EC-8E19BE9CFDBD%7D&Team=&params=itemID=%7B6169FECD-A24F-472B-BF19-C981F0D07444%7D;&UIPartUID=%7B4630C02C-BA51-484F-9013-97702C04A7B8%7D.

49 Data can be found at http://portal.mte.gov.br/data/files/8A7C816A419E9E3401426BEFDF562697/6%20-%20Autoriza%C3%A7%C3%B5es%20concedidas%20pelo%20Conselho%20Nacional%20de%20Imigra%C3%A7%C3%A3o.pdf.

IX. THE ROLE OF MILITARY AND EXTRATERRITORIAL COUNTERTERRORISM ACTIVITIES

Military Justice is grounded in Articles 122 to 124 of its Federal Constitution.[50] It consists of the Supreme Military Court and the military courts and judges. The power of judgment is determined by the Military Criminal Code.[51] This would prevent imprisonment or trials based on laws of war during peacetime because such measures would require a formal declaration of war by the Brazilian government against a foreign state. Such a declaration of war would require an authorization from the National Congress of Brazil (Article 49, II of the Federal Constitution) and an official statement by the president of the republic (Article 84, item XIX of the Federal Constitution).

The military courts' structure differs from that of ordinary criminal courts, as the former consists of a court president named by civil-service examination, and two military judicial officers, appointed by the armed forces and with a temporary term of office.

Brazilian military actions abroad generally relate to requested participation in some sort of international peacekeeping mission. A great example of this trend is the participation of the Brazilian Army, since June 1, 2004, in the United Nations Mission for the Stabilization of Haiti (MINUSTAH), created by Resolution 1542 of the UN Security Council. Brazilian military forces have also taken part in peacekeeping missions in Ivory Coast, Liberia, Cyprus, and Colombia and on the border between Ecuador and Peru.[52]

X. SECRECY AND TERRORISM

All information held by the Brazilian state subject to access restrictions is classified into three levels, according to Law no. 12,527/11:[53] top secret, secret, and confidential.

Such information may thus be classified provided it endangers national defense and sovereignty, or the integrity of the national territory; harms or jeopardizes the conduct of negotiations or international relations undertaken by the country, or if it has been provided in confidence by other states and international organizations; endangers the life, safety, or health of the population; offers high risk to the country's financial, economic, or monetary stability; causes harm or risk to military strategic plans or operations; causes harm or risk to scientific or technological research and development projects, as well as to systems, goods, facilities, or areas of national

[50] http://www.planalto.gov.br/ccivil_03/constituicao/constituicao.htm.

[51] http://www.planalto.gov.br/ccivil_03/decreto-lei/del1001.htm.

[52] http://www.eb.mil.br/missoes-atuais.

[53] http://www.planalto.gov.br/ccivil_03/_ato2011-2014/2011/lei/l12527.htm.

strategic interest; endangers the security of institutions or of senior domestic or foreign authorities and their families; or jeopardizes intelligence activities, as well as investigation and surveillance initiatives in progress and related to the prevention or suppression of offenses.[54]

Top secret information is classified for up to twenty-five years, secret information for up to fifteen years, and confidential information for up to five years.

Such secrecy does not apply to information required for the administrative or legal remedy of fundamental rights. Information or documents regarding conduct underlying the violation of human rights, committed by public officials or by order of public authorities, may not be subject to secrecy claims.[55]

Any citizen can request access to public information, which can even be done through the Internet.[56]

Secret information cannot be used in a prosecution for terrorism; such information would have to be disclosed or revealed to the accused. In addition, secrecy claims by the government cannot be used to hide information that reveals human rights violations by public authorities.

XI. REVIEW AND OVERSIGHT OF COUNTERTERRORISM POWERS

As explained in this chapter, terrorism is not a priority for the Brazilian state. There is no explicit counterterrorism policy, a fact that hinders the development of this subject.

XII. TERRORISM AND NATIONAL SECURITY POLICIES

In the recent past, the discussion about security in Brazil was grounded on what was then called national security doctrine or ideology. Contrary to what one might believe, the concept of national security was placed on the Brazilian agenda even before the last series of military governments. This underlines that there is no unanimity in determining what constitutes national security.

A legislative analysis reveals that already in 1934, the former National Defense Council had become the Higher National Security Council, the name of which featured the first appearance of the term "national security" in Brazilian constitutional history,[57] followed by Law no. 38/35, the first of the National Security Laws.

[54] Article 23 of Law no. 12.527/11.

[55] Article 21 of Law no. 12.527/11.

[56] As in http://www.acessoainformacao.gov.br/acessoainformacaogov/, a website explaining these mechanisms.

[57] Article 159, Federal Constitution of 1934.

Created during the Brazilian constitutional discipline in 1934, the National Security Laws use of the term refers to the powers, arrangement, and organization of the armed forces. But with the enforcement of Law no. 38/35, which provides for the criminalization of conduct against political and social order, for the first time national security and criminal law were associated.

This law[58] was followed by the enforcement of six others, which addressed the same issue and were usually related to the authoritarian regimes ruling Brazil.

It is interesting to observe that there was a significant variation in the definition of national security in the Brazilian laws, a fact that can be explained by the political appropriation of the concept of national security. Moreover, national security was a doctrine, that is, a set of principles on which the idea of the state was based. This doctrine was enforced in the constitutions that supported authoritarian regimes, especially the constitutions of 1937 and 1967; Amendment no. 1 of 1969, and also the National Security Laws, offered a more tangible legal expression of such principles.

Thus, during the democratic period, "national security" meant the defense of the state and its institutions, while during the dictatorship, the term could mean anything that was of the interest to the government.

For instance, national security was mentioned only once in the Federal Democratic Constitution of 1988, in Article 173, curiously while describing the cases where the state could exceptionally explore economic activity. As a rule, the expression used by the constitutional legislator is the defense of the rule of law and democratic institutions, which now hold the position once reserved for national security.

Therefore, the presence of the Brazilian armed forces, mainstay of the previous authoritarian regime, was greatly reduced during the democratic period, and to that account one cannot say an organic national security policy was in force in Brazil.[59] However, national defense actions were being taken, many of them related to the issues of sovereignty and technological development, such as nuclear technology, as well as specific border control actions, carried out by the Brazilian Federal Police.

XIII. COMPENSATION OF THE VICTIMS OF TERRORISM

Brazil has a specific legislative provision for the compensation of victims of terrorist attacks, acts of war, or related events against Brazilian-registered aircraft operated by Brazilian air public transport companies, except for air taxi companies. This

[58] Law no. 136/35, Decree-law no. 428/38, Law no. 1802/53, Decree-law no. 314/67, Law no. 6.620/78, and Law no. 7.170/83.

[59] This can be seen at the Brazilian Ministry of Defense website http://www.defesa.gov.br/. The ministry states that its mission is "to coordinate the integrated defense effort, aiming to contribute to ensuring the sovereignty, the constitutional powers, the law and order, the national heritage, the protection of

provision is represented by Law no. 10,744/03,[60] reserved for cases of terrorist acts against Brazilian aircraft.

Moreover, one should not forget Law no. 10,559/02,[61] which provides for reparations to political amnesty grantees and victims of the Brazilian military regime; this law covers a broader period (from September 18, 1946, to October 5, 1988) than Law no. 10,744/03. Despite not having reparation to victims of terrorism as its specific purpose, this law does encompass victims of acts of terrorism committed by the Brazilian state.

Today terrorism is not a goal to be pursued by the Brazilian armed forces.

XIV. CONCLUSION: A BRIEF ASSESSMENT OF BRAZIL'S ANTITERRORISM LAWS

Brazil still has a long way to go in developing its counterterrorism policy, especially in terms of legislation. The legal system lacks a specific crime category or sentence enhancing factor regarding terrorism. Given concerns about respecting human rights, legislative silence on the issue of terrorism may be the best way for Brazil to deal with such phenomena.

The lack of social concern, which can be explained by the focus of the media and Congress on violent urban crime, create the false impression that terrorism is not a Brazilian problem.

Considering the increasing international prominence of Brazil, it becomes unthinkable that there will not eventually be a proper legal treatment of terrorism in Brazilian law. It is true that social concerns especially relating to fear of using terrorism laws against freedom fighters inhibits Brazil's attempts to criminalize and punish terrorism. Nevertheless, the new criminalization of organized crime, which includes terrorist groups, may inspire the creation of a legal culture surrounding the terrorist phenomenon. It remains to be seen whether Parliament or the courts will use the platform of the 2013 organized crime legislation to provide a satisfactory legal definition of terrorism.

national interests, and the increasing introduction of Brazil in the worldwide scenario." http://www.defesa.gov.br/arquivos/File/2011/portaria_normativa_179.pdf.

60 http://www.planalto.gov.br/ccivil_03/Leis/2003/L10.744.htm.

61 http://www.planalto.gov.br/ccivil_03/leis/2002/l10559.htm.

PART THREE

Europe

6

The United Kingdom

Keith Syrett

I. INTRODUCTION AND CONTEXT

The experience of the United Kingdom (UK) with terrorism is both lengthy and multifaceted. As long ago as the early seventeenth century, a group of Catholic conspirators sought to assassinate King James I by exploding thirty-six barrels of gunpowder in the undercroft beneath the House of Lords on the day of the State Opening of Parliament, 5 November 1605. The discovery and prevention of this 'Gunpowder Plot' is still commemorated in modern times with firework displays and the burning of an effigy of Guy Fawkes, the first plotter to be arrested, on that date every year. More recently, status as a major imperialist power has necessitated response to numerous acts of political violence carried out by nationalist movements both in colonies and within the United Kingdom itself.

Relatedly, but of such significance that it is worthy of special note, one strand of response to British colonisation of Ireland (which had commenced in the mid-sixteenth century) has been the conduct of intermittent campaigns of terrorism in which republican movements, chiefly although far from exclusively the Irish Republican Army (IRA), sought to utilise forms of political violence to achieve their goals. This unstable situation, captured in the seemingly anodyne label, 'the Troubles', presented a particular challenge to the British government from the mid-1960s onward as loyalist paramilitary groups emerged in response to republican activity and the British army and Royal Ulster Constabulary became involved: it has been estimated that there were 3531 deaths in the period from July 1969 to the end of 2001.[1] The 'Good Friday' agreement of 1998 eventually led to the declaration by the

1 See M. Sutton, *Bear in mind these dead... An index of deaths from the conflict in Ireland 1969–1993* (Belfast, Beyond the Pale Publications, 1994) and update available at http://cain.ulst.ac.uk/sutton/book/ (accessed 31 March 2014).

IRA of an end to its armed campaign in July 2005, but sporadic acts of political violence instigated by various paramilitary organisations continue to the present day.

In view of this history, one might expect the legal system in the UK[2] to have been adequately equipped to respond to the 'new' terrorist threat which emerged on 11 September 2001. However, this would be an inaccurate evaluation for two reasons. First, the perception that the nature of terrorist activity had changed necessitated the supplementation of the UK's primary legal counter-terrorism strategy, which has historically centred upon criminal prosecution, with measures designed to pre-empt terrorist activity: this might be said to have particularly been the case following the '7/7 bombings' in London in July 2005. Secondly, the legal basis for responses to terrorism emerging from 'The Troubles' had been afforded by temporary emergency powers legislation, the Prevention of Terrorism (Temporary Provisions) Act 1974, which had been intended to last for six months but which was in fact renewed annually by Parliament for twenty-five years. Shortly prior to the 9/11 bombings, the UK government had accepted the recommendation of a review of counter-terrorism legislation that a permanent statutory framework for counter-terrorism should be enacted;[3] the ensuing law, the Terrorism Act 2000, remains the governing legislation in this field. The attack on the Twin Towers appeared to underline the wisdom of this shift from temporary to permanent legislative powers, suggesting as it did that the threat of terrorism was unlikely to disappear, notwithstanding any amelioration in the Irish situation. However, it is notable that the powers conferred by the 2000 Act were deemed inadequate to respond to the threat posed by Al-Qaeda and other similar groups, and in part as a response to such perceived deficiencies, five further major pieces of legislation were enacted in the ensuing decade. These will be considered in the course of the subsequent discussion.

II. THE DEFINITION OF TERRORISM

An early attempt to define terrorism in law was that contained in section 20(1) of the Prevention of Terrorism (Temporary Provisions) Act 1989, which stated that 'terrorism means the use of violence for political ends and includes any use of violence for the purpose of putting the public or any section of the public in fear'. However, a much more comprehensive definition was set out in section 1 of the Terrorism Act 2000, which remains the applicable law.[4] This provides that the mental element of the act

2 There is no UK-wide legal system: three separate systems operate in England and Wales, Northern Ireland and Scotland. For the purposes of this chapter, the relevant law will be that of England and Wales, although many of the provisions considered apply elsewhere in the UK.

3 *Inquiry into Legislation against Terrorism*, Cm 3240, 1996 ('The Lloyd Report').

4 Note also the Reinsurance (Acts of Terrorism) Act 1993, s.2(2) of which defines 'acts of terrorism' as 'acts of persons acting on behalf of, or in connection with, any organisation which carries out activities

of terrorism (the *mens rea*) constitutes the use or threat of action which is designed to influence the government or an international governmental organisation, or to intimidate the public or a section of the public, and the use or threat being made for the purpose of advancing a political, religious, racial or ideological cause;[5] and that the relevant actions (the *actus reus*) constitute committing serious violence against a person, inflicting serious damage to property, endangering a person's life (other than that of the person committing the act or threat), creating a serious risk to the health and safety of the public or a section of it; or acts designed seriously to interfere with or seriously to disrupt an electronic system.[6] Where firearms or explosives are used (or threatened), it is not necessary to demonstrate that there is intent to influence the government or an international governmental organisation or to intimidate the public or a section of it.[7] The legislation specifies that it applies to acts outside the UK and to attempts to influence governments other than that of the UK (including those in the UK's devolved regions).[8]

This definition is broad: indeed, it has been described as being 'notoriously' so.[9] The term 'violence' in the earlier legislation is extended to cover damage to property, risks to health and safety and disruption to electronic systems, while section 1(1)(b) provides that actions or threats of actions may be classified as terrorism when the motive is merely to *influence* government or an international governmental organisation. Tomkins argues that, taken together, these provisions 'dangerously blur the former distinction between terrorism and other criminal activity governed by regular public order law rather than by the special provisions of terrorism law'.[10]

A particular concern is that political protest – albeit of an extreme form – which is designed to persuade the government (or an international governmental organisation) to alter its policy, might be caught by the legislation. In parliamentary debate upon the Bill which became the 2000 Act, the rhetorical question was posed:

> If someone decided to break into a mink farm in order to release the mink from their cages, or to break into a research station and destroy the animals' cages, that would clearly be an act of serious violence. It would be a criminal act – and one that I deplore. But why should such organisations be classified as terrorist?[11]

directed towards the overthrowing or influencing, by force or violence, of Her Majesty's government in the United Kingdom or any other government *de jure* or *de facto*'.

5 s.1(1). As amended by Terrorism Act 2006, s.34 and Counter-Terrorism Act 2008, s.75.

6 s.1(2).

7 s.1(3).

8 s.1(4).

9 A. Tomkins, 'Legislating against terror: the Anti-Terrorism, Crime and Security Act 2001' [2003] *Public Law* 205, 211.

10 *ibid*, 211–12.

11 House of Commons Debates, 14th December 1999 (D. Hogg).

Notwithstanding such concerns, a review of this statutory definition of terrorism carried out in 2007 by the independent reviewer of terrorism legislation concluded that it was 'useful and broadly fit for purpose',[12] noting that it had 'proved over six years to be effective in covering terrorist activity' and that it was 'understood easily by the police and other agencies working against terrorism at the operational level'.[13] The review did, however, propose that the term 'influence' should be replaced by the term 'intimidate', which was described as 'entirely referable to the most easily understood notions of what terrorism is', and which would have the additional benefit of establishing the same standard in relation to acts directed at government as to the public 'whose embodiment a government should be'.[14] This proposal was rejected by the government for reasons which are not entirely clear, although it would appear that there was concern that the term could not easily apply to government or international governmental institutions.[15]

Rather, the government took the view that 'there is no evidence that the broadness (*sic*) of the definition has caused problems in the way that it has operated'.[16] Its conclusion in this regard was in part based upon the argument that the need to satisfy the various elements contained in the definition meant 'that most actions which would generally be accepted as non-terrorist in nature fall outside the definition'.[17] However, it was conceded that the potential existed for non-terrorist activities to be covered, and here the government indicated that it would place reliance upon the exercise of discretion by police and prosecutorial authorities not to pursue non-terrorist activities under the legislation. This safeguard had also been accorded a high degree of significance by the independent reviewer of terrorism legislation, who had noted both that several offences under the 2000 Act required the consent of the Director of Public Prosecutions before coming to trial,[18] and that 'the continuation of jury trial provides an important protection against prosecutions the public find unreasonable or arbitrary'.[19] Furthermore, the government confirmed that use of the powers, measures and offences contained in the Terrorism Act 2000 would be the exception rather than the norm, occurring only when 'no comparable general offence exists or where specific powers or measures are needed to enable

12 Lord Carlile of Berriew QC, *The Definition of Terrorism*, Cm 7052 (2007), 47.

13 *ibid*, 21.

14 *ibid*, 34. It was further noted that such a change would bring the legislation into line with that used in the Council of Europe Convention on the Prevention of Terrorism (2005).

15 *The Government Reply to the Report by Lord Carlile of Berriew QC, The Definition of Terrorism*, Cm 7058 (2007), 5.

16 *ibid*, 4.

17 *ibid*, 5.

18 Eg Terrorism Act 2000, s.117.

19 Lord Carlile of Berriew QC, above n.12, 35.

them [ie police and other relevant authorities] to investigate or prevent this special category of crime'.[20]

These factors may serve somewhat to diminish disquiet at the breadth of the definition of terrorism in the UK. But an underlying sense of unease is likely to remain for at least two reasons. First, it might be argued that characterising terrorism in such a wide manner, even if prosecution will in practice never ensue, may still have a 'chilling' effect on freedom of expression – as Walker states, it 'remains a concern that the term "terrorism" is inimical to protesters, cranks, and fantasists as much as to terrorists, recognising at the same time that these categories must sometimes be subject to firm policing action'.[21] Secondly, the reliance on discretion is scarcely consonant with the predictability and certainty which resides at the heart of the rule of law.[22] Given that counter-terrorism laws are frequently justified on the basis that terrorist activities present a threat to the rule of law,[23] this would seem to constitute an unfortunate state of affairs.

III. CRIMINAL LAWS AND PROSECUTIONS

Successive United Kingdom governments have maintained that the preferable approach for dealing with terrorists is criminalisation. This has the consequence that the majority of prosecutions for 'acts of terrorism' do not occur in respect of counter-terrorism legislation, but rather take place in the context of trials for murder, explosives offences etc.

A. *Criminal Law*

Part VI of the Terrorism Act 2000 sets out a range of offences specific to terrorist activity. These include engagement in weapons training (including training in biological and chemical weapons and radioactive materials),[24] directing a terrorist organisation,[25] possession of items and materials for terrorist purposes[26] and collection or possession of information for terrorist purposes[27] (including eliciting, publishing

[20] *Government Reply*, above n.15, 4.

[21] C. Walker, *Terrorism and the Law* (Oxford: OUP, 2011), [1.153].

[22] See *eg* J. Raz, 'The Rule of Law and its virtue' (1977) 93 *Law Quarterly Review* 195; T. Bingham, *The Rule of Law* (London: Penguin, 2011), chapter 3.

[23] See *eg* Lord Goldsmith QC, 'Government and the rule of law in the modern age' (2006) 3:1 *Justice Journal* 10.

[24] ss.54, 55. See also Terrorism Act 2006, s.6.

[25] s.56.

[26] s.57.

[27] s.58.

or communicating information about members of the armed forces, intelligence services or police).[28] Further offences are added by Part I of the Terrorism Act 2006: these include publication of statements which directly or indirectly encourage or induce the commission, preparation or instigation of acts of terrorism (including glorification of preparation or commission of such acts),[29] dissemination of terrorist publications,[30] preparation of acts of terrorism,[31] attendance at a place used for terrorist training,[32] making and possession of radioactive devices and materials in connection with an act of terrorism,[33] use of radioactive materials and damage to nuclear facilities in connection with an act of terrorism[34] and terrorist threats relating to radioactive devices and materials and nuclear facilities.[35] Threats and hoaxes are further criminalised by ss.113–114 of the Anti-Terrorism, Crime and Security Act 2001: by contrast to the preceding provisions, these offences are not explicitly linked to commission of acts of terrorism, although the various forms of activity envisaged by s.113 bear close resemblance to the definition of terrorism contained in section 1 of the Terrorism Act 2000 (see Section II).

Outside of anti-terrorism laws, various crimes may be relevant to terrorist activity, including murder, offences against the person, explosives and firearms offences[36] and criminal damage. Treason[37] and treason felony[38] are potentially applicable to terrorist acts,[39] but there has been a reluctance to use such controversial and archaic crimes for this purpose.[40] There may also be relevant offences under domestic legislation which gives effect to international treaties, including those relating to aviation and maritime security, hostage-taking and internationally protected persons.

28 s.58A.

29 s.1.

30 s.2. Both of these sections apply to internet activity: s.3.

31 s.5.

32 s.6.

33 s.9.

34 s.10.

35 s.11.

36 Notably offences under the Explosive Substances Act 1883.

37 Treason Act 1351.

38 Treason Felony Act 1848.

39 See 'Islamic terrorists face treason charges', *The Guardian*, 8 August 2005. No such charges were, in fact, brought.

40 The Independent Reviewer of Terrorism Legislation, 2001–11, Lord Carlile, was reported as stating: 'I do not think there is a lawyer still alive and working who has ever appeared in any part of a treason case and I think we should tread in that historic territory very carefully. Treason tends to apply to war between nations.': 'Use existing laws', *The Guardian*, 9 August 2005.

B. *Terrorism Prosecutions*

The independent reviewer of terrorism legislation has expressed the view that 'the main perpetrators of the most serious acts of terrorism are almost always charged with offences under the ordinary criminal law'.[41] This conclusion is, at least to an extent, borne out by data on prosecutions. These demonstrate that some 45% of convictions in Great Britain in cases where the offence is considered as terrorism-related occurred under the specialist terrorist offences, the remainder being convictions for non-terrorist specific offences. Of the former, 56% were offences under ss.57 and 58 of the Terrorism Act 2000 (possession of items and materials/possession of information); of the latter, 19% were for homicide-related offences, 40% were for property, blackmail, arson or drugs offences, and 38% were for munitions offences. In Northern Ireland, where overall conviction rates remain significantly higher than on the mainland, specific terrorist offences are used less frequently (amounting to some 17% of the total), but the preponderance of convictions also occurs under ss.57 and 58 of the 2000 Act. In respect of non-terrorist specific offences, 56% of Northern Ireland convictions are for munitions offences and only 11% for homicide-related offences.[42]

Prosecutions of the specialist terrorist offences listed in the preceding subsection require the consent of the Director of Public Prosecutions.[43] Otherwise, the legislation contains relatively few special procedures for criminal trial of terrorism-related activity. Outside of Northern Ireland, special courts are not used for terrorism trials;[44] there, a system of juryless 'Diplock courts' remains in place, although these are much less heavily used than was the case at the height of 'the Troubles', and there is an ongoing political commitment to end their use; their deployment is now governed by section 1 of the Justice and Security (Northern Ireland) Act 2007, which enables the Director of Public Prosecutions to issue a certificate that a trial should be conducted without a jury. Such certificates may be issued in situations where there is concern that there will be interference with the trial process, such as tampering with physical evidence or intimidating jurors.

The admission of evidence alleged to have been obtained through torture is considered in Section VII.

It is possible for witnesses to give evidence anonymously, although Article 6 of the European Convention on Human Rights (which forms part of domestic law as a consequence of the enactment of the Human Rights Act 1998) sets out 'a general

41 D. Anderson, QC, *The Terrorism Acts in 2012* (London: The Stationery Office, 2013), [11.1].

42 Walker, above n.21, [5.155], [5.196]. These statistics are for the period 2001–8.

43 Terrorism Act 2000, s.117; Terrorism Act 2006, s.19.

44 Although note that Criminal Justice Act 2003, s.44 does permit the prosecution to make an application for a trial to be conducted without a jury where there is a danger of jury tampering.

and strong rule in favour of unrestricted publicity of any proceedings in a criminal trial'.[45] Decisions have tended to be made on a case-by-case basis,[46] but the matter is now governed by Part 3 of the Coroners and Justice Act 2009, which establishes conditions for granting witness anonymity orders.

C. *Punishment of Terrorism*

Section 30 of the Counter-Terrorism Act 2008 permits more stringent sentencing for specified offences with a 'terrorist connection'. These are non-terrorism–specific sentences, such as homicides and explosives offences. If such a connection is established, the court will treat it as an aggravating factor in respect of commission of the offence.

It is questionable whether this provision has any significant impact in view of the fact that courts have always tended to impose tougher sentences for those engaged in terrorist activity. For example, conviction for the Lockerbie bombing attracted a minimum sentence of twenty-seven years' imprisonment;[47] an attempt to blow up a plane with a bomb hidden in the suitcase of the terrorist's girlfriend yielded a sentence of forty-five years in prison;[48] and the bombing of the Grand Hotel in Brighton during the governing Conservative Party conference led to a minimum jail sentence of thirty-five years.[49]

It seems clear that the major functions of sentencing in this context are deterrence and incapacitation; in *R v Martin*, Lord Bingham observed that 'In passing sentence for the most serious terrorist offences, the object of the court will be to punish, deter and incapacitate; rehabilitation is likely to play a minor (if any) part'.[50] Very occasionally, pursuit of the objective of deterrence results in leniency in sentencing, for example because of a concern that excessive sentences would inflame rather than discourage extremist sentiment.[51]

Section 73 of the Serious Organised Crime and Police Act 2005 sets out the principles relating to reduction in sentences for those who co-operate with the authorities in relation to offences, including those connected to terrorist activity. In Northern Ireland, many paramilitary prisoners were released as part of the 'Good Friday' Agreement, although they remained under licence; 444 prisoners were released on this basis by 14 July 2001.[52] The Northern Ireland Arms Decommissioning

45 *In Re S (A Child) (Identification: Restrictions on Publication* [2005] 1 AC 593, [15] (Lord Steyn).
46 See *eg R v Murphy and Maguire* [1990] NI 306.
47 'Obituary: Abdelbaset al-Megrahi', *BBC News*, 20 May 2012.
48 *R v Hindawi* (1988) 10 Cr App R (S) 104.
49 *R v Anderson* [1988] QB 678.
50 [1999] 1 Cr App R (S) 477, 480.
51 See *R v Rahman, R v Mohammed* [2008] EWCA Crim 1465.
52 Walker, above n.21, [11.71].

Act 1997 further provided for an amnesty period during which firearms, ammunitions and explosives could be yielded up, although individuals might still be prosecuted for offences involving the weapons.

IV. INVESTIGATIVE POWERS

A. *Police Powers*

In considering the powers which are available to police in respect to counter-terrorism, it remains necessary to distinguish the situation in Northern Ireland from that in the rest of the UK. As Walker notes, the Joint Security (Northern Ireland) Act 2007 contains 'vestiges of a startling array of powers, geared to soldiers as well as police officers',[53] although the range of police powers is less broad than was previously the case; it includes powers to stop and question persons or vehicles, to enter property and to conduct searches.

Police in Northern Ireland may also derive power from counter-terrorism legislation applicable to the whole of the UK. The starting-point for analysis of these is, once again, the Terrorism Act 2000. Part IV of the Act confers wide powers relating to 'terrorist investigations', defined to comprise investigations into commission, preparation and instigation of acts of terrorism; acts which appear to have been done for the purposes of terrorism; resources of proscribed organisations; the possibility of making a proscription order; or the commission, preparation and instigation of offences under the 2000 Act or the Terrorism Act 2006.[54] This wording permits police and other authorities to conduct investigations before any act of terrorism is committed, or even any link to terrorism established.

Under s.33, a 'cordoned area' can be designated for the purposes of such investigation – this may be done orally although it must be confirmed in writing as soon as possible. Such designation will usually be undertaken by senior police officers, although police constables can do so in cases of urgency,[55] and it shall not last for more than fourteen days, renewable once for a further fourteen-day period.[56] There are powers to order persons in cordoned areas or premises adjacent to such areas to leave them immediately, to order vehicles to be moved from such areas, to remove or move such vehicles and to prohibit or restrict access by pedestrians or vehicles.[57]

53 *ibid*, [11.39].
54 s. 32.
55 s.34.
56 s.35.
57 s.36.

Part V of the Act contains a range of powers exercisable by police constables in respect to suspected terrorists, defined as those who have committed a range of offences under the 2000 Act, or those who have been concerned in the commission, preparation or instigation of acts of terrorism.[58] These include powers for the police to arrest without a warrant those who are reasonably suspected of being a terrorist,[59] to search premises for a suspected terrorist[60] and to stop and search to discover whether the person searched holds anything in his or her possession which may constitute evidence that the person is a terrorist.[61]

However, the broadest powers are those contained in ss.44–47, which allow police constables to stop and search vehicles (and those within them) and pedestrians, when an authorisation has been issued by a senior police officer (an Assistant Chief Constable or Commander of metropolitan police or London force) in circumstances where the latter 'considers it expedient for the prevention of acts of terrorism'.[62] Such an authorisation must not last longer than twenty-eight days (though this period is renewable), and the senior police officer must inform the Home Secretary of the authorisation as soon as reasonably practicable; it is necessary for it to be confirmed, rejected or amended by the Home Secretary within forty-eight hours.[63] The powers may only be exercised for the purpose of searching for articles of a kind which could be used in connection with terrorism, although they may be exercised irrespective of whether the police constable has grounds for suspecting the presence of such articles.[64]

The controversy to which these provisions can give rise is well demonstrated by the case of R *(on the application of Gillan)* v *Metropolitan Police Commissioner*.[65] Here, under a section 44 authorisation covering the entirety of the London metropolitan police district, a student and a freelance journalist were stopped and searched under s.45 at or near an arms fair taking place in the Docklands area of London, the incidents taking twenty minutes in the case of the former and thirty in the case of the latter. The House of Lords concluded that there had been no deprivation of liberty such that Article 5 of the European Convention on Human Rights was engaged,[66] nor interference with the right to respect for private life under Article 8,[67] Lord Scott observing that 'any invasion of privacy will be shortlived

58 s.40.
59 s.41.
60 s.42.
61 s.43.
62 s.44(3).
63 s.46.
64 s.44(1).
65 [2006] UKHL 12.
66 *ibid*, [25] (Lord Bingham).
67 *ibid*, [28] (Lord Bingham).

and any deprivation of liberty will usually be no more than theoretical'.[68] It also concluded that any infringement of rights would have been 'prescribed by law', as is required to demonstrate that it is 'necessary in a democratic society'. This was the case because the Act and its accompanying procedural code defined and limited the powers and procedure in detail, and in exercising the stop and search power, 'the constable is not free to act arbitrarily'.[69]

However, the European Court of Human Rights disagreed. It considered that Article 8 of the Convention *was* engaged, even in the case of a relatively superficial search: 'the use of the coercive powers conferred by the legislation to require an individual to submit to a detailed search of his person, his clothing and his personal belongings amounts to a clear interference with the right to respect for private life'.[70] Furthermore, it held that the provisions conferred 'an unduly wide discretion on the police, both in terms of the authorisation of the power to stop and its application in practice', and that the safeguards provided by domestic law had not been demonstrated 'to constitute a real curb on the wide powers afforded to the executive so as to offer the individual adequate protection against arbitrary interference'.[71] Consequently, there was a 'clear risk of arbitrariness' in the grant of wide discretion to the police,[72] and the provisions were therefore not 'in accordance with the law'. They amounted to a violation of Article 8. In response to the judgment, the Home Secretary indicated that pedestrians should only be stopped under (the less broad) s.43, with s.44 only being used in cases of 'necessity', not 'expediency'.[73] Subsequently, a Counter-Terrorism Review conducted by the current Conservative-Liberal Democrat Coalition government recommended replacement of s.44 with a more restricted power. This was achieved initially by way of delegated legislation made under the authority of s.10 of the Human Rights Act 1998[74] and subsequently by means of ss.59 and 61 of the Protection of Freedoms Act 2012, which repealed ss.44–47 of the 2000 Act and replaced them with a temporally and geographically more limited power of authorisation, founded upon necessity rather than expediency.

The 2000 Act also confers powers to be exercised at ports and airports, including questioning for the purpose of determining whether a person appears to be a terrorist; stopping a person or vehicle; detaining a person; searching a ship, aircraft, person

68 *ibid*, [63].

69 *ibid*, [35] (Lord Bingham).

70 *Gillan and Quinton v UK* (2010) 50 EHRR 45, [63].

71 *ibid*, [79].

72 *ibid*, [85].

73 For discussion, see J. Ip, 'The reform of counterterrorism stop and search after *Gillan v United Kingdom* (2013) 13 *Human Rights Law Review* 729.

74 Terrorism Act 2000 (Remedial Order) 2011, SI 2011/631.

or baggage and goods; authorising removal from a ship or aircraft; and requiring passenger information to be provided.[75]

B. *Intelligence Agencies*

The legality of various forms of intelligence gathering in the context of terrorism rests primarily upon compliance with the Regulation of Investigatory Powers Act 2000. This is a broad statutory framework which governs public authority use of covert techniques to obtain private information in a number of situations, including crime, public safety and emergencies, as well as terrorism. The Act covers five areas: interception of communications; acquisition of communications data; conduct of covert surveillance in private premises or vehicles (intrusive surveillance) or public places (directed surveillance); use of covert human intelligence sources; and access to electronic data protected by encryption or passwords. A wide range of authorities are covered by the Act, including the police, other law enforcement bodies, security and intelligence services and local government.

The type of authorisation which is required varies according to the nature of the surveillance being carried out. Interception of private communications is regarded as being the most sensitive form of surveillance and generally requires ministerial authorisation; this may also be the case for intrusive surveillance, although in the case of police forces such authorisation may be given by a chief constable. Other forms of activity may be authorised by a senior member of the relevant authority. No prior judicial authorisation is required, except in the case of local authorities.[76] This fact has been heavily criticised by civil liberties organisations.[77]

A controversial aspect of this framework is that s.17 of the Act excludes the process of interception of communications and any material thereby intercepted from admissibility as evidence in legal proceedings. The rationale for this is to preclude disclosure or compromise of sources, 'keeping secret the State's methods of investigation'.[78] This proscription has been subject to some criticism, including from civil liberties organisations:[79] indeed, it has been described as 'the single biggest obstacle to bringing more prosecutions for terrorism'.[80] Although a review ordered by the government recommended that such material should be admissible

75 Schedule 7.

76 Protection of Freedoms Act 2012, ss.37–8.

77 See *eg* Joint Committee on Human Rights, *Counter-Terrorism Policy and Human Rights: 28 Days, Intercept and Post-charge Questioning*, HL Paper 157/HC 394 (2006–07), [159]–[161].

78 Oxford Pro Bono Publico, *Legal Opinion on Intercept Communication* (Oxford: University of Oxford, 2006), 13.

79 See *eg* Liberty, *Reconciling Security and Liberty in an Open Society* (London: Liberty, 2004).

80 Joint Committee on Human Rights, above n.77, [126].

as evidence, subject to various operational requirements judged necessary to protect the public and national security,[81] no legally viable scheme has yet been devised which would meet both the operational requirements and ensure fair trial procedures.[82] Nonetheless, the matter remains on the political agenda.[83]

V. PROSCRIPTION/LISTING OF TERRORIST GROUPS/INDIVIDUALS

The law relating to proscription of organisations is contained in Part II of the Terrorism Act 2000. It will be noted that this legislation precedes the 9/11 attacks, reflecting the origin of the contemporary framework of UK counter-terrorism law in 'the Troubles'. Consequently, Schedule 2 of the Act lists a number of organisations of Northern Irish origin, which had been mentioned in previous legislation, such as the Prevention of Terrorism (Temporary Provisions) Act 1989 and the Northern Ireland (Emergency Provisions) Act 1996. No further domestic organisations have been added to the Schedule, but twenty-one organisations based outside the UK were listed at the point at which the Act came into force.[84] At the end of 2013, sixty-six organisations in total were proscribed under the legislation.[85]

Under s.3(3) of the Act, Schedule 2 can be supplemented (or organisations can be removed from it) by way of delegated legislation made by a minister (in practice, the Home Secretary), subject to approval by Parliament. In order for this to take place, the minister must believe that the organisation is concerned in terrorism,[86] that term being accorded the definition given in section 1 of the 2000 Act (see Section II of this chapter). Section 3(5) provides that being 'concerned in terrorism' constitutes commission or participation in acts of terrorism, preparation for terrorism, promotion or encouragement of terrorism or being 'otherwise concerned in terrorism'. Some criticism has been expressed as to a lack of clarity in the criteria utilised by the minister when exercising discretion on proscription under these provisions, and explanatory guidance has been issued on this matter by the government. This indicates that the factors taken into account are the nature and scale of the organisation's activities, the specific threat that it poses to the UK, the specific threat that it poses to British

81 *Privy Council Review of Intercept as Evidence: Report to the Prime Minister and Home Secretary*, Cm 7324 (2008).

82 *Intercept as Evidence: A Report*, Cm 7760 (2009).

83 See *eg* Interception of Communications (Admissibility of Evidence) Bill, HL Bill 18 (2012–13). The Bill did not proceed beyond First Reading.

84 Terrorism Act 2000 (Proscribed Organisations) (Amendment) Order 2001, SI 2001/1261.

85 https://www.gov.uk/government/publications/proscribed-terror-groups-or-organisations–2 (accessed 31 March 2014).

86 s.3(4).

nationals overseas, the extent of the organisation's presence in the UK and the need to support international partners in the fight against terrorism.[87]

The legislation permits challenges to proscription decisions.[88] An organisation or affected individual[89] must make a written application to the minister requesting that consideration be given to removal from the list of proscribed organisations, with accompanying grounds for the request; a response is required within ninety days. If the application for deproscription is refused, an appeal may be made to the Proscribed Organisations Appeal Commission. This sits in a panel of three persons, at least one of whom holds, or has held, high judicial office; members of the Commission are appointed by the Lord Chancellor, who also makes its procedural rules. These permit oral hearings to be dispensed with in specialised circumstances and enable information to remain undisclosed if this is in the public interest. Legal representation is allowed, but the Commission can exclude persons, including legal representatives, from proceedings. However, a 'special advocate' may be appointed to represent parties; if this occurs, a summary of the reasons and facts relating to the decision and the grounds and evidence for opposing the appeal must be provided to the advocate.

The Commission may overturn a decision of the Home Secretary not to allow an application for deproscription if it considers that such a decision is 'flawed': in practice, this does not permit challenge on the *merits* of the Home Secretary's choice but only on the much more limited grounds which would be applicable in judicial review proceedings. If a challenge is successful, the minister is obliged to give effect to the Commission's decision by laying a draft order before Parliament removing the organisation from the proscribed list: such an order must then be approved by Parliament, or – in urgent cases – issuing an order which immediately lifts the proscription from the organisation (in which instance the order will lapse after forty days unless Parliament approves it). Appeals on points of law from decisions of the Commission can be made to the appeal level of the court hierarchy.[90]

Only one successful challenge to proscription has occurred to date. In *Secretary of State for the Home Department v Lord Alton of Liverpool*,[91] the Court of Appeal upheld the decision of the Commission that the People's Mojahadeen Organisation of Iran was not an organisation 'concerned in terrorism' under section 3 of the 2000 Act. This organisation claimed to have renounced terrorism in 2001 and ceased all

87 Explanatory Memorandum to the Terrorism Act 2000 (Proscribed Organisations) (Amendment Order) 2011, SI 2011/108.

88 ss.4–6.

89 This phrase has been interpreted broadly. See *Secretary of State for the Home Department v Lord Alton of Liverpool* [2008] EWCA Civ 443.

90 s.7.

91 Above n.89.

military activity in 2003. The Home Secretary had argued that terrorist activity had been suspended for pragmatic reasons and might be renewed in the future. However, since there was no evidence that the organisation had sought to re-create any form of structure which would enable it to carry out or support terrorist acts since 2003, nor evidence of any attempt to prepare for terrorism or to encourage others to commit acts of terrorism, the Commission concluded that a reasonable decision-maker could not honestly have entertained the belief that it was concerned in terrorism.[92] The Court of Appeal agreed and the organisation was removed from Schedule 2 of the 2000 Act.

Part II of the Terrorism Act 2000 also sets out offences connected to proscription. Section 11(1) makes it an offence to belong or to profess to belong to a proscribed organisation; section 12 criminalises support for the organisation, including invitation of support; arranging, managing or assisting in arranging or managing meetings connected to proscribed organisations; or addressing a meeting with the purpose of encouraging support for a proscribed organisation. Section 13 establishes offences connected with the wearing of a uniform or the wearing, carrying or display of an article in such a way or in such circumstances as to arouse reasonable suspicion that the individual is a member or supporter of a proscribed organisation.

VI. REGULATION OF TERRORISM FINANCING

As in the case of proscription, the basic legislative framework relating to financing of terrorism is contained in the Terrorism Act 2000, in this instance in Part III. In fact, these provisions extend beyond money and related property to cover 'any resources of a proscribed organisation'.[93] The powers available to the state in this context have been extended by further legislation, notably the Anti-Terrorism, Crime and Security Act 2001 and the Counter-Terrorism Act 2008.

A. *The Regulatory Regime to Counter Terrorism Financing*

The UK possesses a Financial Intelligence Unit which, in addition to dealing with money-laundering, includes a Terrorist Finance Unit. Prior to October 2013, this existed within the Serious Organised Crime Agency; the Agency has now been replaced by a National Crime Agency.[94] The legislation imposes obligations to disclose information acquired in the course of a trade, profession, business or employment to a police officer or an officer of the National Crime Agency as soon as reasonably practicable, where such information gives rise to a belief or suspicion that an offence

[92] *ibid*, [55].

[93] s.14(1)(a).

[94] http://www.nationalcrimeagency.gov.uk/ (accessed 31 March 2014).

has been committed under ss.15–18 of the 2000 Act.[95] This provision extends to those undertaking unpaid employment, for example, the trustees of a charity.[96] Those working in the 'regulated sector' (ie conducting most forms of financial activity) are placed under a particularly onerous obligation in so far as they commit an offence by failing to disclose where there are reasonable grounds for knowing or suspecting that an offence under ss.15–18 has been committed.[97] Disclosure may occur by way of completion of a Suspicious Activity Report, submitted online to the National Crime Agency, which logs the reports on a database.[98]

A Financial Action Task Force report in June 2007 rated the UK as compliant with Special Recommendation II on the criminalisation of terrorist financing.[99]

B. *Criminal Offences of Terrorism Financing*

A number of criminal offences are set out in ss.15–18 of the Terrorism Act 2000. These comprise fund-raising, use and possession of money or property, entering into or being concerned with funding arrangements and money laundering. The various offences have somewhat different standards of *mens rea*: in the case of fund-raising, use or possession and funding arrangements, the individual must either intend that it be used for the purposes of terrorism or have reasonable cause to suspect that it will be so used; while in the case of money laundering, the burden of proof falls upon the defendant to demonstrate that he or she did not know or had no reasonable cause to suspect that the arrangement related to terrorist property. The maximum penalty for commission of any of these offences is imprisonment for fourteen years and/or a fine.[100] In addition to these particular offences, money or property destined for terrorist use may be at issue in trials for other offences such as those under the Theft Act 1968. Such crimes attract more severe sentences when committed in a terrorist context.[101]

Where a conviction is secured under ss.15–18, the court in question may make a forfeiture order under s.23. Forfeiture is also possible in relation to certain other terrorism offences under the 2000 Act and the Terrorism Act 2006 and for certain

95 Terrorism Act 2000, s.19(1).

96 Counter-Terrorism Act 2008, s.77.

97 Terrorism Act 2000, s.21A.

98 http://www.nationalcrimeagency.gov.uk/about-us/what-we-do/specialist-capabilities/ukfiu/the-sars-regime (accessed 31 March 2014).

99 Financial Action Task Force, *Third Mutual Evaluation Report: Anti-Money Laundering and Combating the Financing of Terrorism: United Kingdom of Great Britain and Northern Ireland* (Paris: FATF/OECD, 2007).

100 s.22.

101 See eg *Attorney-General's Reference (No. 5 of 2004) (Potts)* [2004] NICA 27 (blackmail).

non-terrorism offences where the court determines that a terrorist connection exists.[102] Money and property may also be forfeited from a person who receives it as payment or a reward in connection with offences under ss.15–18 of the 2000 Act, even if the person in receipt (such as an accountant) was not the person committing the offence.[103] In order to prevent funds being dispersed in advance of a prosecution, the High Court may issue a 'restraint order' where a forfeiture order has already been made, if it appears that a forfeiture order may arise in ongoing proceedings for the offence, or when a criminal investigation in respect of relevant offences has begun and it appears that a forfeiture order may be issued in subsequent proceedings. Such an order prevents a notified person from dealing with the money or property, and it may be seized by the police to prevent it from being removed from the jurisdiction.

The 2000 Act also includes a power to seize cash, initially limited to seizure at borders, but subsequently extended by the Anti-Terrorism, Crime and Security Act 2001. This power exists whether or not any criminal proceedings have been brought,[104] and relates to cash (including coins and notes in any currency, postal orders, cheques and travellers' cheques, among other instruments)[105] which is intended to be used for purposes of terrorism, consists of resources of a proscribed organisation or is, or represents, property obtained through terrorism.[106]

More extensive, and controversial, powers over terrorist finance and property are contained in the provisions relating to the freezing of assets. Section 4 of the Anti-Terrorism, Crime and Security Act 2001 enables the UK Treasury to make a freezing order – to be laid before and approved by affirmative resolution of Parliament[107] – where it reasonably believes that action to the detriment of the UK's economy (or part of it) or action constituting a threat to the life or property of one or more nationals of the UK or residents of the UK has been or is likely to be taken by the government or a resident of a country or territory outside the UK. Such an order, which has effect for two years,[108] operates to prohibit funds (defined as 'financial assets and economic benefits of any kind')[109] from being made available for the benefit of the specified person(s).[110] Various offences are specified for non-compliance with provisions contained in the freezing order.[111]

[102] Counter-Terrorism Act 2008, Schedule 2.
[103] s.23(7).
[104] Anti-Terrorism, Crime and Security Act 2001, s.1(2).
[105] Schedule 1, para. 1(2).
[106] s.1(1).
[107] s.10.
[108] s.8.
[109] s.5(6).
[110] s.5.
[111] Schedule 3(7).

This power of domestic origin has been relatively little used.[112] By contrast, provisions giving effect to UN Security Council Resolutions 1267 and 1373 (which are implemented in EU law via Council Regulation (EC) 337/2000 of 14 February 2000 and Council Regulation (EC) 2580/2001 of 27 December 2001 respectively) have proved highly contentious. In *HM Treasury v Ahmed*,[113] the Supreme Court quashed the delegated legislation which sought to give effect to UNSCR 1373, the Terrorism (United Nations Measures) Order 2006, in its entirety, and held that the process for listing of individuals and absence of effective legal challenge to such listing, under the Al-Qaida and Taliban (United Nations Measures) Order 2006 (which gave effect to UNSCR 1267) were so unfair as to be unlawful. The court's primary concern was the absence of parliamentary scrutiny. Authority for issuing the delegated legislation was provided by section 1 of the United Nations Act 1946, which requires laying of the legislation before Parliament for information purposes only; however, the process which the section sets out applies when the government considers it 'necessary or expedient' to act in such a way. In the view of Lord Hope, such language was to be interpreted 'on the basis that Parliament did not surrender its legislative powers to the executive any more than must necessarily follow from the words used by it';[114] fundamental rights were not to be overridden by general or ambiguous statutory words,[115] and this amounted to 'a clear example of an attempt to adversely affect the basic rights of the citizen without the clear authority of Parliament'.[116] The President of the Supreme Court was at pains to emphasise that judicial intervention in this case respected, rather than violated, fundamental principles of the British constitutional order, opining that:

> Nobody should conclude that the result of these appeals constitutes judicial interference with the will of Parliament. On the contrary it upholds the supremacy of Parliament in deciding whether or not measures should be imposed that affect the fundamental rights of those in this country.[117]

One might merely note that, in the UK's parliamentary executive system, the distinction may not be as clear-cut as this dictum suggests.

Be that as it may, the quashing of the Terrorism (United Nations Measures) Order 2006 obliged Parliament to respond. It did so by enacting the Terrorist Asset-Freezing

[112] For a notable exception – beyond the counter-terrorism context – see Landsbanki Freezing Order 2008, SI 2008/2668.

[113] [2010] UKSC 2.

[114] *ibid*, [47].

[115] This is the so-called 'principle of legality': for discussion, see *R v Secretary of State for the Home Department, ex parte Simms* [2000] 2 AC 115, 131 (Lord Hoffmann).

[116] [2010] UKSC 2, [61].

[117] *ibid*, [157] (Lord Phillips).

etc. Act 2010. Under the statute, persons are designated by the Treasury or listed under Council Regulation (EC) 2580/2001,[118] either for a final order (which expires after one year unless renewed)[119] or on an interim basis (for no more than thirty days).[120] It is an offence to deal with funds or economic resources owned, held or controlled by a designated person[121] and/or to make funds, financial services or economic resources available to a designated person or to any person for the latter's benefit.[122]

As of 31 December 2013, thirty individuals and eight entities were designated by the Treasury under s.1(1) of the Act and eleven individuals and twenty-six entities under the EU Regulation. The total assets frozen during the quarterly period to that date were £82,000 and £11,000 respectively.[123] These are relatively low figures, and the independent reviewer of terrorism legislation has recommended that further high-level consideration be given to the practical role that the legislation can play in the fight against terrorism.[124]

VII. IMMIGRATION MEASURES

One of the most striking judicial decisions in the UK in recent years, and certainly the most celebrated court case concerned with counter-terrorism, occurred at the interface between immigration and terrorism. *A v Secretary of State for the Home Department*[125] was a highly controversial decision in so far as its ultimate consequence was the substitution by the legislature of one counter-terrorism legislative regime with another, notwithstanding that UK courts possess no 'strike-down' power akin to that which may be exercised by the U.S. Supreme Court and other courts with constitutional review jurisdiction. Furthermore, it has had a wider politico-legal impact, prompting concern within government that the powers conferred upon the judiciary by the Human Rights Act 1998 might operate in such a manner as to impede its choice of strategy to respond to terrorist threats; at the very least, the prospect of an adverse court ruling has given the executive pause to consider its response to perceived

118 s.1.

119 ss.2, 4.

120 ss.6, 8.

121 s.11.

122 ss.12–15. 'Funds' mean cash, cheques, deposits, securities, interest, credit etc; 'economic resources' mean tangible and intangible, movable and immovable assets which are not funds but which can be used to obtain goods, funds and services: s.39.

123 Written Ministerial Statement, *Operation of the UK's Counter-Terrorist Asset Freezing Regime, 1 October 2013 to 31 December 2013* (London: HM Treasury, 2014).

124 D. Anderson QC, *Third Report on the Operation of the Terrorist Asset-Freezing etc. Act 2010* (London: The Stationery Office, 2013), [2.26].

125 [2004] UKHL 56.

national security threats in a manner which is somewhat unfamiliar within the UK constitutional order.[126] In turn, this has caused some politicians – particularly those towards the right of the political spectrum – to express concern as to existing UK human rights legislation,[127] even, in some cases, querying continued UK membership of the machinery of the European Convention on Human Rights (which is in essence 'incorporated' into domestic law by the Human Rights Act 1998).[128] Such issues fall well beyond the scope of this chapter (although they will be returned to in brief in the concluding section), but the decision in A will serve as a thread throughout the present section.

A. *Immigration Detention and Immigration Proceedings and Torture*

The Immigration Act 1971 (as amended) permits refusal of entry to the UK for 'excluded persons', which might include those with links to organisations engaged in terrorist activity.[129] More broadly, the Act permits deportation of persons where the Home Secretary deems this 'conducive to the public good'.[130] The government has explained that this term comprises not only matters relating to national security, but also the expression of views which are considered, *inter alia*, to 'foment terrorism or seek to provoke others to terrorist acts' and/or which 'justify or glorify terrorism'.[131] Schedule 3, paragraph 2 of the Act permits detention pending deportation and establishes no statutory time limit during which an individual may be held. However, certain restrictions have been imposed to ensure compliance with Article 5 of the European Convention on Human Rights, which limits the situations in which liberty and security of the person can be compromised.[132]

Appeals against decisions to exclude or deport are heard by the Special Immigration Appeals Commission Tribunal.[133] There is a presumption that its hearings are conducted openly, but the Tribunal also has a general duty to ensure that 'information is not disclosed contrary to the interests of national security, the international relations of the United Kingdom, the detection and prevention of crime, or in any other circumstances where disclosure is likely to harm the public

[126] See especially *Liversidge v Anderson* [1942] 2 AC 206.

[127] To this end the present Coalition Government set up a Commission to investigate creation of a 'British Bill of Rights': see Commission on a Bill of Rights, *A UK Bill of Rights? The Choice Before Us* (London: Commission on a Bill of Rights, 2012).

[128] See *eg* 'Theresa May: Tories to consider leaving European Convention on Human Rights', *BBC News*, 9 March 2013.

[129] s.8B.

[130] s.3(5)(a).

[131] Home Office, *Exclusion or Deportation from the UK on Non-Conducive Grounds* (London: Home Office, 2005), [7].

[132] See *eg R (on the application of I) v Secretary of State for the Home Department* [2002] EWCA Civ 888.

[133] See Special Immigration Appeals Commission Act 1997.

interest.'[134] To this end, a special advocate may be appointed in closed hearings; this representative is given access to restricted material which the appellant and their legal representative are not permitted to see.

In *A v Secretary of State for the Home Department (No. 2)*,[135] the Commission was asked to consider the admissibility of evidence obtained by torture by appellants subjected to detention. The House of Lords ruled that such an appellant should not be required to prove that the evidence had been obtained by means of torture, given that he or she may not have full access to the necessary information, although it was incumbent upon such an appellant to provide some plausible basis for the claim that torture may have been used (for example, that a particular state was known to practice torture). Such a claim would then oblige the Commission to inquire into the matter and to decide, on balance of probabilities, whether the evidence was obtained under torture, albeit that it would not be necessary for the government to demonstrate that there was no real risk that torture had been used.

The legislative provisions under which detention took place in this case were those which were also at issue in the (similarly named) case of A (otherwise known as the *Belmarsh* case, after the facility in which the detainees were kept), noted in the introduction to this section.[136] Part IV of the Anti-Terrorism, Crime and Security Act 2001 – the UK's response to the 9/11 attacks – contained a range of powers which operated at the interface between immigration and counter-terrorism, the most contentious of which were contained in ss.21–23. Section 21 permitted the Home Secretary to certify status as a 'suspected international terrorist' to those whom the Home Secretary reasonably suspected to be a terrorist and whose presence in the UK was reasonably believed to represent a threat to national security; section 22 permitted refusal or variation of leave to enter or remain in the UK, recommending deportation, taking a decision to make, making and refusing to revoke a deportation order, giving directions for removal from the UK etc, in respect of suspected international terrorists; while section 23 authorised detention of suspected international terrorists under the Immigration Act 1971.

These last two sections were expressed to apply notwithstanding that 'a point of law which wholly or partly relates to an international agreement' temporarily or indefinitely prevented removal or departure from the UK. This curious form of wording was designed to address the decision of the European Court of Human Rights in *Chahal v United Kingdom*,[137] in which the Court had articulated a principle of non-refoulement, in holding that the absolute prohibition on torture or

[134] Special Immigration Appeals Commission (Procedure) Rules 2003, SI 2003/1034, r. 4(4).
[135] [2005] UKHL 71.
[136] Above n.125.
[137] (1997) 23 EHRR 413.

inhuman/degrading treatment or punishment placed a positive obligation upon the state not to deport, even where the state party had argued that the putative deportee represented a threat to national security.[138] Section 23 of the 2001 Act therefore functioned to permit indefinite detention without trial of 'suspected international terrorists' who could not be deported from the UK as a consequence of commitment to non-refoulement.

The compatibility of this provision with the 'Convention Rights' given effect by the Human Rights Act 1998 was explored in the *Belmarsh* case. It should first be noted that the UK government had exercised powers available under section 14 of the Act to issue an order derogating from Article 5(1)(f) of the European Convention on Human Rights (the right to liberty and security of the person) on the grounds that there was a 'public emergency threatening the life of the nation'[139] subsequent to the 9/11 attacks.[140] Such derogation was intended to render indefinite detention without trial under s.23 of the Anti-Terrorism, Crime and Security Act 2001 lawful. The House of Lords was prepared to defer to the executive's expertise on the question of whether the UK's post-9/11 security constituted such a public emergency that it necessitated derogation – this 'being a pre-eminently political judgment'[141] – but any such derogation must nonetheless only 'be to the extent strictly required by the exigencies of the situation'. In this respect, the court considered that the legislative provision amounted to a violation of Article 5(1) and Article 14 (prohibition on discrimination in respect of enjoyment of any of the Convention Rights), given that the detainees 'were treated differently from both suspected international terrorists who were not UK nationals but could be removed and also from suspected international terrorists who were UK-nationals and could not be removed'.[142] As Lord Bingham noted:

> The choice of an immigration measure to address a security problem had the inevitable result of failing adequately to address that problem (by allowing non-UK suspected terrorists to leave the country with impunity and leaving British suspected terrorists at large) while imposing the severe penalty of indefinite detention on persons who, even if reasonably suspected of having links with Al-Qaeda, may harbour no hostile intentions towards the United Kingdom.[143]

Accordingly, the House of Lords issued a declaration under section 4 of the Human Rights Act that s.23 of the 2001 Act was incompatible with Convention Rights. While

[138] See also *Saadi v Italy* (2009) 49 EHRR 30.
[139] European Convention on Human Rights, Article 15(1),.
[140] The Human Rights Act 1998 (Designated Derogation) Order 2001, SI 2001/364.
[141] Above, n.125, [29] (Lord Bingham).
[142] *ibid*, [51] (Lord Bingham).
[143] *ibid*, [43].

such a declaration does not 'affect the validity, continuing operation or enforcement' of the offending legislative provision,[144] the eventual consequence of this judicial decision was, as Walker comments, to 'dislodge a security detention regime from the panoply of immigration law',[145] since the government chose to respond to the declaration by replacing Part IV of the 2001 Act with the system of control orders examined in Section VIII of this chapter.

The principle of non-refoulement was also germane to the long-running legal saga involving the Muslim cleric Omar Othman, better known as Abu Qatada. Qatada had been detained without trial under Part IV of the 2001 Act and was later placed under a control order (see Section VIII). The UK government subsequently sought to deport Qatada to Jordan, having agreed a memorandum of understanding with the Jordanian government, which provided that he would not be subject to torture or inhuman/degrading treatment or punishment contrary to Article 3 of the European Convention. In *OO (Jordan) v Secretary of State for the Home Department*,[146] the House of Lords upheld the decisions of the Court of Appeal and the Special Immigration Appeals Commission that measures set out in the memorandum of understanding could remove the real risk (albeit, not *all* risk) of violation of Article 3 upon return to Jordan. This aspect of the decision was approved by the European Court of Human Rights.[147]

However, that court extended the non-refoulement principle to cover violations of the right to a fair trial under Article 6 of the Convention.[148] It considered that there was a real risk of Qatada being subjected to a flagrant denial of justice as a consequence of the use of torture evidence upon retrial, a conclusion which had been shared by the Court of Appeal,[149] but not the House of Lords, in the UK. In response, extensive negotiations took place between the UK and Jordanian governments, with the latter providing assurances that it would attempt to ensure that any retrial was fair. However, these were regarded as insufficient to enable deportation not to violate the principle of non-refoulement by both the Special Immigration Appeals Commission and the Court of Appeal, the latter noting that 'Torture is universally abhorred as an evil. A state cannot expel a person to another state where there is a real risk that he will be tried on the basis of evidence which there is a real possibility may have been obtained by torture'.[150] Subsequently, the

[144] Human Rights Act 1998, s.4(6).
[145] Above n.21, [7.121].
[146] [2009] UKHL 10.
[147] *Othman (Abu Qatada) v UK* (2012) 55 EHRR 1.
[148] For discussion, see C. Michaelsen, 'The Renaissance of Non-Refoulement? The Othman (Abu Qatada) Decision of the European Court of Human Rights' (2012) *International and Comparative Law Quarterly* 750.
[149] *Othman (Jordan) v Secretary of State for the Home Department* [2008] EWCA Civ 290.
[150] [2013] EWCA Civ 277, [59] (Dyson MR).

UK government concluded a mutual assistance treaty with Jordan,[151] approved by legislatures in both countries in June 2013, and Qatada agreed to return to the country. It has been estimated that the legal costs to the UK government (and, by extension, to UK taxpayers) of this series of challenges amounted to £1,716,306.[152]

VIII. ADMINISTRATIVE/EXECUTIVE MEASURES

In view of the issuing of a declaration of incompatibility in the *Belmarsh* case, the UK government decided to reconsider how best to fulfil its national security objectives while maintaining the commitment to non-refoulement to which the *Chahal* case gave rise. The outcome was the repeal of the detention provisions under Part IV of the Anti-Terrorism, Crime and Security Act 2001 and their replacement by a system of control orders under the Prevention of Terrorism Act 2005. Such orders extended to UK citizens, thus addressing one of the key deficiencies with the detention provisions which was identified in the *Belmarsh* case.

Section 1(1) of the 2005 Act establishes the control order as 'an order against an individual that imposes obligations on him for purposes connected with protecting members of the public from a risk of terrorism'. Those obligations are those considered 'necessary for purposes connected with preventing or restricting involvement by that person in terrorism-related activity'.[153] They are set out in section 1(4), which provides a lengthy catalogue, including restrictions in respect of place of residence or visitors to it; prohibition or restriction on movements; requirement to comply with prohibitions or restrictions on movements as may be imposed for a period not exceeding twenty-four hours; prohibition or restriction on the use of specified articles, substances, services or facilities; restriction with respect to work, occupation or business; restriction on associations or communications; and requirement to report to a specified person at specified times and places. In practice, many of these obligations were combined within a control order.

Orders might be of 'non-derogating' or 'derogating' type. The former, which were issued by the Home Secretary but which required permission from a court, were expected to be the norm; these expired after twelve months but might be renewed.[154] Derogating orders were those which would have such a significant impact upon the liberty of the individual that they would be incompatible with Article 5 of the

[151] *Treaty on Mutual Legal Assistance in Criminal Matters Between the United Kingdom of Great Britain and Northern Ireland and the Hashemite Kingdom of Jordan*, Cm 8612 (2013).

[152] Letter from Rt Hon Theresa May MP, Home Secretary, to the Chair of the Home Affairs Select Committee, 4 June 2013.

[153] s.1(3).

[154] s.2(4).

European Convention on Human Rights. These orders, for which there must be a notice of derogation under Article 15,[155] were issued by courts upon application by the Home Secretary. They were intended to last for six months,[156] but again, could be renewed, provided that the Home Secretary considered that derogation continued to remain necessary.[157] In practice, no orders of this latter type were in fact made under the legislation; almost fifty persons were covered by non-derogating orders during the lifetime of the measure, with a gradual shift from foreign subjects to British citizens.[158]

As with indefinite detention without trial, this strategy also proved highly controversial from a human rights perspective. Various of the Convention Rights were explored in litigation, but those which proved to have most purchase were Articles 5 (right to liberty and security of the person) and 6 (right to a fair trial). As regards the first, the House of Lords ruled in *JJ* that obligations including an eighteen-hour curfew, wearing of electronic tags, authorisation of visits, restrictions on movement beyond a 72 square kilometre radius and prohibition on meeting unauthorised persons amounted to a violation of Article 5, the court succinctly observing that the 'lives [of those subject to the control orders] were wholly regulated by the Home Office... [an] analogy with detention in an open prison was apt, save that the controlled persons did not enjoy the association with others and the access to entertainment facilities which a prisoner in an open prison would expect to enjoy'.[159] The court indicated that the entirety of the circumstances should be considered in order to establish whether there had been a deprivation of liberty: on this basis, it might be 'inappropriate to draw a sharp distinction between a period of confinement which will, and one which will not, amount to a deprivation of liberty, important though the period of daily confinement will be in any overall assessment'.[160] Nonetheless, it was suggested that a period of sixteen hours' curfew might be regarded as acceptable, although this would depend upon all of the circumstances.[161]

In light of this dictum, orders were reissued with maximum sixteen-hour curfews and with averages of thirteen hours.[162] However, in *AP*, a control order which involved a sixteen-hour curfew combined with a move to a town 150 miles from the individual's previous home in North London was held by the Supreme

155 By way of an order made under Human Rights Act 1998, s.14(1)(b).
156 s.4(8).
157 s.6.
158 See 'Q & A: Control Orders', *BBC News*, 3 January 2011.
159 [2007] UKHL 45, [24] (Lord Bingham).
160 *ibid*, [16] (Lord Bingham).
161 *ibid*, [108] (Lord Brown).
162 Walker, above n.21, [7.78].

Court to violate Article 5. Notwithstanding his observations in *JJ*, Lord Brown indicated that there was not a simple sixteen-hour cutoff point: all would depend upon the overall package of control order measures, albeit that the shorter the curfew period, the more severe the other obligations would need to be before a claim of deprivation of liberty under Article 5 could successfully be made out.[163] The judgment was one to be made on a case-by-case basis; but in this instance, the particular difficulties of the family in visiting the individual had a bearing upon compatibility with Article 5 and were deemed to tip the balance towards violation, notwithstanding that they might have been deemed proportionate restrictions under Article 8 (the right to respect for private and family life, home and correspondence).

The system of control orders was also subjected to challenge on the basis of the fairness of the process through which the material justifying the making of a control order was scrutinised, an aspect also pertinent to the discussion in Section X, as it relates in large part to the question of open justice. In *MB and AF*, the material disclosed in open control order proceedings was thin in one case and virtually non-existent in the other. The House of Lords did not consider this to constitute a violation of the limb of Article 6 of the European Convention on Human Rights, which relates to fair trial in criminal proceedings, since proceedings for the making of a control order did not involve the determination of a criminal charge. Nor was there an absolute right to disclosure of all relevant evidence even in such criminal proceedings. However, Article 6 had nonetheless been breached since neither individual had enjoyed 'such measure of procedural protection as is commensurate with the gravity of the potential consequences'.[164] The European Court of Human Rights confirmed in *A v United Kingdom* (in which it considered the *Belmarsh* case) that while it might sometimes be necessary to withhold certain evidence from the defence on public interest grounds, there must exist sufficient opportunity to challenge the allegations in question.[165] This was given effect by the House of Lords in *AF (No. 3)*, the court ruling that, although detailed provision of the evidence justifying the making of a control order is not necessary in order to meet the requirements of a fair trial under Article 6, the individual subject to the control order must be given sufficient information concerning the relevant allegations so as to be able to provide effective instructions to legal representatives in respect of those allegations.[166]

[163] [2010] UKSC 24, [3]–[4].
[164] [2007] UKHL 46, [24] (Lord Bingham).
[165] (2009) 49 EHRR 29.
[166] [2009] UKHL 28.

It might be concluded that cases such as these 'steadily chipped away at the policy on the basis that the control order breaches the subject's human rights'.[167] The system was reviewed by the incoming Coalition government in 2010, and was replaced by a system of Terrorist Prevention and Investigation Measures (TPIMs),[168] operative from January 2012. These have been viewed as 'control orders lite',[169] the range of restrictions contained in Schedule 1 to the Act being somewhat less sweeping than that in the 2005 Act, but nonetheless remaining extensive. As the human rights organisation Justice has noted, TPIM notices continue 'to have a significant impact on a person's liberty, freedom of movement, private and family life, property rights, freedom of expression and association with others',[170] but the maximum curfew which may be imposed is overnight, relocation to another part of the country without consent is not permissible, a TPIM notice may not confine an individual to a particular geographical boundary and it may not prohibit access to the Internet or other communications devices.[171] As with non-derogating control orders, TPIM notices are issued by the Home Secretary, subject to permission of a court.[172] They last for a year, renewable on one occasion,[173] although a further TPIM notice may be issued if the individual is engaged in further terrorism-related activity since the imposition of the original notice.

As at the end of November 2013, eight TPIM notices were in force, all relating to British citizens. Each of these notices had lapsed by 10 February 2014 and had not been renewed.[174] In light of this, and the fact that no new TPIM notice has been issued since October 2012, the Joint Committee on Human Rights has concluded that 'TPIMs may be withering on the vine as a counter-terrorism tool of practical utility'.[175] While the Committee did not feel able to recommend their abolition given insufficient information as to the extent of the threat posed by individuals, it recommended review of the regime early in the life of the next Parliament (*ie*

[167] Liberty, *From "War" to Law: Liberty's Response to the Coalition Government's Review of Counter-Terrorism and Security Powers 2010* (London: Liberty, 2010), 11.

[168] Terrorism Prevention and Investigation Measures Act 2011, ss.1–2.

[169] See Liberty, 'Unsafe, Unfair', http://www.liberty-human-rights.org.uk/campaigning/other-campaigns/unsafe-unfair (accessed 31 March 2014).

[170] Justice, *Terrorism Prevention and Investigation Measures Bill: Briefing for House of Lords Report Stage* (London: Justice, 2011), 7.

[171] *Terrorism Prevention and Investigation Measures Bill: ECHR Memorandum by the Home Office* (2011), [17 (h)].

[172] ss.2, 6.

[173] s. 5.

[174] See 'Terrorism prevention regime not being used', *The Guardian*, 28 March 2014.

[175] Joint Committee on Human Rights, *Post-Legislative Scrutiny: Terrorism Prevention and Investigation Measures Act 2011*, HL Paper 113/HC 1014 (2013–14), [80].

subsequent to the UK general election of May 2015) and prior to the five-year renewal date specified in the legislation.[176]

IX. ROLE OF MILITARY AND EXTRA-TERRITORIAL COUNTER-TERRORISM ACTIVITIES

A. *Military Courts and Detention*

The UK has always shown a preference for utilising criminal laws and criminal justice processes to respond to terrorist activity wherever possible. The consequence is that there has been no significant appetite to utilise the military forces or military courts in counter-terrorism strategy. Of course, this position should not be overstated: the legal framework outlined in this chapter is testament to the perceived need for 'special' laws in specific circumstances. Nonetheless, even during 'the Troubles', primacy was accorded to processes which resembled those utilised in 'ordinary criminal cases' as far as possible.[177] This stands in contrast to the approach adopted in the Republic of Ireland, where Article 38 of the Constitution envisages the establishment of 'special courts' and where a Special Criminal Court, which, *inter alia*, tries offences connected to terrorism, contained military personnel up until 1972.

It follows that the UK does not treat terrorists as combatants in war. Attempts were made to claim prisoner of war status during 'the Troubles': these were resisted by the UK government, although it came to accept that certain international standards (including aspects of the Geneva Conventions) should apply to those imprisoned.[178] More recently, the notion of a 'war on terror' has also been rejected: although in the immediate aftermath of 9/11 Prime Minister Tony Blair declared that the UK was 'at war with terrorism',[179] ministers subsequently stepped back from this position, International Development Secretary Hilary Benn claiming in 2007 that 'in the UK we do not use the phrase "war on terror" because we can't win by military means alone and because this isn't one organized enemy with a clear identity and a coherent set of objectives'.[180] This refutation of a war model applies not only as a matter of political rhetoric but also as a basis for the approach taken under law.

[176] s.21.

[177] For the 'Diplock courts', see section III.

[178] See A. Roberts, 'The laws of war in the war on terror', in F. Borch and P. Wilson (eds.), *International Law and the War on Terror* (Newport: Naval War College International Law Studies Volume 79, 2003) 188.

[179] 'Britain "at war with terrorism"', *BBC News*, 16 September 2001.

[180] 'Briton criticises US's use of "war on terror"', *New York Times*, 17 April 2007. See also D. Miliband, '"War on Terror" was wrong', *The Guardian*, 15 January 2009.

B. *The Extra-Territorial Treatment of Citizens Suspected of Terrorism*

Reference will be made in Section X to litigation involving the UK resident Binyam Mohamed. Mohamed was, in fact, one of seven UK citizens or residents who had been detained in Guantanamo Bay or elsewhere and who claimed damages from the UK government on the basis that the British security services had colluded in torture and/or rendition. In fact, these claims never reached court: the UK government reached an out-of-court settlement with the former detainees in November 2010: the details were confidential, but the figure for Mohamed was rumoured to be in the region of £1 million.[181] From the government's perspective, the settlement avoided the expense and potential risk to security of open court hearings. The allegations were to have been the subject of a judicial inquiry, but this was postponed in 2012 pending further police investigations.[182]

Also germane under this heading are cases in which citizens have sought to utilise the legal process to challenge inaction on the part of the UK government in response to their detention by another state. In *R (on the application of Abassi) v Secretary of State for Foreign and Commonwealth Affairs*,[183] it was claimed that the UK government had failed to seek or require the U.S. government to take various steps to ameliorate the position of the detainee, ranging from release to access to a lawyer. The court held that while no *duty* to protect the citizen could be established, inaction on the state's part could, in principle, be judicially reviewed if it was unlawful (for example, if it failed to meet published standards of conduct), although in this instance the government had not acted unlawfully as it had considered the detainee's request for assistance and made representations to the U.S. government in respect of British citizens held in Guantanamo Bay. A similar challenge failed in *R (on the application of Al Rawi) v Secretary of State for Foreign and Commonwealth Affairs*, the court observing that 'the law accords to the executive an exceptionally broad margin of discretion' in cases such as this which involved the traditionally non-justiciable areas of foreign relations and national security.[184]

C. *Extra-Territorial Terrorism Law Enforcement*

As a member state of the European Union, the UK benefits from a number of mechanisms which may be of assistance extra-territorially in the fight against terrorism.

[181] See 'Guantanamo Bay detainees to be paid compensation by UK government', *The Guardian*, 16 November 2010.

[182] See 'UK inquiry into rendition and torture collusion scrapped', *BBC News*, 19 January 2012.

[183] [2002] EWCA Civ 1598.

[184] [2006] EWCA Civ 1279, [148] (Laws LJ).

Under the Schengen Convention,[185] information is maintained on individuals who are being kept under surveillance for purposes of crime prevention or national security within the EU, and cross-border surveillance operations are permitted. A European Arrest Warrant enables terrorist suspects to be extradited to face trial in the UK (or extradited from the UK).[186] The National Crime Agency is the point of contact for Interpol and Europol: the mandate of the latter includes terrorism, but it acts mainly as an information-gathering, processing and sharing organisation.[187] Joint Investigation Teams enable cross-border police operations to be undertaken.[188] The overall effectiveness of these mechanisms is questionable: O'Neill has observed that 'it is difficult to establish, in this highly secretive area of operation, exactly how the structure works, and how its flaws inhibit cross-border counter-terrorist policing and intelligence led operations'.[189]

As noted in Section VII, Abu Qatada was eventually extradited from the UK to face trial on terror charges in Jordan. The agreement reached between the two countries contained assurances that the court would contain no military appointees as well as provisions precluding the use of evidence obtained by torture. However, the eventual trial was conducted by two civilian judges and one military judge, leading Qatada to claim that he had been 'betrayed' and to state that he did not recognise the court's jurisdiction.[190]

X. SECRECY

Reference has already been made on several occasions in this chapter to instances in which legal provisions preserve some degree of secrecy in the treatment of suspected terrorists. Section III covered the anonymity of witnesses in terrorist trials; in Section V, the possibility of the Proscribed Organisations Appeal Commission precluding information from being disclosed was noted; in Section VII, the possibility of closed hearings before the Special Immigration Appeals Commission Tribunal was addressed; and in Section VIII, litigation on fair process in the making of control orders was discussed.

185 Convention Implementing the Schengen Agreement of 14 June 1985 (1990). See Crime (International Cooperation) Act 2003.

186 See Council Framework Directive of 13 June 2002 on the European Arrest Warrant and the surrender procedures between member states, 2002/584/JHA, [2002] OJ L190/1 and Extradition Act 2003.

187 See M. O'Neill, 'A critical analysis of the EU legal provisions on terrorism' (2008) 20 *Terrorism and Political Violence* 26, 34.

188 See Convention established by the Council in accordance with Article 34 of the Treaty on European Union on mutual assistance in criminal matters between the member states of the European Union (2000), [2000] OJ C197/1, Article 13.

189 Above n.187, 41.

190 See 'Abu Qatada pleads not guilty to terror charges', *BBC News*, 10 December 2013.

Consideration should also be given to the law relating to public interest immunity (PII), which permits suppression of evidence in certain instances. In cases involving terrorist activity, a PII claim will be made by a minister by way of a certificate setting out the nature of the damage to the public interest which would be caused by any disclosure of material. The claim is then assessed by the court, which will seek to balance the public interest in the fair administration of justice (on which basis the courts should have full access to all relevant material) against the need to maintain confidentiality in view of the fact that disclosure would cause real damage to the public interest. In criminal cases, there is a 'golden rule' of full disclosure of material by the prosecution, but if the defendant's interest can be protected without disclosure, or by limited disclosure, this may be permissible provided that there is the minimum of derogation from full disclosure and the trial process remains fair to the defendant.[191] This may mean that a successful claim of public interest immunity necessitates termination of the prosecution.

The position in civil cases was extensively explored in the litigation relating to Binyam Mohamed, who had been detained in Guantanamo Bay subsequent to rendition from Pakistan to Morocco and who claimed tortious damages against the UK government for alleged collusion in unlawful treatment by the CIA. Here, material possessed by the UK government had been transmitted by U.S. authorities on a basis of no further disclosure. The High Court's willingness to give effect to secrecy claims by the government was manifest in the issuance of a closed judgment based upon hearings in private with a special advocate present to represent Mohamed. However, the Foreign Secretary also signed a PII certificate in which he made reference to potential damage to the UK's relationship with the United States if the material was disclosed to Mohamed's lawyers, and requested the removal of seven paragraphs of the first open judgment delivered by the High Court. Once the majority of the material had been made available to the individual's legal team in connection with *habeas corpus* proceedings in the United States, the only remaining issue was the redaction of the seven paragraphs, on the basis that 'the [U.S.] Government will re-evaluate its intelligence sharing relationship with the [UK] with the real risk that it would reduce the intelligence provided ... and this would seriously prejudice the national security of the [UK]'.[192] However, once the relevant information had also entered the public domain as a consequence of the decision of the District Court for the District of Columbia in *Farhi Saeed Bin Mohammed v Barack Obama*,[193] there could be no reason for the continued redaction, the Court of Appeal observing

[191] *R v H and C* [2004] UKHL 3.

[192] *R (on the application of Mohamed) v Secretary of State for Foreign and Commonwealth Affairs* [2010] EWCA Civ 65, [87] (Lord Neuberger MR).

[193] Civil Action No. 05-1347 (GK) (19 November 2009).

that: 'the principle of open justice represents an element of democratic accountability, and the vigorous manifestation of the principle of freedom of expression. Ultimately it supports the rule of law itself. Where the court is satisfied that the executive has misconducted itself, or acted so as to facilitate misconduct by others, all these strands, democratic accountability, freedom of expression, and the rule of law are closely engaged'.[194]

A PII claim may not always be feasible. In *Al Rawi v Security Service*, a further civil claim for damages arising out of alleged mistreatment at Guantanamo Bay and elsewhere, there were 250,000 potentially relevant documents, with potential PII claims in respect of 140,000 of these; the process of determining in respect of which documents PII might be claimed could have taken three years.[195] For this reason, the Security Service argued that, under its inherent powers to regulate its own procedures, the court should substitute a closed material procedure, utilising special advocates, in place of the conventional PII exercise. The Supreme Court declined to take such a course of action, considering that any extension to the existing processes for closed material (as set out, for example, in the Prevention of Terrorism Act 2005 and the Counter-Terrorism Act 2008) was a matter for Parliament, not the judiciary. Such a step has been taken: closed material procedures have been extended into civil litigation by way of Part 2 of the Justice and Security Act 2013. This development is undoubtedly controversial – it has been described as 'anathema to our long-standing common law protection of open, equal and adversarial justice'[196] – but the independent reviewer of terrorism legislation has indicated that he considers that 'in a small but indeterminate category of national-security-related claims, both for judicial review of executive decisions and for civil damages … it is preferable that the option of a closed material procedure – for all its inadequacies – should exist'.[197]

XI. CONCLUSION

As noted in the introduction to this chapter, responding to terrorism is not a novel experience for government or lawmakers in the UK. The period since the enactment of the Terrorism Act 2000 has, however, seen an unprecedented burst of legislative activity, leading the independent reviewer of terrorism legislation to remark that the country possesses 'some of the most extensive and effective counter-terrorism laws in the world'.[198]

[194] Above n.192, [39] (Lord Judge LCJ).

[195] [2011] UKSC 34, [5} (Lord Dyson).

[196] Justice, *Justice and Security Bill (Part 2): Closed Material Procedures; House of Commons Report Stage Briefing* (London: Justice, 2013), [5].

[197] David Anderson QC, cited in Human Rights Joint Committee, *The Justice and Security Green Paper*, HL Paper 286/HC 1777 (2010–12), [73].

[198] David Anderson QC, Press Release, 27 June 2012.

The preceding analysis should serve to demonstrate that the accuracy of the first part of this statement cannot be called into question. Whether the *mode* of legal intervention is best suited to pursuit of the state's objectives in this context is, however, a moot point. The UK possesses a highly complex patchwork of counter-terrorism legislation, an outcome which was not envisaged by those involved in enactment of the 2000 statute. This was 'designed as a consolidating provision, drawing together previous anti-terror laws into a single code that would not need require renewal or re-enactment',[199] although it is notable that much terrorist activity has continued to be dealt with through 'normal' laws, especially criminal laws.

However, the capacity of the 2000 Act to function as a counter-terrorism code was almost immediately scuppered by the 9/11 attacks and the consequent realisation that the primary terrorist threat to the UK lay not with the relatively familiar, albeit destructive, tactics of Northern Irish paramilitaries, but with 'third millennium' terrorism,[200] exemplified by Al-Qaeda. The upshot was two pieces of hastily enacted and poorly deliberated pieces of legislation, the Anti-Terrorism, Crime and Security Act 2001 and Prevention of Terrorism Act 2005; it is surely significant that the central counter-terrorism strategies advanced by each of these (respectively, indefinite detention without trial and control orders) were, in effect, eventually dismantled by the judiciary on human rights grounds. By contrast, Walker evaluates the Terrorism Act 2006 and the Counter-Terrorism Act 2008 as premised upon a 'more calculated approach',[201] reflecting a preference for criminalisation of terrorist activity as distinct from utilisation of immigration or executive measures. Nevertheless, when these are considered alongside the three preceding statutes and the subsequent Terrorism Prevention and Investigation Measures Act 2011, not to mention the array of relevant criminal laws, it is readily apparent that 'counter-terrorism law in the UK is bitty, messy and hard for even its practitioners to comprehend as a whole'.[202] At best, this results in 'untidiness';[203] at worst, it violates the principles of accessibility and clarity which lie at the heart of the rule of law.

As for the operational 'effectiveness' of UK counter-terrorism law, this is more questionable. In part, this may also be a consequence of the unsystematic nature of the legislative framework, which can make it problematic to select the most appropriate response from the many which are available to pre-empt or punish terrorist activity. However, more generally, Walker argues that 'the anti-terrorism laws are often largely

[199] A. Horne, 'Reviewing Counter-Terrorism Legislation' in A. Mellows-Facer (ed.), *Key Issues for the New Parliament 2010* (London: House of Commons Library), 90.

[200] See C. Walker, 'Political Violence and Commercial Risk' (2003) 56 *Current Legal Problems* 531, 534.

[201] Above n.21, [1.157].

[202] D. Anderson QC, *The Terrorism Acts in 2011* (London: The Stationery Office, 2012), [11.2].

[203] *ibid*, [11.3]

peripheral in effect'.[204] It is difficult to offer empirical evidence to support or contradict this statement, although one might note (as does Walker) that the wide range of legislative powers did not prevent the 7/7 bombings in London in 2005, and that the threat level to the UK from international terrorism has never been less than 'substantial', the third highest level – meaning that an attack is a 'strong possibility' – since the alert states were made available to the public from 1 August 2006.[205] Certainly, the argument can be made that the extensive post 9/11 legislative activity has created a 'new suspect community' of Muslims, with attention having shifted away from the 'old suspect community' of the Irish population.[206] If this view is accepted, UK counter-terrorism laws may have counter-productive outcomes, consequent upon:

> a corrosive effect on the relations between Muslim communities and the police. Within this context, the conditions for radicalization are being fomented and the 'flow of information' necessary for effective counter-terrorism policing has been jeopardized. Thus, the very powers that are supposed to promote security are serving to undermine it, whilst Muslim communities continue to endure the spectre of state suspicion.[207]

Beyond the immediate context of its (perhaps double-edged) impact upon security within the UK, the legal framework for counter-terrorism has played a significant role as an arena in which some recalibration of the UK's constitutional order is taking place. In particular, human rights legislation appears to have accorded the judiciary a clear rationale for control over the use of counter-terrorism powers by the executive branch in a manner which does not tally with traditional understandings of the role of the 'least dangerous branch',[208] especially in a system where the principle of the sovereignty of Parliament makes judicial review of legislation constitutionally impermissible. As noted previously,[209] such judicial intervention has often been a source of frustration to politicians, but other – perhaps more objective – observers have welcomed it: for example, the independent reviewer of terrorism legislation has argued that '[court] judgments have in a number of respects affirmed the importance of liberty and due process without, so far as I can judge, causing an unacceptable increase in the level of risk'.[210] Indeed, in more sanguine moments, even government ministers have acknowledged the importance of preserving the

[204] Above, n.21, [1.164].

[205] See https://www.mi5.gov.uk/home/the-threats/terrorism/threat-levels.html (accessed 31 March 2014).

[206] See P. Hillyard, *Suspect Community: People's Experiences of the Prevention of Terrorism Acts in Britain* (London: Pluto Press, 2013).

[207] C. Pantazis and S. Pemberton, 'From the "old" to the "new" suspect community: examining the impacts of recent UK counter-terrorism legislation' (2009) 49 *British Journal of Criminology* 646, 662.

[208] The phrase is that of Alexander Hamilton, but it has been deployed in the UK context: see Lord Steyn, 'The least dangerous branch of government' [1997] *Public Law* 84.

[209] See especially section VII.

[210] Anderson, above n.202, [11.5].

rule of law in the face of the threat of terrorism,[211] suggesting that conflict between the executive and the judiciary in this field is neither unhealthy nor inevitable.

Perhaps the most striking distinction between the legislative responses to 'the Troubles' and those to contemporary international terrorism is the degree of permanence characterising the current legal framework. Counter-terrorism laws are no longer the 'temporary provisions' envisaged by the original Prevention of Terrorism Acts; they are abiding features of the legal and political landscape in the UK. As Walker notes, this aspect is 'increasingly unremarkable',[212] and is common to many countries. It may simply be seen as a reflection of the pervasive and insidious nature of risk in modern society.[213] Of course, this is not to say that the state is entitled to ride roughshod over freedoms and rights in order to pursue a goal of minimising harm to society as a whole. At times, the UK government has veered in this direction, but it has generally been reined back, and there is recent evidence of a 'cautious rebalancing in favour of liberty' as the threat has diminished.[214] In sum, it may be a characteristically British understatement to say of UK counter-terrorism law that 'it could have been much worse',[215] but it is submitted this pithy evaluation nonetheless rather neatly captures the situation.

XII. POSTSCRIPT

The Counter-Terrorism and Security Act 2015[216] received Royal Assent on 12 February 2015. This new addition to the UK's patchwork quilt of legislation followed the raising of the national terrorist threat level to 'severe' in August 2014 and is designed, in particular, to address concerns about persons leaving the country to fight for terrorist organisations or engage in terrorist activity overseas (especially in Syria and Iraq) and subsequently returning to the UK. However, it also altered and supplemented the previously described statutory framework in a number of ways.

The first of these goals is pursued primarily through Parts 1 and 4 of the Act. These respectively set out measures for temporary restrictions on travel (including search for, seizure of and retention of passports[217] and imposition of temporary exclusion orders to control the return to the UK of a British citizen reasonably suspected of involvement in terrorism-related activity outside the UK[218]) and for border and transport security (including powers to require operators of aircraft, ships or trains

[211] See *eg* Miliband, above n.180.
[212] Above n.21, [1.158].
[213] See U. Beck, 'Living in the world risk society' (2006) 35 *Economy and Society* 329.
[214] Anderson, above n.202, 4.
[215] *ibid*, [11.4].
[216] c. 6.
[217] s.1 and Schedule 1.
[218] ss. 2-14

to seek authority to carry certain persons on outbound or inbound journeys[219] and enhanced powers to obtain passenger, crew and service information[220]).

Elsewhere, Part 2 of the Act bolsters the TPIM regime (which, as noted in Section VIII of this chapter, had seemed to be flagging), most notably by enabling the Secretary of State to require an individual to reside in a locality up to 200 miles from the individual's normal residence without the latter's agreement.[221] Part 3 provides powers to require Internet service providers to collect and retain data that would enable identification of the user of a particular internet protocol address,[222] while Part 5 contains preventive measures designed to stop individuals becoming terrorists or supporting terrorism. To this end, it creates a duty for specified bodies – including local government, educational establishments, health bodies and police forces[223] – to have due regard in the exercise of their functions of the need to prevent persons from being drawn into terrorism.[224] Each local authority is also obliged to establish a panel to provide support for those identified by police as being vulnerable to being drawn into terrorism.[225]

The legislation has been criticised by civil liberties organisations, being described by one prominent group as 'continu[ing] the discredited trend of unnecessary and unjust blank cheque powers that have the potential to undermine long-term security'.[226] This might suggest that the 'cautious rebalancing' in the direction of liberty identified by the independent review of terrorism legislation in 2012[227] has come to an abrupt halt in the face of an apparently resurgent terrorist threat to the UK. It is, of course, as yet too early to evaluate whether this legislation will prove any more effective in countering that threat than the statutes that preceded it, and it remains to be seen how the judiciary will respond when called upon to consider the powers that it confers upon the executive. However, what can readily be concluded is that the UK's counter-terrorism framework continues to be characterised by exceptional 'untidiness',[228] as legislation continues to be heaped upon legislation.

219 ss.22-24.
220 s.25 and Schedule 5.
221 s.16.
222 s. 21
223 Schedule 6
224 s.26
225 ss.36-41.
226 Liberty, *Liberty's Second Reading Briefing on the Counter-Terrorism and Security Bill in the House of Lords* (London: Liberty, 2015), 3.
227 Above n.214.
228 See above, n.203

7

Switzerland

Bertrand Perrin and Julien Gafner

I. INTRODUCTION

The prevention of international terrorism has been one of the major concerns of the Swiss authorities for several years.[1] There is no doubt, however, that the terrorist attacks in New York on 11 September 2001 triggered a reinforcement of the methods used to prevent the financial and logistical support, and the propaganda, of terrorist groups and acts.[2]

Switzerland is a party to the United Nations (UN) sectoral conventions and additional protocols on the suppression of terrorism,[3] as well as the topical agreements of the Council of Europe and European Union.[4] It has also concentrated on applying the United Nations Security Council resolutions, particularly Resolution 1373 (2001).[5] As a member of the Financial Action Task Force (FATF), Switzerland also focuses on implementing FATF Recommendations on combating money laundering and terrorist financing. The legislative means available to the Swiss

1 This article was published for the first time, in French, in Lukas Heckendorn Urscheler (éd.), *Swiss Reports Presented at the XIXth Intenationial Congres of Comparative Law*, 2014, Schulthess (www.schulthess.com). The authors thank the editor for his permission.

2 Letter Dated 19 December 2001 from the Chairman of the Security Council Committee Established Pursuant to Resolution 1373 (2001) Addressed to the President of the Security Council, S/2001/1224, p. 4.

3 GAFNER Julien, *L'incrimination du financement du terrorisme*, Schulthess, Geneva/Zurich/Basel 2006, pp. XVI *et seq*.; Swiss international law website: http://www.admin.ch/opc/fr/classified-compilation/international.html; United Nations website: http://treaties.un.org/Pages/DB.aspx?path=DB/studies/page2_en.xml&clang=_en (accessed 6 January 2014).

4 GAFNER Julien, *op. cit.*, note 3, pp. XVI *et seq*; Swiss international law website: http://www.admin.ch/opc/fr/classified-compilation/international.html; Council of Europe website: http://www.coe.int/t/dlapil/codexter/conventions_EN.asp (accessed 6 January 2014); European Union website: http://eur-lex.europa.eu/en/index.htm (accessed 6 January 2014).

5 Federal Council message of 26 June 2002 regarding the International Conventions for the suppression of financing of terrorism and for the suppression of terrorist bombings and regarding the amendment of the Criminal Code and adjustment of other federal laws, *Feuille fédérale* (FF) 2002 V pp. 5019–5021, available at http://www.admin.ch/bundesrecht/00568/index.html?lang=fr (accessed 6 January 2014).

authorities are in keeping with an international co-operation approach, which is essential to the prosecution and punishment of terrorist behaviour.

Generally speaking, there are two aspects of substantive law that need to be mentioned. From the criminal law aspect, only the financing of terrorism has been made a specific offence, while the terrorist act itself is punishable by the mainstream provisions of the Swiss Criminal Code (CrC),[6] such as premeditated murder or hostage taking. On the other hand, in administrative and financial law, Switzerland has a set of rules and measures aimed at effectively combating the financing of terrorism. These measures are also deployed to protect the Swiss financial market from being used for any criminal purposes. Indeed, the Swiss authorities have been much more active on the financial and logistical levels when it comes to the surveillance and investigation of certain individuals and groups.[7] At the moment, Switzerland and the Swiss population do not seem to be subject to concrete terrorist threats in terms of the risks of attacks.[8]

These legal bases define the framework of Switzerland's fight against terrorism. This chapter aims to provide a sufficiently detailed and comprehensive insight to enable a comparative study with other countries.

We will first elucidate the objective and subjective elements (*actus reus* and *mens rea*) of the offence of financing terrorism (Sec. 260^{quinquies} CrC), which will bring us, indirectly, to examine the definition of terrorism in Swiss legislation. We will show the penalties that can be imposed by the courts on both natural persons and legal entities. We will mention the criminal justice authorities responsible for prosecution and judgment, and will then focus on the problems of embargoes, the prevention of money laundering, immigration measures, military law and secrecy in the context of criminal proceedings.

II. TERRORISM AND ITS FINANCING UNDER SWISS CRIMINAL LAW

A. *Criminalisation in Swiss Legislation*

In its Message of 26 June 2002, particularly regarding the International Convention for the Suppression of the Financing of Terrorism, the Swiss Federal Council recommended the adoption of two criminal standards, one punishing terrorism and

6 Recueil systématique du droit suisse (RS) 311.0, available at http://www.admin.ch/bundesrecht/00586/index.html?lang=fr.

7 Federal Intelligence Service (FIS), *Switzerland's Security – Situation Report 2013*, published on 29 April 2013, Berne, available at http://www.vbs.admin.ch/internet/vbs/fr/home/documentation/publication/snd_publ.html (accessed 6 January 2014).

8 *Ibid.*

the other its financing.[9] Parliament, however, chose not to include a general standard on terrorism in the Swiss Criminal Code. It argued that the existing penalties for violent offences were already sufficiently severe and could be used to effectively combat terrorist acts.[10]

The financing of terrorism, on the other hand, was made an independent offence under Section 260^{quinquies} CrC,[11] which now includes the definition of the act of terrorism as follows:

1. A person who collects or provides funds with a view to financing a violent crime that is intended to intimidate the public or to coerce a state or international organisation into carrying out or not carrying out an act shall be liable to imprisonment for a term not exceeding five years or to a fine.
2. If the person merely acknowledges the possibility that the funds may be used to finance terrorism, he does not commit an offence under this section.
3. The act does not constitute the financing of a terrorist offence if it is carried out with a view to establishing or re-establishing a democratic regime or a state governed by the rule of law or with a view to exercising or safeguarding human rights.
4. Paragraph 1 does not apply if the financing is intended to support acts that do not violate the rules of international law on the conduct of armed conflicts.

As we mentioned earlier, the following sections will deal with the concepts of terrorism and its financing. We will then expand on the theme from the prosecution aspect.

B. *The Concept of Terrorism in Swiss Criminal Law*

a. Essential Elements

Sec. 260^{quinquies}(1) CrC defines terrorism as 'a violent crime that is intended to intimidate the public or to coerce a state or an international organisation into carrying out or not carrying out an act'. We will examine what should be understood by a violent crime[12] and what constitutes intimidation or coercion.

[9] FF 2002 V p. 5014; executive summary 02.052 of the Federal Assembly on the ratification of the United Nations Conventions on the suppression of financing of terrorism and the suppression of terrorist bombings, p. 2.

[10] Letter Dated 2 October 2003 from the Chairman of the Security Council Committee Established Pursuant to Resolution 1373 (2001) Concerning Counter-terrorism Addressed to the President of the Security Council, 6 October 2003, S/2003/967, p5.

[11] Entered into force on 1 October 2003.

[12] The French text mentions 'an act of criminal violence'. However, it is more correct to use the term 'violent crime', as was the case in the Swiss Federal Council draft. It is the act that is criminal in nature, not the violence.

VIOLENT CRIME. For an offence to be qualified as terrorist, there must first be a serious felony committed involving the use of violence.[13] Under Swiss law, a felony is an offence that carries a custodial sentence of more than three years (Sec. 10(2) CrC).[14]

Violent acts can fall into any one of three categories of offences in the Swiss Criminal Code, although it should be noted that the use of force, i.e., a physical action, is not a necessary condition,[15] since the propagation of a dangerous virus, for example, could constitute a case to which the provision applies:[16]

- Behaviour directed against individuals, such as intentional homicide (Sec. 111 CrC), murder (Sec. 112 CrC), or assault (Sec. 122 CrC)
- Destruction of property involving a real and serious danger to life and limb, and particularly the use, with criminal intent, of explosives or toxic gases (Sec. 224 CrC) or the transmission of human diseases (Sec. 231 CrC)
- Infringement of freedom with a real risk of causing grievous bodily harm, such as false imprisonment and abduction (Secs. 183 and 184 CrC) or hostage taking (Sec. 185 CrC)

The terrorist act may also fall within the offences set out in Sec. 260bis (acts in preparation of an offence) and Sec. 260ter CrC (participation in or support of a criminal organisation).[17]

INTIMIDATION OR COERCION. The violent crime in question, or the unlawful use of force, must also be such as to intimidate the population or coerce a state or an international organisation into carrying out, or refraining from carrying out, an act. It therefore involves particularly serious violence, specific to the terrorist intent.[18] Although we can clearly qualify the Madrid train bombings on 11 March 2004 as being of a terrorist nature, the qualification of the act in other cases, such as the

[13] FF 2002 V p. 5062.

[14] There are three categories of offences in Swiss criminal law: felonies, misdemeanours (punished by imprisonment not exceeding three years or a fine; Sec. 10(3) CrC), and petty offences or 'contraventions' (punished by a fine of up to CHF 10,000, Secs. 103 and 106(1) CrC).

[15] PERRIN Bertrand, 'L'incrimination du financement du terrorisme en droits canadien et suisse', *Revue générale de droit* (Ottawa), pp. 213–65, No. 1, Vol. 42, 2012, p. 230 ; GAFNER Julien, *op. cit.*, note 2, pp. 30–3.

[16] CASSANI Ursula, 'Le train de mesures contre le financement du terrorisme: une loi nécessaire?' *Revue suisse de droit des affaires*, No. 6-2003, pp. 293, 298.

[17] By way of example, participation in a criminal organisation is liable to imprisonment of five years, and murder is liable to imprisonment for life or for a term of no less than ten years. The provisions of the Swiss Criminal Code, some examples of which are given here, reflect the list of punishable acts in Art. 2(1) of the International Convention of 9 December 1999 for the Suppression of the Financing of Terrorism.

[18] CASSANI Ursula, *op. cit.*, note 16, p. 299; GAFNER Julien, *op. cit.*, note 3, p. 32.

throwing of Molotov cocktails into government administrative buildings,[19] may be less clear-cut.

The intimidation must target a population, that is, a significant number of people, but not necessarily the whole population.[20] In other words, it involves an indefinite number of people and not just one individual.[21] The term 'intimidation' means instilling a climate of fear that arouses concern in a number of people that they will themselves become victims of an attack, thereby giving rise to a feeling of insecurity within the community.[22]

Alternatively, or concurrently with the intimidation of the population, the purpose of the violent crime specified in Sec. 260quinquies(1) CrC may be to coerce a state or an international organisation, or one of its bodies. It is not sufficient that the coercion be used against a public official as an individual.[23]

The purpose of the coercion must either be proclaimed or be known as being a general demand of the terrorist organisation in question. The claims themselves do not necessarily have to be unlawful (e.g., the desire to obtain a region's independence from the central state); it is the means used in attempting to achieve the goals that are.[24] Moreover, under Swiss law, the terrorist act does not have to be committed in the name of a political, religious or ideological cause or objective.[25]

CONCLUSION. As regards terrorism within the meaning of Swiss law, the violent crime may be committed against property or persons, with the use or with the threat of the use of physical force, the determining factor being the creation of a feeling of fear or insecurity and/or an effect causing political destabilisation within a state or international organisation. Swiss legislation has thus adopted a general and progressive definition of terrorism, which leaves it to the court to decide, on the circumstances of the individual case, whether or not the criteria of 260quinquies(1) CrC have been fulfilled.

19 FORSTER Marc, 'Zur Abgrenzung zwischen Terroristen und militanten "politischen" Widerstandskämpfern im internationalen Strafrecht: Am Beispiel des serbisch-kosovo-albanischen Bürgerkrieges', *Revue de la Société des juristes bernois*, pp. 213 *et seq.*, 2005, pp. 215, 237.

20 The word 'population' should be understood in the same way as in Sec. 258 CrC (threats causing fear and alarm among the general public).

21 FF 2002 V p. 5063.

22 *Ibid.*

23 The concept of 'international organisation' concerns intergovernmental organisations and those created by other public sector entities. It also includes organisations for the promotion of regional economic integration, such as the European Union. This definition is given in Sec. 322septies CrC, punishing bribery of foreign public officials, cf. FAVRE Christian, PELLET Marc, STOUDMANN Patrick, *Code pénal annoté*, Bis et Ter, Lausanne 2011, note on Sec. 322septies CrC, p. 760; PERRIN Bertrand, *La répression de la corruption d'agents publics étrangers en droit pénal suisse. Étude de l'article 322septies du Code pénal et de ses enjeux procéduraux*, Helbing Lichtenhahn, Basel 2008, pp. 154–6.

24 FF 2002 V pp. 5063–4.

25 PERRIN Bertrand, *op. cit.*, note 15, pp. 232, 253.

C. *Concept of Financing Terrorism in Swiss Criminal Law (Sec. 260quinquies CrC)*

a. Introduction

The Swiss Criminal Code, in Sec. 260quinquies, provides penalties for the offence of financing terrorism. This subsection aims to set out the objective and subjective conditions of this provision. Later, in Section V, we will see the rules that apply under administrative and financial law, which are intended to prevent the use of the Swiss economic and banking system for terrorist purposes.

b. Objective Elements (*actus reus*)

The objective elements of the offence under Sec. 260quinquies(1) CrC are the terrorist act, which we have just defined, and the collection and provision of funds. With regard to the latter concept, derived from Art. 1(1) of the International Convention of 9 December 1999 for the Suppression of the Financing of Terrorism,[26] it corresponds to the concept of 'assets' defined in Sec. 70 CrC in respect of forfeiture. It involves any pecuniary benefit, and the definition includes tangibles, such as cash or precious stones.[27] It is irrelevant whether the funds are from a lawful or unlawful source.[28]

To collect funds means to gather assets, to amass them for a future use, without a transfer being required.[29] The provision of funds corresponds to the transfer of such funds, resulting from the offender's ability to transfer the power of disposal over the funds to a third party and thereby to support that third party materially. The transfer of actual ownership in the funds is not required.[30]

The administration of assets also falls within the scope of Sec. 260quinquies(1) CrC when its purpose is to enable the use of funds that are intended to serve terrorist objectives.[31] This concept includes management, deposit or any other action that enables or facilitates access to resources that are to be allocated to such purposes.[32]

[26] According to this Convention, the 'funds' may be assets of every kind, whether tangible or intangible, movable or immovable, including claims.

[27] PERRIN Bertrand, *op. cit.*, note 14, p. 238, and cited references; CORBOZ Bernard, *Les infractions en droit suisse*, Vol. II, Staempfli, Berne 2010, N. 5–8 *ad* art. 260quinquies CrC; DUPUIS Michel, GELLER Bernard, MONNIER Gilles, MOREILLON Laurent, PIGUET Christophe, BETTEX Christian, STOLL Daniel, *Petit Commentaire – Code pénal*, Helbing Lichtenhahn, Basel 2012, N. 8 *ad* art. 260quinquies CrC.

[28] FF 2002 V p. 5026.

[29] PERRIN Bertrand, *op. cit.*, note 15, p. 238.

[30] PERRIN Bertrand, *op. cit.*, note 15, p. 238; DUPUIS Michel *et al.*, *op. cit.*, note 27, N. 14–15 *ad* art. 260quinquies CrC.

[31] FF 2002 V p. 5065.

[32] GAFNER Julien, *op. cit.*, note 3, p. 201.

There is no need for a causal relationship between the funds provided and the commission of a crime by the terrorist organisation or for the funds to be actually used for terrorist purposes. Swiss lawmakers have therefore stopped short of considering the offence of financing terrorism as an appendage of the terrorist act.[33]

c. Subjective Essential Elements (*mens rea*)

The financing of terrorism is an intentional offence. Sec. 260^{quinquies}(2) CrC contains a specific element of some importance – recklessness in itself is not sufficient. This means that a person does not commit an offence if he or she merely acknowledges or accepts the possibility that the funds in question may be used to finance terrorism. Under Swiss law, this concept implies that the offender must have had the financing of terrorism as an objective and not merely accepted this possibility should it materialise.[34] Indeed, should the financing of terrorism be an offence in the case of recklessness, everyone who contemplated and accepted the serious risk that some of the funds donated for humanitarian purposes would be used for terrorism[35] – for example, transporting and distributing provisions or funding an educational project in a territory dominated by terrorist groups – could be convicted.

A strict and literal interpretation of Sec. 260^{quinquies} CrC would be that only the financial support of a specific terrorist act may be punished.[36] However, a broader approach would be that this provision is aimed at persons who act with the intention of financing one or more acts of terrorism. This interpretation is justifiable since no causal relationship is required between the act and its financing, and it is not essential that the funds actually be used or a terrorist act actually be committed or attempted.[37] Furthermore, the Swiss Federal Council deemed it necessary to require evidence that the offender's objective was indeed to encourage the carrying out of terrorist operations;[38] this should be understood from the standpoint of overall financial support and not just support for a single act.

33 FF 2002 V pp. 5065 and 5066.

34 PERRIN Bertrand, *op. cit.*, note 15, p. 254; Sec. 12(2) CrC.

35 CASSANI Ursula, *op. cit.*, note 16, p. 297.

36 PERRIN Bertrand, *op. cit.*, note 15, pp. 240, 255–7.

37 CORBOZ Bernard, *op. cit.*, note 27, N. 28 *et seq.*, *ad* art. 260^{quinquies} CP; GAFNER Julien, *op. cit.*, note 2, p. 215.

38 FF 2002 V p. 5066. This interpretation has not as yet been confirmed by the courts. However, it should become recognised in order to comply with Art. 2(1) of the International Convention for the Suppression of the Financing of Terrorism of 9 December 1999 and the UN Security Council Resolution 1373 (2001). Should this not be the case, Sec. 260^{quinquies} CrC would be largely devoid of substance; PERRIN Bertrand, *op. cit.*, note 15, pp. 256 *et seq.*

d. Reservations in Subsections 3 and 4 of Section 260^{quinquies} CrC

The reservation provided by Sec. 260^{quinquies}(3) CrC introduces an exception to criminal liability, in cases where the act of financing terrorism is carried out with a view to establishing or re-establishing 'a democratic regime or a state governed by the rule of law or with a view to exercising or safeguarding human rights'. If the boundaries of the human rights arena are easy to define (European Convention on Human Rights [ECHR], International Covenant on Civil and Political Rights [ICCPR]), the concepts of democracy and a state governed by the rule of law are not easily delimited without causing debate or controversy.

Sec. 260^{quinquies}(4) CrC adds a second exception: the financing of terrorism will not constitute an offence if it 'is intended to support acts that do not violate the rules of international law on the conduct of armed conflicts'.[39]

Because of their political nature, these two exceptions to criminal liability risk interfering with the application of Sec. 260^{quinquies} CrC, since the line between terrorism and legitimate combat is extremely fine. However, these reservations are in fact superfluous, given that the issues covered in the two subsections are already governed by the relevant international conventions.

We would add that the Federal Supreme Court has noted the difficulty of this distinction.[40] According to the Court, extremist parties, political opposition groups and other organisations that attempt to obtain political power in their country, or which lead a fight for freedom against a dictatorial regime, should not be qualified as terrorists.[41] It will inevitably be extremely difficult to draw a clear line, and any decision must respect the principle of proportionality. Exceptions to criminal liability could be acceptable provided that this principle is observed, or more precisely, provided that there is a reasonable relationship between the violence used and the legitimate goal.[42]

e. Comments

Sec. 260^{quinquies} CrC was drafted in line with external and internal security policy considerations.[43] Following the attacks of 11 September 2001, there were

39 Hague Conventions (law of war) and Geneva Conventions (international humanitarian law).

40 Swiss Federal Supreme Court decision (ATF) 128 II 355, consid. 4 (www.bger.ch).

41 ATF 128 II 355, consid. 4.3; ATF 130 II 337, consid. 3; ATF 131 II 235, consid. 2.12 and 3.3.

42 JOSITSCH Daniel, 'Terrorismus oder Freiheitskampf? – Heikle Abgrenzungsfragen bei der Anwendung von Art. 260^{quinquies} StGB', *Revue pénale suisse*, pp. 458 *et seq.*, 2005, pp. 467–9; ATF 130 II 337, consid. 3.3; ATF 131 II 235, consid. 3.3.

43 FORSTER Marc, ‚Die Strafbarkeit der Unterstützung (insbesondere Finanzierung) des Terrorismus', *Revue pénale suisse*, pp. 423 *et seq.*, 2003, p. 441.

compelling reasons to adopt a criminal provision specific to the financing of terrorism in order to be able to eradicate it. But this provision gave rise to significant problems of interpretation, and in this regard its scope is limited considerably by the recklessness exception and the reservations in subsections 3 and 4.[44] Thus, almost ten years after coming into force, Sec. 260^{quinquies} CrC has yet to be applied in judgments.[45]

In practice, the question of financing a terrorist activity or group will entail application of Sec. 260ter CrC, which imposes penalties on the participation and support of a criminal organisation. In this connection, the Federal Supreme Court has ruled that terrorist organisations, such as the Basque ETA, the Italian Red Brigades, or al-Qaeda, fulfil the definition of a criminal organisation.[46] In May 2009, the Federal Attorney General opened an investigation into alleged members of a faction of the Liberation Tigers of Tamil Eelam for belonging to and supporting a criminal organisation (Sec. 260ter CrC),[47] and for money laundering (Sec. 305bis CrC).[48] However, Sec. 260^{quinquies} CrC was not applied at that time.

Nevertheless, the aforementioned elements are sufficient to show that Swiss law fulfils the requirements of Art. 2(1) of the International Convention for the Suppression of the Financing of Terrorism of 9 December 1999, and paragraph 1(a) and (b) of UN Security Council Resolution 1373 of 28 September 2001. Switzerland also fulfils the mandatory requirements of Resolution 1624 of 14 September 2005 in the sense that the Swiss Criminal Code contains provisions suited to preventing incitement to commit terrorism.[49]

44 The content of Sec. 260^{quinquies} CrC seems to have been hurriedly put together after the terrorism provision initially planned in the Federal Council Message (FF 2002 V p. 5062) was abandoned and incorporated in the provision making it an offence to finance terrorism. The adoption of Subsecs. 3 and 4 of the present Sec. 260^{quinquies} CrC was therefore not on the agenda (FF 2002 V p. 5080), and the reason for their introduction is simply unexplainable.

45 At the police level: Office fédéral de la statistique, *Statistique policière de la criminalité (SPC)*, annual reports, available at http://www.bfs.admin.ch/bfs/portal/fr/index/news/publikationen.html (accessed 6 January 2014). Only one offence has been registered so far, in 2009.

46 ATF 125 II 569, consid. 5; ATF 128 II 355, consid. 2.2 and 4.3; Swiss Federal Supreme Court decision (arrêt du TF) 1A.194/2002 of 15 November 2002, consid. 3.5 and 3.7; ATF 132 IV 132, consid. 4.1.2.

47 The concept of criminal organisation assumes the existence of a structured group, of no less than three persons, that demonstrates a certain degree of professionalism in carrying out criminal activities, which consist of the commission of acts of violence or the realisation of economic profits, cf. particularly ATF 129 IV 271, consid. 2.3.1.

48 Sec. 305bis CrC and Sec. 305ter CrC complete the other provisions of the Swiss Criminal Code in respect of countering terrorism and its financing.

49 Sec. 24 CrC provides for punishment of incitement to criminal violence. Sec. 259 CrC punishes the public incitement to commit a felony or violence, which includes terrorism, while Sec. 135 CrC punishes representations of acts of violence.

D. *Penalties and Sanctions for Natural Persons and Legal Entities*

a. Natural Persons

For the punishment of violent crimes of a terrorist nature, one needs to refer to the penalties provided in each case.[50] For example, murder (Sec. 112 CrC) imposes a penalty of imprisonment for life or for a term of not less than ten years. A person who is guilty of financing terrorism risks imprisonment for a term not exceeding five years (Sec. 260^{quinquies}(1) CrC).

Sec. 47(1) CrC stipulates that 'The court shall determine the sentence according to the culpability of the offender. It shall take account of the previous conduct and the personal circumstances of the offender as well as the effect that the sentence will have on his life.' 'Culpability shall be assessed according to the seriousness of the damage or danger to the legal interest concerned, the reprehensibility of the conduct, the motives and aims of the offender, and the extent to which the offender, in view of the personal and external circumstances, could have avoided causing the danger or damage' (subsection 2). From a subjective point of view, the degree of tortious intent and the motives and aims of the offender must be taken into account. In addition, factors concerning offenders themselves – their previous record, their reputation, their personal situation (particularly an offender's professional situation and his or her risk of reoffending), their vulnerability faced with the penalty, as well as their behaviour after the act and during the criminal proceedings, must also be considered.[51] These rules also apply to Sec. 260^{quinquies} CrC.

b. Legal Entities

Legal entities are also subject to criminal sanctions. This concept is broader than that of legal entities. It includes the latter[52] as well as companies or entities that do not have legal personality, such as commercial partnerships or sole proprietorships (Sec. 102(4) CrC). Sec. 102(1) CrC provides for a form of subsidiary responsibility – the undertaking is only liable if, by reason of its inadequate organisation, it is not possible to identify or to punish the natural person who has committed the offence. Sec. 102(2) CrC, which interests us especially, provides for a form of primary responsibility, which is independent of or joined with that of the natural person: the undertaking can be held liable provided it 'is responsible for failing to take all

50 Cf. *supra*, note 16.

51 Among the abundant case law, see for example the decision of the Federal Supreme Court, TF 6B_335/2012 of 13 August 2012, consid. 1.1 and the cited references.

52 Private sector entities (e.g., a foundation, an association, a public limited company, a private limited company or a co-operative) and public sector entities, with the exception of regional bodies.

the reasonable organisational measures that were required' to prevent any of the seven offences exhaustively mentioned, including that of financing terrorism. The undertaking may be punished in addition to the natural person or on its own, if the offender is not identified.[53]

This primary responsibility may be triggered if the two following requirements are fulfilled. On the one hand, the offence – financing of terrorism, for example – must have been committed in the undertaking and in the exercise of its activities and in connection with its objects. On the other hand, the alleged fault of the undertaking must have a causal relationship with the committed offence.

In the event of conviction, the court will punish the undertaking with a fine not exceeding 5 million Swiss francs (Sec. 102(1) CrC). It will assess the fine according to the seriousness of the offence, the organisational inadequacies and the loss or damage caused, based on the undertaking's economic ability to pay the fine (Sec. 102(3) CrC).[54]

Although the Swiss courts have not yet imposed any sentences for financing terrorism, the Federal Supreme Court did rely on Sec. 260^{quinquies} CrC when confirming the validity of mutual legal assistance proceedings with the United States against an alleged provider of funding for al-Qaeda.[55] The Swiss Supreme Court also rejected a request for the release of a person imprisoned by reason of suspected ties with that same terrorist organisation.[56]

E. *Prosecution*

a. Jurisdiction of Swiss Authorities

EXTENT OF FEDERAL AND CANTONAL JURISDICTION. In Switzerland, the prosecution and trial of criminal offences as a rule fall under the jurisdiction of the cantonal authorities (Sec. 22 of the Swiss Code of Criminal Procedure, CCrP).[57]

[53] PERRIN BERTRAND, 'La responsabilité pénale des personnes morales', *Rapports suisses présentés aux XVIIIe Congrès international de droit comparé*, Heckendorn Urscheler Lukas & Peters Annelot (ed.), Schulthess, Geneva/Zurich/Basel 2010, pp. 261-91, 267–8.

[54] Federal Supreme Court decisions have so far not applied Sec. 102(2) CrC. We have no statistics regarding convictions of legal entities and, more generally, of companies. However, on 22 November 2011, the Federal Public Prosecutor, in a summary order, convicted a public limited company on the basis of this provision, in conjunction with Sec. 322^{septies} CrC (bribery of foreign public officials).

[55] FSC decision, TF 1A.147/2004 of 13 September 2004.

[56] FSC decisions TF 1S.3/2004 and 1S.4/2004 of 13 August 2004. We would also mention the case of a person held on remand, by order of the Cour de plaintes Cour des plaintes of the Federal Criminal Court, BH.2013.3 of 2 July 2013, in connection with an investigation into his involvement in the financing of terrorism (the relevant facts are not described).

[57] RS 312.0, available at http://www.admin.ch/opc/fr/classified-compilation/20052319 /index.html.

However, there is an exception with respect to organised crime,[58] financing terrorism and white-collar crime (Sec. 24(1) CCrP), when the offences are to a significant extent committed abroad or in several cantons with no single canton being the clear focus of the criminal activity. In practice, this is generally the case in the field we are concerned with here, considering the transnational character of criminal and terrorist activities.

As a rule, therefore, the offence of financing terrorism is subject to federal jurisdiction. The Federal Attorney General, assisted by the Federal Criminal Police (FCP), is responsible for the preliminary phase of the prosecution. The Federal Criminal Court is the authority competent to hear cases in first instance; as a rule, decisions may be 'appealed' to the Federal Supreme Court. We would add that under Sec. 23(1)(c) CCrP, the taking of hostages in order to exert duress on federal authorities or foreign authorities is also subject to federal jurisdiction.

SWITZERLAND'S UNIVERSAL JURISDICTION AND INTERNATIONAL CO-OPERATION. Sec. 6 CrC is an exception to the traditional principle of territoriality, which stipulates that the Swiss Criminal Code is applicable to 'any person who commits a felony or misdemeanour in Switzerland' (Sec. 3 CrC). Sec. 6(1) provides that the Swiss Criminal Code is applicable to any person who commits a felony or misdemeanour abroad that Switzerland is obliged to prosecute by virtue of an international convention, provided the following:

- The act is also liable to prosecution in the country in which it was committed (double criminality principle) or no criminal law jurisdiction applies at the place of commission.
- The person concerned remains in Switzerland and is not extradited.[59]

Switzerland has adhered to the UN conventions on the prevention of terrorism and its financing, and therefore a Swiss court must, for example, try a person who finances any act of terrorism committed anywhere in the world, provided that he or she is apprehended on Swiss territory and is not extradited.[60] Moreover, as a member of the UN, FATF and the Council of Europe, Switzerland is an active player on

[58] Federal jurisdiction extends to all felonies (not demeanours, cf. *supra*, note 13) committed in connection with a criminal organisation; these involve violent crimes (homicide, hostage-taking, etc.) and the means used to secure gains (e.g., theft, money laundering, drug trafficking); MOREILLON Laurent, PAREIN-REYMOND Aude, *Petit Commentaire – Code de procédure pénale*, Helbing Lichtenhahn, Basel 2013, N. 4 *ad* Sec. 24 CrC.

[59] Moreover, Sec. 6(2) CrC requires the court indirectly to take account of foreign law, to ensure application of the *lex mitior* principle. Moreover, Sec. 6 CrC fulfils the requirements of Art. 7 of the International Convention for the Suppression of the Financing of Terrorism, 9 December 1999.

[60] DUPUIS Michel *et al.*, *op.cit.*, note 27, N. 37 *ad* Sec. 260^{quinquies} CrC and the cited references.

the international scene in the fight against terrorism and its financing. Bilateral agreements with other countries, and with the European Union,[61] also provide the basis for active police and legal co-operation.[62]

Sec. 7 CrC provides another exception to the territoriality principle. This section invests Swiss courts with subsidiary extraterritorial jurisdiction based on the Swiss nationality of the offender or the victim, provided that the double criminality principle is observed, the offender is in Swiss territory or is handed over to the Swiss authorities or the act in question is an extraditable offence but the offender is not extradited (Subsec. 1). Subsec. 2 establishes extraordinary extraterritorial jurisdiction, which does not require the offender or the victim to be Swiss. More precisely, a replacement or substitution jurisdiction is being established here (paragraph (a)), as is universal jurisdiction in the case of a serious felony that is proscribed by the international community (paragraph (b)).

b. Rights of the Accused

Secs. 3 to 11 CCrP set out the general principles governing criminal procedure. With regard to the accused, these provisions contain fundamental rights concerning the respect for human dignity. This comprises in particular the right to a fair trial, that is, the right to be heard, the right to participate in the taking of evidence and the right to be assisted by a lawyer (Secs. 3, 107, 128–32 CCrP). The presumption of innocence is covered in Sec. 10 CCrP.

Every person involved in the proceedings is entitled to these rights, at every stage of the proceedings. They mirror the rights and freedoms that are found in the Swiss Federal Constitution,[63] the ECHR (particularly Art. 6 ECHR) and the ICCPR.

Nevertheless, there are some restrictions. First, documents related to criminal proceedings may be inspected only after the first interview of the accused and the gathering of the most important evidence by the public prosecutor. The right to be heard may also be restricted in the case of abuse of right by the accused or in case of necessity in order to ensure the safety of persons or to safeguard public or private interests in preserving confidentiality (Sec. 108(1) CCrP). This restriction can apply to the accused's counsel, but only as a result of his own conduct (Sec. 108(2) CCrP).

61 Particularly with Europol and Switzerland's association with the Schengen area.

62 GAFNER Julien, *op.cit.*, note 3, pp. 272 *et seq*; website of the Federal Office of Police: http://www.fedpol.admin.ch/content/fedpol/en/home/themen/sicherheit/polizeizusammenarbeit.html (accessed 6 January 2014); website of the Federal Office of Justice: http://www.bj.admin.ch/content/bj/en/home/ themen/sicherheit/internationale_rechthilfe/rechtshilfe_in_strafsache.html (accessed 6 January 2014).

63 Secs. 29–32 Cst (RS 101), available at http://www.admin.ch/opc/fr/classified-compilation/ 19995395/index.html.

Restrictions must be limited in time or to individual procedural acts (Sec. 108(3) CCrP) and therefore comply with the proportionality rule.

Thus, as a matter of principle, the pure prohibition of access to evidence establishing the guilt of the accused is rarely seen in practice, unless there is the need to safeguard the internal or external security of the state, national defence or the economic well-being of the country.[64] The elements put forward to establish the risks for the interests concerned must be concrete and sufficient.[65] Nonetheless, the restriction must be as restrained and as proportionate as possible (e.g., by censoring a single document rather than simply forbidding access to the file or by limiting the duration of the restriction). Sec. 108(4) CCrP states that 'If the reason for imposing the restriction continues to apply, the criminal justice authorities may base their decisions on files that have not been disclosed to a party only if that party has been informed of the essential content thereof.'

c. Protective Measures for Witnesses and Victims

In general, Sec. 149 CCrP provides that everyone implicated in criminal proceedings (victims, witnesses, persons called on to give information, experts, accused persons and interpreters) may benefit from suitable protection measures, if their participation in the investigation and the proceedings exposes them to a serious danger to life and limb or any other serious prejudice. The director of proceedings may therefore give assurance of anonymity (Sec. 150 CCrP) or limit or exclude confrontation hearings between a victim and the accused (Sec. 152 CCrP),[66] providing of course that the defendant's rights are not fundamentally diminished. Sec. 152(4)(a) CCrP stipulates that the confrontation hearing may be ordered if the accused's right to be heard cannot be guaranteed in any other way. In any event, the accused must retain the right to question his or her accuser at least once, whether that person be the victim or a witness, in accordance with the requirements imposed by the European Court of Human Rights and Swiss Federal Supreme Court case law.[67] Alternatives to a direct confrontation hearing, such as audio-visual methods, may be undertaken where possible.[68]

64 BENDANI Yasmina, *Commentaire Romand – Code de procédure pénale suisse*, Kuhn et Jeanneret (eds.), Helbing Lichtenhahn, Basel 2011, N. 6 *ad* Sec. 108 CrC.

65 BENDANI Yasmina, *op.cit.*, note 64, N. 7 *ad* Sec. 108 CrC.

66 With respect to Sec 152 CrC, the concept of 'victim' refers to any person whose rights have been directly violated by an offence and whose physical, sexual or mental integrity has been directly and adversely affected by the offence (Secs. 115 and 116 CCrP).

67 ATF 131 I 476, consid. 2.2.

68 BERSET HEMMER Valérie, *Commentaire Romand – Code de procédure pénale suisse*, Kuhn & Jeanneret (eds.), Helbing Lichtenhahn, Basel 2011, N. 16–18 *ad* Sec. 152 CrC.

Very recently, Switzerland adopted the Federal Act on Extra-procedural Witness Protection (Witness Protection Act), which entered into force on 1 January 2013.[69] In addition to protecting witnesses from the aforementioned exposure to the danger, this law expressly requires that the collaboration of the person concerned must be essential for evidential purposes, that is, the absence of such collaboration would disproportionately hinder the prosecution of the case. According to the Swiss Federal Council, this situation mainly occurs in the fields of organised crime, prevention of terrorism and human trafficking.[70] There are a broad range of concrete protection measures, from safe houses to a new identity and integration in a new life. There are no statistics on the subject, but the number of cases is estimated at between ten and fifteen a year.

III. AUTHORITIES AND INVESTIGATIVE MEANS

A. *Attorney General and the Police*

The prosecution services involved in the area we are dealing with here are the public prosecutors and the criminal police. They are the motors of the first stage of the criminal process, which comprises the preliminary proceedings (Secs. 299–327 CCrP). These generally consist of two stages – the police enquiries and the investigation. The public prosecutor is responsible for leading the proceedings. He oversees the police activities and issues them with instructions or assignments.

The purpose of police enquiries is to determine whether the public prosecutor should open a criminal investigation. Naturally, the police continue to operate throughout the preliminary stage, under the public prosecutor's instructions, in order to gather evidence (e.g., hearing witnesses, carrying out searches or seizing documents).

As we already mentioned, the prosecution of offences related to the financing of terrorism and participation in a criminal organisation is, in principle and in practice, subject to federal, not cantonal, jurisdiction. As such, the Federal Attorney General and the Federal Criminal Police are in charge of investigations in these areas. The activities of the Federal Criminal Police are by nature repressive as well

69 RS 312.2, available at http://www.admin.ch/opc/fr/classified-compilation/20091842/index.html.

70 Federal Council, *Communiqué de presse sur le nouveau service national de protection des témoins*, 7 November 2012, Berne, available at http://www.ejpd.admin.ch/content/ejpd/fr/home/dokumentation/mi/2012/2012-11-072.html (accessed 6 January 2014).

as preventive. The latest report of the Federal Office of Police (Fedpol) briefly states with respect to terrorism:[71]

- In 2012, neither Switzerland nor its citizens were a primary target of attack by militant Islamists – jhadis. However, Swiss citizens can fall victim to an attack by militant groups in Islamic conflict zones at any time.
- People presumed to be jihadis still use Switzerland as a base to provide reinforcements to militant jihadi groups active abroad and to disseminate propaganda. Fedpol is therefore focusing on improving its investigations on the Internet, which obviously serves as a communication platform. A technical surveillance device has been set up to monitor jhadist websites in order to remove any website that might be installed on a server in Switzerland. An example of this was the case of an investigation into two entities suspected of money laundering – the money originated from international drug trafficking and was then laundered in Switzerland before being handed over to a violent extremist organisation in the Arab world.
- Attention is not only focused on terrorism related to Islamic extremism, but also on certain continuing activities of the Kurdistan Workers' Party (PKK) and on representatives of the former Liberation Tigers of Tamil Eelam (LTTE).
- Overall, the investigations initiated by the Federal Criminal Police are aimed primarily at countering support activities for the aforementioned groups.

B. *Federal Intelligence Service*

The Federal Intelligence Service (FIS) is a domestic and foreign security policy instrument. The legal bases for its operations are as follows:

- Federal Act of 3 October 2008 on Responsibilities in the Area of the Civilian Intelligence Service (LFRC).[72]
- Federal Act of 21 March 1997 on Measures to Safeguard Internal Security (LMSI), intended to ensure respect for Switzerland's democratic and constitutional foundations and the protection of the freedoms of its people.[73] This Act confers responsibility on the federal government for taking preventive measures to detect terrorism at an early stage and to counter threats from terrorism. Sec. 3 LMSI provides that information related to the exercise of

[71] Federal Office of Police, *Rapport annuel 2012 – Lutte de la Confédération contre la criminalité*, June 2013, Berne, available at http://www.fedpol.admin.ch/content/fedpol/fr/home/dokumentation/berichte/jb_fedpol.html (accessed 6 January 2014).

[72] RS 121, available at http://www.admin.ch/opc/fr/classified-compilation/20080697/index.html.

[73] RS 120, available at http://www.admin.ch/opc/fr/classified-compilation/19970117/index.html.

fundamental rights, such as freedom of opinion or freedom of association, may be processed if there is a serious presumption of links to the preparation or execution of terrorist acts.
- Sec. 9 LMSI, enables the federal government, after consultation with the FIS, to prohibit a natural person, an organisation or a group from engaging in an activity that would directly or indirectly serve to spread, support or promote terrorist actions, provided that Switzerland's internal or external security is specifically threatened (the prohibition lasts for up to five years but is renewable).

Basically, the FIS is an organisation that uses intelligence tools to collect, analyse, evaluate and disseminate information, with the aim of compiling a comprehensive intelligence picture relevant for decision makers at all levels. Through its operational and preventive services, it contributes directly to Switzerland's security, particularly by detecting threats obtained from the analysis of information that is not publicly accessible. The FIS co-operates closely with various authorities and agencies at the federal and cantonal levels and engages in continuous intelligence co-operation with numerous partner services in other countries.

Among the themes dealt with by the FIS is the fight against terrorism, on the national level and abroad. In this connection, the latest FIS report[74] states that:

- Switzerland is aware of the development of regional branches of al-Qaeda and obviously closely monitors the organisation's potential activities on Swiss territory. Acts of violence are not the major cause of concern, since for the moment Switzerland is not a priority target for jihad-motivated attacks. The acceptance of the popular vote[75] on banning the building of minarets does not seem to have changed the threat level in this regard. Incidentally, as a result of the popular vote, a new subsection (Sec. 72(3)) was added to the Constitution prohibiting such construction.
- However, the risk of politically or terrorist-motivated kidnappings of Swiss citizens abroad is continuing to rise, especially in conflict zones in Islamic regions.
- Across Europe, jihad-motivated travel (for training, for example) to conflict zones is still on the rise and is consequently monitored by the FIS.

[74] Federal Intelligence Service, *Switzerland's Security – Situation Report 2013*, *op.cit.*, note 6.

[75] Secs. 138 and 139 of the Swiss Federal Constitution permits any one hundred thousand persons eligible to vote to request a complete or partial revision of the Constitution. The one hundred thousand signatures must be collected and deposited within eighteen months. The subject of the initiative is then submitted to a vote of the people and the cantons, for acceptance or rejection. Popular votes are the motor of Switzerland's direct democracy, since they do not emanate from either Parliament or the government, but are initiated directly by the citizens.

- As regards ethno-nationalist violent extremism, the FIS is focusing on developments in the PKK and successor organisations of the LTTE; however, they are currently showing little sign of activity in Europe.
- In the area of left- and right-wing extremism, the potential for violence continues but is not on a scale that poses a danger to Switzerland. However, two quite serious acts of violence were committed by the extreme left: one was a letter bomb sent to Swissnuclear[76] in Olten in March 2011, and the other was a thwarted bomb attack on the IBM research centre in Rüschlikon in April 2010.
- Cyber risks are rising substantially and must be monitored more closely since Switzerland is increasingly dependent on information and communication infrastructures that are closely interconnected.

Going forward, the activities of the FIS must be rooted in a new legal basis aimed at strengthening the protection of Switzerland's essential interests, particularly the fight against terrorism. A new Intelligence Service Act is scheduled to become law in the second half of 2015 and will replace the LRFC and LMSI.[77] The primary aim of this new legislation will be to introduce special means for collecting intelligence within Switzerland (monitoring of postal and telecommunications traffic; observation of suspected persons, including on private premises; and infiltration of computers and networks). These means can be implemented rapidly once application for authorisation is submitted to the Federal Administrative Court, which must render a ruling within five days. The incisive nature of these types of measures must always observe the fundamental rights of the individual (as expressed in the Swiss Constitution and by ECHR and ICCPR), as well as the Federal Data Protection Act (DPA).[78]

C. *Investigative Means*

Sec. 6(1) CCrP imposes a basic principle of investigation: 'The criminal justice authorities shall investigate ex officio all the circumstances relevant to the assessment of the criminal act and the accused.' Sec. 139(1) CCrP provides that in order to establish the truth, the authorities 'shall use all the legally admissible evidence that is relevant in accordance with the latest scientific findings and experience.' There is *no restriction on the nature* of evidence taken. It may, in particular, include hearing witnesses, calling on experts and relying on tangible evidence. The criminal justice

[76] A federation of nuclear operators, Swissnuclear, defends the safe and economic operation of nuclear power plants in Switzerland.

[77] Website of the Federal Department of Defence, Civil Protection and Sport, available at http://www.vbs.admin.ch/internet/vbs/fr/home/themen/ndb/uebersicht.html (accessed 6 January 2014).

[78] RS 235.1, available at http://www.admin.ch/opc/en/classified-compilation/19920153/index.html.

authorities may use all methods or resources that could lead to discovery of the material truth.

However, only 'lawfully obtained' evidence may be used. 'The use of coercion, violence, threats, promises, deception and methods that may compromise the ability of the person concerned to think or decide freely are prohibited when taking evidence' (Sec. 140(1) CCrP). Evidence obtained in violation of this rule would not be admissible under any circumstances (Sec. 141(1) CCrP) and would have to be removed from the case documents (Sec. 141(5) CCrP).

The search for truth requires that the evidence must be kept secure, that the attendance of certain persons at the proceedings must be ensured and, finally, that enforcement of the final judgment must be guaranteed. In order to achieve these three objectives, defined in Sec. 196(a) to (c) CCrP, criminal justice authorities may use measures that restrict the fundamental rights of the persons concerned. Swiss legislation uses the expression 'compulsory measures', which are governed by Secs. 196 *et seq.* CCrP.[79] Sec. 197(1) CCrP lists four cumulative conditions that are required before compulsory measures can be taken: they can be ordered if they are permitted by law (paragraph (a)), if there is reasonable suspicion that an offence has been committed (paragraph (b)), if the aims cannot be achieved by less stringent measures (paragraph (c)) and if the seriousness of the offence justifies the compulsory measure (paragraph (d)).

The criminal justice authorities can carry out searches, conduct examinations such as DNA analyses and order the seizure of objects or assets.[80] If necessary, an accused may be placed on remand (Secs. 220 *et seq.* CCrP).

Secs. 269 to 298 CCrP merit a more detailed explanation. They deal with covert surveillance measures, which may be of specific interest in investigations into organised crime and terrorism.

[79] A compulsory measure does not necessarily involve the use of force. It is characterised solely by the restriction of a fundamental right. 'Force may be used as a last resort when carrying out compulsory measures' (Sec. 200 CCrP).

[80] DNA analyses in particular are governed by Secs. 255–9 CCrP and the Federal Act on DNA profiles (RS 363), available at http://www.admin.ch/opc/fr/classified-compilation/20031383/index.html. Seizure methods (Secs. 263–8 CCrP), and forfeiture of assets (Secs. 70–3 CrC) are particularly broad in the case of persons belonging to terrorist organisations, thanks to a lower level of proof required for the investigating authority. Indeed, Sec. 72 CrC introduces a presumption that the criminal (or terrorist) organisation has a power of disposal over the assets belonging to a person who participates in the organisation or supports it. In cases of mutual legal assistance, provisional measures, such as freezing of assets, may be ordered under the provisions of international conventions or, in the absence of such agreements, pursuant to Sec. 18 of the Federal Act on International Mutual Assistance in Criminal Matters (IMAC, RS 351.1), available at http://www.admin.ch/opc/en/classified-compilation/19810037/index.html.

- Surveillance of post and telecommunications (letters, packages, telephone calls, faxes, e-mails) is governed by Secs. 269 to 279 CCrP.[81] This measure may be ordered by the public prosecutor, but requires the authorisation of the Compulsory Measures Court since it restricts fundamental rights. Surveillance may be ordered in the investigation of offences such as financing terrorism, participation in a criminal organisation and any violent crime such as homicide or hostage taking; it may also be ordered for the execution of a request for mutual legal assistance (Sec. 269(2) CCrP).
- Other technical surveillance measures under Secs. 280 and 281 CCrP. These comprise listening to or recording conversations or events in private or in places not generally accessible, as well as establishing the whereabouts of persons or property. The conditions for implementation are identical to those of Secs. 269 to 279 CCrP, which we looked at earlier.
- Covert observation under Secs. 282 and 283 CCrP may be carried out against persons and property in generally accessible locations and permits the making of image or sound recordings. The measure may be ordered by the public prosecutor, and also by the police if it is of short duration not exceeding one month.
- Surveillance of banking relations under Secs. 284 and 285 CCrP is a measure that requires authorisation from the Compulsory Measures Court, at the request of the public prosecutor, for the purpose of investigating felonies or misdemeanours. The measure applies to both banks and other bank-type institutions.
- Undercover investigations are governed by Secs. 285*a* to 298 CCrP.[82] Case law defines this concept as any active or passive contact made with a suspect by a member of a police corps who is not recognisable as such and who acts for the purposes of an investigation independently of the extent of the deception or the extent of the scope of influence permitted.[83] Implementation of this type of measure is subject to the same requirements as for the surveillance of post and telecommunications, and concerns the same catalogue of offences. The

[81] With regard to enforcement, these provisions are supplemented by the Federal Act of 6 October 2000 on the Surveillance of Post and Telecommunications (LSCPT, RS 780.1), available at http://www.admin.ch/opc/fr/classified-compilation/20002162/index.html. Regarding international legal aid, Sec. 18*a* IMAC may apply for the purpose of ordering this type of investigative measure. An amendment of the LSCPT has been adopted and should enter into force shortly (FF 2013 pp. 2379 *et seq.*). Its purpose is to bring the surveillance measures provided by the Act into line with technological developments, thereby ensuring better control.

[82] With regard to the administrative implementation, these provisions are supplemented by the Ordinance of 10 November 2004 on secret investigation (OISec. RS 312.81), available at http://www.admin.ch/opc/fr/classified-compilation/20041820/index.html.

[83] ATF 134 IV 266, consid. 3.5 and 3.6.

undercover agent (a member of a police corps or a person temporarily assigned to police duties) may obtain a false identity and the guarantee of anonymity.
- The FSI can give false identities to its employees and to its informants in sensitive cases related to counter-terrorism, for example. Protective or rehousing measures may also be taken.[84]

Finally, there is Sec. 28*a* CrC, which deals with protection of sources. In certain circumstances, persons who are professionally involved in the publication of information in a periodical medium may not refuse to give evidence in a criminal court regarding their sources. More precisely, the confidentiality of sources does not apply if, without the evidence of such a person, an offence, such as participation in a criminal organisation or financing of terrorism, cannot be solved or if the person suspected of committing the offence cannot be apprehended.

IV. ADMINISTRATIVE FRAMEWORK IN CASE OF INTERNATIONAL EMBARGO: MEASURES AND RESTRICTIONS AGAINST ENTITIES AND INDIVIDUALS LINKED WITH TERRORISM

The UN Security Council Resolution 1267 of 15 October 1999 enabled the implementation of international financial sanctions against the Taliban in Afghanistan.[85] The Swiss federal government, pursuant to Secs. 184(3) and 185(3) of the Federal Constitution, introduced these sanctions into Swiss law in an ordinance of 2 October 2000, imposing measures against persons and entities associated with Osama bin Laden, al-Qaeda or the Taliban. In particular, these measures prohibit the supply of military equipment and similar goods, as well as the freezing of assets and economic resources belonging to or controlled by natural persons and legal entities and to groups and entities listed in the appendix to the ordinance.[86]

[84] Secs. 14*b* and 14*c* LMSI (RS 120) available at http://www.admin.ch/opc/fr/classified-compilation/19970117/index.html.

[85] RS 946.203, available at http://www.admin.ch/opc/fr/classified-compilation/19996052/index.html. Sec. 9 of the Embargo Act (EmbA, RS 946.231) contains criminal provisions in the event of violation of ordinances related to it which are promulgated by the Swiss Federal Council, available at http://www.admin.ch/opc/en/classified-compilation/20000358/index.html. Secs. 33 *et seq.* of the Federal Act on War Material (WMA, RS 514.51) punish any behaviour that fails to comply with licencing requirements; the prohibition of nuclear, biological and chemical weapons; the prohibition of antipersonnel mines; and the prohibition of related financing. Available at http://www.admin.ch/opc/en/classified-compilation/19960753/index.html.

[86] The appendix is managed by the State Secretariat for Economic Affairs, website of the State Secretariat for Economic Affairs (SECO), available at http://www.seco.admin.ch/index.html?lang=en (accessed 6 January 2014); for information cf. also http://www.finma.ch/e/sanktionen/internationale-sanktionen/terrorismuslisten/Pages/default.aspx (accessed 6 January 2014).

The Federal Act on the Implementation of International Sanctions (the Embargo Act, or EmbA) entered into force on 1 July 2003 and provides a legal basis for ordinances issued in connection with international sanctions.[87] The purpose of this Act is to enable the Confederation to enact compulsory measures in order to implement sanctions that have been ordered by the United Nations Organisation, the Organisation for Security and Cooperation in Europe or Switzerland's most significant trading partners, and which serve to secure compliance with international law, especially respect for human rights (Sec. 1 EmbA).

These measures provide, in particular, for the freezing of assets of persons subject to such sanctions. The holding of assets of such individuals or entities thus triggers an obligation to freeze the assets and to disclose them to the Secretary of State for the Economy.[88]

As for the rights of a person or entity concerned by a sanction, Sec. 8 EmbA stipulates that the appeal procedure in respect to rulings made under the Act is governed by the general provisions on the administration of justice at the federal level.

Finally, it should be noted that the legal infrastructure in Switzerland complies with the UN Security Council Resolution 1373 of 28 September 2001 on the obligation of member states to freeze the financial assets of terrorists and terrorist organisations. It also complies with the terms of Art. 8 of the International Convention of 9 December 1999 for the Suppression of Financing of Terrorism.

V. INTEGRATING FINANCING OF TERRORISM IN THE ANTI–MONEY LAUNDERING INFRASTRUCTURE

A. *Introduction*

For over thirty years, Switzerland has been active in the fight to prevent and counter money laundering, though self-regulation and legislative measures. Following the New York attacks of 11 September 2001, the infrastructure in place at the time evolved to incorporate the financing of terrorism. Needless to say, Switzerland is active on the international scene and belongs to keystone bodies such as the Financial Action Task Force and the Basel Committee.

This section will focus particularly on the mechanisms of the fight against money laundering and terrorism funding from the administrative and financial angle, while touching on the Swiss Criminal Code provisions that marked the beginning of the

87 RS 946.231, available at http://www.admin.ch/opc/en/classified-compilation/20000358/index.html.

88 This duty is incumbent on all persons holding assets and does not refer only to financial intermediaries (on this subject, cf. *infra*, Section 5); CASSANI Ursula, *op.cit.*, note 16, p. 308.

anti–money laundering process. The system is not only geared to helping to eradicate these flows, but also to defending the integrity and reputation of Switzerland's role in the global economy.

B. *Legislative Instruments and Self-Regulation*

a. Swiss Criminal Code

As we saw earlier, Sec. $260^{quinquies}$ CrC entered into force on 1 October 2003. Previously, Secs. 305bis and 305ter CrC had come into effect on 1 August 1990.

Aimed at fighting organised crime and making it an offence to potentially endanger the administration of justice (abstract endangerment), Sec. $305^{bis}(1)$ CrC punishes money laundering in the following terms: 'Any person who carries out an act that is aimed at frustrating the identification of the origin, the tracing or the forfeiture of assets which he knows or must believe originate from a felony, shall be liable to imprisonment for a term not exceeding three years or to a fine.'[89] This definition illustrates the difference between money laundering, in which the funds concerned come from a criminal source, and money 'dirtying', which is characteristic of the financing of terrorism. However, funds used to finance terrorism do not always emanate from legal sources; illegal financial resources are also used, in which case there could be coincidence between Sec. $260^{quinquies}$ and Sec. 305bis CP.[90]

Sec. $305^{ter}(1)$ CrC punishes insufficient diligence in financial transactions: 'Any person who as part of his profession accepts, holds on deposit, or assists in investing or transferring assets belonging to a third party and fails to ascertain the identity of the beneficial owner of the assets with the care that is required in the circumstances shall be liable to imprisonment for a term not exceeding one year or to a fine.' It also seeks to protect the functioning of criminal justice, by establishing a duty of vigilance and a right to disclose to the designated authority any observations that indicate that assets originate from a felony (Sec. $305^{ter}(2)$ CrC). This special justification protects persons working in the financial sector from liability for breach of banking or professional confidentiality.[91] The persons particularly affected are professionals in the financial sector, that is, bankers, trustees, fiduciaries, investment advisors, stockbrokers, business lawyers and life insurers. The Anti-Money Laundering Act applies to financial intermediaries, such as casino employees.[92]

89 The penalty may be imprisonment for a term not exceeding five years, particularly in the case of professional money laundering (Sec. $305^{bis}(2)$ CrC).

90 GAFNER Julien, *op.cit.*, note 3, pp. 222–3.

91 DUPUIS Michel *et al.*, *op.cit.*, note 27, N. 26 *ad* Sec. 305ter CrC, and cited references.

92 *Ibid.*, N. 10–18 *ad* Sec. 305ter CrC, and cited references.

b. Money Laundering Act of 10 October 1997

Sec. 305bis CrC was supplemented by an administrative law act, which came into force on 1 April 1998, and which set out the vigilance required of financial professionals who accept and hold third-party financial assets. Entitled the Federal Act on Combating Money Laundering and Terrorist Financing in the Financial Sector (MLA),[93] it applies to financial intermediaries, described in its Sec. 2.[94]

The tasks imposed by the MLA on financial intermediaries are basically the following:

- Due diligence (Secs. 3–8): the duty to verify the identity of the contracting party and to identify the beneficial owner, the duty to repeat these two obligations, the duty to clarify and the duty to establish and retain documents, as well as the requirement to ensure adequate organisation measures.
- Duty in the event of suspicion of money laundering (Secs. 9–11): duty to report (duty of disclosure) to the Money Laundering Reporting Office Switzerland (MROS) and to freeze assets. Thus, a duty to act is imposed on a financial intermediary when it suspects, on good grounds, that assets it knows or has good reason to believe are connected with a criminal organisation, an act of money laundering, a felony or the financing of terrorism. On the one hand, the intermediary must promptly inform MROS and, on the other, it must freeze the suspected assets entrusted to it, without communicating the fact to the persons concerned or to third parties. The assets must remain frozen until the intermediary receives a decision from the competent prosecution authority, but at most they are frozen for five business days from the time of the intermediary's communication to MROS.

There is also a provision for a supervisory system by financial intermediaries aimed at monitoring compliance with the preceding duties (Secs. 12 *et seq.*). The entities responsible for this task are the Swiss Financial Market Supervisory Authority (FINMA), the recognised self-regulatory bodies and the Federal Gaming Board.

Secs. 29 *et seq.* MLA concern administrative co-operation inside Switzerland and with foreign authorities. Finally, Sec. 37 MLA punishes the intentional or negligent violation of the duty of disclosure under Sec. 9 MLA by a fine of up to CHF 500,000.

93 RS 955.0, available at http://www.admin.ch/opc/fr/classified-compilation/19970427/index.html.

94 Those particularly concerned are banks, fund managers, investment companies with variable capital (SICAVs), life insurance institutions, securities dealers, casinos, and persons who on a professional basis accept, hold on deposit or assist in investing or transferring assets belonging to third parties. This concept is aimed particularly at those who carry out credit transactions or provide services related to payment transactions, foreign exchange dealers and asset managers.

The MLA is supplemented by several ordinances, particularly the Swiss Financial Market Supervisory Authority Ordinance on the Prevention of Money Laundering and Terrorism Financing.[95] This ordinance sets out the duties of financial intermediaries in this area and imposes a number of organisational measures on them.

The Swiss government recently presented a bill to implement the revised FATF Recommendations. The main changes to be introduced will affect the system for countering money laundering and terrorism financing, and include in particular the following:[96]

- Improved transparency for legal entities
- Extension of the scope of the MLA (notably in the area of real property, under certain conditions)
- A general duty to identify politically exposed persons
- The inclusion of qualified tax fraud in the area of direct taxation, as a new predicate offence for money laundering
- Extension of mutual assistance in criminal matters to include new tax offences
- Increased powers for the Money Laundering Reporting Office in terms of information exchange with counterpart authorities abroad

c. Self-Regulation

Professionals in the financial sector provided the first regulatory tools in the fight against money laundering. The legislative framework has certainly evolved over the past few years, but the input of financial participants remains an important factor. Self-regulation therefore still plays quite a significant role.

The Agreement on the Swiss banks' code of conduct with regard to the exercise of due diligence (CDB 08) entered into effect on 7 April 2008 between the Swiss Bankers Association and the Swiss signatory banks[97] and provides guidance on the interpretation of legislative acts on money laundering and terrorism financing. The initial version, introduced in 1977, established the duties to verify the identity of

[95] Ordinance of 8 December 2010 of the Swiss Financial Market Supervisory Authority on the Prevention of Money Laundering and Terrorist Financing (AMLO-FINMA, RS 955.033.0), available at http://www.admin.ch/opc/fr/classified-compilation/20101812/index.html; the Ordinance of 18 November 2009 on the Professional Practice of Financial Intermediation (OPPFI, RS 955.071), available at http://www.admin.ch/opc/fr/classified-compilation/20091766/ index.html.

[96] Swiss Federal Council, basic documents on the implementation of the FATF Recommendations revised in 2012, 27 February 2013, Berne, available at http://www.news.admin.ch/NSBSubscriber/message/attachments/ 29775.pdf (accessed 6 January 2014).

[97] Available at http://www.swissbanking.org/en0080410-vsb-cwe.pdf (accessed 6 January 2014).

clients and to identify the beneficial owners. It also prohibited active assistance in the flight of capital and tax evasion.

C. *The Authorities: FINMA and MROS*

The Swiss Financial Market Supervisory Authority and the Money Laundering Reporting Office Switzerland, discussed previously, are the Swiss central administrative authorities in the fight against money laundering and terrorism funding in the financial field.

FINMA is an independent state regulatory body. Its remit is to protect the interests of creditors, investors and insured persons and to ensure the proper functioning of the financial markets. It is invested with extensive powers in respect of banks, insurance companies, stock exchanges, securities dealers and collective investment schemes, as well distributors and insurance intermediaries; it can, in particular, impose sanctions and provide mutual administrative assistance.[98] FINMA also has jurisdiction in matters of money laundering and, correlatively, terrorist financing. In this context, it informs financial intermediaries of financial sanctions imposed on natural persons or legal entities in connection with administrative measures implemented under international embargoes.

MROS, a Financial Intelligence Unit (FIU), is part of the Federal Office of Police (Fedpol). It functions as a relay and filtration point between financial intermediaries and the law enforcement agencies. According to the Money Laundering Act, MROS is responsible for receiving and analysing reports from financial intermediaries on suspicious activity in connection with money laundering and, if necessary, forwarding them to the law enforcement agencies.[99] On the international level, MROS is a member of the Egmont Group, which is an international association of Financial Intelligence Units.

According to the latest MROS report, it received fifteen reports of suspected cases of terrorism financing in 2012, five more than in 2011.[100] This rise is relative, since the cases in 2012 only concerned three separate reports, while in fact twelve others came

[98] FINMA is governed by the Federal Act of 22 June 2007 on the Swiss Financial Market Supervisory Authority (Financial Market Supervision Act, FINMASA, RS 956.1), available at http://www.admin.ch/opc/en/classified-compilation/20052624/index.html.

[99] The operations and duties of MROS are established by Ordinance of 5 August 2004 on the Money Laundering Reporting Office Switzerland (OBCBA, RS 955.23), available at http://www.admin.ch/opc/fr/classified-compilation/20031873/index.html.

[100] Federal Office of Police (Fedpol), *Rapport annuel 2012 du Bureau de communication en matière de blanchiment d'argent* MROS, May 2013, Berne, p. 28, available at http://www.fedpol.admin.ch/content/fedpol/fr/home/ themen/kriminalitaet/geldwaescherei/jahresberichte.html (accessed 6 January 2014).

in the form of two sets of six reports. One of them involved CHF 7.45 million and was therefore by far the most substantial in terms of volume (99.75%).

Over the past ten years (2003–12), a total of eighty-six reported suspected cases were forwarded in connection with the financing of terrorism (between three and eighteen a year), one of which resulted in a conviction and twenty-five of which are still pending. The rest were subject to a no-proceedings order (forty-three), an abandonment of proceedings (seven) or suspension (ten).[101]

VI. IMMIGRATION MEASURES

Legislation governing migration does not deal specifically with terrorism. This section will therefore touch on the general principles of interest to our study, in respect of the law relating to aliens and refugee law.

The first deals with questions concerning the residence or settlement of foreign nationals in Switzerland. As a matter of principle, foreign nationals who wish to enter Switzerland must not pose a threat to public security and order or to Switzerland's international relations (Sec. 5 of the Federal Act of 16 December 2005 on Foreign Nationals, FNA).[102] As such, a person who has violated or represents a threat to public security and order in Switzerland or abroad, or who represents a threat to Switzerland's internal or external security, may be liable to the following measures:

- Revocation of a temporary or permanent residence permit (Sec. 62(c) FNA). Sec. 80 OASA,[103] concerning expulsion, specifically mentions acts of terrorism.
- Ban on entry into Switzerland (Sec. 67(2)(a) FNA). The ban may generally be ordered for a maximum of five years, but may be ordered for an unlimited period in the case of a serious risk.
- Expulsion. The Federal Office of Police, after consultation with the Federal Intelligence Service, may order the expulsion of foreign nationals in order to safeguard the internal or external security of Switzerland. In the case of a serious violation, the expulsion order may be combined with an unlimited ban on re-entry (Sec. 68 FNA).[104]

[101] *Ibid.* It is of note that in 2002, there were fifteen such communications. In 2001, there were ninety-five, most probably because of the high state of alert after the 11 September attacks in New York.

[102] RS 142.20, available at http://www.admin.ch/opc/en/classified-compilation/20020232/index.html.

[103] Ordinance of 24 October 2007 on Admission, Establishment and the Exercise of Lucrative Activities (OASA, RS 142.201), available at http://www.admin.ch/opc/fr/classified-compilation/20070993/index.html.

[104] Federal Intelligence Service, *Switzerland's Security – Situation Report 2013*, *op.cit.* note 6, p. 24: in summer 2012, an entry ban was ordered for the first time on a Jordanian-born man previously resident in Switzerland. According to reliable intelligence, the man was in close contact with the Somali-based terrorist group al-Shabaab, part of the al-Qaeda network, and he wanted to return to Switzerland following his stay in Somalia.

- Considering Switzerland's international human rights commitments, the enforcement of an expulsion order, that is, the return of foreign nationals to their native country or their removal to a third country, is not permitted if such enforcement would be unreasonable. This would apply if the enforcement would seriously endanger the person, for example in cases of war, civil war general violence or medical emergency (Sec. 83(4) FNA).

With regard to asylum law, if there is credible and pertinent information indicating that an asylum seeker has connections with terrorism, the Swiss authorities may apply Sec. 53 of the Asylum Act of 26 June 1998 (AsylA).[105] Under this provision, refugees will not be granted asylum if they are unworthy of it due to serious misconduct.

Sec. 65 AsylA provides for the expulsion of refugees who endanger Switzerland's internal or external security or have seriously violated public order, subject to Sec. 5(1) AsylA. This latter section prohibits the return of persons to a country where their life, physical integrity or freedom are threatened by reason of their race, religion, nationality, membership in a specific social group or political opinion[106] or where they would be at risk of being forced to return to such a country. However, there is an exception to this prohibition in cases where there are substantial grounds for assuming that, because the person invoking it has a conviction for a particularly serious felony or misdemeanour, he represents a threat to Switzerland's security or must be considered a danger to the public (Sec. 5(2) AsylA).

VII. MILITARY AND EXTRATERRITORIAL ACTIVITIES

A. *Military Criminal Law*

Military criminal law has no particular role in the fight against terrorism. On the one hand, the Swiss Military Criminal Code[107] mostly refers to ordinary criminal law provisions, and on the other hand, its application depends on personal conditions. In other words, military criminal law applies only to given categories of persons associated with the army,[108] except in times of war, when it can also apply to civilians.

Like the Swiss Criminal Code, the Swiss Military Criminal Code does not contain offences sanctioning terrorist acts per se or the financing of terrorism. We therefore have to refer to elements we mentioned earlier.

[105] RS 142.31, available at http://www.admin.ch/opc/en/classified-compilation/19995092/index.html.
[106] These are grounds on which refugee status may be granted (Sec. 3 AsylA).
[107] Military Criminal Code of 13 June 1927 (CPM, RS 321.0), available at http://www.admin.ch/opc/fr/classified-compilation/19270018/index.html.
[108] In particular, persons subject to military service and military officials (Sec. 3 MCC).

With regard to offences, military criminal law mainly adopts those dealt with under ordinary criminal law, although it does have some specific characteristics. According to Sec. 8 MCC, 'ordinary criminal law applies to persons subject to military criminal law for offences that are not covered by this Code'. With regard to felonies and misdemeanours specific to the Swiss Military Criminal Code, we would mention offences that could be committed during terrorist acts, namely those against the national defence and the country's defensive power (Secs. 86–107 MCC), such as sabotage (Sec. 86*a* MCC), assisting the escape of detainees or prisoners of war (Sec. 105 MCC) or disclosure of military secrets (Sec. 106 MCC).

With a few exceptions (mainly of an organisational nature), the basic principles of military criminal procedure, for example the right of an accused to defence counsel, are derived from the ordinary rules of law.

B. *Extraterritorial Activities*

Switzerland has no extraterritorial activities with respect to Swiss nationals suspected of terrorism in a foreign country, nor in any other context. Swiss criminal law does not apply abroad, except by virtue of the universality principle (Sec. 6 CrC) and substitution (Sec. 7 CrC) and for felonies or misdemeanours committed abroad against the state or its national security (Sec. 4 CrC).[109] It should also be remembered that Switzerland plays an active part in international co-operation (mutual assistance in police and legal matters and extradition).

With respect to internal and external security matters, intelligence activities, carried out by the Federal Intelligence Service (FIS), must have an impact abroad, if only through the intermediary of similar services in foreign countries.

VIII. SECRECY IN CRIMINAL PROCEEDINGS: TERRORISM

A. *Secrecy in Criminal Procedure*

As we have already mentioned, a person's right to be heard may be restricted under the provisions of Sec. 108 CCrP, although these 'restrictions must be limited in time or to individual procedural acts' (subsection 3). We also saw that the public prosecutor may order an undercover investigation under the provisions of Secs. 285*a* to 298 CCrP. In this connection, measures may be taken to ensure the anonymity of undercover agents (Secs. 151 and 288 CCrP).

However, as a rule, a criminal investigation is not subject to secrecy measures, although it may be in connection with Sec. 73(2) CCrP. This section provides

[109] To our knowledge, Switzerland does not hold any foreign terrorists in prison.

that the director of proceedings may require private claimants and other persons involved in the proceedings (particularly the accused and witnesses, cf. Secs. 104 and 105 CCrP) and their legal counsel, cautioned regarding the penalties under Sec. 292 CrC, to maintain confidentiality with regard to the proceedings and the persons implicated, if the object of the proceedings or a private interest requires it. However, a time limit must be placed on this obligation.

In the context of terrorism cases, we can summarise the preceding elements as follows: secrecy may be ordered in criminal proceedings provided it complies with the proportionality rule and is justified having regard to private and public interests, such as Switzerland's internal or external security. However, as we have seen, 'If the reason for imposing the restriction continues to apply, the criminal justice authorities may base their decisions on files that have not been disclosed to a party only if that party has been informed of the essential content thereof' (Sec. 108(4) CCrP).

B. *Confidentiality of Proceedings and Witness Anonymity*

According to the principle set out in Sec. 69(1) CCrP, proceedings before the court of first instance and the court of appeal, as well as the delivery of oral judgments and orders of these courts, are conducted in public (with the exception of the judges' deliberations). However, the court may partly exclude members of the public from hearings or order hearings in camera if public safety or order, or the legitimate interests of a person involved in the proceedings – in particular, the victim – so require (Sec. 70(1) CCrP). The court must weigh all the interests, while taking into account the respect for the principle of a public hearing. Subject to certain conditions, the court may allow court reporters, or other persons with a legitimate interest, access to in-camera proceedings (Sec. 70(3) CCrP).

We have already mentioned the question of anonymity of witnesses and undercover agents, and simply add that the recent Federal Act of 23 December 2011 on Extra-procedural Witness Protection may prove to be of some use as a measure in terrorism-related investigations. Generally speaking, protective measures and secrecy measures must be ordered only after carefully weighing the interests in the case, that is, those of the persons accused, against those of the security of Switzerland and the other participants in the proceedings.

IX. CONCLUSION

The fight against terrorism has remained a major concern in the twenty-first century. Switzerland has played an active part, essentially by establishing a legal framework capable of hampering its financing. It has an administration of justice system and procedural rules that should allow effective repression, with the key issues being the material resources available to the criminal justice authorities to carry out their important mission, and essential international co-operation.

One point of concern, or at least one question mark, remains. Sec. $260^{quinquies}$ CrC entered into force on 1 October 2003, and so far no convictions have been handed down for financing terrorism. This fact certainly poses a problem in terms of general prevention. There are several possible explanations. First, the provision is still relatively new. In inherently complex matters, we need to allow more time before drawing more definite conclusions. Second, in the fight against terrorism financing, it is often extremely difficult to obtain evidence. As a rule, it is more difficult to prove an unlawful purpose than to show proof of criminal origin. The destination of assets is essentially based on the subjective element of the intent to finance, which seriously complicates the task of the prosecuting authorities. Moreover, the frequent use of informal systems for transferring capital makes the situation even more complex. Finally, there is a tendency at times for authorities to rely on Sec. 260ter CrC, regarding criminal organisation, rather than to apply Sec. $260^{quinquies}$ CrC. Even if this approach is not very satisfactory from the doctrinal point of view, in practice, at least, it overcomes some of the difficulties in applying Sec. $260^{quinquies}$ CrC, which proves to be too restrictive in that it excludes the criminalisation of recklessness.

It is extremely difficult to measure the preventive effect of a criminal provision, particularly in the area we are dealing with here. However, without being overly optimistic, we might realistically assume that some criminals have refrained from using Swiss financial services because of the relative efficacy of its legislative and administrative machinery. At any event, we must continue to deploy our efforts to curtail a phenomenon that impairs fundamental rights and endangers the stability of our societies.

8

Belgium

Anne Weyembergh and Céline Cocq

Warning: On 16 January 2015, following a police intervention in Verviers and in the aftermath of the *Charlie Hebdo* attacks in Paris, the Belgian government announced a series of measures against radicalization and terrorism. They are said to include the extension of terrorist offences, the extension of the use of special investigation techniques, the enlargement of the possibility to withdraw Belgian nationality and to withdraw temporarily the identity cards and passports, the implementation of the freezing of assets at the national level, the possibility to call on the army for specific surveillance missions and the strengthening of the analysis capacities of Belgian intelligence services.

I. INTRODUCTION

A. *Belgian Experience with Terrorism*

Until recently, the terrorist threat with which Belgium was confronted was far more limited than in other Member States (MS) of the European Union (EU), such as Italy, Spain, France, Germany and the United Kingdom.

However, this does not mean that it was totally nonexistent. Like many other Western European states, during the first half of the 1980s, Belgium faced extreme left-wing domestic terrorism, especially the activities of the so-called cellules communistes combattantes (CCC). Although this group committed numerous terrorist attacks that resulted in the death of two firefighters and injury to three others,[1] their seriousness was more limited than those performed by the German Rote Armee Fraktion (RAF) or the Italian Brigate Rosse.[2]

1 See Section III.B.

2 About the CCC's activities and links with RAF and Action directe, see R. Haquin and P. Stéphany, *Les grands dossiers criminels en Belgique*, Bruxelles, ed. Racine, 2005, at 261 and ff.

During the late 1980s and 1990s, no significant terrorist threat was recorded. But the situation changed about ten years ago.

According to intelligence and investigative authorities,[3] the international terrorist threat, especially that related to radical Islamist terrorism, has become a major concern in Belgium.[4] The country serves as an operating base for terrorist Jihadist groups, cells or networks; recruitment and training of terrorists have been organised from Belgium, and Belgium does not escape from the phenomenon of radicalization and homegrown terrorism. In this regard, the existence of more or less organised and structured recruitment network(s) to go to fight in Syria[5] are worrying. Lone wolves and self-radicalisation are also included among Belgian terrorist threats.[6] Action has been taken to face the radicalisation threat, for instance, with the adoption in 2005 of a 'national counter-radicalism plan' and a more recent federal programme of prevention of violent radicalisation.[7]

Even if marginal 'political' terrorism is still present,[8] the anarchistic threat should also be mentioned.

Belgium is not properly speaking a target of separatist terrorist organisations. However, some members of organisations such as ETA or PKK are present and have been arrested[9] on Belgian territory. Belgium does not face an important threat originating from animal rights or environmental eco-terrorist groups.

3 See for instance the annual reports by the Belgian intelligence service, *Sûreté de l'Etat*. Annual report 2011, available at http://justitie.belgium.be/nl/binaries/VSSE_rapportannuel2011_FR_web_tcm265-205216.pdf (accessed on 14 February 2014).

4 In this regard, see the following cases: the *Nizar Trabelsi, Tarek Maaroufi and Amor Sliti case*, also known as the *case of the military barracks of Kleine Brogel*; the *Moroccan Islamic Combatant Group case* (GICM – *Groupe islamique combattant marocain*); the *case of the Iraki kamikaze network*, also called *Muriel Degauque case*; the *case of the Afghan kamikaze network*, also called the *Malika El Aroud* case; the *Ayachi and Ali Tabich* case; the *case of Hasan H. or of the terrorist of Sint-Jansplein*; and the case of the *Syrian and Somali Al-Qaida networks* (about theses cases, see III.B).

5 Belgium is one of the EU Member States from which fighters are more numerous.

6 In this regard, two cases may be mentioned: the attack in March 2012 of a Shiite mosque (*Rida Mosque* in Anderlecht-Brussels) and the attack in June 2012 against police officers in the Brussels' underground (see Section III.B).

7 The prevention programme was launched on 16 April 2013: available at http://www.milquet.belgium.be/sites/default/files/130419-Programme%20de%20prévention%20de%20la%20radicalisation%20violente.pdf (accessed on 14 February 2014).

8 See for instance the *DHKP-C* case (Revolutionary People's Liberation Party–Front) and two other files concerning, on the one hand, the left-wing extremist group parti communiste politico-militaire (PCPM) and, on the other hand, the right-wing extremist group Blood and Honour Vlaanderen (see Section III.B).

9 In this regard, see *e.g.* the *TE-SAT 2011 report* (*EU Terrorism Situation and Trend Report*), at 21 and 37.

B. *Belgian Counter-Terrorism Legislation*

Belgian counter-terrorism legislation has been deeply influenced by EU legislation, specifically the Framework Decision 2002/475/JHA of 13 June 2002 on combating terrorism (hereafter the 2002 FD[10]) and the Framework Decision 2008/919/JHA of 28 November 2008 amending the previous one (hereafter the 2008 FD[11]). These EU instruments have resulted in two Belgian federal/national pieces of legislation:

- First, the law of 19 December 2003 concerning terrorist offences,[12] which mainly aims to implement the 2002 FD and the UN Convention for the repression of terrorism financing of 9 December 1999. It inserted a new Title in Book II CC (Criminal Code), namely *Title Iter. – terrorist offences*, which contains Art. 137 to 141ter. It introduced the 'terrorist offences' (Art. 137 and 138 CC), the 'offences relating to a terrorist group' (Art. 139 and 140 CC) and the 'contribution to the commission of a terrorist offence committed independently from a terrorist group' (Art. 141 CC). This law also revised some provisions of the preliminary title of the Belgian Code d'instruction criminelle (Art. 6 and 10*ter*) and some provisions of the Code d'instruction criminelle (hereafter Code of Criminal Procedure or *CCP*) (Art. 90*ter*).
- Second, the law of 18 February 2013 modifying Book II, Title I*ter* CC,[13] which mainly aims to transpose the 2008 FD and the Council of Europe's Convention of 15 May 2005 on the prevention of terrorism. It inserts new offences (Art. 140*bis* on incitement, 140*ter* on recruitment, 140*quater* on training and 140*quinquies* on being trained) and amends Art. 137 and Art. 138 CC concerning attempts.

II. THE DEFINITION OF TERRORISM

Before the transposition of the 2002 FD, Belgium was among the EU Member States that did not criminalise terrorist offences as such. Terrorism cases were dealt with on the basis of other crimes. The CCC group case[14] and the *military barracks of*

[10] *OJ*, L 164 22 June 2002.

[11] *OJ*, L 330 9 December 2008.

[12] *MB*, 29 December 2003.

[13] *MB*, 4 March 2013.

[14] See especially the attack of 1 May 1985 in front of the head office of the Fédération des entreprises de Belgique (FEB). Four members of the CCC, including P. Carette and B. Sassoye, were tried by the Cour d'assises de Bruxelles in September and October 1988. It resulted in their condemnation to life imprisonment (*réclusion à perpétuité*). However, they were not convicted for terrorist offences, since at the time, the criminal code did not know of this specific offences.

Kleine Brogel case (also known as the *Nizar Trabelsi, Tarek Maroufi and Amor Sliti* case[15]) are good illustrations of this approach.

Terrorist offences were inserted in the CC by the aforementioned law of 19 December 2003. They are defined in Art. 137 CC in a way that is quite similar to the definition of the 2002 FDs. They are composed of three constituent elements, namely the material acts, the particular seriousness and the moral element (*mens rea*) or terrorist intent. It is the latter that gives its specificity to terrorist offences.

The material acts include pre-existing criminal offences such as murder, hostage taking or kidnapping (Art. 137 para 2)[16] as well as new acts that were not previously criminalised and that are punishable only as terrorist offences (Art. 137 para 3).[17] According to the 2002 FD, the mere threat of realising those offences is also to be criminalised. However, according to the explanatory note of the Belgian legislative proposal, such a threat must be *serious*.[18]

To be qualified as terrorist offences, these acts must result in a serious danger: they must be acts that, because of their nature or context, could seriously harm a country or an international organisation.

Finally, terrorist offences include a terrorist intent, which is defined in the same terms as in the 2002 FD: the offence must have been committed 'with the aim of seriously intimidating a population, or unduly compelling a Government or an international organisation to perform or abstain from performing any act, or seriously destabilising or destroying the fundamental political, constitutional, economic or social structures of a country or of an international organisation'.

Two clauses restrict the scope of application of terrorist offences:

- Reflecting the eleventh recital of the preamble to the 2002 FD, Art. 141*bis* excludes from the scope of the offences actions by armed forces during periods of armed conflict as defined by international humanitarian law and, inasmuch as they are governed by other rules of international law, actions undertaken by the state's armed forces in the exercise of their official duties.

[15] They were condemned through a decision in first degree of 30 September 2003 by the Tribunal correctionnel de Bruxelles, which was later on confirmed by a decision of the Cour d'appel de Bruxelles in June 2004.

[16] They also cover homicide, voluntary grievous bodily harm, hostage taking, abduction, massive destructions or damages of constructions (bridges, buildings, dikes, roads, etc.), means of transportation (ships, cars, aircrafts, etc.), computer systems – insofar as such destruction or damages put human lives in jeopardy or produce significant economic losses, etc.

[17] They cover, for example, the fabrication and possession of nuclear and chemical weapons, the use of such arms or biological arms, research and development of chemical arms, release of dangerous substances that put human lives in jeopardy or the disruption of supply of fundamental natural resources that put human lives in jeopardy.

[18] *Doc. parl.*, Chambre, s.o. 2003–4, n°51-258-1, at 11.

- Art. 141*ter* contains a safeguard clause relating to fundamental rights and freedoms, in particular freedom of assembly and association. Its wording has been amended by the law of 18 February 2013. The new version is more developed than the previous one and refers especially to the freedom of expression.

III. CRIMINAL LAWS AND PROSECUTIONS

A. *Criminal Law*

Besides criminalizing terrorist acts (see Section II), Title I*ter* of Book II CC criminalises other acts. Art. 139 and 140 CC concern offences relating to a terrorist group. Art. 139 para 1 first defines such a group. The definition mirrors that of the 2002 FD: 'a structured association of more than two persons, established over a period of time and acting in concert to commit terrorist offences covered by Art. 137'. The notion of 'structured association' is not defined as such; in this regard, reference is made to the definition of Art. 2 para 1 of the 2002 FD. The provision nonetheless stipulates that an organisation whose real purpose is solely of political, trade union or of a philanthropic, philosophical or religious nature, or which solely pursues another legitimate aim, cannot, as such, be considered a terrorist group. Then, Art. 140 CC makes it a criminal offence to participate in the activity of a terrorist group. Such participation can take two forms: participation in the activities of a terrorist group, including by providing information or material resources; or in the financing of the activities of a terrorist group. In both cases, the knowledge that such participation aids the commission of a *crime* or misdemeanours (*délit*) (para 1) is necessary to prosecute these individuals. The fact of directing a terrorist group (para 2) is punished more severely. As specified in Art. 2(2) of the 2002 FD,[19] the requirement that the participant is aware that such assistance aids the commission of an offence is an essential element of the offence that must be proved by the Public Prosecutor. In the absence of such knowledge, participation is not sanctioned by Art. 140. The *travaux préparatoires* are very clear in this respect and follows the requirements of the 2002 FD.[20] This element of knowledge is *a fortiori* required for the act of directing a terrorist group.[21]

Art. 141 CC criminalises the contribution to the commission of a terrorist offence committed independently from a terrorist group. This offence was added to put

[19] Art. 2(2) provides for that 'Each Member State shall take the necessary measures to ensure that the following intentional acts are punishable: (a) directing a terrorist group; (b) participating in the activities of a terrorist group, including by supplying information or material resources, or by funding its activities in any way, with knowledge of the fact that such participation will contribute to the criminal activities of the terrorist group.'

[20] See *Doc. parl.*, Chambre, s.o., 2003–4, n° 258/001, at 13.

[21] *Ibid.*, at 14.

Belgian law in line with the UN Convention for the repression of terrorism financing of 9 December 1999. It punishes persons who, outside the cases provided for in Art. 140, furnish the means, including financial contributions, with a view to commit the terrorist offences of Art. 137.

The law of 18 February 2013 has inserted new specific offences in the CC:

- Art. 140*bis* penalises direct and indirect incitement to commit terrorist offences as defined in Art. 137 (with the exception of threatening to commit a terrorist offence).
- Art. 140*ter* penalises recruitment.
- Art. 140*quater* penalises training.
- Art. 140*quinquies* penalises the fact of being trained.

Whereas the provisions related to incitement and recruitment are quite similar to the provisions of the 2008 FD, those relating to training go beyond the requirements of the European text, in that it inserts the offence of *being trained.*[22]

Besides these offences, it should be borne in mind that aiding or abetting is generally criminalised by provisions belonging to the general part of the CC, namely by Art. 67 to 69. Attempted offences are also punishable, either on the basis of the general part of criminal law (*i.e.*, Art. 51 to 53 CC) or on the basis of Art. 137 para 2 CC.

The first law of 19 December 2003 was criticised by part of the Belgian academy, defence lawyers and nongovernmental organisations (NGOs) working in the field of human rights.[23] One of the main criticisms concerned the vagueness of some constituent elements of the terrorist offences (*i.e.*, the seriousness criteria and the *mens rea*) and the resulting breach of the legality principle. Three NGOs (Ligue des droits de l'homme, Liga voor Mensenrechten and the Syndicat des avocats pour la démocratie) introduced a request for annulment before the Belgian Constitutional Court. The NGOs mainly argued that the definition of terrorist offences established by Art. 137 CC infringes the principle of legality because it uses terms that are too

[22] The insertion of such offence was justified as follows: 'La disposition précédente visant le formateur, et non pas les personnes formées, il convient de manière logique et opérationnelle d'incriminer également la personne qui bénéficie du savoir-faire fourni par le formateur' (*Exposé des motifs*, *Doc. Parl.* Chambre, S.O. 53, 2012–13, doc 2502/001, at 16).

[23] See especially the concerns expressed by Greenpeace and trade unions at the hearings of 9 June 2009 (*Doc. parl.*, Chambre, s.o. 52, 2008–9, 2128, at 59 and ff.) and those expressed by NGOs engaged with the protection of human rights, such as the Ligue des droits de l'homme and the Comité de vigilance en matière de lutte contre le terrorisme (Comité T) (see annual reports of Comité T, available at http://www.liguedh.be. See also M.L. Cesoni, 'Une évaluation des législations antiterroristes: les nouvelles incriminations', avis pour la Commission de la Justice de la Chambre, October 2009; and M. Moucheron, 'Chronique de criminologie – Le terme terrorisme et la construction européenne: une histoire obscure', *Rev. dr. pen.*, 2004, at 889 and ff.

vague and imprecise.[24] By its decision of 13 July 2005, the Court rejected the request after reminding the NGOs that the law aims at transposing the 2002 FD. The Court said that the principle of legality in criminal matters does not prevent the law from conferring a power of discretion to the judges. Even if it confers judges a wide margin of discretion, the law of 19 December 2003 does not give them an autonomous power of criminalisation that would impinge the legislators' competence.[25]

Another criticism concerned the preventive nature of the incriminations. Such criticism addressed especially the criminalisation of the threat to realize a terrorist offence, even if the threat was not followed by any effect (Art.137, para 3, 6°), or the criminalisation of the contribution to an offence that ultimately was not committed or even attempted (Art. 141).[26] More generally, the shift of judicial intervention from a reactive and repressive nature (downstream of the criminal acts) towards a preventive nature (upstream of the criminal acts)[27] or the enlargement of criminal law towards prevention and its consequences, particularly access to specific investigative measures, is a source of concern. Such criticism has also *a fortiori* been addressed to the offences inserted by the law of 18 February 2013,[28] since they have fostered the move of criminal law towards a multiplication of inchoate offences. Because of their broad scope, the definitions of the new offences confer a wide discretionary power to the competent authorities. No doubt their interpretation will be closely followed by numerous observers, and especially by NGOs working on human rights, who are quite critical in this regard.

B. *Terrorism Prosecutions*

Generally speaking, persons who are suspected or accused of terrorist offences are *not* subject to a special regime. They are subject to the same rules and benefit from the same rights as other suspects and accused persons; terrorism prosecutions are conducted in ordinary courts, namely in the Tribunaux correctionnels or in the Cour d'Assises.[29]

However, some particular procedural rules apply to terrorist offences, although they are also applied in other serious crimes. As will be developed later, specific

[24] *Arrêt* 125/2005 : available at http://www.const-court.be (accessed 10 June 2014), paras 4.1. and B.4.

[25] *Arrêt* 125/2005, para B.7 and ff.

[26] See M.L. Cesoni, *op. cit.*, at 4, 13, 14, 17.

[27] See the hearing of D. Vandermeersch, *Doc. parl.*, Chambre, s.o. 52, 2008–9, 2128, p. 43.

[28] See for instance the hearing of the Ligue des droits de l'homme (*Doc. Sénat de Belgique, session de* 2012–13, 5-1905/3).

[29] See the *Rida Mosque case*, which resulted in the death of the Imam Abdoullah Dadouh (*Chambre des Mises en accusation de Bruxelles*, 13 June 2013). On 5 December 2014, the Brussels *Cour d'Assises* found him guilty of arson attack against this mosque with the aggravating circumstance of murder

measures/rules, and especially special investigation techniques, can be used where some of the aforementioned offences are concerned. Terrorist offences are also subject to specific rules concerning extraterritorial jurisdiction (see Section IV.A). Besides, when the good administration of justice so requires, the prosecution may be exercised by the Federal Public Prosecutor (the so-called *parquet fédéral*), whose competence extends to the whole national territory (Art. 144*ter* of the *Code judiciaire*, para 1, 2° and 3°). In practice, centralisation takes place in almost all terrorist cases.[30] Specialised *juges d'instruction* are competent for the offences covered by Art. 137 to 141 CC. Their jurisdiction also extends to the whole Belgian territory.

Since 2005, ninety individuals have been tried before the Belgian courts under terrorism charges.[31] During 2012, there have been twenty-five verdicts (convictions or acquittals). Compared to 2011, the number of arrests increased in 2012, especially those related to religion-inspired terrorism. The number of convictions is also increasing.[32]

So far, only a few cases have concerned the preparation or realization of terrorist attacks in Belgian territory. Two of them have been mentioned earlier – that is, the CCC group case and the *Nizar Trabelsi, Tarek Maaroufi and Amor Sliti case or case of the military barracks of Kleine Brogel* (see Section II). These cases related to facts committed before the entry into force of the 19 December 2003 Belgian law and thus did not concern terrorist offences properly speaking. Two other cases are much more recent. In the case of the attack against three police officers in the Brussels underground, the accused was condemned by the Brussels Tribunal correctionnel by a decision dated 25 June 2013, which confirmed that he was guilty of attempted assassination in the context of a terrorist offence of Art. 137 CC.[33] In the case of the Rida Mosque in Anderlecht-Brussels, the individual was charged by the Federal Public Prosecutor with the terrorist offence of Art. 137 CC, which was finally not confirmed by the jury.

For the rest, most of the criminal proceedings and/or judgments do not involve terrorist offences as such (Art. 137 and 138 CC), but rather offences related to a terrorist group (Art. 139 and 140 CC). That is why most of the relevant cases concern small or larger groups of suspects or accused. The following examples can be mentioned.

against the imam. He was condemned to twenty-seven years in prison. However, the charge of terrorist offence was dropped.

30 See especially *circulaire commune de la ministre de la Justice et du Collège des procureurs généraux relative à l'approche judiciaire en matière de terrorisme* (COL 9/2005), which was several times completed by *addenda*: COL 18/2006 (concerning special investigation judges – *juges d'instruction*) and COL 2/2007(concerning the Organe de Coordination pour l'Analyse de la Menace [OCAM]). On the advantages of such centralisation, see M. Delmulle, *Doc. parl.*, Chambre, s.o. 52, 2008–9, 2128, at 18 and ff., at 52.

31 For numbers, see also those provided in the successive TE-SAT reports from 2008 to 2013.

32 Europol, TE-SAT 2013, at 44.

33 The sentence is seventeen years of imprisonment. This decision has not been subject to appeal.

They concern facts committed after the entry into force of the Belgian law of 19 December 2003:

- The 'Moroccan Islamic Combatant Group' case (GICM)[34]
- The *DHKP-C* case, which resulted in a high number of judicial decisions[35]
- The case of the Iraki kamikaze network, also called Muriel Degauque case[36]
- The Afghan kamikaze network case, also called the Malika El Aroud case[37]
- The Ayachi and Ali Tabich case[38]
- The case of Hasan H. or the terrorist of Sint-Jansplein[39]
- The parti communiste politico-militaire (PCPM) case[40]
- The Blood and Honour Vlaanderen case[41]
- The case of the 'Syrian and Somali Al-Qaida networks'[42]

[34] Brussels Trib. corr. (54th Chamber *bis*), 16 February 2006 and Brussels Appeal Court (12th Chamber), 19 January 2007. Note that in this case, some of the convicted persons brought a case before the European Court for Human Rights (ECtHR), which resulted in the condemnation of Belgium. Indeed, in its decision *El Haski* v. *Belgium*, 649/08, 25 September 2012, the Court considered that the admission in criminal proceedings of statements obtained in violation of Art. 3 automatically rendered the proceedings as a whole unfair and violated Art. 6 of the Convention. So, for these persons, the proceedings are still pending.

[35] *I.e.*, four decisions on the substance of the case and two rulings by the Cour de cassation: Bruges Corr. (14th Chamber), 28 February 2006; Ghent Trib. Corr. (6th Chamber), 7 December 2007; Cass., 19 April 2007, P.06.1605.N/1; Antwerp Trib. Corr. (13th Chamber), 7 February 2008; Cass., 24 June 2008, P.08.0408.N; and Brussels Trib. Corr. (13th Chamber), 23 December 2009.

[36] Brussels Trib. corr. (49th Chamber *bis*), 10 January 2008; and Brussels Court of Appeal (12th Chamber), 26 June 2006.

[37] Brussels Trib. corr. (49ème Chamber), 10 May 2010; and Brussels Court of Appeal (11th Chamber), 1 December 2010.

[38] Brussels Trib. corr., 25 June 2012; Brussels Court of Appeal, 21 February 2013.

[39] Trib. corr. of Mechelen, 5 December 2012; and Antwerp Court of Appeal, 8 January 2014.

[40] Also called *case of the secours rouge international*. This case is still pending. On 19 April 2012, the Chambre du Conseil of Brussels did not retain the qualification of participation in a terrorist activity, but decided the transfer of the four concerned individuals to the Tribunal correctionnel under the qualification of attempted counterfeit. On 24 April 2012, the Federal Prosecutor introduced an appeal against such a ruling. On 28 February 2013, the Chambre des mises en accusation of Brussels decided to refer the case to the Tribunal correctionnel under the qualification of 'participation in a terrorist activity' as well, but this decision was quashed by a decision of the Cour de cassation (*Cass.*, 5 June 2013, P.13.0439.F). The case is still pending.

[41] This case resulted in condemnations on the ground of racism, xenophobia and incitement to discrimination (see especially Trib. Corr. Veurne, 9 March 2011, available on the website of the Centre for Equal Opportunities and Opposition to Racism: http://www.diversite.be/). However, in a case submitted to the Tribunal correctionnel of Termonde, the Federal Office for prosecution prosecuted members of this group on the basis of participation in activities of a terrorist group. The tribunal referred preliminary questions to the Constitutional Court (*Arrêt* 49/2013, 28 March 2013, and comments by B. Michel, 'Le parquet federal, partie intégrante d'un ministère public et indivisible', in *RDPC*, 2013, at 966–83). On 7 February 2014, the Tribunal correctionnel of Termonde convicted some of these members on the basis of participation in activities of a terrorist group.

[42] The first hearing took place the 30 January 2014.

From these cases, it results that, in order to establish the offence of participating in a terrorist group's activities, in most cases, a contribution to the preparation of a concrete terrorist offence is not required. It is sufficient to establish the existence of a terrorist group and of an act of participation to its activities. However, in some cases, some judges gave an extensive interpretation of the offence of participation in the activity of a terrorist group[43] whereas others gave a limited interpretation of such notions.[44] These variations fed the aforementioned criticisms and worries concerning the vagueness of the definition of terrorist offences. This is also why in the *PCPM* case, the defendants asked the Chambre des mises en accusation of Brussels to refer a preliminary ruling to the European Court of Justice (ECJ) to confirm one or the other approach. On 28 February 2013, the Chambre des mises en accusation of Brussels decided to refer the case to the Tribunal correctionnel under the qualification of 'participation in a terrorist activity', without referring a preliminary question to the ECJ. The defence then introduced a *pourvoi en cassation*[45] and the Cour de cassation quashed the decision.[46] It remains to be seen whether a preliminary ruling will eventually be referred to the ECJ.

What is remarkable is the rare use in practice of the new offences inserted in the Belgian CC by the law of 18 February 2013, namely incitement, recruitment and active/passive training (Art. 140*bis* to *quinquies* CC). This may of course be due to its very recent entry into force (14 March 2013). However, it is also due to the fact that, according to the wording of these new provisions, practitioners tend to resort to the offence of participation in the activities of a terrorist group (Art. 139–140 CC) and turn to the new offences only where the others cannot be used. The new offences were expected to apply to the cases of individuals inciting and helping people to travel to Syria for the purpose of training and fighting alongside Al-Qaida and other radical Islamist groups or in the case of persons coming back from Syria (passive training). But, so far, such use seems to remain exceptional, since sooner or later there is a group or a network involved. Nevertheless, a *juge d'instruction* charged a person involved in the organisation of trips to Syria, Jean-Louis le Soumis, with incitement (Art. 140*bis* CC) and training (art. 140*quater*). In the other cases related to the Syrian context, it seems that the offences used are participation in the activities of a terrorist group.[47] It is too early to make an in-depth assessment of the

[43] See *e.g.* in the DHKP-C case the first two Appeal Courts (Bruges and Ghent), which especially elaborated on the notion of direction of such a group.

[44] See in the same case the last two Appeal Courts (Antwerp and Brussels).

[45] Appeal against a final decision before the Court of Cassation (Supreme Court) based on the violation of the law.

[46] *Cour de cass.*, 5 June 2013, P.13.0439.F

[47] See, for instance, the *Jejoen Bontinck* case concerning a young man who stayed eight months in Syria to engage in combat among the rebels against Bashar al-Assad's government and who has been charged with participation in the activities of a terrorist organisation (Art. 139–140 CC).

practical use of the new offences, but it raises of course the sensitive question of their need and utility.

In the first years of implementation of the 19 December 2003 law, charges brought by the Federal Public Prosecutor often included participation in the activities of a terrorist group as well as other offences, such as membership or direction of an *association de malfaiteurs* (Art. 322 to 324 CC) or of a criminal organisation (Art. 324*bis* and ff. CC). This happened, for example, in the *DHKP-C* case. However, it appears that this is becoming less common, and current practice suggests that the Federal Public prosecutor tends to abandon this approach. In any event, it remains true that often,[48] charges of terrorism-related offences are combined with more common offences, such as counterfeiting of official documents, illegal possession of arms, and so on.

C. *Punishment of Terrorism*

A difference is to be made between the main penalties and those that are accessory or complementary.

The main penalties are provided for in the specific provisions of the CC criminalising the various terrorist offences.

When the material acts constituting a terrorist offence are listed among the preexisting offences included in Art. 137 para 1, a system of aggravation of penalties applies: in accordance with Art. 138 para 1 CC, the foreseen criminal sanction corresponds to the aggravated penalty of the offence in question. In turn, Art. 138 para 2 provides the penalties to be applied to the new offences contained in Art. 137 para 2 CC.

According to Art. 140 CC, the penalties for leading a terrorist group are more severe than those foreseen for 'mere' participation: whereas a participant will be sanctioned with an imprisonment sentence of five to ten years and a fine ranging from 550 to 27.500 euros, a leader will be sanctioned with an imprisonment sentence of fifteen to twenty years and a fine ranging from 5.500 to 1.100.000 euros.

The same penalties as those provided for participation in the activities of a terrorist group (i.e., an imprisonment sentence of five to ten years and a fine ranging from 550 to 27.500 euros) are applicable to the offences covered by Art. 140*bis* to 140*quinquies* (incitement, recruitment, training or being trained) and, with some exceptions, to those of Art. 141 CC (contribution to the commission of a terrorist offence committed independently of a terrorist group).

[48] See the *DHKP-C* case, the *Iraki kamikaze network*, etc.

'Accessory' penalties contained in Art. 31 to 34 CC (such as the 'prohibition of certain civil and political rights', such as the right to exercise certain public functions, eligibility rights, the right to vote, etc.) or special confiscation (Art. 42 and 43*quater*) may or must be applied in the light of the general part of the criminal code.

Belgium did not make use of the possibility offered by Art. 6 of the 2002 FD, which allowed Member States to reduce the penalties when the offender renounces terrorist activity and provides administrative or judicial authorities with information that they would not have otherwise managed to obtain. In relation to this, one should however, be reminded that in Belgium, prosecutions are guided by the principle of opportunity, according to which the Public Prosecutor assesses the opportunity to prosecute (Art. 28*quater* para 1 CCP).

The possibility to request rehabilitation[49] is provided for in Art. 621 and ff. of the CCP. Rehabilitation is only possible under the listed conditions. The request must be addressed to the prosecutor of the district where the person lives.[50] Within two months after its reception, the prosecutor submits the request to the *Chambre des mises en accusation*, which shall decide within one month.[51] So far, no claim for rehabilitation seems to have been made in terrorism cases.

IV. INVESTIGATIVE POWERS

Regarding investigative powers in Belgium, a distinction is traditionally made between judicial investigations (Section IV.A), administrative investigations (Section IV.B) and the intelligence and security services missions (Section IV.C).

A. *Judicial Investigations*

In Belgium, police missions are divided in administrative police missions and judicial police missions (*police judiciaire*). Both share the aim of ensuring compliance and contributing to the protection of freedoms and individual rights and the democratic development of society.[52] However, they are different in nature: administrative police missions are public order missions of a preventive nature, whereas judicial police missions aim at bringing offences and their perpetrators to justice and are thus of a more repressive nature. Both types of missions are performed by local and federal police forces.

[49] A mechanism that results in the disappearance or deletion of a conviction and its consequences. It can be provided for by the law, *i.e.*, acquired automatically after a certain period of time, or by the judiciary, *i.e.*, granted by a judicial authority.

[50] Art. 628 CCP.

[51] Art. 630 CCP.

[52] Art. 1, al. 2, Law of 5 August 1992.

In performing their judicial police missions, police forces operate under the control of judicial authorities.

The offences covered by Art. 137 and ff. CC may of course give rise to 'normal' investigatory measures, that is, those that are not specific to a certain category of offences. The offences covered by Art. 137, 140 and 141 CC may also give rise to more specific measures. Indeed, the 19 December 2003 law added those offences to the list of offences of Art. 90*ter* para 2 CCP, for which telephone tapping and other special provisions or measures may apply.

In particular, the offences contained in Art. 137, 140 and 141 CC may give rise to the following:

- Proactive investigations, which consist in the search, collection, recording and treatment of data and information on the basis of a reasonable suspicion that punishable offences yet unknown will be perpetrated or have already been perpetrated (Art. 28*bis* para 2 CCP).
- Special investigation techniques (*méthodes particulières d'enquêtes*, or MPR),[53] formally introduced in the CCP[54] by a law of 6 January 2003 (known as the BOM[55] Law[56]), were subsequently amended.[57] The main MPR are listed in Art. 47*ter* para 1 CCP, namely observation,[58] infiltration[59] and recourse to informers.[60] These measures may also be used in the context of proactive investigations. They are subject to a series of rules, contained mainly in Art. 47*ter*, para 1 to 47*undecies* CPP.[61] They are possible only for the offences listed, among which are the offences defined by Art. 137, 140 and 141 CC.
- Other intrusive investigating measures, such as the interception of communications, are also subject to special conditions (Art. 90*ter* and ff. CCP). Recourse to secret surveillance is also mentioned (Art. 46*quinquies* or 89*ter* CCP).[62]

53 See M. L. Cesoni, 'Terrorisme et involutions démocratiques', *Rev. dr. pén.*, 2002, at 141 and ff.

54 See Art. 47*ter* to 47*undecies* CCP. See M. Franchimont, A. Jacobs and A. Masset, *Manuel de procédure pénale*, Larcier, 2009, at 321 and ff.; M. De Rue and C. De Valkeneer, *Les méthodes particulières de recherche et quelques autres méthodes d'enquête. Commentaire de la loi du 6 janvier 2003 et de ses arrêtés d'application, Bruxelles*, Larcier, 2004.

55 *Loi du 6 janvier 2003 concernant les méthodes particulières de recherche et quelques autres méthodes d'enquêtes*, MB 12 May 2003

56 BOM, *for bijzondere opsporingsmethoden.*

57 For instance by the *Loi du 27 décembre 2005 portant modification diverses au CIC et au CJ en vue d'améliorer les modes d'investigation dans la lutte contre le terrorisme et la criminalité grave et organisée*, MB 30 December 2005.

58 Art. 47*sexies*, para 1 CCP.

59 Art. 47*octies*, para 1 CCP.

60 Art. 47*ter*, para 1 CCP.

61 For example, subsidiarity and proportionality conditions.

62 This provision enables police forces to get into private premises without the owner knowing and without the latter's consent.

- The questioning of anonymous witnesses (Art. 86*bis* to 86*quinquies* CCP) (see Section X.B).
- A prosecutor's request to a bank not to give up debts and engagements linked to bank accounts or to deny access to a safety box during a certain period of time (Art. 46*quater* para 2 b) CCP).

It must be recalled that, because the new offences introduced by the Law of February 2013 (*i.e.*, incitement, recruitment and training) were not included in Art. 90*ter* para 2 CCP, the aforementioned provisions do not apply to them.

Two principles establishing limits to the competent authorities' action are worth mentioning, particularly in the context of MPR. The first is the general prohibition of provocation. In case of provocation, which is defined by the Code, prosecution is inadmissible regarding the concerned facts.[63] Such prohibition is in line with the case law of the European Court of Human Rights (ECtHR).[64] The second principle is the prohibition of police officers committing offences in the execution of MPR.[65] However, it might be necessary to allow the undercover agents to commit offences either for the success of the operation, to be able to get into the criminal circle or to stay in it or to safeguard the officers' own safety or the safety of other persons implicated in the operation.[66] In order to avoid punishment for these offences, an exemption of punishment (*excuse absolutoire*) is provided for, but is subject to strict conditions.[67]

B. *Administrative Investigations*

The administrative police is also active in fighting terrorism, especially in the field of anti-radicalism. However, they do not have access to special investigative techniques. They may collect information without recourse to intrusive means, for instance via informers or by means of open sources. Their activities concern especially the groups listed in the so-called *Liste des groupements à suivre*, which enumerates extreme

[63] According to Art. 30, preliminary Title of the CCP, there is provocation when the criminal intent of the perpetrator is directly borne, strengthened or confirmed although he or she wanted to put an end to it through the intervention of a police officer or a third person acting on the explicit request of this officer.

[64] See ECtHR, 5 Febr. 2008, *Ramanauskas* v. *Lithuania*, 74420/01, para 51,54 and 55; ECtHR, 9 June 1998, *Teixeira de Castro* v. *Portugal*, 25829/94, paras 36 and 38–9. About this case law, see L. Stariene, 'The limits of the use of undercover agents and the right to a fair trial under Article 6(1) of the European Convention on Human Rights' (2009) 3 *Jurisprudencija – Jurisprudence* 117, at 263 and ff.

[65] Art. 47*quinquies* para 1 CCP.

[66] C. De Valkeneer, *La tromperie dans l'administration de la preuve pénale*, Brussels, Larcier, 2000, at 459 and ff.

[67] See Art 47*quinquies* paras 2–3 CCP.

left-wing, extreme right-wing and Islamic radical groups.[68] The main legal basis for these activities lies in Art. 44/1 and ff. of the Law on Police Functions of 5 August 1992. These provisions are currently undergoing an important legal reform. A bill is indeed being discussed before the Belgian Parliament, aiming at strengthening the efficient management of police information and detailing their legal framework. This bill should also provide a legal basis to the aforementioned *Liste des groupements à suivre*.[69]

The aforementioned bill does not aim to provide the administrative police with specific investigatory powers. Thus, it should not be assimilated with a potential proposal for a so-called BAM law,[70] which has been heavily discussed but has not yet materialised. This BAM law would be the third pillar in the field of special investigative techniques and would complete the BOM law (discussed in the previous section) and the BIM law (discussed in the following section).

For the time being, very little has been developed on the administrative side. So Belgium can be considered one of the states where the focus in the fight against terrorism is mostly placed on the judicial actors and proceedings. Whereas some experts assess this as positive, others consider it as a gap and wonder whether such a vacuum will not lead to an overexploitation of judicial actors and proceedings that intervene always more upstream.

C. *Intelligence Agencies*

There are two Belgian intelligence and security services, namely the civil intelligence service or Sûreté de l'Etat, which is of a civil nature, and the General Intelligence and Security Service (Service Général de Renseignements et de Sécurité des Forces Armées, or SGRS), which is of a military nature.[71] Their missions and competences are legally provided for in the Organic Law on the Intelligence and Security Services of 30 November 1998, amended in 2003.[72]

68 This national list existed before the 9/11 attacks. Already in 1998, 146 groups were registered (see *Senate, Questions et Réponses, Bulletin* 1–92, 1998–9, Question n°1409, 28 October 1998. See also *Commission de l'Intérieur, des affaires générales et de la fonction publique, Question* 03.02, 31 January 2007).

69 *Projet de loi modifiant la loi sur la fonction de police, loi du 8 décember 1992 relative à la protection de la vie privée à l'égard des traitements de données à caractère personnel et le Code d'instruction criminelle*, Chamber, doc 53, 3105/001, 4 November 2013, Art. 12.

70 BAM is an acronym for *bijzondere administratieve methoden*.

71 See F. Goossens, 'Les missions et compétences des services de renseignement et de sécurité belges', *JT*, 2002, at 617 and ff.; S. Petermann and W. Claes (eds.), *Les services de renseignement en Belgique et les nouvelles menaces* (Bruxelles, Politeia, 2005).

72 *Loi organique des services de renseignement et de sécurité*, *MB* December 18, 1998, modified by a law of 3 April 2003, *MB*, 12 May 2003.

The Sûreté de l'Etat has different missions, including searching, analysing and exploiting information relating to every activity that threatens or could threaten the internal security of the state, the democratic and constitutional order, the external security of the state and/or its international relations.[73] These activities include individual or collective threatening activities, including terrorism, taking place inside or outside the country.[74] The SGRS is also involved in counter-terrorism activities. It has different missions,[75] including collecting, analysing and exploiting intelligence related to any activity that threatens or could threaten the integrity of the Belgian territory, military defence plans, execution of armed forces' missions, the security of Belgian citizens abroad or any other fundamental interest of the country as defined in the Royal decree following a proposal of the ministerial Committee for Intelligence and Security. Terrorist activities are part of these threats. The SGRS is also in charge of the military security of the personnel operating under the authority of the Ministry of Defence, as well as of the security of military facilities, armament, equipment, plans, documents and communication and information systems. This mission is also related to secrecy pertaining to international agreements with Belgium or to the execution of the missions of the armed forces. All these security-related activities focus on Belgian armed forces and on the allied military facilities in Belgium. If needed, they can be executed for the benefit of Belgian units deployed abroad.

The Law of 4 February 2010 concerning the methods of data collection by intelligence and security services (the so-called BIM law[76]) describes a series of special/exceptional methods for gathering data and affords Belgian intelligence and security services (in case of terrorism, especially the Sûreté de l'Etat) the possibility of using some intrusive measures to collect data (*méthodes de recueil de données*, or MRD). A difference is made between the three following types of measures:

- Ordinary measures (use of open sources, indicators, surveillance of public premises without technical means, etc.) that are not subject to a specific regime
- Specific measures, which are moderately intrusive (surveillance of public premises with technical means, tracking of telecommunication without content

[73] Art. 7 Law 30 November 1998.

[74] Art. 8 Law 30 November 1998.

[75] See Art. 11 Law 30 November 1998.

[76] BIM is an acronym for *Bijzondere inlichtingen methoden*. *Loi du 4 février 2010 relative aux méthodes de recueil des données par les services de renseignement et de sécurité*, MB 10 March 2010. On the practical implementation of the law, see the reports by the Standing Intelligence Agencies Review Committee (*Comité permanent de Contrôle des services de renseignement et de sécurité* (*Comité permanent R*), available at http://www.comiteri.be.

interception, etc.), which are notified to the BIM Commission (composed of three magistrates) and which may be implemented as long as there is no contrary advice

- Exceptional measures, considered exceptional either because of their target (lawyer, physician, journalist) or because of their intrusiveness (interception of telecommunications, observation of private premises, intrusion in a IT system, etc.), which can only be implemented after positive advice of the BIM Commission

With regard to intelligence services, the Law of 10 July 2006 concerning threat analysis should also be mentioned, since it established the Threat Analysis Co-ordination Body (the Organe de coordination pour l'analyse de la menace, or OCAM[77]) and the Royal Decree of 28 November 2006 implementing it.[78] Acting under the joint authority of the Ministers of the Interior and Justice, the OCAM analyses terrorist and extremist threats on the basis of the information and intelligence provided in particular by the General Intelligence and Security Service, the Criminal Investigation Department (*i.e.*, Sûreté de l'Etat) and the federal and local police.

D. *Relations between 'Investigators'*

Security agencies have different aims or objectives. For example, judicial police missions and intelligence services missions are different. Whereas the police services mainly aim to protect citizens and their goods against offences or public order attacks, the intelligence services take care of the protection of the nation and of the general interest. The investigations performed by the judicial police have a judicial finality, while those undertaken by the intelligence services aim to inform the executive power of the existence of threats that may endanger the rule of law or fundamental freedoms.[79]

In spite of such differences, links exist between these actors and their missions.[80] In particular, communication of information by intelligence services to police and judicial authorities is for organised by Art. 19 and 19.1 of the 1998 Law organising the intelligence and security services (see Section X.A). Art. 20 establishes a general

77 Law of 10 July 2006 *relative á l'analyse de la menace*, MB 20 July 2006.

78 *Arréte royal portant exécution de la loi du 10 juillet 2006 relative á l'analyse de la menace, MB*, 1 December 2006.

79 J.-C. Delepière, 'Contrôle démocratique des services de renseignements', *Le Journal de la police*, n°3, March 2006, at 10.

80 See *e.g.* F. Goossens, 'Les missions et compétences des services de renseignement et de sécurité belges', *op. cit.*, at 617 and ff.

duty of ensuring efficient mutual cooperation between intelligence services, police, administrative and judicial authorities. This collaboration must be in accordance with existing agreements and legal requirements.

An approximation of the means or tools available to judicial police, judicial authorities and intelligence services has been observed and results from various elements. Firstly, judicial police and judicial authorities intervene increasingly upstream. This is in particular due to the possibilities offered by proactive investigations and the development of inchoate offences, such as participation in the activities of a terrorist group. Another element to be taken into account is the possibility for the intelligence services to use specific or exceptional measures to collect data (such as MRD) and the fact that such data may be brought before the court (see Section X.A). The question is thus whether this evolution does not create a blur between actors. Such a blur would be worsened if the BAM law were eventually adopted.

E. *Recourse to Data in the Hands of Private Companies*

As is well known, data in the hands of private companies are increasingly being exploited in criminal proceedings. This is especially true in the context of terrorist offences. Besides the ideas developed later in this chapter concerning the fight against terrorism financing, the Belgian implementation of Directive 2006/24/EC of 15 March 2006, covering the retention of data generated or processed in connection with publicly available electronic communications services and public communications networks, and the amending of Directive 2002/58/EC are to be mentioned.[81] This Directive requires operators to retain certain categories of data (identifying users and details of telephone calls and emails, although not the content of those communications) for a period between six months and two years and to make them available, on request, to law enforcement authorities for the purposes of investigating, detecting and prosecuting serious crime and terrorism. The Belgian law implementing the Directive 2002/58/EC[82] amends Art. 126 of the law on electronic communications. A Royal Decree has also been adopted, specifying the data to be retained.[83] As in other Member States, these measures have been severely criticised in Belgium.

[81] Directive 2002/58/EC 12 July 2002 (on privacy and electronic communications) OJL 21, 31 July 2002.

[82] *Loi du 30 juillet 2013 portant modification des articles 2, 126 et 145 de la loi du 13 juin 2005 relative aux communications électroniques et de l'article 90decies du Code d'instruction criminelle.*

[83] Art. 3 to 6, Royal Decree implementing article 126 of Law of 13 June 2005 on electronic communications, MB 8 December 2013, 19 September 2013.

V. PROSCRIPTION AND LISTING OF TERRORIST GROUPS AND INDIVIDUALS

A. *Blacklistings*

The Royal Decree[84] of 28 December 2006 concerning specific restrictive measures against persons and entities in the context of the financing of terrorism is worth mentioning. It was adopted after the first evaluation by Financial Action Task Force (FATF) in 2005.[85] This Royal Decree provides for the freezing of funds and financial resources of the persons and entities listed in EU regulations, which contain the EU's blacklist and implements the UN list.[86] It also provides for the establishment of Belgian blacklists (*i.e.*, of persons and entities listed in Belgium but who are not mentioned in the other lists). The procedure is as follows:

- The OCAM prepares a list on the basis of the threat analysis and available information, in consultation with judicial authorities.
- The list is proposed and adopted by the ministerial committee of intelligence and security.
- In order to become effective, it is then submitted to the Council of Ministers; subsequently all banks and financial institutions must freeze the assets.
- A revision procedure is possible before the Minister of Finance.
- The list is an administrative act, so it is subject to review before the Conseil d'Etat (administrative section).

This Royal Decree is in force, but the mechanism has not yet been 'activated' in the sense that no national blacklist has yet been adopted. This non-activation appears problematic in view of the next evaluation by FATF, which will most likely denounce this situation.

Regarding recourse to the list as evidence of the existence of a terrorist group, it must be noted that, in the *DHKP-C* case, the Ghent Court of Appeal explicitly underlined that the mention of the *DHKP-C* in the EU blacklist does not suffice as evidence and does not exempt the judge from examining whether the concerned organisation satisfies the conditions of a terrorist group as defined by Art. 139 CC.[87]

84 A Royal Decree is an enforceable decision provided for by the executive power, which is represented by the King at the federal level in Belgium. Some laws need a Royal Decree to be enforced. They have a general regulatory purpose.

85 On the 2005 evaluation, see http://www.ctif-cfi.be/website/index.php?option=com_content&view=article&id=56&Itemid=75&lang=en (accessed on 14 February 2014).

86 *Arrêté royal 28 December 2006 relatif aux mesures restrictives spécifiques à l'encontre de certaines personnes et entités dans le cadre de la lutte contre le financement du terrorisme*, MB 17 January 2007.

87 Ghent Court of Appeal, 7 November 2006, at 125–6; See also App. Antwerp, 7 February 2008, at 48

Belgian judicial authorities do seem to clearly separate judicial proceedings from administrative measures such as blacklisting.[88]

B. *Challenges to Listings*

No challenge has been brought against the Belgian list, since it does not exist.

As regards the other lists, the case of the Belgian couple Sayadi and Vinck must be recalled.[89] In 2002, a criminal investigation was launched in Belgium against the two nationals. Soon after, Belgium informed the 1267 Sanctions Committee of the Security Council that the individuals were the director and secretary of the Fondation Secours international, the European branch of an American NGO that was put on the 1267 sanctions list. Within a period of eight days, their names were placed on the lists appended to the Security Council Resolution (23 January 2003), the EU Council Regulation (27 January 2003)[90] and a Belgian ministerial order (31 January 2003),[91] without giving them access to the information used as a basis for their listing. As a consequence, the assets of the two individuals (parents of four children) were frozen. After two years, the criminal investigations had still not led to criminal prosecutions. On 11 February 2005, the Brussels Court of First Instance ordered the government to seek the delisting of the couple. On 19 December 2005, the Brussels Court of First Instance confirmed the plaintiffs' innocence, dismissing the case after more than three years of criminal investigation. Neither of the two decisions was appealed. While the Belgian government sought the delisting of the

88 The Court of Justice of the European Union (CJEU) partially examined the interaction between the blacklisting and criminal proceedings. It established that a criminal conviction on terrorism grounds should be taken into consideration for the purpose of listing (CJEU, 29 June 2010, C-550/09 para 57 and ff.). This decision means that association with a blacklisted organisation cannot form the basis of a criminal prosecution where the listing of that organisation was itself unlawful. But it has not been interpreted as excluding from a criminal prosecution such a list when it is lawful; on the contrary (see especially Cian Murphy, 'Case C-117/06, proceedings brought by Gerda Möllendorf and Christiane Möllendorf-Niehuus, judgment of the European Court of Justice (Second Chamber) of 11 October 2007, [2007] ECR I-8361; Case C-340/08, M & Others v. Her Majesty's Treasury, Judgment of the European Court of Justice (Fourth Chamber) of 29 April 2010, nyr; Case C-550/09, Criminal Proceedings Against E & F, Judgment of the European Court of Justice (Grand Chamber) of 29 June 2010, nyr', *Common Market Law Review* 48, 2011, 243–64; 'Secret evidence in EU security law: special advocates before the Court of Justice?' Working paper 02/2012, Centre of European Law, King's College London.

89 M. Scheinin, 'The ECJ ruling in Kadi incompatible with international law?' *Yearbook of European Law*, 2009, at 638 and ff.

90 Commission Regulation (EC) 145/2003 of 27 January 2003 amending Regulation (EC) 881/2002 for the ninth time.

91 Ministerial order of 31 January 2003 amending the ministerial order of 15 June 2000 implementing the Royal Decree of 17 February 2000 concerning the restrictive measures directed against the Taliban in Afghanistan.

individuals at the UN level, it was unable to obtain the unanimous approval of its request within the 1267 Sanctions Committee. On 22 October 2008, the Human Rights Committee issued its views against the Belgian government, stressing that it had the duty to do everything in its powers to delist these individuals.[92] On 20 July 2009, Sayadi and Vincke were finally removed from the 1267 list as well as from the EU and Belgian list.[93]

C. *Proscription*

For the time being, there is no legal mechanism allowing the proscription of terrorist groups. However, various proposals have been put forward in this regard. On 13 December 2010, a bill was submitted to the Chamber of the Representatives.[94] The proposal aimed at revising and extending the Belgian law of 29 July 1934 on private militia[95] in order to proscribe any organisation or group of individuals that is a danger to democracy because of terrorist, negationist or racist acts in Belgium. This bill has been subject of numerous amendments, especially from Ms. Fonck and M. Dallemagne,[96] which were inspired by another proposal presented by the Minister of Home Affairs, J. Milquet, in the context of her plan against radicalisation,[97] which had been rejected by the Council of Ministers. It must be underlined that the Conseil d'Etat (section de legislation) severely criticized the bill and its amendments on ground of freedom of association, freedom of expression and the principle of legality.[98]

[92] United Nations – Human Rights Committee, Communication 1472/2006, Nabil Sayadi and Patrick Vinck/Belgium on application to have names removed from the Consolidated List of the United Nations Sanctions Committee, 94th session, 22 October 2008, available at http://ccprcentre.org/doc/ICCPR/AR/N1049027.pdf (accessed on 15 January 2014).

[93] Security Council Al-Qaeda and Taliban Sanctions Committee removes names of two individuals from consolidated list, SC/9711, published 21 July 2009. See *e.g.* Didier Bigo, 'Fichage et listing Quelles incidences pour les individus?', *Culture & Conflicts*, n°76, L'Harmattan, Winter 2009, pp. 47–8. See also Christophe Lamfalussy, 'Affaire Sayadi-Vinck: le troisième essai', *La Libre*, 13 December 2000, available at http://www.lalibre.be/actu/international/affaire-sayadi-vinck-le-troisieme-essai-51b8a3e4e4b0de6db9b4de11 (accessed on 16 January 2013).

[94] *Proposition de loi modifiant la loi du 29 juillet 1934 interdisant les milices privées en vue d'interdire les groupements non démocratiques*, submitted by MM. Peter Vandvelthoven and David Geerts, Chamber, doc. 53, 0809/001, 13 December 2010.

[95] Law of 29 July 1934 *interdisant les milices privées en vue d'interdire les groupements non démocratiques*.

[96] See especially Chambre, doc. 53, 0809/004, 25 June 2012.

[97] RTBF, 6 June 2012.

[98] *Conseil d'Etat (CE), avis* 52.522/AG, 19 February 2013, Chamber, Doc. 53, 0809/008.

VI. REGULATION OF TERRORISM FINANCING

A. *The Regulatory Regime to Counter Terrorism Financing*

Setting aside the criminalisation of terrorism financing covered by *Title Iter* of the Book II CC, the Belgian terrorism financing regime is mainly built upon the Law of 11 January 1993 on preventing use of the financial system for purposes of money laundering and terrorist financing.[99] As its title shows, this law covers both terrorism financing and money laundering. It implements the successive EU Directives in the field.[100] It has been revised several times[101] and has been completed by various Royal Decrees.

In the Law of 11 January 1993, 'terrorist financing' is defined as the direct or indirect provision or collection of funds by any means, aiming to be used or in the knowledge that they will be used, in full or in part, by a terrorist or a terrorist organisation or in order to carry out one or more terrorist acts. All acts of terrorism financing are covered, regardless of whether the money has a legal origin or not.[102]

The Law of 11 January 1993 requires that the listed institutions and persons carry out a series of customer due diligence measures, comprising the identification of the customer and the verification of the customer's identity, the identification of the beneficial owner and the verification of its identity. Enhanced due diligence measures are required in situations that, by their nature, present a higher risk of money laundering or terrorist financing. The law also establishes the obligation to report to the competent authorities in the field of money laundering and terrorism financing.

This law established the Belgian FIU, that is, the Cell for Financial Data Processing (CTIF-CFI).[103] This cell is an independent administrative authority with legal personality, in charge of processing and forwarding the necessary information

[99] Law of 11 January 1993, *relative à la prévention de l'utilisation du système financier aux fins de blanchiment de capitaux et du financement du terrorisme*.

[100] Directive 2005/60/EC of the European Parliament and of the Council of 26 October 2005 on the prevention of the use of the financial system for the purpose of money laundering and terrorist financing, OJ L309/15 and Commission Directive 2006/70/EC of 1 August 2006 laying down implementing measures for Directive 2005/60/EC of the European Parliament and of the Council as regards the definition of 'politically exposed person' and the technical criteria for simplified customer due diligence procedures and for exemption on grounds of a financial conducted on an occasional or very limited basis, OJ L214/29.

[101] See *Loi programme* 29 March 2012 (MB 6 April 2012); Law of 18 January 2010 *relatif au dispositif préventif anti-blanchiment et contre le financement du terrorisme instauré par la loi du 11 janvier 1993* (MB 26 janvier 2010).

[102] Art. 5 para 2, Law of 11 January 1993 concerning the prevention of the use of the financial system for money laundering and terrorism financing purposes.

[103] About CTIF, see P. Spreutels and P. De Muelenaere eds.), *La cellule de traitement des informations financiers* (Bruxelles, Bruylant, 2003); CTIF, *Le livre blanc de l'argent noir, 20 ans de lutte contre le*

to combat money laundering and terrorism financing, including the financing of proliferation-sensitive activities or the delivery of nuclear weapon systems.[104] CTIF-CFI, composed of legal and financial experts and a senior officer seconded from the federal police, is placed under the supervision of the Ministries of Justice and Finance and led by a magistrate or his or her temporarily seconded deputy from the Public Prosecutor's Office. Besides performing its advisory and coordinating roles, the CTIF-CFI is responsible for receiving, centralising and analysing the information reported by the institutions and persons listed in the law concerning suspicious transactions. According to the law, the listed institutions have the duty to inform CTIF of every transaction that could be linked to money laundering or terrorism financing or that could give a hint of such activities. The CTIF-CFI may also request the institutions and persons listed in the law to provide any additional information it deems useful for accomplishing its mission, within the time period it determines. It may carry out on-site visits to consult the documents that belong or are in the possession of those institutions or individuals and that could be useful for accomplishing its objectives. Should the information give rise to serious indications of money laundering or terrorist financing activities, such information is forwarded to the Public Prosecutor or to the Federal Public Prosecutor. Among the CTIF-CFI powers, it must be stressed that, if the matter is serious or urgent, it may freeze a transaction. CTIF-CFI determines to what transactions and bank accounts the freezing order applies.[105] This freezing order halts the execution of the transaction for a maximum of five working days. If CTIF-CFI deems that this measure must be extended, it immediately refers the matter to the competent Public Prosecutor or the Federal Public Prosecutor, who will then make a decision on the matter.

The CTIF-CFI's annual reports reveal interesting information. For instance in 2012, CTIF-CFI referred twenty files to the competent judicial authorities because of serious indications of terrorism financing (which amounts to 1.3% of the files reported only), for a total amount of EUR 1.9 million (which represents 0.08% of the total reported amount only).[106] These figures are similar to those of previous years. However, as underlined by the annual report, absolute figures are not a good indicator of the risk that terrorism financing or proliferation entail for society. Terrorism financing seems generally more difficult to detect than money laundering.[107] Information that the CTIF transmits to prosecutors seldom seems to

blanchiment et le financement du terrorisme, 2013, available at http://www.ctif-cfi.be/website/images/FR/annual_report/fr_livre20ans_ctif.pdf (accessed on 28 January 2014).

104 Art. 11 para 1, Law of 11 January 1993.

105 Art. 23 law of 11 January 1993.

106 2012 Annual Report, at 89 and ff.; available at http://www.ctif-cfi.be/website/images/EN/annual_report/annualreport2012.pdf (accessed on 28 January 2013).

107 CTIF, 2012 Annual Report, at 89.

be used to trigger or even to nourish an investigation. In fact, it seems that a transaction is often considered suspicious by the institutions because there is an ongoing investigation.

B. *Criminal Offences of Terrorism Financing*

As stated before, the criminalisation of terrorism financing is covered by Title I*ter* of Book II CC. It is covered by Art. 139–40 when the contributor acts as a member of a terrorist group, and by Art. 141 CC when, outside the cases provided for in Art. 140, a person furnishes the means, including financial contributions, enabling the commission of a terrorist offence as provided for in Art. 137. As seen previously, this last provision aims at implementing the UN Convention for the repression of terrorism financing of 9 December 1999. Although the 2002 FD covered most of the 1999 Convention requirements, the contribution to the commission of a terrorist offence committed independently from a terrorist group had to be added.

It looks like there are only a few judicial files relating to terrorism financing in Belgium and that, for the time being, none have resulted in a condemnation. This is another element that seems to show that the country is not very 'invested' in the fight against terrorism financing.

VII. IMMIGRATION MEASURES

A. *Immigration Law and Terrorists or Suspected Terrorists*

Neither the main Belgian immigration act – that is, the Law of 15 December 1980 sur l'accès au territoire, le séjour, l'établissement et l'éloignement des étrangers – nor the royal decrees complementing it contain specific rules related to terrorists or suspected terrorists. However, three types of provisions are likely to have an impact on terrorists or suspected terrorists.

The first are those referring to non-EU nationals for whom a Schengen Information System (SIS) alert has been issued in order to refuse entry or stay.[108]

The second are those mentioning a danger or a threat to public order or national security. For example, a foreign national can be driven back to the border *(refoulement à la frontière)* if the competent minister, after the advice of the Commission consultative des étrangers (Advisory Committee on Aliens), considers the person a threat to public order or national security.[109] He or she can receive an order to leave the territory *(ordre de quitter le territoire)*.[110] The

[108] E.g. Art. 3, 5° Law of 15 December 1980 (*Loi sur l'accès au territoire, le séjour, l'établissement et l'éloignement des étrangers*).

[109] Art. 3, 7° Law of 15 December 1980. See also Art. 7 3°, 8bis, 20, 21, 22, 43 etc.

[110] Art. 7 3° Law of 15 December 1980. See also Art. 8bis, 19, 20, 21, 22, 43 etc.

person can be removed (*expulsé*) or sent back (*renvoyé*).[111] Public order or national security reasons can also justify the refusal of status of long-term residents to non-EU nationals[112] or a refusal of entry or stay in the territory.[113] According to the 1980 Law, detention is possible under certain conditions.[114] But there is no specific detention in terrorism cases. Nevertheless, the duration of the detention may sometimes be extended in case of danger to public order or national security.[115] In case of danger or threat to public order or national security, the foreigner may be ordered to reside in a specific place.[116] It must be noted that the notion of danger or threat to public order or national security has not been defined by law. Consequently, it is interpreted on a case-by-case basis.[117] The link between the danger or threat to public order or national security and a criminal conviction is made in a few provisions.[118]

The third type of provisions that are likely to have an impact on terrorists or suspected terrorists are those related to the loss of certain status, such as refugee status,[119] subsidiary protection[120] or temporary protection,[121] to any person against whom there are serious reasons to believe that (a) he or she has committed a crime against peace, a war crime or a crime against humanity as defined in the relevant international instruments; (b) the person has committed a serious non-political crime outside the country of refuge prior to his or her admission to that country as a refugee or that the person has committed a serious crime; or (c) he or she has been guilty of acts contrary to the purposes and principles of the UN.[122]

[111] Art. 20 and 21 Law of 15 December 1980.

[112] Art. 15*bis* Law of 15 December 1980.

[113] Art. 19, para 1 and Art. 43, 2° Law of 15 December 1980.

[114] For instance, according to Art. 7 Law of 15 December 1980, pending the execution of an order to leave the territory, the individual who is not authorised to stay more than three months or to establish himself or herself in the country may be detained if less coercive measures may not be applied.

[115] See Art. 7, 29, 74/5 para 3 Law 15 December 1980.

[116] See Art. 22 and 52/4 Law of 15 December 1980.

[117] For an example of such concrete assessment, see the judgment by the CE (*adm. sect.*) of 23 September 1997, 68/259, in the case *Walid Bennani*, which annulled the decision by the Minister of Justice rejecting the urgent request for reexamination introduced by Bennani and addressing him an order to leave the territory in the five days.

[118] See Art. 8 bis on mutual recognition of decisions on the expulsion of third country nationals; Art. 43 Law of 15 December 1980.

[119] Art. 55/2 Law of 15 December 1980.

[120] Art. 55/4 Law of 15 December 1980.

[121] Art. 57/32 Law of 15 December 1980.

[122] About these criteria, see especially CJEU 9 November 2010, *Bundesrepublik Deutschland* v. *B. and D.*, C-57/09 and C-101/09 and Belgian CE (*adm. sect.*), CGRA c. *Lounani Mostafa*, 220/321, 13 July 2012.

Some of the referred provisions explicitly require justification, that is, a statement of the reasons or of facts underlying the decision, unless this is contrary to Belgian security interests.[123]

Concerning practice, in 2013 the Immigration Office (Office des étrangers) worked with justice services to expulse foreign offenders. In March 2013, a joint circular relating to foreign prisoners was signed in order to ease the monitoring and and make more effective the organisation of their removal. Until 14 October 2013, five hundred ex-prisoners had been removed from Belgian prisons to their country of origin.[124] To our knowledge, there are no specific figures concerning terrorism.

B. *Immigration Proceedings and Torture*

As a party to the ECHR, Belgium is bound by the obligation not to deport someone where there are substantial grounds to believe that the person concerned, if deported, faces a real risk of being subjected to treatment contrary to Art. 3 ECHR (*i.e.*, torture or inhuman or degrading treatment).[125] Art. 3 enshrines an absolute right that a person may not suffer any derogation. As a consequence, the deportation prohibition exists independently of any proportionality considerations and is applicable despite the seriousness of the offence of which the person is suspected or has been convicted of committing.[126] These principles found practical application in the Council of State's decisions on expulsion.[127] If Belgian authorities do not respect such non-refoulement obligation, the state is likely to be condemned by the ECtHR.[128]

As a consequence, there are cases of foreigners, who having been condemned of terrorist offences and having served their sentence in Belgium, are set free again and must remain in Belgium in spite of them being considered a threat to public order or national security, because of the risk of torture or inhuman or degrading treatment they would be likely to suffer if they were sent back to their state of origin.

[123] Art. 23 and 46 Law of 15 December 1980.

[124] Available at http://www.deblock.belgium.be/fr/asile-migration-accueil (accessed on 29 January 2014).

[125] See *e.g. Soering v. the United Kingdom*, 7 July 1989, paras 90–1, Series A 161; *Vilvarajah and Others*, para 103; *Ahmed*, para 39; *H.L.R.* v. *France*, 29 April 1997, para 34, *Reports* 1997-III; *Jabari v. Turkey*, 40035/98, para 38; and *Salah Sheekh v. the Netherlands*, 1948/04, para 135, 11 January 2007.

[126] In the case of terrorist offences, see *Saadi v. Italy* (37201/06), 28 February 2008.

[127] See *e.g.* decision 100/001, 22 October 2001, *Chergi Amine* c. *Etat belge* (final decision 135/898, 11 October 2004).

[128] Belgium has already been condemned by the ECtHR for the expulsion decided against Nam Singh and his family (but for an infringement of Art. 13 combined with Art. 3 ECHR): ECtHR, *Singh et al.* c. *Belgique*, 33210/11 (available only in French), 2 October 2012 (def. 2 January 2013), para 91. ECtHR,

VIII. ADMINISTRATIVE AND EXECUTIVE MEASURES

As previously underlined, and setting intelligence and security services' missions aside (see Section V.C), in Belgium the emphasis is placed on judicial measures and proceedings. As a consequence, the anti-terrorism arsenal of an administrative nature is rather limited (see Section V.B).

Blacklisting and asset freezing are among the most relevant administrative measures available in Belgium. However, as has been previously pointed out, there is no Belgian blacklist for the time being (see Section V). The role of administrative police must be recalled, while keeping in mind that they may not resort to special investigation techniques (see Section V.B). Besides its aforementioned task in relation to the collection of information (see Section V.B), the administrative police may, in case of absolute necessity in the exercise of its duties,[129] arrest a person who, for instance, disturbs public peace or is suspected of preparing an offence that would put public peace or security in danger. Once again, there are no specific provisions dealing with administrative arrest in cases of terrorism. Thus, the general rules and conditions[130] apply, including those relating to individual's rights or the maximum length of detention. Detention may not exceed the time needed to achieve its legitimate aim and may not last more than twelve hours.[131] In the event of a combination of an administrative arrest and a judicial arrest – motivated by the detection of an offence or the search of an individual[132] – the length of detention may not exceed twenty-four hours.[133]

IX. THE ROLE OF MILITARY AND EXTRATERRITORIAL COUNTER-TERRORISM ACTIVITIES

A. *Military Courts and Detention*

Since the entry into force of the law of 10 April 2003 on 1 January 2004,[134] military jurisdictions in Belgium were abolished in time of peace. Their competences have been transferred to 'normal' criminal courts.

Boutagni c. *France* (available only in French), 42360/08, 18 November 2010 (def. 18 February 2011), often referred to in the CE jurisprudence; *El Haski* v. *Belgium*, 649/08, 25 September 2012.

[129] See Art. 14 Law of 5 August 1992.

[130] See Art. 31 and 34 Law of 5 August 1992

[131] See Art. 31 Law of 5 August 1992.

[132] Art. 15 1° and 2° Law of 5 August 1992.

[133] Art. 32 Law of 5 August 1992.

[134] See Law of 10 April 2003 *réglant la suppression des juridictions militaires en temps de paix ainsi que leur maintien en temps de guerre*, MB 7 May 2003.

B. *The Extraterritorial Treatment of Citizens Suspected of Terrorism: The Question of Extradition and of the Loss of Belgian Nationality*

a. Examples of Cases Concerning Belgian Nationals

With regard to Belgian citizens arrested abroad on suspicion of involvement in terrorist activities, the case of Moussa Zemmouri and Mesut Sen, who were detained at Guantanamo from 2001 to 2005, is worth mentioning. They had been arrested in Pakistan, detained in Afghanistan shortly after 9/11 and then transferred to Guantanamo Bay. Following their release in April 2005, they returned to Belgium, where the criminal justice authorities examined the case. On 26 May 2009, the Chambre du Conseil of Brussels dismissed the case. In 2010, Moussa Zemmouri filed a complaint before Belgian judicial authorities against Belgium because of its lack of reaction to his detention.

Other cases concerning Belgian citizens should also be mentioned, such as the one of Bahar Kimyongür, involved in the DHKP-C and against whom Turkey has issued several international arrest warrants and extradition requests. Bahar Kimyongür was prosecuted in Belgium in the DHKP-C case, but was finally acquitted by the Brussels Tribunaux correctionnels on 23 December 2009. Had he stayed in Belgium after that, his extradition to Turkey would have been barred, because Belgium does not extradite its nationals to non-EU States.[135] However, he left Belgian territory. In 2006, following his arrest on the basis of an Interpol notice, the Netherlands refused his extradition to Turkey and released him. Subsequently arrested in Spain, he was once again released in June 2013. On 20 November 2013, he was again arrested, this time in Italy. By a decision of the Brescia Court of Appeal, he was released 2 December, but while awaiting a decision of the Italian Prosecutor (expected by the end of March 2014), he was subject to a compulsory residence order. This case has been widely covered in the media. One of the most sensitive questions raised concerns about the scope of protection that the Belgian state owes its nationals. Bahar Kimyongür and his defence lawyers consider that Belgium's duty goes beyond the non-extradition of nationals. According to them, it includes the obligation to intervene in order to avoid other states extraditing him to Turkey or in order to solicit the withdrawal of the Interpol notice.[136]

[135] *Loi sur les extraditions du 15 mars 1874*.

[136] See *e.g.* the request from the FIDH (International Federation for Human Rights) and the Ligue des droits de l'Homme in Belgium, the Unione Forense per la Tutela dei Diritti Umani (UFTUD) and the Human Rights Foundation of Turkey (HRFT) to the Italian Minister of Justice not to extradite Bahar Kimyongür to Turkey, available in French at http://www.fidh.org/fr/europe/belgique/14448-non-a-l-extradition-de-bahar-kimyongur-vers-la-turquie, accessed on 27 January 2014).

A final interesting example is the case of Abdelkader Belliraj, who has dual Belgian and Moroccan nationality and was prosecuted in both states. Arrested in 2008 by the Moroccan police in the course of an investigation against Islamist opponents, he confessed to the six politically motivated crimes allegedly committed by him and his terrorist cell in Brussels back in the late 1980s (among these crimes was the murder of Dr. Joseph Wybran). In 2010, he was sentenced to life imprisonment in Morocco for the crimes committed in Brussels and for terrorist plot. The only key evidence of his involvement in the events of the 1980s is his confession made in Morocco, which is suspected to have been obtained by torture. That explains why, on 10 December 2013, the Belgian Federal Prosecutor asked the Chambre du Conseil of Brussels to dismiss the case. Its decision on the follow-up to reserve to the case and whether to send it to the court is expected on 18 March 2014.

b. The Loss of Belgian Nationality

As mentioned previously, Belgium does not extradite its nationals to non-EU states.

However, according to Belgian law, and under strict conditions, a loss of Belgian nationality is possible. The recourse to such a measure is subject to a series of conditions. It applies only to 'new Belgians' (*i.e.*, those who recently obtained the Belgian nationality) and only as long as it does not result in a stateless situation (*e.g.*, individuals who have a double nationality). The possibility of losing Belgian nationality existed in Art. 23 of the Code of Belgian Nationality, which prescribed the loss of Belgian nationality when it was acquired in a fraudulent manner or through a serious breach of the bearer's duties as Belgian citizen.[137] Until recently, this measure was scarcely used and might seem obsolete. However, it was revived in the context of terrorism. Art. 23 was, for instance, used in the *Kleine Brogel* case mentioned previously, as well as the cases of Tarek Maaroufi,[138] Abdelcrim El-Haddouti and Amor Sliti.

The Law of 4 December 2012 amended the Belgian Nationality Code and inserted Art. 23/1,[139] which complements Art. 23.[140] According to the new provision, the withdrawal of Belgian nationality can also be imposed by the judge at the request

[137] Art. 23 Nationality Code. This article was the focus of an interesting decision by the Constitutional Court (14 May 2009, 85/2009). A preliminary question was asked by the Brussels Court of Appeal in the Abdelcrim El- Haddouti case. The Constitutional Court considered that this article did not violate the principle of non-discrimination and considered that in case of a serious breach of the citizens' duties, it was a 'reasonable' measure (para B.10).

[138] Court of Appeal of Brussels, 26 January 2009.

[139] Art. 20 *Loi modifiant le Code de nationalité belge afin de rendre l'acquisition de la nationalité belge neutre du point de vue de l'immigration.*

[140] See initial Bill, Chambre, doc. 53.0476/001, 27 Oct. 2010.

of the prosecutor to Belgian nationals who have been convicted as perpetrator, co-perpetrator or accomplice to a term of imprisonment of at least five years without parole for one of the listed offences, including the terrorism offences of Art. 137, 138, 139, 140 and 141 CC.[141] The loss of Belgian nationality on this basis is at stake in several pending cases, such as those concerning the convicted persons of the Iraki kamikaze and the Afghan kamikaze networks.

It must be underlined that, whereas recourse to such measure is topical, it is not yet widely used, as the case of the Belgian-Moroccan national Fouad Belkacem (spokesperson of the radical Islamist group Sharia4Belgium) tends to show. Convicted by the Antwerp Court of Appeal for incitement to hatred and violence, the general prosecution service of Antwerp decided not to request the withdrawal of his Belgian nationality.[142]

Recent bills have been introduced to further facilitate and speed up the procedure for withdrawing the Belgian nationality. The terrorism context is not unusual to such projects.[143]

c. Examples of Cases Concerning Foreigners

As explained previously, Belgium is a party to the ECHR and thus must ensure that if a person is to be expelled, returned or extradited, he or she is not returned to a country where there are substantial grounds to believe that the person is at risk of being subjected to torture. The prohibition of torture is absolute and admits no exceptions. This rule of principle has been repeated many times, especially in the context of extradition proceedings seeking to return terrorist suspects to Morocco.[144]

However, in some cases, the Belgian authorities have granted extradition in exchange of diplomatic guarantees. In this regard, the extradition of the Tunisian national Nizar Trabelsi to the United States on 3 October 2013 is worth recalling. As mentioned previously, he had been convicted in Belgium for the preparation of an attack against the military base of Kleine-Brogel in 2004. Furthermore, his extradition was sought by U.S. and Tunisian authorities. Belgian authorities had refused to grant him refugee status and subsidiary protection. Belgium requested and obtained guarantees from U.S. authorities that he would not be subject to the death penalty; that his re-extradition would be contingent on the authorisation of

[141] Art. 23/1, para 1, 1° Nationality Code.

[142] Belga, 6 February 2014.

[143] See *e.g. proposition de loi modifiant le Code de la nationalité belge en ce qui concerne la déchéance de la nationalité, chambre des Représentants*, doc. 53 K2257/001, 13 June 2012.

[144] See *e.g.* CE (adm. sect.), *El Haski* c. *Etat belge*, 215/114, 13 September 2011; *Hakimi* c. *Etat belge*, 216/088, 27 October 2011; *El Haski* c. *Etat belge*, 225/058, 10 October 2013; *El Haski* c. *Etat belge*, 222/731, 5 March 2013.

Belgian authorities; and that, in the event a lifetime imprisonment sentence was passed against him, it could be shortened by an act of grace from the President. On this basis, on 23 November 2011, the Belgian Minister of Justice decided to extradite Trabelsi to the United States and refused his extradition to Tunisia. Due to Trabelsi's application at the ECtHR in December 2009, the President of the Strasbourg's Court requested Belgium to suspend his extradition. In February 2012, Trabelsi sought the annulment of the ministerial extradition decision before the Council of State, but his application was refused on 23 September 2013.[145] A few days later, and in spite of the fact that his case was pending in Strasbourg, he was extradited to the United States. Unsurprisingly, this extradition has been strongly criticized.[146]

C. *Extraterritorial Terrorism Law Enforcement*

Terrorist offences are subject to specific rules of extraterritorial competence, inspired by Art. 9 para 1 of the 2002 FD. With regard to personal jurisdiction over the offences of Title I*ter* CC, Belgium can exercise both the active and passive nationality principle. Thus, Belgium has jurisdiction to prosecute and punish its nationals (as well as jurisdiction over those who have their permanent residence in Belgium) regardless of whether the crime was committed within its territory or abroad.[147] Furthermore, Belgium is also competent if the victim of the offences covered by Arts. 137, 140 and 141 CC is a Belgian national, a Belgian institution or an institution or a body of the EU having its seat in Belgium, regardless of whether the crime was committed within its territory or abroad.[148] However, Art. 12 of the Preliminary Title of the CCP contains an important limit to the exercise of extraterritorial jurisdiction: it is only possible if the indicted person is found in Belgian territory. Since this limit is an important obstacle to the fight against terrorism, the law of 6 February 2012[149] excludes its application to the terrorist offences of Art. 137 CC. For the rest, reference must be made to Art. 12*bis*, according to which Belgian authorities also have extraterritorial jurisdiction when this is imposed under a rule of international or EU law binding on Belgium.

145 CE, *Trabelsi* v. *Etat belge* (adm. sect.), 224/770, 23 September 2013.

146 See *e.g. Ligue des droits de l'homme*, *Rapport alternative* submitted to the Committee against torture, October 2013 (available in French); and Amnesty International, 'Belgium falls short of its obligations on torture and other ill-treatment', EUR 14/003/2013, 27 November 2013.

147 Art. 6, 1°*ter*, Preliminary Title of the CCP.

148 Art. 10*ter* 4°, Preliminary Title of the CCP. For the offences introduced in 2013, see Art. 12bis.

149 Law of 6 February 2012 *modifiant la loi du 17 avril 1878 contenant le titre préliminaire du Code de procédure pénale en ce qui concerne la poursuite de certaines infractions commises à l'étranger*, MB 7 March 2012.

Belgian authorities may 'operate' extraterritorially in the context of a Joint Investigation Team (JIT), which may be organised within the EU.[150] A JIT is an investigation team set up for a fixed period, based on an agreement between two or more EU Member States and/or competent authorities for a specific purpose. It allows the authorities of different Member States to investigate together in the territory of the Member States concerned. Belgian authorities have taken part in JITs operating abroad in terrorism files and has also welcomed JITs in its own territory.

X. SECRECY AND TERRORISM

A. *Secrecy Claims and Secret Evidence*

According to Belgian law, unless a specific rule provides otherwise, evidence is governed by the principle of freedom of proof.[151] The elements of crime can thus be established by all means. This principle is complemented by the rule according to which the judge appreciates freely the weight of the adduced evidence. However, evidence must be subject to contradictory debate. Proof that has not been subject to adversarial cross-examination must be excluded.[152]

Illegally obtained evidence is no longer automatically excluded. The *Antigoon* decision of the *Cour de cassation*[153] established that evidence furnished unlawfully is only to be excluded in the following three cases:

- If the penalty of nullity is legally prescribed for violation of the procedural rules
- If the irregularity affects the reliability of the evidence
- If the use of the illegally obtained evidence violates the right to fair trial[154]

This case law was recently codified in Art. 32 of the Preliminary Title of the CCP.[155] In this regard, it must be recalled that Belgium was condemned by the ECtHR in 2012 in the previously mentioned *El Haski* case, as a result of admitting in a criminal trial statements obtained in violation of Art. 3 ECHR. The ECtHR considered that

[150] The possibility of setting up JITs is provided for in Art. 13 of the Convention on Mutual Legal Assistance in Criminal Matters Between EU MS (*OJ* C197, 12 July 2000) and in the Framework Decision of 13 June 2002 2002/465/JHA on Joint Investigation Teams (*OJ* L162, 20 June 2002).

[151] Cass., 27 February 2002, *Pas.*, 2002, at 598; Cass. 5 March 2002, *Pas.*, 2002.

[152] Cass., 13 February 2007, *T. Strafr.*, 2007, at 315 and footnote.

[153] Cass. 14 October 2003, *RCJB*, 2004, at 405.

[154] See H. D. Bosly, Damien Vandermeersch and Marie-Aude Beernaert, *Droit de la procédure pénale* (Bruges, *La Charte*, 2010) at 1010–15.

[155] According to this new provision, introduced by the Law of 24 October 2013 *modifiant le titre préliminaire du Code de procédure pénale en ce qui concerne les nullities* (MB 12 November 2013).

the use of such evidence rendered the proceedings as a whole unfair and thus found a violation of Art. 6 ECHR.[156]

Art. 29 CCP is of major importance with regard the collaboration between judicial and intelligence services. It establishes the duty of every authority, civil servant or public officer (including those in the intelligence and security services) who find out that a crime or misdemeanour has been committed to inform the Public Prosecutor. Art. 19 and 19/1 of the organic law on security and intelligence services regulates the transmission of information gathered by the intelligence services to other authorities, especially judicial ones. According to Art. 19/1 and to implement Art. 29 CCP, when specific or exceptional measures to collect data reveal serious indications of the commission of a crime or misdemeanour or give rise to reasonable suspicion that punishable acts will be committed or have been committed although they are yet unknown, the intelligence services must communicate them to the BIM Commission (which is in charge of the surveillance of the specific and exceptional methods of data collection by the intelligence and security services provided for by the BIM law). The latter examines the data and, if it so decides, a non-classified report (*procès-verbal non-classifié*) is established and transmitted to the prosecutor. The report must specify the context in which the intelligence mission was carried out, the investigative measure used, the objective pursued and the specific context in which the information that might be used in court has been gathered. Art. 19/1 explicitly provides that this report may not constitute the sole or decisive element grounding a conviction.

Art. 19/1 was the object of an action for annulment before the Constitutional Court, on the ground of a breach of Art. 6 ECHR, understanding that it leads to a violation of the principle of equality of arms because the report in question is not communicated to the defence. The Constitutional Court refused the application considering that there is no absolute right of the defendant to receive communication of the relevant evidence. As stated by the Court:

> … it is necessary to recall that the right to receive the content of all elements of proof is not absolute. In some criminal proceedings, diverging interests such as national security as well as the necessity to ensure the safeguard of witnesses or to keep secret some investigation techniques may be put in balance with the rights of the accused. In some cases, it may be necessary to not divulgue some elements of proof to this party, in order to preserve the fundamental rights of another person or to guarantee important general interest.[157]

[156] ECtHR, *El Haski v. Belgium*, 649/08, 25 September 2012.

[157] Constitutional Court, 145/2011, n°4955 and 5014, 22 September 2011, para B.18.

This opens up the possibility that secret evidence not disclosed to the accused could be used as evidence of guilt, albeit not the sole or decisive evidence of guilt.

In practice, the BIM Commission does not forward non-classified reports to the Public Prosecutor often. Furthermore, the latter seems to scarcely use such reports, avoiding the objections of the defence. The reports are mostly used during the investigation phase, during which the transmitted information is confirmed. It is the result of these judicial investigations that is used in court. That is why some experts argue that the boundaries between intelligence and judicial information are increasingly blurred.[158]

B. *Secrecy in the Courtroom and Anonymous Witnesses*

The Law of 8 April 2002[159] allows the hearing of a witness under partial anonymity, which can take two different forms: either some data relating to the witness' identity are omitted in the hearing report (Art. 155*bis* and 296 CCP) or his or her residence is replaced with an indication of the service address (Art. 155*ter* and 297 CCP). Partial anonymity must either be authorised by the *juge d'instruction* (Art. 75*bis* CCP) or in a latter stage by the tribunal (Art. 155*bis* CCP), because of its necessity to protect the witness or his or her relatives.

If partial anonymity is not sufficient, it is also possible to provide the witness with complete anonymity. This measure must be ordered by the *juge d'instruction* (Art. 86*bis-ter* CCP) or at a latter stage by the Tribunal correctionnel or the President of the Cour d'Assises (Art. 189*bis* and 294 CCP). This measure is available only when there are precise and serious indications that the facts constitute one or several of the offences listed in Art. 90*ter* (which, as said before, include the terrorist offences of Art. 137, 140 and 141 CC). Additionally, the witness or his or her relatives must feel seriously and reasonably threatened, refusing to testify on such grounds. Full anonymity may also be granted where the witness is a police officer, and there are precise and serious indications that the witness or his or her relatives are in danger.

Whereas the probative value of the testimony of a partial anonymous witness is not restricted, the testimony of completely anonymous witnesses has very limited evidentiary value. According to Art. 189*bis* 3rd indent CCP, it may not be the sole or decisive element grounding a conviction. It must thus be corroborated by other

[158] D. Fransen and D. Vandermeersch, 'Les mesures d'investigation et les droits de l'Homme', in L. Hennebel and D. Vandermeersch (dir.), *Juger le terrorisme dans l'Etat de droit* (Brussels, Bruylant, Magna Cart, 2009) at 370.

[159] Law 8 April 2002 *relative à l'anonymat des témoins*.

evidence.[160] This restriction in the weight of the evidence seems to explain why, in practice, fully anonymous witnesses are not used in terrorist files.

XI. CONCLUSION

The 9/11 attacks have indirectly influenced Belgian law with regard to the anti-terrorism legislative frame, that is, via the decisive impact of the 2002 FD. The major role played by the EU in this field was confirmed with the 2008 FD.

Belgian legislation faces serious criticism, especially concerning the multiplication of inchoate offences and the wide margin of discretion left to judges in interpreting terrorist criminal offences. Some cases reveal the awkward situation in which judicial authorities are put when they ought to decide between a restrictive or an extensive interpretation of the criminal offences. Nonetheless, as judicial authorities gain experience in the field, they seem to be developing a prudent approach to the implementation of the law.

Among the main features of Belgian anti-terrorist system is the focus on judicial measures and proceedings and the limited development of the anti-terrorism administrative arsenal. More generally, whereas terrorism has certainly had an impact in fields other than criminal legislation (such as in the field of immigration and asylum), this is not always evident, as often those other norms do not specifically refer to terrorism.

Finally, Belgian nationals going to Syria to fight with jihadist groups and then returning to Belgium pose a very serious challenge ahead. This problem will very likely impact Belgian policy and law.

[160] See ECtHR case law: *e.g.*, ECtHR, *Birutis* v. *Lithuania*, 28 March 2002, para 32.; *Van Mechelen and al.* v. *The Netherlands*, 23 April 1997, para 55; *Doorson* v. *The Netherlands*, 26 March 1996, para 76; *Kostovski* v. *The Netherlands*, 20 November 1989, paras 44–5; in Belgium, GICM case, *op. cit.*

9

Italy

Sabrina Praduroux

I. INTRODUCTION

The age of terrorism in Italy began shortly after the birth of the Republic in 1946. Indeed, Italy experienced acts of terrorism as early as the 1950s. These had Neo-fascist or Neo-nazi origins, except for terrorism that developed in Trentino-Alto Adige, which was rooted in the separatist cause of South Tyrol. Italy faced its most violent wave of terrorist attacks throughout the late 1960s, the 1970s and the early 1980s, which were later labeled the "Years of Lead." During this time, terrorism evolved from the ideological extremism of the revolutionary generation of 1968 and led to the terrorists' revolt against the state, advocating a complete reorganization of society according to socialist or communist principles. On the other hand, terroristic acts such as the 1969 bombing of the Banca Nazionale del Lavoro in Piazza Fontana, Milan, which killed seventeen people and wounded eighty-eight, highlighted the shadowy dealings of sectors of the intelligence community with members who were right-wing extremists and intended to lead the country into chaos and hence create the preconditions for an authoritarian government.

The Years of Lead were characterized by widespread social conflict and unprecedented street violence, armed struggle and acts of terrorism carried out by both right- and left-wing terrorist groups.[1] Between 1968 and 1987, thousands of

[1] The most active left-wing terrorist group was the *Red Brigades* (*Brigate Rosse*). For a narrative of left-wing terrorism in Italy see, among others, R. C. Jr. Meade, *Red Brigades: The Story of Italian Terrorism*, London, Macmillian, 1990;S. G. Tarrow, *Democracy and Disorder: Protest and Politics in Italy, 1965–1975*, Oxford, Clarendon Press, 1989; G. Bocca, *Il terrorismo italiano. 1970–1978*, Milano, Rizzoli, 1978; L. Bonanate, *Dimensioni del terrorismo politico*, Milano, Franco Angeli, 1979. For an attempt to understand the sociological, political, and cultural background of left-wing terrorism in Italy, P. Feltrin, *Il terrorismo di sinistra in Italia (1970–1980)*, Firenze, Libreria Alfani Editrice, 1986; R. Mazzetti, *Genesi e sviluppo del terrorismo in Italia. Il maggio troppo lungo*, Roma, Editore Armando Armando, 1979. On right-wing terrorism, see V. Borraccetti (ed.), *Eversione di destra, terrorismo, stragi: i fatti e l'intervento giudiziario*, Milano, Angeli, 1986; D. Della Porta, *Terrorismi in*

acts of terrorism causing the deaths of hundreds of people were reported. Among the terrorist attacks that had the greatest impact on the Italian collective memory are the following: in 1969, the aforementioned Piazza Fontana bombing at the Banca Nazionale dell'Agricoltura in Milan; in 1976, the killing of Francesco Coco, Public Prosecutor in Genoa; in 1977, the killing of Fulvio Croce, president of the Bar Association of Turin; in 1978, the kidnapping and eventual assassination of Aldo Moro, the five-time premier and candidate for the presidency of the Republic; in 1980, the assassination at the University of Milan of Guido Galli, judge and criminal law professor; and, in the same year, the bombing at Bologna train station, which killed eighty-five people and wounded over two hundred.

Attacks by non-Italian terrorist groups have been rare. Those most relevant ones were two armed attacks by members of an extremist Palestinian organization at the Fiumicino airport in Rome in 1973 and 1985 respectively, and the hijacking, also in 1985, of an Italian ship cruising in the Mediterranean, the Achille Lauro, by Palestinian terrorists.[2]

It is worth mentioning, in this context, Italy's continuing fight against mafia and other forms of organized crime such as the secret criminal organization originating from the area of Naples *(camorra)* and the Calabrian mafia-type organization *('ndrangheta)*. These are to be contrasted with terrorist organizations, because they are not engaged in a political struggle, but aim instead at accumulating and controlling wealth through organized criminal activities damaging the rest of the community. In this respect, mafia and organized criminal associations analogous to it are generally not covered by the specific terrorist offences described in this chapter. Italian legislators have also distinguished mafia and mafia-like activity from common criminal organized crime since 1982 by the introduction of the offence of mafia association under Article 416-*bis* of the Criminal Code. This defines a mafia-type association as an association whose members use the power of intimidation deriving from membership and the conditions of coercion and conspiracy of silence that membership in the association engenders to commit offences; to acquire direct or indirect control of economic activities, licenses, authorizations, public procurement contracts and services; to obtain unjustified profits or benefits for themselves or others; to prevent or obstruct the free exercise of the right to vote; or to procure votes for themselves or others at elections.[3]

Italia, Bologna, Il Mulino, 1984; E. Pisetta, "Per una storia del terrorismo nero" (1983) 5 *Il Mulino* 738–770.

2 This episode culminated in the murder of Leon Klinghoffer, a disabled American citizen, and led to a serious diplomatic crisis between Italy and the United States because of the attempt by the U.S. government to arrest and send to trial in the United States the terrorists under the custody of the authorities. On the reconstruction, and legal analysis, of the facts see A. Cassese, *Terrorism, Politics and Law: the Achille Lauro Affair*, Oxford, Polity Press, 1989.

3 Anti-mafia laws enacted over the years are available on the website of the Minister of the Interior: http://ssai.interno.it/itaindex.php?IdSot=77#AntimafiaLegislazione.

The fight against domestic terrorism has led to the creation of special police units[4] and the adoption of emergency legislation to combat terrorism by introducing new offences, increasing penalties for existing offences, extending the length of pretrial detention and strengthening police powers. However, the most effective antiterrorist measure to date has been the mitigation of sentencing of convicted terrorists who agree to act as police informants or give evidence against fellow terrorists (the so-called *pentiti*).

By the end of the 1980s, all the major terrorist groups had been dismantled. However, the late 1990s and early 2000s witnessed a resurgence of left-wing terrorism with the New Red Brigades, who assassinated two labour law professors acting as government advisors in matters of labour law: Massimo D'Antona in 1999 and Marco Biagi in 2002. The leaders of this new terrorist organization have been arrested, convicted and sentenced.

Today, terrorist threats come mainly from international terrorist groups; however, so far, Italy has not been a specific target for international terrorist attacks in Italy. Nevertheless, various international terrorist groups have established logistics bases in Italy to proselytize, recruit members and raise funds, taking advantage of the presence of Muslim immigrants. In particular, there is a network of Islamic terrorist cells in Italy, which have not yet been associated with a single terrorist organization.[5] In short, the problem of Islamic terrorism arose in Italy after the retreat of the Soviet troops from Afghanistan in 1989, which was celebrated by Osama bin Laden and his followers as a triumph and motivated the fight against the enemies of Islam throughout the world.[6] At first, Al-Qaeda organized its primary command and training facilities in Afghanistan; by the beginning of 2002, however, it lost this sanctuary following the U.S.-led invasion of Afghanistan in 2001. Subsequently, Al-Qaeda pursued a general project of attacking Western states, making use of Islamic fundamentalist terrorists located in different countries. For instance, Rabei Osman Ahmed Ed Sayed was arrested in Milan in 2004 and convicted for being a member of a terrorist organization. He turned out to be a leading figure in the Islamic terrorist world. The Corte d'assise of Milan sentenced him to ten years in

4 In particular, a special anti-terrorism unit was formed and headed by the General of Carabinieri Carlo Alberto Dalla Chiesa, who played a crucial role in the fight against terrorist groups and was murdered, with his wife, by the mafia in 1982.

5 For an overview of the major international terrorist groups in Italy, see A. Spataro, "Le forme attuali di manifestazione del terrorismo nella esperienza giudiziaria: implicazioni etniche, religiose e tutela dei diritti umani," in C. De Maglie, S. Seminara (eds.), *Terrorismo internazionale e diritto penale*, Padova, CEDAM, 2007, especially at pp. 196 ff.

6 As shown by manuals for training terrorists found in the house of suspected terrorists, the main mission of the military organization is to overthrow "godless immoral regimes" and replace them with an Islamic regime. Cfr., A. Spataro, *cit. supra*, p. 175.

prison – reduced to eight years on appeal – for the crime of conspiracy for the purposes of terrorism. He was extradited to Spain in 2007 to be brought to trial on charges relating to the Madrid train bombings of 11 March 2004. On October 2007, the Madrid Court acquitted him of all the charges.

Although the original text of the Criminal Code did not contain specific provisions on terrorist offences, it did enact articles which could apply to terrorism-related offences. For example, Article 270 on subversive associations punishes whoever in the territory of the state promotes, constitutes, organizes or directs associations aimed at violently subverting the economic or social order of the state, or whoever attempts to violently suppress the political and juridical order of the state. Article 306 punishes those who take part to an armed band with the purpose of committing crimes against the state, and Article 284 punishes the crime of armed insurrection against the state. In addition, members of terrorist groups may be punished for the offence of criminal association (Article 416) that aims at illegal immigration, traffic in forged identity documents and other related criminal acts. These articles were introduced into the Criminal Code by Law No. 191/1978 and Law No. 15/1980 (see Section II). Immediately after 11 September 2001, Law No. 348/2001 introduced Article 270-*bis* of the Criminal Code, which specifically provides for the crime of conspiracy for the purposes of terrorism and subversion of democracy.[7]

Other legislation enacted after the terrorist attack to the Twin Towers includes Law No. 415/2001 on sanctions for violations of measures adopted in relation to the Taliban regime[8] and Law No. 431/2001 on urgent measures to fight the financing of international terrorism, which created the Financial Security Committee within the Ministry of Economics and Finance.[9]

Further counterterrorism measures were adopted after the London bombings of 2005. Law No. 155/2005.[10] Among the major changes introduced by this legislation are the possibility to grant a residence permit for the purposes of investigation to former foreign terrorists who collaborate with the authorities; new rules for the deportation and expulsion from the Italian territory of foreigners to prevent of terrorism; the extension from twelve to twenty-four hours of detention to obtain personal identification to cope with the difficulty of quickly ascertaining a person's real identity (especially if he or she comes from outside the European Union) and the authenticity of identity documents; new offences covering recruitment for participation in international terrorist activities (see Article 270-*quater* of the

7 Law No. 438 of 15 December 2001 on urgent dispositions to counteract international terrorism, *Gazz. Uff.* No. 293.

8 Law No. 415 of 27 November 2001, *Gazz. Uff.* No. 277.

9 Law No. 432 of 14 December 2001, *Gazz. Uff.* No. 290.

10 Law No. 155 of 31 July 2005, *Gazz. Uff.* No. 177.

Criminal Code) and training for acts of terrorism (see Article 270-*quinquies* of the Criminal Code, providing punishment of individuals undergoing training); and, finally, a more precise definition of terrorist activities on the basis of Article 1 of the EU Council Framework Decision of 13 June 2002 on combating terrorism[11] (see Article 270-*sexies* of the Criminal Code).

II. THE DEFINITION OF TERRORISM

There is no given definition of the term *terrorism* in Italian legislation. However, Article 270-*sexies* of the Criminal Code enacted in 2005 considers as *conduct for terrorist purposes* conduct that, by its nature and context, is capable of causing serious harm to a state or an international organization, provided that such conduct is carried out with one of the following specific purposes: frightening the population; forcing public powers or an international organization to act or to refrain from acting; or destabilizing or destroying the fundamental political constitutional, economic and social structures of a state or of an international organization. It also includes terrorist conduct under conventions or other provisions of international law to which Italy is bound.

As stated previously, Article 270-*sexies* of the Criminal Code was introduced by Law No. 155/2005, which enacted with amendments legislative decree No. 144/2005.[12] It reproduces almost word for word the definition of conduct for terrorist purposes given in the first sentence of Article 1 paragraph 1 of the EU Council Framework Decision of 2002 referred to previously.[13] However, the Italian legislator opted for leaving out from Article 270-*sexies* the list of intentional acts constituting terrorist offences given by the EU to avoid an excessive typification of criminal conducts, which would prevent the possibility of classifying as terrorist conducts any conduct worthy of being classified as such.

Before terrorism took on an international dimension, the notion of *domestic terrorism* had been defined by Italian courts to include each act of violence aiming at spreading panic and striking terror to undermine citizens' confidence in the state.[14]

[11] *O. J.* L 164, 22 June 2002, p. 3.

[12] Legislative decree No. 144 of 27 July 2005 on urgent measures to fight international terrorism, *Gazz. Uff.* No. 173.

[13] The EU Commission has, however, criticised the implementation of Article 1 of the Framework Decision in Italy because the Italian legislation provides only for a limited number of specific terrorist offences and qualifies common offences by reference to terrorist intent as an aggravating circumstance. See Report from the Commission based on Article 11 of the Council Framework Decision of 13 June 2002 on combating terrorism. http://eur-lex.europa.eu/legal-content/EN/TXT/PDF/?uri=CELEX:52007DC0681&from=IT.

[14] Cfr. Court of Cassation, Criminal Section I, 11 July 1987, (1989) *Cass. Pen.* 41; Court of Cassation, Joint Sections, 23 November 1995, No. 2110 (1996), *Riv. pen.* 723.

Interpreting Article 270-*sexies* of the Criminal Code, the Court of Cassation held that the reference to international conventions means that the definition of terrorist acts must take into account the International Convention for the Suppression of the Financing of Terrorism adopted by the General Assembly of the United Nations on 9 December 1999 and ratified in Italy by Law No. 7/2003.[15] In particular, unlike the EU Council Framework Decision of 2002, the UN Convention of 1999 expressly covers acts carried out in a situation of armed conflict against persons not taking an active part in the hostilities. It follows that those acts also fall within the scope of Article 270-*sexies* of the Criminal Code. Therefore, only acts directed against combatants are not covered by Article 270-*sexies* and, as such, are subject to international humanitarian law.[16]

Acts directed against a military target are considered terrorist acts when there are inevitable and serious consequences to the life and physical integrity of the civilian population. Accordingly, the definition of terrorist acts also covers bombings in crowded places by suicide bombers directed against military targets in the course of an armed conflict.[17]

Finally, the Court of Cassation emphasized that terrorist acts must be carried out for political, religious or ideological considerations.[18] According to the Court of Cassation, there is an international definition of terrorism sufficiently established to be considered as customary and therefore binding on Italian courts, by virtue of Article 10 Cost., which prescribes that national law shall (automatically) comply with customary international law. The Court of Cassation has thus drawn the definition of terrorism from Article 2 of the International Convention for the Suppression of the Financing of Terrorism adopted by the UN General Assembly on 9 December 1999, adding to it the requirement of political, religious or ideological motives. This would be distinctive of every terrorist act as it can – according to the Court – be inferred from several resolutions of the General Assembly, as well as from the International Convention for the Suppression of Terrorist Bombings adopted by the UN General Assembly on 15 December 1997. This interpretation of international norms by the Italian Court of Cassation is, however, misleading. Indeed, international conventions do not include motive elements in the definition of terrorism. As pointed out by Kalliopi K. Koufa, Special Rapporteur on human rights and terrorism, the question of motive has been highly controversial in the debate on the adoption of a universally recognized definition of terrorism.[19]

15 Law No. 7 of 14 January 2003, *Gazz. Uff.* No. 21.

16 Cfr. Court of Cassation, Criminal Section I, 11 October 2006, No. 1072 (2008), 1 *Foro it.* II, 43.

17 See Court of Cassation, Criminal Section V, 18 July 2008, No.75 (2009), 4 *Riv. pen.* 476.

18 See Court of Cassation, Criminal Section I, 11 October 2006, No. 1072, *cit.*

19 See UNCHR (Sub-Commission), "Report by Special Rapporteur Kalliopi K. Koufa on Terrorism and Human Rights," UN Doc E/CN.4/Sub.2/2001/31 (2001). For a discussion on this topic, see B. Saul,

III. CRIMINAL LAW AND PROSECUTIONS

A. *Criminal Law*

From the substantive criminal law perspective, Italian legislation provides a definition of acts committed for terrorist purposes and punishes terrorist conduct both in the form of individual acts and organizational offences.

Criminal offences relating to terrorism are in Book II, Title I of the Criminal Code, which deals with crimes against the state. More specifically, Law No. 15/1980 introduced the offence of carrying out an act of terrorism or subversion under Article 280 of the Criminal Code.[20] This provision punishes anyone who, with the purpose of terrorism or subversion of democracy, threatens the life or safety of another person. The same law introduced the offence of association for the purposes of terrorism or subversion of the democratic order under Article 270-*bis* of the Criminal Code. Originally introduced to cope with the emergence of domestic terrorism, Article 270-*bis* was amended by Law No. 438/2001 to include acts of terrorism against a foreign state, an international institution or an organization. The current version of Article 270-*bis* punishes anyone who promotes, sets up, organizes, manages, finances[21] or takes part[22] in associations whose purpose is the committing of acts of violence intended as terrorism or the subversion of democracy.

As made clear by the Court of Cassation, Article 270-*bis* aims at punishing the mere establishment of an association, whether or not the planned terrorist acts are actually carried out. However, the association must achieve a level of organization such as to make at least realistically possible the execution of the terrorist or subversive plot.[23] Moreover, there must be the intention and ability to use *terrorist methods* within the meaning of Article 270-*sexies* of the Criminal Code.[24]

"The Curious Element of Motive in Definitions of Terrorism: Essential Ingredient – or Criminalising Thought?" Sydney Law School – Legal Studies Research Paper No. 08/123.

20 The original text, abrogated in 1944, provided for the capital punishment of anyone who intended to make an attempt on the life of the head of state. Article 280 was introduced by Law No. 15 of 6 February 1980 on urgent measures for the protection of the democratic order and public safety, *Gazz. Uff.* No. 37.

21 In these cases, the penalty is imprisonment for seven to fifteen years.

22 This conduct is punishable by imprisonment for five to ten years. In all cases, items that served or were destined towards the commission of the crime and any resulting product or profit are confiscated.

23 Court of Cassation, Criminal Section V, 11 June 2008, No. 31389 (2009), 6 *Cass. pen.* 2370; Court of Cassation, Criminal Section VI, 12 July 2012, No. 46308 (2013), 7–8 *Foro it.* II, 434.

24 Court of Cassation, Criminal Section VI, 8 Mai 2009, No. 25863 (2009), *CED Cass. pen.*; Court of Cassation, Criminal Section V, 23 February 2012, No. 12252 (2012), 10 *Cass. pen.* 3329.

For further references to case law, see F. Viganò, "Terrorismo di matrice islamico-fondamentalistica e art. 270-bis c.p. nella recente esperienza giurisprudenziale," 2007 (10) *Cass. Pen.* 3953–987.

Assistance to members of a terrorist organization is punished by imprisonment for up to four years under Article 270-*ter* of the Criminal Code. The offence of assistance to terrorist associations (as distinct from complicity or aiding and abetting[25]) is committed when any person gives refuge or provides sustenance, hospitality, means of transport or instruments of communication to any person who participates in the associations or organizations specified in Articles 270 and 270-*bis* of the Criminal Code, except where the accused gives support to a close relative. Subsequent Articles 270-*quater* and 270-*quinquies* of the Criminal Code criminalize the recruitment of one or more persons for the purpose of committing acts of violence intended as terrorism[26] and training activities directed at domestic or international terrorism.[27] These activities, as set out in Article 270-*quinquies*, include providing instructions for the preparation or use of explosive materials, fire weapons, chemical or biological weapons that are toxic and dangerous and other weapons, as well as of any other technique or method to perform acts of violence or sabotage against utilities. According to the Court of Cassation, Article 270-*quinquies* of the Criminal Code was introduced in 2005 with the aim of suppressing specific conduct directed at the preparation of actual terrorist attacks. In order to strengthen the effectiveness of the fight against international terrorism, the provision criminalizes the dissemination of know-how in the field of terrorist activities. It is therefore intended to suppress teaching activities or the transfer of knowledge of terrorist methods. The following individuals are punishable: the person trained; the trainer (i.e., the person who instructs another in performing a specific task); and the informant (i.e., the person who regularly collects and communicates useful data). A person who is only occasionally a recipient of information is not punishable since, realistically, he or she has not been able to acquire any specific preparation to be capable of performing acts of violence or sabotage.[28]

[25] Complicity (*concorso nel reato*) is addressed under Article 110 of the Criminal Code and covers an individual who is not a member of a terrorist organization but is aware of its goals and consciously contributes to them (Court of Cassation, Criminal Section I, 4 March 2010, no. 16549, *CED Cass. pen.* 2010). Aiding and abetting (*favoreggiamento*) exists when an individual facilitates the task of a member of a criminal organization (Court of Cassation, Criminal Section 1, 11 November 2003, no. 6905, 2005, *Riv. pen.* 1395).

[26] This conduct is punishable by imprisonment for seven to fifteen years.

[27] This conduct is punishable by imprisonment for five to ten years.

[28] See Court of Cassation, Criminal Section VI, 25 July 2011, No. 29670 (2012), 10 *Riv. pen.* 1002. The case concerned an Imam who exchanged information on the use of weapons and explosives, as well as on the use of software capable of destroying websites and evading interception by the police. He also released to mosque frequenters film clips of military actions of suicide bombers and summary executions of soldiers, as well as a PDF file in Arabic containing a handbook providing detailed explanations on techniques for covering up information traces and identifying targets with the aid of satellites. Also see Court of Cassation, Criminal Section I, 12 July 2011, No. 38220 (2011), *CED Cass. pen.* 251363. The two judgments are, however, in opposition as regards the subjective element of the crime. According to the judges of Criminal Section I, general intent (*dolo generico*) is sufficient,

A final specific type of terrorist offence is provided for by Article 289-*bis* of the Criminal Code, which deals with the offence of kidnapping for the purposes of terrorism or subversion of democracy. This Article was added by Law No. 191/1978 after the kidnapping and subsequent assassination of Aldo Moro by a subversive group.[29] This type of offence, however, is no longer common in Italy.

Specific terrorist offences aside, Article 1 of Law No 15/1980 provides for aggravating circumstances for offences for the purposes of terrorism. It applies, in principle, to all offences established by the legislator (except when terrorist purposes are a requirement of the offence), and increases sentencing by 50%.

Finally, the Italian Criminal Code has traditionally punished with imprisonment public instigation to commit a crime (Article 414) as well as incitement of a person to commit a crime (Article 302). In 2005, the former crime was amended to provide that punishment would be increased by 50% for terrorism offences.

B. *Terrorism Prosecutions*

As mentioned previously, a network of Islamic terrorist cells is active in Italy. Up until now, their role has been primarily to provide logistic support and forged documents such as passports, identity cards, residence permits and such for members of the various groups supporting Al-Qaeda. Evidence gathered during investigations shows that counterfeit documents are provided by habitual criminals who do not belong to any terrorist organization but who are fully aware that these documents will be used for terrorist activities. No connection between international terrorist groups and Italian organized crime has been established, and cases in which an Italian citizen is prosecuted for offences related to Islamic terrorism are very rare. Islamic terrorists in Italy are mostly immigrants from North Africa who have been indoctrinated in *Jihad* in Italy, with the jihadists playing on their social marginalization and precarious living conditions.

Numerous trials and investigations concerning offences for the purposes of terrorism and subversion of democracy are, and have been, carried out in Milan, Genoa, Venice, Naples, Perugia, Bologna, Turin, Trento, Brescia as well as other districts.

given that "the purpose of terrorism" mentioned in Article 270-*quinquies* of the Criminal Code is to characterize the acts of violence and sabotage of public services. On the contrary, the judges of Criminal Section VI require specific intent (*dolo specifico*): the training or giving of instructions must be done with a view towards carrying out violent acts of sabotage against public services for the purpose of terrorism. According to scholars, this second approach is to be preferred. See A. Valsecchi, "L'accertamento del (doppio) dolo specifico nel reato di addestramento ad attività con finalità di terrorismo," (2012) 3 *Cass. pen.* 903.

[29] Law No. 191 of 18 May 1978 on criminal and procedural provisions for the prevention and suppression of serious crimes, *Gazz. Uff.* No. 137.

Since 1984, the Ministry of Justice has collected statistics on the number of criminal cases relating to terrorist offences. These reveal that, in the last five years, there have been on average 250 criminal proceedings each year, and 10% of prosecutions result in conviction.[30] Such a low conviction rate can be explained – at least in part – by taking into account certain features of the Italian system of criminal justice, which does not in principle recognize prosecutorial discretion and obliges prosecutors to take action against all prosecutable offenses, to the extent that there is a sufficient factual basis to initiate criminal proceedings against suspects.

Jurisdiction in terrorism cases falls within ordinary courts, and a provision setting up a special court would be unconstitutional under Article 102(2) of the Italian Constitution. According to general rules set out in Articles 6 to 10 of the Criminal Code, Italian courts have jurisdiction when a crime has been committed – even only partially – within the territory of the state. As for crimes committed abroad, the exercise of jurisdiction by Italian courts is possible in the following cases: when the crime has been committed against Italy (Article 7); when the crime has been committed by an Italian citizen, if punished with a minimum of three years of imprisonment, or at the request of the Ministry of Justice (Article 9); when the crime has been committed against an Italian citizen by a non-national and is punished with a minimum of one year of imprisonment; and when requested by the Ministry of Justice, provided that the non-national has been caught in Italy, the crime is punished with a minimum of three years of imprisonment and extradition has not been authorized or accepted (Article 10).

Suspected and accused persons in criminal proceedings for terrorist crimes enjoy the same procedural rights and guarantees that apply to criminal cases in general. In particular, the Code of Criminal Procedure contains principles aiming at safeguarding the moral liberty of persons giving evidence. Under Articles 64(2) and 188, methods or techniques capable of affecting freedom of self-determination or altering the ability to remember and value facts cannot be used during questioning and evidence collection – not even with the consent of the suspect. Any violation of these rules results in inadmissibility of evidence under Article 191 of the Code of Criminal Procedure. Such inadmissibility may be declared *ex-officio* at any stage of the proceedings.

To avoid the risk of intimidation of witnesses and *pentiti*, there is a framework of measures, including the possibility of giving evidence shielded by anonymity, to ensure that they may testify freely.[31] Article 147-*bis* of the implementing provisions of the Code of Criminal Procedure provides that individuals who, by law, are granted protection measures or admitted to a protection program, even of an urgent or

[30] For further details see http://www.giustizia.it/giustizia/it/mg_1_14.wp?facetNode_1=3_1_4&selectedNode=0_10&facetNode_3=0_15_3&facetNode_2=0_15&all=false.

[31] Anonymity as a means of witness protection is also acknowledged by Recommendation No. R (97) 13 concerning the intimidation of witnesses and the rights of defence, adopted by the Committee

provisional nature, shall be heard during criminal proceedings with all necessary precautions to safeguard them. In particular, they may testify from a remote location by means of audio-visual aids showing all the persons present in the room where the witness is located. Anonymous witness evidence is mandatory in criminal proceedings concerning terrorist offences when the person giving evidence has changed his or her identity, unless the court holds that the person's presence in the courtroom is absolutely necessary.[32] In these cases, in order to protect the anonymity of the witness, the court can decide, under Article 472 of the Code of Criminal Procedure, that the hearing will be held without the presence of the public.

C. *Punishment of Terrorism*

As mentioned in Section I, under Italian criminal law the repentance of the offender, if combined with *active collaboration*, can lead to a reduction of the sentence or, for some offences, exemption from punishment.

The first *reward measure (misura premiale)* was enacted by Law No. 191/1978 that, as mentioned previously, introduced Article 289-*bis* of the Criminal Code. Punishing the offence of kidnapping for the purposes of terrorism, this measure provides for a reduction in sentencing for those who, having participated in the offence, dissociate themselves from the other offenders, helping to facilitate the release of the kidnapped person. This provision was the starting point of "reward legislation" adopted in the 1980s to fight terrorism and organized crime. Notably, Law No. 15/1980 provides for a reduction in sentencing for cases where the defendant found guilty of offences committed for the purposes of terrorism or subversion of democracy dissociates himself or herself from the other offenders to prevent additional consequences of the criminal activity, or concretely assists the judicial and police authorities to gather decisive evidence in order to find or arrest accomplices. The provision also provides an exemption from punishment for an offence committed for the purposes of terrorism or subversion of democracy where the defendant voluntarily prevents the accomplishment of the crime and gives decisive evidence for the precise reconstruction of the facts and the location of possible accomplices.

Exemption from punishment is also provided for those who, having committed only offences relating to their membership of a criminal organization or terrorist group, withdraw from the agreement or organization or the terrorist group or bring about its dissolution.[33]

of Ministers on 10 September 1997. Available at http://www.coe.int/t/dghl/standardsetting/victims/recR_97_13e.pdf.

32 See Article 147-*bis* (3.c.) of the implementing provisions of the Code of Criminal Procedure.

33 Article 1 of Law No. 304 of 29 May 1982, on measures for the defence of the constitutional order, *Gazz. Uff.* No. 149.

Further, persons charged with terrorist offences are granted extenuating circumstances if, before conviction, they withdraw from the terrorist organization, make a full confession of the offences committed and effectively cooperate to annul or mitigate the consequences deriving from their criminal acts or to prevent the perpetration of other related types of criminal conduct.[34] Extenuating circumstances (that serve to reduce sentences) apply also to persons charged with terrorist offences who, besides having dissociated themselves from criminal association and confessed to the offences committed, effectively cooperate with judicial authorities in gathering decisive evidence to identify and apprehend the perpetrators of terrorist acts or to find useful information for reconstructing the facts and identifying those responsible.[35]

Finally, Law No. 191/1978 provides for mitigation of sentences for offences committed for the purposes of terrorism or subversion of the constitutional order where the accused or convict has definitively abandoned the organization or the terrorist or subversive movement to which the person belonged.[36]

IV. INVESTIGATIVE POWERS

In the fight against terrorism, the Italian police force co-operates with the national intelligence service. Notably, intelligence bodies are under an obligation to hand over to investigative police any data they receive on possible crimes. However, Public Prosecutors and judges cannot use information from a secret service source as evidence in investigations or trials.

In addition, Law No. 155/2005 provides for the possibility for the Minister of the Interior to set up *ad hoc* counterterrorism units, that is, joint investigation units to carry out criminal police investigation following particularly serious terrorist offences.

A. *Police Powers*

Within the context of counterterrorism, the Italian legislator has adopted laws conferring specific investigative powers on police to deal with suspected terrorists. In particular, Law No. 438/2001 has extended from eighteen to twenty-one months

34 Article 2, Law No. 304/1982. In particular, life imprisonment is replaced by a term of imprisonment of fifteen to twenty-one years, and other terms of imprisonment are reduced by one-third and may not in any case exceed fifteen years.

35 Article 3, Law No. 304/1982.

36 See Law No. 34 of 18 February 1987, on measures in favor of those who disassociate from terrorism, *Gazz. Uff.* No. 43.

the maximum length of preliminary investigations with regard to terrorist offences (see Article 407 of the Code of Criminal Procedure). It also amended Article 226 of the implementing rules of the Code of Criminal Procedure, which deals with wiretapping and preventive communications surveillance, to allow suspected terrorists to be put under police surveillance, and the wiretapping of communications or conversations, also by means of telecommunications systems. Wiretapping must be authorized by the Public Prosecutor. The authorization is valid for a *maximum* period of forty days, which may be extended for additional periods of twenty days by decree of the Prosecutor, issued with a clear explanation of the reasons that make this necessary. Data collected through preventive investigatory activities (e.g., wiretapping carried out before any crime has been committed) cannot be used in criminal proceedings. Moreover, in order to safeguard the secrecy of the investigation, wiretapping and the information gathered from such surveillance cannot be referred to in investigation reports, be the subject of testimony nor otherwise be disclosed.

Police may arrest without a warrant (arrest in *flagrante delicto*) a person who has committed an offence for the purposes of terrorism or subversion of democracy punishable with a term of imprisonment of four to ten years (Article 380 of the Code of Criminal Procedure). Law No. 155/2005 introduced new provisions on arrest and police detention, enabling the detention of a person suspected of having committed an offence for the purposes of domestic or international terrorism or subversion of democracy (Article 384 of the Code of Criminal Procedure). It also extended the scope of Article 18-*bis* of Law No. 354/1975 concerning the possibility of meeting, for investigative purposes, prisoners for collecting information to prevent and suppress organized crime.[37] It is thus possible for the Chief of the provincial Commander of the Police or *Carabinieri*, as well as for investigative police officers charged with investigations relating to terrorism, to meet prisoners to obtain useful information for preventing and suppressing offences committed for the purposes of terrorism, including international terrorism.

Finally, Law No. 146/2006 allows the carrying out of undercover activities during specific police operations, including investigations concerning terrorist acts, to obtain evidence concerning the offences committed.[38]

[37] Law No. 354 of 26 July 1975 on prison rules and the implementation of measures depriving or restricting personal liberty, *Gazz. Uff.* No. 212.

[38] Article 9.b), Law No. 416 of 16 March 2006, on the ratification and execution of United Nations Convention against Transnational Crime and its Protocols, *Gazz. Uff.* No. 85.

B. *Intelligence Agencies*

From an historical perspective, the Italian security intelligence system has ancient roots.[39] The current system, as reformed by Law 124/2007,[40] includes various authorities and organizations responsible for intelligence policies, coordination and operations, which are under the President of the Council of Ministers – that is, the Chief Executive.[41] This President has the exclusive "overall responsibility for security intelligence policy in the interests and defence of the Republic and its underlying democratic institutions as established by the Constitution."[42] To support the President in this task, a special committee – the Department of Security Intelligence (DIS) – has been established within the executive. The DIS coordinates all intelligence activities and operates as a link between intelligence agencies and the armed and police forces, on the one hand, and the state's administrative entities, on the other.[43] The task of defending "the internal security of the Republic and its underlying democratic institutions as established by the Constitution (including in implementation of international agreements) from every threat, subversive activity and form of criminal or terrorist attack," falls within the competence of the Internal Security and Intelligence Agency (AISI).[44]

Intelligence officers enjoy special immunity,[45] however, this does not cover, *inter alia*, the crimes of abduction and terrorism offences. The application of immunity can be challenged before the Constitutional Court.[46]

39 The term *secret service (servizio segreto)* appeared for the first time in official documents in 1855 to refer to military information. See Circolare n. 21 of April 1855, in *Giornale Militare*, namely *Raccolta Uffiziale delle Leggi, Regolamenti e Disposizioni di terra e di mare*, vol. I, published by Ministry of War, Torino, Officina Tipografica e Litografica di Giuseppe Fodratti, 1855, pp. 775–93. However, the establishment of an intelligence system dates back to 1863. For a history of the Italian Intelligence System, see G. De Lutiis, *Storia dei servizi segreti in Italia*, Roma, Editori Riuniti, 1991.

40 Law No. 124 of 3 August 2007 on intelligence systems for the security of the Republic and new provisions governing secrecy, *Gazz. Uff.* No. 187.

41 For an exhaustive analysis of the current intelligence system, see C. Mosca, S. Gambacurta, G. Scandone, M. Valentini, *I servizi di informazione e il segreto di Stato (Legge 3 agosto 2007, n. 124)*, Milano, Giuffrè, 2008.

42 Article 1 a), Law No. 124/2007.

43 Article 4, Law No. 124/2007.

44 Article 7, Law No. 124/2007.

45 According to Article 17 (6) of Law No. 124/2007, intelligence officers who have committed a crime cannot be prosecuted if the unlawful acts (a) were committed either in the exercise or because of the institutional tasks assigned to intelligence agencies and were specifically authorized by the President of the Council of Ministers within the framework of the Security Intelligence System's organizational rules; (b) were indispensable and proportionate to the achievement of otherwise unachievable objectives in an operation; (c) were the result of a thorough and objective balancing of public and private interests involved; and (d) were carried out in such a way as to cause the *minimum* damage possible to affected interests.

46 Article 19, Law No. 124/2007.

For a greater involvement of intelligence services in the fight against terrorism, Law No. 155/2005 has broadened the scope of preventive communications and home surveillance regulated by Article 226 of the implementing rules of the Code of Criminal Procedure. It enables the President of the Council of Ministers to delegate the directors of intelligence authorities to seek from the Chief Appeal Court Prosecutor authorization to carry out surveillance activities when they are necessary for the prevention of terrorist activities or subversion.

V. PROSCRIPTION AND LISTING OF TERRORIST GROUPS AND INDIVIDUALS

A. *Proscription Mechanisms*

In order to implement the UN blacklisting system,[47] Law No. 431/2001 established the Financial Security Committee.[48] Rules on listing processes are in the internal regulation of the Committee.[49] In particular, Article 6 states that the Committee can propose to relevant UN and EU authorities the inclusion of persons or entities in their terrorist lists, on the basis of information provided by the police force, international bodies and foreign states or otherwise acquired. To designate the names to be included in the lists, the Committee may take into account the following: (a) the existence of evidence suggesting an active participation in, or support of, terrorist activities; (b) the existence of pending criminal charges or judicial measures; (c) the suitability of collected data to correctly identify suspects according to reasonable standards; (d) any relationship between the suspect and individuals or entities already included in the lists; (e) the existence of sanctions in accordance with the resolutions of the UN Security Council under Chapter VII of the Charter of the United Nations and the EU Council Common Position to fight terrorism and suppress financing of terrorist activities; and (f) any other relevant information in its possession.

To avoid the risk that a person could be included in the list without any judicial protection, the President of the Financial Security Committee must inform the

47 The Italian legislator expressly refers to Resolutions 1267(1999), 1333(200) and 1373(2001), adopted by the UN Security Council.

48 The Financial Security Committee, chaired by the Director General of the Treasury, includes representatives of the Bank of Italy, the National Commission for Business and the Stock Exchange (CONSOB), the Italian Banking Association, the Italian Exchange Commission, the Police, *Carabinieri* and Financial Corps and the National Anti-Mafia Directorate, as well as representatives of various ministries.

49 Ministerial decree No. 203 of 20 October 2010 on regulation of the functioning of the Financial Security Committee, *Gazz. Uff.* No. 86.

Public Prosecutor in order to start a judicial inquiry.[50] However, since there is no mandatory judicial procedure to ratify inclusion in the lists, there are concerns, such as the indefinite duration of the listing measure and the potential role of the intelligence services in designating the suspected terrorist supporters.[51]

The Financial Security Committee also proposes the removal of a name from the lists to the relevant UN and EU authorities.[52]

B. *Challenges to Proscriptions and Listings*

Decisions of the Financial Security Committee can be challenged before administrative tribunals. When an administrative tribunal, in order to rule on an appeal against a listing decision, needs to know acts covered by state or investigative secrecy, it must suspend proceedings until those acts, or their essential content, may be disclosed. However, suspension cannot last longer than two years, after which the tribunal may fix the date by which the Financial Security Committee shall produce new information or annul the contested measure.[53]

Terrorist blacklists have given rise to a debate concerning the significance in criminal proceedings of the fact of being on such lists. Indeed, initially the Court of Cassation blamed the Tribunal of Naples because it did not take into due account terrorist lists drawn up by international organizations,[54] and then stated that such lists should be considered as a starting point for further inquiry into the scope of such an organization.[55] This approach has been widely criticized by scholars since it would evade rules on evidence by grounding the assessment of *actus reus* (i.e., participation in a terrorist organization, punished under Article 270-*bis* of the Criminal Code) on acts adopted by the executive and international authorities, thus violating the principles of legality and separation of powers enshrined in the Italian Constitution.[56]

[50] Cfr. Article 1-*bis* of Law No. 431/2001, and then Article 3(10) of Legislative Decree No. 109 of 22 June 2007 on measures to prevent, counter and suppress the financing of terrorism and the activities of countries that threaten international peace and security, implementing Directive 2005/60/EC, *Gazz. Uff.* No. 172.

[51] For a closer examination, see, L. G. Bruno, "Misure di prevenzione patrimoniale e congelamento di beni per reati di terrorismo: problemi sostanziali e processuali," (2007) 13 *Diritto penale e processo* 99–108.

[52] Article 3.12 of Legislative Decree No. 109/2007.

[53] Cfr. Article 14 of Legislative Decree No. 109/2007.

[54] Court of Cassation, Criminal Section II, 9 February 2005, No. 10450 (2005), *Foro it.* II, 385.

[55] Court of Cassation, Criminal Section I, 21 June 2005, No. 35427 (2005), 44 *Dir. e giustizia* 79.

[56] On this point see, I. Ingravallo, "L'attuazione in Italia delle 'liste' anti-terrorismo e la loro rilevanza nel processo penale," (2008) 3 *Dir. umani e dir. Int.* 561–80, especially at p. 577; C. Di Stasio, *La lotta multilivello al terrorismo internazionale. Garanzia di sicurezza versus tutela dei diritti fondamentali*, Milano, Giuffrè, 2010, p. 600.

Developing a different approach, the Court of Cassation has made clear that inclusion in a terrorist blacklist derives from a political determination and cannot be considered as evidence in criminal trials.[57] It follows that neither UN nor EU lists may be considered as evidence in criminal proceedings; they are only one among many elements that prosecutors and judges have to take into consideration.[58] Inclusion in the lists therefore has effect only in the administrative sphere, legitimating the imposition of sanctions provided by law; it has no value as evidence in criminal proceedings.[59]

VI. REGULATION OF TERRORISM FINANCING

As a member of the European Union, Italy has developed domestic legislation on terrorism financing on the basis of EC Regulations 2580/2001[60] and 881/2002,[61] as well as EU Council Common Position 2001/931.[62]

A. *Regulatory Regime to Counter Terrorism Financing*

Measures to prevent the use of financial systems for terrorist financing and permit the freezing of funds and economic resources to combat terrorist financing are in Legislative Decree No. 109/2007. In particular, Article 4 establishes that the Minister of the Economy and Finance and the Minister of Foreign Affairs – at the request of the Financial Security Committee – can order the freezing of funds and economic resources held by natural or legal persons, entities or groups before the EU's decision and without involving criminal courts. In so doing, the criteria and procedures established by the UN Security Council or one of its committees under UN Security Council Resolutions under Chapter VII of the UN Charter are followed. Frozen funds and economic resources cannot be subject to any transfer, provision or use; any act committed in violation of this prohibition is null and void.[63]

57 Court of Cassation, Criminal Section I, 15 June 2006, No. 30824 (2006), 44 *Guida al diritto* 60.

58 Court of Cassation, Criminal Section VI, 26 May 2009, No. 33425 (2009), 40 *Guida al diritto* 79.

59 Court of Cassation, Criminal Section I, 11 October 2006, No. 1072 (2007), 4 *Cass. pen.* 1462.

60 Council Regulation (EC) No. 2580/2001 of 27 December 2001 on specific restrictive measures directed against certain persons and entities with a view to combating terrorism (2001) *O J* L 344, 70.

61 Council Regulation (EC) No. 881/2002 of 27 May 2002 imposing certain specific restrictive measures directed against certain persons and entities associated with Osama bin Laden, the Al-Qaida network and the Taliban, and repealing Council Regulation (EC) No 467/2001 prohibiting the export of certain goods and services to Afghanistan, strengthening the flight ban and extending the freezing of funds and other financial resources in respect of the Taliban of Afghanistan (2002) O J L 139, 9.

62 Council Common Position of 27 December 2001 on the application of specific measures to combat terrorism (2001) *O.J.* L 344, 93.

63 Article 5 of Legislative Decree No. 109/2007.

Legislative Decree No. 109/2007, together with Legislative Decree No. 231/2007,[64] also covers the offence of money laundering. Article 648-*bis* of the Criminal Code punishes a person who substitutes or transfers money, goods or other benefits resulting from an unpremeditated crime or carries out other transactions in relation to those assets in such a way as to hinder their identification as the proceeds of a crime, with imprisonment of up to twelve years and a fine. Moreover, Article 648-*ter* of the Criminal Code criminalizes the use of money, goods or other benefits resulting from a crime for economic or financial activities.

Implementing EU law, Italy has enacted measures to counter money laundering practices by prohibiting, among other things, the carrying out of transactions whereby substantial sums of money are transferred using anonymous instruments and making it possible to reconstruct transactions by the identification of customers and recording of data in a special database.

To prevent and combat money laundering and terrorist financing, the Financial Intelligence Unit established at the Bank of Italy in 2008 carries out financial analyses of suspicious transactions reported by financial intermediaries and other entities conducting financial activities, such as banks, post offices, stockbroking firms,[65] asset management companies[66] and variable capital investment funds,[67] as well as by various professionals, including auditors, notaries and lawyers when carrying out financial or real estate transactions in the name and on behalf of their clients and when assisting their clients in certain transactions. In addition, the Unit performs the following tasks: carrying out analyses and studies on individual anomalies traceable to possible cases of money laundering or terrorist financing, on specific sectors of the economy deemed to be at risk and on categories of payment instruments and specific local economic conditions; developing models and patterns of anomalous economic and financial conduct that may be signs of money laundering or terrorist financing; and collaborating with various European and international organizations engaged in preventing and combating money laundering, terrorist financing and the proliferation of weapons of mass destruction.

According to data published in the Annual Report, the Italian Financial Intelligence Unit receives an average of four hundred reports of suspected terrorist financing each year.[68] However, convictions for the offence of financing terrorism

64 Legislative Decree No. 231 of 11 November 2007, on the Implementation of Directive 2005/60/EC on the prevention of the use of the financial system for the purposes of money laundering and terrorist financing and of Directive 2006/70/EC laying down implementing measures for Directive 2005/06/EC, *Gazz. Uff.* No. 290.

65 *Società di intermediazione mobiliare* (SIM).

66 *Società di gestione del risparmio* (SGR).

67 *Società di investimento a capitale variabile* (SICAV).

68 Reports are published on the website of the Bank of Italy: http://www.bancaditalia.it/UIF/pubblicazioni-uif.

have been few. According to data available for years 2000 to 2004, there were only twenty-nine convictions for relating to these activities.[69]

B. *Criminal Offences of Terrorism Financing*

In a report by the Financial Action Task Force (FATF) in October 2005, Italy was rated only partially compliant with recommendations on customers' due diligence and suspicious transaction reporting and was placed under regular follow-up. However, in February 2009, the FATF Plenary decided that Italy had made sufficient progress to move from regular to biennial follow-up. As for the criminalization of terrorist financing, the FATF's report for 2005 pointed out that Italian legislation lacked a definition of the concept of *financing*, including the type of funds and assets that can serve the purposes of financing terrorism. Indeed, Article 270-*bis* of the Criminal Code mentions financing as a conduct that indicates participation in a terrorist association, but it does not provide a definition of the act of financing terrorism. Accordingly, for instance, the Court of Cassation confirmed the holding of the Court of Appeal that established the participation of the accused persons in a terrorist association because they collected funds, provided forged documents and abetted illegal entry into Italy of terrorists.[70]

As noted in the preceding paragraph, the terrorism offence under Article 270-*bis* of the Criminal Code requires specific intent *(dolo specifico)*, namely the accused must be aware of the terrorist nature of the organization he or she intends to support. For a financial transaction to fall within the scope of Article 270-*bis*, the accused must therefore be aware of the purpose of terrorism or subversion of the association to which he or she gave money and must intend to support terrorist activities.

A definition of terrorism financing is now contained in Article 1 of Legislative Decree No. 109/2007. This provision holds that terrorist financing includes any activity of collecting and keeping funds and economic resources with the intention that these should be used, in full or in part, to carry out, commit or facilitate the commission of one or more terrorist offences under the Criminal Code. It is not, however, necessary that the funds are in fact used for carrying out the terrorist offence.

Judicial investigations into suspected terrorist crimes carried out in Italy during recent years have revealed evidence of transfers – sometimes through alternative channels, such as Western Union – of money from individuals who are believed to be

69 See Rapporto dettagliato di valutazione sulle misure di prevenzione del riciclaggio di denaro e del finanziamento del terrorismo, para. 18. http://www.dt.tesoro.it/export/sites/sitodt/modules/documenti_it/prevenzione_reati_finanziari/prevenzione_reati_finanziari/DAR-FMI.pdf.

70 Court of Cassation, Criminal Section V, 4 July 2008, No. 39545, *CED Cass. pen.* 2008.

members of terrorist groups to other suspected terrorists operating often outside Italy or in training camps. Money to finance combatants and terrorist activities have been collected as voluntary contributions from the faithful in compliance with religious norms *(zakāt)*, but also by systematic extortion at the expense of individuals of the Islamic faith. Further, through the declarations of criminals who collaborated to turn evidence to the state (*pentiti*), investigating magistrates have obtained evidence on drug trafficking and money forgery committed for the purpose of financing terrorist activities. Some terrorists have been sentenced for these crimes. Small companies registered under the names of suspects of terrorist activities that probably were used for the illegal financing of such activities have also been exposed.[71]

Money has been confiscated from individuals under investigation on numerous occasions. Indeed, in order to implement UN Resolution 1373, the preventive system of seizure and confiscation of mafia-related assets has been extended to national and foreign suspected terrorists. This means that confiscation of assets can be ordered by administrative authorities outside of criminal proceedings. Lacking evidence that the seized assets have a legitimate origin, they are permanently confiscated within one year.

VII. IMMIGRATION MEASURES

Italian legal provisions on immigration are in Legislative Decree No. 286/1998.[72] Grounds of deportation of non-Italian nationals have been expanded to encompass terrorism. Accordingly, Article 312 of the Criminal Code provides that a EU citizen who is sentenced for a crime against the state (under Title I, Book II, Title I of the Criminal Code) may be deported. Moreover, Article 3 of Law No. 155/2005 grants the Minister of the Interior, or upon delegation the Prefect, the power to order the deportation of a foreign citizen against whom there are well-founded reasons to believe that his or her stay in Italy might in any way facilitate terrorist organizations or activities, at the national or international level. The deportation order prevents the deported person from re-entering Italy for at least five years up to a maximum of ten years.

In general, deportations are ordered where there is evidence that an individual is a threat to national security but the evidence is considered insufficient for prosecution. Some individuals have been deported from Italy by the Minister of

[71] A. Spataro, "Le forme attuali di manifestazione del terrorismo nella esperienza giudiziaria: implicazioni etniche, religiose e tutela dei diritti umani," *cit. supra*, pp. 190 ff.

[72] Legislative Decree No. 286 of 25 July 1998, Unified Text on measures concerning immigration and norms on the condition of foreign citizens, *Gazz. Uff.* No. 191, Supplemento Ordinario No. 139.

the Interior on the basis of investigations into certain Islamist groups and reported attendance at training or combat courses.

Doubts could be cast on the compliance of the deportation procedure under Article 3 of Law No. 155/2005 with the Constitution and the ECHR because of the unfettered discretion conferred to the competent authorities and lack of effective judicial control.[73] Indeed, the deportation order is immediately enforceable because it is not subject to any prior judicial validation, and the regional administrative courts *(Tribunali Amministrativi Regionali)* competent to review its lawfulness cannot order a stay of its execution.[74]

A. *Immigration, Deportation Proceedings and Torture*

The mechanism of deportation of migrants suspected of terrorism under Article 3 of Law No. 155/2005 could jeopardize the prohibition of refoulement,[75] insofar as the deportation order is adopted by the competent authorities without any careful consideration of the risk of torture in the receiving country and is issued without hearing the person concerned. Indeed, Italy was condemned by the European Court of Human Rights (ECtHR) for violation of Article 3 (Prohibition of Torture) in *Saadi v. Italy*.[76] This case concerned a Tunisian citizen, Mr. Nassim Saadi, suspected, among other things, of international terrorism, against whom the Minister of Interior issued a deportation order to Tunisia. The applicant claimed that his deportation to Tunisia would have exposed him to the risk of being subjected to torture or inhuman and degrading treatment contrary to Article 3 ECHR. Considering all the circumstances of the case, the ECtHR held that the Tunisian authorities had not provided the diplomatic assurances requested by the Italian government. Mr. Saadi

[73] Further on this point, A. Saccucci, "The Italian 2005 anti-terrorism legislation in the light of international human rights obligations," (2005) XV, *The Italian Yearbook of International Law*, 167–94, especially at pp. 187 ff.; C. Campeis, "L'espulsione dello straniero ex art. 3 decreto legge 27 luglio 2005 n. 144: una misura di prevenzione mascherata?" in S. Lorenzon, G. Vaccari, V. Zanetti (eds.), *Sicurezza collettiva e diritti fondamentali in tempo di terrorismo. Atti del workshop. Ferrara, 26 settembre 2007*, Roma, Aracne, 2008, especially at pp. 161 ff.

[74] The Constitutional Court ruled that the impossibility of staying the execution of the deportation order does not violate constitutional procedural guarantees. See Constitutional Court, 14 December 2007, No. 432 (2007), *Giur. cost.* 6.

[75] The expulsion of persons who have the right to remain as refugees.

[76] ECtHR [G.C.], 28 February 2008, *Saadi v. Italy*, App. No. 37201/06. In other cases, the ECtHR found that the diplomatic assurances given by the Tunisian authorities were not sufficient to guarantee that the applicant would have been protected against the risk of treatment prohibited by Article 3 ECHR. See, for instance, ECtHR, 24 February 2009, *Ben Khemais v. Italy*, App. No. 246/07; 24 March 2009, *Abdelhedi v. Italy*, App. No. 2638/07; 24 March 2009, *Soltana v. Italy*, App. No. 37336/06; 5 May 2009, *Sellem v. Italy*, App. No. 12584/08; 13 April 2010, *Trabelsi v. Italy*, App. No. 50163/08; 5 April 2001, *Toumi v. Italy*, App. No. 25716/09.

had been sentenced in Tunisia, in his absence, to twenty years of imprisonment for membership in a terrorist organization and incitement to terrorism. Considering, in particular, the numerous and frequent cases of torture and ill treatment meted out to persons accused of terrorist crimes under Tunisian law, the ECtHR considered that the applicant would have been at risk of ill treatment once back in Tunisia. That being so, the ECtHR considered that there were substantial grounds for believing that there was a real risk that the applicant would be subjected to treatment contrary to Article 3 if he were to be deported to Tunisia. Consequently, the ECtHR found that the decision to deport Mr. Saadi to Tunisia would breach Article 3 if it were enforced.

To take into account the ECtHR decision in the *Saadi* case, the Italian Court of Cassation held that any judge deciding on a deportation to Tunisia must adopt an appropriate alternative preventive measure *(misura di sicurezza)*, so as to fully comply with Article 3 ECHR.[77] These measures are listed in Article 215 of the Criminal Code. Probation *(libertà vigilata)* and internment in a penal colony *(casa di lavoro)* are the most likely alternatives.[78]

VIII. ROLE OF THE MILITARY AND EXTRATERRITORIAL COUNTERTERRORISM ACTIVITIES

The main task of the Italian army is the defence of national territory. However, since the end of World War II, the army has co-operated with police forces in controlling the territory to prevent terrorist acts by national and international terrorist organizations. Moreover, the Italian army has been (and still is) involved in missions abroad under the aegis of the UN, NATO and Multinational Forces.

One of the much-discussed operations of the Italian Military Intelligence and Security Service (SISMI),[79] in cooperation with the United States' Central Intelligence Agency (CIA), is the abduction of Hassan Mustafa Osama Nasr, Imam of Milan, also known as Abu Omar, in the context of the U.S. extraordinary renditions program. On 12 February 2003, Omar was walking from his house in

[77] Court of Cassation, Criminal Section VI, 28 April 2010, No. 20514 (2010), 9 *Riv. pen.* 846.

[78] Ufficio di Sorveglianza of Tribunal of Livorno, order of 18 May 2009 (2010), *Corriere del merito* 548; Ufficio di Sorveglianza of Tribunal of Nuoro, order of 16 December 2008. The latter concerned a Tunisian citizen, Mr. Nourreddine Drissi, sentenced to six years in prison for participation in a terrorist association. The judgment provided also that, once he served his sentence, he would have been expulsed to Tunisia. Mr. Drissi appealed against the expulsion. The Tribunal of Nuoro, taking into consideration the case law of the ECtHR, upheld the appeal and ordered the internment in a penal colony *(assegnazione a una casa di lavoro)*. The decision of the Tribunal of Nuoro has been considered in compliance with ECHR law by the ECtHR (see ECtHR (dec.), 28 September 2010, *Drissi v. Italy*, App. No. 44448/08).

[79] In 2007, SISMI was replaced by the External Intelligence and Security Agency.

Milan to the local mosque when he was stopped by a *carabiniere*, immobilized, put in a car, brought to a U.S. airbase in Aviano and then transferred to Egypt. There he was detained in secret for several months for interrogation and allegedly subjected to torture and inhuman and degrading treatment.[80] A criminal trial for the abduction of Abu Omar was held in Milan. The first instance trial in the Tribunal of Milan ended with five-to seven-year sentences for twenty-three CIA agents of U.S. nationality for the crime of abduction; three-year sentences against two Italian SISMI agents for aiding and abetting the kidnapping of Abu Omar; the acquittal of three U.S. citizens for reasons of diplomatic immunity; and the acquittal of five agents of the SISMI because state secrets privilege prevented the assessment of their co-responsibility in the crime.[81] The Court of Appeal upheld the conviction but increased the sentence for the CIA agents.[82] On further appeal, the Court of Cassation upheld the imprisonment of twenty-three U.S. citizens and two Italians and revoked the acquittal of SISMI's agents and three US citizens for reasons of diplomatic immunity.[83] The Court of Appeal, ruling on remand on the charges against the SISMI agents and three U.S. citizens previously acquitted, reversed the judgment of the Tribunal of Milan and sentenced the defendants to six-to-seven-year imprisonment.[84] On 5 April 2013, the Italian President Giorgio Napolitano pardoned Joseph Romano, a U.S. Air Force colonel convicted for his role in the Abu Omar kidnapping.

An application filed by the lawyers of Abu Omar, on behalf of himself and his wife, is now pending before the ECtHR.[85] They claim the violation of Articles 6 (Right to a fair trial); 13 (Right to an effective remedy); 3 (Prohibition of torture); 5 (Right to liberty and security); and 8 (Right to respect for private and family life) ECHR.

80 Further on the Abu Omar case, F. Messineo, "'Extraordinary renditions' and state obligations to criminalize and prosecute torture in the light of the Abu Omar Case in Italy," (2009) 7 *J. Int'l Crim. J.* 1023.

81 Tribunal of Milan, Criminal Section IV, 4 November 2009, No. 5335/2007.

82 Court of Appeal of Milan, Criminal Section III, 15 March 2011, No. 3688/10.

83 Court of Cassation, Criminal Section V, 19 September 2012, No. 46340 (2013), 1 *Riv. dir. int.* 272.

84 Court of Appeal of Milan, Criminal Section III, 1 February 2013, and Court of Appeal of Milan, Criminal Section IV, 12 February 2013, No. 985. Appeal against these judgments was made to the Court of Cassation.

85 App. No. 44883/09, *Hassn Nasr and Ghali v. Italy*. The ECtHR ruled on facts concerning extraordinary renditions in the case *El-Masri v. The Former Yugoslav Republic of Macedonia*. The applicant was a German national of Lebanese origin who was arrested, held in isolation, questioned and ill-treated in a Skopje hotel for twenty-three days, then transferred by CIA agents to a secret detention facility in Afghanistan, where he was further ill-treated for over four months. The ECtHR found a violation of Articles 3, 5, 8 and 13 ECHR. See ECtHR [G.C.] *El-Masri v. The Former Yugoslav Republic of Macedonia*, 12 December 2012, App. No. 39639/09.

IX. SECRECY AND TERRORISM

A. *Secrecy Claims and Secret Evidence*

State secrets privilege (under which the state may exempt evidence from disclosure) is regulated by Law No. 124/2007.[86] In general terms, this privilege covers acts, documents, information, activities and all other things, the knowledge or circulation of which could damage the integrity of the Republic, considering also international agreements to which Italy is a party, the institutions established by the Constitution, the independence of Italy vis-à-vis other states and in its relationships with them or the military defence of Italy. The President of the Council of Ministers – that is, the head of government – is the only authority entitled to assert state secrets privilege, which cannot last for more than thirty years.[87] State secrets privilege prevents judicial authorities from using, either directly or indirectly, information covered by the secret. When the privilege is invoked in the course of criminal proceedings, the judiciary can raise a formal request to the President of the Council of Ministers to ascertain its existence. If the President does not reply within thirty days, the judicial authority can admit as evidence the information for which the request was formulated. If the President of the Council confirms the existence of the privilege, the court must either dismiss the proceedings or continue them without considering the information covered by privilege. Nonetheless, the judicial authority may challenge the privilege asserted by the head of the government by raising a *conflict of attribution*[88] before the Constitutional Court.[89] The Constitutional Court has thus to decide whether the decision to assert the privilege by the head of the government infringed the constitutional prerogatives of the judiciary. As provided by Article 41(7) of Law 124/2007:

> when the Constitutional Court resolves the conflict of attribution denying the assertion of the State secret, the President of the Council [of Ministers] cannot invoke it anymore against the judiciary; when, on the contrary, the Constitutional Court resolves the conflict of attribution by recognizing that the assertion of the State secret was admissible, the judicial authority cannot obtain and make use, either directly or indirectly, of the acts and documents covered by the State secret.

86 For a comprehensive analysis of rules on state secrets privilege, see Mosca et al., *I servizi di informazione e il segreto di Stato (Legge 3 agosto 2007, n. 124), cit.*

87 Article 39 of Law No. 124/2007. Also see Decree of the President of the Council of Ministers No. 31445 of 8 April 2008, on criteria for identification of data, information, documents, records, activities, things and places which may be subject to state secrets privilege, *Gazz. Uff.* No. 90.

88 Under Article 134 of the Italian Constitution, the Constitutional Court shall pass judgment on conflicts arising from the allocation of powers of the state.

89 Article 41 of Law No. 124/2007.

Entrusting the Constitutional Court with the role of final arbiter over the controversy between the judiciary (in charge of punishing crimes) and the executive (having a constitutional duty to defend national security), the Italian legislator has attempted to guarantee a reasonable balance between the assertion of a state secret to defend national security and the rule of law. Law 147/2007, enacted after the Abu Omar case, provides that the state secrets privilege cannot be invoked in criminal investigations concerning, *inter alia*, acts of terrorism and acts directed to subvert the constitutional order;[90] nor can it be invoked to hamper investigations into any unlawful conduct by intelligence officers carried out in violation of rules governing their special immunity. The law also provides that state secrets should not thwart investigations into conduct that harms people or the administration of justice.[91]

The invocation, in the course of the aforementioned Abu Omar trial, of state secrets privilege concerning data collected by Italian intelligence agents – in particular all data obtained following search and seizure at the offices of the SISMI, which revealed the names of foreign agents, secret acronyms of related services and connections between the Italian and foreign intelligence services – generated a cluster of litigation before the Constitutional Court. Indeed, both the Tribunal of Milan and the Office of the Public Prosecutor in Milan brought a conflict of attribution against the decision of the President of the Council of Ministers to check the existence of state secrets regarding the information concerned. The latter, in its turn, started proceedings against the Office of the Public Prosecutor and the judge in Milan for making use of the information subject to state secrets privilege.

The Constitutional Court delivered a decision on the merits of the conflicts of attribution questions in April 2009.[92] The Court ruled that "the official secret never covered the offence of the kidnapping in itself, which could be investigated by the competent courts according to standard procedures, but rather on the one hand the relations between the Italian and foreign secret services, and on the other hand the organization and operational procedures of the SISMi."[93] It then affirmed, consistent with its previous case law, that "any review over the actual exercise of the power to classify material is precluded, since the assessment regarding the means which it is considered must or may be used in order to guarantee the security of the state is a matter for the President of the Council of Ministers, acting subject to parliamentary oversight."[94]

Subsequently, two new conflicts of attribution have been filed by the President of the Council of Ministers against the Court of Cassation, Criminal Section V,

[90] Article 39 (11) of Law No. 124/2007.

[91] Article 204.1-*bis* of the Code of Criminal Procedure.

[92] Constitutional Court, 3 April 2009, No. 106 (2009), 10 *Cass. pen.* 3703.

[93] *Ibidem*, Conclusions on points of law, para. 12.3.

[94] *Ibidem*, Conclusions on points of law, para. 12.4.

with reference to its judgment No. 46340 of 19 September 2012, and the Court of Appeal of Milan, Section IV, with reference to its judgment No. 985 of 12 February 2013 (both referred to previously). The Constitutional Court upheld the position of the President of the Council of Ministers taken against the rulings of these Courts. In its judgment No. 24 of 13 February 2014, the Constitutional Court blamed the Court of Cassation for having, in fact, redefined the scope of state secrets privilege. The Constitutional Court gave preeminence of the *raison d'etat*, reaffirming that, as far as state secrets privilege is concerned, the President of the Council of Ministers enjoys a wide discretionary power. Its exercise is not subject to judicial control by ordinary courts, since the decision on suitable means to ensure national security is an eminently political one.[95] Following this judgment, the Court of Cassation acquitted SISMI's agents.[96]

It is an open question whether these judgments take fully into consideration the warning of the ECtHR that state secrets privilege cannot be invoked to obstruct the search for the truth in investigating allegations of serious human rights violations.[97]

B. *Secrecy in the Courtroom and Anonymous Witnesses*

According to Article 202 of the Code of Criminal Procedure, public officials and civil servants must observe state secrets privilege and cannot testify or give evidence in criminal trials on matters covered by it. Recently, the Constitutional Court ruled that Article 202 applies not only to witnesses but also to suspected *(indagato)* and accused *(imputato)* persons.[98]

When intelligence agencies staff are summoned as witnesses, the judicial authority must adopt appropriate precautionary measures to protect them. When statements have to be taken from a member of the Security Intelligence Services, during the course of investigations, the judicial authority must order their remote hearing.[99]

Finally, to avoid the disclosure of secret information, interception of communications concerning intelligence officers can be used in judicial proceedings only when authorized by the President of the Council of Ministers.[100]

95 Constitutional Court, 13 February 2014, No. 24, Conclusions on points of law, para. 5, (2014) 5 *Cass. pen.* 1510.

96 Court of Cassation, Criminal Section I, 24 February 2014, No. 20447.

97 See *mutatis mutandis*, *El-Masri*, *cit. supra*.

98 Constitutional Court, 23 February 2012, No. 40, Conclusions on points of law, para. 7, *cit.*

99 Article 27 of Law. No. 124/2007.

100 Article 28 of Law No. 124/2007.

X. CONCLUSION

In the Years of Lead, investigating magistrates and public prosecutors proved to be highly effective in fighting domestic terrorism without significantly impairing citizens' rights and freedoms. The fight against today's terrorism is, however, more challenging because of its international dimension. In the immediate aftermath of 11 September 2001, Italy reacted promptly against terroristic threats, under the influence of European and international law, by adopting new legislation on urgent measures to combat international terrorism. Italy thus introduced new criminal offences and broadened police investigative powers.

Some of the new provisions lay themselves open to criticism by reason of their questionable compliance with human rights obligations. This is the case especially for the new statutory rules on the deportation of foreigners. These rules do not effectively protect the deportee against the risk of being subjected to torture or inhuman or degrading treatment in the receiving country, although the Court of Cassation has handed down a decision that takes into account the ruling of the ECHR in the *Saadi* case. On this point, the ECtHR has consistently affirmed that, where there is a real risk of ill treatment in another state, the obligation not to send an individual to that state is absolute. The state therefore cannot claim that public interest reasons for deporting or extraditing an individual outweigh the risk of ill-treatment on the individual's presence in the state where he or she is deported, regardless of the offence or conduct.[101] The Human Rights Committee took the same stand interpreting Article 7 (Prohibition of torture) of the International Covenant on Civil and Political Rights (ICCPR). Indeed, it affirmed that: "States parties must not expose individuals to the danger of torture or cruel, inhuman or degrading treatment or punishment upon return to another country by way of their extradition, expulsion or *refoulement*."[102]

Since the fight against terrorism must respect human rights and the rule of law,[103] it is to be hoped that institutional mechanisms such as state secrets privilege or intelligence officers' special immunity will not be used for escaping accountability for serious violations of human rights.[104] Article 3 ECHR imposes positive obligations on

[101] *Saadi v. Italy*, para. 138, *cit. supra*.

[102] General Comment 20/44 of 3 April 1992, point 9, A/47/40, (1992) *HRC Annual Report*, Annex VI.

[103] See also Guidelines of the Committee of Ministers of the Council of Europe on human rights and the fight against terrorism, adopted by the Committee of Ministers on 11 July 2002, https://wcd.coe.int/ViewDoc.jsp?id=991179.

[104] On 6 October 2011, the Parliamentary Assembly of the Council of Europe adopted Resolution 1838 (2011) on Abuse of state secrecy and national security: obstacles to parliamentary and judicial scrutiny of human rights violations. Point 4 of this Resolution reads: "The Assembly recognises the need for states to ensure effective protection of secrets affecting national security. It considers, however, that information concerning the responsibility of state agents who have committed serious human rights violations, such as murder, enforced disappearance, torture or abduction, does not deserve to be

contracting states, including, *inter alia*, an obligation to provide for effective official investigations capable of leading to the identification and punishment of those responsible of such violations. As recently emphasized by the ECtHR, "an adequate response by the authorities in investigating allegations of serious human rights violations, may generally be regarded as essential in maintaining public confidence in their adherence to the rule of law and in preventing any appearance of collusion in or tolerance of unlawful acts."[105] To this end, the ECtHR recommends that contracting states grant "a sufficient element of public scrutiny of the investigation or its results to secure accountability in practice as well as in theory."[106]

Furthermore, Martin Scheinin, the UN Special Rapporteur on the promotion and protection of human rights and fundamental freedoms while countering terrorism, has voiced concerns about the increasing use of state secrecy provisions and public interest immunities by various European states – including Italy – "to conceal illegal acts from oversight bodies or judicial authorities, or to protect itself from criticism, embarrassment and – most importantly – liability."[107] He maintains that the invocation of the state secrets doctrine jeopardizes the effectiveness of investigation and renders the right to a remedy illusory. This could amount to a breach of Article 2 ICCPR and of the obligation of states to provide judicial assistance to investigations on gross human rights violations and serious violations of international humanitarian law, stated in the Basic Principles and Guidelines on the Right to a Remedy and Reparation for Victims of Gross Violations of International Human Rights Law and Serious Violations of International Humanitarian Law.[108]

In light of such remarks, one could raise doubts about whether the Constitutional Court judgment reaffirming that, as far as state secrets privilege is concerned, the President of the Council of Ministers enjoys a wide discretionary power not to be checked by ordinary courts drew the line in full accordance with the prevailing views over the reach of the current system of protection of human rights in Europe.

protected as secret. Such information should not be shielded from judicial or parliamentary scrutiny under the guise of 'state secrecy'."

105 *El-Masri, cit. Supra*, para. 192.

106 *Ibidem*.

107 UN Doc. A/HRC/10/3, at p. 21. http://daccess-dds-ny.un.org/doc/UNDOC/GEN/G09/106/25/PDF/G0910625.pdf?OpenElement.

108 See principle 12. This document has been adopted and proclaimed by UN General Assembly resolution 60/147 of 16 December 2005. http://daccess-dds-ny.un.org/doc/UNDOC/GEN/N05/496/42/PDF/N0549642.pdf?OpenElement.

10

Spain

Maria Ángeles Rueda and Miguel Ángel Boldova

I. INTRODUCTION

In Spain, the phenomenon of terrorism has generated great alarm because terrorism, unlike individual criminality, attempts to undermine the social and political order. As a consequence, Spanish terrorism law has expanded and restricted fundamental rights. For many years in Spain, different terrorist groups and organizations have operated, which has caused great social upheaval, including many deaths. Consequently, Spanish legislation has tried to provide a harsh response to the challenges posed by domestic and – more recently – international terrorism.

The first record of anti-terrorism legislation in Spain is included in a special criminal legislation of 10 July 1894,[1] which provided for the first time the punishment of those who attack people or cause damage to things, "using substances or explosive devices" (art. 1), with penalties ranging from imprisonment from twelve to twenty years and including the death penalty depending on the production of deaths, injuries to persons or damage to things. Preparatory behaviour was also criminalized, including possession, manufacture, facilitation or sale of explosive substances or equipment that was known or suspected were destined for illegal purposes; conspiracy and attempts to commit such crimes; threats to cause them; provocation by speech, writing or printing, engraving or other means of publication; followed by the commission of these crimes and apology or attempts to justify such terrorist crimes. The 1894 Law established the unlawfulness and the dissolution of those associations that in any way facilitated the commission of felonies covered by

This chapter was translated by Dr. Asier Urruela Mora. We also deeply appreciate Professor Kent Roach's assistance in the translation.

1 See the web page of the BOE (Spanish Official Journal), http://www.boe.es/datos/pdfs/BOE/1894/192/A00155-00156.pdf. About the characteristics of this law, see LAMARCA PÉREZ, *Tratamiento jurídico del terrorismo*, Madrid, Centro de publicaciones del Ministerio de Justicia, Secretaría General Técnica, 1985, page 105ff.

this law. Finally, it was attributed to the Jury Jurisdiction to hear the cases corresponding to the felonies described in the Law of 10 July 1894. Afterwards, a Law of 2 September 1896,[2] temporarily hardened the repression of the crimes introduced in the Law of 10 July 1894, establishing as an unique sanction the death penalty when as result of any of such crimes a person was killed. The 1896 Law also provided the penalty of "expulsion from the Kingdom" of anyone who by speech, writing, printing or other means of publication propagated anarchist ideas or were part of associations that in any way facilitated the commission of crimes included in the law. At a procedural level, the competence to hear such cases was attributed to military jurisdiction.

Afterwards, the Criminal Code of 1928[3] incorporated without substantial amendments the list of crimes related to terrorist acts with explosives previously established in the special criminal legislation, and greater powers were progressively attributed to military courts.[4] After a remarkably turbulent historical period during the Second Republic, a Special Criminal Act of 11 October 1934,[5] was passed. This law has widely been considered the first anti-terrorism law.[6] Art. 1 of the 1934 law established defining elements common to the terrorist phenomenon in certain terrorist attacks: (1) the use of certain violent means (explosive or flammable substances, weapons or use of any other sufficient means to cause serious damages, to cause train accidents or to cause accidents in other means of locomotion by ground or air); (2) the specific purpose of "disturbing public order, frightening the inhabitants of a population or certain of its social classes or concrete sectors or to perform revenge or reprisals of social or political character";[7] and (3) the production of the death of any person or injuries of diverse severity, or property damages or other effects that would constitute felonies. Art. 6 of this law provided that courts of general jurisdiction could try such terrorist cases.

The term "terrorist offences" was legally used for the first time in the Law of 23 November 1935,[8] amending the Law of 4 August 1933, on "Slackers and crooks," adding to art. 2 a paragraph that states that offenders "may also be declared dangerous as anti-socials those that in their activities and propaganda repeatedly incite to the commission of terrorist felonies or robbery and those who publicly make an apology of such crimes."[9] Terrorist felonies are those listed in the Law of 11 October 1934.[10]

[2] See the web page of the BOE, http://www.boe.es/datos/pdfs/BOE/1896/248/A00825-00825.pdf.
[3] See the web page of the BOE, http://www.boe.es/datos/pdfs/BOE/1928/257/A01450-01526.pdf.
[4] See the exhaustive legislative references contained in LAMARCA PÉREZ, *Tratamiento jurídico del terrorismo*, page 109–111, page 114–115.
[5] See the web page of the BOE, http://www.boe.es/datos/pdfs/BOE/1934/290/A00379-00379.pdf.
[6] See LAMARCA PÉREZ, *Tratamiento jurídico del terrorismo*, pp. 120–121.
[7] This subjective element was defined by Law of June 20, 1935, which is available at the web page of the BOE: http://www.boe.es/datos/pdfs/BOE/1935/176/A02411-02411.pdf.
[8] See the web page of the BOE: http://www.boe.es/datos/pdfs/BOE/1935/332/A01715-01715.pdf.
[9] See LAMARCA PÉREZ, *Tratamiento jurídico del terrorismo*, page 123.
[10] See LAMARCA PÉREZ, *Tratamiento jurídico del terrorismo*, page 123.

From 1939 to 1976, General Francisco Franco established his dictatorship in Spain. As stated by Lamarca Pérez, the legal treatment of terrorism is characterized by a certain hesitancy to distinguish the crime of terrorism as a pure political offence. Terrorism is committed for political purposes, but it also involves violence. What distinguishes terrorism in contemporary democratic societies from the one suffered under the dictatorship is that in democracies terrorism is punished primarily because of the violence, even though the violence is seen by the legislature as more objectionable or dangerous, because of its political purposes, whereas during the dictatorship, terrorism was punished mainly because of its political purposes, albeit the use of violence was seen as an aggravating factor.[11] At this stage, we must also highlight the emergence of various groups that use violence to fight against the dictatorial political system established since 1939: ETA, FRAP, MIL, MPAIAC and GRAPO. The actions of these groups resulted in hardening the criminal justice response to crimes of terrorism.

The death of the dictator Franco in 1976 opened a process of profound and important political reforms whose main landmark was the promulgation of the Constitution of 1978.[12] The principal characteristic of this new era was to treat terrorist offences as common criminal offences and to define them more by the nature of the action than by their purpose, with the aim to decouple terrorism from political offenses.[13] The power to prosecute terrorist offences is also attributed to the *Audiencia Nacional*.[14]

The most significant piece of legislation in this period was the Organic Law 9/1984 of 26 December, against the actions of armed gangs as well as the development of art. 52.1 of the Constitution,[15] amending, among other rules, the Criminal Code of 1944. As indicated in its art. 1, this Act applies to people integrated into armed bands or related to terrorist or rebel activities who plan, organize and execute the crimes specified in the following list and who cooperate with them, encourage participation in them or abet those involved. The Law is also applicable to those who make apology of such crimes. The scope of this Act includes the following actions:

a) Crimes against life and integrity of individuals.
b) Assaults on the authority, its agents, civil servants and their families.
c) Unlawful detentions, kidnapping in order to obtain a ransom or under any other condition or with simulation of public functions.

[11] See LAMARCA PÉREZ, *Tratamiento jurídico del terrorismo*, page 126 and page 127.
[12] See the web page of the BOE, http://www.boe.es/boe/dias/1978/12/29/pdfs/A29313-29424.pdf.
[13] See LAMARCA PÉREZ, *Tratamiento jurídico del terrorismo*, page 162ff.
[14] This Court was established by Law-Decree of January 4, 1977.
[15] See the web page of the BOE, http://www.boe.es/boe/dias/1985/01/03/pdfs/A00070-00072.pdf.

d) Attacks against military establishments and of the state police forces, the autonomous communities polices and of the local authorities, facilities and communication centres, trains, ships, aircrafts, cars, public buildings, bank offices, tax collection buildings, commercial establishments or others in which flows are preserved as well as munitions dumps, gunsmiths and health centres.
e) Coercions, threats or extortions.
f) Fire and other damages.
g) Crimes against the head of state and his successor, against high institutions of the nation, against the form of government and crimes against the external security of the state.
h) Rebellion.
i) Holding or storage of arms, ammunition or explosives, as well as purchasing, manufacturing, handling, transportation or supply thereof.
J) The establishment of institutions, organizations, bands or groups formed for the development of terrorist or rebel activities, belonging to them and the acts of cooperation or collaboration with their activities.
k) Any other crimes committed by persons included in number 1, when the commission thereof contributes to rebel or terrorist activities, and related crimes and those committed in cooperation with these activities or individuals.

As for the punishment of such behaviours, art. 3 stated the following:

> The penalties of the felonies covered in Article 1 of this Act will be imposed in their maximum degree, unless they are established in Chapter II of the Act. Inchoate offences will be punished with the same penalties as those indicated for the consummated crime in the course of the statements of paragraphs a) to h) of Section 2 of Article 1.2 of this Law. 2. The provisions of Article 233 of the Criminal Code shall apply to offences against members of the Armed Forces or State Security Forces or Polices of the Autonomous Communities and of the local entities. 3. The offences covered by this law will always entail, besides the penalty prescribed in each case, the absolute barring from holding public office.[16]

Moreover, it was established that instruction, knowledge and judgment of criminal prosecutions for these offences fell within the ordinary jurisdiction of the

[16] In this Organic Law, the following felonies are included: "(1) integration into terrorist or rebel band; (2) felonies of terrorism where those who belong to the terrorist or rebel organization or armed band are punished when they perform any of the criminal acts included in sections (a) to (h) of art. 1, using firearms, bombs, grenades, explosive substances or incendiary devices or media of any kind, irrespective of the result produced, with the penalty of *Prision Mayor* in its maximum degree; (3) felonies of collaboration in terrorist or rebel activities; (4) apology of the felonies established in this Law."

Central Instruction Courts and of the Audiencia Nacional. In connection with the arrest of the suspect, art. 13 also stated that "the detainees, for being included in this Act, shall be made available to the competent court within seventy-two hours of detention. However, pre-trial detention may be extended long enough for research purposes for a maximum period of seven days, provided that the proposal is brought to the attention of the judge, no later than seventy-two hours after the detention. The judge, in the term of twenty-four hours, shall refuse or authorize the proposed extension." Some criminal provisions of this law were amended by Law 3/1988 of 25 May, reforming the Criminal Code.[17]

Finally, the Criminal Code of 1995[18] initially provided a catalogue of offences similar to that discussed previously for Book II, under Title XXII on "Crimes against public order," in its Chapter V "on possession, trafficking and storage of arms, ammunitions or explosives" and "on terrorist crimes," as Section 2. Subsequently, the integration of these criminal acts in the criminal code was rearranged and other new ones were added by the Organic Law 5/2010, of 22 June, amending Chapter V and introducing Chapters VI and VII of the Criminal Code, within Title XXII on "Crimes against public order" (Book II). Chapter V, concerning the possession, trafficking and storage of arms, ammunitions or explosives, includes the punishment of such offences but does not include the crimes of terrorism. Chapter VI includes the criminal regulation of the "criminal organizations and groups" and Chapter VII the criminal regulation of the "terrorist organizations and groups and terrorist offences." In Section III of this chapter, the criminal regulation currently in force in Spain is described in detail.

II. THE DEFINITION OF TERRORISM

In the Spanish criminal legislation, there is no explicit definition of what is meant by terrorism, although a definition of a terrorist organization or group has been incorporated in art. 571 of the Criminal Code by Law 5/2010 of 22 June. However, the regulation contained in art. 571 and in art. 572 and following ones of the Criminal Code allow us to extract the following characteristics of terrorism.[19]

[17] See the web page of the BOE, http://www.boe.es/boe/dias/1988/05/26/pdfs/A16159-16159.pdf.

[18] See the web page of the BOE, http://www.boe.es/boe/dias/1995/11/24/pdfs/A33987-34058.pdf.

[19] See CANCIO MELIÁ, *Los delitos de terrorismo: estructura típica e injusto*, Madrid, Ed. Reus, 2010, page 154ff.; GÓMEZ MARTÍN, "Notas para un concepto funcional de terrorismo," *Terrorismo y estado de derecho*, Serrano-Piedecasas/Demetrio Crespo Dir., Madrid, Iustel, 2012, page 25ff.; LLOBET ANGLÍ, *Derecho penal del terrorismo. Límites de su punición en un Estado democrático*, Madrid, La Ley, 2010, page 55ff.; MUÑOZ CONDE, *Derecho penal, Parte Especial*, 18 ed., Valencia, Tirant lo Blanch, 2010, page 923.

First, terrorism has traditionally been defined as normally carried out through an organized structure of persons, since in almost all terrorist offences the criminalized facts relate to "terrorist organizations or groups." However, this characteristic is not an essential one in the Spanish legal system, as those who do not belong to a terrorist organization or group can also commit terrorist offences.

Second, terrorism has always used violent means of mass intimidation. However, the use of violence is not an exclusive feature of terrorism. Third, terrorism is put in practice with specific purposes. However, the presence of this last characteristic gives autonomy to terrorist offences in comparison to the particular facts constituting criminal offences such as murder or damage, for example. In the following subsections, we will discuss in more detail how each feature of the terrorist phenomenon is established in our criminal justice system.

A. *Need for an Organized Structure of Persons?*

In most of the terrorist offences referred to in Spain's criminal code, it is required that the terrorist belong to an organized structure of persons, what is referred to as the concept of association, band, group or organization.[20] Arts. 570 bis, section 1, second paragraph and 570 ter., section 1, second paragraph of the Spanish Criminal Code, states that "for the purposes of this Code, a criminal organization is construed to be a stable group formed by more of two persons, for an indefinite term, in collusion and co-ordination to distribute diverse tasks or duties in order to commit felonies, as well as to carry out reiterated commission of misdemeanours." Moreover, art. 571, section 3 adds specifically that "for the purposes of this Code, terrorist organizations or groups shall be deemed to be those groups that, fulfilling the characteristics respectively established in Sub-Section 2 of Section 1 of Article 570 bis and in Subsection 2 of Section 1 of Article 570 ter, have the purpose or object of subverting the constitutional order or seriously altering the public peace by committing any of the felonies foreseen in the following Subchapter" related to terrorist offences. A group of two or more persons expresses the tendency of its members towards the commission of certain crimes in a concerted and coordinated manner with a division of responsibilities. This presupposes a certain organization whose components must act in the interests of the group. Hence it follows that individual criminal acts are integrated in the area of activity of the group defined by its objectives and that some stability or permanence does exist. As a result, the

[20] The Spanish Constitutional Court has also concluded that the terrorism of our time, as organized social or political violence, is manifested by an activity of organizations or groups or "bands" in which usually the character of "armed" is present. See Judgment 199/1987 of 16 November.

integration into an organized group also has a criminogenic effect, which is one basis for the danger presented by these terrorist organizations or groups.[21]

However, in the Spanish legal system those who do not belong to a terrorist organization or group can also commit terrorist offences, as provided in art. 577 of the Criminal Code. Although the decision of the Spanish criminal legislator to reject the need in the definition of terrorism for the existence of an organized structure of persons has been criticized,[22] this choice was intended to respond to new manifestations of terrorism, such as the "street terrorism" of "Kale borroka" – street fight – or the "low-intensity terrorism" in the Basque country (Spain), which lacks an organized structure.[23] Therefore, in order to qualify an act as a terrorist one, it is not essential that the subject who commits it to belong to an organized structure of persons.

B. *Using Mass Violent Intimidation?*

The use of mass intimidation has historically been an indispensable and inseparable element of terrorism in all its manifestations. As indicated by Cancio Meliá, terrorism is a communication strategy that involves the massive use of violence to simulate a military capacity to challenge the state in military terms and, especially, to cause certain reactions in the population and state organs. Terrorist organizations cause fear, intimidation or insecurity by selecting randomly the victims of their acts of violence.[24] Such acts of terrorist violence are characterized by the creation of massive intimidation through the use of weapons, explosives, bombs, and such and by the production of extremely serious outcomes such as as death, injury, damage, fire, and so on. On the other hand, the commission of other kinds of actions that would constitute a criminal offence – for example, the placement in the public roads of unforeseeable obstacles or the removal of traffic signals so as to cause a

[21] It has been shown that jihadist terrorism that operates by mean of separate cells that are independent has no hierarchical structure organized vertically. However, it has a flat organization structure that gives it cohesion and permanence. See GÓMEZ MARTÍN, "Notas para un concepto funcional de terrorismo," page 44. See CANCIO MELIÁ, *Los delitos de terrorismo*, page 161; CANO PAÑO, "Reflexiones en torno al "viejo" y "nuevo" terrorismo," *Revista Española de Investigación Criminológica*, www.criminología.net, Número 7, 2009, page 14ff.

[22] See GÓMEZ MARTÍN, "Notas para un concepto funcional de terrorismo," pages 40 and 41; LLOBET ANGLÍ, *Derecho penal del terrorismo*, page 86ff.

[23] On the problems related to the inclusion in the terrorist phenomenon of multiple riots organized by youth groups of ETA and producing high property damage and serious public disorder before the introduction of the art. 577 of the Spanish Criminal Code by Act 7/2000 of 22 December, see CANCIO MELIÁ, *Los delitos de terrorismo*, page 172ff.

[24] See CANCIO MELIÁ, *Los delitos de terrorismo*, pages 167 and 168. See also LLOBET ANGLÍ, *Derecho penal del terrorismo*, page 55ff.

serious risk to road users – can also qualify as terrorist acts, as provided in art. 574 Criminal Code if they subvert the constitutional order or seriously disturb the public peace. Consequently, the use of violence is not necessary to be found guilty of a terrorist crime.

C. *Acting for Certain Purposes*

One last indispensable and inseparable element of terrorism is the aim of subverting the constitutional order or seriously disturbing public peace.[25] The purpose of subverting the constitutional order has a political significance since it refers to the questioning of the decision-making mechanisms established in the state[26] in order to achieve a political goal such as the independence of a part of the territory from the rest of the state to which it belongs.[27] However, this particular purpose or motive impelling the terrorist to commit the crime cannot be subject to criticism, because then terrorist offences should be classified as political offences, and art. 13 Spanish Constitution states that "political crimes are excluded from extradition, not being considered as such the acts of terrorism."[28] In a democratic state, it is possible to defend any political position through established legal and institutional means, and all the political positions that deviate from them, especially if they use violence, undermine the existing constitutional order. Severe disturbance of the public peace has also a political significance[29] and alludes to public safety, defined by doctrine and law as the protection of persons and properties against aggression or violent actions, situations of danger or calamity.[30] We face two important elements of transcendent internal tendency, but it is not necessary that the constitutional order or the public peace be placed in danger. It is sufficient that the conduct infringes the corresponding legal interest protected by the final concrete crime.[31] In any event, the two purposes previously mentioned distinguish terrorist acts from other acts of violence constituting criminal offences such as murder, injury, fire, damage and such.

25 See MUÑOZ CONDE, *Derecho penal, Parte Especial*, page 923.

26 See CANCIO MELIÁ, *Los delitos de terrorismo*, page 184. See also LLOBET ANGLÍ, *Derecho penal del terrorismo*, page 96 ff.

27 See GÓMEZ MARTÍN, "Notas para un concepto funcional de terrorismo," page 45.

28 See GÓMEZ MARTÍN, "Notas para un concepto funcional de terrorismo," pages 45 and 46.

29 See CANCIO MELIÁ, *Los delitos de terrorismo*, page 186.

30 See LAMARCA PÉREZ, "Análisis de las reformas penales en el ámbito de la lucha contra el terrorismo: el caso español," *Terrorismo y estado de derecho*, Serrano-Piedecasas/Demetrio Crespo Dir., Madrid, Iustel, 2012, page 439.

31 See GÓMEZ MARTÍN, "Notas para un concepto funcional de terrorismo," page 37.

III. CRIMINAL LAWS AND PROSECUTIONS

A. *Criminal Law*

Spain's criminal code includes some relevant offenses in Book II, Title XXII on "Crimes against public order," in Subchapter VI, dedicated to "criminal organizations and groups" and in particular, in Subchapter VII, "on terrorist organizations and groups and on felonies of terrorism." Terrorist offences enjoy independence and provide for a more severe penalty than the one corresponding to the respective common crimes such as crimes against persons; crimes against property; fire; havoc; holding; trafficking and storage of arms; ammunitions or explosives; and other crimes. The following subsections discuss behaviours punishable as offences under the Subchapter VII Criminal Code.

a. Conducts That Imply an Advancement of the Punishment Barriers

Art. 571 distinguishes two levels of criminal responsibility. On the one hand (section 1), whoever promotes, forms, organizes or directs a terrorist organization or group shall be punished with imprisonment from eight to fourteen years and barred from public employment and office for a term from eight to fifteen years. On the other hand, Section 2 states that whoever actively participates in the terrorist organization or group, or forms part thereof, shall be punished with imprisonment from six to twelve years and barred from public employment and office for a term from six to fourteen years. We are facing two felonies of abstract danger. The Spanish legislator presumes the danger of all terrorist organizations or groups. The equal response given to the active participation in a terrorist organization or group and to the simple forming part thereof shall be criticized, as they should have a different criminal punishment.[32]

Moreover, art. 573 punishes the deposit of arms or ammunition or possession or storage of explosive, flammable, incendiary or asphyxiating substances or devices or their components, as well as their manufacture, trafficking, transport or supply in any way – and merely placing or using those substances or the appropriate means or devices – with imprisonment from six to ten years when those acts are committed by whoever belongs to, acts in the service of or collaborates with armed gangs, terrorist organizations or groups described in the preceding articles.

[32] According to Muñoz Conde, this equation may lead to an "Offender-based Criminal Law" or to the criminalization of a mere ideological attitude. See MUÑOZ CONDE, *Derecho penal, Parte Especial,* page 919.

b. Behaviours of Terrorist Execution

Executing terrorist acts is punishable according to the production of certain results:

1. Art. 572.1 provides that "those who, while pertaining to, acting in the service of, or collaborating with terrorist organizations or groups, commit the felonies of havoc or arson defined in articles 346 and 351, respectively, shall be punished with a sentence of imprisonment from fifteen to twenty years, without prejudice to the punishment to which they may be subject if they cause loss of life or injury to the physical integrity or health of persons."
2. Section 2 of the stated article specifies that "Those who, while pertaining to, acting in the service of, or collaborating with terrorist organizations or groups commit attacks against persons, shall incur: 1. Sentence of imprisonment from twenty to thirty years if they cause the death of a person;[33] 2. Sentence of imprisonment from fifteen to twenty years if they cause injuries of the kind foreseen in articles 149 and 150 or kidnap a person;[34] 3. Sentence of imprisonment from ten to fifteen years if they cause any other injury or unlawfully detain, intimidate or coerce a person." These aggravations shall be applied when the outcomes of death or injury or arrests, threats or coercions were committed with intention or *dolus* (first degree, second degree or eventual).
3. Art. 572.3 provides specific aggravation if the facts are perpetrated against members of the Cabinet; of the Government Councils of the Autonomous Communities; of the Congress of Deputies, the Senate or the Legislative Assemblies of the Autonomous Communities; of the Local Corporations; of the General Council of the Judiciary or Magistrate of the Constitutional Court; of the armed forces, of the state police and security forces of the Autonomous Communities; or of local corporations. In such cases, the penalty shall be imposed in its upper half (the maximum that the judge may impose).
4. Finally, art. 574 states that "those who, while pertaining to, acting in the service of, or collaborating with terrorist organizations or groups, commit any other felony or misdemeanour for any of the purposes stated in Section 3 of Article 571, shall be punished with the penalty set for the felony or misdemeanour, in its upper half."

[33] The penalty for the crime of murder of art. 139 Criminal Code is imprisonment from fifteen to twenty years. The draft reform of the Criminal Code of 2013, which is currently being discussed in the House of Representatives, establishes the imposition of a sentence of a revisable permanent imprisonment.

[34] The penalties for these offences are imprisonment from six to twelve years (art. 149 Criminal Code), imprisonment from three to six years (art. 150 Criminal Code) and imprisonment for six to ten years in basic kidnapping (art. 164 Criminal Code).

c. Conduct of Funding Terrorist Organizations or Groups

Art. 575 provides that "those who, in order to provide funds to armed gangs, terrorist organizations or groups aforementioned, or in order to favour their activities, attack property, shall be punished with the higher degree punishment that would be applicable for the felony committed without prejudice to the appropriate ones that would be imposed pursuant to what is set forth in the following article for acts of collaboration."

Art. 576 bis states the following:

> 1. Whoever by any means, directly or indirectly provides or collects funds intending them to be used, or knowing they shall be used, fully or partially to commit any of the felonies included in this Chapter or to deliver them to a terrorist organization or group, shall be punished with prison sentences of five to ten years and a fine of eighteen to twenty-four months. Should the funds eventually be used to execute specific acts of terrorism, this shall be punished as co-perpetration or complicity, as appropriate, provided this involves as higher penalty. 2. Whoever, being specifically obliged by law to collaborate with the authorities in the prevention of terrorism financing activities, gives rise, due to serious negligence in the fulfilment of those obligations to any of the conducts described in Section one of this article not being detected or prevented, shall be punished with the penalty lower by one or two degrees to that foreseen herein. 3. When, pursuant to the terms established in article 31 bis of this Code, a legal person is responsible for the offences defined in this article, it shall have the following penalties imposed thereon: a) Fine from two to five years, if the offence committed by a natural person has a punishment of imprisonment foreseen exceeding five years; b) Fine from one to three years, if the offence committed by a natural person has a punishment foreseen of more than two years custodial sentence not included in the preceding Sub-Section. Pursuant to the rules established in article 66 bis of this Code, the Judges and Courts of Law may also impose the penalties established in Sub-Sections b) to g) of Section 7 of article 33.

Section 1 of this article is redundant because the economic cooperation is expressly mentioned in art. 576, which is discussed in the following section.

d. Conducts of Collaboration with the Activities or Purposes of a Terrorist Organization or Group

Art. 576 provides the following:

> 1. Punishment by imprisonment from five to ten years and a fine of eighteen to twenty-four months shall be handed down to whoever carries out, procures or facilitates any act of collaboration with the activities or purposes of a terrorist

> organization or group. 2. Acts of collaboration include information on or surveillance of persons, property or installations; construction, conditioning, assignment or use of accommodation or storage facilities; concealment or transport of individuals related to terrorist organizations or groups; organization of training practices or attending them and, in general, any other equivalent form of co-operation, aid or mediation, economic or of any other kind whatsoever, with the activities of those terrorist organizations or groups. When the information or surveillance of persons mentioned in the preceding Paragraph endangers the life, physical integrity, liberty or property thereof, the punishment shall be imposed as foreseen in Section 1, in the upper half. Should the risk foreseen concur, the act shall be punished as co-perpetration or complicity, as appropriate. 3. The same penalties foreseen in Section 1 of this article shall be imposed on whoever carries out any activity to recruit, indoctrinate, train or induct, aimed at having others join a terrorist organization or group, or at committing any of the offences foreseen in this chapter.

In relation to the specific acts of collaboration, punishment is established for conduct with different levels of gravity, such as, for example, military training of a terrorist group or to host one of its members. This involves a possible violation of the principle of proportionality and also of the principle of legal certainty due to the vagueness of what needs to be understood as an act of collaboration.[35] According to the Supreme Court judgment of 2 February 1987, it is "a preparatory act particularly punishable as favouring act, whose basis for punitive exception to the general rule of impunity for such acts lies … in the importance and danger that such collaborative behaviours have acquired in terrorist activities." Mere support or moral support cannot be punished; that is considered an act of collaboration in the criminal activities of the organization that does not reach the level of membership in the terrorist organization, which has a higher penalty.[36]

e. Conducts of Non-organized Terrorism or "Individual Terrorism"

Art. 577 provides the following:[37]

> those who, without pertaining to an armed gang, terrorist organization or group, and with in order to subvert the constitutional order or seriously alter the public peace, or to contribute to those ends by terrorising the inhabitants of a town or the members of a social, political or professional group, were to commit homicides, injuries of the kind defined under articles 147 to 150, illegal detentions, kidnappings, intimidations or coercion against persons, or who carry out any felonies of arson,

[35] According to Muñoz Conde, the principle of legal certainty is violated by the uncertainty of what is to be understood as an act of collaboration. See MUÑOZ CONDE, *Derecho penal, Parte Especial*, page 927.

[36] See MUÑOZ CONDE, *Derecho penal, Parte Especial*, page 928.

[37] Also known in Spain as low-intensity terrorism.

havoc, damages defined under articles 263 to 266, 323 or 560, or possession, manufacturing, storage, trafficking, transport or supply of arms, ammunition or explosive, flammable, incendiary or asphyxiating substances or devices, or components thereof, shall be punished with the relevant punishment for the act committed, in the upper half.

f. Conducts of Apology or Justification of Terrorism Offences

Art. 578 provides that

> apology or justification by means of public expression or diffusion of the felonies included in articles 571 to 577 of this Code, or anybody who has participated in commission thereof, or in perpetrating acts that involve discredit, distain or humiliation of the victims of terrorist offences or their relatives shall be punished with a sentence of imprisonment from one to two years. In the judgement, the Judge may also order any one or number of the prohibitions foreseen in article 57 of this Code for the term he may set.

The Spanish Constitutional Court has highlighted the vital role that the freedom of speech plays in a democratic society and the need to interpret narrowly criminal felonies that adversely affect it. Nevertheless, the Constitutional Court has not declared unconstitutional Art. 578 relating to speech that attempts to apologize or justify terrorism. As indicated by Magdaleno Alegría,[38] when considering the application of art. 578 Criminal Code the circumstances of the case should be balanced, as well as the context in which they are performed, the seriousness of the statement and the intimidating effect that the statements may have on citizens. In order to balance those circumstances, it is particularly relevant to consider whether the conduct of apology or justification described in art. 578 of the Penal Code takes place "in the context of terrorist activity or simply favoured or predisposed to violence, and when the statements under restriction are capable of causing a particular impact, raising fears of increased disturbances."[39]

g. Conducts Involving Preparatory Acts of Provocation, Conspiracy and Solicitation to Commit Terrorist Offences

Art. 579 specifies the following:

> 1. Provocation, conspiracy and solicitation to commit the offences foreseen in articles 571 to 578 shall be punished with the penalty lower by one or two degrees

[38] See MAGDALENO ALEGRÍA, "Libertad de expresión, terrorismo y límites de los derechos fundamentales," *Revista de Derecho político*, UNED, número 69, 2007, page 206.

[39] See the dissenting opinion formulated by Jiménez de Parga to the Constitutional Court Decision number 136/1999 of 20 July.

> to the relevant one, respectively, for the acts foreseen in the preceding articles. Provided it is not included in the preceding Section or another provision of this Code with a higher penalty, distribution or public diffusion by any means of messages or slogans aimed at provoking, encouraging or favouring commission of any of the felonies foreseen in this Chapter, generating of increasing the risk of them effectively being committed, shall be punished with the penalty of six months to two years' imprisonment.

Finally, art. 580, Criminal Code: International recidivism, provides that "in all felonies related to the activity of armed gangs, terrorist organizations or groups, conviction by a foreign Judge or Court of Law shall be equivalent to judgments by Spanish Judges or Courts of Law for the purposes of application of the aggravating circumstance of recidivism."

B. *Terrorism Prosecutions*

The competence in order to hear and prosecute terrorist offences in Spain is entrusted to the *Audiencia Nacional (Sala de lo Penal)* based in Madrid, as set out in the Transitional Disposition of Law 4/1988.[40] The Audiencia Nacional is a court of the general jurisdiction, and this is clearly stated for our legal system, for example, in art. 117.5 and 6 of the Spanish Constitution (CE), which establishes the principle of jurisdictional unity, the exercise of military jurisdiction within a strictly military framework and the prohibition of Exceptional Courts; and in art. 26 of Law 6 /1985 of 1 July, of the Judiciary Power,[41] which recognizes that the exercise of the judiciary power is attributed to, among other courts, the Audiencia Nacional. The court allows no restriction of the rights of the accused person due to the fact that he or she is being prosecuted by this court

While it is true that the existence of the *Audiencia Nacional* was initially challenged as not being an ordinary court as required in art. 24 Spanish Constitution, the Constitutional Court in its judgment 199/1987, of 16 December, concluded that the *Audiencia Nacional* is organic and functionally, by its composition and method of appointment, an ordinary court, recognized as such by the European Commission on Human Rights in its report on the Barberá case, of 19 October 1986.[42] Moreover, the specific jurisdiction of the *Audiencia Nacional* over the prosecution of terrorist

[40] See the web page of the BOE, http://www.boe.es/boe/dias/1988/05/26/pdfs/A16159-16160.pdf. The Audiencia Nacional is the competent court to hear offences referred to in art. 65 Organic Law 6/1985.

[41] See the web page of the BOE, http://www.boe.es/boe/dias/1985/07/02/pdfs/A20632-20678.pdf, although it has undergone many modifications subsequent to 1985.

[42] See HINOJOSA SEGOVIA, *Derecho procesal penal,* De la Oliva/Aragoneses/Hinojosa/Muerza/Tomé, 7ª ed., Madrid, Editorial Ramón Areces, 2004, page 804.

offences has three advantages: 1) centralization allows the unification of criteria and a certain distance from the scene of conflict; 2) specialization enables a better understanding of the problems that the prosecution of terrorist acts pose, improving efficiency; 3) security can be enhanced by focusing protection in a single seat and in a small number of judges and prosecutors.[43]

The Audiencia Nacional publishes an annual report where a brief display of all cases related to terrorism is collected.[44] The judgments of the court are public, and everybody can access them through the website of the General Council of the Judiciary (Consejo General del Poder Judicial).[45] From a statistical standpoint, the National Institute of Statistics publishes the total number of condemned in Spain each year for a certain number of offences. In 2011, ninety-six people were convicted for terrorism offences, and in 2012, forty-six people were condemned for belonging to terrorist organizations and groups and for committing terrorist offences, although the specific offences for which they are condemned are not specified.

C. *Punishment of Terrorism*

Regarding the repression of terrorism, it is necessary to mention other relevant parts of the Spanish Criminal Code outside the specific penalties applicable to persons convicted for committing a terrorist offence. First, and as provided in art. 579.2 Criminal Code, those responsible for the felonies foreseen in this chapter, without prejudice to the relevant penalties under the preceding articles, shall also be punished with the penalty of absolute barring from public office for a time exceeding that of the term of the custodial sentence duly imposed in the sentence by six to twenty years. The period will be proportional to the crime.

Second, in terrorist felonies the judges and courts of law may impose, giving the reasons in the judgment, a punishment lower by one or two degrees to that stated by the law for the felony concerned when the subject has voluntarily quit his or her criminal activities and has appeared before the authorities to confess the acts in which he or she has participated, has also collaborated actively with the authorities to prevent the felony taking place, has effectively aided in obtaining decisive evidence to identify or capture the others who are responsible or has prevented the action or development of the terrorist organizations or groups to which he or she has belonged or with which he or she has collaborated, as set out in art. 579.4.

43 See SANTOS ALONSO/DE PRADA RODRÍGUEZ, "Protección de testigos en procesos de terrorismo," *Terrorismo, proceso penal y derechos fundamentales*, Madrid, Marcial Pons, 2012, page 152.

44 See the web page http://www.poderjudicial.es/cgpj/es/Poder_Judicial/Audiencia_Nacional.

45 See http://www.poderjudicial.es/search/indexAN.jsp?org=an&comunidad=13.

Third, Law 5/2010 introduced for the first time in the Spanish Criminal Code a measure of security, called probation, for dangerous sex offenders and terrorists. Probation, according to art. 106.1 Criminal Code, consists of the convict being subject to court control and having to fulfil any one or number of measures.[46] According to art. 579.3, those convicted of serious custodial sentences for one or more felonies discussed in this chapter will also have a measure of probation from five to ten years imposed, and one to five years if the sentence of imprisonment is less serious. Notwithstanding the foregoing, in the case of a single offence that is not considered serious committed by a first-time offender, the court of law may hand down the probation measure or not, in view of the lesser or greater dangerousness of the offender. Offences of terrorism do not have a statute of limitations if they have caused the death of a person (art. 131.4), nor do they carry the penalties for offences of terrorism (art. 33.2) if they caused the death of a person.

Moreover, the reform of the Criminal Code of 1995 operated by Organic Law 7/2003 of 30 June on measures for the full and effective enforcement of penalties[47] toughened the conditions for the effective fulfilment of the penalties of deprivation of freedom for certain crimes, among others the felonies of terrorism. Indeed, according to art. 36.2, when the term of prison sentence handed down exceeds five years, the judge or court of law may order that classification of the prisoner in pre-release penitentiary treatment not take place until half of the sentence handed down has been served. In any event, when the term of the prison sentence handed down exceeds five years and is for a felony of those listed in the referred article (among others, felonies of terrorism and those related to terrorist organizations and groups), classification of the convict in pre-release penitentiary treatment may not take place until half the sentence has been served. In art. 76, 1, d), the maximum limit of a sentence to be served reaches forty years when a convict has been found guilty of two or more felonies related to terrorist organizations and groups and offences of terrorism under Section 2 of Chapter VII of Title XXII of Book II of this

[46] The measures are the following: (a) the obligation to always be traceable by means of electronic devices to allow the convict to be traced at all times; (b) the obligation to appear regularly at the place set by the judge or court of law; (c) that of immediately reporting, within the maxim term and by the means stated by the judge or court of law for that purpose, each change of residence or place or post at work; (d) prohibition to leave the place of residence or a specific area without leave from the judge or court of law; (e) prohibition to approach the victim, his or her relatives or other persons determined by the judge or court of law; (g) prohibition to communicate with the victim, his or her relatives or other persons determined by the judge or court of law; (h) prohibition to reside in specific places; (i) prohibition to carry out certain activities that may provide or afford the convict the chance to commit criminal offences of a similar kind; (j) the obligation to participate in labour, cultural, sexual education or other similar training programmes; and (k) the obligation to follow external medical treatment or to submit to periodic medical inspection.

[47] See the web page of the del BOE, http://www.boe.es/boe/dias/2003/07/01/pdfs/A25274-25278.pdf.

Code, and any such felony is punishable by law with a prison sentence exceeding twenty years.[48] Moreover, art. 78 provides that if due to the limitations established in Section 1 of art. 76 the punishment to be served were lower than half the aggregate sum of those imposed, the judge or court of law sentencing shall order (in the case of terrorist offences and felonies related to terrorist organizations and groups) that penitentiary benefits, term-release permits, pre-release classification and calculation of the term to be served prior to probation shall refer to the total penalties imposed in the sentences.

Finally, arts. 90 through 93 toughened conditions for those convicted of terrorist offenses to be granted probation if, among other requirements, the convict shows unequivocal signs of having abandoned the ends and means of the terrorist activity and has also actively collaborated with the authorities, either to prevent other offences being committed by the armed gang, organization or terrorist group; to mitigate the effects of the felony; to identify, capture and prosecute those responsible for terrorist offences; to obtain evidence; or to prevent the activities or development of the organizations or associations to which the convict has belonged or with which he or she has collaborated. This may require a specific declaration of disavowal of the convict's criminal activities and abandoning violence, and specifically apologizing to the victims of this offence. It may also require technical reports accrediting that the convict has really cut off ties with the terrorist organization and the environment and activities of unlawful assemblies and groups that surround these, and that he or she has collaborated with the authorities.[49] The Spanish legislator distrusts of the rehabilitation of the terrorist and has proposed a penal response based on retribution and general deterrence.

In connection with terrorist offences committed by persons under the age of eighteen years, the Organic Law 8/2006, of 4 December, amended Act 5/2000, of 12 January, governing the criminal liability of minors,[50] extended the cases in which measures of closed detention may be imposed. Those can reach a maximum of ten years for those aged sixteen or more and six years for minors between fourteen and sixteen, adding the cases of commission of serious crimes and offenses committed in a group or when the child belongs to or acts in the service of a band, organization or association, including those having temporal character, that conducts such activities.

The jurisprudence of the Supreme Court –Tribunal Supremo (Case no. 197/2006 of 28 February) – and later the Constitutional Court endorsed the so-called "Parot

[48] See BOLDOVA PASAMAR, *Tratado de las consecuencias jurídicas del delito*, Gracia Martín coord., Valencia, Tirant lo Blanch, 2006, page 266ff.

[49] On the regulation under arts. 78 and 90–3 of the Spanish Criminal Code, see GRACIA MARTÍN/ALASTUEY DOBÓN, *Tratado de las consecuencias jurídicas del delito*, Gracia Martín coord., Valencia, Tirant lo Blanch, 2006, page 365ff.

[50] See the web page of the BOE, http://www.boe.es/boe/dias/2006/12/05/pdfs/A42700-42712.pdf.

doctrine," initially applied to terrorists (but then generalized to other types of offenders with multiple convictions) convicted under the criminal Code of 1973. The Parot doctrine was designed to avoid the release of ETA members who, although they had been sentenced to hundreds or thousands of years, had just been released after serving little more than fifteen or twenty years' imprisonment. They had been released under rules of computation based on the maximum effective compliance time (thirty years) and not on all of the penalties imposed. Although the Parot doctrine purported merely to change the meaning of the law and not the law itself, it raised questions about fundamental rights pertaining to democratic rule of law. Indeed, the principle of legality of penalties implies not only that citizens know the legal consequences of their criminal acts, but also that they know at the time of the conviction the maximum penalty that they face by the application of the law. This predictability of the length of the sentence was adversely affected by the Parot doctrine, and this is why the European Court of Human Rights has considered the Parot doctrine contrary to arts 5.1 and 7 of the European Convention on Human Rights in a first judgment dated 10 July 2012, which was subsequently ratified by the Grand Chamber on 21 October 2013.[51]

IV. INVESTIGATIVE POWERS

A. *Police Powers*

According to art. 17.2 CE and art. 520.1 II of the Criminal Procedure Law (*Ley de Enjuiciamiento Criminal*, or LECr.), pre-trial detention may last no longer than the strictly necessary time for the conduct of investigations aimed at the clarification of the facts of the crime. In any event, the detainee must be released or at the disposal of a judicial authority within a maximum period of seventy-two hours. However, the legal regime of detention for terrorist offences includes important restrictions of rights when the arrest is made due to an offence committed by a person integrated or related to armed bands or by terrorists or rebels. In such cases, art. 520 bis LECr. states the following:

> 1. Anyone arrested as alleged participant in any of the offenses established in article 384 bis shall be made available to the competent court within seventy-two hours following the arrest. However, the detention may be extended for the time required for the research purposes, up to a maximum of forty-eight hours more, provided that such extension is requested through motivated communication within the

[51] See the latest resolution cited in http://hudoc.echr.coe.int/sites/eng/Pages/search.aspx#{%22languageisocode%22:[%22ENG%22],%22documentcollectionid2%22:[%22JUDGMENTS%22],%22itemid%22:[%22001–127697%22]}.

> first forty-eight hours of arrest and authorized by the Judge within the following twenty-four hours. Both authorization or denial of the extension shall be adopted in a reasoned judicial decision. 2. Once a person is arrested for the reasons stated in the previous Subsection, the judge may be requested to order his isolation, having to decide on it in a reasoned decision within twenty-four hours. Once the isolation requested, the detainee will stay isolated conserving the right of defence and with full respect of the provisions of articles 520 and 527, until the judge renders the relevant resolution. 3. During detention, the Judge may at any time require information and meet in person or by proxy of the Judge of Instruction of the part of the territory where the detainee is, the arrested person.

Despite the wording of art. 520 bis 2 LECr., it is the police who decide on the isolation once the person detained, and the competent judicial authority limits itself to ratifying an already decreed isolation.[52] This police power was endorsed by the Constitutional Court in its judgment no. 199/1987 of 16 December.

Moreover, the regular term for duration of the isolation of five days may be extended for another period not exceeding five days, according to art. 509.2 LECr. According to this article, in cases where the imprisonment is accorded due to a crime committed by a person integrated in armed band or related to them or by terrorists or rebels or other crimes committed under agreement or in an organized manner by two or more persons, the detention may be extended for another period not exceeding five days. However, in these cases, the competent court or tribunal may order that the prisoner be isolated again, even after being placed in the ordinary communication regime, provided that the further development of the research or of the case would make it necessary. This second isolation shall not exceed, in any case, the term of three days. However, the resolution in which the confinement is accorded or, where appropriate, its renewal, shall state the reasons according to which it was decided. To sum up, in the case of terrorist offences, isolation can be maintained up to thirteen days.[53] The specific scope of the detention is established in art. 527 LECr., which provides that the detainee, while he is isolated, cannot enjoy the rights set forth in Chapter IV of Title VI of the Criminal Procedure Act, except those set out in art. 520, with the following modifications: (a) in all cases, the lawyer will be appointed *ex officio;* (b) the isolated person will not have the right that his or her relatives or person of confidence are informed of the fact of the detention and of the custodial place in which he or she stays in each moment; and

[52] See BERNARDO SAN JOSÉ/DE PADURA BALLESTEROS, "La detención incomunicada por delitos de terrorismo," *Terrorismo, proceso penal y derechos fundamentales*, Madrid, Marcial Pons, 2012, page 111.

[53] See BERNARDO SAN JOSÉ/DE PADURA BALLESTEROS, "La detención incomunicada por delitos de terrorismo," page 112.

(c) the isolated person will not be entitled to have a confidential interview with his or her lawyer at the end of the practice of the proceeding in which he or she had intervened.[54]

As for the intervention of the police officers with persons under isolation due to terrorist offences, since a resolution of 12 December 2006 of the Central Court of Instruction No. 5 of the Audiencia Nacional,[55] certain measures to ensure control of police activity on those detainees have been established, including videotaping of detainees while in police custody, to guarantee them that they can be examined by a doctor of their choice together with the Court's doctor and that they can communicate to their families the place of detention and the transfers that may happen.[56] The referred guaranties include some preventive measures recommended by national and international organizations for the defence of human rights.

The police officers may also immediately arrest people by their own authority in several instances, including cases of exceptional or urgent necessity in the case of alleged perpetrators of crimes committed by persons integrated in an armed band or terrorists or rebels, whatever the location or place where they hide or take refuge. They may also make the registry that, at the time of the arrest, will be made in such places and the confiscation of the effects and instruments that might be found and that could be related to the intended crime. The competent court will be immediately informed on the registry, having the police state the causes for making it and the results obtained therein, with particular reference to the arrests, if any, that had been made. Furthermore, in accordance with art. 553 LECr., the persons involved and the incidents occurred shall be indicated.

Regarding the measure of control of postal, telegraphic or telephonic communications of persons related to whom suspicions of criminal responsibility do exist, as well as the communications that they use for their criminal ends, art. 579.4 LECr. states that in case of emergency, when such investigations are done in relation to crimes connected with the activities of armed bands or of terrorist or rebels, the measure may be ordered by "the Home Minister or, in his absence, the Director of Security of the State, immediately communicating it by written to the competent judge, who, also in a reasoned manner, will revoke or uphold such decision no later than seventy-two hours after the control was ordered."

Art. 582 bis LECr. regulates the figure of the undercover agent who is an officer of the judicial police force authorized by the Judge of Instruction or by the Public

[54] See BERNARDO SAN JOSÉ/DE PADURA BALLESTEROS, "La detención incomunicada por delitos de terrorismo," page 113, 121ff.

[55] This resolution was issued by the Magistrate-Judge of the Court appointed, D. Baltasar Garzón.

[56] For a comprehensive development of the application of the measures referred to, see BERNARDO SAN JOSÉ/DE PADURA BALLESTEROS, "La detención incomunicada por delitos de terrorismo," page 132ff.

Prosecutor, reporting promptly to the Judge, to act under an assumed identity in everything related to a particular investigation connected to organized crime. This undercover agent shall disclose to the person who authorized the investigation the full information that he or she obtains. The undercover agent can also maintain his or her false identity when testifying in the process; this must be accorded by the judicial authority in a reasoned decision, being applicable Law 19/1994 of 23 December on the protection of witnesses and experts in criminal cases.[57] When investigative actions may affect fundamental rights, the undercover agent shall request to the competent court to follow the authorizations established by the Constitution and by the law, as well as to comply with other applicable legal provisions. Finally, the undercover agent shall be exempt from criminal responsibility for those actions that are a necessary consequence of the investigation, provided that they are duly proportionate to the purpose and that they do not constitute an incitement to crime. In order to proceed criminally against the undercover agent by the actions taken for the purposes of the investigation, the competent court shall, immediately on learning of the conduct of any undercover agent thereof, require a report from the agent.[58]

B. *Intelligence Agencies*

Currently, the secret intelligence services of the states have a key role in the fight against terrorism. Consequently, the fight against this kind of crime and, in general, against organized crime would be unthinkable without investigations conducted by these services.[59] Art. 4 of the Law Regulating the National Intelligence Centre[60] specifies the functions of the intelligence services as the following: (a) to obtain, evaluate and interpret information and to disseminate the necessary intelligence to protect and promote the political, economic, industrial, commercial and strategic interests of Spain, and those services may act within or outside the country; and (b) to prevent, detect and enable the neutralization of activities of foreign services, groups or individuals who endanger, threaten or violate the constitutional order, the rights and freedoms of Spanish citizens, sovereignty, integrity and security of the state, the stability of its institutions, national economic interests and welfare of the population.[61] There are, therefore, investigations classified as preventive police

57 See the web page of the BOE, http://www.boe.es/boe/dias/1994/12/24/pdfs/A38669-38671.pdf.

58 See in this regard the presentation by ARAGONESES MARTÍNEZ, *Derecho procesal penal*, De la Oliva/Aragoneses/Hinojosa/Muerza/Tomé, 7ª ed., Madrid, Editorial Ramón Areces, 2004, page 110ff.

59 See GREGORY F. TREVERTON, *Intelligence for an Age of Terror*, Cambridge, 2009, page 15ff.

60 See the web page of the BOE, http://www.boe.es/boe/dias/2002/05/07/pdfs/A16440-16444.pdf.

61 See BACHMAIER WINTER, “Información de inteligencia y proceso penal,” *Terrorismo, proceso penal y derechos fundamentales*, Madrid, Marcial Pons, 2012, page 59ff.

intelligence that afterwards have a direct impact on criminal cases of terrorism in both its initiation and its outcome.[62] Those investigations can provide important information obtained, for example, through monitoring or surveillance devices by agents or informants, or through infiltrated agents who cannot be called in criminal proceedings as witnesses for reasons of safety or due to the permanence of the device.[63] In Spain, however, it is somehow surprising that the need to create mechanisms of connection and cooperation between intelligence and criminal proceedings has not been fully addressed, despite being a country that has a long experience in combating terrorism.[64]

Related to the "evidence of the Intelligence Service Experts" in the criminal process, Spain's Supreme Court, in its Sentence 2084/2001 of 13 December, defined intelligence reports issued by the Guardia Civil members on terrorism as "evidence of Intelligence Service Experts," noting that the reports' function is to give information on the basis of the deep knowledge of the way certain commandos of ETA act and its organization. In the judgment of the Supreme Court no. 783/2007 of 1 October, this kind of evidence is characterized by the following notes: (1) It can be used in some complex proceedings, where special skills are required, not responding to the usual parameters of the more conventional expert evidence; (2) valuation of such reports by the Court is free; and (3) although it is an evidence that has a special nature (which can be defined as being among expert evidence and witness evidence), it is, of course, closer to the expert evidence, as its authors will provide their own knowledge and expertise for the valuation of certain documents or strategies.[65] However, this case law is not uniform, as in other judgments intelligence reports are considered to have the character of circumstantial evidence, as in Case no. 1929/2007 of 16 February.

Moreover, Spain's legal system also requires prior judicial authorization for certain actions of the Secret Intelligence Services, as stated in art. 12 of the Law Regulating the National Intelligence Centre. It affects certain measures concerning the inviolability of the domicile and the secrecy of communications, provided that such measures are necessary for the fulfilment of the functions assigned to the Centre, according to the unique article of the Organic Law 2/2002, of 6 May, regulating the prior judicial control of the National Intelligence Centre.[66] The

62 See BACHMAIER WINTER, "Información de inteligencia y proceso penal," page 61.

63 See BACHMAIER WINTER, "Información de inteligencia y proceso penal," page 99.

64 See BACHMAIER WINTER, "Información de inteligencia y proceso penal," page 48, 62ff.

65 See other judgments of the Supreme Court with the same doctrine as, for example, no. 290/2010 of 31 March; no. 985/2009 of 13 October; no. 124/2009 of 13 February; no. 1097/2011 of 25 October; and no. 156/2011 of 21 March.

66 See the web page of the BOE, http://www.boe.es/buscar/pdf/2002/BOE-A-2002-8627-consolidado.pdf.

adoption of these measures has been criticized by the Spanish Process Law Doctrine because it implies a judicial control without process, without proper parts as such and without any possibility of revision.[67] Nevertheless, it is always better that such control, albeit formal, exist than that it does not exist.[68] Whether these recordings made with prior authorization may or may not acquire the category of evidence in criminal proceedings, the answer is a positive one if we believe that such material has been "lawfully obtained".[69]

V. PROSCRIPTION AND LISTING OF TERRORIST GROUPS AND INDIVIDUALS

The European Union has established a binding EU list of persons, groups and entities involved in terrorist acts, based on investigations by the law enforcement, judicial or police authorities of the countries of the European Union. The list is reviewed at least every six months.[70] The Council of the European Union in its Common Position 2001/931/CFSP includes in its art. 1, Section 2 the requirements to establish what is meant by persons, groups and entities involved in terrorist acts, and in paragraph 3 a definition of terrorist act is established. The inclusion of a person, group or entity in this list is not used explicitly by the Spanish courts to attribute the character of "terrorist" to their violent acts. Terrorism is defined by the existence of certain characteristics described in Section II of this chapter deduced from the Spanish criminal legislation on terrorism, and their presence allows authorities to establish that those individuals, groups or bands perform terrorist acts.[71] However, it is necessary to emphasize that the regulation provided for in Common Position 2001/931/CFSP is consistent with the requirements contained in the Spanish Criminal Code.

67 See DE LA OLIVA, "El control judicial previo de la inteligencia nacional (o de cómo el *remedio* resulta peor que la enfermedad)," *Tribunales de Justicia*, mayo 2003, page 5.

68 See BACHMAIER WINTER, "Información de inteligencia y proceso penal," page 96

69 For a contrary view, however, see BACHMAIER WINTER, "Información de inteligencia y proceso penal," page 97 and 98; the author believes that it would confuse the level of criminal prevention and prosecution. DE LA OLIVA is silent about it, but notes that it is material "lawfully obtained" and that the problem would be the material's classification as official secrets. See DE LA OLIVA, "El control judicial previo de la inteligencia nacional (o de cómo el *remedio* resulta peor que la enfermedad)," page 7.

70 The latest update at the time of writing is in the COUNCIL DECISION 2012/333/CFSP of 25 June 2012 updating the list of persons, groups and entities subject to arts. 2, 3 and 4 of Common Position 2001/931/CFSP on the application of specific measures to combat terrorism and repealing Decision 2011/872/CFSP, published in the Official Journal of the European Union, issue number 165, available on the website http://eur-lex.europa.eu/LexUriServ/LexUriServ.do?uri=OJ:L:2012:165:0072:0074:EN:PDF.

71 See on this point explicitly the Resolution of 26 September 2007 of the Central Economic-Administrative Tribunal.

VI. REGULATION OF TERRORISM FINANCING

A. *The Regulatory Regime to Counter Terrorism Financing*

To prevent terrorist financing activities and prevent the use for that purpose of the financial system in a globalized economy, Spain has enacted Law 12/2003, of 21 May, on blocking the financing of terrorism, the Organic Law 4/2003, of 21 May, complementary to the Law on Prevention and blocking of the financing of terrorism,[72] which amends Law 6/1985 of 1 July, of the Judiciary Power, and Law 29/1998, of 13 July, regulating the Administrative Jurisdiction,[73] and Law 10/2010, of 28 April, to prevent money laundering and financing of terrorism.[74] The Spanish Criminal Code reformed by Law 5/2010, of 22 June, has seen the introduction in the last reform referenced of one offence criminalizing the financing of terrorism, in art. 576 bis. This felony is independent of the criminal offence of money laundering under art. 301 of the Criminal Code, and both offences can be applied together because they protect different individual juridical rights. Moreover, art. 575 establishes that those who – in order to provide funds to armed gangs, terrorist organizations or groups or in order to favour their activities – attack property shall be punished with the higher-degree punishment that would be applicable for the felony committed, without prejudice to the appropriate ones that would be imposed pursuant to what is set forth in art. 576 for acts of collaboration.

The Financial Intelligence Unit (Unidad de Inteligencia Financiera, or UIF) is a central agency in Spain responsible for receiving, analysing and reporting to the competent authorities the cases of money laundering arising from the delivery of financial information related to funds whose origin is suspected to be criminal or of the information required by the national legislation in order to counteract money laundering. The UIF is a point of centralization of information on unusual or suspicious financial transactions and also the recipient of confidential statements made by financial organizations. According to Law 10/2010, it is the competence of the Executive Service of the Commission for the Prevention of Money Laundering and Monetary Offences (SEPBLAC) to prepare the Financial Intelligence Reports regulated in art. 46, which have no value as evidence and cannot be incorporated directly to judicial or administrative diligences. The total number of suspicious transactions reported by SEPBLAC was 2975 in 2011 and 3058 in 2012.[75]

[72] http://www.boe.es/boe/dias/2003/05/22/pdfs/A19490-19494.pdf.

[73] https://www.boe.es/boe/dias/2003/05/22/pdfs/A19486-19487.pdf.

[74] http://www.boe.es/boe/dias/2010/04/29/pdfs/BOE-A-2010–6737.pdf.

[75] See http://www.sepblac.es/espanol/acerca_sepblac/estadisticas/2012/blanqueo_capitales.htm.

B. *Criminal Offences of Terrorism Financing*

The offence established in Spain's Criminal Code on the financing of terrorism in art. 576 bis was not introduced in response to Resolutions 1267 and 1373 of the Security Council of the UN, but was based on the proposed definition contained in Art. 2 of the International Convention for the Suppression of the Financing of Terrorism (New York, 1999). The offence under art. 576 bis presents a problem of evidence because the judge has to infer rationally the intention of providing and collecting money to be used for the terrorist organization or group, or knowing that the money will be used, in whole or in part, to commit terrorist offences or deliver them to the terrorist organization or group. As noted, paragraph 1 of this article is redundant, since economic cooperation is explicitly mentioned in art. 576 and when referred to a specific terrorist act is punishable as authorship or complicity in the act.[76] Moreover, an excessively broad interpretation of this article, which states that "Whoever by any means, directly or indirectly, provides or collects funds intending them to be used, or knowing they shall be used, fully or partially to commit any of the felonies included in this Chapter or to deliver them to a terrorist organization or group," would include the collecting of funds to support terrorist prisoners or their families.[77] As this chapter is being written, there is no jurisprudence on the application of this offence.

Regarding the assets of terrorists condemned for terrorist offences, art. 127.1 Criminal Code establishes that the Judge or Court of Law shall extend the seizure of assets, goods, instruments and gains from criminal activities committed within the setting of a criminal or terrorist organization or group or for an offence of terrorism. For these purposes, the property of each and every one of the persons found guilty of felonies committed within the criminal or terrorist organization that is disproportionate in relation to the revenue lawfully obtained by each one of those persons shall be deemed to have been obtained by the criminal activity. The assets seized (if lawful) shall be sold, applying the sums obtained to covering the civil liabilities of the convict if the law does not foresee otherwise and, if not of lawful trade, the assets shall be applied to the use provided by the laws or, failing that, be destroyed.

VII. IMMIGRATION MEASURES

In the legislation on immigration in Spain – the Organic Law 4/2000 of 11 January on the rights and freedoms of foreigners in Spain and their social integration, as

[76] See MUÑOZ CONDE, *Derecho penal, Parte Especial*, 18 ed., Valencia, Tirant lo Blanch, 2010, page 930.

[77] See MUÑOZ CONDE, *Derecho penal, Parte Especial*, page 930.

amended by various subsequent laws – nothing related to terrorism is contemplated. Moreover, the general scheme of arrest and prosecution for crimes described in the previous sections apply to any foreigner who is involved in a criminal investigation concerning terrorist offences. In any case, if an alien is sentenced to a custodial sentence under six years and is not legally a resident of Spain, the penalty is replaced by the expulsion of the offender from the Spanish territory, according to art. 89 Criminal Code.

VIII. ADMINISTRATIVE AND EXECUTIVE MEASURES

In the Spanish Constitution, there are a number of fundamental rights and public freedoms, which include the right to liberty and security (art. 17), the right to effective judicial protection, the right to an ordinary judge predetermined by law and the right to presumption of innocence (art. 24), that cannot be avoided by the enactment of administrative measures.

IX. ROLE OF EXTRA-TERRITORIAL MILITARY AND COUNTER-TERRORISM ACTIVITIES

The Spanish military law does not provide for any regulation on terrorist offences even in wartime. Currently, the military courts do not hold any competence in the investigation and prosecution of terrorism. Although there have been cases of Spanish citizens who have committed various crimes of terrorism in Spain and France, these persons have been arrested and tried on charges of terrorism in France, and once the sentence has been served, they have been extradited to Spain under the provisions of Law 3/2003 of 14 March on European arrest warrant and the surrender procedures between Member States.

Art. 23.4 Spanish Organic Law 6/1985 of 1 July, of the Judiciary Power, declares the Spanish jurisdiction competent over acts committed by Spaniards or foreigners outside the national territory that may be categorized according to Spanish law as terrorism, among other crimes, as long as it is established that their alleged perpetrators are in Spain, that victims of Spanish nationality exist or that any link of relevant connection with Spain exists. It is also required that no proceeding involving an investigation and effective prosecution of such offences has been initiated in another country or within an international court. This implies that if a Spanish or foreign citizen commits a terrorist offence in another country, Spain would be competent to judge the accused, and his or her extradition cannot be conceded under the provisions of art. 3 of Act 4/1985, of 21 March, of passive extradition: "No Spanish or foreigner shall be extradited for crimes for which the Spanish courts are competent, according to the National legislation."

Finally, and related to Spanish officials who took part in the fight against terrorism abroad, Amnesty International (AI) reported that members of the Spanish police belonging to the Central Information Unit made trips to Guantanamo under the government of President José María Aznar, to attend "illegal" interrogations of prisoners, as it appeared in the testimony of former inmates transferred to Spain. This news sparked considerable controversy in society, but was not confirmed nor denied by any government.

X. SECRECY AND TERRORISM

In Spain, the criminal process ensures the rights of the accused, in particular the principle of contradiction, the principle of publicity, the presumption of innocence and the principle of defence enshrined in the Constitution and procedural laws. The rules of evidence are the same in the prosecution of any offence and there are no exceptions when dealing with terrorist offences. In the trial phase, evidence is collected with full compliance with the principles of publicity, orality, immediacy and contradiction. This accords with the fundamental right to a trial "with all the guarantees" established by art 24.2 of the Spanish Constitution. Therefore, no secret evidence can be presented in criminal proceedings in Spain.

Under Spanish law, the obligation of all citizens to collaborate with judges and courts in the course of a process, according to art. 118 of the Spanish Constitution, implies a number of procedural and criminal consequences if such collaboration is not carried out. Regarding witnesses, some measures of protection and security are included in Organic Law 19/1994 of 23 December on the protection of witnesses and experts in criminal cases. In accordance with art. 1 and 2, when the judicial authority rationally appreciates a serious danger to a witness's person, liberty or property of the person or their family, the following measures may be taken: (a) his or her name, address, workplace and profession or any other information that could serve to identify the witness shall not appear in the proceeding, and to this purpose a number can be used; (b) the witness can appear using any method that prevents normal visual identification; (c) as place of residence for the purpose of citations and notifications, the head office of the intervening judiciary body it can be used, which will transmit them to the addressee. At the request of the prosecution and for the whole process, or once it has ended if the grave danger does continue to exist, witnesses and experts shall be given police protection. In exceptional cases, new identity documents and financial means to change the residence or workplace may be supplied. Witnesses and experts may also be guarded as necessary.

The Judgment of the Constitutional Court no. 64/1994, of 28 February, confirmed the constitutionality of hidden witnesses that give testimony without being seen by the defendants, and the probative value of such testimony was accepted provided the guarantee of contradiction during interrogation was respected in the act of the trial.[78] Spain's procedural law does not limit the anonymity to the investigative phase called temporary partial anonymity. It also accepts the possibility of permanent partial anonymity during the entire procedure, including oral proceedings.[79] However, this anonymity is subjected to control by the judicial body responsible for the prosecution, which must weigh the reasons given by the defendant to know the name of the witness and the need for a concealment technique, using the weighting of interests and rights referred to in art. 4.1 Organic Law 19/1994 of 23 December on the protection of witnesses and experts in criminal cases.[80] Moreover, the maintenance of such partial anonymity should not prevent the defendant from questioning the witness, with full respect of the guarantee of contradiction and the possibility of verifying the statements made at the trial with previous depositions.[81]

XI. CONCLUSION

Related to the assessment of Spanish anti-terrorist legislation, we can establish the following conclusions:

- The Spanish criminal and criminal-procedural terrorism legislation complies with international commitments established under Resolutions 1267 and 1373 of the Security Council of the United Nations,[82] as well as with the Framework Decision 2002/475/JHA of the Council of the European Union on combating terrorism of 13 June 2002, as amended by Framework Decision 2008/919/JHA of 28 November 2008.[83]
- The Spanish legislator has enacted more criminal offences with strict penalties targeting terrorism, including offences against the recruitment, indoctrination

78 See SANTOS ALONSO/DE PRADA RODRÍGUEZ, "Protección de testigos en procesos de terrorismo," page 189.

79 See SANTOS ALONSO/DE PRADA RODRÍGUEZ, "Protección de testigos en procesos de terrorismo," page 188.

80 See SANTOS ALONSO/DE PRADA RODRÍGUEZ, "Protección de testigos en procesos de terrorismo," page 188.

81 See SANTOS ALONSO/DE PRADA RODRÍGUEZ, "Protección de testigos en procesos de terrorismo," page 188.

82 See Global Survey on the Implementation of Security Council Resolution 1373 (2001) by Member States, of September 2011, available at http://www.un.org/en/sc/ctc/docs/2011-globalsurvey1373.pdf.

83 These rules are found in the following website of the *Official Journal of the European Communities*: http://eur-lex.europa.eu/LexUriServ/LexUriServ.do?uri=OJ:L:2002:164:0003:0007:EN:PDF. http://eur-lex.europa.eu/LexUriServ/LexUriServ.do?uri=OJ:L:2002:164:0003:0007:EN:PDF. http://eur-lex.europa.eu/LexUriServ/LexUriServ.do?uri=OJ:L:2008:330:0021:0023:EN:PDF.

or training of future terrorists as well as other preparatory acts for terrorism. These crimes apply to both terrorism committed by organized groups and unorganized individual terrorism. This leads to the conclusion that Spanish criminal law and criminal procedure aimed at terrorism is the epitome of "criminal law against the enemy." If this expansion continues, as appears likely, certain doubts can be raised about the legitimacy of Spanish counter-terrorism law from a constitutional point of view and from the perspective of respect for human rights.[84]

[84] Recent terrorist events such as the terrorists attacks in Paris in January 2015 and concerns about terrorist foreign fighters have given rise to an antiterrorist pact between the principal political parties in Spain (PP and PSOE) on 2 February 2015. As a consequence, new modifications to the different criminal laws related to terrorism will be enacted and likely will expand the punishable behaviors and increase their penalties.

11

Portugal

José Francisco de Faria Costa

I. INTRODUCTION

Portugal has strongly cooperated with counter-terrorism initiatives adopted by the United Nations (UN), the European Council and the European Union (EU). At this level, it is important to note that Portugal is bound by several legal instruments, such as the Security Council Resolution 1624 (2005), the Council of Europe Convention on the Prevention of Terrorism, of May 16th, 2005 (signed, but not yet ratified) and the European Convention on Terrorism Repression (as per Law nr. 19/81, of August 18th). Portugal is also bound to the United Nations Convention on Civil Aviation and Maritime Security regarding prevention and repression of terrorism acts. Finally, it is bound by the "Common Action Plan" dated October 15th, 1996, adopted by the European Council and the European Convention on Extradition (Resolution nr. 23/89 of the Portuguese Parliament).

Terrorism as such was previously regulated in the Portuguese Penal Code, namely Articles 300 and 301 of the Code. The Portuguese Criminal Code also contains provisions on racial or religious discrimination (Article 240); explosive substances or similar substance and weaponry (Article 272); hijack or alteration of course of an aircraft, ship, train or passenger vehicles (Article 287); and incitement to collective disobedience (Article 330). Crimes such as incitement to war (Article 17) or recruitment of mercenaries (Article 18) are now foreseen in Law nr. 31/2004, of July 22nd, amended by Law nr. 59/2007, of July 22nd. Articles 300 and 301 of the Portuguese Criminal Code were revoked, after the transposition of the European Council Framework Decision nr. 2002/475/JAI, dated July 13th, by Law no. 52/2003, dated August, 22nd, which is now the law on the fight against terrorism. There is also a provision foreseeing special conditions of protection of terrorism victims, namely Article 139 of the Portuguese Criminal Procedure Code.

On other matters related to terrorism, Portugal has, since 2007, a new law regulating the conditions of entry, permanence, departure and expulsion of foreigners from the national territory (Law nr. 23/2007, dated July 4th, amended by Law nr. 29/1012, dated August 9th, which revoked Decree-Law nr. 244/98, dated August 8th, amended by Decree-Law nr. 4/2001, dated January 10th, and Decree-Law nr. 34/2003, dated February 25th).

In 2008, a new law on asylum and refugees (Law nr. 27/2008, of June 30th, amended by Law nr. 26/2014, of May 5th) was passed thus revoking the former legal regime of Law nr. 15/98, dated March 26th.

As it pertains to judicial cooperation, and considering that regulations under the UN and EU are directly applicable internally, Portugal has the obligation to deny safe haven to any person linked to any form of terrorism. One thus must regard Law nr. 144/99, dated August 31st (already amended, being the last amendment by Law nr. 115/2009, dated October 12th), as the law on international judicial cooperation in criminal matters, as well as Law nr. 65/2003, dated August 23rd, in transposition of Council Framework Decision nr. 2002/584/JAI, dated June 13th, regulating the European Arrest Warrant. Portugal is also part of the Europol Convention.

There is also important legislation regarding internal security, armed forces and criminal politics. For example, the Internal Security Law (Law nr. 53/2008, dated August 29th) specifically describes the purpose of internal security services as being "to protect the life and the integrity of all citizens and to enforce law and democratic order against terrorism, violent criminality or highly organized criminality..." Recent Resolution nr. 19/2013, dated April 5th, regarding the National Defence Strategic Concept, considers terrorism as one of the global security threats in line with NATO recommendations.

According to the Organic Law of the Intelligence Service (Law nr. 9/2007, dated February 19th, amended by Law nr. 50/2014, of August 13th), the Intelligence Service is entitled to collect information to ensure internal security and when necessary to prevent sabotage, terrorism, espionage and other acts that, by their nature, may affect or destroy the state as constitutionally established. The last Criminal Politics Law adopted according to the Framework Law on Criminal Politics (Law nr. 17/2006, dated May 23rd) considered terrorism and terrorist organizations to be priority crimes for prevention.

Finally, still in the realm of counter-terrorism legislation, one should mention Law nr. 25/2008, dated June 5th, regulating measures of preventive and repressive nature for the fight against money laundering and terrorism financing, transposing Directives nrs. 2005/60/CE of the European Parliament and Council, dated October 26th, and 2006/70/CE, of the Commission, dated August 1st.

All of this comprehensive legislation demonstrates the effort Portugal has made and keeps making in order to comply with its international obligations related to counter-terrorism legislation, and, in particular, with UN Security Council Resolution 1373 enacted after the September 11th terrorist attacks on the United

States and, more recently, terrorism related European legal instruments enacted after the terrorist attacks in Madrid on March 11th, 2004. At the same time, however, Portugal does not have the same experience with terrorism as other countries such as Spain and has fortunately not been a victim of terrorist attacks.

II. THE DEFINITION OF TERRORISM

The first legal definition of terrorism was introduced in the Portuguese Penal Code, enacted in 1982 (Decree-Law nr. 400/82, dated September 23rd). This Code regulated terrorist organizations and terrorism in Articles 288 and 289, respectively.

According to the first of those articles, a person who promoted a terrorist group, organization or association would be punished with five to fifteen years' imprisonment (Article 288, Paragraph 1). Paragraph 2 of Article 288 considered a terrorist group, organization or association to be a group of two or more people who acted together to harm national integrity or independence or impeach; alter or subvert the functioning of state institutions foreseen in the Constitution or force a public authority to abstain from or practice an act; to tolerate the practice of an act; or even to intimidate certain people, groups of people or the population in general through the practice of the following types of crimes:

a. Crimes against human life or integrity or the freedom of people
b. Crimes against the security of transportation and communication
c. Crimes of endangerment, such as arson, release of toxic gas, flood and similar dangers
d. Crimes of sabotage
e. Crimes that involve the use of bombs, grenades or explosives

Note that under Paragraph 5 of this article, the leader of the group would be punished with ten to fifteen years' imprisonment.

Article 289 regulated terrorism. Paragraph 1 of this article dealt with the sentencing of a person who practiced any of the crimes listed in (a) to (d) or with the use of the means described in (e) of Paragraph 2 of the previous article (Article 288), acting with the intent to harm national integrity or independence; impeach, alter or subvert the functioning of state institutions foreseen in the Constitution; force a public authority to abstain from or practice an act or to tolerate the practice of an act; intimidate certain people, groups of people or the population in general. Such a person would be punished with two to ten years' imprisonment or with the penalty foreseen for the corresponding crime.

In the Portuguese Penal Code as per Decree-Law nr. 48/95, dated March 15th, the norms regarding terrorism and terrorist organizations were foreseen in Articles

300 (terrorist organizations) and 301 (terrorism). The legal text suffered some minor changes from the original one but it was revoked by Law nr. 52/2003, dated August 22nd, which established the law on the fight against terrorism (LFAT) which, subject to three amendments, remains the law in force today. One of the amendments in 2007 (Law nr. 59/2007, dated September 4th), included the criminal responsibility of legal persons for such crimes, and another one in 2008 (Law nr. 25/2008, dated June 5th) added provisions regarding the financing of terrorism and one in 2011 (Law nr. 17/2011, dated May 3rd), reinforced penalties for the promoting of terrorist activities.

There are some significant changes in terms of the conduct included under terrorist activities under the LFAT. For example, Article 2 of LFAT enlarges the type of crimes considered in the definition of a terrorist organization and includes as a crime the promotion of terrorist acts. The basis for the definition of terrorist organization is the same (Article 1, Paragraph 1 of LFAT) as it was under the previous criminal legislation, but it now includes reference to acts that destroy or disable the functioning of communications and public facilities or involve chemical or biological weapons or the use of nuclear energy. Such crimes (lines (a) to (f) of Paragraph 1 or Article 2 of LFAT) are able, by nature or context, to seriously affect the state or the population that the organization intends to intimidate.[1]

The leader of the group is now punished with fifteen to twenty years' imprisonment, under Paragraph 3 of Article 2.The LFAT also establishes in Article 4, regarding terrorism, that whoever practices the acts foreseen in Paragraph 1 of Article 2 will be

[1] In order to facilitate the comprehension of this article, we transcribe its Paragraph 1:

It is considered to be a terrorist group, organization or association the group of two or more people that, acting together, have the intent to harm national integrity or independence, impeach, alter or subvert the functioning of State institutions foreseen in the Constitution, force public authority to abstain or practice an act or to tolerate the practice of an act or to intimidate certain people, groups of people of the population in general, through:

a) Crimes against human life or integrity or the freedom of people;

b) Crimes against the security of transportation and communication, including computer, telephone, radio or television;

c) Crimes of endangerment, such as arson, explosion, release of radioactive, toxic or asphyxiating substances, flood or avalanche, destruction of construction, contamination of food or water for human use or spreading of disease, plague, harmful animal or plant;

d) Acts that destroy or make impossible the functioning or divert from their normal ends communication ways, public service facilities or those meant to supply basic needs of the population, definitively or temporarily, totally or partially;

e) Investigation and development of biological or chemical weapons;

f) Crimes that imply the use of nuclear energy, fire, biological or chemical arms, explosives, incendiary means of any kind, rigged packages or letters;

Always that, by their nature or the context they are committed, these crimes are able to seriously affect the State or the population aimed by intimidation.

punished with two to ten years' imprisonment or with the penalty foreseen for the corresponding crime.[2]

An innovation of the LFAT –achieved with the amendment made by Law nr. 17/2011, dated May 3rd – is the concept of international terrorism in Article 5 (combined with Article 3). The original concept of terrorism in criminal law was restricted to the harmful conduct to the integrity or independence of the Portuguese state or of Portuguese institutions or public bodies. This law also considered terrorism to include harmful conduct towards the integrity or independence of a state and the institutions or public bodies of a state or international public organizations. This is a significant enlargement of the concept of terrorism.

In Portugal, there is only one legal definition of terrorism, which is the one in the LFAT. This law is particularly important, since it clearly provides a specific legal regulation for terrorism, thus avoiding difficulties and controversies over the definition. Moreover, the actual definition, although updated and enlarged, is still very coherent with the original definition of terrorism (terrorist organizations) from the Penal Code of 1982. The hallmark of the Portuguese legal definition of terrorism is the intent to harm the integrity or independence of the state and the proper functioning of public institutions as laid down by the Constitution, as well as intent to intimidate (a group of) people.

Other criminal law provisions that can be associated with terrorism are independent crimes. They include racial or religious discrimination (Article 240 of the Portuguese Penal Code); explosive substances or similar substance and weaponry (Article 272 of the Portuguese Penal Code); hijacking or alteration of course of an aircraft, ship, train or passenger vehicles (Article 287 of the Portuguese Penal Code); and incitement to collective disobedience (Article 330 of the Portuguese Penal Code).

III. CRIMINAL LAWS AND PROSECUTIONS

A. *Criminal Law*

As already examined and assessed in Section II of this chapter, terrorism and terrorist organizations are separate crimes from other more general criminal provisions.

There are, however, two aspects to take under consideration. On the one hand, the current LFAT is a special criminal law, meaning that, since 2003, the crimes of terrorism and terrorist organizations are no longer regulated by the Portuguese Penal Code. This decodification allows for a more autonomous regulation on terrorism – already shown by the amendments made to the LFAT – without jeopardizing the

[2] Although aggravated by a third in its minimal and maximal limits if equal or superior to that of two to ten years.

systematization of the Penal Code. It can also underline the importance of these crimes.[3]

On the other hand, the provisions of crimes in the Portuguese Penal Code that can be associated with terrorism can complement the prosecution thereof when not specifically included in the definition of terrorism in the LFAT.

The LFAT has eleven articles. It outlines the concept and punishment of terrorism in four main articles, namely Articles 2 to 5. Article 2, regarding terrorist organizations, gives the main definition.[4] Article 3 regulates other terrorist organizations, where the law extends the scope of the definition to states other than the Portuguese state as well as to international public bodies. Article 4 deals with terrorism and refers to the definition in Article 2. Finally, Article 5 regulates international terrorism, referring to the extension operated by Article 3.

Membership or participation in a terrorist group, organization or association is also considered a crime. Under Paragraph 2 of Article 2, "he who promotes or funds a terrorist group, organization or association, adheres to them or supports them, namely through information or the provision of material means or by any form of financing, shall be punished with eight to fifteen years' imprisonment."

All preparatory acts for the constitution of a terrorist group, organization or association are criminalized in Paragraph 4 of Article 2, and can be punished with one to eight years' imprisonment. This is a special rule regarding the general rule of the Portuguese Penal Code for the crimes – such as homicide or murder – foreseen therein, since, under Article 21 of this Code, preparatory acts are not punishable.

In Article 4, Paragraph 2 of LFAT (under the amendment of 2008), if someone commits the crimes of grand theft, extortion, computer fraud or official document forgery in order to practice the facts described in Paragraph 1 of Article 2, that person will be punished with the penalty foreseen for such crimes, aggravated by a third. This means that here the LFAT treats these crimes as more serious if they are related to terrorism.

The advocating of or incitement to terrorism is also criminalized. In fact, Paragraph 3 of Article 4 of LFAT states that whoever broadcasts a message to the public inciting to the practice of the facts foreseen in Paragraph 1 of Article 2, with the intent therein referred to, will be punished with one to five years' imprisonment.

Also a crime is the recruitment of people for the practice of terrorist acts, according to Paragraph 4 of Article 4 of LFAT. In fact, whoever recruits someone else for the practice of the facts foreseen in Paragraph 1 of Article 2 of LFAT, with the intention therein mentioned, may be sentenced to two to five years' imprisonment.

3 Although, as already stated, this notion of importance can only be related to Portugal's commitment to assist, at an international level and also with national legislation thereto, the fight against terrorism, since terrorism, as such, is not a significant criminal problem – to date – in Portugal.

4 See Section II of this chapter.

Finally, Paragraph 5 of Article 2 of LFAT criminalizes a person who, by any means, trains or instructs someone else on the fabrication or use of explosives, firearms or other dangerous or toxic substances or on other specific methods and techniques to commit terrorist acts.

It is important to note that all three aforementioned paragraphs require the intent specifically mentioned in Paragraph 1 of Article 2 of LFAT.[5]

One important element of the LFAT is the fact that legal persons can be made responsible for terrorism under Article 6 of the LFAT.[6]

In the case of competition of crimes, for example, terrorism and homicide, since terrorism is a special crime, the offender will be punished for terrorism and not for homicide.

B. *Terrorism Prosecutions*

Portugal has not known a large amount of terrorism prosecutions. As previously stated, terrorism is not a national security problem as it is in other states. However, since there are specific terrorism crimes, the very few prosecutions that existed occurred on the basis of these crimes.

The most well-known case of a terrorism prosecution relates to two suspected members of ETA (a Spanish terrorist group). In a search of a house where they were staying in the small village of Óbidos in 2010, a large amount of explosives and other dangerous substances were found, related to the logistics of the possible practice of terrorist crimes. In 2011, two people were prosecuted for terrorism, but there is still no definitive judicial decision regarding this case.[7]

Terrorism prosecutions are conducted in ordinary courts. The legal regime does not foresee special courts or military courts for prosecuting terrorism-associated crimes.

C. *Punishment of Terrorism*

There have not yet been convictions for the crimes of terrorism in Portugal. The Annual Report of Internal Security (ARIS) for 2013[8] shows a total of 20.147 cases

5 Paragraphs 3 to 5 resulted from the amendment made to LFAT by Law nr. 17/2001, dated May 3rd.

6 The Portuguese Penal Code also foresees the criminal responsibility of legal persons for some crimes, according to Article 11.

7 The trial of Andoni Zengotitabengoa Fernandez and Oier Gomez Mielgo started in September 2011, with enhanced court security measures. However, this case did not relate to terrorism against the Portuguese state.

8 Available at http://www.portugal.gov.pt/media/1391220/RASI%202013.pdf.

of violent criminality (a category in which terrorism is included in these reports). However, there are no cases of terrorist organizations or of terrorism listed among those 20.000 cases.

IV. INVESTIGATIVE POWERS

A. *Police Powers*

In Portugal, according to Law nr. 49/2008, dated August 27th (Law on the Organization of Criminal Investigation), there is a reserved competence for the investigation of crimes such as terrorist organizations, terrorism or crimes against the security of the state, given to a specialized security force, namely the Criminal Police (Article 7, Paragraph 2, lines h) and l) of said law).

The Organic Law of the Criminal Police (Law nr. 37/2008, dated August 6th, amended by Law nr. 26/2010, dated August 30th) establishes, in Article 22 thereof, that the Criminal Police has specialized National Units, one of which, according to Article 28, is the National Unit for Counter-Terrorism.

The legal regime of National Units is to be regulated in autonomous legislation. In fact, they are regulated by Decree-Law nr. 42/2009, dated February 12th. Under Article 7 of this Decree-Law, regulating the National Unit for Counter-Terrorism (in Portuguese, Unidade Nacional Contra-Terrorismo, or UNCT), this Unit has competence in cases of prevention, detection, criminal investigation and cooperation with judiciary authorities regarding the following crimes:

a. Terrorist organizations and terrorism
b. Crimes against the security of the state, except those regarding the election process
c. Hijack or attempt on the security of transportation, be it by air, water, railroad or road, which is punishable by more than eight years' imprisonment
d. Crimes carried out with bombs; grenades; explosive devices or substances; firearms or rigged objects; or nuclear, chemical or biological weapons
e. Crimes against the President of the Republic, the President of Parliament, the Prime-Minister, the Presidents of the higher courts and the General Attorney of the State
f. Crimes related to the preceding[9]

[9] The prevention, detection and criminal investigation of crimes such as slavery, kidnapping, arms trafficking, participation in armed riot, and robbery of banks and treasury services are still in UNCT's competence (Article 7, Paragraph 2 of Law nr. 49/2008), because they can also be related to terrorism (here considered in wide terms as criminal phenomena and not in its legal definition).

This Unit has thus special competence for terrorist-related crimes and acts as a centre point for their investigation.

B. *Intelligence Agencies*

In Portugal, there is an Antiterrorism Coordination Unit, which is specifically mentioned in Law nr. 53/2008, dated August 29th (Internal Security Law). In fact, in this Unit there are representatives of the General Secretary of National Security and of the General Secretary of Intelligence Services, as well as the heads of the National Guard, the Police, the Criminal Police, the Borders and Aliens Service, the Strategic Information for Defence Service and the Security Information's Service (Article 23, Paragraph 1 of the Law).[10] This is why, under Paragraph 2 of Article 23 of this law, the Antiterrorism Coordination Unit is competent to ensure the coordination and the sharing of information among all services integrated therein, within the frame of the fight against terrorism.

V. PROSCRIPTION AND LISTING OF TERRORIST GROUPS AND INDIVIDUALS

A. *Proscription Mechanisms*

Article 44 of Law nr. 25/2008, dated June 5th, expressly provides that the Financial Intelligence Unit is responsible for collecting and maintaining updated statistical data on the reported number of suspicious transactions and on money laundering and terrorism financing, as well as on the routing and results of such reports.

These data are then published by the FIU in its annual reports.

Furthermore, Article 44 of the law legally prescribes that the General Directorate for Justice Policy, a department of the Ministry of Justice, shall collect, on an annual basis, all the data referring to the number of cases of money laundering and terrorism financing investigated, the number of persons prosecuted, the number of convictions and the amount of frozen, seized and confiscated property. The Ministry of Justice shall publish this information regularly, according to the same provision.

The General Directorate for Justice Policy is also responsible for publishing the "Statistics on Crime," and the 2012 statistics confirm that there have been no convictions for the crimes of terrorism or in relation to terrorist organizations.[11]

[10] According to Article 25, Paragraph 2 of this law, these are the services that have internal security functions or duties.

[11] See the information available at http://www.siej.dgpj.mj.pt/webeis/index.jsp?username=Publico&pgmWindowName=pgmWindow_635257657010606250.

As a member of the EU, Portugal is obliged by the Council Decision 2009/1004/CFSP of December 22nd to update the list of persons, groups and entities subject to Articles 2, 3 and 4 of Common Position 2001/931/CFSP on the application of specific measures to combat terrorism and take part in compiling the EU terrorist listings.

B. *Challenges to Proscriptions and Listings*

The criminal legal provisions on terrorism and terrorist organizations are not based on any listings of terrorist groups.

VI. REGULATION OF TERRORISM FINANCING

A. *The Regulatory Regime to Counter Terrorism Financing*

The Criminal Police has a special Unit of the National Directorate, namely the Financial Intelligence Unit (under the Organic Law of the Criminal Police, Law nr. 37/2008, dated August 6th), especially dedicated to the collection and analysis of money laundering and tax crimes.

Law Nr. 25/2008, dated June 5th, regulates measures of a preventive and repressive nature for the fight against money laundering and terrorism financing (Law on the Fight Against Money Laundering and Terrorism Financing). It also introduced an amendment to the LFAT, namely Article 5-A, regarding the financing of terrorism.

This law aims to prevent the financial system and some liberal professions (e.g., lawyers) from being used for money laundering or financing of terrorism. In this sense, it establishes a series of duties (identification, dilligence, refusal, cooperation, secrecy or control, among others) for the entities therein considered (for example, financial institutions), foreseeing administrative offenses for failure in compliance.

As far as prevention is concerned, the regulatory structure for money laundering and terrorism financing follows the same standard. For example, the secrecy obligation towards a client regarding an ongoing criminal investigation (of said client) is identical for both money laundering and terrorism (Article 19 of the Law on the Fight Against Money Laundering and Terrorism Financing).

B. *Criminal Offences of Terrorism Financing*

The criminal offense of terrorism financing is provided in, Article 5-A of the LFAT.[12] Under Paragraph 1 of this Article, whoever, by any means, directly or indirectly,

[12] There is a specific criminal offense for money laundering – independent of that of terrorism financing – in Article 368-A of the Portuguese Penal Code.

supplies, holds or receives funds or assets of any type, as well as rights or products that can be transformed into funds, with the intent of them being used, totally or partially, in the planning, preparation or the committing of the terrorist acts foreseen in Paragraph 1 of Article 2 of LFAT, or the practice of those acts with the intent mentioned in Paragraph 1 of Article 3 or in Paragraph 1 of Article 4, can be punished with eight to fifteen years' imprisonment.

It is important to note that for an act to constitute the crime foreseen in the aforementioned paragraph it is not necessary that the funds originate from a third party, nor that the funds have been delivered to whom they were intended or even that these funds were effectively used to commit the crimes (Paragraph 2 of Article 5-A).

On the other hand, Law nr. 5/2002, dated January 11th,[13] establishes measures to fight organized crime and economical and financial crime. This law comprises a special regime for the collection of proof, for the breach of professional secrecy and for the forfeiture of criminal property (in favour of the state) concerning several crimes, in particular money laundering and crimes related to terrorism and terrorist organizations.[14]

According to Article 2 of this law, professional secrecy can be breached whenever a prosecution for these crimes is undertaken and there are reasons to believe that the information is relevant for the discovery of the truth. This breach of secrecy depends on an order issued by the district attorney in charge of the prosecution. However, under Article 5 of this law, every person who comes across this breach of professional secrecy, due to prosecutorial reasons, becomes obliged by judicial secrecy regarding every act that comes to their knowledge due to the prosecution.

In the context of these measures to fight organized crime and economical and financial crime, the collection of voice and image, by any means, without the consent of the envisaged, is authorized in Article 6 when necessary for the investigation of the crimes foreseen in Paragraph 1 of Article 1 of the law. This procedure depends on a previous authorization or order by the court. Although subject to a court order, it is a more lenient regime with regard to the admissibility of evidence than the ordinary procedures under Article 187 of the Portuguese Criminal Procedure Code.

This law also establishes a special regime for the forfeiture of property. Article 7 of the law provides that, in case of conviction, it is presumed for the purposes of forfeiture that the difference between the value of the estate of the defendant and the value of his or her legal income is the result of criminal activity and can

13 Amended by Law nr. 19/2008, dated April 21st; Decree-Law nr. 317/2009, dated October 30th; Decree-Law nr. 242/2012, dated November 7th; and Law nr. 60/2013, dated August 23rd.

14 It also includes other crimes, such as arms smuggling or corruption, under Paragraph 1 of Article 1 of the law.

thus be subject to forfeiture. This is a legal presumption against the defendant, which is an inversion of the legal (and constitutional) principle ruling in criminal matters, namely the *in dubio pro reo* or presumption of innocence principle. Despite the fact that the defendant can, under Article 9 of the law, prove the legal origin of the assets, one can conclude that a lower standard of proof prevails under this law.

VII. IMMIGRATION MEASURES

A. *Immigration Detention*

As a party to the Schengen Agreement, Portugal refuses the entry of foreign citizens indicated in the Schengen Information System. It also denies entry to foreign citizens who constitute a danger to public order or national security (Article 32 of the law that regulates the conditions of entry, permanence, departure and expulsion from the national territory, Law nr. 23/2007, dated July 4th, as amended by Law nr. 29/2012, dated August 9th).

The grounds for the expulsion of foreign citizens from national territory, under Article 134 of this law, is an offence against national security or public order or that the activities of a person in the country constitute a threat to the interests or to the dignity of the Portuguese state or its nationals.

Immigration proceedings are independent from criminal proceedings. In fact, the expulsion proceeding does not prejudice any criminal procedure regarding the offences committed by the foreign citizen (Article 134, Paragraph 2 of Law nr. 23/2007, dated July 4th).

According to Article 3 of Law nr. 27/2008, dated June 30th, asylum is granted to those persecuted or threatened due to their state functions in favour of democracy, social or national liberation, peace among the peoples and liberty and rights of the person in his or her nationality or residence state. Asylum can also be granted to those persecuted due to their race, religion, nationality or political views.

However, under Article 9 of this law, asylum is refused to those suspected of committing crimes against the peace, war crimes or crimes against humanity and crimes punishable by more than three years' imprisonment. It is also refused to those who practiced acts contrary to the objectives and principles of the United Nations.

B. *Immigration Proceedings and Torture*

The Portuguese Constitution expressly prohibits all evidence obtained by torture, coercion and offence to the physical or moral integrity of the person, in Article 32,

Paragraph 8. Therefore, no criminal procedure or any type of procedure can use evidence obtained in such ways.

The aforementioned Article 143 of Law nr. 23/2007, dated July 4th, has a ban on refoulement or deportation to any country where the foreign citizen can be persecuted by reasons that grant asylum under Portuguese law or where such a citizen can be a victim of torture, inhumane or degrading treatment in the meaning referred to in Article 3 of the European Convention on Human Rights.

VIII. ADMINISTRATIVE AND EXECUTIVE MEASURES

Administrative measures are not used as a form of anti-terrorism law alternative to criminal prosecutions or even as a supplement to criminal law.

The cases where administrative offenses are relevant are in certain specific situations, such as regarding the duties to which financial entities are obliged to fulfil – see Section VI – and in order to ensure, at a more efficient level, their compliance with those duties. In these situations, the law provides administrative offenses. As an example, in Law nr. 5/2002, dated January 11th (establishing measures to fight organized crime and economical and financial crime), if a financial institution does not comply with a bank secrecy breach when requested by the competent authorities in the sequence of a terrorism investigation, there is a fine between 750 euros and 750.000 euros. If the failure to comply is persistent or reiterated, this fine can be twice as much.

In the Law on the Fight Against Money Laundering and Terrorism Financing (Law nr. 25/2008, dated June 5th), it is also provided that a fine can, at a maximum, go up to 5.000.000 euros when a financial institution does not comply with the duties established in the context of this law.

On the other hand, under the Portuguese Constitution,[15] Portugal is based upon the rule of law and respect for and effective guarantees of the fundamental rights and freedoms (Article 2 of the Portuguese Constitution). As such, the right to liberty and security (Article 27 of the Portuguese Constitution) expressly states that no one can be deprived of liberty, except as a consequence of a judicial conviction for the practice of an act punished by law with imprisonment.[16] Therefore, no one can be controlled as a suspect of a crime – including that of terrorism – by administrative measures.

[15] Together with other international legal instruments, Portugal has ratified and is obliged to follow, such as the European Convention on Human Rights.

[16] It safeguards the case of detention in *flagrant delicto*.

IX. ROLE OF MILITARY AND EXTRA-TERRITORIAL COUNTER-TERRORISM ACTIVITIES

A. *Military Courts and Detention*

Although terrorism and terrorism-related crimes are prosecuted in ordinary criminal courts, the military plays a role in the fight against terrorism as far as prevention and surveillance are concerned.

The Armed Forces are responsible, according to Articles 273 and 275 of the Portuguese Constitution, for the assurance of the military defence of the Republic from any external threat including terrorism.

In this context, the Navy carries out several tasks of law enforcement and state authority at sea, including the surveillance of suspected vessels crossing Portuguese areas of interest. It is involved in combating multiple crimes such as illegal immigration and drug trafficking, but also terrorism.

The Air Force also keeps a continuous air surveillance system and a quick-reaction fighter aircraft at appropriate readiness state to defend civil aircraft against terrorist attacks. Additionally, procedures between the military air defence and the civil air traffic control have been developed and exercised in accordance with NATO and EUROCONTROL guidance.[17]

The National Guard (Guarda Nacional Republicana, GNR), as a military security force, also helps in the fight against terrorism, especially as a part of the aforementioned Antiterrorism Coordination Unit. However, GNR also contributes to the fight against terrorism through the regular patrols that gather information from the population.

The National Guard also has a Special Intervention Operations Group, which is a unit specially directed to violence and serious crime, including terrorism. It has an Intervention Unit (Article 44 of Law nr. 63/2007, dated November 6th) for the carrying out of missions of maintenance and re-establishment of public order and tactical intervention in situations of organized violence.

B. *The Extra-Territorial Treatment of Citizens Suspected of Terrorism*

There has been no litigation in Portugal with respect to the treatment of nationals detained by another state because of suspicions of their involvement in terrorism.

[17] Annual Exchange of Information on the Code of Conduct on Politico-Military Aspects of Security, Report of the Ministry of National Defence, April 2011.

C. *Extra-Territorial Terrorism Law Enforcement*

Portugal has adopted a posture of useful service to the community of nations, especially within the framework of the EU, NATO, the Organization for Security and Cooperation in Europe (OSCE) and the UN, participating in operations dedicated to the prevention of and the fight against terrorism.[18]

Outside national borders, security forces act in the context of the European Police Services (EUROPOL), and military forces act on the basis of international agreements thereto. As a rule, security forces have territorial competence limited to national territory.

If a suspect of terrorism is found in Portugal, he or she can be arrested by Portuguese security forces and face extradition to the demanding country, under Law nr. 144/99, dated August 31st, which is the law on international judicial cooperation in criminal matters[19] (general context), and under Law nr. 65/2003, dated August 23rd, which is the Law of the European Arrest Warrant[20] (European Union context), in order to face trial or serve the time to which he or she was sentenced.

However, both laws foresee a limit for the extradition or delivery of the suspect, namely if the charge or conviction implies the application of the death penalty. In the case of the law on international judicial cooperation in criminal matters, the limit is provided in Article 6, Paragraph 1, and in the case of the Law of the European Arrest Warrant it is provided in Article 11.

X. SECRECY AND TERRORISM

A. *Secrecy Claims and Secret Evidence*

State secrets are regulated by Organic Law nr. 2/2014, dated August 6th. Under Article 2, Paragraph1, state secrets comprise documents and information the knowledge of which by non-authorized people may put at risk fundamental interests of the state. Paragraph 2 defines those interests as national independence, the unity or integrity of the state, its internal or external security and its economical security, including energy resources and scientific potential.

There are, however, two important aspects relating to criminal procedure. In the first place, under Article 1, Paragraph 4 of the law, the regime of state secrets

[18] Annual Exchange of Information on the Code of Conduct on Politico-Military Aspects of Security, Report of the Ministry of National Defence, April 2011.

[19] As amended by Law nr. 104/2001, dated August 25th; Law nr. 48/2003, dated August 22nd; Law nr. 48/2007, dated August 29th; and Law nr. 115/2009, dated October 12th.

[20] In compliance of the EU Framework Decision nr. 2002/584/JAI, dated June 13th, of the Council.

is not applicable when, under the Constitution and the law, the achievement of its purposes can be accomplished with other less restrictive forms that limit access to the information. In the second place, information and evidence related to the perpetration of crimes against the security of the state must be reported under Article 7 to the competent authorities for their investigation.

All of those people who, due to their functions, have access to classified information are obliged to keep it secret (Article 10, Paragraphs 1 and 2 of the law).

B. *Secrecy in the Courtroom and Anonymous Witnesses*

Under Article 137 of the Portuguese Criminal Procedure Code, witnesses cannot be questioned on facts that constitute state secrets. If the witness invokes state secrets, the Minister of Justice must confirm its existence within thirty days. If this time frame elapses without this confirmation by the Minister of Justice, testimony must be given by the witness.

The Portuguese Criminal Procedure Code also foresees the protection of witnesses in Article 139, regulated in a special law. The Witness Protection Law[21] prescribes a special regime for witnesses who, for reasons of threat or menace to their life, health or liberty due to their contribution to the criminal procedure, have to be protected (Article 1, Paragraph 1 of the Law). Under Article 4 of this Law, the court can decide that the testimony can be given without disclosure of the witnesses' identity, through the use of screens or voice distortion. Exceptionally, and when serious grounds are at stake, the testimony can occur by teleconference, also with non-disclosure of the identity of the witness (Article 5). Criminal procedures are, however, usually public, The public can only be excluded from the inquiry stage, under request, according to Article 86 of the Portuguese Criminal Procedure Code.

XI. OTHER MATTERS

Although one cannot say that Portugal faces a terrorist threat, terrorism law has been developed with an eye to co-operating with other nations and international organizations have. These latter factors have had a very important influence in the development of Portugal's counter-terrorism law.

Article 7 of the Constitution of the Portuguese Republic, regarding the framework of international relations, states that Portugal shall be governed by the principles of the respect for human rights, the rights of peoples, equality between the states, the

[21] Law nr. 93/99, dated July 14, as amended by Law nr. 29/2008, dated July 4th, and Law nr. 42/2010, dated September 3rd.

peaceful settlement of international disputes, non-interference in the internal affairs of other states and cooperation with all other peoples.

Furthermore, under Article 8 of the Constitution, the rules and principles of international law form part of Portuguese law, and rules set out in international conventions or organizations to which Portugal is a party are directly applicable internally. As such, UN Security Council Resolution 1624 and European Union Regulations bind Portugal to the obligations set forth within the legal instruments.

As a consequence, Portuguese counter-terrorism law is strongly influenced by the relations with international organizations and, in particular, by the fact that Portugal is a member of the European Union.

Finally, another relevant aspect regards the extradition of nationals. In fact, according to Article 33, Paragraph 1, the expulsion of Portuguese citizens from Portuguese territory is forbidden. Nonetheless, under Paragraph 3 of this article, the extradition of a Portuguese citizen from national territory is admitted only in reciprocal conditions established in international conventions relating to terrorism and international organized criminality, as long as the legal framework of the demanding state gives assurances of a fair and equitable procedure.

XII. CONCLUSION

After the terrorist attacks of 9/11, a greater emphasis has been placed by international organizations such as the UN, European Union and NATO on combating terrorism. Some aspects of the effort have placed a greater emphasis on state powers, or, put another way, have required compromises between state powers to fight against terrorism and the legal principles on which Portugal is based. One example would be the European Arrest Warrant. Under Article 41, Paragraph 3, of the Portuguese Penal Code imprisonment cannot exceed twenty-five years. Accordingly, the law on international judicial cooperation in criminal matters (under Article 6, Paragraph 1, line f) states that cooperation is denied when it corresponds to a crime punished with life imprisonment. Nevertheless, this domestic restriction does not apply with respect to the European Arrest Warrant.[22] Another example is Law nr. 5/2002, regarding forfeiture of property in favour of the state, where there is a presumption contradicting the *in dubio pro reo* or presumption of innocence principle. Therefore, there should be due care in applying rules to combat terrorism that are not as demanding on the state as the ordinary guarantees of criminal procedure. However, counter-terrorism law in Portugal respects human rights.

[22] Even if, under Article 33, Paragraph 4, of the Portuguese Constitution extradition or delivery of persons to a demanding state where the crime is punished with life imprisonment can be carried out only if that state is a part of an international convention that Portugal is also part of and if the state offers assurances that such punishment shall not be applied.

The major influences of counter-terrorism law in Portugal have indeed been EU legal instruments and recommendations or international organizations, such as the UN Security Council. Given that Portugal is not a victim of a national terrorist threat – at least, not until the present date – and considering that it faces an international terrorist threat, one can state that counter-terrorism laws and the Portuguese legislative framework are adequate. They comply with Portugal's international obligations under international law. Moreover, at a European level, there is a strong legislative harmonization that allows for joint prevention and combating of terrorism.

12

Greece

Georgios Triantafyllou

I. INTRODUCTION

The origins of contemporary Greek terrorism date back to the 1970s. After the collapse of the seven years' colonel's dictatorship (1967–74), some leftist terrorist groups, mainly 17th November, conducted lethal and other violent attacks principally against U.S. diplomats and military officials serving in Greece. Former officials of the dictators' mechanism, Greek entrepreneurs and other prominent persons also figured among the targets of these groups. The attacks were followed by pronunciations sent by the terrorists to certain newspapers which published them in their first pages, thereby securing great publicity. Those pronunciations contained ideological arguments in favor of the attacks, trying to justify the choice of the victims and excuse the use of violence. The role of the United States in general or that of the particular victims during the colonels' dictatorship, the oppressive character of the capitalist state and such were some of the arguments. 17th November managed to stay active until 2001, when most of its members were arrested by the Greek police during a spectacular raid organized in collaboration with foreign police units and intelligence services.

Nevertheless, after a short period following the detection and dismemberment of 17th November and other minor groups such as ELA, terrorist activities resumed and occasionally occur today. A new generation of terrorists has attacked several targets, including embassies, banks, and more. However, it seems that these new groups are less sophisticated, their members being detected or arrested after a short period of action. Currently, several trials of terrorists are pending.

Public attitudes towards the action of 17th November and other terrorist groups have not always been unanimous. Despite the official condemnation expressed by the government and most political parties, a general social disapproval was initially far from clear. The need of special legislation for the repression of terrorism was a topic of fierce political debate among the leading actors of political life. Efforts to introduce counter-terrorism legislation met strong criticism focused on the risks it entailed for civil and political liberties.

Trying to find the main characteristics of the national counter-terrorism regime, one could underline the following:[1]

First, the lack of continuity. Due to different political approaches, specific legislation in that field was not always in force. Political changes always played their role, specifically until 2000. Thus the first anti-terrorism law, No 774/1978, passed by the right-wing party (New Democracy), had led a short life, as it was abolished by the Socialist Party (Pasok) in 1983. A new law passed again by New Democracy in 1990 (No 1916/1990) was abolished by the Socialists in 1993. Only in 2001 did counter-terrorism legislation overcome the obstacles of political antagonism and ideological conflicts, as it was the Socialist Party, which introduced a new article in the Penal Code (PC), namely Article 187A, aiming also at the repression of terrorism. From then on, counter-terrorism legislation has lost most of its political relevance.

Second, the lack of a clear and permanent distinction between terrorism and other forms of organized crime. In some of the aforementioned laws, terrorism was conceived as a form of organized crime, not needing a separate specific regulation. Still, other laws regulated terrorism exclusively, either as a form of organized crime or not. Thus the first law in this field, No 774/1978, "For the depression of terrorism and the protection of the democratic regime," contained no provisions regarding other forms of organized crime. This is also the case currently, with Article 187A of the Penal Code, punishing solely terrorism distinctly from other organized crime, which is punished under Article 187 PC. On the contrary, law No 1916/1991, under the title "For the protection of society from organized crime," although aiming principally at the repression of terrorism, punished generally the formation of and membership in any organized criminal group. Such was also the case with Article 187 A of the Penal Code, which in its initial formulation (2001–4) encompassed all criminal organizations. It was the provisions of that law that were applied by the judgments issued in the case of the terrorist organization 17th November.[2] Nevertheless, the effort to confront terrorism with the legislation on organized crime was regarded to be inefficient, given the differences between those types of criminality.[3]

1 See a detailed presentation of the Greece's anti-terrorist legislative developments by Andreas Banoutsos, "Mapping the Development of Anti-Terror Legislation in Greece in the aftermath of 9/11" in http://www. rimse.gr.

2 See three-member Court of Appeal of Athens, Dec. No, 699, 780, 809, 3244/2003, Poinika Chronika (Law Review) 2004, 993, five-member Court of Appeal of Athens, Dec. No 1149, 1199, 1265, 1299/2005 and Areios Pagos, Dec. No 1413/2010, Poinika Chronika 2010, pp 643ff.

3 See *Mylonopoulos*, "Law no 2928/2001 for the protection of citizens from criminal offences committed by criminal organizations," Poinikos Logos (Law Review) 2001, p. 794. *Mylonopoulos* stresses the fact that individual terrorists may not be covered by the legislation on criminal organizations.

II. TERRORIST AND LINKED OFFENCES: THE DEFINITION OF TERRORISM IN LAW

The first domestic law expressly referring to terrorism, Law No 714/1978, "For the repression of terrorism and the protection of the democratic regime," was marked by a serious deficit in respect of the description of the punishable acts. Although punishing the formation of and participation in "terrorist groups," as well as other acts linked to terrorist activities, the law lacked any definition of terrorism at all. The uncertainty over the meaning of the term "terrorism" raised wide criticism in literature. The criminal provisions of the law, so went the argument, violated the constitutional principle *nullum crimen nulla poena sine lege certa*, requiring the elements of any crime to be expressed in law in clear and unambiguous wording. Consequently, criminal courts should refrain from implementing the penal provisions of the law.[4]

The current domestic provision referring to terrorism, namely Article 187A PC,[5] added by Article 40 § 1 of Law No 3251/2004 and amended by Article 2 § 3 of Law No 3875/2010, has avoided the use of the term "terrorism" as an element of the pertinent offences. The new article reflects principally the provisions of the EU Council Framework Decision (F-D) of 13 June 2002 on combating terrorism (2002/475/JHA) as amended by the EU Council Framework Decision 2008/919/JHA of 28 November 2008 (EU F-D).[6] As a member state of the EU, Greece has transposed the provisions of the F-D into domestic law by adopting in principle the technique of the European legislator in the description of the crimes. Although the domestic provision is entitled "terrorist offences," this term is not used in the description of the punishable acts; nor is the term "terrorism." Instead of applying those vague terms, the law uses a series of objective and personal elements to describe terrorist offences as such or other several crimes related to them. Anyhow, vagueness and uncertainty in the description of the offences still remain.

4 See i.e. G.A. *Mangakis*, Interpretation of Law No 774/1978, "for the repression of terrorism and the protection of the democratic regime," *Nomiko Vima* (law review) 1980, 1018, *I. Manoledakis*, Elements of the crime of the formation of a terrorist group under the Law No 734/1978, *Armenopoulos* (law review) 1981, 360.

5 This provision has been incorporated in Chapter 6 of the Penal Code, punishing offences against public order.

6 In the recitals of the law (Second Part, I), additional international instruments, such as the European Convention on the Suppression of Terrorism of 27.1.1977 or the UN Security Council Resolution 1373, are referred to as sources of international obligations, which led, along with those emanating from the EU F-D, to the enactment of the new law. Nevertheless, the content of the law provisions proves that it was influenced mainly by the Framework Decision.

Article 187A § 1 punishes firstly *terrorist offences* as such, namely acts already punishable in law as felonies or misdemeanors, which are committed under specific circumstances, qualifying them as terrorist.

More specifically, *actus reus* of this crime is made of two elements. The first one is the commission of one of the crimes enumerated in a long list of felonies or misdemeanors already punishable in law.[7] Criminal responsibility does not require commission of the crime by a terrorist group or by a member of such a group. Even a sole terrorist may commit a terrorist offence. Part of the literature has expressed its objection to this provision, claiming that severe penal treatment of terrorism should be restricted solely to terrorist organizations. Individual terrorism is not dangerous enough to justify the severe sentences provided for in counter-terrorism law.[8]

The second element, which differentiates terrorism from other crimes, is commission of the former "in a way, or in an extent or under circumstances that may seriously damage a country[9] or an international organization." This additional qualifying element, which distinguishes a terrorist offence from the corresponding common offence, has raised criticism in terms of its vagueness and imprecise wording. "Countries" consist of a multiple of elements and properties, each one exposed to several possible damages. The law has failed in specifying the elements or properties of countries or international organizations that have to be damaged in order for a crime to be considered as terrorist. Thus, under present law, the possibility of damaging a country or international organization lies in a wide range of acts, which are not foreseeable by reading the law text. The notion of seriousness of damage is equally too vague, to counterbalance that uncertainty.[10]

[7] The list includes most of the offences prescribed in Article 1 of the EU – FD: Manslaughter, serious bodily injury, bodily injury resulting in death, kidnapping, kidnapping of minors, aggravated damage to other's property, causing fires in woods or elsewhere, causing floods or explosions, several acts causing a common danger, possession, supply etc. of weapons, nuclear or chemical weapons etc.

[8] See *Simeonidou – Kastanidou*, The terrorist offence: Provisions of Law No 3251/2004 and their significance for our penal system, Nomiko Vima 2005 [*Simeonidou – Kastanidou* 2005], 623. Contra *Mylonopoulos*, Report of the Scientific Council of the Parliament, Poinikos Logos 2004, [*Mylonopoulos* 2004], 870

[9] Under the concept of "country" fall all states recognized by Greece. See *M. Margaritis*, Penal Code, 3rd ed., 2014, Article 187A, No 22.

[10] See the critic expressed by *Mylonopoulos* (2004), 970, *Simeonidou – Kastanidou*, The law for the European warrant of arrest and the confrontation of terrorism, Poiniki Dikaiosyni (law review) 2004 [*Simeonidou – Kastanidou*, 2004], pp. 784 ff., *Simeonidou – Kastanidou* (2005), 624, *Kaiafa-Gbandi*, The Law for the European warrant of arrest and for terrorism, Poiniki Dikaiosyni 2004, [*Kaiafa-Gbandi*, 2004], p. 838, Kaiafa-Gbandi, Limits in the punishment of terrorism and challenges for a fair criminal law, Poinika Chronika 2005, [*Kaiafa-Gbandi* 2005], 873. *M. Margaritis*, op.cit., No 22, contends that the concept of serious damage may be duly specified by the judge in the course of law enforcement.

As to the *mens rea* of terrorist offences, the law requires that the offender acts with intention. Furthermore, the offence must be committed by him with the additional aim of either seriously intimidating a population or unduly compelling a public authority or an international organization to perform or abstain from performing any act, or seriously destabilizing or destroying the fundamental constitutional, political and economic structures of a country or an international organization.

The law (Article 187A § 2) *exempts* from the notion of terrorist offences the felony of high treason and some other offences linked to it, which are punished separately in other provisions of the Penal Code.[11] Those crimes may in no case be regarded as terrorist offences, even if the qualifying elements of Article 187A occur.[12] The reason seems to lie in the constitutional provisions on judicial competencies in cases of political crimes. Such cases are to be heard by mixed sworn courts, that is, courts composed by a majority of four lay judges and a minority of three professional judges (see Article 97 § 1 of the Constitution). However, under counter-terrorism legislation, defendants in terrorism cases are triable only by courts composed by professional judges (as discussed later in this chapter). In order to abide with the constitutional provisions, the law has exempted high treason and other similar crimes from the scope of terrorist offences.[13] The scope of the crime has thus been determined by procedural necessities.

The law also exempts from the scope of terrorist offences any exercise of fundamental rights and freedoms, namely the struggle to establish or restore democracy, as well as any action supporting freedom or aiming at the exercise of any fundamental human, political or trade union freedom or any right protected in the European Convention of Human Rights (Article 187A § 8). The ratio of this exemption lies in the provision of Article 2 § 2 of the EU F-D, which contains a similar clause in favor of the obligation of the member states to respect fundamental rights. Nevertheless, vague wording of the respective domestic provision has been a point of criticism of this exemption.[14]

What has become clear from the definition of terrorist offence in Article 187A § 1 PC is that this crime is just an aggravated form of other felonies or misdemeanors, committed under the particular circumstances described in Article 187A § 1 PC.

[11] High treason and other offences linked to it are punished in Articles 134–7 PC, included in the First Section of the Special Part of the Penal Code under the title "Offences against the regime."

[12] M. *Margaritis*, op.cit. No 25, holds that terrorist offences are ancillary to the felony of high treason, in the sense that the offender is to be punished for a terrorist offence only when he cannot be held liable for high treason. In my view, subsidiarity to high treason does not exist, given that high treason may in no case constitute a terrorist offence.

[13] See *Simeonidou – Kastanidou* (2004), 785.

[14] *Mylonopoulos* (2004), 970, *Simeonidou – Kastanidou* (2004), 781ff.

Consequently, the sanction provided in law for terrorist offences depends on the sanction provided in general for the felony or misdemeanor committed by the terrorist.[15] Thus for acts normally punished with life incarceration,[16] which is the heaviest sanction presently existing in Greece, the occurrence of the aggravating factor is of no significance with respect to the sentence to be imposed. Notwithstanding that, when a life sentence has been imposed for a terrorist offence, the aggravating instance leads indirectly to the prolongation of the perpetrator's detention. Release on bail in such a case may not be ordered unless the perpetrator has served a term of twenty-five years in prison, whereas for common offenders the term is only twenty years (Article 105 § 1 c PC). Prolongation of time limitation is also a consequence of the aggravating instance, since the most serious terrorist acts, those punishable with life incarceration, are limited to thirty years after their commission, instead of the twenty years provided for common offences.

When the act committed is normally punished with temporary incarceration, the terrorist offence is sentenced with incarceration of not less than ten years, whereas for acts normally punished with imprisonment,[17] the sentence provided for is imprisonment of not less than three years.

Apart from punishing terrorist offences as such, Greek law, in compliance with Article 2 § 2 of the EU F-D, which obliges EU member states to punish certain intentional acts related to terrorist groups, also punishes in Article 187A § 4 establishment or membership in terrorist organizations.[18] Both acts are punishable even if the offender aims at the commission of one terrorist offence only.[19]

15 Self-evidently, the perpetrators may not be punished for both crimes, namely the common offence of the list and its terrorist counterpart. The latter, as special offence, prevails over the general common offence See also the minutes of the Law No 3251/2004, II 2 and *Margaritis*, op.cit. No 25.

16 Incarceration is the principal custodial sentence foreseen in law for felonies (Article 18 PC). Life incarceration is prescribed exceptionally for the most serious felonies, such as homicide, whereas the usual sentence for felonies is "temporary incarceration," which normally may last from five to twenty years, except if otherwise provided in law (Article 52 PC).

17 Imprisonment is the principal custodial sentence provided for misdemeanors and normally may last from ten days to five years (Article 53 PC).

18 In order to define the concept of "terrorist organization," Article 187A § 4 PC has partly adopted the definition of "terrorist group" in Article 2.1. of the EU F-D. A terrorist organization is "a structured group of three or more persons, acting in concert over a period of time, to commit terrorist offences." The key difference of the two definitions is that the domestic one requires *action* over a period of time, whereas European law requires *establishment* over a period of time. According to the recitals of the law (Second Part, II, 5), the definition resembles to a great extent to the definition of criminal organizations in Article 187 § 1 PC. The latter, however, does not include the element of "action in concert," which is an element of terrorist organizations according to the definition of the EU F-D.

19 *Kaiafa-Gbandi*, 2005, 874, proposes that the offender be punishable only when he or she supports intentionally the permanent structure of an organization prepared to commit terrorist offences. Intention to commit one offence is not enough to hold the offender liable.

The sanction provided in law for this felony is incarceration for a term not exceeding ten years. The sentence is reduced[20] if the organization aims at the commission of misdemeanors only or if no crime has been committed at all, whereas it is aggravated in the case of manufacture, acquisition or possession of weapons, explosives, chemical or biological substances or other radioactive substances harmful to a human.

Directing a terrorist group stays as a separate crime, punished under paragraph 5 either with incarceration of not less than ten years or with a reduced sentence (two to twelve years) when the organization aims only at the commission of misdemeanors. Directing may be committed either in the form of a single leadership or by participating in a collective leading organ.[21]

Offences linked with terrorist activities are also punishable under Article 187A. Criminalization of the so-called linked offences is obligatory due to the provisions of Article 3 of the EU F-D. Thus terrorizing by seriously threatening to commit a terrorist offence is punished as a misdemeanor with imprisonment of not less than two years (187 A § 3).[22] The necessity of this provision is far from clear, since the same act falls within the scope of other long-standing provisions of the Penal Code, namely Article 190, punishing disruption of citizens' peace, that is, terrorizing by threatening that felonies or misdemeanors will be committed, or Article 333, punishing threats in general.

Although in principle attempt of terrorist offences as well as of other linked offences is punishable,[23] liability for attempt of terrorizing by seriously threatening is expressly excluded in § 3. Given that the acts described in § 3 may also be punished on the basis of the other provisions just mentioned, whereby punishment for attempt is still possible, the provision of § 3 is of little value.

Also, some other crimes, such as aggravated theft, robbery, forgery of public documents and extortion, are punished heavier (with temporary incarceration or imprisonment of not less than three years in the case of misdemeanors) when they are committed with a view to preparing a terrorist offence (Article 187A § 7). Aggravation, in this case, is not premised on the commission of the terrorist offence, so the intention alone is sufficient. These provisions can reasonably be criticized for disproportionately punishing mere intention.[24]

20 Pursuant to the rules of Article 83 PC, the sentence is reduced to imprisonment of not less than a year or incarceration for a term not exceeding six years.

21 *Margaritis*, op.cit. No 31.

22 This sentence is criticized as not proportional, because it may result in threatening being punished heavier than the attempt of a terrorist misdemeanor. See *Kaiafa-Gbandi*, 2005, p. 877.

23 Attempts of felonies and misdemeanors are punishable pursuant to the general provision of Article 42 § 1 PC.

24 *Simeonidou – Kastanidou* 2004, p. 782; *Kaiafa-Gbandi*, 2005, p. 876.

Another category of linked offences comprises some forms of obstruction of justice in the broadest sense of this term. These are acts directed against public officials, namely the use or threat of violence or the bribery of judges, investigators, judicial officials, witnesses, forensic experts and translators, forestalling the detection, prosecution or punishment of establishment or membership in a terrorist organization (Article 187A § 8 in connection with Article 187 § 4 PC). The sanctions prescribed in law are incarceration for a term not exceeding ten years and a fine of 100.00 to 500.000 euros. Should the act forestall also the detection, prosecution or punishment of a terrorist offence, sanctions are aggravated to temporary incarceration and a fine of 100.000 to 1.000.000 euros.

Article 187 A § 6 punishes as a felony (with incarceration for a term not exceeding ten years) the supply of essential information in order to help a terrorist organization or a sole terrorist in committing one of the felonies listed in the first paragraph of the article. The provision aims at punishing *extranei*, that is, persons who are not members of a terrorist organization, with the sentence provided for the latter. Thus distinguishing the acts of members from the supportive action of third persons has no value in practice.[25] The law requires that the act be committed with knowledge of the fact that the information will be used in the future. Supply of information is also punishable if no terrorist offence is committed at all. In this case, the crime in view is just an attempt to participate in a terrorist offence. It is for that reason that the provision raises doubts in terms of its compatibility with the constitutional principle of proportionality. Attempt of participation in a terrorist offence incurs the same sanction as the participation in a terrorist organization.[26]

A. *Participation*

Pursuant to the provisions of the General Part of the Penal Code, punishable participation in crime may appear in three forms, namely instigation, direct aiding and indirect aiding, the first two of these forms being punishable with the sanction provided for the principal, while indirect aiding is punishable with a reduced sentence. Instigation is any act causing to the principal the decision to commit the illicit act (Article 46 § 1 a PC). Direct aiding, punished in Article 46 § 1 b PC, is the provision of aid during and in the commission of the illicit act, while any other aid to the principal falls within the scope of indirect aiding (Article 47).

[25] *Kaiafa-Gbandi*, 2005, 877.

[26] See *Kaiafa-Gbandi*, 2004, p. 838 with regard to the initial version of this article.

B. *Universal Jurisdiction*

National anti-terrorism law applies not only to offences committed in Greece or by Greek citizens abroad, since terrorist offences have been subjected to the jurisdiction of Greek authorities even if they are committed by foreign citizens abroad (see Article 8 a PC). Jurisdiction of Greek authorities covers all crimes prescribed in Article 187A PC, namely not only terrorist offences and crimes relating to terrorist organizations, but also all other types of linked offences, including terrorism financing.

Combined with the principle of legality of prosecutions,[27] universal jurisdiction obliges Greek authorities to investigate, arrest, prosecute and commit to trial any offender of an act prescribed in Article 187A PC that was committed abroad when he or she enters Greek territory. Courts are also obliged to hear all pertinent cases of international or foreign terrorism, applying Article 187A PC. The side effect of universal jurisdiction consists of the restriction on the obligation to extradite or surrender to third states persons suspected of terrorist offences. Exercise of criminal jurisdiction prevails over the obligation to extradite.

The scope and limits of the jurisdiction established in Article 8a PC are obscure. The wording of the provision supports the view that terrorism is conceived as an international crime. Greek jurisdiction seems to be established even if Greece suffers no harm by a terrorist offence or a terrorist organization. Acts committed all over the world might be punished in Greece if they are found to be contrary to Article 187A PC. Legislation of the country where the act has been committed is of no relevance, since double criminality is not a condition for punishment in Greece. Such an extension of domestic jurisdiction to acts committed abroad raises suspicions of legal paternalism.[28]

III. TREATMENT OF COLLABORATORS OF JUSTICE

Article 187 B PC, referring both to terrorist and other criminal organizations, provides a favorable treatment for dissociating terrorists who decide to collaborate with the authorities. The ratio of the pertinent provisions lies in the effective suppression of criminal organizations. It is for that reason that mere collaboration does not suffice to secure a favorable treatment. An actual damage to the existence or the action of a terrorist organization is also required. In principle, dissociating terrorists are divided

[27] Legality of prosecutions, as opposed to the so-called opportunity principle, is enshrined in Articles 43 § 1 and 47 § 1 CCP. It means that prosecution of crimes falling within domestic jurisdiction is obligatory. Prosecutors are obliged to prosecute when sufficient indices exist that an offence has been committed.

[28] See *Mylonopoulos* 2004, 970.

by law into those who have already committed a terrorist offence and those who have not. Taking into consideration that distinction, paragraph 1 provides that the court shall refrain from imposing a sentence to members of terrorist organizations who, by procuring information for the authorities, contribute either to the prevention of one of the offences already planned or to the dismemberment of the organization. For dissociating members of the organization who have already committed a terrorist offence, contribution to the same goals features as a mitigating factor leading to the reduction of sentence. However, in exceptional circumstances, the court, after taking into consideration all relevant factors of the case, may suspend execution of the imposed sanction for a period of three to ten years. When the suspension period ends, the sanction is not executable (§ 2).

IV. ADMINISTRATIVE SANCTIONS FOR LEGAL PERSONS

Article 7 of the EU F-D obliges member states to take the necessary measures to ensure that legal persons can be held liable for offences referred to in Articles 1 to 4 of the F-D. The F-D does not require that the liability of legal persons be criminal, thus permitting member states, which traditionally acknowledge criminal liability of physical persons only, to impose administrative sanctions.

Greece has opted for administrative sanctions to be imposed in the event of crimes committed by legal persons' employees in the course of exercise of their duties. More specifically, Article 41 § 1 of Law No 3251/2004, as amended by Law No 3875/2010, foresees administrative sanctions to be imposed on legal persons in the event of one of the aforementioned crimes having been committed through, to the benefit of or on behalf of the legal person. The crime must have been committed by anyone acting either individually or as part of an organ of the legal person, who has a leading position, based on one of the following

- A power of representation of the legal person
- An authority to take decisions on behalf of the legal person
- An authority to exercise control within the legal person

The sanctions foreseen are an administrative fine of 50.000–5.000.000 euros and optionally one or more of the following penalties: (a) permanent or temporary revocation or suspension of the authorization to practice a business activity; (b) disqualification from the practice of specific commercial activities or from the establishment of branches or the increase of share capital of a company; or (c) temporary or permanent exclusion from entitlement to public benefits, aids or subsidies and from the assignment of works and services, procurements, advertisement or invitations to tender by the state and legal persons of the public sector.

Furthermore, Article 41 § 2 establishes vicarious liability of the legal person when the lack of supervision or control by a person referred to in paragraph 1 has made possible the commission of any of the offences referred to in Articles 187A PC through, for the benefit of or on behalf of that legal person by a person holding an inferior position.

Liability of legal persons under Article 41 § 1 and 2 does not exclude criminal, civil and disciplinary liability of natural persons referred to therein.

V. PROCEDURAL ISSUES

A. *Investigative Powers*

Investigation of terrorist and other related offences is conducted by the investigating agents (occasionally under the supervision of the public prosecutor) or/and the investigating magistrate according to the general rules of the Code of Criminal Procedure (CCP). Investigating agents act either under the supervision of the prosecutor or, in case of urgency, on their own initiative.

Proactive collection of information and criminal investigation in terrorism cases fall into the competency of special police agents. Pursuant to Article 29 of Presidential Decree No 14/2001, a special part of the Greek police, known also as "the counter-terrorism unit," was set up, having competency for the exercise of these tasks. Agents of this unit may be ordered by the public prosecutors to exercise the investigation powers provided in the CCP.

Police powers for detention of the accused are limited. As prescribed in the Constitution (Article 6 § 1), police may arrest defendants either upon a judicial arrest warrant or, in the absence of a warrant, within strict time limits, that is, not later than the end of the day following its commission. Arrested persons must be produced as soon as possible to the public prosecutor, who has to defer the case either to an investigating magistrate or to the competent court. In any case, arrested persons may stay under detention more than three days, which may be prolonged by the investigating magistrate for two more days. Detention after the arrest is possible only under of a pre-trial detention order issued by the investigating magistrate or by a court judgment convicting the accused.

When police investigation has collected evidence sufficient to support prosecutions, the case, if a felony, is deferred by the public prosecutor to the investigative magistrate, who has the power for further investigation. That magistrate may also order the pre-trial detention of the accused. The detention may not exceed twelve or eighteen months, depending on the sentence foreseen in law for the investigated acts. In the event of misdemeanors, the defendant is directly committed to trial by the prosecutor, without an investigation by the investigating magistrate.

Powers of investigation include investigative acts available in all criminal proceedings. The Code of Criminal Procedure provides nonetheless for some additional investigative techniques, known as "special investigative acts," which may be used during the investigation of terrorist offences. These acts are listed in Article 253A § 1 CCP, which was added by the Law No 2928/2001, initially regulating only the pre-trial investigation of criminal organizations. Later, by the law 3251/2004, which criminalized terrorist offences and terrorist organizations as separate crimes, the same investigative powers were extended to investigations regarding terrorism. Many of these special investigative acts were already known and in special procedural legislation as common investigation techniques available for the detection of certain categories of crimes. Since 2001, these techniques, along with new ones, were regulated in the new Article 253 A CPP.

These special investigative acts are

- Infiltration
- Controlled deliveries
- Telecommunications surveillance
- Recording of activities or other events, occurring outside one's home, by technical devices
- Combination of personal data

Pursuant to Article 253A § 2 CCP, use of these acts is permitted only when there are strong indications that one of the terrorist crimes of Article 187A PC has been committed, detection of which would otherwise be impossible or extremely difficult. It is permitted only upon a reasoned verdict by the competent chamber of accusations of the Court of Appeal, within the time limits set by the Court (Article 253A § 3). Evidence collected by a special investigative act may be used in other proceedings only if the Chamber of Accusations so decides (Article 253A § 4).

After the end of the judicial investigation, the file is submitted to the Chamber of Accusations of the Court of Appeal. The latter decides whether the defendant will be committed to trial or absolved of the accusation (Article 42 § B of Law No 3251/2004).[29]

B. *Trial in Terrorism Cases*

Terrorism cases are heard by ordinary criminal courts. Felonies are tried in the first instance by the three-member Court of Appeal and in the second instance by the

[29] Competency of the Chamber of Accusations of the Court of Appeal is reserved only for serious crimes. Usually this competency is assigned to the public prosecutor or to the Chamber of Accusations of the court of first instance.

five-member Court of Appeal. Revisions are heard by the Supreme Court (Areios Pagos). Given that usually membership in a terrorist organization is a felony, the bulk of terrorist cases are heard by the aforementioned Courts of Appeal. Misdemeanors are heard in first instance either by the single-member or by the three-member Court for Misdemeanors. All these courts are composed by ordinary judges.

Qualification of a crime as a terrorist offence may cause a shift of competency. This is the case not only when a misdemeanor, usually tried by a misdemeanor court, is committed under circumstances that render it a terrorist offence. It is also the case with some felonies, such as homicide, that normally are tried by mixed sworn courts, composed by seven-member courts in which four of the members are lay judges.

This shift in competence had already been adopted by the Law No 2928/2001, which punished formation and membership in a criminal organization. During the three years following its enactment, that law applied also to terrorist organizations in so far as no special legislation on them was in force. Thus offences committed by those organizations were heard by ordinary judges and not by mixed sworn courts. Abolition of mixed courts in terrorist cases seems reasonable given that usually terrorist cases last too long for a lay judge to be in the position to abstain from his normal professional duties. Furthermore, complicated issues raised in terrorism cases require experienced and skillful judges.[30]

Substitution of sworn courts by courts composed by professional judges has raised the problem of its compliance with Article 97 § 1 of the Constitution. The latter establishes mixed sworn courts' competency for political crimes. In the 17th November case, defendants have objected that the offences attributed to them were political crimes, thus falling under the competency of mixed sworn courts. The three-member Court of Appeal of Athens dismissed the defendants' objection, adopting the "objective theory," which regards as political crimes only those that directly attack the state and aim either to subvert or change the established political order. Political motivation, such as the defendants might have had, did not suffice for their offence to be regarded as political.[31]

Presentation and examination of evidence in terrorist cases follow in principle the general rules of the CCP. Exclusionary rules, such as the prohibition of torture or

[30] See Athens Court of Appeal 699, 780, 809, 3244/2003, Poinika Chronika 2004, pp. 999ff. This judgment was issued in the case of the terrorist organization 17th November before the entry into force of the special provisions for terrorist offences (Article 187A PC). Nevertheless, the problem addressed by the Court arises equally under the contemporary regime. The Court dismissed defendants' objection that submission of criminal organizations' cases in the competency of the Court of Appeal was arbitrary and violated the principle of equality. In the Court's view, the legislative decision on this issue was reasonable given the complexity of these cases and the dangerousness of the offenders.

[31] See Athens Court of Appeal, Dec. No 699, 780, 809, 3244/2003, op.cit.

exclusion of evidence obtained by criminal offences (Article 177 § 2 CCP), apply also to terrorist cases. Thus evidence obtained by torture or other degrading treatment is not admissible. Application of that exclusionary rule in terrorist cases was confirmed by the Athens Court of Appeal in the 17th November case. Notwithstanding that, the Court dismissed as not proven several defendants' motions to suppress confessions on the ground that they had been the result of torture.[32]

A difference from other trials in the presentation of evidence may arise in regard with the witness examination (No 2928/2001, Article 9 applying also in terrorist cases). Provisions on the protection of witnesses allow also preservation of their anonymity in the pre-trial phase, as well as their examination in court under a false name (see also the following subsection). Records of their testimony may be anonymous when the public prosecutor so decides. During the trial, anonymous witnesses may be summoned under their false name. Trying to strike a fair balance between witness protection and fair trial rights, the law prohibits conviction based solely on anonymous witnesses' testimonies. However, that evidence rule is of little value, as it is hardly conceivable that the court will not rely on any other corroborative evidence to convict.

Nevertheless, when either the prosecutor, the victim or the defendant request that it do so, the court has to order the disclosure of witness's identity. Thus the general procedural rules on witness cross-examination apply again and exclude any possibility of convictions based on anonymous witnesses' testimonies.

C. *Protection of Witnesses*

Law No 3251/2004 allows in Article 42 § 6 the adoption and implementation of measures aiming at the protection of witnesses in terrorism cases against acts of revenge or intimidation. For the procedure to be followed and the specific measures to be adopted, this paragraph refers to Article 10 of Law No 2928.2001, allowing protection measures in the frame of organized crime cases. Adoption of these measures requires the consent of the witness and may not restrict his or her freedom beyond the necessary degree. The measures' implementation is terminated upon the witness's written request or when he or she does not collaborate for their success. The measures that may adopted are the following (see Law No 2928/2001, Article 10 § 2):

- Guarding with adequately trained police personnel, as well as the following measures aiming at the preservation of witness's anonymity
- Audio or audiovisual recording of statements made by witnesses during the pre-trial investigation

[32] Athens Court of Appeal, Dec. No 699, 780, 809, 3244/2003, op.cit. pp. 1006ff.

- Anonymous statements records, that is, records not including witnesses' name, birthplace and other identity data[33]
- Change of the identity personal details, as well as transfer or secondment of civil servants to new posts

Notwithstanding the need for witness protection in the pre-trial stage, the law respects fair trial rights during the trial phase, thereby enabling defendants to avoid convictions based on anonymous statements. Pursuant to Article 10 § 3 of Law No 2928/2001, anonymous witnesses are summoned to the court under their false name used in their pre-trial statement. Nonetheless, their identity is disclosed upon the defendant's, victim's or the public prosecutor's request. Disclosure may also be ordered by the court *ex proprio motu*. In any event, conviction may not be based solely on anonymous statements (Article 42 § 6 of Law No 3251/2004 referring to Article 9 § 4 of Law No 2928/2001).

D. *Protection of Judges*

In case of majority judgments, the names of the majority and dissenting judges are not revealed (Article. 42 § 6 of Law No 3251/2004). This rule, which applies also in organized crime cases, inserts an exception to the general rule that the names of the dissenting judges must be stated in the decision. The exception, which also has a constitutional basis (see Const., Article 93 § 3) aims at the protection of the judges who have voted for defendant's guilt against acts of revenge.

VI. LISTING OF TERRORIST GROUPS AND INDIVIDUALS

Listing of terrorist groups and individuals is regulated in Law No 3691/2008 "for the combating of money laundering and terrorism financing." Article 49 A § 1 of this law, as amended by law No3932/2011, stipulates that Unit B[34] of the Greek Financial Intelligence Unit (FIU) drafts a list of terrorists, terrorist groups and other persons related thereto. This list serves exclusively for the repression of terrorism financing (discussed later in this chapter). This is clearly stipulated in paragraph 5 of the article, which forbids the use of information supplied or exchanged with the FIU for any other purpose save for the imposition of financial sanctions to terrorists.

The list of Article 49A § 1 has no other probative value in regard with criminal proceedings in terrorism cases. There is not any provision to the effect that persons

[33] Anonymous statements include statements given under a false name.

[34] The Greek FIU consists of three units: Unit A, for the investigation of financial information, Unit B, for pecuniary sanctions on suspects for terrorism and Unit C for the review of statements of financial status.

or other entities included therein should be regarded as terrorists in criminal proceedings. Such a value of the FIU's list would violate the aforementioned exclusionary rule set by Article 49A § 5. It would also contravene the presumption of innocence enshrined in Article 6 § 2 of the European Convention for the Protection of Human Rights (ECHR). Legal presumptions to the detriment of the accused are hardly acceptable under that Convention.

VII. SUPPRESSION OF TERRORISM FINANCING

Terrorism financing is one of the felonies punished by Greek law as a crime related to terrorism. Article 187A § 6 punishes with incarceration for a term not exceeding ten years any person who supplies assets, whether tangible or intangible, movable or immovable; financial instruments of every kind, however acquired, either to a terrorist organization or to a sole terrorist or for the establishment of a terrorist organization or to help someone become terrorist; or collects or manages funds in favor of the aforementioned persons or organizations, whether a terrorist offence has been committed or not. Since commission of a terrorist offence is not needed, terrorism financing is not necessarily a form of participation in crime.[35] The latter presupposes the commission of the principal criminal act either in its complete form or in the form of an attempt.

By enacting this offence, Greece has fulfilled its international obligations stemming from international law, mainly from the International Convention for the Suppression of the Financing of Terrorism ratified by the Law No 3024/2002. However, enforcement of this provision to date, if there has been any at all, is poor given the fact that since its entry into force, there seems to be no conviction based on it.

Apart from that penal provision on terrorism financing, there exists an *administrative regime* aiming to its suppression. As already stated, the mandate of the FIU also covers the repression of that financing. Its main activity in that field lies in the tracing and confiscation of assets related to terrorist activities. For that purpose, the FIU must detect any person or entity domiciled in Greece or possessing assets therein, who has committed, is attempting to commit or participate or is any means facilitating commission of terrorist offences (Article 49A § 1). Detection of those persons is based on information supplied by the Ministry of Home Affairs, prosecutorial authorities and other judicial authorities. The information supplied by all these authorities consists of evidence collected by controls of these persons and

[35] Contra *Margaritis*, op.cit. No 32, who regards the acts described in Article 187A § 6 PC as forms of participation promoted to new crimes.

information on prosecutions or convictions for terrorist offences or for financing of terrorists or terrorist organizations.

The provisions on listing have already been applied with regard to former 17 November members, who have already been convicted for membership in that organization. In its freezing decisions, the Hellenic FIU has accepted that the organization still exists, its former members still possessing their member capacity even though they have been convicted or even released on bail after serving part of their sentence. Areios Pagos has confirmed those decisions dismissing the appeals filed thereof by interested persons.[36]

Registration of a person or entity in the terrorist list leads to the search for assets belonging to that person or entity. If the FIU has traced such assets, it has to freeze them by issuing a freezing decision (Article 49A § 3). The FIU doesn't have the power to confiscate frozen assets. As the law does not determine the duration of the freezing, the question arises, what is the real aim of this freezing? In some cases, listing of terrorists could serve as a preliminary measure for the preservation of assets liable to criminal confiscation. The latter may be imposed by a court only after conviction for a terrorist offence. However, the main reason for the freezing, as expressed in case law, lies in the prevention of assets being available for terrorist activities. Areios Pagos, in line with the FIU, ascribes to it a rather proactive character, lying in the prevention of terrorism financing. In that sense, freezing is considered by Areios Pagos as a measure similar to security measures.[37] This qualification allows, in Areios Pagos' view, the use of freezing decisions even in cases pending before the enactment of the pertinent freezing provisions.[38]

Although not expressly provided in law, Areios Pagos rightly requires that the assets to be frozen should be able to contribute to terrorism financing. In the lack of such evidence, the measure has to be annulled.[39]

Individuals or entities may challenge their registration in the FIU list. For that reason, the registered person has to be notified either of the individual's or the entity's registration or of the decision to freeze the assets. It follows that a person registered in a list may not have knowledge thereof, as long as his or her assets have not been frozen.

36 See Areios Pagos, Dec. No 835/2012 (in chamber), Poiniki Dikaiosyni 2013, pp. 390ff.

37 Security measures are criminal sanctions presupposing the commission of an illicit criminal act. In contrast to sentences, which aim at the punishment of the offender, security measures aim at the protection of the society. Given their non-punitive character, security measures are not liable to the restrictions of the legality principle, mainly to the prohibition of retroactive enforcement of penal laws (see Article 4 § 1 PC).

38 See Areios Pagos, Dec. No 835/2012 (in chamber), Poiniki Dikaiosyni 2013, pp 390ff.

39 See Areios Pagos, Dec. No 835/2012 op.cit, which annulled a freezing of real property, due to lack of any such evidence.

Registered persons or entities may appeal either from the registration or from the freezing decision or both of them. At a first stage, they have to apply to the FIU seeking the revocation of the registration decision. The FIU may also revoke its decision *ex proprio motu* or upon the application of any third interested person (Article 49A § 8).

When the application for the revocation of a registration or freezing decision has not been granted by the FIU, the applicant has the right of appeal to the Supreme Court seeking annulment of the freezing decision (Article 49A § 9). The applicant is summoned and heard before the court reaches its verdict (Article 49A § 10).

Interested persons may also apply for the release of assets necessary to cover general expenses of life, maintenance or functioning (when a legal person is concerned), legal costs and other costs for the maintenance of frozen assets. If their application is dismissed, they may appeal to the administrative courts (Article 49A § 11).

Apart from the list drafted originally by the FIU, the latter keeps also lists of persons or entities based on information transmitted by international organizations. Pursuant to Article 49 § 1 of the Law No 3691/2008, when assets of a person are frozen by resolutions of the Security Council of the UN or regulations and decisions of the EU, the FIU registers that person or entity in separate lists that it keeps. The FIU executes the resolutions, regulations and decisions of the international organizations by freezing the assets of listed persons. Interested persons may appeal to the administrative courts against those freezing orders only on the ground of lack of the legal requirements for freezing (Article 49 § 1 e). It follows that interested person may not challenge the international instrument itself.

VIII. PROTECTION OF VICTIMS

Protection of terrorism victims consists mainly of the financial support granted to them by the state and social security funds. Laws dating back to the 1990s (see Law No 1897/1990) provide for pension and other relief compensation measures to public officials, journalists, union leaders and so on who have been personally injured or suffered damage by a terrorist act directed against them. In the event of lethal attacks against them, those rights are granted to their relatives.

IX. CONCLUSION

Counter-terrorism law in its present form has had only a short life in Greece. It has been shaped on the model of the EU Framework Decision of 13 June 2002, on combating terrorism, as the latter has been amended in 2008. Influence of other universal legal instruments, such as the International Convention for the

Suppression of the Financing of Terrorism, can also be traced, particularly in the field of terrorism financing.

Regarding the substantive law, there are two main deficiencies: first, the vagueness of terms used in the description of the elements of terrorist and linked offences; and second, the disproportionate sanctions foreseen for some of offences.

The short and rare implementation of these criminal provisions in practice does not allow yet a general conclusion concerning their efficacy. Their impact on human rights protection is equally unclear. This is also the case as far as the procedural aspects of the counter-terrorism legislation are concerned. Courts and other judicial authorities will face a challenge of striking a fair balance between efficient enforcement and human rights protection.

13

Croatia

Marissabell Škorić

I. INTRODUCTION

The Republic of Croatia has an integrated approach to the prevention and suppression of terrorism. The legal framework against terrorism includes relevant international and regional documents and provisions of national legislation. At the international level, the Republic of Croatia is an active member of the Global Anti-Terrorism Coalition. As regards the international agreements and conventions concerning the fight against terrorism, the Republic of Croatia has ratified thirteen UN counter-terrorism conventions and protocols:

- Convention on Offences and Certain Other Acts Committed On Board Aircraft (1963)
- Convention for the Suppression of Unlawful Seizure of Aircraft (1970)
- Convention for the Suppression of Unlawful Acts Against the Safety of Civil Aviation (1971)
- Convention on the Prevention and Punishment of Crimes Against Internationally Protected Persons (1973)
- International Convention Against the Taking of Hostages (1979)
- Convention on the Physical Protection of Nuclear Material (1980)
- Convention for the Suppression of Unlawful Acts Against the Safety of Maritime Navigation (1988)
- Protocol for the Suppression of Unlawful Acts of Violence at Airports Serving International Civil Aviation (1988)
- Protocol for the Suppression of Unlawful Acts Against the Safety of Fixed Platforms Located on the Continental Shelf (1988)
- Convention on the Marking of Plastic Explosives for the Purpose of Detection (1991)
- International Convention for the Suppression of Terrorist Bombings (1997)

- International Convention for the Suppression of the Financing of Terrorism (1999)
- International Convention for the Suppression of Acts of Nuclear Terrorism (2005)

At the regional level, Croatia had ratified anti-terrorism conventions, viz. the Council of Europe Convention on the Suppression of Terrorism (1977) with Protocol (2003), the Council of Europe Convention on the Prevention of Terrorism (2005) and the Council of Europe Convention on Laundering, Search, Seizure and Confiscation of the Proceeds from Crime and on the Financing of Terrorism (2008). In the process of alignment of Croatian legislation with the legal norms of the European Union, Croatia has achieved complete harmonization with the Framework Council Decision on Combating Terrorism of June 2002, the Framework Decision on the European Arrest Warrant and other documents of EU's counter-terrorism *acquis*.[1]

At the national level, Croatia uses wide-ranging legislation in order to govern different aspects of the suppression of terrorism. A special place among the anti-terrorist measures belongs to the norms of national criminal law. The Criminal Code sets out the offences that criminalize various forms of terrorism.[2] According to the Criminal Procedure Act, the so-called investigative measures can be applied in all cases of criminal offences related to terrorism.[3] The Act on the Responsibility of Legal Persons for Criminal Offences proscribes criminal liability of legal persons.[4] Moreover, the Act on Proceedings for the Confiscation of Pecuniary Benefit Resulting from Criminal Offences and Misdemeanours has a preventive effect on all forms of organized crime, including terrorist activities.[5]

In 2001, after the events of 11 September, the Croatian government established an Interagency Working Group for Monitoring Implementation of UN Security Resolution 1373 and had took steps to harmonize its legislation with the requirements of Resolution 1373. The Republic of Croatia continued to support actions undertaken pursuant to relevant resolutions of the Security Council, with the aim of suppressing and preventing terrorism. At the beginning of 2002,

1 For a detailed analysis of the European counter-terrorism legal framework, see Wahl, Thomas, The European Union as an Actor in the Fight Against Terrorism, in Wade M. and Maljević A. (eds.), *A War on Terror? The European Stance on a New Threat, Changing Laws and Human Rights Implications* (London, Springer, 2010) pp 107–70. For relationship between international and European legal frameworks in the fight against terrorism, see Pedić, Žana, Odnos međunarodnog i europskog pravnog okvira za suzbijanje terorizma (2012) 1 Zagrebačka pravna revija, pp 57–80.

2 Criminal Code, Official Gazette 125/11, 144/12.

3 Criminal Procedure Act, Official Gazette 152/08, 76/09, 80/11, 121/11, 91/12, 143/12, 56/13, 145/13.

4 Act on the Responsibility of Legal Persons for the Criminal Offences, Official Gazette 151/03, 110/07, 45/11, 143/12.

5 Act on Proceedings for the Confiscation of Pecuniary Benefit Resulting from Criminal Offences and Misdemeanours, Official Gazette 145/10.

the Croatian Parliament adopted the National Security Strategy.[6] The National Strategy highlights the prevention and suppression of terrorism and the active contribution of the Republic of Croatia to the anti-terrorist coalition as one of the Republic's national security priorities. Most importantly, on November 2008 the government of the Republic of Croatia introduced another strategic document, viz. National Strategy for the Prevention and Suppression of Terrorism, with the aim of establishing the systemic prerequisites for the fight against terrorism.[7] In order to implement this strategy, Croatia in 2011 adopted the Action Plan on Prevention and Suppression of Terrorism, which defines in detail roles of all relevant national institutions in the prevention and suppression of terrorism and contains specific operational protocols and procedures.[8] During the preparation of Action Plan, the experiences of the Republic of Croatia as regards terrorism were taken into account. Namely, Croatian experiences regarding terrorism show that its interests and goals were targets of terrorist activity. The brutal murder of twelve employees of Hidroelektra Company in December 1993 in Algeria, which was performed by the Algerian Armed Islamic Group (al-Jama'ah al-Islamiyah al-Musallaha) is considered the first case of terrorism. During and after the Homeland War (1991–5), many acts that were part of the aggression against the Republic of Croatia were introduced as terrorist acts.[9] Finally, a typical act of terrorism occurred in front of the police headquarters in Rijeka in 1995. The car-bomb attack was perpetrated by the Egyptian Islamic Group (al-Gama'al-Islamiyya) as revenge after the Croatian police had captured and extradited the group's leader to the United States. On that occasion, twenty-nine people were injured, whereas the attacker was killed.[10]

II. THE DEFINITION OF TERRORISM

Longstanding efforts of the United Nations to achieve agreement on the definition of terrorism have fallen short of success.[11] Although some UN documents touch

[6] National Security Strategy of the Republic of Croatia, Official Gazette 32/02. See more in Perešin, Anita, Croatian Counter-Terrorism Strategy: Challenges, Prevention and Response System, Research Institute for European and American Studies, no. 160, available at http://www.rieas.gr/images/rieas160.pdf, Committee of Experts on Terrorism (CODEXTER), Profiles on Counter-Terrorist Capacity, Croatia, November 2011, pp 1-3, available at http://www.coe.int/t/dlapil/codexter/Source/country_profiles/CODEXTER_Profiles_2011_Croatia_EN.pdf.

[7] National Strategy for the Prevention and Suppression of Terrorism, Official Gazette 139/08.

[8] Action Plan on Prevention and Suppression of Terrorism, Official Gazette 136/12.

[9] The Republic of Croatia gained its independence on 25 June 1991 in the process of the dissolution of the former Yugoslavia. Shortly after this particular proclamation, the armed conflict had begun. In the light of the warfare between Croatia and the former Yugoslav army, some terrorist acts had been committed as well.

[10] Action Plan on Prevention and Suppression of Terrorism, p 4.

[11] On the many failed attempts by the United Nations to define and criminalize terrorism, see Saul, Ben, *Defining Terrorism in International Law* (Oxford, Oxford University Press, 2006).

upon the definition of terrorism,[12] an internationally agreed-upon definition of terrorism has not been achieved. What was not achieved at the international level was achieved at the regional level. The most important legal framework for the definition of terrorism in the European Union is the Framework Decision of 13 June 2002 on combating terrorism.[13] The Framework Decision distinguishes three types of offences: terrorist offences (art 1), offences relating to a terrorist group (art 2) and offences linked to terrorist activities (art 3). According to the Framework Decision, inciting, aiding or abetting and attempting to commit one of the offences cited in art 1 to 3 must be criminalized in the national legislation of member states.

The Framework Decision obliges all European Union member states to establish in their legal systems minimum rules as regards the constituent elements of terrorism. It also sets out the minimum level of penal sanction for criminal offences. According to art 1 of the Framework Decision, the criminal offence consists of three elements. Firstly, the definition includes offences such as attacks upon a person's life that may cause death; attacks upon the physical integrity of a person; kidnapping or hostage taking; seizure of aircraft or ships; manufacture, possession, acquisition, transport, supply or use of weapons, explosives or nuclear, biological or chemical weapons, as well as research into and development of biological and chemical weapons, and more. Secondly, the aforementioned offences must have the potential to seriously damage a country or an international organization. Finally, an act is considered a terrorist offence when it is committed intentionally and with the aim of seriously intimidating a population, or unduly compelling a government or international organization to perform or abstain from performing any act, or seriously destabilizing or destroying the fundamental political, constitutional, economic or social structures of a country or an international organization.[14]

In the process of aligning its criminal law with the legal norms and provisions of the EU, Croatia achieved complete harmonization with Framework Decisions on combating terrorism.[15]

12 See Security Council Resolution 1566.

13 Council Framework Decision of 13 June 2002 on Combating Terrorism U.N. Doc. 2002/475/JHA, 2002 O. J. (L 164) and Council Framework Decision 2008/919/JHA of 28 November 2008 amending Framework Decision 2002/475/JHA on combating terrorism.

14 Wahl, The European Union as an Actor in the Fight Against Terrorism, pp 122–6, Dumitriu, Eugenia, The E.U.'s Definition of Terrorism: The Council Framework Decision on Combating Terrorism, (2004) 5 *German Law Journal* 5, pp 585–602.

15 For details, see Section III.

III. CRIMINAL LAW AND PROSECUTION

A. *Criminal Law*

The first document in which terrorism was mentioned and defined at the national level was the criminal code. After its independence, Croatia adopted the criminal legislation of the former Yugoslavia, and from the 1991 to 1997 two criminal codes were in force in Croatia, viz. Criminal Code (CC'93) and Basic Criminal Code (Basic CC).[16] Additionally, criminal offences of terrorist activities against the Republic of Croatia were regulated by means of a special code.[17]

The CC'93 stipulates that the act of any person who, with an aim of endangering the constitutional order or the security of the Republic of Croatia, causes an explosion or fire or performs another generally dangerous act or commits some other act of violence, thus causing a feeling of personal insecurity among citizens, is considered a criminal offence of terrorism (art 236). International terrorism was defined in Basic CC (art 135 para 1). The perpetrator of this criminal offence is any person who with intent to harm a foreign state, liberation movement or an international organization kidnaps a person or commits some other act of violence, causes an explosion or fire or by some general dangerous act or device endangers the lives of people and property of considerable value. Apart from these criminal offences, Basic CC prescribes a number of criminal offences by means of which various forms of international terrorist activities are incriminated.[18]

In October 1997, the penal legislation in the Republic of Croatia was modified, and the new, unified Criminal Code (CC'97) was adopted.[19] This Criminal Code also recognizes criminal offence of terrorism (now referred to as anti-state terrorism) and international terrorism, definitions of which are almost identical to the ones from the former criminal codes.[20] Despite certain amendments, CC'97 still criminalized various forms of international terrorist activities.[21]

[16] Basic Criminal Code of the Republic of Croatia (Official Gazette, 31/93, 39/93, 108/95, 16/96, 28/96) and Criminal Code of the Republic of Croatia (Official Gazette, 32/93, 38/93, 16/96, 28/96).

[17] Act on Criminal Offences of Subversive and Terrorist Activities Against the State Sovereignty and Territorial Unity of the Republic of Croatia (Official Gazette, 74/92).

[18] Endangering the safety of internationally protected persons (art 136 Basic CC), taking of hostages (art 137 Basic CC), misuse of nuclear materials (art 199 and 200 Basic CC), hijacking an aircraft (art 191 Basic CC), endangering the safety of international air traffic and maritime navigation (art 192 Basic CC).

[19] Criminal Code, Official Gazette, 110/1997, 27/1998, 50/2000, 129/2000, 51/2001, 111/2003, 190/2003, 105/2004, 84/2005, 71/2006, 110/2007, 152/2008.

[20] Criminal Code, art 141 and 169.

[21] Endangering the safety of internationally protected persons (art 170), taking of hostages (art 171), misuse of nuclear materials (art 172), hijacking an aircraft or a ship (art 179) and endangering the safety of international air traffic and maritime navigation (art 181).

After the events of 11 September 2001, the United Nations and European Union were active in adopting documents for the prevention and suppression of terrorism-related criminal offences. The most important documents that have influenced the Croatian substantive criminal law are Security Council Resolution 1373,[22] Security Council Resolution 1624,[23] Council of Europe Convention on the Prevention of Terrorism[24] and the 2002 European Council Framework Decision on Combating Terrorism. With an aim of incorporating requirements from relevant international documents into the Croatian substantive criminal legislation, the Croatian Parliament adopted a set of important amendments to the CC'97 in 2004, 2006 and 2008, especially as regards the counter-terrorism provisions.[25] Previous articles on anti-state terrorism and international terrorism have been merged in one article named "terrorism," and new offences have been introduced: Public Instigation to Terrorism (art 169a), Recruitment and Training for Terrorism (art 169b) and Financing of Terrorism as a Part of Criminal Offence Association for the Purpose of Committing Criminal Offences Against the Values Protected by International Law (art 187a para 2).

Finally, the new Criminal Code (CC'11) was adopted in 2011, and it entered into force on 1 January 2013.[26] CC'11 further improved previous amendments and introduced important changes with regard to counter-terrorism provisions. Moreover, it is also in line with documents of the United Nations, EU *acquis communautaire*, the Council of Europe's conventions, legal standards of the European Court for Human Rights and other international documents, as well as the best practices of other comparatively relevant legislations.[27] Articles in CC'11 that criminalize terrorism are Terrorism (art 97), Financing of Terrorism (art 98), Public

[22] Security Council Resolution, S/Res/1373 (2001) required states to enact legislation to prevent and suppress the financing of terrorist acts. For critical approach of the Resolution 1373, see Roach, Kent, The 9/11 Effect: Comparative Counter-Terrorism (Cambridge, Cambridge University Press 2011) pp 32–3, Derenčinović, Davor, Essays on Terrorism and Antiterrorism (Zagreb, Pravni fakultet, 2005) p 70.

[23] Security Council Resolution S/Res/1624 (2005) called upon all states to adopt "such measures as may be necessary and appropriate and in accordance with their obligations under international law to prohibit by law incitement to commit a terrorist act or acts." For details, see Roach, The 9/11 Effect: Comparative Counter-Terrorism, pp 55–59.

[24] About the specificity of this Convention, see Derenčinović, Davor, Getoš, Anna-Maria, Cooperation of law enforcement and intelligence agencies in prevention and suppression of terrorism, (2007) 78 Revue internationale de droit penal, pp 93–4.

[25] Law on the Amendments of the Criminal Code, Official Gazette 105/04, 71/06, 152/08.

[26] Criminal Code, Official Gazette, 125/11, 144/12.

[27] Turkalj, Kristijan, Usklađivanje hrvatskog pravnog sustava s pravnom stečevinom EU na području borbe protiv međunarodnog terorizma, in Novi obzori suvremenog terorizma i antiterorizma (Zagreb, Pravni fakultet, Akademija pravnih znanosti Hrvatske, 2012) pp 79–108.

Provocation to Terrorism (art 99),[28] Recruitment for Terrorism (art 100), Training for Terrorism (art 101) and Terrorist Organization (art 102).[29]

A constitutive element of the crime of terrorism is a terrorist objective. The action has to seriously intimidate a population or compel a state or an international organization to do or to abstain from doing an act or seriously destabilize or destroy the fundamental constitutional, political, economic or social structures of a state or an international organization. Acts of committing the criminal offence are specifically mentioned in art 97 para 1 and they include the following:

1. Making an attack upon a person's life that may cause death.
2. Making an attack upon the physical integrity of a person.
3. Kidnapping or taking hostages.
4. Causing destruction to a state or public facility; a transport system; an infrastructure facility, including an information system; a fixed platform located on the epicontinental shelf; a public place; or private property. The destruction must be likely to endanger human life or result in major economic loss.
5. Hijacking an aircraft, vessel or other means of public or goods transport.
6. Manufacturing, possessing, acquiring, transporting, supplying or using weapons, explosives or nuclear, biological or chemical weapons, as well as doing research into and developing nuclear, biological or chemical weapons.
7. Releasing dangerous substances, or causing fires, explosions or floods, the effect of which is to endanger human life.
8. Interfering with or disrupting the supply of water, electricity or any other fundamental natural resource, the effect of which is to endanger human life.
9. Possessing or using radioactive substances or manufacturing; possessing or using a device for the activation, dispersal or emission of radioactive material or ionizing radiation; using or causing damage to a nuclear facility resulting

[28] Before the adoption of Criminal Code 2011, the direct provocation to commit any criminal offence fell under the instigation clause. According to art 37 para 1, "any person who intentionally instigates another to commit a criminal offence shall be punished as if he himself committed it." In the case of terrorism-related offences, the instigator will be punished even if the perpetrator has not attempted to commit the respective criminal offence. It is important to emphasize that instigation always exerts conclusive influence on a specific person to commit a specific criminal offence. In other words, public provocation in the form of distributing a message to the public with the intent of inciting the commission of a terrorist offence, whatever the content of this message may be, wouldn't fall under the scope of art 37 of the CC'97. Derenčinović, Davor, The evolution of the antiterror legal and institutional framework in Croatia, in Wade and Maljević (eds.), A War on Terror?, pp 315–16.

[29] For more details, Munivrana, Maja, Kaznena djela protiv čovječnosti i ljudskog dostojanstva, in Derenčinović, D. (ed.), Posebni dio kaznenog prava (Zagreb, Pravni fakultet, 2013) pp 28–34, Committee of Experts on Terrorism (CODEXTER), Profiles on Counter-Terrorist Capacity, Croatia, November 2011, pp 4–7, available at http://www.coe.int/t/dlapil/codexter/Source/country_profiles/CODEXTER_Profiles_2011_Croatia_EN.pdf.

in the release of radioactive materials or the danger thereof; requesting, by using force or threats, radioactive materials, a nuclear facility or a device for activating, dispersing or emitting radioactive materials.

Such actions may constitute ordinary crimes (for example, bodily injury, serious bodily injury, endangerment of life and property by a generally dangerous act or means, etc.), but their goal and their nature must be such that they could seriously harm a state or an international organization whereby they are transformed into a criminal act of terrorism. The perpetrator of terrorism shall be punished by imprisonment from three to fifteen years. Imprisonment from six months to five years is foreseen for those perpetrators who threaten to commit one of the preceding listed criminal offences (art 97 para 2). An aggravated form of terrorism is provided in paras 3 and 4. Para 3 proscribes extensive destruction and the death of one or more persons as aggravated circumstances and punishable by imprisonment of not less than five years. According to para 4, punishment by imprisonment for not less than ten years or by long-term imprisonment shall be imposed on a perpetrator who intentionally kills one or more persons.

Criminal offences of terrorism can be regarded as criminal offences committed by individuals. But if the perpetrator acts as a part of terrorist association, he or she will be responsible for two criminal offences, terrorism (or another terrorist-related act) and terrorist association (art 102). Namely, terrorist association is regarded as a separate criminal offence. Pursuant to art 102, any person who becomes a member of the criminal association or commits an act which he or she knows contributes to the achievement of the terrorist association's goal is responsible for terrorist association crime. In other words, it is not necessary that the perpetrator becomes a member of a terrorist organization, it suffices that the person takes an action he or she knows contributes to achieving the goals of terrorist organizations. An aggravated form of this offence is organizing or conducting terrorist organizations, the aim of which is to commit a terrorism-related criminal offence.[30]

Other terrorism-related criminal offences provided in the CC are the following: financing of terrorism (art 98),[31] public instigation of terrorism (art 99),

[30] All constitutive elements of crime have to be present in order to establish the crime of terrorist association. Terrorist lists that are regionally and internationally published could be the indicator of connection between a person and terrorist groups. The existence of such lists represents certain obligation for states (see Section V), but these are not sufficient grounds for conviction for any terrorism-related offence. An individual can be convicted for that crime or for being a member of a terrorist association only in criminal procedure and after all constitutive elements of terrorism-related offence have had been proved. This is a reasonable solution, because the method of enlisting a person for a terrorism-related offence is mostly the result of political ideology. States have not reached complete agreement about the criteria that have to be fulfilled for a certain organization to be declared as a terrorist organization. Derenčinović, Essays on Terrorism and Antiterrorism, pp 120–1.

[31] See Section VI.

recruitment for terrorism (art 100), training for terrorism (art 101) and preparing terrorism-related criminal offences.

Pursuant to art 99 of the CC, any person who publicly expresses or promotes ideas directly or indirectly instigating the commission of a terrorism, financing of terrorism and another criminal offences that are related to terrorism is responsible for public provocation to terrorism.[32] Pursuant to this provision, all of the forms and manifestations of encouragement, glorification and apology of terrorism are punishable. Provision of art 99 is in line with art 5 of the Council of Europe Convention on Prevention of Terrorism and Council Framework Decision 2008.[33] Contrary to these documents, the Criminal Code does not require that the provocation causes a danger that one or more terrorist offences might be committed. For the prosecution, it will suffice to prove that there was the intention to instigate another person to terrorist activities. In other words, the Prosecutor cannot prove that the *actus rea* of the perpetrator acting with the intention to instigate another person to commit a criminal offence caused the danger of the commission of the respective offence. This way, the scope of criminalization of public provocation to commit terrorism-related criminal offences is extended.[34] If we keep in mind the fact that the concept of public provocation is very closely related to freedom of expression protected under the European Convention for the Protection of Human Rights and Fundamental Freedoms, it seems that art 99 CC'11 does not represent an appropriate balance between the obligation of the state to protect everyone from terrorism and its obligation to protect freedom of expression as the fundamental human right. Due to that fact, some authors consider that the criminal zone of art 99 is very broad and that this provision should be interpreted in accordance with its international sources.[35]

[32] It includes the following criminal offences: Kidnapping (art 137), Destruction of or Damage to Public-Use Devices (art 216), Misuse of Radioactive Substances (art 219), Attack on an Aircraft, Vessel or Immovable Platform (art 223), Endangering Traffic by a Dangerous Act or Dangerous Means (art 224), Murder, Kidnapping or Attack on an Internationally Protected Person (art 352–5).

[33] Public provocation was the subject of extensive debate in the Council of Europe Committee of Experts Against Terrorism. Due to the fact that the concept of the public provocation has been very closely related to freedom of expression, the main concern was how to find an appropriate balance between protection from terrorism and freedom of expression. For more, see Derenčinović, The evolution of the antiterror legal and institutional framework in Croatia, in Wade M. and Maljević A. (eds.), A War on Terror?, pp 313–16, Derenčinović, D, Suvremeni terorizam na raskrižju – kaznenopravna reakcija vs. "Rat protiv terorizma," in Novi obzori suvremenog terorizma i antiterorizma (Zagreb, Pravni fakultet, Akademija pravnih znanosti Hrvatske, 2012) pp 37–40.

[34] See Council of Europe Convention on Prevention of Terrorism, Explanatory Report, par. 99 and 100.

[35] Munivrana, Kaznena djela protiv čovječnosti i ljudskog dostojanstva, p 33. See Derenčinović, The evolution of the antiterror legal and institutional framework in Croatia, pp 313–19. In practice, up to this point there has been one final judgment for this offence. After an investigation, in 2013 the District Attorney in Split issued an indictment against a Croatian citizen D. M. (1971) for committing

The criminal offence of recruitment for terrorism is provided in art 100 of the CC'11. It foresees the imprisonment from one to ten years for any person who solicits another person to join a terrorist association for the purpose of contributing to the commission of terrorism-related criminal offences. This provision sets forth that the perpetrator has to act intentionally, but does not prescribe that the recruited person actually must join a terrorist organization or commit a terrorism-related activity.

Any person who provides instructions on the making or use of explosive devices, firearms or other weapons, noxious or hazardous substances or on other specific methods or techniques, knowing that the skills provided are intended to be used for the purpose of committing any of the terrorism-related criminal offences is responsible for training for terrorism. The punishment prescribed for training for terrorism is imprisonment from one to ten years.

Finally, according to art 103, preparing criminal offences of terrorism (art 97) is considered a separate criminal offence. This provision provides punishment for all preparatory actions leading to commission of a crime of terrorism.

B. *Terrorism Prosecutions*

Investigating and prosecuting criminal offences present a number of challenges for criminal justice systems. For instance, evidence must be properly obtained in order to be used in court, witnesses may require special security measures and there is a risk of infringing on human rights and fundamental freedoms during the investigation and prosecution of suspects. It is very important to ensure that criminal proceedings are grounded on the rule of law and full respect of human rights.

The legal provisions that are in force in the Republic of Croatia are in line with the European Convention for the Protection of Human Rights and Fundamental Freedoms. The legislation of the Republic of Croatia strictly regulates when and under which conditions human rights may be temporarily limited. The Criminal Procedure Act contains procedural measures that provide the legal framework

the crime of public provocation to terrorism (art 99 in connection to art 97 para 1 sub-para 4 of the Criminal Code). The accused was charged on the grounds of publishing a videotape made in his own home in which, with the intent to disturb citizens of Republic of Croatia and in grave violation of its constitutional, political, economical and social elements, he revealed and directly invited members and followers of the Facebook group to attack objects of special police in Zagreb area, as well as all objects and public institutions (especially the ones with the EU flag hanging at the building), railways, highways, bridges, banks, jewellers, supporters of capitalism, Bruxelles, EU and NATO. His tape was published on YouTube on 13 January 2013. Afterwards, parts of the tape were made public by various media in Croatia. The County Court has sentenced D. M. for the offense of public instigation of terrorism to imprisonment of one year, which was replaced with community service. Besides that, a special obligation to undergo psychosocial therapy was imposed upon the defendant. Decision of the County Court in Split, K-63/2013, 26 March 2014.

for the detection, investigation and prosecution of criminal offences of terrorism by the State Attorney's Office, the police and the courts. Pursuant to art 10, court decisions shall not be founded on illegally obtained evidence (illegal evidence). Illegal evidence is, *inter alia*, evidence obtained by illegal means constituting a violation of the prohibition of torture and cruel or inhuman treatment, these being the rights that are guaranteed by the Constitution, domestic law or international law. Regardless of the gravity of the offence, the possibility that illegally obtained evidence will be considered valid is excluded.

The Criminal Procedure Act provides protection of witnesses (art 294–9) if it is likely that by giving a testimony or by answering any individual question a witness might expose himself or herself or any other person close to the witness to a serious danger to life, health, physical integrity, freedom or property of considerable volume (threatened witnesses). The possibility of witness protection is not related to the gravity of the criminal offence for which the criminal procedure is conducted. In other words, Croatian criminal procedural law does not contain specific provisions that provide additional protection to threatened witnesses in criminal proceedings for terrorism-related criminal offences. Witness protection includes a special manner of questioning a witness and measures for protecting the witness and other persons close to that witness who do not participate in the proceedings. The basic form of protection consists in non-disclosure of identification data of witnesses (i.e., name and surname, his or her father's first name, occupation, place of residence, place of birth, age, personal identification number). Therefore, with this type of protection, witness examination is conducted without publication of his or her personal data (the witness is given a pseudonym). But, the witness is present in the same room as other participants, and the accused is able to see the witness. Another form of protection, by means of which the witness is much more protected, includes, among the aforementioned forms, the non-disclosure of witness's physical appearance. In this case, the examination is conducted by means of technical devices for the transfer of picture and sound. The appearance and the voice of the witness are modified during the examination, and he or she is placed in a room that is separated from the room in which the investigating judge and other persons (including the accused and his or her attorney) attending the examination are situated. The anonymity of the witness is the most effective method of his or her procedural protection, but the implementation of this measure threatens some fundamental rights of the accused. Therefore, the Criminal Procedure Act stipulates some limitations on using the testimony of anonymous witnesses in criminal procedure. Hence, art 298 prescribes that a verdict may not be based only on the testimony of a threatened witness.

The Criminal Procedure Act prescribes subject matter and territorial jurisdiction of the court. According to art 19, criminal cases shall be heard before the municipal courts, county courts, High Criminal Court (since 1 January 2015) and Supreme

Court of the Republic of Croatia. All terrorism-related criminal offences fall under the jurisdiction of County Court (art 19c) as the court before which the proceedings are instituted (the court of first instance). Pursuant to current legislation, the Supreme Court shall have jurisdiction over appeals against decisions of the county courts. All terrorism-related criminal offences are subject to public prosecution whereby the authorized prosecutor is the State Attorney. He or she has the duty to institute the prosecution *ex officio* when there is reasonable suspicion that a certain person had committed a criminal offence that is subject to public prosecution.

In accordance with the official information available in the period from 2001 to 2012, nineteen reports for the crime of counter-state terrorism or terrorism were submitted. Since the perpetrators were unknown, no judgment has been made. No report, accusation or conviction of the crime of international terrorism was recorded in aforementioned period.[36] For the period 1991 to 2000, there are no official statistical data on crimes of terrorism and international terrorism, and accordingly no data on possible reports, accusations or convictions for these crimes. Only the data on all convictions and accusations for all crimes from Chapter XIX (Crimes Against the Republic of Croatia), which comprises crime of terrorism, and crimes from Chapter XV (Crimes Against Humanity and International Law), which comprises crimes of international terrorism, are available. Despite this non-existence of precise information, it has to be emphasized that in the early and mid-1990s, the Republic of Croatia was a target of terrorist attacks.

C. *Punishment of Terrorism*

Pursuant to art 41 of the CC'11, the purpose of punishment is to express public condemnation for the crime committed, raise the confidence of citizens in the legal order based on the rule of law, exert an influence on the perpetrator and all others so that they do not commit criminal offences by raising awareness of the perils of committing criminal offences and of the justness of punishment and allow the perpetrator's readmission into society. Thus, rehabilitation is featured as one of the purposes of punishing the perpetrators of all crimes and, therefore, the perpetrators of crimes related to terrorism.

When determining the type and measure of punishment, the court shall, starting from the degree of guilt and the purpose of punishment, assess all the circumstances affecting the severity of punishment by type and measure of punishment. It is important to mention that the Criminal Code provides the possibility for the court to reduce the punishment of a perpetrator's terrorism-related criminal offence. Pursuant to art 102

[36] Adult offenders of criminal offences, denunciations, indictments and sentences in the period from 2001–12, Central Bureau of Statistics, Zagreb.

para 3, the court may remit the punishment of a person who organizes or conducts terrorist organizations or a person who is a member of the criminal association or commits an act that he or she knows contributes to the achievement of the terrorist association's goal, in two cases: (1) if, by uncovering a terrorist association on time, the person prevents the perpetration of a terrorism-related criminal offence; and (2) if the person who is a member of a terrorist association uncovers the association prior to committing, as its member or on its behalf, a terrorism-related criminal offence.

The Criminal Procedural Act provides cooperation with authorities for the purpose of reduction of sentencing. Art 206 foresees the possibility of achieving an agreement on punishment between the State Attorney and the accused after the accused has confessed that particular crime. In that case, the punishment prescribed by law for the committed offences may be mitigated. The judgment based on such an agreement is possible for all crimes, including terrorism-related criminal offences. But it must be emphasized that the court can reject such an agreement. In that case, the proceeding continues as if there were no agreement at all.

From the beginning of official statistics for each criminal offence in 2001, there were no charges for terrorism-related criminal offences. Since there is no evidence for the period before 2001, no analysis on the sentencing practices after terrorism convictions can be conducted.

IV. INVESTIGATIVE POWERS

A. *Police Powers*

Police authority as one of the subjects of criminal prosecution has duties and powers, *ex officio* or by the order of state attorney. The police can thus undertake inquiries of criminal offences and collect evidence upon the order of state attorney or the court.[37]

During the inquiries police may undertake different activities, *inter alia*, to verify, process and use the data; to verify and establish the identity of persons and objects; to gather data from citizens; to perform polygraph testing; to inspect premises and objects; and to inspect persons, objects and means of transportation. The purpose of these activities is to collect information necessary for the institution of criminal proceeding to reach a decision. It is important to mention that results of these inquiries should not be used as evidence in criminal proceedings.

[37] The police activities have been regulated by the Law on Duties and Powers of the Police and Criminal Procedure Act, Official Gazette, 76/09.

The police authorities are obligated to act upon the order of the State Attorney (the Public Prosecutor), who may order the police authorities to obtain necessary information by making inquiries and undertaking other measures for collecting the data necessary for a decision on the opening of the investigation.[38] The State Attorney may in his or her order to the police authorities determine the content of the inquiry or measure in more detail and order immediate information from the police authorities about the inquiry or measures undertaken.

In order to ensure more efficient prosecution, in all cases of the terrorism-related criminal offences, the following so-called special investigative measures can be applied: (1) surveillance and interception of telephone conversations and other means of remote technical communication; (2) interception, gathering and recording of electronic data; (3) entry to the premises for the purpose of conducting surveillance and technical recording on the premises; (4) covered following and technical recording of individuals and objects; (5) use of undercover investigators and informants; (6) simulated sales and purchases of certain objects, simulated bribe offering and simulated bribe taking; (7) offering simulated business services or closing simulated legal business; and (8) control of the transport and delivery of objects of criminal offences.[39]

Due to the fact that special investigative measures temporarily restrict certain constitutional rights of citizens, the conditions for the applicability of such measures are precisely prescribed. First, these measures can be applied only if the investigation cannot be carried out in any other way or would otherwise encounter significant difficulties. Second, special investigative measures can be applied to the person against whom there are grounds for suspicion that he or she committed or has taken part in committing an offence. Third, these measures may be ordered only for certain criminal offences. Finally, special investigative measures can be carried out upon the order of the court (the judge of investigation) issued on the request of the State Attorney. This order is carried out by the police authorities. Exceptionally, when circumstances require that the actions must be commenced immediately, the State Attorney may issue the order for the term of twenty-four hours. In this case, the State Attorney must deliver the order to the judge of investigation within eight hours from the issuing, and the judge should decide on the legality of the order. If court denies the order, the actions must be immediately ceased, and the data collected pursuant to the order of the State Attorney shall be destroyed. Recordings, documents and objects obtained by special investigative measures may be used as evidence in proceedings against the person suspected of terrorism-related criminal offences.[40]

38 Criminal Procedure Act, art 206.

39 Criminal Procedure Act, art 332 para 1.

40 Criminal Procedure Act, art 332 paras 2–5 and art 338 para 1.

B. *Intelligence Agencies*

The last intelligence system reform in Croatia was carried out in 2006 with the adoption of the Security Intelligence System Act that restructured the previous security services.[41] By the merging of the counter-intelligence agency and intelligence agency, the Security and Intelligence Agency was established, followed by the establishment of the Military Security-Intelligence Agency.

The work of the Security and Intelligence Agency is focused on the prevention of all activities against the constitutional order and those jeopardizing the security of state bodies, citizens and national interests. The Military Security-Intelligence Agency is responsible for supporting the Ministry of Defence and the Army in the execution of defence duties and for collecting and analyzing information that could jeopardize state defence capabilities. The work of the security and intelligence system is directed by the National Security Council, as the highest political body responsible for national security.[42] The oversight of the security intelligence agencies with the aim of decreasing and eliminating possible violations of human rights and freedoms is conducted by the Croatian Parliament and the Office of the National Security Council. In addition, a mechanism of civilian oversight through the Council for the Civilian Oversight of the Security Intelligence Agencies has also been established.[43]

Security intelligence agencies gather information relevant to national security in the civilian and military sectors, processing and analyzing these data and providing information support to policy makers and government bodies that apply the laws in areas of interest to the national security. Within their respective scope of activities, security intelligence agencies gather information from publicly available sources, through communication with citizens and by requesting data from state authority bodies, local authority bodies and regional self-government legal entities, including access to registers and databases and to the official documentation and the application of secret procedures and measures.[44]

[41] Security Intelligence System Act, Official Gazette 79/06, 105/06. For more details, Committee of Experts on Terrorism (CODEXTER), Profiles on Counter-Terrorist Capacity, Croatia, November 2011, pp 9–10, available at http://www.coe.int/t/dlapil/codexter/Source/country_profiles/CODEXTER_Profiles_2011_Croatia_EN.pdf.

[42] National Security Council consists of the President of the Republic, the Prime Minister, member of the government responsible for national security, the minister competent for foreign affairs, the Minister of Justice, the National Security Advisor of the President of the Republic, the Chief of the General Staff of the Armed Forces of the Republic of Croatia, the Director of the Security and Intelligence Agency, the Director of the Military Security-Intelligence Agency and The Head of the Office of the National Security Council (art 4.)

[43] Security Intelligence System Act, art 103.

[44] Security Intelligence System Act, art 25.

The Security Intelligence System Act prescribes that security intelligence agencies may apply measures of secret information gathering that temporarily restrict certain constitutional human rights and basic freedoms, if the information cannot be obtained in any other way or if the collection thereof is linked with disproportionate difficulties. Measures of secret information gathering include the following:

1. Secret surveillance of telecommunication services, activity and traffic:
   (a) Secret surveillance of the communication content
   (b) Secret surveillance of the telecommunication traffic data (intercept-related information)
   (c) Secret surveillance of the location of the user
   (d) Secret surveillance of international telecommunications
2. Postal censorship
3. Secret surveillance and technical recording of the interior of facilities, closed spaces and objects
4. Secret surveillance and monitoring, with recording of images and photos of persons in open and public spaces
5. Secret surveillance and monitoring, with audio recording of the content of communication between persons in open and public spaces
6. Secret purchase of documents and objects

The following measures can be taken only upon submitting the request to the Supreme Court: secret surveillance of the communication content; postal censorship; secret surveillance and technical recording of the interior of facilities, closed spaces and objects; and secret purchase of documents and objects.[45] The written justified proposals for the application of these secret measures are submitted by the directors of the security intelligence agencies. These measures may last up to four months, although this deadline may be extended. Exceptionally, when there is a risk that an important opportunity may be missed due to administrative procedures, covert measures can be temporarily approved by the director of the security agency that is bound to obtain the approval of the judge of the Supreme Court. If the judge refuses to issue a written warrant for the application of the measure, the security intelligence agency must destroy all the data collected during the application of the measures.[46]

The data collected by security and intelligence agency upon the order of the Supreme Court judge, as well as data obtained by order of the director of security

45 Application of other measures is approved by a written and justified warrant issued by the directors of the security intelligence agencies (art 38).

46 Security Intelligence System Act, art 33, 36–8.

and intelligence agencies, may not be used as evidence in proceedings against the person suspected of criminal offences.[47] Exceptionally, according to art 185 para 5, personal data used to determine the identity of the defendant, collected by the security intelligence services, may be used as evidence only in processes for the most serious criminal offences, such as terrorism, financing of terrorism and terrorist association, and for punishment of the most severe forms of criminal offences against the Republic of Croatia.

V. PROSCRIPTION AND LISTING OF TERRORIST GROUPS AND INDIVIDUALS

The designation of individuals and entities as "terrorists" on the international and regional level in order to sanction such entities is a new phenomenon. In the aftermath of 9/11, the United Nations and European Union agreed upon establishing the terrorist lists. In addition, some EU member states[48] have established their own national terrorist lists. Croatia has not been one of them, but as a member of the United Nations and European Union, it has obligation to implement lists of these organizations.

The main sanction regime was established in 1999 by UN Security Council Resolution 1267 concerning Al-Qaida and the Taliban and associated individuals and entities. The regime aims at cutting off financial and material support for the target group. The Security Council Sanctions Committee has been established by this Resolution, with the mandate to oversee the implementation of the sanctions against aforementioned targets and to review and extend lists of those individuals and entities.[49] On 28 September 2001, UN Security Council adopted Resolution 1373 imposing the obligations to freeze and seize funds associated with terrorism. Unlike the Resolution 1267, Resolution 1373 does not contain an annexed list. It only sets out the general objective of fighting against terrorism, without identifying the particular targets itself. However, it could be considered the most sweeping

47 Where the collected data indicate that a criminal act that is prosecuted *ex officio* is being planned or committed, the security intelligence agencies shall notify the Public Attorney's Office thereon.

48 For example, United Kingdom, The Netherlands and Spain. An overview of lists in the United States, the UN and Europe, see Thorne, Kristina, "Terrorist" lists–a brief overview of lists and their sanctions in the US, UN and Europe, Centre for Humanitarian Dialogue, June 2006 available at http://www.hdcentre.org/uploads/tx_news/140_Terroristlists-AbriefoverviewoflistsandtheirsanctionsintheUSUNandEurope.pdf.

49 A number of UN resolutions that followed Resolution 1267 reinforced the obligations of the member states and renewed the lists. See Security Council Resolution 1333 (2000), 1390 (2002), as reiterated in resolutions 1455 (2003), 1526 (2004), 1617 (2005), 1735 (2006), 1822 (2008), 1904 (2009), 1989 (2011) and 2083 (2012). The list was last updated on 6 January 2014.

sanctioning measures ever adopted by Security Council.[50] The list that is based on UN Security Council Resolution 1267 has been incorporated into EU law by Regulation 337/2000. This EU list includes the names of persons and organizations that are associated with Osama Bin Laden, the Al-Qaida network and the Taliban. The second EU list, which is based on UN Security Council Resolution 1373, was established by EU Common Position 2001/931 of 27 December 2001 on the application of specific measures to combat terrorism and Council Regulation (EC) No 2580/2001 on specific restrictive measures directed against certain persons and entities with a view towards combating terrorism.[51] This list was drawn up autonomously by the EU and includes persons, entities and groups involved in terrorist activities.[52]

Creation of the lists of organizations and individuals suspected to be members of terrorist organizations or participants in their financing has been harshly criticized for breaching the most fundamental procedural rights and stigmatizing persons on the lists. Namely, listing of terrorists is mostly the result of political decisions.[53] The individuals and groups listed in that way have very limited possibilities to challenge the facts that are the basis for the restriction of their fundamental human rights. Therefore, there are many examples of the long-term preventive freezing of assets of suspected persons without valid legal basis. Individuals on UN terrorist lists do not have at disposal any judicial remedy at the UN level.[54] Those persons listed and sanctioned by the European Union have a right of access to justice before European Court of Justice and European Court of Human Rights.[55] But the problem arises from the fact that European Courts are faced with the lack of relevant information because member states are unwilling to share the necessary information on why

[50] Christina Eckes, Trapped between courts and how terrorist suspects lost their right to remedy, in Follestal, Wessel, Wouters (eds.), Multilevel Regulation and the EU: The Interplay Between Global, European and National Normative Processes (Leiden, Martinus Nijhoff, 2008) p 266.

[51] Council Regulation (EC) No 2580/2001 of 27 December 2001 provides for a freezing of all funds, other financial assets and economic resources belonging to the persons, groups and entities concerned and ensuring that no funds, other financial assets and economic resources may be made available to them, whether directly or indirectly.

[52] See more in Wählisch, Martin, EU Terrorist Listing, an Overview About Listing and Delisting Procedure, Berghof Peace Support, 2010, available at http://www.berghof-peacesupport.org/publications/RLM_EU_Terrorist_Listing.pdf.

[53] For details on the listing procedure of the autonomous EU terrorism list regime, see Wählisch, EU Terrorist Listing, p 6.

[54] Based on the objection that human rights have not been respected, attempts have been made to reform the listing and delisting procedure. Roach, The 9/11 Effect, pp 59–63.

[55] For more details see, Eckes, Christina, The Legal Framework of the European Union's Counter-Terrorist Policies, Full of Good Intentions, University of Amsterdam, pp 14–22, available at http://papers.ssrn.com/sol3/papers.cfm?abstract_id=2092789.

someone is considered to be a terrorist. This makes it impossible for the courts to rule on the merits and provide effective judicial protection.[56]

VI. REGULATION OF TERRORISM FINANCING

The accumulation of financial resources is the main prerequisite for the preparation of terrorist actions. Therefore, the financing of terrorism is a high-priority problem that has to be resolved. Croatia has adopted extensive legal basis with the aim to prevent the financing of terrorism.

A. *The Regulatory Regime to Counter Terrorism Financing*

The responsibility for the prevention of money laundering and terrorist financing in the Republic of Croatia does not lie with one institution but with a system that determines the roles of the participants, their interaction and cooperation. It consists of prevention bodies (banks, housing savings banks, exchange offices, insurance companies, brokers, lawyers, public notaries, tax advisors, the Office for Money Laundering Prevention as the central analytics service, etc.), supervisory bodies (the Financial Inspectorate, the Tax Administration, the Croatian National Bank, the Croatian Financial Services Supervisory Agency) and criminal prosecution authorities (the police, the State Attorney's Office and the judiciary).

The Anti-Money Laundering Law entered into force on 1 November 1997.[57] The enactment of this Act and the establishment of the Office for the Prevention of Money Laundering as an autonomous and independent financial intelligence unit within the Ministry of Finance set the basis for development of anti-money laundering system.

Unlike money laundering, which is always preceded by an unlawful activity, terrorism may be financed by lawful activities of humanitarian organizations, various associations, donations and so on. This makes detection of terrorist financing very difficult, even more so if we bear in mind the fact that the amounts of terrorist financing transactions often tend to be smaller than the amounts that according to the law have to be reported to the anti-money laundering office. As the measures taken to prevent money laundering are not sufficient in the fight against terrorist financing, they have to be supplemented by special measures. For that

56 About the negative consequences of placing individuals and organizations on the list of terrorists on human rights system, see Derenčinović, D., Essays on Terrorism and Antiterrorism, p 121, Eckes, Christina, EU Counter-Terrorist Policies and Fundamental Rights – the Case of Individual Sanctions, Oxford, Oxford University Press, 2010; Gargantini, Giulia, European cooperation in counter-terrorism and the case of individual sanctions (2011) 3, *Perspectives on Federalism*, 3, p 163.

57 Anti-Money Laundering Law, Official Gazette 69/97, 106/97, 67/01 i 114/01, 117/03, 142/03.

purpose and in order to harmonize national legislation with the EU *acquis*[58] and Council of Europe Convention on Laundering, Search, Seizure and Confiscation of the Proceeds from Crime and on the Financing of Terrorism of 16 May 2005, the Croatian Parliament adopted in 2008 the new Anti Money Laundering and Terrorist Financing Law.[59] This law prescribes measures and actions in banking and non-banking financial operations and money-related and other operations undertaken for the purpose of the prevention and detection of money laundering and other activities of individuals, legal persons, groups and organizations in relation with terrorist financing.[60]

According to the Anti-Money Laundering and Terrorist Financing Act, the Anti-Money Laundering Office, as an administrative organization within the Ministry of Finance, performs different tasks aimed at preventing money laundering and terrorist financing. As a national financial intelligence unit, the Office collects, analyses and submits data, information and documentation on suspicious transactions to competent government bodies for further proceedings.[61] In preventing money laundering and terrorist financing, this Office cooperates with the State Attorney's Office, the Ministry of the Interior, the Croatian National Bank, the Security-Intelligence Agency, the Ministry of Justice and other state authorities. When it has a reason for suspicion that money laundering or terrorist financing is connected with some transaction or person, the Office shall report it to the competent domestic or foreign body. In a case when the Office has to take urgent action to verify data on a suspicious transaction or a person or when it believes that a transaction or a person is linked with money laundering or terrorist financing, the Office may issue a written order that instructs the reporting entity to suspend the execution of the suspicious transaction temporarily for the maximum of seventy-two hours. Exceptionally, the Office may give to the same entity a verbal order to suspend temporarily the execution of the suspicious transactions. In this case, the written

58 Notably Directive 2005/60/EC of the European Parliament and of the Council of 26 October 2005 on the prevention of the use of the financial system for the purpose of money laundering and terrorist financing.

59 Anti-Money Laundering and Terrorist Financing Law, Official Gazette 87/08, 25/2012. For more details, see Committee of Experts on Terrorism (CODEXTER), Profiles on Counter-Terrorist Capacity, Croatia, November 2011, pp 11–21, available at http://www.coe.int/t/dlapil/codexter/Source/country_profiles/CODEXTER_Profiles_2011_Croatia_EN.pdf.

60 In addition, relevant legislation in this field also includes Croatian National Bank Act, Credit Institutions Act, Foreign Exchange Act, Payment System Act, Act of the Financial Inspectorate, Act on Proceedings for the Confiscation of Pecuniary Benefit Resulting from Criminal Offences and Misdemeanours, etc.

61 In 2012, the Office received 572 notices about suspicious activities. Republic on Croatia, Ministry of Finance, Anti-Money Laundering Office, available at http://www.mfin.hr/adminmax/docs/GODISNJE%20IZVJESCE%202012.-28.08.pdf.

order has to be issued within twenty-four hours. The Office must notify the State Attorney's Office about all issued orders. After the expiration of the aforementioned deadline, the transaction may be suspended only by the court decision according to the provisions of the Criminal Procedure Act.[62]

B. *Criminal Offences of Terrorism Financing*

Based on the adopted international obligations under UN Security Council Resolution 1373, the International Convention for the Suppression of the Financing of Terrorism and the Council Framework Decision 2002, the Republic of Croatia has criminalized the financing of terrorism and terrorist operations.

Terrorism financing has been a criminal offence in the Republic of Croatia since 2004. Article 187a on Planning Criminal Offences Against Values Protected by International Law in para 2 provides imprisonment from one to five years to any person who procures or collects financial means being aware that they shall be used totally or partially for the perpetration of the terrorism-related criminal offences.[63] Further amendments to the Criminal Code prescribe sanctions for the perpetrator who, in whatever manner, directly or indirectly, gives or raises funds knowing that they will, fully or partially, be used for the purpose of committing terrorism-related criminal offences. The perpetrator shall be punished irrespective of whether the funds have been fully or partially used for the purpose of committing the criminal offence and irrespective of whether the act has only been attempted.[64]

In order to fully harmonize the Croatian criminal law with international legal documents, the new Criminal Code has prescribed the financing of terrorism as a separate criminal offence. According to art 98 para 1 CC'11, any person who directly or indirectly provides or collects funds with the intention that they be used or with the knowledge that they will be used, in full or in part, in order to carry out one or more terrorism-related criminal offences will be sentenced to imprisonment for one to ten years. The perpetrator shall be punished irrespective of whether the funds have been fully or partially used for the purpose of committing the criminal offence and irrespective of whether the act has been attempted. The same punishment is

[62] Relevant international institutions for anti-money laundering and counter-terrorist financing systems monitoring have evaluated Croatian activities in this field on several occasions. A special team of experts Council of Europe Select Committee of Experts on the Evaluation of Anti-Money Laundering Measures (MONEYVAL) was in Croatia in 2012 and collected data on harmonization of Croatian legislation and practice in this field with FATF recommendations. The mutual evaluation report on the fourth assessment visit of Croatia was adopted at MONEYVAL's 42nd Plenary, available at http://www.coe.int/t/dghl/monitoring/moneyval/Countries/Croatia_en.asp.

[63] Law on the Amendments of the Criminal Code, Official Gazette 105/04.

[64] Law on the Amendments of the Criminal Code, Official Gazette 71/06, 152/08.

prescribed in para 2 to any person who directly or indirectly provides or collects funds with the intention that they be used or in the knowledge that they will be used, in full or in part, by terrorists or terrorist associations. The funds referred to in paragraphs 1 and 2 shall be confiscated.

One of the main principles of criminal substantive law is that no one may retain a pecuniary advantage acquired through illegal means. The CC'11 prescribes the conditions and manner of confiscation of pecuniary advantage.[65] Moreover, the Act on Proceedings for the Confiscation of Pecuniary Benefit Resulting from Criminal Offences and Misdemeanours entered into force on 1 January 2011. This Act has had not only a direct but also a preventive effect on all forms of organized crime as well as on terrorist activities.

VII. IMMIGRATION MEASURES

The attacks of 9/11 had an effect on European Union's policies in the field of asylum and immigration as well as other policies related to free movement of persons. In effect, a more restrictive approach on the issues of asylum, immigration and border security was taken with the aim to ensure a high level of internal safety against terrorism. Access to the territory is limited by the right of states to control the entry, stay and expulsion of foreign nationals on their territory. Croatia has followed up on all relevant regional and international documents about immigration policy and has been harmonizing national legislation with the EU *acquis*.

In Croatia, different measures are used to limit access to the territory and deter foreigners from entering the country, for example, visa policy, a network of immigration and airport liaison officers, biometric and IT databases, cross-border cooperation and so on. The border police of the Ministry of the Interior prevents the movements of potential terrorists and persons who could be connected to them across the state border in accordance with the State Border Surveillance Act.[66] The primary Croatian legislation related to the area of immigration consists in two acts: the Aliens Act[67] and the Asylum Act.[68] These acts provide an additional legal basis for countering terrorism from the perspective of controlling the residence and migration of foreigners in the Republic of Croatia. The Aliens Act regulates conditions for the entry, movement, stay and work of aliens in the Republic of Croatia. A security check on an alien for the purpose of the national security reasons is carried out by the Security and Intelligence Agency. In the decision rejecting or

65 Art 5, 77 and 78.
66 State Border Surveillance Act, Official Gazette 83/13.
67 Aliens Act, Official Gazette 130/11, 74/13.
68 Asylum Act, Official Gazette 79/07, 88/10, 143/13.

terminating the stay of an alien or expelling an alien on the grounds of national security, an elaboration of the grounds decisive to adopt the decision is not included.

The basic legislation that regulates the right to asylum in the Republic of Croatia is the Asylum Act, which came into force on 1 January 2008. The provisions of this Act ensure that asylum seekers have not been involved in terrorist activity before granting refugee status. Pursuant to art 6 of the Asylum Act, asylum shall not be granted to an alien for whom there are serious reasons for considering that he has committed, encouraged or in any other way participated in committing (1) a crime against peace, a war crime or a crime against humanity as defined by provisions of the international instruments; (2) a serious non-political crime outside the Republic of Croatia, before his or her arrival in the Republic of Croatia, also including particularly cruel acts, even if committed with an allegedly political objective; and (3) acts contrary to the purposes and principles of the United Nations as set out in the Preamble and Articles 1 and 2 of the Charter of the United Nations.

VIII. ADMINISTRATIVE AND EXECUTIVE MEASURES

The Croatian Parliament adopted in 2008 International Restrictive Measures Act.[69] This Act enables a more comprehensive and efficient implementation of the sanctions, including of existing counterterrorism sanctions that are adopted within the framework of the UN and the European Union. According to this Act, the Republic of Croatia implements, enforces or removes international restrictive measures against persons, countries, international organizations and territorial entities associated with terrorism. The government of the Republic of Croatia adopts the decision on the introduction of restrictive measures, prescribing the application of the restrictive measures on a case-by-case basis and determining the type of the restrictive measure, the manner of its application, the duration period and supervision of its application.[70]

The legal basis for the application of international restrictive measures is the International Restrictive Measures Act and some special decisions of the Croatian government. They represent the basis for freezing of assets of individuals, groups, economic subjects and entities listed on terrorist lists, made in correspondence with the UN Security Council resolutions and the corresponding EU Common Position.[71]

[69] International Restrictive Measures Act, Office Gazette 139/08.

[70] International Restrictive Measures Act, art 4.

[71] The Government of the Republic of Croatia has adopted Decision on the manner of implementing international restrictive measures against asset disposal (Official Gazette, 78/2011) and Decision on the implementation of measures imposed by the UN Security Council Resolutions 1267 (1999), 1333 (2000), 1363 (2001), 1373 (2001), 1390 (2002), 1452 (2002), 1455 (2003), 1526 (2004), 1617 (2005),

Some restricted measures are determined by the International Restrictive Measures Act, such as restriction upon entry into the country and restricted disposal of assets. The entry into or transit through the territory of the Republic of Croatia is forbidden for the persons included on the terrorist list.

The measure of restricted disposal of assets is conducted by implementation of assets freezing through (a) freezing all the assets owned, held or belonging in any other way to the entity to which the measures are applied, controlled or supervised by that entity; and (b) making the assets unavailable, directly or indirectly, to the entity to which the measures are applied.[72]

IX. ROLE OF MILITARY AND EXTRA-TERRITORIAL COUNTER-TERRORISM ACTIVITIES

International cooperation between states is one of the fundamental prerequisites of the successful fight against terrorism. This cooperation could be realized on different levels. One is the participation of the military forces in different operations such as those that support peace or respond to crisis, humanitarian operations and other activities abroad.[73] Concerning international military tasks and missions in the prevention and fight against terrorism, the Republic of Croatia has actively participated in International Security Assistance Force (ISAF) operation in Afghanistan since 2002.[74] During the participation in those missions, the members of military forces have a duty to obey the rules of international war and humanitarian law, always and under all circumstances. If there is a suspicion that they have committed a criminal offence, they should be under jurisdiction of the criminal courts.

The institute of extradition has a special place concerning the international cooperation between states in the fight against terrorism. In Croatia, the issue of extradition is regulated by the Act on International Legal Assistance in Criminal Matters[75] and the Act on Mutual Assistance in Criminal Matters Between the Member States of the European Union.[76] Besides following these two acts, Republic

1735 (2006), 1822 (2008) and 1904 (2009) regarding sanctions against the members of the Al-Qaida organization, Osama bin Laden, the Taliban and other individuals, groups, undertakings and entities associated with them (Official Gazette 89/2010 i 80/11).

72 International Restrictive Measures Act, art 11 para 1.

73 The Croatian Parliament decides how Croatian armed forces can operate across the borders on the proposal of the government with the prior approval of the Croatian President. Art 49 para 1 of the Law of Defence, Official Gazette, 73/13.

74 The Republic of Croatia annual information exchange on national implementation of the code of conduct on politico-military aspects of security, 2013, available at http://www.osce.org/fsc/1032135.

75 The Act on International Legal Assistance in Criminal Matters, Official Gazette 178/04.

76 The Act on Mutual Assistance in Criminal Matters Between the Member States of the European Union Official Gazette, 91/10, 81/13, 124/13.

of Croatia has the obligations as a member party of numerous international multilateral and bilateral agreements that apply in the case of extradition. Despite the legislation, the application of the institute of extradition has not been successful enough, especially concerning terrorist criminal offences. Namely, states have not been willing enough to extradite the perpetrators of these crimes, considering them as political offences. The first important step in the process of depoliticizing terrorism was the adoption of the European Convention of the Suppression of Terrorism.

Explanatory Report to the Convention clearly states that "certain crimes are so odious in their methods or results in relation to their motives, that it is no longer justifiable to classify them as 'political offences' for which extradition is not possible."[77] In spite of good intentions of the Convention's creators, the possibility for member parties to make reservation on certain clauses led to the fact that extradition still depends on subjective interpretation of the notion of political criminal offence. Therefore, states rarely call upon states to extradite people for terrorism-related activities. Events that happened after 11 September 2001 instigated states to work on the revision of the Convention in order to further depoliticize the provision of the Convention and harmonize the opinions of the member states concerning the notion and content of the terrorism in relation to the political criminal offences.[78]

Traditional systems of extradition continue to show numerous shortcomings. Among them, two should be emphasized: complexity and delay. This is especially significant when the EU member states are concerned. The shortcomings but also the worldwide treatment of terrorism after the events of September 11 gave rise to the adoption of the Council Framework Decision on the European arrest warrant and surrender procedures between member states.[79] The European arrest decision was enacted by the Council of the European Union, and has been in force since 1 January 2004.

77 Explanatory Report to the European Convention of the Suppression of Terrorism, para 2, available at http://conventions.coe.int/Treaty/EN/Reports/Html/090.htm.

78 In May 2003, the Council of Europe updated the Convention with the Protocol "wishing to strengthen the fight against terrorism while respecting human rights." According to the Protocol, the member states have the right to reject a request for extradition if there is a risk of death penalty or life imprisonment without the possibility of release on probation in the requesting state. This Protocol differs from the original Convention in several main issues. Firstly, the list of offences not regarded as "political crimes" in case of extradition was extended to all acts incriminated by the UN Conventions from 1973. Secondly, a simplified amendment procedure has been introduced that enables the list of criminal acts to be extended without initiating a special procedure for adopting a new protocol. Thirdly, the Convention has been opened to accession by the observers to the Council of Europe.

79 Council Framework Decision of 13 June 2002 on the European arrest warrant and the surrender procedures between Member States, available at http://eur-lex.europa.eu/LexUriServ/LexUriServ.do?uri=OJ:L:2002:190:0001:0018:EN:PDF.

One of the most important provisions of the Framework Decision concerns the specification of the criminal offences that lead to the execution of the European arrest warrant order without the verification of the double criminality of the act, which was, until now, one of the fundamental prerequisites in traditional extradition law. In other words, after receiving the European arrest warrant, an EU member state has to execute it, even if the warrant concerns an offence that is not punishable by the law of the concerned state. This rule is applicable to thirty-two listed offences, among them the criminal offence of terrorism. Despite some difficulties in the implementation of the Framework Decision, experience shows that the process of extradition in the territories of the EU member states is now significantly more efficient, less complex and faster.[80]

Duty to respect human rights and fundamental freedoms has been guaranteed in numerous national constitutions and international agreements. In the jurisprudence of the European Court of Human Rights, individuals have often referred to art 3 of the European Convention for the Protection of Human Rights and Fundamental Freedoms, which prescribes the absolute prohibition of torture or inhuman or degrading treatment or punishment. Also, the Framework Decision prescribes in its Preamble that "no person should be removed, expelled or extradited to a State where there is a serious risk that he or she would be subjected to the death penalty, torture or other inhuman or degrading treatment or punishment." Regarding the obligatory national and international instruments, the Republic of Croatia has a duty to refuse the extradition if there is a danger of violation of human rights or fundamental freedoms.

X. SECRECY AND TERRORISM

Pursuant to the Criminal Procedure Act, criminal courts shall reach their judgments only on the facts and evidence presented at the trial.[81] If the statement of the person is the evidence in the trial, it should be taken by issuing a summons and examining the person. According to positive law, every person summoned as witness is bound to comply with the summons and, if not otherwise prescribed by the Criminal Procedure Act, this person is also bound to testify. The Criminal Procedure Act has prescribed the duty of data protection as one of the basic duties. Pursuant to art 284, a person who would violate a legally binding confidentiality obligation by giving

[80] About the European arrest warrant, see Sievers, Julia, "Too Different to Trust? First Experiences with the Application of the European Arrest Warrant," in Geyer, Florian, Guild Elspeth (eds.) *Security Versus Justice?: Police and Judicial Cooperation in the European Union* (Aldershot, Ashgate, 2008) pp 109–26.

[81] Criminal Procedure Act, art 450 para 1.

a statement may not testify as a witness until the competent authority releases the person from this obligation. The Data Secrecy Act regulates a protection of data collected by the state authorities.[82]

This Act classifies degrees of secrecy for data as top secret, secret, confidential and restricted.[83] Data whose unauthorized disclosure would result in exceptionally grave damage to national security and vital interests of the Republic of Croatia are protected under different degree of secrecy: top secret, secret or confidential. When there is a public interest, the data owner shall determine the proportionality between the right for data access and damage that the protected values would suffer by the public disclosure of information. Accordingly, the owner will decide on maintaining the degree of secrecy, changing the degree of secrecy or seeking declassification or exemption from the obligation to keep data secret, based on the opinion of the National Security Council Office.

Therefore, data that represent a secret could be disclosed and used as the evidence in a criminal proceeding if a competent body that is the data's owner has declassified the secret data. The court may exclude the public from the trial completely or partially if it deems it necessary as for, *inter alia*, the protection of the security and defence of the Republic of Croatia or if the confidentiality of the information could be jeopardized by a public hearing.[84] As discussed previously, the Criminal Procedure Act regulates the terms under which the statement of a witness can be anonymous.[85]

XI. CONCLUSION

The Republic of Croatia is an active member of the global anti-terrorism coalition. Activities and development of the Croatian counter-terrorism system can be divided into two phases, the first ending with the twentieth century and second beginning with the twenty-first century.

In 1991, the year when Croatia gained its independence, the war operations had started. Consequently, the national security system was organized according to the conditions of war. The problem of terrorism was observed through the prism of violent acts within an armed rebellion.[86] After the war ended in the middle of 1990s, development of a modern democratic national security system started. Despite the fact that Croatia had adopted the relevant international documents concerning the

82 Data Secrecy Act, Official Gazette 79/07, 86/12.

83 Previous Data Secrecy Act (Official Gazette 108/96) has distinguished four types of secrets: state secret, official secret, military secret and professional secret.

84 Criminal Procedure Act, art 388 para 2.

85 See Section III.

86 Perešin, Croatian Counter-Terrorism Strategy, p 15.

fight against terrorism and harmonized the national legislation, terrorism was not a focus for state authorities because it was not seen as a threat to national security.

At the beginning of the new century, terrorism was recognized as one of the most dangerous phenomena for the national security. Therefore, it was necessary to develop the complete system of measures for fight against terrorism. It became clear that the problem of terrorism could not be solved within the national borders and that the cooperation of the states is *condition sine qua non* not only in preserving regional and international security, but also in preserving the national security of every state. In 2002, the first strategic document, the National Security Strategy, was adopted. It defines terrorism not only as an internal, but also as an international, threat. The Republic of Croatia has accepted all relevant international anti-terrorist documents and built, at the national level, a wide-ranging legal system in order to cover different aspects of the suppression of terrorism.

Activities in the field of criminal law were especially important. Besides the criminal offence of terrorism, financing of terrorism and terrorist association, in Croatian substantive criminal legislation were also integrated the criminal offences of public provocation to terrorism, recruitment for terrorism and training for terrorism. With the adoption of those criminal offences, the national criminal legislation was completely harmonized with relevant international and regional documents. At the same time, it should be emphasized that in these criminal offences the border of crime and punishment has been moved to an earlier phase, preceding the attempt to commit a terrorist attack. Therefore, the modern standards of protection of fundamental human rights have to be respected while proscribing this type of offences. The Croatian legislator has widened the scope of criminalization of public provocation to terrorism (art 99) according to the relevant international and regional documents. It seems that art 99 CC'11 does not represent an appropriate balance between the duty of the state to protect everyone from terrorism and its obligation to protect freedom of expression as the fundamental human right.

In spite of the whole range of activities that have been taken with the goal to prevent terrorism, some shortcomings could be found in the Croatian perception of the terrorism. It has been recognized only as a global threat to international peace and security that indirectly jeopardizes the interests of the Republic of Croatia.[87] In other words, terrorism is not seen as a direct danger to the national security of Croatia. Such optimism cannot be accepted.[88] Based on the perception that terrorism is a global threat, an elaborate system of terrorism prevention has been built, with the state as the main actor. This system has yet to be used, and no terrorism prosecution has been recorded. The Croatian system is focused on the

87 Action Plan on Prevention and Suppression of Terrorism, p 5.

88 Derenčinović, The evolution of the antiterror legal and institutional framework in Croatia, p 318.

criminal law, but ignores some other important issues. Development of cultural dialogue, promotion of human rights and especially the protection of minorities are crucial, as is the role of every citizen and non-government organization (NGO). Although they are recognized in the National Strategy for the Prevention and Suppression of Terrorism as important holders in the fight against terrorism, measures and instruments that are alternatives to criminal prosecutions have been implemented very slowly in Croatia.

14

Slovenia

Vasilka Sancin and Maša Kovič Dine

I. INTRODUCTION

Slovenia's international legal framework for its counter-terrorism activities consists of treaties binding upon it and rules of customary law, which according to Slovenia's Constitution[1] prevail over any domestic laws and regulations. It is also worthwhile mentioning that 'legal acts and decisions adopted within international organizations to which Slovenia has transferred the exercise of part of its sovereign rights shall be applied in Slovenia in accordance with the legal regulation of these organizations.'[2]

Slovenia is, among others, a member of the UN and its specialized agencies (e.g., the International Civil Aviation Organization [ICAO], the International Maritime Organization [IMO], the International Atomic Energy Agency [IAEA]), Interpol, the European Union (EU), the Council of Europe and participating states of the Organization for Security and Cooperation in Europe (OSCE).

A. *Slovenia's Treaty Status*

The following table details the treaties to which Slovenia is a party. All treaties that Slovenia succeeded to after former Yugoslavia (SFRY) are effective in Slovenia since 25 June 1991 (Day of Independence of Slovenia).[3]

[1] Article 8 of the Constitution of the Republic of Slovenia reads, 'Laws and regulations must comply with generally accepted principles of international law and with treaties that are binding on Slovenia. Ratified and published treaties shall be applied directly', and Article 153, § 2 states ' Laws must be in conformity with generally accepted principles of international law and with valid treaties ratified by the National Assembly, whereas regulations and other general legal acts must also be in conformity with other ratified treaties.' Official Gazette of the Republic of Slovenia Nos. 33/91-I, 42/97, 66/2000, 24/03, 69/04, 68/06, and 47/13.

[2] Article 3a, § 3. This article was added by the Constitutional Act Amending Chapter I and Articles 47 and 68 of the Constitution of the Republic of Slovenia, 27 February 2003 (Official Gazette RS No. 24/03).

[3] In a letter dated 1 July 1992, received by the Secretary-General of the United Nations on the same date and accompanied by a list of multilateral treaties deposited with the Secretary-General, the government

Treaty	International Organization	Signature by Slovenia	Ratification by Slovenia	Accession by Slovenia	Succession by Slovenia
Convention on the Prevention and Punishment of Crimes Against Internationally Protected Persons, Including Diplomatic Agents; New York, 14. 12. 1973	UN				6 July 1992 Effective date: 25 June 1991
International Convention Against the Taking of Hostages; New York, 17. 12. 1979	UN				6 July 1992 Effective date: 25 June 1991
International Convention for the Suppression of Terrorist Bombings; New York, 15. 12. 1997	UN	30 Oct 1998	25 Sep 2003		
International Convention for the Suppression of the Financing of Terrorism; New York, 9. 12. 1999	UN	10 Nov 2001	23 Sep 2004		
International Convention for the Suppression of Acts of Nuclear Terrorism; New York, 13. 4. 2005	UN	14 Sep 2005	17 Dec 2009		
Convention on Offences and Certain Other Acts Committed on Board Aircraft; Tokyo, 14. 9. 1963	ICAO				18 Dec 1992 Effective date: 25 June 1991
Convention for the Suppression of Unlawful Seizure of Aircraft; Hague, 16. 12. 1970	ICAO				27 May 1992 Effective date: 25 June 1991

(continued)

Treaty	International Organization	Signature by Slovenia	Ratification by Slovenia	Accession by Slovenia	Succession by Slovenia
Convention for the Suppression of Unlawful Acts Against the Safety of Civil Aviation; Montreal, 23. 9. 1971	ICAO				27 May 1992 Effective date: 25 June 1991
Protocol on the Suppression of Unlawful Acts of Violence at Airport Serving International Civil Aviation Supplementary to the Convention for the Suppression of Unlawful Acts Against the Safety of Civil Aviation; Montreal, 24. 2. 1988	ICAO				27 May 1992 Effective date: 25 June 1991
Convention on the Marking of Plastic Explosives for the Purpose of Detection; Montreal, 1. 3. 1991	ICAO			5 June 2000[a] Effective date: 4 Aug 2000	
Convention on the Suppression of Unlawful Acts Relating to International Civil Aviation; Beijing, 10. 9. 2010	ICAO				
Protocol Supplementary to the Convention for the Suppression of Unlawful Seizure of Aircraft; Beijing, 10. 9. 2010	ICAO				
Convention on the Physical Protection of Nuclear Material; Vienna, 3. 3. 1980	IAEA				7 July 1992 Effective date: 25 June 1991

Amendments to the Convention on the Physical Protection of Nuclear Material; Vienna, 8. 7. 2005	IAEA		1 Sep 2009	
Convention for the Suppression of Unlawful Acts against the Safety of Maritime Navigation; Rome, 10. 3. 1988	IMO			18 July 2003 Effective date: 16 Oct 2003
Protocol of 2005 to the Convention for the Suppression of Unlawful Acts Against the Safety of Maritime Navigation; London, 14. 10. 2005	IMO			
Protocol for the Suppression of Unlawful Acts Against the Safety of Fixed Platforms Located on the Continental Shelf; Rome, 10. 3. 1988	IMO			18 July 2003 Effective date: 16 Oct 2003
Protocol of 2005 to the Protocol for the Suppression of Unlawful Acts Against the Safety of Fixed Platforms Located on the Continental Shelf; London, 14. 10. 2005	IMO			
European Convention on the Suppression of Terrorism; Strasbourg, 27. 1. 1977	Council of Europe	28 March 2000	29 Nov 2000 Effective date: 1 March 2001	
European Convention on the Transfer of Proceedings in Criminal Matters; Strasbourg, 15. 5. 1972	Council of Europe	24 June 2002		

(continued)

Treaty	International Organization	Signature by Slovenia	Ratification by Slovenia	Accession by Slovenia	Succession by Slovenia
European Convention on the Compensation of Victims of Violent Crimes; Strasbourg, 24. 11.1983	Council of Europe				
Convention on Cybercrime; Budapest, 23. 11. 2001)	Council of Europe	24 July 2002	8 Sep 2004 Effective date: 1 Jan 2005[b]		
Additional Protocol to the Convention on Cybercrime, concerning the criminalization of acts of a racist and xenophobic nature committed through computer systems; Strasbourg, 28. 1. 2003	Council of Europe	26 Feb 2004	8 Sep 2004 Effective date: 1 March 2006		
Protocol Amending the European Convention on the Suppression of Terrorism; Strasbourg, 15. 5. 2003	Council of Europe	15 July 2003	11 May 2004		
Council of Europe Convention on the Prevention of Terrorism; Warsaw, 16. 5. 2005	Council of Europe	19 May 2006	18 Dec 2009 Effective date: 1 April 2010		
Council of Europe Convention on Laundering, Search, Seizure and Confiscation of the Proceeds from Crime and on the Financing of Terrorism; Warsaw, 16. 5. 2005	Council of Europe	28 March 2007	26 April 2010[c] Effective date: 1 Aug 2010		

[a] Declaration, in accordance with Article XIII, § 2, of the Convention, that Slovenia is not a producer state, i.e., a state in whose territory explosives are manufactured (as defined in Article 1, point 6 of the Convention).

[b] In declarations to the Convention, Slovenia made the following designations:

- the Ministry of Foreign Affairs as the authority responsible for making or receiving requests for extradition in the absence of a treaty;
- the Ministry of the Interior, Criminal Investigation Police Directorate, International Police Cooperation Section as the authority responsible for making or receiving requests for provisional arrests in the absence of a treaty (period covered: 20/12/2006–);
- the Ministry of Justice as the central authority responsible for sending and answering requests for mutual assistance, and as a point of contact available on a twenty-four-hours-a-day, seven-days-a-week basis.

  Ministry of the Interior, Criminal Police Directorate, International Police Cooperation Division, Email: interpol.ljubljana@policija.si (period covered: 20/12/2006 –)

[c] Upon ratification, Slovenia made three declarations and a reservation. The declarations accomplished the following:

- designated the Ministry of Finance – Office for Money Laundering Prevention the central authority responsible for sending and answering requests made under the Chapter IV, executing such requests or transmitting them to the authorities competent for their execution;
- declared that Slovenia is ready to accept and execute requests received electronically or by other means of communication under the condition that the request was sent by a secure e-mail, in an encrypted form (e.g., Pretty Good Privacy [PGP] key or other equivalent commonly accepted mode of encoding) or by a protected network, such as Egmont Secure Web (ESW) and FIU-net;
- reserved the right to require that the requests and documents supporting such requests addressed to the central authority of the Republic of Slovenia be accompanied by a translation into Slovenian or the English language;
- declared that, without its prior consent, information or evidence provided by it under the Chapter IV may not be used or transmitted by the authorities of the requesting party in investigations or proceedings other than those specified in the request.

In its reservations, Slovenia declared that it reserves the right not to apply Article 3, § 4, of the Convention (period covered: 1 August 2010 to the present); see http://www.conventions.coe.int/Treaty/Commun/ListeDeclarations.asp?NT=198&CM=8&DF=28/01/2014&CL=ENG&VL=1.

Slovenia is also a party to the following:

- Four Geneva Conventions from 1949 and the three additional protocols (1977 and 2004), applicable to situations of armed conflicts
- The International Covenant on Civil and Political Rights and International Covenant on Economic, Social and Cultural Rights of 1966
- The Convention on the Elimination of All Forms of Discrimination Against Women
- The Convention Against Torture and Other Cruel, Inhuman or Degrading Treatment or Punishment
- The United Nations Convention Against Illicit Traffic in Narcotic Drugs and Psychotropic Substances
- The Convention on the Rights of the Child
- The Rome Statute for the International Criminal Court
- The Protocol to Prevent, Suppress and Punish Trafficking in Persons, Especially Women and Children, supplementing the United Nations Convention Against Transnational Organized Crime
- The Protocol Against the Smuggling of Migrants by Land, Sea and Air, supplementing the United Nations Convention Against Transnational Organized Crime
- The United Nations Convention Against Transnational Organized Crime
- The Protocol Against the Illicit Manufacturing of and Trafficking in Firearms, Their Parts and Components and Ammunition, supplementing the United Nations Convention Against Transnational Organized Crime
- The United Nations Convention Against Corruption
- The Convention Relating to the Status of Refugees
- The Protocol Relating to the Status of Refugees
- The European Convention on Human Rights and Fundamental Freedoms and its Protocols

(footnote 3 continued)
of the Republic of Slovenia notified the UN of the following: 'When declaring independence on 25 June 1991, the Parliament of the Republic of Slovenia determined that international treaties which had been concluded by the SFRY [Socialist Federal Republic of Yugoslavia] and which related to the Republic of Slovenia remained effective on its territory (Article 3 of the Constitutional Law on the implementation of the Constitutional Charter on the Independence and Sovereignty of the Republic of Slovenia…). This decision was taken in consideration of customary international law and of the fact that the Republic of Slovenia, as a former constituent part of the Yugoslav Federation, had granted its agreement to the ratification of the international treaties in accordance with the then valid constitutional provisions. The Republic of Slovenia therefore in principle acknowledges the continuity of treaty rights and obligations under the international treaties concluded by the SFRY before 25 June 1991, but since it is likely that certain treaties may have lapsed by the date of independence of Slovenia or may be outdated, it seems essential that each treaty be subjected to legal examination…' https://treaties.un.org/pages/HistoricalInfo.aspx?#"Slovenia".

- The European Convention on Extradition
- The European Convention on Mutual Assistance in Criminal Matters
- The Additional Protocol to the European Convention on Mutual Assistance in Criminal Matters
- The Treaty of Lisbon amending the Treaty on European Union and the treaty establishing the European community

Slovenia is also a party to the Convention between the Kingdom of Belgium, the Federal Republic of Germany, the Kingdom of Spain, the French Republic, the Grand Duchy of Luxembourg, the Kingdom of the Netherlands and the Republic of Austria on the stepping up of cross-border cooperation, particularly in combating terrorism, cross-border crime and illegal migration[4] (the so-called Prüm Convention) adopted mainly to enable the parties to exchange data regarding DNA, fingerprints and vehicle registration of suspicious persons and to cooperate against terrorism. In addition, Slovenia concluded a number of bilateral treaties concerning *inter alia* combating terrorism.[5]

[4] Official Gazette RS – International Agreements, No. 5/07.

[5] For example, the Agreement between the government of the Republic of Slovenia and the government of the Republic of Croatia on cooperation in combating terrorism, illicit traffic in and abuse of drugs as well as against organized crime (Official Gazette RS – International Agreements, No. 3/94), the Agreement between the Ministry of the Interior of the Republic of Slovenia and the Federal Minister of the Interior of the Republic of Austria on cooperation in the suppression of international organized crime, international illicit drug traffic and international terrorism (Official Gazette RS – International Agreements, No. 4/96), the Agreement between the government of the Republic of Slovenia and the government of the Republic of Albania on cooperation in combating terrorism, illicit traffic in drugs and organized crime (Official Gazette RS – International Agreements, No. 18/94), the Agreement between the government of the Republic of Slovenia and the government of the Republic of Macedonia on cooperation in combating terrorism, illicit traffic in drugs and organized crime (Official Gazette RS – International Agreements, No. 18/94), the Agreement between the government of the Republic of Slovenia and the government of the Slovak Republic on cooperation in combating terrorism, illicit traffic in drugs, psychotropic substances and their precursors and organized crime (Official Gazette RS – International Agreements, No. 6/95), the Agreement between the Republic of Slovenia and the United States of America for the Exchange of Terrorism Screening Information (Official Gazette RS – International Agreements, No. 12/2011), the Agreement between the government of the Republic of Slovenia and the Government of the Czech Republic on cooperation in combating illicit traffic in drugs, psychotropic substances and organized crime and combating terrorism (Official Gazette RS – International Agreements, No. 9/99), the Agreement between the government of the Republic of Slovenia and the government of the Hellenic Republic on cooperation in fighting crime, especially terrorism, illicit drug trafficking and organized crime (Official Gazette RS – International Agreements, No. 29/2003), the Agreement between the government of the Republic of Slovenia and the government of the Kingdom of Sweden on cooperation in the fight against organized crime, illicit drug trafficking in drugs and precursors, terrorism and other serious crimes (Official Gazette RS – International Agreements, No. 11/2005), the Agreement between the government of the Republic of Slovenia and the government of Malta on cooperation in the fight against organized crime, trafficking in illicit drugs, psychotropic substances and precursors, terrorism and other serious crimes (Official Gazette RS – International Agreements, No. 29/2003), the Agreement between the government of the Republic of

Slovenia, as a European state, is a part of a developed regional counter-terrorism architecture.[6] The EU, the Council of Europe and the OSCE offer a wide range of counter-terrorism programs, activities and initiatives that complements Slovenia's legal and policy framework established by various parts of the UN system. Among various EU acts adopted to counter-terrorism,[7] it is the creation of European Arrest Warrant (EAW) that importantly facilitates extradition (also of terrorist suspects) among EU members, including Slovenia.[8] Slovenia also benefits from activities and support of Eurojust and Europol.

Slovenia and the government of the Republic of Bulgaria on cooperation in the fight against organized crime, illicit drugs, psychotropic substances and precursors trafficking, terrorism and other serious crimes (Official Gazette RS – International Agreements, No. 7/2002), the Agreement between the government of the Republic of Slovenia and the government of the Republic of Cyprus concerning cooperation in the fight against terrorism, illicit drug trafficking and organized crime (Official Gazette RS – International Agreements, No. 29/2003), the Agreement between the government of the Republic of Slovenia and the government of the Republic of Montenegro on cooperation in the fight against organized crime, people trafficking and illegal migrations, trafficking in illicit drugs and precursors, terrorism and other crimes (Official Gazette RS – International Agreements, No. 6/2007), the Agreement between the government of the Republic of Slovenia and the government of the Republic of Estonia on cooperation in the fight against organized crime, illicit drugs, psychotropic substances and precursors trafficking and terrorism (Official Gazette RS – International Agreements, No. 1/2004), the Agreement between the government of the Republic of Slovenia and the government of the Republic of Poland on the cooperation in combating terrorism, organized crime, illicit traffic in drugs, psychotropic substances and their precursors (Official Gazette RS – International Agreements, No. 3/97), the Agreement between the government of the Republic of Slovenia and the government of the Republic of Turkey on Cooperation in the fight against organized crime, illicit drugs trafficking, international terrorism and other serious crimes (Official Gazette RS – International Agreements, No. 7/2005), the Agreement between the government of the Republic of Slovenia and the government of Romania on cooperation in fighting against organized crime, illicit drugs, psychotropic substances and precursors trafficking, terrorism and other serious crimes (Official Gazette RS – International Agreements, No. 6/2001), the Agreement between the government of the Republic of Slovenia and the government of the Russian Federation concerning the cooperation in the fight against organized crime, illicit drug trafficking, terrorism and other forms of crime (Official Gazette RS – International Agreements, No. 26/2001), the Agreement between the government of the Republic of Slovenia and the federal government of the Federal Republic of Yugoslavia on cooperation in the fight against organized crime, illicit drugs, psychotropic substances and precursors trafficking, terrorism and other serious crimes (Official Gazette RS – International Agreements, No. 17/2001), the Agreement between the government of the Republic of Slovenia and the government of the Republic of Latvia on cooperation in combating terrorism, organized crime, illicit trafficking in narcotic drugs, psychotropic substances and precursors and other serious crimes (Official Gazette RS – International Agreements, No. 8/2006).

6 Anton Du Plessis: A *snapshot of international criminal justice cooperation against terrorism since 9/11* in: Larissa Van Den Herik and Nico Schrijver (eds.) *Counter-Terrorism Strategies in a Fragmented International Legal Order* (Cambridge: Cambrdige University Press, 2013) at 52.

7 Council of the European Union, Declaration on Combating Terrorism (2004); European Union Counter Terrorism Strategy, Doc. 14469/4/05 REV 4 (2005); European Union Strategy for Combating Radicalization and Recruitment to Terrorism, Doc. 14781/1/05 REV 1 (2005); Council of the European Union, Fighting Against Terrorist Financing: Six Months Report, Doc. 11948/2/07 REV 2 (2007).

8 Slovenia implemented it through the Act on the European Arrest Warrant and Surrender Procedures adopted in 2004 (Official Gazette RS, No. 37/2004 and 102/2007).

II. THE DEFINITION OF TERRORISM

The Slovenian Criminal/Penal Code[9] (hereafter Criminal Code) defines terrorism in Article 108, paragraph 1, which stipulates the following:

> Whosoever with the intention to destroy or severely jeopardize the constitutional, social or political foundations of the Republic of Slovenia or another country or international organization, to arouse fright among the population or to force the government of the Republic of Slovenia or another country or international organization to perform or stop performing something, performs or threatens to perform one or more of the following actions:
>
> - assault on life or body or human rights and freedoms,
> - taking hostages,
> - considerable destruction of state or public buildings or representations of foreign states, transport system, infrastructure, information system, secured platforms in the continental shelf, public place or private property,
> - hijacking of an aircraft, ship or public transport,
> - production, possession, purchase, transport, supply or use of weapons, explosives, nuclear, biological or chemical weapons,
> - research and development of nuclear, biological or chemical weapons,
> - endangering security by releasing hazardous substances or causing fires, floods or explosions,
> - disturbance or termination of the supply of water, electrical energy or other basic natural resources, which could endanger human life, shall be sentenced to imprisonment for between three and fifteen years.

The subsequent paragraphs of Article 108 address also the use of nuclear and radioactive substances; aid in committing crimes of terrorism; intent to cause death; death as a consequence of the carried-out crimes; and membership, participation or founding of a criminal group with the intention to carry out the aforementioned acts from Article 108.

The act of terrorism as a separate criminal act was added to the Slovenian Criminal Code in 1995, initially differentiating between domestic terrorism and international terrorism.[10] This differentiation is based on the division of the 1995 Criminal Code into separate chapters on criminal acts against the security of the Republic of Slovenia on one hand and criminal acts against humanity and international law on the other. Thus, the criminal act of domestic terrorism encompassed only acts that

9 Criminal Code, Official Gazette RS, No. 63/94 from 13.10.1994 and its subsequent changes.

10 The Criminal Codes of the Socialist Federal Republic of Yugoslavia and the Socialist Republic of Slovenia prior to dissolution of the former Yugoslavia did not criminalize terrorism or acts related to terrorism as a separate crime.

would threaten or destroy the constitutional order or security of the Republic of Slovenia, while the act of international terrorism stipulated acts directed towards a foreign state or international organizations. The financing of terrorism was added as a new crime in a 2004 amendment to the Criminal Code.

In 2008, the Slovenian Criminal Code was revised and redrafted, leading to changes in the definition of the act of terrorism and the addition of related criminal acts. Thus, the division between domestic and international terrorism was abandoned and the preceding definition of terrorism was adopted. Beside the criminal act of financing of terrorism (Article 109), two other activities related to terrorism were added as separate criminal offences: incitement and praising of terrorist acts (Article 110) and recruitment and training for terrorism (Article 111).[11] The definition of terrorism and the addition of new criminal acts related to terrorism are based on the European Union Council Framework Decision on Combating Terrorism from 2002,[12] the amended European Union Council Framework Decision on Combating Terrorism from 2008[13] and in parts also the Council of Europe's Convention on the Prevention of Terrorism.[14]

The comprehensive legal definition of the criminal act of terrorism in the Slovenian Criminal Code has not been followed in other legal acts addressing terrorism. The Act on the Prevention of Money Laundering and Financing of Terrorism[15] refers to the definition of terrorism as defined in Article 2 of the International Convention for the Suppression of the Financing of Terrorism.[16] The Act on Prevention of Money Laundering and Financing of Terrorism was adopted in order to implement the EU Directive on the prevention of the use of the financial system for the purpose of money laundering and terrorist financing.[17] It is interesting

[11] In December 2014, a proposal was made for the addition of the definition of "foreign terrorist fighters" in the Criminal Code. The proposal was not supported by the government of the Republic of Slovenia, which claimed that the elements of the definition were already included in the articles of the current Criminal Code, so the proposal was thus rejected in the Parliament.

[12] Council Framework Decision of 13 June 2002 on Combating Terrorism (2002/475/JHA), OJ L 164, 22.6.2002, at 3.

[13] The preparation of the proposal for the 2008 revision of the Slovenian Criminal Code was carried out in parallel with the process for the amendment of the Framework Decision of 2008, thus the proposal for the Slovenian Criminal Code includes also the proposed amendments of the Framework Decision. Council Framework Decision 2008/919/JHA of 28 November 2008 amending Framework Decision 2002/475/JHA on combating terrorism, OJ L 330, 9.12.2008, at 21.

[14] Council of Europe's Convention on the Prevention of Terrorism, 16 May 2005, ETS No. 169.

[15] Act on Prevention of Money Laundering and Financing of Terrorism, Official Gazette RS, No. 60/2007 from 6.7.2007 and subsequent changes.

[16] International Convention for the Suppression of the Financing of Terrorism, Resolution A/RES/54/109, UNTS 2178, at 197.

[17] Directive 2005/60/EC of the European Parliament and the Council of 26 October 2005 on the prevention of the use of the financial system for the purpose of money laundering and terrorist financing, OJ L 309/15, 25.11.2005.

that while the directive refers to the EU Council Framework Decision[18] to provide a definition of terrorism, Slovenian legislators decided to refer to the UN convention. The definition of terrorism under the International Convention for the Suppression of the Financing of Terrorism defines terrorism as any act that constitutes an offence under the treaties enumerated in the annex[19] to the convention or any "act intended to cause death or serious bodily injury to a civilian, or to any other person not taking an active part in the hostilities in a situation of armed conflict, when the purpose of such act, by its nature or context, is to intimidate a population, or to compel a government or an international organization to do or to abstain from doing any act." A careful look at the two definitions (the definition of the crime of terrorism in Article 108 of the Criminal Code and the definition of the terrorist act in the Act on Prevention of Money Laundering and Financing of Terrorism) indicates that certain acts can be considered as terrorism under one definition and not the other. The definition of terrorism adopted in the Act on Prevention of Money Laundering and Financing of Terrorism differs from the definition in the Criminal Code. It does not include, for example, the acts of destruction of public buildings, interference with the electronic information systems or release of hazardous substances, which are included in Article 108 of the Criminal Code. At the same time, it includes other acts omitted from the Criminal Code, such as acts related to the safety of fixed platforms located on the continental shelf. This may cause inconsistencies, as the financing for a performance of one act can be considered illegal as a crime of financing of terrorism, while the actual performance of this act does not fall under the definition of a crime of terrorism in the Criminal Code.[20] It may however, be considered a different crime. Thus, the Council of Europe's Committee of Experts on the Evaluation of Anti–Money Laundering Measures and the Financing of

[18] Directive 2005/60/EC, Article 1, § 4.

[19] These treaties are: Convention for the Suppression of Unlawful Seizure of Aircraft, Convention for the Suppression of Unlawful Acts against the Safety of Civil Aviation, Convention on the Prevention and Punishment of Crimes against Internationally Protected Persons, including Diplomatic Agents, adopted by the General Assembly of the United Nations, International Convention against the Taking of Hostages, adopted by the General Assembly of the United Nations, Convention on the Physical Protection of Nuclear Material, Protocol for the Suppression of Unlawful Acts of Violence at Airports Serving International Civil Aviation, supplementary to the Convention for the Suppression of Unlawful Acts against the Safety of Civil Aviation, Convention for the Suppression of Unlawful Acts against the Safety of Maritime Navigation, Protocol for the Suppression of Unlawful Acts against the Safety of Fixed Platforms located on the Continental Shelf, International Convention for the Suppression of Terrorist Bombings, adopted by the General Assembly of the United Nations.

[20] This was confirmed also by the Council of Europe's Committee of Experts on the Evaluation of Anti–Money Laundering Measures and the Financing of Terrorism (MONEYVAL), Council of Europe, Committee of Experts on the Evaluation of Anti–Money Laundering Measures and the Financing of Terrorism (MONEYVAL) (hereafter MONEYVAL Report), Slovenia, Report on Fourth Assessment Visit, 17 March 2010, at 32.

Terrorism (hereafter MONEYVAL) in its last report on Slovenia (the fourth report from March 2010) suggested the extension of the definition of the crime of terrorism in the Criminal Code to include all the elements of terrorist acts recognized by the International Convention for the Suppression of the Financing of Terrorism.[21] The same report also suggested that the definition be extended also to include among the elements of the crime of terrorism, the acts referred to in the Second Protocol to the Convention for the Suppression of Unlawful Acts Against the Safety of Maritime Navigation,[22] such as seizing or exercising control over a fixed platform by force or threat thereof or any other form of intimidation, performing an act of violence against a person on board a fixed platform if that act is likely to endanger its safety and causing damage to the fixed platform that is likely to endanger its safety.[23]

Although the legislators' intention was to transpose the 2002 and 2008 EU Council Framework Decision, they nevertheless adopted a restrictive definition of the crime of terrorism, providing an exhaustive list of acts that compose the crime of terrorism. It is interesting that the legislators did not use a blanket norm with reference to international law for defining the act of terrorism, as they did, for example, with the crime of piracy.[24] Such an approach would eliminate the aforementioned inconsistencies with the definition of terrorism under the Act on Prevention of Money Laundering and Financing of Terrorism.

III. CRIMINAL LAWS AND PROSECUTIONS

The crime of terrorism, as defined in Slovenia's Criminal Code, includes all the elements of terrorism (both objective and subjective) from the EU Council Framework Decision. As the latter was influenced by UN Security Council

[21] The report suggested that the financing of a terrorist and the financing of a terrorist organization should be separately incriminated in the Criminal Code. "The offence of terrorism defined in Article 108 of the Slovenian Criminal Code has an overarching condition while under UN Conventions, the funding of the acts that constitute an offence is to be prohibited regardless of such condition (…). Therefore the criminalization of the terrorist financing act is not as broad as required by the convention." MONEYVAL Report, at 32.

[22] Second Protocol to the Convention for the Suppression of Unlawful Acts Against the Safety of Maritime Navigation, LEG/CONF.15/21, 1.11.2005.

[23] Council of Europe, Committee of Experts on the Evaluation of Anti–Money Laundering Measures and the Financing of Terrorism (MONEYVAL), Slovenia, Report on Fourth Assessment Visit, 17 March 2010, at 32.

[24] Criminal Code, Article 374: "(1) Whoever by force or serious threat of force, or violation of the rules of international law, takes over command of an aircraft or of a sea vessel shall be sentenced to imprisonment for not less one and not more than ten years. (2) The same sentence shall be imposed on the member of the crew of an aircraft or of a sea vessel who undertakes a mutiny and takes over the command of the aircraft or sea vessel. (3) If the offence under §s 1 or 2 of this Article entails the death of one or more persons or a substantial loss of property, the perpetrator shall be punished by imprisonment of not less than five and not more than fifteen years."

IV. INVESTIGATIVE POWERS

The Counter-Terrorism and Extreme Violence Division within the Ministry for the Interior is responsible for criminal investigation of offences related to terrorist crimes. The division also deals with risk analysis and contributes to threat assessments.[48] It is the police contact point for the national co-coordinator for counter-terrorism, which is the Director of the Slovene Intelligence and Security Agency.[49]

The Police Act[50] grants police no special powers in regard to criminal investigations of the crime of terrorism. According to Article 3, police officers may conduct anti-terrorist searches of premises, buildings, facilities and areas in order to ensure the general safety of persons and property on particular premises, in buildings and at facilities. An anti-terrorist search as defined in the Police Act is comprised of an explosives search, a chemical-bacteriological-radiological search and a search for electronic surveillance devices.[51] Article 36b allows the police to carry out covert surveillance of individuals involved in activities that could be regarded as crimes of terrorism, financing of terrorism, incitement and praising of terrorist acts and recruitment and training for terrorism. However, this is not exclusive to acts related to terrorism, but can be approved also for thirty-seven other acts, such as murder or piracy.

Furthermore, Article 149a of the Code on Criminal Procedure stipulates that secret surveillance of a certain person may be ordered if there are reasonable grounds for suspecting that the person has committed, is committing, is preparing to commit or is organizing the commission of any of the criminal offences specified in the fourth paragraph of the article; if it is reasonable to conclude that police officers would be unable to uncover, prevent or prove this offence using other measures; or if these other measures would give rise to disproportionate difficulties.[52] The crime of terrorism is not specifically referred to in this article, but falls under the category of crimes for which a sentence of imprisonment over five years is prescribed. Secret surveillance may also, under exceptional circumstances, be ordered with respect to a person who is not a suspect if it is reasonable to conclude that surveillance of this person will lead to the identification of a suspect whose personal data are unknown.[53] Such surveillance can be carried out by continuous or repeated observation or tracking with the use of technical devices, including those for recording of

48 Ministry of Foreign Affairs of the Republic of Slovenia, Information exchange on the Code of Conduct of the Politico-Military Aspects of Security (hereafter Information exchange) FSC.EMI/77/12, 12 April 2012, http://www.osce.org/fsc/89681, at 9.

49 Protiteroristični koordinator, Information exchange, at 9.

50 Police Act, Official Gazette RS, No. 49/98 from 3.7.1998 and subsequent changes.

51 Police Act, Article 40.

52 Code on Criminal Procedure, Article 149a, § 1.

53 Code on Criminal Procedure, Article 149a, § 2.

sound, photography and video; the surveillance must be focused on the location, movement and activities of the surveilled person.[54] Surveillance may take place in public locations and private locations with the consent of the owner.[55] The state prosecutor may permit secret surveillance on the basis of a written order and at the written request of the police.[56] The investigating judge must issue an order in cases where the surveillance includes recording of sounds, secret positioning of technical devices for determining the movement of the suspect in closed/private locations, use of private locations for surveillance or surveillance of an individual who is not a suspect.[57] In exceptional cases, if written orders cannot be obtained in time and if a delay would present a risk, the state prosecutor may, at the verbal request of the police, allow the measure to commence on the basis of a verbal order.[58] Application of a measure may last for a maximum of two months; if due cause is adduced, it may be extended every two months by means of a written order.[59]

Article 150 stipulates that for crimes against the security of the Republic of Slovenia and its constitutional order and for crimes against humanity and international law for which a sentence by imprisonment of five years and more is prescribed, including the crime of terrorism and crimes related to terrorism, the surveillance of communications systems, including the computer system of a bank or institution that provides financial services, may be granted.[60] In these cases, only the investigating judge may grant the power of surveillance upon a written request by the state prosecutor. The police shall cease surveillance measures as soon as the reason for their necessity is no longer in place.[61] The police shall send the body that ordered the measure a monthly report on the progress of the measure and the information obtained and shall notify it of the cessation of surveillance without delay.[62] The police must carry out secret surveillance in a way that encroaches in the least possible manner on the rights of persons who are not suspects.[63] If any of these surveillance activities have been carried out in contravention to the aforementioned restrictions, the results cannot be used as evidence against the suspect.[64] Similar rules apply also to undercover operations.[65]

54 Code on Criminal Procedure, Article 149a, § 3.
55 Code on Criminal Procedure, Article 149a, § 3.
56 Code on Criminal Procedure, Article 149a, § 5.
57 Code on Criminal Procedure, Article 149a, § 6.
58 Code on Criminal Procedure, Article 149a, § 8.
59 Code on Criminal Procedure, Article 149a, § 10.
60 Code on Criminal Procedure, Article 150.
61 Code on Criminal Procedure, Article 149a, § 11.
62 Code on Criminal Procedure, Article 149a, § 11.
63 Code on Criminal Procedure, Article 149a, § 13.
64 Code on Criminal Procedure, Article 154, § 4.
65 CODEXTER Report.

The police also control the Slovenian border in accordance with the State Border Control Act.[66] To carry out its tasks of control, the police may perform personal checks, vehicle checks and goods checks, as well as identity checks at international traffic connections and facilities relating to cross-border traffic.[67] Furthermore, it may also adopt special measures in specific cases to prevent risks that constitute a direct threat to public safety and order, particularly to the life and health of people and property.[68] In order to protect the state border efficiently, the police may keep records of persons subject to border checks and records of persons subject to an identification procedure.[69]

The Slovene Intelligence and Security Agency (SISA) is the only Slovenian government agency with a mandate to collect intelligence information in the field of counter-terrorism. Its main tasks are to collect and analyze data and information on the preparations for and the commission of terrorist and other violent acts by individuals, organizations and groups on the territory of Slovenia or by abusing its territory.[70] The SISA reports directly to the Prime Minister; however, it also forwards to the relevant ministers and other officials information relating to their field of work in order for the competent authorities to take and adopt necessary measures.

In 2003, a special interdepartmental working group on transnational threats, including a special group focusing on the terrorist threat to Slovenia, was established by the National Security Council. The group is chaired by the Director of SISA and is composed of representatives of the SISA, the Ministry of the Interior, the police, the Ministry of Justice, the Ministry of Foreign Affairs, the Intelligence and Security Service of the Ministry of Defense, the General Staff of the Slovenian Armed Forces, the Office for Money Laundering Prevention and the Customs Administration.[71] A year later, the government created the post of Counter-Terrorism Coordinator, which is also held by the Director of the SISA.[72]

The National Security Council sets the requirements for the collection of information and performance of analysis by SISA.[73] Other duties and responsibilities of SISA are defined in the Act on Slovene Intelligence and Security Agency.[74] If the Agency establishes that grounds exist for suspecting that a certain person has committed, or is preparing or organizing, a crime of terrorism or facilitating in the

66 State Border Control Act, Official Gazette RS, No. 60/2007 from 6. 7. 2007 and subsequent changes.

67 State Border Control Act, Articles 28–9, 35a–b.

68 State Border Control Act, Article 6.

69 State Border Control Act, Articles 40–3.

70 CODEXTER Report at 5.

71 Information exchange, at 9.

72 Information exchange at 9.

73 CODEXTER Report, at 5.

74 Act on Slovene Intelligence and Security Agency, Official Gazette RS, No. 23/1999 from 8. 4. 1999 and subsequent amendments.

preparation of performance of this crime, SISA must notify the competent authorities (the police or the state prosecutor) about it.[75] The SISA cooperates in this area with the Ministry of the Interior and the police, the Ministry of Defense and also, if necessary, the competent State Prosecutor's Office or other competent institutions (e.g., the Office for Money Laundering Prevention).[76] The information that SISA gathers can be used in criminal proceedings conditioned upon the requirements of evidence gathering in the Code of Criminal Proceedings described in Section II.

V. PROSCRIPTION AND LISTING OF TERRORIST GROUPS AND INDIVIDUALS

Slovenia does not have a national mechanism for proscription or listing of terrorists or terrorist groups and adoption of restrictive measures directed against them.[77] In 2006 Slovenia adopted the Act Relating to Restricting Measures Introduced or Implemented in Compliance with Legal Instruments and Decisions Adopted Within International Organizations,[78] which grants it the legal basis for issuing of regulations to implement United Nations Security Council Resolutions 1267 (1999) and 1373 (2001) and the EU Regulation on specific restrictive measures directed against certain persons and entities with a view to combating terrorism.[79] For the act's implementation, the Decree concerning restrictive measures for certain persons and entities with a view to combating terrorism was adopted, according to which persons should inform the Ministry of Foreign Affairs of attempts to act contrary to the prohibitions laid down in the EU Regulation, as well as of any measures taken for the implementation of the provisions of the EU Regulation.[80] The issued regulations specify the type, implementation method and the duration of restrictive measures, their supervision and sanctions for violation.[81] The restrictive measures automatically terminate or cease to apply when the corresponding EU and UN legal acts cease to apply.[82] The proposals for issuing of these regulations and monitoring of their implementation are carried out by the Interdepartmental Working Group for Implementation of Restricting Measures and Monitoring of

75 Act on Slovene Intelligence and Security Agency, Article 8, § 2.
76 CODEXTER Report, at 5.
77 CODEXTER Report, at 4; Information exchange, at 6.
78 Act Relating to Restricting Measures Introduced or Implemented in Compliance with Legal Instruments and Decisions Adopted Within International Organizations, Official Gazette RS, No. 127/2006 from 7. 12. 2006, Article 3, § 1.
79 Council Regulation (EC) No 2580/2001 of 27 December 2001 on specific restrictive measures directed against certain persons and entities with a view to combating terrorism, OJ L 344/70 from 28.12.2001.
80 CODEXTER Report, at 4.
81 MONEYVAL Report, at 35.
82 MONEYVAL Report, at 35.

Activities Related to Combating Terrorism established under Article 7 of the Act Relating to Restricting Measures Introduced or Implemented in Compliance with Legal Instruments and Decisions Adopted Within International Organizations, headed by a representative of the Ministry of Foreign Affairs and consisting of representatives from other ministries and institutions.[83] This group can also propose the introduction of restrictive measures in regard to domestic terrorists; however, all the restrictive measures currently in place are based on the United Nations Security Council (UNSC) and EU instruments.[84]

As no national listing of terrorists or terrorist organizations has yet been adopted, there have also been no challenges to the listings. Article 8 of the Act Relating to Restricting Measures Introduced or Implemented in Compliance with Legal Instruments and Decisions Adopted Within International Organizations[85] enables persons and entities to apply to the relevant ministry in respect to matters arising from the regulations on restrictive measures made under the Act. The Slovenian authorities have recognized that this provision is wide enough to include applications made in respect to the exceptions allowed by the UN and EU regarding access to funds for humanitarian needs, delisting requests, or people or entities wrongly identified as a person or entity on the relevant UN or EU lists.[86] Such applications are dealt with according to the general administrative procedure.[87]

VI. REGULATION OF TERRORISM FINANCING

Financing terrorism is a criminal offence defined in Article 109 of the Criminal Code:

> (1) Whoever provides or collects money or assets with the intention of this being used partly or entirely for the perpetration of the crime referred to in Article 108 of this Code [the crime of terrorism] shall be punished by imprisonment of one to ten years.
>
> (2) The same sentence shall apply to the perpetrator of an act referred to in the preceding paragraph also where money or assets provided or collected for the intended purpose were not actually used for the perpetration of crimes set out in the preceding paragraph.

[83] MONEYVAL Report, at 36.

[84] MONEYVAL Report, at 36.

[85] Act Relating to Restricting Measures Introduced or Implemented in Compliance with Legal Instruments and Decisions Adopted Within International Organizations, Official Gazette RS, No. 127/2006 from 7. 12. 2006.

[86] MONEYVAL Report, at 36–7.

[87] MONEYVAL Report, at 36–7.

(3) If such act referred to in the preceding paragraph of this Article was perpetrated within an organized crime group, the perpetrator shall be punished by imprisonment of three to fifteen years.

(4) Money and assets referred to in the preceding paragraphs shall be seized.

This article was added to the Criminal Code in response to the UN Security Council Resolution 1373, International Convention on the Suppression of the Financing of Terrorism and the EU Council Framework Decision on Combating Terrorism. Article 109 criminalizes any collection or provision of money that is used with the special intent to perform a terrorist act. It is thus a preparatory crime. Crucial is the special/subjective intent of the perpetrator to use the funds for the performance of an act of terrorism. It is irrelevant whether the funds are collected legally or or illegally. This special/subjective intent differentiates this preparatory crime from other general preparatory crimes.[88] The article criminalizes the actual provision or collection of funds regardless of whether the act of terrorism has been performed or not.

The general provisions of the Criminal Code apply also to the crime of financing terrorism, which means that the attempt to commit a crime of financing terrorism, participating as an accomplice or organizing or directing the crime of financing of terrorism is also criminalized.

The issue of financing of terrorism is further defined in the Act on Prevention of Money Laundering and Financing of Terrorism, which was adopted in 2007, and where the aforementioned elements of the act of financing of terrorism are clarified.[89] Additionally, for its own purpose, the Financing Act also defines the terms "terrorist" and "terrorist organization." As discussed previously, it defines terrorism in accordance with the 1999 Convention on the Financing of Terrorism and not as defined in the Criminal Code. According to the Financing Act, a terrorist is someone who in any way performs or tries to perform a terrorist act, participates in the performance of the terrorist act as an accomplice, facilitator or aide; organizes the performance of a terrorist act; or intentionally contributes to the performance of a terrorist act of a group of people that act with a common aim, with the intention to contribute to the continuous performance of a terrorist act or with awareness of the intention of the group to perform the terrorist act.[90] These same elements also define the terrorist organization, as a group of terrorists, that is, individuals who satisfy the aforementioned elements of the definition of a terrorist.[91] It needs to be pointed

[88] Polona Mozetič: Kaznivo dejanje financiranja terorizma: zlo preprečevanja zla, *Pravna praksa*, No. 26 (2008), at 18–19.

[89] See Section II of this chapter.

[90] Act on Prevention of Money Laundering and Financing of Terrorism, Article 2, § 4.

[91] Act on Prevention of Money Laundering and Financing of Terrorism, Article 2, § 5.

out that the Financing Act provides the only definition of a terrorist organization in the Slovenian legislation. Paragraphs 6 through 8 of Article 108 of the Criminal Code criminalize only membership, participation or founding of a criminal group with the intention to carry out crimes of terrorism, but do not specifically define the group. The third report of MONEYVAL recommended to the Slovenian authorities that the legislation should differentiate between the crime of financing an individual terrorist and a crime of financing a terrorist group.[92] This has not yet been addressed in the legislation.

The 2007 Act on Prevention of Money Laundering and Financing of Terrorism was adopted to implement the EU Directive 2005/60/EC on the prevention of the use of the financial system for the purpose of money laundering and terrorist financing.[93] The preparation of the Act was based on the following documents: 40 FATF Recommendations on money laundering from 2003,[94] IX Special FATF Recommendations on Financing of Terrorism from 2001 and 2004 (Special FATF Recommendations),[95] Council of Europe Convention on Laundering, Search, Seizure and Confiscation of the Proceeds from Criminal Offences, including Financing of Terrorism from 2005,[96] EU Regulation No. 1781/2006 on Data on Payer Accompanying Transfers of Funds[97] and EU Regulation No. 1889/2005 on cash control by entering or leaving the EU.[98] The Act has replaced the previous one on the prevention of money laundering and harmonized national law with respect to the provisions of the revised anti–money laundering legal instruments. It also added the crime of financing of terrorism, thus bringing Slovenian legislation in line with the new standards on countering the financing of terrorism.[99] The same year, Slovenia also signed the Council of Europe Convention on Laundering, Search,

[92] MONEYVAL Report, at 16; OMLP Report 2012, http://www.uppd.gov.si/fileadmin/uppd.gov.si/pageuploads/deloUrada/letno_porocilo_2012_tiskovno.pdf, at 32.

[93] Directive 2005/60/EC of the European Parliament and of the Council of 26 October 2005 on the prevention of the use of the financial system for the purpose of money laundering and terrorist financing, OJ L 309/15, 25. 11. 2005.

[94] Financial Action Task Force on Money Laundering, The Forty Recommendations, 20 June 2003, http://www.fatf-gafi.org/media/fatf/documents/recommendations/pdfs/FATF%20Recommendations%202003.pdf.

[95] Financial Action Task Force on Money Laundering, FATF IX Special Recommendations, http://www.fatf-gafi.org/media/fatf/documents/reports/FATF%20Standards%20-%20IX%20Special%20Recommendations%20and%20IN%20rc.pdf.

[96] Council of Europe Convention on Laundering, Search, Seizure and Confiscation of the Proceeds from Criminal Offences, Including Financing of Terrorism, CETS No. 198, 16 May 2005.

[97] Regulation (EC) No. 1781/2006 of the European Parliament and Council from 15 November 2006 on information on payer accompanying transfers of funds, OJ L 345/1 from 18.12.2006.

[98] Regulation of European Parliament and Council No. 1889/2005 from 26 October, 2005 on controls of cash by entering or leaving the Community, OJ L 309/9 from 25.11.2005.

[99] CODEXTER Report.

Seizure and Confiscation of the Proceeds from Crime and on the Financing of Terrorism, which was ratified in August 2010.

With the changes to the Act on Prevention of Money Laundering and Financing of Terrorism the Office for Money Laundering Prevention (OMLP)[100] gained the mandate in the areas of detection and prevention of the financing of terrorism in addition to money laundering. Since 2005 to 2012, the notification of suspicious money transactions to the OMLP quintupled, as has the number of transfers suspicious to the prosecutor.[101] However, so far only thirteen of the notifications received by the office were related to the offence of financing terrorism under Article 109 of the Criminal Code. In 2009, the first notification was received in which the office confirmed the suspicion of financing of terrorism and transferred all the information and data to the competent authorities.[102] In 2010 and 2011, another such notification was received that was transferred to the police and the Slovenian intelligence unit[103] and the state prosecutor[104] respectively. No information is available from the police or the state prosecutor regarding these cases. The other notifications were received by the office in 2009 (4), 2010 (1), 2011 (3) and 2012 (1); however, the office denied the existence of reasonable grounds for suspicion of the crime of financing of terrorism.[105]

Since 1995 to 2012, a total of 265 judicial proceedings were initiated for the crime of money laundering, however, none for the crime of financing of terrorism. By 31 December 2012, 103 of these cases were concluded with the force of *res judicata*.[106] Among these, fifty cases were dismissed by the prosecutor; thirteen cases were acquitted; in nine cases, a judgment of conviction was issued; in three cases, a

[100] Act on Prevention of Money Laundering and Financing of Terrorism, Articles 53–72.

[101] From 2005 to 2012, the number of reported suspicious transactions rose from 116 to 559. Similarly, the number of suspicious transactions that were transferred by the Office for Money Laundering Prevention to the state prosecutor rose from 32 in 2005 to 175 in 2012. MONEYVAL Report, at 16; Office of Money Laundering Prevention, Data from the Report of the Office of Money Laundering Prevention for year 2012 (hereafter OMLP Report), http://www.uppd.gov.si/fileadmin/uppd.gov.si/pageuploads/deloUrada/letno_porocilo_2012_tiskovno.pdf, at 6.

[102] OMLP Report 2009, http://www.uppd.gov.si/fileadmin/uppd.gov.si/pageuploads/deloUrada/letno_porocilo_2009_tiskovno.pdf, at 8.

[103] OMLP Report 2010, http://www.uppd.gov.si/fileadmin/uppd.gov.si/pageuploads/deloUrada/letno_porocilo_2010_tiskovno.pdf, at 8.

[104] OMLP Report 2012, http://www.uppd.gov.si/fileadmin/uppd.gov.si/pageuploads/deloUrada/letno_porocilo_2012_tiskovno.pdf, at 11.

[105] OMLP Report 2009, http://www.uppd.gov.si/fileadmin/uppd.gov.si/pageuploads/deloUrada/letno_porocilo_2009_tiskovno.pdf, at 8; OMLP Report 2010, http://www.uppd.gov.si/fileadmin/uppd.gov.si/pageuploads/deloUrada/letno_porocilo_2010_tiskovno.pdf, at 8; OMLP Report 2011, http://www.uppd.gov.si/fileadmin/uppd.gov.si/pageuploads/deloUrada/letno_porocilo_2011_tiskovno.pdf, at 7; OMLP Report 2012, http://www.uppd.gov.si/fileadmin/uppd.gov.si/pageuploads/deloUrada/letno_porocilo_2012_tiskovno.pdf, at 11.

[106] OMLP Report 2012, http://www.uppd.gov.si/fileadmin/uppd.gov.si/pageuploads/deloUrada/letno_porocilo_2012_tiskovno.pdf, at 19.

judgment of conviction for the crime of concealment of money laundering was issued; in twenty-four cases, either the prosecutor withdrew from the proceedings or the court discontinued the case; and four cases were referred to other countries.[107] For the rest of the 162 cases, the prosecutor has either not yet adopted a decision or they are in pre-trial procedure.[108]

The OMLP is a body under the responsibility of the Ministry of Finance. The office receives, collects, analyzes and disseminates information on any money transaction in the amount above 30,000 euros, money transfers over the Slovenian border in the amount above 10,000 euros or suspicious money transaction or parties for which there are reasonable grounds to believe the crime of money laundering or financing of terrorism is taking place.[109] If the office upon the analysis of the received and requested data believes that the crime of money laundering or financing of terrorism has been performed, the office forwards a written notification with all the information on the suspected crime to the competent authorities, which are the police or state prosecutor.[110] In such cases, the office may also issue a written request to put the money transfer on hold for maximum of seventy-two hours.[111] Additionally, the office can forward to the competent authorities information on other suspicion criminal activities that might be related to money laundering and financing of terrorism such as creation of criminal groups, corruption or other serious crimes with a sentence of imprisonment of five years or more.[112] The office also manages a database of all acts of money laundering and financing of terrorism[113] and may exchange information with other countries on financial transactions and adopt agreements on cooperation with its counterparts.[114] Hence, the office is one of the founding offices of the international Egmont group of offices of money laundering prevention.[115] By 30 September 2012, the office had signed thirty-eight memoranda of understanding on cooperation and exchange of information for money laundering prevention with thirty-eight foreign offices.[116]

107 OMLP Report 2012, http://www.uppd.gov.si/fileadmin/uppd.gov.si/pageuploads/deloUrada/letno_porocilo_2012_tiskovno.pdf, at 19.

108 OMLP Report 2012, http://www.uppd.gov.si/fileadmin/uppd.gov.si/pageuploads/deloUrada/letno_porocilo_2012_tiskovno.pdf, at 20.

109 Act on Prevention of Money Laundering and Financing of Terrorism, Article 4, 38, 49.

110 Act on Prevention of Money Laundering and Financing of Terrorism, Article 61.

111 Act on Prevention of Money Laundering and Financing of Terrorism, Article 58.

112 Act on Prevention of Money Laundering and Financing of Terrorism, Article 62.

113 Act on Prevention of Money Laundering and Financing of Terrorism, Article 70.

114 Act on Prevention of Money Laundering and Financing of Terrorism, Article 64–9.

115 OMLP Report 2012, http://www.uppd.gov.si/fileadmin/uppd.gov.si/pageuploads/deloUrada/letno_porocilo_2012_tiskovno.pdf, at 24–5.

116 Signed Memorandums of Understanding with FinCEN (USA), CTIF/CFI (Belgium), UIC and Guardio di Finanza (Italy), USPN (Croatia), FAU (Czech Republic), ONPCSB (Romania), Ofic

The office also regularly on a monthly basis examines its own database on money transactions, suspicious transactions and transfers of cash to the EU and from it, to detect whether any individuals or organizations on the EU Consolidated List of Persons, Groups and Entities subject to EU Financial Sanctions carried out any financial transactions in Slovenia. The EU directives and United Nations resolutions have adopted certain financial sanctions against listed individuals or groups.[117] So far, no such cases have been detected.[118]

The work of the office is closely related to and, in many instances, bound by instructions of the Council of Europe's MONEYVAL and the European Commission's Committee on Prevention of Money Laundering and Financing of Terrorism.[119] Slovenia is not a member of the Financial Action Task Force (FATF). The OMLP is also the central body to receive requests and application from other countries for information regarding money laundering, search, seizure and confiscation of proceeds under the ratified Council of Europe Convention on Laundering, Search, Seizure and Confiscation of the Proceeds from Crime and on the Financing of Terrorism.[120]

As mentioned previously, so far the Office for Money Laundering Prevention has in three instances confirmed the existence of reasonable grounds for the crime of financing terrorism. The cases have been transferred to the police, state intelligence units or the state prosecutor, but no information is available on their handling. According to paragraph 4 of Article 109 of the Criminal Code, confiscation of

UFP (Slovakia), BFI (Bolgaria), MOKAS (Cyprus), KDFIU (Latvia), FCIS (Lithuania), SICCFIN (Monaco), MLPD (Macedonia), DCFML (Albania), General Inspector of Financial Information (Poland), AUSTRAC (Austalia), State Department for Financial Monitoring within Ministry of Finance (Ukraine), Uprava za spečavanje pranja novca (Serbia), Money Laundering Information Bureau (Estonia), IMPA (Israel), Federal Service for Financial Monitroing (Russia), Uprava za spečavanje pranja novca (Montenegro), Financial Monitoring Service (Georgia), Financial Report and Analysis Centre (Canada), Financial Analysis Unit (Chile), Financial Intelligence Department of the State Investigation and Protectiona Agency (Bosnia and Herzegovina), Ufficio Antiriciclaggio, banca Centrale della Repubblica di San Mario (San Marino), Meldpunt Ongebruikelijke Transacties (Dutch Antilles), Centre for Combating Economic Crime and Corruption (Moldova), Financial Itelligence Analysis Unit (FIAU) (Malta), Financial Intelliegence Centre (Kosovo) and Reporting Center Unusual Transactions (Aruba) and with counterparts in Honduras, Islamic Republic of Iran, Mongolia, Kingdom of Saudi Arabia and Sri Lanka.

117 OMLP Report 2012, http://www.uppd.gov.si/fileadmin/uppd.gov.si/pageuploads/deloUrada/letno_porocilo_2012_tiskovno.pdf, at 11.

118 OMLP Report 2012, http://www.uppd.gov.si/fileadmin/uppd.gov.si/pageuploads/deloUrada/letno_porocilo_2012_tiskovno.pdf, at 11.

119 *See* OMLP Report 2012, http://www.uppd.gov.si/fileadmin/uppd.gov.si/pageuploads/deloUrada/letno_porocilo_2012_tiskovno.pdf, at 21–3.

120 Act of Ratification of the Council of Europe Convention on Laundering, Search, Seizure and Confiscation of the Proceeds from Crime and on the Financing of Terrorism, Article 3; OMLP Report 2012, http://www.uppd.gov.si/fileadmin/uppd.gov.si/pageuploads/deloUrada/letno_porocilo_2012_tiskovno.pdf, at 24.

property gained with the performance of the crime of financing terrorism is mandatory even when the case does not end in conviction.[121] While the wording of Article 498a of the Code of Criminal Proceedings limits the state's right to confiscate money or property when the case does not end in a conviction only to the crime of money laundering and crimes connected with bribery and corruption, this right is extended to the crime of financing terrorism, as the crime of financing terrorism is a predicate offence to money laundering.[122] For this same reason, the Article 25 of the Liability of Legal Entities for Crimes Act can be applied recognizing criminal responsibility of legal persons for the crime of financing terrorism.[123] Regardless of the legal provisions, the Slovenian authorities have been reluctant to confiscate property benefits that might have arisen from money laundering or terrorism financing offences. MONEYVAL has recognized this lack of effort to confiscate property as the greatest deficiency in the Slovenian system.[124] Administrative bodies do not have the authority to request forfeiture of terrorist property.

Slovenian legislation does not recognize any exemptions for the provision of funds to finance legitimate and humanitarian activities by terrorist groups.

VII. IMMIGRATION MEASURES

Slovenia's immigration legislation is harmonized with that of the EU. The Aliens Act[125] addresses all the questions regarding immigration matters for foreign individuals. Pursuant to Article 43 a foreign individual shall not be granted a temporary or permanent residence permit in Slovenia if there is suspicion that he or she might present a threat to public order and safety or to the international relations of Slovenia, of if there is a suspicion that the alien's residence in the country will be associated with the commission of other violent acts, illegal intelligence activities, drug trafficking or other similar criminal offences. Residence may be denied also to a family member of a resident in Slovenia if any threats of the aforementioned acts are confirmed.[126] Additionally, any individual under any of the previously mentioned grounds of suspicion may be denied entry to Slovenia even if he or she does not need a residence permit or a visa to stay in Slovenia for as long as three months.[127] If any of the aaforementioned grounds for suspicion arise after the foreign individual has received his or her residence in Slovenia, the residence permit can

[121] Code of Criminal Proceedings, Article 498a.
[122] MONEYVAL Report, at 31.
[123] Liability of Legal Entities for Crimes Act, Official Gazette RS, No. 59/99 from 23. 7. 1999, Article 25.
[124] MONEYVAL Report, at 34.
[125] Aliens Act, Official Gazette RS, No. 61/99 from 30. 7. 1999 and the subsequent changes.
[126] Aliens Act, Article 93k.
[127] Aliens Act, Article 93b.

be revoked and the individual deported.[128] Under the Aliens Act, Slovenia can also deny residence to victims of human trafficking on its territory if there are reasons to believe that the victim's residence in Slovenia could be related to terrorist activity.[129] Police can also request that a Slovenian citizen be denied the issue of a passport if he or she has been at least twice sentenced with imprisonment for the commission of the crime of terrorism, financing of terrorism, incitement and praising of terrorist acts or recruitment and training for terrorism.[130]

The Asylum Act denies the right to asylum to individuals for whom there are reasonable grounds to believe that they committed crimes against peace, war crimes or crimes against humanity as defined by international acts, graves crimes of a non-political nature outside Slovenia before being accepted into the country as refugees or acts counter to the aims and principles of the United Nations.[131] The article does not specifically describe terrorism, but the acts addressed can be included under the terrorism definition of Article 108 of the Criminal Code. As a party to the Convention Relating to the Status of Refugees[132] and the Protocol Relating to the Status of Refugees,[133] Slovenia has to respect its international obligations, including the right to non-refoulement and the ban on deportation to torturing countries.

While Slovenia has been widely criticized for its policy in denying asylum to asylum seekers, so far only one case has been reported where the asylum was denied on the grounds of terrorism. An international arrest warrant for terrorism was issued against the asylum seeker, but before appropriate actions could be taken, the individual voluntarily left the Asylum Centre.[134]

VIII. ROLE OF THE MILITARY AND EXTRA-TERRITORIAL COUNTER-TERRORISM ACTIVITIES

According to the national legislation, the Slovenian Armed Forces have no direct accountability and responsibility in preventing and combating terrorism.[135] Nonetheless, the Ministry of Defense and the Slovenian Armed Forces are an indispensable element in the fight against terrorism in Slovenia. The Ministry of Defense is responsible for the work of the Intelligence and Security Service of the Ministry and for the organization, preparation and implementation of the system

[128] Aliens Act, Aricle 93u and 93z.
[129] Aliens Act, Article 38a.
[130] Passport Act, Official Gazette RS, No. 65/2000 from 21. 7. 2000 and subsequent changes, Article 26.
[131] Asylum Act, Official Gazette RS, No. 61/99 from 30. 7. 1999 and subsequent changes, Article 4.
[132] Convention relating to the Status of Refugees, UNTS 189, at 137;
[133] Protocol relating to the Status of Refugees, UNTS 606, at 267.
[134] Report of the Republic of Slovenia on the implementation of counter-terrorism measures in line with United Nations Security Council Resolution 1624 (2005), UN Doc. S/2006/552, 21 July 2006, at 5.
[135] Information exchange, at 8.

for civil protection and disaster relief. The Slovenian Armed Forces addresses terrorism issues through the position of the Assistant Chief of General Staff for counter-terrorism.[136]

Both the Ministry of Defense and the Slovenian Armed Forces contribute to international security and stability by implementing UN, EU, NATO and OSCE decisions and guidelines.[137] Slovenia is also a contributor in peacekeeping operations, and in November 2009 the government adopted the Strategy of the Participation of the Republic of Slovenia in International Operations and Missions,[138] which recognizes participation in international operations and missions as an integral part of the comprehensive provision of security, international peace and stability.

The Slovenian Armed Forces are not involved in combating terrorism until the specific circumstances of a serious terrorist act with broad consequences requires their intervention. In case of such a terrorist act, the Parliament of Slovenia is entitled to declare an emergency in the country and activate additional units of the Armed Forces to be deployed to consolidate the situation.[139] In the first stage, the best-trained and best-equipped units of the rapid reaction forces will be used.[140] Once the perpetrators of the crime of terrorism and crimes related to terrorism are captured, a direct and close cooperation with neighboring countries will be established to determine the goals of the perpetrators and their background.[141] In case of terrorism appearing in the region outside the territory of Slovenia, a reinforced cooperation between secret services is established and special measures to distribute information will be taken in order to help the state concerned.[142]

The Code of Criminal Procedure regulates the provision of mutual legal assistance (legal aid, judgments passed by foreign courts, the surrendering of criminal prosecution and extradition).[143] However, the provisions of the Code of Criminal Procedure apply only in the absence of an international agreement.[144] The Code also stipulates that international legal aid in criminal matters is administered directly between national and foreign authorities that participate in criminal proceedings under the condition that reciprocity is applied or if so stipulated by an international

[136] Information exchange, at 9.

[137] Information exchange, at 16.

[138] Strategy of the Participation of the Republic of Slovenia in International Operations and Missions. Official Gazette RS, No. 19/2010 from 12. 3. 2012.

[139] Bojan Potočnik: *The Role of Slovenian Armed Forces in the Fight Against Terrorism*, http://www.zmne.hu/dokisk/hadtud/slovenia2.pdf, at 4.

[140] *Ibidem*.

[141] *Ibidem*.

[142] *Ibidem*.

[143] Code of Criminal Procedure, Articles 514–37.

[144] Code of Criminal Procedure, Article 514.

agreement.[145] Otherwise, the aid is administered through diplomatic channels.[146] In emergency cases, petitions for legal aid under the condition of reciprocity may be transmitted through the Ministry of the Interior and Interpol's system or through the competent authority for the prevention of money laundering in money laundering cases.[147]

The Act on Cooperation in Criminal Matters with the European Union Member States implements the broad European legislation on mutual assistance in criminal matters[148] and thus regulates surrender procedures, the transfer of proceedings, the transfer of sentenced persons, cooperation with Eurojust and the European Judicial Network (EJN), as well as specific procedures for the execution of foreign decisions on freezing, seizure and confiscation.

The extradition of an individual found guilty of a crime by a foreign court is possible only if it is provided by an international agreement or if other measures of reciprocity are available.[149] Extradition to an EU member state is regulated by the aforementioned Act on Cooperation in Criminal Matters with EU Member States, and extradition to other countries has to be carried out in respect of the Council of Europe's European Convention on Mutual Legal Assistance in Criminal Matters with its additional protocol,[150] the Council of Europe's European Convention on Extradition with its additional protocols,[151] the Schengen Convention,[152] the Council

[145] Code of Criminal Procedure, Article 515, § 3.

[146] Code of Criminal Procedure, Article 515, § 1.

[147] Code of Criminal Procedure, Article 515, § 2.

[148] Council Framework Decision of 13 June 2002 on the European arrest warrant and the surrender procedures between the member states, OJ L 190/1 from 18. 7. 2002; Council Framework Decision of 13 June 2002 on joint investigation teams, OJ L 162/1 from 20. 6 2002; Council Decision 28 February 2002 setting up Eurojust with a view to reinforcing the fight against serious crime, OJ L 63/1 from 6. 3. 2002; Council Framework Decision 2005/214/JHA of 24 February 2005 on the application of the principle of mutual recognition to financial penalties, OJ L 337/102 from 16.12.2008; Council Framework Decision 2003/577/JHA of 22 July 2003 on the execution in the European Union of orders freezing property or evidence, OJ L 196/45 from 2. 8. 2003; Council Framework Decision 2005/212/JHA from 24 February 2005 on Confiscation of Crime-Related Proceeds, Instrumentalities and Property, OJ L 68/49 from 15. 3. 2005; Council Framework Decision 2006/783/JHA from 6 October 2006 on the application of the principle of mutual recognition of confiscation orders, OJ L 328/59 from 24. 11. 2006; Convention implementing the Schengen Agreement of 14 June 1985, OJ L 239/19 and subsequent; Council Act of 29 May 2000 establishing in accordance with Article 34 of the Treaty on European Union the Convention on Mutual Assistance in Criminal Matters Between the Member States of the European Union Convention on Mutual Legal Assistance Between the Member States of the EU, OJ C 197/1 from 12. 7. 2000.

[149] Code of Criminal Procedure, Article 521.

[150] Council of Europe, European Convention on Mutual Legal Assistance in Criminal Matters, ETS No. 30, 13 December 1957, http://conventions.coe.int/Treaty/en/Treaties/Html/030.htm.

[151] Council of Europe, European Convention on Extradition, ETS No. 24, 13 December 1957, http://conventions.coe.int/Treaty/en/Treaties/Html/024.htm.

[152] Convention implementing the Schengen Agreement of 14 June 1985, OJ L 239/19 and subsequent.

of Europe's Convention on the Transfer of Sentenced Persons,[153] bilateral treaties on mutual legal assistance and extradition and the Act on Criminal Procedure,[154] which all apply the principle of subsidiarity. The decision to extradite an individual is passed by the senate of the district court where the individual is located who confirms whether the conditions for extradition are met.[155] The individual may appeal this decision at the court of second instance.[156] The decision of the court of second instance is forwarded to the Minister of Justice, who makes the final decision on the extradition.[157] The Minister of Justice may reject extradition if the individual enjoys the right of asylum, if a military or political criminal offence is in question, or for other reasons defined in international agreements.[158]

IX. CONCLUSION

As the overview illustrates, Slovenia strongly condemns terrorism in any form. It has adopted national legislation that mirrors international and European requirements on combating terrorism and is an active participant in activities that strengthen the capabilities on the international and European plane to counter terrorist activities. Slovenia continuously supports counter-terrorism initiatives and measures put forward by the UN, EU, NATO, OSCE, the Council of Europe and others. As the introductory section of this chapter indicates, Slovenia is a party to numerous bilateral and multilateral treaties on the fight against terrorism. It also supports the further universalization of counter-terrorist instruments, strengthened implementation of the UN Global Counter-Terrorism Strategy and an expedited conclusion of negotiations on the Comprehensive Convention on International Terrorism. However, Slovenia also strongly calls for the necessary respect of human rights in combating terrorism.

Slovenia has so far dealt with only a minor number of local terrorism cases. However, these cases have forced the competent authorities in Slovenia to develop new measures, mechanisms and practices continuously to be able to respond successfully to terrorist attacks and most importantly prevent them. Major progress has been achieved since 2004, when the national Criminal Code was amended to

[153] Council of Europe, Convention on the Transfer of Sentenced Persons, ETS No. 112, 21 March 1983, http://conventions.coe.int/Treaty/en/Treaties/Html/112.htm.

[154] Ministry of Foreign Affairs of the Republic of Slovenia, Information exchange on the Code of Conduct of the Politico-Military Aspects of Security, FSC.EMI/77/12, 12 April 2012, http://www.osce.org/fsc/89681, at 10–11.

[155] Code of Criminal Procedure, Article 527.

[156] Code of Criminal Procedure, Article 528.

[157] Code of Criminal Procedure, Article 529.

[158] CODEXTER Report, at 6.

include the new crime of terrorism and the Act on Prevention of Money Laundering and Financing of Terrorism was extended to include the financing of terrorism. These two acts also address the majority of concerns in the area of counter-terrorism and are well suited to provide the measures for prosecuting crimes of terrorism and crimes related to terrorism. With the small number of terrorism cases and a sufficient regulatory basis, there is no need for the establishment of special procedures to prosecute these crimes, or even special courts.

15

Poland

Piotr Daranowski

I. INTRODUCTION

The first stage of counter-terrorism law on Poland occurred in the socialist era, which lasted until 1989; the second stage, dates from the moment of gaining independence to 11 September 2001; the third stage dates from 9/11 to Poland's accession to the European Union (on 1 May 2004); and the fourth and last stage continues to the present day.

The first stage, is characterized by actions undertaken by Polish People's Republic to become bound by five multilateral United Nations sector conventions. They outline the body of antiterrorist acts[1] that has been extended to the full catalogue of the present era (thirteen conventions in total[2]). That impulse of the Polish People's Republic to partake in fulfilling the rules of universal jurisdiction towards acts pointed out at the conventions was proceeded by enacting in 1969, as a part of the new Polish Penal Code (PPC), a clause stating *expressis verbis* the existence of duty, flowing from international treaties, to prosecute perpetrators of terrorist acts – aliens – within

The Report presented herein is the outcome of the common effort of the following: Lodz University / Law and Administration Faculty – team: Prof. Piotr Daranowski, PhD (I, II, V, VI, XII); Prof. Witold Kulesza, PhD (III. A.); Prof. Jacek Izydorczyk, PhD (III.B.1; IV); Jan Kulesza, PhD (III.B.2.); Dominika Drożdż, PhD (VI); Dorota Głowacka, MA (VII); Joanna Połatyńska, PhD; Marek Wasiński, PhD (IX, X); Joanna Kulesza, PhD (XI). Final drafting of this Report – Prof. Piotr Daranowski, PhD.

1 Convention on Offences and Certain Other Acts Committed on Board Aircraft, concluded at Tokyo, on 14 September 1963 – Official Journal of Laws of the Republic of Poland (Dziennik Ustaw RP, abbreviated hereafter as OJ) of 1971 No 15, location 147 [OJ 1971 – 15/147]; Convention for the Suppression of Unlawful Seizure of Aircraft, signed at the Hague on 16 December 1970 – OJ 1972 – 25/181; Convention for the Suppression of Unlawful Acts Against the Safety of Civil Aviation, concluded at Montreal on 23 September 1971 – OJ 1976 – 8/37; Convention on the Prevention and Punishment of Crimes Against Internationally Protected Persons, Including Diplomats Agents, adopted in New York on 14 December 1973 – OJ 1983 – 37/168; Convention on the Physical Protection of Nuclear Material, adopted in Vienna on 3 March 1980 – OJ 89 – 17/94.

2 United Nations Treaty Collection – Text and Status of the United Nations Conventions on terrorism – https://treaties.un.org/Pages/DB.aspx?path=DB/studies/page2_en.xml.

the Polish legal system.[3] Practical implementation of the conventions through the penalization of the defined acts had not occurred in the first stage.

The *second* stage embraced the widening of the catalogue of antiterrorist treaty obligations – all universal in their character – by the subsequent three UN conventions,[4] and also after Poland's accession to the Council of Europe (on 26 November 1991)[5] – by the antiterrorist conventions of that organization.[6]

What needs to be underscored, however, are certain autonomous changes in the Polish legal system whose sole purpose are antiterrorist in nature. Also, it seems essential to bear in mind the practical dimension of the duty to grant EU regulations the necessary expression as a part of body of Polish law,[7] including, what seems to be obvious, the regulations that have a potentially antiterrorist dimension.

There has been a broadening of *universal jurisdiction* by explicit inclusion of Polish citizens in the new Polish Penal Code (PPC), established in 1997,[8] in its Article 113.[9] This article, in its disposition referring to "a Polish citizen," constitutes a very important – from the standpoint of the realization of duty to penalize *delicta iuris*

3 Art. 115 PPC stating that "Notwithstanding regulations in force in the place of commission of the offence, the Polish penal law shall be applied to an alien in the case of the commission: (...) 2) an offence the Republic of Poland is obliged to prosecute under international agreements." – OJ 1997 – 88/553.

4 International Convention Against the Taking of Hostages, adopted in New York on 17 December 1979 – OJ 2000 – 106/1123; Convention for the Suppression of Unlawful Acts Against the Safety of Maritime Navigation, done at Rome on 10 March 1988 – OJ 1994 – 129/636; Protocol for the Suppression of Unlawful Acts Against the Safety of Fixed Platforms Located on the Continental Shelf, done at Rome on 10 March 1988 – OJ 1992.

5 OJ 1994 – 118/565.

6 European Convention on the Suppression of Terrorism (27.01.1977) – OJ 1996 – 117/557.

7 Europe Agreement (1991) – OJ 1994 – 11/38 – Chapter III Approximation of laws Art. 68 "The Contracting Parties recognize that the major precondition for Poland's economic integration into the Community is the approximation of that country's existing and future legislation to that of the Community. Poland shall use its best endeavors to ensure that future legislation is compatible with Community legislation."

8 OJ 1997 – 88/554.

9 Art. 113. "Notwithstanding regulations in force in the place of commission of the offence, the Polish penal law shall be applied to a Polish citizen or an alien, with respect to whom no decision on extradition has been taken, in the case of the commission abroad of an offence which the Republic of Poland is obligated to prosecute under international agreements." Analyzing Article 113, what needs to be highlighted is that although Poland assumed the obligation to prosecute certain crimes regulated in the conventions, bringing the perpetrators to justice in Poland still requires the existence of a substantive law basis in Polish law. Those substantial law foundations are set in Chapter 16 of the PPC, which puts together and classifies offences named in its title – "Offences against peace, and humanity, and war crimes" – (Articles 117–26). Juxtaposition of the dispositions laid out in the anti-terrorist conventions with Article 113 and the catalogue of crimes presented in Chapter 16 of the PPC is the basis of penalization and proves the thesis that "Poland [is] fulfilling its international obligations penalizes all the behaviors defined in the ratified treaties." See Polish Penal Code – General Regulations – Commentary to Articles 32–116 (hereafter The Commentary), vol. II, M. Królikowski, R. Zabłocki (eds.), Munich 2010, p. 904.

gentium (acts defined as crime by international law) – exception to the cardinal rule of Polish law, according to which a Polish citizen can be held responsible for the offences committed abroad only if the requirement of dual criminality has been met.

Considering the consequences flowing from the duty of a candidate state aspiring to join the EU structures to harmonize its legislation with the Union regulations of antiterrorist character, Polish law anticipated the Union regulations targeting money laundering[10] practices, which could also serve the purpose of blocking possible acts of terrorism financing.

The fact that the Police Act has introduced "antiterrorist sub-units"[11] as one of the components of the forces – even though the essential range of their operation has not been set – can also be considered a response to the terrorist threat.

The UN Security Council Resolution No 1373 opens the *third* stage. The duty to execute its provisions became an impulse for deep and complex changes. However, the first action that the Republic of Poland took after the reception of the Security Council Resolution was to ask whether the existing body of law allows for any countermeasures against the terrorist threat, the scope and subject of which had been indicated in the Resolution.[12] The result was a preliminary list of acts[13] and an assessment of their adequacy.[14]

[10] Which found its expression in the Council Framework Decision 2001 /500/JHA of 26 June 2001 on money laundering and the identification, tracing, freezing, seizing and confiscation of instrumentalities and the proceeds of crime – OJ L 182/1. – and in the solutions of the earlier enacted Act of 16 November 2000 on counteracting the introduction to financial transactions of property values originated from illegal or unclear sources. (OJ 2000 – 116/1216) (hereafter The 2000 Act].

[11] The Police Act of 6 April 1990 (OJ 1990 – 30/179) – Chapter 2. Article 4.1.

[12] In general – as for the main issues tackled – the Security Council Resolution No 1373 in its narration requires (i) prevention and suppression of direct or indirect financing of terrorist acts in the widest sense of the term; (ii) blocking recruitment of terrorist groups members and exchanging information on terrorists' migrations; (iii) elimination of the supply of weapons to terrorists; and (iv) penalization of terrorist acts. Thus the tailored contents of the Resolution have delineated the main course and dimension of antiterrorist – also legislative – measures.

[13] As far as the fundamental regulations were concerned, the juxtaposition embraced (i) the 2000 Act – see footnote 10 – seen as a tool that allowed terrorist acts to be subject to total control of "responsible institutions," which include banks, and also allowed the acts to be qualified as "money laundering" directly named and penalized in the PPC; (ii) the Act of 29 November 2000 on international exchange in goods, technologies and services of strategic importance for the safety of the state, and the maintenance of international peace and safety that allows the blocking of "terrorist" weapon exchange; (iii) collating sequence of PPC regulations so that they could give grounds to penalization of "(...) several instances of penalization of the behavior that possesses characteristics of terrorist acts", especially dispositions of Articles 140, 163, 165, 171, 185 and 258 of the PPC – applicable apart from the realization of the *universal jurisdiction* rule; (iv) and, last but not least, giving the Republic of Poland the ability to prevent terrorist acts as an effect of the information concerning imminent threats that can be exchanged between the responsible institutions, with operations made possible on the basis of international agreements targeting organized crime prevention and to which Poland is a party.

[14] The early Polish reports (2001–2) submitted to the Security Council Counter-Terrorism Committee were the first indication of the ability to counteract terrorist threats on the grounds of the existing legal solutions – *see also* http://www.un.org/en/sc/ctc/resources/countryreports.html.

Step number two was making independent changes in the internal law, which were carried out by the Polish legislator in order to execute the obligations flowing from Resolution 1373. The outcome was the amendment to the 2000 Act[15] introduced on 27 September 2002, adopting measures for "the prevention of the financing of terrorism."

In turn, the process of implementation of the *basic European Union regulations* constituted the next set of changes: rules that concern, directly or indirectly, the actions aiming at eradicating terrorism.[16] The process's key effect was the implementation, by means of a new Act of 16 April 2004, into the PPC,[17] the resolutions of Council Framework Decision 2002/475/JHA.[18] The Act resulted in introduction of an offence of terrorist character into Article 115 § 20.[19] The promulgation of the rules set in Article 115 § 20 of the PPC was accompanied by the significant extension of the provision set in Article 110 § 1 of the PPC by a passage that allows Polish penal law to be applied "(...) to aliens who have committed a terrorist offence abroad."[20] In the operational sense, the modified Article 110 § 1 determined the responsibility of an alien in Polish law for terrorist offences committed abroad. It also informs the jurisdiction of Polish courts in case where it would not be possible to hold such person responsible on the basis of the *universal jurisdiction* provided in the PPC.[21]

The implementation of the remaining Framework Decisions issued in 2002 by the Council was also carried out by means of the aforementioned Act of 2004.[22]

15 See footnote 10.

16 Council Framework Decision of 13 June 2002 on combating terrorism (2002/475/JHA) – OJ EU L 164; Council Framework Decision of 13 June 2002 on joint investigation teams (2002/465/JHA) – OJ EU L 162; Council Framework Decision of 13 June 2002 on the European arrest warrant and the surrender procedures between member states (2002/584/JHA) – OJ EU L 190; Council Framework Decision of 28 February 2002 setting up Eurojust with a view to reinforcing the fight against serious crime (2002/187/JHA) – OJ EU L 063.

17 OJ 2004 – 93/889.

18 OJ EC L 164/3.

19 See also Section III of this chapter.

20 Article 110 § 1 had been worded as follows: "The Polish penal law shall be applied to aliens who have committed an offence against the interests of the Republic of Poland, a Polish citizen, a Polish legal person or a Polish organizational unit not having the status of a legal person and to aliens who have committed abroad a terrorist offence."

21 See also: The Commentary p. 890.

22 The Act had developed Chapter 62 of the Polish Criminal Procedural Code [PCPC], titled: "Mutual Legal Assistance and Summons in Penal Cases," set from Articles 589b to 589f, also implementing Council Framework Decision on combating terrorism (2002/475/JHA) and adding two subsequent chapters, 65a and 65b, to Part XIII of the PCPC. The first of the aforementioned chapters regulates procedure that is to be followed when a Polish court puts forward a request to a member state for handing over the person under prosecution, whereas the other chapter regulates a request of an EU member state for handing over the perpetrator for whom a European arrest warrant has been issued, thus implementing the Council's decision on the European arrest warrant and the surrender procedures between member states (2002/584/JHA). See also M. Wróblewski, *Wspólne zespoły*

At the same time, the following government agencies that come under the authority of the Prime Minister were set up and regulated in a separate bill – the Agency of Internal Safety (Agencja Bezpieczeństwa Wewnętrznego, or ABW) and Intelligence Agency (Agencja Wywiadu, or AW). The task of these agencies (among others) was "preventing and eliminating terrorism (the crimes of terrorism)."[23] Also, the signal for the necessity of fighting those crimes, in broader all-European dimension, found its reflection in the accession by Poland to Europol on 1 November 2004.[24] The sign of changes in quality of the law was also the act of introducing into the bills – enacted in the year 2002 – concerning states of emergency (that is, *martial law*,[25] *state of emergency*,[26] and *state of emergency in case of natural disaster*),[27] special clauses stating that such circumstances can also be "caused by terrorist actions."[28]

The *fourth* stage is the period of Poland's operations as an EU member state fulfilling the guidelines of the EU Counter-Terrorism Strategy, adopted in 2005. During this stage Poland implemented the Strategies[29] – *prevent, protect, pursue, respond* –in the analogous Strategies of the Republic of Poland – *National Security Strategy of the Republic of Poland*;[30] *National Counter-Terrorism Programme of the Republic Poland 2012–2016*;[31] and *Polish Foreign Policy Priorities 2012–2016*.[32]

Contemplating the motifs *prevent and protect*, the following achievements of the legislation have to be mentioned. First, an amendment of the 2000 Act[33] introduced on 25 June 2009 was dedicated to the "prevention of money laundering and terrorism financing."[34] The amendment introduces, in the text of Article 165a,[35] a new provision to the PPC, the aim of which is to penalize any acts of "financing of the terrorism." The offence implements recommendations set forth by the UN Security Council Counter-Terrorism Committee that monitors the execution of Resolution

dochodzeniowo-śledcze (Mutual Investigation and Inquiry Teams), in *Prokuratura i Prawo (Prosecutor's Office and the Law)* 9, 2006, pp. 74–85.

23 The Act of 24 May 2002 on the Agency of Internal Safety and the Intelligence Agency – OJ 2002 – 74/676.

24 OJ 2005 – 29/243.

25 The Act of 29 August 2002 – OJ 2002 – 156/1301.

26 The Act of 21 June 2002 – OJ 2002 – 113/985.

27 The Act of 18 April 2002 – OJ 2002 – 62/558.

28 Article 2.1. of both Acts.

29 *The European Union Strategy for Combating Radicalization and Recruitment to Terrorism* (2005); *The EU Internal Security Strategy – Towards a European Security Model* (2010).

30 http://www.iniejawna.pl/pomoce/przyc_pom/SBN_RP.pdf (in Polish).

31 http://zbrojnie.pl/wp-content/uploads/2013/06/Narodowy_Program_Antyterrorystyczny_na_lata_2012-2016.pdf (in Polish).

32 http://www.msz.gov.pl/resource/d31571cf-d24f-4479-af09-c9a46cc85cf6:JCR.

33 See also footnote 10.

34 See also Section VI of this chapter.

35 See also Section III of this chapter.

1373, as well as the obligations Poland has under Article 2.1 of the UN International Convention for the Suppression of the Financing of Terrorism.[36] At the same time, the terrorism financing offence also implements Article 1.4 of the Directive 2005/60/EC of the European Parliament and of the Council of 26 October 2005 on the prevention of the use of the financial system for the purpose of money laundering and terrorist financing.[37] The amendment also represents statutory acceptance of the Financial Action Task Force recommendation that aims at terrorism suppression.[38]

Furthermore, it is necessary to mention the amendment of 25 May 2012 to the Act of 29 November 2000 on international exchange in goods, technologies and services of strategic importance for the safety of the state and for the maintaining international peace and security. It specifically requires blocking the supply of terrorist weapons, in compiiance with EU decisions.[39] Following EU Council Common Positions, Criterion No 6 requires an assessment of "behavior of the buyer country with regard to the international community, as regards in particular its attitude to terrorism (...)" Therefore, the Act (per its Article 16.2.3) indicates that the circumstance in which "(...) final destination country; a) supports terrorism and international organized crime" constitutes grounds for the refusal of weapon transfer.

Another bill has been enacted, namely, the Act of 26 April 2007 on *critical management*.[40] It opens the possibility to undertake indirect actions in the face of threats that need to be combated with the use of resources that go beyond the scope of the basic forces and measures, but do not require resorting to the tools of a state of emergency. The array of such threats – according to the text of the amended law[41] – include "acts terrorist in character" (Article 3. 11) that "shall be (...) understood as situations being the effect of an offence described in Article 115 § 20 (...) of the PPC (...)"

The Antiterrorist Centre of ABW[42] coordinates actions of all the forces and institutions that take part in securing the Republic of Poland against the terrorist threat, not only in the information-analytical scope of operations, but also by support of the decisional process of the state executives based on the information obtained.[43]

36 See also Section VI of this chapter.

37 OJ EU L 309/15.

38 See also footnote 71.

39 Council Common Position 2008/944/CFSP of 8 December 2008 defining common rules governing control of exports of military technology and equipment (OJ EU L 335/99).

40 OJ 2007 – 89/590.

41 OJ 2013 – 1166.

42 The Prime Minister's Order No 102 – in: Monitor Polski 2008 – 69/622.

43 See also A. Makarski, *Centrum Antyterrorystyczne Agencji Bezpieczeństwa Wewnętrznego. Geneza, zasady działania oraz doświadczenia po pierwszym roku funkcjonowania (Antiterrorist Centre of the Internal Safety Agency)*, in *Przegląd Bezpieczeństwa Wewnętrznego (Internal Safety Review)* No 2 (2) 2010, pp. 101–12.

Also, an amendment to the Act on Border Guards adds to the catalogue of the guards' tasks by adding antiterrorist actions.[44] In the case of the Police forces, the amendment implies the antiterrorist scope of tasks by means of the construct that "[the Police] carries out tasks flowing from the legal regulations of the EU as well as international contracts and agreements on grounds and in accordance with the rules contained therein."[45]

In terms of taking on international antiterrorist treaty obligations, the preceding process has been supplemented by the act of ratifying four subsequent UN conventions[46] and the Council of Europe conventions.[47] The practice of penalizing numerous variants of terrorist acts described in those documents by applying *universal jurisdiction* rule had not occurred in the analyzed stage.

II. THE DEFINITION OF TERRORISM

The first attempt at defining terrorism in the law of the Republic of Poland was the amendment in 2002 to the 2000 Act on Counteracting Introduction into Financial Circulation of Property Values Originating from Illegal or Undisclosed Sources. The change of title of the 2000 Act indicated that its goal became, aside from preventing money laundering, also combating acts that aim at financing terrorist activity. Article 2.7 defined the essence of the "financed" actions, stating that "any time the Act mentions a terrorist action, it shall be understood as crimes against peace, humanity, as well as war crimes, crimes against universal safety and those described in Articles 134 and 136 of the PPC."

It would be difficult, however, to recognize the rule stated in the Article 2.7 of the Act as a legal definition of terrorism, because it describes a terrorist act by enumerating a closed catalogue of offences classified in the regulations of the Penal Code.[48] Thus, it has to be concluded that the amendment to the PPC of 16 April

[44] The Act of 12 October 1990 on Border Guards (OJ 1990 -78/462) – from 2007 (OJ 2007 – 82/558); in its Article 1.2.5, it states that one of the tasks of the Border Guards is, among others, "carrying out activities in order to recognize and counteract terrorist threat."

[45] OJ 2010 – 164/1108.

[46] International Convention for the Suppression of the Financing of Terrorism, adopted in New York on 9 December 1999 – OJ 2004 – 263/2620; Protocol for the Suppression of Unlawful Acts of Violence at Airports Serving International Civil Aviation, done at Montreal on 24 February 1988 – OJ 2005 – 48/348; International Convention for the Suppression of Terrorist Bombings, adopted in New York on 15 December 1997 – OJ 2007 – 66/438; Convention on the Marking of Plastic Explosives for the Purpose of Identification, done in Montreal on 1 March 1991; OJ 2007 – 135/948.

[47] European Convention on the Prevention Terrorism (16.05.2005) – OJ 2007 – 191/1364; European Convention on Laundering, Search, Seizure and Confiscation of the Proceeds from Crime and on the Financing of Terrorism (16.05.2005) – OJ 2008 – 165/1028; see also footnote 137.

[48] Included in Chapter 16 of PPC, which puts together and classifies behaviors listed in its title – "Offences against peace, and humanity and war crimes" – behaviors (Articles 117–26) that allow the

2004 for the first time introduced into the Polish body of law the legal definition of terrorism. It remains regulated in the text of Article 115 § 20 of the PPC.

Art. 115 An offence of a terrorist nature

§ 20 An offence of a terrorist nature is an act subject to punishment of deprivation of liberty, with the upper limit of at least five years, committed for:

1) a serious intimidation of many persons,
2) compelling the public authority of the Republic of Poland or of the other state or of the international organization to undertake or abandon specific actions,
3) causing serious disturbance to the constitutional system or the economy of the Republic of Poland, of the other state or international organization and a threat of the commitment of such act.

By means of this amendment, the Republic of Poland has implemented the Framework Decision No 2002/475/JHA of the Council, fulfilling its recommendation obligating the member states of the European Union to pass a uniform definition of a crime that is terrorist in character.

III. CRIMINAL LAWS AND PROSECUTIONS

A. *Criminal Law*

The 2004 PPC discussed in the preceding section defined an offence of a terrorist nature with reference to two criteria that need to be met cumulatively: a substantive one and a formal one. It is assumed that the offence has been defined as to its substance, similarly to the meaning of Article 1 § 1 of the Framework Decision, although with a different wording. The definition contained in Article 115 § 20 PPC names as the substantive criteria a particular aim, which must accompany the perpetrator for him to commit an offence of a terrorist nature. Such an aim driving the culprit of an offence of a terrorist nature ought to be (1) seriously intimidating many persons; (2) compelling the public authority of the Republic of Poland, another state or an international organization to undertake or abandon specific actions; or (3) causing serious disturbance to the constitutional system or to the economy of the Republic of Poland, another state or an international organization. The second

Republic of Poland to fulfill the act of *universal jurisdiction* (see also footnote 8) – supplemented by the provisions for penalization of an assassination attempt against "the President of the Republic of Poland" (Article 134 PPC) and perpetrating on the Polish territory an "active attack against the head of a foreign state or the accredited chief of diplomatic mission of such state or any person benefiting from similar protection on the basis of internal legal acts, agreements or universally recognized international customs" (Article 136 PPC).

criteria – unlike the Framework Decision – does not contain an enumeration of particular kinds of crimes, such as attacking human life; kidnapping or taking hostages; causing damage to governmental or public utility buildings; hijacking an air vessel or other means of transportation; producing, supplying or using weapons; propagating hazardous substances; causing fires or explosions; or interfering with or interrupting water or energy supplies in a way threatening to human life. Instead of such an enumeration, Polish lawmakers introduced a formal criteria by defining an offence of a terrorist nature is (any) prohibited act committed for one of the three aforementioned purposes, subject to imprisonment with the upper limit of at least five years. Because in the PPC each of the crimes named in the Framework Decision is subject to imprisonment with the upper limit of at least five years and in many cases of a much higher limit, the definition of an offence of a terrorist nature covers in its scope all the categories of crimes named in the Framework Decision.

The use of a formal criteria (of the act being subject to imprisonment with the upper limit of at least five years) in the definition of an offence of a terrorist nature by the Polish lawmakers instead of including a list of such crimes (when the perpetrator acts under a specific aim) enabled for a concise wording of Article 115 § 20 PPC. This regulation is much shorter than Article 1 § 1 of the Framework Decision, which ought to be recognized as a virtue of the legislative technique used. As a vice of such a method, one might recognize the fact that the scope of an offence of a terrorist nature covers also acts not included in the original definition of the Framework Decision, making the Polish definition broader than that of the Framework Decision. As one example, one might mentioned the disclosure of secret information aimed at forcing an organ of state power to undertake or refrain from taking a certain action. A criminal act of disclosing information designated as "top secret" or "secret" is subject to punishment of deprivation of liberty from three months to five years (Article 265 § 1 PPC[49]). Therefore, when both criteria are met, the substantive criterion – that is, the perpetrator acting to force state authorities, Polish or foreign, to undertake a certain action – next to the formal one – the prohibited act being subject to imprisonment with the upper limit of at least five years – in light of Polish criminal law an offence of a terrorist nature has been committed. As an illustration of such an event, one might consider a person who reveals a secret document about using illegal methods of surveillance or the existence of a secret prison where torture is deployed; the person is committing the crime of revealing secret information in order to force public authorities to refrain from such practice, so he or she will be recognized as a "terrorist." Although the preceding example is purely of academic nature, it serves to show that the verbal interpretation of Article 115 § 20 PPC may

[49] Chapter XXXIII Offences against information protection – art. 265 § 1 PPC.

lead to a broader understanding of "an offence of a terrorist nature" than the one included in the Framework Decision, which does not name the act of revealing state secrets as an act of terror.

When assessing the acts of a culprit who committed an offence of a terrorist nature, the court is obliged to decide upon a sentence of deprivation of liberty above the lower limit foreseen in the act of law; it may, however, increase the upper limit of the sanction by half (Article 64, Article 65 PPC).

Criminal responsibility will also be faced by those who take part in an organized criminal group or association (art. 258 PPC[50]), "aiming at committing offences of a terrorist nature" (art. 258 § 2 PPC), when they do not themselves commit a terrorist crime. A member of such a group or association is subject to punishment of prison from six months up to eight years. A particularly severe prison sentence (of at least three years) will be the responsibility of those who "create or manage a terrorist group or association" (art. 258 § 4 PPC). The notion of "taking part" ought to be understood as membership in such a group or association, accepting its rules, executing orders or tasks designated by individuals holding leading positions, taking part in meetings, planning criminal acts, providing resources needed for the fulfillment of its tasks, seeking hideouts, giving shelter, enabling transportation, donating money, as well as undertaking actions disabling the identification of group's or association's members. It is understood that an "organized group" ought to include at least three individuals who act to achieve a joint goal that is the commission of an offence of a terrorist nature. It is punishable by law to participate in such a group, even if it was created for the commission of just one crime. The traits of an "association" include its durable formation, the existence of an identifiable leadership and the internal discipline of its members.

B. *Terrorism Prosecutions*

Poland has not been directly threatened by terrorist attacks. But we cannot completely exclude the increased interest in Poland on the part of terrorist organizations, especially in the context of Polish involvement, among others, in Afghanistan (and in the past, in Iraq). As in the case of Poland, the threat of terrorism in Central Europe is currently low. However, in regions neighboring the EU (the North Caucasus, Central Asia and the Maghreb countries), we observe the activity of extremist/terrorist groups of varying intensity.[51]

[50] Art. 258 Contribution in an organized criminal group or criminal association.

[51] This is an official statement of the Ministry of Foreign Affairs of the Republic of Poland (1 October 2013); see http://www.msz.gov.pl/en/foreign_policy/security_policy/international_terrorism/). There are some statistical data on different issues, such as criminal trials during a year, periods of criminal trials, etc.

Fortunately, because there is no direct threat, there are currently no such crimes under prosecution in Poland. Information on crimes and criminal trials are available, for example, on the website of the Ministry of Justice of Republic of Poland.[52]

There are no specialized courts for terrorism prosecution in Poland. Because of the legal definition of a terrorism crime (the PPC, section 115 § 20) and so-called nature of such crimes (for example, manslaughter, kidnapping, possession of a weapon), potential offenders would be prosecuted by a public prosecutor and their cases would be sent to a district court (in Poland, we have criminal courts, so-called common courts and military courts; and there are three levels of courts and two legal instances of a criminal trial).

Of course, in Poland there is no possibility to obtain evidence through torture or degrading treatment in any case. There are no exceptions in Polish law, and everyone who overuses his or her power would face a criminal prosecution because of such an unlawful act.

A regulation in the Polish Criminal Procedural Code (PCPC) of 1997 (section 184) allows a witness to testify anonymously. But this regulation is only for "protection of a witness's life, health, freedom and his/her belongings in a wide scale" in all criminal cases. Moreover, according to the Polish Supreme Court's jurisprudence, such anonymous testimony cannot be the sole evidence for an indictment (in every criminal trial).[53] All procedural regulations are established for all criminal cases (for example, rules of the Polish criminal trial, i.e., [1] *Lex retro non agit* [law doesn't act back]; [2] *Nullum crimen, nulla poena sine praevia lege poenali* [no crime and no punishment without law]; [3] *Nullum crimen sine culpa* [no crime without guilt]; [4] *The rule of humanitarian punishments*; [5] *The right to appeal*; [6] *The material truth*; [7] *The free evaluation of evidence*; [8] *The objectivism*; [9] *The directness*; [10] *The accusatorial process*; [11] *The contestability*; [12] *The equality of parties*; [13] *The mandatory prosecution* [of legalism]; [14] *The presumption of innocence*; [15] *In dubio pro reo* [irresolvable doubts in favor of defendant]; [16] *Onus probandi* [burden of proof]; [17] *The right to defence*; [18] *The public trial* [open for people and media]; [19] *The oral and (or) in writing process*; and [20] *The concentration of a criminal trial*).

A theoretical issue, recently gaining in significance around the world, as well as in Poland, is the question of legitimate means for solving so-called *ticking bomb scenarios* without infringing national legal norms.[54] This is a question of the

[52] See: http://ms.gov.pl/en/.

[53] See also Section X of this chapter.

[54] J. Kulesza, *Czy państwo może mordować własnych obywateli? Zestrzelenie samolotu typu renegade w świetle prawa karnego – zarys problemu (Can a State Murder Its Own Citizens? The Renegade Aircraft Shootdown in the Light of Penal Law – Outline of the Problem)*, in *Czasopismo Prawa Karnego i Nauk Penalnych (Penal Law and Penal Sciences Periodical)* 2009, no. 3, pp. 5–33; J. Kulesza, *Legalne tortury*

possibility of applying torture and other cruel, inhuman or degrading treatment towards a person suspected of contributing to a terrorist act, if such treatment would offer a chance for saving human life. Torture and other cruel, inhuman or degrading treatment is generally considered prohibited under Article 3 of the European Convention on Human Rights and Article 40 of the Polish Constitution.[55] It might, however, be considered admissible in the light of necessary self-defence (Article 25 PPC) or force majeure (Article 26 PPC). Those acting in their official capacity should not be able to take advantage of such defences, but they might apply when an officer is off duty.[56] This is supported by conclusions that the binding norms on states under Article 3 of the European Convention on Human Rights[57] and Article 40 of the Polish Constitution ought not be applied horizontally to individuals not acting in their official capacity. A private individual may therefore use the aforementioned means in the name of self-defence in order to obtain information on the hiding place of a kidnapped person or an active explosive. Fulfilling the legally proscribed prerequisites for self-defence, such as the reality of a threat, its directness and the illegality of a violation, raises no doubt. The methods used to obtain the aforementioned information ought to be assessed as per the regulations of Article 25 PPC, in particular the proportionality towards the risk of a prevented violation.

The applicability of force majeure, as per Article 26 PPC, in the preceding situation is doubtful, primarily due to the need of its subsidiarity, which in the circumstances of force majeure means the necessity to address appropriate law enforcement authorities, as well as the applicability of Article 25 PPC, which relates particularly to situations where two competing legal interests are contested and that of the wrongdoer is to be sacrificed in order to preserve that of the victim.

(Legal Torture), in *Problemy wymiaru sprawiedliwości karnej. Księga jubileuszowa Profesora Jana Skupińskiego (Problems of Penal Judiciary. Professor Jan Skupiński's Jubilee Book)*, J. Jakubowska-Hara, A. Błachnio-Parzych, H. Kuczyńska, J. Kosonoga, (eds.), Warsaw 2013, pp. 882–93.

55 http://www.sejm.gov.pl/prawo/konst/angielski/kon1.htm

56 Decision of the Polish Supreme Court (Postanowienie Sądu Najwyższego) of Oct. 27, 1994, case number III KRN 144/94, Orzecznictwo Sądu Najwyższego, Izba Karna i Wojskowa 1995, no 1–2, position 3, with commentaries from M. Dąbrowska-Kardas and P. Kardas, Palestra 1996, no. 7–8, p. 275 ff; M. Filar, in: Kodeks karny. Komentarz, M. Filar (Ed.), Warsaw 2012, p. 91; J. Lachowski, in *Kodeks karny (Penal Code). Część ogólna (General Provisions)*. Vol. I. Komentarz (Commentary), R. Zawłocki, M. Królikowski (eds.), Warsaw 2011, pp. 791–2; Decision of the Appelate Court for Katowice from May 15, 2008, case number II AKa 13/08, Krakowskie Zeszyty Sądowe 2008, No 9, position 40.

57 More on that, see L. Garlicki, in *Konwencja o Ochronie Praw Człowieka i Podstawowych Wolności (The European Convention on Human Rights)*, Vol. I, L. Garlicki (ed.), Warsaw 2010, pp. 135–6.

IV. INVESTIGATIVE POWERS

In Polish law, there are no special investigative powers in terrorism cases given to the police, intelligence agencies and the military. All criminal proceedings are under the same rules, for example (see Section III.B): the presumption of innocence, the criminal nature of torture or degrading treatment, the right to defence, the right to appeal and so on). Poland does obey both – the international law and its own constitutional law.

A. *Police Powers*

The Polish police handling terrorism cases have no special or extra powers unavailable in ordinary criminal investigations and cases. There are no special preventive arrests, pretrial detention powers or similar powers.

B. *Intelligence Agencies*

Polish intelligence agencies have no special powers in terrorism cases unavailable in ordinary criminal investigations and cases. Of course, they can use some legal measures (for example, electronic surveillance), but all powers in criminal prosecutions and criminal trials are the same for every case and against every person.

V. PROSCRIPTION AND LISTING OF TERRORIST GROUPS AND INDIVIDUALS

As far as proscription is concerned, creation of "antiterrorist" listings by the authorities of the Republic of Poland, in principle, is not provided for in the Polish law.

Registering groups, persons and entities that are subject to special terrorism combating restrictive measures – which are included in the law of the Republic of Poland – is a consequence of putting those "groups, persons and entities" on the appropriate lists. The lists are created by the UN Security Council, as well as implemented by means of the EU decisions,[58] or are put together by the EU within the framework of an independently realized antiterrorist strategy of the Union.[59] In

[58] Council Regulation (EC) No 881/2002 of 27 May 2002 – OJ L 139; Council Regulation (EC) No 596/2013 of 24 June 2013 amending Regulation No 881/2002 imposing certain specific restrictive measures directed against certain persons and entities associated with the Al-Qaida network – OJ EU L 172/1 – 25.6.2013.

[59] Council Common Position of 27 December 2001 on the application of specific measures to combat terrorism – 2001/931/CFSP – OJ L 344/93. Council Regulations (EC) of 27 December 2001 on specific restrictive measures directed against certain persons and entities with a view to combating terrorism – No 2580/2001 – OJ L 344/70.

the case of the latter, the action is performed by means of the lists approved (since 2001) according to the procedure amended in 2007.[60]

Those specific restrictive measures directed against persons and entities that are on the lists contain, first of all, the necessary measures to combat any form of financing for terrorist activities.[61] But it does not exhaust the phenomenon of restrictive measures.

The lists are used with respect to various restrictive measures, including migration/immigration control and possible arms trade transactions blocking. Creating such tools also reflects the realization of the general obligation to exchange information concerning terrorist threats by proper forces, both in the national and international (Europol) dimensions. The scale of those operations is unknown due to their confidentiality.[62]

The self-executing character of the lists means that all forces involved in antiterrorist activities (including the Prosecutor's Office, ABW [the Antiterrorist Centre of ABW], Central Anticorruption Bureau [Centralne Biuro Antykorupcyjne, or CBA], the police and Border Guards) are aware of their content and of the duty to take them into consideration in the course of undertaken operations.

International (UN/EU) lists of persons can potentially be supplemented by the autonomous immigration/migration decisions of Polish authorities in the case of building lists of persons whose presence on the territory of the Republic of Poland is undesired.[63]

VI. REGULATION OF TERRORISM FINANCING

The regulation of terrorism financing after 11 September 2001 has depended on a 2000 Act concerned with money laundering.[64] The 2000 money laundering law was amended on 27 September 2002. The title as well as the scope of the regulation was widened by the provisions concerning the prevention of "terrorism financing." In the Act, the legislator – not referring to the contents of international debates on terrorist financing – defined independently the notion of a "terrorist act."[65]

60 Council of EU – 10826/07 Restraint – 21 June 2007; see also http://eeas.europa.eu/cfsp/sanctions/consol-list_en.htm.
61 See also Section VI of this chapter.
62 See also Section X of this chapter.
63 See also Section VII of this chapter.
64 See also footnote 10.
65 See also Section II of this chapter.

A subsequent amendment of 25 June 2009 changed the title of the Act; from that moment on, it has been the Act "on *prevention of money laundering and terrorism financing*." It implements the UN-member obligations[66] and the Union Directive 2005/60/WE of the European Parliament and of the council on the prevention of the use of the financial system for the purpose of money laundering and terrorism financing.[67] The most crucial consequence in Article 9 of the amended Act was to create a terrorism financing offence in Article 165a of the PPC. Before that amendment, such an offence was unknown in Polish penal law. The offence provides:

> **Art. 165a. Gathering, transferring or offering legal tenders for the purposes of financing a terrorist act**
>
> Whoever gathers, conveys or offers legal tenders, financial instruments, securities, foreign currencies, property rights or other unmovable property for the purpose of financing a crime of a terrorist nature, shall be subject to penalty of deprivation of liberty from 2 to 12 years.

Consequently, in the present legal state, the PPC in its Article 115 § 20 and Article 165a provides for critical antiterrorist regulations.

The aforementioned Act, in its many provisions, refers to the contents of Article 165a of the PPC, indicating that "whenever 'terrorism financing' is mentioned, it shall be understood as an offence defined in Article 165a of the PPC." In principle, the aim of referring to the PPC is to facilitate recognition of the acts that constitute terrorism financing, but it is also an obvious sign of the legislators' will to unify the interpretation of the notion of "terrorism" in the law of the Republic of Poland in general. The interpretation of law has to be carried out in accordance with the basic standard set in the PPC. The standard determines the practice of application of the Act as much as other statutory regulations that contain antiterrorist provisions.

The prevention of money laundering and prevention of terrorism financing are two separate subject matters, yet they both are regulated and treated with equal determination.[68] The main mechanism used to reveal an act of "terrorism financing" are the procedures that disclose money laundering acts. Those procedures were

66 See also Section I of this chapter.

67 OJ EU L 309/15 – and Commission Directive 2006/70/EC (1.08.2006) laying down implementing measures for Directive Parliament and of the Council as regards the definition of "politically exposed person" and the technical criteria for simplified customer due diligence procedures and for exemption on grounds of financial activity conducted on an occasional or very limited basis.

68 A. Golonka, *Polskie rozwiązania prawne w zakresie przeciwdziałania finansowania terroryzmu (Polish Legal Solutions Within the Scope of Terrorism Financing Prevention)*, in *Prokuratura i Prawo (Prosecutor's Office and the Law)* No 3, 2013, pp. 95–110.

adopted in the 2000 Act. They currently include verification of the source of the origin of money accumulated in a bank account and the responsibilities of over twenty "obligated authorities," including banks, accountants and attorneys/notaries,[69] to report any transaction that exceeds the value of 15.000 euros to the Undersecretary of State at the Ministry of Finance – the General Inspector of Financial Information (Generalny Inspektor Informacji Finansowej, or GIIF). They must also report "suspicious transactions," which remain connected to the acts of terrorism financing, as activities bearing characteristics of the offence defined in the text of Article 165a of the PPC.

The degree of ability with which the obliged entity is capable to perform the proper assessment of the occurrence of "terrorism financing" *ergo* "'suspicious transactions," remains an open question. Statistics published by GIIF in 2010[70] indicated 15,357 reports of information about "suspicious transactions," but only 16 of them related to suspicion of terrorism financing. A risk assessment and customer due diligence are carried out by the obligated entity to determine whether a transaction is "suspicious." Such a determination may result in account blocking, transaction withholding and the freezing of funds.

On the grounds of the provisions of the Act, the procedure devoted to terrorism financing prevention also includes the GIIF's competence to request from the state authorities (the Prosecutor's Office, ABW [Antiterrorist Centre of ABW], CBA, etc.), the disclosure of information about all cases of open investigations that concern terrorism financing acts along with the cases where only suspicion of those acts has been demonstrated. In turn, the GIIF is obliged to disclose to those authorities any obtained data, as indicated in the Act, that remain connected with the information provided by those organs.

The Act, in harmony with the premises of the Convention/Directive, presents a reliable regulation that limits terrorism financing. This demonstrates the fundamental conformity of the Polish law with international obligations in that matter as it has been outlined in the latest periodical MONEYVAL Report.[71]

69 See A. Kołaczek, *Księgowi a przeciwdziałanie praniu pieniędzy i finansowaniu terroryzmu (Accountants and Money Laundering and Terrorism Financing Prevention)*, in: Rachunkowość (Bookkeeping) 10/2009, pp. 9–16.

70 Information available on http://www.mf.gov.pl/_files_/giif/publikacje/spr_2010_v2g_final_23.pdf.03; see also Report of the General Inspector of Financial Information on the implementation of the Act of 16 November 2000 on *counteracting money laundering and terror financing* in 2011; see http://www.mf.gov.pl/en/documents/764034/1223641/spr_2011_ANG.pdf.

71 See Report on Fourth Assessment Visit – *Executive Summary* – Anti-Money Laundering and Combating the Financing of Terrorism – Poland – 13 April 2013 – Key findings, pp. 5–7.

VII. IMMIGRATION MEASURES

Although Poland is a country in which there appears to be an insignificant level of immigration,[72] its geographical location and legal conditions arising from the EU membership, including the Schengen area, make it often a transit country for migrants on their way to western and northern Europe. This also applies to citizens of the "dangerous countries" *(kraje wysokiego ryzyka)*, which – according to the Ministry of Foreign Affairs – may be a factor fostering terrorist activities on the territory of Poland.[73] The government highlights in this respect the need to "conduct consistent and coherent migration and asylum policy, which may prevent the emergence of terrorist threats."[74]

In the Polish legal system, there is a number of regulations in the field of immigration law that can be used to combat terrorism. These are in particular the rules governing residence permits and visas to foreigners and provisions related to granting international protection and protection of borders. This short text provides an overview of these regulations, sometimes combined with their critical analysis, as well as examples of their practical application.

A. *Law on Foreigners*

In the Polish legal system, the Law on Foreigners is the basic legal act that regulates such issues as third-country citizens' entry into, stay in or expulsion from the Polish territory.[75] The Law does not explicitly refer to the threat of terrorism. It does, however, refer to more general terms, such as a threat to "national security" or "security and public order." These premises are examined in the course of proceedings on the legalization of stay. The immigration body assesses whether the entry or stay of a particular migrant does not constitute a threat to the aforementioned values. The "national security" or "protection of security and public order" clauses can be used in proceedings conducted against persons suspected of terrorist activity.

The task of granting residence titles *(tytuły pobytowe)* lies within the remit of voivods. Prior to granting a given residence title, the voivod[76] submits a motion to the

[72] J. Godlewska, *Migracje i imigranci w Polsce – skala, podstawy prawne, polityka (Migrations and migrants in Poland – scope, legal basis, policies)*, Polish Committee of the European Net Against Poverty EAPN (Polski Komitet Europejskiej Sieci Przeciwdziałania Ubóstwu EAPN), 2010.

[73] See also footnote 30.

[74] See also footnote 30.

[75] Law on Foreigners of 13 June 2003 (OJ 2003 – 128/1175).

[76] Voivode (wojewoda) is a local government office governing the terrirory of a voivodship and the head of united government administration there.

Border Guard Unit Commander, the Voivodship Police Commander, the Chief of the ABW, and sometimes also the consul competent with respect to the foreigner's last place of residence abroad, to provide information on whether the foreigner's entry into or stay in the Polish territory constitutes a threat to the defence or security of the state or protection of security and public order. Data of those foreigners who are eventually classified by immigration bodies as posing such a threat can be entered into the index of persons whose stay in the territory of the Republic of Poland is undesirable (Article 128 § 6). The index is a national information system, existing beside the European Union's Schengen Information System (SIS). It is maintained by the Head of the Office for Foreigners. A record in the index entails a refusal of entry into or stay in the Polish territory within the period covered by the record. In particular, the inclusion of the foreigner's data in the index vests immigration bodies with the authority to refuse the entry into the territory of the Republic of Poland, refuse to grant a visa, refuse to grant a limited-time residence permit, refuse to grant a permit to settle, issue an expulsion decision or establish a prohibition on the part of the foreigner of reentry into the Polish territory. Furthermore, a record in the index results in the inclusion of the foreigner's data in SIS, which prevents the foreigner from entering any of the countries belonging to the "Schengen area."

If an entry into the index of undesirable persons was based on the premise of constituting a threat to the defence and security of the state or protection of security and public order or a violation of the interest of the Republic of Poland (Article 88 § 1 pt. 5), the foreigner's data are stored in the register for the longest period provided in the Law, that is, five years (in the event when an index entry is based on other premises, this period – as a rule – lasts from six months to three years, according to Article 99b).

In practice, it is difficult to estimate the number of index entries that concern persons undesirable on the premises of "national security" or "security and public order" and which relate specifically to foreigners posing a terrorist threat. This is the case because, first and foremost, the aforementioned clauses also encompass threats to national interests that are of a character other than terrorist. Secondly, the existence of a threat to the "defence and security of the state" or "security and public order" allows immigration bodies not to substantiate their decisions issued in proceedings conducted on the basis of the Law on Foreigners (Article 8 § 1). In those circumstances, factual bases for inclusion in the index of undesirable persons are not disclosed either (Article 128 § 1 pt. 6). Secrecy stretches onto case files of such proceedings (e.g., the opinion and documents provided to the voivod by ABW), which are usually covered by the confidentiality clause due to protection of classified state or professional information. A foreigner who is the subject of proceedings has no possibility of learning the particular premises that underpin their classification as a person posing, for example, a threat to national security. Such a foreigner does not have the possibility – either directly or through a proxy (even one authorized to access classified information) – of examining evidence gathered against him or her in the course of such proceedings. If the clauses of "national security" and "security and public order" are used in the cases of persons suspected of terrorism, the public learns this only from unofficial information disclosed by the media. By way of example, one may point out the case of a Yemeni national, Imam Ahmed Ammar,[77] who was subject to expulsion from Poland, or the case of a Cracow Polytechnic graduate from Morocco, Chakib Marakchi.[78]

The case of Chakib Marakchi adequately illustrates the arbitrariness of the previously described residence procedure. The Moroccan, who had been living in Poland for eight years, was refused a limited-time residence permit pursuant to Article 57 § 1 pt. 5 on the grounds of protection of national security or security and public order. The voivod issued such a decision upon receiving a negative opinion concerning the foreigner from ABW. Subsequently, Chakib Marakchi was included in the index of undesirable persons and ordered to leave the territory of the Republic of Poland. His data were also entered into SIS, which prevented him from going to France, where he was to begin doctoral studies. The foreigner filed an (eventually ineffective) appeal against the voivod's decision with the Head of the Office for Foreigners; then he lodged a complaint with the administrative court. In the application, Chakib Marakchi argued that due to the lack of detailed explanations of decisions issued against him and the classified character of case files, which could not be accessed by a professional proxy representing him either, he did not have a possibility of disputing the charges brought against him effectively and on the merits. The applicant also argued that administration bodies did not verify the accuracy of information on the alleged threat to national security and public order provided by ABW. The Voivodship Administrative Court dismissed the case[79] (the judgment is not final; the applicant lodged a cassation appeal with the Supreme Administrative Court and is awaiting its consideration).

It should be noted that, in the current shape, the provisions of the Law on Foreigners do not correspond to international standards as developed by the European Court of Human Rights (ECtHR; see judgments in the cases *Lupsa against Romania*,[80] *Al-Nashif and others against Bulgaria*[81] and *Chahal against*

[77] W. Czuchnowski, *"He encouraged to Jihad?" ("Wzywał do dżihadu?")*, *Gazeta Wyborcza*, 26 May 2004.

[78] *Absolwent Politechniki Krakowskiej terrorystą? ABW: "To możliwe" (Graduate of the Cracow Technical University is a terrorist? ABW: it's possible")*, *Gazeta Wyborcza*, 22 February 2010, http://wiadomosci.gazeta.pl/wiadomosci/1,114873,7587961,Absolwent_Politechniki_Krakowskiej_terrorysta__ABW_.html.

[79] Judgment of the Administrative Court in Warsaw of 28 December 2012, No. V SA/Wa 173/12.

[80] *Lupsa against Romania*, ECtHR judgment of 8 June 2006 r., No. 10337/04.

[81] *Al-Nashif and others against Bulgaria*, ECtHR judgment of 20 June 2002, No. 50963/99.

the United Kingdom[82]) and the Court of Justice of the European Union (CJEU; see judgment in case C 300/11[83]). In their case law, both courts have established a series of procedural conditions for issuing decisions on expulsion of foreigners on the basis of national security threats. According to those conditions, the national procedure has to provide particular safeguards against arbitrary actions of state bodies. It is crucial to ensure not only that the decisions issued are formally evaluated, but also that the evidence is reviewed by an independent organ. Furthermore, ECtHR and CJEU point out that a procedure is unacceptable when neither the person under expulsion nor his or her legal representative are allowed to acquaint themselves with the reasons for expulsion (besides a general indication of being a threat to national security). Such a procedure makes it impossible for a foreigner to present his or her stance in the case and effectively enjoy the right to a fair trial. Classifying proceedings should be accompanied by the foreigner's right to the assistance of a special lawyer with a certificate of access to classified information (a *security-cleared counsel*) who will represent the foreigner's interests in proceedings (the institution of a "special advocate" was introduced, for example, in the United Kingdom after the Chahal case, which was decided by ECtHR).

In conclusion, it is justified to express a critical view of Polish law, which lacks procedural solutions enabling the person under expulsion (or his or her legal representative) to build effective defence. Such a situation results from the refusal of access to classified case files and a refusal to provide appropriately detailed justifications for immigration decisions. In the light of international standards, these practices, in cases such as that of Chakib Marakchi, could be considered by ECtHR to be a violation of Article 6 and 13 of the European Convention on Human Rights and Article 1 of Protocol 7 to the Convention (which concerns procedural safeguards referring to expulsion of foreigners). The problem has been noted by Polish commentators on legal doctrine.[84] It has also been singled out repeatedly by non-governmental organizations that offer legal aid to foreigners.[85]

82 *Chahal against the United Kingdom*, ECtHR judgment of 15 November 1996, No. 22414/93.

83 *Z.Z. against Secretary of State for the Home Department*, CJEU judgment of 4 June 2013, No. C 300/11.

84 I. C. Kamiński, *Procedural safeguards concerning the expulsion of foreigners posing state security threat – Chakib Marakcji case (Proceduralne gwarancje związane z wydaleniem cudzoziemca ze względów bezpieczeństwa państwa – uwagi na kanwie sprawy Chakiba Marakchiego)*, in *Problemy Współczesnego Prawa Międzynarodowego, Europejskiego i Porównawczego*, 2012, vol. X.

85 Comments of the Helsinki Foundation for Human Rights to the periodic report by the government of the Republic of Poland presented on the basis of the International Covenant on Civil and Political Rights. Commentary to answers, 15 September 2010, http://www.hfhr.org.pl/pliki/komentarz_hfpc .pdf.

B. *Amnesty Law*

In 2012, Poland granted an "amnesty" for irregular migrants, allowing them to legalize their stay. It was introduced by the Law on legalization of the stays of some foreigners on the territory of the Poland and the Act amending the Act on granting protection to foreigners on Polish territory and the Law on Foreigners.[86] One of the conditions for the use of the amnesty mechanism by a migrant was the absence of contraindications for legalization of their stay because of the threat to national defence or national security or the protection of public order and safety or interests of the Republic of Poland (Article 3. 2 point 5). The amnesty was also not available for the foreigners whose data were included for the aforementioned reasons in the index of undesirable persons (Article 3. 2, point 6).

C. *The Regulations for Granting Refugee Status*

The fact that the migrant poses a threat to the state security can also be the basis – according to the Act on granting protection to foreigners on the territory of the Poland[87] – for refusing them refugee status or for granting other forms of international protection (such as a tolerated stay or subsidiary protection). The Act also does not expressly refer to the risks associated with terrorist activity. This makes it difficult to determine how often this provision is in fact used as a reason for denying the refugee status to migrants constituting a terrorist threat.

D. *The Border Guard Act*

Under the Border Guard Act[88] and the Act on the Protection of the State Borders,[89] the Border Guard plays an important role in responding to migration-related terrorist threats. The Border Guard is a unified, uniformed and armed law enforcement formation set up for the purpose of land and maritime border protection and border traffic control in accordance with national security interests. The specific role of the Polish Border Guard in Europe results from the obligation to safeguard one of the longest sections of external land border of both the European Union and NATO.

86 An Act on legalization of stay of some foreigners on the territory of the Poland, amending the Act on granting protection to foreigners on Polish territory and the Act on foreigners of 28 July 2011 (OJ 2011 No -191/1133).

87 Act on granting protection to foreigners on the Polish territory of 13 June 2003 (OJ 2003 – 128/1176).

88 Border Guard Act of 12 October 1990 (OJ 2005 – 234/1997).

89 Act on the Protection of the State Borders of 12 October 1990 (OJ 2005 – 226/1944).

In contrast to the Law on Foreigners, the Border Guard Act explicitly recognizes the power of the Border Guard to "conduct operations to identify and counter threats of terrorism" (Article 1.2 point 5d). This provision was added in 2007 by the amendment that expanded the competences of the Border Guard in the area of national security and public order.[90] The amendment was introduced in connection with the planned abolition of controls at the borders of Poland representing the internal borders of the European Union, which took place in 2008 (according to the Schengen Agreement).

Specific duties of the Border Guard regarding counter-terrorism include, in particular:

- Maintaining law and order within the territorial border crossings, including the protection of objects owned or used by the Border Guard against terrorist attacks
- Monitoring environments and clusters of migrants and their criminal activity in the territory of the Republic of Poland
- Collecting, processing and analyzing information related to potential terrorist threats
- Implementing operational activities related to the recognition and prevention of terrorist threats
- Cooperating in countering terrorist threats with the ABW, the Intelligence Agency, the Police Service of Counterintelligence, the Military Intelligence Service and the Military Police and border authorities of neighboring countries

The Border Guard is also to prevent illegal transporting across the border of waste, harmful chemicals, nuclear and radioactive materials, drugs and psychotropic substances, arms, ammunition and explosives. An important obligation of the Border Guard is to ensure the safety of international transport by conducting security checks of passengers, their baggage as well as sapper-pyrotechnic activities at airports, train stations and harbors for the purposes of crime prevention (including terrorist activity).

The role of the Border Guard in the fight against terrorism was highlighted in the *National Security Strategy of the Republic of Poland*.[91] This document emphasizes the further development of the intelligence and monitoring competencies of the Border Guard in relation to the prevention of terrorist activities. As underlined in the Strategy, "monitoring and control of migration of foreigners on the territory of the whole country is a very important task and should be performed also in the

[90] Act amending the Border Guard Act and other acts of 13 April 2007 (OJ 2007 – 82/558).

[91] Signed by the President of Poland on 13 November 2007, §§ 36, 108.

preventive manner. Both the Police and the Border Guard should constantly monitor the terrorist threats and cooperate with other services in this respect."

Measures taken by the Border Guard aimed at preventing terrorist attacks sometimes raise doubts. In 2011, there was an interesting trial in Poland for the protection of personal rights against the Commander of the Border Guard brought by a citizen of the United Kingdom, Shaminder Puri. Puri is a Sikh who during security checks at the airport in Warsaw was ordered to remove his turban. When he refused, citing religious reasons, he was fined by the Border Guards. Puri argued during the court proceedings that the inspection carried violated his dignity and freedom of religion. Moreover, he referred to the violation of the principle of proportionality – Border Guard officers immediately demanded taking down his turban without applying less invasive methods of control in a first place (for example, the body scanner or metal detector). Polish courts found, however, that the Border Guard officers acted within their statutory competences and the lawsuit was finally dismissed.[92] It is important to note that this case triggered a public debate in Poland over the absence of any rules governing the conduct of the Border Guard officers with respect to religious minorities during security checks at airports.

E. *Summary*

Based on the discussed legislation, it is difficult to determine clear trends in the development of regulatory efforts such as the tightening of immigration policy because of the increasing terrorist threat in Poland. Besides the extension of the competence of the Border Guard associated with Poland's full implementation of the Schengen Agreement, there have not been any significant legislative changes introduced in this area in the recent years. Most discussed legislation contains only general regulations aimed at countering threats to national security or public order that cover *inter alia* the fight against terrorism. We cannot rule out the possibility that these provisions are today being employed to implement more restrictive practices to combat terrorist threats. The problem of confidentiality of proceedings against migrants suspected of terrorist activities and the lack of reasons given in such cases by immigration authorities, however, make it is difficult to estimate the real scale of the phenomenon.

Some procedural solutions adopted in Polish immigration law raise certain doubts regarding their conformity with international standards for the protection of human rights. As indicated previously, the Act on Foreigners lacks procedural solutions that provide the migrant (being under expulsion from Poland due to suspicion of

[92] Judgment of the Appeal Court in Warsaw of 12 February 2012, No. I ACa 499/12.

terrorist activity) or his or her attorney an effective remedy against these allegations. Consequently, the law does not guarantee a fully effective right to a fair trial.

Although the role of immigration laws in preventing and combating terrorism seems to be gaining in importance, it should be noted that this problem is only to a small extent included in the government documents specifying the conditions for the development of legal regulations concerning state security and protection against terrorist threats. These issues were only very briefly tackled in the aforementioned *National Security Strategy of the Republic of Poland*' (2007).[93] A little bit more attention to this problem was paid in the *National Counter-Terrorism Programme of the Republic of Poland for 2012–2016*.[94] In the context of immigration measures, this document calls for the improvement of the mechanism of mandatory consultation with the relevant enforcement agencies (such as ABW) by the immigration authorities prior to delivering decisions on visas and residence permits. It also stresses the need for introduction of more effective integration programmes for foreigners in Poland in order to prevent the radicalization of their attitudes and vulnerability to recruitment into extremist groups. Moreover, the document urges development of electronic databases to facilitate the exchange of information between different institutions dealing with immigration issues (there is currently no central database of foreigners in Poland; each of the institutions operates its own information system). Finally, the document previews the introduction of biometric residence permits and visas to facilitate the control of migration processes.

The key document, *Polish Migration Policy – the Current State and Proposed Actions*, adopted by the Polish government in July 2012,[95] sets out the national priorities on immigration policy and legal changes in this respect, but does not discuss counter-terrorism.

VIII. ADMINISTRATIVE AND EXECUTIVE MEASURES

No use of such measures have been observed either in practice or in doctrinal discussion.

IX. ROLE OF MILITARY AND EXTRA-TERRITORIAL COUNTER-TERRORISM ACTIVITIES

Criminal cases involving terrorism offences are decided by common courts of general jurisdiction. A personal exception applies, however: courts-martial composed

93 See footnote 30.
94 See footnote 31.
95 http://emn.gov.pl/ese/news/8765,dok.html.

of military judges are competent to hear cases involving soldiers in active service, civilian employees of the armed forces, soldiers of the armed forces of foreign states present in the territory of the Republic of Poland and civilian members of their personnel.[96] Procedural guarantees of the right to the fair trial apply equally before common courts and courts-martial.[97]

Four Polish Military Contingents (PMCs) acted outside national territory in 2013. In all instances, their missions were inseparably linked to international operations either with a clear antiterrorist mandate (the International Security Assistance Force in Afghanistan)[98] or exposed to a terrorist threat during performance of their stabilization or training functions (the European Union Force ALTHEA in Bosnia and Herzegovina, the European Union Training Mission in Mali and the Kosovo Force in the Republic of Kosovo, the former Yugoslav republic of Macedonia and Bosnia and Herzegovina).

The Ministry of National Defence (MND) asserts that PMCs have not conducted any antiterrorist operations and have performed only peacekeeping and training duties. Nonetheless, there were instances of apprehension and short-term detention in Afghanistan and Iraq (PMC-Iraq formed a part of the NATO Training Mission – Iraq, completed in December 2011) when security of the mission so required. In cases involving short-term detention, detainees were transferred to relevant local authorities after an unspecified time, but allegedly pursuant to military procedures applicable to PMCs. MND claims no statistics in this respect available and information on relevant military procedures are classified. Detained individuals did not try to challenge detention before domestic or international courts.[99]

In early December 2002, at least two suspected high-ranking al-Qaeda members (Saudi Arabia national Abd Al Rahim Hussayn Muhammad al Nashiri and stateless Palestinian Zayn Al-Abidin Muhammad Husayn, a.k.a. Abu Zubaydah), both in custody of the U.S. Central Intelligence Agency (CIA), were allegedly transferred covertly to Poland and detained in a secret CIA detention centre at the Stare Kiejkuty intelligence training base. Throughout six and nine months incommunicado detention respectively, the two suspects were supposedly ill-treated by CIA agents, thereafter transferred from Poland to other CIA "black sites" and finally to the Internment Facility at the U.S. Guantanamo Bay Naval Base in Cuba. It is claimed that Polish Military Information Services (MIS)[100] had oversight of

[96] Article 647 of PCPC, Article 22 and 54 Court-Martial Act of 1997 – O.J. 2012 – 952.

[97] Art. 646 of PCPC.

[98] Security Council's Resolution S/RES/2069 (2012).

[99] A note by MND of 5.06.2013 on file with authors.

[100] MIS (Wojskowe Słuzby Informacyjne) was a separate and specialized intelligence agency of the Polish Armed Forces (PAF), established to strengthen the state defence and security of the PAF and supervised by the lower house of the Polish Parliament (Sejm), pursuant to Article 1 of an Act of 9

the operation with an authorization given by high-ranking officials of the Republic of Poland (e.g., the President, the Minister of National Defence and the Head of Military Intelligence).[101] The existence of a secret prison in Poland was disclosed in November 2005 by Human Rights Watch (HRW).[102] In the same month, the Parliamentary Assembly of the Council of Europe launched an investigation of the issue, resulting in three reports prepared in 2006,[103] 2007[104] and 2011[105] by a Swiss senator, Dick Marty, confirming HRW allegations.

In November and December 2005, the Polish Parliamentary Committee for Special Services initiated an inquiry on the matter. The Committee generally worked *in camera* and without minutes. It held a one-day meeting on 21 December 2005 to discuss the allegations of secret CIA prisons in Poland. The only public indication given by the Committee was that there had not been any CIA prisons in Poland.[106]

On 14 February 2007, the European Parliament (EP) adopted the Resolution on the alleged use of European countries by the CIA for the transportation and illegal detention of prisoners (2006/2200(INI), deploring *inter alia* "the glaring lack of cooperation by the Polish government with EP temporary committee," and "encouraging the Polish Parliament to establish a proper inquiry committee, independent of the government and capable of carrying out serious and thorough investigations."[107]

On 11 March 2008, the District Prosecutor's Office in Warsaw instituted proceedings on the alleged existence of so-called secret CIA detention facilities in Poland as well as the illegal transport and detention of persons suspected of terrorism. The Prosecutor' Office granted injured party status in these proceedings to Al Nashiri and Abu Zubaydah in October 2010 and January 2011 respectively. The proceedings have not reached a trial stage yet and are to be conducted by the Appellate Prosecutor's Office in Cracow.[108] Until June 2013, the investigation has

July 2003 on MIS (OJ.2003.139.1326). MIS was liquidated in 2006 by Sejm amidst allegations of its extralegal conduct as revealed in the Report of the Chairman of the Verification Commission: http://web.archive.org/web/20071008104447/http://raport.gov.pl/Raport_jawny_16022007.pdf (in Polish).

101 See note 9 (II Marty Raport) §§ 168, 174.

102 Statement on U.S. Secret Detention Facilities in Europe, http://www.hrw.org/news/2005/11/06/human-rights-watch-statement-us-secret-detention-facilities-europe.

103 AS/Jur (2006) 16 Part II,7 June 2006, http://assembly.coe.int/Main.asp?Link=/CommitteeDocs/2006/20060606_Ejdoc162006PartII-FINAL.htm.

104 AS/Jur (2007) 36, 7 June 2007, http://assembly.coe.int/ASP/Doc/XrefDocDetails_E.asp?FileID=11555.

105 Report | Doc. 12714 | 16 September 2011, http://assembly.coe.int/ASP/XRef/X2H-DW-XSL.asp?fileid=12952&lang=EN.

106 2011 Marty Report, § 40.

107 http://www.europarl.europa.eu/sides/getDoc.do?type=TA&language=EN&reference=P6-TA-2007-32, par. 167, 178.

108 http://www.hfhr.pl/en/odpowiedz-prokuratury-na-pytania-o-przebieg-postepowania-ws-tajnych-wiezien-cia/.

been extended nine times and remains pending without a clearly defined date for its completion. The bulk of the case files are classified.[109]

On 19 February 2010, the Human Rights Council of United Nations released the *Joint Study on Global Practices in Relation to Secret Detention in the Context of Countering Terrorism of the Special Rapporteur on the Promotion and Protection of Human Rights and Fundamental Freedoms While Countering Terrorism*, appreciating the fact that an investigation had been opened on the existence of places of secret detention, but, at the same time, deploring the lack of transparency into the investigation.[110] The UN Human Rights Committee, in its concluding observations of the sixth periodic report on the Republic of Poland of 27 October 2010, expressed its concern that secret detention centre had reportedly existed at Stare Kiejkuty and that the domestic investigation was not yet concluded.[111]

On an unspecified date, presumably on 10 January 2012, the Warsaw Prosecutor of Appeal charged Z. Siemiątkowski, the Head of the Intelligence Agency from 2002 to 2004, with abuse of power and with violation of international law by "unlawful detention" and "imposition of corporal punishment" on prisoners of war.[112]

Al Nashiri and Abu Zubaydah lodged applications against Poland to the European Court of Human Rights on 6 May 2011[113] and 28 January 2013[114] respectively, both communicated to the Polish government. The applicants allege violation of numerous provisions of the European Convention on Human Rights as a result of their ill-treatment in Poland while in U.S. custody, their unconditional transfer from Poland by U.S. agents and Poland's failure to conduct an effective investigation into the circumstances surrounding their ill-treatment, detention and transfer from the Polish territory. In July 2014, the European Court of Human Rights found Poland had violated Article 3, prohibiting torture and inhumane treatment, in both its procedural and substantive aspects; Article 5, relating to liberty and security; Article 6, relating to fair trial in regard to its knowledge of transfers to Guanantamo Bay; Article 8, relating to privacy and family life; and Article 13, relating to effective investigation and remedy. The Court awarded each applicant 100,000 euros in non-pecuniary damages and ruled that Poland take steps to ensure that the United States would not impose the death penalty on Al Nashiri.[115]

[109] http://www.hfhr.org.pl/cia/images/stories/Odpowiedz%20PA%20Krakow_marzec%202013.pdf (in Polish).

[110] A/HRC/13/42, 26 January 2010, § 118.

[111] CCPR/C/POL/CO/6, § 15,http://www2.ohchr.org/english/bodies/treaty/CD_Concl_Obs_2010/CCPR/100th%20session/CCPR-C-POL-CO-6%20(e).pdf.

[112] ECHR, Application no. 7511/13 Zayn Al-Abidin Muhammad HUSAYN (ABU ZUBAYDAH) against Poland lodged on 28 January 2013, § 143.

[113] Application no. 28761/11.

[114] Application no. 7511/13.

[115] Al Nashiri v. Poland Application no. 28761/11 Judgment of the Former Fourth Section 24 July, 2014; Husayn Abu Zabaydah v. Poland Application no. 7511/13 Judgment of the Former Fourth Section 24 July, 2014.

X. SECRECY

Cases involving terrorist offences are subject to general rules of Polish criminal procedure as provided in the PCPC, the law of 5 August 2010 on protection of classified data (hereafter the 2010 Act)[116] and the Ordinance of the Minister of Justice of 20 February 2012 on the handling of transcripts of questioning and other documents or items covered by the duty to maintain secrecy of classified information or the duty of secrecy related to the exercise of a profession or function (hereafter the 2012 Ordinance).[117]

The courts are to base their judgments in such cases solely on facts and evidence disclosed during the main trial.[118] An accused's access to classified files, documents and items may be conditioned (but not refused), as they shall be made available to parties, counsel and representatives only on the basis of an order issued by the court or its president or, at the investigation stage, by the prosecutor. Such an order should indicate the person authorized to study evidence and specify its scope, manner and place. If the person concerned asks for the creation of a bound set of documents for the purposes of taking notes, such a bound set of documents are to be made and classified appropriately. The set will be deposited and made available only in the court's or the prosecution's secret registry.[119] However, judges may not impose conditions on disclosure such that only the accused's lawyer and not the accused see a classified file, document or item.

As a rule, the hearing shall be held in open court unless otherwise provided by the law.[120] The court may permit the media to make video and sound recordings during the trial if the public interest so requires, the hearing is not obstructed thereby and it is not contrary to any important interest of a participant in the proceedings.[121] On the other hand, the court shall exclude the public from all or part of the trial when, for example, the hearing may disclose circumstances that should remain secret to protect interests of the state.[122] Moreover, when classified files, documents and items are referred to in open decisions or judicial writs, classified data should be replaced by an evidentiary number of such evidence.[123] If all or part of the trial is held in

[116] The Act of 5 August 2010 on the protection of classified data – OJ 2010 – 182/1228.

[117] The Order of the Minister of Justice of 20 February 2012 on the procedure of managing the interrogations protocols and other documents or objects which are protected by the duty to maintain secrecy of the classified data and/or to maintain the secrecy of profession or office, OJ 2012 – 219.

[118] Article 410 of PCPC.

[119] § 6 The Ordinance.

[120] Article 355 of PCPC.

[121] Article 357. § 1 of PCPC.

[122] Article 360. § 1.3 of PCPC.

[123] § 11 of the 2012 Ordinance

closed session, the announcement of the statement of reasons for the judgment may be also made in closed session.[124]

A notable ambiguity exists as to the conflict between the right to defence in criminal proceedings and the protection of classified information. Article 265 § 1 of the PPC provides that whoever discloses or, in violation of the 2010 Act, uses information rated as "secret" or "top secret" shall be subject to the penalty of deprivation of liberty for a term of between three months and five years. An unconditional wording does not exclude an accused intending to use classified information in a statement at any stage of the proceedings.[125] A doctrine in its majority takes a different stand, however, advancing systematic and functional interpretation to the effect that if only classified information is relevant in a given case, an accused is not legally barred from using such information even if not duly cleared to do so.[126]

On the other hand, witnesses (e.g., intelligence service members), experts, translators and court experts obliged to preserve information rated as "secret" or "top secret" may be examined as to the circumstances to which this obligation extends only if cleared by an authorized superior agency or, if clearance not granted, by a relevant central administration agency.[127] Such clearance, on the request of the court or prosecutor, may be refused only if the giving of evidence might result in serious damage to the state's interest.[128] This rule applies to documentary evidence accordingly.[129] Therefore, judges and prosecutors lack the power to balance the competing claims of secrecy and disclosure in individual cases, as the competence is granted solely to the relevant superior agency or the central administration agency.

Witnesses (e.g., intelligence service members) may testify in terrorism prosecutions anonymously in accordance with general rules of Polish criminal procedure.[130] In particular, if there is a justified concern for safety of life, health, freedom or considerable property loss of the witness or his or her next-of-kin, the court (or at the pretrial stage, the prosecutor) may issue an order classifying as secret personal data of such witness. Such personal data shall be known exclusively to the court, the prosecutor and, when necessary, a police official at the pretrial stage. Consequently,

[124] Article 364 § 2 of the PCPC.

[125] See e.g. Polish Supreme Court's Judgment of 11.04.1983, no. I KR 393/82, unpublished.

[126] M. Klejnowska, *Oskarżony jako osobowe źródło informacji o przestępstwie (The Accused as a Personal Source of Information About the Offence)*, Zakamycze, 2004; P. Hofmański, S. Zabłocki, *Elementy metodyki pracy sędziego w sprawach karnych (Elements of Judge's Work Methodology in Penal Cases)*, Zakamycze 2006; Michał Leciak, *Tajemnica państwowa w wyjaśnieniach oskarżonego w procesie karnym (State Secret in Explanations of the Accused in Penal Proceedings)*, in *Prokuratura i Prawo (Prosecutor's Office and the Law)* 11/2005, p. 56.

[127] Article 179 § 1 I n conjunction with Article 197 § 3, 204 § 3 and 206 § 1 of PCPC.

[128] Article 179 § 2 of PCPC.

[129] Article 226 in conjunction with Article 179 of PCPC.

[130] Article 184 of PCPC.

records of interrogations of the witness may be made available to the accused or counsel redacted to prevent identification of the witness.

XI. OTHER MATTERS

A. *Poland's Anti-Cyberterrorism Strategy*

Following its access to the NATO Cooperative Cyber Defence Centre of Excellence in 2011, Poland enhanced its work on an effective cybersecurity strategy.

The baseline for such a strategy may be found in the 2007 Act on critical management, which defines the critical infrastructure as systems and functionally connected objects composite thereof, including building objects, facilities, installations and services crucial to state security and that of the country's citizens and allowing for effective operation of public administration bodies, as well as institutions and entrepreneurs. The Act was followed by a *2012 National Critical Management Plan*[131] adopted by the Council of Ministers, identifying four stages of crisis management, including prevention, preparation, reaction and restoration. Each of those stages rests in the competences of different public authorities. The division of those competences was described in more detail within the *White Book on National Security of the Republic of Poland (2013)*,[132] presented by National Security Office (Biuro Bezpieczeństwa Narodowego, or BBN).

The *White Book* assigns the task of counter-cyberespionage to BBN. Yet, according to the *White Book*, due to the fast pace of information innovation, cybercrime and cyberterrorism prevention and monitoring follow no uniform methodology in Poland. To meet new challenges posed by cyberterrorism, the Ministry of Administration and Digitalization was created in 2011 and fully authorized to manage national information and communication policies, including management of telecommunication networks and critical infrastructure functioning within it, as well as the development of the information society. Its competence over critical infrastructure management is to ensure a high level of integrity and confidentiality of information transmitted and processed through such networks. Also within the BBC a specialized unit was created, the Governmental Counter Unit for Computer Incidents (CERT.GOV.PL), responsible for prompt reactions to any attempted cyberattack against critical infrastructure located within Poland's jurisdiction. According to the *White Book*, Poland struggles with shortages of highly educated computer staff allowing for effective protection of national critical infrastructure from cyberthreats. Another challenge is the diffusion of responsibility for national

[131] http://rcb.gov.pl/eng/?p=403.
[132] WhiteBook_NationalSecurity_PL_2013.pdf.

information security among different governmental entities, resulting in the lack of a sustainable system for coordinating the exchange of information.

With all those challenges in mind, the 2011 amendments of numerous acts on states of emergency, including the martial law act amendment, made significant contributions to increased national cybersecurity.[133] The latter includes a definition of cyberspace – possibly the only legal definition of cyberspace in modern state legislation worldwide. According to Article 2 § 1b of the Act of 29 August 2002 on martial law, cyberspace is to be understood as the space of processing and exchanging information created by teleinformation systems, including their interconnections and relationship with users. The amended act allows the General Commander to introduce martial law in case of threats to Poland's security originating from cyberspace.

The aforementioned documents were supplemented by the *2013 National Programme on Critical Infrastructure Protection*[134] presented by the Government Centre for Security, based on Article 5b of the Act on critical management (2007). According to that document, Poland as a developed country needs to ensure the security of services, allowing for a certain standard of living in a modern society, available through what is referred to in the report as "critical infrastructure." All human and natural threats to critical infrastructure must be prevented. According to this document, critical infrastructure includes all systems needed for supplying energy and fuel, communications, telecommunication services, financial services, food and water supply, health care, transportation as well as emergency services, and allowing for the continued operation of state administration and production and storing of chemical and radioactive substances, including pipelines for hazardous substances. Following the stipulations of the *2010 Regulation of the Council of Ministers on the National Critical Infrastructure Protection Programme* § 1, a critical infrastructure operator is identified as the owner or an owner-like possessor of objects, installations, facilities and services of critical infrastructure.[135] Among the addressees of the programme were various entities, including governmental bodies; private business, with particular emphasis on critical infrastructure operators; academia; and civil society. The document invites individual entities, in particular critical infrastructure operators, to provide risk assessments for the infrastructure they operate. When combating terrorist threats, critical infrastructure operators are required to rely on information provided to them by state agencies. Such information should be used to produce detailed analysis of threats to individual

[133] OJ 2011 – 222/1323.
[134] http://rcb.gov.pl/eng/?p=791.
[135] http://rcb.gov.pl/eng/wp-content/uploads/2011/03/REGULATION-on-NATIONAL-CRITICAL-INFRASTRUCTURE-PROTECTION-PROGRAMME-AB.pdf.

objects, installations or systems. Such scenarios need to indicate areas of potential insecurity and risk factors and corresponding security decisions which need to be taken. Such scenarios need to be credible, factually correct, consequential, functional and simple. All instructions included in the programme strongly rely on European Union regulations dealing with European critical infrastructure as defined within the *European Programme for Critical Infrastructure Protection* based on the Communication from the Commission of 12 December 2006 on a European Programme for Critical Infrastructure Protection,[136] followed by the Council Directive 2008/114/EC of 8 December 2008 on the identification and designation of European critical infrastructures and the assessment of the need to improve their protection.[137]

Summarizing the current endeavors, Poland enhanced its efforts in combating cyberthreats to national security by defining the components subject to cyberthreats and by introducing legislation to combat such threats. At the same time, however, Poland still lacks coherent procedures and methodology for recognizing and preventing cyberterrorism.

XII. CONCLUSION

This chapter bears testimony to the fact that coordinated, complex, autonomous counter-terrorism legislative measures in the Republic of Poland have been developed in the aftermath of the World Trade Center (WTC) attacks and, consequently, the absorption of the EU regulations observed in Polish law. As a result, the powers of the government and its institutions to counteract and suppress acts of terrorism have been emphasized and strengthened. The adopted regulations and their application do not indicate any disregard for human rights. The lack of terrorist activity cases in the territory of the Republic of Poland also gives rise to the assumption that the regulations along with the process of their adoption shall be deemed reliable and fully effective. Counter-terrorist law embraces the domain of penal law, financial law regulations, immigration law, the Acts regulating matters of international exchange between states and other legal subjects indicated in the rules, as has been comprehensively signaled in this chapter.[138] This illustrates the significant influence of "counter-terrorism law" – after 11 September 2001 – on "other branches of the law." From the comparative perspective, Poland is a thoroughly responsible partner in antiterrorist actions.

136 COM (2006) 786 final – OJ C 126 of 7.6.2007.

137 OJ EU L 345/75.

138 See also www.coe.int/terrorism – Council of Europe – Committee of Experts on Terrorism (Codexter) – Profiles on Counter-Terrorist Capacity – Poland (February 2012).

16

The Czech Republic

Veronika Bílková

I. INTRODUCTION

A. *Basic Information about the Czech Republic*

The Czech Republic is a medium-sized country situated in Central Europe. After the fall of communism in 1989, it undertook a process of political and economic transition turning it into a democratic country with a free market economy. Since 2004, the Czech Republic has been a member of the European Union. It is also a member of other international organizations, such as the United Nations, the Council of Europe, NATO and the Organization for Security and Cooperation (OSCE) as well as a host of specialized international organizations (the World Trade Organization, World Health Organization, UNESCO, etc.). Over the years, the Czech Republic has signed and ratified, or acceded to, various anti-terrorist instruments adopted by these organizations.

The Czech Republic belongs to the continental legal system (civil law).[1] The main source of law is a written act. The legal order of the Czech Republic forms a normative pyramid. The top of this pyramid is occupied by the Constitution (1993), which defines the Czech Republic as a "sovereign, unitary and democratic, law-abiding State, based on respect for the rights and freedoms of man and citizen" (Article 1, par. 1). The Constitution sets principles of the division of power and introduces various checks and balances. The Constitution is part of the so-called constitutional order of the Czech Republic, which also encompasses the *Charter of Fundamental Rights and Freedoms* (1993), the main domestic human rights instrument, and a series of constitutional acts (for instance, the *Constitutional Act on the Security of the Czech Republic* of 1998, Act No. 110/1998 Coll.), enjoying the same legal force as the Constitution. Other sources of law are ordinary acts adopted

[1] For more details, see European Judicial Network, *Legal Order – Czech Republic*. Online – http://ec.europa.eu/ civiljustice/legal_order/legal_order_cze_en.htm (retrieved on 23 August 2013).

by the Parliament and executive acts adopted by the government (government regulations), ministries (ministerial decrees) and municipalities (local ordinances).

The Czech Republic has a well-established judicial system. The system consists of four levels of courts encompassing district courts, regional courts, high courts and two supreme courts: the Supreme Court of the Czech Republic (civil and criminal proceedings) and the Supreme Administrative Court of the Czech Republic (administrative proceedings). Decisions of these courts are not a general source of Czech law, nor do they have precedential value. A special position within the judiciary is reserved to the Constitutional Court, which reviews the constitutionality of legal acts and protects the constitutional order and fundamental rights guaranteed to individuals. Decisions issued by the Constitutional Court are "binding upon all agencies and individuals" (Article 89, par. 2 of the Constitution).

The Czech Republic uses a mixed approach, with elements of both monism and dualism, with respect to international law. Article 10 of the Constitution stipulates that "promulgated international treaties, the ratification of which has been approved by the Parliament and which are binding on the Czech Republic, shall constitute a part of the legal order; should an international treaty make provision contrary to a law, the international agreement shall be applied." These so-called presidential international treaties, the list of whose categories is provided in Article 49 of the Constitution, thus become part of the Czech legal order. Other – so-called governmental and ministerial – international treaties are not directly applicable in the territory of the Czech Republic. If they are to produce legal effects within the country, they need to be transformed or adapted through a domestic legal act (usually an act of the Parliament).

B. *The Czech Republic's Experience with Terrorism*

Fortunately for its inhabitants, the Czech Republic does not have a very rich experience with terrorism. Its predecessor, Czechoslovakia, knew a wave of extreme left-wing, anarchist terrorism shortly after its establishment in 1918. In 1919, there was an attempted murder of the prime minister of Czechoslovakia, Karel Kramář, committed by an anarchist, but the prime minister escaped unharmed. Four years later, in 1923, another anarchist attacked the minister of finances of Czechoslovakia, Alois Rašín, who died as a result of the attack. During the communist period (1948–89), Czechoslovakia offered training to left-wing and nationalist terrorist groups operating in the Middle East and in Latin America.[2] Communist Czechoslovakia was also involved in at least one terrorist attack, namely the attack

[2] Ministry of the Interior of the Czech Republic, *Terorismus a jeho projevy v někdejším Československu a dnešní České republice* (Terrorism and its Manifestations in former Czechoslovakia and in the current

against the building of the European Steel and Coal Community in Strasbourg in 1957. The attack, which cost the life of the Strasbourg mayor's wife, was planned by the Czechoslovak intelligence service with the aim of hampering the integration processes in Western Europe. After the fall of communism, two intelligence agents allegedly responsible for the attack were prosecuted, but neither of the proceedings resulted in a conviction (due to the death of the first agent and serious health problems of the second agent).[3]

The Czech Republic, established after the dissolution of Czechoslovakia in 1993, has been so far spared any serious terrorist attack.[4] According to the information provided by the Ministry of the Interior of the Czech Republic,[5] the country has witnessed about twenty incidents in the 1990s, originally qualified as acts of terrorism. These incidents usually included the use of explosives in a public place.[6] Most of them, however, turned out to either be acts of groups of organized crime, settling accounts with other groups of the same type, or acts of mentally disturbed people. Some of the incidents have remained unexplained. None of them have been claimed by any terrorist group. No similar database on occurrences of terrorism in the Czech Republic exists for the period since 2000.

The record, however, would be largely similar to that of the 1990s, with occasional use of explosives mostly attributable to organized crimes groups.[7] There have also been several incidents of blackmailing of politicians and one incident in which a fake attack by means of a plastic gun was committed against the president of the Czech Republic, Václav Klaus, in September 2012.[8] There have also been several terrorist

Czech Republic). Online – http://www.mvcr.cz/clanek/terorismus-a-jeho-projevy-v-nekdejsim-ceskoslovensku-a-dnesni-ceske-republice.aspx (retrieved on 3 April 2013).

3 Teroristický útok v režii StB zůstane bez trestu, rozhodl soud (A terrorist attack directed by the State Security will remain without punishment, the court decided), *iDnes*, 2 April2013.

4 See Oldřich Krulík, *Česká republika v boji proti terorismu. Terorismus a organizovaný zločin ve střední a východní Evropě* (The Czech Republic in the Fight Against Terrorism. Terrorism and Organized Crime in Central and Eastern Europe), Brno, Ústav strategických studií, 2003.

5 Ministry of the Interior of the Czech Republic, *Terorismus a jeho projevy v někdejším Československu a dnešní České republice* (Terrorism and its Manifestations in former Czechoslovakia and in the current Czech Republic). Online – http://www.mvcr.cz/clanek/terorismus-a-jeho-projevy-v-nekdejsim-ceskoslovensku-a-dnesni-ceske-republice.aspx (retrieved on 3 April 2013).

6 The most serious incidents of the 1990s occurred still under Czechoslovakia, in 1990. In June 1990, a homemade bomb exploded in the Old Town Square in the centre of Prague – a German tourist lost an eye in the explosion, and about ten other people suffered light injuries. In August 1990, another homemade bomb went off in the dam of Hostivař, at the outskirts of Prague, resulting in several light injuries. Perpetrators of, and motivation for, these incidents have never been discovered.

7 TV Nova, *Výbuchy, které otřásly Prahou. Přehled explozí za 20 let* (Explosions which have shattered Prague. The Overview of explosions for the past 20 years). Online – http://tn.nova.cz/zpravy/cernakronika/vybuchy-ktere-otrasly-prahou-prehled-explozi-za-20-let.html (retrieved on 20 August 2013). See also TV NOVA, *Blast injures eighteen people in the centre of Prague*, 2 August 2004.

8 Fox News, *Man arrested for firing plastic gun at Czech president*, 28 September 2012.

attacks against the members of the Czech armed forces in Iraq and Afghanistan. One citizen of the Czech Republic died during the terrorist attack in Sharm El Sheikh, Egypt, in 2005. Moreover, reports indicate that the Czech Republic has been used as a transit country, through which terrorists as well as weapons and materials have been transferred from non-European regions, especially the Middle East, to Western Europe. According to Europol, eight persons affiliated with Al-Qaeda were arrested in the territory of the Czech Republic in 2011.[9]

Despite the low exposure to terrorism, the Czech Republic considers terrorism one of the most serious security threats. The recent Security Strategies of the Czech Republic, adopted in 2011 and 2015, rank terrorism at the top of the list of security threats.[10] Such a prioritization of terrorism is a rather new phenomenon, characterizing the period after 2001. In fact, until 2002, the Czech Republic had no special instrument relating to the fight against terrorism. The drafting of such an instrument began in 2000. After the attacks of 11 September 2001, the Draft was amended in light of the common European anti-terrorist strategy and finally adopted as a *National Action Plan to Combat Terrorism* in April 2002.[11] From 2002 to 2008, the *National Action Plan* was updated several times.[12] In 2010, this instrument was replaced by the *Counter-Terrorism Strategy*.[13] The updated version of this Strategy, adopted in 2013,[14] is the main instrument defining the key principles of counter-terrorism in the Czech Republic.

The Czech Republic conceptualizes terrorism as a "worldwide, latent, permanent, and omnipresent threat."[15] Although it is a country in which open manifestations of domestic or international terrorism are not common, the Czech Republic believes that it needs to remain vigilant with respect to terrorism for two main reasons. First, "the potential risk of a politically motivated attack against the Czech Republic or its interests abroad (led by the international terrorists) could be closely related to the foreign policy orientation of our country."[16] Secondly, the country supports the fight against terrorism as an expression of its international solidarity with countries exposed to this threat and with individual victims of terrorism.

9 Arrests in 2011 per member state and per affiliation, in Europol, *TE-SAT 2012, EU Terrorism Situation and Trend Report*, European Police Office, 2012, p. 37.

10 Government of the Czech Republic, *Security Strategy of the Czech Republic*, 2011; and Government of the Czech Republic, *Security Strategy of the Czech Republic*, 2015, p. 8.

11 Government Regulation No. 385 of 10 April 2002 (for 2002).

12 Government Regulations No. 361 of 14 April 2003 (for 2003), No. 479 of 19 May 2004 (for 2004) and No. 1466 of 16 November 2005 (for 2005–2007), No. 129 of 11 February 2008 (for 2007–9).

13 Ministry of the Interior of the Czech Republic, *Counter-Terrorism Strategy, 2010–2012*, Prague, 2010.

14 Ministry of the Interior of the Czech Republic, *Counter-Terrorism Strategy, from 2013*, Prague, 2013.

15 *Ibidem*, p. 29.

16 *Ibidem*.

The Czech Republic uses two main strategies to counter terrorism. The first is the law enforcement strategy, which is mainly preventative in nature, aimed at preventing radicalization (in the long run) and at thwarting activities of existing terrorist organizations (in the short run). The second is the military strategy, which is reflected in the support of, and occasional involvement in counter-terrorist military operations led by its allies, especially the United States (Afghanistan, Iraq). So far, the fight against terrorism has only rarely been conceptualized as an issue relating to immigration.[17] This can be explained by the prevailing nationality of immigrants (Slovaks, Ukrainians and Vietnamese) and the lack of any important immigrant communities from regions connected with terrorism (especially the Middle East).[18]

II. THE DEFINITION OF TERRORISM

Terrorism, as such, is not defined under the Czech legal order. There is, however, a definition of a "terrorist attack" contained in the *Criminal Code* and a working (non-legal) definition of the same term contained in the *Counter-Terrorism Strategy*. The latter states that "a terrorist attack should be understood as politically motivated violence intended to spread fear in the society (besides resulting in direct victims and in damage to property)."[19] This definition is used solely for operational purposes and it has no legal implications. The only legal definition of a "terrorist attack" in the Czech legal order is that present in Section 311 of the *(New) Criminal Code* (Act No. 40/2009 Coll., as amended). It is a criminal law definition aimed at permitting criminal prosecution of an individual who:

> with the intention of damaging the Republic's constitutional system or defence capability, of undermining or destroying the fundamental political, economic or social structures of the Republic or those of an international organization, of seriously intimidating the population or of unlawfully compelling the government or another body of public power or an international organization to perform, omit or tolerate an act,

[17] This might however easily change. There has been opposition by the Czech public to the government's plan to accept war refugees from Syria. See Martin Fendrych, Uprchlíky ze Sýrie? Teroristy? Ne. Pomáhat se má přece nám (Accepting Refugees from Syria? Terrorists? No. It Is Us Who Needs Help) *Aktuálně.cz*, 2 December 2014.

[18] One exception to this rule relates to the presence in the territory of the Czech Republic of immigrants (refugees) from Chechnya. Although the Czech Republic has shown sympathy to these immigrants, the Czech public perceives them as security threat. The fear of the Chechens has also a somewhat funny aspect in that the Czechs and the Chechens are occasionally confused. See, for instance, Charlie Campbell, *Czech Republic Forced to Remind the Internet That Chechnya Is in Different Country After Boston Bombing*, News Feed, 23 April 2013.

[19] Ministry of the Interior of the Czech Republic, *Counter-Terrorism Strategy, From 2013*, Prague, 2013, p. 3.

a) commits an attack against the life or health of a person with the intention of causing death or serious bodily harm;
b) takes hostages or commits an abduction;
c) destroys or seriously damages public utilities, transport or telecommunication systems, including information systems, fixed platforms on the continental shelf, electric energy and water supplies, the health service or other important facilities, public sites or public property with the intention of endangering human life, the safety of the facilities, systems or sites, or of exposing such property to the risk of major damage;
d) disrupts or stops the supply of water, electric energy or other basic natural resources with the intention of endangering human life or of exposing property to the risk of major damage;
e) seizes or controls an aircraft, vessel or other means of passenger or freight transport, and/or destroys, seriously damages or seriously interferes with the operation of navigation systems or facilities; or provides false information on important facts, thus endangering human life and health, the safety of the means of transport or exposing property to a risk of major damage;
f) without due authorization, manufactures or otherwise acquires, stores, imports, transports, exports or otherwise delivers or uses explosives, nuclear, biological, chemical or other weapons of mass destruction; and/or engages in unauthorized research into and development of nuclear, biological, chemical or other weapons or combat means or explosives prohibited by law or by an international treaty; or
g) exposes human beings to a danger of death or serious bodily harm, or exposes the property of other persons to a risk of major damage by causing a fire or flood or the harmful effects of explosives, gas, electricity or similarly dangerous substances or forces; or commits a similarly dangerous act; or aggravates an imminent danger or obstructs efforts to counter or alleviate it.

This definition is inspired by the EU definition of a "terrorist offence" enshrined in the EU Council Framework Decision of 13 June 2002 *on combating terrorism* (2002/485/JHA). The offence of "terrorist attack" was included in the *(Old) Criminal Code of the Czech Republic* (Act No. 14/1961 Coll.)[20] in 2004 (Act No. 537/2004 Coll., amending the *Criminal Code*[21]). The explanatory memorandum indicates that the primary rationale for the inclusion was the need to implement, in the Czech legal order, instruments adopted by the organs of the European Union (the Council of the EU) within the third pillar, which are binding upon all member states of

[20] See Section 95 of the *(Old) Criminal Code*.
[21] The amendment entered into force on 21 October 2004.

the EU.[22] The memorandum also refers to some of the UN legal instruments that, however, are not directly relevant for the definition of a "terrorist attack," but rather for the extent of auxiliary offences. For instance, the *UN International Convention for the Suppression of the Financing of Terrorism* (1999) has been implemented in the Czech Republic through the auxiliary offence of providing financial, material or other support to a terrorist attack, a terrorist or a member of a terrorist group.

The definition of a "terrorist attack" in the *Criminal Code* is a rather complex one. The *actus reus* of the offence can consist of any of the acts enumerated under (a). The *means rea* requires that the offence be committed intentionally and that it have a specific intention (that of damaging the Republic's constitutional system or defence capability; of undermining or destroying the fundamental political, economic or social structures of the Republic or those of an international organization; or of seriously intimidating the population or of unlawfully compelling the government or another body of public power or an international organization to perform, omit or tolerate something). There are no exceptions to the definition made in favour of, for instance, certain groups of people or individuals acting for specific motives. Generally speaking, the definition of a "terrorist attack" is not controversial in the Czech Republic. There have never been any discussions on the political scene or within the academic community about the definition in the *Criminal Code*. Nor have any requirements to exclude certain acts or individuals from its scope of application been ever made.

III. CRIMINAL LAWS AND PROSECUTIONS

A. *Criminal Law*

Under the Czech legal order, terrorism – or, more exactly, a terrorist attack – is a separate offence enshrined in Section 311 of the *(New) Criminal Code* (Act No. 40/2009 Coll., as amended). The provision is part of Chapter IX relating to *Criminal offences against the Czech Republic, a foreign state or an international organization*. Section 311 criminalizes not only the commission of a terrorist attack (Section 311, par. 1) but also a series of auxiliary offences. These offences include the threat to commit a terrorist attack (Section 311, par. 2); the public incitement of a terrorist attack (Section 311, par. 2); the provision of financial, material or other support to a terrorist attack, a terrorist or a member of a terrorist group (Section 311, par. 2); and the preparation of a terrorist attack (Section 311, par. 4). Whereas the threat, provision and preparation have been included in the section since its

[22] See Parliament of the Czech Republic, Tisk č. 514, *Důvodová zpráva* (Explanatory Memorandum), 2003.

adoption in 2004, the offence of public incitement was added in 2011[23] in reaction to changes in the EU law.[24] The inclusion of this new offence did not give rise to any public debate or public criticism. Under the general rules of the *Criminal Code*, the attempt to commit a terrorist attack is criminalized in the same way as the commission of such an offence (Section 21). The participation in the commission or attempted commission of a terrorist attack, consisting of the organization of the offence, the incitement of the offence and the facilitation of the offence, also gives rise to criminal responsibility (Article 24).

In addition, the *Criminal Code* criminalizes, as separate forms of criminal collaboration, the following acts: the public approval of a terrorist attack and the public praise of a perpetrator of such an offense (Section 365); favouritism consisting of helping the perpetrator of a terrorist attack to escape criminal prosecution or a criminal sentence (Section 366); the non-thwarting of a terrorist attack, on the preparation or commission of which the person has reliable information (Section 267); and the non-reporting of a terrorist attack, on the perpetration of which the person has reliable information (Section 268). It is a separate offence to establish, participate in the activities of or support any criminal group, especially if such a group is aimed at committing terrorist attacks (Section 361). Since the Czech Republic does not maintain its own list of terrorist organizations, it would be for a court to determine that a certain organization is a terrorist (criminal) one and that an individual supported it intentionally and with knowledge of its terrorist (criminal) character. The offence of a terrorist attack is subject to universal jurisdiction (Section 7). It is excluded from the application of statutes of limitations, if "it is committed in such circumstances as to amount to a war crime or a crime against humanity under international law" (Section 35, par. b).

Perpetrators of a terrorist attack may be sentenced to a term of imprisonment of five to fifteen years, along with the forfeiture of property. The same sentence is imposed on those having committed auxiliary offences. In qualified cases, perpetrators may be sentenced to a term of imprisonment of twelve to twenty years and even to the exceptional punishment of twenty to thirty years or life imprisonment, along with the forfeiture of property. The qualified cases are cases, in which (a) the offender acts as a member of an organized group; (b) he or she causes serious bodily harm or death; (c) as a result of his or her act a considerable number of people are made homeless; (d) the offender causes serious disruption to the transportation system; (e) he or she causes very considerable damage by the act; (f) the offender commits such a crime with the intention of acquiring great benefit; (g) he or she, by the act, endangers the

[23] Act No. 330/2011 Coll., amending the *Criminal Code*.

[24] See Council Framework Decision of 28 November 2008, *amending Framework Decision 2002/475/JHA on combating terrorism* (2008/919/JHA).

international position of the Czech Republic or of an international organization of which the Czech Republic is a member; and/or (h) the offender commits the act during a state of emergency or state of war. Individuals sentenced for a terrorist attack may not be conditionally released before the expiration of two-thirds of the sentence (Section 88). The fact that an offence is committed with the intention of facilitating the commission of a terrorist offence is, with respect to certain offences, considered to be a qualified case, entailing a higher sentence for the given offence.[25]

The *Criminal Code* also contains other offences which are either similar to the terrorist attack or could be applied to some terrorist acts in its stead. The former category encompasses other offences in Chapter IX (criminal offences against the Czech Republic, a foreign state or an international organization), namely high treason, subversion of the Republic, terror, and sabotage. High treason is committed by citizens of the Czech Republic who, in contact with a foreign power or a foreign agent, commit one of the other offences (subversion, terrorist attack, terror or sabotage; Section 309). Subversion of the Republic consists of violent acts committed with the intent of undermining the constitutional order, territorial integrity or defence capability of the Czech Republic or at destroying its independence (Section 310). Terror consists of the intentional (or attempted) killing of a person, committed with the intent to undermine the constitutional order (Section 312). Sabotage is committed by persons who, acting with the intent to damage the constitutional order or defence capability of the Czech Republic, abuse their position or office or commit some other act for the purpose of frustrating or obstructing the fulfilment of an important task by a state organ or the armed forces (Section 314).

The latter category encompasses ordinary criminal offences such as murder (Section 140), robbery (Section 173), hostage-taking (Section 174), extortion (Section 175), common danger (Section 272), damage and endangerment of public utilities (Section 276), unauthorized arming (Section 279), endangering the safety of an aircraft or civil vessel (Section 291), unlawful taking of an aircraft abroad (Section 292) or spreading of an untrue alert message (Section 357). The offence of a terrorist attack is *lex specialis* with respect to these general offences. One terrorist attack may nonetheless result in the commission of several separate offences and, of course, a person can commit various offences progressively (for instance, a person can commit a robbery and a terrorist attack or two different terrorist attacks). In such a case, the offender can be charged with several offences at the same time, but he or she would be sentenced to an aggregate (not cumulative) punishment determined by

[25] This applies to the following offences: Robbery – Section 173, Extortion – Section 175, Theft – Section 205, Embezzlement – Section 206, Unlawful Use of Foreign Property – Section 207, Fraud – Section 209, Insurance Fraud – Section 210, Credit Fraud – Section 211, Grant Fraud – Section 212, Falsification of a Public Document – Section 368 of the *(New) Criminal Code*.

the penalty foreseen for the most serious offence; the commission of other offences would, however, usually be considered as an aggravating circumstance.

Since 1 January 2012, the Czech Republic has known not only the criminal responsibility of natural persons, but also the criminal liability of legal persons.[26] The concept was introduced into the Czech legal system partly under the pressure of the European Union, and partly in order to be able to better implement obligations stemming from various international instruments, including several UN and Council of Europe counter-terrorism treaties. The Act on Criminal Liability of Legal Persons and the Proceedings makes it a criminal offence for a legal person to commit, by means of an act carried out on its behalf, in its interest or in the framework of its activities by its statutory organs or its employees, certain criminal offences and minor offences. Offences of Chapter IX of the *Criminal Code* are not included in the list of such offences, with one exception: that of the terrorist attack (Section 311 of the *Criminal Code*). Thus, legal persons may be held liable for a terrorist attack (Section 7 of the Act). Moreover, this offence is subject to universal jurisdiction (Section 4 of the Act) and it is, as the only offence under the Act, excluded from the application of statutes of limitations, on the condition that "it were committed in such circumstances as to amount to a war crime or a crime against humanity under international law" (Sections 13 and 25 of the Act).

B. *Terrorism Prosecutions*

Due to scarcity of cases relating to terrorist attacks in the Czech Republic, it is difficult to speak about any consolidated prosecution and/or sentencing practices. In principle, it is possible to distinguish two periods: the period before 21 October 2004, when the Czech legal order did not have a separate offence of a terrorist attack; and the period after this date, when such an offence has been introduced. During the first period, perpetrators of terrorist attacks had to be prosecuted for ordinary crimes. That is what happened, for instance, in the case of Marian Monczka, a Czech citizen who, in 1998, planted two bombs into garbage bins situated in public places in Prague (April 1998) and Ostrava (September 1998). He threatened to plant more explosives unless he was provided with a certain sum of money. When arrested, Monczka was charged with common danger, extortion and causing of serious bodily harm, and sentenced by the Municipal Court in Prague to a term of imprisonment of fifteen years.[27]

In the second period, that is, since 2004, it has been possible to charge perpetrators of terrorist acts with the special crime of terrorist attack. Such charges, however,

[26] Act No. 418/2011 Coll., *on criminal liability of legal persons and the proceedings against them.*

[27] There was a film about Monczka, entitled *Výbuch* (Explosion), shot in 2000.

have been made only very rarely. According to the data provided by the Ministry of Justice of the Czech Republic,[28] only one person has been convicted for the offence of a terrorist attack, by virtue of Section 95, par. 2(a) of the *(Old) Criminal Code*. The person – a man born in 1984 – sent several letters to leading Czech politicians threatening to use violence against them unless certain political conditions were met. The man was sentenced to five years in prison.[29] The media reports, moreover, indicate that perpetrators originally suspected of having committed terrorist attacks are in most cases still charged with ordinary crimes. This was, for instance, the case of Pavel Vondrouš, who committed a fake attack on the president of the Czech Republic, Václav Klaus, by means of a plastic gun, in the town of Chrastava in September 2012. In spite of voices calling for this act to be qualified as a terrorist attack (Section 311 of the *Criminal Code*),[30] Vondrouš was charged with disorderly conduct (Section 358 of the *Criminal Code*) and sentenced to a term of imprisonment of six months, with a one-year probation.[31]

In the absence of relevant practice, it is only possible to describe what the prosecution of a suspected terrorist should look like based on the legal regulation, not what it looks like in reality. Perpetrators of terrorist acts, regardless of whether they are charged with ordinary offences or with the offence of a terrorist attack, would be prosecuted by ordinary courts. In fact, there are no other courts in the Czech Republic, since the system of military courts established in the 1950s[32] was abolished in 1993.[33] The determination of the character of an act (ordinary offence vs. terrorist attack) may, however, have an impact upon the level at which the act would be adjudicated. While many ordinary crimes fall within the competence of district courts, the offence of a terrorist attack falls within that of regional courts (Section 17 of the *Criminal Procedural Code*, Act No. 141/1961 Coll., as amended).[34] Persons charged with offences relating to terrorism are entitled to the same procedural guarantees as any other persons (Section 33 of the *Criminal Procedural Code*).

Section 89 of the *Criminal Procedural Code* states that "it shall be possible to use as evidence anything that may contribute to properly clarifying the matter and

[28] See http://cslav.justice.cz/InfoData/uvod.html (retrieved on 10 October 2013).

[29] Municipal Court in Prague, *Case No. 63 T 4/2005*, 21 December 2005.

[30] *Vyjádření starosty města Chrastava ze dne 1. 10. 2012* (Declaration by the mayor of Chrastava dated 1 October 2012). Online – http://www.klaus.cz/clanky/3202 (retrieved on 12 April 2013).

[31] Prague Daily Monitor, *Klaus shooter gets suspended sentence*, 7 June 2013.

[32] See Act No. 66/1952 Coll., *on the organization of courts*.

[33] The Constitution of the Czech Republic stipulated that military courts would cease their existence by 31 December 1993 (Article 110).

[34] Regional courts are competent to adjudicate cases involving criminal offences that entail the minimum term of imprisonment of five years or for which an exceptional punishment may be imposed. This means that most ordinary criminal offences that could be applied to terrorist attacks (murder, hostage-taking, etc.), would also be adjudicated by regional courts.

that has been obtained in a lawful manner from the means of evidence" (par. 2). The section adds that "evidence obtained by means of unlawful duress or threat of duress cannot be used in the proceedings with the exception of the case when it is to be used as evidence against a person who used duress or threat of duress" (par. 3). Evidence obtained through torture or inhuman or degrading treatment would therefore be considered inadmissible in terrorism prosecutions. Its use, moreover, could amount to the violation of Article 3 of the *European Convention on Human Rights* and Article 7 of the (domestic) *Charter of Fundamental Rights and Freedoms*. So far, there has not been any terrorism-related case in which this provision would have been applied.

Under Section 97 of the *Criminal Procedural Code*, all persons have an obligation to "appear when summoned and to give a witness testimony about his/her knowledge of the crime and the offender, or of the circumstances relevant for criminal proceedings." As a rule, the identity of a witness shall be disclosed and established before his or her examination. If, however, there is "a justified fear that disclosing the identity or the domicile and/or the whereabouts of a witness could put his or her life, health, bodily integrity in danger or if such danger exists for a person close to him or her, the witness may be allowed not to give his or her personal data" (Section 101, par. 4). The authorization to proceed in such a way is issued by the presiding judge or, in pre-trial proceedings, by a prosecutor. The materials that make it possible to establish the identity of such a witness shall be deposited with the Prosecutor's Office and, in judicial proceedings, with the presiding judge. These materials shall be included in the file only if the danger no longer exists. Before examining an anonymous witness, the court has to "exclude the public from the hearing and take other measures to provide for the witness's safety" (Section 101, par. 5). At the main hearing, an anonymous witness shall make a statement as to how he or she gained knowledge of the facts he or she reports. If necessary, the witness may also be asked questions concerning the facts related to his or her credibility, in particular questions about his or her relation to the accused or to the injured.

C. *Punishment of Terrorism*

The range of sentences to which persons charged with the offence of a terrorist attack would be subject to was indicated previously. Under the general rules of sentencing, the court, when determining the type and extent of punishment, shall take into consideration the nature and gravity of the offence, the personal situation of the offender, the possibility of the offender reforming, as well as his or her behaviour after the act, including the offender's efforts to remedy the harm and his or her contribution to the disclosure of the offence committed by an organized group (Section 39 of the *Criminal Code*). The court may also apply mitigating and aggravating circumstances. Mitigating circumstances include, among others, the fact that the offender himself or herself reported the crime, assisted the appropriate organs in clearing up the offence, or assisted in clearing up criminal acts committed as part of a criminal conspiracy (Section 41 of the *Criminal Code*). Aggravating circumstances include, for instance, the fact that the offender committed the crime for a particularly contemptible motive; committed the crime in a brutal manner, insidiously, with special cunning or in a similar manner; caused major damage by his crime; committed the crime as its organizer, a member of an organized group or a member of a conspiracy; or had already been sentenced for a crime (Section 42 of the *Criminal Code*).

IV. INVESTIGATIVE POWERS

A. *Police Powers*

The powers of the Police in the area of counter-terrorism are governed by the *Act on the Police Force of the Czech Republic* (Act No. 273/2008 Coll., the Police Act). The Act entered into force on 1 January 2009, replacing the previous Police Act (Act No. 283/1991 Coll.). Unlike the previous Act, the 2008 Police Act does not explicitly rank "the fight against terrorism" (§ 2(1)(c) of the 1991 Act) among the tasks of the Police. This can be easily explained by the fact that the 2008 Police Act fails to include a provision enumerating the tasks of the Police. The 2008 Police Act nonetheless refers to the fight against terrorism several times, thus confirming that it is part of the tasks of the Police. The references are all made with the aim of conferring upon the Police certain special powers, which primarily relate to access to protected data (banks, health insurance, communication networks, taxes, etc.). These are the only special powers that the Czech Police have while fighting terrorism. In 2009, a special *National Contact Point for Terrorism* (NKBT) was established within the Police to coordinate counter-terrorist activities and gather, in cooperation with the intelligence services, information about terrorist threats. The NKBT also serves as a national contact point in the area of terrorism with respect to Interpol, Europol and Eurojust.

The access by the Police to protected data is regulated by Sections 71 and 71a of the Police Act. Under Section 71, the Police may, in order to prevent or detect a concrete threat in the area of terrorism, demand, to the extent necessary, (a) access to the operational and localization data administrated by natural or legal persons maintaining public communication networks or providing publicly accessible services of electronic communication; (b) access to the bank data relating to the time and place of the use of a means of payment; and (c) access to the data administrated by health insurance companies and companies providing health care and relating to the time and place of the provision of health care. Access to communication data is further regulated by the *Act on the Electronic Communications* (Act No. 127/2005 Coll.). Under Section 71a of the Police Act, the Police may require the tax administrator, for the purposes of an ongoing prosecution or in order to be able to start such prosecution, to provide information obtained in the administration of taxes, if such information is necessary to fulfil a concrete task related to the fight against terrorism.

B. *Intelligence Agencies*

There are three different intelligence services operating in the Czech Republic: the Security Information Service (SIS, civilian counterintelligence); the Office for Foreign Relations and Information (OFRI, civilian intelligence); and the Military Intelligence Service (MI, military intelligence and counterintelligence). All are governmental bodies responsible for the acquisition, collection and evaluation of information important for the protection of the interests of the Czech Republic. Their activities are regulated by the *Act on Intelligence Services of the Czech Republic* (Act No. 153/1994 Coll.). Under Section 5, par. e) of this Act, securing "information concerning organized crime and terrorism" falls within the competence of the SIS.[35] The other two services, however, are of relevance too. The OFRI secures information originating abroad that is important for the protection of the foreign political and economic interests of the Czech Republic.[36] The MIS secures information originating abroad that is important for the defence and security of the Czech Republic.[37] In both cases, the relevant information may relate to terrorism.

Similar to the Police, the intelligence services are entitled by virtue of Section 11a of the *Act on Intelligence Services* to demand access to bank data, when fulfilling concrete tasks in their competence relating to the fight against financing of terrorism. They get the access on the basis of an authorization by the president of the Senate of the High Court in Prague and only "if securing the required data by other means would be inefficient or highly difficult or impossible in the case" (Section 11a, par. 2). The authorization must contain information allowing the identification of the client as well as the determination of the relevant period of the access and the reasons for granting it. The relevant period shall not exceed three

35 The SIS is the main intelligence service operating within the territory of the Czech Republic. Its activities are regulated by the *Act on the Security Information Service* (Act No. 154/1994 Coll.). It is financed from a separate chapter of the state budget.

36 The OFRI is subordinated to the Ministry of Interior and is also financed from a separate budget chapter.

37 The MIS is subordinated to the Ministry of Defence. Its activities are regulated by the Act on the Military Intelligence (Act No. 289/2005 Coll.).

months, but it can be repeatedly prolonged, always by three months maximally. The intelligence service has the duty to inform the court regularly about whether the reasons for the authorization are still valid. The court is entitled to withdraw the authorization at any moment. No appeal is available against any of the decisions of the court (authorization or withdrawal). It is possible to use intelligence collected by intelligence agencies in terrorism prosecutions, although no relevant practice exists in this respect.

V. PROSCRIPTION AND LISTING OF TERRORIST GROUPS AND INDIVIDUALS

A. *Proscription Mechanisms*

The Czech Republic does not have its own internal system of listing or proscribing terrorist groups or individuals. It is, however, involved in the listing and proscribing systems of the UN and of the European Union. The freezing of funds on the basis of international obligations was originally implemented in the Czech Republic by virtue of the *Act on Measures in Relation to the Afghan Taliban Movement* (Act No. 48/2000 Coll.) and the *Act on the Implementation of International Sanctions for the Maintenance of International Peace and Security* (Act No. 98/2000 Coll.). In 2006, these two acts were replaced by the *Act on the Implementation of International Sanctions* (Act No. 69/2006 Coll.). Sanctions relating to the fight against terrorism are explicitly mentioned among the types of sanctions covered by this new act.

The Act regulates sanctions imposed on the basis of international obligations stemming from UN Security Council resolutions adopted by virtue of Article 41 of the UN Charter and from secondary acts of the European Union. EU acts that are directly applicable in the territory of the Czech Republic do not require any implementing act; all other international acts, including the UN Security Council resolution, need to be implemented by means of *case-by-case* government regulations.[38] The same mechanism is used with respect to international sanctions adopted against states and those directed against individuals and non-state actors. In practice, the Czech Republic uses the *Consolidated List of Persons, Groups and*

[38] See the *Government Regulation on the Implementation of Special Measures to Fight Against Terrorism* (No. 210/2008 Coll.). The Regulation was adopted to implement Common Position of the Council of the EU 2001/931/CFSP on the application of specific measures to combat terrorism. The Regulation contains the list of persons, groups and entities involved in terrorist acts that are based in the EU. The Regulation has been amended once, in 2009, when thirteen natural persons mostly related to the Basque Homeland and Freedom (ETA) group were added to the list (Government Regulation No. 88/2009 Coll.).

Entities Subject to EU Financial Sanctions,[39] as adopted and regularly updated by the EU. It also implements other sanctions adopted by the EU.

The *Act on the Implementation of International Sanctions* foresees various areas in which restrictions upon states or natural and legal persons may be imposed. Such areas encompass trade and services, financial transactions, transport, communications, technical infrastructure, scientific contacts, cultural contacts and sport contacts. Important decisions relating to sanctions shall be adopted by the Ministry of Finances. If the sanction relates to property, the decision shall be adopted within thirty days after receiving information on the presence of the property subject to the UN/EU sanctions in the territory of the Czech Republic. The decision may be appealed (the appeal is called *rozklad* [analysis]). Unless provided otherwise by the Act, the appeal does not have a suspensory effect. The property that is the object of sanctions shall be administrated by the Ministry of Finances. The Act also establishes several exceptions to the sanction regime that relate, for instance, to humanitarian assistance, health care or the subsistence of dependent persons. An exception may be granted at the request of the person concerned or without such request, *ex officio*. It is decided upon by the Ministry of Finances which, however, may grant an exception only if such an option is foreseen by the relevant international act. The Ministry is also competent to abolish the exception, if it is no longer applicable to the case. Non-compliance with the sanction by the person subject to it or by any third persons qualifies as a minor offence (natural persons) or as an administrative offence (legal persons) and shall be sanctioned accordingly.

B. *Challenges to Proscriptions and Listings*

So far, there has been no recorded practice relating to the proscription or listing of terrorist groups or individuals suspected of involvement in terrorism in the Czech Republic.

VI. REGULATION OF TERRORISM FINANCING

A. *The Regulatory Regime to Counter Terrorism Financing*

The Czech Republic is party to the *UN International Convention for the Suppression of the Financing of Terrorism* (1999)[40] and implements the UN Security Council

[39] The Consolidated List is available online – http://eeas.europa.eu/cfsp/sanctions/consol-list_en.htm (retrieved on 11 November 2013).

[40] The Czech Republic signed the Convention in 2000 and ratified it in 2005.

Resolution 1373 (2001) as well as various Financial Action Task Force (FATF) recommendations.[41] The main institutions playing a role in the fight against the financing of terrorism are the Ministry of Finances of the Czech Republic and its Financial Analytical Unit (FAU), the Czech National Bank, the Police of the Czech Republic and the Prosecutor's Office. Under the guidance of the Ministry of Finances, an interdepartmental group known as the Clearing House of the Czech Republic was established in 2002. The group, which includes members from state institutions, coordinates state policy in the fight against financial crime in general (financing of terrorism, money laundering, etc.). There is no separate financial intelligence service in the Czech Republic. The FAU, however, serves as an intelligence unit within the Ministry of Finances.

The legal framework regulating the fight against the financing of terrorism is set out by the *Act on selected measures against legitimization of proceeds of crime and financing of terrorism* (Act No. 253/2008 Coll.), which entered into force in 2008.[42] The Act defines the financing of terrorism as "gathering or providing financial or other assets knowing that such assets will be, in full or in part, used to commit a crime of terror, terrorist attack or a criminal activity intent to facilitate or support such a crime, or to support an individual or a group of individuals planning such a crime" (Section 3, par. 2(a)) and "acting with the intention to remunerate or compensate a person who has committed an act of terror, terrorist attack or a crime intended to facilitate or support such a crime, or to an individual close to such a person as defined by the *Criminal Code*, or collecting assets to pay such remuneration or compensation" (Section 3, par. 2(b)). The Act establishes the obligation to report suspicious transactions to the Ministry of Finances, which may inform the Police and the prosecutor.

The legal regulation against the financing of terrorism applies to any cases of financing of terrorism regardless of whether persons accused of this activity are listed on any terrorist list or not. Listing is, however, important in that transactions involving persons or property on which international sanctions binding upon the Czech Republic are imposed automatically qualify as suspicious transactions under Section 6 of the 2008 Act. The same regulatory framework is used for financing of terrorism and for money laundering (the 2008 Act). The financing of terrorism and money laundering are, however, not the same offence (see Sections 216 and 217 of the *Criminal Code* for money laundering and Section 311 par. 2 of the Criminal Code for financing of terrorism). In practice, instances of money laundering are detected in the Czech Republic from time to time. On the contrary,

[41] The Czech Republic is not a member of the FATF but implements its recommendations.

[42] The English translation of the Act is available online – http://www.coe.int/t/dghl/monitoring/moneyval/National_ legislation/CZE_AMLCFT2008.pdf (retrieved on 24 January 2013).

cases of the financing of terrorism have not so far been detected in the country; there have been several suspicious cases, but none of them have been confirmed. Since 2001, the Czech legal regulation on the financing of terrorism has been subject to regular scrutiny by the Council of Europe Committee of Experts on the Evaluation of Anti–Money Laundering Measures and the Financing of Terrorism (Moneyval).[43]

B. *Criminal Offences of Terrorism Financing*

The financing of terrorism is criminalized in the Czech Republic under Section 311, par. 2 of the *(New) Criminal Code*. By virtue of this provision, persons providing "financial, material or other support to a terrorist attack, a terrorist or a member of a terrorist group" may be sentenced to a term of imprisonment of five to fifteen years, along with the forfeiture of property. The provision is part of the offence of terrorist attack, which was included in the Czech legal order in 2004,[44] primarily to implement in the Czech legal order instruments adopted by the organs of the European Union (the Council of the EU) within the third pillar.[45] The offence of the financing of terrorism requires proof of the knowledge of the terrorist nature of the supported activity or actors; it also requires a subjective intent to support such activities or persons.

There are no exceptions foreseen by the Czech legal order for the provision of funds to finance legitimate and humanitarian activities by a terrorist group, but the motivation could play a role in the determination of the intent. The theory that funds given for the humanitarian activities of a terrorist organization should be prohibited because they free up funds for the group's terrorist activities has never been publicly discussed in the Czech Republic. The financing of terrorism qualifies as a criminal offence not only for natural persons but also, since 1 January 2012, for legal persons.[46] So far, there has been no prosecution of either natural or legal persons for the financing of terrorism. The forfeiture of property may be imposed as a criminal sanction, determined as part of a criminal prosecution, upon both natural and legal persons.

[43] Moneyval, *Anti-Money Laundering and Combating the Financing of Terrorism. Report on Fourth Assessment Visit of the Czech Republic*, 12 April 2011.

[44] See Act No. 537/2004 Coll., amending the *Criminal Code*.

[45] See Parliament of the Czech Republic, Tisk č. 514, *Důvodová zpráva* (Explanatory Memorandum), 2003.

[46] Act No. 418/2011 Coll., *on criminal liability of legal persons and the proceedings against them*.

VII. IMMIGRATION MEASURES

A. *Immigration Detention*

There is no information indicating that immigration laws would have been used against suspected terrorists in the Czech Republic. The legal status of foreigners staying in the territory of the Czech Republic is determined by the *Act on the Residence of Foreign Nationals in the Territory of the Czech Republic* (Act No. 326/1999 Coll.)[47] and the *Act on Asylum* (Act No. 325/1999 Coll.).[48] The former Act makes it possible to expel foreigners constituting a security threat to the Czech Republic (Sections 154–5). This regulation could be applied to persons suspected of terrorism, but so far no indication exists that this has happened. The latter Act makes it possible to reject an application for asylum (or, rather, for a refugee status) submitted by suspected terrorists, but only if their acts would qualify as crimes under international law; serious, non-political crimes; or acts contrary to the purposes and principles of the United Nations (Section 1(F)). Again, no indications exist that this provision would have ever been applied. For instance, in the case of Oussama Kassir (see Section IX), the application for asylum was rejected simply because he did not meet the criteria of a refugee.

Expulsion of foreigners may take place either on the basis of an administrative decision taken by the Police, under the *Act on the Residence of Foreign Nationals*, or as a part of criminal proceedings, under the *Criminal Code*. Any expulsion has to take place while respecting international obligations binding upon the Czech Republic as well as Article 14 of the (domestic) *Charter of Fundamental Rights and Freedoms*, which states that "a foreigner may be expelled only in cases specified by the Law" (par. 5).

Administrative expulsion can be imposed upon a foreigner if there is a serious suspicion that he or she constitutes a security threat. Collective expulsion of foreigners is prohibited (Section 118, par. 3 of the *Act on the Residence*). Moreover, a foreigner cannot be expelled if he or she, when returned to the country of his or her citizenship, would face a real danger of harm consisting of the death penalty, torture or inhuman and degrading treatment or punishment or serious threat to life and human dignity caused by arbitrary violence in the situation of international or internal armed conflict, or if the expulsion would conflict with

[47] The English translation of the Act is available online – http://www.czechlegislation.com/en/326-1999-sb (retrieved on 12 December 2013).

[48] The English translation of the Act is available online – http://www.mvcr.cz/mvcren/article/procedure-for-granting-international-protection-in-the-czech-republic.aspx (retrieved on 12 December 2013).

the international obligations of the Czech Republic (Section 179). Thus, the principle of non-refoulement is sanctioned by the Czech legal order. This principle may be disregarded on the condition that the foreigner committed a crime under international law or an especially serious offence. Perpetrators of terrorist acts would in most cases fall within this exception. They would nonetheless be provided with a sixty-day period to seek refuge in any other state.

The criminal sanction of expulsion can be imposed upon any non-citizen of the Czech Republic found guilty of a criminal offence, if the expulsion "is required to ensure security of people or property" (Section 80 of the *Criminal Code*). It can be imposed together with other sanctions or as the only sanction and can extend from a period of one year to an indeterminate period. It is not possible to expel foreigners who are permanent residents of the Czech Republic, have been granted asylum status or are citizens of the EU with a close link to the Czech Republic. Moreover, it is not possible to expel a foreigner if "there is a risk that in the state to which he or she should be expelled, he or she would be persecuted on the basis of his or her race, allegiance to an ethnic group, nationality, allegiance to a certain social group, political or religious conviction, or if the expulsion would put him or her at risk of torture or another inhuman or degrading treatment or punishment" (Section 80, par. 3(d)). This is another instance in which the principle of non-refoulement is confirmed in the Czech legal order. The procedure for expulsion is regulated by the *Criminal Procedural Code* (Section 350b-j).

In the course of the procedure of (administrative or criminal) expulsion, foreigners may be detained. Administrative detention takes place by virtue of Section 124 of the *Act on the Residence of Foreign Nationals*. The Police are entitled to detain foreigners only if the proceeding of expulsion has already been started and there is a risk that the foreigner could pose a threat to security or to other protected values. The detention period cannot exceed 180 days (90 days in the case of a juvenile) and it may be appealed in courts (Section 2000 of the *Civil Procedural Code*). The detention takes place in so-called detention installations, which are located in Velké Přílepy, Velké Přílepy-Jezová, Poštovná, Balková and Frýdek-Místek. Criminal detention may be imposed by virtue of Section 350c of the *Criminal Procedural Code*. The presiding judge may authorize it if there is a risk that a person sentenced to expulsion could run away or go into hiding. The detention cannot extend more than one to four years depending on the severity of the committed crime. The necessity of the detention is monitored by the court.

B. *Immigration Proceedings and Torture*

There is no specific prohibition on the use of evidence obtained through torture or cruel and degrading treatment in immigration proceedings. Such a use is explicitly prohibited only in criminal trials the *Criminal Procedural Code.*, Section 89 of the Code stipulates that "evidence obtained by means of unlawful duress or threat of duress cannot be used in the proceedings with the exception of the case when it is to be used as evidence against a person who used duress or threat of duress" (par. 3). The lack of such a provision in immigration legislation can be easily explained by the fact that the term "evidence" is not used in immigration proceedings. It is nonetheless probable that the use of information obtained through torture or cruel and degrading treatment in immigration proceedings would be considered a violation of Article 3 of the *European Convention on Human Rights* and Article 7 of the (domestic) *Charter of Fundamental Rights and Freedoms*. There have been no public concerns expressed in this respect.

The Czech legal order, as already stated, upholds the principle of non-refoulement. This principle is enshrined in Section 80, par. 3(d) of the *Criminal Code* and Section 179 of the *Act on the Residence of Foreign Nationals*. The principle is also, on a more general level, recognized by several international instruments binding upon the Czech Republic, such as the *Convention Against Torture* (Article 3), the *Convention for the Protection of Refugees* (Article 33) and the *European Convention on Human Rights* (Article 3, implicitly). The issue of non-refoulement arose in practice in the case of Oussama Kassir (see Section IX), but after diplomatic assurances were provided by the United States, the extradition was granted in this case.

VIII. ADMINISTRATIVE AND EXECUTIVE MEASURES

Administrative and executive measures are not used in the Czech Republic to control the activities of people suspected or convicted of terrorism. It is considered, also due to the scarcity of relevant cases, that ordinary measures applicable to any other criminal activities are adequate and no need exists to resort to special measures. Moreover, some of these measures would be prohibited by the (domestic) *Charter of Fundamental Rights and Freedoms* (1993). The Charter stipulates that

> (a) … a person accused or suspected of having committed a criminal act may be detained only in cases specified by law. A person who is detained shall be immediately informed of the grounds for the detention, questioned, and within forty-eight hours at the latest, either released or turned over to a court. A judge must question the detained person and decide, within twenty-four hours of receiving her, whether the person shall be placed in custody or released (Article 8, par. 3).
>
> (b) A person accused of a criminal act may be arrested only on the basis of a warrant issued by a judge in writing and stating the grounds for the arrest. The arrested person shall be turned over to a court within twenty-four hours. A judge shall question the arrested person and decide, within twenty-four hours, whether the person shall be placed in custody or released (Article 8, par. 4).

(c) Nobody may be placed in custody, except on the grounds and for the period of time laid down in a law, and only on the basis of a judicial decision (Article 8, par. 5).

IX. ROLE OF MILITARY AND EXTRA-TERRITORIAL COUNTER-TERRORISM ACTIVITIES

A. *Military Courts and Detention*

The military plays no role in the domestic enforcement of terrorism acts. Military courts, which existed in Czechoslovakia,[49] were abolished in 1993, the year of the creation of the Czech Republic.[50] The possibility of establishing military or any other special courts has never been discussed in the Czech Republic. There is also no need for them due to the scarcity of terrorism-related cases. The Czech Republic has so far not used the law of armed conflicts to detain suspected terrorists on its territory. It does, on the contrary, use this law when detaining suspected terrorists in war areas in which its army operates, especially in Afghanistan. No detailed information is available as to what happens to such persons and what legal status is granted to them. Yet media reports indicate that they are usually handed over to the allied forces or to the local authorities.[51] No suspected terrorists detained outside the Czech Republic have so far been transferred to its territory and prosecuted there.[52]

B. *The Extra-Territorial Treatment of Citizens Suspected of Terrorism*

No nationals of the Czech Republic have so far been detained by another state because of suspicions of their involvement in terrorism. No Czechs, consequently, have been detained at Guantanamo, Bagram or any other similar detention installation.

C. *Extra-Territorial Terrorism Law Enforcement*

The Czech Republic supports the global effort to eradicate terrorism. It is, and wants to be, a close ally of the United States and has always had an understanding

49 See Act No. 66/1952 Coll., *on the organization of courts.*

50 By virtue of Article 110 of the Constitution of the Czech Republic, military courts ceased their existence by 31 December 1993.

51 ČTK, *Čeští vojáci v Afghánistánu osvobodili rukojmí a zajali velitele* (Czech soldiers in Afghanistan liberated a hostage and detained a commander), 7 November 2013.

52 The Czech Republic is party to all the four 1949 Geneva Conventions and the two 1977 Additional Protocols to the Geneva Conventions.

for the extra-territorial counter-terrorist operations of this state. It is also a close ally of Israel and, again, largely supports its counter-terrorist activities. The Czech army has taken part in the military operations in Afghanistan and Iraq. Moreover, the Czech Police and intelligence services cooperate with their counterparts from other countries, especially other EU and NATO members, and engage in joint activities. No further details on such activities are available. As already noted, the Czech Republic, although not a frequent target of terrorists, is often considered to be one of the transit countries through which terrorists and their weapons and materials are transferred to Western Europe. The issue of extradition of suspected terrorists has therefore already arisen in the country in several instances.

The best-known case is that of the Swedish citizen of Lebanese origin, Oussama Kassir, who was arrested at the Prague Ruzyně airport in December 2005 while travelling from Stockholm to Beirut, pursuant to a U.S. arrest warrant and an Interpol Red Notice. He was suspected of conspiracy to provide material support to terrorists in connection with the planned establishment of an Islamist terrorist training camp in Bly, Oregon. The United States requested the extradition of Kassir. Kassir objected, claiming that if sent to the United States, he would face the death penalty, torture and other serious violations of human rights. He also applied for political asylum in the Czech Republic. His application was denied, and in September 2007 the Municipal Court in Prague decided to grant the U.S. request. At the end of September 2007, Kassir was extradited to the United States,[53] where he was sentenced in 2009 to life imprisonment for providing material support to Al-Qaeda.[54] Before the extradition, the United States provided the Czech Republic with diplomatic assurances guaranteeing that Kassir would not face the death penalty in the United States. These assurances have been respected.

X. SECRECY AND TERRORISM

A. *Secrecy Claims and Secret Evidence*

The protection of classified information in the Czech Republic is regulated by the *Act on the Protection of Classified Information and on Security Eligibility* (Act No. 412/2005 Coll.). The Act distinguishes four degrees of protection of classified information and sets conditions for access to this information. It contains no provisions on the use of classified information in terrorism trials. This matter is regulated by the *Criminal Procedural Code* (Act No. 141/1961 Coll.). Under Section

[53] The Local, *Swedish terror suspect extradited to United States*, 25 September 2007.

[54] See U.S. Attorney's Office, Southern District of New York, *Swedish Citizen Oussama Kassir Found Guilty of Providing Material Support to al Qaeda*, 12 May 2009.

51b of the Code, if classified information is to be used in a trial, all persons involved must be informed about this fact and about the consequences of the disclosure of classified information, by a police officer or prosecutor (in the pre-trial period) or by judge (during the trial). Under these conditions, both the prosecutor and the accused have the right to gain access to classified information, if it is necessary for the defence of their rights.[55] The necessity is considered by the organ making the decision in the matter. Secret evidence not seen by the accused cannot be used as incriminating evidence in a terrorism trial. The disclosure of classified information devoid of a legal basis may entail administrative or criminal sanctions.[56]

B. *Secrecy in the Courtroom and Anonymous Witnesses*

It is prohibited to ask witnesses about circumstances relating to classified information, unless they are released from the obligation to keep this information secret (Section 99, par. 1 of the *Criminal Procedural Code*). The need to protect classified information has to be taken into account by the Court when it authorizes access to case records (Section 65, par. 5). In the trial, it is possible to exclude the public, if its presence could endanger classified information (Section 200, par. 1). Intelligence service members may testify at terrorism prosecutions. They may testify anonymously if conditions stated in Section 55, par. 2 of the Code are met. Under this provision, the identity and appearance of a witness may be kept secret if "there are circumstances indicating that the witness or a person close to the witness might face the threat of harm to health or of any other serious violation of fundamental rights." Anonymity may be granted at the request of the witness or without such a request, *ex officio*. The Code contains a specific provision relating to the anonymity of police witnesses. Under this provision, Section 102a of the Code, anonymity is granted to police officers who serve as agents or carry out feigned transactions. Such anonymity may be waived in specific cases.

XI. OTHER MATTERS

The issues relating to terrorism and counter-terrorism have been discussed in the Czech Republic, both at the political level and within the academic community.[57] One of the aspects giving rise to contentions is the impact of counter-terrorism

[55] Such access, under the same conditions, may be granted within civil or administrative proceedings.

[56] The 2009 *Criminal Code* contains three relevant offences, namely espionage (Section 316), endangerment of classified information (Section 317) and endangerment of classified information by negligence (Section 318).

[57] See also Miroslav Mareš, *Terorismus v ČR* (Terrorism in the Czech Republic), Centrum strategických studií, Brno, 2005.

measures on human rights. This aspect, however, is mainly discussed with respect to measures adopted by other states, not those of the Czech Republic itself.[58] No important reorganization of governmental departments has taken place over the past years, but the increased emphasis placed upon counter-terrorism has manifested itself in the establishment of several new organs, such as the *National Contact Point for Terrorism* operating within the Police of the Czech Republic. The treatment of victims of terrorism has not been an issue in the Czech Republic, largely due to the absence of such victims in the country. The Czech counter-terrorism legal framework has been primarily shaped by EU standards and regulations, although other international standards (the UN, the Council of Europe) have also had an impact upon it.

XII. CONCLUSION

The Czech Republic has not so far faced serious terrorist threats. Despite that, the country takes the risk of terrorism seriously and has therefore sought to create a counter-terrorism legal framework that is effective and at the same time respects human rights and international law. Although some counter-terrorist measures were already in place in the 1990s, the counter-terrorism system as it exists now has largely been built since 2001. The first *National Action Plan to Combat Terrorism* was adopted in April 2002. After several updates, it was finally replaced in 2010 by a *Counter-Terrorism Strategy*; an updated version of this Strategy, adopted in 2013, defines the main principles of the current counter-terrorism policy of the Czech Republic.¨

The criminal offence of a terrorist attack was added to the *Criminal Code* in 2004, in the implementation of EU instruments. So far, only one person has been convicted for having threatened to commit a terrorist attack. Several other persons who have committed acts exhibiting features of terrorism have been convicted for other, more general offences (murder, common danger, etc.).

In the Czech Republic, the fight against terrorism is primarily considered a law enforcement matter falling within the competence of the Police, the courts and the Ministries of Justice and of the Interior. The legal framework has been amended in the post-2001 period, to give state organs competences and to make it possible for the Czech Republic to implement international obligations stemming from counter-terrorism treaties, UN Security Council resolutions, EU acts and other normative instruments. The increase in state powers has not, however, been

[58] See also Veronika Bílková, Boj proti terorismu z pohledu ochrany lidských práv (Fight Against Terrorism and the Protection of Human Rights), Aleš Čeněk, Praha, 2014.

really substantive. The legal framework moreover does not seem to pose any serious challenges with respect to human rights.

It is difficult to assess the effectiveness of the Czech Republic's response to the terrorist threats. On the one hand, the scarcity (or almost an absence) of terrorist attacks in the post-2001 period might indicate that the Czech policy is an efficient one. One the other hand, the Czech Republic did not experience any wave of terrorism prior to 2001 either. Counter-terrorism legal regulation has not had any major impact upon other areas of national legal order. It has nonetheless made it easier for the Czech Republic to cooperate with other states and international organizations.

17

Romania

Raluca-Ioana Mocanu and George Antoniu

I. INTRODUCTION

There are some notorious examples from Western Europe of political assassinations that could be characterized as terrorism.[1] Romania has not been immune from political violence. Between 1930 and 1940, the Iron Guard was involved in the assassination of Romania's prime-minister I. Gh. Duca, Armand Călinescu and eleven other important political leaders or state personalities.[2]

Terrorist acts were criminalized for the first time and labelled explicitly as "terrorist offences" in 2001 but with major subsequent amendments in 2004 and 2014. Since that time, the Romanian courts have adjudicated three terrorist cases. In each case, the prosecutor's accusations were confirmed in court, and the defendants were convicted for terrorist acts.

II. THE DEFINITION OF TERRORISM

The events surrounding 9/11 have revealed major "silent zones" from the international community regarding the intent to build a common framework and the willpower to adopt a unique convention against terrorism. This convention remains a work in progress. There is no legal instrument that defines terrorism or delineates terrorist acts at the international level. Terrorist offences were not punished as such and must therefore be drawn from the vast sphere of all forms of political violence.

Before the terrorist attacks in 2001, Romanian criminal law did not contain any provisions targeting terrorist acts. Despite signing the Convention Against the Taking of Hostages (New York, 17 December 1979) and criminalizing such acts at

1 Please note that Professor Antoniu was not able to participate in all of the writing of this chapter because of his unfortunate death in 2014.

2 L. Weinberg *Introduction to Political Terrorism* (New York: McGraw-Hill, 1989) at 31.

the national level, Romania never specified them as acts of terrorism. The challenge of properly identifying the sphere in which this criminal conduct belongs therefore fell to national legal scholars.

Only after 9/11 did Romania join other states in working to prevent and combat terrorism through enacting legislation. Between 2001 and 2004, Romania's domestic law was characterized by repeated attempts to develop anti-terrorist legislation. Romania quickly adopted several laws aimed at criminalizing terrorist acts and associated activity.

On 25 October 2001, the Romanian government adopted Emergency Ordinance n°. 141 regarding terrorist acts and other acts against public order.[3] This ordinance was a special law exclusively containing criminal law and related procedural provisions. The ordinance was approved by the Romanian Parliament on 9 July 2002 and adopted as Law no. 472/2002.[4] The law as enacted by the legislature did not contain radical amendments to the ordinance initially promulgated by the executive.

The ordinance and the law were conceived in the wake of 9/11 as a response to the need to convict terrorist acts domestically. However, they failed to meet the prerequisites of anti-terrorist legislation. This, coupled with the European Union's adoption of Council Framework Decision 2002/475/JHA, affirmed the need to reshape the ordinance and legislation quickly enacted after 9/11. Accordingly, the Romanian Parliament adopted Law no. 535/2004, aimed at preventing and combating terrorism.[5] The preamble of the new legal provision does not indicate that it was modelled on the 2002 European Union Council Framework Decision, but its influence is easily recognizable.

A simple comparative exercise underlines the complexity of Law no. 535/2004. In addition to criminal law and procedural provisions, the act contains provisions describing particular public institutions that are to be involved in preventing and combating terrorism. Law no. 535/2004 was modified by article 159 from the Law no. 187/2012. The amendments entered into force on 1 February 2014.

It is well known that there is no generally accepted definition of terrorism. Pending the discovery of a "magical formula" and given the seeming impossibility of defining terrorism, the 2004 law sought the easy path in describing terrorism based on its intrinsic characteristics. A definition of terrorism must include a wide variety of terrorist attacks. This fundamental feature – the dynamic evolution of terrorism – risks rendering any definition partial given the evolving and expansive nature of terrorism.

[3] M. Of. no. 691/ 31.10.2001.
[4] M. Of. no. 524/18.07.2002.
[5] M. Of. no. 1.161/8.12. 2004.

Scholars argue that terrorism is difficult to define because there is no single form of terrorism but rather several types that share common features. What characterizes one form of terrorism does not necessarily apply to others. There are more forms of terrorism today than there were thirty years ago, many quite different from what was formerly considered to be terrorism. Consequently, certain acts can no longer be described as "terrorism." In the future, new terms will be found for new forms of terrorist behaviour.[6] We tend to agree with this point of view because it is reinforced by the persistent creation and reinvention of terrorist activity – most recently, "cyber-terrorism."

Romanian criminal law first defined "terrorism" in 2004, when Law no. 535/2004 entered into force. The very first article contains the following definition:

> Terrorism is the assembly of actions and/or threats which represent a public risk and affect national security, having the following characteristics:
>
> a) they are committed in a premeditated manner by terrorist entities, motivated by extremist conceptions and attitudes, hostile towards other entities against which they act through violent and/or destructive ways;
> b) are following specific political objectives;
> c) aim to hit human and/or goods from public authorities, public institutions, civilians, or other segment of those sectors;
> d) intend to produce a powerful psychological impact on the population, meant to draw attention to their purposes.

In our opinion, this is a hybrid definition that tries to reflect the main characteristics of the phenomenon and the elements that distinguish terrorism from the vast sphere of terrorist activity. The preceding definition was not designed according to classical rules of logic – proximal case and specific differences. Instead, the Romanian legislature opted for a descriptive definition, identifying specific features of terrorism.

The definition does not follow each specific element that may be used to distinguish and extract terrorism from other forms of political violence, such as guerrilla war or a national liberation fight. It is obvious that the definition does not communicate the Romanian legislature's view of terrorism as a type of asymmetrical conflict (a tactic used by non-state actors in pursuit of their political objectives). On the contrary, it emphasizes terrorism as criminal conduct, though it is not completely detached from its intrinsic ideology.

One Romanian scholar maintains that "in the preamble of article 1 there is a general definition of terrorism, pointing out the implications and major

[6] W. Laquer *The New Terrorism* (New York: Oxford University Press, 1999), at 7.

consequences of terrorism, underlining the risk represented for public order as well as how it affects national security."[7]

Obviously, this definition is not above reproach: "not all terrorist activities and their method of violent manifestation affect national security, some of them not even indirectly; therefore, it cannot be sustained that an act which does not affect national security is not terrorist in nature."[8]

In our opinion, the existing definition provided by Romanian law is designed to describe terrorism seen as a whole rather than each terrorist act. A terrorist act is a single expression of violence that may or may not jeopardize national security.[9] Terrorism as a phenomenon constitutes the systematic use of different forms of violence with a political motive.

One of terrorism's features, reflected by the Romanian definition, is the premeditated nature of violent acts. In general, the attacks are rigorously prepared to guarantee their success. Terrorism and terrorist acts are incompatible with impulsive or irrational behaviour. It was stated that "Every terrorist act is conceived to spread a message and such a task requires careful preparation."[10]

The Romanian legislature considers terrorist acts to be committed by "terrorist entities." This excludes, in our opinion, isolated acts carried out by individuals acting independent of a terrorist group.

The specific trigger for members of terrorist entities, identified by the Romanian legislature as the members' motivation, is the extremism animating their ideas and attitudes. Extremism cannot be detected or measured according to an objective and unfailing system of values; it must be evaluated according to the subjective criterion of the targeted state that has labelled them "extremists."

Terrorist organizations usually question the constitutional values and major institutions of the targeted state and concentrate their efforts on undermining it through a violent and systematic struggle. As a result, the ideology that propels them has a negative polarity compared to the rule of law of the contested state. Terrorism is beyond the legal limits of political life and involves violent action rather than general and abstract "extremism." It is difficult to evaluate extremism, because political, social or judicial order is constantly changing. What is extreme at one point in time may not be extreme at another. Nonetheless, certain forms of

7 D. V. Diaconu, *Privire critică de ansamblu asupra prevederilor Legii nr. 535/2004 pentru prevenirea şi combaterea terorismului*, în Pandectele Române nr. 3/2005, at. 241.

8 *Idem*, p. 241.

9 For instance, a suicide bomber attack without any victim as the effect of a wrong moment of the explosion wouldn't affect national security, while hijacking a plane and crashing it into a nuclear facility dramatically endangers the targeted state.

10 Russel D. Howard et al. *Terrorism and Counterterrorism: Understanding the Security Environment: Readings and Interpretations* (Guilford, Connecticut: McGraw-Hill, 2003), at. 37.

violent extremism must be banned where they cannot be tolerated despite serving a noble cause.

In our opinion, extremism should not be a defining feature of terrorism. It is redundant to use this criterion while the definition also requires a political purpose[11] for any terrorist attack (according to article 1). It is difficult to find objective criteria to help distinguish terrorism and extremism. An important difference is the inherently violent nature of terrorism, which is not necessarily a feature of extremism.

Extremism may be related to terrorism when extremists choose to express their political demands in a violent manner. As a consequence, the annual reports of Europol count as terrorist acts those offences labelled by certain states as extremist conduct if committed with the aim of seriously undermining or destroying the fundamental political, economic or social structure of a state.[12] Thus, in the aforementioned reports, politically motivated violent acts committed by extreme right movements or those that advocate for animal rights are often lumped together with terrorist offences based on their extremist values.[13]

Another defining feature of terrorism is the psychological impact of each attack. This is not a collateral or indirect effect of a terrorist act. For terrorists, spreading panic amongst the population is as important as the success of the attack itself.

In our opinion, defining terrorism in domestic law is not necessary in order to develop a comprehensive anti-terrorist law, convict terrorists or prevent future attacks.

Though defining terrorism remains a central objective at the international level, one should bear in mind that any definition may be highly subjective, reflecting the political values of the party who proposes it.

The Council Framework Decision 2002/475/JHA is the European Union's most relevant legal instrument. The European legislature tried to address the difficulties of defining terrorism. The Framework Decision timidly limited its functions to a demonstrative statement, without any intention of engineering legal change: "terrorism is one of the most serious breaches of principles and values upon which the European Union is built."[14] Though the Law nr. 535 has been enacted in order to comply with the 2002 EU Framework Decision, some other amendments were later adopted. For instance, the original incrimination of terrorist acts was not a neat transposition of the similar elements in the EU definition. As a result of the new amendment of 1 February 2014, the definition of terrorist offence implemented in

[11] According to article 32 paragraph 1 from the Law no. 535/2004, after the amendment entered into force on 1 February 2014, certain ordinary crimes are terrorist acts if committed in order to follow a political purpose.

[12] E.U. Terrrorist Situation and Trend Report – TE-SAT 2010 at. 9.

[13] TE-SAT 2007 at. 11.

[14] According to paragraph 1 of the Preamble of Framework Decision.

the domestic legal definition of terrorist now includes the same definition of terrorist purpose from the EU Framework Decision.

In our opinion, Professor Cherif Bassiounni has articulated one of the clearest and most complete definitions of terrorism available. Reflecting specific objective and subjective elements, Bassiounni states, "terrorism is an ideologically-motivated strategy of internationally prescribed violence designated to inspire terror within a particular segment of a given society in order to achieve a power-outcome or to propagate a claim or a grievance irrespective of whether its perpetrators are acting for and on behalf of themselves or a state."[15]

III. CRIMINAL LAWS AND PROSECUTIONS

A. *Criminal Law*

In Romanian criminal law, terrorist acts and other acts related to terrorist activity are criminalized pursuant to articles 32 to 38 of Law no. 535/2004 regarding the prevention of terrorism.

The provisions of article 32 criminalize terrorist acts. The text of article 33 provides for the criminalization of other aspects of terrorist activity. The provisions of article 35 criminalize the act of forming and leading a terrorist group. Article 36 sanctions terrorist financing.

Alongside "classical" terrorist offences, domestic law contains some other offences that mirror the Council Framework. On 1 February 2014, new provisions entered into force. Article 33^1 contains legal provisions criminalizing special activities related to terrorism, such as recruitment of new members in order to execute terrorist attacks, whereas article 33^2 provides new provisions related to propaganda for terrorist purposes.

The text of article 34 is of general application. It includes special provisions concerning particular criminal law institutions, such as attempts to commit a terrorist offence, as well as "preparatory acts." Neither attempts nor preparatory acts will be punishable in every case and will depend on the seriousness of the particular act.

Romanian law also contains provisions criminalizing conduct beyond actual terrorist acts. The provisions of article 37 criminalize threats to use weapons of mass destruction or the use of substances endangering the environment. The last offence (found in article 38) involves falsely alerting the authorities about a potential harm to the population.

15 M. Ch. Bassiouni *International Criminal Law*, vol. I CRIMES (New York: Transnational Publishers, 1999) at. 777.

a. Terrorist Offences (Article 32)

Early versions of Romanian terrorism laws criminalized only a limited number of activities related to political violence.

After Law no. 535/2004 entered into force, terrorist acts were criminalized either as complex offences (article 32 paragraph 1 contains terrorist acts reported to other common offences) or as simple, autonomous offences (article 32 paragraph 2).

In order to distinguish terrorist offences from ordinary crimes, the definition of terrorist offences was amended to include a specific constitutive element or, rather, a set of essential conditions.

The definition of terrorist offences was modified again on 1 February 2014. The constitutive elements were refined to facilitate interpretation and preclude overlap with texts criminalizing ordinary crimes. This latest amendment to Romanian legislation transposes the "terrorist purpose" defined in the Framework Decision 2002/475/JHA. In accordance with this new definition, ordinary offences (murder, serious injuries, kidnapping, destruction, threatening, seizure of aircraft, destruction of a fixed platform located on the continental shelf etc.) committed with the aim of "seriously intimidating a population, or unduly compelling a government or international organization to perform or abstain from performing any act, or seriously destabilizing or destroying the fundamental political, constitutional, economic or social structures of a country or an international organization" may be considered terrorist offences. The 2014 amendments closely follow the 2002 EU Framework Decision.

Article 32 provides the following:

> (1) Terrorist acts punishable with imprisonment – aggravated with a third added to the penalty of the simple offence it refers to, and with the complementary penalty of suspending certain civil rights – are the following acts which, by nature or context, seriously endanger a country or an international organization, if they are committed with the purpose of seriously intimidating a population, or unduly compelling a government or international organization to perform or abstain from performing any act, or seriously destabilizing or destroying the fundamental political, constitutional, economic or social structures of a country or an international organization:
>
> a) murder, aggravated murder, serious injuries;
>
> b) threatening or kidnapping;
>
> c) destruction, including arson;
>
> d) communicates information which the accused knows to be false, thereby endangering the safety on an aircraft in flight;
>
> e) performs, with the help of a device, arm or substance, an act of violence against a person from a civilian airport, if that act is likely to endanger the

safety or the security of that airport; performs an act of physical or moral violence against a person on board an aircraft in flight;

f) destroys or seriously damages, with the help of a device, a weapon or a substance, navigation facilities of a civilian airport or of an aircraft in or out of service, grounded on an airport or causes damage to the aforementioned, whereby rendering it incapable of flight, or endangering its safety in flight, as well as the interruption of services of an airport, if such an act may jeopardize the safety of the airport;
g) destroys or damages air navigation facilities or interferes with their operation, if such an act is likely to endanger the safety of an aircraft in flight;
h) places on an aircraft in service, by any means, whatsoever, a device, or a substance likely to destroy the aircraft or to cause damage to incapacitate it or to endanger the safety in flight;
i) unlawfully, by any means, seizes an aircraft or exercises control of it;
j) seizes a ship or a fixed platform or exercises control over it by force or threat;
k) performs an act of violence against a person on board a ship or a fixed platform if that act is likely to endanger its safety;
l) destroys a fixed platform or a ship or causes damage to a platform or the laden of the ship, which is likely to endanger its safety;
m) places on a ship or a fixed platform, by any means whatsoever, a device or substance likely to destroy it or to cause damage to the ship, the fixed platform or the laden, likely to endanger its safety;
n) destroys or causes serious damage to a fixed platform or navigation facilities or interferes with their operation, if such an act is likely to endanger the safety of a fixed platform or a ship;
o) disobeys the rules of holding weapons or ammunition, nuclear, radioactive or explosive materials;
p) attempts which are likely to endanger state security, attempts to endanger a community, acts of diversion;
q) computer frauds, credit-card payment frauds, offences against the informatics system;
r) seizure of means of public or goods transport.

(2) For offences provided in paragraph 1 the fine penalty does not apply.

(3) Any and all of the following acts with the same purpose mentioned at paragraph (1) are also considered terrorist acts punishable with imprisonment from 7 to 15 years and the suspension of certain civil rights:

a) the manufacturing, obtaining, possession, transportation, delivery, or transfer to another person, directly or indirectly, of chemical biological weapons, explosive devices whatsoever, as well as research into, and development of such weapons or devices;

b) the introduction or release into the atmosphere, on the ground, underground or in the water of products or substances, materials of any kind, microorganisms or toxins likely to endanger human or animal health, or the environment, in order to cause fires, floods or explosions, the effect of which are to endanger human lives;

c) the interference with or disruption of the supply of water, power, or any other fundamental natural resource the effect of which is to endanger human lives.

The preceding text indicates that terrorist acts are built as complex offences based on ordinary crimes if they are committed with a special intention and certain purposes. Acting in accordance with an inner purpose is insufficient. Domestic law preserved another provision from the Framework Decision stating that the act must seriously endanger the country or the international organization.

As mentioned, terrorist offences are also criminalized as simple offences in three situations imagined (by the Romanian legislature) only as terrorist acts, without being based on a subsequent ordinary crime: some acts relate to potential means of obtaining or producing weapons of mass destruction and other types of weapons designed to harm life on a large scale; the use of these weapons against the population or the environment; and the interference with or disruption of the water supply, power or any other fundamental natural resource that endangers human life. These are independent harms that do not build on offences already existing in Romanian criminal law.

b. Offences Related to Terrorist Acts (Article 33)

Although the provisions of the Romanian law concerning terrorist offences are, in our opinion, extremely vast (the text is intended to be exhaustive), article 32 is incomplete absent the provision found in article 33, which criminalizes a large set of actions not termed "terrorist" acts, yet still related to terrorism. The first version of the text labelled these as "acts related to terrorist acts." The legislature reversed this in its last amendment. The doctrine will delineate the limits of terrorist offences and those found in article 33.

The source of the text is found in the provisions of article 3 of the 2002 European Union Framework Decision.

In analyzing the content of what this text criminalized, we may easily discern a heterogeneous text that subsumes many acts, diverse in concept and execution, within the same large sphere of terrorism. The heterogeneous character of the offences assembled in a single text complicates the understanding of the text.

According to article 33:

(1) The following acts punishable with imprisonment from 5 to 12 years and the suspension of certain civil rights, if committed in one of the purposes mentioned in article 32 paragraph 1, are considered offences:
   a) obtaining, possessing, manufacturing, transporting or delivering products or technologies with double use or military products or explosive substances or ignitable substances, in order to produce destructive means or explosive devices of any kind, as well as chemical, biological, radiological or nuclear substances the effect of which endangers human and animal lives or the environment;
   b) training or preparing a person to use or produce firearms, ammunition, explosives, explosive devices, chemical, biological, radiological or nuclear weapons, or any equipment designed to these weapons.

(2) The following acts will be considered offences punishable with imprisonment from 2 to 5 years and the suspension of certain civil rights:
   a) cross-border helping, housing, the help to enter into a zone aimed to be targeted by a person who participated in or had committed or will participate or will commit one of the offences provided for in article 32 paragraph 1 or 3 and one of the offences provided for in the previous paragraph;
   b) collection of information, detention of information in order to transmit those pieces of information concerning targeted places to a terrorist entity;
   c) forgery of official documents in order to commit one of the offences described in the present law;
   d) extortion committed in order to sustain a terrorist act;
   e) participation in the training for the use of destructive methods, toxic or dangerous substances, firearms, explosive devices of any kind, ammunition, explosives, chemical, biological, radiological or nuclear weapons in order to commit terrorist acts;
   f) aggravated theft committed in order to sustain one of the acts provided for in the present law.

The preceding provisions of article 33 were not initially the same. The text underwent several amendments, the most significant being the attachment of a constitutive element. Although these are not cited as "terrorist offences," the legislature attached the same "terrorist scope." Consequently, the amendment, which entered into force on 1 February 2014, has had the effect of diluting the differences between the provisions of articles 32 and 33.

In our opinion, the new provisions are vulnerable to criticism, and there is some overlap between attempts to commit a terrorist act (article 32) and completed offences (for instance, article 33 paragraph 2 lett. b). To support this contention, we will refer to article 3 of the Framework Decision used as a model by the Romanian legislature, but not completely transposed, consequently generating the aforementioned overlap in offences.

The text itself is divided into two paragraphs. The first paragraph covers activities preceding a terrorist act, including the production of weapons of mass destruction and other highly destructive weapons, as well as training militants to use those weapons. In the second paragraph, the legislature criminalized elements of terrorist activity (committed before or after a terrorist act), which were extracted from the core of this activity, creating autonomous offences. Absent an express provision, they would remain acts of complicity (collecting and possessing information concerning objectives targeted by terrorist organizations) or abetting (helping to cross the border, housing a terrorist etc.).

c. Recruiting a Person in Order To Commit Terrorist Acts or Other Offences Related with Terrorism (Article 33^1)

This article entered into force on 1 February 2014 and criminalizes the recruitment of new members for terrorist organizations in order to commit either terrorist acts or other acts related to terrorism.

This is not a new offence: article 33 previously named "Offences assimilated with terrorist acts" contained a similar disposition to paragraph. b) relating to recruiting and training terrorists. After the Council Framework Decision 2008/919/JHA was adopted by the European Union, the Romanian legislature removed the aforementioned name of article 33, and this provision is now part from the text of article 33^1.

According to article 33^1: "Recruiting a person in order to commit a terrorist act or other acts related to terrorism is punishable with imprisonment from 5 to 12 years."

Following these revisions, the legislature criminalized both activities: recruiting and training future terrorists. It also criminalized the implication of the recruiters in any and all activities necessary to become initialized in terrorist activities.

d. Propaganda for a Terrorist Organization (Article 33^2)

According to article 33^2:

(1) Public provocation to commit a terrorist act or other offences from the present law through verbal, written or any other means is punishable with imprisonment from 6 months to 3 years or a fine. The penalty should not be more severe than the one provided for the offence which was the object of the instigation.

(2) If the aforementioned offence is committed by a person in public office, the penalty will be imprisonment from 1 to 5 years and the suspension of civil rights. The penalty cannot be more severe than the one provided for the offence which was the object of the instigation.
(3) If the offence which was the object of the instigation has been committed, the penalty for the incitement act is the same as the one for the incited offence.
(4) Promoting a propaganda message committed publicly, by any means, in order to instigate for one of the offences provided for in article 32 paragraph (1) and paragraph (3) and article 33 paragraph (1) and paragraph (2) lett. e), irrespective of the fact that the message directly sustains terrorism or of the fact that the offences were actually committed, is punishable with imprisonment from 6 months to 3 years.

The provisions contained in Romanian law, though not identical, are lifted from the provisions of article 3 paragraph 2 lett. a) of the Framework Decision 2002/475/JHA/2002 following the amendments adopted by the Framework Decision 2008/919/JHA. In particular, the Romanian offence does not require that the provocation create a risk that a terrorism offence will occur as a result of the public provocation.

The new public provocation offence is necessary given how the Internet has transformed our world. All terrorist organisations are using the Internet to broadcast "on-line executions" or last statements by suicide-bombers. These messages spread fear among civilians, amplify security concerns and facilitate recruitment. Though terrorist organizations are highly secretive, they began using not only modern weapons technology, but also modern methods of communication, such as e-mail, instant messages and social media. Internet propaganda is as dangerous as terrorism itself because it foments hatred and revenge among future recruits, glorifying violence as the best way to achieve political objectives. The ability of a terrorist group to generate persuasive propaganda is crucial in obtaining financial support and recruiting the members required to guarantee their continued operation.[16] For all these reasons, it was necessary to enact an offence against public provocation of a terrorist act, as the Romanian legislature did in 2014.

e. Offences Related to a Terrorist Group (Article 35)

According to article 35:

(1) The association or the intent to constitute an association aimed at committing acts of terrorism, as well as the adhesion or support, by any means, of a said

[16] TESAT 2010 – at 15.

association is punishable with imprisonment from 5 to 12 years and the suspension of certain civil rights, without surpassing the penalty provided for the offence which was the object of the association.

(2) Leading a terrorist entity is punishable with imprisonment from 7 to 15 years and the suspension of certain civil rights.

The provisions of article 35 are divided according to two situations: forming a terrorist group and leading an existing group.

After forming a terrorist entity, the group develops and operates with the goal of being considered a "terrorist organization" or "terrorist group" whose members are accordingly labelled "terrorists." This offence requires a minimum number of perpetrators – at least two or three must be acting for same purpose in order to form a terrorist group. This is typically a "collective" offence.

The second hypothesis that was criminalized is the act of "directing" a terrorist organization.

Legal authors have argued that: "as long as terrorism implies violence put into practice by a small group of persons, it may mislead us to believe that terrorist groups consist in a reduced number of persons. Such a conclusion is valid just for terrorist units involved in attacks."[17] To put into practice, some types of terrorist acts, such as seizure of airplanes or hostage taking, "obviously [need] a number of highly skilled people."[18]

Terrorist groups are typically formed from cells. This presents two possible interpretations of "directing a terrorist entity": the individual either leads the whole terrorist entity or simply is a part of it (e.g., the cell). Though we have not found any proposed definition of those small units which execute terrorist attacks, there are similarities between the description of the "structured group" (in the Romanian domestic provisions) and the "structured association" (in the 2002 Framework Decision).

We can identify an important difference between the definition proposed by European legal instruments and existing Romanian law. The offence outlined in the Framework Decision concerns only the directing of a "terrorist group," whereas the domestic provisions apply the offence more broadly to include any formation of a terrorist group. In this way, the Framework Decision operates as a minimum basis for criminalization, and the Romanian legislature has enacted broader offences than strictly required by the EU Framework Decisions.

[17] "There are well-known terrorist groups with a small number of members, while others have a huge number, like Palestinian Liberation Organisation which gathered around 15.000 members in the '70s." Cited in L. Weinberg *Introduction to Political Terrorism* (New York: McGraw-Hill, 1989) at 107.

[18] *Idem* at. 107.

Despite the amendments made to the text of article 35, none aimed to change the "rank" of this offence. In other countries, offences related to terrorist groups were also labelled terrorist offences. However, Romanian legislation does not treat the same offences in this manner. For instance, according to article 421-2-1 of the French Criminal Code, activity that consists of participating in an existing terrorist group or involvement in the commission of a terrorist attack is also a terrorist act. The necessity of the special incrimination found in the French doctrine was explained as follows: "criminal law sometimes had to create genuine offences allowing the state to repress a perpetrator independent of subsequent acts irrespective of the fact that the latter were committed."[19] Similar provisions may be found in other European Criminal Codes.[20]

f. Offences Consisting of Threatening to Commit Some Terrorist Acts (Article 37)

According to article 37 provisions, the Romanian legislature has criminalized some forms of threatening to commit terrorist acts, as follows:

> (1) The threatening by any means of a natural or moral person or a collective entity by using firearms, nuclear, chemical, biological weapons, nuclear installations or ionized radiation generating devices, by provoking a nuclear explosion or a nuclear accident or by spreading or using products, substances, microorganisms, toxins or materials of any kind, capable to endanger the health of people or animals or of the environment, or to cause extremely grave consequences, threat committed in the purpose prescribed in article 32 para. (1), constitutes a crime punishable with imprisonment from 1 to 5 years.
>
> (2) If the aforementioned threat was addressed to a state or an international organization, the act is punishable with imprisonment from 2 to 7 years and the suspension of certain civil rights.

While the Framework Decision refers to a "general" threat – committed by means of any type of terrorist act – the Romanian text has criminalized only the act of threatening to commit certain types of dangerous attacks. In this instance, the Romanian legislature has defined the offence more narrowly than the EU directive.

19 Philippe Chrestia *La loi du 23 janvier 2006 relative à la lutte contre le terrorisme. Premières observations* (Paris: Recueil Dalloz, 2006) at 1409.

20 Art. 270-bis (Associazioni con finalita' di terrorismo anche internazionale o di eversione dell'ordine democratico); (Art. 129 a) – Forming Terrorist Organizations.

g. Offences Consisting of False Alarming of the Authorities About a Terrorist Threat (Article 38)

Pursuant to article 38:

> (1) Alarming, by any means and without a justifiable reason, a natural or moral person or a collective entity, an institution specialized in emergency intervention, an institution with attributions in the field of national security or in the safeguard of public order, with regards to the usage of firearms, nuclear, chemical, biological, radiological weapons or to the spreading or the usage of products, substances, microorganisms, toxins or materials of any kind, capable of endangering the lives, bodily integrity or health of people or animals or of the environment or of causing extremely grave consequences, is punishable with imprisonment from 3 months to 2 years or with a fine.

The last act criminalized in Romanian anti-terrorist law is falsely alarming the authorities about various forms of terrorism, an act considered by the legislator to present a certain degree of public threat. This offence recognizes that falsely alerting the competent authorities spreads anxiety amongst targeted people and may mislead the competent authorities from a real terrorist risk unknown to the authorities.

B. *Terrorism Prosecutions*

There have only been three important terrorism cases in Romania where the court decided to imprison the culprits. In each case, the perpetrators were accused and convicted for multiple charges. We will briefly present the facts and the final decision in each of these terrorist cases:

- C.D. was accused and ultimately convicted of committing several terrorist offences and other ordinary crimes.[21] In the investigation file, the facts were described as follows: in August 2002, C.D. stole some grenades and projectiles from a military deposit. In November 2002, C.D. threw a grenade into a schoolyard, injuring five children and destroying several cars and the high school building. C.D. later sent two threatening letters to the acting prime minister from the high school attended by his sons. On 14 March 2003, C.D. armed a second grenade and left it in an intensely travelled alley near a central park. The court convicted C.D. of committing several terrorist offences (attempts to murder several victims, attempts to destruction), stealing of arms and threatening to commit terrorist attacks. C.D. was found guilty and

[21] Decision no. 975/2007, Criminal Section, High Court of Justice and Cassation. (not public).

sentenced to eighteen years in prison. The convictions also suspended his civil rights.

- L.F.I. was convicted of attempting to commit a terrorist attack in 2008 – an attempt to commit aggravated murder against multiple victims and an attempt to destruction. He was also convicted for committing propaganda for a terrorist purpose.[22] The prosecutor's indictment sustained those facts: the alleged offender created a website for Muslims who had decided to kill for Islam and in the name of Allah, pretending that during 1993 through 1995 he had fought as a volunteer in Bosnia in the Muslims Brigades and converted to Islam. Using this website, he promoted ideas, conceptions and a behaviour meant to support the cause and the activities of Islamic terrorist entities. He cited from the Quran and spread arguments invoked by notorious terrorist organization leaders, such as Osama bin Laden or Fawaz bin Muhammad. L.F.I. was also accused of trying to produce an improvised explosive device to be detonated in a public place in Timişoara. The perpetrator intended to kill more civilians and destroy the area where the device would explode. In preparation, the perpetrator created a video message similar to those broadcast by terrorist organizations. The message, conceived to announce threats to Romanian people, was sent to several commercial TV providers from Romania and abroad. Because of some technical problems, its content was not received properly and could not be seen except at his personal e-mail address. The perpetrator also bought two gas containers, with the intention of detonating them. However, he was taken into custody by the authorities before he was able to execute his plan.
- The last case, which we will synthesize, is the conviction of O.H. for inciting others to commit terrorist acts.[23] Though prosecutors in several ordinary criminal cases had previously investigated O.H., he was first convicted only after contacting M.M. and convincing him to kidnap three Romanian citizens while visiting Iraq. Based on O.H.'s plans, three Romanian journalists were kidnapped in Iraq and kept hostage by a terrorist organization for almost two months. Their release was conditioned on the withdrawal of Romanian troops from Iraq.

The procedure used in terrorism investigations and trials follows the ordinary procedures, with some exceptions. According to the provisions of article 12 paragraph 1 lett. c) of Law no. 508/2004,[24] the prosecutors qualified to investigate terrorist

[22] Decision no. 386/2008, Criminal Section, High Court of Justice and Cassation. (not public).

[23] Decision no. 611/2008, Criminal Section, High Court of Justice and Cassation. (not public).

[24] Law no. 508/2004 with regards to the organization and functioning of Direction for Investigating Organized Crime and Terrorism.

offences are specialized prosecutors from the Direction for Investigating Organized Crime and Terrorism.

Anti-terrorist law provides the most important derogative dispositions. Article 20 of Law no. 535/2004 outlines all special measures that may be taken in order to collect information or evidence in terrorism cases: provisions related to intercepting and recording communication, as well as special provisions regarding search warrants. Articles 21 and 22 provided detailed regulation of these measures, but they were abrogated on 1 February 2014. However, the same provisions are now part of Law no. 51/1991 concerning national security (article 12^{1}–12^{10}). These measures do not affect the right to an equitable trial because the constitutional framework restrains derogative criminal proceedings.

According to article 148 from New Procedural Criminal Code, in terrorism cases (as in serious organized crime cases), the public prosecutor may use undercover operations to obtain information or evidence, for a period no longer than sixty days, and only if there is a reasonable suspicion that a crime is to be committed or has already been committed (article 148 paragraph 1 C.p.p.). The use of undercover operations are exceptional measures to be used only when necessary and where there is no other way of gathering evidence about a serious crime (article 148 paragraph 1 lett.c C.p.p.). In addition, any restraint of fundamental rights and liberties has to be proportionate with the importance of the information or evidence that may be gathered from an undercover operation (article 148 alin. 1 lett.b C.p.p.).

Article 40 of Law no. 535/2004 authorizes the Appeals Court to try terrorism cases. The resulting sentence may be contested at the High Court of Justice and Cassation. These provisions are not unique: cases dealing with offences against national security are handled in the same way. Therefore, Romania does not have special courts for terrorism cases, which would in any event be banned by constitutional norms.

The New Romanian Procedural Criminal Code (which also entered into force 1 February 2014) contains new provisions addressing illegal evidence: "evidence obtained by torture, as well as subsequent evidence obtained from such evidence, is not allowed to be used in the criminal trial" (article 102 paragraph 1 C.p.p.). These provisions conclude: "evidence obtained through illegal methods is not allowed to be used in the criminal trial"(article 102 paragraph 2 C.p.p.). The previously cited provisions affect the whole criminal process – the investigation phase, proceedings and court trial. In order to guarantee the defendant's rights to a proper defence and fair trial, the Code also provides that evidence considered to be illegal must be excluded from the accused's file (article 102 paragraph 3 C.p.p.).

Therefore, if investigators have used any violence (or the interrogation techniques tend towards violence), evidence obtained through such methods must be excluded in all criminal cases, including those involving terrorism.

Romanian law has no special provisions regarding the protection of witnesses, other than those applicable in any case using the deposition of protected witnesses. (Provisions from article 125 to article 129 regulate the special statute of protected witnesses and the procedure of hearings.) If the life or the safety of a witness is somehow endangered by his or her testimony, the prosecutor or the court may accept the testimony of a witness using a pseudonym, testimony provided through audio/video technology that distorts the witness's voice and image, recordings or transcripts (during investigations). The lawyers and other participants involved in the criminal process may address questions to the witness.

C. *Punishment of Terrorism*

There is limited jurisprudence regarding terrorism. The three major cases examined in the preceding section resulted in severe sentences (eighteen, twelve and twenty years of prison), but the sentences are proportionate to the gravity of each offence.

The same conditions apply to the rehabilitation of terrorists as they do for any sentence with a penalty that meets a certain threshold. Neither the Romanian Criminal Code nor the anti-terrorist law derogate from the conditions that must be satisfied by individuals convicted of terrorist offences in order to undertake rehabilitation.

Law no. 535/2004 does not have any special provisions to reduce penalties by taking into account mitigating circumstances or cooperation with authorities conducting the investigation. Such a provision exists in the European Union Framework Decision 2002/475/JHA, but it was not transposed into domestic law. At the same time, Romanian criminal law was familiar with the system of reducing the penalties for those who cooperate with the authorities, and such mitigation could be used in terrorism cases. This may be precluded, however, by new criminal terrorism offences that have mandatory minimum punishments and provide for no special circumstances that may mitigate such penalties.

IV. INVESTIGATIVE POWERS

The state, including the police, intelligence agencies and the military, are often given special investigative powers in terrorism cases that are unavailable in other criminal proceedings.

A. *Police Powers*

The national law provides for "special" police officers who participate in terrorist cases, working in units specialized in combating organized crime and terrorism.

They exercise identical powers in both organized crime cases and terrorist cases, derogating from the general framework of investigative powers.

Neither the Romanian Procedural Criminal Code nor the anti-terrorist Law include any provision regarding preventive arrest in terrorist cases. As previously stated, there are no special powers regarding interrogations. Pre-trial detention is subject to the same conditions governing ordinary cases.

Article 148 of the Romanian Procedural Criminal Code, which also entered into force on 1 February 2014, allows the use of undercover investigators or collaborators with protected identities in criminal proceedings regarding serious crimes and terrorist cases. There must be a reasonable suspicion that a terrorist offence is being planned or committed. This proceeding supposes a preliminary authorization from the prosecutor. This method of collecting information is restricted to exceptional circumstances where there is no other way to collect evidence or locate a suspect.

Both police officers and intelligence agents may execute undercover operations (article 148 paragraph 4 C.p.p.). If the investigator collects evidence in the form of photos or audio or video recordings, the prosecutor must obtain a preliminary warrant for technical surveillance from the judge for civil rights and liberties (article 148 paragraph 3 C.p.p.).

B. *Intelligence Agencies*

Law no. 535/2004 contained a special chapter titled "Measures to be taken in order to collect information," which was later amended by the Romanian Criminal Procedural Law, which entered into force on 1 February 2014. Those provisions remain a part of Law no. 51/1991 regarding national security (also amended the last time by Law no. 255/2013; the amendments entered into force on 18 March 2014).

According to these provisions (13–23[25] from the Law no. 51/1991), if a competent authority in counter-terrorism considers that the activity of a terrorist organization threatens national security, that authority must submit, according to article 15 paragraph 2 from Law no. 51/1991 a request to the General Prosecutor of the High Court of Justice and Cassation in order to perform specific activities related the collection of information. These activities include intercepting and recording of communications; seeking information, documents or objects; and searching for documents or objects (article 13 from Law no. 51/1991).

[25] Law no. 51/1991 was republished in the Official Monitor from 18 March 2014, and articles 12^1 to 12^{10} introduced by Law no. 255/2013 were renumbered from 13 to 23. These articles contain mainly provisions regarding criminal investigation of terrorism cases and other serious crimes jeopardizing the security of the state.

A strict procedure governs the authorization of operations to collect information. For instance, authorities qualified to collect information must submit a written request to the General Prosecutor of the High Court of Justice and Cassation, as previously mentioned. According to article 15 paragraph 1 the request must identify the activities to be authorized, the existence of a threat to national security justifying this authorization, the identity of the person whose communications must be intercepted (if the identity of the person is known), the identity of the person who will be searched and the duration of surveillance activity.

Upon receipt, the General Prosecutor designates which prosecutor(s) is/are in charge to analyze the legality of the request and give a disposition if the requested authorization is justified. If the prosecutor does not consider such a request to be justified, the prosecutor denies the authorization in a motivated ordinance (article 15 paragraph 3).

If the request is justifiable, a written proposal will be sent to the President of the High Court of Justice and Cassation within twenty-four hours, in order to authorize the collection of information (article 15 paragraph 4).

Judges appointed by the President of the High Court of Justice and Cassation will make a special decision either in favour or against the requested authorization. If rejected, this decision is communicated to the prosecutor. If the judges deem the reasons sufficient to sustain the request, they will issue a warrant authorizing the collection of information (article 15 paragraphs 6 and 7).

The warrant may be valid for as long as to six months and can be prolonged by three months, but cannot be extended more than two years (article 17 paragraph 4). A judge appointed by the President of the High Court of Justice and Cassation must reevaluate the reasons for prolonging the warrant and need not extend authorization if he or she reasonably doubts the continued necessity for the investigative activities authorized by the warrant.

There are also provisions that refer to the objectives pursued while collecting information and the relationship between the intelligence agencies involved. The law stipulates that they must inform the General Prosecutor of the High Court of Justice and Cassation about the results of authorized activities and the measures undertaken and the procedure that regulates the regime of evidence gathering (article 20 paragraph 3 and article 21 paragraph 1).

However, there is a possible derogation from the general framework: in exceptional cases, intelligence agents may collect information without preliminary authorization. This is permitted only for the purpose of eliminating an imminent threat to national security. Even in this situation, a request for authorization must be submitted to the prosecutor or court within forty-eight hours (article 19 paragraph 1).

V. PROSCRIPTION AND LISTING OF TERRORIST GROUPS AND INDIVIDUALS

A. *Proscription Mechanisms*

After the 9/11 attacks, Romania adopted Government Ordinance no. 159/2001 regarding the freezing of assets of terrorist organizations and suspected persons. The completed ordinance includes an annex reproducing the list from the UN Security Council Resolution 1267/2001.

B. *Challenges to Proscriptions and Listings*

Romania did not directly use the proscription or listing of terrorist groups in order to criminalize terrorist offences or combat international terrorism. In accordance with article 23 of Law no. 535/2004, the Romanian legal system implemented the list from UN Security Council Resolution 1267/2001.

In order to prevent financial support of terrorist organizations, the law forbids all financial or bank operations between residents or non-residents and moral or natural persons listed in Government Ordinance no. 159/2001.

VI. REGULATION OF TERRORISM FINANCING

The Romanian legislature has criminalized the financing of terrorism based on the understanding that it increases the power of terrorist organizations and facilitates terrorist attacks.[26] The offence is linked to the entire anti-terrorist legislation and was not adopted as a response to the UN Security Council Resolutions 1267 or 1373.

While financing of terrorism became a major problem only at the end of 1999, legal scholars emphasized as early as the late 1980s that "modern terrorists, compared to their predecessors, do not live with enthusiasm, they require large amounts of money. It is usually expensive to prepare important operations; they need to fund logistical support, buy weapons and information, and pay the terrorists themselves who have no other income."[27]

[26] Developments in financing of terrorist organizations have been as interesting as the evolution of terrorism itself. Narodnaya Volya's modest financial support was received from sympathizers in Russia. The anarchists were poor and were rarely assisted by financing. One exception was the Spanish anarchist Francisco Ferrer receiving a million francs from his French lover. W. Lacquer, ed., *The Age of Terrorism (A Completely Revised and Expanded Study of National and International Political Violence, Based on the Author's Classic Terrorism)* (New York: Little, Brown, 1987), p. 96.

[27] *Ibid.*

According to article 36:

> (1) Financing the collection (directly or indirectly) of licit or illicit funds, knowing that those funds will be used in total or in part to commit terrorist offences or to sustain a terrorist entity, constitutes the offence of terrorism.

The second paragraph of article 36 contains a special provision that imposes a major penalty on those who obtain funds knowing that those funds will be used for terrorist purposes.

Romanian law does not exempt funds used to finance the legitimate and humanitarian activities of a terrorist group.

We are not aware of any terrorist financing cases being prosecuted in Romania.

There is no special provision concerning the forfeiture of terrorist property, apart from the general framework of confiscation or seizure. Romanian legislation recently adopted procedures for the extensive confiscation of property; this also applies to terrorist cases. Again, we know of no terrorist case where these forfeiture powers have been used.

VII. IMMIGRATION MEASURES

Immigration law has not been used against suspected terrorists in Romania. There are no special or derogatory procedures for taking suspected terrorists into custody or deporting them.

A. *Immigration Proceedings and Torture*

Romanian legislation contains no prohibition on the use of evidence obtained through torture or cruel and degrading treatment in immigration proceedings. However, immigration proceedings are subject to the existing prohibition on obtaining evidence by violent means. The problems of using secret evidence perhaps obtained by torture in immigration cases have not appeared in Romania.

VIII. ADMINISTRATIVE/EXECUTIVE MEASURES

Alternative executive or administrative measures have sometimes been used as a form of anti-terrorism law, as a less restrictive alternative to criminal prosecutions or to supplement to criminal law.

In some cases, certain suspects, under the monitoring of national security services for being involved in activities against national security, were declared as undesirable to remain on Romanian ground and banned from returning in the next five to fifteen years. The decision was rendered by the Bucharest Appeal Court's administrative section.[28]

IX. ROLE OF MILITARY AND EXTRA-TERRITORIAL COUNTER-TERRORISM ACTIVITIES

A. *Military Courts and Detention*

Military courts do not have jurisdiction over terrorism cases. Romania has never detained any alleged terrorist based on the law of war.

B. *The Extra-Territorial Treatment of Citizens Suspected of Terrorism*

There are no reports of any Romanian litigation or other proceedings with respect to the treatment of Romanian nationals detained by another state because they are suspected terrorists.

C. *Extra-Territorial Terrorism Law Enforcement*

We have no knowledge of the extra-territorial counter-terrorism activities of Romania or state officials outside the country.

Based on our records, Romania has not extradited any alleged terrorists. Regardless of the circumstances, Romania cannot extradite a national or non-national to a country where a convicted person could face the death penalty.

X. SECRECY AND TERRORISM

A. *Secrecy Claims and Secret Evidence*

The new Romanian Procedural Criminal Code established explicit norms regarding classified information and provisions applicable to any serious crime case (not only acts of terrorism). If the dossier contains classified information essential to the case, the court has several options: it may urgently request a total declassification (disclosure), a partial declassification or lower degree of the classified information.

[28] Such an example may be Decision no. 3450/07.11.2013 of the Bucharest Appeal Court, the Administrative Section, regarding M.S.G., A.K., A.F. and A.S., Afghan citizens, declared undesirable for security reasons as they were under suspicion of involvment in terrorism. They were forced to leave Romania and banned from returning for fifteen years. Similarly, Decision 2339/22.08.2013 of the Bucharest Appeal Court, the Administrative Section, declared G. T., a Tunisian citizen, undesirable for security reasons and forced the subject to leave Romania, banning his return for fifteen years.

The court may also allow the defendant's lawyer to access declassified information (article 352 paragraphs 11 from the Romanian Procedural Criminal Code).

The court itself cannot disclose classified information (this falls under the jurisdiction of the issuing authority). Therefore, if the issuing authority does not allow the defendant's lawyer to access to classified information, the court cannot convict, withdraw or postpone punishment based on secret information not disclosed to the accused's lawyer (article 352 paragraph 12 from Romanian Procedural Criminal Code).

B. *Secrecy in the Courtroom and Anonymous Witnesses*

According to general procedural provisions, court proceedings are public. The prosecutor may request, as an exception, a closed courtroom if the public courtroom risks compromising confidential information from the file. The court may opt for a non-public courtroom once it has heard from all the participants in the case. Intelligence service members may testify anonymously.

XI. CONCLUSION

Violence has existed throughout history, and its complete eradication is unrealistic. The more feasible goal of modern societies is to take effective measures to diminish or prevent violence.

After interstate conflicts or civil wars, terrorism represents the most acute form of violence. Unfortunately, terrorism has adapted well to the modern age, and globalization has worked to its advantage. As globalization improved international economic and cultural networks among civilized societies, it was also used by terrorists to export violence, create cells in more countries than ever before and establish constant, rapid communication between members. This has heightened a sense of insecurity among states that see themselves as vulnerable targets.

Unfortunately, experts have not exaggerated the likelihood of future terrorist attacks. Prevention has become a central goal of state cooperation in this matter, with efforts focused on the discovery and annihilation of terrorist organizations.

Using judicial instruments to prevent terrorism is one of the most important issues on the European Union's agenda. Following the creation of "Justice, Freedom and Security," there was a constant need to protect member states from internal and external risk.

Though the Romanian legislature has chosen to criminalize terrorist acts through anti-terrorism law containing a wide variety of provisions, we maintain that a better treatment of terrorism would be the use of preexisting ordinary offences under the Romanian Criminal Code. The fact that the vast majority of legislation from the continental system has criminalized terrorist acts and related offences in their Criminal Code, rather than through special law, lends support to this proposal. This approach would avoid the difficult and perhaps impossible task of defining terrorism.

We tend to be very critical of Romania's existing provisions criminalizing terrorism. Eight offences can be grouped under three main branches of terrorism or banned activities associated with terrorism: terrorist offences, forming or leading a terrorist group and other offences related to terrorist activity.

In our opinion, terrorist offences may be further subdivided into "classical" terrorist acts (murder, hostage taking, aircraft seizure, etc.) and new types of terrorist offences (obtaining dangerous substances, experimenting or using weapon of mass destruction or cyber-crimes used for terrorist purposes).

We would emphasize that Romanian legislation regarding terrorism has continued to evolve since 2001. The current provisions appear to offer a better response to the EU's Framework Decisions than the 2001 ordinance and 2002 legislation. For instance, all acts from the EU Framework Decisions have been criminalized, and the provisions themselves have been reformulated in both the 2004 law and the 2014 amendments to that law.

Romanian law has transposed the provisions from the EU Framework Decision 2002/475/JHA in several steps. After more than eleven years, we have finally completed the harmonization process. For instance, terrorist acts consisting in "seizure of means of public or goods transport" and "the interference with or disruption of the supply of water, power or any other fundamental natural resource the effect of which is to endanger human lives" were criminalized only after the amended process of Law no. 535/2004, which entered into force in 2014.The first configuration of the text was extremely complicated because articles 32 and 34 criminalized terrorist acts, while article 33 criminalized acts associated with terrorism. This became more coherent on 1 February 2014, when the amendments confined the criminalization of terrorist acts to a single article (article 32).

Unfortunately, the text still needs improvement. In its effort to create exhaustive legislation, the legislature produced an enormous text containing too many prohibited acts. This has resulted in undesirable overlap, illustrated by comparing the provisions of article 32 paragraph 3 lett.a), lett.b) with those of article 33 paragraph 1 lett.a). The legislature did not intend to produce a convoluted text, but it should be amended. The problem of overlap is more dangerous when the law criminalizes not only the completed terrorist act. but also attempts and preparatory acts. Trying to cover everything has made completed acts nearly indistinguishable from attempted or preparatory acts and has undermined the integrity of the criminal law.

We do not understand why the Romanian legislature, in order to transpose in a more accurate manner the EU Framework Decision, has not criminalized a "threat to commit a terrorist act" instead of criminalizing a "threat" as an ordinary crime with a terrorist purpose – article 32 paragraph 1 lett.b). In our opinion, defining terrorist acts as a "threat" to commit any ordinary crime, instead of limiting the threat to those acts already identified as terrorist acts while committed with a political purpose, is too vague. Such a broadly worded offence departs from the specificity that should be seen in prohibiting terrorism as a severe and extraordinary crime.

In our opinion, certain provisions in the new Romanian counter-terrorism law appear useless, such as those enumerations found in article 32 paragraph 1 lett.e)-n), which repeats a simple set of acts – the seizure of ships and any violence against person or the destruction of a fixed platform.

In our opinion, the acts, from article 32 paragraph 1 lett.q), of "computer frauds, credit-card payment frauds," do not represent terrorist acts, and therefore we believe that the legislature should not criminalize them as terrorist acts together with other typical terrorist offences. To our knowledge, no similar provision exists in other legislation. We strongly believe that computer fraud and credit-card payment fraud can indeed be acts supporting terrorism, but they should be treated as distinct crimes.

One major problem remaining after all the amendments of the law is that the Romanian provisions criminalizing terrorist activity and terrorist groups do not clearly state whether terrorist offences have to be considered collective offences. Since the amendments entered into force on 1 February 2014, the definition of terrorist acts is no longer linked to article 4 of the Law no. 535/2004 (which contains the definitions of terrorist entities as "terrorist," "terrorist group," "structured group" and "terrorist organization"). Other European legislation has resolved the bias raised by this question in different ways. Consider article 129 a) from the German Criminal Code, which clearly communicates the legislature's vision of a collective offence, while French law, in article 421-1, defined terrorist acts as those committed individually or through a collective effort. We consider the provision in the Austrian Criminal Code (article 278 lett a-c) to be the most refined. It stipulates that a terrorist association is a union of more than two people aiming to commit one or more terrorist criminal offences by one or more members of the association.

Our final criticism relates to the provisions found in article 38 (falsely alarming the authorities about a terrorist threat). In our opinion, this article is unrelated to anti-terrorist legislation as long as it remains neither a terrorist act nor an act in preparation for a terrorist activity.

We believe there is an immediate need to refine Romanian counter-terrorism law so that experts and citizens alike may more easily understand it.

PART FOUR

Middle East and Africa

18

Israel

Shiri Krebs

I. INTRODUCTION: LAW AS THE CONTINUATION OF WAR BY OTHER MEANS

October 13, 1953, 1:30 A.M.; a squad of infiltrators from Jordan crosses the border into Israel and throws a grenade into the home of a sleeping family.[1] The explosion kills the mother, thirty-nine-year-old, pregnant Suzanne Kinyas and two of her children: Shoshana, a three-year-old girl, and her baby brother, Benny.[2] Another child, Yitzhak, was wounded; he died three years later.[3] His younger brother, Eli, who was only six years old the night of the murder, still suffers from chronic PTSD (post-traumatic stress disorder) and has attempted suicide several times in the years that passed.[4] The savage attack shocked the Israeli public; yet it was not an isolated event.[5] By 1953, the five-year-old state of Israel was already experienced with terror attacks directed against its citizens.[6]

Zuckerman Fellow, Law and Security Fellow, Stanford Center on International Security and cooperation (CISAC); Christiana Shi Stanford Interdisciplinary Graduate Fellow, Stanford University; JSD Candidate, Stanford Law School. I wish to thank editors Liora Lazarus and Ryan Goss for their valuable comments, and my advisers, Jenny Martinez and Mariano-Florentino Cuéllar, for their advice, guidance and encouragement. I am grateful for the inspiring environment and financial support I received from the Stanford Center on International Security and Cooperation (CISAC).

1 Original phrase coined by Carl von Clausewitz: "War is a mere continuation of policy by other means," On War, trans. Col. J.J. Graham (London: Kegan Paul, Trench, Trubner & C., 1918), at vol. 1, para 24.

2 Avichai Becker, The Kinyas children, *Ha'aretz*, January 6, 2003 [in Hebrew], available at http://www.haaretz.co.il/mobile/1.853441 (last accessed August 26, 2013).

3 *Id.*

4 *Id.*

5 Benny Morris, The Israeli Press and the Qibya operation, 1953, 25(4) *Journal of Palestine Studies* 40 (1996), pp. 40.

6 Martin Gilbert, *The Routledge Atlas of the Arab-Israeli Conflict*, 8th ed. (Routledge: New York, 2005), p. 58.

The Israeli response to the attack was quick and brutal: in the spirit of random retaliatory counter-measures that was adopted by the Israeli government in the early 1950s, the Palestinian village of Qibya was chosen as a target.[7] Unit 101, the special commando unit led by Major Ariel ("Arik") Sharon, was chosen for the mission (together with Paratroop Battalion 890 and a mortar unit).[8] Their instructions were "to carry out destruction and maximum killing with the aim of driving the inhabitants of the village from their homes."[9] On the night of October 14, the assaulting units entered Qibya, moving from house to house, blowing in doors, throwing grenades through the windows and "cleaning out" the rooms with light weapons fire. Inhabitants who tried to flee their homes were gunned down in the alleyways. Subsequently, the paratroops blew up forty-five of the village's houses. Altogether some sixty villagers – most of them women and children – were killed.[10]

The Qibya massacre ("Operation Shoshana") was a turning point in Israel's early counter-terrorism policy.[11] At the time, it was widely and unequivocally supported by almost all of the Israeli newspapers.[12] It made sense: it was impossible to know the precise identities of the infiltrators responsible for various acts of terror, and so the Israeli Defense Forces (IDF) took action against villages screened by Israeli intelligence, from which infiltrators were assumed to be operating.[13] But the retaliatory policy had severe political implications, undermining Israel's already fragile international status.[14] The international reaction to the Qibya massacre,[15] including the UN Security Council condemnation,[16] forced Israel to rethink its retaliatory early counter-terrorism policy:

7 Morris, *supra* note 4, at 41.

8 *Id.*

9 *Id.*

10 *Id.*

11 Benny Morris, *Righteous Victims: A History of the Zionist-Arab Conflict 1881–2001* (New York: First Vintage, 2001), at 279. Vardi argues that the actual turning point in Israeli policy (theoretically, if not practically) was triggered by another operation – the Samaria operation – which occurred in 1956 and was directed against Qalqilya police forces (which about one hundred of whom were killed in the operation, along with seventeen Israeli Defense Forces soldiers). Gil-li Vardi, "Pounding their feet': Israeli military culture as reflected in early IDF combat history, 31(2) Journal of Strategic Studies 295 (2008), at 300.

12 Morris, The Qibya Operation, *supra* note 4, at 51.

13 Vardi, *supra* note 11, at 300.

14 As Vardi points out, such a retaliatory policy had several important negative implications, including weakening King Hussein's position in Jordan, cut across Israel's political interests, and provoked international anger and denunciations of Israeli aggression. *Id.*

15 Neil J. Mitchell, Agents of Atrocity: Leaders, Followers and the Violation of Human Rights in Civil War (New York: Palgrave MacMillan, 2004), at 81.

16 U.N. doc. S/INF/8, Nov. 24, 1953, available at: http://avalon.law.yale.edu/20th_century/mid009.asp (last accessed: August 28, 2013).

> After Qibya the IDF switched from civilian to military targets. Arab civilian casualties declined markedly, reducing Western condemnation of "indiscriminate" Israeli reprisals. But the sorties increased in size and firepower: Many more troops and guns were needed to conquer a well-fortified military camp or police fort than to overrun a village.[17]

In the sixty years that passed from the Qibya massacre to this day, much has changed in the strategic and tactical policies adopted by Israel to cope with the threats of terrorism. The terrorist threats themselves have changed in many ways. But the main legal, moral, ethical and even strategic dilemmas remained very much the same and are still alive and unsettled. These dilemmas include fundamental issues such as the very definition of terrorism, as well as more practical questions concerning the applicable legal framework and the balance between national security and personal liberties. Moreover, the Israeli reaction to the terrorist attack against the Kinyas family captures the complexity of the phenomenon of terrorism (a horrible crime against an individual family and at the same time a bloody battle in an ongoing protracted armed conflict); and the versatility of the applicable legal regimes: from international humanitarian law and the use of force, to domestic law enforcement regimes. The following sections will focus on the domestic law enforcement regime in Israel and on the particular ways Israeli legislators adopted to cope with the threats of terrorism. While analyzing specific law enforcement counter-terrorism means and methods, this chapter focuses on "law as the Continuation of war by other means," and demonstrates the impact of the "*war* on terror" on counter-terrorism *law* and practice.

II. DEFINITION OF TERRORISM

Despite the historical roots and the long time Israel has been struggling with terrorism (and maybe because of it), to date there is no comprehensive legislation governing terrorism and counter-terrorism measures in Israel.[18] Different laws govern different contexts and circumstances, using inconsistent definitions and leaving several lacunas and unresolved issues (including the fundamental question of what constitutes "an act of terrorism.")[19] The oldest (yet very much alive) Israeli

[17] Morris, *Righteous Victims*, at 279. Vardi adds that After Qibya, operations focused on enemy military and police bases, and a clear pattern of larger and ever more organised attacks against Arab military targets emerged. Vardi, *supra* note 11, at 300.

[18] A new comprehensive terror bill, which will be dealt with in length hereinafter, was recently approved by the Ministerial Committee for Legislation, but has not passed all stages of the legislation process yet. Counter-terrorism bill, 2011 [Hebrew], available at http://www.justice.gov.il/NR/rdonlyres/77CD3245-3A1D-4F8E-AA54-5D8C25344888/29272/611.pdf (last accessed: February 9, 2015).

[19] Ido Rosenzweig and Yuval Shany, New comprehensive counter-terrorism memorandum bill, 17 Terrorism and Democracy (2010).

legislation concerning terrorism is the Prevention of Terrorism Ordinance 5708-1948 (hereinafter: *Ordinance*).[20] A modern and more nuanced definition of terrorism is found in the Prohibition on Terror Financing Law 5765-2004 (hereinafter: *Terror Financing Law*), which constitutes, together with the Ordinance, the main legislative tools concerning terrorism.[21] Due to their limited scopes, the Ordinance and the Terror Financing Law are supplemented with various provisions of the criminal code and administrative measures, such as the Defense (Emergency) Regulations of 1945, which date back to the British mandate over Palestine; the Incarceration of Unlawful Combatants Law 5762-2002, which was legislated to enable easy and indefinite preventive detention of Palestinians from Gaza Strip; and the Criminal Procedure (Detainee Suspected of Security Offense) (Temporary Order) Law, 2006, which allows the state to hold criminal prosecution hearings without the presence of the defendant.

A. *"Act of Terrorism"*

The Prevention of Terrorism Ordinance defines "acts of terrorism" as

> [A]cts of violence calculated to cause death or injury to a person or to threats of such acts of violence.[22]

This definition is anachronistic, outdated and fails to distinguish between the unique phenomenon of terrorism and other forms of organized crime. The terror financing law provides a modern, narrower and more refined definition for a terrorist act:

> (a) an act that constitutes an offence or a threat to commit an act that constitutes an offence that was committed or was planned to be committed in order to influence a matter of policy, ideology or religion if all of the following conditions are fulfilled:
>
> (1) it was committed or was planned to be committed with the goal of causing fear or panic among the public or with the goal of coercing a government or another governing authority, including the government or governing authority of a foreign country, to take action or to refrain from taking action; for the purposes of this paragraph – foreseeing, as a nearly certain possibility, that the act or the threat will cause fear or panic among the

[20] The official English translation of this law is available at http://mfa.gov.il/MFA/MFA-Archive/1900–1949/Pages/Prevention%20of%20Terrorism%20Ordinance%20No%2033%20of%205708–19.aspx (last accessed December 18, 2013).

[21] An unofficial English translation of this law is available at www.justice.gov.il/NR/rdonlyres/4FE9E898-1264-4561-B7AA-0957F6DEA67A/0/ProhibitionTerroristFinancing.doc (last accessed December 18, 2013).

[22] Ordinance, article 1.

public is equivalent to having a goal to cause fear or panic among the public;

(2) the act that was committed or that was planned or the threat included:

(a) actual injury to a person's body or his freedom, or placing a person in danger of death or danger of grievous bodily injury;

(b) the creation of actual danger to the health or security of the public;

(c) serious damage to property;

(d) serious disruption of vital infrastructures, systems or services;

(b) if the aforementioned act or threat was committed or was planned to be committed using weapons as defined in Section 144(c)(1) and (3) of the Penal Law, excluding a weapon part or accessory, it will be considered an act of terrorism even if the conditions of paragraph (1) of subsection (a) are not met, and if it was committed or planned to be committed using chemical, biological or radioactive weapons that are liable, due to their nature, to cause actual mass harm – even if the conditions set forth in paragraphs (1) and (2) of subsection (a) are not met;

The main elements of this definition are an *illegal act* (or threat thereof), which is committed in order to *influence a matter of policy, ideology or religion*, with the specific goal of *causing fear* among the public or *coercing a government*. The act must include *actual injury* (or danger thereof), *actual danger to the health or security of the public*, *serious damage to property or serious disruption of vital infrastructures*. The law relinquishes the goal element in cases where the illegal act or threat was committed using weapons, and it relinquishes both the goal and injury/damage requirement in cases where the act was committed using chemical, biological or radioactive weapons. For example, a threat to use chemical weapons to protest against governmental health policy is considered a terrorist act with no other elements required. Similarly, throwing a grenade at an empty military facility or vehicle, in order to protest against the military's gender policies, is considered an act of terrorism.

In June 2013, a new counter-terrorism bill, prepared by the Israeli Ministry of Justice, was approved by the Ministerial Committee for Legislation after a brief fifteen-minute discussion.[23] The comprehensive 105-page bill, officially titled the Counter-terrorism bill, 2011 [hereinafter: *bill, counter-terrorism bill*], is intended to consolidate current Israeli counter-terrorism legislation into one coherent document. The counter-terrorism bill suggests some important changes to the definition of a terrorist act, including adding another motive of racism; replacing the

[23] Jonathan Lis, Israeli lawmakers blast Livni for rushing anti-terror bill through committee, *Haaretz*, June 11, 2013, available at http://www.haaretz.com/news/national/.premium-1.529200 (last accessed December 18, 2013).

goal of coercing a government to act or refrain from acting with a wider and vaguer alternative of "motivating" a government (or international organization) to act or refrain from acting; adding, alongside causing (or endangering with) severe damage to property, an alternative of causing (or putting at risk of) damage to property that might cause severe financial damage or severe harm to governmental institutions; and finally, adding a tautological presumption according to which an act that was committed by a terror organization will be considered an act of terrorism (as long as it includes one of the required injuries/damages). Meaning, any act committed by a *member* of a *terror organization* (both defined very broadly by the bill, as will be elaborated hereinafter) is considered an act of terrorism, as long as it includes an element of injury/damage or a putting placing at risk of such, as specified in section 3 of the definition. For example, a threat to burn a flag (damage to property that might harm governmental institutions) will be considered an act of terrorism, as long as such a threat was affiliated with a member of a terror organization. Similarly, a member of terror organization who threatens his or her neighbor with violent acts is committing an act of terrorism. Combining this definition with the bill's broad definitions of "terror organization" and "membership in a terror organization" sets an even lower, more ambiguous and overly broad bar for an "act of terrorism" than the current definitions.

B. *"Terror Organization"*

The terror financing law defines a "terror organization" as

> [A]n association of people which acts to perpetrate an act of terrorism or has as its goal enabling or promoting the perpetration of an act of terrorism.[24]

The new counter-terrorism bill suggests supplementing this definition with another group of organizations: "auxiliary" or "dawah" organizations. Dawah organizations include charitable societies and other social organizations that are connected to terror organizations (such as Hamas in Gaza or the Muslim Brotherhood in Egypt) and function as their community services system by providing educational, medical and welfare services to its supporters and to the general population.[25] Under the new bill, the Minister of Defense is authorized to declare any dawah organization a terror

[24] Terror financing law; the Prevention of Terrorism Ordinance defines a "terrorist organization" as a "body of persons resorting in its activities to acts of violence calculated to cause death or injury to a person or to threats of such acts of violence."

[25] The explanatory note to articles 2–3 of the counter-terrorism bill. And see also Israeli Security Agency, *"Dawa" – Hamas' Civilian Infrastructure and its Role in Terror Financing*, available at http://www.shabak.gov.il/English/EnTerrorData/Reviews/Pages/Dawa%E2%80%93Hamas-report.aspx (last accessed December 19, 2013).

organization.[26] The philosophy underlying such a broad definition is that auxiliary organizations are meant to generate public support for terrorist organizations, such as Hamas, through the humanitarian activities they conduct.[27] Nonetheless, defining such auxiliary organizations as terror organizations incriminates charitable activities and harms poor populations who are in need of their services. By adopting such broad definitions of "terror organizations," a truck driver who delivers food to the needy becomes a terrorist, and so are those making the food or providing shelter for the poor.

C. "*A Member of a Terrorist Group*"

The Ordinance defines a "member of a terrorist organization" very broadly, to include not only those participating in its activities, but also those who publish propaganda in favour of a terrorist organization or collect money for the benefit of a terrorist organization.

The terror financing law adopted a narrower definition, describing a "terrorist activist" as:

> [A] person who is active in perpetrating an act of terrorism or aids or solicits the perpetration of an act of terrorism or a person who takes an active role in a terrorist organization that has been declared as such pursuant to paragraph (1) of the definition of a declared terrorist organization.

Nonetheless, the new counter-terrorism bill seeks to broaden this active definition with a passive one: according to the bill, a person will be considered a terrorist if he or she actively participated in the activities of a terror organization, if that person expressed his or her consent to join the organization to someone who is associated with that organization, or if that person presented himself or herself as a member of the organization. The bill contains other problematic aspects, including a presumption that a person who was once a member of a terrorist organization remains a member of such organization (if the member was sixteen years old or younger at the time that he or she agreed to become a member of such an organization, the presumption will be valid for only five years.) In other words, a seventeen-year-old boy or girl who bragged to a friend about being a member of a terror organization (including auxiliary organizations) will be presumed to be a member of that organization for years to come, unless he or she can prove otherwise.

[26] Counter-terrorism bill, article 3.
[27] Rosenzweig and Shany, *supra* note 19.

III. CRIMINAL LAWS AND PROSECUTIONS

The Israeli legislation includes three main categories of criminal terrorism-related prohibitions: prohibitions on membership in terror organizations; prohibitions on terror activities; and prohibitions on supporting terror organizations. The next few subsections will explore these various offenses.[28]

A. *Criminal Prohibitions Concerning Membership in a Terror Organization*

According to regulation 58(d) of the Defense (Emergency) Regulation, 1945 (hereinafter: *the Defense Regulations*), a person shall not "be a member of any group or body of persons, any one or more of whom has committed while as a member of the group or body or is committing an offence against this regulation." Strikingly, the penalty attached to this prohibition is death. Section 84 of the Defense Regulations criminalizes membership in an unlawful association, which includes, among terror acts and other activities, the "bringing into hatred or contempt of, or the exciting of disaffection against" the Israeli government or a member of its secretaries. This offense applies not only with regard to membership in an unlawful association, but also to anyone who "does any work or performs any service for an unlawful association." The penalty associated with this offense is one or ten years, depending on the court at which the prosecution was filed. Article 3 of the Terrorism Prevention Ordinance includes a specific offense of "membership in a terror organization," which has a five-year imprisonment penalty. According to this article, "membership" includes passive membership (the mere expression of agreement to join the organization), as well as publication of propaganda supporting a terror organization. In the Kawasma case, the Military Court of Appeals determined that:

> Concerning membership, this is normally done in a way of "proposal and acceptance;" a senior member approaches an individual who is not a member and proposes that he join the organization, and if that individual agrees, from that moment on he is considered a member for all intents and purposes. It should be emphasized that becoming a member does not require that the new member will be tasked with any duties, and the mere agreement to join the organization is enough to constitute the crime of membership.[29]

This is a very broad definition, which significantly widens the scope of the crime of membership. And if that is not enough, the military courts infused into this legal

[28] The terrorism financing law includes additional, more specific prohibitions, relating to financing of terrorism, which will be explored in Section IV of this chapter.

[29] 56/00 *Kawasma v. the Military Prosecutor* [2000], Military Court of Appeals (Judea, Samaria and the Gaza Strip) [in Hebrew], p. 2.

regime a presumption according to which once an individual has expressed his or her will to join an unlawful organization, the person shall be considered a "member" of the named organization indefinitely, unless he or she can prove otherwise. In the Kawasma case, the Military Court of Appeals states that:

> We are permitted to presume that whoever decided to join an unlawful organization identifies with its ideas and intends to continue being a member in that organization until it will fulfill its objectives and goals.[30]

Interestingly, this ruling was later adopted by the District Court of Jerusalem, with regard to a student who joined a student association and was appointed the head of the "dawah" and education committees.[31] Both the civil and military courts have continued to follow this ruling in numerous cases during the years.[32] In a recent case, given in late 2011, the military court took this presumption one step forward, applying it not only to a large and well-known terror organization, but also to smaller and unknown groups (in this case, the "unlawful organization" referred to several instances of communication between the accused and another person while they were imprisoned together).[33]

B. *Criminal Prohibitions Concerning Support of a Terror Organization*

According to the ordinance, an individual who supports a terror organization will be subject to three years of imprisonment. This includes not only those who provide the organization material support, but also anyone "who publicizes, in writing or orally, words of praise, sympathy or a call for help or support for a terrorist organization; or who holds propaganda material for the benefit of a terrorist organization." In the *Jabarin* case, the Israeli Supreme Court limited the scope of this offense, determining that it applies only to cases of support of a terror organization and not to support of private actions.[34] But later on, the Israeli legislator amended the Criminal Code to include "support of any terror or violent acts" as a part of the general

[30] *Id*, at p. 7.

[31] 6815/04 *The State of Israel v. Barkat* [2004], District Court of Jerusalem [in Hebrew].

[32] See, for example, 1019/10 *Archimi v. The Military Prosecutor* [2010], Military Court of Appeals (Judea and Samaria) [in Hebrew]; 4030/08 *The Military Prosecutor v. Tzuman* [2009], Military Court (Judea) [in Hebrew]; 1970/09 *Shana'a v. The Military Prosecutor* [2009], Military Court of Appeals (Judea and Samaria) [in Hebrew]; 2472/08 *The Military Prosecutor v. Salach* [2008], Military Court of Appeals (Judea and Samaria) [in Hebrew]; 2906/05 *The Military Prosecutor v. Al-Hadana* [2005], Military Court of Appeals (Judea and Samaria) [in Hebrew].

[33] 1935/11 *The Military prosecution v. Awad* [2011], Military Court of Appeals (Judea and Samaria) [in Hebrew].

[34] AHC 8613/96 *Jabarin v. the State of Israel*, 54(5) PD 193.

prohibition on incitement.[35] In one of the cases, the Magistrate Court judge (who is now Justice of the Supreme Court of Israel) convicted a person of the crime of supporting a terror organization and sentenced him to five months' imprisonment) based on the fact that the accused called "Hezbollah, destroy Kiryat Shmona" and "kill the Jews" while participating in a parade of people who were denied access to pray in the mosque of Al Aqsa.[36] In another case, the Magistrate Court convicted a person of supporting a terror organization based on waving the organization's flag and wearing a shirt with its symbols and slogans.[37] In yet another case, the defendant was convicted of this crime after he was seen raising a photo of Hassan Nasrallah, the leader of Hezbollah, and in his room were found news articles with photos of suicide bombers and other terrorists.[38]

The new counter-terrorism bill wishes to broaden the crime of supporting a terror organization even more and adds a new criminal offense of "negligent support" of acts of terrorism. According to the bill, individuals who provide resources or services, when there is a reasonable ground to suspect that such activity may help the commission of an act of terrorism (or to escape after the commission of such act), will be incarcerated for two years.

Another peculiar new offense that the counter-terrorism bill wishes to introduce is a crime of "failing to act reasonably to prevent a crime," which occurs when an individual has information that gives rise to a concrete suspicion that an act of terrorism is about to be committed. In case that person has further information, including the identity of the potential offender, he or she is required to contact the Israeli authorities immediately. Failure to abide by this rule results in a three-year imprisonment.

C. *Criminal Prohibitions Concerning Terror Activities*

In addition to proscribing membership in and support of terrorist organizations, the Ordinance prohibits "activity within a terror organization" (which includes making a public speech on behalf of a terror organization). The penalty attached to this prohibition is twenty years' imprisonment.

The new counter-terrorism bill wishes to add another – more severe – offense to this category: "managing/leading a terror organization." Under article 17 of the bill, a person who manages a terror organization (which could be, under the bill, a charity

[35] Article 144D2, the Criminal Code, 1979. For a further discussion of this issue, see The Counter-Terrorism Bill, 2010: Israeli Democracy Institute Critical Review [2010], at p. 15, available at http://en.idi.org.il/analysis/articles/the-counter-terrorism-memorandum-bill/.

[36] 4577/00 *The State of Israel v. Lavan* [2003], Jerusalem Magistrates Court [in Hebrew].

[37] 4299/04 *The State of Israel v. Herskowitz* [2005], Jerusalem Magistrates Court [in Hebrew].

[38] 2212/02 *The State of Israel v. Basal* [2002], Nazareth Magistrates Court [in Hebrew].

or social organization linked to a terror organization) or a branch of such a terror organization will be incarcerated for twenty-five years. The bill does not require managing or directing the *criminal* activities of the organization and is satisfied with penalizing those who generally manage or lead the organization.

IV. INVESTIGATIVE POWERS AND CRIMINAL PROCEDURES

This section will explore the main issues relating to the investigative and procedural aspects of terror investigations, including torture, criminal detentions pending trial and the accused right to be present during his or her judicial hearings.

A. *Torture*

In its investigations of terror suspects, the Israeli Security Agency (ISA) made use of methods that included subjecting suspects to "moderate physical pressure" in circumstances in which such pressure was immediately necessary to save human life. Petitions were submitted to the Supreme Court, sitting as High Court of Justice, challenging the legality of these methods. In 1999, five years after the submission of the petitions, the Supreme Court gave its unanimous decision, ruling that the ISA did not have the authority to employ physical interrogation methods.[39] Nonetheless, the nine Justices avoided dealing with the substantive moral dilemmas relating to the issue of interrogational torture, and based their declaratory judgment on other grounds.[40] The judgment's main conclusion was that while there might be a justification for using exceptional interrogation measures in order to save lives, as the lesser evil, and while the concept of lesser evil is embodied in the criminal defense of necessity, the government is nevertheless not authorized to use such means in the absence of explicit legislation to that effect.[41]

Although determining that it is mainly the legislator's prerogative to decide on investigatory methods, the Court unanimously ruled that the executive branch's power to interrogate, like any administrative power, is designed for a specific purpose and must be exercised in conformity with the basic principles of the democratic regime. With regard to the general limitations on interrogational methods, derived by the core principles of democracy, the Court explicitly stated the following:

39 HCJ 5100/94 *Public Committee Against Torture v. Government of Israel* [1999] 53(4) IsrSC 817 (hereinafter: the *Torture* case). Available at http://elyon1.court.gov.il/files_eng/94/000/051/a09/94051000.a09.pdf (last accessed February 1, 2014).

40 For a critical analysis of this judicial approach, see M. Kremnitzer & R. Segev, *The Legality of Interrogational Torture: A Question of Proper Authorization or a Substantive Moral Issue?*, 34 ILR 509 (2000) (hereinafter: *The Legality of Interrogational Torture*).

41 The *Torture* case.

> A democratic, freedom-loving society does not accept that investigators may use any means for the purpose of uncovering the truth. A reasonable investigation is necessarily one free of torture, free of cruel, inhuman treatment and free of any degrading conduct whatsoever. There is a prohibition on the use of "brutal or inhuman means" in the course of an investigation.... This conclusion is in accord with international treaties, to which Israel is a signatory, which prohibit the use of torture, "cruel, inhuman treatment" and "degrading treatment".... These prohibitions are "absolute." There are no exceptions to them and there is no room for balancing. Indeed, violence directed at a suspect's body or spirit does not constitute a reasonable investigation practice.[42]

With regard to the specific interrogation methods discussed in the petitions – including shaking the suspect, using excessively tight handcuffs and placing him or her in the "Shabach" position[43] or in the "Frog Crouch" position[44] – the Court determined that these are prohibited investigation methods. With regard to "Shaking," the Court emphasized that:

> Clearly, shaking is a prohibited investigation method. It harms the suspect's body. It violates his dignity. It is a violent method which cannot form part of a legal investigation.[45]

With regard to the "Frog Crouch" method, the Court held that:

> This is a prohibited investigation method. It does not serve any purpose inherent to an investigation. It is degrading and infringes an individual's human dignity.[46]

With regard to the "Shabach" position, the Court stated that:

> This is a distorted and unnatural position. The investigators' safety does not require it. Similarly, there is no justification for handcuffing the suspect's hands with especially small handcuffs, if this is in fact the practice. The use of these methods is prohibited.[47]

Finally, the Court determined that:

> All these methods do not fall within the sphere of a "fair" interrogation. They are not reasonable. They infringe the suspect's dignity, his bodily integrity and his basic

[42] *Id.*

[43] A suspect investigated under the "Shabach" position has his or her hands tied behind his or her back. The suspect is seated on a small and low chair, whose seat is tilted forward, towards the ground. One hand is tied behind the suspect and placed inside the gap between the chair's seat and back support. The second hand is tied behind the chair, against its back support. The suspect's head is covered by a sack that falls down to his or her shoulders. Loud music is played in the room.

[44] This refers to consecutive, periodical crouches on the tips of one's toes, each lasting for five-minute intervals.

[45] The Torture case, *supra* note 39.

[46] *Id.*

[47] *Id.*

rights in an excessive manner. They are not to be deemed as included within the general power to conduct interrogations.

In spite of these strong and clear words, absolutely forbidding any use of torture (in the wide sense) during investigations conducted by the ISA, the Court opened a window for the executive to continue using torture in extreme circumstances, in the form of the criminal defense of necessity. At the end of its decision, the Court stated that in rare and extreme circumstances the investigator may enjoy – *ex post facto* – the necessity defense to bar individual criminal liability.[48] The decision was therefore justly criticized for creating – and allowing for – a gap between the general and absolute norm prohibiting torture and the practical immunity that could be given to torturers.[49]

Nonetheless, this decision is both brave and important: brave because this unpopular decision was given at a sensitive time, when suicide bombers attacked Israeli buses and cafes regularly, leading to many civilian casualties; important because at least theoretically it stated out loud that torture should be interpreted widely and that there is no exception to the prohibition on torture. The Court used this opportunity to annul an important executive authority and to redefine the limits of the government's authorities in a sensitive and contested national security issue.

B. *Criminal Pre-trial Detentions*

Criminal detentions are at the heart of both the rule of law doctrine and the judicial power. Normally, pretrial detention can be order for a period of no more than fifteen days, which can be extended for no more than fifteen days at a time, for a period of up to thirty days (unless approved by the attorney general).[50] If the arrest warrant was issued *ex parte*, the detainee must be brought before a judge within twenty-four hours.[51] The warrant itself must be in writing and must include all of the relevant details, including the reason for the arrest.[52] The detainee has a right to meet with his or her attorney, and that meeting can be delayed for only several hours (or up to forty-eight hours in extreme circumstances).[53] Nonetheless, if the detainee is

[48] *Id.*

[49] See, for example, M. Kremnitzer & R. Segev, *The Legality of Interrogational Torture: A Question of Proper Authorization or a Substantive Moral Issue?*, 34 *Israel Law Review* 509 (2000); Barak Cohen, Democracy and the misrule of law: The Israeli legal system's failure to prevent torture in the occupied territories, 12 *Ind. Int'l & Comp. L. Rev.* 76 (2002). For a different approach, see Yuval Shany, The prohibition against torture and cruel, inhuman, and degrading treatment and punishment: Can the absolute be relativized under existing international law?, 56 *Cath. U. L. Rev.* 840 (2007).

[50] The Criminal Procedure Law (Enforcement Powers – Detentions), 2006, article 17 [hereinafter: *detentions law*].

[51] *Id*, at article 17.

[52] *Id*, at article 18.

[53] *Id*, at article 34.

accused with security-related offenses (including violations of the infiltration law that applies to unlawful immigrants), the meeting with his or her lawyer can be postponed for a period of up to twenty-one days.[54]

In 2006, the Israeli legislator introduced a "temporary law" amending some of the detentions law rules with regard to suspected terrorists. This "temporary law," which is still is force and will soon celebrate its eighth birthday,[55] was enacted as a temporary law (for a period of eighteen months) in order to constitute a legal framework for the detention of Gaza residents, similar to the one that was in force in Gaza under the Israeli military law (which was in force until Israel withdrew from Gaza in September 2005). However, the temporary order's scope of application included any individual who is charged with a security-related offense and did not limit itself to Gaza residents only.

The Criminal Procedure Law (Detainee Suspected of Security Offenses) (Emergency Order), 2006 (hereinafter: *Security Offenses Law*) allows the state to interrogate the suspect – without bringing him or her before a court – for a period of ninety-six hours. The security offenses law also allows the state to detain a suspect for a period of thirty-five days before he or she is officially charged with anything (the maximum length of each detention order will not exceed twenty days).

Pursuant to section 3 of the security offenses law, security suspects may be detained for up to ninety-six hours before being brought before a judge, as opposed to forty-eight hours in other cases. The law also provides for a subsequent judicial remand hearing in the absence of the detainee for up to twenty days.

On February 2010, the Israeli Supreme Court gave an important decision to strike down the provision that enabled courts to conduct detention hearings *in abstentia* in cases involving suspects charged with security offenses.[56] This was the seventh time in the Court's history that it declared a law enacted by parliament as unconstitutional and only the second time that it revoked security-related legislation. The case involved A, who was detained as a suspected member of an unlawful association. The state requested to conduct the proceedings to prolong the suspect's criminal detention *in abstentia*, under the regime of the security offenses law, and its request was granted by the Magistrate Court (and later upheld by the District Court). A appealed this decision before the Israeli Supreme Court. Among other claims, A argued that this provision is unconstitutional, as it infringes on basic

54 *Id*, at article 35.

55 This "temporary order" has been extended again and again, and is now in force at least until 2015 (when it could be extended once again). The Criminal Procedure Law (Detainee Suspected of Security Offenses) (Emergency Order), 2006.

56 CHR [Criminal Hearing Request] 8823/07 Ploni v. State of Israel [2010] (not published) [in Hebrew] (hereinafter: the *Criminal Detention* case).

human rights and that it is also contrary to Israel's obligations under international humanitarian law.[57]

In its decision, the Supreme Court unanimously found the provision to be unconstitutional and in violation of the due process requirements.[58] Still, the decision to strike down the article was accepted by a majority of eight to one, the sole dissenting Justice opining that the revocation of the article should be postponed by six months in order to allow the legislature to take appropriate steps to remedy the legislation in question.[59] With regard to the constitutionality of the provision, the Court held that the defendant's right to be present at his or her criminal trial is part of the due process rights, which are an essential part of the constitutional right to liberty, established in Basic Law: Human Dignity and Liberty.[60] After examining the compliance of the provision with the terms of the Basic Law's limitation clause (limitation by law, compatibility with the values of the state, an aim to further a worthy cause and proportionality), the Court found that the provision does not meet the tests of proportionality and, hence, must be annulled.[61]

Furthermore, the Court discussed the connection between the right to be present in the Court's proceedings and interrogation methods.[62] In its arguments, the state claimed that without this provision the success of security offenses' interrogations would be in danger. The Court rejected this argument and held that in a democratic society, the effective interrogation of a subject in detention must include meaningful judicial review. Therefore, the methods of interrogation must be modified in order to allow effective and fair judicial review. The Court concluded its decision by noting that constitutional order must be protected even in the face of counter-terrorism imperatives, because the rule of law is integral to the strength of democratic societies.[63]

In her dissenting opinion, Justice Naor agreed that this provision is unconstitutional, but opined that it should not be immediately annulled but rather the Court should allow the Knesset a period of six months to amend the provision and to set narrower restrictions on its application.[64] According to Justice Naor, the state should be

57 For a more elaborated description of the proceedings in this case, see Ido Rozenzweig and Yuval Shany, Israeli Supreme Court decision: A suspect charged with security offenses must be allowed to attend judicial detention hearings, 14 *Terrorism and Democracy* (2010), available at http://en.idi.org.il/analysis/terrorism-and-democracy/issue-no-14/israeli-supreme-court-decision-a-suspect-charged-with-security-offenses-must-be-allowed-to-attend-judicial-detention-hearings (last accessed February 1, 2014).

58 Criminal Detention case, *supra* note 56.

59 *Id*, per Justice Naor's opinion.

60 *Id*, per Justice Rivlin's opinion, writing for the majority.

61 *Id*.

62 *Id*.

63 *Id*.

64 *Id*, per Justice Naor's opinion.

allowed to resort to the provision in the rare cases of an unequivocal need to conduct detention proceedings *in absentia* in order to prevent risking lives (such as "ticking bomb" situations).

The Supreme Court rarely issues decisions that strike down legislation, especially when dealing with security-related issues. This decision, therefore, may signify a greater willingness of the Court to review security measures that compromise human rights, especially in cases that endanger the due process and the fairness of judicial proceedings and that interfere with the Court's domain.

Nonetheless, the new counter-terrorism bill wishes to reintroduce this harmful legislation, with some constraints (mainly, that the *in absentia* hearing will be reserved for cases in which it is necessary to prevent terror activities).

V. PROSCRIPTION AND LISTING OF TERRORIST GROUPS AND INDIVIDUALS

Article 2 of the Terror Financing Law authorizes the Security Cabinet to declare a foreign association to be a terrorist organization based on a relevant designation by a foreign country or by the United Nations Security Council.[65] Article 4 of the terror financing law allows individuals designated as terrorists, organizations designated as terrorist organizations or anyone else who has been directly affected by the Security Cabinet's declarations to petition the Advisory Committee at the Ministry of Justice to request the revocation of the declaration. Declarations by the Security Cabinet obligate Israeli banks and financial institutions to monitor accounts and financial transactions linked to the designated organizations and to report any suspicious activity to the Israel Money Laundering and Terror Financing Prohibition Authority.[66]

VI. REGULATION OF TERRORISM FINANCING

In April 2002, the International Convention for the Suppression of the Financing of Terrorism, of which Israel is a member, entered into force. To fulfill its obligations under the convention, the state of Israel adopted, in 2004, the financing of terrorism law described earlier. The law did not quash the previous legislation (which included, mainly, the Prevention of Terrorism Ordinance and the Defense Regulations), and it only adds new tools to the existing legislation. Regulation 84(2) of the Defense Regulations authorizes the search and confiscation of any asset that is used by or intended to be used by an unlawful association. The regulation requires

65 Prohibition on Terror Financing Law 5765-2004, article 2.

66 For further discussion of this issue, see Ido Rozenzweig and Yuval Shany, Israeli Security Cabinet declared 50 groups to be "terrorist organizations"11 *Terrorism and Democracy* (2009).

anyone – including third parties – to provide information on any such assets.[67] The regulation further vests other significant powers with the Minister of Finances, including entry and search.[68] In applying these powers, there is no requirement to

[67] The full language of regulation 84 states:
(1) In this part, the expression "unlawful association" means any body of persons, whether incorporated or unincorporated and by whatsoever name (if any) it may from time to time be known, which –
(a) by its constitution or propaganda or otherwise advocates, incites or encourages any of the following unlawful acts, that is to say – (i) the overthrow by force or violence of the constitution of Palestine or the Government of Palestine; (ii) the bringing into hatred or contempt of, or the exciting of disaffection against, His Majesty's Government in the United Kingdom or the Government of Palestine or the High Commissioner in his official capacity; (iii) the destruction of or injury to property of His Majesty's Government in the United Kingdom or of the Government of Palestine; (iv) acts of terrorism directed against servants of His Majesty's Government in the United Kingdom or against the High Commissioner or against servants of the Government of Palestine; or which has committed or has claimed to have been responsible for, or to have been concerned in, any such acts as are mentioned in sub-paragraph (ii), (iii) or (iv) of this paragraph; or
(b) is declared by the High Commissioner to be an unlawful association and includes a branch, centre, committee, group, faction or institution of any such body.
(2) On coming into force of a declaration by the High Commissioner under paragraph (b) of subregulation (1) that any body of persons is an unlawful association, the following consequences shall ensue, that is to say:–
(a) every person having in his possession, custody or control any property (which expression means moveable and immoveable property of all kinds) of the association, and every person with whom the association has any account or deposit or by whom any sum is or will be payable to the association, shall, within forty-eight hours, send a written notice of that fact (giving true and full particulars thereof) to the Financial Secretary by registered post;
(b) the Financial Secretary may give directions to any such person (whether or not that person has complied with subregulation (1)) forfeiting any such property, or the amount due on any such account or the deposit or amount payable to the High Commissioner and requiring such person to transfer, surrender, pay or otherwise make the same available to the High Commissioner in such manner as may be provided in the directions;
(c) no person shall remove, deal with or part with the possession, custody or control of any property, account, deposit or sum payable as mentioned in paragraph (a), otherwise than in accordance with directions given under paragraph (b), without permission given by or on behalf of the Financial Secretary;
(d) any police officer and person generally or specially authorized by the Financial Secretary may enter any premises in which he may have cause to believe that there is any property, or any document relating to any property or account or deposit or sum payable, which is mentioned in paragraph (a) and may search the said premises and may examine and take possession of and retain any such property or document pending the directions of the Financial Secretary under paragraph (b);
(e) every person shall give truthfully any information in his possession which is demanded by, or by any person acting under the general or special orders of, the Financial Secretary regarding any property, account, deposit or sum payable which is mentioned in subregulation (a);
(f) any person who contravenes any provision of this sub-regulation, or of any direction or requirement thereunder, shall be guilty of an offence against these Regulations.

[68] Defense (Emergency) Regulations, 1945, Regulation 82(2)(6).

prove any connection to specific terror activities – all that is required is that the assets are linked to an unlawful association, no matter what their specific purpose or use.[69] In the past, the Minister of Defense declared not only terror organizations as unlawful associations according to regulation 84, but also with regard to organizations that are involved in financing of terrorism.[70]

In addition to confiscation, the Defense Regulations include criminal prohibitions relevant to financing of terrorism, with a penalty of up to ten years' imprisonment. These prohibitions include holding possessions belonging to or benefiting an unlawful association;[71] receiving donations on behalf of an unlawful association;[72] or providing a service to an unlawful association.[73] In addition to these preventative measures, the Defense Regulations include a punitive confiscation measure, allowing the confiscation of any asset belonging to a person who participated, assisted or attempted to participate in a violation of the regulation, including acts of violence or terrorism.[74]

The prevention of terrorism ordinance includes several other measures that are directly relevant to the financing of terrorism. The ordinance adopted a wide definition of membership in a terror organization (up to five years' imprisonment), which specifically includes individuals who collect money or property for the benefit of the terror organization. The ordinance further criminalizes supporting of a terror organization (up to three years' imprisonment) and specifically includes in this prohibition individuals who provide money or property to a terror organization.

The ordinance authorizes the general inspector of the police to order the seizure of any property belonging to a terror organization and to request a District Court to approve its final confiscation. The ordinance includes a presumption that any assets or property that are found in a place used by the terror organization (even sporadically or on a certain occasion) or at the premises of a member of a terror organization will be considered a terror organization property unless proven otherwise.

While confiscation according to the Defense Regulations is an administrative power, the confiscation according to the ordinance includes a judicial review process by a District Court. Another importance difference between the two processes is that the ordinance does not allow confiscation of property that was *intended* for a terror organization.[75]

69 Gilad Noam, *The Legal Battle Against the Financing of Terrorism in Israel*, 79 IDI Policy Paper (2009), at p. 55.

70 *Id.*

71 Defense (Emergency) Regulations, 1945, Regulation 85(1)(6).

72 Defense (Emergency) Regulations, 1945, Regulation 85(1)(8).

73 Defense (Emergency) Regulations, 1945, Regulation 85(1)(3).

74 Defense (Emergency) Regulations, 1945, Regulation 120.

75 For elaboration on these and other differences between the Defense Regulations and the ordinance, see: Noam, *The Legal Battle Against the Financing of Terrorism*, *supra* note 69, at p. 61.

After Israel joined the Financing Convention in 2003, it became obvious that both the Defense Regulations and the ordinance are not sufficient to fulfill its obligations under the International Financing Convention. Therefore, the parliament adopted, in 2005, a new legislation that seeks to complement the exciting tools with new methods to address issues stemming from international terrorism that are not necessarily linked to the state of Israel.[76] Therefore, the financing of terrorism law does not require criminal jurisdiction and is satisfied with "double criminality," meaning that the act should be a crime in both Israel and the place in which it was committed.[77]

As a part of the effort to integrate the international efforts to fight terrorism in Israeli legislation, the financing law authorizes the ministerial committee, when deciding on declarations of terror organizations, to rely on external declarations (made by foreign states or organizations).[78] While the law includes a process to challenge a declaration made according to the committee, this administrative process is complicated and puts an even harder burden on those infringed by the declaration than the judicial process adopted by the ordinance.[79]

The financing of terrorism law includes three criminal offenses relating to property: the use of property for purposes of terrorism (ten years' imprisonment);[80] the use of terror property or the use of property to aid or finance a terror activity or providing property for the use of a terror organization (seven years' imprisonment);[81] and violating duties of reporting property activities (one year imprisonment).[82] This last criminal prohibition is extremely wide and vague; does not exclude attorney-client privileges from the duty to report; applies not only to bankers but to every person who is involved with acts concerning property (including buying or selling a used car); and is satisfied with reasonable suspicion that the act may aid a terror activity.[83]

Lastly, the financing of terrorism law includes three distinct mechanisms for confiscating property: a judicial confiscation after a conviction in a criminal prosecution; a judicial confiscation as a part of a civil case involving a terror organization or terror activities that have no linkage to Israel; and an administrative seizure of terror property concerning a terror organization or activity that has no linkage to Israel.

76 *Id*, p. 65.
77 Prohibition on Terror Financing Law 5765-2004, article 1.
78 *Id*, article 2.
79 Noam, *The Legal Battle Against the Financing of Terrorism*, *supra* note 69, at footnote 220.
80 Prohibition on Terror Financing Law 5765-2004, article 8.
81 *Id*, article 9.
82 *Id*, article 10.
83 For a thorough analysis of this prohibition, see Noam, *The Legal Battle against the Financing of Terrorism*, *supra* note 69, at pp. 84–98.

VII. IMMIGRATION MEASURES

The state of Israel uses several laws to deal with the phenomenon of illegal immigration. One of the central legal tools in this area is the Prevention of Infiltration Act, which was enacted in 1954 to address the problem of Palestinian *fedayeen*, armed militia members who attempted to infiltrate to attack Israeli targets, which was considered to be a security threat at the time; the symbolic significance of applying this particular "securitization discourse" to all asylum seekers should not be underestimated.[84]

This law was recently revived, as refugees, asylum seekers and other illegal immigrants from Africa started entering Israel through its southern border with Egypt. In 2012, the Israeli parliament passed an amendment to the Prevention of Infiltration Act. The amended act defines any person who is not a resident of Israel and who enters Israel without authorization as an "infiltrator." The new legislation thus defines all persons entering Israel through Israel's southern border, many of whom are prospective asylum seekers, as "infiltrators."[85] More importantly, the amendment authorized their immediate and automatic detention for a period of up to three years. Concurrently, Israel established in the south large detention facilities with the capacity to detain thousands of illegal immigrants.[86]

On September 16, 2013, the Israeli Supreme Court, sitting as the High Court of Justice, unanimously quashed Amendment 3 of the Prevention of Infiltration Act, holding it to be unconstitutional, as it violates the constitutional right to liberty.[87] Nonetheless, immediately after quashing this three-year detention regime and holding it to be unconstitutional, the parliament amended the law again, this time allowing for a shorter period, of "only" one year, to detain without trial asylum seekers (and other illegal immigrants).[88] The state further designates the new detention facility as an "open residence facility," with a requirement to report in the facility three times a day to ensure that its residents are not working outside its walls.

In response to these developments, the United Nations High Commissioner for Refugees (UNHCR) issued a statement expressing its concern that the new

84 Ruvi Zigler, *The New Amendment to the "Prevention of Infiltration" Act: Defining Asylum-Seekers as Criminals*, Israel Democracy Institute, January 16, 2012. Available at http://en.idi.org.il/analysis/articles/the-new-amendment-to-the-prevention-of-infiltration-act-defining-asylum-seekers-as-criminals (last accessed January 10, 2014).

85 *Id.*

86 *Id.*

87 HCJ 7146/12 *Adam v. The Knesset* [2013], available at http://elyon1.court.gov.il/files/12/460/071/b24/12071460.b24.pdf (last accessed January 10, 2014).

88 Omri Efraim, *State Ratifies Amendment to Prevention of Infiltration Law*, *Ynet News*, November 24, 2013. Available at http://www.ynetnews.com/articles/0,7340,L-4457427,00.html (last accessed January 10, 2014).

detention regime, including its three-times-per-day reporting requirement and other discipline measures, puts serious restrictions on asylum seekers' freedom of movement. Since the detention facility is housing people who cannot be returned to their countries of origin for reasons of non-refoulement, the organization further expressed its concern that this facility could, in effect, result in indefinite detention, with no release grounds.[89] The statement emphasized that:

> Under the latest Amendment, new asylum-seekers arriving in an irregular manner will automatically be detained for at least a year, as will people whose conditional release visas have expired. Difficulties in renewing visas are meanwhile growing, with renewal possible in four cities and for a few hours each week. Long queues have been reported in some of these locations.[90]

VIII. SECRECY: PREVENTIVE (SECURITY) DETENTIONS AS A CASE STUDY

Since its founding in 1948, the state of Israel has used several security detention regimes to cope with various national security threats.[91] Over the years, Israel held thousands of individuals – mostly Palestinians from the West Bank and Gaza – in security detention for periods ranging from several months to several years.[92] The highest number of security detainees was documented during the first intifada. In November 1989, Israel was holding 1,794 Palestinians in security detention.[93] During the 1990s, the number of security detainees dramatically decreased, and at the end of the decade there were no more than a few dozen security detainees.[94] In December 2000, ten weeks after the second intifada had erupted, Israel held twelve Palestinians in security detention.[95] However, in April 2002, during Operation

89 UNHCR, *UNHCR is concerned at new Amendment to Israel's Law on the Prevention of Infiltration,"* January 10, 2014, available at http://www.unhcr.org/52cfe2a09.html (last accessed January 10, 2014).

90 *Id.*

91 This section is based on some of my previous studies: Shiri Krebs, Lifting the veil of secrecy: Judicial review of administrative detentions in the Israeli Supreme Court (2012) 45(3) *Vanderbilt J of Transnational L* 639; National security, secret evidence and preventive detentions: The Israeli Supreme Court as a case-study, in David D. Cole, Federico Fabbrini, Arianna Vedaschi (eds.) *Secrecy, National Security and the Vindication of Constitutional Law* (Cheltenham, UK: Edward Elgar Publishing, 2013); and Shiri Krebs, The secret keepers: Judges, security detentions, and secret evidence, in Liora Lazarus and Ryan Goss (eds.) Reasoning Rights (London: Hart Publishing, 2014).

92 These numbers were provided to the Israeli non-governmental organization (NGO) B'Tselem by the Israeli Prison Service (IPS), according to its obligations under the Freedom of Information Act of 1998. Hamoked Ctr. for the Def. of the Individual & B'tselem, *Without Trial: Administrative Detention of Palestinians by Israel and the Incarceration of Unlawful Combatants Law* (2009), p. 13, available at http://www.btselem.org/ Download/200910_Without_Trial_Eng.pdf.

93 *Id.*

94 *Id.*

95 *Id.*

Defensive Shield, Israel detained hundreds of Palestinians in the West Bank.[96] By the end of the year, more than 900 Palestinians were detained.[97] Since then, the number of security detainees has constantly decreased,[98] and only 204 detainees remained in December 2010.[99] Today the number of security detainees stands at 147. Over the years, Israel has also held a few Israeli citizens in security detention, both Arabs and Jews.[100] However, these cases were scarce, and most of the Israeli detainees were held for short periods.[101]

The resort to such an expansive security detention regime was justified by Israel as a "state of emergency" necessity.[102] At its founding in 1948, Israel applied a "state of emergency" legal regime in its territory, a state of affairs that is valid and implemented in Israel to this day.[103] In 1991, when Israel joined the International Convention on Civil and Political Rights of 1966, it informed the Secretary General of the United Nations that a state of emergency existed within the state and accordingly declared derogation from the right to personal liberty, as enshrined in the Convention.[104] In its declaration dated October 3, 1991, Israel stated that:

> [T]he State of Emergency which was proclaimed in May 1948 has remained in force ever since. This situation constitutes a public emergency within the meaning of article 4 (1) of the Covenant. The Government of Israel has therefore found it necessary, in accordance with the said article 4, to take measures to the extent strictly required by the exigencies of the situation, for the defence of the State and for the protection of life and property, including the exercise of powers of arrest and detention. In so far as any of these measures are inconsistent with article 9 of the Covenant, Israel thereby derogates from its obligations under that provision.[105]

This legal regime enables the state, under certain conditions, to derogate from the right to personal liberty.[106] Arguably, under this derogation regime, the state

96 *Id.*

97 *Id.*

98 One of the main reasons for the dramatic decrease in the numbers of detainees was probably the decision of the Israeli Supreme Court in the Mar'ab case, which prohibited the practice of mass detentions without prompt judicial review. HCJ 3239/02 *Mar'ab v IDF Commander in the West Bank* 57(2) PD 349 [2002] (Isr).

99 B'Teselm, Statistics on Administrative Detention, available at http://www.btselem.org/english/administrative_detention/Statistics.asp (last accessed August 20, 2013).

100 Hamoked Ctr. for the Def. of the Individual & B'Tselem, *supra* note 93, at 66.

101 *Id.*

102 Status: International Covenant on Civil and Political Rights, United Nations Treaty Collection (1 March 2012), available at http://treaties.un.org/pages/ViewDetails.aspx?src=TREATY&mtdsgno=IV-4&chapter=4&lang=en (stating Israel's reservations to the Covenant).

103 *Id.*

104 *Id.*

105 *Id.*

106 International Covenant on Civil and Political Rights, art. 4(1), opened for signature 19 December 1966, 999 U.N.T.S. 171, 174 (entered into force March 23, 1976).

is not limited to the use of criminal detentions, but can also confront individual "dangerousness" by the use of security detentions, if criminal proceedings are not feasible, for various reasons.[107]

Currently, Israel employs three different security detention regimes to detain Israelis, Palestinians from the West Bank and foreign "unlawful combatants." The main differences among these legal regimes relate to the maximum length of each individual detention order, the authority that issues the detention order, the courts that review them and the promptness and frequency of the judicial review. Generally, the detention regime least harmful to individual freedom is the regime that applies in the Israeli territory; a more harmful regime is the one employed by the Israeli military in the West Bank, and the most harmful is the detention regime that applies to alien unlawful combatants.

In Israeli territory, the Emergency Powers (Detentions) Law of 1979 (IDL) applies.[108] Under the IDL regime, the Minister of Defense is vested with the authority to order a person's detention without trial for the protection of state security and public safety for a period of up to six months. The detention may be extended indefinitely by issuing repeat orders.[109] The IDL mandates judicial review by the civilian court system;[110] initially, within forty-eight hours from the time of arrest[111] and then repeatedly every three months.[112] Since detention orders are often based on secret evidence, the IDL specifies that while assessing the secret evidence, the reviewing judge is not bound by the regular rules of evidence.[113] In particular, the judge may "admit evidence not in the presence of the detainee or his representative, or without revealing it to them," if he or she is convinced that disclosure of the evidence is liable to "harm the security of the region or public security."[114]

In the West Bank (and until recently also in Gaza) – an area regarded by Israeli courts as subject to belligerent occupation – military law applies and independently authorizes preventive detention.[115] The most recent military order governing

107 HCJ 3239/02 *Marab v IDF Commander in the West Bank* 57(2) PD 349, paras. 21–4 [2002] (Isr); HCJ 7/48 *Al-Karbuteli v Minister of Defence* 2(1) PD 5, 97 [1949–50] (Isr), para 13; see also HCJ 5784/03 *Salama v IDF Commander in Judea and Samaria* 57(6) PD 721, para 7 [2003] (Isr).

108 Emergency Powers (Detention) Law, 5739-1979, 33 LSI 89 (1979) (Isr).

109 *Id*, § 2(a).

110 Mara Rudman and Mazen Qupty, The Emergency Powers (Detention) Law: Israel's courts have a mission – should they choose to accept it? (1989) 21 *Columbia Human Rights L Rev* 469, 470–1 (1989); see also Itzhak Zamir, Preventive detention (1983) 18 *Israel L Rev* 150, 153.

111 Emergency Powers (Detention) Law § 4(a).

112 *Id*, § 5.

113 *Id*, § 6. For discussion on secret evidence in Israeli preventive detention proceedings, see Daphne Barak-Erez and Matthew Waxman, Secret evidence and the due process of terrorist detentions, 48 *Colum. J. Transnat'l L.* 3, 20–1 (2009), p. 19.

114 Emergency Powers (Detention) Law § 6(c).

115 See, e.g., HCJ 7957/04 *Mara'abe v Prime Minister of Isr.*, 45 I.L.M. 202, 207 (2006) (Isr.); HCJ 2056/04 *Beit Sourik Vill. Council v Gov't of Isr.* 58(5) PD 807, para 23 [2005] (Isr.); HCJ 3799/02 *Adalah*

preventive detentions in the West Bank is Preventive Detentions Order No. 1591 (MDO).[116] The MDO authorizes IDF's military commanders to detain a person for a maximum period of six months when there is "a reasonable basis to believe that the security of the region or public security" requires it.[117] Here too, the detention may be extended indefinitely, six months at a time.[118] The detainee must be brought before a military judge within eight days to determine whether the detention is justified.[119] Similar to the IDL regime, the MDO includes a provision permitting the use of secret evidence that is not revealed to the detainee or his or her representative and permits deviations from the regular rules of evidence.[120] The military court's decision may be appealed in the Military Court of Appeals (MCA) by either the detainee or the military commander.[121] Although, according to the MDO, the decision of the MCA should be the last instance of review for the military commander's decision, a practice has developed over the years of submitting *habeas corpus* petitions to the Israeli Supreme Court, sitting as High Court of Justice, to review the decisions of the MCA.[122]

In 2002, the Israeli parliament introduced a new security detentions law: the Incarceration of Unlawful Combatants Law of 2002 (UCL).[123] The UCL gives state authorities the power to detain "unlawful combatants," who are as defined in § 2 of the law as persons who have taken part in hostilities against the state of Israel, directly or indirectly, or who are members of a force carrying out hostilities against Israel, and who do not satisfy the conditions of prisoner of war status under international humanitarian law.[124] According to the UCL, persons identified as unlawful combatants may be subject to preventive detention for an unlimited period of time if the Chief of Staff believes that their release will harm state security.[125] Article 5(a) determines that within fourteen days from the date of arrest, the

Legal Ctr. for Arab Minority Rights in Isr. v GOC Cent. Command, 45 I.L.M. 491, 498 (2006) (Isr.); see also Aharon Barak, A judge on judging: The role of a Supreme Court in a democracy (2002) 116 *Harvard L Rev* 16, 148–60; Daphne Barak-Erez, Israel: The security barrier – between international law, constitutional law, and domestic judicial review (2006) 4 *Intl J of Constitutional L* 540, 542–8.

116 Military Order Regarding Preventive Detention (Judea and Samaria) (No. 1591), 5767-2007, § 1 (Isr.), available at www.btselem.org/sites/default/files/ preventive_detention_military_order_1591_eng.pdf.

117 *Id*, § 1(a).

118 *Id*, § 1(b).

119 *Id*, § 4(a).

120 *Id*, §§ 7–8.

121 *Id*, § 5.

122 Esther Rosalind Cohen, Justice for occupied territory? The Israeli High Court of Justice Paradigm (1986) 24 *Columbia J of Transnational L* 471.

123 Incarceration of Unlawful Combatants Law, 5762–2002, SH No. 1834 p. 192, reprinted in Yoram Dinstein and Fania Domb (eds), *Israeli Year Book on Human Rights*, vol. 32 (Leiden, Netherlands: Brill-Nijhoff, 2003), 389.

124 *Id*, art 2.

125 *Id*, art 3(a).

detainee must be brought before a District Court judge to determine whether the detention is justified.[126] A District Court judge must then review the detention every six months.[127] Article 5(e) permits the court to depart from the rules of evidence, including the admittance of evidence without the presence of the detainee or the detainee's lawyer.[128]

All three security detention regimes include a judicial review process before the Israeli Supreme Court. The judicial review process is held in a unique manner: due to the importance of the right to personal liberty, and unlike other appellate proceedings, the Court examines the *case de novo*, assessing all of the relevant information and analyzing all of the relevant evidence, in spite of the fact that it is either an appeal to reverse the District Court's decision (under the IDL and UCL regimes) or a petition to reverse the MCA decision (under the MDO regime).[129] Whether the case is being heard by a sole Justice (IDL and UCL) or by a panel of three Justices (MDO), both the state and the detainee are allowed to plead their case before the court and to present the court with all of the relevant materials.[130] They are not restricted to legal matters or to appellate claims.

After both parties plead their case, the court then conducts, in most cases, an *ex parte* hearing in which the state attorney presents the secret evidence that is meant to justify the detention.[131] In the absence of the detainee or his or her attorney, the court is the one to independently examine the secret evidence and investigate the ISA representatives who collected and assessed the secret evidence.[132] This process has crucial significance in these cases, since in most instances the court's decision is based on these twenty minutes of *ex parte* hearing, and on the credibility, variety, and strength of the secret evidence presented.[133]

From its establishment in 1948 to this day, and out of hundreds of *habeas corpus* petitions, the Israeli Supreme Court ordered the release of security detainees from their preventive detention in six cases, all of which were decided more than a decade ago: the *first* and *second* releases came as early as 1949[134] and 1950[135] – only a year or two after the foundation of the state of Israel, when its security situation

126 *Id*, art 5(a).
127 *Id*, art 5(c).
128 *Id*, art 5(e).
129 This description of the process is based on both interviews with Supreme Court Justices, state attorneys and defense lawyers and on personal observation of dozens of such court hearings.
130 Krebs, *supra* note 92, at 667.
131 *Id.*
132 *Id.*
133 The data were provided to me by the Registrar of the Israel Supreme Court.
134 Ilan Saban, Theorizing and tracing the legal dimensions of a control framework: Law and the Arab-Palestinian minority in Israel's first three decades (1948–1978) (2011) 25 *Emory Intl L Rev* 299, 335 (citing HCJ 7/48 *Al-Karbuteli v Minister of Def.* 2(1) PD 5, paras 14–15 [1949–50] (Isr.)).
135 *Id* (citing HCJ 95/49 *Al-Khouri v Chief of Staff* 4(1) PD 34, 41, 48 [1949] (Isr.)).

was arguably more unstable and while the Israeli state was literally fighting for its existence. Interestingly, neither decision was based on substantial reasons relating to the justifications for, or necessity of, the detentions, but rather on procedural flaws such as a failure to specify in the detention orders the detainee's place of arrest. (In contrast to these decisions, in a recent UCL case, the court identified four different procedural flaws before upholding the detention order.[136]) The *third* and *fourth* decisions to release detainees were given in the 1980s.[137] In *Kawasma*, the Court emphasized the importance of internal State oversight and stated that "[T]he minister of defense should not be a rubber stamp of the ISA [.]"[138] The *fifth* decision is a unique case from 1990 – the only recorded case in which the Israeli Supreme Court ordered the release of an MDO detainee. In its brief decision, the Court held that the secret evidence did not justify the continuation of the detention and

136 Salach was detained in Gaza on January 4, 2009, during Operation Cast Lead. Only twelve days later, an arrest warrant against him – under the UCL detention regime – was issued and signed by the state authorities. The warrant was vague and did not state the reasons for detention or any of the specific allegations against Salach. It took two more days to bring Salach before an IDF officer for an initial hearing. The hearing was brief, and it was unclear whether a translator was present. On January 27, twenty-three days after his initial arrest, a judicial review process before the District Court was first held. In the hearing, the state authorities refused to share any of the information – including his own (alleged) confession – with Salach or his lawyer, and stated that it would be presented to the court during the *ex parte* hearing. On February 3, the detention order was upheld by the District Court. Based on these many procedural flaws, Salach appealed to the Supreme Court. Only on March 30, a day before the Supreme Court hearing, was Salach first interrogated by the police in order to examine the possibility of initiating criminal proceedings against him. The Supreme Court, after considering these many procedural flaws, criticized the way in which the detention process was conducted in this case and set instructions for the future. It criticized the state for refusing to give Salach a gist or even a paraphrased version of his own confession and for failing to consider a criminal prosecution instead of using preventive detention (in light of the existing evidence in Salach's case). Furthermore, the Court stressed that the state authorities should examine the twelve-day gap between the initial arrest and the issue of the detention order and do their best to prevent such incidents in the future. It also stated that it "assumes" that the state authorities will investigate Salach's allegations that he and his son were abused by IDF soldiers following his arrest. The Court further emphasized the importance of holding a meaningful hearing immediately after the arrest, providing the detainee with some information on the accusations against him or her and allowing the detainee to respond to these accusations. It criticized the state for holding back information and for failing to provide Salach with the main accusation against him – that he belongs to the Palestinian "popular front" organization – until late in the proceedings, and for conducting the first police investigation of Salach only a day before the Supreme Court hearing. Considering these flaws, and especially the possibility of initiating criminal proceedings against Salach, the Court ordered the District Court to review the case again in three months time (instead of the mandatory six months.) At the same time, the Court denied the appeal and upheld the detention order, based on the secret evidence that was presented during the *ex parte* stage of the hearing and in spite of determining that the dangerousness of the appellant "is not of a high level." ADA 1949/09 *Salach v State of Israel* [2009] (unpublished decision) (Isr.).

137 ADA 7/88 *A v Minister of Def.* 42(3) PD 133 [1988] (Isr.); ADA 1/82 *Kawasma v Minister of Def.* 36(1) PD 666 [1982] (Isr.).

138 *Kawasma* 36(1) PD at 668–69.

therefore ordered the release of the detainee.[139] The *sixth* and final decision is the *Bargaining Chips* case, where the Court ordered the release of Lebanese detainees that were detained under the IDL as "bargaining chips."[140] All of these decisions were given before the "war on terror" era.

After September 11, 2001, the Court granted only two petitions, and in neither case was a release order given. In the *Marab* case, the Court invalidated military orders that authorized IDF officers in the West Bank to order the detention of a detainee for a period of twelve days (under one order) and eighteen days (under another order), without judicial review.[141] However, this declaration of nullification was suspended for a six-month period, and the Court did not actually order the release of any of the thousands of individuals who were detained according to these orders.[142] In the *Mahmad* case – the only case in the last decade in which the Court reversed a Military Court of Appeals decision – the Court granted the state's petition to reverse the MCA's decision to release a detainee.[143] Farhat As'aad Abdullah Mahmad was detained from February 2003 until September 2005 based on secret intelligence information according to which he was an active member of the Hamas terror organization. In July 2006, less than a year after his release, he was arrested again, based on similar accusations. His security detention was approved by the military court. Mahmad appealed, and the MCA accepted his claims and ordered the state to release him from custody. The decision to release him was based on three main reasons: *first*, the non-military nature of the spokespersonship activities that were attributed to him; *second*, the public nature of these activities, which allowed authorities to follow his moves and collect evidence for criminal trial; and *third*, a rejection of the state's assumption that he would necessarily resume his military activities within Hamas. In an unusual and even extreme move, the state decided to submit a petition to the Supreme Court, sitting as High Court of

139 HCJ 907/90 *Zayad v Military Commander in the W. Bank* [1990] (unpublished decision) (Isr.).

140 The petitioners in this case were Lebanese citizens held by Israeli authorities as bargaining chips in an attempt to obtain the release of an Israeli navigator from captivity. In its decision – reversing its previous judgment on the matter – the Supreme Court held that the desire to release Israelis from captivity does not justify administrative detention. The Court explained that the only legal way to administratively detain the petitioners was under the IDL regime, which only allows for detention that is justified by *individual dangerousness*. Therefore, the Court determined that without individual dangerousness there is no legal basis to continue detaining the petitioners. This judgment motivated the Knesset (the Israeli parliament) to introduce a new security detention regime – UCL – which was discussed earlier. CrimFH 7048/97 *Anonymous Persons v Minister of Def.* 54(1) P.D. 721, 743 [2002] (Isr.).

141 *Military Commander in the W. Bank v Military Court of Appeals* [2007] (unpublished decision) (Isr.); HCJ 3239/02 *Marab v IDF Commander in the W. Bank* 57(2) PD 349 [2002] (Isr.).

142 *Id*, para 36.

143 HCJ 1389/07 *Commander of IDF Forces in the Judea & Samaria Area v Military Court of Appeals* [2007] (Isr.).

Justice (henceforth the Supreme Court), to overrule the decision of the MCA. The Supreme Court, with the consent of both parties, returned the case to the MCA to rehear the security experts and reconsider its previous ruling. After rehearing the state's arguments and reexamining the intelligence information, the MCA decided, again, that the secret evidence did not justify the detention and ordered his release. The state returned to the Supreme Court, insisting that the Court hear the case on its merits. Deviating from its well-founded precedent that the Court will only intervene in rare and unique cases, and that the Court will not replace the MCA's judgment with its own, the Court reversed the release decision based on its own interpretation of the secret evidence. In its final decision, the Supreme Court determined that the MCA's decision was "extremely unreasonable," since the secret evidence indicated that Mahmad's activities within the Hamas organization extended beyond mere spokespersonship. The Court did not elaborate on those other activities and stated only its impression that the activities of the respondent were diverse and embodied significant danger to the safety of the area and the public.[144] This case is the only one in a decade in which the Israeli Supreme Court intervened in an MCA decision in individual detention cases.

In other cases throughout the years, the Court nonetheless shortened the length of the detention orders;[145] reversed a part of the District Court's legal analysis, thus setting out a binding legal framework for the lower court in accordance with the detainees' legal arguments;[146] shortened the time periods between judicial reviews;[147] and included general instructions on security detentions, such as instructions to the state to interrogate detainees immediately after their arrest (invalidating the state's practice of holding Palestinians in preventive detention for long periods of time without conducting any interrogation).[148]

[144] *Id*, para 5.

[145] ADA 10198/09 *Anonymous v State of Israel* [2010] (unpublished decision) (Isr.); ADA 2627/09 *Osama Rashek v State of Israel* [2009] (unpublished decision) (Isr.).

[146] ADA 4794/05 *Ufan v Minister of Def.* para 41 [2005] (unpublished decision) (Isr.); ADA 4414/02 *Anonymous v State of Israel* 57(3) PD 673, 677 [2002] (Isr.); ADA 7750/08 *A. v State of Israel* [2008] (unpublished decision) (Isr.).

[147] ADA 2595/09 *Sofi v State of Israel para* 27 [2009] (unpublished decision) (Isr.) (ordering to hold the next judicial review process within three months); ADA 6409/10 *Al-Amudi v State of Israel* para 5 [2010] (unpublished decision) (Isr.); ADA 6406/10 *Sarski v State of Israel* para 5 [2010] (unpublished decision) (Isr.); ADA 2156/10 *Anonymous v State of Israel* para 13 [2010] (unpublished decision) (Isr.); ADA 9257/09 *Anonymous v State of Israel* para 6 [2009] (unpublished decision) (Isr.). In the last four cases, the Court did not intervene in the timing of the judicial review process *per se*, but ordered the state security authorities to review the necessity of the detention every month.

[148] See, e.g., HCJ 1546/06 *Gazawi v Military Commander in the W. Bank* para 6(3) [2006] (unpublished decision) (Isr.); HCJ 6068/06 *El-Afifi v Military Commander in the W. Bank* para 6(5) [2006] (unpublished decision) (Isr.); HCJ 9015/06 *Taweel v Military Commander in the W. Bank* para 4(2) [2006] (unpublished decision) (Isr.).

A recent case, decided on in 2013, demonstrates the impact of the use of secret evidence on the judicial review process and on the widening gap between the Israeli Supreme Court's rigorous reasoning and its reluctance to act on this reasoning and actually order the release of detainees in appropriate cases. In the *Aberah* case,[149] the Israeli Supreme Court, sitting as High Court of Justice, upheld a detention order based on secret evidence in spite of severe flaws, including the refusal of state authorities to provide the detainee with significant unclassified information. Israeli security authorities suspected Aberah of being a member of, and taking part in the activities of, the Hamas terror organization. Aberah denied these accusations. The evidence the state obtained was not sufficient for criminal proceedings. Therefore, the state issued a security detention order against him, based on secret intelligence information.

Aberah challenged the detention order before the military court. In an effort to refute the secret evidence, his lawyer asked the military prosecutor many questions concerning the reason for the arrest, the type of activity that was attributed to his client, the length of his alleged activity and so forth. The prosecutor did not answer these questions, but instead laconically stated that everything would be presented to the Court during the *ex parte* hearing. After the *ex parte* hearing, the Court determined that the secret evidence was reliable and convincing and affirmed the detention order.

Aberah appealed to the MCA, which was sympathetic to his claims, and emphasized the increased duties of the state authorities in security detention proceedings. Furthermore, the MCA determined that these increased duties included answering questions concerning the secret evidence to the maximum extent possible without endangering sources and confidential information. Nonetheless, after examining the secret evidence, the MCA found that there was reliable and up-to-date information suggesting that Aberah is involved in "dangerous activity that is intended to harm state security." While finding the state's interpretation of the secret evidence "correct and appropriate," the Court did suggest that this conclusion required a "certain interpretation" of the secret evidence. Therefore, the MCA upheld the military court's decision to affirm the detention order against Aberah.

Aberah submitted a petition to the Israeli Supreme Court. Interestingly, the decision was given by Justice Shoham, who was appointed to the Supreme Court in 2012 and who had previously served on the MCA. In his decision, Justice Shoham reiterated the MCA's determination that the military court, as well as the military prosecution, has "increased duties" to inspect the secret evidence carefully and to offer the defense all possible information, providing that it will not harm state

149 HCJ 317/13 *Aberah v The Military Commander in the West Bank* (unpublished decision from January 27, 2013).

security. He emphasized the Court's role as the detainee's lawyer during the *ex parte* hearing, serving as the detainee's mouth and scrutinizing the secret evidence in a deep, thorough and comprehensive manner. Once again, the Court emphasized the priority that should be given to criminal proceedings, whenever it is possible, as well as the duty to conduct meaningful investigation at an early stage.

After considering the secret evidence and the nature of the information requested by the defense in this case, the Court determined that there was no reason to abstain from answering the defense's questions, since to do so did not risk revealing secret information that would harm state security. The Court determined that neither the military prosecution nor the military court fulfilled their duties to the detainee by providing him with all relevant and necessary information. The Court stated that in future cases, the military prosecutor should be well briefed by the security agency investigators and be prepared to answer the detainee council's questions in a sincere and genuine effort to provide the defense with the full information, without compromising the secrecy of the confidential material.

Nonetheless, the Court did not return the case to the Military Court for rehearing, this time with proper defense. Rather, it dismissed the petition and upheld the detention order. While disclosing most of the information to Aberah, the Court did not seem to think that this new development had any impact on the judicial review process. Moreover, the Court examined, *ex parte*, the judicial evidence and determined that the secret evidence was clear and required no "interpretation" in order to conclude that Aberah was dangerous and should remain behind bars.

The decision of the Israeli Supreme Court in the *Aberah* case emphasizes the impact of secret evidence on the judicial review process: the Court interprets the secret evidence without any involvement or participation by the detainee, without allowing the detainee to defend himself or herself and without tools to assess properly the credibility and meaning of the secret evidence. Moreover, the fact that the Court decided the case based on information that should have been delivered to the detainee and his counsel, without allowing the detainee and his counsel to use the information and to respond to it, undermines basic principles of participation and fairness. Of deep concern is that the Court discounted the possibility that information that was wrongfully withheld from the detainee could potentially have been useful for his defense.

Inherently, the design of the Israeli judicial management model downplays participation and bolsters the judges' ability to determine whether disclosure matters. It builds on an assumption that the judges are capable to determine, independently and without hearing the detainee, whether disclosure matters. Unfortunately, as was revealed in a prior study, it is now evident that even the utmost professional judges are limited in their ability to interpret secret intelligence evidence. It may well be that the Court's decision in *Aberah* was the right one and that its interpretation of the information was correct. Perhaps the information would not have been useful for the detainee and his counsel and would not have made any difference. The point is, we shall never know.

IX. CONCLUSION

The Israeli counter-terrorism laws and policies have a long and bloody history. So long is that history that it is rarely remembered that the early counter-terrorism instruments (which are still in force) were designed to deal with Jewish terrorism: the Defense Regulations, which were enacted by Britain to deal with Jewish resistance to the British mandate over Palestine; and the terrorism prevention ordinance, which was enacted by the four-month-old state of Israel, in response to the assassination of UN peace mediator Count Bernadotte by Jewish terrorists. Interestingly, the newborn Israeli government decided to adopt the same emergency policies that were targeted and designed against its own members. But the assassins of Bernadotte (whose identities were known to the Israeli authorities) were never prosecuted or punished, and in the years that followed the Israeli counter-terrorism policy became an important tool in the Israeli–Palestinian conflict. The new counter-terrorism bill openly renounces these historical roots and clearly defines Palestinian terrorism as its main target.

The Qibya massacre, which signaled a turning point in Israel's early counter-terrorism policy (and the beginning of the end of the policy of reprisals against civilians) also signaled the vague boundaries between the law of war and the law enforcement regimes in the "war on terror." And as it became clear that the world will not tolerate reprisals against civilians in the law of war context, the law enforcement model became more and more tolerant of extreme measures being used against civilians. Current Israeli counter-terrorism laws include "temporary" orders that allow the state to hold criminal proceedings without the presence of the accused; secret evidence has emerged as a convenient tool to justify indefinite preventive detentions of suspected terrorists; and asylum seekers have been treated as infiltrators and as security risks that justify long-term detentions. The new counter-terrorism bill goes further than that and wishes to broaden the definition of terrorism to include humanitarian aid organizations (and other charities and auxiliary organizations) and to treat school teachers and drivers, physicians and cooks, as violent and dangerous terrorists.

"The war against terror is a war of the law against those who seek to destroy it,"[150] determined Justice Aharon Barak, former Chief Justice of the Israeli Supreme Court. But when the law is modified and broadened to adopt draconian and intolerant measures, law becomes a mere continuation of war by other means. The new bill

[150] HCJ 3451/02 *Almadani v. Minister of Defence* [2002] 56(3) IsrSC 30, at 34.

introduces vague and broad criminal prohibitions, vast use of secret evidence and *ex parte* proceedings, long-term preventive detention regimes and severe limitations on freedom of speech. If approved by the Knesset, Israeli counter-terrorism policy would come a full circle, allowing, once again, harm to civilians as a part of an official governmental counter-terrorism policy.

19

South Africa

Jamil Ddamulira Mujuzi

I. EXPERIENCE WITH TERRORISM

The issue of whether or not South Africa has experienced terrorism should be understood in the context of its political history. It is beyond the scope of this chapter to deal with the political history of South Africa. However, it should be noted that the Apartheid government in South Africa used terrorism laws as one of the ways to repress those who were opposed to its racist and oppressive laws and policies. This was clear from the manner in which the 1967 Terrorism Act was introduced.[1] The Act was published on 27 June 1967, but its section 9(1) provided that the Act '…shall be deemed to have come into operation on the twenty-seventh day of June 1962…'. The effect of section 9 was that 'the Act was deemed to have been in force five years before it was adopted and published.'[2] Section 2 of the 1967 Terrorism Act provided for the offence of participating in terrorist activity. There were cases from South African courts in which people were convicted of terrorism on the basis of the Terrorism Act.[3] The High Court observed that there was a 'plethora of prosecutions' under the Terrorism Act.[4] In 1977, the Public Security Act[5] was enacted; one of the offences it created was that of terrorism, and some people were convicted of terrorism on the basis of the Public Security Act.[6] In 1982, the Internal Security Act[7]

1 Terrorism Act 83 of 1967.
2 Christo Botha, Statutory Interpretation : An Introduction for Students (2012) p 56.
3 See, for example, *S v Tuhadeleni and Others* 1969 (1) SA 153 (A) (the appellants were sentenced to lengthy prison terms of terrorist acts committed outside South Africa, that is, in the territory of South-West Africa).
4 *Zuma v National Director of Public Prosecutions* 2009 (1) BCLR 62 (N) para 78.
5 Public Security Act 30 of 1977.
6 See, for example, *S v Ndzamela and Another* 1990 (2) SACR 282 (TKA) (they were convicted of planting a bomb in a casino).
7 Internal Security Act 74 of 1982.

was enacted, and one of the offences it created was that of terrorism.[8] There were also cases from South African courts where people were convicted of terrorism on the basis of the Internal Security Act.[9]

In 2004, South Africa enacted the Protection of Constitutional Democracy Against Terrorist and Related Activities Act.[10] The preamble of this Act specifically mentions the United Nations Security Council Resolution 1373/2001 and provides that this resolution is 'binding on all Member States of the United Nations', including South Africa. This is evidence that this resolution was considered in drafting the Act. The Protection of Constitutional Democracy Against Terrorist and Related Activities Act is the most used counter-terrorism law in South Africa.

II. DEFINITION OF TERRORISM

Section 1(xxv) of the Protection of Constitutional Democracy Against Terrorist and Related Activities Act defines a terrorist activity to mean:

> a) any act committed in or outside the Republic, which – (i) involves the systematic, repeated or arbitrary use of violence by any means or method; (ii) involves the systematic, repeated or arbitrary release into the environment or any part of it or distributing or exposing the public or any part of it to – (aa) any dangerous, hazardous, radioactive or harmful substance or organism; (bb) any toxic chemical; or (cc) any microbial or other biological agent or toxin; (iii) endangers the life, or violates the physical integrity or physical freedom of, or causes serious bodily injury to or the death of, any person, or any number of persons; (iv) causes serious risk to the health or safety of the public or any segment of the public; (v) causes the destruction of or substantial damage to any property, natural resource, or the environmental or cultural heritage, whether public or private; (vi) is designed or calculated to cause serious interference with or serious disruption of an essential service, facility or system, or the delivery of any such service, facility or system, whether public or private, including, but not limited to – (aa) a system used for, or by, an electronic system, including an information system; (bb) a telecommunication service or system; (cc) a banking or financial service or financial system; (dd) a system used for the delivery of essential government services; (ee) a system used for, or by, an essential public utility or transport provider; (ff) an essential infrastructure facility; or (gg) any essential emergency services, such as police,

8 See section 54 of the Act.

9 See, for example, *S v Francis* 1991 (1) SACR 198 (A); *Rapholo v State President and Others* 1993 (1) SACR 421 (T); In *S v Mngomezulu* 1991 (2) SACR 212 (A) the appellant was convicted of terrorism in that he had recruited people to membership of the African National Congress, instructed them in the use of firearms and established arms' caches.

10 Protection of Constitutional Democracy Against Terrorist and Related Activities Act No. 33 of 2004

> medical or civil defence services; (vii) causes any major economic loss or extensive destabilisation of an economic system or substantial devastation of the national economy of a country; or (viii) creates a serious public emergency situation or a general insurrection whether the harm contemplated in paragraphs (a) (i) to (vii) is or may be suffered in or outside the Republic, and whether the activity referred to in subparagraphs (ii) to (viii) was committed by way of any means or method; and (b) which is intended, or by its nature and context, can reasonably be regarded as being intended, in whole or in part, directly or indirectly, to – (i) threaten the unity and territorial integrity of the Republic; (ii) intimidate, or to induce or cause feelings of insecurity within the public, or a segment of the public, with regard to its security, including its economic security, or to induce, cause or spread feelings of terror, fear or panic in a civilian population; or (iii) unduly compel, intimidate, force, coerce, induce or cause a person, a government, the general public or a segment of the public, or a domestic or an international organisation or body or intergovernmental organisation or body, to do or to abstain or refrain from doing any act, or to adopt or abandon a particular standpoint, or to act in accordance with certain principles, whether the public or the person, government, body, or organisation or institution referred to in subparagraphs (ii) or (iii), as the case may be, is inside or outside the Republic; and (c) which is committed, directly or indirectly, in whole or in part, for the purpose of the advancement of an individual or collective political, religious, ideological or philosophical motive, objective, cause or undertaking.

The Preamble to the Protection of Constitutional Democracy Against Terrorist and Related Activities Act refers to international and regional instruments on terrorism. This shows the influence those instruments had on its drafting. There are exceptions to the definition of terrorism. The exceptions are provided for under section 1(4), which provides that:

> Notwithstanding any provision of this Act or any other law, any act committed during a struggle waged by peoples, including any action during an armed struggle, in the exercise or furtherance of their legitimate right to national liberation, self-determination and independence against colonialism, or occupation or aggression or domination by alien or foreign forces, in accordance with the principles of international law, especially international humanitarian law, including the purposes and principles of the Charter of the United Nations and the Declaration on Principles of International Law concerning Friendly Relations and Cooperation among States in accordance with the said Charter, shall not, for any reason, including for purposes of prosecution or extradition, be considered as a terrorist activity, as defined in subsection (1).

Terrorism is not defined differently in different forms of law in South Africa. There is only one definition of terrorism, and it is the preceding one.

III. CRIMINAL LAWS AND PROSECUTION

A. *Criminal Law*

Terrorism is a separate crime provided for under section 2 of the Act, which is to the effect that 'Any person who engages in a terrorist activity is guilty of the offence of terrorism.' As indicated previously, United Nations Security Council Resolution 1373/2001 was influential in drafting the Act, and therefore the punishments were formulated to reflect that resolution. Section 3 deals with the offences associated with or related to terrorist activities. It is to the effect that:

> (1) Any person who – (a) does anything which will, or is likely to, enhance the ability of any entity to engage in a terrorist activity, including to provide or offering to provide a skill or an expertise; (b) enters or remains in any country; or (c) makes himself or herself available, for the benefit of, at the direction of, or in association with any entity engaging in a terrorist activity, and who knows or ought reasonably to have known or suspected, that such act was done for the purpose of enhancing the ability of such entity to engage in a terrorist activity, is guilty of the offence associated with a terrorist activity.
>
> (2) Any person who – (a) provides or offers to provide any weapon to any other person for use by or for the benefit of an entity; (b) solicits support for or gives support to an entity; (c) provides, receives or participates in training or instruction, or recruits an entity to receive training or instruction; (d) recruits any entity; (e) collects or makes a document; or (f) possesses a thing, connected with the engagement in a terrorist activity, and who knows or ought reasonably to have known or suspected that such weapons, soliciting, training, recruitment, document or thing is so connected, is guilty of an offence connected with terrorist activities.

Ordinary criminal laws are not applied to terrorist crimes. There is no evidence that suspected terrorists have been prosecuted for other offences. However, there is a case where a person who was charged with the offence of harbouring and concealing terrorism suspects was convicted of harbouring and concealing escaped prisoners in terms of the Correctional Services Act.[11] Section 14(d) provides for, inter alia, the offence of inciting terrorism. It is to the effect that any person who 'aids, abets, induces, incites, instigates, instructs or commands, counsels or procures another

[11] *S v Bogaards* [2012] 1 All SA 376 (SCA).

person to commit an offence in terms of this chapter, is guilty of an offence.'[12] This provision has not been used.

B. *Terrorism Prosecutions*

There has been one case of terrorism prosecution since the commencement of the Act. This is the case of *S v Okah*,[13] in which the High Court convicted the accused of terrorism[14] for the terrorist acts that were committed in Nigeria. The Court invoked section 14 of the Act and held that it had jurisdiction although the offences were committed outside South Africa. The judge added that '[t]o the extent that it may be held that I am wrong in having found the accused guilty on the main charges, I am of the view that the evidence in any event clearly discloses that the accused conspired with some or all of the individuals mentioned in the indictment to commit the various charges' of terrorism.[15] As indicated previously, the prosecution was conducted in an ordinary High Court as opposed to a specialised court. The Act does not provide for specialised courts for terrorism suspects.

Section 35(5) of the South African Constitution provides that: 'Evidence obtained in a manner that violates any right in the Bill of Rights must be excluded if the admission of that evidence would render the trial unfair or otherwise be detrimental to the administration of justice.' South African courts have developed rich jurisprudence on section 35(5). What is important to note for the purposes of this chapter is that South African courts have held that evidence obtained through torture is inadmissible. The Constitutional Court of South Africa held that if

> ... derivative evidence is obtained as a result of torture there might be compelling reasons of public policy for holding such evidence to be inadmissible even if it can be proved independently of the accused. Otherwise, the ends might be allowed to justify the means. The admission of evidence in such circumstances could easily bring the administration of justice into disrepute and undermine the sanctity of the constitutional right which has been trampled upon.[16]

The South African Supreme Court of Appeal held that evidence obtained through torture, whether the torture was inflicted on the accused or a third party, is inadmissible.[17] Although the preceding two cases did not deal with terrorism, the

[12] Section also section 15(4), which deals with the issue of courts' jurisdiction with respect to the offence of inciting terrorism.

[13] *S v Okah* (SS94/2011) [2013] ZAGPJHC 6 (21 January 2013).

[14] *S v Okah* (SS94/2011) [2013] ZAGPJHC 6 (21 January 2013) para 106.

[15] *S v Okah* (SS94/2011) [2013] ZAGPJHC 6 (21 January 2013) para 105.

[16] *Ferreira v Levin NO and Others; Vryenhoek and Others v Powell NO and Others* 1996 (1) SA 984 (CC); 1996 (1) BCLR 1 para 150.

[17] See *S v Mthembu* 2008(2) SACR 407(SCA).

principle remain the same – evidence obtained through torture is inadmissible in South African law irrespective of the seriousness of the offence. However, courts are yet to pronounce on the admissibility or otherwise of evidence obtained through degrading treatment. Such evidence, like any other evidence, would have to be assessed on the basis of section 35(5) of the Constitution for the Court to determine whether or not it is admissible. In my opinion, like evidence obtained through torture, evidence obtained through degrading treatment should be automatically inadmissible. This is because practice from international human rights bodies such as the Human Rights Committee[18] and the Committee Against Torture[19] is to the effect that such evidence should be inadmissible. Witnesses can testify anonymously without their names being identified in terrorism cases. In *S v Okah*,[20] the Court allowed the main state witness to testify anonymously. The Court justified that decision in the following terms:

> The main witnesses for the State were the accused's two principal accomplices in planning and executing the bombings in Warri and Abuja. The state was granted an application to retain the anonymity of these witnesses for fear of reprisal by those who are still loyal to the accused. The application was also granted as these two witnesses were expected to testify in the trials of other accused currently charged in Nigeria with similar offences arising from the same two bombings in Warri and Abuja. Their identities were, however, verified by myself upon checking exhibits of their respective statements.[21]

Section 35(3)(i) of the South African Constitution provides that an accused person has a right to a fair trial, which includes the right to adduce and challenge evidence. This means, inter alia, that a person accused of terrorism can invoke that section to challenge the evidence of anonymous witnesses. The judge, as it happened in the Okah case, has to verify that such witnesses indeed exist.

Section 18 of the Act provides for the sentences that a court may impose on a person convicted of terrorism. The maximum sentence that a court can impose on a person convicted of terrorism is life imprisonment. It should be recalled that the sentence of life imprisonment is the severest sentence under South African law, as the death penalty was abolished. In *S v Okah*,[22] the offender was sentenced to twenty-four years' imprisonment. The Court held that the sentence it imposed 'should … send the necessary deterrent message to would-be terrorists, wherever they may be.'[23]

18 Concluding Observations of the Human Rights Committee on Austria's fourth periodic report, CCPR/C/AUT/CO/4, 30 October 2007 para 5(a).

19 Concluding Observations of the Committee against Torture on the fourth and fifth combined periodic reports of Austria, CAT/C/AUT/CO/4-5, 20 May 2010, para 5(a)(i).

20 *S v Okah* (SS94/2011) [2013] ZAGPJHC 6 (21 January 2013).

21 *S v Okah* (SS94/2011) [2013] ZAGPJHC 6 (21 January 2013) para 92.

22 *S v Okah* (SS94/2011) [2013] ZAGPJHC 6 (21 January 2013).

23 *S v Okah* (SS94/2011) [2013] ZAGPJHC 6 (26 March 2013) (sentence) para 32.

Thus, the purpose of the sentence was general deterrence. The court did not mention retribution or rehabilitation not even specific deterrence.

C. *Investigative Powers*

In investigating terrorism cases, the police do not have special powers not available in ordinary criminal investigations or cases. In *Minister of Safety and Security and Others v Mohamed and Another*,[24] the applicants were suspected of committing terrorism and contravening 'several sections of the Protection of Constitutional Democracy against Terrorist and Related Activities Act',[25] and the police invoked sections 20 and 21 of the Criminal Procedure Act to obtain a warrant to search their premises and seize several articles. Section 40(a) of the Criminal Procedure Act empowers a peace officer, including a police officer, to arrest any person 'who commits or attempts to commit any offence in his presence.' Section 35(1)(d) of the Constitution provides that 'Everyone who is arrested for allegedly committing an offence has the right to be brought before a court as soon as reasonably possible, but not later than (i) 48 hours after the arrest; or (ii) the end of the first court day after the expiry of the 48 hours, if the 48 hours, expire outside ordinary court hours or on a day which is not an ordinary court day.' This section is applicable to anyone including terrorism suspects. The South African Supreme Court of Appeal held that the police have no right to detain a person for forty-eight hours.[26]

However, there are circumstances in which the forty-eight-hour rule might be extended, and the fact that someone is suspected of terrorism or any other serious offence is not one of the grounds upon which the forty-eight-hour period may be extended.[27] Section 22 of the Act provides for special investigatory powers in terms of which the prosecuting authority is allowed to work hand in hand with the police in investigating alleged or suspected terrorist activities. This power is important because it is prosecution-driven. In other words, unlike in normal circumstances where the police investigate crime without the knowledge of the prosecuting authority, in this case the prosecuting authority initiates the investigation and the police come on board to continue with what the prosecuting authority initiated.

[24] *Minister of Safety and Security and Others v Mohamed and Another* 2012 (1) SACR 321 (SCA).

[25] *Minister of Safety and Security and Others v Mohamed and Another* 2012 (1) SACR 321 (SCA) para 25.

[26] In *Mashilo and Another v Prinsloo* 2013 (2) SACR 648 (SCA) para 16, the Supreme Court of Appeal held that 'The outer limit of 48 hours envisaged in the subsection does not, without more, entitle a policeman to detain someone for that entire period without bringing him to court if it could be done earlier. The subsection obliges police authorities to bring someone before court as soon as is reasonably possible. This is so, whether or not the 48 hour expires before or during the weekend. Expedition relative to circumstances is what is dictated by the subsection and the Constitution. Deliberately obstructive behaviour…is not tolerated.'

[27] See generally *Mashilo and Another v Prinsloo* 2013 (2) SACR 648 (SCA).

Section 12 imposes a duty of any person to report the presence of a person suspected of intending to commit an offence of terrorism, and failure to report such a person is an offence. The law that governs that use of traps and undercover operations is section 252A of the Criminal Procedure Act.[28] Evidence that has been obtained through traps and undercover operations is admissible unless the court decides to exclude it on the basis of section 35(5). Although there are many cases on the issue of evidence obtained through entrapment and undercover operations,[29] the author is not aware of any case that has dealt with the issue of terrorism.

Electronic surveillance collected by intelligence services may be used as evidence in terrorism prosecutions. This is on the basis of section 47 of the Regulation of Interception of Communications and Provision of Communication-Related Information Act,[30] which provides that:

> (1) Information regarding the commission of any criminal offence, obtained by means of any interception, or the provision of any real-time or archived communication-related information, under this Act, or any similar Act in another country, may be admissible as evidence in criminal proceedings or civil proceedings as contemplated in Chapter 5 or 6 of the Prevention of Organised Crime Act.
>
> (2) Any information obtained by the application of this Act, or any similar Act in another country, may only be used as evidence in any criminal proceedings or civil proceedings as contemplated in Chapter 5 or 6 of the Prevention of Organised Crime Act, with the written authority of the National Director, or any member of the prosecuting authority authorised thereto in writing by the National Director.

[28] Section 252A(1) provides that 'Any law enforcement officer, official of the State or any other person authorised thereto for such purpose (hereinafter referred to in this section as an official or his or her agent) may make use of a trap or engage in an undercover operation in order to detect, investigate or uncover the commission of an offence, or to prevent the commission of any offence, and the evidence so obtained shall be admissible if that conduct does not go beyond providing an opportunity to commit an offence: Provided that where the conduct goes beyond providing an opportunity to commit an offence a court may admit evidence so obtained subject to subsection (3).' Section 252A(3)(a) provides that '(3) (a) If a court in any criminal proceedings finds that in the setting of a trap or the engaging in an undercover operation the conduct goes beyond providing an opportunity to commit an offence, the court may refuse to allow such evidence to be tendered or may refuse to allow such evidence already tendered, to stand, if the evidence was obtained in an improper or unfair manner and that the admission of such evidence would render the trial unfair or would otherwise be detrimental to the administration of justice.'

[29] See, for example, *S v Odugo* 2001 (1) SACR 560 (W); *Amod v S* 2001 (4) All SA 13 (E); *S v Kotzè* 2010 (1) SACR 100 (SCA); *S v Van der Berg and Another* 2009(1) SACR 661(C); *S v Nnasolu And Another* 2010 (1) SACR 561 (KZP); *S v Zürich* 2010 (1) SACR 171 (SCA).

[30] Regulation of Interception of Communications and Provision of Communication-Related Information Act No. 70 of 2002.

IV. PROSCRIPTION AND LISTING OF TERRORIST GROUPS AND INDIVIDUALS

Section 25 of the Act provides that

> The President must, by Proclamation in the Gazette, and other appropriate means of publication, give notice that the Security Council of the United Nations, under Chapter VII of the Charter of the United Nations, has identified a specific entity as being – (a) an entity who commits, or attempts to commit, any terrorist and related activity or participates in or facilitates the commission of any terrorist and related activity; or (b) an entity against whom Member States of the United Nations must take the actions specified in Resolutions of the said Security Council, in order to combat or prevent terrorist and related activities.

On the basis of section 25 and in line with UN Security Council Resolution 1267, different South African presidents have issue notifications on the entities identified by the UN Security Council as 'entities that commit, or attempt to commit, any terrorist and related activity or participate in or facilitate the commission of any terrorist and related activity; or entities against whom Member States of the United Nations must take the actions specified in the Resolutions of the said Security Council, in order to combat or prevent terrorist and related activities.'[31] All these notifications give effect to the UN Security Council lists of Al-Qaeda individuals or groups associated with Al Qaeda. I am not aware of any challenges to the listing process and the change of a listing decision in response to a court challenge.

V. REGULATION OF TERRORISM FINANCING

Section 4 of the Act criminalises terrorism financing. Section 4(1) provides that

> (1) Any person who, directly or indirectly, in whole or in part, and by any means or method – (a) acquires property; (b) collects property; (c) uses property; (d) possesses

[31] Proclamation by the President of the Republic of South Africa, Notification by President in Respect of Entities Identified by the United Nations Security Council: Section 25 of the Protection of Constitutional Democracy Against Terrorist and Related Activities Act, 2004, No. R. 51, 2006, 22 December 2006; Proclamation by the President of the Republic of South Africa, Notification by President in Respect of Entities Identified by the United Nations Security Council: Section 25 of the Protection of Constitutional Democracy Against Terrorist and Related Activities Act, 2004, No. R. 14, 2006, 22 March 2006; Proclamation by the President of the Republic of South Africa, Notification by President in Respect of Entities Identified by the United Nations Security Council: Section 25 of the Protection of Constitutional Democracy Against Terrorist and Related Activities Act, 2004, No. R. 13, 2006, 22 March 2006; Proclamation by the President of the Republic of South Africa, Notification by President in Respect of Entities Identified by the United Nations Security Council: Section 25 of the Protection of Constitutional Democracy Against Terrorist and Related Activities Act, 2004, No. R. 40, 2013, 20 September 2013; Proclamation by the President of the Republic of South Africa, Notification

property; (e) owns property; (f) provides or makes available, or invites a person to provide or make available property; (g) provides or makes available, or invites a person to provide or make available any financial or other service; (h) provides or makes available, or invites a person to provide or make available economic support; or (i) facilitates the acquisition, collection, use or provision of property, or the provision of any financial or other service, or the provision of economic support, intending that the property, financial or other service or economic support, as the case may be, be used, or while such person knows or ought reasonably to have known or suspected that the property, service or support concerned will be used, directly or indirectly, in whole or in part – (i) to commit or facilitate the commission of a specified offence; (ii) for the benefit of, or on behalf of, or at the direction of, or under the control of an entity which commits or attempts to commit or facilitates the commission of a specified offence; or (iii) for the benefit of a specific entity identified in a notice issued by the President under section 25, is guilty of an offence.

As indicated earlier, UN Security Council Resolution 1373 is mentioned in the preamble to the Act. This means that it influenced the drafting of section 4 of the Act. Section 17(4) of the Act provides an exception to section 4. It provides that 'Nothing in section 4 makes it an offence to provide or collect funds intending that they be used, or knowing or while a person ought reasonably to have known or suspected that they are to be used, for the purpose of advocating democratic government or the protection of human rights.' There have not been prosecutions stemming from allegations of terrorist financing alone. In *S v Okah*,[32] although it was alleged that the offender had financed terrorism,[33] it is not one of the offences of which he was convicted. This is because he was convicted of the main charges of terrorism.

Section 19 of the Act deals with the forfeiture of terrorist property. Section 19(1) provides that:

(1) Whenever any person is convicted of an offence under this Act, the court in passing sentence must, in addition to any punishment which that court may impose in respect of the offence, declare any property which is reasonably believed to have been used – (a) in the commission of the offence; or (b) for the purpose of or in connection with the commission of the offence, and which was seized under any power exercised under section 22, or is in the possession or custody or under the control of the convicted person, to be forfeited to the State.

by President in Respect of Entities Identified by the United Nations Security Council: Section 25 of the Protection of Constitutional Democracy Against Terrorist and Related Activities Act, 2004, No. R. 41, 2013, 20 September 2013.

32 *S v Okah* (SS94/2011) [2013] ZAGPJHC 6 (21 January 2013).

33 *S v Okah* (SS94/2011) [2013] ZAGPJHC 6 (21 January 2013) para 3.

It is evident from the preceding provision that the forfeiture of terrorist property is imposed as part of a criminal prosecution. The court does not have a discretion on the issue of whether or not to order that the property in question should be forfeited to the state. It is obliged to make that order. This is not the case when a person is convicted of a crime other than terrorism.[34] Money laundering is dealt with under the section 4 of the Prevention of Organised Crime Act.[35]

South Africa has a financial intelligence unit known as the Financial Intelligence Centre (FIC), which was established by the Financial Intelligence Centre Act.[36] Section 3(1) of the Financial Intelligence Centre Act provides that '[t]he principal objective of the [Financial Intelligence] Centre is to assist in the identification of the proceeds of unlawful activities and the combating of money laundering activities and the financing of terrorist and related activities.' Section 3(1) thus makes it clear that the mandate of the Financial Intelligence Centre covers both money laundering and terrorism. Section 4 of the Financial Intelligence Centre Act provides for the following functions of the Financial Intelligence Centre:

> (a) process, analyse and interpret information disclosed to it, and obtained by it, in terms of this Act;
> (b) inform, advise and cooperate with investigating authorities, supervisory bodies, the South African Revenue Service and the intelligence services;
> (c) monitor and give guidance to accountable institutions, supervisory bodies and other persons regarding the performance by them of their duties and their compliance with the provisions of this Act;
> (d) retain the information referred to in paragraph (a) in the manner and for the period required by this Act.

Information from the Financial Intelligence Centre indicates the number of reports of suspicious transactions that it receives annually from financial institutions and other entities. In its 2011/2012 Annual Report, the Financial Intelligence Centre reported on suspicious transactions as follows:

> As a result of the enhanced compliance regime and co-operation by entities obliged to report under the FIC Act, the FIC received 53 506 suspicious transaction reports (STRs) during 2011/12 – a 45 per cent increase on the prior year. The vast majority came from financial institutions. Since the FIC was established, the number of STRs has increased annually in line with growing collaboration with the banking sector. During the reporting period the FIC evaluated about 15 000 STRs and 4 million electronic funds transfers (EFTs). As a result of these reports and the

[34] See, for example, 35 of the Criminal Procedure Act.

[35] Prevention of Organised Crime Act No. 121 of 1998.

[36] Financial Intelligence Centre Act 38 of 2001.

Schedule 1: Item No.	Number of Cash Threshold Reports	No. of Suspicious Transaction Reports	Number of Terror Property Reports	Total Number of Reports
Attorneys	1 677	105	0	1782
Trust companies	95	8	0	103
Estate agents	1413	6	0	1419
Authorised user of an exchange (and stock exchange)	87	183	0	270
Unit trusts (collective investment scheme managers)	1 233	17	1	1 251
Banks	5 228 592	70 090	18	5 298 700
Mutual banks	1606	1	0	1607
Long-term insurance	400	91	0	491
Gambling institutions	603 909	753	0	604 662
Foreign exchange	166 769	46 349	0	213 118
Moneylenders against the security of securities	151	1	0	152
Investment advisors or intermediaries, approved person by registrar of stock exchanges (asset managers), and Registrar of financial markets (asset managers)	5 750	4 696	2	10 448

Issuers of traveller's cheques and money orders	1 437	1 434	0	2 871
Post bank	18 626	288	35	18 949
Ithala	133	3	0	136
Money remitters	18 655	23 459	0	42 114
SCHEDULE 3: ITEM NUMBER				
Motor vehicle dealers	42 177	259	0	42 436
Krugerrand dealers	698	1	0	699
GRAND TOTAL	**6 093 408**	**147 744**	**56**	**6 241 208**

Source: Financial Intelligence Centre 2012/2013 Annual Report (2013) p 28.

analysis of other data, the FIC identified various direct connections between criminal conduct and financial benefit, and froze 482 bank accounts that were believed to be harbouring the proceeds of unlawful activities. The freezing of bank accounts is one component of the FIC's activities; most of the FIC's work that spotlights potentially illicit activity, including corruption, is reflected in its reports to other State agencies, which pursue further investigation, up to and including prosecution.[37]

In its 2012/2013 Annual Report, the Financial Intelligence Centre summarises the reports it received in 2012 and 2013, as the following table shows:

In its 2011/2012 Annual Report,[38] the Financial Intelligence Centre sums up the suspicious transaction reports it has received since 2002. The figures are as follows:

Financial year	Number of STRs
2002/03	991
2003/04	7 480
2004/05	15 757
2005/06	19 793
2006/07	21 466
2007/08	24 580
2008/09	22 762
2009/10	29 411
2010/11	36 990
2011/12	53 506

The Financial Intelligence Centre reports on the Financial Action Task Force (FATF) as follows:

After the FATF adopted revised international standards in February 2012, the focus shifted to assessing whether countries are implementing the standards. In February 2013, the FATF adopted a new methodology for assessment. Although technical compliance will still be assessed, equal weight will be given to the effectiveness of applying the standards across various sectors. South Africa will be assessed within the next few years, and its systems to combat money laundering and the financing of terrorism will need to demonstrate enhanced effectiveness in line with the revised standards.[39]

37 Financial Intelligence Centre 2011/2012 Annual Report (2012) p 18.
38 Financial Intelligence Centre 2011/2012 Annual Report (2012) p 19.
39 Financial Intelligence Centre 2012/2013 Annual Report (2013) p 33.

The report adds that the Financial Intelligence Centre

> … participated in the FATF's process to improve its global reach by becoming involved in the newly formed Global Network Co-operation Group. Co-chaired by the FIC's Legal and Policy head, this group facilitates collaboration between the FATF and regional organisations that subscribe to the global standards. In addition, the FIC facilitated participation by South African authorities in a number of FATF projects, such as a typology study on the illicit tobacco trade, which was led by a SARS [South African Revenue Service] official….[40]

The Financial Intelligence Centre also reports that the February 2009 FATF and the Eastern and Southern Africa Anti–Money Laundering Group Mutual Evaluation Report states, inter alia, that '[s]ince 2003, South Africa has taken numerous steps to address many of the recommendations that were made in its first FATF mutual evaluation report.'[41] The preceding examples show that South Africa has been subject to and responded to an adverse FATC report with respect to terrorism financing.

VI. IMMIGRATION MEASURES

Section 29 of the Immigration Act[42] provides that:

> (1) The following foreigners are prohibited persons and do not qualify for a visa, admission into the Republic, a temporary or a permanent residence permit:
> (a) Those infected with or carrying infectious, communicable or other diseases or viruses as prescribed;
> (b) anyone against whom a warrant is outstanding or a conviction has been secured in the Republic or a foreign country in respect of genocide, terrorism, murder, torture, drug-related charges, money laundering or kidnapping;
> (c) anyone previously deported and not rehabilitated by the Director-General in the prescribed manner;
> (d) a member of or adherent to an association or organisation advocating the practice of racial hatred or social violence;
> (e) anyone who is or has been a member of or adherent to an organisation or association utilising crime or terrorism to pursue its ends; and
> (f) anyone found in possession of a fraudulent residence permit, passport or identification document. (2) The Director-General may, for good cause, declare a person referred to in subsection (1) not to be a prohibited person.

One of the factors that have to be considered in determining whether or not a person should be granted a South African visa or residence permit is whether he is or has

[40] Financial Intelligence Centre 2012/2013 Annual Report (2013) p 33.
[41] Financial Intelligence Centre 2009/2010 Annual Report (2010) p 7.
[42] Immigration Act No. 13 of 2002.

been 'a member of or adherent to an organisation or association utilising crime or terrorism to pursue its ends.'[43] I am not aware of any case in which section 29 has been applied to terrorism suspects. However, it has been invoked in cases of drug-related convictions to deport foreign nationals from South Africa.[44]

Section 12(d) of the South African Constitution prohibits torture. South Africa is also a state party to the Convention Against Torture, which, under article 3, prohibits the return of a person to a country where there is a risk that he or she would be subjected to torture. Article 3 of the Convention Against Torture was domesticated[45] in South African law by section 8 of the Prevention and Combating of Torture of Persons Act,[46] which provides that:

[43] See Immigration Regulations (made under section 7 of the Immigration Act 2002) No. R. 413 22 May 2014.

[44] See, for example, *Udoh v Minister of Home Affairs* [2012] JOL 28812 (ECP) (where the High Court dismissed the applicant's application challenging his deportation from South Africa on the basis of section 29 on the ground that he had been convicted of dealing in drugs).

[45] In *Glenister v President of the Republic of South Africa and Others* 2011 (3) SA 347 (CC) at 374–5 Justice Ngcobo of the South African Constitutional Court detailed the process through which international law becomes part of South African law as follows:

> [89] The constitutional scheme of s 231 is deeply rooted in the separation of powers, in particular the checks and balances between the executive and the legislature. It contemplates three legal steps that may be taken in relation to an international agreement, with each step producing different legal consequences. First, it assigns to the national executive the authority to negotiate and sign international agreements. But an international agreement signed by the executive does not automatically bind the Republic, unless it is an agreement of a technical, administrative or executive nature. To produce that result, it requires, second, the approval by resolution of Parliament.[90] The approval of an agreement by Parliament does not, however, make it law in the Republic, unless it is a self-executing agreement that has been approved by Parliament, which becomes law in the Republic upon such approval, unless it is inconsistent with the Constitution or an Act of Parliament. Otherwise, and third, an 'international agreement becomes law in the Republic when it is enacted into law by national legislation'.[91] The approval of an international agreement, under s 231(2) of the Constitution, conveys South Africa's intention, in its capacity as a sovereign State, to be bound at the international level by the provisions of the agreement. As the Vienna Convention on the Law of Treaties provides, the act of approving a convention is an 'international act … whereby a State establishes on the international plane its consent to be bound by a treaty'. The approval of an international agreement under s 231(2), therefore, constitutes an undertaking at the international level, as between South Africa and other States, to take steps to comply with the substance of the agreement. This undertaking will, generally speaking, be given effect by either incorporating the agreement into South African law, or taking other steps to bring our laws in line with the agreement, to the extent they do not already comply.[92] An international agreement that has been ratified by resolution of Parliament is binding on South Africa on the international plane. And failure to observe the provisions of this agreement may result in South Africa incurring responsibility towards other signatory States. An international agreement that has been ratified by Parliament under s 231(2), however, does not become part of our law, until and unless it is incorporated into our law by national legislation. An international agreement that has not been incorporated in our law cannot be a source of rights and obligations.'

[46] Act 13 of 2013.

(1) No person shall be expelled, returned or extradited to another State where there are substantial grounds for believing that he or she would be in danger of being subjected to torture.
(2) For the purpose of determining whether there are such grounds, all relevant considerations must be taken into account, including, where applicable, the existence in the State concerned of a consistent pattern of gross, flagrant or mass violations of human rights.

In *Arwah Abdi v Minister of Home Affairs*, where the Department of Home Affairs attempted to deport two Somali nationals to Somalia, the South African Supreme Court of Appeal held that it would be unlawful to deport the applicants to Somalia because of, inter alia, the fact that:

> The appellants would face a real risk of suffering physical harm if they were forced to return to Somalia. It is obvious that no effective guarantee can be given that the appellants would not be persecuted or subjected to some form of torture or cruel, inhuman and degrading treatment if they are compelled to re-enter that country. It is the prevention of this harm that the [Refugee] Act[47] seeks to address by prohibiting a refugee's deportation. Deportation to another state that would result in the imposition of a cruel, unusual or degrading punishment is in conflict with the fundamental values of the Constitution.[48]

The South African Constitutional Court held that immigration laws cannot be invoked to extradite or deport a suspect to a country where, if convicted, he or she could be sentenced to death unless there are guarantees that the death sentence will not be imposed or if imposed will not be executed.[49] In the light of the preceding jurisprudence and legislation, South African authorities cannot lawfully deport or return terror suspects to countries where they would be subjected to torture. I am not aware of any case in which South African authorities have deported or alleged to have deported non-citizens to torture. Evidence obtained through torture is automatically inadmissible. However, evidence obtained through cruel and degrading treatment could be admitted on the basis of section 35(5) of the Constitution.

47 The Refugee Act 130 of 1998.

48 *Arwah Abdi v Minister of Home Affairs* [2011] ZASCA 2 (15 February 2011) para 26. Footnotes omitted.

49 See *Minister of Home Affairs v Tsebe, Minister of Justice and Constitutional Development v Tsebe* 2012 (5) SA 467 (CC); *Mohamed v President of the Republic of South Africa* 2001 (3) SA 893 (CC). (In this case, South African Home Affairs officials surrendered a terrorist suspect, a Tanzanian national, to the U.S. authorities for his prosecution for committing terrorist attacks against the U.S. Embassy in Tanzania. There was a danger that if convicted he could be sentenced to death. The Constitutional Court held that the surrender was unlawful.)

VII. ROLE OF THE MILITARY AND EXTRA-TERRITORIAL COUNTER-TERRORISM ACTIVITIES

The military has not played a role in the domestic enforcement of terrorism laws.[50] The enforcement is done by the police. Military courts are not used with respect to terrorism prosecutions. This is because the Defence Act does not confer such jurisdiction to military courts. South Africa does not detain suspected terrorists on a law of war basis. The detention of any person as a prisoner of war is regulated by the Implementation of the Geneva Conventions Act,[51] which stipulates clearly the circumstances in which a person may be detained as a prisoner of war.

The principle laid down by the Constitutional Court in the case of *Kaunda and Others v President of the Republic of South Africa and Others*[52] on the issue of diplomatic protection of South African nationals who are detained abroad is applicable to South African terrorism suspects detained abroad. In this case, South African nationals were arrested and detained in Zimbabwe on the basis that they were planning to overthrow the government of Equatorial Guinea. Zimbabwe set in motion the process of extraditing them to Equatorial Guinea. They were also detained in inhumane conditions in Zimbabwe. They argued, inter alia, that their extradition would be contrary to the South African Constitution as there was a risk that if convicted they could be sentenced to death, yet the death penalty was unlawful in South Africa. The Court observed that the issue to be decided was:

> … whether the Constitution binds the State to take steps to protect the applicants in relation to the complaints they have concerning their conditions of detention in Zimbabwe and the prosecution they face there, as well as the possibility of their being extradited to Equatorial Guinea to face charges which could result, if they were to be convicted, in their being sentenced to death.[53]

The Court added that '[t]he relief they claim is in effect a mandamus ordering the government to take action at a diplomatic level to ensure that the rights they claim to have under the South African Constitution are respected by the two foreign governments.'[54] The Court held that the South African Constitution has no

[50] However, section 19(1) of the Defence Act 42 of 2002 provides that 'The Defence Force may be employed in co-operation with the South African Police Service in terms of section 201 (2) (a) of the Constitution in the prevention and combating of crime and maintenance and preservation of law and order within the Republic.'

[51] Implementation of the Geneva Conventions Act, No. 8 of 2012.

[52] *Kaunda and Others v President of the Republic of South Africa and Others* 2005 (4) SA 235 (CC).

[53] *Kaunda and Others v President of the Republic of South Africa and Others* 2005 (4) SA 235 (CC) para 19.

[54] *Kaunda and Others v President of the Republic of South Africa and Others* 2005 (4) SA 235 (CC) para 22.

application beyond South African borders.[55] The Court did not find it necessary to resolve the issue of whether South African law and in particular the Bill of Rights limits the actions of South African officials outside South Africa. It observed that:

> During argument hypothetical questions were raised relating to South African officials abroad, to South African companies doing business beyond our borders, to the government itself engaging in commercial ventures through State-owned companies with bases in foreign countries, and to what the State's obligations might be in such circumstances. There is a difference between an extraterritorial infringement of a constitutional right by an organ of State bound under s 8(1) of the Constitution, or by persons bound under s 8(2) of the Constitution, in circumstances which do not infringe the sovereignty of a foreign State, and an obligation on our government to take action in a foreign State that interferes directly or indirectly with the sovereignty of that State. Claims that fall in the former category raise problems with which it is not necessary to deal now. They may, however, be justiciable in our courts, and nothing in this judgment should be construed as excluding that possibility.[56]

In the light of the preceding reasoning, the argument can be made that South African domestic law limits the actions of state officials outside of South Africa. Their actions have to be in line with the South African Constitution. On the issue of diplomatic protection, the Court held that:

> South African nationals facing adverse State action in a foreign country are … entitled to request the South African government to provide protection against acts which violate accepted norms of international law. The government is obliged to consider such requests and deal with them appropriately. Decisions made by the government in these matters are subject to constitutional control. Courts required to deal with such matters will, however, give particular weight to the government's special responsibility for and particular expertise in foreign affairs, and the wide discretion that it must have in determining how best to deal with such matters.[57]

VIII. SECRECY AND TERRORISM

As of the time of writing, South Africa had not conducted a prosecution of terrorism in which the issue of state secrets arose. However, the South African law of evidence

[55] *Kaunda and Others v President of the Republic of South Africa and Others* 2005 (4) SA 235 (CC) para 36.

[56] *Kaunda and Others v President of the Republic of South Africa and Others* 2005 (4) SA 235 (CC) para 45. Footnotes omitted.

[57] *Kaunda and Others v President of the Republic of South Africa and Others* 2005 (4) SA 235 (CC) para 144 (5 and 6).

governs the use of privileged evidence (state privilege).[58] Secret evidence not seen by the accused may not be used as incriminating evidence in a terrorism trial, as this would be contrary to section 35(3)(i) of the Constitution, which provides for the accused's right to challenge evidence. The accused has a right to access information contained in the police docket if that information is necessary for the fairness of the trial. In *Shabalala and Others v Attorney-General of the Transvaal and Another*, the Constitutional Court held that:

1. The "blanket docket privilege" ... is inconsistent with the Constitution to the extent to which it protects from disclosure all the documents in a police docket, in all circumstances, regardless as to whether or not such disclosure is justified for the purposes of enabling the accused properly to exercise his or her right to a fair trial in terms of section 25(3).
2. The claim of the accused for access to documents in the police docket cannot be defeated merely on the grounds that such contents are protected by a blanket privilege....
3. Ordinarily an accused person should be entitled to have access to documents in the police docket which are exculpatory (or which are prima facie likely to be helpful to the defence) unless, in very rare cases, the State is able to justify the refusal of such access on the grounds that it is not justified for the purposes of a fair trial.
4. Ordinarily the right to a fair trial would include access to the statements of witnesses (whether or not the State intends to call such witnesses) and such of the contents of a police docket as are relevant in order to enable an accused person properly to exercise that right, but the prosecution may, in a particular case, be able to justify the denial of such access on the grounds that it is not justified for the purposes of a fair trial. This would depend on the circumstances of each case.
5. The State is entitled to resist a claim by the accused for access to any particular document in the police docket on the grounds that such access is not justified for the purposes of enabling the accused properly to exercise his or her right to a fair trial or on the ground that it has reason to believe that there is a reasonable risk that access to the relevant document would lead to the disclosure of the identity of an informer or State secrets or on the grounds that there was a reasonable risk that such disclosure might lead to the intimidation of witnesses or otherwise prejudice the proper ends of justice.
6. Even where the State has satisfied the Court that the denial of access to the relevant documents is justified on the grounds set out in paragraph 5 hereof,

[58] Schwikkard and Van der Merwe *Principles of Evidence* (3rd Edition) 156–78.

> it does not follow that access to such statements, either then or subsequently, must necessarily be denied to the accused. The Court still retains a discretion. It should balance the degree of risk involved in attracting the potential prejudicial consequences for the proper ends of justice referred to in paragraph 5 (if such access is permitted) against the degree of the risk that a fair trial may not enure for the accused (if such access is denied). A ruling by the Court pursuant to this paragraph shall be an interlocutory ruling subject to further amendment, review or recall in the light of circumstances disclosed by the further course of the trial.[59]

The fairness of the trial is the most important factor that the court will consider in determining whether or not secret information should be disclosed to the accused. It is not for the state or the prosecution to decide which evidence should or should not be disclosed to the accused. This decision is for the court to make. The accused who wants access to the police docket has to write to the prosecutor.[60] Section 153 of the Criminal Procedure Act provides a mechanism to protect state secrets at the actual trial. Section 153(1) is to the effect that:

> ... if it appears to any court that it would, in any criminal proceedings pending before that court, be in the interests of the security of the State or of good order or of public morals or of the administration of justice that such proceedings be held behind closed doors, it may direct that the public or any class thereof shall not be present at such proceedings or any part thereof.

Section 154(1) regulates the publication of information or evidence given at a trial which was held behind closed doors. It is to the effect that:

> Where a court under section 153 (1) on any of the grounds referred to in that subsection directs that the public or any class thereof shall not be present at any proceedings or part thereof, the court may direct that no information relating to the proceedings or any part thereof held behind closed doors shall be published in any manner whatever: Provided that a direction by the court shall not prevent the publication of information relating to the name and personal particulars of the accused, the charge against him, the plea, the verdict and the sentence, unless the court is of the opinion that the publication of any part of such information might defeat the object of its direction under section 153 (1), in which event the court may direct that such part shall not be published.

There has not been a trial of terrorism in South Africa where intelligence service members have testified. However, whether or not they will be called as state witnesses

[59] *Shabalala and Others v Attorney-General of the Transvaal and Another* 1995 (12) BCLR 1593; 1996 (1) SA 725 para 72.

[60] Schwikkard and Van der Merwe *Principles of Evidence* (3rd Edition) 174.

will depend on whether the prosecution thinks that they should be witnesses.[61] But if an intelligence official reported his suspicion to the police in terms of section 12 of the Act, the question of whether or not he will give evidence at the proceedings is governed by section 17(8) of the Act, which provides that 'A person who has made, initiated or contributed to a report in terms of section 12 (1) concerning a suspicion that any other person intends to commit or has committed an offence referred to in section 4 is competent, but not compellable, to give evidence in criminal proceedings arising from the report.' It should also be recalled that under South African law, a court has wide discretion to admit hearsay evidence if it thinks that it is in interest of justice to admit such evidence. However, such evidence should be used in addition to other evidence.[62]

IX. TERRORISM AND NATIONAL SECURITY POLICY

The South African government is in the process of developing a national security policy. In May 2013, the Minister of State Security informed the Parliamentary Extended Public Committee that:

> In 2013 the government and the ruling party have directed us to expedite the process of the development and finalisation of the National Security Strategy. The SSA [State Security Agency] and the Justice, Crime Prevention and Security, JCPS, Cluster have already covered a lot of ground in preparing the draft document and we hope to submit it for Cabinet approval within the next three months. Thereafter it is critical to canvass inputs and buy-in by all South Africans. We hope that this Parliament will also drive public consultations.
>
> It is our considered view that this strategy, within the South African historical context, must unpack what we mean by national security, and we think that we should follow a broad human security approach. We must reach consensus on what we mean by national security. This strategy must deepen our national consensus around national security challenges – what are the threats? – and provide a long-term framework for their mitigation and management. It must also propose critical structures for the effective and integrated upholding of national security. It must highlight the important role of the citizens as owners and beneficiaries of national security.[63]

In the same address, the Minister also emphasised that terrorism will be one of the issues to be addressed in the national security policy.

[61] In South African law, the prosecution is the master of the case.

[62] See, generally, J. D. Mujuzi, "Hearsay evidence in South Africa: should courts add the 'sole and decisive rule' to their arsenal?" (2013) 17 *International Journal of Evidence & Proof* 347–66.

[63] See Debate on Vote No 10 – National Treasury (State Security), 14 May 2013 at http://www.pmg.org.za/hansard/20130514-debate-vote-no-10-national-treasury-state-security.

X. COMPENSATION OF THE VICTIMS OF TERRORISM

The Protection of Constitutional Democracy Against Terrorist and Related Activities Act is silent on the issue of compensating victims of terrorism. However, section 300 of the Criminal Procedure Act provides that, 'Where a person is convicted by a superior court, a regional court or a magistrate's court of an offence which has caused damage to or loss of property (including money) belonging to some other person, the court in question may, upon the application of the injured person or of the prosecutor acting on the instructions of the injured person, forthwith award the injured person compensation for such damage or loss.' This provision could be invoked in a case where a terrorism survivor has also lost property. Another important provision is section 342 of the Criminal Procedure Act, which provides that 'A conviction or an acquittal in respect of any offence shall not bar a civil action for damages at the instance of any person who has suffered damages in consequence of the commission of that offence.' This could be invoked by surviving victims of terrorism against a person convicted or acquitted of terrorism.

PART FIVE

Asia and Australia

20

Japan

Takeyoshi Imai

I. INTRODUCTION

Terrorism has been a serious problem in Japan for several decades. Before 9/11, several terrorist groups perpetrated hideous acts of terrorism against Japanese and other nationals. For example, members belonging to the Japanese Red Army hijacked the Japan Airlines Flight 472 at Mumbai Airport on 28th of September 1977. The terrorists made the plane fly to Dhaka and forced the Japanese government to release prisoners who were their colleagues. In addition, they demanded ransom (6 million U.S. dollars). The government could not help accepting the illegal requests. Another (in)famous instance was a series of wrongdoings by Aum Shinrikyo. This was a Japanese religious cult group that was responsible for the 1995 sarin gas attack on the Tokyo subway.

After 9/11, the risk of the international terrorism has been more widely recognised in Japan. As a result, several laws have been drafted in accordance with the international tendency. For example, to meet the demand of the International Convention for the suppression of the financing of terrorism and UN Resolution 1373, the Act for Punishment of the Financing of Criminal Activities for the Purpose of Intimidation of the General Public and of Governments (Act No. 67 of 2002), was enacted in 2002. Provision or collection of funds with the intention that they should be used or in the knowledge that they are to be used in order to carry out terrorism was also added as a predicate offence for money laundering in the Act on Punishment of Organised Crimes and Control of Crime Proceeds.

In addition, in the light of the 9 Special Recommendations of the Financial Action Task Force (FATF), the following laws were enacted: the Act that obliges financial institutions to identify customers (2004) and the Act on Prevention of Transfer of Criminal Proceeds (2007).

II. THE DEFINITION OF TERRORISM

There is not a uniform definition of terrorism in Japanese law. One important definition is, however, contained in section 1 of the Act for Punishment of the Financing of Criminal Activities for the Purpose of Intimidation of the General Public and of Governments enacted in 2002. The definition of terrorism in this act is heavily influenced by the 1999 International Convention for the Suppression of the Financing of Terrorism. The common characteristics of the terrorism acts defined by section 1 are as follows:

Activities which fall in one of the following categories and to be done for intimidation of the general public and of governments:

1) murder, serious injury with armed forces, kidnap or taking of hostages with armed forces
2) hijacking, its attempt and its preparation with armed forces as well as destruction of planes or ships
3) explosion of, setting fire to or destruction of vehicle for public transportation (such as train or car), public space (such as road, park or station), electricity, gas or water supply facilities and buildings for public use

There are other older definitions of terrorism in Japanese law. Section 38(4) of the Ordinance regarding establishment of the National Police Agency (1954) defined terrorism as terroristic subversive activity and as one of the acts to be supervised for the sake of national security. Now this section has been amended to define terrorism as the same activities mentioned in the Act on the Control of Organisations Which Committed Indiscriminate Mass Murder, which is discussed later in this chapter.

III. CRIMINAL LAWS AND PROSECUTIONS

Membership or participation in a terrorist group and incitement of terrorism are not crimes in Japanese criminal law. Typical acts to be penalised by the Act for Punishment of the Financing of Criminal Activities for the Purpose of Intimidation of the General Public and of Governments are as follows: providing or collecting funds with the intention that they should be used or in the knowledge that they are to be used in order to carry out terrorism. If this act were applied to an actual case of terrorism, it is possible that the accused might be penalised simultaneously by the ordinary offences, such as aiding and abetting murder, causing serious injury and so on.

On the other hand, providing material benefits other than funds (e.g., land, house, things or services) is not penalised. Also, providing funds or material benefits with the secondary participants in the principal's act is not a crime. The government has proposed that the bill include these acts as crimes. This bill has not yet been approved by the Diet, Japan's Parliament.

Crimes of preparation for or facilitation of terrorism are broader than those for other "ordinary" crimes because the former shall be penalised as long as these acts were done with the intention that they should be used or in the knowledge that they are to be used in order to carry out terrorism. In other words, the former are crimes that can be committed without accomplices. The relationship between principal (i.e., terrorists) and others need not be proved.

Ordinary criminal laws covering crimes such as murder, kidnapping and conspiracy are to be applied to terrorist crimes. Suspected terrorism is sometimes prosecuted for other offences in part because forming a terrorist association does not constitute an offence in Japan.

Offences related to terrorist acts can overlap. For example, offences of financing of terrorism and of preparation for murder by a terrorist can be applied simultaneously. This overlap reflects the different purposes of the offences. For example, the offence of financing of terrorism is to protect the society from the risk of terrorism, while murder is to protect the life of the victim. In theory, offences in the 2002 Act and ordinary crimes can be applied to the same defendant simultaneously. Nevertheless, there has not been an actual case where the offence of financing of terrorism and another ordinary offence such as murder have been applied concurrently to the same defendant. In fact, there has not been any case where a conviction for terrorism financing under the 2002 has been obtained.

A. *Terrorism Prosecutions*

In many cases of terrorism, defendants were charged with murder or kidnapping. Multiple charges and multiple accused are common in this area. For example, preparation of murder, offences in the Law to Control the Possession of Firearms and Swords and money laundering have been used simultaneously. In fact, these offences were used for prosecution of the defendants in the case of *Aum Shinrikyo*.[1]

After the case of *Aum Shinrikyo*, the Act on Prevention of Bodily Harm by Sarin and Similar Substances was enacted, and this law could apply today.

Terrorism prosecutions would be conducted in normal courts in Japan. Evidence that could have been obtained through torture or degrading treatment would not be admissible in terrorism prosecutions. The courts in Japan have excluded illegally

[1] Judgments of the Supreme Court, 21st of November 2011, which dismissed the appeal of the defendant, who had been sentenced to death.

obtained evidence, and this rule should apply to case of terrorism. There are, however, no actual cases where such a rule has had to be applied.

In terrorism prosecutions, a witness must identify himself or herself before being asked to testify on his or her experience. However, the witness's identity can be protected in ways different from the ordinary ones. For example, the witness may be identified simply with a card so that his or her personal information cannot be revealed to the defendants. This procedure can help protect witnesses in terrorism cases.

B. *Punishment of Terrorism*

The sentencing practices in terrorism cases are not different from those in normal cases. This means that rehabilitation can be considered only as a mitigating factor in deciding a defendant's sentence even in a terrorism case. In reality, most of the defendants in terrorism cases have been sentenced to prison without a stay of execution.

As the number of terrorism cases is not ample in Japan, it is not so easy to survey the actual sentences ordered by court to such cases. So the sentencing in a recent typical case will serve as example. In the *Amu Shinrikyo* case, the most horrifying terrorism case in the last two dacades, thirteen defendants were given the death penalty in the ordinary court and five were given life imprisonment. Among other defendants (i.e., twenty-two people), the average length of imprisonment was 9.5 years.

In theory, sentencing reductions for those who co-operate with authorities could be made. There is no law providing for such a practice, so any reduction of sentencing would be done on a case-by-case basis.

IV. INVESTIGATIVE POWERS

A. *Police Powers*

In terrorism cases, Japanese police do not have special powers not available in ordinary criminal investigations and cases. For example, they do not have special preventive arrest powers nor special powers with respect to interrogations, pre-trial or investigatory detention, searches, use of informers and electronic surveillance. In addition, the state cannot compel those with information about a terrorist act to provide the information. There are also no laws or regulations to govern the use of undercover operations in terrorism or other criminal cases. Entrapment or other defences based on abuse of police powers have not been argued in terrorism prosecutions so far.

B. *Intelligence Agencies*

Intelligence agencies with respect to counter-terrorism are the Counter International Terrorism Division in the National Police Agency (NPA). It coordinates criminal investigations conducted by the local police departments. The NPA is also responsible international terrorism investigations.

Intelligence collected by intelligence agencies can be used as evidence in terrorism prosecutions as long as it was not obtained illegally. The exclusionary rule would be applied to illegally obtained evidence, including that obtained through torture. Intelligence could be provided to the court either orally or in writing. The identity of the intelligence operative would not be made public. The intelligence operative would not be cross-examined by the accused.[2]

There are no special laws regarding electronic surveillance by intelligence services. However, by applying the Act on Wiretapping for Criminal Investigation, telephone calls, e-mails or faxes that are suspected of being linked to murder or other serious offences by criminal organisations can be intercepted by the investigating authorities. If there is a reasonable suspicion that a terrorist group has committed a particular offence, such as murder, injury, use of bombs or explosive materials or arson, then information related to the suspicion can be monitored and stored as evidence. An authorisation cannot be obtained simply on the basis of membership in a terrorist or organised crime group.

V. PROSCRIPTION AND LISTING OF TERRORIST GROUPS AND INDIVIDUALS

Since 2003, Japan has had a mechanism for listing and freezing the asset of terrorist groups and terrorists. This law is intended to implement United Nations Security Council Resolutions 1267, 1333, 1373, 1390, 1988 and 1989. The mechanism is the Foreign Exchange and Foreign Trade Act enacted on the 6th of January 2003. According to this Act, inspection of the assets possessed by those who are found to be foreign terrorists are to be checked and can be frozen. In addition, as a preparatory measure for such dispositions, financial institutions are obliged to identify customers more strictly than before.

As of the 23th of July 2014, 352 individuals and 89 groups that are listed as terrorists by the United Nations Security Council Resolutions (1267, 1333, 1390, 1988, 1989) are also listed as the objects of the Japanese system. As explained previously,

[2] In this area, the discussion as to the fair trial for terrorist suspects has just began. Therefore, my explanation is no more than the description of the expected legal framework.

the domestic listing process in Japan is almost the same one conceived under UN Security Council Resolution 1267 for those associated with al-Qaeda.

A listing decision is based on the United Nations Security Council Resolution. As a result, the decision in Japan can be based on speech or advocacy of terrorism as opposed to direct or indirect participation in terrorist activities as long as the United Nations Security Council Resolution took such a stance.

A. *Challenges to Proscriptions and Listings*

So far, there have been no challenges to a terrorist listing, and neither the courts, the legislature nor the executive have changed a listing decision in response to a challenge. The decision to list an individual or a group is based on the judgment of the United Nations Security Council Resolution. Thus, in theory, the Japanese authorities could defend a listing decision just on the basis of the UN's judgments. At the same time, there are sections of the Foreign Exchange and Foreign Trade Act that would allow a member of a listed group to challenge the listing decision. A court could in theory revoke a listing if it found an illegality.

The definition of a terrorist group in criminal offences is not based in part or wholly on the proscription or listing of terrorist groups, and the court would determine the existence of a terrorist connection on the basis of evidence submitted to it.

VI. REGULATION OF TERRORISM FINANCING

A. *The Regulatory Regime to Counter Terrorism Financing*

In Japan, the Criminal Investigation Bureau in the National Police Agency serves as a financial intelligence agency. Its mandate covers both money laundering and terrorism. The number of reports of suspicious transactions that the Japanese financial intelligence unit (FIU) receives is shown in the following table:[3]

Year	2005	2006	2007	2008	2009	2010	2011	2012	2013
Number of reported cases	165747	185101	256670	381590	462074	502955	572177	645841	645862

Source: http://www.npa.go.jp/sosikihanzai/jafic/nenzihokoku/data/jafic_2013j.pdf, p38.

[3] The number includes the reported cases based on suspicion of money laundering as well as other related offences (especially terrorism financing and its aiding and abetting). It is not possible to separate the number for respective offences.

To tackle terrorism financing more robustly, attempts have been made to subject informal money transfer systems, such as *hawalas*, to the terrorism financing regime. At the same time, however, there are few cases involving *hawalas*, though Pakistani suspects were arrested in connection with *hawalas* in 2004 and 2005.

In spite of the dedication of the Japanese financial intelligence unit, Japan has been subject to and has responded to an adverse FATF report with respect to terrorism financing. To respond to these criticisms, the Japanese government has been planning to amend the sections in the Punishment of the Financing of Criminal Activities for the Purpose of Intimidation of the General Public and of Governments first enacted in 2002. The planned revisions are as follows. Firstly, the Act will be expanded to apply not only to money but other interests, such as land, houses, things, services and other equivalent support for terrorism. Secondly, the Act wll be expanded to cover indirect as well as direct support for terrorism. These amendments to the 2002 law have not yet been approved by the Diet.

B. *Criminal Offences of Terrorism Financing*

The Act on Punishment of the Financing of Criminal Activities for the Purpose of Intimidation of the General Public and of Governments enacted in 2002 to comply with UN Security Council Resolution 1373 has made terrorism financing an offence. The offence requires proof of a subjective intent or knowledge with respect to terrorist acts. In addition to calling for the intention of committing the respective offence, the Act requires the purpose of terrifying the public. Section 2 applies to providing money to terrorists, and section 3 applies to collecting funds for terrorists There is no exemption for the provision of funds to finance legitimate and humanitarian activities by a terrorist group. Thus far, no terrorism financing prosecutions have occurred that were not coupled with other terrorism charges.

The 2002 terrorism financing law does not have specific provisions for the forfeiture of terrorist property, but sections 19 and 1902 of the Penal Code, which are general provisions for the forfeiture of property, could apply to terrorist property but only as part of an ordinary criminal prosecution.

VII. IMMIGRATION MEASURES

A. *Immigration Detention*

Immigration law has been used against suspected terrorists. In December 2001, under the amended Immigration Control and Refugee Recognition Act, for example, five Afghans were detained by the Immigration Bureau on suspicion of being terrorists in December 2001. Thereafter, they were deported.[4] In 2006, the Immigration Control and Refugee Recognition Act was revised to include new sections by which foreigners who hope to enter Japan are asked to provide information for personal identification, such as their fingerprints. Immigration proceedings have been used as an alternative to criminal prosecutions. In many cases, the detainees will be given the evidence that is the basis for their detention and deportation, but in a case where a suspect seems to have relationship with terrorists, this procedure might not be observed for the sake of the social security. The detainee could ask for a judicial review of the case in which case the judge could review the secret evidence. However, this is hypothetical because there are no cases in Japan that have questioned the use of secret evidence against terrorist suspects.

B. *Immigration Proceedings and Torture*

As explained previously, evidence that has been obtained through torture or degrading treatment is not admissible in terrorism prosecutions. The exclusionary rule of the illegally obtained evidence should also be applied in immigration cases. Japan also maintains a ban on refoulement or deportation to torture, but deportation to countries that employ or have employed torture has not emerged as an issue in cases where a suspected terrorist may be a citizen of such a country and face a substantial risk of torture.

VIII. ADMINISTRATIVE AND EXECUTIVE MEASURES

In Japan, a number of administrative measures are used to control the activities of people suspected or convicted of terrorism. The Anti-Subversive Activities Act regulates terroristic subversive activity. For example, rioting by extreme far-right or far-left groups are regulated, and those who instigated the activities are punished. In this sense, this Act has a penal provision, but its main purpose is to supervise and prevent the activities of the groups administratively. For example, under this Act, the Public Security Examination Commission can hear applications to dissolve subversive groups.

The Act on the Control of Organisations Which Committed Indiscriminate Mass Murder is designed to prevent the commission of indiscriminate mass murder by a cult group or the extreme right or left groups. It has been applied to the Aum Shinrikyo and its successor. This Act also provides for the observation of suspected terrorist groups. There has not been any use of administrative measures after acquittals or reversals of convictions in terrorism cases

4 Recently, such cases have not been reported publicly.

Under both these administrative acts, it is not necessary to prove guilt beyond a reasonable doubt as in a criminal case. In other words, what is needed under these administrative measures is only proof on a balance of probabilities. Secret evidence not disclosed to the affected person, however, cannot be used to justify the use of the administrative measures. There has so far been no legal or political controversy with respect to the use of administrative or executive measures.

IX. ROLE OF MILITARY AND EXTRA-TERRITORIAL COUNTER-TERRORISM ACTIVITIES

A. *Military Courts and Detention*

The military does not exist in Japan. Therefore, questions as to the role of the military against terrorist activities cannot be answered.

B. *The Extra-Territorial Treatment of Citizens Suspected of Terrorism*

There have not been litigation or review proceedings in Japan with respect to the treatment of Japanese nationals who may be detained by another state because of suspicions of their involvement in terrorism.

C. *Extra-Territorial Terrorism Law Enforcement*

The NPA has a close relationship with Interpol. Through this channel, the NPA can acquire sensitive but indispensable information regarding possible terrorism. Such activities of NPA are not limited by domestic laws.

So far, terrorist suspects have not been extradited from Japan to face terrorism prosecution in another country.

X. SECRECY AND TERRORISM

A. *Secrecy Claims and Secret Evidence*

Generally speaking, state secrets related to terrorism are not given special treatment in terrorism prosecutions. However, such secrets shall be kept hidden to the public. According to a section in the Act on the Protection of Specially Designated Secrets, information that is related to prevention of terrorism and is not known to the public shall be deemed as Specially Designated Secrets and be kept hidden for not exceeding thirty years. This term shall be extended for another thirty years if needed.

There has not been a terrorism trial where evidence not seen by the accused has been used as incriminating evidence in Japan.

In connection with the Act on the Protection of Specially Designated Secrets, a person who leaks the secret without good reason shall be penalised. In a trial for the accused of this offence, the alleged secret material as specifically designated shall be presented and be tried *in camera* (section 223–6 of the Civil Proceedings Act).

Before a case is brought to the court, the accused can request for examination of whether data should be regarded as secret. In this procedure, again, the case shall be reviewed *in camera* (section 9-1 in the Act for Establishment of the Information Disclosure and Personal Information Protection Review Board).

As long as the Act on the Protection of Specially Designated Secrets shall be applied, the state restricts normal rights of the accused to access or disclose information held by the state if that information is claimed classified or subject to a judicial determination that it is secret. If the accused and others intend to use in a terrorism prosecution information that might be considered a state secret, they are responsible for notifying the prosecutor or other state representative of their intention. In such cases, the accused would have to establish that the information cannot be classified as Specially Designated Secrets under the Act.

The procedure for determining whether information claimed to be secret can be disclosed to the accused or the accused's lawyer is regulated by sections 223–6 in the Civil Proceedings Act or the section 9-1 in the Act for Establishment of the Information Disclosure and Personal Information Protection Review Board.

In such cases, judges have the power to balance the competing claims of secrecy and disclosure, but they must also obey the conditions in the aforementioned sections. As a result, judges cannot redact or edit the information to protect secrets. Judges also cannot ask the government to request that other states allow the disclosure of information protected under the third-party rules. In addition, judges cannot impose conditions on disclosure, such as that only the accused's lawyer and not the accused may see the information or that it not be disclosed to the press and the public.

Viewed from the objective rule for fact finding, evidentiary rules or privileges should not prevent the disclosure of intelligence sources and methods.

B. *Secrecy in the Courtroom and Anonymous Witnesses*

There are mechanisms to protect state secrets at the actual trial or judicial proceedings in Japan. State secrets that a public officer acquired in the due course of his or her duties cannot be presented to the courts unless their uses in the court were approved by the Ministry under which he or she works (section 100 of the National Public Service Act). If the Ministry approved their use, they might be used in closed courtrooms or court exhibits that cannot be published in the media. It is conceivable that intelligence service members might testify at terrorism prosecutions, but this has not occurred so far. Anonymous witnesses cannot testify in terrorism prosecutions.

XI. CONCLUSION

As explained in this chapter, the UN resolutions and similar international initiatives such as those undertaken by the FATF have had a great impact on Japan's policies against terrorism. Several news laws, such as the Act for Punishment of the Financing of Criminal Activities for the Purpose of Intimidation of the General Public and of Governments (Act No. 67 of 2002), have been enacted in response both to 9/11 and UN Security Council Resolution 1373. The predicate offences for money laundering have been enlarged in view of the development of the legal framework of counter-terrorism. Counter-terrorism law in Japan is in line with the desirable tendencies in international society.

There have been few cases or controversy over protecting human rights while preventing terrorism in Japan. It is important that human rights be protected, but it should also be recognised that the potential harm caused by terrorism could easily surpass the traditional harms of ordinary crime. The lack of controversy may reflect that there has not yet been serious cases of terrorism in Japan since 9/11.

As to the challenges and major issues facing counter-terrorism law in Japan in the near future, one threat that may occur, perhaps in relation to the Olympic Games to be held in Tokyo, is the threat of terrorism committed by foreign nationals. Japanese immigration law has already been strengthened, and the necessity of introducing much stricter screening, detection and prevention of the those who seemingly have radical ideas and might become terrorists in Japan is being discussed. There are also proposals before the Diet to strengthen terrorism financing laws in response to criticisms by the FATF. Before the Olympic Games scheduled for 2020 in Tokyo, more counter-terrorism laws should be considered and implemented while taking care to respect human rights.

21

China

Li Zhe

I. INTRODUCTION

Terrorism has long been a key issue influencing world peace and development. Terrorist attacks have become more and more frequent and serious in China in the past few years. From April 2013 to July 2014, twelve influential and large-scale terrorist attacks have occurred in China, including several cities of Xinjiang Uygur Autonomous Region, where the terrorists are based,[1] as well as some big cities in China, such as Beijing[2] and Kunming.[3] During the aforementioned terrorist attacks, altogether 181 persons were killed and 397 seriously injured, and costly property damage was inflicted, including at the Goldwater Bridge of Tian'an Men Square.[4]

The Chinese government had made great efforts to combat terrorist crimes nationally and internationally. It has joined twelve international anti-terrorism conventions under the framework of the United Nations; promoted the establishment of the Shanghai Cooperation Organization, of which it is a member; and carefully enforced the resolutions of the Security Council in policy, legislation and administration. Although there is no special anti-terrorism law, several laws, regulations and amendments to current laws have been added to implement Security Council resolutions, in particular Resolutions 1373 and 1624, in an attempt to better combat terrorist-related crimes.

The anti-terrorism law in China includes criminal law, military law, administrative law as well as administrative regulations and judicial explanations. The most important laws include the Criminal Law, the Criminal Procedure Law,

1 Cities had suffered terrorist attacks in China in recent years: http://news.163.com/special/attacked_city/.
2 Police cracked the "10·28" violent terrorist attack: http://news.xinhuanet.com/legal/2013-10/30/c_117938784.htm.
3 Kunming violent terrorist attack caused 29 people killed: http://www.chinanews.com/gn/2014/03-02/5899255.shtml.
4 The data were calculated by the author based on the news reports covering such terrorism.

the Anti-money Laundering Law, the Exit and Entry Administration Law and the Martial Law. The issuing organs concerning the administrative regulations with respect to anti-terrorism are the Ministry of Public Security, the Ministry of National Security, the Ministry of Justice, the People's Bank of China, and so on. The judicial explanations concerning terrorism include the guidelines and ordinances issued by the Supreme People's Court and the Supreme People's Procuratorate.[5]

Another important document is the Decision on Issues Concerning Strengthening Anti-Terrorism Work, published by the Standing Committee of the National People's Congress (DISAW) on October 29, 2011. This decision is not of a legislative nature since it is not a document issued under the order of the President of the People's Republic of China (PRC). But the DISAW has provided important guidance on some issues urgently needed in the anti-terrorism area, such as the definition of several terrorist-related norms, the listing of terrorist groups and individuals and the freezing of assets used to finance terrorist activities. Moreover, several administrative regulations were issued based on the DISAW.

The Standing Committee of the National People's Congress of PRC on November 3, 2014 released the Anti-Terrorism Law (Draft) (hereinafter referred to as Draft AT)[6] and the Ninth Amendment to Criminal Law (Draft)(hereinafter referred to as Draft Amendment)[7] for public comment. The inquiry ended on December 3, 2014, and the second reading of the Draft AT was conducted on February 25, 2015. It is estimated that these two legal documents will be promulgated and come into force before the end of 2015. The main focus of the Draft AT is the preventive measures and working mechanisms of the anti-terrorism organizations in China, while the Draft Amendment adds to the criminal law on terrorism.

The Anti-Terrorism Law (Draft) is a comprehensive law, containing 10 chapters and 106 articles. According to Article 106, once the new law is effective it will abolish the previous DISAW articulated in October 2011. The aim of the draft law is to prevent and combat terrorism and protect state safety, public security and the safety of the lives and properties of the public (Article 1 of the Draft AT). The law will place counter-terrorism in an unprecedented important position in China. Anti-terrorism work will be included in the state security strategy. Political, economic, legal, cultural, educational, advocacy, technological, diplomatic and military measures

[5] According to Article 129 of the Constitution of the PRC, the people's procuratorates of the People's Republic of China are state organs for legal supervision. The guidelines and ordinances issued by the People's Procuratorates are deemed as providing judicial explanation.

[6] Chinese version of the Draft is available at the official website of the National People's Congress, http://www.npc.gov.cn/npc/xinwen/lfgz/flca/2014-11/03/content_1885027.htm, last visit on February 15, 2015.

[7] Chinese version of the Draft is available at the official website of the National People's Congress, http://www.npc.gov.cn/npc/xinwen/lfgz/flca/2014-11/03/content_1885029.htm, last visited on February 15, 2015.

will be applied collaboratively to prevent and combat terrorism (Article 3 of the Draft AT). Anti-terrorism organizations will be set up at the national, provincial and municipal level to coordinate anti-terrorism efforts (Article 9 of the Draft AT).

II. THE DEFINITION OF TERRORISM

Defining "terrorism" is a difficult issue in China as it is throughout the world. A definition of "terrorism" cannot be found in Chinese legislation, although several related terms, such as "terrorist act" or "terrorism organization" have been used several times in Chinese laws and legal documents. In the future, if a special counter-terrorism law is drafted, the definition of "terrorism" will still be one of the hardest issues to resolve, as several opinions have already been put forward regarding the definition of terrorism in the academia.[8]

Article 8 of the Implementing Rules of the National Security Law of PRC, effective from June 4, 1994, was the first legal provision that mentioned the word "terrorist act" in China. This article listed "organizing, planning or implementing a terrorist act" as one of the "other acts endangering the national security." In the criminal law, which has been effective since October 1, 1997, the offence of "organizing, leading or participating in terrorist organizations" was regulated. Although this law uses terms related to "terrorism," such as "terrorist act"[9] and "terrorist organization," and expressly incriminated the "terrorist act," it still did not include any definition of "terrorism," "terrorist act" or "terrorist organization." After the criminal law was enacted, several amendments were made concerning terrorist crimes, but there is still no clear definition of "terrorism," "terrorist act" and "terrorist organization."

It was not until the announcement of the DISAW on October 29, 2011, that the definitions of "terrorist," "terrorist activity" and "terrorist organization" first appeared in a legal document. Before the announcement of DISAW by the Standing Committee of the National People's Congress, the Shanghai Convention

[8] There are several opinions about the definition of "terrorism." One opinion is that terrorism is a crime. See Wang Yan, Wu Dawei: Probe on the Definition of "Terrorism Crime," Journal of Henan Public Security College, No.4, 2003, P.52. Another opinion is that terrorism is a concept of ideology; see Yang Xinyu, Ding Yi: Discussion on the Definition of Terrorism and Related Concepts, Contemporary Law Review, No.3, 2003, P.33. Other opinions consider terrorism a system of terrorist activities; see Wang Yizhou: Investigate the Origin of Terrorism, Beijing, Social Science Academic Press, 2002. Still others classify terrorism as dual nature from criminology and criminal law review; see Tong Weihua: On Defining Terrorism Crimes, Journal of Gansu Political Science and Law Institute, No.4, 2002, P.77. Also, related discussion can be found: Du Miao, Zhao Bingzhi: Summary of Topics of Terrorism Crimes, Beijing, Chinese People's Public Security University Press, 2008.

[9] Since there is no clear definition of "terrorist act" or related terms, the textbooks in China have made their own definitions. "Terrorist act refers to those organized crimes, such as murder, injury, poisoning, kidnapping, for the purpose to arouse the terror from the society and the public." Gao Mingxuan, Ma Kechang: Criminal Law, Beijing, Peking University Press 2010, P.387.

on Combating Terrorism, Separatism and Extremism (hereinafter referred to as the "Shanghai Convention"),[10] approved by China in 2001, had established a clear definition of "terrorism."[11] During the drafting of DISAW, the aforementioned international and regional documents were deeply researched as a reference to the terrorist-related norms defined in DISAW.[12]

According to Article 2 of the DISAW, "terrorist activities" are activities conducted by violence, destruction, intimidation and other means to create social panic, endanger public security or threaten state organizations or international organizations; cause or attempt to cause casualties, grave property loss, damage to public facilities, disruption of social order and other severe social harm; as well as acts to assist the aforementioned activities by instigation, financing or any other means. This is a broader definition than contained in the Shanghai Convention.

The definitions of "terrorist organization" and "terrorist" in the DISAW are based on the regulation of "terrorist activity" defined in the same document. "Terrorist organizations" are criminal groups formed for conducting terrorist activities, and "terrorists" are individuals who organize, plan or conduct terrorist activities and are members of terrorist organizations. The terrorist activities are differentiated from other criminal activities from the perspectives of concrete activities and criminal results, as opposed to requirements of proof of a political or religious motive or the intimidation of populace or government requirements. There is no exemption for expressive and associational activities or for national liberation struggles.

The November 2014 Draft AT proposed China's first binding definition of terrorism.[13] According to Article 104 of the Draft AT, Terrorism refers to ideology, speech or action with the intent to cause social panic or terror, influence national decision making, create racial hatred, subvert state power or divide the country by

[10] The Shanghai Convention was drafted and signed in June 2001 after the establishment of Shanghai Cooperation Organization. The member states of the Shanghai Convention include the Republic of Kazakhstan, the People`s Republic of China, the Kyrgyz Republic, the Russian Federation, the Republic of Tajikistan and the Republic of Uzbekistan.

[11] According to Article 1 of the Shanghai Convention, "terrorism" means: "(a) any act recognized as an offence in one of the treaties listed in the Annex to this Convention and as defined in this Treaty; and (b) other act intended to cause death or serious bodily injury to a civilian, or any other person not taking an active part in the hostilities in a situation of armed conflict or to cause major damage to any material facility, as well as to organize, plan, aid and abet such act, when the purpose of such act, by its nature or context, is to intimidate a population, violate public security or to compel public authorities or an international organization to do or to abstain from doing any act, and prosecuted in accordance with the national laws of the Parties. Also, section 2 of this Article provides that this Article shall not affect any international treaty or any national law of the Parties, that provides or may provide for a broader application of the terms used in this Article."

[12] Yang Huanning: Explanation to the Draft of "the Decision on Issues Concerning Strengthening Anti-Terrorism Work," National People's Congress Standing Committee Bulletin, No. 7, 2011, P.659.

[13] Although Article 2 of DISAW contains a definition of terrorism, due to the nature of DISAW, the definition serves only as a working definition.

means of violence, destruction or intimidation. Article 104 of the Draft AT also defines extremism, which is "the ideology, speech or action which distorts religious teachings, promotes religion extremism, violence, hostility to society or against humanity, or others." This definition was revised[14] in the Second reading of the Draft by the Standing Committee of the National People's Congress, PRC. The revised definition makes only two changes in the aspects of special intentions and the manifestations of terrorism. The original reference to "ideology, speech or acts" was changed to "advocacy or acts." This would exclude mere thoughts from the definition of terrorism. As to the special intentions, "create social panic, endanger public safety, or compel state organs or international organisations" was provided instead of "cause social panic or terror, influence national decision-making, create racial hatred, subvert state power, or divide country." Moreover, the position of the definition was adjusted from the original Chapter 10 "Supplementary Provisions" to the very beginning of the Draft AT.[15]

III. CRIMINAL LAWS AND PROSECUTIONS

A. *Criminal Law*

The criminal punishment of terrorism has undergone some progress since 1997, when the Criminal Law of China was largely revised based on the 1979 Criminal Law. In the 1997 Criminal Law,[16] terrorist activities were declared a separate crime that would be punished together with other ordinary crimes committed during the process of terrorist activities, such as murder, detonation of explosives or kidnapping, according to the regulations for punishing multiple crimes. In order to more rigorously and effectively combat criminal terrorist activities and to better respond to the requirement of the UN Security Council Resolution 1373,[17] some amendments were made in the Criminal Law, which included Amendment III to

[14] The revised definition of terrorism can be read as: "Terrorism is the advocacy or acts, which will create social panic, endanger public safety, or compel state organs or international organisations, by means of violence, destruction or intimidation."

[15] People's Daily, February 26, 2015, http://www.npc.gov.cn/npc/xinwen/lfgz/2015-02/26/content_1905617.htm.

[16] Article 120 of the Criminal Law of China in 1997 states: "Whoever forms, leads or actively participates in a terrorist organization shall be sentenced to fixed-term imprisonment of not less than three years but not more than ten years; other participants shall be sentenced to fixed-term imprisonment of not more than three years, criminal detention or public surveillance. Whoever, in addition to the crime mentioned in the preceding paragraph, commits other crimes of homicide, explosion or kidnap shall be punished in accordance with the provisions on combined punishment for several crimes."

[17] Report by China on the Implementation of Security Council Resolution 1373 (2001), S/2001/1270, P.4.

the Criminal Law of China in December 2001 and Amendment VIII to the Criminal Law of China in 2011.

According to Amendment III to the Criminal Law, more severe punishments were placed into the criminal law for terrorist-related crimes. The first paragraph of Article 120 was revised to read: "Whoever forms or leads a terrorist organization shall be sentenced to fixed-term imprisonment of not less than 10 years or life imprisonment; persons who actively participate in a terrorist organization shall be sentenced to fixed-term imprisonment of not less than 3 years but not more than 10 years; other participants shall be sentenced to fixed-term imprisonment of not more than 3 years, criminal detention, public surveillance or deprivation of political rights."[18] This 2001 amendment has greatly increased the punishment of those who form or lead a terrorist organization up to life imprisonment, whereas under the 1997 Criminal Law, the upper sentencing limit for such crimes was ten years' imprisonment. It also provides for mandatory minimum punishments for terrorist crimes. The possibility of multiple punishments applied to terrorist-related crimes still remains in section 2 of Article 120 of the Criminal Law, which provides: "Whoever, in addition to the crime mentioned in the preceding paragraph, commits other crimes of homicide, explosion or kidnap shall be punished in accordance with the provisions on combined punishment for several crimes."

Another important change made by Amendment III to the Criminal Law is the new offence of "terrorist funding." Article 120a was added to provide: "Whoever provides funds to any terrorist organization or individual who engages in terrorism shall be sentenced to fixed-term imprisonment of not more than five years, criminal detention, public surveillance or deprivation of political rights, and shall also be fined; if the circumstances are serious, he shall be sentenced to fixed-term imprisonment of no less than five years, and he shall also be fined or his property shall be confiscated."[19] The organization can also be the subject of such an offence.[20]

Amendment VIII to the Criminal Law of China was promulgated in 2011. It has changed the provisions for recidivism concerning some serious crimes. If a criminal has been convicted of a terrorist-related crime accordingly to Article 120 of the Criminal Law, then he or she will be treated as recidivist if the criminal commits such a crime again at any time.[21] According to the Criminal Law of China, recidivists

[18] Para.3, Order of the President No.64, Amendment III to the Criminal Law of the People's Republic of China, http://english.gov.cn/laws/2005–10/11/content_75958.htm.

[19] Amendment III to the Criminal Law of the People's Republic of China, Order of the President No.64, Para.4, http://english.gov.cn/laws/2005–10/11/content_75958.htm.

[20] Section 2 of Article 120a of Criminal Law of China states, "Where a unit commits the crime mentioned in the preceding paragraph, it shall be fined, and the persons who are directly in charge and the other persons who are directly responsible for the offence shall be punished in accordance with the provisions of the preceding paragraph."

[21] Accordingly to the Amendment VIII to the Criminal Law of China, Article 66 of the Criminal Law is amended as: "A criminal committing the crime threatening national security, the crime of terrorist

shall be given a heavier punishment; no suspension of sentence or parole shall be granted to recidivists.[22]

The November 2014 draft Amendment IX to Criminal Law in China would amend Article 120 to add property-related punishment for criminal offences of forming, leading or participating in terrorist organizations. Articles 120b, 120c, 120d and 120e would be added as new criminal offences. They would apply to acts that propagate terrorism or extremism or instigate violent and terrorist activities by way of preparing or distributing materials, releasing information and teaching face to face or through audio, video, information network, and so on (Article 120b); to acts that instigate or coerce the general public to disrupt the implementation of marriage, judicial, education and social management systems and other systems, by making use of extremism (Article 120c); to the possession of the articles, books or audio or video materials that propagate terrorism or extremism with serious circumstances (Article 120d); and to the refusal to provide relevant information or evidence to judicial investigating authorities when a person is clearly aware that any other person has committed the crime of terrorist activities or the crime of extremism (Article 120e). Also, a paragraph will be added in Article 251 of Criminal Law to punish those who force others to wear in public places the clothing or signs promoting terrorism and extremism, by violence or coercion.

In summary, the terrorist-related crimes in the current Chinese Criminal Law include the crimes to form, lead, actively participate or participate in terrorist organizations and provide financial assistance towards terrorist activities. The Draft Amendment to Criminal Law has added new terrorism or extremism offences relating to incitement to terrorism or extremism, possession of terrorist or extremist materials in serious circumstance and refusal to supply authorities with information. The punishments for terrorist-related crimes are more serious than for ordinary crimes.

In the collective crimes that require the gathering of a crowd for certain activities, such as those "gathered to forcibly seize public or private money or property" (Article 268 of Criminal Law), "gathered to seriously disturb the public order" (Article 290 of Criminal Law), "gathered to engage in affrays" (Article 292 of Criminal Law) and "gathered to assault a military restricted zone" (Article 371 of Criminal Law), only those who lead or actively participate in the gathering of a crowd or have played a substantial role shall be punished; ordinary participation shall not be liable for criminal punishment. For terrorist-related crimes, all the participants, including

activities or the organized crime with gang nature shall all be treated as a recidivist if committing any of the above-mentioned crimes at any time after serving the sentence or being granted a pardon."

22 Articles 65, 74 and 81 of the Criminal Law.

those engaged in ordinary participation in terrorist organizations, will be deemed as criminals and be liable for a criminal punishment.

As to the legal regulations to prohibit and prevent the incitement of a terrorist act or acts, there was already general provision in the 1997 Criminal Law. It provided that those who incite others to commit any crime should bear criminal liability.[23] The International Convention for the Suppression of Terrorist Bombings and the Shanghai Convention on Combating Terrorism, Separatism and Extremism, both of which China has acceded to, carry clauses on the prohibition and prevention of inciting one or more terrorist activities. All these provisions had greatly helped in combating the inciting of terrorist activity crimes in China.[24] After the UN Security Council Resolution 1624 in 2006, there has been no further reaction with regard to the incitement crimes in this regard.[25] The 2014 Amendment to Criminal Law would, however, include indictment to terrorism and extremism, apply to certain forms of speech and create crimes based on extremism in writings, recordings and teachings.

B. *Terrorism Prosecutions*

The most commonly prosecuted terrorism crimes in China are the crimes to form, lead or participate in a terrorist organization and to fund a terrorist organization. These crimes are usually prosecuted together with the crime of murder,[26] bombing[27] or inciting to subvert state power[28] under the multiple punishment principle. The

[23] Article 29 of the Criminal Law provides, "Anyone who instigates another to commit a crime shall be punished according to the role he plays in a joint crime. Anyone who instigates a person under the age of 18 to commit a crime shall be given a heavier punishment. If the instigated person has not committed the instigated crime, the instigator may be given a lighter or mitigated punishment."

[24] Fifth Report by China on the Implementation of Security Council Resolution 1373 (2001), S/2006/470, P.20.

[25] According to Decision on the Terrorist Crime Cases Handled by the Public Security Organizations issued by the Ministry of Security in August 2012, incitement, finance or other means of assistance to terrorist activities shall be investigated. It is not in fact a new provision, just a declaration to pay attention not only to the actual activity of the terrorist, but also the incitement, finance or other means of assistance to the terrorist. This regulation is not a legal document in China, but in fact it plays a very important role in the law enforcement practice since it has binding effect to security organizations all over China.

[26] Article 232 of Criminal Law provides that whoever intentionally commits homicide shall be sentenced to death, life imprisonment or fixed-term imprisonment of not less than ten years; if the circumstances are relatively minor, he or she shall be sentenced to fixed-term imprisonment of not less than three years but not more than ten years.

[27] Article 114 of Criminal Law indentifies as criminals anyone who commits arson; breaches a dike; causes an explosion; spreads poisonous or radioactive substances, infectious-disease pathogens or other substances; or uses other dangerous means, thereby endangering public security but causing no serious consequences. Anyone who commits such a crime shall be sentenced to fixed-term imprisonment of not less than three years but not more than ten years.

[28] Article 105 of Criminal Law provides that among those who organize, plot or carry out the scheme of subverting the state power or overthrowing the socialist system, the ringleaders and the others who

trial of such cases will be confidential and closed, while the sentencing shall be open to the public.[29] There are no statistical data about the number of terrorist cases, but for the individual cases, especially those very influential cases, the judgment can be easily found in China. Accordingly to the reports made by the Higher People's Court of Xinjiang Uygur Autonomous Region[30] in 2012 and 2013, terrorist cases are tried very quickly. In 2011, "Terrorism, Separatism and Extremism" crimes and crimes committed by the illegal organization Yitzhak Bout were severely punished; most of the leaders were sentenced to death. From 2003 to 2008, there were altogether 1,003 cases of endangering public safety, including terrorist cases.[31]

The procedures for terrorist crimes are almost the same as with other cases, but there are some differences. No special court is available for terrorism cases. Both the ordinary courts and the military courts are eligible for the trial of terrorist cases; the courts that are used depends on whether the criminal is a military staff member or not. Also, as in other cases, the evidence obtained through torture or degrading treatment cannot be used against the accused in terrorist cases. According to Article 62 of the Criminal Procedure Law, with regard to crimes endangering state security, those involving terrorist activities, organized crimes committed by groups in the nature of criminal syndicates, drug-related crimes and the like, if the personal safety of the witnesses, experts or victims or their close relatives is threatened due to their testimony in lawsuits, the people's courts, people's procuratorates and public security organs shall keep confidential the real names, addresses, employers and other personal information of the aforesaid persons. To guarantee fully the defence of such testimony, the defence lawyer can apply to check whether anonymous names were used with a signed undertaking to keep the information confidential during the trial process.[32]

commit major crimes shall be sentenced to life imprisonment or fixed-term imprisonment of not less than ten years; the ones who take an active part in it shall be sentenced to fixed-term imprisonment of not less than three years but not more than ten years; and the other participants shall be sentenced to fixed-term imprisonment of not more than three years of criminal detention, public surveillance or deprivation of political rights. Whoever incites others by spreading rumours or slanders or any other means to subvert state power or overthrow the socialist system shall be sentenced to fixed-term imprisonment of not more than five years of criminal detention, public surveillance or deprivation of political rights; and the ringleaders and the others who commit major crimes shall be sentenced to fixed-term imprisonment of not less than five years.

29 See Article 11, 183 and 196 of the Criminal Procedure Law of China.

30 According to the news of China, we can get a rough idea that most of the terrorist crimes were committed in Xinjiang Uygur Autonomous Region.

31 http://news.ifeng.com/mil/special/kongbu/doc/200807/0720_4117_663335.shtml.

32 Article 12 of the Decision on the implementation of criminal procedure law, which is a judicial explanation issued by Supreme People's Court, Supreme People's Procuratorate, Ministry of Public Security, Ministry of National Security, Ministry of Justice, the Legislative Affairs Commission of the NPC Standing Committee, effective from January 1, 2013.

C. *Punishment of Terrorism*

The same court that convicts terrorists also sentences them. Terrorist offenders will usually be sentenced to a quite long-term imprisonment according to the Criminal Law of China. For example, whoever forms or leads a terrorist organization shall be sentenced to a fixed-term imprisonment of not less than ten years or life imprisonment; persons who actively participate in a terrorist organization shall be sentenced to fixed-term imprisonment of not less than three years but not more than ten years; other participants shall be sentenced to fixed-term imprisonment of not more than three years' criminal detention, public surveillance or deprivation of political rights. Also, whoever provides funds to any terrorist organization or individual who engages in terrorism shall be sentenced to a fixed-term imprisonment of not more than five years' criminal detention, public surveillance or deprivation of political rights, and shall also be fined; if the circumstances are serious, he or she shall be sentenced to a fixed-term imprisonment of not less than five years, and the offender shall also be fined or his or her property shall be confiscated.

According to the General Part of Criminal Law of China, if any criminal, including anyone involved in terrorist crimes, surrenders voluntarily or performs meritorious services such as exposing an offence committed by another (and the offender's information is verified through investigation) or producing important clues for solving other cases, the offender may be given a lighter or mitigated punishment (Articles 67 and 68 of Criminal Law). The public prosecutor may also consider deciding not to prosecute the defendant based on the discretionary power of the prosecution office under such circumstances.[33]

IV. INVESTIGATIVE POWERS

The investigative powers in terrorist crime cases are carried out mainly by the public security organs and the state security organs. According to Article 3 and 4 of the Decision on the Terrorist Crime Cases Handled by the Public Security Organs,[34] terrorist crime cases are mainly investigated by the anti-terrorism unit of the public security organs. If such a case is involved with international terrorism, then the anti-terrorism unit shall assist the state security organs with the investigation.

[33] Section 2 of Article 173 of Criminal Procedure Law of China provides that "with respect to a case that is minor and [where] the offender need not be given criminal punishment or need be exempted from it according to the Criminal Law, the People's Procuratorate may decide not to initiate a prosecution."

[34] The Decision on the Terrorist Crime Cases Handled by the Public Security Organs was issued by the Ministry of Public Security on August 1, 2012, after the DIASW was announced in October 2011. The purpose of this Decision by the Ministry of Public Security is to better organize the investigation of terrorist cases based on the DISAW.

A. *Police Powers*

There is no special law or a special chapter in the Criminal Procedure, but there are some special provisions concerning terrorist cases regulated in some chapters of the Criminal Procedure Law of China. In general, the police powers of investigating terrorist cases are similar to the powers in other cases; no special preventive arrest powers and interrogation powers are available for terrorist cases, which is also a concern of China during the discussion for the draft of a special anti-terrorism law.

The right of the suspect to meet with the defence lawyer during the investigation period is restricted in terrorist cases. During the investigation period for crimes involving terrorist activities, defence lawyers shall obtain the approval of the investigating organs before meeting with the criminal suspects (Article 37 of Criminal Procedure Law).

More severe compulsory measures may apply to suspects involved in terrorist activities. For a criminal suspected to be implicated in a crime involving terrorist activities, residential surveillance at the domicile of the criminal suspect or defendant may impede the investigation; residential surveillance may, upon approval by the People's Procuratorate or the public security organs at the next higher level, be enforced at a designated place of residence, provided that residential surveillance is not enforced in a detention house or a special venue for case investigation (Article 73 of Criminal Procedure Law). In other words, a terrorist suspect can be detained before conviction of a terrorist crime. The notification to family members of the suspect may be deferred after arrest in terrorist cases. If the detainee is involved in crimes involving terrorist activities, and such notification may hinder the investigation, then the family of the detainee shall not be notified of the detention within twenty-four hours after the detention, but the family of the detainee shall be notified of relevant information immediately after the circumstances impeding investigation have been eliminated (Article 83 of Criminal Procedure Law).

Also, some technical measures and undercover investigations[35] may apply in terrorist crime cases (Articles 148 and 151 of Criminal Procedure Law), the evidence obtained through such methods will be discussed in detail in Section X.

B. *Intelligence Agencies*

There are no specific anti-terrorism intelligence agencies in China. The intelligence agencies of the public security organs and the national security organs are responsible

[35] There are no special laws or regulations about undercover investigation. Undercover investigation is regulated in the Criminal Procedure Law and some judicial explanations issued by the Supreme People's Procuratorate and the Supreme People's Court, as well as some regulations or guidelines issued by the Ministry of Public Security.

for intelligence collection concerning terrorist crimes. The intelligence agencies of the public security organs are divided into several streams, including those of the crime investigation department, the economic crime investigation department, the drug crime investigation department and so on.[36] The evidence collected by the intelligence agencies can be used as evidence in the criminal procedure if it is permitted by the Criminal Procedure Law. In judicial practice, most of the information collected by the intelligence agencies is used as clues for the public security organs to collect more evidence submitted to the court. However, according to Article 41 of the Draft AT, an intelligence agency, the National Anti-Terrorism Intelligence Center will be founded under the direction of the National Anti-Terrorism Work Leading Organ. The National Anti-Terrorism Intelligence Center will set up the information platform, coordinating interdepartment information exchange and sharing.

The information collected through electronic surveillance can be used as evidence according to the Criminal Procedure Law in China. However, according to the second reading of the Draft Anti-Terrorism Law, such measures shall be subject to strict approval procedure, and the evidence obtained can be used only for anti-terrorism purposes.[37] Article 152 of the Criminal Procedure Law provides that materials collected by technical investigations may be used as evidence in criminal proceedings. Where the use of such evidence may threaten the personal safety of relevant personnel or result in other serious consequences, protective measures shall be adopted to avoid the exposure of the applied technical measures and the true identity of such personnel, and when necessary, judges may verify the evidence outside courtrooms.[38]

V. PROSCRIPTION AND LISTING OF TERRORIST GROUPS AND INDIVIDUALS

A. *Proscription Mechanisms*

The DISAW provides that the lists of prohibited terrorist groups and terrorist individuals should be verified and adjusted by the National Anti-Terrorism Work Leading Group[39] based on Article 2 of DISAW. The lists of terrorist groups and

[36] See Li Benxian and other authors: Frame Design on the Anti-Terrorism Information and Early Warning System in China, Journal of China People's Public Security University, No. 4, 2012, P.118.

[37] People's Daily, February 26, 2015, http://www.npc.gov.cn/npc/xinwen/lfgz/2015-02/26/content_1905617.htm.

[38] Some procedural guarantees for the fairness and truthfulness of such cases are regulated in the Criminal Procedure Law and some judicial explanations in China, which will be discussed in detail in Section X.

[39] As introduced by the leader and Minister of Public Security, Guo Shengkun, the team will fully mobilize governmental resources and make every effort to fight against terrorism before attacks happen to avoid the risk of social damage, according to a statement on the ministry's official website.

individuals shall be announced by the public security organs of the PRC State Council. Until the end of 2013, altogether three lists were announced by the Ministry of Public Security.[40] The second reading of the Draft Anti-Terrorism Law would allow the Courts in China to list terrorists or terrorist groups during the criminal procedure, and also enable the Ministry of Foreign Affairs to apply for the listing of terrorists and terrorist groups.[41]

According to the DISAW, the regulation on the verification of the terrorist groups and individuals should be issued by the PRC State Council. However, there has been no such regulation open to the public up to now. Based on the lists announced already by the Ministry of Public Security, the terrorist groups and individuals are mainly listed according to Chinese priorities in combating terrorism. Meanwhile, the lists of terrorist groups and individuals announced by the Security Council of the United Nations should be verified by the National Anti-Terrorism Work Leading Group via the Ministry of Foreign Affairs. Thus, the lists announced by the UN Security Council and the lists announced by the Chinese government are both valid in China. The draft 2014 terrorism law also provides for the listing of individual terrorists and terrorist groups.

The listing criteria of the terrorist groups or individuals are based on a broader definition than existing crimes relating to terrorism. As explained by Zhao Yongchen, the Vice Director of the Anti-terrorism Bureau of the Ministry of Public Security, while announcing the first list of terrorist groups and individuals on December 15, 2003, not only those who directly or indirectly participate the terrorist activities but also those who involved in "organizing, planning, inciting or instigating" the enforcement of terrorist activities can be listed.[42] According to Article 5 of DISAW, when publishing the lists of terrorist organizations and people involved in terrorist activities, the public security department under the State Council shall at the same time decide to freeze the funds or other assets related to the relevant terrorist organizations and people involved in terrorist activities. However, such listings cannot be used in a criminal prosecution; whether the listed person or organization has actually been involved in terrorist acts shall be proved before the court in due process. This will not change under the 2014 Draft Anti-Terrorism Law.

[40] The first list, published on December 15, 2013, included four "East Turkistan" terrorist organizations and eleven terrorists; the second list, published on October 21, 2008, includes eight terrorists; and the third list, published on April 5, 2012, includes six terrorists.

[41] People's Daily, February 26, 2015, http://www.npc.gov.cn/npc/xinwen/lfgz/2015-02/26/content_1905617.htm.

[42] See Xinhua Net, http://news.xinhuanet.com/legal/2003–12/15/content_1232510.htm.

B. *Challenges to Proscriptions and Listings*

Until now, there has been no individual challenge against the listing decisions of the Chinese government. When the lists are announced by the Chinese government, the factual grounds for such listings are disclosed, but there is no special procedure and tribunals dealing with the challenges against such listings. However, according to the Draft Anti- Terrorism Law, the listed individual terrorists and terrorist groups can apply for a review to the National Anti-Terrorism Leading organization.

It should be noticed that to put some terrorist group or individual on the listing does not necessary mean that the organization or person is deemed to be terrorist in the sense of law. If a person listed was accused in the criminal procedure, then he or she can defend by himself or herself and be defended by a defence attorney. The facts disclosed together with the list cannot be used as evidence against the defendant in the criminal procedure. As introduced by famous anti-terrorism expert Mei Jianming, when the Chinese government announced the third list of terrorists, the listing resulted in the freezing of the funds or other assets related to the relevant terrorist organizations and people involved in terrorist activities at the same time. Also, the listing shows the positive attitude and ability of the Chinese government in gathering intelligence regarding terrorist acts and promotes international cooperation in combating terrorism.[43] Article 71 of the Draft Anti-Terrorism Law confirms the practice of freezing the funds and other assets of the listed terrorist individuals and groups. Meanwhile, if the terrorist individual is a foreigner, he or she can be arrested, extradicted or prosecuted.

VI. REGULATION OF TERRORISM FINANCING

As a permanent member of the Security Council of the UN, China plays an important role in combating terrorism financing. Some regulations on the combating of terrorism financing were issued to set up gradually the counter-terrorism financing system in China, such as Provisions on Anti–Money Laundering of Financial Institutions (PALFI), Measures for the Administration of Financial Institutions' Report on Large and Suspicious RMB Transactions and Payments (MAFIRLSRTP), Measures for the Administration of Financial Institutions' Report on Large and Suspicious Foreign Exchange Transactions (MAFIRLSFET), the Anti–Money Laundering Law, Measures for the Administration of Financial Institutions' Report Involving Suspicious Transactions of Terrorist Financing Activities (MAFIRSTTFA) and Notice of the People's Bank of China on Implementing the Notice of the Ministry of Foreign Affairs on Implementing Relevant Resolutions

[43] http://epaper.jinghua.cn/html/2012-04/07/content_777349.htm.

of the Security Council (NBINFAIRRSC). On January 10, 2014, Measures for the Administration of Freezing of Assets Involved with Terrorist Activities (MAFAITA) was issued by the People's Bank of China, the Ministry of Public Security and the Ministry of National Security, which has improved anti-terrorism financing legislation in China.

A. *The Regulatory Regime to Counter Terrorism Financing*

The terrorism financing regime was set up on the basis of the listing of terrorist groups and individuals verified in China. The NBINFAIRRSC provides that Chinese financial institutions should take corresponding financial restriction measures based on the list of terrorist groups and personnel forwarded by the financial supervision unit, which was issued by the Ministry of Foreign Affairs according to Resolutions 1267 and 1373 by the Security Council of the UN. Meanwhile, Article 3 of the MAFAITA specifies that the financial institutions and other certain entities should take corresponding asset-freezing measures based on the list of terrorist groups and personnel and the decisions to freeze the assets issued by the Ministry of Public Security.

Unlike some other countries, there is no special administrative regulation concerning terrorism financing and money laundering in China. In the area of criminal law, financing terrorist activities and money laundering are two separate offences in the Criminal Law. Terrorism financing is regulated in Article 120 of the Criminal Law, while money laundering is regulated in Article 191 of the Criminal Law. But the two offences are closely related in that the resources for money laundering include the money earned through crimes of a terrorist nature (Article 2 of the Anti–Money Laundering Law).

In 2003, the Anti–Money Laundering Bureau was set up inside the People's Bank of China, whose mandate covers the organizing and coordinating of anti–money laundering and anti-terrorism. In 2004, the China Anti–Money Laundering Monitoring and Analysis Centre was established under the leadership of the People's Bank of China, with the duty to collect and analyze big amounts and suspicious transactions reported by financial institutions and other entities. After careful screening, the suspicious transaction information is submitted to the Anti–Money Laundering Bureau of the People's Bank of China. Then the Anti–Money Laundering Bureau transfers the information, which may be related to crimes, for criminal investigation. According to the data published by the website of the People's Bank of China, quite a lot of key clues in the form of suspicious transactions were found every year. In 2008, 1,932 cases were discovered from of a large number of suspicious transaction clues. In 2009, the number was 1,082; in 2010, the number was 1,038; in 2011, the number was 1,593. In 2012, altogether, 4,800 suspicious transaction reports were collected and received, and 530 reports were used to file a case for an anti–money laundering investigation.[44]

In 2005, China was invited to be an observer of the Financial Action Task Force (FATF). In 2006, the FATF carried out an overall field evaluation towards the anti–money laundering and anti-terrorism financing progress in China. In 2007, China became a member of the FATF, and a follow-up report was submitted to the FATF in 2012.[45]

B. *Criminal Offences of Terrorism Financing*

Article 120a, "the offence of financing terrorist activities," was added to Article 120 in 2001 in response to Security Council Resolutions 1267 and 1373. Article 120a states that "whoever provides funds to any terrorist organization or individual who engages in terrorism" shall be liable for such crime, which means that a subjective fault element is needed to convict a suspect of financing terrorist activities. However, the sentencing for terrorism financing is lighter compared to the "offence of forming, leading and participating in terrorist organizations." The criminal convicted of terrorism financing shall be sentenced to fixed-term imprisonment of not more than five years' criminal detention, public surveillance or deprivation of political rights and shall also be fined; if the circumstances are serious, he or she shall be sentenced to fixed-term imprisonment of not less than five years, and also be fined or have his or her property confiscated.

The funds given to finance legitimate and humanitarian activities by a terrorist group can also be deemed as financing terrorist activities because the illegal nature of the organization still remains. There is no discussion yet as to whether the funds given for humanitarian activities of a terrorist organization should be prohibited or not since so far no such case has occurred in China.

Another way to forfeit terrorist property was established in the newly amended Criminal Procedure Law, which went into effect starting January 1, 2013. Article 280 of the Criminal Procedure Law provides that a people's procuratorate may apply with a people's court for confiscation of illegal gains in a case of grave crimes, such as corruption, bribery or terrorist activities where the criminal suspects or defendants have absconded and have not been found one year after the public arrest warrants were issued or where the criminal suspects or defendants have died, and the illegal gains and other property involved in the case shall be confiscated pursuant to the Criminal Law.

[44] See website of the People's Bank of China, http://www.pbc.gov.cn/publish/fanxiqianju/3295/index.html.

[45] See the website of the FATF, http://www.fatf-gafi.org/countries/a-c/china/.

VII. IMMIGRATION MEASURES

Illegal immigration has been heavily combated by the Chinese government. A series of criminal and administrative laws and regulations have been improved to set up a legal foundation for the prevention and combating of illegal immigration in China, which includes the Exit and Entry Administration Law (EEAL) of PRC, the Law of the People's Republic of China on Penalties for Administration of Public Security (LPAPS), the Nationality Law of PRC, the Criminal Law, Administration on the Examination and Approval of Permanent Residence of Foreigners in China (AEAPRFC) and Regulation on the Exit and Entry of Foreigners (REEF).

A. *Immigration Detention*

The Exit and Entry Administration Law (EEAL), effective from July 1, 2013, had no special provisions on the exit and entry of terrorists, but put terrorists into the category of those who "endanger China's national security and interests." For example, Articles 21 and 25 of the EEAL provide that if foreigners may endanger China's national security and interests, disrupt social and public order or commit other crimes, then the foreigners shall not be issued with China visas or shall not be allowed to enter China. Article 49 of EEAL provides that if a foreigner endangers China's national security and interests, the Ministry of Public Security shall decide to cancel the foreigner's permanent residence in China.

Regarding the procedures for handling such suspects, both immigration procedures regulated in the EEAL, which is an administrative measure in nature, and the criminal procedure in the Criminal Procedure Law may apply accordingly depending on the nature of the violation. According to Article 88 of the EEAL, where violations of the law constitute crimes, criminal liabilities shall be prosecuted in accordance with the law, which means that if the violator has already committed a crime, then the criminal procedure may apply with priority; if no criminal law was involved, and then the immigration procedure shall apply.

Some compulsory measures may be applied to the suspected foreigners during the immigration procedure regulated by the EEAL, which include on-the-spot interrogation and continued interrogation,[46] investigative detention[47] and movement

[46] Article 59 of the EEAL provides that on-the-spot interrogation and continued interrogation according to the People's Police Law may be carried out upon those who may endanger public security and interests.

[47] Article 60 of the EEAL specifies that if a foreigner still cannot be cleared of suspicion and needs to be further investigated after on-the-spot interrogation or continued interrogation, relevant organs may detain them for investigation. Periods of detention for investigation shall not exceed thirty days; if cases are complicated, periods may be extended to sixty days upon approval by public security organs under local people's governments at the next-highest level or exit-entry frontier inspection organs.

restriction.[48] When foreigners are detained for investigation, relevant organs shall show written decisions on detention for investigation, but no evidence requirement is written in the EEAL. After the detention or movement restriction, a decision of repatriation may be made upon the foreigner under question. Repatriated personnel shall not be allowed to enter China within one to five years from the date of repatriation. Possible remedy may be sought against the aforementioned measures. Foreigners who refuse to accept continued interrogation, detention for investigation, movement restriction and repatriation imposed on them in accordance with the EEAL may apply for administrative reconsideration in accordance with the law, and decisions of such administrative reconsideration shall be final (Article 62 of the EEAL).

If a foreigner engages in activities not corresponding to the purposes of his or her stay or residences or is involved in circumstances that make it inappropriate for the foreigner to continue staying or residing in China because of violation of Chinese laws and regulations, he or she may be ordered to exit China within a given time limit. Where foreigners' violations of this law are serious but have not constituted crimes, the Ministry of Public Security may deport them. The ministry's punishment decisions shall be final. Deported foreigners shall not be allowed to enter China within ten years from the date of deportation (Article 81 of the EEAL).

B. *Immigration Proceedings and Torture*

The EEAL includes no specific discussion about torture and the use of evidence obtained through torture in immigration proceedings. But if a person was tortured during the immigration procedure and an unfair compulsory measure or decision was made regarding that person, then he or she may apply for an administrative reconsideration, where the torture may be considered as a cause to nullify or change the decision. According to Article 62 of the EEAL, foreigners who refuse to accept continued interrogation, detention for investigation, movement restriction and repatriation imposed on them in accordance with this law may apply for administrative reconsideration in accordance with the law. While in Article 28 of the Administrative Reconsideration Law in China, if a specific administrative act is taken in violation of statutory procedures or if authority is exceeded or power is abused, the administrative decision shall be nullified or declared illegal. In such cases, the defending party shall be ordered to take another specific administrative act within a time limit. Thus, if torture or

[48] Article 61 of the EEAL states that under some special circumstances, such as being ill with a serious disease, pregnant or breast feeding, under the age of sixteen or over the age of seventy, the detention for investigation may not apply to foreigners and their movements may be restricted.

cruel and degrading treatment is used in immigration proceedings, the foreigner can forward this issue to the administrative reconsideration organs and use it as a ground to nullify or change the decision.

China is one of the state parties of the United Nations Convention Against Torture and Other Cruel, Inhuman or Degrading Treatment or Punishment. Article 3 of the aforementioned convention provides that no state party shall expel, return ("refouler") or extradite a person to another state where there are substantial grounds for believing that he or she would be in danger of being subjected to torture. There is no direct national legislation maintaining a ban on refoulement or deportation to torture, nor were there any reports of such individual cases in the mass media in China. But in the Extradition Law of China, such a ban on possible torture is clearly required. Article 8 of the Extradition Law provides that the request for extradition made by a foreign state to the People's Republic of China shall be rejected if the person sought has been or will probably be subjected to torture or other cruel, inhumane or humiliating treatment or punishment in the requesting state.

VIII. ADMINISTRATIVE AND EXECUTIVE MEASURES

As is guaranteed in Article 12 of the Criminal Procedure Law in China, no person shall be found guilty without being judged as such by a People's Court according to the law. No conviction can be made outside the courts. However, some alternative measures can be taken before or after the criminal procedure as a supplement to the criminal law.

Before a person is filed as the suspect of a criminal case concerning terrorist-related crimes, the police can make an on-the-spot investigation and continued investigation, which are administrative measures in nature, according to the People's Police Act and the Exit and Entry Administration Law of China. In order to maintain public order, the people's police officers of public security organs may, upon producing an appropriate certificate, interrogate and inspect the person suspected of having violated a law or committed a crime. After interrogation and inspection, the person may be taken to a public security organ for further interrogation upon approval of this public security organ, if he or she is under any of the following circumstances: (1) being accused of a criminal offence; (2) being suspected of committing an offence on the scene; (3) being suspected of committing an offence and being of unknown identity; and (4) carrying articles that were probably obtained illegally. The period of time for holding the interrogated person shall be not more than twenty-four hours, counting from the moment he or she is taken into the public security organ. In special cases, this time limit may be extended to forty-eight hours upon approval by the public security organ at or above the county level, and the interrogation record shall be kept on file.[49] If further interrogation of the person is not approved, he or she shall be released immediately. If, through further interrogation, a public security organ considers it necessary to detain the interrogated person or adopt other compulsory measures against him or her according to law, a decision shall be made within the aforementioned period of time. If the decision cannot be made within that period, the interrogated person shall be released immediately (Article 9 of the People's Police Law).

The Draft Anti-Terrorism Law has made some detailed regulations concerning the investigative powers of the police (Article 47 and 48). It allows the public security organs to check bank information and supervise terrorist-related funds (Article 50) and to engage in search and seizure (Article 51). Meanwhile, according to Article 52 of the Draft AT, the public security organs can apply one or more of the following administrative measures to restrict terrorist suspects: the prohibition on leaving a designated domicile or area without prior approval; the prohibition on attending mass activities or commercial activities; the prohibition on taking public transportation or entering specific public places; the prohibition on accepting specific public services or on purchasing or using specific facilities or goods; the prohibition on meeting or communicating with specific people; requirements to report the activities and income resources to the public security organs at fixed periods; and requirements to submit travel documents, ID or drivers licence to such authorities.

If an acquittal or a reversal of conviction in a terrorism case was ordered by a court, then some administrative measures may be taken after the judicial process. The main legislative grounds are the Law of the People's Republic of China on Penalties for Administration of Public Security (LPAPS) and the Exit and Entry Administration Law. According to Article 2 of LPAPS, if a person disturbs public order, endangers public safety, infringes on the rights of person and property or hampers social administration in a manner that is harmful to the society and constitutes a crime according to the Criminal Law of China, he or she shall be investigated for criminal responsibility according to law; and if such an act is not serious enough for criminal punishment, the public security organ shall impose on the person a penalty for administration of public security, according to this law. Thus, if a suspect involved

[49] According to Article 9 of the People's Police Act (1995), if further interrogation of the person is approved, his or her family or the organization in which he or she works shall be notified without delay. The "interrogation" here is deemed as an administrative measure to ensure public security, not "interrogation" in the criminal procedure. However, according to the newly revised Criminal Procedure Law of 2012, if a suspect involved in terrorist acts is detained for interrogation in the criminal procedure, the notice of such detention to the family may be exceptionally delayed if such notice will hinder the investigation. It is suggested by the author that the notice of detention with administrative nature regulated in the People's Police Act shall also be delayed if such notice may hinder the investigation.

in a terrorist crime cannot be found guilty in a criminal procedure, administrative measures, such as a warning, administrative detention and a fine may still apply to the person. To a foreigner who acts against the administration of public security, departure from the country within a time limit or deportation attached to a penalty may be applicable (Article 10 of the LPAPS). Some compulsory measures, such as on-the-spot interrogation, continued interrogation, detention and movement restriction, as well as the administrative measures of departure from the country within a time limit or deportation may also be applied to a person outside the criminal procedure, according to the EEAL, which has already been discussed in Section VII.

As to the requirement of evidence, there are not a lot of provisions in comparison with what is required for the criminal procedure. Under the LPAPS, due process of collecting evidence is required. Article 79 of the LPAPS provides that public security organs and the people's police shall investigate cases of public security according to law. Extorting confessions by torture or collecting evidence by such illegal means as intimidation, enticement or deception is strictly prohibited. Evidence collected by illegal means shall not be used for conviction.

Other than the measures against the freedom of the person, some administrative measures against the property related to terrorist crimes are regulated in Chinese law as well, which include the freezing of assets related to terrorist crimes, restriction of transactions and confiscation of illegal income.[50]

IX. ROLE OF MILITARY AND EXTRA-TERRITORIAL COUNTER-TERRORISM ACTIVITIES

A. *Military Courts and Detention*

There is no special legislation in the anti-terrorism law concerning enforcement by the military forces.[51] The participation of military forces in combating terrorist activities is mainly regulated in the Martial Law of the PRC. Article 2 of the Martial Law provides that the state may decide to apply martial law when such a state of emergency as unrest, rebellion or grave riot occurs that seriously endangers unification and security of the state or public security and under which public order cannot be maintained and safety of people's lives and property cannot be ensured unless extraordinary measures are taken. Under the status of martial law, the State Council may make a suggestion

[50] For reference, see Article 26 of the Anti–Money Laundering Law, Article 3 of the Measures for the Administration of Freezing of Assets Involved with Terrorist Activities; Article 3 of the Notice of the People's Bank of China on Implementing the Notice of the Ministry of Foreign Affairs on Implementing Relevant Resolutions of the Security Council; Articles 72, 74, 79 and 80 of the Exit and Entry Administration Law.

[51] See Liu Renshan: Research on Legal Issues of International Terrorism, Beijing, China Democracy and Legality Press, 2011.

to the Central Military Commission that it dispatch troops of the People's Liberation Army (PLA) to help perform martial law tasks (Article 8 of the Martial Law). The martial law–enforcing officers have the right to detain the persons who are committing an offence that endangers state security or disrupts public order or who are strongly suspected of such an offence immediately and to search the person of the detainees, the houses of criminal suspects and the places where criminal offenders, criminal suspects or weapons, ammunition and other dangerous articles are suspected of being concealed (Articles 24 and 25 of the Martial Law). During the period of martial law, the procedures and time limit for detention and arrest may be free from the restrictions of the relevant provisions of the Criminal Procedure Law of the People's Republic of China, except that an arrest shall be subject to approval or decision of a People's Procuratorate (Article 27 of the Martial Law).

Besides the participation of anti-terrorism activities during the martial period, the military courts have jurisdiction over terrorist-related crimes after the investigation and prosecution by the military police and military procuratorate. The security departments of the Army shall exercise the power of investigation with respect to criminal offences that have occurred in the Army. The handling of criminal cases by the security departments of the Army shall be governed by the relevant provisions of the Criminal Procedure Law in China (Article 290 of the Criminal Procedure Law).

Although the criminal procedures for the ordinary courts and the military courts are almost the same, the appointment and removal of military judges are quite different. Accordingly to Article 11 of the Judges Law of the PRC, the measures for the appointment or removal of the presidents, vice-presidents, members of the judicial committees, chief judges and associate chief judges of divisions and judges of the Special People's Courts such as the military courts shall be formulated by the Standing Committee of the National People's Congress separately.

B. *The Extra-Territorial Treatment of Citizens Suspected of Terrorism*

The nationality principle of jurisdiction applies to the Chinese Criminal Law. Article 7 of the Criminal Law provides that this law shall be applicable to any citizen of the People's Republic of China who commits a crime prescribed in this law outside the territory and territorial waters and space of the People's Republic of China.[52] Any person who commits a crime outside the territory of China may still be investigated for his or her criminal responsibility, even if that person has already been tried in a foreign country. However, if he or she has already received criminal punishment in the

[52] However, if the maximum punishment to be imposed is fixed-term imprisonment of not more than three years as stipulated in this law, the citizen may be exempted from the investigation for his or her criminal responsibility.

foreign country, the person may be exempted from punishment or given a mitigated punishment (Article 10 of the Criminal Law). Thus, even if a Chinese national had been detained by another state because of suspicions of involvement in terrorism, he or she may still be investigated and tried by Chinese courts.

C. *Extra-Territorial Terrorism Law Enforcement*

Some reports can be found about the joint anti-terror exercises carried out by Chinese military forces with other countries, such as India, Pakistan and the member states of Shanghai Cooperation Organization.[53] There is no legislation about the extra-territorial investigations in terrorist-related cases, but some similar legislation issued by the Ministry of Public Security was found as a reference. According to Articles 6, 7 and 11 of the Temporary Regulations on the Extra-territorial Arrest Enforced by the Economic Crime Investigation Department of the Public Security Organs, arrest and evidence collection outside of China shall be carried out in accordance with the extradition treaties signed with related countries, agreements of judicial assistance, agreements about combating crimes among the governments and other regulations. If no such regulations are available, the arrest and evidence collection can be carried out via diplomatic channels under the principle of reciprocity or through the channel of the International Criminal Police Organization. The arrest and evidence collection shall be carried out by means of extradition, deportation, bilateral or multilateral law enforcement assistance and other legal channels.

Cooperation between China and foreign countries in the area of extradition is conducted in accordance with related extradition treaties or on the basis of equality and reciprocity. In the absence of treaties, extradition is to be conducted through diplomatic channels, and the Ministry of Foreign Affairs of the People's Republic of China is the communicating authority thereof. Procedures for submission of extradition requests to China by foreign countries, and to foreign countries by China, are specified in Chapters II and III of the Extradition Law of the People's Republic of China.[54] Thus far, no extradition case regarding a suspect or criminal involved in terrorist crimes has been reported in China. The Extradition Law of China includes no provisos regarding the extradition of those who may be sentenced to the death penalty after being extradited.

[53] See http://news.ifeng.com/mil/data/detail_2010_09/02/2418647_0.shtml. Also see http://www.china.org.cn/english/China/193029.htm.

[54] Fifth Report by China on the Implementation of Security Council Resolution 1373 (2001), S/2006/470, P.16.

X. SECRECY AND TERRORISM

A. *Secrecy Claims and Secret Evidence*

Defence lawyers can obtain access to the evidence even involving state secrets. They have the right to apply for access to the evidence collected by the prosecution office, as well as to meet and communicate with the suspect even if the case involves state secrets. If the defence attorney is not a lawyer,[55] however, the public prosecution office may reject the application of the non-lawyer defence attorney on such a request (Article 48 of the Guideline for the People's Procuratorate in the Criminal Procedure [GPPCP]). Also, if the public prosecutor has edited interrogation videos to protect state secrets, such editing should be announced to the court in the trial (Article 75 of the GPPCP).

Whether the defence attorney can pass the information obtained in the case file, including state secrets, to the accused, there are still different opinions in the judicial areas and between academics. Moreover, there is no clear legislation about this in the criminal procedure law in China. However, the defence lawyers may verify the facts with the suspect during the meeting with him or her without the presence of police. If the cases involve terrorist crimes, such meetings between defence lawyers and the accused may be denied by the investigation organs (Article 37 of the Criminal Procedure Law).

B. *Secrecy in the Courtroom and Anonymous Witnesses*

State secrets cannot be made open to the public during the process of criminal procedure. Article 52 of the Criminal Procedure Law of China requires that evidence involving state secrets, trade secrets or personal privacy shall be kept confidential. A people's court shall try cases of first instance in open court sessions, except for the cases involving state secrets or personal privacy (Article 183 of the Criminal Procedure Law).

There are several regulations in the Chinese Criminal Procedure Law to keep the evidence involving state secrets confidential. The public prosecutor shall suggest the production of evidence involving state secrets only with the court, prosecutors, investigators, accused and defence attorney being present (Article

[55] The defence attorney in China is not necessarily a lawyer with a lawyer's license. Article 32 of the Criminal Procedure Law provides that, in addition to exercising the right to defend himself or herself, a criminal suspect or a defendant may entrust one or two persons as his or her defenders. The following persons may be entrusted as defenders: (1) lawyers; (2) persons recommended by a public organization or the unit to which the criminal suspect or the defendant belongs; and (3) guardians or relatives and friends of the criminal suspect or the defendant.

75 of the GPPCP). If a public prosecutor, accused or victim produces evidence involving state secrets, then the court shall prevent the production. Where such evidence is indeed relevant to the case, the people's court may, depending on actual circumstances, decide to change the trial of the case to a closed court session or to conduct a judicial investigation of relevant evidence in a non-public manner. Also, if a case is tried in an open court session, the relevant people's court shall stop the defendant from making final statements that involve state secrets, personal privacy or commercial secrets.[56]

Intelligence service members who have investigated terrorist-related cases may be asked to testify anonymously or be questioned by the judge outside of the court.

Article 62 of the Criminal Procedure Law provides the protective measure of "keeping confidential the real name, address, employer and other personal information" of the witnesses, who include the intelligence service members serving as a witness. If the people's courts, people's procuratorates or public security organs decide not to disclose the real names, addresses, employers and other personal information of the witness, they may use an assumed name or other means to replace the witness's personal information in the written record (Article 12 of the Provisions of the Supreme People's Court, the Supreme People's Procuratorate, the Ministry of Public Security, the Ministry of State Security, the Ministry of Justice and the Commission of Legislative Affairs of the National People's Congress on Certain Issues Related to the Implementation of the Criminal Procedure Law [PCIICPL]).

According to Article 152 of the Criminal Procedure Law, the materials collected by technical means, including electronic surveillance and undercover investigation, may be used as evidence in criminal proceedings. Where the use of such evidence may threaten the personal safety of relevant personnel or result in other serious consequences, protective measures are adopted to avoid the exposure of the applied technical measures and the true identity of such personnel, and when necessary, judges may verify the evidence outside courtrooms. If an intelligence service member testifies in court, then he or she can testify anonymously.

However, there are some guarantees or safeguard measures for the aforementioned procedures. Firstly, the use of wiretapping, undercover investigation and other technical measures should be open to access by the defence attorneys.[57] Secondly, if an anonymous witness is used, the use of such assumed names shall be explained in writing, and such legal documents and evidentiary materials shall be marked

[56] Article 68, 235 of the Interpretations of the Supreme People's Court on the Application of the "Criminal Procedure Law of the People's Republic of China"(ICACPL).

[57] Article 20 of the PCIICPL provides that where any materials collected using technical investigation measures are adopted as evidence, the legal documents approving the adoption of the technical investigation measures shall be attached to them. Defence attorneys may consult, excerpt and reproduce such legal documents and present them in court during court sessions.

with the classification thereof and put on file separately. A defence attorney who accesses the information about the use of an assumed name with regard to a witness, expert witness or victim upon approval by a court shall sign a written non-disclosure commitment (Article 12 of the PCIICPL).Thirdly, the evidence obtained by verification outside the courtroom shall be admitted as the basis for deciding the case only after cross-examination in court, unless both the accused and the prosecution have raised no objection when being consulted outside the courtroom. Relevant situations shall be recorded in writing (Article 220 of the ICACPL).

XI. OTHER MATTERS

Under the "one country, two systems" formula, the legislation and judicial systems of Hong Kong and Macao are quite different from that of Mainland China. The constitutional framework for the legal system is provided by the Hong Kong Basic Law and Macao Basic Law accordingly. The anti-terrorism laws in the two Special Administrative Regions (SARs) are different from the anti-terrorism law in Mainland China.

A. *Anti-Terrorism Law in the Hong Kong SAR*

The United Nations (Anti-Terrorism Measures) Ordinance (hereinafter referred to as "Ordinance") was promulgated by the Legislative Council of the Hong Kong Special Administrative Region in 2002. In response to the UN Security Council Resolutions 1373(2001) and the recommendations against terrorist financing by the FATF, several amendments were made in 2004, such as the definition of terrorist groups, the regulatory measures on terrorism financing and more. On April 1, 2012, the Anti–Money Laundering and Counter-Terrorist Financing (Financial Institutions) Ordinance came into effect in Hong Kong to better combat money-laundering and terrorist financing.

"Terrorist act" is defined in Hong Kong with reference to the UK and Canadian definition.[58] The intention for the use or threat of terrorist action includes not only the compelling effect on the government or an international organization (which is similar to Mainland China's definition), but also to the public or a section of the public (which is not regulated in the laws of Mainland China at least until the 2014 Draft Anti-Terrorism Law, which, if enacted, would cover acts and threats that

[58] Report of the Bills Committee on the United Nations (Anti-terrorist Measures) Bill, § 14, at http://www.legco.gov.hk/yr01-02/english/bc/bc59/reports/bc590710cb2-rpt-e.pdf; Section 1 Terrorism Act (2000), at: http://www.legislation.gov.uk/ukpga/2000/11/section/1; Anti-terrorism Act (2001), S.C. 2001, Ch. 41.

cause "social panic").[59] The terrorist act shall be made for the purpose of advancing a political, religious or ideological cause, which is not required in Mainland China and Macao. Terrorist-related crimes are regulated in the Ordinance in Hong Kong as well, such as provision or collection of property to commit terrorist acts, supply of weapons to terrorists and terrorist associates, recruitment of terrorists, false threats of terrorist acts and bombing of prescribed objects relating to ships and fixed platforms. The definitions of terrorism-related terms, such as "terrorists," "terrorist associates," "terrorist assets property" and "terrorist acts," are regulated in the Ordinance. "Terrorist" is defined in a broader way, which includes a person who attempts to commit a terrorist act. Any property used to finance or assist the commission of a terrorist act is deemed as terrorist property.

As to the regulation of terrorism financing, the newly promulgated Anti–Money Laundering and Counter-Terrorist Financing (Financial Institutions) regulation has played a very important role. The financial institutions shall help to supervise the activities suspicious of money-laundering and terrorism financing. The Anti–Money Laundering and Counter-Terrorist Financing (Financial Institutions) Review Tribunal was set up to review disciplinary decisions made by the relevant authorities under the Ordinance against financial institutions, as well as licensing decisions made by the Commissioner of Customs and Excise in respect of money service operators.

The immigration measures of Hong Kong can also serve anti-terrorism functions. The process of issuing Hong Kong identification cards and passports is very rigorous to make counterfeiting extremely difficult. Hong Kong already has numerous laws in effect criminalizing the forgery of travel documents issued under the regulations governing entry into the Special Administrative Region.

B. *Anti-Terrorism Law in Macao SAR*

"The law on Prevention and Suppression of Terrorism Crimes" and "The law on Prevention and Suppression of Money Laundering Crimes" were promulgated in 2006. These laws have criminalized terrorist-related activities, such as establishing, forming, participating in or supporting terrorist organizations. Moreover, a very specific anti–money laundering rule was set up based on Macao's status as a gaming and gambling centre.

The establishment and forming of and participation in terrorist organizations, the financing of terrorist organizations and the incitement of terrorist activities and even preparations to form terrorist organizations are punished under Macao law.

59 Para.1, The United Nations (Anti-Terrorism Measures) Ordinance.

The definition of "terrorism organization" is clearly written in Macao law, which refers to any association of two or more persons acting in concert to impede, alter or subvert, by means of violence, the operation of the political, economical or social system of the Macao SAR, to compel a public authority to do or refrain from doing any act or to tolerate it, or to intimidate certain persons, group of persons or the population in general, through the commission of certain prohibited acts.[60] As discussed previously, the intention of a terrorist act in Macao is similar to that in Hong Kong. Also, the concrete acts that may be deemed as terrorist acts in Macao are much broader than Hong Kong and Mainland China. According to Article 4 of "The law on Prevention and suppression of Terrorism Crimes," besides the ordinarily regulated acts of terrorist crimes, "the research and development of nuclear, biological or chemical," and "the use of nuclear energy, fire weapons, biological or chemical weapons, explosives, incendiary media of any kind, parcels or mails containing extremely dangerous devices or substances" shall be deemed terrorist acts as well, together with other required elements.

The law concerning the combating of terrorist financing is made based on the characteristics of the gaming industry. The obligated entities for the supervision of terrorist financing include not only those traditional institutions, such as credit institutions, financial corporations, insurance, precious metals dealers, lawyers, solicitors, notaries, registrars, auditors, accountants and tax advisers, but also some special entities. These include the entities that operate games of chance, lotteries, betting and promoter's games of chance in casinos, money exchange companies and entities that offer fast delivery of securities in cash.

In terms of immigration measures, Macao law allows certain designated persons to be denied entry. For example, all persons whose names appear on the list of terrorists provided by the Counter-Terrorism Committee of the Security Council will be refused entry without exception. Customs and immigration officials can read all documents released by the government in that regard. The process of issuing a Macao travel document has also been perfected; it is divided into several phases, each of which is the responsibility of a different person. The document contains the holder's photograph and fingerprints. The system for issuing Macao travel documents has been certified under the ISO9001:2000 standard. Macao also has advanced technological means at its disposal for identifying forged documents.[61]

[60] Article 4 Law no. 3/2006 of 30 March 2006, *Boletim Oficial* I, No. 15, 10 April 2006, 433. For an unofficial English translation see Law no. 3/2006, on the prevention and suppression of the crimes of terrorism, at www.gif.gov.mo/web1/doc/gif/law-3-2006.pdf.

[61] Report by China on the Implementation of Security Council Resolution 1373 (2001), S/2001/1270, P.13.

XII. CONCLUSION

Many terrorist attacks in China are part of the terrorism activities of Al-Qaeda, especially one branch of it, known as the East Turkestan Islamic Movement (ETIM). As announced by the State Council of the PRC, over 200 terrorist attacks were performed by ETIM or with the support of ETIM, 162 people killed and more than 440 wounded in Xinjiang, China, from 1990 to 2001.[62] ETIM was listed as terrorist organization by the Security Council of the UN on September, 11, 2002,[63] and was recognized as one of the first four terrorist organizations in China in December 15, 2003.[64] The Afghanistan Taliban and Osama Bin Laden's Al-Qaeda provided both financial and technical support to ETIM. ETIM sent its personnel for military and terrorism training in Afghanistan with the Taliban and Al Qaeda, and such personnel came back to China for terrorist activities such as explosions, assassination and poisoning.[65] In 1998, Osama Bin Laden funded the East Turkestan Liberation Organization with millions of U.S. dollars to support them in engaging in religious extremist and violent terrorist activities.[66] Instigation of terrorism and teaching of violent techniques via online videos has become a new method of ETIM to provoke terrorist attacks in China. Starting from 2013, ETIM has increased the frequency and quantity of terrorism videos via the Internet, spreading violent terrorist and extreme religious thoughts such as Jihadi ideology, which had become an important precipitating factor of terrorist attacks in China. As revealed by the State Internet Information Office, almost all the criminals of the terrorist attacks that happened during these few years have admitted that they were encouraged and influenced by the online terrorism videos, most of which were manufactured and spread by ETIM.[67]

The rapid increase of terrorist attacks has aroused greater attention from the Chinese government.[68] As was discussed by the Minister of Public Security, Guo Shengkun, anti-terrorism is now an issue concerned with state safety, public safety and public order and is closely connected with the fundamental interests of the public.[69] The Chinese government has invested greater effort to combat

[62] http://www.people.com.cn/GB/shizheng/20020121/652705.html.

[63] http://www.un.org/sc/committees/1267/NSQE08802E.shtml.

[64] http://www.mps.gov.cn/n16/n983040/n1988498/1988540.html.

[65] http://www.gov.cn/gongbao/content/2002/content_61790.htm.

[66] http://www.mps.gov.cn/n16/n983040/n1988498/1988553.html.

[67] http://news.xinhuanet.com/politics/2014-06/24/c_1111293608.htm.

[68] For example, a very recent terrorist attack in a railway station in the southwest Chinese city of Kunming killed dozens of people and wounded more than one hundred. http://edition.cnn.com/2014/03/02/world/asia/china-railway-attack/.

[69] See the website of Ministry of Public Security, http://www.mps.gov.cn/n16/n894593/n895609/3883656.html.

terrorist-related activities. In August 2013, the National Anti-Terrorism Work Leading Group was set up to facilitate the anti-terrorism efforts of different organs in China and to improve the efficiency and quality of counter-terrorism. Guo was appointed the group leader, and the unit members of the National Anti-Terrorism Work Leading Group include the public security organ, the national security organ, the military, the foreign affairs organ, the armed police, and more. Another high-level organization is the National Security Committee, which was set up in January 2014 according to the resolution of the Third Plenary Session of the eighteenth Central Committee of the Communist Party of China. Xi Jinping, the President of China, is the chair of the committee. All these organizational changes have shown great resolution by the Chinese government to combat terrorist activities, which have been increasing and becoming more serious.

At the legislative level, China has made much progress in recent years. The progress includes the amendments to the Criminal Law, the amendment of the Criminal Procedure Law, the promulgation of the Anti–Money Laundering Law and the Exit and Entry Administration Law and the issuing of several administrative regulations mentioned in this chapter. The draft of a special anti-terrorism law had been scheduled as far back as 2005. In September 2005, the Vice Director of the Anti-terrorism Bureau of the Ministry of Public Security, Zhao Yongchen, announced that the framework of the anti-terrorism law in China had been completed.[70] Until now, the Standing Committee of the People's Congress has not put the draft of the anti-terrorism law onto its legislative schedule. On October 24, 2011, the Vice Minister of Public Security, Yang Huanning, introduced the 23th meeting of the 11th Standing Committee of National People's Congress a draft of the Decision on Issues Concerning Strengthening Anti-Terrorism Work (DISAW), which was announced by the Standing Committee of the National People's Congress on October 29, 2011. As was introduced by Vice Minister Yang, after broad investigation and thorough discussion, it was decided that the chance for the promulgation of a special anti-terrorism law was not yet mature.[71] Nevertheless, in the wake of increasing terrorist attacks in China, a draft Anti-Terrorism Law was released in November 2014 for public comment; the second reading of the Draft Anti-Terrorism Law was completed in February 2015 and may be enacted in the near future.

70 http://www.chinanews.com/news/2005/2005-09-06/8/621874.shtml.

71 Yang Huanning: Explanation to the Draft of "the Decision on Issues Concerning Strengthening Anti-Terrorism Work," National People's Congress Standing Committee Bulletin, No. 7, 2011, P.659.

22

Singapore

Eugene K. B. Tan

Fortunately, Singapore has not suffered a terrorist attack in recent years...
But the threat has not disappeared, and we remain a target.
From time to time, we hear reports of terrorists in our region wanting to attack Singapore or Singapore assets in our neighbourhood.
We must never let our guard down.[1]

I. INTRODUCTION

The arrest and detention of thirty-six terrorist suspects, most of whom were members of a homegrown Jemaah Islamiyah (JI)[2] terrorist cell in Singapore, under the Internal Security Act[3] in late 2001 and early 2002 created an atmosphere of mutual suspicion and distrust between Malay-Muslims and non-Muslims.[4] The Malay-Muslims, comprising 14 per cent of Singapore's 3.2 million citizen population in 2000, were themselves confronted by self-doubt and ambivalence at the latest doubts cast over their faith and their loyalty to Singapore. The government was deeply worried about the negative impact the JI arrests would have on Singapore's multiracial and multireligious society. In January 2003, during the parliamentary debate over

1 Speech delivered by Singapore Prime Minister Lee Hsien Loong at the International Conference on Terrorist Rehabilitation and Community Resilience, 26 March 2013.

2 *Jemaah Islamiyah* means "Islamic Community." The JI's ultimate goal is to create a region-wide *Daulah Islamiyah* or "Islamic State" made up of Malaysia, Indonesia, southern Philippines, Brunei and Singapore. The JI has links to Al-Qaeda. Selected JI members were sent for military training at Al-Qaeda camps in Afghanistan since the 1990s.

3 Cap. 143, 1985 Rev Ed.

4 William Case, "Singapore in 2002: Economic Lassitude and Threats to Security," (2003) 43(1) *Asian Survey* 167–73; Barry Desker, "The *Jemaah Islamiyah* (JI) Phenomenon in Singapore," (2003) 25(3) *Contemporary Southeast Asia* 489–507; Andrew Tan, "Terrorism in Singapore: Threats and Implications," (2002) 23(2) *Contemporary Security Policy* 1–18.

the 'The Jemaah Islamiyah Arrests and the Threat of Terrorism' White Paper,[5] the discussion of the terrorist threat in Singapore was notable for the articulation of a subtle moral panic that obliquely linked increased Muslim religiosity and perceived Malay-Muslim separateness with increased susceptibility towards terrorism. The official articulation highlighted the concern with the Muslims' supposed exclusionary practices and self-segregation and the formation of an isolated "micro-community" accompanied by the unilateral closing of common space. This panic prompted the then-president of the Islamic Religious Council of Singapore (MUIS), a government statutory board, to observe:

> Not only did it [the Muslim-Singaporean community] have to grapple with the shocking revelation that some members of the community were involved in insidious activities that threatened society's peace and harmony, it also had to contend with unrelenting public scrutiny over the tenability of Islamic practices in a modern, secular and multiethnic polity.[6]

On another occasion, the Minister-in-charge of Muslim Affairs, Yaacob Ibrahim, remarked that:

> Practices of the Malay community, which have evolved naturally, became the subject of scrutiny. There was even some questioning as to whether these practices were desirable or otherwise. A community, which had hitherto lived peacefully with other communities, found itself the subject of discussion by all – with some participants taking their reference points from outside the Singapore context. The local context did not matter as we were swathed with exciting stories of terrorism and extremism prefaced by the word 'Islamic' supplied by overnight experts. There were increased concerns and questions about the implications of overt symbols and signs of Muslim identity and beliefs. Some wondered why Muslims needed to consume food that was *halal* (or permitted) as though it was a radical behavioural departure. Observing religious practices became a short of shorthand for hovering at the edge of terrorism.[7]

Quite evidently, the key challenge post-9/11 is to manage adeptly the terrorism threat. In the aftermath of 9/11, Southeast Asia was described in the Beltway as the "second front" in the "war against terror."[8] Unsurprisingly, Malay-Muslim Singaporeans' increased religiosity, their perception of being under siege, as

[5] Cmd. 2 of 2003, 7 January 2003. The White Paper is available at http://www.mha.gov.sg/publication_details.aspx?pageid=35&cid=354.

[6] MUIS, *Making the Quantum Leap* (MUIS Annual Report) (Singapore: MUIS, 2002), 2. MUIS advises the President and the government on matters relating to Islam.

[7] Yaacob Ibrahim, Speech by the Minister for Community Development and Sports and Minister-in-charge of Muslim Affairs, at the Wee Kim Wee seminar on Cross-Cultural Understanding, Singapore Management University, 2 August 2003.

[8] John Gershman, "Is Southeast Asia the Second Front?" (2002) 81 *Foreign Affairs* 60–74.

well as the non-Muslim apprehension, fears and misunderstanding of Islam and Muslim-Singaporeans, contributed to the overall unease in Singapore. The tenor of the political leadership's exhortations has consistently been that the Muslim community practices its faith in the context of a multiracial society with moderation as the defining attribute.[9]

Today, the rise of the self-styled "Islamic State" amid the Syrian and Iraqi crises has increased the terrorism threat to Singapore.[10] A key challenge identified by the Singapore government is to counter the radical propaganda used by the terrorists and radical ideologues to recruit foreign fighters. The Singapore government sees the issue as an ideological battle between those who distort Islam for their violent political ends and those who uphold the tenets of Islam as a religion of peace. However, the government is also mindful that this issue must not be seen as being confined to the Muslim-Singaporean community. Instead, it has consciously sought to characterize the challenge of terrorism as a national one since it is what happens after a terrorist attack that could severely undercut social cohesion. After all, governments do not defeat terrorism; it is the people who will determine whether a multiracial, multireligious society is resilient and cohesive enough to withstand the divisive effects of terrorism.

II. THE DEFINITION OF TERRORISM

The main legislation used to deal with terrorism and suspected terrorists is the Internal Security Act (ISA), a legacy of British colonial rule when the predecessor law was used primarily to deal with the communist threat.[11] The ISA has been described as the "power of the Government to deal with extra-constitutional threats."[12] This highlights the Singapore government's perspective that the terrorist threat, as an extra-constitutional threat, cannot be satisfactorily dealt with through constitutional means. The ISA, however, does not define terrorism, although in section 2 of the Act, "terrorist" is statutorily interpreted as follows:

"terrorist" means any person who –

9 See Eugene K. B. Tan, "Norming 'Moderation' in an 'Iconic Target': Public Policy and the Regulation of Religious Anxieties in Singapore," (2007) 19(4) *Terrorism and Political Violence* 443–62.

10 Reply to parliamentary question on the Islamic State in Iraq and the Levant (ISIL) by Teo Chee Hean, Deputy Prime Minister, Coordinating Minister for National Security, and Minister for Home Affairs, 7 October 2014.

11 The origins of the ISA are the Emergency Regulations introduced by the British in Malaya and Singapore in 1948 to combat communists, subversives and racial and religious extremists. In 1955, the Preservation of Public Security Ordinance replaced the Emergency Regulations.

12 Speech by Minister for Law K. Shanmugam at the New York State Bar Association Rule of Law Plenary Session, 29 October 2009; available at https://www.mlaw.gov.sg/content/minlaw/en/news/speeches/speech-by-minister-for-law-k-shanmugam-at-the-new-york-state-bar-association-rule-of-law-plenary.html.

(a) by the use of any firearm, explosive or ammunition acts in a manner prejudicial to the public safety or to the maintenance of public order or incites to violence or counsels disobedience to the law or to any lawful order;
(b) carries or has in his possession or under his control any firearm, ammunition or explosive without lawful authority therefor; or
(c) demands, collects or receives any supplies for the use of any person who intends or is about to act, or has recently acted, in a manner prejudicial to public safety or the maintenance of public order.

The definition coheres with the understanding of the communist insurgency tactics of the 1950s to 1970s. This definition does not capture any ideological imperative that motivates the alleged terrorist. In any case, the ISA's draconian approach enables the government to detain terrorist suspects preventively and without trial for renewable two-year periods. The ISA sanctions the detention of terrorist suspects "with a view to preventing that person from acting in any manner prejudicial to the security of Singapore or any part thereof or to the maintenance of public order or essential services therein."[13]

Similarly, the Terrorism (Suppression of Financing) Act or TSOFA, adopts a broad definition of "terrorist."[14] It also defines "terrorism financing offence" as: (i) providing or collecting property for terrorist acts, (ii) provision of property and services for terrorist purposes, (iii) use or possession of property for terrorist purposes, and (iv) dealing with the property of terrorists.[15] It covers the conspiracy or attempt or the aiding, abetting, counseling or procuring of the commission of any of those offences. Enacted in 2002 to counter terrorism financing in Singapore, the TSOFA gives effect to the UN International Convention for the Suppression of the Financing of Terrorism (1999)[16] and the UN Security Council Resolution (UNSCR) 1373 (2001), which call on states to work together to prevent and suppress acts of terrorism, including terrorism financing.

The TSOFA defines a "terrorist entity" as "any entity owned or controlled by any terrorist or group of terrorists and includes an association of such entities." Such entities are set out in the First Schedule of the TSOFA. Currently, the Taliban and Al-Qaida are the two only scheduled entities.[17] It should be noted that this definition of "terrorist" in TSOFA broadens the definition of "terrorist" as membership in or association with specified "terrorist entities," and would automatically make a person with such membership or association fall within the technical definition of

[13] Internal Security Act, s. 8(1).
[14] Terrorism (Suppression of Financing) Act, (Cap. 325, 2003 Rev Ed), s. 2.
[15] Terrorism (Suppression of Financing) Act, ss. 3–6.
[16] 2178 UNTS 256.
[17] See First Schedule of TSOFA.

a "terrorist" under the law. This is regardless of whether or not the person actively participates in or facilitates the commission of specific acts of terrorism.

In January 2008, Singapore enacted the Terrorism (Suppression of Bombing) Act[18] to give effect to the International Convention for the Suppression of Terrorist Bombings.[19] Following the approach taken in many international conventions, "terrorist" is not defined, although "terrorism bombing" is.

The most comprehensive definitions, albeit in the form of subsidiary legislation, is probably attempted in the United Nations (Anti-Terrorism Measures) Regulations[20] on who is a terrorist and what is a terrorist act. For instance, "terrorist," "terrorist," and "terrorist acts" are defined accordingly:

"terrorist" means any person who –

(a) commits, or attempts to commit, any terrorist act; or
(b) participates in or facilitates the commission of any terrorist act, and includes any person referred to in the Schedule;

"terrorist act" means the use or threat of action –

(a) where the action –
 (i) involves serious violence against a person;
 (ii) involves serious damage to property;
 (iii) endangers a person's life;
 (iv) creates a serious risk to the health or the safety of the public or a section of the public;
 (v) involves the use of firearms or explosives;
 (vi) involves releasing into the environment or any part thereof, or distributing or otherwise exposing the public or any part thereof to –
  (A) any dangerous, hazardous, radioactive or harmful substance;
  (B) any toxic chemical; or
  (C) any microbial or other biological agent, or toxin;
 (vii) is designed to disrupt any public computer system or the provision of services directly related to communications infrastructure, banking and financial services, public utilities, public transportation or public key infrastructure;

18 Cap. 324A, 2008 Rev Ed.

19 2149 UNTS 256.

20 Rg 1, enacted in November 2001 pursuant to section 2(1) of the United Nations Act (Cap. 339, 2002 Rev Ed). Interestingly, the parent legislation, the United Nations Act, does not define "terrorism." The long title of the Act reads: "An Act to enable Singapore to fulfil its obligations respecting Article 41 of the Charter of the United Nations." Article 41 provides that the United Nations Security Council may decide on measures not involving the use of armed force to give effect to its decisions.

(viii) is designed to disrupt the provision of essential emergency services such as the police, civil defence and medical services; or
(ix) involves prejudice to public security or national defence; and

(b) where the use or threat is intended or reasonably regarded as intending to –
(i) influence the Government or any other government; or
(ii) intimidate the public or a section of the public.

The slew of counter-terrorism laws enacted in the past decade ensures that Singapore is in compliance with its treaty obligations relating to terrorism. The laws seek to reinforce Singapore's ability to deal with not just the acts or attempts at terrorism but also the precursor acts or acts preparatory to a terrorist attack, such as financing and non-financial support, including the provision of safe houses, by which terrorists use to commit terrorist acts. While preventive detention is the preferred method for dealing with alleged terrorists, criminal law is principally used for non-direct perpetrators of terrorist acts. TSOFA is one such example; it does not target terrorists *per se*. While the ISA remains the primarily legislation to deal with terrorism, laws enacted post 9/11 are crafted as criminal legislation. Yet, they are also endowed with provisions that take them beyond the criminal law framework. This may make it difficult for the courts to regulate the proper use of the legislation or for an accused person to have the full protection that the criminal law regime normally provides.[21]

Nonetheless, terrorism remains broadly defined in Singapore's statute books, and the influence of the British definition of terrorism is evident in the recent counter-terrorism legislation in the past decade.[22] The various but similar definitions found in the different laws are consistent in that they do not include any ideological imperative that may motivate an alleged terrorist. The global experience has been the difficulty in defining "terrorist" and "terrorism" satisfactorily. As it is often said, "one man's freedom fighter is another man's terrorist." The transnational dimension of terrorism adds to the complexity. As it stands, the various but similar definitions of terrorist and terrorism in Singapore's statute books are broad and tautological. This unsatisfactory state of definition means that the law is potentially more exposed to the increased possibility of abuse by the executive, willfully or otherwise, through the overzealous determination to deal with a grave threat.

Overall, Singapore's laws relating to terrorism are fairly all-embracing, and the definitional issue remains unchanged in that the ideological dimension as to why threats and/or acts of violence are used is still not dealt with in the various legislation.[23]

[21] See further Section V on regulation of terrorism financing.

[22] See, for example, UK's Terrorism Act 2000 (c. 11).

[23] Put another way, the tautological definitions of "terrorist" and "terrorism" in the various pieces of legislation are akin to the authorities saying, "Trust us, although we can't define them specifically, we

The definitional ambivalence in Singapore is made more complicated by the fact that terrorism is neither completely within nor outside of Singapore's criminal law framework.

Singapore's uncompromising approach of terrorism is weighted in favour of enabling the government to deal swiftly and pre-emptively with any threat to public order and national security.[24] Despite the definitional challenges, the definition of terrorism has not been controversial thus far in Singapore. The courts have not had the occasion to tackle the difficult issue of the definition of terrorism found in different pieces of legislation in Singapore's statute books. Similarly, and unsurprisingly, in the aftermath of 9/11, Singapore has been ready and comfortable to embrace a broader definition of "terrorism" to include property destruction and serious disruptions of essential services. However, Singapore's broad definitions of "terrorism" do not always seek to bring terrorist activities wholly within the criminal law framework even as the same laws enable the executive to mount investigations and to exercise pre-emptive powers of detention.

Currently, Singapore has no plans to promulgate a comprehensive anti-terrorism legislation to consolidate the various legislation that relate to terrorism. The government prefers the current arrangement, one in which there is:

> [A] range of Acts and provisions across different pieces of legislation that enable us to act against terrorism, whether it is pre-emptively or on an *ex-post* basis. And indeed, one could argue that whilst this may not be elegant from a legislative point of view, it does give us the flexibility to take calibrated and targeted action depending on which piece of legislation is most appropriately used in the context of the actions that are required. Having said that, I will not rule this out but it is certainly not on the agenda at this point."[25]

III. CRIMINAL LAWS AND PROSECUTIONS

A. *Criminal Law*

In Singapore, while terrorism is regarded seriously as a grave threat to national security and social cohesion, the direct actions of terrorism are generally not treated

know a terrorist, a terrorist act and terrorism when we see one and so need a broad enough definition for us to act against them."

24 Michael Hor, "Terrorism and the Criminal Law: Singapore's Solution" [2002] *Sing. J.L.S.* 30.

25 Clarification by S. Iswaran, Second Minister for Home Affairs, to a supplementary question by the author (in the capacity as a Nominated Member of Parliament) at the Second Reading of the Terrorism (Suppression of Financing) (Amendment) Bill, 12 August 2013. The debate on the Bill can found in the *Singapore Parliament Reports*, vol. 90; available at http://sprs.parl.gov.sg/search/topic.jsp?currentTopicID=00004877-WA&currentPubID=00004837-WA&topicKey=00004837-WA.00004877-WA_3%2Bid-712a6bee-bc24-4ab1-a048-0eb494325747%2B.

as criminal offences in which the normal criminal process applies. Certainly, in the aftermath of 9/11 and the discovery of a homegrown terrorist cell in Singapore, terrorist crimes were created, amended, expanded or made subject to more punishment in response to UNSCR 1373 (2001). This concerted action to ensure that the legislative arsenal was sufficiently broad to cater to the terrorism supply chain is not surprising given the abiding fear of the government that Singapore is an "iconic" target for terrorists.[26] Thus, new legislation such as the Terrorism (Suppression of Terrorist Bombings) Act, the Terrorism (Suppression of the Financing) Act and the United Nations Act was enacted in 2007, 2002 and 2001 respectively, to give effect to the relevant international conventions as well as the UN Security Council resolutions in the aftermath of 9/11.

These recent terrorism laws criminalize the facilitation and preparation for terrorist acts but they do not provide for preventive detention for such indirect actions of supporters of terrorism. Preventive detention of alleged terrorists remains within the sole domain of the ISA. Given that there have not been any successful terrorist attacks in Singapore post-9/11, it is unclear whether ordinary criminal laws such as those relating to murder, kidnapping and conspiracy, if applicable, would be applied as well. It is likely that where intelligence and official secrets would be compromised, the greater is the likelihood that only the ISA would be used.

The general legal tenor is not to treat direct terrorist activities as criminal acts as this would require the government to prosecute the suspects in open court and to provide the requisite evidence to the "beyond a reasonable doubt" standard of proof. Membership or participation in a terrorist group will render a person liable to detention or restriction orders under the ISA. Thus far, all terrorist suspects have been dealt with under the ISA, signalling a clear preference for direct terrorist activities to be treated as *sui generis* and not as criminal activities. Given that alleged terrorists are not criminally tried for alleged terrorist activities, it is unlikely that suspected terrorists would be prosecuted for other criminal offences.

As for laws to deal with those who incite violence by glorifying violence, the government's position is that the existing laws are inadequate. In response to a parliamentary question, the government indicated that there were three legislative provisions that could be used in this regard. First, section 153 of the Penal Code[27] makes it an offence for any person to provoke rioting. In addition, the Sedition Act[28] makes it an offence to promote feelings of ill-will and hostility between different races or classes of the population of Singapore. "These laws have proven adequate over the years to deal not only with those who encourage terrorism but also any

[26] "Threat of Terror Strike Far from Over," *The Straits Times*, 28 August 2004.

[27] Cap. 224, 2008 Rev Ed.

[28] Cap. 290, 2013 Rev Ed.

others who threaten our racial and religious harmony through their inflammatory actions or words."[29] Likewise, in determining whether a publication is objectionable and so runs foul of the Undesirable Publications Act,[30] the consideration of whether publication "promotes or encourages criminal acts or acts of terrorism" is pertinent.[31] Thus far, there are no known instances where there has been prosecution for the advocacy of terrorism and for the incitement of terrorism.

B. *Terrorism Prosecutions*

As indicated earlier, Singapore has generally preferred to deal with internal security threats through the use of preventive detention, rather than criminal prosecution. This preference persists and strengthens as the threat has shifted from communism (1950s to 1980s) to faith-inspired terrorism today. The government's oft-cited reasons for this preference include the ability of preventive detentions to safeguard sensitive intelligence information and the identity of witnesses who might otherwise not be prepared to testify in open court, as well as the likelihood that valuable additional information might be obtained from detainees who are kept out of the criminal process that would result in a fixed custodial sentence (regardless of whether they have been successfully rehabilitated).

As Singapore's legal system does not treat direct acts of terrorism as crimes, there are no terrorism prosecutions to speak of for persons alleged to have been planning terrorist attacks.[32] Alleged terrorists are typically not charged for any criminal activity. Instead, as mentioned earlier, they are detained without trial under the ISA. Under section 19 of the ISA, where a person is detained under the Act, there "shall be without prejudice to the taking of any criminal proceedings against such person, whether during or after the period of his detention." This means that an ISA detainee may be charged for a crime during or after his or her detention. It appears, however, that such a provision has never been used.

Under the ISA, a person can only be held for no more than thirty days from the date of arrest to facilitate investigation. Before this arrest period expires, the Internal Security Department (ISD) will have three options before it:

[29] *Singapore Parliament Reports*, vol. 81, cols. 307–9 (28 February 2006) per Senior Minister of State for Home Affairs Assoc. Prof. Ho Peng Kee; available at http://sprs.parl.gov.sg/search/topic.jsp?currentTopicID=00001809-WA&currentPubID=00004714-WA&topicKey=00004714-WA.00001809-WA_1%2B%2B.

[30] Cap. 338, 1998 Rev Ed.

[31] Undesirable Publications Act, s. 4(2)(iii).

[32] Indirect activities that support terrorism, such as terrorism financing and harbouring of terrorists, are criminal offences that are dealt with by specific laws or under general criminal law such as the Penal Code.

- Detain such a person under an Order of Detention (OD) not exceeding two years; or
- Issue such a person with a Restriction Order (RO) not exceeding two years, or
- Release such a person unconditionally.

Under Article 151(4) of the Constitution,[33] if the decision is to serve an OD or a RO on a person, the President's assent must be sought before the expiry of the thirty-day period. Under section 8(1)(b) of the ISA, the RO can take various forms in restricting a person's activities and movement. For example, the RO may restrict a person's activities and the places of his or her residence and employment.[34] The RO may prohibit a person from being outdoors during specific times.[35] The RO may require a person to notify the relevant authority of his or her movements.[36] The RO can prohibit a person from addressing public meetings, holding office in or taking part in the activities of or acting as advisor to any organization or association or from taking part in any political activities.[37] Finally, the RO may prohibit a person from travelling out of Singapore unless prior permission has been obtained.[38]

Under section 8(2) of the ISA, the President may extend the OD or RO for "a further period or periods not exceeding two years at a time." This means that such orders can be renewed multiple times with no limitation.[39] Given the draconian powers afforded to the executive under the ISA, the government has, from time to time, sought to explain the safeguards to assure Singaporeans that it is not used to quell political dissent.[40]

a. Review of OD and RO by the Advisory Board

As provided for in section 13 of the ISA, every order of detention and restriction order is reviewed annually. Each OD and RO must be reviewed by an independent Advisory Board (AB), which comprises a Supreme Court judge and two qualified

33 1985 Rev Ed, 1999 reprint.
34 S. 8(1)(b)(i), ISA.
35 S. 8(1)(b)(ii), ISA.
36 S. 8(1)(b)(iii), ISA.
37 S. 8(1)(b)(iv), ISA.
38 S. 8(1)(b)(v), ISA.
39 The longest ISA detainee is Chia Thye Poh. He was arrested and detained under the ISA in October 1966. Never charged or tried for any offence, Chia was on conditional release between May 1989 and November 1998 before he was released unconditionally. The Singapore government attributed Chia's detention to his alleged membership in the Communist Party of Malaya (CPM) and involvement in violent subversive activities, allegations that Chia has denied.
40 See, for instance, the parliamentary speech on the Internal Security Act by Teo Chee Hean, Deputy Prime Minister, Coordinating Minister for National Security, and Minister for Home Affairs, 19 October 2011; available at http://www.mha.gov.sg/news_details.aspx?nid=MjEzMg%3D%3D-as%2B9gJeLXQ0%3D.

citizens appointed by the President in consultation with the Chief Justice. Constituted under Article 151(2) of the Constitution, the Advisory Board has all the powers of a court of law for summoning and examining witnesses, compelling the production of documents and evidence that it deems relevant, examining a detainee's representations, as well as examining ISD officers and statements of witnesses.[41] The Advisory Board has to consider the representation of an ISA detainee within three months of the date of his or her OD; it subsequently makes its recommendation to the President.[42]

At the hearings of the Advisory Board, usually held at the Supreme Court, the Advisory Board hears the representations of detainees, examines ISD officers and statements of witnesses and reviews the evidence and investigation. The government and its officers are not required to disclose facts or to produce documents whose disclosure or production the Home Affairs Ministry considers to be against the national interest.[43] All proceedings before an Advisory Board shall be dealt with *in camera*.[44] Following its review, the Advisory Board will submit its findings and recommendations to the President. After considering the Advisory Board's recommendations, the President will then direct the Minister for Home Affairs on the detention or release of the detained person. Where the Advisory Board recommends the release of the detained person, the person shall not be detained further without the President's concurrence.[45]

The Ministry of Home Affairs has indicated that a number of detainees have been released from their OD earlier than the stipulated date, on the Advisory Board's recommendation. However, the Advisory Board should not be treated as a judicial body, even though its workings seek to allay concerns that there are inadequate safeguards due to the exclusion of judicial review for the substantive grounds of detention under the ISA.[46] Further, section 8B(1) stipulates that the law applicable to judicial review of any decision made or act done in pursuance of any power conferred upon the President or the Minister under the ISA "shall be the same as was applicable and declared in Singapore on the 13th day of July 1971; and no part of the law before, on or after that date of any other country in the Commonwealth

41 Section 14, ISA. See also s 11(3) of the ISA and also Internal Security (Detained Persons Advisory Board) Rules, R2.

42 Section 12(1), ISA. See Home Affairs Ministry's press statement, "ISA Advisory Board's Recommendation 30 May 02," available at http://www.mha.gov.sg/news_details.aspx?nid=NDAz-qtFYiGsfQAw%3D.

43 Section 16, ISA.

44 Internal Security (Detained Persons Advisory Board) Rules, R5.

45 See further the government's news release of 25 February 2002 on the ISA arrests of alleged JI terrorists, available at http://www.mha.gov.sg/news_details.aspx?nid=MzAx-%2FGE4QRun%2BNo%3D.

46 Section 8B(2) of the ISA reads: "There shall be no judicial review in any court of any act done or decision made by the President or the Minister under the provisions of this Act save in regard to any question relating to compliance with any procedural requirement of this Act governing such act or decision." This provision has not been judicially challenged thus far.

relating to judicial review shall apply."[47] The Singapore Court of Appeal, in the landmark case of *Chng Suan Tze v The Minister of Home Affairs & Ors and other appeals*,[48] had decided that the subjective approach, which supported judicial non-interference with ministerial discretion in matters of national security, was no longer sustainable and abandoned it in favour of the objective approach.[49] However, Singapore's legislature moved swiftly to overrule the decision in *Chng* legislatively.[50] By "freezing" the law, this legislative intervention mandates the retreat from the objective test in *Chng*. Furthermore, it significantly reduces the scope and intensity of any judicial review to determining whether the executive is subjectively of the view that the detainee should be detained as a national security threat.[51] Judicial review of ISA detention cases is strictly confined to procedural matters only. Ministerial satisfaction is jealously guarded and ring-fenced and remains the exclusive domain of the executive.

b. Detainees' Right of Representation

Under section 9 of the ISA, a detainee must be informed of the grounds of detention and allegations made against him or her. The detainee has the right to make representations against his or her OD to the Advisory Board. For the purpose of enabling the detainee to make representation, he or she is furnished with a written statement of the grounds on which the OD was made, as well as the allegations of facts on which the OD was based, and any other particulars that he or she may, in the opinion of the Minister, reasonably require to make his or her representations against the OD.[52] The detainee is free to engage a lawyer or any person of his or her choosing who is not involved in the case to assist the detainee in his or her representation to the Advisory Board.[53]

47 Ibid.

48 [1988] 2 SLR(R) 525.

49 Under the subjective test, the courts in ISA detention cases only had to consider whether the executive was in fact satisfied (subjectively) that the detainee posed a threat to national security, The courts did not have to concern themselves with whether there were reasonable (objective) grounds to justify that belief.

50 Judgment in *Chng* was handed down on 8 December 1988. The first reading of the Constitution of the Republic of Singapore (Amendment) Bill and the Internal Security (Amendment) Bill was on 16 January 1989, with the second and third readings on 25 January 1989. The constitutional amendment was effective 27 January 1989, while the ISA amendments came into force on 30 January 1989.

51 For the debate, see *Singapore Parliament Reports*, vol. 52, cols. 463–556 (25 January 1989).

52 Section 11(2)(b), ISA.

53 Article 9(3), Singapore Constitution; and R 4(1) of the Internal Security (Detained Persons Advisory Board) Rules.

c. Veto Power of the Elected President

As alluded to earlier, an important check on the abuse of the ISA is the veto power of the President. This is provided for in Article 151(4) of the Singapore Constitution. Should the Advisory Board recommend the release of any detainee, he or she cannot be further detained by the government without the President's concurrence. Under Article 21(2)(g) of the Singapore Constitution, this is a decision that the President makes in his or her own discretion, and the President is not bound to consult the Council of Presidential Advisers, though of course the President may do so if he or she sees fit (Article 21(4)). This veto power was accorded to the President in 1991 through amendments to the Constitution and the ISA.

d. Board of Inspection

There is a Board of Inspection (BOI) made up of volunteers from community and civic groups to inquire into the well-being of ISA detainees. Members of the Board of Inspection are empowered to make unannounced visits to the ISD detention centre. The BOI comprises more than fifty Justices of the Peace and community leaders, and two different members visit the detention centre every month to inspect the place and speak to any of the detainees without ISD officers being present. Detainees are able to convey requests and complaints to these BOI members, who will report them, along with any other recommendations, to the Minister for Home Affairs. Besides the BOI, a detainee also has access to a number of persons unassociated with the ISD to whom he or she can raise a complaint of any nature. These include family members, the AB, legal advisors, religious counsellors, doctors and nurses. Detainees are also provided safeguards such as visits entitlement from legal advisers and family and friends, access to medical and dental care, access to books and paper, avenues to make complaints and petitions, provision of food in accordance with the detainee's religious obligations and specific dietary/medical needs.[54] There are no known reports of serious allegations of mistreatment of the detainees.

Section 10 of the ISA provides that the Minister may issue a Suspension Direction (SD) to suspend the operation of an existing OD. The SD can be made subject to the execution of a bond and to such conditions as the Minister sees fit. The conditions may include restrictions regarding a person's residence, employment, movements and activities. The SD lapses when the OD expires. An RO may be issued upon the expiry of the SD/OD. The Minister may revoke the SD if the ex-detainee fails

[54] See, generally, the Internal Security (Detained Persons) Rules. The approach under the ISA regime is not to treat detainees as criminals.

to observe any condition imposed on him or her or it is otherwise necessary in the public interest to revoke the SD.

C. *Punishment of Terrorism*

Since alleged terrorists have all been detained under the ISA instead of being prosecuted, there are no sentencing practices to speak of. As indicated earlier, alleged terrorists can either be detained under the ISA or subjected to restriction orders. These orders are normally of two-year duration and can be renewed indefinitely. It should be noted that the ISA regime for detainees is not regarded as punishment since the focus of detention is to rehabilitate and reintegrate detainees into mainstream society even as it protects society.[55] For those convicted of offences under other terrorism legislations, a range of penalties ranging from fines and/or jail terms is applicable.

While in detention, detainees undergo counseling with a voluntary group of *ulamas* and *asatizahs* (Islamic scholars and religious teachers) from the Religious Rehabilitation Group (RRG). Officially launched on 23 April 2003, the RRG was formed with the primary objective of countering the ideological misunderstanding of the JI members through counselling. RRG's main and primary focus is towards rehabilitating the JI detainees and their families. For the JI detainees, this rehabilitation by a non-state entity is crucial as the process seeks to correct the offender's misinterpretation of religious concepts and way of thinking by those with the requisite authority, knowledge and legitimacy. As the RRG articulates, "In other words, the rehabilitated detainee is expected, not only to refrain from committing criminal acts, but also to recognize and accept that their understanding of Islam has been misled (sic). In addition, since the JI's ideology has affected their family members, their family need (sic) to be guided, so as to avoid and disrupt such a violent cycle."[56]

Singapore Prime Minister Lee Hsien Loong notes:

> The idea for the RRG arose after we arrested members of the *Jemaah Islamiyah* (JI) in Singapore in December 2001. We realised from our investigations that just arresting the JI members was not enough. JI members had misinterpreted key Islamic concepts, and convinced themselves that terrorism was "righteous" and "legitimate." We needed to counter, at source, this radical and wrong-headed misinterpretation of Islam. We had to offer convincing alternative interpretations of key doctrines central to this ideology. We also needed an effective rehabilitation

55 R 88(1) of the Internal Security (Detained Persons) Rules describes the place of detention as "a place for the rehabilitation of detained persons."

56 See http://rrg.sg/about-us.

programme and support structure to help those who had got involved with terrorism integrate back into society after their release.[57]

Besides ISA detainees and those subjected to restriction orders under the ISA, persons found guilty of terrorism financing offences will be required to undergo counselling. Furthermore, persons found to be ideologically indoctrinated to support terrorism activities will be encouraged to undergo religious counselling as part of their rehabilitation.[58] The RRG also engages in outreach efforts to the wider community, especially Muslims. Such outreach seeks to convey the anti-extremist messages, to explain why certain interpretations – which could lead people towards extremism – are not the correct teachings and to guide the wider community along the right path. Such efforts aim to marginalize militant ideas and prevent them from gaining a foothold within the wider community. In this regard, the salience of "moderation" in the practice of Islam is subtly emphasized. If the detainees renounce their jihadist beliefs and are assessed by ISD to pose no threat to society, they are released from detention. There may be conditions attached to the release, including continuing to receive counselling. However, for the "hard-core elements" who remain in detention, counselling is provided only when they are receptive.[59]

IV. INVESTIGATIVE POWERS

In Singapore, there is no separate regime for terrorism investigations. Investigations into terrorism are multi-agency, involving the ISD, the police and other intelligence agencies. These investigations are led by the ISD, a department under the Ministry of Home Affairs, whose predecessor institution, the Special Branch, was created by the British colonial government specifically to deal with communist subversion. The

57 Speech by Prime Minister Lee Hsien Loong at the International Conference on Terrorist Rehabilitation and Community Resilience, 26 March 2013; available at http://www.pmo.gov.sg/content/pmosite/mediacentre/speechesninterviews/primeminister/2013/March/speech_by_prime_ministerleehsienloongattheinternationalconferenc.html#.VAqt80sxL8s.

58 S. Iswaran, Second Minister for Home Affairs, at the Second Reading of the Terrorism (Suppression of Financing) (Amendment) Bill, 12 August 2013. The debate on the Bill can found in the *Singapore Parliament Reports*, vol. 90; available at http://sprs.parl.gov.sg/search/topic.jsp?currentTopicID=00004877-WA&currentPubID=00004837-WA&topicKey=00004837-WA.00004877-WA_3%2Bid-712a6bee-bc24-4ab1-a048-0eb494325747%2B.

59 Id. It was reported in 2011 that with the help of RRG, two-thirds of those detained were successfully rehabilitated. There were also those who were not detained whom the RRG "helped guide onto the right path before they got into deeper concerns." See "DPM Teo: Regional Terror Groups Are Top Security Threat," *The Straits Times*, 10 September 2011. Since then, the rehabilitation rate has improved. As of 9 July 2014, more than four-fifths of those detained under the Internal Security Act since January 2002 for their involvement in terrorism-related activities have since been released after they were assessed to have been rehabilitated. Information provided by the Ministry of Home Affairs, Singapore, on 24 September 2014 (correspondence on file with author).

ISD has both (domestic) intelligence collection and executive functions. It collects and analyses intelligence and presents its assessments and policy recommendations to the government. It also investigates and, where necessary, takes direct action in relation to the defined security threats of terrorism or politically motivated violence, foreign subversion, espionage and communal extremism.[60]

The operational charter of the ISD is confined within the sovereign territory of Singapore – it is not empowered to operate overseas. Within Singapore, the ISD's powers of investigation and arrest are identical to police powers and are likewise regulated and governed by the laws of the land, in particular the Criminal Procedure Code,[61] the Official Secrets Act,[62] the Internal Security Act and the Maintenance of Religious Harmony Act.[63]

A. *Police Powers*

ISD officers who hold warrants as police officers exercise the same police powers as ordinary police officers.[64] Part IV of the ISA stipulates that the various powers of police officers in an ISA case are provided with the same set of rights and powers as other police officers. They do not possess special powers of investigation, search and arrest for investigation into terrorism cases. Section 74 of the ISA provides for a police officer to arrest without warrant and to detain any person whom the officer has reason to believe that there are grounds that would justify the person's detention under section 8, and that he or she has acted, is about to act or is likely to act in any manner prejudicial to the security of Singapore or any part thereof. In effecting an arrest, the police officer may use such force as, in the circumstances of the case, may be reasonably necessary, including the use of lethal weapons.[65] Section 63(1) of the Criminal Procedure Code (CPC) provides that "Any police officer who has reasonable grounds to suspect that any offence may be committed may intervene for the purpose of preventing and must, to the best of his ability, use all lawful means to prevent the commission of the offence." Section 63(2) of the CPC empowers a police officer to "act in any manner (including doing anything likely to cause the death of, or grievous hurt to, any person) if the police officer has reasonable grounds to believe that the person (whether acting alone or in concert with any other person) is doing or about to do, something which may amount to a terrorist act." There is no doubt that where draconian powers are needed in the face of clear and present

[60] See ISD website at http://www.mha.gov.sg/isd/abt-isd.htm.
[61] Cap. 68, 2012 Rev Ed,
[62] Cap. 213, 2012 Rev Ed
[63] Cap. 167A, 2001 Rev Ed.
[64] See generally the Criminal Procedure Code.
[65] Section 75(1), ISA.

danger posed by terrorism, the constitutional and legislative framework permits such use of heightened police powers that could potentially infringe upon constitutional freedoms.[66] For instance, Part XII of the Singapore Constitution is concerned with special powers against subversion and with emergency powers. This derogation from the rule of law is justified on the basis of necessity and extraordinary circumstances to deal with emergencies and subversion.

In Singapore, there are no special laws or regulatory regime to govern undercover operations. The usual laws apply. As ISA operations are subject to the Official Secrets Act and arrests and detentions are not subject to open court trials, little is known about the methods that the ISD and other agencies deploy in their operations. For example, in Singapore's fifth report in response to the United Nations Counter-Terrorism Committee, Singapore did not respond to the Committee's query on the kind of special investigation techniques, such as interception of communications on the Internet and other communication facilities, that are used in conducting undercover operations, tracking the funds of criminal groups and breaking the chain of communication in terrorist groups.[67]

It is not known whether entrapment or other defences based on abuse of police powers have been argued in the ISA Advisory Board hearings (which are all held in camera).[68] There are no known judicial review applications based on the entrapment or the abuse of police powers in connection with ISA cases involving JI terrorist suspects.

B. *Intelligence Agencies*

As is the case for undercover operations, there are no special laws or publicly known regulatory regime to govern legal powers and roles of intelligence agencies with respect to counter-terrorism. Both ISD and the Security and Intelligence Division are regulated and governed by the laws of the Singapore. Hardly anything is available in the public domain on the extra-legal regulatory framework governing clandestine operations by Singapore's intelligence agencies domestically and abroad. There are established work processes and communication channels to share information among the local agencies.[69] What is clear, in the context of ISA detentions of terrorism suspects, is that intelligence gathered by intelligence agencies are used to support such detentions. Depending on their probative value, there is no reason

66 These fundamental liberties are found in Part IV of the Singapore Constitution.

67 Singapore's response to the request by the Counter-Terrorism Committee for Singapore's fifth report, S/2006/120, 15 February 2006, para 1.8 at p. 8; available at http://daccess-dds-ny.un.org/doc/UNDOC/GEN/N06/253/52/IMG/N0625352.pdf?OpenElement.

68 The decisions of the ISA Advisory Board are not published.

69 *Singapore National Money Laundering and Terrorist Financing Risk Assessment Report* 2013, p. 5.

why electronic and other surveillance collected by intelligence agencies would not be used.[70] It was disclosed in Parliament that the Singapore authorities are aware of Singapore nationals who had joined other foreign fighters to fight in Syria, joining various entities including terrorist groups such as the Al-Qaida-linked Jabhat Al-Nusra or the Al-Nusra Front and the former Al-Qaida affiliate Islamic State of Iraq and the Levant (ISIL), which has renamed itself the Islamic State (IS). The Singapore government knows of a handful of Singaporeans who have gone to Syria to take part in the conflict as well as other Singaporeans who had intended to travel to Syria or other conflict zones to engage in the fighting in those areas but were detected before they could proceed with their plans. The government is aware of others who have expressed interest in going to Syria to join in the fighting, and these individuals are presently under investigation.[71]

In this regard, electronic surveillance collected by intelligence services would almost certainly form part of the decision whether to use the ISA on alleged terrorist suspects.[72] There are no laws in Singapore that explicitly prohibit the use of wiretaps and other forms of surveillance, including electronic ones. Neither are there laws that prohibit the use of such surveillance information as evidence in investigations, for preventive detentions and for criminal prosecutions (subject to meeting the evidentiary requirements stipulated by the relevant laws). It is an open question whether intelligence agencies are required to apply for judicial warrants from the courts. If such warrants are needed, it appears that the warrants are also granted without the requirement of hearing from the other side. It is also possible that a judicial warrant is not needed if the telecommunications corporation, which holds the data, consents to its release.[73]

It would appear that the security and intelligence agencies only need ministerial authorization for their surveillance domestically and in foreign jurisdictions.[74]

70 See also section 15A of the Computer Misuse and Cybersecurity Act (Cap. 50A, 2007 Rev Ed).

71 Reply by Deputy Prime Minister and Home Affairs Minister Teo Chee Hian to parliamentary questions on security threat posed by militants who travel overseas to fight, *Singapore Parliament Reports*, vol. 92 (9 July 2014).

72 On mass surveillance and the use of big data technologies in Singapore, see Shane Harris, 'The Social Laboratory,' *Foreign Policy* (July/August 2014, Issue 207), pp. 64–71; available at http://www.foreignpolicy.com/articles/2014/07/29/the_social_laboratory_singapore_surveillance_state. This essay was reproduced in *The Straits Times* (Singapore) of 9 August 2014. See Peter Ho, "RAHS Programme Not Out to Spy on Singaporeans," *The Straits Times*, 10 August 2014: The writer, a former head of the Singapore Civil Service, was referred to in the *Foreign Policy* article. RAHS is an acronym for the Risk Assessment and Horizon Scanning programme.

73 Section 58 of the Telecommunications Act (Cap. 323, 2000 Rev Ed) empowers the Communications and Information Minister to give directions to a telecommunications licensee, where it is "requisite or expedient to do so ... on the occurrence of any public emergency, in the public interest or in the interests of public security, national defence, or relations with the government of another country."

74 For instance, the Schedule to the Constitution of the Republic of Singapore (Responsibility of the Minister for Home Affairs) Notification 2011, S. 299 of 2011, charges the Home Affairs Minister with

Furthermore, Singapore's Constitution does not provide for a constitutional right to privacy. As such, questions of whether the conduct of intelligence agencies intrudes upon reasonable expectations of privacy and infringes a person's privacy rights have not arisen, and may encounter difficulty in finding legal expression in an opaque regulatory regime for intelligence agencies.

V. PROSCRIPTION AND LISTING OF TERRORIST GROUPS AND INDIVIDUALS

A. *Proscription Mechanisms*

The main legislation that is used to proscribe and list terrorist groups and individuals thought to be associated with terrorist groups is the United Nations Act[75] and the Terrorism (Suppression of Financing) Act. Currently, the United Nations Act provides for the proscription to apply to "All individuals and entities belonging to or associated with the Taliban and the Al-Qaida organization in the 1267 List."[76] The Terrorism (Suppression of Financing) Act proscribes "All individuals and entities belonging to or associated with the Taliban in the Taliban List, and all individuals and entities belonging to or associated with the Al-Qaida organization in the Al-Qaida List." In short, the Taliban and Al-Qaida and their related or associated entities as well as individuals belonging to or associated with these two organizations are proscribed under Singapore's counter-terrorism laws.[77] It would appear that Singapore takes the lead on proscription from the United Nations, with the current terrorist listings very much aligned with Singapore's international obligations with regards to counter-terrorism measures. There does not appear to be a separate domestic listing and process. Theoretically, it is possible that a listing decision can be based on speech or advocacy of terrorism as opposed to direct or indirect participation in terrorist activities.

the responsibility, *inter alia*, for the subject of "homeland security," which includes counter-terrorism, border security, national emergency preparedness, civil contingency planning and crisis and consequence management. Likewise, the Defence Minister is charged with the broad subject matter of "defence and security": see Constitution of the Republic of Singapore (Responsibility of the Minister for Defence) Notification 2011, S. 305 of 2011.

75 Cap. 332, 2002 Rev Ed.

76 See First Schedule of the Terrorism (Suppression of Financing) Act listing of terrorists and terrorist entities. The "1267 List" refers to the consolidated list of individuals and entities belonging to or associated with the Taliban and the Al-Qaida organization. The United Nations 1267 Committee updates this list from time to time.

77 "Entity" means a person, group, trust, partnership or fund or an unincorporated association or organization.

The two acts do not stipulate a specific mechanism for proscribing or listing terrorist groups. Under section 38(a) of the Terrorism (Suppression of Financing) Act, the (Home Affairs) Minister may, by order published in the *Gazette*, amend, add to or vary the First Schedule (which lists terrorists and terrorist entities). This means that the act of proscription is an executive one for which the Minister does not need to refer to nor seek the approval of Parliament. An Inter-Ministry Committee on Terrorist Designation is the designated authority to implement terrorist designations; the Committee oversees the listing and delisting of terrorists and coordinates the freezing and unfreezing of terrorist funds and assets in accordance with the relevant United Nations Security Council resolutions.[78]

B. *Challenges to Proscriptions and Listings*

The legislation does not lay out any appeal process against a proscription decision. Thus, it would appear that any challenge to a proscription decision would be by way of judicial review. There are no known instances of any proscribed individual challenging his or her listing. There is no doubt that the process is essentially an executive decision that can be made without the affected person being found guilty by a court of law for a terrorism or terrorism-related offence. Such decisions are made without prior reference or notice to the listed person, and the executive is not required to provide that person with the requisite evidence used to justify the listing. Although concerns over the propriety and efficacy of listing have not arisen in Singapore, the government is mindful that such listings should not create undue hardship, particularly to the family of the listed person.

VI. REGULATION OF TERRORISM FINANCING

A. *The Regulatory Regime to Counter Terrorism Financing*

Singapore is an important global and regional financial leader: the International Monetary Fund ranks Singapore as one of twenty-five systemically important financial centres in the world. Given the large size of the financial sector, the high volume of transactions and wide international reach, the government is alive to the reality that countering money laundering (ML) and terrorism financing (TF) requires a coordinated national response in which every stakeholder has a critical role to play.[79] Singapore's national anti–money laundering and countering the

78 *Singapore National Money Laundering and Terrorist Financing Risk Assessment Report 2013*, p. 9.

79 See, for instance, International Monetary Fund's *Singapore Staff Report for the 2014 Article IV Consultation*, 8 September 2014, paras 24–36 and 39; available at http://www.imf.org/external/pubs/ft/scr/2014/cr14312.pdf.

financing of terrorism (AML/CFT) regime includes laws and regulations, as well as supervisory and enforcement frameworks. In addition, given that TF is a cross-border phenomenon, Singapore has established formal cooperation channels with other jurisdictions for both supervisory and law enforcement purposes, with the additional focus on AML/CFT, as part of the process to better manage cross-border ML/TF risks. The financial sector is regulated by the Monetary Authority of Singapore (MAS), Singapore's *de facto* central bank. Thus, section 27B of the Monetary Authority of Singapore Act (Cap. 186, 1999 Rev Ed) authorizes the MAS to issue such directions or make such regulations concerning any financial institution or class of financial institutions it considers necessary for the prevention of money laundering or for the prevention of the financing of terrorism.

Singapore's counter-terrorism financing regime is not solely dependent on the proscription or listing decisions discussed in Section V, although that process is an important part of dealing with the terrorism threat. In essence, TF is the act of soliciting, collecting or providing funds, from both legal and illicit sources, with the intention of supporting terrorist activities or organizations. While a money launderer's main aim is to conceal the *source* of funds, a terrorist financier aims mainly to conceal the *use* of funds. Given Singapore's advanced financial system, Singapore is potentially an attractive conduit for foreign TF.

Enforcement and investigation work comes under the jurisdiction of the Suspicious Transaction Reporting Office (STRO), a branch of the Financial Investigation Division of Commercial Affairs Department, Singapore Police Force. The Financial Investigation Division is in charge of enforcing the AML/CTF in Singapore. Confidentiality of suspicious transaction reports (STRs) is secured under legislation by section 56 of the Corruption, Drug Trafficking and Other Serious Crimes (Confiscation of Benefits) Act [CDSA] (Cap. 65A, 2000 Rev Ed). In addition, there are also internal controls within the STRO to ensure confidentiality of the STRs received.

To date, there have been no charges or convictions for terrorism financing. It has also been reported that there has been no evidence of TF being committed in Singapore or of funds being raised domestically for terrorism-related activities in Singapore or abroad. There is also little evidence of foreign funds flowing into Singapore for terrorist activities or of Singapore being used as a conduit for TF.[80] Singapore is also aware that terrorist organizations, in the guise of charitable relief, have misused charities and other non-profit organizations to raise funds in other jurisdictions. Charities in Singapore, mostly domestically oriented, must be registered and are regulated by the Charities Act[81] which provides ample

80 *Singapore National Money Laundering and Terrorist Financing Risk Assessment Report 2013*, at 31 and 38.

81 Cap. 37, 2007 Rev Ed.

safeguards to ensure that funds raised are not misused. Besides meeting registration requirements, the charities are required to submit their annual reports and financial statements, which have to be audited or reviewed by external auditors or independent examiners. Separately, there are also concerns that terrorist elements are continuing to use the international banking and financial networks to launder illicit funds for terrorism-related purposes.[82] As such, the Casino Regulatory Authority, which oversees the casino gaming industry in Singapore, is empowered by section 200(2)(t) of the Casino Control Act[83] to make regulations on the requirements to detect or prevent money laundering and the financing of terrorism.

The key legislation regulating terrorism financing is the Terrorism (Suppression of Financing) Act.[84] Sections 3 to 6 of the Act comprehensively cover the scope of criminal activities set out in Article 2 of the International Convention for the Suppression of the Financing of Terrorism. Section 3 of the Act provides that it is an offence for any person to provide or collect property for a terrorist act. Section 4 makes it an offence for any person to provide or collect property for a terrorist purpose, while section 5 stipulates that it is an offence for any person to use or possess property for terrorist purposes. Section 6 provides that it is an offence to deal with terrorist property. Section 35 of the Terrorism (Suppression of Financing) Act, which gives effect to Article 5 of the International Convention for the Suppression of Financing of Terrorism, declares that if a body corporate commits an offence under the Terrorism (Suppression of Financing) Act, the "director, manager, secretary or other similar officer or partner of the company, firm, society, [etc.]" shall be guilty of that offence unless that person can show that the offence was committed without his or her consent or connivance and that he or she had exercised due diligence.

In August 2013, to strengthen the Act's deterrent effect, TSOFA was amended to enhance the maximum penalties for terrorism financing offences: fines were increased from $100,000 to $500,000 for individuals and $1 million for entities. The maximum imprisonment term remains unchanged at ten years.[85] The 2013 amendments to TSOFA also includes new provisions that (i) make it an offence to disclose, by one person to another, information which is likely to prejudice the investigation of a terrorism financing offence; and (ii) protect the identity of informers against disclosure and discovery during legal proceedings. Overlapping provisions in the MAS (Anti-Terrorism Measures) Regulations and the UN (Anti-Terrorism Measures) Regulations were also migrated to the TSOFA, so as to

[82] *Singapore National Money Laundering and Terrorist Financing Risk Assessment Report 2013*, 38.
[83] Cap. 33A, 2007 Rev Ed.
[84] Cap. 325, 2003 Rev Ed.
[85] The enhancement of financial penalties was to bring them in line with the maximum fines for money laundering offences under sections 46 and 47 of the Corruption, Drug Trafficking and Other Serious Crimes (Confiscation of Benefits) Act (Cap. 65A, 2000 Rev Ed).

simplify and streamline the CFT regime.[86] Taken together, the 2013 amendments serve to strengthen Singapore's CFT regime and to further align it with the Financial Action Task Force (FTAF) Recommendations.[87]

In addition, effective 1 November 2014, professional accountants, including public accountants, have to abide by enhanced mandatory requirements on implementing controls and procedures for AML and CFT. The enhanced requirements are contained in the recent Ethics Pronouncement 200, "Anti-Money Laundering and Countering the Financing of Terrorism – Requirements and Guidelines for Professional Accountants in Singapore," issued by the Institute of Singapore Chartered Accountants (ISCA). This pronouncement is also being adopted by the Accounting and Corporate Regulatory Authority (ACRA) and will be applicable to public accountants and accounting entities registered under the Accountants Act[88] who are regulated by ACRA.[89]

B. *Criminal Offences of Terrorism Financing*

Under section 7(1) of the Terrorism (Suppression of Financing) Act, the Minister may exempt any person in Singapore, or any citizen of Singapore outside Singapore, from any specified activity or transaction or a class of specified activities or transactions carried out by the person or citizen. This provision, passed in 2013, permits the provision of property and services, including financial services such as loans, to the affected person. This exemption, it was explained in Parliament, is invoked to cover cases where the provision of such property or financial services would support the subsistence or rehabilitation of a terrorist, as well as the subsistence of his or her family. The exemptions granted, of course, will not extend to the provision of property and services for terrorist purposes. The law also streamlines the process for granting exemptions for transactions relating to basic expenses. Prior to the 2013 amendment, the Minister would make a separate exemption order for each transaction that is for the purpose of meeting basic expenses. With the amendment, a general exemption order will be made by the Minister upfront, with the definition

86 See also Notice 3001 Prevention of Money Laundering and Countering the Financing of Terrorism (for both Money-Changing & Remittance Licensees), July 2014; available at http://www.mas.gov.sg/Regulations-and-Financial-Stability/Regulations-Guidance-and-Licensing/Money-Changing-and-Remittance-Businesses/Notices/2014/Prevention-of-Money-Laundering-and-Countering-the-Financing-of-Terrorism.asp.

87 The FATF's website is at http://www.fatf-gafi.org. Singapore's country reports to the FATF can be found at http://www.fatf-gafi.org/countries/s-t/singapore/.

88 Cap. 2, 2005 Rev Ed.

89 See ACRA and ISCA joint press release of 29 October 2014; available at http://www.news.gov.sg/public/sgpc/en/media_releases/agencies/acra/press_release/P-20141029-1/AttachmentPar/0/file/Press%20release_Ethics%20Pronouncement_291014.pdf.

of basic expenses (such as payment for foodstuff, rent, mortgage, medicine and public utility charges) stipulated in the order, to exempt automatically transactions undertaken to meet stipulated basic expenses.[90] This legislative refinement seeks to support the rehabilitation efforts of the alleged terrorist and his or her family, particularly if the person is under detention, even as procedural safeguards are in place to ensure that the exemptions are not channeled towards terrorist activities. The exemptions can include conditions and requirements, such as regular reporting. Since 2006, about sixty exemption orders have been granted.

VII. IMMIGRATION MEASURES

A. *Immigration Detention*

Thus far, immigration law has not been used against suspected terrorists. The issue has not arisen yet as all the suspects were Singapore citizens. As such, immigration proceedings are inapplicable, and certainly would not be used as an alternative to criminal prosecutions. Where a non-citizen is involved, the Singapore authorities may use the ISA, which will keep the suspect on Singapore's territory. Alternatively, the authorities could extradite the suspect using either the Extradition Act[91] or deport such persons under the Immigration Act.[92] In this regard, there are no known special immigration procedures that have been established for the deportation of suspected terrorists.

Using other immigration cases as a proxy where the revocation of visa status had been challenged, it would appear that the courts have been receptive to "evidence" obtained through intelligence. Such secret evidence had not been seen by the applicant or his or her legal representatives and were used against the applicant in immigration proceedings. Legally, a challenge to the evidence can be mounted under judicial review, but such challenges have not been successful. The courts have deferred to the executive on matters of immigration such as prohibiting or limiting entry into Singapore "in the interests of public security or by reason of any economic, industrial, social, educational or other conditions in Singapore."[93]

Under Article 129(3)(a) of the Singapore Constitution, a Singapore citizen by naturalization shall cease to be such a citizen if he or she is deprived of his or her citizenship by an order of the government made in accordance with this constitutional

90 The definition of basic expenses would be consistent with that in the United Nations Security Council Resolution 1452 (2002), which allows funds and resources for such expenses to be exempted from financial sanctions.

91 Cap. 103, 2000 Rev Ed.

92 Cap. 133, 2008 Rev Ed.

93 Section 9(1)(a), Immigration Act.

provision. There are two grounds for such deprivation of citizenship: (i) where the person has shown himself or herself by act or speech to be disloyal or disaffected towards Singapore; or (ii) that the person has, during any war in which Singapore is or was engaged, unlawfully traded or communicated with an enemy or been engaged in or associated with any business which to the person's knowledge was carried on in such manner as to assist an enemy in that war. Under Article 129(3)(b)(ii) of the Constitution, a Singapore citizen by registration or by naturalization may be deprived of his or her Singapore citizenship if the government is satisfied that such a person has, at any time after registration or naturalization, been engaged in any activities that are prejudicial to the security of Singapore; the maintenance of public order therein; the maintenance therein of essential services; or any criminal activities that are prejudicial to the interests of public safety, peace or good order. However, under Article 129(7), no person shall be deprived of his or her citizenship unless the government is satisfied that it is not conducive to the public good that that person should continue to be a citizen of Singapore, and that as a result of the deprivation he or she would not be a citizen of any country (that is, the person becomes stateless). Thus far, no JI detainee or ex-detainee has been deprived of his Singapore citizenship on account of the detainee's alleged terrorist activity.

B. *Immigration Proceedings and Torture*

There have been no cases dealing with the prohibition on the use of evidence obtained through torture or cruel and degrading treatment in immigration proceedings. However, it is unlikely that the Singapore courts will allow such evidence to be admissible. There is case authority for this in *Nguyen Tuong Van v. Public Prosecutor*,[94] where the Court of Appeal, Singapore's apex court, ruled that torture, as well as other cruel, inhuman or degrading treatment or punishment, when practiced as state policy, were violations of customary international law. The Court also stated that a customary international law rule had to be "clearly and firmly established" before it would be adopted by the domestic courts.[95]

Singapore has extradition treaties in force with the United States, Germany and Hong Kong. Singapore also has extradition arrangements in force with forty Commonwealth countries and territories pursuant to the London Scheme for Extradition Within the Commonwealth. The Mutual Assistance in Criminal

[94] [2005] 1 SLR(R) 103. This case was a Misuse of Drugs Act (Cap. 185, 2001 Revised Edition) offence of drug trafficking for which the mandatory death penalty applied upon conviction.

[95] The Court of Appeal also held that there was insufficient state practice to justify that there was a specific customary international law prohibition against hanging as a mode of execution.

Matters Act (MACMA)[96] allows Singapore authorities to provide, on a case-by-case basis, coercive forms of mutual legal assistance to a requesting country that does not have a mutual legal assistance treaty in force with Singapore, if that country provides an undertaking that it will comply with a future request by Singapore for similar assistance involving a similar offence. This enables Singapore to provide mutual legal assistance to requesting states for terrorism-related offences, in accordance with the provisions of MACMA, even in the absence of an extradition treaty.

Although the issue of whether Singapore subscribes to a ban on refoulement has not arisen in Singapore courts, it is highly unlikely for Singapore to deport a terrorist suspect to a state in which he or she faces the threat of torture or any other form of cruel or inhuman treatment or punishment. It may well be that well be that where there is such a deportation or extradition request, assurances and undertakings would be sought from the receiving country that torture would not be used.

VIII. ADMINISTRATIVE AND EXECUTIVE MEASURES

Executive or administrative measures, effected primarily through the Internal Security Act, are the main mode by which to detain suspected terrorists and to manage the activities of people suspected of terrorism. The Singapore Constitution permits the use of such measures.[97] Ordinarily, Part IV of the Singapore Constitution provides for the fundamental liberties such as freedom of speech, association, assembly (Article 12) and the liberty of the person (Article 9). However, such constitutional freedoms are not unrestricted and are subject to provisos that impose restrictions on the exercise of such freedoms when the Singapore Parliament regards such restrictions as necessary or expedient in the interest of the security of Singapore, public order or morality. The use of the ISA is reinforced by Part XII of the Singapore Constitution, which legalizes the special powers against subversion and emergency powers even if they are inconsistent with the fundamental liberties provided for in Part IV of the Constitution. Tremendous latitude is thus given to legislation designed against subversion.

As discussed earlier, such executive or administrative measures are used as the primary form of anti-terrorism law. Criminal prosecutions have not been exercised on those suspected of terrorist activities. Instead, executive or administrative measures are very much the mainstay of action against terrorists or suspected terrorists in the first instance. In this regard, executive or administrative measures are not conceived

[96] Cap. 190A, 2001 Rev Ed.

[97] See Part XII of the Singapore Constitution, especially Article 149. Part XII of the Constitution provides for special powers against subversion, as well as emergency powers that can be resorted by the executive.

as a supplement to criminal law. Neither are such measures regarded as an alternative to criminal law.

As it is not sitting as a judicial body, the ISA Advisory Board in reviewing detention and restriction orders is not bound by the criminal standard of proof, that is, beyond all reasonable doubt. The standard of proof required by the Advisory Board is, conceivably, the same as that used in civil cases, which is on the balance of probabilities. The detainee and his or her lawyers are also prohibited by law from seeing the evidence that the executive presents to the Advisory Board. It is generally presumed that the release of such evidence even in closed-door settings would be detrimental to national security and/or the safety of the witnesses. There is also no provision to challenge the secret evidence as legal challenges to ISA cases are confined to procedural challenges only. In short, the judicial regime for ISA cases is not designed for adversarial challenges.[98] The subjective judgment of the executive that a detention or restriction order is necessary is sufficient to meet the legal thresholds in the ISA regime.

A piece of legislation such as the ISA is bound to generate political controversy. There are regular calls for the ISA to be abolished, although such calls have not gained significant traction. However, the government will have to continue to justify the existence of such draconian legislation as the ISA, particularly when security threats are perceived to have weakened over the years. The aftermath of 9/11 and the renewed and new concerns of terrorism with the ISIS/ISIL have given the ISA a tentative extension of its shelf life and renewed its relevance.

This is notwithstanding that Malaysia has replaced its ISA with new legislation in 2012.[99] Earlier in September 2011, after Malaysia had announced that it would replace its Internal Security Act with new legislation aimed at preventing "subversive action, organised violence and criminal acts," the Singapore Home Affairs Ministry released a press statement, extracts of which follow:

> 3. The Singapore Government has used the ISA sparingly. The ISA has only been used against individuals who have acted in a manner prejudicial to the security of Singapore or to the maintenance of public order or essential services therein. No person has ever been detained only for their political beliefs.
>
> 4. The ISA in Singapore has only been used to deal with threats of subversion, racial and religious extremism (such as inciting racial or religious hatred, strife and violence), espionage and terrorism. These threats continue to be salient today, especially in the last ten years against the threat of terrorism, where the

[98] See, generally, Internal Security (Detained Persons Advisory Board) Rules.

[99] The issue of liberal democracies defending themselves from extremists who stay within the law but seek to undermine public order and national security has generated debate over proposed anti-terrorism measures, such as anti-foreign subversion law, in the UK and Australia.

> Government's priority is to act swiftly to prevent an attack from taking place. The arrests made under the ISA in Dec 2001 thwarted the imminent suicide bombings against establishments in Singapore that were planned by Al-Qaeda operatives assisted by several of the arrested Jemaah Islamiyah members, preventing the loss of innocent lives. The ISA continues to be relevant and crucial as a measure of last resort for the preservation of our national security.[100]

It is clear that the Singapore government's approach is to demonstrate the ISA's relevance in light of the evolving national security threats including terrorism, and that abolishing the Act would fundamentally undermine Singapore's ability to deal with such threats.[101] Over the years, Singapore has put in place a variety of laws to deal with threats to national security, such as those posed by racial and religious conflicts. These include the Sedition Act, the Penal Code (revised in 2007) and the Maintenance of Religious Harmony Act.

The ISA is part of this legislative arsenal to deal with threats in a calibrated manner. The non-ISA laws do not provide for renewable two-year periods of preventive detention without trial nor prohibition orders, including restrictions on movement, political activities and overseas travel. Specifically, it is this power to detain without trial that makes the ISA such a harsh piece of legislation, but also enables the government to deal with egregious security threats where the means to prosecute through the legal process present formidable challenges, ranging from evidential difficulties to releasing classified information that would compromise security operations and intelligence sources. Indeed, in the post-9/11 era, it is notable that criticism from the United States and Europe over the use of the ISA has become quite muted. Law enforcement agencies elsewhere have been disadvantaged by the lack of an equivalent ISA-type legislation.

Following the landmark 1989 case of accused Marxist co-conspirator *Chng Suan Tze*, where the Court of Appeal decided in the appellant's favour on a technical ground, Parliament moved to legislatively overrule the court's decision. The Constitution and ISA were promptly amended, confining judicial review only to questions relating to compliance with the ISA's procedural requirements. However, allowing the judges to review both procedural requirements and the substance of the ISA orders would bolster public confidence. This does not mean that judges would ultimately decide what is good or necessary for national security or public safety, as they would likely defer to the executive on what national security entails. However, the key principle is that the executive should not have extensive discretionary powers

[100] Ministry of Home Affairs press statement, 16 September 2011.

[101] See, for example, the Ministry of Home Affairs' 2002 booklet, *A Singapore Safe for All*, on the necessity of the ISA and the safeguards against its use. The booklet is available online at http://www.mha.gov.sg/publication_details.aspx?pageid=35&cid=348.

that are not subject to judicial review. The introduction of more safeguards would go far in reassuring the public.

Even so, more safeguards and the exceptional, judicious use of the ISA may not provide sufficient assurance in a society that seeks to be governed by the rule of law. Here, the concern is not so much the fear that the executive would abuse the ISA. Instead, such a draconian piece of legislation lends itself completely to the expectation of abuse.[102] Although the Singapore government had in its 16 September 2011 media statement stated that "No person has ever been detained only for their political beliefs," the likelihood that it could be used to counter political threats is not a mere theoretical possibility.[103] The utility of the ISA to the executive is not at all in question. Writing extrajudicially, Singapore's Chief Justice noted that the ISA is "philosophically entirely different from the conventional criminal law – it is first preventive and prophylactic, next rehabilitative and redemptive."[104] He added that the "counter-terrorism efficacy of the ISA has rarely been questioned," and urged for the ISA to be "assessed for the balance it has sought to achieve between the right to security and the right to liberty."[105]

The consistent use of the ISA since 9/11 against suspected Islamist terrorists has obviated the need for public trials. In "the context of a history of delicate racial and religious relations" between Singapore's non-Muslim majority and its Muslim's minority, Michael Hor has argued that:

> [T]he spectacle of a public trial against alleged Malay Muslims accused of extremism and terrorism might polarize the different communities in Singapore to an unacceptable degree. People are bound to take sides and the side that they take is likely to follow the racial and religious divide. It would also be an uphill task to try to persuade the Malay Muslim minority that the majority are not oppressing them out of racial or religious prejudice. Also, it would not be fanciful to predict that a public trial might feed existing racial or religious prejudice on the part of the majority, or even create prejudice where it did not exist before.[106]

Yet, it is also important to note that the use of the ISA to detain suspected Islamist terrorists since 9/11 could also give rise to fears that the ISA can be used as a tool

[102] *Cf* A *Singapore Safe for All* (at p. 28), the Ministry of Home Affairs states that "As Singapore is a parliamentary democracy, the Government is elected by the people. The Government will be held responsible by all Singaporeans if it abuses the powers of the ISA. The people of Singapore are therefore the greatest check on any abuse of the ISA's powers of preventive detention."

[103] For instance, critics note that Operation Spectrum, which was an ISD operation against alleged Marxist conspirators in the 1980s, created a political chill that continues to colour Singapore politics.

[104] Sundaresh Menon, "International Terrorism and Human Rights" (2014) 4 *Asian Journal of International Law* 1–33 at 28.

[105] Sundaresh Menon, "International Terrorism and Human Rights," (2014) 4 *Asian Journal of International Law* 1–33 at 25–6.

[106] Michael Hor, "Terrorism and the Criminal Law: Singapore's Solution" [2002] *Sing. J.L.S.* 30 at 49.

for religious repression. "Religion" can easily morph into a national security threat. While that concern is not a real one in the current circumstances, the ISA remains controversial even if the contention remains latent and inchoately articulated.

IX. ROLE OF MILITARY AND EXTRA-TERRITORIAL COUNTER-TERRORISM ACTIVITIES

A. *Military Courts and Detention*

During peacetime, the Singapore Armed Forces (SAF) does not play a role in the domestic enforcement of terrorism law. However, if there is a proclamation of emergency in Singapore pursuant to Part XII of the Singapore Constitution, the military can be deployed as part of the larger scheme of enforcing the terrorism laws. Similarly, section 201C of the Singapore Armed Forces Act[107] provides for the deployment of the SAF for land operations, in aid of civilian authorities, in the event of a terrorist attack in Singapore. The SAF has conducted joint counter-terrorism exercises with other militaries, including the Indonesian National Defence Forces (TNI)[108] and China's People's Liberation Army (PLA).[109] Military courts are not at all used with respect to terrorism prosecutions either domestically or extra-territorially. Thus far, Singapore has not detained any suspected terrorists on a law of war basis.

B. *The Extra-Territorial Treatment of Citizens Suspected of Terrorism*

While there have been Singapore nationals arrested and/or detained abroad because of suspicions of their involvement in terrorism, there have been no litigation or review proceedings in Singapore with respect to their treatment while in detention by another state. The Singapore approach is very much to let the foreign state, seized with proper jurisdiction, allow the laws take their course. Singapore stands ready to provide appropriate consular assistance to its nationals. When such a person is subsequently deported to Singapore by the foreign state, he or she may be detained under the ISA.

107 Cap. 295, 2000 Rev Ed.

108 See Ministry of Defence (MINDEF) press release of 26 July 2012, "SAF and TNI Conclude Joint Counter-Terrorism Exercise"; available at http://www.mindef.gov.sg/imindef/press_room/official_releases/nr/2012/jul/16jul12_nr.html#.VAvfftzGB8c.

109 See MINDEF report, "SAF, PLA conclude joint counter-terrorism training exercise," 24 November 2010; available at http://www.mindef.gov.sg/imindef/resourcelibrary/cyberpioneer/topics/articles/news/2010/november/24nov10_news.html#.VAvgOdzGB8c.

C. *Extra-Territorial Terrorism Law Enforcement*

The operational charters of the Internal Security Department and the police do not enable them to participate in operational extra-territorial counter-terrorism activities. Singapore's external intelligence operations are conducted by the Security and Intelligence Division (SID), which comes under the purview of the Ministry of Defence. Little is known about the SID's operational work, and no specific law regulates the roles and activities of the SID. However, given the transnational nature of terrorism, intelligence is vital as part of Singapore's overall counter-terrorism efforts as it is in other jurisdictions. Prime Minister Lee gave an indication of this when he said, "We need to be able to pick up intelligence leads, pursue them thoroughly, and nip emerging threats in the bud. Keeping Singapore safe is a constant cat-and-mouse game, as terrorist organizations become more and more sophisticated."[110]

No terrorist suspect is known to have been extradited from Singapore to face terrorism prosecutions in another country. Assuming that such an extradition request was made, the Extradition Act would presumably apply.[111] In addition, the Terrorism (Suppression of Financing) Act (TSOFA) includes provisions that allow the International Convention for the Suppression of the Financing of Terrorism to serve as a basis for mutual legal assistance under MACMA and for extradition under Singapore's laws.[112] As such, Singapore is likely able to make and accommodate requests for mutual legal assistance and extradition involving other Convention parties. Similarly, Singapore's Terrorism (Suppression of Bombings) Act, which implements the International Convention for the Suppression of Terrorist Bombings, provides for either extraditing or prosecuting persons accused of committing or aiding in the commission of terrorist bombings.

In most, if not all, circumstances, an act of terrorism is likely to be offence in most jurisdictions. As Singapore's penal laws still provide for the death penalty and preventive detention permitted under the ISA, extradition of alleged offenders to countries where there is the death penalty or the use of military detention or trial is not likely to pose a significant legal hurdle. However, given Singapore's preferential and exclusive use of the ISA rather than prosecution against alleged terrorists, this could complicate cooperation with other countries in the prosecution of terrorist suspects. This is because information that Singapore considers sensitive intelligence, if shared with countries intending prosecutions, could result in that information

110 Speech by Singapore Prime Minister Lee Hsien Loong at the International Conference on Terrorist Rehabilitation and Community Resilience on 26 March 2013.

111 See also discussion in Section VI.B.

112 Part V of TSOFA.

being made public and/or shared with other parties (such as defence lawyers). This may be beyond the comfort level of the Singaporean authorities.

X. SECRECY AND TERRORISM

A. *Secrecy Claims and Secret Evidence*

As prosecutions are not the main mode by which alleged terrorists are dealt with, the risk that state secrets could be compromised is less of a concern in the case of Singapore. As indicated earlier, in the review of ISA detentions by the ISA Advisory Board (AB) secret evidence not seen by the accused can still be used as incriminating evidence for the purposes of a detention order. Although the AB has all the powers of a court of law in summoning and examining witnesses, compelling the production of documents and evidence that it deems relevant and examining a detainee's representations, as well as examining ISD officers and statements of witnesses, the AB does not operate as a judicial body. Furthermore, it is restricted to reviewing only the procedural grounds for the detention. The state can restrict normal rights that the accused may have to access information, or the state may hold disclosure of information if it claims or classifies that information as secret.

The emphasis on secrecy in terrorism-related cases is also strong in the TSOFA. Section 10A of TSOFA seeks to protect the information and identity of an informer by stipulating that such information shall not be admitted in evidence in any criminal or civil proceedings. This provision, introduced in 2013, would make it onerously difficult for an accused person to mount a defence in such circumstances. The Minister, in moving the amendment bill, replied that:

> [W]e need to strike a balance in the public interest between giving the accused unlimited access to all available information for his defence, and protecting informants so that they will not be afraid to provide much needed intelligence to prevent terrorist attacks. This does not absolve our enforcement agencies from conducting proper investigations and gathering the requisite evidence to prove all the elements of the offence. But the key point here is this balance is an important one and this Bill seeks to strike a balance in the context of what we have experienced in Singapore today.[113]

The key takeaway is not the Minister's emphasis on striking a balance between the public interest and the prevention of terrorist attacks, which is not unusual in its own right, but rather that prevention of terrorism must take overriding precedence. The judges are not asked and are effectively prohibited from determining where

[113] *Singapore Parliament Reports*, vol. 90 (12 August 2013) per Second Minister for Home Affairs S. Iswaran. Note the use of "gathering the requisite evidence to prove all the elements of the offence."

the balance ought to lie between competing claims of secrecy and disclosure in individual cases. Such evidentiary rules privilege and prevent the non-disclosure of intelligence sources and methods.

XI. OTHER MATTERS: RELIGION, SECURITY AND CITIZENSHIP AS INDIVISIBLE

Post 9/11, religion and national security are now even more intimately linked. Religion and state security are taken seriously in Singapore, although there has been no overt religious conflict since its hurried independence in August 1965. In some respects, 9/11 and its aftermath have driven home the message that the terrorism threat is best dealt with not by indiscriminately clamping down on religion. Even as national security comes under threat, the better approach is to ensure that the citizens' religious identities, especially that of Muslims, remain secure. Such a paradoxical approach also entails that civil society play a bigger role in ensuring that the state and religion are both secure. In short, looking at religion merely as a security threat is manifestly inadequate in keeping both state and society safe.[114] The vast majority (99 per cent) of the indigenous Malays are Muslims. The minority (Malay-)Muslim community's importance is constitutionally recognized, and the community enjoys several privileges not accorded to the other races or religions.[115] Besides being governed by *Shariah* law in personal matters, the community enjoys free tertiary education (qualified through means testing in 1989); state support for various aspects of its religious life, including the mosque-building programme and the *haj* (pilgrimage to Mecca); and the appointment of a Minister-in-Charge of Muslim Affairs in the Cabinet.

Aware of the power of religion to mobilize, motivate and enforce behaviour, values and norms among the faithful, the Singapore political leadership has even mobilized religion to facilitate aspects of nation-building.[116] The government has become more conscious and responsive to civil society's role in strengthening

[114] For a more detailed analysis, see Eugene K. B. Tan, "From Clampdown to Limited Empowerment: Hard and Soft Law in the Calibration and Regulation of Religious Conduct in Singapore," (2009) 31(3) *Law and Policy* 351–79.

[115] Article 152(2) of the Constitution recognizes the "special position of the Malays who are the indigenous people of Singapore." Limited legal pluralism is facilitated by Article 153 of the Constitution and enabled by the Administration of Muslim Law Act (Cap. 3, 2009 Rev Ed), which provides for Muslim religious affairs to managed by the Islamic Religious Council of Singapore (MUIS), a statutory board constituted to advise the President and the government in matters relating to the Muslim religion. Article 153 is the only constitutional provision that specifically mentions a religion.

[116] See Eugene K.B. Tan, 'Keeping God in Place: The Management of Religion in Singapore,' in Lai Ah Eng (ed.), *Religious Diversity in Singapore* (Singapore: Institute of Southeast Asian Studies and the Institute of Policy Studies, National University of Singapore, 2008), pp. 55–82.

interfaith engagement and understanding and the thickening of social fabric. In countering the terrorist threat, the approach has evolved rapidly from a "whole-of-government" to a "whole-of-society" approach, a significant recognition of terrorism as being "by far the most serious [security problem] that we have faced since the communist problem."[117] This is a tacit acknowledgment that the security of the state, government and society are all interlinked. The terrorism threat requires not just a security response but a holistic one, one which seeks to align the hearts and minds of the faith communities to the societal objective of harmony and peace.

Institutional efforts to deal with the terrorism threat are in essence a collective action challenge: How do societies prevent the terrorist ideology from establishing and gaining traction within a community? What can multicultural societies such as Singapore do to cope with the aftermath of a terrorist attack? How can societies fortify themselves to come out resiliently against the forces that seek to divide and destroy? The government is right to conclude that the graver threat to society is not whether a terrorist attack is successful but rather how society responds to a terrorist attack.

In Singapore, the government established the Inter-Racial and Religious Confidence Circles, better known as IRCCs, as government-affiliated grassroots organizations that function as local-level interfaith platforms in every constituency to promote racial and religious harmony. As "networks of trust," the IRCCs

> serve as important bridges between religious, ethnic and community groups at the local level. Leaders from various religious, ethnic and other community organizations have come together to join the IRCC networks to build friendships and trust. The IRCCs also aim to deepen people's understanding of the various faiths, beliefs and practices through inter-faith and inter-ethnic themed activities such as inter-faith heritage trails, inter-faith talks and dialogues and various ethnic and religious celebrations. The IRCCs are also primed to respond quickly to incidents with racial and religious tensions and to project solidarity on the ground during crises.[118]

In this regard, IRCCs function as informal redress mechanisms to ensure that relational disputes do not flare up to increase tensions.

The work of the IRCCs is an integral part of the larger effort to ensure that society is resilient enough in the face of terrorist threats and attacks. In this regard, the government launched the Community Engagement Programme (CEP) in 2006. The CEP seeks to strengthen the understanding and ties between people of different

[117] "Not the Terror, but the Fallout," *Today* (Singapore), 10 February 2006.
[118] See generally http://www.ircc.sg/about.php.

races and religions and aims to develop Singaporeans skills and knowledge in coping with emergencies, in particular, terrorist attacks.[119] As the CEP website observes,

> The 11 September 2001 attack in the United States and other attacks after that have shown that terrorism is now largely linked to religious extremism. The terrorists use religion as a reason to commit violence against others. The arrests of Jemaah Islamiyah (JI) members for plotting bombings in Singapore in 2001 showed that Singapore can be a target of these terrorists as well. It also showed us that there were Singaporeans who have been misled by these terrorists.... Terrorism is a long-term threat to Singapore, so we have to prepare ourselves to prevent attacks and to manage the consequences should there be an attack.... If terrorists successfully launch an attack in Singapore, they will not just want to kill people and destroy property. Their true intention is to create suspicion, tension and strife between the different racial and religious groups in Singapore. We must not allow this to happen. A crisis such as a terrorist incident is a national problem, not one of any particular race or religion. We must face any such crisis united as one nation and one people.[120]
>
> This is why the Community Engagement Programme is NOT just another anti-terrorist emergency planning effort. It is a lot more. We want to find ways to ensure that our society stays strong and united during and after such a crisis, so that as a society we can recover quickly, and as Singaporeans we can continue to work, study and live together in peace and harmony.
>
> Through the Community Engagement Programme, the community will be involved in response plans that will be activated when a crisis, e.g. a terrorist incident, does occur. These plans aim to help Singaporeans cope with the shock and to stay calm and resilient. This will ensure that our society stays together, and we can continue with our daily lives as quickly as possible.[121]

In the immediate aftermath of the initial rounds of JI arrests, the government had adopted a privatized approach to what was and is essentially a mutual existential threat. The collective security approach, which hitherto had laid the substratum for stable ethnic relations in Singapore, was sidelined. Instead, the Malay-Muslim community was expected to shoulder the brunt of the concern and responsibility. It was, to all intents and purposes, held solely responsible for the radicalization of a small minority of Muslims, and for any terrorist act and its subsequent fallout.

The government had expressed its fears of the Muslim community's perceived exclusion and self-segregation from Singaporean society on religious grounds.

[119] On the CEP, see Asad-ul Iqbal Latif, *Hearts of Resilience: Singapore's Community Engagement Programme* (Singapore: Institute of Southeast Asian Studies, 2011). See also the CEP's "Singapore United" portal, at www.singaporeunited.sg.

[120] See http://www.singaporeunited.sg/cep/index.php/web/About-CEP/Why-the-need-for-CEP/ (language).

[121] See http://www.singaporeunited.sg/cep/index.php/web/About-CEP/What-is-CEP.

Unfortunately, this was accompanied by unrelenting and uninformed public scrutiny over the tenability of Islamic practices and increased religiosity in Singapore. There were concerns and questions over the overt symbols and signs of Muslim identity and beliefs, which hitherto did not arouse concern. This led the Minister-in-charge of Muslim Affairs to remark that, "Observing religious practices became a shorthand for hovering at the edge of terrorism."

Before the launch of the Community Engagement Programme in February 2006, the public discourse on the terrorist threat was inflected with a moral panic that linked increased Islamic religiosity and perceived Malay-Muslim separateness with increased susceptibility towards terrorism. These developments demonstrated that sole reliance on coercive legislation to deal with the terrorism threat was woefully inadequate.

Although the government intended to rally the Muslim community into action, this privatized approach can have the unintended effect of isolating the mainstream community, thereby threatening mutual security and undermining ethnic relations. The government quickly realized that such a privatized, finger-pointing approach would neither help to isolate the terrorists nor ensure that the terrorist ideology did not acquire wider support. Given the nature of the terrorist threat and its dependence on a sympathetic constituency to draw support and recruits to the cause, the non-discriminating, clamping-down strategy more often than not marginalizes, if not alienates, the very bedrock of the Muslim community that is depended upon to form the bulwark against creeping radicalization.

Furthermore, given that people rather than governments defeat terrorism, policy makers have to fortify and prepare society by having all communities work together in ensuring that society does not unravel in the aftermath of a terrorist strike through mutual suspicion and distrust. Hence, the privatized approach gave way to a communitywide or a "whole-of-society" approach. Isolating the terrorists, both politically and on religious grounds, is the dominant approach now. Consequently, the overwhelming hard law emphasis has conceded space for a soft law approach, recognizing that the terrorism threat needs a collective and holistic response from governments and societies alike. The previous narrow framing of terrorism as being a "Malay-Muslim problem" was abandoned. Terrorism is now being framed as a "national problem," requiring a solution in which all Singaporeans, regardless of their racial and religious allegiance, have a role to play. The Prime Minister issued this timely corrective when he launched the CEP, the centerpiece of Singapore's social cohesion and counter-terrorism endeavors:

> … [W]e must know that this is not a Malay-Muslim problem. This is a national problem and non-Muslims also have to play your part, for example, by preserving the space for minorities in the majority-Chinese society by upholding the ideals

> of meritocracy and equal opportunity and treatment, regardless of race, language and religion and by clearly distinguishing the small number of extremists who are a threat to us from the majority of moderate, rational, loyal Muslim Singaporeans with whom we work together to tackle a shared problem. And this way, we can build confidence and trust between the different communities and the best time to do that is now when we don't have a crisis. This is because building trust takes time. . . .[122]

The CEP aims to mobilize Muslim and non-Muslim communities to work together in tackling the terrorist threat. In this regard, the tolerance mode, manifested in the oft-mentioned "live and let live" dictum, is inadequate. While draconian legislation may be apt in the event of a crisis, it does not assist in the building of inter-ethnic ties during peaceful conditions. Nor do they do help society to get back on its feet in the aftermath of a terrorist attack. Enforcing draconian legislation is reactionary, with little didactic and normative value. To be sure, the Singapore government believes in the utility and necessity of coercive legislation. It also continues to insist that the Muslim community practice its faith in the context of a multiracial society with moderation as the defining attribute. But the government is also convinced that legislation alone is insufficient to keep the deleterious effects of radicalism and the social consequences of a terrorist attack at bay. Singapore's then–Foreign Minister put it aptly: "There is a limit to what laws can do. We can legislate against extremism but we can't legislate harmony."[123] It is indeed highly questionable whether governments can ever out-law extremism.

The trouble with the primacy of a hard law approach is that it abrogates to the state and policy makers the power to control and define the "problem." It obfuscates the reality and the urgency of building ties between a devout Muslim minority and a non-Muslim majority within a political structure that sanctions secular political governance. Hard law also denies the sociopolitical and religious dimensions present in terrorism. Ironically, hard law can secure the state, but its overemphatic use ultimately impoverishes the very security of the state and society. With soft law, a putative mechanism of norms, institutions and structures can buttress the framework to sustain religious harmony.

The focus of Singapore's response to terrorism post-9/11 has been to reach out to the "moderate, mainstream" Muslims as a bulwark against societal implosion. This broad-based endeavor pivots on "religious moderation."[124] While coercive draconian

122 Speech by Prime Minister Lee Hsien Loong at the Community Engagement Programme Dialogue, Singapore, 9 February 2006.

123 Speech by Foreign Minister George Yeo, at the Jamiyah Seminar, "Towards Peace, Intercultural, Interfaith Harmony and Justice," Singapore, 1 September 2006.

124 See Eugene K. B. Tan, "Norming Moderation in an 'Iconic Target': Public Policy and the Regulation of Religious Anxieties in Singapore" (2007) 19(4) *Terrorism and Political Violence*, 443–62.

legislation remains the mainstay against extremists and radicals, the mobilization of soft law, aspirational norms and values are consciously woven into the state's endeavors to enhance society's resilience and cohesion.

Following 9/11 and the discovery of a homegrown terrorist cell in Singapore, the belief in interfaith dialogue and understanding received a boost. When an issue involving religion arises, the trust and confidence enables the various religious leaders to communicate with each other directly. Continuing this dialogue and keeping communication lines open are also practiced between the government and the individual major religious communities. As the Deputy Prime Minister and Home Affairs Minister reported in Parliament recently:

> Government and religious leaders meet regularly on public occasions such as community functions, religious events and activities under our Community Engagement Programme. Government and religious leaders also regularly meet privately, individually or in groups. Both Government and religious leaders know that when sensitive issues arise that they wish to discuss in confidence, they can do so candidly behind closed doors. This approach has worked well. These interactions help to build mutual understanding and trust, and have enabled our religious leaders to become valued and vital partners of the Government in maintaining religious harmony in Singapore.[125]

XII. CONCLUSION

The threat to Singapore from terrorism remains real; it has acquired the complexion of an existential challenge.[126] The fact that there has been no successful terrorist attack in Singapore may give rise to a false sense of security. At the same time, there is an almost irresistible, evocative appeal in the label of "terror," "terrorism," and "terrorist." The mere use of any one or all of these "T-words" brings us into the realm of the extra-criminal world with all the attendant fears, dangers, moral panic and even a crisis. Nevertheless, to maintain a functioning society, the government also strives to strengthen the societal resolve not to allow Singapore to be paralyzed by the terrorist threat, and not to allow its social cohesion and order to be undermined by a terrorist attack.

[125] *Singapore Parliament Reports*, vol. 89, 15 October 2012.

[126] Singapore co-sponsored UN Security Council Resolution 2178, passed on 24 September 2014, which obliges UN member states, *inter alia*, to counter the violent ideologies that fuel radicalism and prevent the international flow of terrorist fighters to and from conflict zones. At the UN General Assembly on 29 September 2014, Singapore condemned the terrorist actions of ISIS "in the strongest possible terms. ISIS will continue to target those who do not conform to its extremist agenda." See speech by the Minister for Foreign Affairs and Minister for Law K Shanmugam at the United Nations General Assembly 69th session general debate; available at http://www.mfa.gov.sg/content/mfa/media_centre/press_room/pr/2014/201409/press_20140930.html.

The current legal framework provides tremendous leeway and special powers to the authorities to deal with the scourge of terrorism. The use of special powers such as the ISA must be strictly constrained and properly justified. In fighting terrorism, it is absolutely essential that this operational imperative be balanced by the critical need to ensure that the values a society holds dear are not compromised or undermined by the operational imperative. Values such as rule of law, due process and protection of fundamental freedoms provided for in the Singapore Constitution. To be sure, the prudent and principled use of discretionary powers by the various executive agencies in the various anti-terrorism legislation will go a long way towards maintaining the legitimacy of the various laws on the statute books. But it is also impossible to legislate that those upon whom such discretionary powers are vested will exercise such powers with utmost scruples, responsibility and wisdom. The need to exercise discretion properly is fundamental to maintaining public confidence in any anti-terrorism legislation, especially when the counter-terrorism regime provides for detention without trial. The Judiciary performs the ultimate check-and-balance role. Singapore's counter-terrorism regime must be cognizant of the need for fettered discretion on the part of the executive when it exercises discretionary power.

Although there is no violent religious conflict connected with terrorist activity in Singapore, the Singapore government has indicated that the threat posed by faith-inspired terrorist groups remain a real one. Since the 11 September 2001 attacks in the United States, Islam has come under very close scrutiny globally. In Singapore, there were several rounds of arrests and detention of Jemaah Islamiyah (JI) and "self-radicalized" terrorist suspects in Singapore. These arrests of "homegrown" terrorist suspects had unsettled the Singapore polity, with anecdotal evidence suggesting that ethnic relations were strained, if not shrouded in suspicion, during the initial crackdown between 2001 and 2004. The Malay-Muslims were themselves confronted by self-doubt and ambivalence. The backdrop of the government's apprehensions over the loyalty of Muslim-Singaporeans to Singapore is a long-standing issue that gnaws at the relationship between the community and the government.

While it is misleading to equate the increased religiosity of the Muslim-Singaporean community as sympathy with or support for violent extremism, the government has always been concerned that primordial loyalties of faith and ethnicity would take precedence over civic and secular loyalties to the Singapore nation-state. In particular, the government's concern with the perceived, growing exclusivity of the Malay-Muslim community was amplified with the discovery of homegrown Islamist terrorist suspects post-9/11.

Singapore's earlier focus on dichotomizing the moderate and radical elements of Islamic faith perhaps exaggerated the image and perception of Muslim-Singaporeans as being susceptible to religious radicalism. Fortunately, this discourse has now taken a backseat, and a more inclusive approach has been adopted. Had the government persisted in putting the terrorist threat at the feet of the Muslim community, it would have marginalized the "moderates" who are needed to form the bulwark in the proverbial battle for the hearts and minds of Muslims. The violent extremist tendencies of the detained terrorist suspects should not be treated as being inherent in Islam nor equated as bearing the endorsement of the larger Muslim-Singaporean community. As terrorist tendencies are too often conflated with broader Muslim sympathies, this distinction is crucial and must be constantly reiterated in Singapore.

The terrorism threat persists today and for the foreseeable future with no clear resolution in sight. While counter-terrorism laws are necessary to keep a society safe, they are not sufficient to counter the threat. More importantly, such laws do not ensure that society remains cohesive and resilient in such challenging times. The urgent need to counter violent extremist ideas and ideologies must be an integral part of any sustainable action plan against the scourge of terrorism. As Singapore's Deputy Prime Minister Teo Chee Hean puts it, "It's an evolving threat, requires constant vigilance and it's paradoxical. The temptation to become complacent is always there, and the longer we go without actually having a successful attack, the greater the temptation. You believe it will never happen."[127]

127 See "DPM Teo: Regional Terror Groups are Top Security Threat," *The Straits Times*, 10 September 2011.

23

Australia

Fergal Davis, Nicola McGarrity and George Williams

I. INTRODUCTION

On 15 and 16 December, 2014, Man Haron Monis held eighteen people hostage in the Lindt Café, Martin Place, Sydney. By the end of the siege, two hostages and the hostage taker were dead. Prior to those events, Australia had enjoyed a history relatively free of terrorist attacks on domestic soil. Before December 2014, the most infamous terrorist act was the bombing of the Commonwealth Heads of Government Meeting at the Hilton Hotel in Sydney in 1978. These historically low levels of terrorism go some way towards explaining why Australia did not have any national laws dealing specifically with terrorism when the attacks on the United States occurred on 11 September 2001.

While the full response to the Martin Place siege is yet to become apparent, the impact of 9/11 on Australian counter-terrorism law is clear. A decade after 9/11, the Federal Parliament has enacted over sixty anti-terrorism laws.[1] These deal with such topics as defining terrorism, criminalizing a range of terrorism-related activities, expanding the investigatory powers of law enforcement and intelligence agencies and, finally, creating alternative mechanisms for restricting the liberty of terrorist suspects.[2] One catalyst for these laws was the requirement in United Nations Security Council Resolution 1373 (Resolution 1373) that states '[t]ake necessary steps to prevent the commission of terrorist acts' by ensuring that they 'are established as serious criminal offences in domestic laws and regulations'. Australia undoubtedly already had laws in place that could have been used to *prosecute* individuals for acts of terrorism. However, new anti-terrorism laws were said to be needed on the basis

[1] George Williams, 'The Legal Legacy of the "War on Terror"' (2013) 12 *Macquarie Law Journal* 3, 6–7.

[2] See George Williams, 'Anti-Terror Legislation in Australia and New Zealand' in Victor Ramraj et al. (eds), *Global Anti-Terrorism Law and Policy* (Cambridge University Press, 2nd ed, 2012) 541; George Williams, 'A Decade of Australian Anti-Terror Laws' (2011) 35(3) *Melbourne University Law Review* 1136.

that the existing law was insufficient to *prevent* such acts from occurring in the first place.[3]

II. THE DEFINITION OF TERRORISM

Australia's new anti-terrorism laws define a 'terrorist act' as an action or threat of action made with two intentions.[4] The first is the intention to advance a political, religious or ideological cause; the other is the intention to coerce or influence by intimidation a government or to intimidate the public or a section of the public. The action or threat of action must also cause one of the listed harms, ranging from death and serious bodily harm to endangering a person's life, seriously interfering with electronic systems or creating a serious risk to the health or safety of a section of the public. The definition excludes advocacy, protest, dissent or industrial action so long as there is no intention to cause personal harm.

The Australian definition has much in common with those employed in other common law jurisdictions.[5] That said, Saul has argued that 'Australia's legal definition of terrorism is actually amongst the most tightly-defined and human rights-respecting definitions in the domestic laws of any country'.[6] However, this opinion is not universally shared. Syrota has written that the definition is 'imperfect' and 'in need of serious revision'.[7] In 2009, the Australian Greens Party proposed significant changes to the definition of a terrorist act.[8] Its proposal would have excluded threats of action, narrowed the harm element to personal harm only,

[3] For example, in 2007, the then–Attorney-General Phillip Ruddock championed the role of prevention in Australia's counter-terrorism policy, arguing that the government ought to 'prevent rather than to react to terrorist offences': see Phillip Ruddock, 'Law as a Preventative Weapon Against Terrorism' in Andrew Lynch, Edwina Macdonald and George Williams (eds), *Law and Liberty in the War on Terror* (Federation Press, 2007) 4. For further discussion on the role of prevention in Australian counter-terrorism law, see Tamara Tulich, 'Prevention and Pre-emption in Australia's Domestic Anti-Terrorism Legislation (2012) 1(1) *International Journal of Crime and Justice* 52.

[4] *Criminal Code Act 1995* (Cth) s 100.1(1)-(3).

[5] Ben Golder and George Williams, 'What Is "Terrorism"? Problems of Legal Definition' (2004) 27 *University of New South Wales Law Journal* 270; Jessie Blackbourn, Fergal Davis and Natasha Taylor, 'Academic Consensus and Legislative Definitions of Terrorism: Applying Schmid and Jongman' (2013) 34(3) *Statute Law Review* 239; Keiran Hardy and George Williams, 'What Is "Terrorism"? Assessing Domestic Legal Definitions' (2011) 16 *UCLA Journal of International Law and Foreign Affairs* 77.

[6] Ben Saul, Submission [no number available], Council of Australian Governments Review of Counter-Terrorism Legislation, *Council of Australian Governments Review of Counter-Terrorism Legislation*, 4 December 2012, 2.

[7] George Syrota, 'The Definition of "Terrorist Act" in Part 5.3 of the Commonwealth Criminal Code' (2007) 33(2) *University of Western Australia Law Review* 307, 348.

[8] Explanatory Memorandum, Anti-Terrorism Laws Reform Bill 2009 (Cth), 3. For a discussion of this Bill, see Senate Legal and Constitutional Affairs Legislation Committee, Commonwealth Parliament, *Anti-Terrorism Laws Reform Bill 2009* (2009) 3–5, 13–16.

excluded action committed within the context of an armed conflict and removed the political, religious or ideological cause element.[9]

The 2013 report of the Council of Australian Governments Review of Counter-Terrorism Legislation (COAG Review) generally agreed with Saul's positive assessment of the definition.[10] However, it nevertheless acknowledged that some amendments were appropriate.[11] Amendments were also proposed in the 2012 annual report of the Independent National Security Legislation Monitor (INSLM).[12] Both the COAG Review and the INSLM recommended that acts committed during armed conflicts governed by international law should be excluded from the definition.[13] The COAG Review also recommended removing 'threat of action' from the definition and replacing it with a separate offence of 'threatening to commit a terrorist act'.[14] The INSLM was critical of the cause element in the definition and noted that 'the requirement to prove religious motive in terrorism offences comes too close to pursuing a case against a religion'.[15] To date there has been no government response to the reports of either the COAG Review or the INSLM.

III. CRIMINAL LAWS AND PROSECUTIONS

A. *Criminal Law*

a. Federal Criminal Law

The Federal Parliament has enacted legislation criminalising a wide range of activities connected with terrorism.[16] Federal terrorism offences fall into five broad

9 The United Nations Human Rights Committee has also criticised the vagueness of the Australian definition of a terrorist act and recommended that it 'ensure that its application is limited to offences that are indisputably terrorist offences': United Nations Human Rights Committee, *Concluding Observations: Australia*, 95th sess, UN Doc CCPR/C/AUS/CO/5 (7 May 2009) [11].

10 Council of Australian Governments Review of Counter-Terrorism Legislation, *Report of the Council of Australian Governments Review of Counter-Terrorism Legislation* (2013) 7–8.

11 Ibid 8.

12 Independent National Security Legislation Monitor, *Declassified Annual Report* (2012).

13 Council of Australian Governments Review of Counter-Terrorism Legislation, *Report of the Council of Australian Governments Review of Counter-Terrorism Legislation* (2013) 10; Independent National Security Legislation Monitor, *Declassified Annual Report* (2012) 124.

14 Council of Australian Governments Review of Counter-Terrorism Legislation, *Report of the Council of Australian Governments Review of Counter-Terrorism Legislation* (2013) 8.

15 Independent National Security Legislation Monitor, *Declassified Annual Report* (2012) 115. The COAG Review acknowledged the position of the INSLM but respectfully disagreed: Council of Australian Governments Review of Counter-Terrorism Legislation, *Report of the Council of Australian Governments Review of Counter-Terrorism Legislation* (2013) 8.

16 For an overview of the approach taken under federal criminal law, see Edwina MacDonald and George Williams, 'Combating Terrorism: Australia's *Criminal Code* Since September 11, 2001' (2007) 16(1) *Griffith Law Review* 27.

categories. The first is the offence of engaging in a terrorist act in s 101.1 of the *Criminal Code Act 1995* (Cth) (*Criminal Code*). This offence carries a maximum penalty of life imprisonment.

The second category of offences contains the preparatory terrorism offences in div 101. The main focus of the terrorism offences introduced into the *Criminal Code* was upon the pre-emption of terrorist acts. In *Lodhi v R*, Spigelman CJ of the Supreme Court of New South Wales noted that:

> Preparatory acts are not often made into criminal offences. The particular nature of terrorism has resulted in a special, and in many ways, unique, legislative regime. It was, in my opinion, the clear intention of Parliament to create offences where an offender has not decided precisely what he or she intends to do. A policy judgment has been made that the prevention of terrorism requires criminal responsibility to arise at an earlier stage than is usually the case for other kinds of criminal conduct, e.g. well before an agreement has been reached for a conspiracy charge.[17]

These offences criminalise particular acts – providing or receiving training, possessing a thing and collecting or making a document – connected with preparation for, the engagement of a person in or assistance in a terrorist act.[18] The maximum penalty for these offences differs depending upon whether the act is done knowingly (twenty-five or fifteen years) or merely recklessly (fifteen or ten years). Division 101 of the *Criminal Code* also contains a catch-all offence of doing any act in preparation for, or planning, a terrorist act.[19] This offence – like that of engaging in a terrorist act – carries a maximum penalty of life imprisonment.

The terrorist organisation offences in Division 102 make up the third category of offences. The purpose of these offences is to restrict the flow of human and financial resources to terrorist organisations. With that in mind, they criminalise directing the activities of, being a member of, recruiting for, providing training to or receiving training from, providing funding to or receiving funding from, providing support or resources to and associating with a member of a terrorist organisation.[20] The maximum penalty for these offences ranges from three to twenty-five years. There are two means by which an organisation may be characterised as a terrorist organisation. The first is that it satisfies the definition of a terrorist organisation in s 102.1, that is, it 'is directly or indirectly engaged in, preparing, planning, assisting in or fostering the doing of a terrorist act (whether or not a terrorist act occurs)'. This determination is made by a jury in the course of the prosecution of an individual for a terrorist organisation offence. The second is the listing of an organisation in a

[17] [2006] NSWCCA 121 [66] (Spigelman CJ).

[18] *Criminal Code Act 1995* (Cth) ss 101.2, 101.4 and 101.5.

[19] Ibid s 101.6.

[20] Ibid s 102.2–8.

regulation made by the Governor-General. This serves as conclusive proof at trial that the organisation is in fact a terrorist organisation. The listing process will be discussed in more detail later in this chapter. However, it is relevant here to note that, although glorifying terrorism is not an offence in Australia, an organisation may be listed as a terrorist organisation if it 'advocates' committing a terrorist act.

The penultimate category of offences consists of the terrorist financing regimes in Division 103 of the *Criminal Code* and in the *Charter of the United Nations Act 1945* (Cth) (*UN Charter Act*). These will be discussed in more detail later in this chapter. The categorisation of the final set of offences, being the 'urging violence' – originally 'sedition' – offences in Part 5.1 of the *Criminal Code*, as terrorism offences is controversial. Scholars have suggested that at least some of these offences would be more appropriately placed within the framework of anti-vilification legislation.[21] Section 80.2 makes it an offence punishable by seven years' imprisonment to urge the overthrow of the Australian Constitution or government by force or violence or to urge interference in parliamentary elections.[22] It is also an offence to urge violence against a group or an individual on the basis of his or her race, religion or political opinion.[23]

b. State and Territory Criminal Offences

For the most part, the role of the states and territories in the criminalisation of activities related to terrorism has been limited. This is because – shortly after September 11 – they decided to refer their power to legislate on terrorism to the Federal Parliament.[24] Such a move was necessary both to ensure that the constitutional foundations of federal anti-terrorism legislation were secure and also that there was consistency in the criminal law across the various Australian jurisdictions. There are a couple of exceptions. First, the Northern Territory was the only jurisdiction in Australia – federal, state or territory – to have a specific offence of engaging in a terrorist act prior to September 11.[25] This jurisdiction also criminalised the obtaining or supply of anything with the intention that it be used, or knowing that it is intended to be used, for or in connection with the preparation or commission of an act of terrorism. These offences still remain on the statute books in the Northern Territory in largely

[21] Australian Law Reform Commission, *Fighting Words: A Review of Sedition Laws in Australia*, Report No 104 (2006) 207–10.

[22] *Criminal Code Act 1995* (Cth) s 80.2(1).

[23] Ibid ss 80.2A–B.

[24] See, eg, *Terrorism (Commonwealth Powers) Act 2003* (Vic). For a more detailed discussion, see Andrew Lynch, 'State Referrals and Terrorism Law Reform Paralysis: Cause and Effect?' (2010) 21 *Public Law Review* 155.

[25] *Criminal Code Act* (NT) Sch 1 pt III div 1.

the same terms. Furthermore, s 310J of the *Crimes Act 1900* (NSW) contains a mirror offence to that in the *Criminal Code* of being a member of a terrorist organisation. Section 310K makes it clear that the New South Wales offence is meant to play a subsidiary role to its federal equivalent. A person may be punished for the former offence only if he has not already been convicted for the latter.

B. *Terrorism Prosecutions*

Terrorism prosecutions in Australia are conducted in largely the same way as those for traditional criminal offences.[26] Trials are held in the Supreme Court of the state or territory in which the offences were alleged to have been committed – in each case to date, New South Wales or Victoria. The decision maker is a jury made up of at least twelve members of the community. This is necessary in order to comply with the constitutional requirement of trial by jury for indictable federal offences.[27] In terms of the procedures adopted by these courts, there are only two unusual aspects. The first is the requirement that exceptional circumstances must be established before a person charged with a terrorism offence – excluding the association offence in s 102.8 – may be released on bail.[28] Another is the expansive rules relating to the giving of evidence via video-link in terrorism and related proceedings.[29]

Putting to one side the legislation enacted by the Federal Parliament for the disclosure of national security information in court proceedings (discussed later in this chapter), there is only one special rule of evidence that applies to terrorism prosecutions. This is the requirement in s 25A of the *Foreign Evidence Act 1994* (Cth) that the court must allow the prosecution to adduce foreign material as evidence in a trial for a designated offence unless it would have a substantial adverse effect on the defendant's right to a fair trial. In general terms, however, trial judges and appellate courts have been careful to ensure that all material admitted at trial complies strictly with the traditional rules of evidence. For example, in 2006, the Court of Appeal of the Supreme Court of Victoria controversially quashed the conviction of Joseph Thomas for receiving funds from a terrorist organisation.[30] Thomas had been detained in Pakistan for a significant period of time and, whilst there, was threatened and suffered significant physical and psychological abuse. Although Australian officials were not directly involved, the Court found that he

[26] An overview of the terrorism trials conducted in Australia is contained in Nicola McGarrity, '"Testing" Our Counter-Terrorism Laws: The Prosecution of Individuals for Terrorism Offences in Australia' (2010) 34(2) *Criminal Law Journal* 92.

[27] *Australian Constitution* s 80.

[28] *Crimes Act 1914* (Cth) s 15AA.

[29] *Crimes Act 1914* (Cth) pt IAE.

[30] *R v Thomas* [2006] VSCA 165. This offence is contained in *Criminal Code Act 1995* (Cth) s 102.6.

was still under the influence of this mistreatment when he made various admissions. This meant that the admissions had not been made voluntarily and could not be relied upon by the prosecution at trial.[31]

Terrorist suspects in Australia have historically been prosecuted under the ordinary criminal law. Even today – after the enactment of specific terrorism offences – it is still possible to identify some examples of this approach being adopted. For example, in 2008, John Amundsen was gaoled for six years in relation to a plot to set off explosives outside the home of his ex-girlfriend's parents. The ten charges to which he pleaded guilty included those of obtaining the explosives by fraud, possessing the explosives in his vehicle and using a telecommunications service to make a threat to kill.[32] It is clear, however, that use of the ordinary criminal law to prosecute terrorists is regarded by prosecutors as a second-best approach. This approach is adopted only when it is clear that an element of the terrorism offences is not satisfied. In addition to the aforementioned offences, Amundsen was originally charged with possessing a thing connected with preparation for a terrorist act.[33] This charge was withdrawn after it was realised that his motivation for the act was personal – namely, to win back his ex-girlfriend's love – rather than political, religious or ideological, as the definition of a terrorist act requires.[34]

Since their enactment in 2002, the specific terrorism offences have been aggressively enforced. The Australian Federal Police (AFP) testified before a parliamentary committee in October 2007 that it had been directed to 'lay as many charges under the new terrorist legislation against as many suspects as possible because we wanted to use the new legislation'.[35] Thus, as of February 2014, thirty-eight people – all men and virtually all identifying as Muslims – had been charged with terrorism offences. To date, no one has been charged with the offence of engaging in a terrorist act. The focus of law enforcement agencies and prosecutors has instead been upon the prevention of such acts by charging people with offences under either Division 101 or Division 102 of the *Criminal Code*. A particular trend – as evidenced by the three most recent trials – has been to charge people with a combination of the inchoate offence of conspiracy and that of doing an act in preparation for, or planning, a terrorist act. In total, the terrorism trials conducted in Australia have resulted in the conviction of twenty-six people – including nine guilty pleas – with one person yet to face trial.

[31] Similar reasoning underpinned the decision of the Supreme Court of New South Wales to exclude admissions that Izhar Ul-Haque had made: *R v Ul-Haque* [2007] NSWSC 1251.

[32] Commonwealth Director of Public Prosecutions, *Annual Report 2007–08* (2008) 47.

[33] *Criminal Code Act 1995* (Cth) s 101.4.

[34] Jason Gregory, '6 Years for Amundsen Bomb Plot', *The Courier-Mail*, 24 February 2008.

[35] Sally Neighbour, 'Charge Suspects to Test Terror Laws', *The Australian*, 13 November 2007.

It is worthwhile noting that terrorism charges have been withdrawn prior to trial on several occasions. Possibly the most notorious example was the case of Mohamed Haneef – an Indian doctor working in Australia – who was charged with intentionally providing resources to a terrorist organisation. This related to his gifting of a partially used subscriber identity module (SIM) card to his second cousin, Kafeel Ahmed, at the end of a visit to the United Kingdom. Ahmed was subsequently involved in – and died of injuries sustained during – the terrorist attack upon Glasgow Airport. Haneef was intercepted at Brisbane Airport on 2 July 2007 and detained for twelve days without charge under the controversial 'dead time' provisions of the *Crimes Act 1914* (Cth). However, once he was finally brought before the courts, he was released upon bail by Magistrate Payne. Her Honour was highly critical of the prosecution case, noting that there was no allegation that Haneef had any direct association with a terrorist organisation or any evidence that his SIM card was used or associated with a terrorist act (other than being in a vehicle that was used in a terrorist attack).[36] Similarly critical remarks were subsequently made by the Hon John Clarke QC during an independent inquiry into the behaviour of intelligence agencies, the police and prosecutors in relation to Haneef. He wrote that 'I have no doubt that if the proper advice had been given Dr Haneef would have been released'.[37] The Commonwealth Director of Public Prosecutions then withdrew the charges against Haneef on the basis that 'there are no reasonable prospects of proving all of the elements of the offence'.[38] Instead, the Commonwealth decided to use immigration law to facilitate his deportation from Australia. This will be discussed in more detail later in this chapter.

Suspected terrorists have generally been charged in groups – for example, thirteen people in the Benbrika trial and nine in the Elomar trial – and have often faced multiple charges. The practice of laying multiple charges has been challenged in several of the terrorism trials. For example, one of the defendants in the Benbrika trial, Fadl Sayadi, claimed that the double jeopardy principle was violated by his conviction for being a member of a terrorist organisation as well as providing resources to a terrorist organisation.[39] The Court of Appeal of the Supreme Court of Victoria, however, held that 'there was no abuse of process involved in laying multiple charges which contained different elements, and where one charge was not wholly included within the other'.[40] There has only been one successful challenge to the practice of laying multiple charges in the terrorism

[36] The Hon John Clarke QC, *Report of the Clarke Inquiry into the Case of Dr Mohamed Haneef* (2008) 146.

[37] Ibid x.

[38] Commonwealth Director of Public Prosecutions, *Media Release re Dr Haneef* (27 July 2007).

[39] *Criminal Code Act 1995* (Cth) ss 102.3 and 102.7.

[40] *Benbrika and Ors v The Queen* [2010] VSCA 281 [427] (the Court).

context. The background is that four of the men convicted in the Benbrika trial were subsequently tried for an additional charge of conspiring to do an act in preparation for, or planning, a terrorist act.[41] The trial judge, Forrest J, ordered that a permanent stay of the trial should be granted on the basis that it was oppressive. It was recognised that this 'is an extraordinary remedy to be exercised only in extreme and incurable circumstances'.[42] The matters that his Honour took into account included the avoidable nature of the second trial; the financial cost to be met by the community; the very poor circumstances in which the defendants were detained during the first trial; the considerable overlap of evidence; and the very low level of additional unpunished criminality.

C. *Punishment of Terrorism*

The legislative framework for the sentencing of convicted terrorists is – in large part – the same as that which applies to ordinary criminals. The principles that must be taken into account by the courts in setting a sentence are contained in s 16A of the *Crimes Act 1900* (Cth). The overarching one is that the sentence must be 'of a severity appropriate in all the circumstances of the offence'. The only significant difference between the legislative framework for the sentencing of convicted terrorists and ordinary criminals relates to s 19AG of the *Crimes Act 1914* (Cth). This requires that the non-parole period must be no less than three quarters of the head sentence.

In practice, however, the courts have taken quite a different approach to the sentencing of convicted terrorists.[43] They have given particular emphasis to two sentencing factors, namely, denunciation and deterrence. This is because of their assessment of the intrinsic seriousness of any involvement – even where it is only preparatory – in terrorism-related activities.[44] In *Lodhi v R*, Whealy J stated that:

> [T]he obligation of the Court is to denounce terrorism and voice its strong disapproval of activities such as those contemplated by the offender here.... In my view, the courts must speak firmly and with conviction in matters of this kind. This does not of course mean that general sentencing principles are undervalued or that matters favourable to an offender are to be overlooked. It does mean, however,

[41] *Criminal Code Act 1995* (Cth) ss 11.5 and 101.6.

[42] *R v Benbrika and Ors (Ruling No 3)* [2011] VSC 3342 [6] (Forrest J).

[43] See Anthony Pyne, 'The Mood and Temper of the Public: *R v Lodhi* and the Principles of Sentencing in the War on Terror' (2011) 23(2) *Current Issues in Criminal Justice* 163; Robert Diab, 'Sentencing for Terrorism Offences: A Comparative Review of Emerging Jurisprudence' (2011) 15 *Canadian Criminal Law Review* 267; Nicola McGarrity, '"Let the Punishment Match the Offence": Determining Sentences for Australian Terrorists' (2013) 2(1) *International Journal for Crime and Justice* 1.

[44] See, eg, *Benbrika and Ors v R* [2010] VSCA 281 [557] (the Court).

> that in offences of this kind, as I have said, the principles of denunciation and deterrence are to play a substantial role.[45]

In contrast, the prospects of rehabilitation of the defendant have played a subsidiary role at best. It is only in cases where a defendant has pleaded guilty that the court has been prepared to find that there has been 'a drawing back by the offender from the extremist views that motivated the commission of the offences'.[46] Evidence from psychologists and other experts on this issue has been given very little weight.[47]

The sentences that have been imposed upon convicted terrorists in Australia have varied widely. This is unsurprising given that the maximum penalties set out in the legislation also vary widely – from three years to life imprisonment. The longest sentences that have been imposed have been for the offence of conspiring to do an act in preparation for, or planning, a terrorist act.[48] This carries a maximum penalty of life imprisonment. The five men convicted in the Elomar trial were sentenced to between twenty-three and twenty-eight years imprisonment (with non-parole periods ranging from seventeen to twenty-one years). In determining the sentence to be imposed, particular emphasis was given by Whealy J to the seriousness of conspiracy charges. His Honour wrote that 'the level of criminality involved in the present conspiracy was far more substantial than the criminality involved in the individual acts of each offender'.[49] This is because it 'is much more difficult to shut down … [and] the overall extremist zeal of a group venture is more enduring, more fanatical, more determined, more resourceful and ultimately more likely to be successful than an individual acting alone'.[50]

In contrast, Whealy J and other trial judges have been reluctant to give much weight to the proximity of the preparatory acts to the commission of the ultimate terrorist act. The 'main focus of the assessment of objective seriousness must [instead] be the offender's conduct and the offender's intention at the time the crime was committed'.[51] This includes consideration of whether the defendant had selected a target, the method that would be used to carry out the terrorist act and whether it would be likely to result in a loss of human life. In the Elomar trial, for example, Whealy J stated that '[w]hile I cannot be satisfied beyond reasonable doubt that any of the offenders intended directly to kill or take human life, it is clear beyond argument that the fanaticism and extremist position taken by each offender countenanced the possibility of loss of life, if that were to occur'.[52]

45 (2006) 199 FLR 364 [91]-[92] (Whealy J).

46 *R v Sharrouf* [2009] NSWSC 1002 [74] (Whealy J).

47 See, eg, *R v Fattal and Ors* [2011] VSC 681 [99] (King J).

48 *Criminal Code Act 1995* (Cth) ss 11.5 and 101.6.

49 *R v Elomar and Ors* [2010] NSWSC 10 [64] (Whealy J).

50 Ibid.

51 *Lodhi v R* (2007) 179 A Crim R 470, 530 (Price J).

52 *R v Elomar and Ors* [2010] NSWSC 10 [60] (Whealy J).

IV. INVESTIGATIVE POWERS

A. *Police Powers*

In Australia, the police have broad powers to investigate ordinary – and especially serious – criminal offences. It is unsurprising that legislation was enacted after September 11 to extend these powers to the investigation of terrorism offences. For example, s 5D of the *Telecommunications (Interception and Access) Act 1979* (Cth) includes the terrorism offences within the definition of a 'serious offence'. This means that telecommunications interception warrants may be issued to assist with the investigation of terrorism offences. It is notable here that a warrant may be sought not only in relation to suspects but also any person who is 'likely to communicate' with him or her.[53] Material gathered by means of a telecommunications interception warrant has been heavily relied upon by the prosecution in many of the terrorism trials conducted in Australia.

The police also have extensive powers to engage in undercover or 'controlled' operations under Part IAB of the *Crimes Act 1914*. These powers have frequently been used in Australia to infiltrate and gain information about the activities of terrorist organisations. For example, evidence from an undercover officer that he had offered to sell chemicals to the defendants and instruct them in the use of explosives was an important part of the prosecution case in the Benbrika trial.[54] These undercover operations have been highly controversial. In one case, defence counsel made an application under s 138 of the *Evidence Act 1995* (Cth) to exclude conversations that the defendant had with an undercover police officer posing as a journalist.[55] Whilst the evidence was found to have been obtained improperly, the court nevertheless exercised its discretion in favour of admission because 'the police acted in good faith, in circumstances where they had legitimate concerns as to a pending terrorist act of considerable magnitude'.[56] A different approach was taken by one of the defence counsel in the trial of Wissam Fattal and four others. He argued that his client was not guilty of the charged offence because he had been incited by a Victorian police officer, 'Hamza', into making extremist statements about jihad and going to Holsworthy Army Barracks to conduct reconnaissance. The guilty verdict ultimately handed down by the jury indicates that it did not accept this.

The main purpose of this section is not to look at the powers of the police generally to investigate criminal offences. Rather, it is to examine the additional – or

[53] This amendment was made by the *Telecommunications (Interception) Amendment Act 2006* (Cth).

[54] *R v Benbrika and Ors* [2009] VSC 21 [34]-[37] (Bongiorno J).

[55] *R v Mallah* [2005] NSWSC 358.

[56] Ibid [138] (Wood CJ at CL).

expanded – powers that the police have been given to investigate terrorism offences specifically. There are three such powers of particular note that will be discussed in turn in this section.

First, the police have been given the power to conduct warrantless searches.[57] The *Anti-Terrorism Act (No 2) 2005* (Cth) allowed the police to conduct warrantless searches of people, their property and vehicles in certain circumstances. These were (a) where a person is in a Commonwealth place and the police officer reasonably suspects that he or she might have committed, might be committing or might be about to commit a terrorist act; or (b) where the person is in a zone that has been prescribed by the Minister because he or she believes that it would assist in preventing a terrorist act from occurring or responding to a terrorist act that has occurred. The *National Security Legislation Amendment Act 2010* (Cth) extended the powers of the police to warrantless searches of premises. An officer may enter premises without a warrant in order to prevent a thing from being used in connection with a terrorism offence and where there is a serious and imminent threat to a person's life, health or safety. Whilst on the premises, police officers have the power to seize any other 'thing' if they suspect on reasonable grounds that doing so is necessary to protect someone's health or safety or where the circumstances are 'serious or urgent'.[58]

Secondly, the circumstances under which a person may be detained without charge by the police are different for terrorism offences. Of particular note is that the maximum period of detention is double that for ordinary criminal offences – twenty-four instead of twelve hours.[59] Furthermore, in the case of a terrorism offence, certain periods of time are disregarded for the purpose of calculating whether the maximum period of detention has been reached. This includes when the detainee is resting, receiving medical attention or intoxicated, or where the police need to arrange for an identification parade. It also, most controversially, includes any period of time that is specified by a magistrate as 'reasonable' under s 23DB(9)(m). It was this provision that enabled the detention of Mohamed Haneef for twelve days without trial. In response to an independent inquiry conducted by the Hon John Clarke QC into the circumstances of Haneef's detention, the *National Security Legislation Amendment Act 2010* (Cth) imposed a seven-day limit on the amount of 'dead time' that may be disregarded during the investigation of terrorism offences.[60]

57 *Crimes Act 1914* (Cth) pt IAA, div 3A.
58 *Crimes Act 1914* (Cth) s 3UEA.
59 Compare ibid ss 23C and 23DA with ss 23DB and 23DF.
60 Ibid s 23DB(11).

Thirdly, in addition to updating security protocols for airports, aircraft, ports and ships, anti-terror legislation has also vested customs and transport security officers with a number of specific powers.[61] Customs officers now have the power to make an arrest without a warrant where a person resists or obstructs their functions or makes a threat to cause serious harm.[62] Airport security guards have the power to physically restrain a person suspected of committing an offence, and screening officers have a general power to frisk search a person in order to carry out a proper search.[63]

B. *Intelligence Agencies*

Arguably the most controversial of the anti-terrorism laws enacted by the Federal Parliament was the *Australian Security and Intelligence Organization Amendment (Terrorism) Act 2003* (Cth), which introduced a new Part III div 3 into the *Australian Security Intelligence Organisation Act 1979* (Cth).[64] This Part empowers the Australian Security Intelligence Organisation (ASIO) to apply for a warrant to question – for up to twenty-four hours – or question and detain – for up to a week – a person who is not suspected of having committed or even being likely to commit any criminal offence. The test is simply whether 'there are reasonable grounds for believing that the warrant will substantially assist the collection of intelligence that is important in relation to a terrorism offence'.[65] There is a legal obligation upon the person being questioned to comply with the warrant, that is, it is a criminal offence, carrying a lengthy term of imprisonment, to fail to attend for questioning, to refuse to answer questions or provide documents or things or to give false or misleading information. This is so even if the information might tend to incriminate the person subject to the questioning or questioning and detention warrant. Information that is obtained during questioning may not be used against the defendant in criminal proceedings (other than proceedings for an offence under Part III div 3). However, there is no *derivative* use immunity. The prospect of a warrant being issued is not merely a hypothetical one. Over the last decade, sixteen questioning warrants have

[61] See generally *Aviation Transport Security Act 2004* (Cth); *Maritime Security Transport Act 2003* (Cth); *Maritime Security Transport Amendment Act 2005* (Cth).

[62] See *Customs Act 1901* (Cth) s 210 (power triggered by offences in the *Criminal Code* ss 147.1–147.2, 149.1). This provision was introduced by *Border Security Legislation Amendment Act 2002* (Cth) sch 11.

[63] See *Aviation Transport Security Act 2004* (Cth) ss 95C–96. Section 95C was introduced by *Aviation Transport Security Amendment (Additional Screening Measures) Act 2007* (Cth) sch 1 item 5.

[64] See Lisa Burton, Nicola McGarrity and George Williams, 'The Extraordinary Questioning and Detention Powers of the Australian Security Intelligence Organisation' (2012) 36(2) *Melbourne University Law Review* 415.

[65] *Australian Security Intelligence Organisation Act 1979* (Cth) ss 34E(1)(b) and 34G(1)(b).

been issued. In contrast, no detention warrant has even been requested by ASIO, let alone actually issued.

V. PROSCRIPTION AND LISTING OF TERRORIST GROUPS AND INDIVIDUALS

The proscription of organisations deemed to pose a threat to Australian democracy can be traced back to the early years of the federation.[66] The *Unlawful Associations Act 1916* (Cth), for example, was targeted at the Industrial Workers of the World. Part IIA was then introduced into the *Crimes Act 1914* (Cth) by the *Crimes Act 1926* (Cth). This adopted a similar proscription mechanism with the aim of defeating 'the nefarious designs of the extremists in our midst.'[67] Most notably, the conservative government of Prime Minister Robert Menzies steered the *Communist Party Dissolution Act 1950* (Cth) through the Federal Parliament. This legislation declared the Communist Party to be unlawful. It also provided for the Governor-General to declare other organisations associated with the Communist Party to be unlawful. The consequence of such a declaration was that these organisations were dissolved, membership became a criminal offence and the property belonging to the organisations was forfeited to the Commonwealth. The Act was subsequently declared by the High Court of Australia to be unconstitutional.[68]

A. *Proscription Mechanisms*

On 11 September 2001, the only federal regime enabling the proscription of organisations were the 'unlawful associations' provisions of Part IIA of the *Crimes Act 1914* (Cth).[69] That situation quickly changed. In response to Resolution 1373, Australia adopted the *Charter of the United Nations (Anti-terrorism Measures) Regulations 2001* (Cth). These regulations were later superseded by changes to the *UN Charter Act* made by the *Suppression of the Financing of Terrorism Act 2002* (Cth).

[66] See Andrew Lynch, Nicola McGarrity and George Williams, 'Lessons from the History of the Proscription of Terrorist and Other Organisations by the Australian Parliament' (2009) 13 *Legal History* 25.

[67] Information and Research Services, 'Terrorism and the Law in Australia: Legislation, Commentary and Constraints' (Research Paper No 12, Australian Parliamentary Library, Parliament of Australia, 2001–2002) 12, citing Stanley Bruce PM, 'Policy Speech' (Speech delivered at Dandenong, Victoria, 5 October 1925).

[68] *Australian Communist Party v Commonwealth* (*Communist Party Case*) (1951) 83 CLR 1.

[69] Andrew Lynch, Nicola McGarrity and George Williams, 'The Proscription of Terrorist Organisations in Australia' (2009) 37(1) *Federal Law Review* 1, 4.

Under the *UN Charter Act*, there are two separate proscription mechanisms. Each of these is relatively limited in that the decision maker is bound by the terms of international instruments or decisions of the United Nations Security Council. Under s 15, the Minister for Foreign Affairs must proscribe an organisation, person, asset or class of assets if satisfied that it falls within paragraph 1(c) of Resolution 1373. Under s 18, the Governor-General (on the advice of the Attorney-General) may make regulations proscribing persons or entities if satisfied that the proscription would give effect to a decision (a) that the Security Council has made under Chapter VII of the Charter of the United Nations; and (b) that Article 25 of the Charter requires Australia to carry out; (c) that relates to terrorism and dealings with assets; and (d) under which the person or entity is identified (whether in the decision or using a mechanism established under the decision) as a person or entity to which the decision relates.

Division 102 of the *Criminal Code* contains additional powers to proscribe organisations. These were introduced by the *Security Legislation Amendment (Terrorism) Act [No 2] 2002* (Cth). As first enacted, the Attorney-General was not granted a unilateral power of proscription but was only permitted to proscribe organisations identified as terrorist organisations by the United Nations Security Council.[70] This limitation was removed by the *Criminal Code Amendment (Terrorist Organisations) Act 2004* (Cth). Under Division 102 as it currently exists, an organisation may be proscribed by regulation made by the Governor-General. The effect of such a regulation is to furnish conclusive proof in court proceedings that the organisation is in fact a terrorist organisation. The Attorney-General may advise the Governor-General to make a regulation if satisfied on reasonable grounds that the organisation either (a) 'is directly or indirectly engaged in, preparing, planning, assisting in or fostering the doing of a terrorist act' or (b) 'advocates the doing of a terrorist act(whether or not the terrorist act has occurred or will occur)'.[71] The definition of 'advocates' includes directly or indirectly urging, counselling or providing instruction on the doing of a terrorist act or even if the organisation 'directly praises the doing of a terrorist act in circumstances where there is a risk that such praise might have the effect of leading a person (regardless of his or her age or any mental impairment that the person might suffer) to engage in a terrorist act'.[72] The scope of this definition is extremely wide and problematic. It is arguable,

[70] George Williams, 'Anti-Terror Legislation in Australia and New Zealand' in Victor Ramraj et al. (eds), *Global Anti-Terrorism Law and Policy* (Cambridge University Press, 2nd ed, 2012) 541, 550.

[71] *Criminal Code Act 1995* (Cth) s 102.1(2).

[72] Ibid s 102.1(1A). The *Classification (Publications, Films and Computer Games) Amendment (Terrorist Material) Act 2007* (Cth) also introduced a new section 9A into the *Classification (Publications, Films and Computer Games) Act 1995* (Cth). This provides that a publication, film or computer game that advocates committing a terrorist act must be refused classification (that is, banned). The definition of 'advocates' is in the same terms as s. 102.1(1A).

for example, that an organisation could be proscribed as a terrorist organisation if just one member of that organisation praised liberation struggles in East Timor or against a colonial power.

The key similarity between the mechanisms in Division 102 and the *UN Charter Act* is that they are dominated by the executive branch of government. This, combined with an absence of procedural fairness and the limited avenues for independent review, has generated considerable concern amongst academics and practitioners.[73] However, there are also important points of distinction between the proscription mechanisms under Division 102 and the *UN Charter Act*. For example, the latter regime allows the proscription of not only organisations but also individuals, assets and classes of assets. These differences have resulted in the substantially different content of the proscription lists. The Division 102 list currently contains eighteen names,[74] whereas that under the *UN Charter Act* contains over one thousand.[75]

B. *Challenges to Proscriptions and Listings*

The proscription of an organisation under the *UN Charter Act* may be revoked by the Minister if he or she is 'satisfied that the listing is no longer necessary'.[76] In addition, a 'listed person or entity may apply to the Minister to have the listing revoked'.[77] There has not been any successful challenge to the proscription of an organisation under the *UN Charter Act*. Division 102 of the *Criminal Code* is an improvement in that it imposes a positive obligation on the Attorney-General to make a declaration where he or she 'ceases to be satisfied' of the criteria necessary for listing an organisation under that proscription regime.[78] The effect of such a declaration is that the regulation listing the organisation would no longer apply. In addition, an organisation or individual may apply to the Attorney-General for the organisation to be de-listed on the ground that there is 'no basis' for the Attorney-General to be satisfied that the organisation meets

73 See, eg, Joo-Cheong Tham, 'Possible Constitutional Objections to the Powers to Ban "Terrorist" Organisations' (2004) 27 *University of New South Wales Law Journal* 482; Roger Douglas, 'Proscribing Terrorist Organisations: Legislation and Practice in Five English-Speaking Democracies' (2008) 32 *Criminal Law Journal* 90; Andrew Lynch, Nicola McGarrity and George Williams, 'The Proscription of Terrorist Organisations in Australia' (2009) 37 *Federal Law Review* 1.

74 Attorney-General's Department, *What Governments Are Doing: Listing of Terrorist Organisations* (14 January 2014) Australian National Security http://www.nationalsecurity.gov.au/agd/www/nationalsecurity.nsf/AllDocs/95FB057CA3DECF30CA256FAB001F7FBD?OpenDocument.

75 See, eg, Department of Foreign Affairs and Trade, Australian Government, www.dfat.gov.au/icat/regulation8_consolidated.xls.

76 *Charter of the United Nations Act 1945* (Cth) s 16.

77 Ibid s 17.

78 *Criminal Code Act 1995* (Cth) s 102.1(4). See Andrew Lynch, Nicola McGarrity and George Williams, 'The Proscription of Terrorist Organisations in Australia' (2009) 37(1) *Federal Law Review* 1, 9–10.

the definition of a 'terrorist organisation'.[79] However, 'a fundamental flaw in Division 102 … is that it does not specify the factors or material that the Attorney-General must take into account, the process that the Attorney-General must follow in considering a de-listing application or the time-period within which the decision must be made'.[80] It is therefore unsurprising that no organisation has as yet been de-listed.

There is some potential for judicial review of a decision of the Attorney-General to make a regulation or to refuse to de-list an organisation.[81] However, such review 'does not permit an investigation of whether a proscribed organisation *in fact* meets the definition of a terrorist organisation'.[82] It is limited to an assessment of the legality and not the merits of the Attorney-General's decision, for example, whether the decision was made in bad faith or at the direction of another person or is so unreasonable that no reasonable person could have exercised the power.[83] Two of the authors of this chapter have frequently noted that such review is further impeded by judicial deference and the limited access to material that characterises cases involving national security.[84]

An additional source of review of the proscription powers in Division 102 is by the Federal Parliament. The Parliamentary Joint Committee on Intelligence and Security (PJCIS) was required to conduct a one-off review of the operation, effectiveness and implications of Division 102 in 2007.[85] Furthermore, the PJCIS has the discretion to review any regulation as soon as possible after it is made and to report its comments and recommendations to each House of Parliament before the end of the fifteen-day parliamentary disallowance period.[86] Finally, 'either House of the Commonwealth Parliament has 15 sitting days after a regulation is tabled in that House to disallow the regulation'.[87] A motion of disallowance has the effect of repealing the regulation. Problematically, however, disallowance does not have retrospective effect and thus 'all action taken by the executive in accordance with the

79 *Criminal Code Act 1995* (Cth) s 102.1(17).
80 Andrew Lynch, Nicola McGarrity and George Williams, 'The Proscription of Terrorist Organisations in Australia' (2009) 37(1) *Federal Law Review* 1, 10.
81 This is available under the *Administrative Decisions (Judicial Review) Act 1977* (Cth) ('*ADJR Act*') or s 75(v) of the *Constitution* and s 39B of the *Judiciary Act 1903* (Cth).
82 Andrew Lynch, Nicola McGarrity and George Williams, 'The Proscription of Terrorist Organisations in Australia' (2009) 37(1) *Federal Law Review* 1, 10.
83 *Administrative Decisions (Judicial Review) Act 1977* (Cth) s 5.
84 Andrew Lynch, Nicola McGarrity and George Williams, 'The Proscription of Terrorist Organisations in Australia' (2009) 37(1) *Federal Law Review* 1, 11.
85 *Criminal Code Act 1995* (Cth) s 102.1A(2). See also Parliamentary Joint Committee on Intelligence and Security, Parliament of Australia, *Inquiry into the Terrorist Organisation Listing Provisions of the* Criminal Code Act 1995 (2007).
86 *Criminal Code Act 1995* (Cth) s 102.1A(1).
87 Andrew Lynch, Nicola McGarrity and George Williams, 'The Proscription of Terrorist Organisations in Australia' (2009) 37(1) *Federal Law Review* 1, 11.

regulation (for example, a prosecution instituted against a person for membership of a terrorist organisation) prior to the disallowance resolution remains valid'.[88]

VI. REGULATION OF TERRORISM FINANCING

A. *The Regulatory Regime to Counter Terrorism Financing*

The *Anti–Money Laundering and Counter-Terrorism Financing Act 2006* (Cth) (AML/CTF Act) sets out the main aspects of the regulatory regime for money laundering and terrorist financing in Australia.[89] This is supplemented by supporting regulations and legally binding *Anti–Money Laundering and Counter-Terrorism Financing Rules Instruments* issued by the Chief Executive Officer of the Australian Transaction Reports Analysis Centre (AUSTRAC). AUSTRAC is also Australia's Financial Intelligence Unit (FIU). It does not have any law enforcement or prosecutorial powers and is therefore best described as an 'administrative' FIU.[90] The AML/CTF Act requires financial services, money services businesses, the gambling sector and bullion dealers to provide reports to AUSTRAC on suspicious financial activity, high-value cash transactions and international electronic transactions.[91] The low number of federal prosecutions for money laundering was criticised by the Financial Action Task Force (FATF) in a 2005 report.[92] However, the situation has significantly improved since; the Australian Institute of Criminology calculated that seventy-four people had between prosecuted between 2006–2007 and April 2010.[93]

B. *Criminal Offences of Terrorism Financing*

a. Legislative Framework

The complex nature of the criminal terrorist financing regime in Australia is – in large part – a consequence of the reactive manner in which it has

[88] Ibid 12.

[89] The *Financial Transactions Reports Act 1988* (Cth) provides the regulatory framework for businesses that are not covered by the AML/CTF Act.

[90] Australian Institute of Criminology, *Anti-Money Laundering and Counter-Terrorism Financing Across the Globe: A Comparative Study of Regulatory Action* (2011) 8, 10. The other models of FIU are law enforcement, judicial (prosecutorial) and hybrid.

[91] In total, in 2008–9, there were more than 19 million reports provided to AUSTRAC. See Australian Institute of Criminology, *Anti-Money Laundering and Counter-Terrorism Financing Across the Globe: A Comparative Study of Regulatory Action* (2011) 66.

[92] Financial Action Task Force, *Third Mutual Evaluation Report on Anti–Money Laundering and Combating the Financing of Terrorism* (2005) 6.

[93] Australian Institute of Criminology, *Anti–Money Laundering and Counter-Terrorism Financing Across the Globe: A Comparative Study of Regulatory Action* (2011) 67.

been developed.[94] One of the first pieces of legislation passed by the Federal Parliament in response to the September 11 terrorist attacks was the *Suppression of the Financing of Terrorism Act* (2002). This was described as implementing both the Convention for the Suppression of the Financing of Terrorism and also para 1(b) of Resolution 1373. It added a new Division 103 to the *Criminal Code*. This Division – which has been amended on several occasions – makes it an offence to provide funds, collect funds, make funds available to another person, or collect funds for or on behalf of another person, being reckless as to whether they will be used to facilitate or engage in a terrorist act.

There are two other sets of offences relating to terrorist financing. Unlike those in Division 103, which concentrate upon the purpose for which the funding may be used, these other offences criminalise the provision of funds to particular individuals or organisations. As originally enacted in response to Security Council Resolution 1373, the *Security Legislation Amendment (Terrorism) Act 2002* (Cth) introduced into the *Criminal Code* two offences relating to the receipt of funds from, or making of funds available to, a terrorist organisation (whether directly or indirectly). The *Anti-Terrorism Act (No 2) 2005* (Cth) expanded the offences to cover also the situation where a person collects funds for, or on behalf of, a terrorist organisation (whether directly or indirectly). The Explanatory Memorandum to the Anti-Terrorism Bill (No 2) 2005 (Cth) stated that this amendment was 'in response to the FATF requirement that the wilful *collection* of funds for terrorist organisations be explicitly covered by terrorist financing offences'.[95]

The final set of offences is contained in the *UN Charter Act*. These were intended to implement para 1(c) of Resolution 1373 concerning the freezing, seizure and confiscation of the assets of terrorists and terrorist organisations. Section 20 of the *UN Charter Act* makes it an offence for a person or body corporate who holds a 'freezable asset' to use or deal with the asset, allow the asset to be used or dealt with or facilitate the use or dealing with the asset, where the use or dealing is not in accordance with a s 22 notice. A 'freezable asset' is defined broadly as a listed asset, an asset owned or controlled by a proscribed person or an asset derived or generated from an asset in either of the previous two categories.[96] Section 21 makes it an offence for a person or body corporate to make an asset available to a 'proscribed person or

94 The information in this section is taken from Nicola McGarrity, 'The Criminalisation of Terrorist Financing in Australia' (2012) 38(3) *Monash University Law Review* 55.

95 Explanatory Memorandum, Anti-Terrorism Bill (No 2) 2005 (Cth) 12 (emphasis added). In its 2005 country evaluation report, the FATF identified the absence of such a provision as a significant gap in Australia's counter-terrorism financing regime and instructed Australia to remedy this: see Financial Action Task Force, 'Third Mutual Evaluation Report on Anti-Money Laundering and Combating the Financing of Terrorism: Australia' (14 October 2005) 6, 32–3.

96 *Charter of the United Nations Act 1945* (Cth) s 14.

entity' where it is not done in accordance with a s 22 notice. The maximum penalty for each of these offences is ten years' imprisonment.

Possibly the most controversial aspect of the terrorist financing offences is the fault elements attaching to them. For the vast majority of the offences, recklessness – rather than knowledge or intention – attaches to at least one of the physical elements. That is, it is only necessary to prove that the defendant was aware of a significant risk that the organisation is a terrorist organisation or that the funds would be used to facilitate or engage in a terrorist act. The primary effect of the fault element of recklessness is to place a very heavy burden upon a person to conduct rigorous investigations before providing money to any organisation (especially one that is located overseas). Even then, it is likely that uncertainty would remain as to where the boundaries of the offences lie. It may be, for example, that the recklessness standard would be satisfied where the defendant is simply aware that the organisation is located in the same geographical area as a terrorist organisation or that it is an Islamic organisation.

b. Prosecutions for Terrorist Financing

To date, no one has been charged with the offences in Division 103 of the *Criminal Code*. This is probably unsurprising given that they impose a greater burden upon the prosecution by requiring proof of the defendant's recklessness as to the *purpose* for which the funds were to be used. Instead, the prosecution has relied upon the terrorist financing offences in s 102.6 of the *Criminal Code* and ss 20 and 21 of the *UN Charter Act* in the prosecution of seven people. Four men – Joseph Thomas and three of the defendants in the Benbrika trial – were charged with a combination of the s 102.6 offences and other general terrorism offences. Three others – Aruran Vinayagamoorthy and two co-accused – were charged with a combination of the s 102.6 offences and the *UN Charter Act* offences.

Reliance by the prosecution upon the s 102.6 offences has had a relatively low success rate. Only three of the seven men – the Benbrika defendants – were convicted. They were sentenced to either four or five years imprisonment each. The low success rate is likely due to the problems the prosecution faces in proving that an organisation satisfies the definition of a terrorist organisation. It will be a rare case in which the prosecution is able to rely upon the listing of an organisation under the *Criminal Code*; as noted previously, this list contains the names of very few organisations. Reliance upon the offences in the *UN Charter Act* would seem to be much simpler. However, there is a different downside to relying upon these, namely, the sentences that are likely to be imposed. Vinayagamoorthy pleaded guilty to two counts of offences under the *UN Charter Act* – one relating to making monies, and the other to making electronic components worth $97 000, available to the Liberation Tigers of Timil Eelam (LTTE) – and the two co-accused each pleaded guilty to one count of making monies available to the LTTE.[97] At the time that they were sentenced, the maximum penalty for the offences was five years. It has since been increased to ten years. The sentencing judge, Coghlan J, commented that the offences fell in either the low or middle range of seriousness and sentenced the defendants to between one year and eighteen months' imprisonment. He further determined that it was appropriate in all the circumstances to suspend the sentences for all three men. He released the men on a recognisance release order in the sum of $1000 to be of good behaviour for four years in the case of Vinayagamoorthy and three years for the other two men.[98]

c. Forfeiture of Terrorist Property

The *Proceeds of Crime Act 2002* (Cth) provides two broad mechanisms for the confiscation of assets. One of these is civil in the sense that it does not depend upon the institution of criminal proceedings. The Commonwealth Director of Public Prosecutions may apply to the relevant state or territory court for a person-directed forfeiture, assets-directed forfeiture, pecuniary penalty or literary proceeds order on the basis that the assets that are the subject of the application are the proceeds of crime.[99] This must be proven on the balance of probabilities.[100] The other mechanism for the confiscation of assets depends upon the conviction of the person after criminal proceedings. In particular, automatic forfeiture of proceeds is available where a person has been convicted of a 'serious offence', that is, an indictable offence punishable by imprisonment for three or more years.[101] This avenue is available only where the proceeds have already been made the subject of a restraining order issued by the relevant state or territory court. In essence, a restraining order prohibits the subject of the order from dealing with certain property.[102] It must be made by a court where there are reasonable grounds to suspect that a person has committed a serious offence or where he or she has been convicted of or charged with an indictable offence or where it is proposed that the person be charged with an indictable offence.

97 *R v Vinayagamoorthy* [2010] VSC 148 (31 March 2010) [1]–[3] (Coghlan J).
98 Ibid.
99 *Proceeds of Crime Act 2002* (Cth) pts 2.2 (forfeiture orders), 2.4 (pecuniary penalty orders) and 2.5 (literary proceeds orders).
100 Ibid s 317.
101 Ibid s 92.
102 Ibid ss 17–18.

VII. IMMIGRATION MEASURES

In December 2003, a former Qantas baggage handler, Zeky Mallah, became the first person charged with offences under Australia's new anti-terrorism laws.[103] He was charged with two counts of 'doing an act in preparation for a terrorist act' under s 101.6(1) of the *Criminal Code Act 1995* (Cth) *(Criminal Code)*.[104] Prior to that, in 2002, Mallah had applied to the Department of Foreign Affairs and Trade for an Australian passport to travel to Lebanon. In interviews with ASIO, Mallah 'denied that he had any intention of participating in any violent action [in Lebanon], but then stated that if Jihad was declared, the Koran would require him to take part'.[105] Perhaps unsurprisingly, his application was refused on the basis of an adverse security assessment: ASIO found that Mallah was likely to engage in conduct that might prejudice the security of Australia or a foreign country.[106] The denial of a passport to Mallah is mirrored in recent reports that ASIO has sought to prevent Australia citizens from taking part in the conflict in Syria by ensuring that they are either refused passports or their renewal.[107] Under s 22(1) of the *Passports Act*, the Minister has a general power to cancel a person's passport. In addition, s 22(2) identifies a number of specific situations in which this power may be exercised – including where a 'competent authority' has made a request for such cancellation.[108]

The Haneef case provides an even more direct example of immigration law being used as a tool of counter-terrorism. As was noted earlier in this chapter, following the collapse of the criminal prosecution of Haneef, the federal government sought to utilise immigration law to facilitate his removal from Australia. Immediately after he was granted bail, the Minister of Immigration and Citizenship cancelled his visa under s 501(3) of the *Migration Act 1958* (Cth) *(Migration Act)*.[109] That decision

[103] For a discussion of this case, see Bernadette McSherry, 'The Introduction of Terrorism-Related Offences in Australia: Comfort or Concern' (2005) 12(2) *Psychiatry, Psychology and Law* 279, 283–6; Miriam Gani, 'How Does it End? Reflections on Completed Prosecutions under Australia's Anti-Terrorism Legislation' in Miriam Gani and Penelope Mathew, *Fresh Perspectives on the 'War on Terror'* (ANU E-Press, 2008) 269, 276, 284–7; Nicola McGarrity, '"Testing" Our Counter-Terrorism Laws: The Prosecution of Individuals for Terrorism Offences in Australia' (2010) 34(2) *Criminal Law Journal* 92, 95–6.

[104] *R v Mallah* (2005) 154 A Crim R 150 [1]-[2] (Wood CJ).

[105] Alex Conte, 'Terror Meets Tyranny? The Interface Between Counter-Terrorism and Human Rights' (2002) 9(3) *Murdoch University Electronic Journal of Law* 38 [25].

[106] *R v Mallah* [2005] NSWSC 317 [4]-[5] (Wood CJ).

[107] ABC News, 'ASIO Cancels Passports of Muslim Men "over Jihad War Fears"' (9 December 2013); http://www.abc.net.au/news/2013-12-08/asio-cancels-passports-of-muslim-men/5142884.

[108] *Passports Act* 2005 (Cth) s 22(2)(d). See Sangeetha Pillai, 'The Rights and Responsibilities of Australian Citizenship: A Legislative Analysis' (forthcoming) *Melbourne University Law Review*.

[109] The Hon John Clarke QC, *Report of the Clarke Inquiry into the Case of Dr Mohamed Haneef* (2008) 146.

was challenged in the Australian courts. The Federal Court of Australia held that the decision was not authorised by the *Migration Act*. Counsel for the Minister submitted that s 501(6)(b) of this Act allows revocation of a visa where the 'the visa holder has "an association with" the person, group or organisation that the Minister reasonably suspects has been involved in criminal conduct'.[110] The Minister cited the case of *Minister for Immigration and Multicultural Affairs v Kuen Chan* as a precedent for its claim that an 'association' could include an 'innocent association'.[111] However, the Federal Court held that '*Chan* was wrongly decided. It is not correct to consider the words "an association with a person or group" by themselves, and then consider, as a separate question, whether the person or group is reasonably suspected of involvement in criminal activity'.[112] The Full Court of the Federal Court of Australia rejected an appeal by the Minister against this decision.[113] In terms of the wider implications of this case, it is worth noting that the Federal Court accepted that if the Minister had applied the correct test, there was enough material to support cancellation of Haneef's visa. It cited the fact that the was a person of interest to the United Kingdom counter-terrorism services and had been charged with providing resources to a terrorist organisation.[114] In effect, the Federal Court actually upheld the potential to revoke a visa – with all that such a decision entails – on the basis that an individual is of interest to the authorities in another jurisdiction.

VIII. ADMINISTRATIVE AND EXECUTIVE MEASURES

One of the most significant changes to Australian law has been the introduction of control order and preventative detention order (PDO) regimes by the *Anti-Terrorism Act (No 2) 2005* (Cth).[115] Division 104 of the *Criminal Code* permits an AFP officer, with the consent of the Commonwealth Attorney-General, to apply to the court for a control order. Before granting either an interim or confirmed control order, the court must be satisfied either that making the order would substantially assist in preventing a terrorist act; or the person subject to the order has provided training to or has received training from a terrorist organisation.[116] It must also be satisfied that any obligations, prohibitions or restrictions imposed on a person under a control

[110] *Haneef v Minister for Immigration and Citizenship* (2007) 161 FCR 40 [156] (Spender J).

[111] (2001) 34 AAR 94.

[112] *Haneef v Minister for Immigration and Citizenship* (2007) 161 FCR 40, Explanatory Statement (Spender J).

[113] *Minister for Immigration and Citizenship v Haneef* (2007) 163 FCR 414.

[114] *Haneef v Minister for Immigration and Citizenship* (2007) 161 FCR 40 [261]-[264] (Spender J).

[115] George Williams, 'Anti-Terror Legislation in Australia and New Zealand' in Victor Ramraj et al. (eds), *Global Anti-Terrorism Law and Policy* (Cambridge University Press, 2nd ed, 2012) 541, 554.

[116] *Criminal Code Act 1995* (Cth) ss 104.4 and 104.14.

order are both reasonably necessary and reasonably appropriate and adapted for the purpose of protecting the public from a terrorist act.

Since 2005, only two control orders have been issued. Australia's first control order was issued against Joseph Thomas in August 2006. This was issued after Thomas's conviction for receiving money from Al Qa'ida was overturned by the Court of Appeal of the Supreme Court of Victoria. The conditions of Thomas's control order included a ban on communicating with a member of a terrorist organisation or any one of fifty specified people, including Osama bin Laden. The second control order was issued against David Hicks. After training with Lashkar-e-Taiba in Pakistan, Hicks was captured by the Northern Alliance in Pakistan in December 2001 and sold to the United States military. He was rendered to Guantanamo Bay and became one of the first people there to be charged with terrorism offences. Hicks ultimately pleaded guilty before a military commission to providing material support for terrorism. In April 2007, he was returned to Australia to serve the remaining nine months of a seven-year sentence.[117] Hicks became the second subject of an Australian control order upon his release in December 2007. The use of the control order regime in these two cases has been criticised on the ground that the government 'is willing to use these schemes in addition to the normal trial process, and even to have a second attempt at detaining a person where there has not been a conviction'.[118] The control orders against both Thomas and Hicks have since expired, and there are currently no control orders in force in Australia.

The constitutionality of the control order regime was challenged in *Thomas v Mowbray (Thomas)*.[119] The Australian Constitution specifies three arms of federal government: a legislature, executive and judiciary. That structural fact, combined with s 71 of the Australian Constitution, which establishes the independence of the federal judiciary, has resulted in a particularly strict separation of the judiciary from the other arms of government. Despite that, in *Thomas*, a majority of the High Court of Australia concluded that the power to make interim control orders did not infringe on the separation of powers.[120]

The preventative detention order regime in Division 105 of the *Criminal Code* has never been used.[121] The COAG Review noted the Australian preventative detention order regime and the United Kingdom's 'preventive warrantless arrests'[122] differ

117 Andrew Lynch, Nicola McGarrity and George Williams, Inside Australia's Anti-Terrorism Laws and Trials (NewSouth Publishing, 2015), 183.

118 Edwina MacDonald and George Williams, 'Combating Terrorism: Australia's Criminal Code Since September 11, 2001' (2007) 16 *Griffith Law Review* 27, 50.

119 (2007) 233 CLR 307.

120 For a detailed analysis of this case, see Andrew Lynch, '*Thomas v Mowbray*: Australia's "War on Terror" Reaches the High Court' (2008) 32 *Melbourne University Law Review* 1182.

121 George Williams, 'Anti-Terror Legislation in Australia and New Zealand' in Victor Ramraj et al. (eds), *Global Anti-Terrorism Law and Policy* (Cambridge University Press, 2nd ed, 2012) 541, 554.

122 *Terrorism Act 2000* (UK) s 41.

markedly from each other (although they are each executive administrative orders based on prevention and protection of the public).[123] Australia's preventative detention orders enable the AFP to detain a person on the basis that detention will either aid in preventing the commission of an act of terrorism expected to occur within the next fourteen days or preserve evidence of a terrorist act that has occurred within the last twenty-eight days. The regime imposes strict time limits upon the period of detention – an initial order (which is issued by a senior AFP officer) lasts up to twenty-four hours and a continued order (which is issued by retired judges, tribunal members or federal judges acting in their personal capacity) may last for a further period not more than forty-eight hours from the time the person was first detained. The regime was framed in this manner to avoid constitutional challenges based on the separation of powers doctrine in the Australian Constitution. However, complementary regimes in the Australian States and Territories, which are not so constrained by that doctrine, permit an application to be made to a judge for a person to be detained for up to fourteen days.[124]

The restrained use of control orders and preventative detention orders is welcome; however, their existence is nevertheless troubling. Both 'orders enable significant restrictions on individual liberty. This is more than a breach of the old "innocent until proven guilty" maxim: it ignores the notion of guilt altogether'.[125] In his first substantive report, the INSLM strongly criticised the control order regime.[126] In addition, both the INSLM and the COAG Review urged the repeal of the preventative detention order regime. The COAG Review argued that '[i]f any form of preventive detention were to be retained, it would require a complete restructuring of the legislation at Commonwealth and State/Territory level, a process which, in the view of the majority of the Committee, may further reduce its operational effectiveness'.[127] The INSLM was equally forthright, arguing that:

> [t]here is no demonstrated necessity for these extraordinary powers, particularly in light of the ability to arrest, charge and prosecute people suspected of involvement in terrorism. No concrete and practical examples of when a PDO would be necessary to protect the public from a terrorist act because police could not meet the threshold to arrest, charge and remand a person for a terrorism offence have been provided or imagined.[128]

[123] Council of Australian Governments Review of Counter-Terrorism Legislation, *Council of Australian Governments Review of Counter-Terrorism Legislation* (2013) 64.

[124] See, eg, *Terrorism (Police Powers) Act 2002* (NSW) pt 2A.

[125] Andrew Lynch and George Williams, *What Price Security? Taking Stock of Australia's Anti-Terror Laws* (2006) 42.

[126] Independent National Security Legislation Monitor, *Declassified Annual Report* (2012) ch II.

[127] Council of Australian Governments Review of Counter-Terrorism Legislation, *Report of the Council of Australian Governments Review of Counter-Terrorism Legislation* (2013) 67.

[128] Independent National Security Legislation Monitor, *Declassified Annual Report* (2012) 67.

As noted previously, successive federal governments have failed to respond to the reports of either the INSLM or the COAG Review. However, both measures are subject to sunset clauses and will require renewal in 2016.[129] It is possible that the existing criticisms will result in the measures lapsing rather than being renewed at that time. On the other hand, however, the lack of use of these regimes perversely appears to have been an impediment to their repeal to date. It has resulted in a lack of controversy and a resulting lack of public concern about the regimes.

IX. ROLE OF MILITARY AND EXTRA-TERRITORIAL COUNTER-TERRORISM ACTIVITIES

A. *Military Courts and Detention*

The role of the military in matters of domestic law enforcement has historically been very limited. Doogan writes that although Australia was established as a penal colony under military administration, 'the evolution of the … political system ensured a clear distinction between military powers and civil powers'.[130] The military courts are not used for the prosecution of terrorism either domestically or extra-territorially. Furthermore, although s 119 of the Australian Constitution gives the federal government a power to call out the military to protect the states and territories, there has been only one instance of this during the twentieth century. This was in response to the Hilton Hotel bombing in 1978.

However, the Sydney 2000 Olympics provided the 'catalyst'[131] for legislation that considerably expanded the powers of the federal government to call out the military on domestic soil.[132] A review of these powers was commissioned in the aftermath of the September 11 terrorist attacks. Then, shortly before the Melbourne 2006 Commonwealth Games, legislation was enacted that further expanded the powers of the federal government to call out the military.[133] The most significant way in which these powers differ from that under s 119 of the Australian Constitution is that the agreement of the relevant state or territory is not necessary. The Prime Minister,

[129] *Criminal Code Act 1995* (Cth) ss 104.32, 105.53 See Nicola McGarrity, Rishi Gulati and George Williams, 'Sunset Clauses in Australian Anti-Terror Laws' (2012) *Adelaide Law Review* 307.

[130] Christopher Doogan, 'Defence Powers Under the Constitution: Use of Troops in Aid of State Police Forces – Suppression of Terrorist Activities' (1981) 31 *Defence Force Journal* 31.

[131] Federal Parliament, *Parliamentary Debates*, House of Representatives, 28 June 2000, 18413 (Stephen Martin).

[132] *Defence Legislation Amendment (Aid to Civilian Authorities) Act 2000* (Cth). See Michael Head, 'The Military Call-Out Legislation – Some Legal and Constitutional Questions' (2001) 29 *Federal Law Review* 273.

[133] *Defence Legislation Amendment (Aid to Civilian Authorities) Act 2006* (Cth). See Michael Head, 'Military Call-Out Powers Expanded' (2006) 31(2) *Alternative Law Journal* 83.

the Minister of Defence and the Attorney-General may, for example, advise the Governor-General to call out the military where domestic violence is occurring or is likely to occur and the relevant state or territory is incapable of protecting federal interests.[134] The military is then entitled to engage in a wide range of activities, such as taking control of buildings, detaining people, searching premises and seizing possessions.[135] Where the three Ministers decide to declare a 'general security area', the military may also conduct personal searches, erect barriers and stop means of transport.[136] On top of this, if a 'designated area' is declared within a general security zone, the military is empowered to halt and control all movements of traffic and people, issue directions to individuals and compel people to comply with directions.[137]

B. *Extra-Territorial Terrorism Law Enforcement*

Two Australian citizens – Mamdouh Habib and David Hicks – have been detained by the United States at Guantanamo Bay. Habib was captured by United States forces in Afghanistan and then detained in Pakistan by Pakistani authorities during October 2001. He was rendered to Egypt the following month and held there for a further six months. In 2002, Habib was rendered to Guantanamo Bay. He was released without charge and repatriated to Australia in 2005. The circumstances in which Hicks was captured and detained were discussed earlier in this chapter.

Both Habib and Hicks claimed that they were abused and even tortured during their detention. Shortly after his return to Australia, Habib commenced proceedings in the Federal Court in relation to the involvement of Australian officials in his mistreatment. He alleged that they had aided, abetted, counseled or procured the commission of federal offences – including the prohibition on torture – by Pakistani, Egyptian and United States officials.[138] More than five years after the proceedings were commenced, in 2010, the federal government offered to settle the case. Habib was awarded an undisclosed financial payment in return for forgoing all future claims. The timing of the settlement suggests that it was intended to avoid the content of two witness statements presented by Habib's legal team – one from an Egyptian military officer who worked in the prison that he was held in and another from a fellow prisoner – coming to light at trial. However, a subsequent report presented by

[134] *Defence Act 1903* (Cth) s 51A.
[135] Ibid s 51I.
[136] Ibid ss 51L, 51O and 51P.
[137] Ibid s 51R.
[138] *Habib v Commonwealth of Australia* [2010] FCAFC 12 [2]-[3] (Black CJ). See Stephen Tully, '*Habib v Commonwealth*: Clarifying the State of Play for Acts of State?' (2010) 32 *Sydney Law Review* 711.

the Inspector-General of Intelligence and Security found that no Australian official had 'engaged in acts of mistreatment ... or had knowledge of any actual or intended mistreatment by others'.[139]

Hicks also brought proceedings against the federal government in the Federal Court.[140] These related to the failure of the federal government not to request his release and repatriation from Guantanamo Bay.[141] An application by the federal government for summary dismissal of the proceedings was rejected. Justice Tamberlin stated that '[i]t is clear in the case before me that the deprivation of liberty for over five years without valid charge is an even more fundamental contravention of a fundamental principle, and is such an exceptional case as to justify proceeding to hearing by this Court'.[142] However, the proceedings were ultimately rendered moot by Hicks' decision to enter a guilty plea before the United States military commission. This secured his release from Guantanamo Bay without the need for the intervention of the federal government.

X. SECRECY

A. *Secrecy Claims and Secret Evidence*

Until very recently, the primary mechanism for dealing with state secrets in the courtroom was the doctrine of public interest immunity. As codified in s 130(1) of the *Evidence Act 1995* (Cth), this doctrine provides that:

> If the public interest in admitting into evidence information or a document that relates to matters of state is outweighed by the public interest in preserving secrecy or confidentiality in relation to the information or document, the court may direct that the information or document not be adduced as evidence.[143]

The critical point about this doctrine is that, if a claim is successful, the evidence is excluded from the trial. It cannot be relied upon by the prosecution. This means that a case may be 'unable to proceed due to a lack of admissible evidence or because withholding information from a defendant may prevent them from

139 Inspector-General of Intelligence and Security, *Inquiry into the Actions of Australian Government Agencies in Relation to the Arrest and Detention Overseas of Mr Mamdouh Habib from 2001 to 2005* (2011) 6.

140 *Hicks v Ruddock* [2007] FCA 299. See Marley Zelinka, 'Hicks v Ruddock versus The United States v Hicks' (2007) 29 *Sydney Law Review* 527.

141 *Hicks v Ruddock* [2007] FCA 299, Explanatory Statement (Tamberlin J).

142 Ibid [91] (Tamberlin J).

143 Section 130(4) of the *Evidence Act 1995* (Cth) provides guidelines as to when information 'relates to matters of state'. Section 130(5) sets out the facts that the court is to take into account for the purpose of determining the balance on the public interest.

mounting a full defence and receiving a fair trial'.[144] On the other hand, if a claim is unsuccessful:

> [T]he Commonwealth may face the unpalatable decision of whether to risk disclosing sensitive information relating to national security or to protect this information by abandoning a prosecution, even where the alleged crimes could themselves have grave consequences for our national security.[145]

The *National Security Information (Criminal and Civil Proceedings) Act 2004* (Cth) *(NSIA)* was enacted to address these problems.[146] A party to court proceedings must notify the federal Attorney-General if the party knows or believes that he or she or a witness will disclose national security information.[147] In practical terms, the broad definition of 'national security' means that the parties to a terrorism trial would probably need – in order to be certain of avoiding sanctions – to provide a list of virtually all evidence that might be adduced.[148] The Attorney-General then has a power to issue a non-disclosure or witness exclusion certificate.[149] Such a certificate triggers a requirement for the court to hold a closed hearing to determine whether the information should be excluded, disclosed in full or disclosed in a particular form (such as a summary or statement of the facts).[150] There are two particularly controversial aspects of the regime. The first is the potential for the court to exclude the defendant and even his or her legal representative from the hearing.[151] Secondly, in deciding whether and in what form to admit the evidence, the judge or magistrate must give the 'greatest weight' to the interests of national security over and above the defendant's right to a fair trial.[152]

The *NSIA* has been the subject of a constitutional challenge on the ground that it permits a person charged with terrorism offences to be tried through a process incompatible with the exercise of judicial power. However, Whealy J held that the legislation was not incompatible because it did not impinge 'in any fundamental way upon the ordinary process of the establishment of guilt or innocence by judge

[144] Australian Government, Attorney-General's Department, *National Security Information (Criminal and Civil Proceedings) Act 2004: Practitioners' Guide* (2008) 6.

[145] Parliament of Australia, House of Representatives, *Hansard*, 27 May 2004, 29307 (Philip Ruddock).

[146] These problems were highlighted by the case of *R v Lappas & Dowling* [2001] ACTSC 115.

[147] *National Security Information (Criminal and Civil Proceedings) Act 2004* (Cth) ss 24(1) and 25(1).

[148] This is defined in s 8 as 'Australia's defence, security, international relations or law enforcement interests'. See Stephen Donoghue, 'Reconciling Security and the Right to a Fair Trial: The National Security Information Act in Practice' in Andrew Lynch, Edwina MacDonald and George Williams (eds), *Law and Liberty in the War on Terror* (Federation Press, 2007) 87–8.

[149] *National Security Information (Criminal and Civil Proceedings) Act 2004* (Cth) ss 26 and 28.

[150] Ibid ss 27(5) and 31(2), (4)-(5).

[151] Ibid s 29.

[152] Ibid s 31(8).

and jury'.[153] Rather, it simply sets down a procedure for determining the pre-trial disclosure of evidence.

Despite the controversy surrounding it, the *NSIA* has had a limited effect upon terrorism prosecutions in Australia. This is because s 22 of the Act provides that the parties may, at any time during the trial, agree to a different arrangement about the disclosure, protection, storage, handling or destruction of national security information. The practice in terrorism trials, in particular, has been to rely upon this provision so as to avoid the cumbersome and time-consuming procedures under the Act.[154]

B. *Secrecy in the Courtroom and Anonymous Witnesses*

Courts in Australia have wide powers to restrict disclosure of national security information at trial. These are part of the inherent jurisdiction of the courts to control proceedings before them. At one extreme, the courtroom may be completely closed to the public. Even where the court remains open, the judge may disguise the identity of a witness or informant; issue a suppression order preventing publication of the whole or a particular aspect of the court proceedings; prevent the public from hearing aspects of the evidence (for example, by giving headsets to the judge, jury, parties and lawyers or by ordering documents to be handed up to the court but not read into the public record); require confidentiality undertakings for counsel or others who deal with national security information; or allow access to the information only to counsel with a security clearance. Many of these measures have been utilised by the courts in the terrorism trials conducted in Australia to date. One of the most commonly used is to allow police and intelligence officers engaged in ongoing undercover investigations to give evidence via video-link. To protect their identities from disclosure to the defendants and other members of the public, Bongiorno J in the Benbrika trial ordered that their facial features should be pixelated.[155]

XI. CONCLUSION

Three major lessons emerge from the decade of anti-terrorism lawmaking in Australia. The first is that the Federal Parliament needed – both for strategic reasons and also in order to comply with its international obligations – to enact specific anti-terrorism laws in the aftermath of the September 11 terrorist attacks. Unfortunately, however,

[153] *R v Lodhi* [2006] NSWSC 571 [85] (Whealy J).

[154] Independent National Security Legislation Monitor, *Declassified Annual Report* (2013) 127–8, 154–5.

[155] *R v Benbrika and Ors (Ruling No 23)* [2008] VSC 137.

the laws that were actually enacted reflect major problems of process and political judgment. This is the second lesson. Australia's anti-terrorism laws were often drafted as a reaction to catastrophic terrorist attacks overseas. As a consequence, they were – for the most part – pushed through the Federal Parliament in great haste and without adequate consideration of their impact upon civil liberties. Such concerns about the process by which anti-terrorism laws were enacted are not restricted to Australia. However, the failings of the Federal Parliament were exacerbated by the situation that Australia is the only democratic country in the world without a national human rights framework. The third lesson is that reliance upon representative and responsible government provides an inadequate check upon lawmaking in the anti-terrorism context. Additional protection may be offered by either a statutory or a constitutional bill or rights at the federal level.

XII. POSTSCRIPT

In the second half of 2014, three tranches of national security legislation were introduced into Australia's federal Parliament.[156] Together, they represent the most significant package of anti-terrorism measures enacted in Australia since the 2005 London bombings. The first two measures have been passed by Parliament, with the third coming on for debate in early 2015. Key information about the changes is as follows:

National Security Legislation Amendment Act (No 1) 2014 (Cth)

- The Act allows ASIO officers operating under a single 'computer access warrant' to access data held on multiple computers and computer networks. The legislation does not define 'computer network', leading some to argue that this could mean that a warrant could grant access to all computers connected to the Internet (as the Internet is a 'network of computer networks').
- It creates a 'special intelligence operations' regime that grants ASIO officers immunity from civil and criminal liability for unlawful acts done in the course of specially approved undercover operations. Immunity will not be available for acts that cause death or serious injury, involve the commission of a sexual offence, cause serious property damage or constitute torture. Concerns about freedom of speech and of the press have been raised in respect of a provision that imposes a maximum penalty of five years' imprisonment where a person (a) discloses information, and (b) the information relates to a special intelligence operation (SIO). The person need only be 'reckless' as to

[156] These and other more recent developments are examined in Andrew Lynch, Nicola McGarrity and George Williams, *Inside Australia's Anti-Terrorism Laws and Trials* (NewSouth, 2015).

whether the information relates to an SIO (that is, the person must be aware of a 'substantial risk' that the information relates to an SIO and then decide to publish that information anyway). There is also an aggravated offence, punishable by ten years' imprisonment, where the disclosure endangers health or safety or prejudices an SIO or where the person intends such results to occur.

- The Act significantly strengthens existing offences for the disclosure of classified information by intelligence officers and creates new offences that apply to the copying or recording of classified information. It also penalises the disclosure of any information relating to a special intelligence operation, which poses a risk to journalists reporting on ASIO's activities.

Counter-Terrorism Legislation Amendment (Foreign Fighters) Act 2014 (Cth)

- Three controversial counter-terrorism powers – control orders, PDOs and ASIO's questioning and detention warrant powers – were due to expire under sunset clauses in late 2015 and mid-2016. This Act delays the expiry of these measures until September 2018 and, in the case of control orders, greatly expands their possible operation. Further expansion of the grounds on which control orders can be issued was also made subsequently by the Counter-Terrorism Legislation Amendment Bill (No. 1) 2014 (Cth). Control orders now may be issued for grounds, including engaging in hostile activity in a foreign country or supporting such activity.
- The amendment creates an offence of entering or remaining in a 'declared area'. No other physical elements of the offence are required. It is a defence to show that the person travelled to the area solely for a legitimate purpose (such as conducting official duties or visiting family members), although many other legitimate purposes for travel are not included in the list of exemptions (such as undertaking a religious pilgrimage, conducting business or commercial transactions or visiting friends).
- The Act creates an offence of 'advocating' terrorism, which applies where a person urges, counsels, encourages or promotes the doing of a terrorist act or terrorism offence. The offence is likely to target a range of legitimate speech acts, and in this respect it raises similar problems to the discredited (and now amended) sedition offences introduced by the Howard government in 2005.

Telecommunications (Interception and Access) Amendment (Data Retention) Bill 2014 (Cth)

- If passed, this amendment will establish a mandatory data retention regime requiring communications service providers to retain metadata for two years.
- The metadata to be retained are not specified in the Bill, and will remain unspecified until regulations are made. However, the Bill does provide some

guidance on the types of information that can be specified by the regulations – such as the source, destination, duration and location of a telephone call or e-mail.
- Which agencies will have access to metadata will be subject to declarations made by the Attorney-General. Such agencies will be able to access metadata without a warrant where doing so is reasonably necessary for the purpose of investigating criminal offences, missing persons or laws that impose pecuniary penalties or protect the public revenue.

In the wake of this new legislation, major anti-terrorism raids were conducted across Australia, as authorities made greater use of their anti-terrorism powers. Forty-two people, all men, have now been charged with terrorism offences in Australia. On 19 December 2014, two interim control orders were issued. Four days later, one of the men was charged with breaching his order. He allegedly used a public telephone and a mobile phone that did not belong to him in breach of a prohibition on the use of certain telecommunications devices. This is the first time that a person has been charged with the offence of breaching a condition in a control order.

PDOs were issued for the first time on 18 September 2014. This was done by the New South Wales Supreme Court in respect of three unnamed men detained after raids that day. Nothing of substance can be determined about these PDOs, as they are the subject of a nonpublication order by the Court.

24

Thematic Conclusions and Future Challenges

Kent Roach

I. INTRODUCTION

The previous chapters have provided much information on the rapid evolution of counter-terrorism laws in a number of important jurisdictions. It is important to learn lessons from the post-9/11 decade as there is every indication that new counter-terrorism laws will be enacted in the near future. Security Council Resolution 2178, much like Resolution 1373 enacted immediately after 9/11, has called for new counter-terrorism laws and actions, in this case in relation to foreign fighters who wish to join the brutal forces of the Islamic State in parts of Syria and Iraq. Like Resolution 1373, it leaves the definition of terrorism to domestic states while also encouraging states to counter violent extremism and radicalization that promotes recruitment of terrorists. It also confirms a commitment to terrorist listing for the purpose of travel bans and terrorist financing measures, despite concerns about both the fairness and efficacy of listing regimes.

With some exceptions, including the United States,[1] many countries are responding to the rise of terrorist foreign fighters and to domestic terrorists attacks in late 2014 and early 2015 in Ottawa, Sydney, Paris and Copenhagen with new legislation. Australia[2] and

[1] The lack of an American legislative response to foreign terrorist fighters is consistent with that country's executive-dominated approach to counter-terrorism and its comparative reluctance to adopt legislative measures with respect to matters such as preventive detention, deprivation of citizenship or regulation of speech associated with terrorism. See Kent Roach *The 9/11 Effect: Comparative Counter-Terrorism* (Cambridge: Cambridge University Press, 2011) at ch. 4.

[2] Counter-Terrorism Legislation Amendment (Foreign Terrorist Fighters) Act 2014, No 116, 2014; National Security Legislation Amendment Act (No 1) 2014 No. 108, 2014. The Australian government has also indicated an intent to enact more legislation in 2015, including legislation similar to that enacted in Canada to deprive some people convicted of terrorism offences of citizenship. Tony Abbott, "Australian Leader Outlines Crackdown on Terrorism" New York Times February 24, 2015. A Canadian bill follows 2014 Australian legislation in proposing increased counter-terrorism powers for civilian security intelligence agencies and proposing a new offence of advocating terrorism. Bill C-51, Anti-Terrorism Act, 2015 1st reading January 30, 2015.

France,[3] have already responded with new counter-terrorism laws designed to counter not only terrorism but extremism and terrorist activities abroad. The UK has enacted the Counter-Terrorism and Security Act, 2015, with measures to strengthen terrorism prevention and investigation measures (TPIMs) to include residence relocation; to have temporary but renewable exclusion orders for citizens involved in terrorism abroad; and to impose obligations on various sectors to counter radicalization.[4] In September 2014, China issued new instructions to police, prosecutors and courts reminding them that those involved in "religious extremism" may be guilty of offences such as participating in a terrorist group or advocating succession. China also released a broad draft terrorism law in November 2014 that included provisions on speech that propagates terrorism or extremism.[5] The challenges of crafting effective responses without sacrificing freedoms will only increase as nations respond to extremism and radicalization as well as actual acts of terrorism.

This concluding chapter will identify some common themes that emerge from the chapters examining counter-terrorism law in twenty-two different jurisdictions. It will identify areas of convergence and divergence in both laws and practices. It will explore how some terrorism measures such as targeting killing may be substituted for other measures such as military detention and trial. It will also continue the discussion of comparative law method started in the first chapter, including the important role of scholars in evaluating both the propriety and efficacy of counter-terrorism measures on the basis of the information in the public domain.

II. THE CHALLENGE OF EVALUATING THE EFFICACY OF COUNTER-TERRORISM MEASURES

Laura Donohue has expressed skepticism about whether scholars will ever know about counter-terrorism success stories given the need to maintain secrecy.[6] Bertrand Perrin and Julien Gafner make a similar point in suggesting that "it is extremely difficult to measure the preventive effect of a criminal provision,"[7] especially those dealing with terrorism. These are important and valid points. Nevertheless, it is doubtful that scholars can or should ignore the efficacy of counter-terrorism measures.

3 French National Assembly XIV E Legislature Loi no. 406 (September 2014). In the wake of January 2015 terrorist attacks in Paris, additional legislation has been promised. "France Vows Forceful Measures Against Terrorism" New York Times January 21, 2015.

4 Counter-Terrorism and Security Act, 2015 c.6

5 "China Focus: Judicial Explanation Clarifies Law on Terrorism" *Shanghai Daily* 21 September 2014; Human Rights Watch "China Draft Counterterrorism Law a Recipe for Abuse" January 20, 2015.

6 Laura Donohue *The Costs of Counter-Terrorism* (Cambridge: Cambridge University Press, 2008)

7 Chapter 7, "Switzerland" infra at 233.

Countries have made massive investments in counter-terrorism and intelligence since 9/11, but the terrorist threat has by most accounts increased with the rise of the Islamic State. Governments, citizens and courts all need to be in a better position to make judgments about what counter-terrorism measures have been effective. Such judgments are also necessary in determining whether limits on human rights can be justified. They are also important in deciding whether some counter-measures can be abandoned and whether some counter-measures may actually be counterproductive. It is especially important to ask the last question with respect to new counter-measures against extremism and speech because they pose a special danger if they are seen as an attack on Islam or a disparagement of legitimate grievances that may be felt by many Muslims.

Questions of propriety and compliance with human rights cannot always be divorced from questions of effectiveness. Modern human rights law is largely based on the central question of whether limits on rights can be justified as proportionate and necessary to achieve important social objectives such as combating terrorism. Arguably the most important judicial precedent of the post-9/11 era – the decision of the UK House of Lords and subsequently the European Court of Human Rights[8] that indeterminate detention of non-citizens suspected of involvement with terrorism could not be justified – was in no small part based on the judgment that such an approach would be ineffective because the terrorist threat to the UK was not limited to non-citizens. This conclusion was tragically confirmed by the 2005 London bombings. It is even more true in light of the radicalization of citizens in democracies who wish to join or commit acts of terrorism on behalf of the Islamic State. Some states, including France after the January 2015 Paris attacks and Denmark after the February 2015 Copenhagen attacks, are starting to recognize that exclusive reliance on hard strategies such as imprisonment may produce their own problems in terms of feeding radicalization. Western democracies that have so far taken an almost exclusively punitive approach towards terrorism must question the effectiveness of such strategies. They can perhaps learn from countries such as Singapore that, as discussed in Chapter 22, have supplemented incapacitation with rehabilitative de-radicalization strategies.[9]

Determinations about the proportionality of counter-terrorism measures that violate human rights necessarily require some examination of the efficacy of those measures. We know that the terrorism financing laws that so many countries enacted after 9/11 have considerable costs. These costs are financial costs often externalized onto financial institution, but also human rights costs implicit in problematic listing procedures, misidentification of Muslims as terrorists and the chill that these laws

8 A. v. Secretary of State [2004] UKHL 56 affd 2009 E.H.RR. 1

9 Chapter 22, "Singapore" infra at 642ff.

place on Islamic charitable efforts. Terrorism financing laws, however, might be acceptable if there was evidence that they were effective in stopping terrorism. Unfortunately, however, the available evidence, including data examined in this collection, suggests that terrorism financing laws have produced few measureable successes in countering terrorism. Such conclusions should be considered by courts, governments and society when evaluating whether these measures should be maintained.

III. THE CHALLENGE OF COUNTERING RADICALIZATION

Another pressing challenge is the need to respond to the phenomena of radicalization that is producing new recruits for both the Islamic State and al Qaeda. With the important exception of pentiti practices, originated in Italy to encourage those within terrorist groups to assist the state in the apprehension of other terrorists, the emphasis in most democracies has been on punishment to deter, denounce and incapacitate terrorists. An important challenge for the future will be determining how effective such strategies have been and whether alternative means to rehabilitate and incapacitate potential terrorists are available. Nationals from as many as eighty countries are participating in the brutal activities of the Islamic State in parts of Syria and Iraq, and there are growing concerns that they may return to their countries of citizenship and present a danger. It is of course possible to criminalize their activities, especially given the willingness to give counter-terrorism laws extra-territorial application. Nevertheless, the effectiveness of strategies based on deterrence and punishment remains partial. There may be a need in the future to stress softer approaches that attempt to rehabilitate extremists and counter extremist propaganda.

One of the advantages of comparative law is that it allows for the expansion of our legal and policy imaginations. Comparative law may be particularly valuable when it examines jurisdictions that are quite different from those which are usually examined.[10] The consensus among Western democracies about the need to prosecute and punish terrorism is so deep that it may be necessary to examine jurisdictions outside of the mainstream to explore alternatives. The global South, including more developed and prosperous parts of that area, is often neglected in comparative law scholarship. The chapters in this collection about Brazil and Colombia demonstrate some significant divergences from the approach taken in many Western democracies. Brazil stands almost alone among developed democracies in not yet adopting

[10] For a timely critique of the usual "World Series" approach to comparative law that focuses only on a few Western democracies, see Ran Hirshl *Comparative Matters: The Renaissance of Comparative Constitutional Law* (Oxford: Oxford University Press, 2014) ch. 5.

terrorism-specific laws.[11] That fact alone should make scholars re-think the necessity of criminalizing terrorism as terrorism.

Colombia has many strong anti-terrorism laws, but it has engaged with terrorism both militarily and through peace talks with FARC in which questions of amnesties are very much alive.[12] Questions of terrorism look different when viewed through the lens of war, peace and transitional justice as opposed to the more individualized and less complex lens of the criminal law. This does not mean that we should attempt to negotiate with the Islamic State, Al-Shabaab or al Qaeda, but it should open our imaginations to alternative approaches to countering terrorism other than simple reliance on the criminal law and the threat of punishment.

Asia is often underrepresented in comparative law scholarship, and there is much that can be learned from that region.[13] Although the government of China punishes terrorism in the Xinxiang region harshly, including with the death penalty, and could impose martial law to quell separatism, it also has recently engaged in some attempts to increase understanding between the largely Muslim population of that region and the non-Muslim majority in China.[14] At the same time, its criminalization and harsh punishment of "separatism" and its refusal to accept religious freedoms should also make us cautious about how the new mandate to counter "extremism" promoted by Security Council Resolution 2178 will be implemented in China. This is especially true because of China's focus on "extremism," and not necessarily the "violent extremism" that is identified in Resolution 2178. The global North and the global South each have much to learn from the other with respect to counter-terrorism strategies. Indeed, such learning should focus on past failures in counter-terrorism as opposed to the search for acontextual "best practices."

Singapore has extensive and sophisticated experience in combining hard law against terrorism with softer and more social efforts to counter extremism and terrorism. As Eugene Tan notes in Chapter 22, the government of Singapore placed pressures on its significant Muslim minority (14% of that city-state's population) to rehabilitate suspected terrorists and to participate in "an ideological battle between those who distort Islam for their violent political ends, and those who uphold the tenets of Islam as a religion of peace."[15] Singapore's largely successful experience with the rehabilitation of terrorists and their families deserves greater attention.[16]

[11] Chapter 5, "Brazil" at 148ff.

[12] Chapter 4, "Colombia" at 120ff.

[13] For an exception which examines a number of Asian jurisdictions including India, Indonesia and the Philippines not examined in this collection, see Victor Ramraj et al. eds. *Global Anti-Terrorism Law an Policy* 2nd ed (Cambridge: Cambridge University Press, 2012).

[14] Chapter 21, "China" infra at 608. See also Fu Hualing "Responses to Terrorism in China" in Ramraj et al. *Global Anti-Terrorism Law and Policy* 2nd ed.

[15] Chapter 22, "Singapore" infra at 612.

[16] Ibid.

To be sure, the facts that Singapore allows indefinite detention without trial and highly regulates expression and religion cannot be ignored, but its linkage between discouraging extremism and terrorism while also promoting greater understanding, respect and trust in its Muslim minority should not be disparaged by Western democracies increasingly concerned about Muslim radicalization. The difficulties of translating these concepts to Western democracies should not be underestimated. They are underlined by controversies in the UK over whether universities, along with schools, prisons, health authorities and local councils, should be included as authorities with duties to prevent people from being drawn into terrorism.[17]

IV. THE CHALLENGE OF ACCOUNTABILITY

The immediate focus after 9/11 was on breaking down walls within and between governments to facilitate greater co-operation and sharing of intelligence about suspected terrorists. Most countries today take a "whole of government" approach to the prevention of terrorism. This reflects the use of multiple laws to counter terrorism, including customs, financial regulation, telecommunications regulation, immigration, administrative, military and criminal law. There is a need for central co-ordination of the multiple departments of government with counter-terrorism responsibilities. Countries also need to ensure that they respect their growing international and regional obligations with respect to counter-terrorism. Foreign affairs and central government departments often must report to bodies such as the UN's Security Council and the Financial Action Task Force (FATF) regarding their country's counter-terrorism efforts. Increased international co-operation in counter-terrorism often invites central co-ordination of counter-terrorism efforts.

Although Brazil has not enacted a terrorism law, it has an integrated "whole of government" approach to security that includes intelligence agencies and the ministries of justice, defence, foreign affairs, finance, labour, health, social security, science, environment, civil defence, agriculture, transport, aviation, communication and mines.[18] Such an approach has the potential to avoid an exclusive and perhaps disproportionate focus on terrorism as a threat to human security. It has the potential to distribute resources more equitably over the range of security threats, including epidemics and natural and man-made disasters faced by the society. In 2004, on the heels of an epidemic, Canada adopted an all-risks approach to national security that included but was not limited to terrorism.[19] It has more recently focused

[17] They were included but with added references to their duties with respect to freedom of speech and academic freedom. See *Counter-Terrorism and Security Act, 2015* c. 6 part 5.

[18] Chapter 5, "Brazil" infra at 157ff.

[19] For a defence of such an approach, see Kent Roach *September 11: Consequences for Canada* (Montreal: McGill Queens, 2003) ch. 7.

on a British-style program that focuses on preventing and pursuing terrorism and preparing and protecting society against attack.[20] An important issue that should not be ignored is whether societies are overinvesting in counter-terrorism because of the visibility and horror of terrorism and underinvesting in less visible threats such as climate change.[21]

A 2008 law created an Anti-Terrorism Coordination unit in Portugal that brings together a "whole of government" approach to terrorism that includes policing, intelligence, military and immigration agencies.[22] Slovenia also established a whole of government interdepartmental working group on terrorism in 2003 that includes representatives of defence, money laundering, customs, intelligence and police officials with an overall Counter-Terrorism Co-Coordinator.[23] In 2009, the Czech Republic established a National Contact Point for Terrorism to co-ordinate counter-terrorism activities between the police and intelligence agencies and to interact with Interpol, Europol and Eurojust.[24] A 2013 law in Colombia provides for co-ordination of counter-terrorism activities, including those involving the military, police and intelligence.[25] The chapters in this collection demonstrate a general trend towards whole of government security co-ordination.

Poland has an anti-terrorist centre that co-ordinates intelligence sharing and other counter-terrorism activities, and its Border Guard is increasingly working with police and intelligence agencies on counter-terrorism. Accountability within Poland seems weak, with a legislative committee concluding after a secret inquiry that the CIA did not operate detention centres in Poland,[26] something later contradicted by inquiries by the European Parliament and decisions of the European Court of Human Rights.[27] Both the 9/11 Commission[28] and Canada's Inquiry into the Air India bombing[29] underlined the dangers of a lack of co-ordination in counter-terrorism. Both commissions found that there was intelligence that may have prevented both

20 UK Contest Strategy Cm 8123 July, 2011; Canada *Building Resilience Against Terrorism: Canada's Counter-Terrorism Strategy* 2nd ed (2013).

21 Cass Sunstein "On the Divergent American Reactions to Terrorism and Climate Change" (2007) 107 *Columbia Law Review* 503.

22 Chapter 11, "Portugal" infra at 327.

23 Chapter 14, "Slovenia" infra at 411.

24 Chapter 16, "The Czech Republic" infra at 469.

25 Chapter 4, "Colombia" infra at 125ff.

26 Chapter 15, "Poland" infra at 446.

27 Al Nashiri v. Poland Application no. 28761/11 Judgment of the Former Fourth Section 24 July, 2014; Husayn Abu Zabaydah v. Poland Application no. 7511/13 Judgment of the Former Fourth Section 24 July, 2014.

28 National Commission on Terrorist Attacks Against the United States *The 9/11 Report* (New York: Norton, 2004) ch.13

29 Commission of Inquiry into the Bombing of Air India Flight 182 *A Canadian Tragedy* (Ottawa: Supply and Services, 2010) Vol 1 ch. 7

acts of terrorism but that the intelligence was not shared with front-line officials in a position to take preventive action. These findings go a long way to justifying "whole of government" approaches to terrorism that increase intelligence sharing. At the same time, however, increased co-ordination can be dangerous if it is not accompanied by increased and coordinated accountability measures. In early 2015, the Canadian government introduced a bill that would allow seventeen federal departments and agencies to receive broadly defined security information and then share it with others, but without matching these increased powers with increased whole of government review and accountability for information sharing.[30] Governments have taken whole of government approaches to security in the twenty-first century, but have often retained outdated and stove-piped twentieth century approaches to accountability.

Although increased co-ordination of counter-terrorism within and among governments has the potential to help prevent acts of terrorism, it challenges traditional accountability mechanisms which in many countries are tied to specific ministries or agencies of government and are in any event limited to the domestic arena. Sudha Setty, in Chapter 2, notes that concerns have been raised that intelligence fusion centres with municipal, state and federal employees in the United States have invaded privacy and other civil liberties while at the same time "wasting taxpayer funds."[31] Her comments underline how a lack of accountability can result in counter-terrorism activities that both abuse human rights and are inefficient and potentially counterproductive in terms of preventing terrorism. Professor Setty also places the revelations about massive surveillance by the National Security Agency in the light of concerns about the adequacy of congressional committees and of the Foreign Intelligence Surveillance Court as accountability mechanisms.

In Chapter 3, Robert Diab reveals how Canada created a new Department of Public Safety after 9/11 in order better to integrate counter-terrorism activities, including those involving customs and immigration, and to work better with the similarly integrated U.S. Department of Homeland Security. The Canadian

[30] Bill C-51, Anti-Terrorism Act, 2015 part 1 Security of Canada Information Sharing Act. 1st reading January 30, 2015. The Canadian government had previously appointed a public inquiry with extraordinary jurisdiction to examine the conduct of all Canadian officials involved in Maher Arar's rendition and torture in Syria. The inquiry examined the conduct of Canadian intelligence, police, customs and consular access officials. The same inquiry recommended better integrated and enhanced review powers. See Commission of Inquiry into the Activities of Canadian Officials in Relation to Maher Arar A *New Review Mechanism for the RCMP's National Security Activities* (Ottawa: Public Works, 2006). For a critique of the proposed Canadian information sharing legislation on the basis that it defines security too broadly and does not provide for enhanced whole of government review, see Kent Roach and Craig Forcese "Backgrounder 3 Sharing Information and the Lost Lessons of the Maher Arar Experience" February 16, 2015, available at www.antiterrorlaw.ca along with other analysis of Canada's proposed Anti-Terrorism Act, 2015.

[31] Chapter 2, "The United States" infra at 57.

government subsequently appointed two inquiries to examine Canadian complicity in the torture of four Canadians held in Syria on suspicion of terrorism. These inquiries, headed by judges, were appointed at the discretion of the Canadian government and were given special jurisdiction to examine the activities of all Canadian officials involved in the cases. Such ad hoc inquiries appointed at the discretion of governments cannot make up for the fact that police and intelligence agencies are subject to different review mechanisms in Canada and that the reviewers cannot share secret information with each other. Moreover, customs, border and foreign affairs officials and many other security officials in Canada are not subject to dedicated independent review at all.[32] The UK appointed a similar ad hoc inquiry to examine whether intelligence, military and foreign affairs officials were complicit in torture at Guantanamo and in Libya, but that inquiry was abandoned in favour of less transparent police investigations.[33]

A few ad hoc inquiries and legislative committees have a "whole of government" mandate, but they remain the exception to the rule. Even where there is extraordinary "whole of government" accountability, there is a lack of accountability for transnational counter-terrorism. Canada's inquiry into the Maher Arar case asked the governments of the United States and Syria to explain their actions, but both governments exercised their sovereign right to refuse to co-operate with the Canadian inquiry. There are also accountability gaps at the supra-national level. The European Court of Justice (ECJ) has been able to impose some accountability for the fairness of the European Union (EU) process of listing terrorists,[34] but there is no similar judicial forum at the UN level for individuals who seek remedies for terrorist listing and other counter-terrorism activities. A couple suspected of terrorist financing in Belgium was only delisted by the UN 1267 committee in July 2009 despite 2005 findings by Belgian courts and 2008 findings by a UN Human Rights Committee that they should be delisted.[35] The Security Council and its committees are attempting to be more rights-friendly and have created an ombudsperson who has enjoyed some success with respect to delisting persons who had been listed on the basis of secret intelligence as associated with al Qaeda. Nevertheless, much work remains to be done in ensuring accountability for transnational security activities.

[32] Chapter 3, "Canada" infra at 107ff.

[33] Kent Roach "Public Inquiries as an Attempt to Fill Accountability Gaps Left by Judicial and Legislative Review" in Fergal Davies and Fiona de Londras eds. *Critical Debates on Counter-Terrorist Judicial Review* (Cambridge: Cambridge University Press, 2014).

[34] Kadi 2008 C 402 /05 P; Kadi II (2013) Joined Cases C-584/10 P, C-593/10 P and C-595/10 P. But on the limits of such review, see Cian Murphy "Counter-Terrorism Law and Judicial Review: The Challenge for the Court of Justice of the European Union" in Davies and de Londras eds. *Critical Debates on Counter-Terrorist Judicial Review*.

[35] Chapter 8, "Belgium" infra at 254.

Fundamental accountability gaps mean that much "whole of government" and transnational counter-terrorism will escape independent review. This combined with the secrecy of much counter-terrorism activity creates a danger that illegal abuses of human rights may not be detected. Leaks by Edward Snowden and others have revealed much, but they are hardly a reliable or legal method of achieving accountability. The inability of accountability mechanisms to keep pace with better coordinated counter-terrorism threatens human rights, but it also increases the danger that inefficient counter-terrorism activities will be tolerated.

V. ARE BROAD DEFINITIONS OF TERRORISM FIT FOR THEIR PURPOSE?

As examined in Chapter 1, one important trend in counter-terrorism law is towards broad definitions of terrorism that go beyond threats to life and health and include various forms of property damage and disruptions of essential services. These broad definitions of terrorism reflect the vulnerabilities of modern interconnected societies, but they also present threats to dissent and human rights.

As examined in Chapter 1, a few definitions, including the definition of terrorism in the Terrorism Act, 2000, Egypt's 1992 definition and the European Council's 2002 Framework Decision, have been influential, though states have placed their own stamp on these definitions, sometimes restraining them and sometimes broadening them. This raises interesting issues with respect to the harmonization of law and the appropriate balance between international co-operation and domestic democracy and sovereignty. Many but not all European states have transposed broad EU definitions into their domestic laws, but concerns about overbreadth and vagueness remain.[36] Some but not all nations qualify broad definitions of terrorism with exemptions for protests and strikes, and even fewer address the difficult question of freedom fighters and state terrorism.

It will be interesting to see if the few states that have not defined terrorism, as represented by Brazil and China in this collection, will be able to resist global trends towards broad definitions of terrorism. As discussed in Chapters 1 and 21, a very broad definition of terrorism in China's November 2014 draft terrorism law can extend to attempts to subvert or influence the state and to split the country through intimidation. Moreover, the draft law often equates terrorism with "extremism." China's proposed definition has most in common with Egypt's broad definition, but it also draws on concepts such as "extremism" and "speech" found in Security Council Resolution 2178. Brazil has so far resisted enacting an anti-terrorism law in large part because of scepticism about adequately defining the term, but Professor Rodrigo de Souza Costa warns that this may soon change.[37]

[36] See, for example, Chapter 12, "Greece" at 348 and Chapter 17, "Romania" at 498.

[37] Chapter 5, "Brazil" infra at 164.

The definition of terrorism is a tricky and long-standing issue but it cannot be ignored. The reach of broad definitions of terrorism is often enhanced because they trigger a broad array of criminal offences and investigative powers and they often apply to offences committed outside of the enacting jurisdiction. There is a possibility that the focus on violent extremism and radicalization in Security Council Resolution 2178 may lead to even broader definitions of terrorism in the future. This begs the question of whether our broad definitions of terrorism do more harm than good.

The Independent Reviewer of Terrorism Legislation in the UK, David Anderson Q.C., has called for reforms to that country's influential definition of terrorism. He has noted that Parliament has expanded the already-broad definition in the Terrorism Act, 2000 by targeting people who are "involved' in "terrorist activity" or "terrorism-related activity."[38] The UK Supreme Court has called on Parliament to provide some exceptions for armed conflict,[39] and another recent decision has confirmed that the politically motivated Snowden leaks could constitute terrorism if they endanger life.[40] Mr. Anderson has provocatively argued that a newspaper publishing politically or religiously motivated advocacy against vaccinations could be proscribed and have its assets frozen as a terrorist organization. Moreover, all associated with the newspaper could be prosecuted under broad offences relating to advocating terrorism, preparing for terrorism and possessing items that may be useful for terrorism.[41] Polish law would reach a similar result by including the leakage of secrets as one of the possible crimes that could, if committed with certain aims, constitute a terrorist crime.[42]

To be sure, the Independent Reviewer did not maintain that the UK's broad definition of terrorism was likely to be abused in a manner that threatened dissent in that society, but as illustrated in the first chapter of this volume, the broad UK definition has been influential in many other countries who do not share the UK's democratic and rule of law traditions. Even in the UK, questions can be raised whether overbroad definitions of terrorism dilute the denunciatory force of the term among some people. This is not simply an academic debate given the willingness of significant numbers of people in established democracies to risk the terrorism label by joining extremist groups at home and abroad. A more restrained and focused definition of terrorism that focuses on the murder and maiming of

[38] David Anderson QC The Terrorism Acts in 2013 July 2014 at 10.56 citing Terrorist Asset-Freezing &c. Act 2010 s.2 and Terrorism Prevention and Investigation Measure Act 2011 ss.3 and 4.

[39] R. v. Gul [2013] UKSC 64.

[40] David Miranda v SSHD and MPC [2014] EWHC 255 (Admin).

[41] David Anderson QC The Terrorism Acts in 2013 July, 2014 at 4.20ff.

[42] Chapter 15, "Poland" infra at 433ff.

innocent people might augment the stigma of the term and perhaps even assist with counter-radicalization campaigns that attempt to deglorify terrorism.

Overbroad terrorism laws that have a pedigree in established democracies can threaten human rights when they migrate to other jurisdictions. As examined in the first chapter, Pakistan, Malaysia and Singapore were quick to adopt parts of the broad definition of terrorism in the UK's Terrorism Act, 2000 into their own laws. The chapter on Israel also reveals how that country is debating replacing some of its older terrorism laws with a comprehensive law that, like its 2004 terrorism financing law, draws on the UK's Terrorism Act, 2000. Comparative lawyers have an important role to play in examining the migration of terrorism laws and in revealing how similar laws can have different effects when administered in a different legal, political and social context. In other words, comparative law scholars must be as interested in the law in action and in context as in the books.

VI. CRIMINAL LAWS AND PROSECUTIONS

The criminal law remains the main form of law used to respond to terrorism, despite increased use of administrative, immigration and military detention. Building on the trend towards broad definitions of terrorism, there is a global trend to multiple and overlapping criminal offences. There is also a trend, one that may intensify given the focus on violent extremism and radicalization in Security Council Resolution 2178, to create criminal offences for speech that advocates or condones terrorism. The growing range of terrorism offences allows the state to intervene well before any completed act of terrorism and to punish various forms of preparation for terrorism and participation in terrorist groups as crimes as well as speech associated with terrorism. Such broad laws raise issues of fair labelling and proportionate punishment. It has also created very complex terrorism laws that may be difficult for police, prosecutors and judges including lay juries to apply.

There are more significant differences in the practice of actual terrorism prosecutions than in broad and overlapping terrorism offences that are now found in most jurisdictions. Some jurisdictions frequently rely on the prosecution of ordinary non-terrorism offences while others place greater reliance on the use of terrorism charges. Some jurisdictions, including China, the UK and the United States, bring significant numbers of terrorism prosecutions, but most jurisdictions represented in this collection report low numbers of prosecutions.

A. *The Ordinary Criminal Law*

Keith Syrett reports that the majority of terrorism prosecutions in the UK involve ordinary criminal offences relating to matters such as explosives and murder as opposed to many newer terrorism offences.[43] The utility of the ordinary criminal law is sometimes ignored because not enough attention is paid to the expansive nature of inchoate or anticipatory liability based on conspiracy, attempts or incitement to commit crimes, especially in common law countries. The denunciatory and deterrent objectives of the criminal law can be fulfilled by the ordinary criminal law. For example, the ordinary criminal law offence of conspiracy to commit murder was applied to condemn those who attempted a second London bombing on 21 July 2005 and those who were involved in the 2006 Liquid Bomb plot to bring down as many as ten Transatlantic planes.[44] It is a mistake to conclude that the ordinary criminal law can only be used after an act of terrorist violence.

The use of the ordinary criminal law avoids some of the problems associated with uncertainty and even lack of legitimacy of broad definitions of terrorism. Some countries such as Brazil and Greece continue to rely on the ordinary criminal law as the only response to terrorism, though Greece provides for increased punishment if the commission of pre-existing offences satisfies criteria of terrorism as defined in the 2002 EU Framework Decision. Switzerland and Japan have enacted new terrorism financing offences in response to supra-national pressures, but still rely on the ordinary criminal law with respect to all other forms of terrorism.[45] Although intentional financing of terrorism could generally result in accomplice liability under the ordinary criminal law, most jurisdictions have enacted terrorism financing offences.

In some cases, the ordinary criminal law will not be available to deal with apprehended acts of terrorism. Indonesia, for example, has a Penal Code influenced by Dutch criminal law that does not have general offences of conspiracy. Moreover, it defines attempts narrowly to require that an act be under way and interrupted by unexpected circumstances. Given the narrow ambit of inchoate offences under the ordinary Indonesian criminal law, it is understandable why specific crimes related to preparation for terrorism were created in Indonesia in 2002, albeit only after the 2002 Bali bombings.[46]

B. *Treason and Sedition*

Although the ordinary criminal law continues to be used against terrorists in some jurisdictions, treason and sedition offences have rarely been used.[47] There has been

43 Chapter 6, "The United Kingdom" infra at 173.

44 R. v. Ibrahim [2008] EWCA 880; R. v. Abdullah Ahmed Ali, *The Times* 9 September 2008 (Woolwich Crown Ct); see Clive Walker *Terrorism and the Law* (Oxford University Press, 2011) at 5.167.

45 Chapter 7, "Switzerland" at 204–205; Chapter 20, "Japan" at 570.

46 Kent Roach "Militant Democracy and Terrorism: Some Eastern and Western Comparisons" in Andras Sajo ed. *Militant Democracy* (Amsterdam: Eleven Publishing, 2004)

47 Walker *Terrorism and the Law* supra at 5.169–5.178. In Italy, pre-9/11 legislation that is still in force punishes terrorism and "subversion." Chapter 9, "Italy" infra at 277.

an increase in sedition prosecutions in Malaysia since its 2012 repeal of its Internal Security Act. Australia expanded its offence of treason in 2002 to include acts to assist not only other countries but "organisations" engaged in armed hostilities with Australian Defence Forces. In 2005, Australia expanded its sedition offence to speech that urged people to commit such actions. These offences could apply to those who supported terrorist groups and others fighting against Australian Forces in Afghanistan and Iraq. They suggest that Australia is perhaps more comfortable than other democracies with a legal war against terrorism that has echoes of old-style security based on notions of betrayal of the state.[48] In 2010, Australia changed the archaic label of the sedition offence to urging violence and expanded it to include situations where a person urges violence against another person on the basis of group membership. This demonstrates a merging of anti-hate and anti-terrorism rationales for speech regulation.

Other democracies have not used or expanded treason and sedition to cover support of terrorist groups.[49] This might, however, change, and more countries may follow the Australian example given the current focus on the Islamic State, which has more of a territorial presence than al Qaeda. There may, however, be continued reluctance to use old and vague offences of treason and sedition against terrorists. For example, Greece has exempted treason from its list of pre-existing offences that can qualify as terrorism because of concerns that treason might be classified as a political offence that would not be subject to extradition.[50]

C. *Inchoate Liability and Statutory Inchoate Offences*

Modern terrorism law involves the creation of new statutory offences that overlap with and merge into inchoate and accomplice liability under the ordinary criminal law. The Supreme Court of Canada has referred to a new crime of participating in a terrorist group as a "statutory inchoate offence."[51] Australian courts have similarly recognized that the many preparatory terrorism offences contained in their Commonwealth Code constitute a "unique, legislative regime" because it was "the clear intention of Parliament to create offences where an offender has not decided

[48] Kent Roach *The 9/11 Effect: Comparative Counter-Terrorism* (Cambridge: Cambridge University Press, 2011) at 326–7.

[49] Kent Roach "Old and New Visions of Security: Article 23 Compared to Post-September 11 Security Laws" in Fu Hualing, Carole Petersen and Simon Young eds. *National Security and Fundamental Freedoms: Hong Kong's Article 23 Under Scrutiny* (Hong Kong: Hong Kong University, 2005) at 122ff discussing a failed attempt to resurrect offences related to treason, sedition and subversion in an aborted security bill introduced in Hong Kong in 2003. See also George Fletcher *Romantics at War: Glory and Guilt in the Age of Terrorism* (Princeton: Princeton University Press, 2002) ch. 6.

[50] Chapter 12, "Greece" infra at 348.

[51] R. v. Khawaja [2012] SCC 69 at paras 60–1.

precisely what he or she intends to do."[52] In these contexts, courts accepted the intent of the legislature when enacting new terrorism crimes to go beyond what would traditionally qualify as criminal conduct under the general principles of inchoate and accomplice liability of the ordinary criminal law. This allows the state to intervene earlier in terrorist plots, but it can also challenge principles of fair labeling and proportionate punishment.

Vasilka Sancin and Maša Kovič Dine suggest that the enactment of separate offences to comply with Article 4 of the 2002 EU Framework Decision requiring member states to ensure that inciting, attempting and aiding and abetting terrorism have resulted in a sui generis approach to liability for terrorism in Slovenian criminal law.[53] José Francisco de Faria Costa argues that Portugal's enactment of a 2003 law against terrorism separate from the Penal Code achieved a "decodification" that allows for "more autonomous regulation of terrorism without jeopardizing the systematization of the Penal Code."[54] The separate Portuguese terrorism law allows the act of preparation for terrorism to be punished even though the Portuguese Penal Code, like the Dutch-derived Indonesia Penal Code discussed previously, does not generally punish acts of preparation.

Comparative lawyers should be attentive to how domestic systems receive terrorist crimes that may not easily fit into their own systems. The Portuguese approach of "decodification" minimizes the disruptive influence of new statutory terrorism crimes. The Slovenian approach of accommodating new terrorism offences in the Penal Code results in a blurring and overlap of statutory offences and offences under general principles of inchoate and participatory liability. It will also be important to study how legislators, administrators and courts receive new types of terrorism crimes. There may be a reluctance to use novel and alien crimes and a countervailing use of the ordinary criminal law. In Portugal, for example, only one prosecution under the new terrorism law has been reported, and it has still not yet been resolved.

Acceptance of new forms of liability for terrorism may place legislatures under pressure to use similarly broad offences to deal with other crimes, such as organized crime. In Canada, some new terrorism offences enacted in 2001 were patterned after offences for organized crime enacted in 1997. Innovations made in one area may spread to attempts to control other serious crimes.

There is a danger that overlapping and multiple terrorism crimes may collapse under their own weight. The administration of such a complex and dynamic regime will challenge police, prosecutors and judges.

[52] Lodhi v. R. [2006] NSWCA 122 [66].
[53] Chapter 14, "Slovenia" infra at 406.
[54] Chapter 11, "Portugal" infra at 330.

D. *Multiple and Overlapping Terrorism Crimes*

Most jurisdictions examined in this collection have a broad range of overlapping terrorist crimes. Article 2 of the 2002 EU Framework Decision[55] required each member state to have offences related to directing a terrorist group and participating in the activities of a terrorist group, including supplying material resources, funding or information with knowledge that such participation will contribute to the criminal activities of the terrorist group.

The 2002 EU Framework Decision implicitly rejected the approach taken in s.11 of the UK's Terrorism Act, 2000 of making it a criminal offence to belong to or profess membership in a terrorist group. Chapter 13 on Croatia notes, however, that the new participation in a terrorist group offence can be broader than a membership offence because under the former offence, "it is not necessary that the perpetrator becomes a member of a terrorist organization."[56] Robert Diab reaches similar conclusions. He finds that Canada's participation in a terrorist group offence is broader than a membership offence. He also notes that the Supreme Court of Canada has found the participation offence not to be vague, overbroad, arbitrary, disproportionate or otherwise unconstitutional because it goes beyond ordinary principles of inchoate or accessory liability.[57] The UK's membership offence may be an example of an older security paradigm, and new offences that target any participation in a terrorist group may actually be broader than the older style of membership offences.

EU Framework Decisions in 2002 and 2008 have encouraged EU member states to enact many new terrorist offences. Romania, for example, enacted many new terrorism offences in 2004 in order to comply with the 2002 mandate. It also enacted new offences relating to recruitment, training and terrorist propaganda in 2014 as contemplated in the 2008 Framework Decision. Romania's response has raised concerns that too many separate acts are now included in overlapping terrorist crimes.[58] Belgium also enacted legislation to comply with the 2008 Framework Decision, but also included a slightly broader offence that applied to a person who received terrorist training.[59] A Polish law enacted in 2004 is also broader than the EU directive in including all crimes punishable in the Polish Criminal Code by at least five years' imprisonment and not only those crimes listed in the 2002 Framework Decision.[60] This raises an interesting question of whether EU Framework Decisions should be seen as the minimum that member states should enact or the maximum.

55 2002/475/JHA 13 June 2002.
56 Chapter 13, "Croatia" infra at 370.
57 Chapter 3, "Canada" infra at 83 in reference to R. v. Khawaja [2012] 3 S.C.R. 555.
58 Chapter 17, "Romania" infra at 488ff.
59 Chapter 8, "Belgium" infra at 239.
60 Chapter 15, "Poland" infra at 432.

The former position allows each state to determine whether it wants to exercise its sovereignty to enact additional and broader terrorism laws. At the same time, however, broader laws may pose a risk to human rights.

A 2009 law of the Czech Republic includes many of the offences contemplated in the 2002 directive. In 2011, the Czech Republic enacted a public provocation of terrorism offence to comply with the 2008 EU Framework Decision. An interesting feature of Czech terrorism law is that statutes of limitations do not apply if the terrorist crimes amount to war crimes or crimes against humanity in international law.[61] Even while criminalizing terrorism, the Czech approach recognizes that war crimes and crimes against humanity have more settled and established meanings than terrorism in international law. This helps explain why terrorism remains outside of the jurisdiction of the International Criminal Court. It may also suggest that especially in monist jurisdictions, the legitimacy of the terrorism label may be contested.

Overlapping offences are not limited to EU member states. Davis, McGarrity and Williams note that Australian courts have accepted multiple and overlapping charges in terrorism cases so long as "one charge was not wholly included within the other."[62] Takeyoshi Imai suggests that terrorists could also be charged with overlapping offences in Japan, including those related to new terrorism financing offences enacted in 2002.[63] The overlapping nature of many terrorist crimes combined with their broad nature can place pressures on principles of proportionate punishment. Countries may also have incentives to enact multiple terrorist offences in order to demonstrate their commitment to combating terrorism, but then find that the overlapping and complex nature of the offences make terrorism prosecutions more difficult.

E. *Frequently Charged Offences*

Even when there are multiple offences, there are some offences that are used more often by prosecutors. Setty indicates how various offences relating to the material support of terrorism are favoured in American terrorism prosecutions. Material support offences have been broadened in the United States to include matters such as supplying expertise to benefit a terrorist group.[64] In the United Kingdom, offences of

[61] Chapter 16, "The Czech Republic" infra at 464.

[62] Benbrika and Ors v. The Queen [2010] VSCA 281 [427] as quoted in Chapter 23, "Australia" infra at 657. One listing of terrorist offences in Australia, Canada, New Zealand and the United Kingdom in 2009 takes up almost sixty single-spaced pages. Alex Conte *Human Rights in the Prevention and Punishment of Terrorism* (Heidelberg: Springer, 2010) at 743–804.

[63] Chapter 20, "Japan" infra at 571.

[64] Chapter 2, "The United States" infra at 53.

possessing things or having a document connected with terrorism under ss.57 and 58 of the Terrorism Act, 2000 are the most frequently charged terrorism offences.[65] The British courts have stopped short of requiring that the accused "actually possessed the fertilizer for a purpose connected with the commission of an act of terrorism. That would be to impose on the Crown a requirement that is not to be found in section 57(1)."[66] In 2006, Parliament raised the maximum period of imprisonment for these frequently prosecuted but very broad offenses from ten to fifteen years, thus placing pressure on principles of proportionate punishment. The most frequently charged terrorism offences in both the UK and the United States have at best only a remote connection to the commission of actual terrorist violence. The breadth of these commonly charged offences presents challenges to be examined in this chapter for fair labelling and proportionate punishment.

F. *The Failure of Fault Requirement to Restrain Modern Terrorism Offences*

It is not a coincidence that the most frequently charged terrorism offences in both the UK and the United States are broad offences that do not require proof that the accused has a purpose or specific intent to engage in terrorism. In *Holder v. Humanitarian Law Project*,[67] the United States Supreme Court decided that people could be guilty of the offence of material support of a foreign terrorist group even if their only purpose was to assist in the humanitarian activities of the organization. Chief Justice Roberts rejected imposing a terrorist purpose requirement because it would be "inconsistent with the text of the statute… Congress plainly spoke to the necessary mental state for a violation… and it chose knowledge about the organization's connection to terrorism, not specific intent to further the organization's terrorist activities."[68] The British courts have similarly held that one could be guilty of possession of items related to terrorism or attending terrorist training even in the absence of a purpose to engage in terrorism.[69] Professor Clive Walker has concluded that broad British terrorism offenses could be applied to journalists or others who attended training sites for legitimate purposes.[70] Professors Hodgson and Tadros go further and argue that the UK approach can "make a terrorist out of nothing."[71] These findings are

[65] Chapter 6, "The United Kingdom" infra at 173.

[66] *R. v. G. and J.* [2009] UKHL 13, [68].

[67] 130 S.Ct. 2705 (2010).

[68] Ibid at at 2717.

[69] The Court of Appeal concluded that section 8 of the Terrorism Act 2006 "creates an offence of attending at terrorist training even for a person who does not have the intention of putting it to terrorist purposes. In such a case he should not be there." *R. v. Da Costa* [2009] EWCA Crim. 482, [21].

[70] Walker, *Terrorism and the Law* (2011), para. 5.21.

[71] Victor Tadros and Jacqueline Hodgson, "How to Make a Terrorist out of Nothing," (2009) 72 *Modern LR* 984.

even more significant given the emphasis in Security Council Resolution 2178 on ensuring that terrorist recruitment and training are serious offences. Broad terrorism offences may not only strain principles of proportionate punishment and fair labeling, but also encourage defiance by people who are attracted to such activities in the genuine belief that they are assisting people in need. Broad offences may sap the terrorism label of some of its denunciatory force, especially among radicalized groups.

In 2012, the Australian High Court upheld a conviction of making a document connected with assistance in a terrorist act in a case of a journalist and commentator on Islamic affairs who spent three days downloading, annotating and writing a preface for a book on the "rules of jihad" that outlined various terrorism techniques, including assassinations. One judge explained that while the evidence "suggests a reasonable possibility that the [accused] lived a useful and blameless professional life," it was not sufficient to suggest that the accused "acted, in this particular instance, with an intention other than facilitating assistance in a terrorist act."[72] There is a danger that overbroad terrorism offences that are not restrained by requirements of a terrorist purpose may deprive terrorist convictions of some of their denunciatory force. Concerns about the legitimacy of the terrorism label may increase as states focus more on preventing radicalization.

G. *Extra-Territorial Jurisdiction*

Article 9 of the 2002 EU Framework Decision encouraged countries to enact terrorism offences that could apply to conduct that takes place outside their jurisdictions. This recognition of the international nature of terrorism was already reflected in the UK's influential Terrorism Act, 2000, which defined terrorism to apply to acts against governments anywhere in the world. Some countries place limits on extra-territorial jurisdiction by requiring some connection to their jurisdiction. Georgios Triantafyllou argues in Chapter 12 on Greece that it would raise "suspicions of legal paternalism" if a country prosecuted a terrorist offence if there was no connection between the act and the prosecuting jurisdiction.[73]

Despite the trend to the assertion of extra-territorial jurisdiction, none of the authors in this collection report problems of countries competing to prosecute the same acts of terrorism. There are some examples of integrated prosecutions. The first prosecution under Canada's Anti-Terrorism Act was of a Canadian citizen who plotted with British citizens who were successfully prosecuted in the UK. The Canadian prosecution also involved a witness who had been prosecuted in the

[72] Queen v. Khazaal [2012] HCA 26, para. 110.

[73] Chapter 12, "Greece" infra at 352.

United States.[74] As will be examined later in this chapter, extradition proceedings are important in allowing jurisdictions with the closest connection to an offence or perhaps the harsher penalties to prosecute terrorist offences. Canadian courts, for example, have rejected challenges that suspected terrorists who could be prosecuted in Canada should not be extradited to face terrorist charges in the United States simply because they will face harsher penalties if convicted in the United States.[75]

The extra-territorial application of counter-terrorism law can place the freedom fighter issue discussed in Chapter 1 in stark relief. People have been convicted of terrorism offences in the UK for fighting against the Ghaddifi regime in Libya.[76] The UK Supreme Court has recognized the potential harshness of convicting people of terrorism who have fought against repressive regimes outside of the UK, but has simply asked Parliament to address this issue,[77] something that Parliament has not done. Criminal prosecutions can be blunt and problematic tools when applied to complex conflicts in foreign lands. There is a danger that some extra-territorial uses of terrorism laws may undermine the denunciatory force and legitimacy of terrorism prosecutions and even be counterproductive as an approach to combating radicalization.

Extra-territorial prosecutions could also be used against those who leave their home countries in Europe or North America to fight for the Islamic State in Iraq and Syria. The possibility of prosecution provides the state with another instrument but could potentially complicate and even hinder anti-radicalization programs designed to prevent people from joining foreign terrorist organizations or to prevent them from engaging in violence after they have returned from fighting with foreign terrorist organizations.

H. *Speech Offences Related to Terrorism*

The post–London bombing trend towards criminalizing speech associated with terrorism may intensify in the future given the focus on violent extremism and radicalization in Security Council Resolution 2178. Nevertheless, it is significant that the trend towards criminalizing speech associated with terrorism followed patterns started by non-democratic regimes. For example, Tunisia under the rule of Ben Ali enacted new terrorism laws in 2003 that drew a link between speech and terrorism. Article 6 of the 2003 law also provided that "acts of incitement to hatred or religious

74 R. v. Khawaja 2012 SCC 69; Khyam v. The Queen (2008) WWCA 1612 (C.A.).

75 Sriskandarajah v United States of America [2012] 3 S.C.R. 609; United States v Muhammad 'Isa, 2014 ABCA 256

76 Chapter 6, "The United Kingdom" infra at 171.

77 R. v. Gul supra

fanaticism shall also be dealt with as terrorist offences."[78] This law demonstrates how some counter-terrorism laws were motivated both by a concern about hatred and religious extremism and a concern about preventing terrorism. Laws against hatred and against the incitement or condoning of terrorism will also play a role in new strategies to counter violent radicalization. For example, Australia enacted a new offence of advocating terrorism in 2014 and a similar offence is proposed in Canada.[79] Such criminalization strategies have to co-exist with softer persuasion and education-based strategies targeting radicalization. More needs to be known about the effectiveness and interaction of both types of strategies.

Responding to concerns about extremism in the wake of the 2005 London bombings, the UK played a lead role in UN Security Resolution 1624. The Resolution called on all nations to ensure that incitement of terrorism was treated as a serious crime. The UK's Terrorism Act, 2006 prohibits statements that intentionally or recklessly directly or indirectly encourage acts of terrorism anywhere in the world. This includes statements that glorify the commission or preparation of acts of terrorism, including those in the past. There are, however, some restraints, and the offence is not as sweeping as first proposed by Prime Minister Blair. The glorification of past acts of terrorism must be done in a manner that reasonably could be expected to encourage listeners to emulate the act in existing circumstances. The British approach reflects a desire to criminalize ideologies that are associated with terrorism regardless of their connection with actual terrorism. It also blurs the counter-terrorism rationale of prohibition of extremist speech with the related but somewhat different rationales of countering hate speech and promoting a militant democracy that is intolerant of those who oppose and disparage democracy.

In 2008, the EU Council responded to Security Council Resolution 1624 with a Framework Decision requiring member states to criminalize the public provocation of terrorism.[80] The EU approach was more restrained than the UK's approach because it required that the public provocation cause a danger that terrorism offences would be committed. At the same time, it was somewhat less restrained

[78] Lynn Welchman "Anti-Terrorism Law and Policy in Arab States" in Ramraj et al. *Global Anti-Terrorism Law and Policy* 2nd ed supra at 648.

[79] National Security Legislation Amendment Act (No 1) 2014 No. 108, 2014 adding s.80.2C to the Criminal Code creating an offence of advocating a terrorist act while being reckless that others will commit a terrorism offence. The Canadian Anti-Terrorism Act, 2015 Bill C-51 1st reading January 30, 2015, would add s.83.221 to the Criminal Code, creating an offence of knowingly advocating or promoting terrorism offences in general while being reckless that a person may commit a terrorist offence as a result of the communication.

[80] 2008/475/JHA 28 November 2008. This framework decision also contributed to the overlapping nature of terrorism offences by requiring the enactment of offences relating to recruitment for terrorism, training for terrorism, aggravated theft, extortion and the drawing up of false administrative documents for terrorist purposes.

than a competing declaration from the European Parliament that would have required that the incitement "manifestly causes a danger." In general, the European Parliament has been more concerned with human rights compliance than the more executive-dominated European Union Council. This is an important reminder that comparative law analysis should be filtered through attention to the separation of powers.[81] As will be seen, the executive has also dominated many other aspects of counter-terrorism law, including terrorism financing, terrorist listing, immigration law and administrative measures, even though there is a legislative basis for most of these measures. Supra-national requirements to enact terrorism laws encourage executive domination of even nominally legislative acts. The frequent fusion of legislative and executive action highlights the importance of the judiciary as a potential counterweight.

The 2008 Framework Decision on public provocation of terrorism came after a number of decisions of the European Court of Human Rights accepting that prosecution of speech connected to terrorism constituted reasonable and proportionate limits on such rights.[82] The lack of strong judicial counterweights can lead to excessive and even repressive state use of power. Cian Murphy has criticized the 2008 Framework because it criminalizes "a broad range of political action and provides weak safeguards for legitimate political action."[83] The weak protection of dissent and fundamental freedoms may reflect executive domination of the legislative process and a willingness of the judiciary to accept limitations on freedom of expression. The effectiveness of laws against speech associated with terrorism in preventing terrorism, however, remains unclear.

A few European states such as Italy and Switzerland relied on general provisions on incitement of all criminal offences, but many others enacted new offences to comply with the 2008 Framework Decision. For example, the Czech Republic added the offence of public incitement of terrorism in 2011. Veronika Bilková observes that this new offence "did not give rise to any public debate or public criticism," perhaps as a result of the EU decision. This raises the question of whether the more hierarchical European approach to harmonization stifles democratic debate. Slovenia's criminal law was amended in 2008 to include an offence of inciting and praising terrorist acts.[84] Croatia also enacted an incitement of terrorism offence in response to the 2008 EU Framework Decision, but this offence is broader than the EU mandate because it does not require that the act of encouragement, glorification or apology create a danger that a terrorism offence will be committed. This example indicates

81 Daphne Barak Erez "Terrorism Law Between the Executive and Legislative Models" (2009) 57 *American Journal of Comparative Law* 877.

82 Cian C. Murphy *EU Counter-Terrorism Law* (Oxford: Hart Publishing, 2012) at 70–1.

83 Ibid at 74

84 Chapter 14, "Slovenia" infra at 464.

how expansion beyond the parameters of a EU Framework Decision can place pressure on human rights. Marissabell Škorić expresses concerns that the resulting Croatian offence does not strike the appropriate balance "between the obligation of the state to protect everyone from terrorism and its obligation to protect freedom of expression as a fundamental human right."[85]

a. *American Exceptionalism on Speech*

As Sudha Setty notes in Chapter 2, the United States told the Counter-Terrorism Committee of the Security Council that the First Amendment constrained its ability to respond to Security Council Resolution 1624 with respect to the criminalization of the incitement of terrorism. As she notes, "the United States government maintains … that the majority of the terrorist propaganda found on the Internet today," including "a website advocating committing acts of terrorist violence," could not be prosecuted under the First Amendment in the absence of proof of "imminent lawless action."[86] Restrained at home by its Bill of Rights, the American state often acts abroad. A recent example of this phenomena is the key role that the United States played in the enactment of Security Resolution 2178, which indicates a "strong determination" to use UN processes to list those who recruit entities associated with al Qaeda "through information and communications technologies, such as the Internet, social media, or any other means…"[87] The United States has used its powers on the Security Council to encourage other states to take actions in their domestic laws against recruitment and radicalization that would at home be prohibited by the First Amendment.

American constitutional restraints may help explain some aspects of American exceptionalism. In the United States, immigration law more directly targets expressive and associational activities than domestic criminal law.[88] Similar constitutional restraints on criminal justice and in particular restrictions on preventive detention and the ban on the use of secret evidence may have played a role in the U.S. decision to emphasize military detention and trial in the immediate aftermath of 9/11.[89] One intriguing aspect of American exceptionalism is how tight restraints on the state's domestic powers may encourage the American state to rely on its considerable and largely unrestrained foreign and military powers abroad. Rather than enact new offences against speech associated with terrorism, the United States has relied on a Congressional Authorization of the Use of Military Force to authorize a range

85 Chapter 13, "Croatia" infra at 371.
86 Chapter 2, "The United States" infra at 54.
87 S/Res/ 2178 at para 7 (2014).
88 David Cole *Enemy Aliens* (New York: New Press, 2003).
89 Roach *The 9/11 Effect* ch.4.

of measures, including military detention and trial of suspected terrorists captured abroad, rendition, mass surveillance of foreign communications, targeted killing and bombings of foreign terrorist fighters in Iraq and Syria.

I. *Terrorism Prosecutions*

China, the United States, the United Kingdom and Italy are jurisdictions represented in this collection that report high levels of terrorism prosecutions in the hundreds or thousands.[90] In contrast, Portugal, Slovenia, Poland, Brazil, Japan, Singapore, the Czech Republic, Romania and South Africa report very small numbers or even no recent terrorism prosecutions. Other jurisdictions such as Australia, Belgium, Canada, Croatia and Spain report an intermediate number of terrorist prosecutions.[91] In continental Europe, Japan and South Africa, the lack of prosecutions may speak to the fact that much terrorism law has been enacted mainly to comply with supra-national demands. In Singapore, the lack of prosecutions can be explained by the use of alternative and more secretive measures in the form of indeterminate detention without trial under the Internal Security Act. In Brazil, the lack of terrorism convictions reflects a principled but now perhaps wavering refusal to attempt to define terrorism by enacting terrorism offences.

A 2011 study recorded over thirty-five thousand terrorism prosecutions since 9/11, with Turkey accounting for a third of these convictions and Turkey and China accounting for more than a half of them.[92] Another study recorded about three hundred terrorism convictions in the United States in the decade after 9/11 with an 87% conviction rate and an average sentence of fourteen years. This is a similar conviction rate to all federal cases, but about a third of terrorism cases go to trial as opposed to less than 4% of non-terrorist cases in the U.S. federal criminal justice system. Over 40% of the American terrorism prosecutions involved an informant.[93] Sudha Setty in Chapter 2 raises concerns that American juries have never accepted a successful entrapment defence despite the extensive and largely unregulated use

90 In China, there were 1003 convictions of endangering public safety between 2003 and 2008, and these include terrorism convictions. Chapter 21, "China" infra at 588.

91 In Australia, forty-two people, all men and virtually all Muslims, have been charged with terrorism offences since 9/11; Chapter 23, "Australia" infra at 682. In Belgium, ninety individuals have been prosecuted since 2005 with twenty-five verdicts; Chapter 8, "Belgium" infra at 241. In Spain, ninety-six people were convicted of terrorism offences in 2011 and forty-six were convicted in 2012; Chapter 10, "Spain" at 311. In Canada, about seventeen people have been convicted of terrorism offences since 2001. Chapter 3, "Canada" at 85.

92 Martha Mendoza "Nations Turned to Anti-Terrorism Laws as a Shield – and a Sword – After 9/11" *Seattle Times* 4 September 2011 available at http://seattletimes.com/avantgo/2016104402.html.

93 NYU Center for Law and Security *Ten Years Later: Terrorist Trial Report Card 2001–2011* available at http://www.lawandsecurity.org/Portals/0/Documents/TTRC%20Ten%20Year%20Issue.pdf.

of informers to persuade people to engage in terrorist acts.[94] At the opposite end, Sabrina Praduroux reports that only 10% of terrorism prosecutions in Italy have resulted in convictions.[95] These striking differences can, Praduroux suggests, partially be explained by the nature of the Italian criminal process, which obligates the Italian prosecutor to start an investigation and a prosecution when there is evidence of a terrorist act, as compared to the American system, which grants both prosecutors and grand juries discretion to decide whether a case is worth prosecuting.

Data from the UK indicate that between September 2001 and the end of August 2012, 2,297 people were arrested on terrorism charges, with 838 of these people being charged. This indicates substantial attrition between arrest and prosecution.[96] These statistics also suggest that police may be using arrests as a form of disruption even when prosecutors find there is not enough evidence to justify a prosecution. One prominent Australian case involved the arrest and detention of an Indian doctor, Mohammed Haneef, whose charges of providing resources to a terrorist organization were subsequently withdrawn.[97] Of the 838 people charged in the UK, 241 were convicted and of those 56% received sentences under five years.[98] This suggests a conviction rate closer to the low Italian one than the high American rate. It also indicates how sentencing judges in the majority of cases must have concluded that the offences were relatively minor despite their connection with terrorism. This suggests that sentencing discretion can be used to mitigate the effects of overbroad terrorism offences. It also raises concerns that broad terrorism offences combined with a broad definition of terrorism may be undermining some of the denunciatory and stigmatizing force of the terrorist label. The short sentences given after many terrorism convictions mean that prison radicalization and the possibly counterproductive effects of prison cannot be ignored, especially in light of information that some of the 2015 Paris attackers and the Copenhagen attacker had spent time in prison.

In many of the countries that report few if any terrorism prosecutions, there is a sense that new terrorism laws have been enacted primarily to comply with supra-national demands. Singapore has since 9/11 enacted new criminal laws against terrorism financing, terrorist bombings and hostage taking, but Eugene K. B. Tan suggests in Chapter 22 that these laws have not been used.[99] In South Africa, there

94 Chapter 2, "The United States" infra at 54–55.

95 Chapter 9, "Italy" infra at 278.

96 Home Office Terrorist Arrests – analysis of sentencing and charging outcomes by religion 12 September 2013 at https://www.gov.uk/government/publications/terrorism-arrests-analysis-of-charging-and-sentencing-outcomes-by-religion/terrorism-arrests-analysis-of-charging-and-sentencing-outcomes-by-religion.

97 Chapter 23, "Australia" at 657.

98 See *supra* 96.

99 Chapter 22, "Singapore" at 617.

has only been one conviction since the creation of terrorist crimes in 2004, with the accused, a Nigerian national resident in South Africa, being sentenced to fourteen years for financing and conspiring with respect to two fatal car bombings in Nigeria.[100] The court rejected the accused's argument that his campaign against the Nigerian government was a struggle for self-determination and national liberation against colonialism that is exempted from South Africa's otherwise very broad definition of terrorism. The conviction also relied on testimony from anonymous witnesses who said they were accomplices of the accused based in Nigeria.[101]

Poland enacted broad new terrorism offences in 2004 as it entered the European Union, but there have been no prosecutions under these offences.[102] In the Czech Republic, there has only been one terrorism conviction since the creation of terrorist crimes in 2004. The conviction resulted in a five-year sentence for a man who wrote letters threatening to use violence against politicians "unless certain political conditions were met." Other cases that might have been considered terrorism have been prosecuted as ordinary crimes.[103] In Romania, there have been only three terrorism convictions.[104] In Slovenia, there were only a few reports of terrorism prosecutions, the first being in 2008. The most high-profile conviction was the conviction of a Croatian man who was given an eleven-year sentence in relation to a plot to assassinate Slovenia's Prime Minister.[105] In most countries, the bark of broad terrorism laws has been much louder than the actual bite of terrorism prosecutions.

a. Exceptional Courts?

The vast majority of jurisdictions in this collection conduct terrorism prosecutions in ordinary criminal courts. The use of exceptional courts, such as the use of military commissions at Guantanamo, can be controversial.[106] Countries with aspects of exceptional courts often take pains to categorize the courts as not exceptional. There is a specialized terrorist court in Spain, but when it was constitutionally challenged, the courts classified it as an ordinary court.[107] The exclusion of lay judges in Greece has also been challenged in terrorism cases but has been upheld on the basis that terrorism does not constitute a political crime, which under the Greek constitution

[100] Chapter 19, "South Africa" at 547, citing R. v. Okah 2013 ZAGPJHC 6.
[101] Ibid at para 8.
[102] Chapter 15, "Poland" infra at 435.
[103] Chapter 16, "The Czech Republic" at 467.
[104] Chapter 17, "Romania" at 497–498.
[105] Chapter 14, "Slovenia" at 407.
[106] See generally Fionnuala ni Aolain and Oren Gross eds. *Guantanamo and Beyond: Exceptional Courts in Comparative Context* (New York: Cambridge University Press, 2013).
[107] Chapter 10, "Spain" at 310.

requires the use of lay judges. In addition, the courts have concluded that complex terrorism trials require professional judges.[108] Jury-less Diplock courts are used much less frequently in the UK in part because of perceptions that they were not legitimate.[109] In Canada, terrorism prosecutions are decided by the ordinary courts, but specialized designated judges with expertise in security matters make decisions that bind criminal trial judges about whether information should not be disclosed because of national security confidentiality. The Supreme Court of Canada has upheld the constitutionality of this regime by stressing that ordinary criminal trial judges can still stop proceedings if they conclude that non-disclosure has made a trial unfair.[110] China uses the ordinary courts in terrorism cases, but in security cases only the sentencing is conducted in public.[111]

J. *Punishment of Terrorism*

There is almost a universal trend towards ensuring that those convicted of terrorism crimes be punished seriously. One exception is the ability in many jurisdictions, pioneered in Italy, to reduce punishment to encourage perpetrators to co-operate and give evidence for the state in terrorism prosecutions. Another exception is Singapore, which has not relied upon the heavy penalties, including the death penalty, available under its criminal laws for terrorist acts, but has instead subjected suspected terrorists to indefinite detention under its Internal Security Act.[112] A Rand study found that forty of sixty terrorist suspects were released in Singapore after being detained on average for four years and that only one of those released had been rearrested.[113] In Chapter 22 Professor Tan reports an even higher 80 percent rate of success. Although the context of detention and rehabilitation in Singapore is distinct, Western democracies can no longer continue to ignore issues of rehabilitation.

a. Mandatory Minimum Sentences

Article 5 of the 2002 EU Framework Decision required member states to ensure that crimes committed with terrorist purposes be subject to greater punishment

[108] Chapter 12, "Greece" at 356.
[109] Chapter 6, "The United Kingdom" at 173.
[110] Chapter 3, "Canada" at 104, in reference to R. v. Ahmad [2011] 1 SCR 110.
[111] Chapter 21, "China" at 588.
[112] Chapter 22, "Singapore"; Roach *The 9/11 Effect* supra at 140–2.
[113] Angel Rabasa et al. *Deradicalizing Islamic Extremists* (Santa Monica, CA: Rand Corporation, 2010) at 100–4. See Chapter 22, "Singapore" at 624, footnote 59 reporting 80 per cent success in rehabilitation of those detained under the Internal Security Act.

than similar ordinary crimes unless the ordinary crime was already subject to a jurisdiction's maximum punishment. It provided that the crime of directing a terrorist group be subject to a maximum sentence of not less than fifteen years' imprisonment[114] and that participation in a terrorist group be subject to a maximum sentence of not less than eight years. A number of EU states have complied, but some, including Spain, have also added minimum sentences that are not present in the EU directive.[115] China added mandatory minimum sentences of three and ten years in 2001 to terrorism offences first created in 1997.[116] Mandatory minimum sentences of imprisonment stress the penal objectives of general deterrence and denunciation of terrorism over the specific deterrence and rehabilitation of individual offenders. They can prevent the sentencing judge from ensuring that the sentence fits the particular crime and offender. As seen from the preceding, terrorism crimes are quite broad and may involve offenders without prior criminal records who are followers rather than leaders. The combination of broad offences and mandatory minimum punishments can challenge principles of proportionate punishment. Mandatory sentences can also prevent reduction of punishment as a reward for an offender's co-operation with authorities, a topic examined later in this chapter.

b. Anxiety and Struggle over Release: The Parot Case

Many jurisdictions experience anxiety at the prospect that terrorists will be released after serving their sentence. The Spanish courts attempted to prevent the release of Henri Parot after he had served thirty years in prison in relation to terrorism by ETA, the Basque terrorist group. The Grand Chamber of the European Court of Human Rights held that the Parot doctrine, designed to ensure Parot's continued detention on his original sentence of thousands of years' imprisonment, violated articles 5 and 7 of the European Convention on Human Rights relating to liberty and prohibitions of retroactive or illegal punishment.[117] This decision demonstrates how some punitive and populist sanctions for terrorism may violate human rights.

A recurring theme in this volume is that courts often do not have the last word when they make decisions defending human rights in the terrorism context. Shortly after the European Court of Human Rights decision, Spain introduced in 2010 a

114 The only exception is that the mandatory minimum sentence need only be eight years if the directing offence relates only to threats to commit underlying offences such as murder, kidnapping and explosives.

115 Greece, for example, imposes minimum sentences of three and ten years' imprisonment for terrorist offences; Chapter 12, "Greece" at 350.

116 Chapter 21, "China" at 585.

117 Rio Prado v. Spain Application 42750/09.

new sanction of community supervision for dangerous sex offenders and terrorists that can potentially extend ten years beyond the end of an imprisonment sentence. As Boldova and Rueda note in Chapter 10: "The Spanish legislator distrusts the rehabilitation of the terrorist and has proposed a penal response based on retribution and general deterrence."[118] The lack of interest and confidence in rehabilitation of terrorists also helps to explain a growing trend to provisions that place restrictions on terrorists who have served their sentences. For example, the UK's Counter-Terrorism Act, 2008[119] provides for a notification scheme that can last for thirty years after a terrorist offender is released and can also include prohibition on foreign travel.[120] The anxiety over the release of offenders is connected to the neglect of the need to rehabilitate terrorists as well as understandable anxiety about terrorist attacks in early 2015 by people who had been released from prison.

c. The Death Penalty

The United States used the death penalty with respect to the 1993 Oklahoma City bombings, and Japan used the death penalty with respect to thirteen people connected to the 1995 Amu Shinrikyo Sarin gas terrorists attacks.[121] Neither country, however, has used the death penalty in a terrorist case since 9/11, though the United States is seeking the death penalty in the Boston marathon bombing case. China is the only jurisdiction examined in this collection that frequently uses the death penalty in terrorism cases. India hanged a person convicted in relation to the 2008 Mumbai terrorist attacks. The effects of using the death penalty in high-profile terrorism cases are speculative. On the one hand, it can be argued that the death penalty might have counterproductive effects that might make some sympathize with terrorist groups. On the other hand, it can be argued that terrorist groups such as al Qaeda and the Islamic State may see the reluctance to use the death penalty as a sign of the weakness of the West. Even if that is true, democracies must be aware of the harm that use of the death penalty might cause to themselves, including the possible harm of executing innocent people who have been wrongly convicted of terrorism.[122]

d. Rehabilitation

Not all Western democracies have rejected the penal objective of rehabilitating those convicted of terrorism. As Robert Diab notes, the Supreme Court of Canada

118 Chapter 10, "Spain" at 313.
119 c. 28, Part IV.
120 Ibid Part V.
121 Chapter 20, "Japan" at 572.
122 Kent Roach and Gary Trotter "Miscarriages of Justice in the War Against Terror" (2005) 109 *Penn. State Law Review* 967.

rejected the idea expressed by lower courts that rehabilitation had no place when sentencing terrorists.[123] At the same time, however, the Court upheld a life sentence for a terrorist who had expressed no remorse. Canadian officials have so far demonstrated little interest in rehabilitation, housing most convicted terrorists together in a high-security special handling unit and starting proceedings to deport those who are non-citizens after they have served their sentences.[124]

Both the UK and Canada have provided that in some cases those convicted of terrorism offences can be deprived of citizenship. This suggests a continued tendency to define terrorism as an external threat. It also correlates with the willingness of those countries to use immigration law for anti-terrorism purposes, which will be examined in Section X of this chapter. There have also been populist demands for such citizenship stripping in the United States, but it would almost surely be found to be unconstitutional.[125] Yaser Hamdi renounced his American citizenship as part of a deal that allowed him to be released from Guantanamo and allowed to return to Saudi Arabia. American citizens may not be vulnerable to citizenship stripping, but they can be subject to targeted killing if they leave the United States.[126] The common thread is that Western democracies are more comfortable in defining terrorists as an external threat that must be defeated rather than as citzens who must be rehabilitated. This may change in the wake of the foreign terrorist fighters, but it will require substantial adjustments in most Western democracies.

In the wake of the January 2015 terrorist attacks in Paris, France is considering reviving a post–World War II national dignity law that would allow convicted terrorists, like Nazi collaborators, to be deprived of voting and other political rights.[127] Such an act, like attempts to deprive terrorists of citizenship, symbolizes a desire to remove convicted terrorists from the political community. Such ideas are understandable in light of the horror of terrorist acts and terrorists' rejection of non-violent pluralism, but they also implicitly reject the idea that terrorists can be rehabilitated and can eventually return as law-abiding members of the community.

e. Pentiti Practices

The only exception to the Western trend to increased punishment of terrorists are pragmatic reductions in punishment given for co-operating with terrorism prosecutions. Article 6 of the 2002 EU Framework Decision accommodates the

[123] Chapter 3, "Canada" at 90.
[124] Namouh v. Canada (Public Safety and Emergency Preparedness), 2012 FC 1545.
[125] Afroyim v. Rusk 387 U.S. 253 (1967).
[126] Al-Aulaqi v. Obama 727 F. Supp. 2d 1 (2010).
[127] "France Vows Forceful Measures Against Terrorism" *New York Times* January 21, 2015.

system started in Italy in 1978[128] of reducing sentences for co-operating terrorists by providing that members states may (not must) take steps to reduce sentences if the offender renounces terrorist activities and co-operates with authorities to prevent terrorism or help bring offenders to justice. These provisions also contemplate a largely unregulated process of encouraging those prosecuted as terrorists to assist the authorities and to inform on other terrorists. Such practices may provide valuable information that could help prevent terrorism, but they may also produce false information that could contribute to the wrongful conviction of the innocent.

Strategic reductions in punishment for terrorists have proven attractive both within and outside the EU. In the UK, s.73 of the Serious Organized Crime and Police Act 2005[129] provides for reductions of sentences if there are written co-operation agreements with prosecutors. This provision allows such reductions of sentences even below statutory minimum sentences. China relies on general provisions under Articles 67 and 68 of its Penal Code to provide reduced punishment for those who surrender or assist authorities, and these could be applied to those convicted of terrorism.[130] Spain also provides for reduced punishments for those who assist authorities. A 2003 law makes it necessary for those serving terrorist sentences to renounce terrorism, apologize to victims and assist authorities before being granted parole or controlled release during a sentence of imprisonment.[131] In Greece, co-operating suspects may have their punishment suspended.[132] In Slovenia, witness protection seems to be linked to whether the witness has co-operated with authorities.[133] In North America, reductions of punishment for co-operation would be achieved through the largely unregulated process of plea bargaining. This is a reminder to comparative lawyers that the absence of a formal provision may only mean that similar results are achieved through informal practice.

Brazil and Colombia have contrasting approaches to the reduction of punishment. Colombia has a 2005 law that provides a means of reintegrating members of armed groups into society and allows judges to reduce sentences. Such reductions are not available, however, if terrorist crimes constitute a crime against humanity. This prohibition was upheld in a 2007 decision of the Constitutional Court.[134] Brazil has a more lenient regime. Judges can reduce punishment in all cases of co-operation, but a 2013 law on organized crime has special provisions providing for pardons or reductions of sentence by up to two-thirds if an accused helps the state with

128 Chapter 9, "Italy" at 279.
129 C. 15.
130 Chapter 21, "China" at 589.
131 Chapter 10, "Spain" at 313.
132 Chapter 12, "Greece" at 352.
133 Chapter 14, "Slovenia" at 408.
134 Chapter 4, "Colombia" at 137.

respect to a criminal organization, including a terrorist group. Such reductions in punishment raise interesting tensions between the utilitarian and retributive uses of criminal law.

K. *Summary*

Western democracies have largely ignored the rehabilitation of terrorists. Concerns about prisoner radicalization[135] will increase in the wake of terrorist attacks in Europe by ex-prisoners in early 2015. There seems to be a shortsighted tendency to devote more energy to introducing post-sentence controls on offenders than to trying to rehabilitate and de-radicalize them. Singapore stands out as the jurisdiction included in this collection that has been most concerned with rehabilitation. Its successful program should be studied, albeit with due regard to the distinct context of Singapore. One challenge in the future may be the integration of counter-radicalization programs in prisons and the larger community. The possibility that the almost-universal trend to harsh punishment of terrorism may in some cases be counterproductive cannot be dismissed.

VII. INVESTIGATIVE POWERS

The main divide with respect to investigative powers is between countries that have a special regime for terrorism investigations and those that rely on existing powers. The special investigative regimes in the UK, Australia and Canada have been controversial. Many are designed to be temporary and many have been challenged as infringing various human rights. Some other countries including Brazil, China, Greece and South Africa have special investigative powers for organized crime that can be used in terrorism investigations. Many countries in continental Europe, as well as Japan, China and Singapore, rely on regular investigative powers in terrorism cases. Reliance on ordinary investigative powers obviously begs the question of baseline positions, and countries such as China and Singapore tend to give police and intelligence agencies broad powers with respect to all crimes and threats to security. As Eugene Tan points out in Chapter 22, in Singapore it is not possible to know whether police and intelligence agencies have abused their powers in terrorism investigations because proceedings under that country's Internal Security Act are secret.[136] The United States has only a few terrorism-specific investigative powers, generally related to surveillance, but this must also be viewed against the backdrop of aggressive use of pre-textual law enforcement and undercover stings. The USA

[135] Mark Hamm *The Spectacular Few: Prisoner Radicalization and the Evolving Terrorist Threat* (New York: New York Press, 2014).

[136] Chapter 22, "Singapore" at 624ff.

PATRIOT Act did not include powers of preventive arrests, but material witness warrants were abused after 9/11 to achieve a similar effect.[137] Comparative lawyers must focus not simply on special laws for terrorism, but the wider institutional and criminal justice context and de facto special powers used to investigate terrorism.

Some investigative powers are subject to ex ante legislative and judicial control, while others are only subject to ex post controls. For example, the use of undercover sting operations are subject to prior judicial authorization and supervision in many European countries but are only subject to the ex post control of the entrapment defence in the United States and Canada. The latter approach maximizes executive discretion and can even merge with the controversial extra-legal approach advocated by Oren Gross by allowing security officials to decide how far they wish to go in a terrorism investigation subject only to the uncertain possibility of sanctions being imposed ex post.[138] Such an approach also can limit democratic debate about counter-terrorism activities by keeping them secret.

A. *Police Powers*

Although many European countries rely on ordinary powers for terrorism investigations, it would be wrong to conclude that there are no special investigative powers. Some of the countries with the most extensive experience with terrorism have enacted special investigative powers. For example, Spain has long had powers to allow for extra detention and isolation procedures for suspected terrorists. The specialized Spanish terrorist court has also imposed some restraints on this special investigative regime, including videotaping, notification of relatives and examination by a doctor of the detainee's choice. Spanish legislation also allows executive authorization of electronic surveillance in emergency cases involving the activities of terrorists, armed bands or rebels but subject to judicial ratification within seventy-two hours.[139] Italy enacted warrantless arrest provisions in 2005 in relation to domestic or international terrorism.[140] Croatia has special investigative powers for terrorism, including electronic surveillance, use of undercover investigators and specific forms of limited law breaking. These techniques must be authorized by a judge, but in extraordinary circumstances they can be authorized by a state attorney for a limited twenty-four-hour period. Material obtained with judicial approval can be used as evidence.[141] Those suspected of terrorism are subject to

[137] Chapter 2, "The United States" at 56.

[138] Oren Gross "Chaos and Rules: Should Responses to Violent Crisis Always Be Constitutional?" (2003) 112 *Yale L.J.* 1011.

[139] Chapter 10, "Spain" at 314.

[140] Chapter 9, "Italy" at 281.

[141] Chapter 13, "Croatia" at 376.

special investigative powers in Belgium, including powers of observation and the use of informers. The civilian intelligence agency also has access to a range of special investigative powers in the case of suspected terrorism.[142]

A number of countries rely on special investigative powers for organized crime in terrorism investigations. Brazil has not enacted a terrorism law, but it has enacted a 2013 law that provides for various forms of electronic surveillance; infiltration by the police, including limited law breaking by undercover officers; and sharing of information in organized crime investigations that can include terrorism investigations. Under this legislation, the police have warrantless access to subscriber information but require judicial authorization for access to the content of information and to bank and other financial data.[143] South Africa has followed a somewhat similar route. Special investigative powers were controversial and dropped from its terrorism bill before it became law in 2004. These investigative powers are, however, available under the general powers available for investigating organized crime including terrorism.[144] Article 148 of China's Criminal Procedure Law provides for wiretapping, undercover agents, and controlled delivery of substances if the case involves crimes endangering state security; crimes of terrorist activities; organized crimes committed by groups such as criminal syndicates; major drug-related crimes; or other crimes seriously endangering the society. In 2004, Greece amended a 2001 law so that judicially authorized powers, including infiltration, controlled deliveries, electronic surveillance and combination of personal data can be used in terrorism cases as well as organized crime cases.[145] The merging of special investigative powers into general organized crime legislation may make such powers less controversial, but may also facilitate the spread of special investigation powers.

a. Preventive Arrests

The UK has the most elaborate and perhaps most controversial system of special investigative powers reserved for terrorism cases. This reflects in part the UK's long experience with terrorism, but also its commitment to exposing such measures to legislative and political debate.

The UK used preventive arrests as an instrument to respond to terrorism in Northern Ireland, and it was prepared to derogate from the European Convention of Human Rights to maintain this power. Section 41 of the Terrorism Act, 2000 continued powers of preventive arrest but accepted increased judicial review of those

[142] Chapter 8, "Belgium" at 246.
[143] Chapter 5, "Brazil" at 153.
[144] Chapter 19, "South Africa" at 549.
[145] Chapter 12, "Greece" at 355.

powers so as to avoid the necessity of a derogation. It empowered a police constable to arrest without a warrant a person reasonably suspected of being a terrorist. This is a lower standard than used for arrests under the ordinary criminal law. This power has facilitated arrests for investigative and intelligence-gathering reasons, with only about a third of cases resulting in charges.[146] The period of preventive arrest can be extended after forty-eight hours by judicial order when necessary for investigative purposes. Under the European Convention on Human Rights, judicial review is supposed to restrain the use of preventive arrests, but the UK legislation limits the judicial role to determining issues of investigative necessity rather than determining the likelihood and strength of the charge. The accused can participate in the extension hearing, but also can be excluded from the hearing for security related reasons.[147] From 1974 to 2003, the maximum period of preventive arrest was seven days. In 2003, the maximum period was raised to fourteen days and in 2006 to twenty-eight days. The government wanted to raise the maximum period to ninety or forty-two days in the wake of the 2005 London bombings but Parliament would only accept the twenty-eight-day period. The maximum period was reduced to fourteen days in 2011. As Clive Walker notes, the twenty-eight-day period is very long, but comparisons are difficult to make given long periods of detention during judicial as opposed to police investigations in continental Europe.[148] This is another important reminder that comparative lawyers need a wide lens in order to understand how different laws may play a similar functional role in different systems.

Australia and Canada enacted milder forms of preventive arrest than in the UK. Preventive arrests introduced in Canadian law after 9/11 can last only seventy-two hours, but could also trigger a judicially imposed year-long peace bond to control behaviour in the community. The Canadian provision was never used before it was allowed to sunset in 2007. The power was revived in 2013, and in the wake of two "lone-wolf" terrorist attacks in October 2014, the Canadian government is proposing to raise the maximum period to seven days, with judicial approvals required after three and five days. The fact remains that preventive arrests have never been used in Canada. Moreover, by definition, they are a temporary solution. An accused charged with a terrorism offence may be subject to longer periods of pre-trial detention. In Canada, an accused charged with a terrorism offence must establish that bail is consistent with attendance at trial, public safety and public confidence in the administration of justice.[149] The denial of bail can last much longer than even enhanced periods of preventive arrest.

[146] Walker *Terrorism and the Law* at 4.37.

[147] Ward v. Police Services for Northern Ireland [2007] UKHL 50.

[148] Walker *Terrorism and the Law* at 4.84–4.90.

[149] Kent Roach "Be Careful What You Wish? Terrorism Prosecutions in Post 9/11 Canada" (2014) 40 *Queens L.J* 99 at 105–13 examining bail laws and practices in Canadian terrorism prosecutions.

The Australian approach to preventive detention is complex. Since 2005, a terrorist suspect could be subject to seventy-two hours of preventive detention under federal law, but can also be subject to fourteen days of preventive detention under the laws of most Australian states.[150] As in Canada, officials in Australia have tended to rely on arrest and bail practices in terrorism cases.[151] As Davis, McGarrity and Williams note in Chapter 23, Dr. Mohamed Haneef was arrested for providing resources to a terrorist organization in July 2007 and detained for twelve days under controversial "dead time" provisions that allowed terrorist suspects to be detained longer than other suspects. In response to criticisms of this incident, Australian law was amended in 2010 to limit such detention to seven days.[152] This is a reminder of the need to examine special investigative powers for terrorism in their broader criminal justice context. Preventive detention powers in terrorism laws raise red flags, but the ordinary criminal law often also authorizes pre-trial detention.

b. Stop and Search Powers

As outlined in Keith Syrett's Chapter 6, the UK's Terrorism Act, 2000 contained wide and controversial police stop and search powers related to terrorism. Sections 44 to 47 allowed senior police officers and the Home Secretary to authorize stop and search of pedestrians and vehicles for terrorism-related articles when expedient to prevent acts of terrorism. In 2006, the House of Lords in the Gillan case held that such stops and searches did not deprive people – in that case, a protester and journalist in London – of liberty. On appeal, however, the European Court of Human Rights held that the law was an arbitrary invasion of privacy. It raised concerns about the discriminatory use of such powers.[153] In 2012, these powers were repealed in the Protection of Freedom Act, 2012[154] and replaced with more limited warrantless search powers based on executive determinations of necessity rather than expediency. A similar power in South African legislation requires judicial authorization on necessity grounds,[155] perhaps reflecting the presence of a constitutional bill of rights in that jurisdiction. The 2012 UK legislation reflects a recurring theme of the legislature responding to judicial decisions with new powers that are often only slightly more restrained than those found to have violated human rights.

[150] Chapter 23, "Australia" at 657.
[151] Three preventive detention orders were issued in September 2014. Chapter 23, "Australia" at 682.
[152] National Security Legislation Amendment Act 2010 s.23DB(11).
[153] Gillan v. Commissioner of the Police 2006 UKHK 12 rev'd Gillan v. UK 2010 50 EHRR 45.
[154] c.9 Part IV.
[155] Protection of Constitutional Democracy Act, 2004 s.24.

As with the Act's definition of terrorism, the broad investigative powers in the UK Terrorism Act, 2000 has been influential in former British colonies. A 2002 Zimbabwe Public Order and Security Act[156] has a similar stop and search power to the UK Act. As in the UK, this power is authorized by a senior police officer and not a judicial official. The power in Zimbabwe, however, applies not just in terrorism cases, but on any grounds related to "public disorder or public violence." Pakistani terrorism legislation also has similar stop and search powers based on a senior police officer's determination that such powers are "expedient for the purpose of a terrorist investigation."[157] Australian legislation enacted in 2005 allows warrantless searches in zones designated by Ministers on terrorism prevention grounds and also by police officers on grounds of reasonable suspicion.[158] The migration of police powers of warrantless stops and searches from the UK to other countries raises issues similar to those discussed in Chapter 1. The Australian powers, let alone those found in Zimbabwe and Pakistan, are not subject to judicial review in the European Court of Human Rights, which was concerned in the Gillan case with unnecessary and perhaps discriminatory use of police powers.

With some exceptions, the United States does not have special statutory investigative powers in terrorism cases. In this area, American police powers are initiated by the executive and subject to ex post review by the judiciary, whereas British police powers are more likely to be subject to ex ante legislative and executive controls as well as judicial review after the fact. The American courts have upheld stops and searches for counter-terrorism purposes.[159] This is another reminder that comparative lawyers must be attentive to background differences in legal systems. The UK approach reflects a legal culture where police actions are quite closely regulated by legislation, while the U.S. approach reflects an American system that often relies on ex post judicial regulation of all police powers.[160]

c. Undercover Operations and Entrapment

The pattern of European ex ante regulation compared to North American ex post regulation is also reflected in undercover operations, which can play a vital role in terrorism investigations. For example, undercover agents in Spain must be authorized to act undercover and report their activities to a judge. This authorization

156 Public Order and Security Act, Act 1 of 2002 s.33.

157 Anti-Terrorism Act, 1997 as amended s.21A(2) available at https://www.unodc.org/tldb/showDocument.do?documentUid=7788&q=cordon&edit_btn=SEARCH.

158 Chapter 23, "Australia" at 661.

159 MacWade v. Kelly 460 F 3d 260 (2nd cir 2006); Cassidy v. Chertoff 471 F 3d 67 (2d cir 2006).

160 On the limits of ex post judicial controls throughout the American justice system, see Craig Bradley *The Failure of the Criminal Procedure Revolution* (Philadelphia: University of Pennsylvania Press, 1993).

also allows judicial authorization of necessary and proportionate law breaking by the undercover agent.[161] A 2006 Italian law similarly regulates undercover operations subject to judicial authorization.[162] In Slovenia, undercover operations, including surveillance, are regulated by the Code of Criminal Procedure and have to be authorized by the prosecutor or an investigative judge.[163]

In contrast to the preceding European examples, undercover agents and informers are used extensively in American and Canadian terrorism investigations without any ex ante legislative or judicial regulation. The only regulation is ex post determinations of whether the prosecution must be stopped because of the existence of entrapment. The American federal entrapment defence focuses on whether the suspect was predisposed to commit a crime before he or she was approached for what are often elaborate and sustained sting operations. In theory, an American federal prosecutor must prove beyond a reasonable doubt that the accused was predisposed to commit a terrorist crime before he or she is subject to stings.[164] The 2nd Circuit recently held that an accused's desire to "inflict harm on the U.S." and "to be willing to die like a martyr" was sufficient predisposition to justify a prolonged and sophisticated sting. One judge argued in dissent that the accused's grievances are common among Muslims and in most cases will "never combust" unless accompanied, as in the case, with a year-long campaign of inducements by an informer.[165] The restraints of the entrapment defence are illusory, because as Sudha Setty notes, American juries have rejected entrapment defences in all terrorism cases where they have been raised.[166] Human Rights Watch has reported that elaborate terrorism stings in the United States have undermined the legitimacy of some criminal convictions by targeting those with mental disabilities and involving appeals to both the religion and the economic interests of those who are targeted. Its report also raises concerns that juries have been exposed to prejudicial evidence about the accused's religious and political views.[167]

The British and Canadian courts, as well as the European Court of Human Rights,[168] apply a more demanding test for entrapment than American courts. The objective approach used by these courts is more attentive to the legitimacy of the initial decision to target the accused for a terrorist sting than the subjective test used by American federal courts. At the same time, British and Canadian courts have

161 Chapter 10, "Spain" at 317.
162 Chapter 9, "Italy" at 281.
163 Chapter 14, "Slovenia" at 409.
164 Jacobson v. U.S., 502 U.S. 540 (1992).
165 U.S. v. Cromitie, 727 F.3d. 194 2nd Cir, 2013.
166 Chapter 2, "The United States" at 54.
167 Human Rights Watch *Illusion of Justice: Human Rights Abuses in US Terrorism Prosecutions* July 2014.
168 Teixeira de Castro v. Portugal (1998) 28 EHRR 101.

left the door open to "random virtue testing" based on the person's presence at a suspicious or high-crime area.[169] Perceptions of random targeting of Muslims could undermine the legitimacy of some terrorism prosecutions.[170] Reliance on ex post regulation of state conduct in terrorism investigations is also affected by the drastic nature of ex post remedies which if applied would stop the prosecution of suspected terrorists.

d. The Use of Intelligence as Evidence

In some countries, electronic surveillance is authorized by the executive, while in others it is authorized by judicial order. Keith Syrett notes how under the UK's Regulation of Investigatory Powers Act 2000[171] even the most intrusive form of surveillance requires only ministerial authorization. An important feature of the UK regime is that electronic surveillance generally cannot be used as evidence. There has been much interest in using intelligence as evidence, but the overall conclusion has been that this cannot be done without sacrificing secrecy deemed essential by the security services.[172] Although electronic surveillance collected by intelligence agencies in Australia and Canada could be used as evidence, there are also secrecy concerns. Intelligence agencies in those countries often provide tips and encourage the police to conduct their own activities so as to maximize the secrecy of the intelligence agency's sources and methods. There is a danger that such an approach may result in inefficient and duplicative terrorism investigations. Canada's inquiry into the Air India bombing concluded that intelligence agencies must become more comfortable with new evidentiary obligations in terrorism investigations while police must become more accepting of using information from intelligence agencies and more sensitive to legitimate secrecy interests.[173]

Concerns about secrecy do not seem to be a barrier for many countries in continental Europe when they use intelligence as evidence. A 2007 Spanish judicial decision accepted intelligence reports as a form of expert evidence.[174] The Constitutional Court of Belgium decided in 2011 that because of the importance of protecting witnesses, secret evidence not disclosed to the accused could be used in national security cases.[175] Courts in Romania also have the discretion of

169 R. v. Barnes [1991] 1 SCR 449; R. v. Loosely [2001] UKHL 53.
170 Kent Roach "Entrapment and Equality in Terrorism Prosecutions" (2011) 80 *Mississippi Law Journal* 1455.
171 C. 23.
172 Chapter 6, "The United Kingdom" at 178.
173 Commission of Inquiry into the Investigation of the Bombing of Air India Flight 182 *Air India Flight 182 A Canadian Tragedy* Vol 3 (Ottawa: Public Works, 2010) at 91–9.
174 Chapter 10, "Spain" at 318.
175 Chapter 6, "Belgium" at 266.

whether to use classified information despite the accused not being able to see it.[176] Swiss criminal procedure also contemplates the use of evidence not seen by the accused, but only if the accused has been informed of "the essential content" of the information.[177] The use of specialized terrorism courts in countries such as France and Spain may also facilitate the use of intelligence as evidence if only as background.

Intelligence can have evidentiary value, especially in relation to broad terrorism offences that target remote forms of preparation and association with terrorists. Nevertheless, the use of intelligence as evidence is problematic when the intelligence is not subject to full adversarial testing. As will be seen, similar problems emerge in the context of terrorist listings and administrative and immigration detention.

e. Electronic Surveillance and Metadata

The PATRIOT Act expanded the ability to obtain warrants under the Foreign Intelligence Surveillance Act so long as a significant but not necessarily sole purpose of the warrant remained the collection of foreign intelligence. The PATRIOT Act also updated the 1978 FISA act to provide for roving warrants, searches of emails and delays in notifying people that they had been subject to invasions of privacy. Sudha Setty details in Chapter 2 how the U.S. National Security Agency has collected telephonic subscriber or meta data of U.S. persons under s.215 of the PATRIOT Act. She notes how the Edward Snowden leaks revealed "a nonpublic body of law that allowed the NSA to amass the metadata (time, location, duration and other information not containing content) for all domestic and some international phone calls."[178] These revelations cast doubt on the restraining effects of the need for prior judicial authorization. They have led to calls for reforms to allow security-cleared special advocates to challenge the government's requests for judicial warrants to authorize surveillance. As Professor Setty notes, the result has been some changes in executive policies, but so far no legislative reform. This accords with a trend observed elsewhere of the United States relying more on executive than legislative regulation of counter-terrorism powers.

Metadata about subscriber information is also a contentious issue in Europe. An EU directive enacted in response to the 2004 Madrid and 2005 London bombings required the retention of data by telecommunication companies for six to twenty-four months. This directive was found to violate domestic constitutional protections in

[176] Chapter 17, "Romania" at 506.
[177] Chapter 7, "Switzerland" at 216.
[178] Chapter 2, "The United States" at 59.

a number of countries, including by the German Constitutional Court,[179] but was upheld by the European Court of Justice in 2009[180] on jurisdictional grounds. In 2014, however, the European Court of Justice held that the directive was an unjustified violation of privacy. It stressed the ability of subscriber information to reveal the identity of both sides of communications and the length of the communication. In this way, access to metadata violated privacy even though it did not reveal the content of the communications. The European Court of Justice held that the data retention directive was a disproportionate infringement of privacy in part because it allowed subsequent access with respect to the investigation of all serious crime and not just terrorism, and also because the directive provided no measures to prevent abuse, especially if the data were transferred outside the EU.[181] As is frequently the case, this judicial decision left the door open to the enactment of better tailored and less rights-restrictive counter-terrorism measures.

The UK Parliament responded to ECJ decision with emergency legislation requiring the retention of data but also establishing some role of oversight by a reviewer of anti-terrorism law.[182] The emergency legislation has, however, been criticized for allowing extra-territorial data retention orders and for allowing data retention for a broad range of reasons, including those relating to the economic well-being of the UK. It remains to be seen whether this new law will be upheld when it is challenged in court. This episode underlines the reality that courts often may not have the last word on matters related to the proportionality of counter-terrorism measures.

f. Intelligence Agencies and the Collection of Human Intelligence and Evidence

Intelligence agencies rely not only on electronic surveillance but the collection of intelligence from human sources. The Supreme Court of Canada has recently rejected an attempt to extend police informer privilege to the human sources of the Canadian Security Intelligence Service, but the government quickly responded with a legislated privilege that can only be overcome if the accused's innocence is at

179 Cian Murphy notes that such decisions place member states in a position where compliance with domestic constitutional norms would put them in violation of EU directives. Murphy *EU Counter-Terrorism Law* supra at 173. Such conflicts raise issues discussed in Chapter 1 of this collection about whether the European project of harmonization of counter-terrorism laws is desirable or possible.

180 Ireland v. European Parliament and Council [2009] ECR 1–593.

181 Digital Rights Ireland v. Minister of Communications Joined Cases C-293/12 and C-594/12.

182 Data Retention and Investigatory Powers Act, 2014 c.27.

stake.[183] New legislation in Malaysia and Singapore attempts to ensure that identities of informers always remain secret.[184] Nevertheless, it is easy to see that in some cases the identity of an informer must be known to ensure fairness if the intelligence is used as evidence to impose legal consequences on people.

A controversial 2003 law allows the Australian Security and Intelligence Organization (ASIO) to apply for a judicial warrant to detain and question a person for up to twenty-four hours if there are reasonable grounds to believe that questioning will substantially assist in the collection of important intelligence in relation to a terrorism offence. It is an offence not to answer questions or to give misleading answers. The legally compelled answers are generally not admissible in subsequent proceedings, but there is no limit on the admissibility of derivative evidence. The questioning is carried out before an executive authority because of concerns that having judges act as investigators would be inconsistent with the separation of powers and limits on the judicial functions. Davis, McGarrity and Williams report sixteen uses of these extraordinary provisions, though the numbers have been declining.[185] The law was supposed to sunset in 2016 but has been extended until 2018, thus rejecting proposals by the independent monitor of terrorism laws that the powers should be abolished.[186]

The ASIO warrants can be compared to a similar controversial power in Canada: investigative hearings. Investigative hearings also require people on pain of criminal penalty to answer questions relevant to a terrorism investigation. Unlike ASIO hearings, Canadian investigative hearings are carried out before a judge who the Supreme Court of Canada has determined should apply the rules of evidence and apply the presumption of an open court. There is a prohibition on using both the answers and evidence derived from the answers in subsequent criminal proceedings except perjury. The Supreme Court of Canada upheld the constitutionality of these controversial powers in 2004 in the only case in which they have been used, but dissenters argued that they violated the separation of powers and the independence of the judiciary by requiring judges to preside at what is effectively a police investigation.[187] As Robert Diab notes in Chapter 3, these powers were allowed to sunset in 2007 but were re-enacted in 2013 subject to a renewable five-year sunset.[188]

183 Canada v. Harkat 2014 SCC 37. For arguments that the new privilege may unintentionally make it more difficult for human sources to be transferred from intelligence agencies to police forces for purposes of prosecutions and that the innocence at stake exception is underinclusive given the use of intelligence as evidence in immigration law, see Kent Roach "The Problems with the New CSIS Human Source Privilege in Bill C-44" (2014) 61 *Criminal Law Quarterly* 451.

184 Chapter 22, "Singapore" at 631.

185 Chapter 23, "Australia" at 662.

186 Counter-Terrorism Legislation Amendment (Foreign Terrorist Fighters) Act, 2014. No 116, 2014.

187 Re Section 83.28 of the Criminal Code [2004] 2 S.C.R. 248; Re Vancouver Sun [2004] 2 S.C.R. 332.

188 Chapter 3, "Canada" at 87.

Although a number of anti-terrorism laws are enacted as temporary laws, the trend seems to be towards renewal of such laws.

An alternative to either the Australian or Canadian approach is to make it an offence for a person not to disclose information that would be relevant to a terrorism investigation. Such offences were first used in Northern Ireland but were repealed when the Terrorism Act, 2000 was originally enacted. They were reinserted in the UK in 2001 and are also found in some recent legislation in Singapore.[189] The existence of such an offence may facilitate the coercive recruitment of human sources in a manner that is less visible and controversial than under the Australian and Canadian provisions.

There is a danger that intelligence agencies may respect human rights less than police services because intelligence, unlike evidence, is produced for preventive purposes and is not generally reviewed in courts. Shiri Krebs in Chapter 18 on Israel notes how the intelligence service was authorized to use harsh interrogation techniques before the Israeli Supreme Court in a landmark 1999 decision held that techniques such as stress positions and shaking were not legally authorized. Krebs notes, however, that:

> In spite of these strong and clear words, absolutely forbidding any use of torture (in the wide sense) during investigations conducted by the ISA, the Court opened a window for the executive to continue using torture in extreme circumstances, in the form of the criminal defense of necessity. At the end of its decision, the Court stated that in rare and extreme circumstances, the investigator may enjoy – *ex post facto* – the necessity defense to bar individual criminal liability. The decision was therefore justly criticized for creating – and allowing for – a gap between the general and absolute norm prohibiting torture, and the practical immunity that could be given to torturers.[190]

The Israeli Supreme Court prohibited ex ante attempts by the executive to regulate harsh interrogation, but it left open the possibility that courts might excuse harsh interrogation after the fact by means of the necessity defence. Individual interrogators were left to decide how far they should go in interrogations. Although some posit that the threat of criminal prosecution might deter harsh interrogations,[191] the interrogators could easily conclude that they were unlikely to be prosecuted, and that if prosecuted they might be excused or pardoned. Kreb's warnings are both important and depressing because they suggest that a celebrated anti-torture legal precedent

[189] Anti-Terrorism Crime and Security Act, 2001 s.117; Terrorism Suppression of Financing Act, 2003 s.10; Terrorism (Suppression of Bombings Act, 2007 s.4; Hostage Taking Act, 2010 s. 5.

[190] Chapter 18, "Israel" (footnotes omitted) at 523.

[191] Oren Gross "Chaos and Rules: Should Responses to Violent Crisis Always Be Constitutional?" (2003) 112 *Yale L.J.* 1011

might have had substitution effects that encouraged extra-legal harsh interrogation. This is another important reminder that students of comparative counter-terrorism law must be aware of both the law in the books and the law in action, including substitution effects between multiple counter-terrorism instruments. Such insights are part of what makes the study of comparative counter-terrorism law such a challenging and dynamic subject.

VIII. PROSCRIPTION AND LISTING OF TERRORIST GROUPS AND INDIVIDUALS

Proscription or listing of terrorist groups and individuals presents challenges to the separation of powers and human rights because it often involves an executive decision made on the basis of secret intelligence. These decisions are made without prior notice to the listed person, and they do not provide that person with a right to know or challenge the evidence (often intelligence) used to justify the listing. The executive act of listing often has severe consequences on individuals such as freezing their assets and imposing travel bans.

All twenty-two jurisdictions represented in this collection have various listing regimes, generally tied to listings by the UN Security Council and the EU. Even Brazil, which has not criminalized terrorism,[192] uses such international lists. The Security Council has taken steps to make the listing process fairer by appointing an ombudsperson to assist with delisting, but the process remains secret and dominated by both the executive within the UN and the executive and security services of those on the Security Council. The Security Council's 2014 affirmation and expansion of terrorist listing in Security Council Resolutions 2178, 2161 and 2160 raise concerns about the effectiveness of listing as a process for imposing travel bans and asset freezes. Listing has always been a process that is one step behind the evolving nature of terrorism. This was true of al Qaeda, but it may be even more true with respect to the recruitment of tens of thousands of foreigners who have joined the forces of the Islamic State in Syria and Iraq.

The UK's Terrorism Act, 2000 allows the Secretary of State to list and proscribe organizations that are "concerned with terrorism." There are appeals to a Proscribed Organisations Appeal Commission that can consider secret evidence not disclosed to representatives of the listed organization but subject to challenge by a security-cleared special advocate. Professor Syrett indicates that there are sixty-six proscribed organizations in the UK, but that only one group has successfully challenged its listing on the grounds that it had renounced terrorism.[193]

[192] Chapter 5, "Brazil" at 159.
[193] Chapter 6, "The United Kingdom" at 179.

In the UK, there are separate offences under the Terrorism Act, 2000 relating to membership in a proscribed terrorist organization. Israel also has similar offences for being a member of, supporting or attending a meeting of a proscribed organization. In this way, both British and Israeli law have residues of old forms of security based on the banning of subversive groups. This older form of security is now being modernized in the guise of modern terrorism laws. As Krebs discusses, a counter-terrorism bill in Israel would allow the Minister of Defence to list not only terrorist groups but auxiliary or dawah organizations, including "charitable societies and other social organizations that are connected to terror organizations (such as Hamas in Gaza or the Muslim Brotherhood in Egypt) and function as their community service system by providing educational, medical and welfare services to its supporters and to the general population."[194] Krebs raises concerns that such a broad approach to defining a terrorist organization could stop humanitarian assistance to the poor. Such an approach would find support in the U.S. Supreme Court's 2010 *Holder v. Humanitarian Law Project*[195] decision, which held that financial support for the humanitarian activities of a listed terrorist group was a crime on the basis that such support freed up funds for commission of terrorist activities by the group.

Listing in many countries is implemented through subordinate laws that allow for the implementation of international obligations. Such listing by way of regulation under the UK's *United Nations Act* was held by the UK Supreme Court to be deficient in *HM Treasury v. Ahmed*[196] because the rights of citizens should not be interfered with without clear parliamentary authorization. Parliament then promptly provided such clear authorization.[197] Parliamentary authorization of terrorist listing does not provide a full answer to the fairness concerns about listing a person on the basis of secret evidence. This episode again demonstrates the ability of legislatures quickly to reassert and refashion their interest in counter-terrorism measures found deficient by the court.

Most states in continental Europe have listing mechanisms tied to UN and EU lists. A 2003 Swiss law only contemplates the implementation of UN international sanctions, such as those of the 1267 committee, which lists entities associated with the Taliban and al Qaeda, and not the EU listing, because Switzerland is not a member of the European Union.[198] A 2001 law in Italy established a Financial Security Committee chaired by the Director General of the Treasury, who proposes listing

[194] Chapter 18, "Israel" at 516.

[195] 130 S. Ct. 2705 (2010). Interestingly, this seems inconsistent with other U.S. Supreme Court decisions that provides that people are free under the First Amendment to give money to domestic political groups. Citizens United v. Federal Election Commission 130 S.Ct. 876 (2010).

[196] [2010] UKSC 2.

[197] Terrorist Asset Freezing Act, 2010 c.38.

[198] Chapter 7, "Switzerland" at 203.

and delisting. Sabrina Praduroux notes that there are concerns about "the indefinite duration of the listing measure" and its use of intelligence without any "mandatory judicial procedure." The Italian courts have also retreated from using listings by the executive as proof in criminal trials.[199] Listing was a "new phenomenon" for Croatia, as it was for many states, before the UN Security Council and the Council of the European Union effectively required member states to adopt it. Marissabell Škorić argues that listing "is mostly the result of political decisions."[200]

Under a 2006 Royal Decree, Belgium has a procedure for implementing EU listings. Belgium has not yet implemented a national list, something that in Chapter 8 Anne Weyemberg and Celine Cocq predict will be criticized by the next review conducted by the FATF. At the same time, Belgium has a reason to be cautious about lists because it has had experience with wrongly listed people. It initially failed to obtain the delisting of a couple, Sayadi-Vinck, from the UN 1267 list of persons associated with al Qaeda or the Taliban. This came after the couple was found innocent in 2005 after two years of court investigation in Belgium during which their assets were frozen. The couple was eventually removed from the UN list in 2009 after a favourable 2008 ruling from the UN Human Rights Committee.[201] The ultimate authority with respect to delisting lies not with domestic courts or the Human Rights Committee but with the committee formed under UN Security Council Resolution 1267. The Security Council has responded to fairness criticisms of its listing process by creating an ombudsperson who can make delisting recommendations subject to a veto by the 1267 committee. The reluctance of countries to share intelligence that might support the listing makes it difficult to review listings on their merits. The European Court of Justice has in a series of cases invalidated listings on the procedural basis that not enough information has been disclosed to allow the listed person to defend himself or herself.[202] Such reviews, however, stop short of merits-based review of the secret intelligence that was said to justify the listing in the first place. As such, they may not always be effective in clearing a wrongly listed person's name.

Terrorist listings can have drastic effects on those whose assets are frozen and travel is banned. The Czech Republic adopts UN and EU listings but also has a provision for humanitarian exemptions from the effects of listing.[203] Listing mimics an intelligence process of watch listing. Listed entities that challenge their listing or seek humanitarian exemptions run the risk of attracting more attention from the authorities. Section 10 of the UK's Terrorism Act, 2000 recognizes this reality by

[199] Chapter 9, "Italy" at 284.
[200] Chapter 13, "Croatia" at 380.
[201] Chapter 8, "Belgium" at 252.
[202] Kadi 2008 C 402 /05 P; Kadi II (2013) Joined Cases C-584/10 P, C-593/10 P and C-595/10 P.
[203] Chapter 16, "The Czech Republic" at 472.

providing that actions in relation to attempts to become delisted should not be used as evidence of membership or support of a proscribed group, but similar provisions are often lacking in the laws of other countries.

Sudha Setty indicates that the U.S. Secretary of State's ability to list foreign terrorist organizations "has been an important tool for U.S. counterterrorism efforts."[204] A listing, which can be done on the basis of involvement or incitement of terrorism, triggers asset freezing, increased surveillance and criminal material support prosecutions for those who support the organization. There are internal reviews of listings as well as the possibility of judicial challenge, but these must be undertaken within thirty days of listing. The executive can supplement its defence of a listing with classified information not disclosed to the applicant.

Both Australia and Canada allow listing under multiple laws. In Australia, over one thousand individuals and nineteen groups are listed.[205] The basis for listing has expanded over time and is no longer tied to the UN listing. Davis, McGarrity and Williams find the Australian approach to listing to be "extremely wide and problematic. It is arguable, for example, that an organisation could be proscribed as a terrorist organisation if just one member of that organisation praised liberation struggles in East Timor or against a colonial power."[206] In contrast, Diab suggests that a group could not be listed in Canada "solely on the basis of speech or advocacy of terrorism."[207] This, however, does not mean that listing is infallible in Canada. Diab recounts a 2009 case where a Canadian citizen listed by the UN 1267 committee had to seek judicial relief to be allowed to return to Canada from Sudan.[208] The man was subsequently delisted by the UN near the end of 2011. Listing on the basis of secret intelligence is a fallible process, and its effects on a wrongly listed person can be severe.

In both Australia and Canada, listing by the executive is intended to be conclusive proof in legal proceedings that a listed group is in fact a terrorist group, something that would not be allowed in most European jurisdictions. As Professor Diab notes in Chapter 3, this substitutes an executive decision on the basis of secret evidence for proof beyond a reasonable doubt with public evidence.[209] Listing has, however, played a minimal role in Canadian terrorism prosecutions, which have almost all involved homegrown, self-radicalized groups. Listing processes seem to be one step behind the terrorists and an example of fighting the last war.

[204] Chapter 2, "The United States" at 60.
[205] Chapter 23, "Australia" at 645.
[206] Chapter 23, "Australia" at 665.
[207] Chapter 3, "Canada" at 92.
[208] Abdelrazik v. Canada (Minister of Foreign Affairs), [2010] 1 FCR 267, 2009 FC 580.
[209] Chapter 3, "Canada" at 92.

Despite a growing number of successful legal challenges to the fairness of listing, as well as concerns that listings may not capture the dynamic of homegrown and self-radicalizing terrorism, listing of terrorist individuals and groups is a common feature in all the jurisdictions examined in this collection. Moreover, it is required under various supra-national mandates and was reaffirmed by the UN Security Council in September 2014 as a instrument to respond to the growing number of foreign terrorist fighters. At the same time, unfairness of executive listing based on secret evidence is increasingly being acknowledged by courts, including the European Court of Justice. The next question is whether such unfairness can be justified as necessary to prevent terrorism. The answer in large part depends on the effectiveness of laws that try to prevent terrorism by targeting its financing.

IX. TERRORISM FINANCING

The international and domestic listing processes examined in the preceding section cannot be fully understood outside the context of laws against terrorism financing. Such laws require financial institutions and others that handle money and property to report financial transactions involving suspected terrorists and to take steps to freeze their assets and assist in their forfeiture. Lists of suspected terrorists are necessary to assist in these processes. They are also necessary to assist in the enforcement of travel bans.

In the immediate aftermath of 9/11, the UN Security Council and the United States stressed the need for laws against terrorist financing. This may have been a product of bin Laden's reputation as a financier, one that the 9/11 Commission found was exaggerated. The Commission also found that terrorism financing laws would not have detected the half million American dollars that financed the four hijackings.[210] Despite evidence of the limited efficacy of elaborate laws against terrorism financing and concerns about the fairness of the listing regime, the Security Council reaffirmed its faith and commitment to the listing regime in 2014 as a response to the growing number of foreign terrorist fighters joining the Islamic State.[211]

Terrorism financing laws generally create a broad range of crimes for supporting or dealing with terrorist property, provide in rem remedies against property and funds believed to be associated with terrorism and operate as a means to collect intelligence about the flow of resources involving suspected terrorists. The United

[210] National Commission on the Terrorist Attacks Against the United States *The 9/11 Report* supra at 5.4.

[211] The Security Council in S/Res/2160 and S/Res 2161 in June 2014 reaffirmed its commitment to the listing of entities associated with al Qaeda and accompanying travel bans and asset freezing, and also reiterated its determination to use the listing regime against foreign terrorist fighters in S/Res/2178 at para 7 issued in September 2014.

States took the lead on terrorism financing after 9/11. As Professor Setty notes in Chapter 2, the PATRIOT Act amended bank secrecy laws to require more reporting of suspicious transactions. As in many other countries, there have been large increases in the reporting of suspicious transactions in the United States. The U.S. model relies more on criminal prosecutions under various material support offences and less on administrative regulation such as is used in the UK, especially with regards to charities.[212] Professor Setty reports that material prosecutions have been "an effective, if highly controversial" device.[213] The U.S. Supreme Court affirmed in its 2010 *Holder v. Humanitarian Law Project* decision that a person can be guilty of providing material support to a listed foreign terrorist organization simply for providing assistance for the humanitarian activities of the group. The majority of the Court held that this very broad offence did not violate the First Amendment because people could still voice their support for proscribed organizations.[214]

China enacted a new terrorist financing offence in 2001. Li Zhe reports that "the funds given to finance legitimate and humanitarian activities by a terrorist group can also be deemed as financing terrorist activities since the illegal nature of the organization still remains."[215] This follows the logic of the *Holder v. Humanitarian Law Project* case. China established an Anti–Money Laundering Bureau in 2003 that considers suspicious transactions reports. China became a member of the FATF in 2008, underlining the significant influence of that organization and the increasing need for comparative lawyers to be attentive to non-state actors that influence the content of laws. The FATF is a voluntary organization emerging from the G7 group of nations. It originally monitored only money laundering laws, but added terrorism financing to its mandate after 9/11 despite the fact that terrorism financing often involves only small amounts of funds often derived from legitimate sources, whereas money laundering involves large amounts of funds from illegitimate sources. As will be seen, the number of suspicious transactions in relation to terrorism financing in every country is dwarfed by the reporting of suspicious transactions in relation to money laundering. This raises concerns about the efficacy of terrorism financing laws.

Some data contained in this collection suggest that the terrorism financing regime is not achieving particularly impressive results. For example:

[212] Mark Sidel "Choices and Approaches: Anti-Terrorism Law and Civil Society in the United States and the United Kingdom After September 11" (2011) 61 *University of Toronto Law Journal* 119.

[213] Chapter 3, "The United States" at 62.

[214] Holder v. Humanitarian Law Project, 130 S. Ct. 2705, 2717 (2010).

[215] Chapter 21, "China" at 595.

- In the European financial centre of Switzerland in 2012, there were only fifteen cases of suspected terrorism financing in relation to three incidents involving less than $8 million Swiss francs. From 2003 to 2012, there were eighty-six terrorism financing reports to the Swiss financial intelligence centre with only one conviction so far being recorded. There are twenty-five cases still pending and ten suspended cases, but fifty have been the subject of a no-proceeding order or have been abandoned.[216]
- In the Asian financial centre of Singapore, there has been no terrorism financing charges or convictions.[217]
- Japan has had no terrorism financing prosecutions since enacting its terrorism financing law in 2002, even though its financial intelligence agency reported over sixty-four thousand suspicious transactions for money laundering or terrorism financing offences in 2012.[218]
- South Africa has a financial intelligence centre that as in most countries covers both money laundering and terrorist property. It has received over 6 million suspicious transaction reports but no terrorism financing convictions.[219]
- There has been no terrorism financing conviction in Belgium, and its financial intelligence agency in 2012 referred only twenty files representing $1.9 million to judicial authorities with regards to terrorism financing.[220]
- There has been no terrorism financing conviction in Slovenia, and only 13 reports to its financial intelligence centre involved suspected terrorism financing.[221]
- Romania has broad terrorism financing laws but no convictions.[222]
- Greece has recorded no terrorism financing convictions since enacting its terrorism financing law in 2008.[223]
- In Poland in 2010, only 16 of 15,357 suspicious transactions were related to terrorism financing.[224]
- There is "no jurisprudence" under Spain's terrorism financing offence.[225]

[216] Chapter 7, "Switzerland" at 229.
[217] Chapter 22, "Singapore" at 630.
[218] Chapter 20, "Japan" at 574–575.
[219] Chapter 19, "South Africa" at 552–555.
[220] Chapter 8, "Belgium" at 256.
[221] Chapter 14, "Slovenia" at 411.
[222] Chapter 17, "Romania" at 504.
[223] Chapter 12, "Greece" at 359.
[224] Chapter 15, "Poland" at 440.
[225] Chapter 10, "Spain" at 321.

To be sure, there are more terrorist financing convictions in some countries. Italy has had twenty-nine terrorism financing convictions between 2000 and 2004.[226] This number may have increased after Italy enacted a specific terrorism financing offence in 2007 after being rated only partially compliant by the FATF. There are about four hundred reports of suspicious terrorist financing each year. Partially through co-operating suspects, Italy has prosecuted a broad range of terrorism financing acts involving charity or zakat, small companies and illegal activities, including drug trafficking and forgery.

Prosecutions should not be the only measure of the effectiveness of terrorism financing laws. Even though it does not have laws against terrorism financing, Brazil collects intelligence about suspected terrorism financing through a financial intelligence centre designed to combat money laundering.[227] Italy has also made use of asset freezes that are not dependent on prosecution or conviction.[228] Georgios Triantafyllou argues that the freezing of assets can be defended as a preventive measure against terrorism.[229] At the same time, this raises the question discussed previously about the difficulty of obtaining effective remedies for those who may be wrongly listed on the basis of secret but perhaps unreliable intelligence.

Convictions for terrorism financing raise complex issues about appropriate punishment. Material support of terrorism offences often results in long terms of imprisonment in the United States even though a person may not have the intent to assist terrorism. Professor Setty reports that such prosecutions have been "an effective, if highly controversial" device that has deterred charitable giving, especially to Islamic charities.[230] Australia and Canada have taken a more lenient approach. Australian judges have provided suspended sentences to men who pled guilty to supplying money to the LTTE, also known as the Tamil Tigers. A similar case in Canada attracted a six-month sentence that was upheld after a prosecutorial appeal.[231] The sentences in these cases underline the difficulty of defining terrorism in relation to a civil war in Sri Lanka. They also suggest that despite the "terrorist" label, terrorist financing convictions may not always merit significant punishment.

A few striking conclusions emerge from the information in this collection about terrorism financing laws. The first is the similarity of the terrorism financing regimes in countries with very different legal traditions. In this respect, there is much less difference in terrorism financing regimes than found among domestic definitions of

[226] Chapter 9, "Italy" at 287.
[227] Chapter 5, "Brazil" at 159.
[228] Chapter 9, "Italy" at 289.
[229] Chapter 12, "Greece" at 361.
[230] Chapter 2, "The United States" at 62.
[231] R. v. Thambaithurai 2011 BCCA 137.

terrorism examined in Chapter 1. This underlines the "off the rack" quality of many terrorism financing regimes. For example, Indonesia and Egypt enacted terrorism financing laws after 9/11 that bore little resemblance to how their domestic legal systems treated terrorism.[232]

Another conclusion is that many countries have been responsive to criticisms from the FATF that their terrorism financing regime was deficient. For example, Italy created a specific terrorist financing offence in 2007 after FATF had criticized its prior approach, which was to consider terrorism financing as part of the offence of participating in a terrorist group.[233] Singapore increased the maximum penalties for terrorism financing in 2013 and included provisions to protect the identity of informers in any terrorism financing prosecution, even though there have been no prosecutions in that jurisdiction.[234] Japan's terrorism financing regime has also been criticized as deficient by the FATF, and there are legislative proposals before the Diet to expand the law to apply to the provision of goods other than money to terrorist organizations and to apply to indirect forms of financing terrorism.[235] These amendments may strengthen Japan's terrorism financing regime, but the results from other countries with compliant regimes suggest that terrorism financing convictions might well continue to be rare under even a strengthened regime.

Terrorism financing laws in large part depend on listing of suspected terrorists, and there is increasing recognition of the unfairness of listing based on secret intelligence. To the extent that financial institutions enforce terrorism financing laws, there may be concerns about profiling those who may share names with the listed, and terrorism financing laws have disproportionate effects on Muslim charities. The possibility that the terrorism financing regime may have counterproductive effects by playing into a narrative of discriminatory profiling of Muslims cannot be dismissed.

Terrorism financing is difficult to control. Professor Perrin and Dr. Gafner in Chapter 7 on Switzerland acknowledge that there have been no terrorism financing convictions in that country, but argue that the laws may still deter terrorism financing.[236] A recurring problem, however, is that terrorism financing laws have been tacked on to and are dwarfed by money laundering laws aimed at organized crime. Terrorism unfortunately requires limited funds, and the funds can be generated by legitimate means. Although most jurisdictions have broad terrorism financing offences, few report many successful prosecutions. The nominal sentences given by both Australian and Canadian courts to Sri Lanka ex-patriates

[232] Roach *The 9/11 Effect* supra ch.3.
[233] Chapter 9, "Italy" at 286.
[234] Chapter 22, "Singapore" at 629–633.
[235] Chapter 20, "Japan" at 571.
[236] Chapter 7, "Switzerland" at 233.

who provided money to the LTTE reflects the difficulties of defining terrorism and of prosecuting terrorism financing as a serious criminal offence. The UN Security Council, led by the United States, invested heavily in regulating terrorism financing after 9/11. More recently, it has doubled down and confirmed its commitment to using listing, asset freezing and travel bans to combat foreign terrorist fighters associated with the Islamic State. Unfortunately, this commitment has been made despite growing evidence showing that listing and terrorism financing laws harm human rights by treating people unfairly while also not being obviously effective in countering terrorism.

X. IMMIGRATION MEASURES

The United States, the UK, Israel, Canada, Australia and Japan were attracted after 9/11 to using immigration law as a form of counter-terrorism law even though the ultimate remedy in immigration law – deportation – would export terrorists to another country. This trend was encouraged by Security Council Resolution 1373,[237] which highlighted the dangers of terrorists abusing refugee status even though none of the 9/11 hijackers applied for asylum and democracies could not send terrorists who sought refugee status back to countries where they would be killed or tortured. Many others countries, including many in continental Europe, did not focus on using their immigration regimes for counter-terrorism purposes. This finding again underlines the importance for comparative lawyers to examine the law in action and not simply the national security provisions that most countries have as part of their immigration laws.

The focus on immigration law as a response to terrorism was often motivated by a sense that the terrorist threat was a foreign threat. This perception has eroded in the years since 9/11, as many countries have encountered homegrown terrorism, including that inspired by al Qaeda and more recently the Islamic State. At the same time, some countries, including the UK and Canada, still are devoting substantial energies to attempting to deport non-citizens who are perceived to be security threats. Such efforts are complicated by the danger that a person deported to Middle Eastern countries on the basis of allegations of involvement in terrorism will often be at risk of being tortured. This affirms the interdependency of counter-terrorism regimes in different countries and the need to study counter-terrorism in a comparative manner.

Security Resolution 2178 now places greater emphasis on preventing citizens from leaving Western democracies to become foreign terrorist fighters or placing

[237] S/Res/1373 para 3(f)(g).

restrictions on those who may return after engaging in foreign terrorism. Western democracies will struggle with these issues because citizens often have more rights than non-citizens. The concluding part of this section, however, will suggest that some democracies are starting to use measures inspired by immigration law – travel restrictions and deprivation of citizenship – and to apply them to citizens suspected of involvement in terrorism.[238]

A. *Post-9/11 Uses of Immigration Law as Anti-Terrorism Law*

Some of the most draconian laws against terrorism are immigration laws that apply only to non-citizens. Immigration laws are even more vague and broad than broad terrorism criminal offences. They have lower burdens of proof and often allow the use of secret evidence or intelligence not disclosed to the non-citizen. Although democracies after 9/11 thankfully stopped short of internment of people on the basis of their race, religion or national or ethnic origin, they employed laws against suspected terrorists who were non-citizens that would not have been accepted if applied to citizens.

Section 412 of the PATRIOT Act authorizes the detention of aliens certified by the Attorney General of the United States as engaged in terrorism or otherwise a danger to U.S. national security. The initial detention period was for seven days, but detention could be renewed for six-month periods as long as removal or criminal proceedings had been started and the Attorney General certified that release would threaten national security or the safety of the community. Given the difficulties of removal to countries such as Egypt and Syria that torture terrorist suspects, this provision could have amounted to indefinite executive-certified preventive detention. This was aggressive post-9/11 legislation especially because the U.S. Supreme Court had disapproved of indeterminate detention of non-citizens shortly before 9/11.[239] In any event, Section 412 was not used because pre-9/11 immigration laws provided sufficient and often pre-textual grounds for detention and removal of foreign nationals suspected of involvement in terrorism. This serves as a reminder of the need for students of comparative counter-terrorism law to be aware of how the ordinary law as well as special measures can be used against terrorist suspects.

As Professor Setty notes in Chapter 2, immigration laws fail to provide guarantees such as the right to a lawyer, the right to a speedy trial, the confrontation clause the prohibits secret evidence and the presumption of innocence that were all constitutionally guaranteed in the American criminal justice system. Immigration

[238] David Cole warned of this type of migration of measures in 2003. See David Cole *Enemy Aliens* (New York: New Press, 2003).

[239] Zadvydas v. Davis 533 U.S. 678 (2001).

hearings were held in secret for a period after 9/11. There was also a special registration program for males from twenty-five countries, all Muslim countries with the exception of North Korea. There were also concerns about abuse in detention facilities. Professor Setty concludes: "Muslims in the immigration system have been subjected to possibly abusive preventive detention, exclusion based on political views, heightened surveillance and arguably unconstitutional racial profiling."[240]

The UK was also active in using immigration law as anti-terrorism law. The UK has broad powers to detain and deport non-citizens for reasons related to the public good, including concerns about involvement in terrorism. Appeals are heard by the Special Immigration Appeal Commission, which can base its decision on secret evidence not disclosed to the non-citizen but challenged by a security-cleared special advocate. Despite these robust pre-existing powers[241], Part IV of the Anti-Terrorism, Crime and Security Act, 2001 provided for the indeterminate detention of suspected non-citizen terrorists who could not deported because of concerns that they would be tortured in their country of citizenship. In order to achieve this result, the UK government became the only country after 9/11 to declare an emergency and derogate from provisions of the European Convention on Human Rights that allow detention only pending deportation. The UK government recognized that deportation of many suspected terrorists to their country of citizenship often in the Middle East was not feasible given the absolute prohibitions on deportation to torture or degrading treatment under both the European Convention and international law.

In 2004, the House of Lords in a landmark decision accepted that there was an emergency threatening the life of a nation as required for a derogation, but held that the derogation was both disproportionate and discriminatory towards non-citizens given that the threat of terrorism extended to citizens.[242] The highest court in the UK issued a non-binding declaration of incompatibility under its statutory bill of rights, but the UK government decided to accept this ruling, which was subsequently affirmed by the Grand Chamber of the European Court of Human Rights.[243] In 2005, the UK government repealed the offending section in its 2001 legislation. At the same time, however, the UK enacted administrative measures called control orders that allowed the liberty of both citizens and non-citizens to be restricted while they remained in the community. These control orders were then applied to all the non-citizens who had formally been detained under the repealed provision of the 2001 Act as well as other non-citizens and citizens. Thus the boldest judicial decisions of the post-9/11 era did not constitute the final word, and the UK

[240] Chapter 2, "The United States" at 65.
[241] Secretary of State v. Rehman [2001] UKHL 47.
[242] A. v. Secretary of State [2004] UKHL 56 (often known as the Belmarsh case after the prison where the non-citizens were subject to indeterminate detention).
[243] A. v. United Kingdom (2009) 49 EHRR 1 (Grand Chamber).

enacted controversial control orders that were nevertheless more proportionate in not authorizing imprisonment and less discriminatory because they applied to both citizens and non-citizens.

With the repeal of indeterminate detention on non-citizens, greater emphasis was placed on the ability to deport suspected terrorists. The UK government tried to deport Abu Qatada, who had been detained under the repealed 2001 law, to Jordan. The European Court of Human Rights accepted that while assurances had reduced the risk of torture, there was still an unacceptable risk that a Jordanian trial would be made unfair by the use of evidence derived from torture.[244] This resulted in the successful negotiation of a treaty between the UK and Jordan.[245] Abu Qatada was eventually tried and acquitted of terrorism charges in Jordan even though he alleged he had not received a fair trial because of the admission of a confession obtained under alleged mistreatment and because of the composition of the court. This case and the non-refoulement principle illustrate the interdependence of countries in combating international terrorism. The human rights situation in Jordan and other countries is very relevant to the treatment of international terrorist suspects in Western democracies.

As Robert Diab explains in Chapter 3, Canada was particularly active in using immigration law for counter-terrorism purposes. Between 2001 to 2003, five male non-citizens, some of whom had been granted refugee status, were apprehended and detained under security certificates as suspected associates of al Qaeda. These men were detained indefinitely even though the deportation was unlikely because it would result in their torture in their countries of citizenship: Egypt, Syria, Morocco and Algeria. Three of the men remain today under security certificates and restricted liberty. One of the five certificates was quashed as unreasonable, and another was abandoned to avoid disclosure of secret information.[246]

In January 2002, the Supreme Court of Canada ruled that those held under security certificates generally could not be deported to a risk of torture. At the same time, the Court articulated the so-called *Suresh* exception, which stated that non-citizens could be deported to a risk of torture under "exceptional circumstances" while also recognizing that such a decision would put Canada in breach of international human rights law.[247] The UK government subsequently attempted without success to persuade the European Court of Human Rights to accept the *Suresh* exception.[248] The Canadian government has relied on it as an alternative argument in the security certificate cases involving the five men. Professor Diab also notes that the *Suresh*

[244] Othman (Abu Qatada) v. UK (2012) 55 EHRR 1.

[245] Mutual Legal Assistance Treaty Between Jordan the UK, April 2013 Cmnd 8612.

[246] Chapter 3, "Canada" at 97–99.

[247] Suresh v. Canada [2002] 1 S.C.R. 3.

[248] Saadi v Italy (2008) 47 EHRR 17.

exception has been applied to rule inadmissible to Canada a person suspected of membership in an Angolan terrorist group.[249] The *Suresh* exception is a regrettable product of post-9/11 North American anxiety about the possibility of a "second attack" being launched from beyond its shores. It reflects a time and a place that resulted in cultural product such as the television series 24, which had its debut in November 2001, shortly before the January 2002 *Suresh* decision, and which celebrated torture as a necessary counter-terrorism measure. Although the *Suresh* exception has been sparingly used, it, like the infamous *Korematsu*[250] decision approving of the wartime internment of Japanese Americans, is a "loaded weapon" that can still be used by the Canadian government and courts against non-citizens.

Security certificates were successfully challenged under the Canadian Charter in 2007, with the Court holding that the government had a year to enact new legislation to provide some form of adversarial challenge to secret evidence used to determine whether the detainee was a security threat.[251] The government enacted a system of security-cleared special advocates similar to that used in the UK. This system was upheld by the Supreme Court in 2014 from a second constitutional challenge.[252] The Court, however, stressed that enough evidence should be made public to allow the detainees to respond to the case against them and that judges should exercise their powers to allow the special advocates to contact others, including the detainee, after having seen the secret evidence if such contact was necessary to ensure the fairness of the proceedings. Since that decision, however, the government has proposed legislation that could make it difficult for special advocates to identify human sources that provide secret intelligence in immigration cases even while the legislation accepts that the innocence at stake exception to the privilege must be made in criminal cases.[253]

Security certificates have been used in Canada for over a decade as a de facto indeterminate detention/control order regime for the three remaining men who are now free but subject to conditions. The remaining certificates may return to their immigration roots if the government persists in its attempts to deport the three men to Egypt and Algeria. The use of immigration law as anti-terrorism law will then run into the harsh reality that many suspected terrorists hold citizenship in countries with poor human rights records. The government will argue that the courts should

[249] Chapter 3, "Canada" at 100, citing *Nlandu-Nsoki v. Canada (Minister of Citizenship and Immigration)*, 2005 FC 17 at para 22.

[250] 323 U.S.214 (1944).

[251] Charkaoui v. Canada [2007] 1 S.C.R. 350.

[252] Canada v. Harkat 2014 SCC 37.

[253] Kent Roach "The Problems with the New CSIS Human Source Privilege in Bill C-44" (2014) 61 *Criminal Law Quarterly* 451. New legislation amending immigration law may also have the effect of reducing the background disclosure received by special advocates. Bill C-51 supra note 2 part 5.

defer to their conclusion that the men could be deported without a substantial risk of torture.[254] The Canadian government may try to negotiate assurances with Egypt and Algeria, as the UK has done with Jordan, but it may have to rely on the controversial *Suresh* exception that would allow the men to be deported to torture.

Israel uses immigration law as anti-terrorism law. In 2012, Israel amended the Prevention of Infiltration Act, first enacted in 1954, to presume that all illegal migrants were infiltrators and to subject them to an automatic three years' detention. As Shiri Krebs notes in Chapter 18, this was an example of the securitization of migration that has also been observed in many Western democracies in the post-9/11 era. The Israel Supreme Court in 2013 held that the three years of indeterminate detention violated Israel's Basic Law on human rights. As in many other human rights cases involving security laws, the legislature quickly responded to the adverse judicial decision. It did not repeal the law, but reduced the three years of detention to one year of detention in an open detention facility that allows non-citizen detainees to leave in order to work. As Krebs notes, however, the UN has raised concerns that the one-year limit on detention may prove unrealistic given that many detainees may not be returned to their country of citizenship because of concerns that they might be tortured. The Israeli Supreme Court found in 2014 that detention still violated rights and ordered the release of over two thousand asylum seekers, mainly from Sudan and Eritrea, in ninety days. The government, however, has indicated its continued desire to keep the Holot detention centre open.[255]

The recent Israeli episode reveals a pattern seen in other states since 9/11. Courts have not been completely deferential to security measures enacted by legislatures, but legislatures have also been active in reasserting their interests in security after adverse judicial decisions. Professors Ewing and Tham argue such legislative replies underline the futility of judicial protection of human rights in general and of the courts' particular inability to curb the security state.[256] My own view, however, is that legislative replies in the UK, Canada and Israel have often followed the logic of judicial proportionality doctrines. These doctrines give courts confidence that they can strike down overbroad security laws with minimal damage to the important objective of preventing terrorism.[257] In any event, judicial review of security matters remains contentious, as other commentators argue that courts lack the knowledge

[254] The courts have previously held that it was patently unreasonable to rely on assurances from Egypt that it would not torture suspected terrorists, in part relying on findings by UN rights committees that Sweden was complicit in torture when it relied on similar assurances. Re Mahjoub 2006 FC 1503.

[255] Chapter 18, "Israel" at 530–531. "Israel Orders Closure of Detention Facility for African Asylum Seekers" *Shanghai News* 23 September 2014; "Israel to Release 138 Detained Asylum Seekers" *The Times of Israel* 6 November 2014.

[256] Keith Ewing and Joo-Cheong Tham "The Continuing Futility of the Human Rights Act" (2008) *Public Law* 668.

[257] Kent Roach "Judicial Review of the State's Counter-Terrorism Activities: The Post 9/11 Experience and Normative Justifications for Judicial Review" (2009) 3 *Indian J of Constitutional Law* 138.

and expertise in security matters to know whether security goals can be as effectively achieved through less rights-invasive means.[258] More damaging than legislative replies, however, would be government defiance of judicial decisions or judicial orders to release people such as the asylum seekers held in Israel. Robust legislative replies at least are transparent and demonstrate some commitment to legality.

Australia also has used immigration law as counter-terrorism law. Davis, McGarrity and Williams report how denial of passports and revocations of visas have been used as less demanding alternatives to criminal prosecutions and are facilitated by legislation enacted in 2014.[259] The Australian High Court has tolerated indeterminate detention of non-citizens somewhat similarly to the Canadian courts.[260] In contrast, courts in the UK, the United States and Israel have ruled against indeterminate detention, thus providing an example of divergence within similar common law legal systems.[261] The Australian and Canadian decisions also suggest that courts may not always be united in enforcing human rights restrictions, often drawn from international law, on the national security state.[262]

Japan has also used immigration law to counter terrorism. Takeyoshi Imai outlines how secret evidence can be used to detain and deport a non-citizen from Japan. Unlike in common law countries, however, there have been no legal or political controversies over the use of immigration law in this manner.[263] This lack of controversy could perhaps be related to Japan's respect for the ban against deportation to torture and the ban against the use of illegally obtained evidence derived from torture. It may also reflect the lack of power and vulnerable status of non-citizens in that country. Similar concerns about the fairness of immigration law are raised in Chapter 15 on Poland where Piot Darnowski expresses concerns that the use of secret evidence in immigration proceedings against suspected terrorists may not accord with human rights standards.[264]

B. *Countries That Have Not Used Immigration Law as Anti-Terrorism Law*

Most other countries in this collection report little use of immigration law as anti-terrorism law. Most European states have laws that would allow for non-citizens involved with terrorism to be denied refugee status and to be detained and deported

[258] Adrian Vermeule and Eric Posner *Terror in the Balance* (Oxford University Press, 2008).

[259] Chapter 23, "Australia" at 671.

[260] Al-Kateb v. Godwin 2004 HCA 37.

[261] Rayner Thwaites *The Rights of Non-Citizens* (Oxford: Hart Publishers, 2014) at 15–20.

[262] Contrary to the predictions in Eyal Benvenisti "United We Stand: National Courts Reviewing Counterterrorism Measures" in Andrea Bianchi and Alexis Keller eds. *Counterterrorism: Democracy's Challenge* (Oxford: Hart Publishing, 2008) 251.

[263] Chapter 20, "Japan" at 576.

[264] Chapter 15, "Poland" at 441–448.

on that basis. For example, a 2008 law in Croatia provides that non-citizens can be denied asylum because they have engaged in terrorist activities.[265] Portugal allows foreigners to be expelled as a threat to national security.[266] Non-citizens suspected of being a threat to national security in Belgium can be detained or made to reside at a certain location before being removed. There is no precise definition of what constitutes a threat to national security, and the concept is interpreted on a case-by-case basis. At the same time, Belgium respects its non-derogable and absolute obligations under the European Convention not to remove non-citizens to torture or degrading treatment. Indeed, some convicted terrorists have been allowed to remain in Belgium after serving their sentences on this basis.[267]

Non-citizens can be detained and removed from China on grounds that they "may endanger China's national security and interests and disrupt social and public order, or commit other crimes."[268] These are broad grounds, but not broader grounds than found in many Western democracies. A person sought to be deported from China can request administrative reconsideration. China has international law but no explicit domestic law obligations not to expel a person to torture, though such a provision does exist in Article 8 of its Extradition Law. South Africa has not used immigration law against terrorist suspects and in 2013 enacted an ordinary statute affirming its international law obligation not to expel or extradite a person if there is a danger of torture.[269]

C. *The Continued Vulnerability of the Right Not to Be Deported to Torture*

Almost all of the countries represented in this volume purport to respect the absolute right of a person not to be deported to torture or degrading treatment, but the struggle to maintain this fundamental right should not be underestimated. Sabrina Praduroux raises concerns about deportation of suspected terrorists from Italy. She notes that a deportation order made by the executive because of security concerns is "immediately enforceable" without judicial validation and may not involve "any careful consideration of the risk of torture in the receiving country and without hearing the person concerned."[270] In the famous 2008 case of *Saadi v. Italy*, the European Court of Human Rights found that Italy had violated the European Convention on Human Rights by trying to deport a suspected terrorist to Tunisia despite the risk of torture. This case affirmed the absolute nature of the

[265] Chapter 13, "Croatia" at 385.
[266] Chapter 11, "Portugal" at 337.
[267] Chapter 8, "Belgium" at 257–259.
[268] Chapter 21, "China" at 596.
[269] Prevention and Combating Torture of Persons Act Act 13 of 2013 s.8.
[270] Chapter 9, "Italy" at 289.

norm of non-refoulement to torture and implicitly rejected the Canadian *Suresh*[271] exception to torture. At the same time, it also demonstrated how the Italian executive attempted a deportation without adequate assessment of the risk of torture. Judicial enforcement of the right against refoulement to torture is an important human rights safeguard, but it depends on non-citizens having adequate legal representation and judges being prepared not to defer to state arguments that the risk of torture is minimal.

Veronika Bílková reports that while the international law principle of non-refoulement is reflected in Czech law, it "may be disregarded on the condition that the foreigner, for instance, committed a crime under international law or an especially serious offence. Perpetrators of terrorist acts would in most cases fall within this exception. They would nonetheless be provided with a sixty-day period to seek refuge in any other state."[272] As in Italy and Canada, the right not to be deported to torture or degrading treatment may not be entirely secure in the Czech Republic.[273]

D. *The Continued Vulnerability of Other Rights of Non-Citizens*

Although some have criticized it,[274] the Belmarsh case[275] stands for the important principle that a focus on immigration law as anti-terrorism law may violate the equality rights of non-citizens and be influenced by fears and prejudice towards non-citizens. A UK citizen, Shaminder Puri, challenged the proportionality of a request by a Polish border guard that he remove his turban. His legal challenge was unsuccessful, but the case "triggered a public debate in Poland."[276] Polish law allows non-citizens to be denied entry or expelled on grounds relating to national security, public order or violating Polish interests. Another non-citizen in Poland, a Moroccan national who has lived eight years in Poland, has appealed, so far without success, in an attempt to gain access to secret evidence said to justify his deportation as a security threat.[277] Abuses of human rights in Morocco raise the risk of possible deportation to torture and also that some of the secret evidence that the Polish state uses from Morocco may not be reliable. The

271 [2002] 1 S.C.R. 3.

272 Chapter 16, "The Czech Republic" at 476.

273 For arguments that even such basic norms need constant reaffirmation not only by courts but by governments and interested publics, see Stephen Toope and Jutta Brunee *Legitimacy and Legality in International Law* (Cambridge University Press, 2011).

274 Compare John Finnis "Nationality, Alienage and Constitutional Principle" (2007) 123 *Law Quarterly Review* 430 with Ronald Dworkin "The Threat to Patriotism" *New York Review of Books* 28 February 2002 for differing views about the relevance of equality rights in evaluating counter-terrorism laws that limit rights.

275 [2004] UKHL 56.

276 Chapter 15, "Poland" at 447.

277 Chapter 15, "Poland" at 443.

fairness critique of the use of immigration law as anti-terrorism law is well known, but deportation of a person with terrorist ties may also be ineffective if that person truly is prepared to engage in acts of international terrorism.

E. *The New Vulnerability of the Rights of Citizens to Travel Restrictions, Citizenship Revocation and Exclusion Orders*

With the rise of the Islamic State and the focus in Security Council Resolution 2178 on foreign terrorist fighting, there may be increasing attempts to use quasi-immigration law to limit the rights of even citizens suspected of involvement in terrorism. Singapore can already revoke citizenship and restrict citizens from leaving, but other countries seem to be catching up. In 2013, Canada enacted four new criminal offences that apply to those who attempt to leave Canada to participate in terrorism abroad. In 2014, Australia enacted an even broader offence of being in a declared area such as parts of Syria and Iraq. These offences are criminal offences that require proof of guilt beyond a reasonable doubt in a criminal trial. Canada followed their enactment with a 2014 law that allowed dual citizens convicted of terrorism offences to be deprived of their citizenship and presumably deported,[278] and Australia is considering similar laws.[279] In 2012, Belgium revived the loss of citizenship for criminal offences and applied it to those convicted of terrorism. This approach may be intensified in the wake of the January 2015 Paris attacks and subsequent terrorism arrests in that country.[280] The UK has also amended laws in 2006[281] and again in 2014 to make it easier to deprive people of citizenship. These powers have been used in a number of cases of suspected involvement in terrorism, including with respect to naturalized citizens who have left the UK to join the Islamic State. In two reported cases, such denaturalized citizens were killed abroad. In one case, the UK Supreme Court overruled a deprivation of citizenship on the basis that it would leave the suspected terrorist stateless only to have the Home Secretary remove citizenship again.[282] The United States again appears exceptional in its constitutional protections against involuntary loss of citizenship.[283] One less restrained form of compensation, however, is the targeted killing of its own citizens suspected of terrorism when they

278 Strengthening Canadian Citizenship Act S.C. 2014 c. 22 s 8. For criticisms and arguments that this act may be unconstitutional, see Craig Forcese "A Tale of Two Citizenships Citizenship Revocation for 'Traitors and Terrorists'" (2013) 39 *Queens L.J.* 551; Audrey Macklin "Citizenship Revocation, the Privilege to Have Rights and the Production of the Alien" (2014) 40 *Queens L.J.* 1.

279 "Tony Abbott, Australian Leader Outlines Crackdown on Terrorism" *New York Times* February 24, 2015.

280 Chapter 8, "Belgium" at 262–263.

281 Immigration, Asylum and Nationality Act, 2006; Immigration Act, 2014.

282 Home Secretary v Al-Jedda [2013] UKSC 62; "Terror Suspect Hilal al-Jedda Stripped of UK Citizenship" 2 December 2003 BBC News at http://www.bbc.com/news/uk-25190305.

283 Afroyim v. Rusk 387 U.S. 253 1967

leave the United States not only for places where armed conflicts exist but also for countries that do not enforce counter-terrorism laws.[284]

The UK's Counter-Terrorism and Security Act, 2015 allows the executive to issue renewable two-year exclusion orders on the basis of reasonable suspicion that a UK citizen or resident has been involved in terrorism-related activity abroad and that such an order is necessary to guard against "a risk of terrorism." Conditions similar to those available under TPIMs can be imposed on the person's return to the UK. Returning to the UK in breach of a temporary exclusion order can be punished by up to five years' imprisonment.[285] This bill exposes citizens to some of the travel restrictions that democracies impose on non-citizens and is even broader than citizenship-stripping provisions because it applies to all citizens and not only those who hold dual citizenship. Given the influence of other UK counter-terrorism law, exclusion orders could become a template for other laws in the Commonwealth and beyond to deal with the foreign terrorist fighter problem associated with the rise of the Islamic State.[286]

F. *Summary*

The heavy use of immigration law as anti-terrorism law in the United States, the UK, Canada and Israel in the post-9/11 era suggests that some developed countries are attracted to using immigration law, with its lower standard of proof and its tolerance for secret evidence, as a form of counter-terrorism law. This occurs even though the ultimate immigration law remedy – deportation – may simply export terrorism problems to less developed countries. Most other states report little use of immigration law as anti-terrorism law. In doing so, they have avoided both the fairness and efficacy problems that often accompany this problematic counter-terrorism measure.

The current focus on foreign terrorist fighters suggests that some of the methods of immigration law are starting to be employed against citizens. There is renewed interest in stripping dual citizens convicted of terrorism offences of citizenship

[284] Al-Aulaqi v. Obama 727 F. Supp. 2d 1 (2010).

[285] Counter-Terrorism and Security Act, 2015 c. 6, ss.1–15.

[286] Attempts to exclude citizens and residents from returning could be challenged in court. For example, a Canadian citizen suspected of involvement in terrorism had to secure judicial relief to be allowed to return to Canada from Sudan. Abdelrazik v. Canada 2009 FC 580 He has subsequently been delisted by the UN as a person associated with al Qaeda and is suing the Canadian government, alleging that it was complicit in his torture in Sudan. A current bill in Canada does not follow the UK model but contemplates that judges could authorize a Canadian intelligence agency to take measures in violation of domestic and foreign laws and Charter rights, including the Charter right of citizens to leave and return to Canada. Bill C-51, First Reading January 30, 2015 part 4. For analysis and criticism of this and other parts of Bill C-51, see www.antiterrorlaw.ca.

with legislation being enacted in Belgium, Canada and the United Kingdom. Such offenders would presumably be deported after having served their sentences. They would then become some other country's problem if they have not been rehabilitated. It is noteworthy how Western democracies have stubbornly held on to the idea that terrorism is or can be made a foreign threat even in the face of rising levels of homegrown self-radicalization and terrorism by citizens. The UK 's Counter-Terrorism and Security Act, 2015 allows citizens and residents suspected of being involved in terrorism to be kept out of the UK for renewable two-year periods and allowed to return only under controlled conditions. Such temporary exclusion orders, like deportations, raise questions about the risk that suspected terrorists excluded from a democracy may be exposed to death or mistreatment in foreign lands. Exclusion orders may complement growing military efforts against foreign terrorist fighters, especially the more than fifteen thousand people from eighty countries, including an estimated five hundred people from the UK, who are believed to have gone to Iraq and Syria under the banner of the Islamic State. This again underlines the need for students of comparative counter-terrorism law to be sensitive to how multiple counter-terrorism instruments interact with each other.

XI. ADMINISTRATIVE AND EXECUTIVE MEASURES

Administrative or executive measures, like immigration law and listing processes, have been used as a less restrained alternative to criminal prosecutions. Executive domination of anti-terrorism measures not only represents a concentration of power but also often involves the use of secret intelligence that is not disclosed to the affected person. A particular challenge is that executive measures may not adequately be reviewed by the courts. The best-known executive measures are those associated with detention, but Security Council Resolution 2178 may increase the use of other executive measures, such as denial of passports to those suspected of involvement in terrorism and the creation of executive measures designed to prevent people from travelling to or returning from foreign terrorist fights.[287]

The chapters on the vast majority of European states,[288] as well as those on Colombia and Brazil, report no use of administrative measures to combat terrorism.

287 A Canadian court has upheld the denial of passport to a suspected terrorist on the basis that "common sense dictates that the possible collective harm outweighs the real individual harm." Canada v Kamel 2009 FCA 21 at para 67. On the use of secret intelligence to deny passports and comply with no fly lists in the United States, see Jeffrey Kahn *Mrs Shipley's Ghost: The Right to Travel and Terrorist Watchlists* (Ann Arbour: University of Michigan Press, 2013).

288 One European exception is the power under section 9 of a 1997 law on Measures to Safeguard Internal Security that allows the Swiss federal government, after consulting with the Swiss federal intelligence agency, to "prohibit a natural person, an organisation or a group from engaging in an

Indeed, many of the countries that report no use of administrative measures also report no use of immigration law. This suggests that at least some decisions not to use both administrative and immigration measures against terrorist suspects may reflect not simply migration patterns but a principled commitment to and confidence in using the criminal law against terrorists. In the wake of the January 2015 terrorist attacks in Paris, this reluctance to use executive measures may be challenged. There will be pressures to restrict the ability of people to travel to foreign terrorist fights through the suspension of passports and other administrative measures. There will be increased pressure to monitor travel and to disable Internet sites that may help recruit and train foreign terrorist fighters. As in the UK, executive measures may be used to attempt to prevent those who have left for foreign terrorist fights from returning. This may be particularly pressing for France, where an estimated nine hundred people have left to fight for the Islamic State. The use of executive measures has the potential to facilitate quick action, but it may also mean that the action will be guided by intelligence. There will be pressure to keep the intelligence secret and not to allow full adversarial challenge of its reliability.

It is interesting that in Colombia, the use of the criminal law as opposed to either administrative or war measures is also seen as a means of denouncing terrorism as crime as opposed to giving suspected terrorists either combatant status or the status of those who have suffered human rights violations.[289] Both Canada and Australia have pursued a criminalization strategy with respect to foreign terrorist fighters by making it an offence to attempt to leave the country to participate in terrorist activities or, in the case of Australia, even to be in designated areas. A criminalization strategy places demands on officials to convert secret intelligence into public evidence, but it may be more effective in denouncing terrorism and demonstrating a commitment to treat people fairly than reliance on administrative measures. The use of immigration law security certificates in Canada were very controversial in part because they could be fairly criticized as "secret trials."[290] Similar concerns led some in the UK to conclude that the use of internment without trial in Northern Ireland actually assisted the cause of terrorists and that military detention at Guantanamo and other abuses helped recruit people to terrorist causes. This raises the possibility that some violations of human rights in countering terrorism may be both normatively wrong

activity that would directly or indirectly serve to spread, support or promote terrorist actions, provided that Switzerland's internal or external security is specifically threatened." Such prohibitions can be up to five years but are also renewable. Chapter 7, "Switzerland" at 219.

289 Chapter 4, "Colombia" at 133.

290 See Kent Roach "The Law Working Itself Pure? The Canadian Experience with Exceptional Courts and Guantanamo" in Fionnuala Ni Aolain and Oren Gross eds. *Guantanamo and Beyond: Exceptional Courts and Military Commissions in Comparative Perspective* (Cambridge: Cambridge University Press, 2013) ch. 9.

and counterproductive. More specifically, it raises the question of whether reliance on new administrative measures in Europe and elsewhere to counter real security threats, as underlined by the Paris and Copenhagen attacks in early 2015, might potentially be counterproductive to deradicalization strategies. In crafting new measures, policy makers need to be aware of the often unhappy historical legacy of administrative measures.

A. *Administrative Measures in Asia*

Japan, China and especially Singapore use administrative measures against suspected terrorists with minimal judicial review and little apparent controversy. Malaysia has attempted to move away from reliance on its Internal Security Act, but has more recently used similar measures.

Japan's Anti-Subversive Activities Act can be used to supervise and even dissolve the existence of groups on "the extreme right or left."[291] Another administrative measure, the Act on the Control of Organizations Which Committed Indiscriminate Mass Murder, has been applied to Aum Shinrikyo and successor groups. Administrative measures are easier to use than criminal prosecutions in Japan because they require only proof on a balance of probabilities as opposed to proof beyond a reasonable doubt. The use of such measures in Japan has so far not caused legal or political controversy.[292]

China has a range of administrative measures that can apply to suspected terrorists before or after criminal proceedings or as an alternative to criminal proceedings. Administrative measures can apply in China if a terrorist suspect "cannot be found guilty in a criminal procedure."[293] They include up to fifteen days' administrative detention, a warning or a fine or deportation in the case of a non-citizen. China is not alone in contemplating that administrative measures can be used after an acquittal in a criminal case. In the UK, the Secretary of State issued a control order in at least one case after the accused was acquitted of a terrorist plot in relation to the bombing of multiple transatlantic flights.[294] Administrative measures allow the state to restrict the liberty of suspected terrorists more quickly and on the basis of less evidence than in criminal proceedings. China's new Draft Anti-Terrorism Law includes a broad array of administrative measures, including "house arrest" orders, orders restricting the use of public transportation, attendance at certain places,

[291] Chapter 20, "Japan" at 576.
[292] Chapter 20, "Japan" at 577.
[293] Chapter 21, "China" at 600.
[294] Secretary of State v AY 2009 EWCA 3053 (Admin).

associations with certain people and surrender of official documents, including travel documents.[295]

Singapore has relied almost exclusively on administrative measures in the form of indeterminate detention without trial and controlled release under that country's Internal Security Act (ISA). One of the advantages of the ISA for the state is that it avoids public trials that could reveal secrets and cause disharmony. It also allows for decisions to be made about detention both by an Advisory Board and ultimately by the President on the basis of evidence that is not disclosed to the detainee. The review board is chaired by a Supreme Court judge with hearings held in the Supreme Court, and the detainee has the right to make representations to the board. Nevertheless, Professor Tan warns that the Advisory Board "should not be treated as a judicial body,"[296] both because of restrictions on the ability of the courts to review the process and because the President retains the right to veto any recommendation that the Advisory Board makes to release a detainee. Release under the ISA is not an all-or-nothing matter. A person can be placed on restriction orders that limit his or her travel, associations and possession of materials. As will be seen, there are modern echoes of such restriction orders in the UK's control orders and Terrorism Prevention and Investigation Measures (TPIMs), which will also be integrated into its new temporary exclusion order regime. This is another reminder that comparative lawyers should be attentive to history and the evolution of various measures over time as well as between countries.

As Professor Tan notes, there are no plans in Singapore to repeal the ISA. The ISA as well as severe restrictions on judicial review of detention under the Act is entrenched in Singapore's constitution. The government of Singapore has rebranded the ISA as necessary anti-terrorism legislation in the wake of the detention of about sixty members of Singapore's Muslim minority in late 2001 and 2002 on the basis that they were part of an al Qaeda affiliate responsible for the 2002 Bali bombings that killed over two hundred people. Continued support for the ISA may be related to the fact that a Board of Inspection visits the detention centre, there are rules governing the conditions of detention that include visits from families and lawyers and there have been no public complaints about mistreatment of the detainees. Moreover, about two-thirds of suspected terrorists detained under the ISA since 9/11 have been released after convincing authorities that they have been rehabilitated. The chief justice of Singapore has recently suggested that "criticisms of the ISA scheme are relatively muted in today's post 9/11 context as commentators increasingly become aware of, or, indeed, even laud, the objectives of the ISA."[297]

295 Chapter 21, "China" at 599.

296 Chapter 22, "Singapore" at 620.

297 Sundarish Menon "International Terrorism and Human Rights" (2014) 4 *Asian Journal of International Law* 1 at 32

Malaysia, like Singapore, inherited an Internal Security Act from its time of British colonial rule and constitutionally entrenched both the ISA and limited judicial review of indeterminate detention under it.[298] Malaysia repealed its ISA in 2012 but replaced it with a broad, modern terrorism law that made generous allowance for secrecy and a twenty-eight-day period of preventive detention. By 2015, the ISA was restored in all but name, so that an executive board can order renewable two-year detention orders, as were available under the ISA. Judicial review is again restricted to procedural matters.[299] Even when countries have been prepared to repeal controversial executive measures, such measures appear to be depressingly durable.

B. *Administrative Measures in Israel*

Israel has multiple forms of administrative detention, with the 1945 Defence Emergency regulations having their origins, as in Singapore and Malaysia, in British colonial rule. Israel also has a 2002 Detention of Unlawful Combatant Act patterned after controversial post-9/11 U.S. practices of military detention. As Shiri Krebs explains, the rationale for the use of administrative measures stems from Israel's permanent state of emergency. Common features include detention on the basis of executive decisions usually by military officials, detention on the basis of secret evidence not disclosed to the detainee and the availability of indefinite detention through renewable detention orders, often for renewable six-month periods.

Israel's most recent administrative regime, the 2002 Detention of Unlawful Combatants Act, attempts to deny a new category of "unlawful combatants" the rights that combatants or civilians would ordinarily have under the laws of war and crime. In this respect, it has some similarities to the U.S. approach to detention at Guantanamo Bay. This law also fits into a pattern of robust legislative responses to court judgments vindicating human rights because it was enacted in response to an Israel Supreme Court decision that held it was unlawful to use detainees as "bargaining chips" for hostages. The 2002 law was upheld in 2008 by the Israel Supreme Court, which rejected the controversial category of unlawful combatants, but also stressed that the state enjoyed "a relatively broad margin of appreciation" on security matters.[300]

[298] Therese Lee "Malaysia and the Internal Security Act" (2002) *Singapore Journal of Legal Studies* 56.

[299] Malaysian Bar Press Release "Amendments to the 1959 Prevention of Crime Act are Regressive and a Blow to the Rule of Law in Malaysia" 3 October 2013, at http://www.malaysianbar.org.my/press_statements/press_release_amendments_to_the_prevention_of_crime_act_1959_are_regressive_and_a_blow_to_the_rule_of_law_in_malaysia.html; Prevention of Terrorism Act, 2015 s.19.

[300] Iyyad v. Israel in *Judgments of the Israeli Supreme Court* Vol 3 at 286.

Judicial review of military and administrative detention is more readily available in Israel than in Singapore or Malaysia. The Israeli Supreme Court reviews detentions de novo and questions secret material presented to the Court by the state in the absence of detainees or their lawyers.[301] In this way, Israel relies on the inquisitorial ability of its judges, as opposed to the UK and Canada, which allow security-cleared special advocates to challenge secret evidence while also requiring that at least the gist of the allegations be made public to allow the detainee to respond. Shiri Krebs reports that only six release orders have been issued with respect to administrative detention in Israel and suggests that Israel's judicial management case discounts the ability of detainees to participate in their own defence.[302] The Israeli approach certainly falls short of the UK and Canada's combination of requiring the gist of allegations to be disclosed and allowing secret evidence not seen by the detainee to be challenged by special advocates. Such comparisons underline how comparative counter-terrorism law may factor into proportionality-based judicial review and how the Israeli system may be vulnerable to successful judicial challenge in the future unless the courts decide that Israel's security needs are significantly different from those of the UK or Canada.

C. *The UK's Control Orders and TPIMs*

The UK enacted executive measures known as control orders in the Prevention of Terrorism Act, 2005. This act was a response to the Belmarsh case[303] and the government's decision to repeal the scheme for indeterminate detention of non-citizens suspected of terrorism who could not be deported because of torture concerns. Henceforth, terrorist suspects, including citizens and non-citizens of the UK, could be subject to executive controls in the community. Control orders were issued by the executive and often on the basis of secret evidence not disclosed to the controlee. As Keith Syrett suggests, control orders were "highly controversial from a human rights perspective,"[304] even though the UK never used its powers under the 2005 act to derogate from the right to liberty under Article 5 of the European Convention on Human Rights. Over fifty control orders were used. The House of Lords held that control orders with a eighteen-hour curfew violated the right to liberty, and the European Court of Human Rights held that Article 6's right to a fair trial would be violated if sufficient evidence was not publicly disclosed to the

[301] Chapter 18, "Israel" at 535–541.
[302] Ibid. For a more qualified defence of the judicial management model, see Daphne Barek-Erez and Mathew Waxman "Secret Evidence and the Due Process of Terrorist Detentions" (2009) 48 *Columbia J of Transnational Law* 3.
[303] A. v. Secretary of State [2004] UKHL 56.
[304] Chapter 6, "The United Kingdom" at 191.

detainee to allow the detainee to defend himself or herself.[305] In this way, the courts imposed case-by-case restrictions on control orders in the name of human rights.

Control orders were eventually replaced with Terrorist Prevention and Investigation Measures (TPIMs) in 2011. Unlike control orders, TPIMs could not last more than two years. The use of such administrative measures declined in the UK so that none were imposed by the summer of 2014. The Counter-Terrorism and Security Act, 2015, however, strengthened TPIMs to include residence relocation and travel restrictions in an attempt to deal with threats associated with people in the UK leaving to fight for the Islamic State or returning after such foreign terrorist fights.[306] In some cases, terrorist suspects subject to control orders or TPIMs could be prosecuted under expanded and extra-territorial crimes for preparation for terrorism and participation in terrorist groups. This raises the question of the comparative strengths and weaknesses of executive and criminal measures. Lord Macdonald, a former Director of Public Prosecutions, argued that criminal prosecutions were preferable to the more controversial use of administrative measures.[307] Unlike criminal prosecutions, administrative measures allow the use of secret evidence. As the courts placed more restrictions on the use of secret evidence, administrative measures become less attractive to the state. According to this reasoning, criminal offences that would apply to foreign terrorist fighters might be more effective and less controversial than administrative measures.[308]

Australia enacted control orders in 2005 that were modeled on British control orders. Although used much less than in the UK, they were used in the "Jihad Jack" Thomas case after a suspected terrorist had his criminal terrorism conviction overturned because of concerns about statements obtained from Thomas in Pakistan. The reversal of the criminal conviction was controversial given Thomas's admissions that he had attended an al Qaeda training camp. The magistrate who imposed the control order relied on the same statements taken in Pakistan that the criminal courts had found suspect. This control order was eventually upheld by the Australian High Court as a legitimate exercise of the defence power and as a similar judicial function to allowing judges to deny bail and issue peace bonds on

[305] United Kingdom v. A (2009) 49 EHRR 1.

[306] Counter-Terrorism and Security Act, 2015 c. 6, ss.9, 16–20.

[307] Lord Macdonald *Review of Counter-Terrorism and Security Powers* January 2011 cm. 8003 at 9.

[308] In 2013, Canada enacted new terrorist offences that punish leaving Canada to participate in the activity of a terrorist group, leaving Canada to facilitate terrorist activity, leaving Canada to commit offences for a terrorist group and leaving Canada to commit an offence that is a terrorist activity. S.C. 2013 c.9. At the same time, Bill C-51 supra note 2, part 3 would make it easier for the state to obtain recognizances that are similar to control orders in placing controls on a suspected terrorist in the community. Breach of the conditions of a recognizance, which can include travel bans, non-association orders and orders not to use computer systems, would be punishable by up to four years' imprisonment.

preventive grounds. Justice Kirby dissented and stressed that control orders were not necessary given the many new terrorism crimes, and Justice Hayne dissented and warned about the dangers of judges making decisions about a person's liberty on the basis of fragmentary intelligence.[309] This decision was less searching than the multiple and frequently successful challenges to control orders in the UK. As Andrew Lynch has argued, a facially similar control order regime in Australia was less restrained than in the UK because of the absence of effective judicial review mechanisms, including review in the European Court of Human Rights.[310]

D. *American Exceptionalism: No Legislative Authorization and Limited Judicial Review*

In the aftermath of 9/11, the United States engaged in administrative preventive detention of thousands of non-citizens under immigration law. Officials also used material witness warrants as a de facto form of preventive arrest. The American approach was exceptional not in its use of less restrained administrative measures, but in its refusal to authorize such measures in legislation, including in its PATRIOT Act. The American approach of pre-textual law enforcement was defended by Attorney General John Ashcroft, who argued that "aggressive detention of lawbreakers and material witnesses is vital to preventing, disrupting or delaying new attacks."[311] Because administrative measures in the United States were not explicitly authorized in legislation, they were shrouded in secrecy until they were revealed by the American free press. Those detained under material witness warrants and held in immigration detention after 9/11 have sought damages from Ashcroft, but the courts have generally rejected their claims on the basis that executive officials must be able to respond vigorously to security threats.[312] The American approach relies on executive initiative,[313] but the lack of effective accountability for executive actions means that it often condones extra-legal behavior.

Another form of American executive action that was not sanctioned by legislation was its extraordinary rendition program. Renditions were used by the United States before 9/11 but mainly as an extra-legal means to extradite suspects to face trial in the United States. American courts condoned such practices as not depriving them

309 Thomas v. Mowbray (2007) 233 CLR 307 (H.C.).

310 Andrew Lynch "Control Orders in Australia: A Further Case Study of the Migration of British Counter-Terrorism Law" (2008) 8 *Oxford University Commonwealth Law Journal* 159.

311 Cole *Enemy Aliens* at 36.

312 Ashcroft v. Iqbal 129 S.Ct. 1937 (2009); Ashcroft v. Al Kidd 131 S.Ct. 2074 (2011)

313 Daphne Barak Erez "Terrorism Law Between the Executive and Legislative Models" (2009) 57 *American Journal of Comparative Law* 877

of jurisdiction when a suspect was illegally taken to the United States for trial.[314] After 9/11, however, Sudha Setty in Chapter 2 explains that extraordinary rendition involving illegal kidnappings was used to capture over one hundred terrorist suspects and transfer them to foreign countries, including Egypt and Syria. Renditions were undertaken by the executive without legislative or judicial authorization. They were also shrouded with official secrecy, which has been somewhat penetrated by investigative reporting. Many of those tortured as a result of such renditions have brought suit in American courts, but their cases have all been dismissed on procedural grounds related to matters such as state secrets and non-justiciability.[315] As discussed later in this chapter, there were some prosecutions of American officials in Italy and some of the rendition victims have brought suits in other countries that had more peripheral involvement in their renditions but more accommodating legal systems.

E. *Summary*

Executive or administrative measures are used against suspected terrorists in only a minority of the jurisdictions represented in this volume. Singapore, Israel and the United Kingdom have the most developed regimes of administrative measures. These measures are clearly authorized in legislation and subject to varying degrees of judicial review. In some cases, judicial review has restrained such measures, but in others it has sustained and legitimated such measures. Keith Syrett in Chapter 6 on the UK tends to the former view, whereas Shiri Krebs in Chapter 18 on Israel tends to the latter view. My own view is somewhat between these two views. Judicial review in the UK has made administrative measures less attractive to the state by requiring the disclosure of more information. If executive measures are used, there should be some judicial check on power. On the other hand, the government has frequently prevailed in judicial challenges to administrative detention, especially in Israel. It is intriguing that the two jurisdictions with the least robust form of judicial oversight, Singapore and Australia, have been relatively restrained in their use of administrative measures. The lesson for comparative lawyers seems to be that they must carefully evaluate the strengths and weaknesses of judicial review and must also be aware of social and political factors that help determine how legal powers are used.

The problem of terrorist foreign fighters has already resulted in a strengthening of various administrative measures in the UK and other countries. It will be tempting for countries to use executive measures in an attempt to prevent foreign terrorist travel and to mitigate threats that radicalized people present to the community. Past

[314] US v. Alvarez-Machain 504 U.S. 655 (1992). A civil suit by the rendered fugitive was subsequently dismissed in Sosa v. Alvarez-Machain 542 U.S. 692 (2004).

[315] Chapter 2, "The United States" at 76.

experience suggests that such measures may be controversial and that courts may moderate some of their more extreme effects. Countries should also be alive to the possibility that administrative measures may work less well with the most recalcitrant and radicalized individuals and that community supervision orders may not always command public confidence. Criminalization strategies may be preferable both in terms of incapacitation and denunciation, but may not always be possible given the difficulties of converting secret intelligence that often informs administrative measures into public evidence that can prove guilt beyond a reasonable doubt.

The American approach to administrative measures is exceptional because it allows executive action without either legislative or judicial authorization. Post-9/11 measures such as mass and pre-textual immigration detention, abuse of material witness warrants and renditions would have remained secret were it not for the work of the free press. Although the United States has a constitutional bill of rights and an active human rights bar that challenged these executive measures once they came to light, American courts have consistently deferred to the executive and the need to preserve state secrets. In the next section, a particularly robust form of executive measure, military detention, will be examined.

XII. THE ROLE OF THE MILITARY

Before 9/11, the use of military courts and detention against suspected terrorists was generally reserved for notoriously authoritarian regimes.[316] Since 9/11, however, the United States has been aggressive in its use of military detention and military trials of suspected terrorists. As will be seen, military detention and trials have also been used in Colombia and Israel. The legal rationale for America's actions is Congress's Authorization of the Use of the Military Force (AUMF), issued a few days after 9/11. The AUMF authorized the President to use "all necessary and appropriate force" against those who aided, committed or harboured the attackers and "in order to prevent future acts of international terrorism against the United States by such nations, organizations or persons."[317] The AUMF was the start of the U.S. war against terrorism and was used to authorize military strikes starting in September 2014 against the Islamic State on the basis that it is an al Qaeda affiliate.

[316] Syria and Egypt are two countries notorious for trying terrorism cases before military courts. Military courts in China would have jurisdiction over terrorism offences if martial law was declared in a region. Military officers would have special powers of search and detention if a person "endangers state security or disrupts public order" or are "strongly suspected" of offences. Restrictions on detention and arrest in the Criminal Procedure Law would not apply during martial law. See Chapter 21, "China" at 600–601. As in the United Kingdom and Israel, powers to declare martial law in certain territories opens up the possibility of different legal regimes in different parts of the country.

[317] 115 Stat 224.

The AUMF mainly has implications for non-American citizens suspected of terrorism, but it was used in a few cases against American citizens such as Jose Padilla. Padilla was initially detained under a material witness warrant after he was arrested in Chicago. Padilla was transferred to military custody in June 2002 upon the order of President Bush. In 2004, the U.S. Supreme Court dismissed Padilla's habeas corpus claim on the technical basis that he brought proceedings where he had been held on the material witness warrant and not in the judicial district where he was held and subject to extreme interrogation by the military.[318] A subsequent lower court held that Padilla as an American citizen should face a criminal trial rather than a military trial, but the Fourth Circuit Court of Appeals reversed this judgment on the grounds that the criminal justice system might compromise intelligence gathering and permit Padilla to "return to battle."[319] Padilla was eventually charged with conspiracy to commit acts of terrorism shortly before the Supreme Court was to determine whether the AUMF authorized the detention of American citizens as enemy combatants. Padilla was convicted in criminal courts despite his arguments that he had been tortured while in military custody. He was sentenced to seventeen years' imprisonment, but the sentence was increased to twenty-one years on the grounds that his time in military custody should not count against his criminal sentence. The Padilla episode is a disturbing example of experimentation and manipulation of law in a manner that seems designed to deny suspected terrorists rights that they would be entitled to under either criminal law or the law of war.

A. *Detention and Trial at Guantanamo Bay*

The AUMF and presidential authority was used to justify military detention and trial at the American military base at Guantanamo Bay, Cuba. As Sudha Setty suggests in Chapter 2, the Bush administration chose Guantanamo Bay to avoid habeas corpus review by American courts. The U.S. Supreme Court, however, held in 2004 that habeas corpus would apply to Guantanamo detainees.[320] In a pattern observed throughout this chapter, the legislature did not simply accept this judicial decision. Congress responded by enacting 2005 legislation denying habeas relief even to those who had already commenced litigation to seek "the great writ." In 2006, the Supreme Court held as a matter of statutory interpretation that Congress's habeas stripping law could not be applied retroactively.[321] It also held that the military commissions

[318] 542 U.S. 426.
[319] Hanft v. Padilla 423 F. 3d 388 (4th Cir. 2005).
[320] Rasul v. Bush 542 U.S. 466 (2004).
[321] Hamdan v. Rumsfeld 548 U.S. 557 (2006).

at Guantanamo were unlawful because they violated the Uniform Code of Military Justice and Common Article 3 of the Geneva Conventions in part because they contemplated the use of secret evidence not disclosed to the detainee. Congress responded to this ruling with the Military Commissions Act, 2006, which provided a code for proceedings at Guantanamo and again attempted to deny habeas corpus to the Guantanamo detainees. This latter part of the law was ruled unconstitutional by the Supreme Court in 2008.[322] That ruling, however, applies only to Guantanamo. The American military adjusted to the ruling and increasingly held detainees at Bagram Air Base in Afghanistan, where American courts had refused to extend habeas corpus.[323] The state can respond to rights-friendly judicial decisions by using other counter-terrorism measures. The idea that habeas corpus extends to Guantanamo but not Bagram also represents the case-by-case minimalism of many American constitutional rulings that undercuts some of the force of the American Bill of Rights.[324]

The effects of the extension of habeas corpus review to Guantanamo should not be overstated. Lower courts have been deferential in reviewing the detentions and have often presumed that the intelligence used to justify continued detention was reliable. In some cases, courts have granted habeas corpus, but the detainee has not been released. There are also cases where concerns have been raised about refoulement to torture of Guantanamo detainees. Congress has prohibited the transfer of Guantanamo detainees to the United States either for detention or trial despite the criminal conviction of the one Guantanamo detainee who faced criminal trial before civilian criminal courts. Five detainees were used as “bargaining chips” to obtain the release of U.S. Sergeant Bowe Bergdahl, who had been detained by the Taliban in Afghanistan.[325] In a somewhat similar case, the Israel Supreme Court disapproved of the use of military detainees as bargaining chips on human dignity grounds.[326] This was a controversial decision in Israel, but it was accepted. In contrast, American concerns about the Bergdahl trade have focused on whether the soldier had been loyal to his country and whether the released Guantanamo detainees would attack the United States.

The population of Guantanamo has been reduced from a high of 684 detainees in June 2003 to 122 as of January 2015. Most of these releases were a result of executive

[322] Boumediene v. Bush 128 S.Ct. 2239 (2008).

[323] Al Maqaleh v. Gates 605 F. 3d. 84 (D.C. Cir. 2010).

[324] This approach has been defended as minimizing the counter-majoritarian difficulty of unelected judges imposing decisions on the elected branches of the government. See Cass Sunstein *One Case at a Time* (Cambridge, MA: Harvard University Press, 2006)

[325] “Obama Defends Decision to Trade 5 Guantanamo Detainees for Bergdahl” *Washington Post* 3 June 2014.

[326] Chapter 18, “Israel” at 537.

and not judicial decisions. There are continuing concerns about conditions of confinement, suicides and hunger strikes among the remaining detainees. Professor Setty observes:

> There have been consistent reports of widespread abuse, torture, and violations of the prisoners' human rights. Almost two-thirds of the prisoners joined an ongoing hunger strike in February 2013, which has led to military resorting to force-feeding several prisoners. Federal district courts have declined to intervene on behalf of the prisoners, despite widespread condemnation by the United Nations and international human rights groups that the force-feeding constitutes torture.[327]

The Obama administration continues to use military commissions, which as Setty notes in Chapter 2 have lower standards of fairness towards the accused than both criminal courts and military courts-martial. In particular, they do not guarantee defendants the right to remain silent, speedy trials or the exclusion of coerced statements. The jury is composed of members of the military and does not have to be unanimous in non-capital cases.

Australian David Hicks and Canadian Omar Khadr pled guilty before their military commissions in successful attempts to facilitate their release from Guantanamo. There have been very few completed trials before military commissions, and some of the convictions, including Hicks' conviction, have been overturned by American courts on the basis that offences such as material support of terrorism under the Military Commissions Act are not war crimes within the jurisdiction of the military justice system[328] or on the basis of the creation of retroactive crimes.[329] In any event, a person who was acquitted by a military commission could still be detained by the executive, much as is the case with the use of administrative detention after acquittals in criminal trials. The Military Commissions Act represents legislative authorization of what started as an executive measure, but it remains an uneasy and novel blend of military and criminal justice concepts. As such, it can perhaps best be explained as a de facto form of administrative detention. It represents an experimental and so far unsuccessful attempt to create a third model that denies suspected terrorists rights that they would have in either the traditional military or criminal justice systems.[330]

[327] Chapter 2, "The United States" (footnotes omitted) at 69–70.

[328] Hamdan v. United States 696 F. 3d 1238 (D.C. Cir, 2012).

[329] Al Bahlul v. United States 767 F.3d 1 D.C. Cir, 2014; Hicks v. United States. United States Court of Military Commission Review February 18, 2015.

[330] Ulrich Sieber, "Blurring the Categories of Criminal Law and the Law of War – Efforts and Effects in the Pursuit of Internal and External Security" in S. Manacorda and A. Nieto Martín eds. *Criminal Law Between War and Peace – Justice and Cooperation in Criminal Matters in International Military Interventions* (Cuenca, Universidad de Castilla-La Mancha, 2009) at 35–69.

B. *Targeted Killing*

Military detention and trials continue at Guantanamo, but the Obama administration currently stresses targeted killing as a method to deal with suspected al Qaeda terrorists. Targeted killing of suspected terrorists, including American citizens, is authorized by the AUMF and is apparently not limited to armed conflicts. Attempts to subject targeted killing to judicial review have failed, with courts holding that judicial review is precluded on a number of grounds, including state secrets and non-justiciable political questions.[331] This demonstrates the same type of deferential approach by American courts as seen in the cases examined in the last section challenging pre-textual uses of immigration and material witness warrant detention. As suggested previously, the deference of American courts to executive action can condone extra-legal action.

Israel and the United States both use their military as a prime counter-terrorism actor, but the Israeli courts have been more active in reviewing military actions than the American courts. The Israel Supreme Court reviews military detention de novo and has also prohibited the use of military detainees as bargaining chips. It has also reviewed the use of targeted killing by applying a form of proportionality analysis in a case brought by the same civil society group that challenged the use of harsh interrogation techniques by Israeli intelligence agents.[332] The Court accepted the use of targeted killing against those who planned or directed acts of terrorism but not against those involved in terrorist financing or propaganda. The decision has been both praised for promoting ex ante and ex post accountability and criticized for diluting the protections afforded to citizens under international law.[333] The possibility that judicial review may legitimate controversial counter-terrorism activities cannot be dismissed, and domestic review in Israel may be an attempt to head off possible international war crime prosecutions.[334] The targeting decisions made by the Israeli military and the possibility of war crimes investigations and prosecutions for disproportionate

331 Al-Aulaqi v. Obama 727 F.Supp 1 (2010).

332 Public Committee against Torture v. Israel HCJ 769/02 in Judgments of the Israel Supreme Court Vol 3. Such a public interest group would never be granted standing in the United States. For example, an attempt to review surveillance by the National Security Agency (NSA) before the Snowden revelations was denied on the grounds that the Amnesty International did not have standing. Clapper v. Amnesty International 133 S.Ct. 1138 (2013).

333 Compare "On Target? The Israeli Supreme Court and Targeted Killings"(2007) 116 *Yale L.J.* 187; and Antonio Cassese "On Some of the Merits of the Israeli Judgment on Targeted Killings" (2007) 5 *International Journal of Criminal Justice* 339.

334 Amichai Cohen and Yuval Shany "A Development of Modest Proportions" (2007) 5 *International Journal of Criminal Justice* 310.

killing of civilians has emerged as an issue after over one thousand civilians were killed in Gaza during the summer of 2014. The decision is another reminder that students of comparative counter-terrorism law must examine the complex interactions between domestic and international law.

C. *Executive Action and Constitutionalism*

The reluctance of U.S. courts to review many executive counter-terrorism measures, including targeted killing, means that such actions are subject to review only within the executive branch. The most notorious examples of the limits of such review are the so-called torture memos that held that extreme interrogation techniques were legal. These memos were eventually leaked to the press and rescinded by the Office of the Legal Counsel.[335] At the same time, executive interpretation of legal norms continue to be the main restraint on American executive and military counter-terrorism measures. A recently declassified legal memo reveals that the Obama administration has rejected arguments made by the UN's Special Rapporteur on extra-judicial killings that targeted killings should be limited to places of armed conflict, such as Afghanistan.[336] The memo concludes that targeting killings are authorized by the post-9/11 AUMF and that they are consistent with the laws of war and do not constitute murder even when executed by the Central Intelligence Agency against an American citizen in Yemen.[337] Some have defended the approach on the basis that the United States applies tests of necessity and proportionality that would prevent the use of drones against al Qaeda suspects in the developed world,[338] but the fact remains that these tests are applied by lawyers within the executive and not by the independent judiciary. Another problematic factor is that targeted killing is based not simply on legal analysis by the executive but secret intelligence of unknown reliability.

D. *The Treatment of (Unlawful) Combatants, Civilians and Peace Talks*

Luz E. Nagle outlines in Chapter 4 how the Colombian military is used against the Revolutionary Armed Forces of Colombia, better known as FARC. FARC

335 See generally Karen Greenberg and Joshua Dratel *The Torture Papers* (New York: Cambridge University Press, 2005).

336 Philip Alston, *Report of the Special Rapporteur on Extrajudicial, Summary or Arbitrary Executions* at 18 (United Nations Human Rights Council, Fourteenth Session, Agenda Item 3, May 28, 2010).

337 "Court Releases Large Parts of Memo Approving Killing of American in Yemen" *New York Times* 23 June 2014.

338 David Cole "The Drone Memo: Secrecy Made It Worse" *New York Review of Books* 24 June 2014 at http://www.nybooks.com/blogs/nyrblog/2014/jun/24/awlaki-secret-drone-memo/?insrc=wbll.

functions as an army, an organized crime group and a terrorist group with revenues between $80 million and $350 million. Despite the use of armed forces against FARC, Professor Nagle reports that the official Colombian response has been to treat terrorism as a crime in part to ensure that there is no recognition of belligerent status for FARC. Keith Syrett similarly indicates that the UK has historically denied terrorists combatant or prisoner of war status.[339]

It will be interesting to see whether adherents of the Islamic State and other foreign terrorist fighters will be accorded combatant status, but the recent past suggests a reluctance to do so. Not according terrorists combatant status in situations of armed conflict often results in an attempt to create a third body of law outside the established laws of war and crime based on the concept of unlawful combatants who do not receive the same protections as either civilians or combatants. Courts in both Israel and the United States have expressed discomfort at such incoherent experimentation that seems designed to deny terrorists the benefits that they would receive under the law of war and the law of crime.[340] The Colombian and Northern Ireland examples, however, also suggest the reality that states will when confronted with long-standing domestic terrorism use peace negotiations and reform measures as a means to reduce the number of terrorist attacks. Such options appear less realistic when applied to international terrorism associated with al Qaeda or the Islamic State.

E. *Summary*

The United States has certainly been the most active country represented in this collection in using the military to prevent terrorism, but it is not alone in this regard. The United States with a number of allies, including Australia, Canada, Jordan and some European countries have bombed Islamic State targets in Iraq and Syria since September 2014. One difference from other post-9/11 wars is an increased challenge in confining warlike approaches and attitudes to the theatre of armed conflict. Canada's Prime Minister Stephen Harper conflated war and crime when he defended a counter-terrorism bill introduced in the wake of a lone wolf September 2014 attack on Canada's parliament on the basis that "violent Jihadism in not a human right, it is an act of war, and our government's new legislation

339 Chapter 4, "Colombia" at 130, Chapter 6, "The United Kingdom" at 194.

340 The Israel Supreme Court upheld the 2002 Detention of Unlawful Combatants Act, but by holding that the detention of civilians and not "unlawful combatants" was justified. Iyaad v. Israel, 2008 in Judgments of the Israeli Supreme Court Vol 3. The Military Commissions Act in the United States has been repeatedly challenged on a variety of bases, including the inclusion of crimes that may not be war crimes and on the basis of retroactively creating crimes. See, for example, Hamdan v. United States 696 F. 3d 1238 (D.C. Cir, 2012).

fully understands the difference."[341] This rhetoric is politically popular, but it ignores that even supporters of the Islamic State retain due process and expressive rights in Western democracies even if they become legitimate military targets when they travel to armed conflict zones in Iraq and Syria.

Even in war, there are laws. Much of the American military response, including the offensive against the Islamic State, has been based on Congress's AUMF issued immediately after 9/11. Nevertheless the Obama administration is seeking new authorization from Congress. The American courts have extended habeas corpus to review military detention at Guantanamo (but refused to extend it to Bagram Air Force Base in Afghanistan) and have also enforced some basic human rights and constitutional standards on military trials. The U.S.'s Military Commission Act has frequently been successfully challenged for its incoherent blend of law of war and criminal justice concepts. It seems designed to deny detainees some of the rights they would normally enjoy in both military and criminal courts. In any event, few trials have been completed under it. American courts have refused to review targeted killing or the use of military detainees as bargaining chips, even though the Israeli courts have. The American courts have also not heard claims by Guantanamo detainees and others who alleged they were abused in American custody, but as will be discussed in the next section, a number of other courts, including the European Court of Human Rights, are now undertaking such reviews.

XIII. EXTRA-TERRITORIAL ISSUES

The growing emphasis on international terrorism has raised many issues concerning the extra-territorial application of laws prohibiting terrorism and of domestic human rights norms. Many countries have asserted universal jurisdiction over terrorism crimes, though some have expressed preference for prosecuting crimes committed beyond their territory only if they involve their own citizens or interests. As discussed in the first chapter, the assertion of universal jurisdiction has raised issues of prosecuting people for terrorism for supporting the use of violence against despotic regimes abroad. Nevertheless, problems of universal jurisdiction do not appear to have caused major practical problems despite the theoretical possibility of states all asserting universal jurisdiction and competing to prosecute suspected terrorism.

341 "Stephen Harper Makes His Case for New Powers to Combat Terror" CBC News January 30, 2015, at http://www.cbc.ca/news/politics/stephen-harper-makes-his-case-for-new-powers-to-combat-terror-1.2937602.

A. *Extradition and Deportation and the Increasing Interdependence of Legal Systems*

A more live issue has been how human rights concerns should affect transnational processes such as deportation and extradition. Most states have affirmed their absolute commitment not to deport a person to torture. The European Court of Human Rights has affirmed this obligation in a case where it concluded Italy was improperly trying to deport a suspected terrorist to torture in Tunisia.[342] As Keith Syrett notes in Chapter 6 on the United Kingdom, the European Court of Human Rights has accepted that Abu Qatada could be deported to Jordan without a substantial risk of torture, but in the same case extended the non-refoulement obligation to prohibit extradition if it would result in the use of evidence obtained by torture.[343] The UK subsequently negotiated a treaty with Jordan in an attempt to ensure basic fair trial rights, and Abu Qatada was subsequently acquitted of terrorism charges in Jordan.[344] This case reaffirms the interdependence of legal systems. It will be interesting to see whether temporary exclusion orders under the Counter-Terrorism and Security Act, 2015[345] will be challenged as infringing the excluded person's right to life if that person is effectively kept in areas of armed conflict in Iraq or Syria or whether courts will accept the orders as a proportionate measure to deal with the terrorist foreign fighter problem. In any event, exclusion orders, like extradition and deportation, demonstrate how conditions in one jurisdiction impact and can provide a basis for legal challenges of counter-terrorism measures in another jurisdiction.

Conditions attached to extradition and deportation affect the way that countries implement counter-terrorism measures. European and other states will seek assurances from the United States that it will not apply the death penalty[346] and increasingly life imprisonment without parole to suspected terrorists.[347] Canada has also secured assurances that a person extradited to the United States to face terrorism charges for attacks on American troops in Iraq will not be subject to military custody or trial at Guantanamo.[348] Canadian courts have refused to extradite Abdullah Khadr to face terrorism charges with respect to activities in Afghanistan because of its findings that American officials were complicit in his mistreatment when he was

[342] Saadi v Italy supra.

[343] Othman (Abu Qatada) v UK (2012) 55 EHRR 1.

[344] Chapter 6, "The United Kingdom" at 190.

[345] C. 6.

[346] The Czech Republic deported a Swedish citizen to face terrorism charges in the United States, again with assurances that the death penalty would not be applied. He was eventually sentenced to life imprisonment in the United States. Chapter 16, "The Czech Republic" at 479.

[347] Trabelsi v. Belgium App no 140/10.

[348] United States v Muhammad 'Isa, 2014 ABCA 256 at para 19.

originally captured in Pakistan.[349] At the same time, however, Canadian courts have allowed extradition to the United States even though an accused would face a much harsher sentence for terrorism in the United States than in Canada.[350] Assurances may temper the application of some of the United States' most controversial counter-terrorism policies. Extradition and deportation proceedings increasingly provide a venue for examining and challenging how other countries conduct terrorism investigations and trials. As such, they reaffirm the theme seen throughout this chapter of the increasing interdependence of legal systems.

Chapter 13 on Croatia raises concerns about the time-consuming nature of extradition proceedings and the continued danger that states may characterize acts of terrorism as political crimes not subject to extradition. It notes that the EU has attempted to "depoliticize" terrorism. For example, Greece chose not to characterize treason as a terrorist crime in part because of fear that it might be characterized as a political offence.[351] The European Arrest warrant that applies to thirty-two crimes, including terrorism, provides a quicker and simpler alternative to formal extradition proceedings.[352] The European Arrest Warrant is only permissive, and some member states such as Spain and Portugal have prohibitions on the extradition of their own citizens.[353] Extradition and deportation proceedings implicate the competing demands of co-operation and harmonization and allowing each country to apply its own domestic norms. They play an increasingly important role in counter-terrorism law and underline the interdependence of different legal systems and the dialogue that occurs between different legal systems.

B. *Diplomatic Requests*

Courts are increasingly comfortable in enforcing human rights by stopping or placing conditions on extradition or deportation. They are, however, less comfortable in requiring governments to make diplomatic representations to assist nationals being detained as terrorists in other states. Following Constitutional Court jurisprudence, South Africa would not extradite a person to face the death penalty or torture. At the same time, however, the Constitutional Court of South Africa refused to order that the executive make diplomatic representations to Zimbabwe about the conditions faced their by South African citizens suspected of terrorism.[354]

[349] United States v. Abdullah Khadr 2011 ONCA 358. For further discussion of this case, see Kent Roach "Uneasy Neighbors: Comparative American and Canadian Counter-Terrorism" (2012) 38 *William Mitchell Law Review* 1701 at 1769ff.

[350] Sriskandarajah v. United States of America, 2012 SCC 70, [2012] 3 S.C.R. 609.

[351] Chapter 12, "Greece" at 348.

[352] Chapter 13, "Croatia" at 387.

[353] Chapter 10, "Spain" at 322, Chapter 11, "Portugal" at 342.

[354] Kaunda v. President 2005 (4) SA 235 (CC).

The Supreme Court of Canada reversed an order that would have required Canada to make diplomatic representation on behalf of Omar Khadr, who had been held by the United States at Guantanamo since he was fifteen years of age.[355] The British courts reached similar results in earlier cases dealing with both UK citizens and permanent residents detained at Guantanamo.[356] One exception to this trend is a 2012 order by British courts that required the UK government to ask the United States to release Yunis Rahmatullah from American custody at Bagram, where the British courts held that he had been transferred contrary to the Geneva Conventions and understandings between the UK and the United States about prisoners captured in Iraq.[357] The U.S. government refused this request. This case, however, is part of a growing trend of non-American courts being asked to review controversial American counter-terrorism activities.

C. *Substitute Justice: Non-American Courts Reviewing American Counter-Terrorism Activities*

As observed by Professor Setty, most lawsuits seeking damages for unlawful counter-terrorism activities by the American executive have been dismissed on grounds of state secrets and lack of justiciability.[358] This underlines the limited nature of judicial review of the American state's national security activities. In what I have described elsewhere as an imperfect form of "substitute justice,"[359] courts in other countries have attempted to fill the accountability gap left by American courts.

The European Court of Human Rights has held that Macedonia violated Article 3 of the European Convention on Human Rights prohibiting torture or inhumane and degrading treatment by its complicity in the CIA's rendition of El-Masri, including his "disappearance," his "hooding," his "forced undressing" and the painful and involuntary administration of a suppository in his anus. The Court awarded him 60,000 euros in damages. The judgment is most notable for its review and condemnation of U.S. extraordinary rendition practices, in contrast to

355 Khadr v. Canada [2010] 1 S.C.R. 44.

356 Abbasi v. Secretary od State 2002 EWCA 1598; R. (Al Rawi) v. Sec'y of State for Foreign & Commonwealth Affairs, [2006] E.W.C.A. (Civ.) 1279.

357 Secretary of State v. Ramatullah 2012 UKSC 48.

358 Chapter 2, "The United States" at 74–76.

359 See Kent Roach "Substitute Justice? Challenges to American Counter-Terrorism Activities in Non-American Courts" (2013) 82 *Mississippi Law Journal* 907, outlining the role of Australian, British and Canadian courts in indirectly reviewing American counter-terrorism activities in cases involving their own nationals. Italian courts have also played a role in convicting CIA and Italian agents for their role in kidnapping Abu Omar and rendering him to Egypt. He also has complaints pending before the European Court of Human Rights. Chapter 9, "Italy" at 290–293.

the U.S. courts, which dismissed El-Masri's lawsuit on state secrets grounds.[360] The European Court of Human Rights also found that Poland violated the European Convention by its complicity in the torture of Abu Zabaydah and Al Nashiri at CIA black sites in Poland and their subsequent transfer to Guantanamo. They awarded both applicants 100,000 euros in damages. These cases featured judgments of more than two hundred pages based on the public information about American counter-terrorism practices.[361] The Court noted that CIA documents reveal how the black site program was designed "to strip" detainees "of any safeguards afforded by both the US Constitution and international law."[362] These important cases underline the need for comparative lawyers to study how actions in one legal order may stimulate countervailing actions in other legal systems. The reluctance of American courts to review American executive measures has resulted in non-American courts indirectly reviewing the effects of American actions on human rights. The existence of multiple and interdependent legal orders greatly complicates the task of the student of comparative law, but it also ensures that human rights challenges that fail in one legal order can be reformulated in another.

D. *The Rule of Law and Extra-Territorial Counter-Terrorism Activities*

The ultimate issue is whether the rule of law will apply to extra-territorial counter-terrorism activities. The Canadian courts held that Canada's Charter of Rights applied extra-territorially to actions by Canadian officials because they breached international law when they interrogated Omar Khadr in 2003 and 2004, when he was detained without access to habeas corpus at Guantanamo.[363] They, however, retreated from the logic of respecting international human rights abroad when they held that the Canadian constitution was not violated even if Canadian forces in Afghanistan transferred their detainees to torture in Afghan custody.[364] This approach raises concerns that extra-territorial counter-terrorism activities will escape human rights review.[365] Indeed, there are concerns that the United States may continue to use extra-territorial counter-terrorism activities such as renditions

[360] Compare El-Masri v. The former Yugoslav Republic of Macedonia, Application No. 39630/09 (Eur. Ct. H.R. Dec. 2012), ¶¶ 208–10, 221, 221, 240 & 270 and El-Masri v. United States, 479 F.3d 296, 300–01 (4th Cir. 2007).

[361] Abu Zabaydah v. Poland Application 7511/13; Al Nashiri v. Poland Application 28761/11.

[362] Abu Zabaydah v. Poland Application 7511/13 at para 524.

[363] Khadr v. Canada [2008] 2 S.C.R. 125; Canada v. Khadr [2010] 1 S.C.R. 44.

[364] Amnesty International v. Canada 2009 FCA 401.

[365] Recent terrorism bills in Canada take a different approach and propose that judges can authorize Canadian security officials to act "without regard to any law, including any foreign law" when they act abroad. Canadian Security Intelligence Act R. S.C. 1985 c. C-23 ss.21. 3.1, 21.1 4 as amended by S.C. 2015 c. 9 and Bill C-51 supra note 2.

and targeted killings in part because they are not as restrained by American or international law as domestic activities are.[366]

E. *Summary*

The European Court of Human Rights and other courts are reviewing American rendition and black site detention practices even though American courts have refused to do so, often for reasons related to state secrets or a refusal to prosecute. The effectiveness of such indirect regulation of the American security state and whether it can be extended to new American practices such as targeted killing is debatable. What is not debatable is that counter-terrorism law is an excellent site for comparative lawyers to examine the increasing interdependence and interaction of different legal systems. Extradition and deportation hearings, requests for judicial orders of diplomatic requests and substitute justice actions that seek indirect review of American counter-terrorism actions in non-American courts provide an important venue for courts in one country to review whether terrorism investigations and trials in another country are conducted in accordance with human rights and to balance such human rights concerns with other concerns, including the need to co-operate in preventing terrorism.

The extra-territorial nature of many measures against international terrorism presents acute challenges for the rule of law. This is especially true if countries take the position that their domestic laws do not apply when security or military officials act beyond their territory and if the United States maintains the view that it is not even bound by international law when its security officials act abroad. As discussed previously, many states are unwilling to grant terrorists combatant status under the laws of war. Fears of a legal black hole for extra-territorial counter-terrorism activities are only enhanced by the likelihood that such activities, already quite prevalent, will intensify as measures are taken against foreign terrorist fighters.

366 The Obama administration's policy on extraordinary renditions is not clear, but one former counsel for the Central Intelligence Agency has argued that such practices could still be used in large part because the Convention Against Torture would not apply extra-territorially and because of the lack of domestic penalties. See Daniel L Pines "Rendition Operations: Does US Law Impose Any Restrictions?" (2011) 42 *Loyola University Chicago Law Journal* 523. However, Harold Koh, as the senior lawyer in the Department of State, argued in a 2013 memorandum that the United States should be bound by the Convention Against Torture when acting abroad. Harold Koh Memorandum January 21, 2013, at https://www.documentcloud.org/documents/1053901-state-department-cat-memo .html. The official position of the U.S. government, however, is not clear but seems to favour the idea that it is not bound by the Convention Against Torture when engaged in extra-territorial action. Charlie Savage "U.S. seems unlikely to Accept That Rights Treaty Applies to Its Actions Abroad" *New York Times* March 6, 2014.

XIV. SECRECY

Secrecy is a constant challenge in evaluating a state's counter-terrorism laws or activities. States and in particular intelligence agencies have an interest in keeping secret their sources and methods as well as information shared with foreign partners. Intelligence agencies often have particularly intense interests in secrecy because their prime objective is to provide confidential warnings of security threats to governments as opposed to providing evidence that may eventually be disclosed in a public trial. In Poland, the Border Guard is increasingly working with the police and intelligence agencies on counter-terrorism, but the secrecy of its operations makes it difficult to know the propriety of many of its actions.[367] Similarly in Singapore, the secrecy of ISA's proceedings means that little is known about counter-terrorism activities in that city-state.[368] In contrast, leaks in the United States have placed much information about black sites, renditions, surveillance and harsh interrogation into the public domain. A public inquiry into Canadian complicity into the U.S.'s 2002 rendition of Maher Arar to Syria found that the government of Canada had engaged in a pattern of overclaiming secrecy in part to protect the Canadian government from embarrassment.[369] Successful assertions of secrecy can hide misconduct and provide impunity for abuse by security officials.

In some cases, courts have questioned governmental claims of secrecy. The UK courts scrutinized secrecy claims made by Ministers in the Binyam Mohammed litigation brought by former Guantanamo detainees and stressed the importance of open justice. The litigation also revealed that the United States threatened the UK with decreased intelligence sharing if the UK allowed intelligence to be disclosed.[370] The UK Supreme Court stressed the importance of open justice and the problems created by secret evidence by refusing to allow the use of secret evidence in civil proceedings.[371] Parliament responded to this ruling with the Justice and Security Act, 2013,[372] which authorizes the use of closed proceedings and special advocates in civil proceedings. This reflects a recurring pattern in the UK of rights-friendly judicial decisions quickly being replaced by security-based legislative replies. In addition, as Keith Syrett notes, there is a trend for new UK legislation to be made permanent.[373]

367 Chapter 15, "Poland" at 475–477.

368 Chapter 22, "Singapore" at 624–628.

369 Chapter 3, "Canada" at 106.

370 R (on application of Mohamed) v. Secretary of State [2010] EWCA 65 [39}. For an incisive analysis of this litigation, see Adam Tomkins "National Security and Due Process of Law" (2011) 64 *Current Legal Problems* 215.

371 Al Rawi v. Security Service [2011] UKSC 34.

372 2013 c.18.

373 Chapter 3, "The United Kingdom" at 198.

Italy has a broad state secrets law that generally does not allow judicial review on the merits,[374] but a 2007 law places limits on the invocation of state secrets in cases where security agents have acted in a way that harms persons or the administration of justice. These amendments likely have the origins in the prosecutions of American and Italian security officials in relation to the kidnapping of Abu Omar from Milan and his subsequent rendition to Egypt. Sabrina Praduroux raises concerns, however, that secrecy claims in Italy may still protect executive misconduct.[375] This is true, but the 2007 law demonstrates some legislative concern that state secrets not be allowed to shelter serious illegalities by security officials. In the United States, a broad state secrets doctrine has effectively prevented all civil lawsuits arising from American conduct, including extraordinary renditions and abusive forms of interrogation.[376] A comparison of the American and Italian approaches is another reminder of the need to study the law in action as applied to particular acts of abuse. There have been successful prosecutions of American and Italian security officials in Italy for Abu Omar's kidnapping and extraordinary rendition[377] even though the courts have had a very limited role in reviewing the executive's secrecy claims, whereas there have been no successful civil actions or criminal prosecutions for abuse by American security officials in the United States despite the greater role of American courts in reviewing secrecy claims.

Despite the continued ability of secrecy to hide counter-terrorism activities, the study of comparative counter-terrorism has been greatly assisted in the last decade by official and unofficial decisions to place more information about security activities into the public domain. Much more is now known about activities that once were secret. The American First Amendment tradition has helped ensure that more is known about problematic American practices than is known about the practices of other states. Denials by Polish officials about a CIA black site were effectively contradicted by inquiries by the European Parliament and judgments of the European Court of Human Rights.

374 Commentators have observed that the Italian Constitutional Court's "jurisprudence indicates that it has resigned from the role of reviewer" and simply confirms whether the executive and legislature have confirmed the secrecy claim. Arianna Vedaschi "Arcana Imperii and Salus Rei Publicae: State Secrets Privilege and the Italian Legal Framework" in David Cole, Federico Fabbrini and Arianna Vedaschi eds. *Secrecy, National Security and the Vindication of Constitutional Law* (Cheltenham: Edward Elgar, 2013) at 109.

375 Chapter 9, "Italy" at 292–294.

376 Chapter 2, "The United States" at 74–76.

377 In at least one case, however, the Italian prime minister pardoned an American official in order to protect relations with the United States. Helen Duffy "Accountability for Counter-Terrorism Challenges and Potential in the Role of the Courts" in Davies and de Londras eds. *Critical Debates on Counter-Terrorism Judicial Review* (Cambridge: Cambridge University Press, 2014) at 331–3. See also Human Rights Watch "Italy Stands Alone on Justice for CIA Abuses" March 12, 2014, at http://www.hrw.org/news/2014/03/12/dispatches-italy-stands-alone-justice-cia-abuses.

A. *Secrecy and the Criminal Courts*

Criminal courts have generally resisted the use of secret evidence in terrorism trials.

In *Hamdan v. United States*,[378] the United States Supreme Court decided that the use of secret evidence not disclosed to the detainee would violate Common Article 3 of the Geneva Conventions and the U.S. Uniform Code of Military Justice. The prohibition on the use of secret evidence helps protect fair trials, but may also encourage the state to use other counter-terrorism instruments such as targeted killing and renditions that will not require the disclosure of secret intelligence. This is another reminder of the need for counter-terrorism scholars to be aware of the possibility that restraints on one counter-terrorism measure may simply encourage states to use other less restrained measures.

Although the criminal courts of most countries resist the use of secret evidence not disclosed to the accused,[379] it is a mistake to think that secrecy does not affect criminal trials. Most countries allow non-disclosure of unused but possibly relevant material to the accused in terrorism trials. This can shelter intelligence investigations and co-operation with foreign countries that precede most criminal investigations of international terrorism from disclosure, but also deny the accused access to information that might demonstrate innocence, a rights violation or the lack of reliability of some of the evidence that the state uses in legal proceedings.

In the United States, the Classified Information Procedures Act allows judges to grant non-disclosure orders and provide summaries or non-classified substitutes for the disclosure of otherwise secret material to the accused. The Military Commissions Act, used to govern military trials of suspected terrorists at Guantanamo Bay, also encourages judges to use similar devices to balance the state's interests in disclosure and non-disclosure. The UK uses a system of public interest immunity orders under the common law. This allows criminal trial judges to balance the competing interests in disclosure and non-disclosure with respect to secret material that is not being used in the prosecution. In the UK, secret evidence not seen by the accused would not be used in a criminal trial, but is used in proceedings involving administrative measures and, since 2013, in civil trials.

[378] 548 U.S. 557 at 665 (2006).

[379] But see infra notes 174–177 outlining how some criminal courts in continental Europe allow intelligence to be used as evidence in a manner that is perilously close to the use of secret evidence. Li Zhe reports that intelligence agents in China can testify anonymously "or be questioned by the judge outside of the court." This latter possibility raises concerns about the use of secret information that is never subject to adversarial challenge. Chapter 21, "China" at 607. Eugene Tan explains how Singapore has not used criminal proceedings against terrorism in part because of the ISA allows its legal system to use secret evidence. Chapter 22, "Singapore" at 624.

Australia and Canada follow the British system of public interest immunity, but with some interesting statutory twists. Davis, McGarrity and Williams examine how Australian judges who review an executive certificate that material should not be disclosed to the accused are instructed to give the "greatest weight" to the state's interest in national security as opposed to the accused's interest in a fair trial. This legislative weighting of the balance of interests has been held upheld from a constitutional challenge as not inconsistent with the judicial function.[380] Canada only allows specially designated Federal Court judges to decide national security confidentiality issues, even though such judges do not have jurisdiction to conduct criminal trials. The constitutionality of this awkward scheme, which reflects Canada's anxieties as a net importer of intelligence, has been upheld with the Supreme Court stressing that the trial judge remains free to stay proceedings if a fair trial is not possible as a result of the Federal Court's non-disclosure order.[381] Canadian courts will not be able to reveal identifying information about the human sources of both the police and intelligence agencies unless they have been convinced that the accused's innocence is at stake.

There is an important law in action dimension to secrecy issues. Intelligence agencies are having to adjust to the reality that their secret intelligence has increased evidential value given the enactment of broad new terrorism offences and other post-9/11 developments such as terrorist listings.[382] If intelligence agencies resist the disclosure of their material, this may require states to make secrecy claims that can slow down or collapse a criminal prosecution or use other proceedings such as administrative measures that allow the use of secret evidence. Traditional intelligence concerns about sources, methods and information obtained from third parties may make it difficult to transition from secret intelligence to a public prosecution. Secrecy proceedings provide a glimpse into the competing mandates and practices of policing and intelligence agencies.

B. *Anonymous Witnesses*

European states generally accept the use of anonymous witnesses. For example, partial or full anonymity may be granted to witnesses in both Belgium and Italy.[383]

380 Chapter 23, "Australia" at 678.

381 R. v. Ahmed 2011 SCC 6, discussed in Chapter 23, "Canada" at 104.

382 A Canadian commission of inquiry in 2010 found that a continued reluctance by intelligence agencies to disclose material still adversely affected terrorism investigations and trials. Commission of Inquiry into the Bombing of Air India Flight 182 A *Canadian Tragedy vol. 3 The Relationship Between Intelligence and Evidence and the Challenges of Terrorism Prosecutions* (Ottawa: Supply and Services, 2010).

383 Chapter 8, "Belgium" at 267; Chapter 9, "Italy" at 269.

The European Court of Human Rights regulates the use of anonymous witnesses and would not allow a conviction if the bulk of evidence were from an anonymous witness. In contrast, an anonymous witness would likely be absolutely prohibited in the United States given the constitutional right of the accused to challenge witnesses. This may be another example of how American domestic due process restraints indirectly encourage the use of less restrained counter-terrorism instruments such as renditions and targeted killing.

C. *Summary*

Any serious examination of counter-terrorism law must grapple with issues of secrecy if only to be aware that scholars may never know the full truth about the state's counter-terrorism activities. The study of secrecy should also make scholars aware of the state's ability to switch counter-terrorism instruments so as to avoid disclosure of intelligence. The criminal trial is the instrument most resistant to the use of secret evidence, but secrecy can still adversely affect the amount of a disclosure of unused material that an accused receives. Administrative, immigration and military detention may be more attractive if it allows the use of secret evidence. The wide variety of counter-terrorism instruments available to the state ensures that counter-terrorism law will of necessity be both a broad and dynamic field of inquiry.

XV. CONCLUSION

New terrorism laws were adopted in many countries after 9/11 in order to comply with various supra-national mandates. Laws enacted mainly for external consumption may have weak roots. Veronika Bílková in Chapter 16 stressed that the Czech Republic does not face serious terrorist threats, and its "counter-terrorism law has not had any major impact upon other areas of national law. It has nonetheless made it easier for the Czech Republic to co-operate with other states and international organizations."[384] Poland has enacted new counter-terrorism laws to ensure that it is "a thoroughly responsible partner in anti-terrorist actions"[385] both at the EU and international levels. Similarly, one of "the major influences"[386] on terrorism laws in Portugal has been the need to comply with various UN and EU directives. Singapore has enacted three post-9/11 terrorism laws relating to terrorist financing, bombings and hostage taking, but relies on its older Internal Security Act to detain suspected terrorists. Japan enacted a terrorism financing law in 2002 in response to

[384] Chapter 16, "The Czech Republic" at 482.
[385] Chapter 15, "Poland" at 456.
[386] Chapter 11, "Portugal" at 343.

UN Security Council Resolution 1373 and is proposing to strengthen it in response to FATF criticism, but has yet to record one terrorism financing conviction.[387] The only "holdout" country examined in this collection that has not enacted a law to criminalize terrorism and terrorism financing is Brazil. Nevertheless, Rodrigo de Souza Costa concludes that given its increased international prominence, "it becomes unthinkable"[388] that Brazil will not eventually enact terrorism legislation. This suggests that counter-terrorism law has become an international imperative, but one with weak roots in many societies. This may, however, change as countries react to the fact that nationals from eighty countries are reported to have joined the forces of the Islamic State and other foreign terrorist groups. The legislative reaction to this emerging terrorist threat has already started and may eventually turn out to be as significant as the legislative response to 9/11.

One of the fundamental challenges of counter-terrorism law is the difficulty of defining terrorism in a satisfactory manner that accommodates domestic dissent and freedom fighting against repressive regimes. The UN Security Council offered little guidance on this critical subject when in Resolution 1373 it demanded immediately after 9/11 that all states treat terrorism and terrorist financing as serious crimes. In Resolution 2178, targeting foreign terrorist fighters, the Security Council has again left it to individual states to define terrorism and has encouraged them to pursue measures aimed at combating the even vaguer harms of "violent extremism" and "radicalization." As discussed in the first chapter, a number of definitions of terrorism have been extremely influential, but there are concerns that all of them could capture domestic dissent. Moreover, few of the definitions exempt "freedom fighters" who attack repressive regimes or who fight in situations of armed conflict that should be governed by the laws of war. In a draft anti-terrorism law released in November 2014, China has defined terrorism very broadly and equated it with "extremism" in a manner that may legitimate repression of minorities such as the Muslim Uighurs.

Potentially overbroad definitions of terrorism in turn are reflected in broad terrorism offences that criminalize preparation, financing, association and incitement of terrorism. The freedom fighter issue is magnified by the fact that these broad offences often apply to extra-territorial conduct against any government in the world. Marissabel Škorić concludes that a new Croatian offence of public provocation of terrorism "does not represent an appropriate balance between the obligation of the state to protect everyone from terrorism and its obligation to protect freedom of expression as the fundamental human right." She also suggests that the criminal approach to terrorism may not give adequate weight to "cultural

[387] Chapter 20, "Japan" at 575.
[388] Chapter 5, "Brazil" at 164.

dialogue, promotion of human rights and especially the protection of minorities."[389] Rueda and Boldova raise concerns that counter-terrorism law in Spain is becoming an autonomous but expansive form of "enemy criminal law" that challenges both constitutionalism and human rights.[390] These strong criticisms reflect the executive orientation of counter-terrorism law that even when passed by legislatures is often designed to respond to demands of executive-dominated groups in the UN Security Council, the Council of the European Union and the Financial Action Task Force.[391] In this respect, it is noteworthy that the 2006 Counter-Terrorism Strategy of the General Assembly of the United Nations stresses issues such as human rights and respect for the rule of law that are often downplayed in executive-dominated forms of counter-terrorism. Broad offences based on broad definitions of terrorism allow the state to intervene long before any violence is imminent, but such offences may be less useful in denouncing and stigmatizing terrorism and establishing a narrative that counters radicalization and successfully equates terrorism with the murder and maiming of innocent civilians.

One executive-dominated form of counter-terrorism that was heavily promoted since 9/11 has been the listing of terrorists to enforce terrorism financing laws and travel bans. In recent years, there have been increasing and successful challenges to the fairness of terrorist lists. The European Court of Justice has been particularly active in holding that listed entities are treated unfairly because they do not know the basis for their listing. To be sure, efforts have been made to improve the transparency and fairness of the listing and delisting processes, but merits-based review of listing depends on the willingness of intelligence agencies to disclose material that may reveal their sources and methods. In any event, the material examined in this collection suggests that after more than a decade, the public accomplishments of listing and terrorism financing regimes are very modest. Nevertheless, the UN Security Council in Resolution 2178 has reaffirmed its commitment to listing as a means to deal with the growing number of foreign terrorist fighters. This area underlines the need for scholars critically to evaluate both the human rights propriety and the efficacy of counter-terrorism measures. Listing is an unfair process, but there is also very little reason to think it has been effective in countering al Qaeda, let alone the Islamic State. Indeed, there is a danger that listing may even be counterproductive to stopping radicalization and terrorism to the extent it is perceived to discriminate against Muslim individuals and charities.

Unlike measures against terrorism financing, which are quite similar in most of the world, there tends to be more diversity with respect to other counter-terrorism measures. An important theme that runs throughout the collection is that states have

389 Chapter 13, "Croatia" at 371.
390 Chapter 10, "Spain" at 325.
391 Murphy *EU Counter-Terrorism Law* supra at 79

a broad range of counter-terrorism instruments at their disposal. These instruments cross traditional disciplinary boundaries within legal scholarship. The multiplicity of counter-terrorism instruments requires that those who study counter-terrorism law be familiar with immigration, administrative and military law as well as the criminal law. There may be a temptation to conclude that this makes the field of counter-terrorism law too broad, but this temptation must be resisted. If the states are breaking down silos and taking a whole of government approach to security, so too must the scholars. Such a broad approach is also necessary to understand how states may substitute some measures, such as military or administrative detention, for other measures, such as criminal trials.

This collection reveals much diversity in whether countries are prepared to use immigration law as a form of counter-terrorism law. The UK relied on immigration law in the aftermath of 9/11 and was prepared to derogate from the European Convention on Human Rights to do so. The use of immigration law as anti-terrorism law was deemphasized somewhat after the House of Lords' landmark 2004 Belmarsh ruling, which found that the UK's focus on non-citizens was both disproportionate and discriminatory. The Abu Qatada case, however, reveals a continued desire by the UK to deport terrorist suspects as well as the difficulties of deporting suspects to countries with poor human rights records. Australia, Canada, Israel, Italy and the United States have all used immigration law as anti-terrorism law, but many states in continental Europe report no such use of the law. Some of the techniques of immigration law- administrative measures based on secret evidence, travel restrictions and even denial of citizenship for dual nationals- are now being employed against citizens because of concerns about foreign terrorist fighting. Common challenges include the fairness of using secret evidence not disclosed to the detainee and the international law prohibition on one country being complicit in threats to life, torture or degrading treatment in another country. Moreover, it should never be forgotten that approaches to terrorism that rely on or are inspired by immigration law at the end of the day simply export terrorism to another country.

The exceptionalism of the American war on terror has been widely noted in the literature. Without detracting from such critiques, including that of Sudha Setty in Chapter 2 on the United States, the chapters in this collection illustrate that the United States is not the only country to use the military as an important agent of counter-terrorism. The military has been used against terrorism in Colombia and Israel. At the same time, however, as Luz E. Nagle illustrates in Chapter 4, Colombian authorities have been careful not to grant FARC terrorists belligerent status and have recognized that the criminalization of terrorism has some strategic advantages. Shiri Krebs outlines the fundamental role of the military in counter-terrorism in Israel, but also the frequent review of military detention by the Israeli Supreme Court.

The extent to which judicial review has restrained or legitimated counter-terrorism can be debated. American courts have frequently refused to review American counter-terrorism actions, including increased use of targeted killing, but other courts, including the Israeli Supreme Court, have attempted such review. The European Court of Human Rights as well as domestic courts in the United Kingdom and elsewhere have increasingly been asked indirectly to review American counter-terrorism activities. Such substitute justice litigation is a reaction to the unwillingness of American courts to review such activities because of concerns about state secrets and justiciability. This litigation, including recent judgments by the European Court of Human Rights for victims of U.S. practices of extraordinary renditions, demonstrates that not even the United States is immune from attempts to assert the rule of law. In addition, countries are also asking for assurances that the United States will not employ some of its more controversial counter-terrorism practices, such as military detention and trial as a precondition for counter-terrorism co-operation. One of the most important themes of this collection, and of comparative counter-terrorism law in general, is the interdependence of nations when they attempt to deal with the menace of international terrorism.

Another important theme in the study of comparative law generally is the interaction of universal imperatives with those that are particular to the legal system and history of each country.[392] The field of counter-terrorism law, especially since 9/11, has been driven by supra-national demands for various counter-terrorism laws and activities. This has resulted in many countries developing elaborate counter-terrorism laws even when they have very little experience with terrorism and even when they make little or no use of their new counter-terrorism laws. Supra-national and especially regional demands for counter-terrorism laws have often served as agents of convergence, for example, producing similar counter-terrorism laws throughout much of the European Union.

At the same time, the influence of national legal traditions and cultures and the different experiences that different countries have with terrorism are also very evident in the material contained in this collection. The exceptionalism of the American response to terrorism has frequently been noted, but there are pockets of exceptionalism in many other countries' terrorism laws. For example, Italian counter-terrorism law bears the mark of that country's successful use of rewards in its battle with terrorism in the 1980s. Singapore's counter-terrorism reflects the entrenched nature of indeterminate detention without trial in that country, but also its concerns about maintaining harmonious relations with its significant Muslim minority. The United Kingdom's counter-terrorism law has been shaped by its extensive experience with terrorism as well as its frequent legislative responses

[392] Mark Tushnet *Weak Courts Strong Rights* (Princeton: Princeton University Press, 2008) at 10–15.

and pushback to judicial decisions applying the European Convention on Human Rights.

Even when countries follow the examples of other countries, their own political and social context and legal traditions will make a difference. EU countries have stopped short of full harmonization of counter-terrorism law, and some elements of legal nationalism are found in those countries' laws. Canada borrowed heavily from British laws, but modified them to ensure consistency with Canada's constitutional bill of rights. Australia has been even more heavily influenced by British counter-terrorism law, but even its laws have made some accommodations for domestic Australia constitutional law requirements, especially those relating to the limits on judicial power. Even when Australia has enacted similar laws to the UK, such as control orders, Australia's laws have different effects given the absence of a national bill of rights in that country.

Despite significant evidence of convergence, there remains considerable diversity in counter-terrorism law. At one end, Brazil continues to resist enacting terrorism laws in part because of past abuses of terrorism laws in that country. At the other side of the spectrum, South Africa stands as an example of a country that was willing to enact a very broad counter-terrorism law in 2004 despite past abuses of terrorism laws during the apartheid regime. The South African approach seems to be one that relies on a combination of executive discretion and human rights vigilance by the courts to discipline the use of very broad terrorism laws. Indeed, much of the world is left in a similar position to South Africa given the global post-9/11 trend to the enactment of broad counter-terrorism laws.

The interplay of broad counter-terrorism laws and human rights challenges in the courts will continue as countries respond to Security Council Resolution 2178 and the increasing threat of foreign terrorist fighters. Courts will eventually respond to increased use of administrative measures designed to prevent radicalized persons from leaving to join foreign terrorist fights or returning after having participated in them. Courts will also have to decide whether new offences targeting extremist speech are consistent with democratic freedoms.

Counter-terrorism law will continue to evolve. Laws and practices in one country will continue to influence those in others. Supra-national institutions, including the UN Security Council, the EU and FATF will continue to play an important role. All in all, counter-terrorism will continue to be particularly dynamic. An important constant is that counter-terrorism law will continue to be a subject worthy of sustained comparative study because of its profound effects on security, human rights, democracy and the rule of law.

APPENDIX

Guidelines for Country Reports on Counter-Terrorism Law

Purpose of the Guidelines: These guidelines are intended to provide some basic structure to assist in the preparation and subsequent publication of the country and general reports. They are not intended to prevent each country reporter from explaining what is most important in understanding the counter-terrorism law of his or her country.

In some cases, specific questions may not be relevant to each country. At the same time, it may be important to explain why an issue that has become important in the law of other countries has not become important in your country.

Feel free to address specific questions under each bolded section in the order that seems most logical to you.

If this outline omits something that you believe is important, please feel to add it under the headings other matters.

Some Sources: Each reporter will obviously be in the best position to identify relevant sources, but you may want to consult the publicly available reports (up to 2006) that your country filed with the Counter-Terrorism Committee created by UN Security 1373, available at http://www.un.org/en/sc/ctc/resources/countryreports.html

Translations of many relevant international, regional and national documents are also available from the UN Office on Drugs and Crime: https://www.unodc.org/tldb/en/index.html

The International Commission of Jurists also has a good library of developments in their e bulletins on terrorism and human rights searchable at http://www.icj.org/

The Financial Action Task Force (FATF) at http://www.fatf-gafi.org has information on terrorism financing including country reports.

Overall Structure: One of the challenges of the study of comparative counter-terrorism law is the breadth of the scope of terrorism law. Counter-terrorism law "crosses boundaries between states and conventional divisions between domestic, regional and international law." It also "crosses traditional disciplinary boundaries between administrative, constitutional, criminal, financial, immigration, international and military law, as well as the law of war." "Introduction" in Victor Ramraj et al. *Global Anti-Terrorism Law and Policy* 2nd ed. (Cambridge University Press) at 1. Terrorism is often investigated and prosecuted as an ordinary crime by police in ordinary courts. At the same time, however, intelligence agencies, the military and specialized courts are also involved with the prosecution of terrorism in many countries. The following structure is proposed for each country report, though as noted below, some overlap and cross-referencing between the different sections is inevitable.

I. Introduction: Brief Overview of Your Country's Experience with Terrorism and Terrorism Law
II. The Definition of Terrorism
III. Criminal Laws and Prosecutions
IV. Investigative Powers
V. Proscription/Listing of Terrorist Groups/Individuals
VI. Regulation of Terrorism Financing
VII. Immigration Measures
VIII. Administrative/Executive Measures
IX. Role of Military and Extra-Territorial Counter-Terrorism Activities
X. Secrecy
XI. Other Matters (if necessary)
XII. Conclusion: Assessment of Your Country's Anti-Terrorism Laws

This is a challenging array of topics, but one that is necessary to do justice to the breadth, complexity and high stakes of anti-terrorism law.

I. INTRODUCTION: BRIEF OVERVIEW OF YOUR COUNTRY'S EXPERIENCE WITH TERRORISM AND TERRORISM LAW

One of the important themes in the study of comparative counter-terrorism law and indeed comparative law generally is the interaction of universal imperatives with those that are particular to the legal system and history of each country. Mark Tushnet *Weak Courts Strong Rights* (Princeton: Princeton University Press, 2008) at 10–15. In a short introduction of a few paragraphs, each country report should inform the reader about relevant experience with terrorism in your country and provide a brief overview of the most important elements and developments in terrorism law. It may be helpful to note whether there were specific responses to UN Security Council Resolution 1373 enacted after the 11 September 2001 terrorist attacks on the United States. This brief overview may also alert the reader to the most important and used forms of counter-terrorism law in the country, whether they be criminal, immigration or military law.

II. THE DEFINITION OF TERRORISM

The difficulty of defining terrorism is an important theme in counter-terrorism law.

How is terrorism defined in the laws of your country? When was terrorism first defined in law? What were the influences on the definition whether in the law of other states or regional/international instruments? How is terrorism differentiated from other crimes (e.g., political or religious motive, intimidation of populace or government requirements)? Are there any exemptions from the definition of terrorism, for example, for expressive or associational activity or for national liberation struggles? Is terrorism defined differently in different forms of law in your country? Are some offences or laws (i.e., murder, bombing, etc.) used to avoid the difficulties and controversies of defining terrorism?

III. CRIMINAL LAWS AND PROSECUTIONS

A. *Criminal Law*

Is terrorism a separate crime? Is some definition of terrorism or terrorist activities incorporated into substantive criminal law? Note there is no need to repeat the description and assessment of the definition of terrorism examined in Section II.

Were terrorist crimes created, amended, expanded or made subject to more punishment in response to UN Security Council Resolution 1373? Is membership or participation in a terrorist group a crime? What forms of facilitation, preparation and participation for terrorist acts are criminalized? In general, are crimes of preparation for or facilitation of terrorism broader than those available for other "ordinary" crimes such as murder? Note that some of the details of the specific offences can be relegated to footnotes.

Are ordinary criminal laws such as murder, kidnapping and conspiracy applied to terrorist crimes? Is suspected terrorism sometimes prosecuted for other offences, and if so, why?

Are terrorist crimes overlapping and what rule, if any, restrains multiple convictions?

If your country is a federation, are there both state and national laws on terrorism, and if so, how do they compare and interact?

Is there a crime of advocacy/apology/incitement of terrorism? Was it enacted in response to UN Security Council Resolution 1624 or in response to some other supranational instrument? Has the provision been used? Has it been controversial and/or challenged under a human rights instrument?

B. *Terrorism Prosecutions*

What crimes are most frequently charged in terrorism prosecutions? Are multiple charges and multiple accuseds typical? What information is available about the result of terrorism prosecutions, including whether trials were held? If possible, provide a brief description of some of these prosecutions.

Are terrorism prosecutions conducted in specialized courts, and if so, describe the specialized court and how it differs from ordinary courts in your country. If used, are specialized courts controversial or is their legitimacy generally accepted? Are accused persons subject to fewer (or more) rights as a result of the use of specialized regime? Please include both historical examples of specialized courts and possible future examples that are being proposed. Note that if military courts are used for terrorism prosecutions, these should be noted here but more fully described in Section IX. Similarly, specialized provisions relating to secrecy should be discussed in Section XI.

Would evidence that could have been obtained through torture or degrading treatment be admissible in terrorism prosecutions? Have there been any examples of such evidence being excluded or other proceedings and methods (immigration, extradition laws etc.) used to avoid this prospect?

Can a witness testify anonymously and without his or her name being identified in terrorism prosecutions? If so, what are the safeguards or limits of such testimony?

C. *Punishment of Terrorism*

What are the sentencing practices after terrorism convictions? Does rehabilitation play a role in sentencing terrorists? Are there sentencing reductions for those who co-operate with authorities?

IV. INVESTIGATIVE POWERS

The state including the police, intelligence agencies and the military are often given special investigative powers in terrorism cases that are not available in other criminal proceedings.

A. *Police Powers*

Do the police have special powers not available in ordinary criminal investigations and cases? In particular, are there special preventive arrest powers? Are there special powers with respect to interrogations, pre-trial or investigatory detention, searches, use of informers and electronic surveillance?

Can the state compel those with information about a terrorist act to provide the information, and if so, what if any safeguards apply?

Are there special laws or regulations to govern the use of undercover operations?

Has entrapment or other defences based on abuse of police powers been successfully argued in terrorism prosecutions?

B. *Intelligence Agencies*

What are the legal powers and roles of intelligence agencies in respect to counter-terrorism?

Is intelligence collected by intelligence agencies also used as evidence in terrorism prosecutions? In particular, can electronic surveillance collected by intelligence services be used as evidence in terrorism prosecutions? Note that provisions relating to secrecy during criminal prosecutions may be more fully described in Section XI.

V. PROSCRIPTION/LISTING OF TERRORIST GROUPS/INDIVIDUALS

Many terrorism laws including at the international and regional level have processes for proscribing and listing terrorist groups and individuals thought to be associated with terrorism groups.

A. *Proscription Mechanisms*

Is there a mechanism for proscribing or listing terrorist groups and/or listing? Is the process governed by primary legislation or subordinate/administrative regulations?

What is the relation between the domestic listing process and that used under UN Security Council Res 1267 for those associated with al Qaeda? Can a listing decision be based on speech or advocacy of terrorism as opposed to direct or indirect participation in terrorist activities? Have either the courts, the legislature or the executive changed a listing decision in response to a challenge?

B. *Challenges to Proscriptions and Listings*

Have there been any challenges to the proscription or listing of terrorist groups, and if so, what was the result? Can the government defend a proscription or listing decision on the basis of evidence not disclosed to the listed group or individual?

If so, is there some procedure that allows some form of adversarial challenge such as the use of a security-cleared special advocate? Is the listing decision subject to review by a specialized judge or review tribunal?

Is the definition of a terrorist group in criminal offences based in part or wholly on the proscription/listing of terrorist groups? If so, can and has this listing/proscription be challenged in a criminal prosecution on the basis that listing by the executive is substituted for proof in a criminal trial that a group is a terrorist group?

VI. REGULATION OF TERRORISM FINANCING

The UN Security Council and other transnational bodies have stressed the need to combat terrorism financing, though concerns have also been raised about the fairness and the efficacy of such measures.

A. *The Regulatory Regime to Counter Terrorism Financing*

Does the terrorism financing regime in your country depend on proscription or listing decisions discussed in Section V? Note there is no need to repeat descriptions of the listing regime or challenges to it in this section.

Is the same offence and regulatory structure used for terrorism financing and money laundering? Is there a financial intelligence unit in your country? Does its mandate cover both money laundering and terrorism? Briefly describe the activities of the financial intelligence unit, such as the number of reports of suspicious transactions that it receives yearly from financial institutions and other entities. Have attempts been made to subject informal money transfer systems, such as hawalas, to the terrorism financing regime? Has your country been subject to and responded to an adverse Financial Action Task Force (FATF) report with respect to terrorism financing?

B. *Criminal Offences of Terrorism Financing*

Are there criminal offences against terrorism financing? If so, were they passed in response to UN Security Council Resolutions 1267 or 1373? Do they require proof of a subjective intent or knowledge with respect to terrorist acts? Is there any exemption for the provision of funds to finance legitimate and humanitarian activities by a terrorist group? Is there acceptance of the theory that funds given for humanitarian activities of a terrorist organization should be prohibited because it frees up funds for the group's terrorist activities?

Have there been prosecutions stemming from allegations of terrorist financing that were not coupled with other terrorism charges? What were the results in terms of convictions and sentences? Have the sentences for terrorist financing been as severe as those for other terrorist crimes?

Are there provisions for the forfeiture of terrorist property? If so, are these imposed as part of a criminal prosecution or as an administrative measure perhaps subject to a lower standard of proof?

VII. IMMIGRATION MEASURES

Immigration law has frequently been used as a form of anti-terrorism law in regards to international terrorism.

A. *Immigration Detention*

Has immigration law been used against suspected terrorists? If so, on what basis? Have immigration proceedings been used after or as an alternative to criminal prosecutions? Are there special immigration procedures providing for the detention and/or deportation of suspected terrorists? Can secret evidence not seen by the detainee be used against them in immigration proceedings? If so, is there an alternative vehicle to allow the evidence to be challenged?

B. *Immigration Proceedings and Torture*

Is there a prohibition on the use of evidence obtained through torture or cruel and degrading treatment in immigration proceedings and are there concerns that such forms of evidence might be used?

Does your country maintain a ban on refoulement or deportation to torture? Has deportation to a substantial risk of torture emerged as an issue in cases of suspected terrorists who may be citizens of countries that employ or have employed torture? If so, what steps have been taken to resolve this issue? For example, the negotiation of assurances with other countries that they not use torture, long-term detention within your country, release subject to conditions or criminal prosecution within your country of non-citizens suspected of being involved in terrorism?

VIII. ADMINISTRATIVE/EXECUTIVE MEASURES

Alternative executive or administrative measures have been used as a form of anti-terrorism law sometimes as a less restrained alternative to criminal prosecutions and sometimes as a supplement to criminal law.

Are administrative measures used to control the activities of people suspected or convicted of terrorism? If not, why? For example, would constitutional norms preclude their use? Has there been any use of administrative measures after acquittals or reversals of convictions in terrorism cases?

Describe the administrative measures that have been used and are now used with respect to terrorist suspects. How does the standard of proof compare to that used in criminal law? Can secret evidence not disclosed to the affected person be used to justify the use of administrative measures? If so, is the secret evidence challenged by specialized judges and/or security-cleared advocates who can act in an adversarial manner? Is there legal or political controversy with respect to the use of administrative/executive measures?

IX. ROLE OF MILITARY AND EXTRA-TERRITORIAL COUNTER-TERRORISM ACTIVITIES

A. *Military Courts and Detention*

Does the military play a role in the domestic enforcement of terrorism law? Are military courts used with respect to terrorism prosecutions either domestically or extra-territorially? If so, how do military courts differ from ordinary criminal courts with respect to their personnel and procedures?

Does your country detain suspected terrorists on a law of war basis? Has this detention proven to be controversial? Has it been challenged either domestically or through regional or international venues or in the courts of other countries, and if so, with what results?

B. *The Extra-Territorial Treatment of Citizens Suspected of Terrorism*

Has there been litigation or review proceedings in your country with respect to the treatment of nationals of your state who may be detained by another state because of suspicions of their involvement in terrorism, for example, in relation to those detained by the United States at Guantanamo or Bagram?

C. *Extra-Territorial Terrorism Law Enforcement*

What is known about the extra-territorial counter-terrorism activities of your state officials, including police, intelligence and military? Do domestic laws limit the actions of your state's officials outside of their country?

Have terrorist suspects been extradited from your country to face terrorism prosecutions in another country? If so, what conditions have been placed on extradition, for example, with respect to the application of the death penalty or the use of military detention or trial?

X. SECRECY AND TERRORISM

A. *Secrecy Claims and Secret Evidence*

How are state secrets treated in terrorism prosecutions? Can secret evidence not seen by the accused be used as incriminating evidence in a terrorism trial? Can the state restrict normal rights that the accused may have to access or have disclosure of information held by the state if that information is claimed, classified or subject to a judicial determination that it is secret? Does the accused and others have responsibility to notify the prosecutor or other state representative if they intend to use information in a terrorism prosecution that might be considered a state secret?

What is the procedure for determining whether information claimed to be secret can be disclosed to the accused or the accused's lawyer? Do judges have the power to balance the competing claims of secrecy and disclosure in individual cases? Can judges redact or edit the information to protect secrets? Can judges ask the government to request that other states allow the disclosure of information protected under the third-party rules? Do evidentiary rules or privileges prevent the disclosure of intelligence sources and methods?

Can judges impose conditions on disclosure, such as only the accused's lawyer and not the accused may see the information or that it not be disclosed to the press and the public?

B. *Secrecy in the Courtroom and Anonymous Witnesses*

Are there mechanisms to protect state secrets at the actual trial or judicial proceedings? Does this include closed courtrooms or court exhibits that cannot be published in the media?

Do intelligence service members testify at terrorism prosecutions? Can they testify anonymously or with their identity hidden? Can anonymous witnesses testify in terrorism prosecutions? If so, has this happened and are there limits on the use of anonymous witnesses?

XI. OTHER MATTERS

Have other important issues not covered by the preceding emerged in your country, especially over the last decade or so? For example, have their been controversies over failures to prevent terrorism and/or human rights abuses in countering terrorism, including complicity in terrorism? Has there been important reorganization of governmental departments or review structures that has influenced the enforcement of counter-terrorism law? Has the treatment of the victims of terrorism emerged as an important issue in your country? Have relations with other nations or regional or international organizations been an important influence in the development of your country's counter-terrorism law?

It is not necessary to report under this heading if the outline is comprehensive for your country, but readers should be aware of the major legal issues confronting your country's response to terrorism.

XII. CONCLUSION: ASSESSMENT OF YOUR COUNTRY'S ANTI-TERRORISM LAWS

Provide your own overall assessment and conclusions about your country's counter-terrorism law. Has there been a greater emphasis on state powers to prevent terrorism since the events of 11 September 2001? Should the law better respect human rights? Has it been effective in responding to the terrorist threat faced in your country? What have been the major influences on the development of counter-terrorism law? In turn, has counter-terrorism law influenced other parts of law, or will it? What are your own conclusions about your country's counter-terrorism law in comparative perspective? What do you think will be the challenges and major issues facing counter-terrorism law in your country over the next decade or so?

Index

Lightning Source UK Ltd.
Milton Keynes UK
UKHW021226260420
362095UK00010B/342